Lecture Notes in Computer Science 7265

Commenced Publication in 1973
Founding and Former Series Editors:
Gerhard Goos, Juris Hartmanis, and Jan van Leeuwen

Lecture Notes in Computer Science

Esra Erdem   Joohyung Lee   Yuliya Lierler
David Pearce (Eds.)

Correct Reasoning

Essays on Logic-Based AI in Honor of Vladimir Lifschitz

Springer

Volume Editors

Esra Erdem
Sabanci University
Faculty of Engineering and Natural Sciences
Orhanli, Tuzla 34956, Istanbul, Turkey
E-mail: esraerdem@sabanciuniv.edu

Joohyung Lee
Arizona State University
School of Computing, Informatics and Decision Systems Engineering
P.O. Box 878809, Tempe, AZ 85287, USA
E-mail: joolee@asu.edu

Yuliya Lierler
University of Kentucky
Department of Computer Science
329 Rose Street, Lexington, KY 40506, USA
E-mail: yuliya@cs.uky.edu

David Pearce
Politechnical University of Madrid
Department of Artificial Intelligence
Campus de Montegancedo, 28660 Boadilla del Monte, Madrid, Spain
E-mail: david.pearce@upm.es

ISSN 0302-9743
e-ISSN 1611-3349
ISBN 978-3-642-30742-3
e-ISBN 978-3-642-30743-0
DOI 10.1007/978-3-642-30743-0
Springer Heidelberg Dordrecht London New York

Library of Congress Control Number: 2012938501

CR Subject Classification (1998): F.4.1, I.2, F.3, I.2.3, D.2.4, F.4

LNCS Sublibrary: SL 1 – Theoretical Computer Science and General Issues

Typesetting: Camera-ready by author, data conversion by Scientific Publishing Services, Chennai, India

Printed on acid-free paper

Springer is part of Springer Science+Business Media (www.springer.com)

Vladimir Lifschitz

Preface

Vladimir Lifschitz was born in Moscow, Russia, on May 30, 1947. The present volume is a Festschrift in his honor to celebrate the 65th birthday of an outstanding scholar of computer science, logic and artificial intelligence. It comprises 44 contributions by no less than 87 authors. They include many of Vladimir's students, colleagues, co-authors and friends. Their topics cover many of the scientific areas where Vladimir has made a lasting and profound contribution: logic programming, circumscription, default logic, action theory, planning, causal reasoning and of course answer set programming.

On approaching scholars to contribute to this Festschrift, we received an overwhelming, positive response. It became clear that Vladimir is admired, liked and held in esteem throughout the scientific community the world over. The enthusiasm with which authors responded to our request was delightful and infectious. It became clear that we could have produced several volumes of this size, and only time and practical concerns prevented us from doing so. We heartily thank all the contributors for their fine efforts, and we apologize sincerely to the many colleagues that we were not able to approach. We are especially grateful to Jack Minker for contributing a personal piece on Vladimir's life and work. The reader will also find a collection of personal reminiscences on Vladimir Lifschitz as teacher, as lived by his students. Our warm thanks also go to Springer for their support of this initiative and the editorial process.

We shall not dwell further here on the scientific achievements of Vladimir Lifschitz the scholar, since they are visible time and again in the pages that follow. For Vladimir Lifschitz, colleague and friend, we close by wishing you a very happy 65th birthday! We are sure we speak on behalf of all the present contributors in wishing you many more years in the business of correct reasoning.

March 2012

Esra Erdem
Joohyung Lee
Yuliya Lierler
David Pearce

Table of Contents

To Vladimir Lifschitz on His 65th Birthday

Jack Minker

Department of Computer Science and
Institute for Advanced Computer Studies,
University of Maryland,
College Park, Maryland 20742

1 Introduction

I am honored to have been invited by the editors of this Festschrift to write an article in honor of Vladimir Lifschitz on the occasion of his 65th birthday. In this article I describe some of the major contributions that Vladimir has made in his exceptional career. I provide background material about Vladimir in the Former Soviet Union (FSU), where he was born; discuss his beginning years in the United States (US); how I became aware of his research; his work on stable models with Michael Gelfond, and some of my work in related areas; and describe some of the many contributions Vladimir has made in formalizing ad hoc approaches in artificial intelligence to a formal basis of logic-based analysis.

2 Vladimir Lifschitz in the Soviet Union

Vladimir Lifschitz was born in Moscow in the Former Union of Soviet Socialist Republics (USSR) on May 30, 1947 to Jewish parents. His family moved to Leningrad when he was five. The USSR had a long history of discrimination against their Jewish citizens not only by USSR citizens, but by the state as a whole. This became especially severe under the regime of Joseph Stalin who, in 1922, won the most powerful post in the USSR, general secretary of the party. His reign lasted until March 5, 1953. Under Stalin, thousands USSR citizens had been brutally killed by orders of the state without legal process, and millions incarcerated without due process.

Following the death of Stalin, subsequent general secretaries of the party were less brutal. However state anti-Semitism still existed. Jewish students were discriminated against and were prevented from attending the best universities. Vladimir was too good a scholar to be denied entry to one of the best universities in the USSR, and was accepted to Leningrad State University in 1963. In fact, he was a kind of "child prodigy": he learned calculus on his own, and audited advanced college courses, when he was in high school. At the age of 19, he presented his original research at the International Congress of Mathematicians in Moscow, and he published nine more papers on mathematical logic during the next three years. Fate would have it that Michael Gelfond, also enrolled at the same time and both majored in mathematics. They took many courses together and became friends forever.

While still an undergraduate student, Vladimir met a charming and intelligent young woman, Elena Donskaya at a holiday resort for writers and their families where they

E. Erdem et al. (Eds.): Correct Reasoning, LNCS 7265, pp. 1–13, 2012.

spent some time during winter break. Elena was also a student at Leningrad University and studied English literature. Vladimir's father was a famous playwright who wrote under the name Alexander Volodin. His mother had a degree in chemistry. Elena and Vladimir were married when Vladimir was 20 years old. They have a son Alexander, and a granddaughter Sonya.

As a high school student, Vladimir attended seminars and discussions of the logic group at the famous Steklov Mathematical Institute in Leningrad. The Steklov Institute was known for its work in mathematical logic and mechanical theorem proving. In 1968, under the direction of the famous logician Nikolai Alexandrovich Shanin, Vladimir completed and defended his thesis, "Constructive Counterparts of Gödel's Completeness Theorem." In spite of anti-Semitism, he was able to find eventually a really good position at a research institute of the Academy of Sciences in Leningrad.

Elena recalls their decision to emigrate from the USSR as follows

> The main reason why we decided to emigrate was our general disgust for the totalitarian Soviet system, our desire to live as free people. There were two choices there: either to repeat slavishly the lies of the official propaganda or to become outspoken dissidents and to spend years in prisons and labor camps. We didn't like either option, and this is why we chose the difficult path of emigration.

In 1974, Vladimir and Elena applied for an exit visa and became refuseniks. A refusenik is generally a Jewish person in the USSR who was denied an exit visa. According to the Universal Declaration of Human Rights passed by the United Nations on December 10, 1948, every individual has the right to leave their country. Vladimir and Elena received their exit visa in 1976 and immigrated to the US. At the time they applied, Vladimir was employed. When someone in the USSR applied for an exit visa, they were generally dismissed from their job. However, Vladimir decided to leave on his own terms and resigned. He did not want to cause trouble for those who had hired him. His boss, Boris Pittel, eventually immigrated to the US where Vladimir wrote several papers with him.

3 Vladimir Lifschitz's Early Years in the United States

After Vladimir arrived in the US in 1976, he was fortunate to find a temporary position at Stanford University working with Patrick Suppes on computer-aided learning. In 1977 he found a two year position at Brigham Young University in the Mathematics Department as an assistant professor. In 1979 he found a tenure track position as an assistant professor in the Mathematics Department at the University of Texas, El Paso (UTEP). Shortly after Vladimir was at UTEP, he was instrumental in attracting Michael to UTEP. As with many universities at that time, UTEP had a computer science program as part of its mathematics department and decided to upgrade the program to a Department of Computer Science. Michael and Vladimir contributed to developing a Plan of Organization for the new department and were among its first members.

Since Vladimir was in a computer science department, he decided to broaden his knowledge in computers. While he was at UTEP, he enrolled in a summer course in computer science and artificial intelligence (AI) offered at Stanford University. One of the courses he attended was by John McCarthy, where he learned about circumscription. He was very impressed with the idea and its potential and introduced his friend Michael to circumscription. Vladimir wanted to find out more about circumscription and decided to go to California to be near McCarthy. He found a position at San Jose University and attended McCarthy's seminars at Stanford University. Vladimir Lifshitz is undoubtedly now the leading exponent on circumscription. Michael and I both believe that John McCarthy, may he rest in peace, was instrumental in Vladimir's change of interest to work in nonmonotonic reasoning and logic-based artificial intelligence. It is a perfect fit for someone who had been trained as a logician. Vladimir is one of the few researchers in nonmonotonic research, a field so dependent upon logic, who is a trained logician.

4 Vladimir Lifschitz's Scientific Contributions

It is not possible to cover the depth and scope of all of Vladimir's research. Primarily, I will discuss some of his work related to nonmonotonic reasoning and some other work of general interest, that I believe to be significant. In particular, I discuss a book he wrote on mechanical theorem proving developments in the USSR; his work on stable model semantics and answer set programming; his solution to McCarthy's 1959 AI planning problem; work in complexity; circumscription; reasoning about actions; semantics of logic programs; and the mathematics of logic programming.

4.1 Mechanical Theorem Proving in the USSR

I do not recall when I first became aware of Vladimir's research activities. It may have been in 1984 or 1985, when he wrote his first papers on circumscription. I was aware of Vladimir's work when I received a request to review a book some time in 1984-1986 that he wrote, **Mechanical Theorem Proving in the USSR: The Leningrad School** [30]. As I recall, some government organization had commissioned Vladimir to write the book. Since I had done some work in mechanical theorem proving, the government organization requested that I read the book and give them my comments. The book was of interest to me, as I had known that the Leningrad School had done excellent work in mechanical theorem proving, but the work was not well-known in Western countries. In 1971 I had read papers on work by S. Ju. Maslov [25], [42] and was interested in learning more about his work. I found the book to be well-written, and provided a great deal of information that was unknown in the West. The Leningrad School was located at the branch of the Steklov Mathematics Institute in Leningrad. Vladimir's book made the work accessible to those who read English. I realized after reading the book that Vladimir Lifschitz was someone whose work I should follow. Since his book was not generally accessible or known to the theorem proving community, he wrote an article, "What Is the Inverse Method?" [33]. In the article he described the relationship between the inverse method and J. Alan Robinson's resolution method [64] used in theorem proving in Western countries.

4.2 Stable Model Semantics for Normal Logic Programs

The field of logic programming was dominated in early days with work on Horn clauses. The efficiency of dealing with Horn clauses was fundamental to the development of

Prolog [6]. In 1978 at a workshop organized in Toulouse, France in 1978, by Herve Gallaire, Jack Minker, and Jean-Marie Nicolas [22], two important papers on negation in Horn clause theories appeared: Reiter's closed world assumption [61], and Clark's negation-as-failure and completion theory [7]. These were the first papers written, based on Horn clauses, that provided a semantics for default negation that was based on logic.

It became clear to me a few years after the Toulouse workshop, that non-Horn clauses (also referred to as disjunctive clauses) were needed for work in knowledge bases and other AI applications. Hence, there was a need to develop a semantics for default negation in theories with disjunctive clauses. I believe that the generalized closed world assumption [46] that I developed in 1982, motivated by Reiter's work, may have been the first treatment of negation in disjunctive clauses.

Although Prolog had a default negation operator, there was a need to extend default negation in Horn theories. In 1986, I organized a workshop in Washington, DC. At that workshop, three papers related to the semantics of default negation in Horn theories were developed. Apt, Blair, and Walker [1] and independently, Van Gelder [12], showed how to handle Horn clause programs with default negation in the body of clauses that extended the work where there was no recursion through negation in the program. This work is referred to as stratified clauses. Apt et al. proved that a unique fixpoint exists that represents the semantics. The unique fixpoint is referred to as *perfect model* by Przymusinski [59]. Papers from the workshop were published in a book I edited, [47].

In the area of normal programs that are not stratified, that is, there may be negation through recursion, several competing theories were developed at roughly the same time: the theory of *stable models* developed by Gelfond and Lifschitz [16]; the theory of *well-founded semantics* developed by Van Gelder, Ross and Schlipf [23], and elaborated upon by Przymusinski [60]; the theory of *generalized well-founded semantics* by Baral, Lobo and Minker [4] and the theory of *stable classes* developed by Baral and Subrahmanian [5]. As shown by Baral and Subrahmanian [5], the concept of stable classes is able to capture both the notion of stable models and the well-founded semantics.

In an invited talk I presented at the First International Workshop on Logic Programming and Non-monotonic Reasoning, Washington, D.C., July 23, 1991, I provided a comprehensive survey of work in nonmonotonic reasoning and its relation to logic programming. (The survey was extended and published in the Journal of Logic Programming under the title, "An overview of nonmonotonic reasoning and logic programming" [48].) I discussed the various semantics that had been developed, together with complexity results that had been obtained for various theories and how the logic programming theories related to the three nonmonotonic theories: autoepistemic reasoning [51], circumscription [45], and default logic [62].

In the question/answer period following the talk, I was asked which semantics was the most appropriate. I answered cautiously and said that it would probably depend upon the application and the user. A voice from the back of the room, with a Russian accent, 'quietly said', **STABLE MODEL SEMANTICS!** I was taken by surprise by this 'modest' statement, and answered that time will tell. Now, after more than 20 years, I can convincingly say that it is **NOT** stable model semantics, but Answer Set Programming (ASP). Yes, I must admit that Vladimir Lifschitz, the voice from the back of the room was correct, stable model semantics is the most appropriate semantics - renamed by Vladimir and Michael as ASP. I have known this for many years and I have acknowledged this in several lectures and in a paper [50].

The past years have seen a veritable explosion of research and implementations of ASP systems. In addition, the Gelfond and Lifschitz paper on stable model semantics was deemed the Most Influential Paper in 20 Years Award from the Association for Logic Programming (2004). It is interesting that the paper was first sent to a conference in 1987, but was rejected. No, Michael and Vladimir, I was not one of the reviewers of the paper! Vladimir, in an article in the *Association for Logic Programming Newsletter* [35] wrote about how the stable model semantics was developed, and the rejection of the paper. With respect to the rejection he said, "The reason, I suspect, was simply that the referees couldn't believe in what we had demonstrated – that the definition of an iterated least fixed point can be replaced by something quite simple, and, at the same time, more general." Michael in [13] also wrote about his work related to stable model semantics. The outstanding survey article by David Pearce, "Sixty Years of Stable Models [58], provides an interesting discussion of how Gelfond and Lifschitz devised the stable model semantics and a history of stable models.

A brief description of how they came to stable model semantics is through work by Michael in autoepistemic logic and by Vladimir in minimal models. As Vladimir wrote in the *ALP Newsletter*, Gelfond had the idea of characterizing the meaning of a logic program by translating it into autoepistemic logic or default logic. Gelfond, in the paper "On stratified autoepistemic theories" [11], proposed to insert a modal operator after every occurrence of negation in a logic program, and to interpret the resulting set of formulas in accordance with the semantics of autoepistemic logic, that is to say, in terms of stable expansions. The intuition behind this translation is that negation in a logic program is understood as "is not believed." If the given program is stratified then Michael's translation produces the same result as the iterated least fixpoint semantics [1], with the advantage that there is no need to worry about stratifications – the "right" minimal model is automatically produced by the definition of a stable expansion." After discussing this with Gelfond, they devised the concept of stable model semantics. The paper is significant in that, as Vladimir stated eloquently, above, it introduced a simple explanation of stable model semantics and the definition of stable model semantics is independent of Autoepistemic Logic.

4.3 Disjunctive Theories and Negation

The work by Apt et al. [1] motivated me to return to work I started in 1982 on disjunctive theories. I first started to develop a theory for disjunctive theories that gave a semantics similar to what had been done by van Emden and Kowalski [66] for Horn logic programs. That is, a semantics for disjunctive programs without default negation in the body of clauses. I realized that to find a mapping, I had to map positive disjuncts to positive disjuncts rather than a mapping from atoms to atoms as in Horn theories. Together with Arcot Rajasekar, we formalized the fixpoint, proof theoretic and model theoretic semantics for disjunctive clauses [52].

Work in disjunctive theories started to expand both by me and my students [36] and elsewhere. Efforts were made to include disjunctive clauses with negated atoms in the body of these clauses. At about the same time as Rajasekar and I developed the semantics for positive disjunctive theories, in 1990 Gelfond and Lifschitz [17] extended the definition of a stable model to programs that contain disjunction, default and classical negation. This was an important development with respect to disjunctive logic programs. A uniform approach for Horn and disjunctive programs now existed. They also changed the terminology from stable models to "answer sets", which has now become the standard in logic programming.

A veritable industry has grown up with respect to Answer Set Programming. ASP systems have been developed that permit large sets of clauses, applications have been implemented and the concept of stable models was extended to more general syntax. Two important extensions are the development of choice rules and cardinality constraints by Niemelä and Simons [55] which allows for more expressive programs. A second important development is equilibrium logic developed by Pearce [57]. The logic provides more expressive power.

Efficient ASP systems have been developed by Leone et al. [38], DLV; Niemelä, Simons, and Soininen [55], [54], [65], Smodels; and by Schaub et al. [15], CLASP, as well as others. The CLASP system has outperformed all other systems in tests run by the Dagstuhl Initiative [2]. The systems are available for applications and provide many novel features of use for knowledge representation and reasoning.

In addition to his two major contributions to stable model semantics and its extension to disjunctive theories including default and logical negation, Vladimir has made other contributions. Among these contributions is his work with Ferraris and Lee [9] where they present a new approach to semantics of stable models which is not based on grounding and a fixpoint definition. This establishes closer ties of stable model semantics and circumscription. In addition it provides a uniform approach to the definition of semantics of choice rules, conditional literals, and aggregates.

4.4 McCarthy's 1959 AI Planning Problem and Its Solution in 2010

In his 1959 paper on common sense reasoning, John McCarthy [43] defined and proposed a solution to a planning problem. In a critique by the philosopher and mathematician Yehoshua Bar Hillel [3], he noted that the formal commonsense reasoning used by McCarthy, was oversimplified and that a proper formalization would be more complex. McCarthy acknowledged the correctness of the critique. The problem became known as "the oldest planning problem in artificial intelligence", and can be stated as follows: "At home, your car is in the garage, and you want to get to the airport. How do you make a plan to get there?" Forty-one years later, Vladimir Lifschitz et al. [37] provided an interesting analysis of Bar Hillel's objections and presented the first solution to the problem.

The reason it took so long to provide an adequate solution is due to the need for a combination of results that needed to be developed in nonmonotonic reasoning. The results needed that led to the solution were: Reiter's default logic [62]; a modification of Clark's [7] completion semantics of negation-as-failure in logic programming by McCain and Turner [53]; the formalization of Reiter's closed world assumption that can be viewed as the use of McCarthy's circumscription; Reiter's solution to the frame problem in the situation calculus; and action languages by Gelfond and Lifschitz [19].

4.5 Early Study of Complexity Issues

Some of Vladimir's early work was in the area of complexity. In contrast to other work in complexity that studied worst-time complexity, he studied other measures and developed interesting results.

In [27] Vladimir demonstrates that a simple algorithm for solving the knapsack problem is shown to perform much better than 2^n, which it requires in the worst case.

In "The worst-case performance and the most probable performance of a class of set-covering algorithms", Lifschitz and Pittel [28] show that asymptotically almost certainly, the computation time of these important algorithms is of a considerably lower order than that in the worst case.

4.6 Contributions to McCarthy's Theory of Circumscription

Vladimir is undoubtedly the leading authority on McCarthy's theory of circumscription. Amongst his significant contributions is the paper, "Circumscription" [34], where he noticed difficulties with the use of circumscription in examples similar to those of the Yale shooting problem earlier than Hanks and McDermott [24]. Instead of concluding that nonmonotonic theories such as circumscription could not solve the problem, Vladimir considered circumscription with ordering relations on sets different from the simple subclass relation and investigated properties of these new formalisms and their applicability to knowledge representation.

Computing with circumscriptive theories is difficult since they are second order formulas. In the paper, "Computing circumscription" [29], (reprinted in [14]), Vladimir defined a class of formulas for which a second order formula for circumscription can be reduced to a first-order formula.

Another approach to computing circumscription was suggested in, "Compiling circumscriptive theories into logic programs" [26], where Vladimir and Michael mapped some circumscriptive theories into Prolog.

4.7 Reasoning about Actions

One of the more important topics in artificial intelligence is how to reason in worlds where actions take place. The world changes when objects move and real-world problems have to be accounted for. The classic book by Ray Reiter, **Knowledge in Action** [63], provided the first systematic approach to deal with such problems. Reiter's approach was based on McCarthy's situation calculus [44]. Together with McCarthy, Reiter, and others, Lifschitz and Gelfond were among the first to develop logical approaches to such problems.

Fikes and Nilsson in 1971 [10] developed STRIPS, the first action language. However, its logical semantics has always been questionable. There have been several variations on STRIPS. Lifschitz, in 1987 gave the first accurate logical semantics to the "original" action language STRIPS [32].

Vladimir [31] (reprinted in [14]) gave one of the first in-depth studies of applications of circumscription to formalizing effects of actions. Among other things the paper presents a solution to the Yale Shooting Problem. The paper demonstrated the use of nonmonotonic reasoning to solve a problem considered by the proposers of the problem to be not amenable to be handled by nonmonotonic reasoning.

In [21], Gelfond, Lifschitz, and Rabinov, provide a natural extension of the situation calculus capable of reasoning with parallel actions and other features previously believed to be impossible to express in this framework.

A problem of considerable importance is that of representing action and change in logic programs. In [18], Gelfond and Lifschitz present the first provably correct formalization of actions in logic programming. The method of proof, based on action language $\mathcal{A}$ introduced in this paper, was later used by many authors to prove the correctness of their formalization.

Giunchiglia and Lifschitz [20] introduced an action language $\mathcal{C}$ based on the theory of causality developed by McCain and Turner [53]. $\mathcal{C}$ and its extensions are now widely used for a large variety of applications. Lifschitz and Ren [40] then developed a powerful modular extension of $\mathcal{C}$.

4.8 Mathematics of Logic Programming

Vladimir made several important contributions to the mathematics of logic programs: splitting of a logic program; the investigation of strongly equivalent programs; mathematical foundations of answer set programming; and the investigation of loop formulas.

Splitting a Logic Program. In 1994, Lifschitz and Turner [41] observed that in many cases, a logic program can be divided into two parts, so that one of them, the "bottom" part, does not refer to the predicates defined in the "top" part. The "bottom" rules can be used to evaluate the predicates that they define, and the computed values can be used to simplify the "top" definitions. They discuss this idea of splitting a program in the context of the answer set semantics. The main theorem shows how computing the answer sets for a program can be simplified when the program is split into parts. The programs covered by the theorem may use both negation as failure and classical negation, and their rules may have disjunctive heads. The theorem became one of the major tools for mathematical investigation of logic programs.

Strongly Equivalent Logic Programs. In 1966, David Pearce [56] introduced the concept of equilibrium logic. Using the idea of equilibrium logic, Lifschitz, Pearce, and Valverde [39], investigated the problem of strong equivalence of logic programs. A logic program P1 is said to be equivalent to a logic program P2 in the sense of the answer set semantics if P1 and P2 have the same answer sets. They address the stronger condition: for every logic program, P, P1 ∪ P has the same answer sets as P2 ∪ P. The study of strong equivalence is important, because one can simplify a part of a logic program without looking at the rest of it. The main theorem shows that the verification of strong equivalence can be accomplished by checking the equivalence of formulas in a monotonic logic, called the logic of here-and-there (also referred to as equilibrium logic), which is intermediate between classical logic and intuitionistic logic. They show that equilibrium logic is an approach to nonmonotonic reasoning that generalizes the stable model and answer set semantics for logic programs. They present a method to implement equilibrium logic and, as a special case, stable models for logic programs with nested expressions, based on polynomial reductions to quantified Boolean formulas.

The introduction and investigation of the notion of strong equivalence gave rise to studies of various notions of equivalence in logic programming. Ferraris and Lifschitz [8] describe some other results.

Loop Formulas. In "Why there are so many loop formulas?", Lifschitz and Razborov [40] show that any equivalent translation from logic programs into propositional formulas involves a significant increase in size. This provides some explanation to the fact that logic programs lead to more compact formalizations of knowledge than propositional logic.

5 Closing Remarks

This brief overview of Lifschitz's research demonstrates some of the significant contributions he has made to nonmonotonic reasoning and logic-based artificial intelligence. It is an impressive body of work that ranges over a wide variety of topics.

Vladimir's efforts in this field were stimulated by John McCarthy, who sadly died recently. Had he not met and learned about McCarthy's work on circumscription, he might have contributed to other areas. The field of nonmonotonic reasoning and logic-based artificial intelligence benefited immensely from Lifschitz's work in this field.

Vladimir was wise to realize that he had no future in the Former Soviet Union, a country that did not appreciate his capabilities because he was Jewish. Denied the possibility to work on areas of interest to him in the Soviet Union, he decided to immigrate to the United States. The Soviet Union lost a scientist who would have contributed significantly to his country, but refused to allow Jews to flourish because of state anti-Semitism. The United States, the country that welcomed him and allowed him to thrive, gained a world-class scientist.

Vladimir is a warm, caring person. When he was at the University of Texas at El Paso (UTEP), he recruited his friend Michael Gelfond, also an immigrant to the US from the FSU, who was working in industry, not commensurate with his talents. There then began a collaboration of research between the two that led to the stable model semantics, judged by the Association for Logic Programming in 2008 as the most significant paper in logic programming in 20 years. As noted by David Pearce [58], "This has since become one of the most cited works in declarative programming. It led to a new approach to non-monotonic reasoning and eventually paved the way to establish a vibrant new programming paradigm: ASP of answer set programming."

As noted in this paper, Vladimir has also made many outstanding contributions to many different topics in nonmonotonic reasoning and logic-based artificial intelligence. He has worked with Gelfond on many of these efforts, as well as with his students, and other colleagues. As discussed in the short essays by some of his students (Fangkai Yang, Wanwan Ren, Joohyung Lee, Yulia Lierler, Neelakantan Kartha, and Esra Erdem) in this Festschrift, Vladimir was revered as a teacher, an adviser, a colleague, and a friend. He and Elena provided a welcoming family to all his students and particularly those who were away from their homes.

My early work in developing the first formalization of default negation in disjunctive theories, the generalized closed world assumption, and, together with my student Rajasekar, in formulating the semantics for disjunctive deductive logic programs may have been instrumental in starting efforts in disjunctive theories. This work has been overtaken by work of others, especially by Vladimir and Michael's research in stable model semantics and ASP programming.

Mazal Tov, Vladimir, on your 65th birthday. I am honored to be your friend and colleague. You still have many years of research ahead of you. I look forward to continue to follow your outstanding research.

Acknowledgements. I am indebted to Michael Gelfond who provided me personal information about Vladimir and Elena Lifschitz. He graciously pointed me to some of Vladimir's important research and sent me comments on the paper. Michael was a vital resource who helped to shape this paper. Elena Lifschitz shared some of her memories with me also. I also wish to thank the editors, Esra Erdem, Joohyung Lee, Yuliya Lierler, and David Pearce for inviting me to contribute to the Festschrift.

References

1. Apt, K.R., Blair, H.A., Walker, A.: Towards a Theory of Declarative Knowledge. In: Minker, J. (ed.) Foundations of Deductive Databases and Logic Programming, pp. 89–148. Morgan Kaufmann Pub., Washington, D.C (1988)
2. Borchert, P., Anger, C., Schaub, T., Truszczyński, M.: Towards Systematic Benchmarking in Answer Set Programming: The Dagstuhl Initiative. In: Lifschitz, V., Niemelä, I. (eds.) LPNMR 2004. LNCS (LNAI), vol. 2923, pp. 3–7. Springer, Heidelberg (2003)
3. Bar-Hillel, Y., McCarthy, J., Selfridge, O.: Discussion of the paper: Programs with common sense. In: Lifschitz, V. (ed.) Formalizing Common Sense: Papers by John McCarthy, pp. 17–20. Ablex, London (1990)
4. Baral, C., Lobo, J., Minker, J.: Generalized Well-founded Semantics for Logic Programs. In: Stickel, M.E. (ed.) CADE 1990. LNCS, vol. 449, pp. 102–116. Springer, Heidelberg (1990)
5. Baral, C., Subrahmanian, V.S.: Stable and Extension Class Theory for Logic Programs and Default Logics. Journal of Automated Reasoning 8(3), 345–366 (1992)
6. Colmerauer, A., Kanoui, H., Pasero, R., Roussel, P.: Un systeme de communication homme-machine en francais. Technical report, Groupe de Intelligence Artificielle Universitae de Aix-Marseille II, Marseille (1973)
7. Clark, K.L.: Negation as Failure. In: Gallaire, H., Minker, J. (eds.) Logic and Data Bases, pp. 293–322. Plenum Press, New York (1978)
8. Ferraris, P., Lifschitz, V.: Mathematical foundations of answer set programming. In: Artemov, S., Barringer, H., Avila Garcez, A.S., Lamb, L.C. (eds.) We Will Show Them! Essays in Honour of Dov Gabbay, vol. 1, pp. 615–664. King's College Publications, London (2005)
9. Farris, P., Lee, J., Lifschitz, V.: A new perspective on stable models. In: Proceedings IJCAI 2007, pp. 372–379 (2007)
10. Fikes, R.E., Nilsson, N.J.: STRIPS: A new approach to the application of theorem proving to problem solving. Artificial Intelligence 2, 189–208 (1971)
11. Gelfond, M.: On Stratified Autoepistemic Theories. In: Proc. AAAI 1987, pp. 207–211 (1987)
12. Van Gelder, A.: Negation as Failure Using Tight Derivations for General Logic Programs. In: Minker, J. (ed.) Foundations of Deductive Databases and Logic Programming, pp. 1149–1176. Morgan Kaufmann (1988)
13. Gelfond, M.: Answer sets in kr: a personal perspective. Association for Logic Programming 19(3) (2006)

14. Ginsberg, M.L. (ed.): Readings in Nonmonotonic Reasoning. Morgan Kaufmann Pub. (1987)
15. Gebser, M., Kaufmann, B., Schaub, T.: The Conflict-Driven Answer Set Solver *clasp*: Progress Report. In: Erdem, E., Lin, F., Schaub, T. (eds.) LPNMR 2009. LNCS, vol. 5753, pp. 509–514. Springer, Heidelberg (2009)
16. Gelfond, M., Lifschitz, V.: The Stable Model Semantics for Logic Programming. In: Kowalski, R.A., Bowen, K.A. (eds.) Proc. 5th International Conference and Symposium on Logic Programming, Seattle, Washington, August 15-19, pp. 1070–1080 (1988)
17. Gelfond, M., Lifschitz, V.: Logic programs with classical negation. In: Proc. 5th International Conference on Logic Programming, pp. 579–597 (1990)
18. Gelfond, M., Lifschitz, V.: Representing action and change by logic programs. Journal of Logic Programming 17(2/3&4), 301–321 (1993)
19. Gelfond, M., Lifschitz, V.: Action languages. Electronic Transactions on Artificial Intelligence 2, 193–210 (1998)
20. Giunchiglia, E., Lifschitz, V.: An action language based on causal explanation: preliminary report. In: Proceedings AAAI 1998, pp. 623–630 (1998)
21. Gelfond, M., Lifschitz, V., Rabinov, A.: What are the limitations of the situation calculus? In: Boyer, R.S. (ed.) Automated Reasoning: Essays in Honor of Woody Bledsoe. Automated Reasoning Series, pp. 167–180. Kluwer Academic Publishers (1991)
22. Gallaire, H., Minker, J. (eds.): Logic and Databases. Plenum Press, New York (1978)
23. Van Gelder, A., Ross, K.A., Schlipf, J.S.: Unfounded Sets and Well-founded Semantics for General Logic Programs. In: Proc. 7th Symposium on Principles of Database Systems, pp. 221–230 (1988)
24. Hanks, S., McDermott, D.: Default reasoning, nonmonotonic logics and the frame problem. In: AAAI, pp. 328–333 (1986)
25. Kuehner, D.: A Note on the Relation Between Resolution and Maslov's Inverse Method. In: Meltzer, B., Michie, D. (eds.) Machine Intelligence 6, pp. 73–76. American Elsevier Publishing Company (1971)
26. Lifschitz, V., Gelfond, M.: Compiling circumscriptive theories into logic programs. In: Proceedings AAAI-1988, pp. 455–459 (1988)
27. Lifschitz, V.: The efficiency of an algorithm of integer programming: a probabilistic analysis. Proceedings of the American Mathematical Society 79(1) (1980)
28. Lifschitz, B., Pittel, V.: The worst and the most probable performance of a class of set-covering algorithms. SIAM Journal of Computing 12(2), 329–346 (1983)
29. Lifschitz, V.: Computing circumscription. In: Proceedings of the 9th International Joint Conference on Artificial Intelligence 1985, pp. 121–127. Morgan Kaufmann (August 1985)
30. Lifschitz, V. (ed.): Mechanical Theorem Proving in the USSR: The Leningrad School. Delphic Associates, Falls Church, Virginia (1986)
31. Lifschitz, V.: Formal theories of action. In: Brown, F. (ed.) The Frame Problem in Artificial Intelligence. Morgan Kaufmann, San Mateo (1987)
32. Lifschitz, V.: On the semantics of STRIPS. In: Georgeff, M.P., Lansky, A.L. (eds.) Reasoning about Actions and Plans, San Mateo, California. Morgan Kaufmann (1987)
33. Lifschitz, V.: What is the inverse method? Journal of Automated Reasoning 5(1), 1–23 (1989)
34. Lifschitz, V.: Circumscription. In: Gabbay, D., Hogger, C., Robinson, J. (eds.) Handbook of Logic in Logic Programming and Artificial Intelligence, vol. 3, pp. 89–148. Oxfrod University Press, Washington, D.C. (1993)
35. Lifschitz, V.: Inventing stable models: a personal perspective. Association for Logic Programming 19(3) (2006)
36. Lobo, J., Minker, J., Rajasekar, A.: Foundations of Disjunctive Logic Programming. MIT Press (1992)

37. Lifschitz, V., McCain, N., Remolina, E., Tacchella, A.: Getting to the airport: The oldest planning problem in AI. In: Minker, J. (ed.) Logic-Based Artificial Intelligence, ch.7, pp. 157–165. Kluwer Academic Publishers, Boston (2000)
38. Leone, N., Pfeifer, G., Faber, W., Eiter, T., Gottlob, G., Perri, S., Scarcello, F.: The DLV system for knowledge representation and reasoning. ACM Transactions on Computational Logic (TOCL) 7(3) (2006)
39. Lifschitz, V., Pearce, D., Valverde, A.: Strongly equivalent logic programs. ACM Transactions on Computational Logic 2(4), 526–541 (2001)
40. Lifschitz, V., Ren, W.: A modular action description language. In: Proceedings AAAI (2006)
41. Lifschitz, V., Turner, H.: Splitting a logic program. In: Proceedings ICLP 1994, pp. 23–37 (1994)
42. Maslov, S.J.: Proof-Search Strategies for Methods of the Resolution Type. In: Meltzer, B., Michie, D. (eds.) Machine Intelligence 6, pp. 77–90. American Elsevier Publishing Company (1971)
43. McCarthy, J.: Programs with common sense. Mechanization of Thought Processes 1 (1959)
44. McCarthy, J.: Situations, actions and causal laws (1963); Memo 2
45. McCarthy, J.: Circumscription - a form of non-monotonic reasoning. Artificial Intelligence 13(1 and 2), 27–39 (1980)
46. Minker, J.: On Indefinite Databases and the Closed World Assumption. In: Loveland, D.W. (ed.) CADE 1982. LNCS, vol. 138, pp. 292–308. Springer, Heidelberg (1982)
47. Minker, J. (ed.): Foundations of Deductive Databases and Logic Programming. Morgan Kaufmann Pub. (1988)
48. Minker, J.: An overview of nonmonotonic reasoning and logic programming. Journal of Logic Programming 17(2, 3 and 4), 95–126 (1993)
49. Minker, J.: Homage to Michael Gelfond on His 65th Birthday. In: Balduccini, M., Son, T.C. (eds.) Logic Programming, Knowledge Representation, and Nonmonotonic Reasoning. LNCS, vol. 6565, pp. 1–11. Springer, Heidelberg (2011)
50. Minker, J.: Reminiscences on the anniversary of 30 years of nonmonotonic reasoning. In: Brewka, G., Marek, W., Truszczynski, M. (eds.) Nonmonotonic Reasoning. Essays Celebrating its 30th Anniversary, pp. 295–334. College Publications (2011); A volume of papers presented at NonMOn at 30 meeting, Lexington, KY, USA (October 2010)
51. Moore, R.C.: Semantical considerations on nonmonotonic logic. Artificial Intelligence 25(1), 75–94 (1985)
52. Minker, J., Rajasekar, A.: A fixpoint semantics for disjunctive logic programs. Journal of Logic Programming 9(1), 45–74 (1990)
53. McCain, N., Turner, H.: Causal theories of action and change. In: AAAI/IAAI, pp. 460–465 (1997)
54. Niemelä, I.: Logic programs with stable model semantics as a constraint programming paradigm. Annals of Mathematics and Artificial Intelligence 25(3/4), 241–273 (1999)
55. Niemelä, I., Simons, P.: Extending the Smodels system with cardinality and weight constraints. In: Minker, J. (ed.) Logic-Based Artificial Intelligence, ch.21, pp. 491–521. Kluwer Academic Publishers, Boston (2000)
56. Pearce, D.: A New Logical Characterization of Stable Models and Answer Sets. In: Dix, J., Przymusinski, T.C., Moniz Pereira, L. (eds.) NMELP 1996. LNCS (LNAI), vol. 1216, pp. 57–70. Springer, Heidelberg (1997)
57. Pearce, D.: Equilibrium logic. Annals of Mathematics and Artificial Intelligence 47, 3–41 (2006)
58. Pearce, D.J.: Sixty Years of Stable Models. In: Garcia de la Banda, M., Pontelli, E. (eds.) ICLP 2008. LNCS, vol. 5366, p. 52. Springer, Heidelberg (2008)

59. Przymusinski, T.C.: On the declarative semantics of deductive databases and logic programming. In: Minker, J. (ed.) Foundations of Deductive Databases and Logic Programming, ch.5, pp. 193–216. Morgan Kaufmann Pub., Washington, D.C (1988)
60. Przymusinski, T.C.: Stationary semantics for disjunctive logic programs and deductive databases. In: Debray, S., Hermenegildo, M. (eds.) Proc. of the North American Conference on Logic Programming, Austin, Texas, pp. 40–62 (October 1990)
61. Reiter, R.: On Closed World Data Bases. In: Gallaire, H., Minker, J. (eds.) Logic and Data Bases, pp. 55–76. Plenum Press, New York (1978)
62. Reiter, R.: A Logic for Default Reasoning. Artificial Intelligence 13(1 and 2), 81–132 (1980)
63. Reiter, R.: Knowledge In Action. The MIT Press, Cambridge (2001)
64. Robinson, J.A.: A machine-oriented logic based on the resolution principle. J.ACM 12(1), 23–41 (1965)
65. Simons, P., Niemelä, I., Soininen, T.: Extending and implementing the stable model semantics. Journal of Artificial Intelligence 138(1/2), 181–234 (2002)
66. van Emden, M.H., Kowalski, R.A.: The Semantics of Predicate Logic as a Programming Language. J.ACM 23(4), 733–742 (1976)

Vladimir Lifschitz — A Youth at 65

Neelakantan Kartha, Esra Erdem, Joohyung Lee, Paolo Ferraris, Wanwan Ren, Yuliya Lierler, Fangkai Yang*, and Albert Rondan**

Lifschitz's School of Computational Logics and Knowledge Representation

Reminiscences of Working with Vladimir Lifschitz

Neelakantan Kartha (graduated in 1995)

My first meeting with Vladimir was somewhat accidental. What prompted the meeting was that I was assigned by the computer science department at University of Texas at Austin to work as his teaching assistant for the graduate course he was teaching on Mathematical Logic. When we met for the first time in his office, he explained what he was planning to cover during the semester, gave me the book that he was planning to teach from and asked me to sit in on the course so that I would know what he was teaching each week. I agreed to sit in on the course, but without much enthusiasm because I believed that I already knew the content he was planning to teach.

Once I started attending, I was struck by the clarity and elegance of his lectures, and found that I was getting new insights about the material I thought I already knew. Thereafter, I became an enthusiastic attendee of his course. That semester Vladimir was also teaching another course on knowledge representation and commonsense reasoning and although I had missed the first few lectures I decided to sit in on that course as well. I had become convinced from my experience in his logic course that attending the course would be rewarding. My expectations were fully met and I was again struck by Vladimir's ability to precisely articulate the subtle issues that arise in commonsense reasoning, and by his approach to addressing these issues in a clear and mathematically sophisticated fashion. Afterwards, I decided to work with him for my dissertation and he accepted my request to be my doctoral advisor.

My initial idea for a thesis topic was to formalize what is meant by a good solution to the frame problem since several existing approaches to the frame problem had been found to be unsatisfactory in that they worked as expected on a few motivating problems, but failed to work on minor modifications of the problems. Vladimir then suggested studying the formalization problem in the context of Action Languages (which he was developing with Michael Gelfond). This suggestion turned out to be quite fruitful in understanding the strengths and weaknesses of different and new approaches to the frame problem and became the core of my dissertation.

* Coordinated the co-authors.

** Kindly proofread these essays.

E. Erdem et al. (Eds.): Correct Reasoning, LNCS 7265, pp. 14–23, 2012.

Regarding his advising style, he would generally start our regularly scheduled weekly meeting by asking *What's new?* I would then outline what I had done during the previous week, which would lead to a brainstorming session and a discussion on what to do next. Any time during the week when I wanted to discuss something with him, he was always available. His way of indicating that he liked something I had done was to say *Very interesting. Continue!* He also gave detailed feedback on my papers; improving their clarity, organization and even typography.

Vladimir organized a weekly reading group where the group of students working with him (Norman McCain, Hudson Turner and I) and other interested students met and discussed new papers, both published and unpublished. Each week a participant volunteered to read a new paper and report on it while the other participants (who were also expected to read the paper in advance) could ask any questions and critique the paper if they felt it had any shortcomings. Vladimir actively participated in the discussions and he often provided a broader perspective to best view the work in. The weekly reading group was a great learning experience in critically reading research literature and in understanding how to improve the exposition of one's own papers.

From Vladimir, I learned not to be satisfied with the initial formulation of a problem or result, but to strive for clarity and elegance, paying close attention to notation and technical details. Through his papers and talks, Vladimir taught by example the importance of motivating and situating one's research and of conveying new ideas and results concisely while at the same time backing up the results with detailed proofs.

Vladimir, I wish you a very happy 65th birthday, and many many years of great contributions ahead!

Being a Part of Lifschitz's School

Esra Erdem (graduated in 2002)
Sabanci University, Istanbul, Turkey

Working with Vladimir brings about various privileges starting from the very first meeting and continuing even after graduation.

When I started working with Vladimir, Norm McCain told me: *Among many things, you will definitely learn how to write a research paper.* Indeed, writing a research paper with Vladimir is more than summarizing the results of some work with concise and clear sentences; it is a process of learning and perfecting those results. On one occasion, after proving a theorem and writing it clearly, Vladimir noticed that the proof can be made more elegant using some mathematical concepts. Since I did not know about those concepts, he picked a book from his library and we studied every chapter of the book together for several months before revising the proof.

Vladimir is extremely enthusiastic about his research. You can see his enthusiasm from sparks in his eyes, and feel it from his positive energy while he is talking about his work! After Hudson Turner defended his Ph.D., I was the "research group" of Vladimir for a while. We often had long research meetings, sometimes with short breaks to the coffee houses on the drag (a popular street that runs along the side of the campus). At all of these meetings, from the very beginning to the end, I have not only observed his enthusiasm about research but also felt it very deeply. When Enrico Giunchiglia visited us in Austin, he told me: *You talk about your research like Vladimir, and I think with a little bit of Russian accent.* Whenever I talk to other students of Vladimir, I remember what Enrico said. I still feel Vladimir's enthusiasm for research that he conveyed to me, like all other students of his.

Vladimir also encourages his students to investigate problems that are not necessarily in his research agenda. When I told him the possibility of applying answer set programming to wire routing and to phylogenetics, he was excited! Although we were working on some theoretical problems at that time, he encouraged me to work on these applications on the side and emphasized the importance of linking these applications to theoretical results. It is wonderful to work with Vladimir on both theoretical and application-oriented problems.

Lifschitz's school is not only about studying interesting research problems and learning various aspects of being a researcher and a teacher. It is also like a family; You can sincerely feel that Vladimir and his wife Elena care about you. At LPNMR/ICLP 1999 (the first conference I attended), Wolfgang Faber asked me rhetorically, *So, being away from your family, I guess he is like a father figure to you as well?* Indeed, Vladimir has been a family and a friend to all of us.

I know that all students of Lifschitz's school have had such privileges, and there is some Vladimir Lifschitz in each of us. Even now as a faculty member, I appreciate these privileges even more. Thank you Vladimir, and happy birthday!

An Ideal Advisor

Joohyung Lee (graduated in 2005)
Arizona State Univeristy, USA

When I started my Ph.D. program just after receiving a Bachelor's degree, I knew that Artificial Intelligence was an area that I wanted to study, but did not know where to start. I took a seminar course offered by Vladimir... and loved it. Still I was not sure; At the Open House, I signed up for an individual meeting with Vladimir, but did not have time to talk to him because I was interviewing Esra Erdem and Norm McCain about how wonderful their (former) advisor is.

Soon after I started working with Vladimir, I was offered to move in to the room next to his office. It was in fact a room that connects his office to the corridor. I was hesitant because my office then was on the 20th floor of the UT tower with a wonderful scenery, but being able to sit next to Vladimir was not comparable. It was a privilege! Like young children who keep trying to talk to their parents, we, the students of Vladimir, were eager to tell him about any progress we were making. Once Vladimir had 6-7 students and not have much time of his own. Still he seldom turned us down when we knocked at his door. In fact, the door was almost always open when he was in. I was surprised to learn that he himself did not have the same kind of opportunity with his Ph.D. advisor.

Vladimir encouraged each of us in his unique way. When I found some small errors from the work of some established researchers, he seemed more excited than me! When he encountered the idea of strong equivalence he gave a simple related problem to the class he was teaching. Many students - including me - attempted to prove the conjecture. As usual, Vladimir patiently looked at my proof attempt and asked me to explain some steps, which I could not do. When I came back with another attempt, he pointed out another gap, and so on. He already knew that there was no proof, but did not discourage. Weekly individual meetings with him were a joy, not a stress (like some other students may feel towards their advisor). With that said, was able to deepen my knowledge about the internals of mathematical structures, and this is what I want to teach to my students now. Once I found out that some work that I had been doing had been very recently published, Vladimir told me what is more important is what was proven than who proved it.

A Ph.D. program is long enough for ups and downs. My wife and I had those too. But Vladimir and Elena's love and care gave us strength to overcome them.

I learned many things from Vladimir, and was eager to practice them when I started teaching. I know it is challenging, but I have confidence because I've seen and experienced first-hand how effective his methods are.

I haven't learned tricks from him but principles. I often think *What would Vladimir do in this case?* That makes me feel like I am not alone, and brings me courage to do things the right way.

Thank you Vladimir, and Happy Birthday!

Keeping Things Simple

Paolo Ferraris (graduated in 2007)
Google Inc, USA

I met Vladimir Lifschitz for the first time in 2000, when I visited him and his research group in Austin, Texas just after graduating with a BS/MS degree in Italy. In my 3-month visit I was only supposed to complete the research that I did for my Masters' thesis, but I also had the chance of learning what the team was doing. During this stay, I was able to write a draft of a joint-paper that was then published a few years later. In 2001, I joined the University of Texas as a Ph.D. student and Vladimir became my research advisor.

The 6 years that I spent as a Ph.D. student at Austin were wonderful. Vladimir's academic teaching and advising style worked perfectly for me. It evolved along my Ph.D.; at the very beginning, when I had a shallow knowledge of mathematical logic, his didactic approach of advising helped me ramp up pretty quickly. Later, he had a more collaborative approach. He has always been available when I needed. There is no need for me to say how important his contribution to research is, but I want to emphasize his abilities in communicating; I consider some of his classes probably the best that I have ever taken in all my studies and I am always amazed in seeing how well-written his scientific papers are.

I am not in research any more (unfortunately) but what I have learned from Vladimir is still invaluable for my current career. I have learned to have a mathematical approach to engineering when possible, how to write technical documents, and how to make public presentations effective. But, more importantly, I've learned how essential it is to keep things simple.

I am happy to dedicate this note to celebrate Vladimir's 65th birthday! Happy birthday, Vladimir!

Happy Birthday, Vladimir!

Wanwan Ren (graduated in 2009)
Oracle America Inc, USA

When I was first enrolled in the Master's program in Computer Science at the University of Texas at Austin in 2000, I needed to select a course in each of the three categories: theory, system, and application. Some senior students recommended I register in the theory course, "Introduction to Mathematical Logic" providing me with the following reasons; First, deduction in logic was an interesting subject, second, workload was not heavy, and third, the instructor was very well-organized and friendly which made the class a lot of fun. The name of the instructor was Vladimir Lifschitz.

Unfortunately I registered for this class relatively late and therefore could not be added into the class. With a little bit of hope, I talked to Vladimir. He explained to me that the number of students must be limited because the major part of the class was students' presentations of their solutions to the problems and discussions. Such structure of a course would not be possible for a large group of students. Missing this opportunity, I was forced to wait another year to take his logic class, and this time I was lucky to get an early assigned time slot for registration. After I received my Ph.D. in the area of computational logics and knowledge representation, I wish I could have had a chance to be in his class earlier so that I could have started my research with him earlier.

Once I took his class in Fall, 2001, I began to know Vladimir little by little, and I enjoyed his class very much. His teachings showed the beauty of Logic, with which I was totally intoxicated — he is a great teacher. Being in his class, I understood why it always became full quickly. I also took Artificial Intelligence course in the same semester, where Joohyung Lee was a teaching assistant. Joohyung was already working with Vladimir on his dissertation, and frequently talking to Joohyung enabled me to know more of Vladimir's research from his student's side. From Joohyung I learnt that he was an excellent advisor to work with and so after taking his logic class, I decided to work with Vladimir.

Soon after I began working with him, I became deeply impressed by his intellectual superiority as a mathematician by training. For instance, one day after a few hours' work, I thought a problem had been solved perfectly. I checked my solution again and again and had been sure that all technical details were correct.

However, when the solution was presented to Vladimir, it took him only a few minutes to figure out a pitfall. This was not occasional and I gradually made progress with his patience and help. It was always a great pleasure to have discussions with Vladimir. Sometimes we talked about high-level issues, and sometimes about a specific step in a proof. No matter what we were discussing, he could always be counted on. In this process, not only were mathematical conjectures proved, but my ability of solving logic problems was greatly strengthened as well.

Being his student offered me the opportunity to talk to him almost any time. I could stop by his office to ask a quick question, and when writing a paper or my dissertation, we would work together for hours every day to edit sentence by sentence, word by word. By revising a few papers and my dissertation with him, I had improved my writing skills as well.

While Vladimir is very strict with details of logical deductions, as a person he is not as serious as a mathematical proof and has a full sense of humour. In his class, our research seminar, or our group dinners he always talked a lot about interesting subjects and made jokes. Once in his class, a student was presenting a solution and noticed that a proof was missing a part. She added the missing part while saying, "oops". Later when she realized the same thing should be added again somewhere else in the solution, Vladimir said, "here we also need an oops".

Furthermore, I have genuinely felt the love and care from him and his wife Elena. He has always encouraged us and offered tea and snacks at our group seminars.

It has always been a fortune for me to do research under Vladimir's supervision. I have learned a lot in many aspects while working with Vladimir for a few years. This has benefit me in both my career and my life. Thank you Vladimir, and Happy Birthday!

A Cool Advisor

Yuliya Lierler (graduated in 2010)
University of Kentucky, USA

> "Men have forgotten this truth," said the fox. "But you must not forget it. You become responsible, forever, for what you have tamed"
>
> *Antoine de Saint-Exupery, The Little Prince*

These words by de Saint-Exupery are great to start a note attributed to the occasion of Vladimir's 65th Birthday. It has been an absolute privilege to be a student, a colleague, and a friend of Vladimir because he belongs to a class of men who have not forgotten this wisdom. Once I attended a talk by researcher Mary Lou Soffa on mentoring students. One of the things she said was that the job of an advisor is not over with a student's graduation. In other words; advisor is a position for life and that is how Vladimir treats this role.

Vladimir's ability to think deeply, notice details, and express himself concisely and clearly both in speaking and writing, has always fascinated me. *Correct reasoning is our business* and *Pay attention to detail* are logos on his websites. They could easily be logos for every single conversation, paper, or email of his.

Vladimir is a remarkable story teller: he often explains things and events using a story or an anecdote from his own experiences or from what he has read about. One of his recent stories that found a place in his weekly seminar was about Soviet cosmonaut Georgy Grechko who was once asked *What is the hardest part of being in Space?* Grechko replied that *The most difficult thing in Space is the same as on Earth: To tell the Truth.* During lectures Vladimir would often find time to tell students about history of scientific developments and scientists thus sharing his appreciation and excitement about science and, in particular, mathematics. As for his personal life, Vladimir is a man who stands for his values and freedom. Not many people possess the courage to abandon 29 years of their lives; Vladimir did just that by being one of the very few who emigrated from the Soviet Union.

I would like to conclude with one of my warmest memories from my first year as a Ph.D. student. After the reception at the AAAI symposium Vladimir approached me and offered to sing together as *it is customary for tipsy Russian people*[1]. Graduate students from another lab who happened to observe the occasion mentioned afterwards that *they do not sing with their advisors.* I have been blessed to have a cool advisor!

Happy Birthday, Vladimir!

A Youth at 65

Fangkai Yang, current Ph.D. student
University of Texas at Austin, USA

Vladimir will turn 65 in 2012? This is astonishing!

In my impression, Vladimir displays endless energy that makes it hard to believe that he is over 60 years old. He walks, drives and talks quickly. He even has an advanced treadmill and a swimming pool at his house, indicating that he regularly exercises. Every Tuesday and Thursday afternoon when we walk together from our offices to the classroom where he teaches, I find it hard to follow him!

The truth is, Vladimir perfectly combines the energy of a youth and the wisdom of an elder — a youth at 65.

No one can disagree that the energy and enthusiasm he shows in his work is typical for a person in their 30s. He works in his office from 11am to 5pm on weekdays, during which he is always fully scheduled. He arrives at his office and holds his office hour until midday, during which he meets students from his class. Afterwards, he has a brief 15 minute lunch, prepares class for about half an hour, and then meets with his graduate students until he needs to teach or host his

[1] Vladimir is Jewish and the author of this essay is Belarusian.

weekly seminars. Then he may work in the office alone; either on a paper draft or a proof of his conjecture, or continuing to meet with his graduate students. As his student, I have the privilege of discussing things with him at almost any time. Dropping by his office, I have knocked at his door and said *Hi, Vladimir, do you have a minute?* — no appointment is needed at all. Usually he smiles and replies with an exciting and loud *Yes* without hesitation, even though he may be working on a draft or composing an email. A one minute discussion may last as long as three hours and he never ends the meeting unless a conclusion is drawn or my concern is fully addressed. When working on composing a paper or polishing a long proof for a theorem, we usually work together on the draft from morning to late afternoon with a short lunch break in the middle. Sometimes when I find my brain has stopped working and needs a break, he continues to speak, think and type as clearly and fluently as at the beginning of the day. When he works at home, he sends out emails to me from as early as 7am to as late as 11pm, and my emails are usually addressed within half an hour. I can only imagine he spends the whole day in his study.

In addition to his youthful energy, Vladimir has an energetic heart. He is eager to learn research work outside his own area. Once in a while he invites internationally renowned scientists in related areas to our department where they give talks in the Forum for Artificial Intelligence. People such as Chitta Baral, Marc Denecker, Matthew Ginsberg, Judea Pearl, Bart Selman are on his list of speakers. Furthermore, he encourages his students to pursue topics that they find interesting and supports them as much as he can. For instance, after he learned that I was interested in logic-based agent reasoning and planning, he introduced me to Michael Gelfond, an expert on logic-based agent architecture with whom we've had several teleconferences and emails exchanged, and later helped me establish a joint project with a professor working on autonomous agents and robotics, Peter Stone. Vladimir also encourages me to look for internships as long as I can find companies with interesting projects to work on, and is eager to learn whatever my project is about.

On top of that, Vladimir exhibits insightful vision towards scientific research that can only be found from a maestro scientist, and he imparts his invaluable experience and perspective to his students without any reservation. A scientist at heart, he regards scientific research as a part of his life and he educates me to enjoy the process of exploration by curiosity instead of chasing for publications and benefits; as a mathematician by training, he has a motto of "paying attention to details," and never tolerates the smallest imperfections including inappropriate punctuation in his work. As a fan of fine arts, he expects the theory and proof in his work to show artistic, mathematical beauty and simplicity and elegance. As a son of a famous dramatist and poet, he wrote research papers with clarity, balance, and eloquence. What's more, he is happy to share such an exciting journey of scientific discovery with his students by getting them involved in all aspects of his research work; from attitude of scientific research, statement of motivation, forming a conjecture and a counterexample, proof technique and details to presentation and organization of a paper and therefore sets up a role model for them to emulate — the best way I can imagine for a graduate student. I consider it a privilege and fortune to receive meticulous instructions, advice and suggestions that are fully tailored to myself.

In addition to research excellence that can be justified by his age, Vladimir treats his students as his children in the full sense of the word, and generously offers them fatherly love and care. As an international student far away from my homeland, I could not have appreciated it more when Vladimir invited me to his house to celebrate my birthday with his wife Elena, Yuliya Lierler and Frank Lierler. Elena prepared delicious food, birthday cake and candles and Vladimir and Yuliya gave me birthday gifts and cards. This is a deeply moving event in my life because for the first time I felt I had a new home in a country where I don't have any blood relatives. Even our weekly seminars are like a family gathering, where Vladimir prepares cookies and Turkish tea (thanks to Selim Erdogan!) and the first 15 minutes of the seminar is "exchange of the news".

To me, it is a blessing to be Vladimir's student. When I get my degree, I can be honourably linked to an academic genealogy with him and other brilliant names in human civilization such as Karl Weierstrass and Carl Friedrich Gauss. What I really learned from him is fundamental; stick to important problems with maximal scientific values, dedicate to and enjoy the process of scientific exploration, pay attention to details, and be open to other important directions. He teaches me how to be a genuine scientist as well as a decent gentleman.

I honourably dedicate this essay to Vladimir's 65th birthday, with the most sincere wishes for his health, longevity, fortune! Happy birthday, Vladimir!

Endless Wisdom

Albert Rondan (Undergraduate in Computer Science)
University of Texas at Austin

What is there to say about a man who speaks so elegantly for himself? Quite a lot as it turns out, especially during the commemoration of his 65th Birthday!

To me, Vladimir Lifschitz has been the source of an uncountably infinite amount of wisdom, courage, and perspective throughout my undergraduate career. One of my first college courses (discrete mathematics) was taught by him. The class was an incredible learning experience due to his style of teaching; there was no book and each student was required to work on their own and do their best to come up with solutions. Then, during class, students would attempt to present their solution while Vladimir patiently listened and corrected them, providing useful insights along the way. Coming from a public school system where exams are the only metric for performance, I found this drastic change in environment enticing and it led me to dive deeper into the world of mathematics and logics where the chalkboard is king, and the chalk reveals all truths. Near the end of that semester, I received an email about research opportunities and Vladimir Lifschitz's name popped out at me immediately. Little did I know that from that day forward, I would be embarking on an academic and intellectual journey that is still stretching my boundaries today.

Starting off with one on one meetings, Vladimir would teach me the very basics of not only Answer Set Programming but formal languages too. At first, I was intimidated by his accent and his intensity, but as time passed I saw that the intensity was really his passion for his teachings and the science behind it all. His clairvoyance and attention to detail was what really inspired me to continue in the field of Artificial Intelligence, and after taking his *Logic Based Reasoning* course, the inspiration continued. Vladimir's weekly seminars were (and still are!) a chance to witness his energy and charisma as he offers tea and cookies and catches up with attendees. Then, while discussing a research paper, he frequently provides additional, relevant information as well as a more general point of view about the topic to highlight its importance. All of this is done with a smile on his face, or a look of genuine excitement!

I have not worked with Vladimir as extensively as the fine people who authored the essays above me but even so he has offered me his time, an invaluable privilege. I once came to him to present a practical application of Answer Set Programming with scheduling type problems and not only did he listen to my presentation and respond with enthusiasm at the ideas, but he also suggested improvements and exposed interesting theoretical aspects that could be further researched. He, Yulia, and Fangkai also made helpful remarks and suggested research papers to read in order to further my goals. It is during these moments that I really am grateful to be surrounded by these incredibly intelligent people who also have hearts of gold and scientific progress at mind. I simply can not wait to work more with Vladimir et al in the future! None of these experiences I have shared would be possible without Vladimir Lifschitz, so I must exclaim with utmost gratitude, respect, and enthusiasm; Happy Birthday, Vladimir!

A "Conservative" Approach to Extending Answer Set Programming with Non-Herbrand Functions

Marcello Balduccini

Kodak Research Laboratories,
Eastman Kodak Company,
Rochester, NY 14650-2102 USA
marcello.balduccini@gmail.com

Abstract. In this paper we propose an extension of Answer Set Programming (ASP) by non-Herbrand functions, i.e. functions over non-Herbrand domains. Introducing support for such functions allows for an economic and natural representation of certain kinds of knowledge that are comparatively cumbersome to represent in ASP. The key difference between our approach and other techniques for the support of non-Herbrand functions is that our extension is more "conservative" from a knowledge representation perspective. In fact, we purposefully designed the new language so that (1) the representation of relations is fully retained; (2) the representation of knowledge using non-Herbrand functions follows in a natural way from the typical ASP strategies; (3) the semantics is an extension of the the semantics of ASP from [9], allowing for a comparatively simple incorporation of various extensions of ASP such as weak constraints, probabilistic constructs and consistency-restoring rules.

1 Introduction

In this paper we describe an extension of Answer Set Programming (ASP) [9,13,2] called ASP{f}, and aimed at simplifying the representation of non-Herbrand functions.

In logic programming, functions are typically interpreted over the Herbrand Universe, with each functional term $f(x)$ mapped to its own canonical syntactical representation. That is, in most logic programming languages, the value of an expression $f(x)$ is $f(x)$ itself, and thus strictly speaking $f(x) = 2$ is false. This type of functions, the corresponding languages and efficient implementation of solvers is the subject of a substantial amount of research (e.g. [7,4,14]).

When representing certain kinds of knowledge, however, it is sometimes convenient to use functions with *non-Herbrand domains* (*non-Herbrand functions* for short), i.e. functions that are interpreted over domains other than the Herbrand Universe. For example, when describing a domain in which people enter and exit a room over time, it may be convenient to represent the number of people in the room at step s by means of a function $occupancy(s)$ and to state the effect of a person entering the room by means of a statement such as

$$occupancy(S + 1) = occupancy(S) + 1$$

where S is a variable ranging over the possible time steps in the evolution of the domain.

E. Erdem et al. (Eds.): Correct Reasoning, LNCS 7265, pp. 24–39, 2012.

Of course, in most logic programming languages, non-Herbrand functions can still be represented, but the corresponding encodings are not as natural and declarative as the one above. For instance, a common approach consists in representing the functions of interest using relations, and then characterizing the functional nature of these relations by writing auxiliary axioms. In ASP, one would encode the above statement by (1) introducing a relation $occupancy'(s, o)$, whose intuitive meaning is that $occupancy'(s, o)$ holds iff the value of $occupancy(s)$ is o; and (2) re-writing the original statement as a rule

$$occupancy'(S + 1, O + 1) \leftarrow occupancy'(S, O). \tag{1}$$

The characterization of the relation as representing a function would be completed by an axiom such as

$$\neg occupancy'(S, O') \leftarrow occupancy'(S, O),\ O \neq O'. \tag{2}$$

which intuitively states that $occupancy(s)$ has a unique value. The disadvantage of this representation is that the functional nature of $occupancy'(s, o)$ is only stated in (2). When reading (1), one is given no indication that $occupancy'(s, o)$ represents a function – and, before finding statements such as (2), one can make no assumption about the functional nature of the relations in a program when a combination of (proper) relations and non-Herbrand functions are present. As a consequence, the declarativity of the rules is penalized.

In comparison to other methods allowing for a direct representation of non-Herbrand functions, we view the language proposed in this paper as an extension of ASP that is "conservative" from a knowledge representation standpoint, and that is achieved by a rather small modification of the original semantics. By conservative we mean that the proposed language not only allows for a representation of non-Herbrand functions that is natural and direct, but also retains the key properties of the underlying language of ASP. In particular, we designed our language so that:

- The ease of representation of ASP is retained;
- It is possible to represent, and reason about, incomplete information regarding both relations and non-Herbrand functions;
- The representation of knowledge regarding non-Herbrand functions follows formalization strategies similar to those used in ASP. For example, the encoding of a default "normally $f = 2$" should be syntactically similar to the encoding of a default "normally p."
- The semantics of the new language is a modular extension of the semantics of ASP as defined e.g. in [9].

The last requirement allows for a comparatively simple incorporation into our language of extensions of ASP, such as weak constraints [5], probabilistic constructs [3] and consistency restoring rules [1]. Although discussing the implementation of the proposed language is outside the scope of the present paper, it is worth noting that the last requirement also opens the door to the implementation of the language within most state-of-the-art ASP solvers.

The other requirements may seem straightforward, but they are in one way or another violated by most approaches to extending ASP with non-Herbrand functions that are found in the literature. Some simple examples of this are presented next, while a more thorough discussion can be found later in the paper.

The existing approaches can be categorized into two groups, depending on whether they allow for partial functions or not. The approaches described in [10], [12], [15] and [8] define languages that deal with total functions, whereas [6] uses partial functions.

One limitation of the approaches that require total functions is that they force one to model lack of knowledge by means of multiple answer sets, whereas in ASP one is free to model lack of knowledge *either* with multiple answer sets (such as $\{p\}$, $\{\neg p\}$) *or* by the lack of the corresponding literals in an answer set (e.g. answer set $\{q\}$ states that q is believed to be true, and that nothing is known about p and $\neg p$). Not only this in itself involves a substantial difference in knowledge representation strategies and limits one's ability to represent and reason about incomplete information, but it also favors the derivation of *unsupported conclusions*: literals that are not in the head of any rule, and yet occur in an answer set. This is a drastic change of direction from ASP, in which supportedness is a fundamental property.

The language of [6] allows for the representation of partial functions, and in this respect allows for an approach to knowledge representation that is closer to that of ASP. That language however does not allow strong negation. The lack of strong negation appears to force the introduction of a special comparison operator $\#$ to express the fact that the two functions being compared are not only different, but also both defined. A further difference is that the semantics of the language of [6] is based on Quantified Equilibrium Logic rather than on [9].

The rest of the paper is organized as follows. The next two sections describe the syntax and the semantics of the proposed language. In the following section we discuss the topic of knowledge representation with non-Herbrand functions, both in ASP$\{$f$\}$ and in other comparable languages from the literature. Next, we discuss the relationship between the proposed language and ASP and use such relationship to establish some important properties of ASP$\{$f$\}$. Finally, we draw conclusions and discuss future work.

2 The Syntax of ASP{f}

In this section we define the syntax of ASP$\{$f$\}$. Because in this paper we focus exclusively on non-Herbrand functions, from now on we drop the "non-Herbrand" attribute. (Allowing for Herbrand functions does not involve technical difficulties, but would lengthen the presentation.)

The syntax of ASP$\{$f$\}$ is based on a signature $\Sigma = \langle \mathcal{C}, \mathcal{F}, \mathcal{R} \rangle$ whose elements are, respectively, sets of *constants*, *function symbols* and *relation symbols*. A *term* is an expression $f(c_1, \ldots, c_n)$ where $f \in \mathcal{F}$, and c_i's are 0 or more constants. An *atom* is an expression $r(c_1, \ldots, c_n)$, where $r \in \mathcal{R}$, and c_i's are constants. The set of all terms (resp., atoms) that can be formed from Σ is denoted by $\mathcal{T}$ (resp., $\mathcal{A}$). A *t-atom* is an expression of the form $f = g$, where f is a term and g is either a term or a constant. We call *seed t-atom* a t-atom of the form $f = v$, where v is a constant. Any t-atom that is not a seed t-atom is a *dependent t-atom*. Thus, given a signature with $\mathcal{C} = \{a, b, 0, 1, 2, 3, 4\}$ and $\mathcal{F} = \{occupancy, seats\}$, expressions $occupancy(a) = 2$ and $seats(b) = 4$ are seed t-atoms, while $occupancy(b) = seats(b)$ is a dependent t-atom.

A *regular literal* is an atom a or its strong negation $\neg a$. A *t-literal* is a t-atom $f = g$ or its strong negation $\neg(f = g)$, which we abbreviate $f \neq g$. A *dependent t-literal* is any t-literal that is not a seed t-atom. A *literal* is a regular literal or a t-literal. A *seed literal* is a regular literal or a seed t-atom. Given a signature with $\mathcal{R} = \{room\_evacuated\}$, $\mathcal{F} = \{occupancy, seats\}$ and $\mathcal{C} = \{a, b, 0, \ldots, 4\}$, $room\_evacuated(a)$, $\neg room\_evacuated(b)$ and $occupancy(a) = 2$ are seed literals (as well as literals); $room\_evacuated(a)$ and $\neg room\_evacuated(b)$ are also regular literals; $occupancy(b) \neq 1$ and $occupancy(b) = seats(b)$ are dependent t-literals, but they are not regular or seed literals.

A *rule* r is a statement of the form:

$$h \leftarrow l_1, \ldots, l_m, not\ l_{m+1}, \ldots, not\ l_n \tag{3}$$

where h is a seed literal and l_i's are literals. Similarly to ASP, the informal reading of r is that a rational agent who believes $l_1, \ldots, l_m$ and has no reason to believe $l_{m+1}, \ldots, l_n$ must believe h. Given a signature with $\mathcal{R} = \{room\_evacuated, door\_stuck, room\_occupied, room\_maybe\_occupied\}, \mathcal{F} = \{occupancy\}, \mathcal{C} = \{0\}$, the following is an example of ASP{f} rules encoding knowledge about the occupancy of a room:

$$\begin{array}{l} r_1 : occupancy = 0 \leftarrow room\_evacuated,\ not\ door\_stuck. \\ r_2 : room\_occupied \leftarrow occupancy \neq 0. \\ r_3 : room\_maybe\_occupied \leftarrow not\ occupancy = 0. \end{array}$$

Intuitively, rule r_1 states that the occupancy of the room is 0 if the room has been evacuated and there is no reason to believe that the door is stuck. Rule r_2 says that the room is occupied if its occupancy is different from 0. On the other hand, r_3 aims at drawing a weaker conclusion, stating that the room *may* be occupied if there is no explicit knowledge (i.e. reason to believe) that its occupancy is 0.

Given rule r from (3), $head(r)$ denotes h; $body(r)$ denotes $\{l_1, \ldots, not\ l_n\}$; $pos(r)$ denotes $\{l_1, \ldots, l_m\}$; $neg(r)$ denotes $\{l_{m+1}, \ldots, l_n\}$.

A *constraint* is a special type of rule with an empty head, informally meaning that the condition described by the body of the rule must never be satisfied. A constraint is considered a shorthand of:

$$\bot \leftarrow l_1, \ldots, l_m, not\ l_{m+1}, \ldots, not\ l_n, not\ \bot$$

where $\bot$ is a fresh atom. Thus, the constraint

$$\leftarrow room\_occupied,\ door\_stuck.$$

states that it is impossible for the room to be occupied when the door is stuck.

A *program* is a pair $\Pi = \langle \Sigma, P \rangle$, where Σ is a signature and P is a set of rules. Whenever possible, in this paper the signature is implicitly defined from the rules of Π, and Π is identified with its set of rules. In that case, the signature is denoted by $\Sigma(\Pi)$ and its elements by $\mathcal{C}(\Pi)$, $\mathcal{F}(\Pi)$ and $\mathcal{R}(\Pi)$. A rule r is *positive* if $neg(r) = \emptyset$. A program Π is *positive* if every $r \in \Pi$ is positive. A program Π is also *t-literal free* if no t-literals occur in the rules of Π.

For practical purposes, it is often convenient to use variables in programs. In ASP{f}, variables can be used in place of constants and terms. The *grounding of a rule* r is the set of all the syntactically valid rules obtained by replacing every variable of r with an element of $\mathcal{C} \cup \mathcal{T}$. The *grounding of a program* Π is the set of the groundings of the rules of Π. A syntactic element of the language is *ground* if it is variable-free and *non-ground* otherwise. Thus, the fact that a room is unoccupied at a any step S in the evolution of a domain whenever the room is not accessible can be expressed by the non-ground rule:

$$occupancy(S) = 0 \leftarrow not\_accessible(S).$$

Given possible time steps $\{0, 1, 2\}$, the grounding of the rule is:

$$\begin{array}{l} occupancy(0) = 0 \leftarrow not\_accessible(0). \\ occupancy(1) = 0 \leftarrow not\_accessible(1). \\ occupancy(2) = 0 \leftarrow not\_accessible(2). \end{array}$$

3 Semantics of ASP{f}

The semantics of a non-ground program is defined to coincide with the semantics of its grounding. The semantics of ground ASP{f} programs is defined below. In the rest of this section, we consider only ground terms, literals, rules and programs and thus omit the word "ground."

A set S of seed literals is *consistent* if (1) for every atom $a \in \mathcal{A}$, $\{a, \neg a\} \not\subseteq S$; (2) for every term $t \in \mathcal{T}$ and $v_1, v_2 \in \mathcal{C}$ such that $v_1 \neq v_2$, $\{t = v_1, t = v_2\} \not\subseteq S$. Hence, $S_1 = \{p, \neg q, f = 3\}$ and $S_2 = \{q, f = 3, g = 2\}$ are consistent, while $\{p, \neg p, f = 3\}$ and $\{q, f = 3, f = 2\}$ are not. Incidentally, $\{p, \neg q, f = g, g = 2\}$ is not a set of seed literals, because $f = g$ is not a seed literal.

The *value* of a term t w.r.t. a consistent set S of seed literals (denoted by $val_S(t)$) is v iff $t = v \in S$. If, for every $v \in \mathcal{C}$, $t = v \notin S$, the value of t w.r.t. S is *undefined*. The value of a constant $v \in \mathcal{C}$ w.r.t. S ($val_S(v)$) is v itself. For example given S_1 and S_2 as above, $val_{S_2}(f)$ is 3 and $val_{S_2}(g)$ is 2, whereas $val_{S_1}(g)$ is undefined. Given S_1 and a signature with $\mathcal{C} = \{0, 1\}$, $val_{S_1}(1) = 1$.

A seed literal l is *satisfied* by a consistent set S of seed literals iff $l \in S$. A dependent t-literal $f = g$ (resp., $f \neq g$) is *satisfied* by S iff both $val_S(f)$ and $val_S(g)$ are defined, and $val_S(f)$ is equal to $val_S(g)$ (resp., $val_S(f)$ is different from $val_S(g)$). Thus, seed literals q and $f = 3$ are satisfied by S_2; $f \neq g$ is also satisfied by S_2 because $val_{S_2}(f)$ and $val_{S_2}(g)$ are defined, and $val_{S_2}(f)$ is different from $val_{S_2}(g)$. Conversely, $f = g$ is not satisfied, because $val_{S_2}(f)$ is different from $val_{S_2}(g)$. The t-literal $f \neq h$ is also not satisfied by S_2, because $val_{S_2}(h)$ is undefined. When a literal l is satisfied (resp., not satisfied) by S, we write $S \models l$ (resp., $S \not\models l$).

An *extended literal* is a literal l or an expression of the form *not* l. An extended literal *not* l is satisfied by a consistent set S of seed literals ($S \models$ *not* l) if $S \not\models l$. Similarly, $S \not\models$ *not* l if $S \models l$. Considering set S_2 again, extended literal *not* $f = h$ is satisfied by S_2, because $f = h$ is not satisfied by S_2.

Finally, a set E of extended literals is satisfied by a consistent set S of seed literals ($S \models E$) if $S \models e$ for every $e \in E$.

We begin by defining the semantics of ASP{f} programs for *positive* programs.

A set S of seed literals is *closed* under positive rule r if $S \models head(r)$ whenever $S \models pos(r)$. Hence, set S_2 described earlier is closed under $f = 3 \leftarrow g \neq 1$ and (trivially) under $f = 2 \leftarrow r$, but it is not closed under $p \leftarrow f = 3$, because $S_2 \models f = 3$ but $S_2 \not\models p$. S is closed under Π if it is closed under every rule $r \in \Pi$.

Finally, a set S of seed literals is an *answer set* of a positive program Π if it is consistent and closed under Π, and is minimal (w.r.t. set-theoretic inclusion) among the sets of seed literals that satisfy such conditions. Thus, the program:

$$\begin{array}{l} p \leftarrow f = 2. \\ f = 2. \\ q \leftarrow q. \end{array}$$

has an answer set $\{f = 2, p\}$. The set $\{f = 2\}$ is not closed under the first rule of the program, and therefore is not an answer set. The set $\{f = 2, p, q\}$ is also not an answer set, because it is not minimal (it is a proper superset of another answer set). Notice that positive programs may have no answer set. For example, the program

$$\begin{array}{l} f = 3 \leftarrow not\ p. \\ f = 2 \leftarrow not\ q. \end{array}$$

has no answer set. Programs that have answer sets (resp., no answer sets) are called *consistent* (resp., *inconsistent*).

Positive programs enjoy the following property:

Proposition 1. *Every consistent positive program Π has a unique answer set.*

Next, we define the semantics of arbitrary ASP{f} programs.

The *reduct* of a program Π w.r.t. a consistent set S of seed literals is the set Π^S consisting of a rule $head(r) \leftarrow pos(r)$ (the *reduct* of r w.r.t. S) for each rule $r \in \Pi$ for which $S \models body(r) \setminus pos(r)$. From Proposition 1 it follows that the reduct w.r.t. a given set has a unique answer set.

Example 1. Consider a set of seed literals $S_3 = \{g = 3, f = 2, p, q\}$, and program Π_1:

$$\begin{array}{l} r_1 : p \leftarrow f = 2, not\ g = 1, not\ h = 0. \\ r_2 : q \leftarrow p, not\ g \neq 2. \\ r_3 : g = 3. \\ r_4 : f = 2. \end{array}$$

and let us compute its reduct. For r_1, first we have to check if $S_3 \models body(r_1) \setminus pos(r_1)$, that is if $S_3 \models not\ g = 1, not\ h = 0$. Extended literal $not\ g = 1$ is satisfied by S_3 only if $S_3 \not\models g = 1$. Because $g = 1$ is a seed literal, it is satisfied by S_3 if $g = 1 \in S_3$. Since $g = 1 \notin S_3$, we conclude that $S_3 \not\models g = 1$ and thus $not\ g = 1$ is satisfied by S_3. In a similar way, we conclude that $S_3 \models not\ h = 0$. Hence, $S_3 \models body(r_1) \setminus pos(r_1)$. Therefore, the reduct of r_1 is $p \leftarrow f = 2$. For the reduct of r_2, notice that $not\ g \neq 2$ is not satisfied by S_3. In fact, $S_3 \models not\ g \neq 2$ only if $S_3 \not\models g \neq 2$. However, it is not difficult to show that $S_3 \models g \neq 2$: in fact, $val_{S_3}(g)$ is defined and $val_{S_3}(g) \neq 2$.

Therefore, *not* $g \neq 2$ is not satisfied by S_3, and thus the reduct of Π_1 contains no rule for r_2. The reducts of r_3 and r_4 are the rules themselves. Summing up, $\Pi_1^{S_3}$ is:

$$\begin{array}{l} r_1' : p \leftarrow f = 2. \\ r_3' : g = 3. \\ r_4' : f = 2. \end{array}$$

Finally, a consistent set S of seed literals is an *answer set* of program Π if S is the answer set of Π^S.

Example 2. By applying the definitions given earlier, it is not difficult to show that the answer set of $\Pi_1^{S_3}$ is $\{f = 2, g = 3, p\} = S_3$. Hence, S_3 is an answer set of $\Pi_1^{S_3}$. Consider instead $S_4 = S_3 \cup \{h = 1\}$. Clearly $\Pi_1^{S_4} = \Pi_1^{S_3}$. From the uniqueness of the answer sets of positive programs, it follows immediately that S_4 is not the answer set of $\Pi_1^{S_4}$. Therefore, S_4 is not an answer set of Π_1.

Most properties of ASP programs are also enjoyed by ASP{f}, such as:

Proposition 2. *For every ASP{f} program Π and set of constraints C formed from $\Sigma(\Pi)$, S is an answer set of $\Pi \cup C$ iff S is an answer set of Π that does not satisfy the body of any constraint from C.*

4 Knowledge Representation with Non-Herbrand Functions

In this section we demonstrate the use of ASP{f} for knowledge representation, and compare the corresponding formalizations with those from the existing literature. We start our discussion by addressing the encoding of defaults.

Consider the statements: (1) the value of $f(x)$ is a unless otherwise specified; (2) the value of $f(x)$ is b if $p(x)$ (this example is from [10]; for simplicity of presentation we use a constant as the argument of function f instead of a variable as in [10], but our argument does not change even in the more general case). These statements can be encoded in ASP{f} as follows:

$$P_1 = \begin{cases} r_1 : f(x) = a \leftarrow \textit{not } f(x) \neq a. \\ r_2 : f(x) = b \leftarrow p(x). \end{cases}$$

Rule r_1 encodes the default, and r_2 encodes the exception. It is worth stressing that the informal reading of r_1, according to the description given earlier in this paper, is "if there is no reason to believe that $f(x)$ is different from a, then $f(x)$ must be equal to a", which is essentially identical to the original problem statement. We argue that this representation of the default is, at least by ASP standards, natural and direct. Moreover, it is not difficult to see that the formalization follows a strategy similar to that of the formalization of defaults in ASP. Consider the statement "$q(x)$ holds unless otherwise specified". A common way of encoding it in ASP is with a rule $q(x) \leftarrow \textit{not } \neg q(x)$. Not only the informal reading of this rule ("if there is no reason to believe that $q(x)$ is false, then it must be true") is close to the informal reading of r_1, but the rules themselves have a similar structure as well. On the other hand, this is not the case of the language of weight constraint programs with evaluable functions [15], where a substantially different representation strategy is adopted, in which the default is encoded as:

$$f(x) = a \leftarrow [f(x) \neq a : 1]0.$$

In this case there is arguably little similarity between the body of this rule and the body of the default for $q(x)$, both syntactically *and* conceptually.

In the language of IF-programs [10], the default for $f(x)$ has an encoding rather similar to that of r_1:

$$f(x) = a \leftarrow \neg(f(x) \neq a)$$

Note that, in the language of IF-programs, $\neg$ has a meaning similar to that of *not* here. Where the language deviates from ASP is in the fact that in the language of IF-programs the above rule is equivalent to:

$$f(x) = a \ \vee \ f(x) \neq a.$$

The equivalence of the two encodings is somewhat problematic from the point of view of the language requirements that we are seeking to satisfy in this paper. In fact, in ASP the epistemic disjunction operator $\vee$ denotes a non-deterministic choice between two alternatives: a statement $p \ \vee \ q$ in ASP means that p and q are equally acceptable alternatives. In the language of IF-programs, instead, the disjunction operator appears to express a preference for the left-hand-side expression. In this sense, the representation of disjunctive knowledge in ASP and in [10] follows two very different strategies. (It is not difficult to show that ASP{f} can be naturally extended to allow for disjunction with a semantics following closely that of ASP).

Another language that allows for a direct representation of functions is that of CLINGCON [8]. However, the representation of defaults involving functions in CLINGCON may yield rather unintended results if one follows the typical ASP knowledge representation strategies.

Consider a modification of the default discussed earlier in which the value of $f(x)$ is 1 by default (CLINGCON only supports functions with numerical values), and let us assume that $f(x)$ ranges over the set $\{0, 1\}$. One might be tempted to encode it in the language of CLINGCON as:

$$\begin{array}{l} \$domain(0..1). \\ f(x) \,\${==}\, 1 \leftarrow \textit{not}\ f(x) \,\$!{=}\, 1. \end{array}$$

where the first statement specifies the domain of the functions and the second statement formalizes the default, with prefix \$ denoting equality and inequality of functions. As one would expect, this program has an answer set, $\{f(x) = 1\}$, in which $f(x)$ has its default value of 1. However, the program also has a second, unintended answer set, $\{f(x) = 0\}$, in which $f(x)$ is assigned the non-default value of 0. Clearly, in CLINGCON defaults cannot be represented using the typical ASP techniques.

As mentioned in the Introduction, a difference between languages with partial functions and languages with total functions is the way incomplete or uncertain information can be encoded. Suppose we know that function $f(x)$ ranges over $\{a, b\}$, but we do not know its value. In ASP, this could be encoded by the program:

$$
\begin{array}{l}
f'(x,a) \leftarrow not\ f'(x,b). \\
f'(x,b) \leftarrow not\ f'(x,a). \\
\leftarrow f'(x,a),\ f'(x,b).
\end{array}
\tag{4}
$$

The first two rules informally say that we know that the value of $f(x)$ is either a or b, but we do not know which one it is; the last rule characterizes $f'(x,v)$ as a function. It is not difficult to show that this program has two answer sets, $\{f'(x,a)\}$ and $\{f'(x,b)\}$, each corresponding to one possible assignment of value to $f(x)$. Alternatively, the same scenario can also be encoded in ASP by the program:

$$
\begin{array}{l}
\leftarrow f'(x,a),\ f'(x,b). \\
\leftarrow f'(x,V),\ V \neq a,\ V \neq b.
\end{array}
\tag{5}
$$

where the first constraint is as before, and the second constraint restricts the domain of $f(x)$ to $\{a,b\}$. This program has a unique, empty answer set. The fact that no literal of the form $f'(x,v)$ occurs in the answer set implies that the value of $f(x)$ is not known.

Similarly, in languages that support partial functions, such as ASP{f} and [6], both methods can be applied for the representation of incomplete information about functions. For instance, in ASP{f} an equivalent of (4) is:

$$
\begin{array}{l}
f(x) = a \leftarrow not\ f(x) = b. \\
f(x) = b \leftarrow not\ f(x) = a.
\end{array}
\tag{6}
$$

whose answer sets, along the lines of those of the ASP formalization, are $\{f(x) = a\}$ and $\{f(x) = b\}$. A formalization equivalent to (5) is an empty program (with a suitable signature), which has an empty answer set. According to the semantics defined earlier, an empty set entails that statements such as $f(x) = a$ and $f(x) \neq a$ are neither true nor false, implying that the value of $f(x)$ is unknown.

On the other hand, in languages that only allow for total functions, such as [10], [12], [15] and [8], the incompleteness of information about functions can only be represented by means of multiple answer sets. For example, in the language of [12] an empty program together with a specification of domain $\{a,b\}$ for $f(x)$ yields two answer sets, $\{f(x) = a\}$, $\{f(x) = b\}$. Because the functions specified by the formalizations are required to be total, there is no way to describe uncertainty about $f(x)$ by means of answer sets where the value of $f(x)$ unspecified.

Extending a common ASP methodology, the technique used in (6) to formalize the choice between a and b can also be easily extended to represent functions whose domains have more than two elements and to incorporate default values. Consider the statements (adapted from [10]): (1) the value $f(X)$ is a if $p(X)$; (2) otherwise, the value of $f(X)$ is arbitrary. Let the domain of variable X be given by a relation $dom(X)$, and let the possible values of $f(X)$ be encoded by a relation $val(V)$. A possible ASP{f} encoding of these statements is:

$$
r_1 : f(X) = a \leftarrow\ p(X),\ dom(X).
$$

$$
r_2 : f(X) = V \leftarrow\ dom(X),\ val(V),\ not\ p(X),\ not\ f(X) \neq V.
$$

Rule r_1 encodes the first statement. Rule r_2 formalizes the arbitrary selection of values for $f(X)$ in the default case. It is important to notice that, although r_2 follows a strategy of formalization of knowledge that is similar to that of ASP, the ASP{f} encoding is more compact than the corresponding ASP one. In fact, the ASP encoding requires the introduction of an extra rule formalizing the fact that $f(x)$ has a unique value:

$$r'_1 : f'(X) = a \leftarrow p(X),\ dom(X).$$

$$r'_2 : f'(X, V) \leftarrow dom(X),\ val(V),\ not\ p(X),\ not\ \neg f'(X, V).$$

$$r'_3 : \neg f'(X, V') \leftarrow val(V),\ val(V'),\ V \neq V',\ f'(X, V).$$

Not only having to write r'_3 is rather inconvenient, but this kind of rule may also have quite a negative impact on the performance of the ASP solvers used to compute the answer sets of the program. In fact, it is not difficult to show that the grounding of r'_3 grows proportionally to the square of the size of the domain of $f(x)$. For functions with large domains, this growth can cause performance problems (and cause the grounding of rules like r'_3 to become substantially larger than the grounding of the rest of the program). On the other hand, the grounding of the corresponding ASP{f} program does not suffer from such a growth, and a solver could in principle take advantage of that and compute the program's answer sets substantially faster.

A similar use of defaults is typically associated, in ASP, with the representation of dynamic domains. In this case, defaults are a key tool for the encoding of the law of inertia. Let us show how dynamic domains involving functions can be represented in ASP{f}. Consider a domain including a button b_i, which increments a counter c, and a button b_r, which resets it. At each time step, the agent operating the buttons may press either button, or none. A possible ASP{f} encoding of this domain is:

$$r_1 : val(c, S+1) = 0 \leftarrow pressed(b_r, S).$$

$$r_2 : val(c, S+1) = N + 1 \leftarrow pressed(b_i, S),\ val(c, S) = N.$$

$$r_3 : val(c, S+1) = N \leftarrow val(c, S) = N,\ not\ val(c, S+1) \neq N.$$

Rules r_1 and r_2 are a straightforward encoding of the effect of pressing either button (variable S denotes a time step). Rule r_3 is the ASP{f} encoding of the law of inertia for the value of the counter, and states that the value of c does not change unless it is forced to. For simplicity of presentation, it is instantiated for a particular function, but could be as easily written so that it applies to arbitrary functions from the domain. Rule r_3 follows the same encoding strategy used for relations in ASP, where the inertia law for a relational fluent p typically takes the form:

$$\begin{aligned} p(S+1) &\leftarrow p(S),\ not\ \neg p(S). \\ \neg p(S+1) &\leftarrow p(S),\ not\ p(S). \end{aligned} \tag{7}$$

The only difference is in the fact that (7) uses two rules because p and $\neg p$ are treated separately due to syntactic restrictions of ASP. Incidentally, it is not difficult to see that (7) is also a valid encoding of inertia for relational fluents in ASP{f}.

Let us now consider a typical ASP encoding for the above domain:

$$r'_1 : val(c, S+1, 0) \leftarrow pressed(b_r, S).$$

$$r'_2 : val(c, S+1, N+1) \leftarrow pressed(b_i, S),\ val(c, S, N).$$

$$r'_3(a) : val(c, S+1, N) \leftarrow val(c, S, N),\ not\ \neg val(c, S+1, N).$$

$$r'_3(b) : \neg val(c, S, N') \leftarrow val(c, S, N),\ N \neq N'.$$

Rules r'_1, r'_2 are similar to their ASP{f} counterparts. The only difference is that, taken out of context, r'_1 and r'_2 do not provide any indication that val is a function, and that as a consequence only one of $\{val(c, s, 0), val(c, s, 1), \ldots\}$ can hold at any step s. As mentioned earlier, this difference is rather important from a knowledge representation perspective, as it reduces the declarativity of the rules. Rule $r'_3(a)$ encodes the law of inertia. Because this encoding represents functions by means of relations, the rule depends on a suitable definition of the axioms of the uniqueness of value for val, formalized by $r'_3(b)$. As we discussed in the previous example, the grounding of $r'_3(b)$ can grow quite substantially – in fact, in practice, it can grow even more dramatically than in the previous example, because of the extra argument for the time step. The ASP{f} representation is thus not only more natural, but also potentially more efficient.

Coming back to the comparison between languages that allow partial functions and languages that do not allow them, another important distinguishing feature is the fact that in the languages with partial functions all conclusions are supported. A conclusion, i.e. a literal l from an answer set A of a program Π, is *supported* if it is in the head of some rule r whose reduct with respect to A has its body satisfied by A. In ASP, as well as in ASP{f} and [6], all conclusions enjoy this property. Both from a practical perspective and from the standpoint of knowledge representation, this feature has the advantage that a programmer can look at a program and rather easily understand which literals may be in the program's answer sets, and which ones cannot be in any answer set. Similarly, it is not difficult, given a literal from an answer set, to identify which rules may have caused its derivation. In languages with total functions, on the other hand, conclusions are not required to be supported. To highlight the ramifications of this difference from a knowledge representation perspective, let us consider the graph coloring problem (see e.g. [6,12]). In this problem, one must assign a color to each node of a graph so that no two adjacent nodes have the same color. A possible ASP{f} formalization is:

$$color(X) = V \leftarrow node(X),\ available\_color(V),\ not\ color(X) \neq V.$$

$$\leftarrow arc(X, Y),\ color(X) = color(Y).$$

The first rule states that each node can be assigned an arbitrary color, thus making *color* a total function. The second rule says that two adjacent nodes are not allowed to have the same color. In the language of [12], the graph coloring problem admits a solution that is even more compact:

$$\leftarrow arc(X, Y),\ color(X) = color(Y). \tag{8}$$

The reason why this is a solution to the graph coloring problem is because in [12] functions are total. Therefore, there is no need for an extra statement that forces $color(X)$ be defined. But at the same time, conclusions such as $color(n_1) = red$ will occur in the answer sets of (8) without occurring in the head of any rule. In this sense, (8) does not follow the typical knowledge representation strategies of ASP. In fact, it follows a quite opposite representation strategy: consider the ASP program consisting of a definition R of relation arc and of:

$$\leftarrow arc(X,Y),\ color(X,C),\ color(Y,C). \tag{9}$$

Because relation $color$ does not occur in the head of any rule, one can immediately conclude that the constraint is never triggered and that the program has thus a unique answer set consisting only of the definition of relation arc. Therefore, the color of any node X is unknown. That is, although program $R \cup (9)$ is syntactically very similar to $R \cup (8)$, their meanings are very different!

Finally, as pointed out in [6], in languages that allow for the representation of partial functions a statement such as "Louis XIV is not the king of France" may be intended in either one of two ways: (1) "whether France has a king or not, definitely Louis XIV is not the king of France", and (2) "France has a king, and it is not Louis XIV." The difference between the two readings is that in the second case the statement is true only if France is known to have a king (i.e. if the function is defined), whereas in the first case the statement is true even if we have no knowledge about France having a king. In [6], the apartness operator $\#$ is introduced, which informally states that the functions being compared (1) are defined and (2) have different values. So, the first reading of the sentence is encoded as $not\ king(france) = louisXIV$, whereas the second reading is encoded as $king(france)\ \#\ louisXIV$. In ASP{f}, on the other hand, one can achieve the same result by combining default negation and strong negation, as is normally done in ASP. More precisely, the first reading can be expressed in ASP{f} by the statement:

$$not\ king(france) = louisXIV \tag{10}$$

which, as explained earlier, has the informal reading of "there is no reason to believe that LouisXIV is the king of France". The second reading can be encoded as

$$king(france) \neq louisXIV. \tag{11}$$

which informally states "the king of France is different from Louis XIV" (recall that in ASP{f} $king(france) \neq louisXIV$ is an abbreviation of $\neg(king(france) = louisXIV)$). According to the semantics of ASP{f} defined earlier, (10) is satisfied by a consistent set S of seed literals if $king(france) = louisXIV$ is not satisfied by S. Because $S \models king(france) = louisXIV$ iff $val_S(king(france))$ is defined and $val_S(king(france))$ is $louisXIV$, it follows that (10) is satisfied if either $val_S(king(france))$ is undefined, or $val_S(king(france))$ is different from $louisXIV$. On the other hand, (11) is satisfied by S iff $val_S(king(france))$ is defined *and* different from $louisXIV$. It is worth stressing that $king(france) \neq louisXIV$ is just a syntactic variant of $\neg(king(france) = louisXIV)$, which implies that, in ASP{f} as well, the use of default and strong negation allows avoiding the introduction of an ad-hoc comparison operator.

5 Relationship with ASP

In this section we establish some useful formal relationships between ASP{f} and ASP, and use them to derive some important properties of ASP{f}.

To distinguish between the definitions given above in the context of ASP{f} and the corresponding definitions in the context of ASP, in this section we prefix ASP{f}-related terms with ASP{f}. So, if literal l is satisfied by a consistent set S of seed literals, we say that it is *ASP{f}-satisfied*. Similarly we say that S is *ASP{f}-closed* under a rule r. When we refer to the traditional ASP definitions, we use prefix ASP and say for example *ASP-satisfied* and *ASP-closed*. We introduce a similar distinction in the notation, and use symbols $\models_{ASP\{f\}}$ and $\models_{ASP}$ respectively.

For t-literal free programs, it is not difficult to prove that the following proposition holds:

Proposition 3. *For every t-literal free program Π, A is an answer set of Π under the ASP{f} semantics iff A is an answer set of Π under the ASP semantics.*

Because of this result, when in this section we use the term "answer set", we leave the semantics implicitly defined by whether the corresponding program is t-literal free or not. With similar reasoning, we do not explicitly refer to a semantics when referring to the reduct of a program.

Let us now consider arbitrary ASP{f} programs. An ASP{f} extended literal e can be mapped into an ASP extended literal (defined, as usual in ASP, as a literal l or the expression *not* l) by replacing every occurrence of a t-literal $f = x$ (resp., $f \neq x$) in e by $eq(f,x)$ (resp., $\neg eq(f,x)$), where eq is a fresh relation symbol. We denote the *ASP-mapping* of e by $\alpha(e)$. The notion of ASP-mapping is extended to sets of extended literals ($\alpha(\{e_1,\ldots,e_k\})$), rules ($\alpha(r)$), and programs ($\alpha(\Pi)$) in a straightforward way. The inverse of the α mapping is denoted by α^{-1}.

Now, let Π be an ASP{f} program. We define the *ASP-completion of Π* to be $\gamma(\Pi) = \alpha(\Pi) \cup \sigma_r(\Pi)$ where $\sigma_r(\Pi)$ is formed as follows:

- For every term t from $\Sigma(\Pi)$ and $v, v' \in \mathcal{C}(\Pi)$ such that $v \neq v'$, $\sigma_r(\Pi)$ contains a rule $\neg eq(t,v') \leftarrow eq(t,v)$.
- For every pair of terms f, g from $\Sigma(\Pi)$, every $v, v_f, v_g \in \mathcal{C}(\Pi)$ such that $v_f \neq v_g$, $\sigma_r(\Pi)$ contains the rules:

$$eq(f,g) \leftarrow eq(f,v),\ eq(g,v). \qquad \neg eq(f,g) \leftarrow eq(f,v_f),\ eq(g,v_g).$$

The next definition will be used later to link answer sets of ASP{f} programs and of their ASP-completions. Let $\Sigma = \langle \mathcal{C}, \mathcal{F}, \mathcal{R} \rangle$ S be a set of seed literals from Σ. The *ASP-completion* of S ($c(S)$) is:

$$\begin{aligned}
c(S) = {} & \alpha(S) \ \cup \\
& \{\neg eq(t,v') \mid t = v \in S \wedge v \in \delta(t) \wedge v' \in \delta(t) \wedge v \neq v'\} \ \cup \\
& \{eq(f,g) \mid f = v \in S \wedge v \in \delta(f) \wedge g = v \in S \wedge v \in \delta(g)\} \ \cup \\
& \{\neg eq(f,g) \mid f = v_f \in S \wedge v_f \in \delta(f) \wedge g = v_g \in S \wedge v_g \in \delta(g) \wedge v_f \neq v_g\}
\end{aligned}$$

Intuitively, the ASP-completion of a set S of seed literals adds to S the dependent t-literals that are ASP{f}-entailed by S.

We are now ready to state the main results of this section on the relationship between ASP and ASP{f}.

Proposition 4. *For every ASP{f} program Π and every consistent set A of seed literals, $\alpha(\Pi^A) = \alpha(\Pi)^{c(A)}$.*

Proposition 5. *For every ASP{f} program Π: (1) if A is an answer set of Π then $c(A)$ is an answer set of $\gamma(\Pi)$; (2) if B is an answer set of $\gamma(\Pi)$ then there exists A such that $B = c(A)$ and A is an answer set of Π.*

From Propositions 4 and 5, the following properties follow:

Proposition 6. *The task of deciding whether a consistent set of seed literals is an answer set of an ASP{f} program is coNP-complete. The task of finding an answer set of an ASP{f} program is Σ_2^P-complete.*

The same propositions also allow to extend the Splitting Set Theorem [11] to ASP{f}. Let us call *splitting set* for an ASP{f} program Π a set U of seed literals such that, for every rule $r \in \Pi$, if $head(r) \cap U \neq \emptyset$, then $body(r) \subseteq U$. The set of rules of $r \in \Pi$ such that $body(r) \subseteq U$ is denoted by $b_U(\Pi)$. The *partial evaluation*, $e_U(\Pi, X)$ of Π with respect to U and set of seed literals X is the set containing, for every $r \in \Pi$ such that $pos(r) \cap U \subseteq X$ and $neg(r) \cap U$ is disjoint from X, a rule r', where $head(r') = head(r)$, $pos(r') = pos(r) \setminus U$ and $neg(r') = neg(r) \setminus U$. We say that a *solution* to Π with respect to U is a pair $\langle X, Y \rangle$ of sets of seed literals such that (1) X is an answer set for $b_U(\Pi)$; (2) Y is an answer set for $e_U(\Pi \setminus b_U(\Pi), X)$; (3) $X \cup Y$ is consistent.

Proposition 7. *A set A of seed literals is an answer set of ASP{f} program Π if and only if $A = X \cup Y$ for some solution $\langle X, Y \rangle$ to Π with respect to U.*

6 Conclusions and Future Work

In this paper we have defined the syntax and semantics of an extension of ASP that supports the direct use of non-Herbrand functions. As we have discussed throughout the paper, the ability to represent directly non-Herbrand functions has important advantages from both a knowledge-representation perspective, a practical perspective, and the perspective of solver performance. Compared to other approaches for the introduction of non-Herbrand functions in ASP, our language is more "conservative", in that it is intentionally defined so as to allow for the use of the same knowledge representation strategies of ASP. Because the definition of the semantics of ASP{f} is based on the one from [9], it allows for a comparatively simple incorporation in the new language of certain extensions of ASP such as weak constraints, probabilistic constructs and consistency-restoring rules. The simplicity of the modification of the original semantics makes it also relatively straightforward to extend properties of ASP programs to ASP{f} programs.

Although the results from the previous section could in principle be used to implement an ASP{f} solver, the simplicity of our modification to the semantics from [9] makes it possible to extend state-of-the-art ASP solvers to provide direct support for

ASP{f}. We have implemented an ASP{f} solver using this strategy and compared its performance to the performance obtained with the translations to normal logic programs described in [6] and [10]. In our preliminary experimental results, the performance of our ASP{f} solver is consistently more than an order of magnitude better than the performance obtained with the translation to normal logic programs.

A topic that is not addressed in this paper, is that of expressions with nested non-Herbrand functions. For example, in the language of [6] it is possible to write an expression such as $mother(father(mother(X)))$, and in the language of [12] one can write a rule such as $reached(hc(X)) \leftarrow reached(X)$. Although these expressions can be encoded in ASP{f} using additional variables (e.g. $reached(Y) \leftarrow reached(X),\ Y = hc(X)$), we believe that a more direct support for expressions with nested non-Herbrand functions in ASP{f} could not only allow for more compact rules, but could also be effectively exploited for an efficient implementation of the ASP{f} solver.

Acknowledgments. We would like to thank Michael Gelfond, Daniela Inclezan and Stefan Woltran for useful feedback and suggestions.

References

1. Balduccini, M., Gelfond, M.: Diagnostic reasoning with A-Prolog. Journal of Theory and Practice of Logic Programming (TPLP) 3(4-5), 425–461 (2003)
2. Baral, C.: Knowledge Representation, Reasoning, and Declarative Problem Solving. Cambridge University Press (January 2003)
3. Baral, C., Gelfond, M., Rushton, N.: Probabilistic reasoning with answer sets. Journal of Theory and Practice of Logic Programming (TPLP) 9(1), 57–144 (2009)
4. Baselice, S., Bonatti, P.A.: A Decidable Subclass of Finitary Programs. Journal of Theory and Practice of Logic Programming (TPLP) 10(4-6), 481–496 (2010)
5. Buccafurri, F., Leone, N., Rullo, P.: Adding Weak Constraints to Disjunctive Datalog. In: Proceedings of the 1997 Joint Conference on Declarative Programming APPIA-GULP-PRODE (1997)
6. Cabalar, P.: Functional Answer Set Programming. Journal of Theory and Practice of Logic Programming (TPLP) 11, 203–234 (2011)
7. Calimeri, F., Cozza, S., Ianni, G., Leone, N.: Enhancing ASP by Functions: Decidable Classes and Implementation Techniques. In: Proceedings of the Twenty-Fourth Conference on Artificial Intelligence, pp. 1666–1670 (2010)
8. Gebser, M., Ostrowski, M., Schaub, T.: Constraint Answer Set Solving. In: Hill, P.M., Warren, D.S. (eds.) ICLP 2009. LNCS, vol. 5649, pp. 235–249. Springer, Heidelberg (2009)
9. Gelfond, M., Lifschitz, V.: Classical Negation in Logic Programs and Disjunctive Databases. New Generation Computing 9, 365–385 (1991)
10. Lifschitz, V.: Logic Programs with Intensional Functions (Preliminary Report). In: ICLP11 Workshop on Answer Set Programming and Other Computing Paradigms, ASPOCP 2011 (July 2011)
11. Lifschitz, V., Turner, H.: Splitting a logic program. In: Proceedings of the 11th International Conference on Logic Programming (ICLP 1994), pp. 23–38 (1994)
12. Lin, F., Wang, Y.: Answer Set Programming with Functions. In: Proceedings of the International Conference on Principles of Knowledge Representation and Reasoning (KR 2008), pp. 454–465 (2008)

13. Marek, V.W., Truszczynski, M.: Stable Models and an Alternative Logic Programming Paradigm. In: The Logic Programming Paradigm: a 25-Year Perspective, pp. 375–398. Springer, Berlin (1999)
14. Syrjänen, T.: Omega-Restricted Logic Programs. In: Eiter, T., Faber, W., Truszczyński, M. (eds.) LPNMR 2001. LNCS (LNAI), vol. 2173, pp. 267–279. Springer, Heidelberg (2001)
15. Wang, Y., You, J.-H., Yuan, L.-Y., Zhang, M.: Weight Constraint Programs with Functions. In: Erdem, E., Lin, F., Schaub, T. (eds.) LPNMR 2009. LNCS, vol. 5753, pp. 329–341. Springer, Heidelberg (2009)

The Inverse Lambda Calculus Algorithm for Typed First Order Logic Lambda Calculus and Its Application to Translating English to FOL

Chitta Baral, Marcos Alvarez Gonzalez, and Aaron Gottesman

School of Computing, Informatics, and Decision Systems Engineering, Arizona State University, Tempe, AZ

Abstract. In order to answer questions and solve problems that require deeper reasoning with respect to a given text, it is necessary to automatically translate English sentences to formulas in an appropriate knowledge representation language. This paper focuses on a method to translate sentences to First-Order Logic (FOL). Our approach is inspired by Montague's use of lambda calculus formulas to represent the meanings of words and phrases. Since our target language is FOL, the meanings of words and phrases are represented as FOL-lambda formulas. In this paper we present algorithms that allow one to construct FOL-lambda formulas in an inverse manner. Given a sentence and its meaning and knowing the meaning of several words in the sentence our algorithm can be used to obtain the meaning of the other words in that sentence. In particular the two algorithms take as input two FOL-lambda formulas G and H and compute a FOL-lambda formula F such that F with input G, denoted by $F@G$, is H; respectively, $G@F = H$. We then illustrate our algorithm and present soundness, completeness and complexity results, and briefly mention the use of our algorithm in a NL Semantics system that translates sentences from English to formulas in formal languages.

1 Introduction

Our overall goal is to translate English to formal logics and Knowledge Representation (KR) languages. In this, our approach is to use λ-calculus formulas [1] to represent the meaning of words, phrases and sentences as previously done in [2], [3], [4] and [5]. To construct the meaning of a sentence from the meaning of its constituent words and phrases we use Combinatory Categorial Grammar (CCG) [6]. A big challenge in the above approach is to come up with the λ-calculus formulas that represent the meaning of the words. In some of the above mentioned works, they were either constructed by the authors or generated by a hand crafted set of rules. However, such an approach is not scalable. By analyzing how a human would come up with the λ-calculus formulas of words we noticed that at times a human, given G and H, would try to construct a formula F such that $F@G = H$ or $G@F = H$.

E. Erdem et al. (Eds.): Correct Reasoning, LNCS 7265, pp. 40–56, 2012.

We illustrate the basic idea of inverse application of FOL-λ-calculus formulas and how they can be used in constructing the FOL-λ-calculus expressions of words through the following example. Here we take an example from the database querying domain of [7] that is presented in Table 1.

Table 1. CCG and λ-calculus derivations for "Texas borders a state"

Texas	borders	a	state
NP	$(S\backslash NP)/NP$	NP/NP	NP
NP	$(S\backslash NP)/NP$	NP	
NP	$(S\backslash NP)$		
	S		

Texas	borders	a	state
texas	$\lambda w.\lambda x.(w@\lambda y.borders(y,x))$	???	$\lambda x.state(x)$
texas	$\lambda w.\lambda x.(w@\lambda y.borders(y,x))$	???	
texas	???		
	$\exists x.[state(x) \wedge borders(x, texas)]$		

In Table 1 it is assumed that one knows the meaning or translation of the sentence "Texas borders a state" and knows the FOL-λ-calculus formulas for "Texas", "borders", and "state". But the semantic representation for the word "a" is not known. The first step to compute this missing semantic representation is to take the meaning of the sentence "Texas borders a state" and the meaning of the word "Texas" to compute the semantic representation of "borders a state". But to do that one needs to know or a-priori decide whether it is appropriate to use the meaning of "Texas" as an input to the meaning of "borders a state" or vice versa. Traditional grammars such as Context Free Grammars do not help us in this. On the other hand, Combinatory Categorial Grammars (CCGs) [8] provide us directionality information that can be used in deciding which is the input and which is the function.

In Table 1 the top part gives a CCG parse of the sentence "Texas borders a state". The various symbols correspond to basic categories; "S" represents a sentence, "NP" represents a noun phrase; and more complex categories are formed using "\" and "/" slashes which specify directionality. For instance, the category "$S\backslash NP$" specifies that when a phrase corresponding to that category is concatenated on the left with a phrase of category "NP" , then the resulting phrase is of the category "S"; i.e., a sentence. Intuitively, a non-transitive verb has a category "$S\backslash NP$", meaning that if a noun phrase is added on the left, we get a sentence. Similarly, the category "NP/NP" means that a phrase of that category concatenated on the right by a phrase of category "NP" results in a phrase of the category "NP".

The phrase "Texas" has a category "NP" and it is being applied from the right to "borders a state". Therefore, if we take H as the meaning of the sentence and G as the meaning of "Texas", we can see by inspection that an F, the meaning of "borders a state", such that $F@G = H$ can be $F = \lambda y.\exists x.[state(x) \wedge borders(x, y)]$.

Now we can take H as the meaning of "borders a state" and G as the meaning of "borders", which has category $(S\backslash NP)/NP$, and we can can find the meaning of F, for "a state". Since "a state" has category NP and is applied to the right of "borders", we need to find F such that $G@F = H$ which can be $F = \lambda y.\exists x.[state(x) \wedge y@x]$. Finally, with H being the expression for "a state" and G being the expression for "state", with category NP, we can obtain F, a representation for "a", with category NP/NP. Therefore, we need $F@G = H$, which can be $F = \lambda z.\lambda y.\exists x.[z@x \wedge y@x]$. This is the typed first-order λ-calculus representation for the simple word "a". But how exactly did we compute it?

The main goal of this paper is to address that and present algorithms which are capable of automatically computing F such that $F@G = H$ or $G@F = H$. It is this task we refer to as the *Inverse λ-Problem* and our algorithms as *Inverse λ-Algorithms.* The algorithm that computes F such that $F@G = H$, we call $Inverse_L$, while the second algorithm which computes F such that $G@F = H$, we call $Inverse_R$. Although our algorithms are defined in a way that they can be useful with respect to multiple KR languages, in this paper we focus on First-Order Logic as the KR language.

To help in showing the correctness and applicability of our $Inverse_L$ and $Inverse_R$ algorithms we need to recap the notion of typed λ first order theories and the notion of order in such theories, as these notions will be used when we present the soundness, completeness and complexity results of our Inverse λ-Algorithms. For example, the completeness result is with respect to typed first order theories up to the second order. This recapping is done in Section 2.

The rest of this paper is organized as follows. In Section 3 we present the Inverse λ-Algorithms. In Section 4 we illustrate our algorithms with respect to several examples. In Section 5 we show a use case example. In section 6 we present the complexity, soundness and completeness results. In Section 7 we discuss related work and other approaches in solving the Inverse λ-Problem. Finally, in Section 8 we conclude and briefly mention the companion learning based natural language semantics system that uses our algorithms as described in [9].

Overall, the main contributions of this paper are the development of the Inverse λ-Algorithms for typed λ first order theories and the presentation of soundness, completeness and complexity results for these algorithms.

2 Background

Montague, [10], was the first to suggest that natural languages need not be treated differently from formal languages and they could have formal semantics. The approach of using λ-calculus to represent the meaning of words and λ-application as a mechanism to construct the meaning of phrases and sentences is also considered to originate from Montague. As mentioned before, that is also our approach.

However, to further ground the notion of "meaning" (or semantics) it is useful to have a notion of models of λ-calculus expressions. Such notions also allow us to evaluate our natural language meaning representations. Both untyped and typed

λ-calculus can be characterized using models, but the one that has had the most impact on natural language semantics is typed λ-calculus, as creating models for typed λ-calculus theories is somewhat simple. When we refer to model, we are looking for a semantic tool that can give us two elements: the entities that we have in our domain, and for every element in our signature, the semantic value associated with it.

We will use the "Simply Typed Lambda Calculus" of Church (1940), since it is most commonly used in linguistics. In this theory, there is only one type constructor, $\rightarrow$, to build function types and each term has a single type associated with it [11]. The books [12] and [13] are good reference points for typed lambda calculus.

2.1 Typed First-Order Logic Lambda Calculus

First-Order Logic has been widely studied and used for many years. Since a large body of research in natural language semantics has focused on translating natural language to first-order logic we focus our Inverse λ-Algorithms on it, particularly on Typed First-Order Logic Lambda Calculus. For obtaining formal results, we need to define the signature of our language, the construction of typed terms and typed formulas, and the notion of sub-terms of a typed term in the language.

We start by introducing the signature of the Typed First-Order Logic Lambda Calculus Language (Typed FOL Lambda Calculus). It consists of:

- The lambda operator (also called the lambda-abstractor) λ, the lambda application @, the parenthesis (,), [,].
- For every type a, an infinite set of variables $v_{n,a}$ for each natural number n and a (possibly empty) set of constants c_a.
- The quantifiers $\forall$ and $\exists$, the equality symbol $=$, the connectives $\neg$, $\vee$, $\wedge$, $\rightarrow$.
- Predicates symbols and function symbols of any arity n.

Next, we introduce the set of types that are going to be used with Typed FOL Lambda Calculus, in conjunction with the definition of the semantics of types assigned to the different expressions of the language. We will follow the principles presented in [14], where D_a represents the set of possible objects (*denotations*) that describe the meanings of expressions of type a. Thus, denotations are the objects of the language that correspond to a given type.

The *set of types* Δ is defined recursively as follows:

- e is a type.
- t is a type.
- If a and b are types, then $(a \rightarrow b)$ is a type.

Let E be a given domain of entities. Then the semantics of the types are defined as:

- $D_e = E$.
- $D_t = \{0, 1\}$ the set of truth values.
- $D_{a \to b}$ = the set of functions from D_a to D_b.

These letters are commonly used in the linguistics literature. An expression of type e denotes individuals that belong to the domain of our model, expressions of type t denote truth values and they will be assigned to expressions that can be evaluated to a truth value in our model. Expressions of type $(a \to b)$ denote functions whose input is in D_a and whose output values are in D_b. For example, the type $e \to t$ corresponds to functions from entities to truth values.

We continue with the definitions for FOL typed term and FOL typed λ-calculus formula. A *FOL atomic term* is a constant or a variable of any type a. If $t_1, ..., t_n$ are FOL atomic terms, and f is a function symbol, $f(t_1, ..., t_n)$ is also a FOL atomic term of type e.

Definition 1. *The elements of the set Δ_α of FOL typed terms of type α are inductively defined as follows:*

1. *For each type a, every FOL atomic term of type a belongs to Δ_a.*
2. *If P is a predicate symbol of arity n and $t_1, ..., t_n$ are FOL atomic terms, then $P(t_1, ..., t_n)$ is a FOL typed atomic formula that belongs to Δ_t.*
3. *For any types a and b, if $\alpha \in \Delta_{a \to b}$ and $\beta \in \Delta_a$, then $\alpha @ \beta \in \Delta_b$.*
4. *For any types a and b, if u is a variable of type a and $\alpha \in \Delta_b$ has free occurrences of the variable u, then $\lambda u.\alpha \in \Delta_{a \to b}$ and the free occurrences of u are now bound to the abstractor λu.*[1]
5. *If $\alpha \in \Delta_t$ and $\beta \in \Delta_t$, then $\alpha \vee \beta$, $\alpha \wedge \beta$ and $\alpha \to \beta \in \Delta_t$.*
6. *If $\alpha \in \Delta_t$, then $\neg\, \alpha \in \Delta_t$.*
7. *If α and $\beta \in \Delta_e$, then $(\alpha = \beta) \in \Delta_t$.*
8. *For any type a, if $\alpha \in \Delta_t$, and u is a variable of type a, then $\forall u \alpha$ and $\exists u \alpha$ $\in \Delta_t$.*

A *typed FOL λ-calculus formula* is a FOL typed term of type a where every variable is bound to an abstractor (quantifier variables may not) and every abstractor binds to a variable. These conditions ensure that first-order formulas are obtained when the typed FOL λ-calculus formula is in β-normal[2] form and there are no more λ-operators. They also correspond to the definition of closed and λI terms from classical lambda calculus theory.

Let us show an example. Consider the typed FOL formula $\lambda x.person(x)$, which has type $e \to t$. In this case, the variable x is a typed variable ranging over the entities of the domain and therefore it has type e. When an individual from the domain, such as the typed constant of type e, "John", is applied to the formula, we obtain a First Order Formula $person(John)$ which is of type t. The formula is no more than a function from individuals to truth values.

[1] An occurrence of a variable x in a typed term P is bound iff it is in the scope of an occurrence of λx in P, otherwise it is free. Occurrence is defined in Definition 2.

[2] A typed FOL λ-calculus formula is in β-normal form if no β-redex occurrence is possible. An example of a β-redex is a typed term of the form $(\lambda v.v)@(John)$.

This illustrates the signature for Typed FOL λ-calculus and shows how we can specify a model with a domain of entities and a function to assign semantics to elements of the signature. With such a model, we can choose an interpretation for the formula $\lambda x.person(x)$ where only those entities of the domain that belong to the set of the predicate *person* would return the value *true* as output of the function. Therefore the interpretation of $\lambda x.person(x)@John$ would be the same as the one for $person(John)$ in the model. This is assured by the well-typed application that takes place between the formula $e \to t$ and the argument e, where a well-typed application is one where the type of the argument is the same as the "input" type of the function receiving it. In general, types are in charge of regulating which applications are possible and when both argument and function have the correct types, we have a *well-typed* expression.

We end this sub-section with three more definitions that will be used by the Inverse λ-Algorithms.

Definition 2 (Occurrence). *The relation P occurs in Q is defined by induction on Q as follows:*

- *A FOL typed term P occurs in P.*
- *If P occurs in M or in N, then P occurs in M@N.*
- *If P occurs in M, then P occurs in* $\lambda x.M$.
- *If P occurs in* ϕ *or P occurs in* ψ, *then P occurs in* $\phi \vee \psi$, $\phi \wedge \psi$, $\phi \to \psi$.
- *If P occurs in* ϕ, *then P occurs in* $\neg\phi$.
- *If P occurs in* ϕ, *then P occurs in* $\forall u\phi$ *and* $\exists u\phi$.
- *If P occurs in* ϕ *or P occurs in* ψ, *then P occurs in* $\phi = \psi$.
- *If P occurs in any typed term* t_i, *then P occurs in* $f(t_1, ..., t_n)$. *Where f is a predicate symbol or a function symbol.*

A *sub-term* of a λ-calculus term F is any term P that occurs in F [13].

Example 1. Consider the typed FOL λ-calculus formula $J = \lambda w.\lambda u.(man(John) \wedge w@\lambda z.(loves(z,u)))$. The typed terms $loves(z,u)$, $man(John)$, $\lambda z.(loves(z,u))$, and w occur in J, and hence, are some of the sub-terms of J. However, λw is not a sub-term.

Definition 3 (FOL λ-component). *Constants, quantifier variables, connectives* $\neg$, $\wedge$, $\vee$ *and* $\to$, *quantifiers* $\exists$ *and* $\forall$, *predicates and function symbols, and the equality symbol = are denoted as FOL* λ*-components. The set of FOL* λ*-components of a formula J is identified as* $LC(J)$.

Basically, all elements of the typed FOL λ-calculus signature except for the λ-application symbol, λ-abstractor and their corresponding bound variables, are considered FOL λ-components.

Example 2. Consider the typed FOL λ-calculus formula $J = \lambda w.\lambda u.(man(John) \wedge w@\lambda z.(loves(z,u)))$. $LC(J) = \{man, John, \wedge, loves\}$.

2.2 Type Order

So far we have introduced typed λ-calculus and the different types that will be assigned to typed terms. We now define the notion of an order that is associated with these types and that separates typed λ-calculus formulas to several classes. We will use the notion of orders to show that the Inverse λ-Algorithm is a complete algorithm for typed λ-calculus formulas up to order two. We start with a definition of type order and some intuition behind it:

Definition 4. *The order of a type is defined as:*

- *Base types e and t have order 0.*
- *For function types,* $order(a \rightarrow b) = max(order(a) + 1, order(b))$.

This definition is almost identical to the one introduced in [15], where base types have order one. We, however, follow the intuition introduced in [2]. Some examples of typed FOL λ-calculus formulas of different orders are the following:

- Order zero: $man(Vincent)$. It has type t.
- Order one: $\lambda v.\lambda u.(v \rightarrow u)$. It has type $e \rightarrow (e \rightarrow t)$.
- Order two: $\lambda v.\lambda u.(v@Mia \wedge u@Vincent)$. It has type $(e \rightarrow t) \rightarrow ((e \rightarrow t) \rightarrow t)$.
- Order three: $\lambda w.(w@(\lambda z.(happy(z))))$. It has type $((e \rightarrow t) \rightarrow t) \rightarrow t$.

With these simple examples, one can see the intuition behind the order of typed FOL λ-calculus formulas. Formulas of order zero correspond to expressions with base types. Formulas of order one correspond to expressions which start with a series of λ-abstractors followed by a FOL formula with variables bound to the initial λ-abstractors.

Formulas of order two extend the expressions allowed in order one by including applications. Formulas of order zero can be applied to variables inside the formula. Formulas of order three extend those present in order two by allowing λ-abstractors inside the expression after the initial λ-abstractors. In this case, formulas of order one can be applied to variables, this is why now, we can find λ-abstractors at the beginning and in the middle of the formulas. These claims can be easily proved by contradiction using the given definitions.

3 The Inverse λ-Algorithms

We start this section by presenting a lemma and some properties that are important for the Inverse λ-Algorithms and that are helpful to understand its completeness. After this introduction, the Inverse λ-operators of the Algorithm will be defined along with the explanation of its different parts. We start by presenting a lemma based on Lemma 1B1.1 from [13].

Lemma 1. *Given typed FOL λ-calculus formulas H, G and F, if G@F β-reduces*[3] *to H, then LC(G@F) = LC(H).*

Proof. Our definition of typed FOL λ-calculus formulas implies that all variables that appear in a formula are bound (except quantifier variables). Therefore, when one formula is applied to another and β-contractions are performed, none of the λ-components of those formulas will be modified by the application due to the definition of application in λ-calculus. In case of clashes with quantifier variables, α-conversion[4] would be used as usual. □

With this lemma, it can be shown that given typed FOL λ-calculus formulas H, G and F such that $H = G@F$ or $H = F@G$, any FOL λ-component of H must be contained in either F or G (since we obtain H from these two formulas), and it can not be the case that a FOL λ-component in F or G will not appear in H (since there would be no proper second formula in the application that gives us H). This characteristic of the structure of the application is an essential part of the Inverse λ-Algorithms and the way in which it constructs the missing formula out of the other two. Also, by the way we defined typed FOL λ-calculus formulas, we eliminated the case where we set F to be $\lambda v.H$ which does not provide any semantic meaning to the expression that F represents but would be a valid classic λ-calculus formula for the application. Our aim is to keep the semantic information between F and G, which combined, give the semantics of H. By assuring that the information in G will lead us to obtain the semantics of H, we are providing F with a semantic representation that contains the value we are looking for.

3.1 The Inverse λ-Operators

This sub-section presents the formal definition of the two components of the Inverse λ-Algorithms, $Inverse_L$ and $Inverse_R$. First, some definitions and explanations necessary to help understand the terminology used in defining $Inverse_L$ and $Inverse_R$ will be introduced. The objective of $Inverse_L$ and $Inverse_R$, is that given typed λ-calculus formulas H and G, the formula F is computed such that $F@G = H$ and $G@F = H$. The different symbols used in the algorithm and their meanings are defined as follows:

- Let G, H and J represent typed λ-calculus formulas, J^1,J^2,...,J^n represent typed terms; and v, w and v_1,...,v_n represent variables. Typed terms that are sub-terms of a typed term J^i are denoted as J^i_k.

If the formulas being processed within the algorithm do not satisfy any of the conditions, then the algorithm returns *null*.

[3] A typed term P β-reduces to Q if one can obtain Q after a finite sequence of β-contractions from P allowing for substitution of bound variables. The typed term $(\lambda v.v)@John$ β-reduces to $John$. We refer the reader to [12,13] for additional lambda calculus definitions.

[4] α-conversion allows one to change the bound variables of a λ-expression if doing so does not affect the meaning of the expression. For example $\lambda x.x$ α-converts to $\lambda y.y$.

Definition 5 (operator :). *Consider two lists (of same length) of typed λ-calculus formulas $A_1, ..., A_n$ and $B_1, .., B_n$, and a typed FOL λ-calculus formula H. The result of the operation $H(A_1, ..., A_n : B_1, .., B_n)$ is defined as:*

1. *find the first occurrence of formulas $A_1, ..., A_n$ in H.*
2. *replace each A_i by the corresponding B_i.*
3. *find the next occurrence of formulas $A_1, ..., A_n$ in H and go to 2. Otherwise, stop.*

Next, we present the definition of the two inverse operators:

Definition 6 ($Inverse_L(H, G)$). *Given G and H:*

1. *G is $\lambda v.v$*
   - $F = \lambda v.(v@H)$
2. *G is a sub-term of H*
   - $F = \lambda v.H(G : v)$
3. *G is not $\lambda v.v$, $(J^1(J_1^1, ..., J_m^1), J^2(J_1^2, ..., J_m^2), \ ... \ , J^n(J_1^n, ..., J_m^n))$ are sub-terms of H, and $\forall J^i \in H$, G is $\lambda v_1, ..., v_s.J^i(J_1^i, ..., J_m^i : v_{k_1}, ..., v_{k_m})$[5] with $1 \leq s \leq m$ and $\forall p$, $1 \leq k_p \leq s$.*
   - $F = \lambda w.H(J^1, ..., J^n : (w@J_{k_1}^1, ..., @J_{k_m}^1), ..., (w@J_{k_1}^n, ..., @J_{k_m}^n))$ *where each J_{k_p} maps to a different v_{k_p} in G.*
4. *H is $\lambda v_1, ..., v_i.J$ and $f(\sigma_{i+1}, ..., \sigma_s)$ is a sub-term of J, G is $\lambda w.J(f(\sigma_{i+1}, ..., \sigma_s) : w@\sigma_{k_1}@...@\sigma_{k_s})$ with $\forall p$, $i + 1 \leq k_p \leq s$.*
   - $F = \lambda w \lambda v_1, ..., v_i.(w@\lambda v_{i+1}, ..., v_s.(f(\sigma_{i+1}, ..., \sigma_s : v_{k_1}, ..., v_{k_s})))$

Definition 7 ($Inverse_R(H, G)$). *Given G and H:*

1. *G is $\lambda v.v@J$*
   - $F = Inverse_L(H, J)$
2. *J is a sub-term of H and G is $\lambda v.H(J : v)$*
   - $F = J$
3. *G is not $\lambda v.v@J$, $(J^1(J_1^1, ..., J_m^1), J^2(J_1^2, ..., J_m^2), \ ... \ , J^n(J_1^n, ..., J_m^n))$ are sub-terms of H and G is $\lambda w.H(J^1(J_1^1, ..., J_m^1), ..., J^n(J_1^n, ..., J_m^n) : (w@J_{k_1}^1, ..., @J_{k_m}^1),$
   $..., (w@J_{k_1}^n, ..., @J_{k_m}^n))$ with $1 \leq s \leq m$ and $\forall p$, $1 \leq k_p \leq m$.*
   - $F = \lambda v_1, ..., v_s.J^1(J_1^1, ..., J_m^1 : v_{k_1}, ..., v_{k_m})$.
4. *H is $\lambda v_1, ..., v_i.J$ and $f(\sigma_{i+1}, ..., \sigma_s)$ is a sub-term of J, G is $\lambda w.\lambda v_1, ..., v_i.(w@ \lambda v_{i+1}, ..., v_s.(f(\sigma_{i+1}, ..., \sigma_s : v_{k_1}, ..., v_{k_s})))$ with $\forall p$, $i + 1 \leq k_p \leq s$.*
   - $F = \lambda w.J(f(\sigma_{i+1}, ..., \sigma_s) : w@\sigma_{k_1}@...@\sigma_{k_s})$

---

[5] When the formula G is being generated, the indexes of the abstractors $\lambda v_1, ..., v_s$ must be assigned to bind the variables from $v_{k_1}, ..., v_{k_m}$ in such a way that G is a valid formula.

4 Examples

In this section we illustrate with examples each of the different conditions of the two algorithms. In each example λ-calculus formulas G and H are given and we want to find F using the given case of the Inverse λ-Algorithms. This section shows how the algorithms apply pattern matching to calculate F in the various cases. A use case example follows in the next section.

Inverse$_{\mathbf{L}}$ - Case 1
$H = woman(Mia)$ and $G = \lambda x.x$. Then,
$F = \lambda x.(x@H)$, and in this case $F = \lambda x.(x@woman(Mia))$.
To demonstrate correctness we now apply G to F to get H:
$F \ @ \ G = \lambda x.(x@woman(Mia)) \ @ \ \lambda x.x$
$\quad = (\lambda x.x@woman(Mia)) = woman(Mia) = H.$

Inverse$_{\mathbf{L}}$ - Case 2
$H = \lambda u.(man(Vincent) \wedge u \rightarrow man(Vincent))$ and $G = man(Vincent)$.
G is a sub-term of H. Therefore,
$F = \lambda v.H(G : v)$, which in this case yields $F = \lambda v.H(man(Vincent) : v)$.
We substitute every appearance of G in H by the variable "v" obtaining
$F = \lambda v.\ \lambda u.(v \wedge u \rightarrow v)$.

Inverse$_{\mathbf{L}}$ - Case 3
$H = \lambda u.(woman(Mia) \wedge happy(Mia) \wedge man(Vincent) \wedge happy(Vincent)$
$\wedge\ loves(Mia, u))$, and $G = \lambda v.\lambda w.(v \wedge happy(w))$
G is not $\lambda v.v$. That satisfies the first condition.
To match the formula of G, the following are assigned the subterms of H:
$J^1 = woman(Mia) \wedge happy(Mia)$
$\quad J^1_1 = woman(Mia)$ and $J^1_2 = Mia$ (from $happy(Mia)$).
$J^2 = man(Vincent) \wedge happy(Vincent)$
$\quad J^2_1 = man(Vincent)$ and $J^2_2 = Vincent$ (from $happy(Vincent)$).
That satisfies second condition.
The third condition is satisfied since $\forall J^i \in H$, $G = \lambda v_1.\lambda v_2.J^i(J^i_1, J^i_2 : v_1, v_2)$.
For example, for J^1:
$\quad G = \lambda v_1.\lambda v_2.J^1(woman(Mia), Mia : v_1, v_2) = \lambda v.\lambda w.(v \wedge happy(w))$.
Thus, $F = \lambda x.H((J^1 : x@J^1_1@J^1_2), (J^2 : x@J^2_1@J^2_2))$, which yields
$F = \lambda x.H((J^1 : x@woman(Mia)@Mia), (J^2 : x@man(Vincent)@Vincent))$,
$F = \lambda x.\lambda u.(x@woman(Mia)@Mia \wedge x@man(Vincent)@Vincent \wedge loves(Mia, u))$.

Inverse$_{\mathbf{L}}$ - Case 4
$H = \lambda u.(happy(Mia) \rightarrow lovesBefore(Mia, Vincent, u))$
$G = \lambda v.(happy(Mia) \rightarrow v@Vincent@Mia)$.
$H = \lambda v_1.J$ with $J = happy(Mia) \rightarrow lovesBefore(Mia, Vincent, v_1)$ and
$\quad f(\sigma_2, ..., \sigma_s) = lovesBefore(Mia, Vincent, u)$ where
$\quad \sigma_2 = Mia$ and $\sigma_3 = Vincent$, chosen to match the variable v in G.
Therefore, G can be seen to be $\lambda v.J(f(\sigma_{1+1}, \sigma_3) : v@\sigma_{k_{1+1}}@\sigma_{k_3})$.

Thus, $G = \lambda v.J(f(\sigma_2, \sigma_3) : v@\sigma_3@\sigma_2)$, which in this case yields
$G = \lambda v.J(f(Mia, Vincent) : v@Vincent@Mia)$.
Thus, both conditions are satisfied. So, F can be calculated as follows:
$F = \lambda w \lambda v_1(w@\lambda v_{1+1}, ..., v_3.(f(\sigma_{1+1}, ..., \sigma_3 : v_{k_{1+1}}, ..., v_{k_3}))),$
$F = \lambda w \lambda v_1(w@\lambda v_2, v_3.(f(\sigma_2, \sigma_3 : v_{k_2}, v_{k_3}))),$
$F = \lambda w \lambda v_1(w@\lambda v_2, v_3.(f(\sigma_2, \sigma_3 : v_3, v_2))),$
$F = \lambda w.\lambda v_1.(w@\lambda v_2, \lambda v_3.lovesBefore(v_3, v_2, v_1)).$

Inverse$_{\mathbf{R}}$ - Case 3
$H = loves(Mia, Vincent) \wedge loves(Mia, Robert)$
$G = \lambda v.(v@Mia@Vincent \wedge v@Mia@Robert)$
G is not $\lambda v.v@J$, since $J = Mia@Vincent \wedge v@Mia@Robert$ cannot be a formula by the definition. That satisfies the first condition.
From H, and chosen to match the input to the variable v of G, one has the following formulas that are sub-terms:
$J^1 = loves(Mia, Vincent)$
 $J^1_1 = Mia,\ J^1_2 = Vincent$
$J^2 = loves(Mia, Robert)$
 $J^2_1 = Mia,\ J^2_2 = Robert$
Therefore, G can be seen to be of the form:
$G = \lambda x.H((J^1(J^1_1, J^1_2) : x@J^1_{k_1}@J^1_{k_2}), (J^2(J^2_1, J^2_2) : x@J^2_{k_1}@J^2_{k_2}),$
$G = \lambda x.H((J^1(J^1_1, J^1_2) : x@J^1_1@J^1_2), (J^2(J^2_1, J^2_2) : x@J^2_1@J^2_2),$
$G = \lambda x.H((loves(Mia, Vincent) : x@Mia@Vincent), (loves(Mia, Robert) : x@Mia@Robert))$. Thus, the second condition of case 3 is satisfied.
Therefore, one can now calculate F:
$F = \lambda v_1, v_2.J^1(J^1_1, J^1_2 : v_1, v_2)$ and so $F = \lambda v_1.\lambda v_2.loves(v_1, v_2)$

5 Use Case Example

In this section, we revisit our earlier example and give another example to show how we can use the Inverse λ-Algorithms to obtain semantic representations for words when we have a sentence with its logical representation in typed first-order logic λ-calculus, the syntactic categories from CCG parsing and some semantic information. We again use an example from the database querying domain of [7].

Let us start with the sentences: "Texas borders a state.", and "What state borders Texas?". We will consider that our initial lexicon includes the semantics for simple nouns and verbs. If we obtain the output of a simplified CCG parsing with two categories "S" and "NP", and we add the semantics from our lexicon, we obtain what is presented in Table 2.

One can see in Table 2 that we are missing the semantic representation for the words "a" and "What". These two words are not part of our initial lexicon but using the Inverse λ-Algorithms we will be able to compute their corresponding typed first-order λ-calculus representation. Let us start with the first sentence. We can take the meaning of the sentence and the meaning of "Texas" to calculate the representation of "borders a state".

Table 2. CCG and λ-calculus derivations for "Texas borders a state.","What state borders Texas?".

Texas	borders	a	state	What	state	borders	Texas
NP	$(S\backslash NP)/NP$	NP/NP	NP	$S/(S\backslash NP)/NP$	NP	$(S\backslash NP)/NP$	NP
NP	$(S\backslash NP)/NP$	NP		$S/(S\backslash NP)/NP$	NP	$S\backslash NP$	
NP	$(S\backslash NP)$			$S/(S\backslash NP)$		$S\backslash NP$	
	S			S			

Texas	borders	a	state
texas	$\lambda w.\lambda x.(w@\lambda y.borders(y,x))$	???	$\lambda x.state(x)$
texas	$\lambda w.\lambda x.(w@\lambda y.borders(y,x))$	???	
texas	???		
	$\exists x.[state(x) \wedge borders(x, texas)]$		

What	state	borders	Texas
???	$\lambda x.state(x)$	$\lambda y.\lambda x.borders(x,y)$	texas
???	$\lambda x.state(x)$	$\lambda x.borders(x, texas)$	
???		$\lambda x.borders(x, texas)$	
$\lambda x.state(x) \wedge borders(x, texas)$			

We can see in the CCG tree that "borders a state" has category $(S\backslash NP)$ and therefore the λ-calculus expression will receive the word "Texas" from the left. Following this, if we take H as the meaning of the sentence and G as the meaning of "Texas", we can use $Inverse_L(H, G)$ to obtain the expression for "borders a state". In this case, option one of the algorithm is satisfied with *texas* as formula J and $F = \lambda y.\exists x.[state(x) \wedge borders(x, y)]$.

Now we have the expression for "borders a state" and "borders", we can calculate the expression of "a state" calling $Inverse_R(H, G)$ with H being the meaning for "borders a state" and G being "borders". Option four of the algorithm is satisfied and we obtain F as $\lambda y.\exists x.[state(x) \wedge y@x]$. Finally, we call $Inverse_L(H, G)$ with H being the expression for "a state" and G being "state" to obtain the desired representation for "a". In this case, option two of the algorithm is satisfied and $F = \lambda z.\lambda y.\exists x.[z@x \wedge y@x]$. This is the typed first-order λ-calculus representation for the simple word "a".

The process to obtain the word "What" from the second sentence follows the same idea as shown above. First we call $Inverse_L(H, G)$ with H being the meaning of the sentence and G being "borders Texas" to obtain the meaning of "What state". Option two of the algorithm is satisfied and $F = \lambda y.\lambda x.(state(x) \wedge y@x)$. Next, we call $Inverse_L(H, G)$ again with "What state" and "state" to obtain the desired meaning of "What". Option two of the algorithm is satisfied and $F = \lambda z.\lambda y.\lambda x.(z@x \wedge y@x)$.

Using the Inverse λ-Algorithms we have easily added to our lexicon the λ-calculus representation for the words "a" and "What".

6 Theorems

Theorem 1 (Soundness). *Given two typed FOL λ-calculus formulas H and G in β-normal form, if $Inverse_L(H, G)$ returns a non-null value F, then $H = F @ G$.*

Theorem 2 (Soundness). *Given two typed FOL λ-calculus formulas H and G in β-normal form, if* $Inverse_R(H, G)$ *returns a non-null value F, then* $H = G @ F$.

Theorem 3 (Completeness). *For any two typed FOL λ-calculus formulas H and G in β-normal form, where H is of order two or less, and G is of order one or less, if there exists a set of typed FOL λ-calculus formulas* Θ_F *of order two or less in β-normal form, such that* $\forall F_i \in \Theta_F$, $H = F_i@G$, *then* $Inverse_L(H, G)$ *will give us an F where* $F \in \Theta_F$.

Theorem 4 (Completeness). *For any two typed FOL λ-calculus formulas H and G of order two or less in β-normal form, if there exists a set of typed FOL λ-calculus formulas* Θ_F *of order one or less in β-normal form, such that* $\forall F_i \in \Theta_F$, $H = G@F_i$, *then* $Inverse_R(H, G)$ *will give us an F, where* $F \in \Theta_F$.

Theorem 5 ($Inverse_L$ complexity). *The* $Inverse_L$ *Algorithm runs in exponential time in the number of variables in G and polynomial time in the size of the formulas H and G.*

Theorem 6 ($Inverse_R$ complexity). *The* $Inverse_R$ *Algorithm runs in exponential time in the number of variables in G and polynomial time in the size of the formulas H and G.*

Due to space constraints, we will only comment on how the complexity, soundness and completeness proofs are structured. $Inverse_L$ has worst-case complexity in case 3. For every subterm of H it is necessary to check if a partial permutation of its subterms can be used to generate G. If G has k variables, then the number of permutations that needs to be checked is in worst case $\frac{n!}{(n-k)!}$ where n is the length of H. When k is small, as it is in most of the applications we have tested (see Section 8 below), the number of permutations becomes approximately $O(n^k)$.

The complexity of $Inverse_R$ is the same as $Inverse_L$ since $Inverse_L$ is called as a subroutine in case 1. All other cases of $Inverse_R$ run in polynomial time. Note that case 3 of $Inverse_R$ has polynomial complexity since the formulas given as input to the applications in G can be used to find the subterms of H that can generate them. Therefore, we do not have to search all permutation of the subterms as in $Inverse_L$.

The soundness proof shows how in each of the four cases of $Inverse_L$, the typed FOL λ-calculus formula H is obtained by applying F to G. The application $F@G$ is computed using the expressions from the algorithm for F and G, generating the expression for H given in the algorithm. The same reasoning is followed for $Inverse_R$.

The completeness proof is divided to six cases, which correspond to the six possible valid combinations of orders that H, F and G may have, such that the order of the terms will be less than 2. These are shown in Table 3. For each case, it is proven by contradiction that $Inverse_L$ and $Inverse_R$ return a formula F if one such F exists. It is done by assuming that they return a *null* value and

Table 3. Possible order combinations for F, G and H formulas, with $H = F@G$

H	F	G	FOL type examples for formula F
0	1	0	$e \to t$
1	1	0	$e \to (e \to t)$
2	2	0	$e \to ((e \to t) \to t)$
0	2	1	$(e \to t) \to t$
1	2	1	$(e \to t) \to (e \to t)$
2	2	1	$(e \to t) \to ((e \to t) \to t)$

reaching a contradiction at the end of the proof. In the process, each of the four conditions of the algorithms are analyzed, where it is shown that at least one of the conditions of the algorithm has been satisfied for each of the six cases.

7 Related Work

The problems solved by the Inverse λ-Algorithms are similar to two problems referred to in the literature as "higher-order matching" and "Interpolation problem". This problem consists of determining if a λ-calculus term, in the simply typed λ-calculus, is an instance of another. It can also be understood as solving the equation $M = N$ where M and N are simply typed λ-terms and N is a closed[6] term. More intuitively, the problem is to find a substitution σ assigning terms of consistent types to the free variables of M such that $\sigma(M)$ admits N as its normal form. A proof that third-order matching is decidable is presented in [16]. In literature about higher-order matching, the order of atomic types is generally 1. This slightly differs from the definition presented in this work. Thus, third order in [16] has to be understood as second order in this research.

The higher-order matching and interpolation problems are defined with respect to an extension of λ-calculus denoted as $\beta\eta$-calculus[7], while the Inverse λ-Algorithms follow the theory of β-calculus, since it is the theory most commonly used in linguistics. Another important difference is that in the case of $Inverse_L$ and $Inverse_R$, terms G,F and H are typed λ-calculus formulas that, by definition, have been set as closed and λI terms, and are also considered in β-normal form. The higher-order matching and interpolation problems do not enforce these restrictions in the terms involved. However, in essence, both approaches deal with the same problem. Thus, we argue that $Inverse_R$ and $Inverse_L$ can be considered special cases of the matching and interpolation problems , respectively (when we restrict the problem to β-calculus and only try to substitute for one variable in M).

However, the Inverse λ-Algorithms provide an important contribution. As it is stated in [15], the higher-order matching problem, in the general case, is undecidable when using β-calculus, as shown in [17]. $Inverse_R$ is an algorithm for

[6] A λ-expression is closed if no free variables occur in it

[7] $\beta\eta$-calculus allows for η-conversions as well as β-reductions. An η-conversion converts between $\lambda x.f@x$ and f whenever x does not appear as a free variable in f.

computing a subset of the third order matching problem under β-calculus. Also, the higher-order matching algorithm proposed in [16], where a set of solutions to a third order matching problem are enumerated, will not terminate if the problem admits no such set. In the case of $Inverse_R$, the algorithm will simply return a *null* value and terminate.

Another related work, [18,19], discusses two algorithms that solve the problem of learning word-to-meaning mappings extended to the field of typed λ-calculus. In [19], the algorithm introduced considers β-calculus and closed λI terms. This definition is very closely related to the $Inverse_R$ definition. However, the author refers to the problem that the algorithm presents with incompatibility between meaning of words already known and meaning of words obtained by the algorithm. Our approach does not present such problem. Another key difference refers to the assumptions made before executing the algorithm. In [18,19], there is a first phase where the learner, in some way, obtains the set of constants that form each word. In the case of the Inverse λ-Algorithms, the unknown representation of words in a sentence is obtained using the meaning of the sentence and the meaning of known words. There is no previous information needed about the unknown meaning.

The comparison with the works [15,16,18] is leading us to research the possible benefits of defining the Inverse λ-Algorithms in terms of $\beta\eta$-calculus, in order to use useful related results. This step will be approached in future work.

A more general notion of higher-order matching is the notion of "higher-order unification". The difficulty of higher-order unification is studied in [20,21]. In [22] a restricted version of higher-order unification is defined and used. They describe an algorithm which given h, finds pairs of logical expressions (f, g) such that either $f(g) = h$ or $\lambda x.f(g(x)) = h$. Note that in our Inverse λ-Algorithms the input consists of two expressions and the output is a single expression.

8 Implementation Success and Evaluation

The usefulness of the two Inverse λ-Algorithms is validated in the natural language learning system [9], which learns the semantic representations of words from sentences. The results obtained by the system in [9] are quite promising. A summary is presented in Table 4. The system outperforms earlier systems on F-measure for the two standard corpora GEOQUERY and CLANG.

In the table, *Inverse* and *Inverse+* are two different versions of the system. *Inverse* uses the two Inverse λ-Algorithms, $Inverse_L$ and $Inverse_R$ and a process called *generalization*, which generalizes the meaning of unknown words from known words based on the syntactic information received from the CCG parser. *Inverse+* adds trivial inverse results for some words and "on demand" *generalization*. *Inverse+i* considers the semantic representations "definec" and "definer" of the training data as the same element, with respect to CLANG.

The evaluation of the data was performed using 10 fold cross validation and the *C&C* parser from [6]. An equal number of train and test sentences were arbitrarily selected from the GEOQUERY and CLANG corpora. For more details about this system and its results, we refer the reader to [9].

Table 4. Performance results for GEOQUERY and CLANG

GEOQUERY	Precision	Recall	F-measure
Inverse+	93.41	89.04	91.17
Inverse	91.12	85.78	88.37

CLANG	Precision	Recall	F-measure
Inverse+i	87.67	79.08	83.15
Inverse+	85.74	76.63	80.92

9 Conclusion

In this work, we have presented two Inverse λ-Algorithms and have shown their application to typed first-order logic λ-calculus. With this algorithm we are able to automatically obtain semantic representations of unknown words using the information already available from known sentences and words. These two algorithms not only work for first-order logic, but with minor changes work for a group of other Knowledge Representation languages such as Answer Set Programming, and Linear Temporal Logic and Dynamic Logic; but formal results with respect to those languages need to be proven. For the algorithms we have developed a completeness proof up to second order expressions. Blackburn and Bos in [2] mention that natural language semantics rarely requires types above order three. Completeness results for third order expressions is the next step to extend this work and is part of our immediate future plans.

Acknowledgement. We thank Vladimir Lifschitz, Yuliya Lierler and Johan Bos for introducing us to the use of λ-calculus in characterizing natural language. We thank Juraj Dzifcak for implementing the inverse λ-Algorithms, building the system mentioned in Section 8 and doing the evaluations mentioned in that section. We thank Peter Schueller for his valuable comments. We acknowledge support by NSF (grant number 0950440), IARPA and ONR-MURI for this work.

References

1. Gamut, L.T.F.: Logic, Language, and Meaning. The University of Chicago Press (1991)
2. Blackburn, P., Bos, J.: Representation and Inference for Natural Language: A First Course in Computational Semantics. Center for the Study of Language (2005)
3. Zettlemoyer, L.S., Collins, M.: Online learning of relaxed ccg grammars for parsing to logical form. In: Proceedings of the 2007 Joint Conference on Empirical Methods in Natural Language Processing and Computational Natural Language Learning, pp. 678–687 (2007)
4. Baral, C., Dzifcak, J., Son, T.C.: Using answer set programming and lambda calculus to characterize natural language sentences with normatives and exceptions. In: AAAI 2008: Proceedings of the 23rd National Conference on Artificial Intelligence, pp. 818–823 (2008)
5. Dzifcak, J., Scheutz, M., Baral, C., Schermerhorn, P.: What to do and how to do it: translating natural language directives into temporal and dynamic logic representation for goal management and action execution. In: Robotics and Automation, ICRA 2009, pp. 4163–4168 (2009)

6. Clark, S., Curran, J.R.: Wide-coverage efficient statistical parsing with ccg and log-linear models. Computational Linguistics 33 (2007)
7. Zettlemoyer, L.S., Collins, M.: Learning to map sentences to logical form: Structured classification with probabilistic categorial grammars. In: 21th Annual Conference on Uncertainty in Artificial Intelligence, pp. 658–666 (2005)
8. Steedman, M.: The syntactic process. MIT Press (2000)
9. Baral, C., Dzifcak, J., Gonzalez, M.A., Zhou, J.: Using inverse lambda and generalization to translate english to formal languages. In: Proceedings of the 9th International Conference on Computational Semantics, ICWS 2011 (2011) (to appear)
10. Montague, R.: Formal Philosophy. In: Selected Papers of Richard Montague. Yale University Press, New Haven (1974)
11. Barendregt, H.: Lambda Calculi with Types, Handbook of Logic in Computer Science, vol. II. Oxford University Press (1992)
12. Hindley, J.: Introduction to Combinators and Lambda-Calculus. Cambridge University Press (1986)
13. Hindley, J.: Basic Simple Type Theory. Cambridge University Press (1997)
14. Barbara, H., Partee, A.T.M., Wall, R.E.: Mathematical Methods in Linguistics. Kluwer Academic Publishers (1990)
15. Stirling, C.: Decidability of higher-order matching. To appear Logical Methods in Computer Science 5(3) (2009)
16. Dowek, G.: Third order matching is decidable. Annals of Pure and Applied Logic 69(2-3), 135–155 (1994)
17. Loader, R.: Higher-order beta-matching is undecidable. Logic Journal of IGPL 11(1), 51–68 (2003)
18. Kanazawa, M.: Learning word-to-meaning mappings in logical semantics. In: Proceedings of the Thirteenth Amsterdam Colloquium, pp. 126–131 (2001)
19. Kanazawa, M.: Computing word meanings by interpolation. In: Proceedings of the Fourteenth Amsterdam Colloquium, pp. 157–162 (2003)
20. Huet, G.: The undecidability of unication in third order logic. Information and Control 22(3), 257–267 (1973)
21. Huet, G.: A unication algorithm for typed calculus. Theoretical Computer Science 1, 27–57 (1975)
22. Kwiatkowski, T., Zettlemoyer, L., Goldwater, S., Steedman, M.: Inducing probabilistic ccg grammars from logical form with higher-order unification. In: Proceedings of the Conference on Empirical Methods in Natural Language Processing, EMNLP (2010)

Parameterized Splitting: A Simple Modification-Based Approach*

Ringo Baumann[1], Gerhard Brewka[1], Wolfgang Dvořák[2], and Stefan Woltran[2]

[1] Leipzig University, Informatics Institute, Postfach 100920, 04009 Leipzig, Germany
{baumann,brewka}@informatik.uni-leipzig.de
[2] Vienna University of Technology, Institute of Information Systems, Favoritenstraße 9–11, A-1040 Vienna, Austria
{dvorak,woltran}@dbai.tuwien.ac.at

Abstract. In an important and much cited paper Vladimir Lifschitz and Hudson Turner have shown how, under certain conditions, logic programs under answer set semantics can be split into two disjoint parts, a "bottom" part and a "top" part. The bottom part can be evaluated independently of the top part. Results of the evaluation, i.e., answer sets of the bottom part, are then used to simplify the top part. To obtain answer sets of the original program one simply has to combine an answer set of the simplified top part with the answer set which was used to simplify this part. Similar splitting results were later proven for other nonmonotonic formalisms and also Dung style argumentation frameworks.

In this paper we show how the conditions under which splitting is possible can be relaxed. The main idea is to modify also the bottom part before the evaluation takes place. Additional atoms are used to encode conditions on answer sets of the top part that need to be fulfilled. This way we can split in cases where proper splitting is not possible. We demonstrate this idea for argumentation frameworks and logic programs.

1 Introduction

In an important and much cited paper Vladimir Lifschitz and Hudson Turner have shown how, under certain conditions, logic programs under answer set semantics can be split into two disjoint parts, a "bottom" part and a "top" part. The bottom part can be evaluated independently of the top part. Results of the evaluation, i.e., answer sets of the bottom part, are then used to simplify the top part. To obtain answer sets of the original program one simply has to combine an answer set of the simplified top part with the answer set which was used to simplify this part.

Splitting is a fundamental principle and has been investigated for several other nonmonotonic formalisms, including answer-set programming [13,7], default logic [15] and most recently argumentation [3,4,12]. It has important implications, both from the theoretical and from the practical point of view. On the the theoretical side, splitting allows for simplification of proofs showing properties of a particular formalism. On the practical side, splitting concepts are useful for solving since the possibility to compute

* This work has been funded by Vienna Science and Technology Fund (WWTF) through project ICT08-028.

E. Erdem et al. (Eds.): Correct Reasoning, LNCS 7265, pp. 57–71, 2012.

solutions of parts of a program, and then to combine these solutions in a simple way, has obvious computational advantages.

In this paper we present a simple generalization of the "classical" splitting results for argumentation and logic programming. Generalizations for the latter have been investigated in depth in [11]. In fact, Janhunen et al. describe an entire rather impressive module theory for logic programs based on modules consisting of rules together with input, output and hidden variables. To a certain extent some of our results can be viewed as being "implicit" already in that paper. Nevertheless, we believe that the constructions we describe here complement the abstract theory in a useful manner. In particular, we present a generalized approach to splitting which is based on simple modifications of the components that are obtained through splitting. The general idea is to add certain constructs (new atoms in case of logic programs, new arguments in case of argumentation frameworks) representing meta-information to the first component. Solutions computed for the augmented first component thus will contain meta-information. This information is used, together with the standard propagation of results known from classical splitting, to modify the second component. The aim is to guarantee that solutions of the second part match the outcome for the first component. The main advantage of this approach is practical: standard solvers can directly be used for the relevant computations.

The outline of the paper is as follows. In Sect. 2 we provide the necessary background on classical splitting for logic programs and argumentation frameworks. Sect. 3 introduces quasi-splittings for argumentation frameworks and shows how stable extensions of AFs can be computed based on them. Sect. 4 defines quasi-splittings for normal logic programs and treats the computation of answer sets in a similar spirit. Finally, in Sect. 5 we propose a general theory of splitting abstracting away from concrete formalisms and take a closer look at computational issues concerned with quasi-splitting. We conclude the paper with a brief summary and an outlook on future work.

2 Background

In this section we give the necessary background on argumentation frameworks and logic programs.

Argumentation Frameworks. Abstract argumentation frameworks (AFs) have been introduced by Dung [6] and are widely used in formal argumentation. They treat arguments as atomic entities, abstracting away from their structure and content, and focus entirely on conflict resolution. Conflicts among arguments are represented via an attack relation. Different semantics have been defined for AFs. Each of them singles out sets of arguments which represent reasonable positions based on varying principles. We start with some notation.

Definition 1. *An* argumentation framework (AF) *is a pair $F = (A, R)$ where A is a finite set of arguments and $R \subseteq A \times A$ is the attack relation. For a given AF $F = (A, R)$ we use $A(F)$ to denote the set A of its arguments and $R(F)$ to denote its attack relation R. We sometimes write $(S, b) \in R$ in case there exists an $a \in S$, such that $(a, b) \in R$; likewise we use $(a, S) \in R$ and $(S, S') \in R$.*

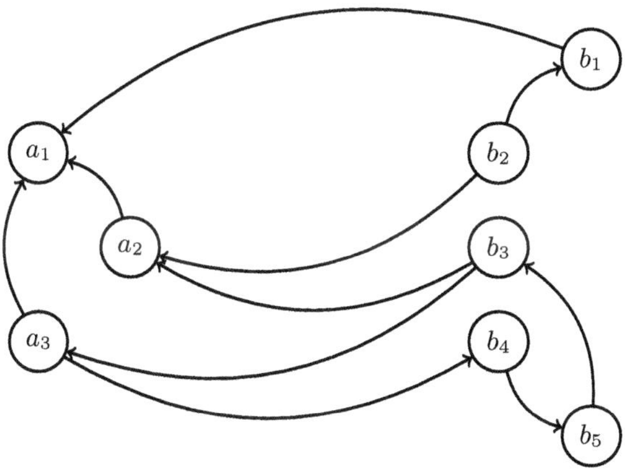

Fig. 1. An argumentation framework which is our running example

Given $F = (A, R)$ and a set $S \subseteq A$, we write $F|_S$ to denote the AF $(S, R \cap (S \times S))$ induced by S. Furthermore, $S_R^{\oplus} = \{b \mid (S, b) \in R\}$ and $S_R^{\ominus} = \{a \mid (a, S) \in R\}$; as well $S_R^{+} = S \cup S_R^{\oplus}$ and $S_R^{-} = S \cup S_R^{\ominus}$.

Several semantics for argumentation frameworks have been studied in the literature, see e.g. [1,2]; we focus here on the stable semantics as introduced already in [6], not the least due to its close connection to the ASP semantics. Intuitively, a set S of arguments is a stable extension if no argument in S attacks another argument in S, and moreover all arguments not in S are attacked by an element of S.

Definition 2. *Let $F = (A, R)$ be an AF. A set $S \subseteq A$ is* conflict-free (in F), *denoted as $S \in cf(F)$, iff there are no $a, b \in S$, such that $(a, b) \in R$. Moreover, S is called a stable extension of F iff $S \in cf(F)$ and $S_R^{+} = A$. The set of all stable extensions of F is given by $stb(F)$.*

Example 1. Figure 1 shows an example AF with stable extensions $\{a_3, b_2, b_5\}$ and $\{a_1, b_2, b_3, b_4\}$.

Logic Programs. We restrict the discussion in this paper to normal logic programs. Such programs are sets of rules of the form

$$a \leftarrow b_1, \ldots, b_m, \text{ not } c_1, \ldots, \text{ not } c_n \tag{1}$$

where a and all b_i's and c_j's are atoms. Intuitively, the rule is a justification to "establish" or "derive" that a (the so called *head*) is true, if all default literals to the right of $\leftarrow$ (the so called *body*) are true in the following sense: a non-negated atom b_i is true if it has a derivation, a negated one, not c_j, is true if c_j does not have one. Variables can appear in rules, however they are just convenient abbreviations for the collection of their ground instantiations.

The semantics of (ground) normal logic programs [8,9] is defined in terms of answer sets, also called stable models for this class of programs. Programs without negation in the bodies have a unique answer set, namely the smallest set of atoms closed under the rules. Equivalently, this set can be characterized as the least model of the rules, reading $\leftarrow$ as classical implication and the comma in the body as conjunction.

For programs with negation in the body, one needs to guess a candidate set of atoms S and then verifies the choice. This is achieved by evaluating negation with respect to S and checking whether the "reduced" negation-free program corresponding to this evaluation has S as answer set. If this is the case, it is guaranteed that all applicable rules were applied, and that each atom in S has a valid derivation based on appropriate rules. Here is the formal definition:

Definition 3. *Let P be a normal logic program, S a set of atoms. The Gelfond/Lifschitz-reduct (GL-reduct) of P and S is the negation-free program P^S obtained from P by*

1. *deleting all rules $r \in P$ with not c_j in the body for some $c_j \in S$,*
2. *deleting all negated atoms from the remaining rules.*

S is an answer set of P iff S is the answer set of P^S. We denote the collection of answer sets of a program P by $AS(P)$.

For convenience we will use rules without head (constraints) of the form

$$\leftarrow b_1, \dots, b_m, \text{ not } c_1, \dots, \text{ not } c_n \tag{2}$$

as abbreviation for

$$f \leftarrow \text{ not } f, b_1, \dots, b_m, \text{ not } c_1, \dots, \text{ not } c_n \tag{3}$$

where f is an atom not appearing anywhere else in the program. Adding rule 2 to a program has the effect of eliminating those answer sets of the original program which contain all of the b_is and none of the c_js.

For other types of programs and an introduction to answer set programming, a problem solving paradigm based on the notion of answer sets, the reader is referred to [5].

3 Quasi-splittings for Argumentation Frameworks

In this section we develop our approach for argumentation frameworks under stable semantics. We start with the definition of quasi-splittings.

Definition 4. *Let $F = (A, R)$ be an AF. A set $S \subseteq A$ is a* quasi-splitting *of F. Moreover, let $\bar{S} = A \setminus S$, $R^S_{\rightarrow} = R \cap (S \times \bar{S})$ and $R^S_{\leftarrow} = R \cap (\bar{S} \times S)$. Then, S is called*

- k-splitting *of F, if $|R^S_{\leftarrow}| = k$;*
- *(proper)* splitting *of F, if $|R^S_{\leftarrow}| = 0$.*

Note that above definition also allows for trivial splittings, i.e. $S = \emptyset$ or $S = A$. In what follows, we often tacitly assume quasi-splittings to be non-trivial.

A quasi-splitting S of F induces two sub-frameworks of F, namely $F_1^S = F|_S$ and $F_2^S = F|_{\bar{S}}$, together with the sets of links $R_{\rightarrow}^S$ and $R_{\leftarrow}^S$ connecting the sub-frameworks in the two possible directions.[1] All these components are implicitly defined by S. For this reason specifying this set is sufficient.

Our goal is to use - under the assumption that k is reasonably small - a k-splitting to potentially reduce the effort needed to compute the stable extensions of F. The case $k = 0$, that is proper splitting, was considered by Baumann [3][2].

The basic idea is as follows. We first find a stable extension of F_1^S. However, we have to take into account that one of the elements of S may be attacked by an argument of F_2^S. For this reason we must provide, for each argument a in F_1^S attacked by an argument in F_2^S, the possibility *to assume it is attacked*. To this end we add for a a new argument $att(a)$ such that a and $att(a)$ attack each other. Now we may choose to include the new argument in an extension which corresponds to the assumption that a is attacked. Later, when extensions of F_2^S are computed, we need to check whether the assumptions we made actually are satisfied. Only if they are, we can safely combine the extensions of the sub-frameworks we have found.

Definition 5. *Let $F = (A, R)$ be an AF, S a* quasi-splitting *of F. A conditional extension of F_1^S is a stable extension of the modified AF $[F_1^S] = (A_S, R_S)$ where*

- $A_S = S \cup \{att(a) \mid a \in A^+_{R_{\leftarrow}^S}\}$, *and*
- $R_S = (R \cap (S \times S)) \cup \{(att(a), a), (a, att(a)) \mid a \in A^+_{R_{\leftarrow}^S}\}$.

In other words, $[F_1^S]$ is obtained from F_1^S by adding a copy $att(a)$ for each argument a attacked from F_2^S, and providing for each such a a mutual attack between a and $att(a)$. For a k-splitting we thus add k nodes and $2k$ links to F_1^S - a tolerable augmentation for reasonably small k. For a proper splitting S, note that $[F_1^S] = F_1^S$.

Example 2. Consider $S = \{a_1, a_2, a_3\}$, a splitting of our example AF F, and the resulting frameworks $[F_1^S]$ and F_2^S as depicted in Figure 2. We have $R_{\rightarrow}^S = \{(a_3, b_4)\}$ and $R_{\leftarrow}^S = \{(b_1, a_1), (b_2, a_2), (b_3, a_2), (b_3, a_3)\}$. The set of the grey highlighted arguments $E = \{att(a_1), att(a_2), a_3\}$ is a conditional extension of F_1^S, i.e. a stable extension of the modified framework $[F_1^S]$. Further stable extensions of $[F_1^S]$ are $E_1 = \{a_1, att(a_2), att(a_3)\}$, $E_2 = \{att(a_1), a_2, att(a_3)\}$, $E_3 = \{att(a_1), a_2, a_3\}$ and $E_4 = \{att(a_1), att(a_2), att(a_3)\}$.

Each conditional extension E of F_1^S may contain meta-information in the form of $att(x)$ elements. This information will later be disregarded, but is important to verify the assumptions extensions of F_2^S need to fulfill so that E can be augmented to an

[1] Unlike Lifschitz and Turner we enumerate the sub-frameworks rather than calling them bottom and top framework. For quasi-splittings there does not seem to be a clear sense in which one is below the other.

[2] Note that Baumann used a more involved definition of a splitting. The definition we use here is not only simpler but also closer to the one used by Lifschitz and Turner.

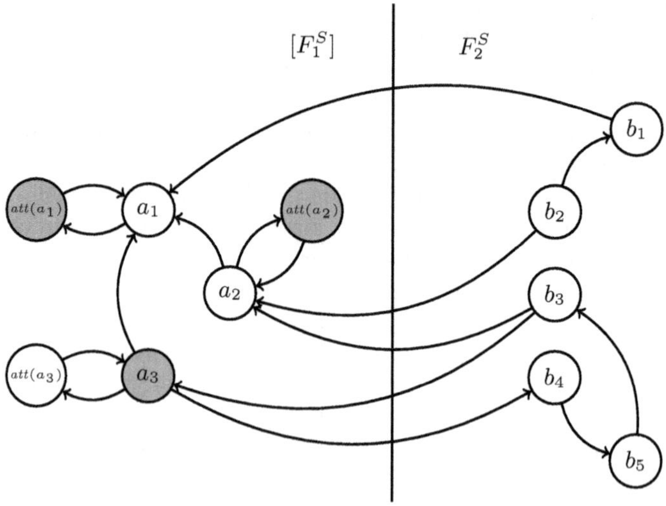

Fig. 2. A splitting of our example framework

extension of the entire argumentation framework F. As in [3], E will be used to modify F_2^S accordingly, thus propagating effects of elements in E on F_2^S. In the generalized case we also need to take the meta-information in E into account to make sure the assumptions we made are valid. In particular,

- if $att(a)$ is in E yet a is not attacked by another element in $E \cap S$, then we know that a must be externally attacked from an element of F_2^S. In other words, we are only interested in extensions of F_2^S which contain at least one attacker of a.
- if b is in E yet it is attacked by some argument in F_2^S, then we are only interested in extensions of F_2^S not containing any of the attackers of b.

Before we turn these ideas into a definition we present a useful lemma which helps to understand our definition.

Lemma 1. *Let $F = (A, R)$ be an AF. Let further B and $C_1, \ldots, C_n$ be sets s.t. $B, C_1, \ldots, C_n \subseteq A$, and $D = \{d_1, \ldots, d_n\}$ s.t. $D \cap A = \emptyset$. The stable extensions of the AF*

$$F' = (A \cup D, R \cup \{(b, b) \mid b \in B \text{ or } b \in D\} \cup \{(c, d_j) \mid c \in C_j, 1 \leq j \leq n\})$$

are exactly the stable extensions E of F containing no element of B and at least one element of every C_i, i.e. $C_i \cap E \neq \emptyset$ for every $i \in \{1, \ldots, n\}$.

Proof. Let $E \in stb(F)$, s.t. E does not contain an element of B (+) and $C_i \cap E \neq \emptyset$ for every $i \in \{1, \ldots, n\}$ (*). We observe $E \in cf(F')$ because of $E \subseteq A$ and (+), and furthermore, $E^+_{R(F')} = E^+_{R(F)} \cup D = A \cup D$ because of (*). Thus, $E \in stb(F')$.

Assume now $E \in stb(F')$. We observe that $E \cap B = \emptyset$ since conflict-freeness has to be fulfilled. Furthermore, $C_i \cap E \neq \emptyset$ for every $i \in \{1, \ldots, n\}$ has to hold because

$E^+_{R(F')} = A \cup \{d_1, \ldots, d_n\}$ and only arguments in C_i attack the argument d_i by construction. Obviously, $E \subseteq A$ since the elements of D are self-attacking. Furthermore, $E \in cf(F)$ because $R(F) \subseteq R(F')$. Consider now the attack-relation $R(F')$. We obtain $E^+_{R(F)} = E^+_{R(F')} \setminus D = (A \cup D) \setminus D = A$ which proves $E \in stb(F)$. □

Based on the lemma we can now define the modification of F_2^S that is needed to compute those extensions which comply with a conditional extension E, capturing also the assumptions made in E. First, we can eliminate all arguments attacked by an element of E. This step corresponds to the usual propagation needed for proper splittings as well. In addition, we make sure that only those extensions of the resulting framework are generated which (1) contain an attacker for all externally attacked nodes of S, and (2) do not contain an attacker for any element in E. For this purpose the techniques of the lemma are applied.

Definition 6. *Let $F = (A, R)$ be an AF, S a* quasi-splitting *of F, and let E be a conditional extension of F_1^S. Furthermore, let*

$$EA(S,E) = \{a \in S \setminus E \mid a \notin (S \cap E)^{\oplus}_R\}$$

denote the set of arguments from F_1^S not contained in E because they are externally attacked. An (E, S)-match of F is a stable extension of the AF $[F_2^S]_E = (A', R')$ where

- $A' = (\bar{S} \setminus E^+_{R^S_\rightarrow}) \cup \{in(a) \mid a \in EA(S,E)\}$*, and*
- $R' = (R \cap (A' \times A')) \cup \{(in(a), in(a)), (b, in(a)) \mid a \in EA(S,E), (b,a) \in R^S_\leftarrow\} \cup \{(c,c) \mid (c,E) \in R^S_\leftarrow\}$.

In other words, we take the framework F_2^S and modify it w.r.t. a given conditional extension E of F_1^S. To this end, we remove those arguments from F_2^S which are attacked by E via $R^S_\rightarrow$ but we make a copy of each argument a in F_1^S externally attacked by F_2^S via $R^S_\leftarrow$. These additional self-attacking arguments $in(a)$ are used to represent the forbidden situation where an externally attacked argument a actually remains unattacked. Finally, we exclude those arguments in F_2^S from potential extensions which attack an argument in E located in F_1^S; these are the self-loops (c, c) for arguments s with $(c, E) \in R^S_\leftarrow$. Again the size of the modification is small whenever k is small: we add at most k nodes and $2k$ links to F_2^S.

Example 3. We continue our running example with Figure 3. On the right-hand side we have the modification of F_2^S w.r.t. the conditional extension $E = \{att(a_1), att(a_2), a_3\}$, i.e. the AF $[F_2^S]_E$. Observe that $EA(S,E) = \{a_2\}$ because a_2 is not an element of E and furthermore, it is not attacked by an argument in $E \cap S = \{a_3\}$. Hence, we have to add a self-attacking node $in(a_2)$ to F_2^S which is attacked by the attackers of a_2, namely the arguments b_2 and b_3. The argument a_3 (which belongs to the extension E) is attacked by the argument b_3 and attacks the argument b_4. Hence, we have to add a self-loop for b_3 and further, we have to delete b_4 and its corresponding attacks. The set of the light-grey highlighted arguments $E' = \{b_2, b_5\}$ is an (E, S)-match of F, i.e. a stable extension of $[F_2^S]_E$; in fact, it is the only (E, S)-match of F. Recall that

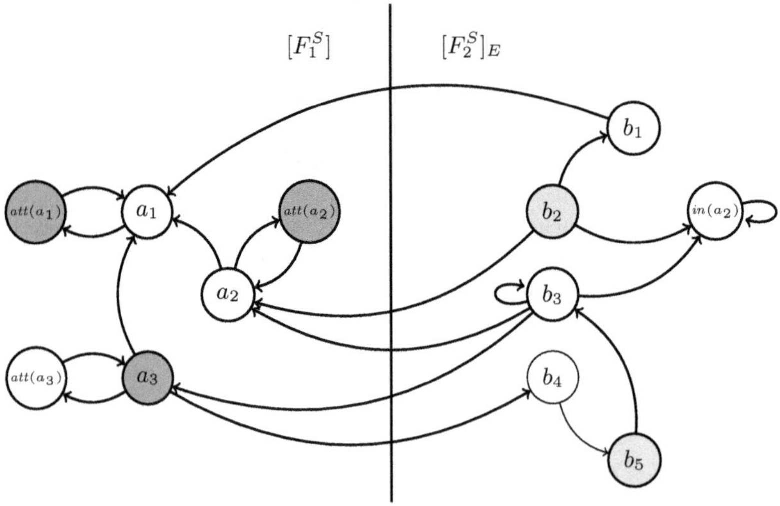

Fig. 3. Propagating conditional extensions to the second AF

$(E \cap S) \cup E' = \{a_3, b_2, b_5\}$ is a stable extension of the initial AF F; we will below show this result in general. One can further check that $\{b_2, b_3, b_4\}$ is an (E_1, S)-match of F with E_1 as given in the previous example. On the other hand, for the remaining conditional extensions of F_1^S, no corresponding matches exist. Take, for instance, $E_2 = \{att(a_1), a_2, att(a_3)\}$; here we have to put self-loops for b_2 and b_3, but b_2 remains unattacked in $[F_2^S]_{E_2}$. Thus no stable extension for $[F_2^S]_{E_2}$ exists.

Theorem 1. *Let $F = (A, R)$ be an AF and let S be a* quasi-splitting *of F.*

1. *If E is a conditional extension of F_1^S and E' an (E, S)-match of F, then $(E \cap S) \cup E'$ is a stable extension of F.*
2. *If H is an extension of F, then there is a set $X \subseteq \{att(a) \mid a \in A^+_{R^S_{\leftarrow}}\}$ such that $E = (H \cap S) \cup X$ is a conditional extension of F_1^S and $H \cap \bar{S}$ is an (E, S)-match of F.*

Proof. ad 1. First we will show that $(E \cap S) \cup E' \in cf(F)$. Given that E is a conditional extension of F_1^S we deduce $E \in cf([F_1^S])$. Consequently, $E \cap S \in cf([F_1^S])$ (less arguments) and thus, $E \cap S \in cf(F_1^S)$ (less attacks). Finally, $E \cap S \in cf(F)$ since $(F_1^S)|_S = F|_S$ holds. Let E' be an (E, S)-match of F, i.e. $E' \in stb([F_2^S]_E)$. According to Lemma 1, $E' \in stb(F')$ where $F' = (\bar{S} \setminus E^{\oplus}_{R^S_{\rightarrow}}, R(F) \setminus (E^{\oplus}_{R^S_{\rightarrow}}, E^{\oplus}_{R^S_{\rightarrow}}))$. Thus, $E' \in cf(F)$. Obviously, $(E \cap S, E') \notin R(F)$ since $E \cap S \subseteq S$ and $E' \subseteq \bar{S} \setminus E^{\oplus}_{R^S_{\rightarrow}}$. Assume now $(E', E \cap S) \in R(F)$. This means, there are arguments $e' \in E'$ and $e \in E \cap S$, s.t. $(e', e) \in R$. This contradicts the conflict-freeness of E' in $[F_2^S]_E$ because $R([F_2^S]_E)$ contains the set $\{(c, c) \mid (c, E) \in R^S_{\leftarrow}\}$. Thus, $(E', E \cap S) \notin R(F)$ and $(E \cap S) \cup E' \in cf(F)$ is shown.

We now show that $((E \cap S) \cup E')^+_{R(F)} = S \cup \bar{S} = A$. Let us consider an argument s, s.t. $s \notin ((E \cap S) \cup E')^+_{R(F)}$. Assume $s \in S$. Consequently, $s \in EA(S, E)$.

Since E' is an (E, S)-match of F, by Lemma 1, $E \in stb(F')$ such that $(E, in(s)) \in R(F')$. By definition of F' we have $R(F') \subseteq R(F)$ and thus $(E, in(s)) \in R(F)$ contradicting the assumption. Assume now $s \in \bar{S}$. Obviously, $s \in \bar{S} \setminus E^{\oplus}_{R^S_{\rightarrow}}$. Since E' is an (E, S)-match of F we deduce by Lemma 1 that E' is a stable extension of F' as defined above. Thus, $s \in (E')^+_{R(F)}$ contradicting the assumption. Altogether, we have shown that $(E \cap S) \cup E'$ is a stable extension of F.

ad 2. Let $(H \cap S)^+_{R(F)} \dot{\cup} B = S$. Since $H \in stb(F)$ is assumed it follows $B \subseteq (H \cap \bar{S})^+_F$. This means, $B \subseteq A^+_{R^S_{\leftarrow}}$. Consider now $X = \{att(b) \mid b \in B\}$. It can be easily seen that $E = (H \cap S) \cup X$ is a conditional extension of $[F^S_1]$. Note that $B = EA(S, E)$. Since $H \in stb(F)$ it follows $H \cap \bar{S} \in stb(F')$ where F' is as above. Furthermore, there is no argument $c \in H \cap \bar{S}$, s.t. $(c, d) \in R^S_{\leftarrow}$ with $d \in E$. Remember that $B = EA(S, E)$. Hence, for every $b \in B$, $(H \cap \bar{S}) \cap \{b\}^{\oplus}_{R^S_{\leftarrow}} \neq \emptyset$, since $H \in stb(F)$. Thus, Lemma 1 is applicable which implies that $H \cap \bar{S}$ is an (E, S)-match of F. □

4 Quasi-splittings for Logic Programs

We restrict ourselves here to normal logic programs. A splitting S can then be defined as a set of atoms dividing a program P into two disjoint subprograms P^S_1 and P^S_2 such that no head of a rule in P^S_2 appears anywhere in P^S_1.

One way to visualize this is via the dependency graph of P. The nodes of the dependency graph are the atoms in P. In addition, there are two kinds of links, positive and negative ones: whenever b appears positively (negatively) in a rule with head c, then there is a positive (negative) link from b to c in the dependency graph. A (proper) splitting S now is a set of atoms such that the dependency graph has no links - positive or negative - to an atom in S from any atom outside S.[3]

Now let us consider the situation where a (small) number k of atoms in the heads of rules in P^S_2 appear negatively in bodies of P^S_1. This means that the dependency graph of the program has a small number of negative links *pointing in the wrong direction.* As we will see methods similar to those we used for argumentation can be applied here as well.

In the following $head(r)$ denotes the head of rule r, $At(r)$ the atoms appearing in r and $pos(r)$ (respectively $neg(r)$) the positive (respectively negative) atoms in the body of r. We also write $head(P)$ for the set $\{head(r) \mid r \in P\}$ and $At(P)$ for $\{At(r) \mid r \in P\}$.

Definition 7. *Let P be a normal logic program. A set $S \subseteq At(P)$ is a* quasi-splitting *of P if, for each rule $r \in P$,*

- *$head(r) \in S$ implies $pos(r) \subseteq S$.*

Let $\bar{S} = At(P) \setminus S$ and $V_S = \{c \in \bar{S} \mid r \in P, head(r) \in S, c \in neg(r)\}$. S is called

- k-splitting *of P, if $|V_S| = k$;*
- *(proper)* splitting *of P, if $|V_S| = 0$.*

[3] An argumentation framework F can be represented as a logic program P as follows: for each argument a with attackers $b_1, \ldots, b_n$, P contains the rule $a \leftarrow$ not $b_1, \ldots,$ not b_n. Now the graph of F corresponds exactly to the dependency graph of P with all links negative.

Analogously to AFs where a splitting induces two disjoint sub-frameworks, here the set S induces two disjoint sub-programs, P_1^S having heads in S and P_2^S having heads in $\bar{S}$. Whenever $|V_S| \neq 0$, there are some heads in P_2^S which may appear in bodies of P_1^S, but only in negated form. This is not allowed in standard splittings which thus correspond to 0-splittings.

Note an important distinction between splittings for AFs and for logic programs: an arbitrary subset of arguments is an AF splitting, whereas a splitting S for a program P needs to fulfill the additional requirement that for each rule $r \in P$ with its head contained in S, also the entire positive body stems from S.

Example 4. Consider the following simple program

(1) $a \leftarrow$ not b
(2) $b \leftarrow$ not a
(3) $c \leftarrow a$

The program does not have a (nontrivial) classical splitting. However, it possesses the quasi-splitting $S = \{a, c\}$ (together with the complementary quasi-splitting $\bar{S} = \{b\}$). P_1^S consists of rules (1) and (3), P_2^S of rule (2). It is easily verified that $V_S = \{b\}$.

For the computation of answer sets we proceed in the same spirit as before by adding rules to P_1^S which allow answer sets to contain meta-information about the assumptions which need to hold for an answer set. We introduce atoms $ndr(b)$ to express the assumption that b will be underivable from P_2^S.

Definition 8. *Let P be a normal logic program, let S be a quasi-splitting of P and let P_1^S, respectively P_2^S, be the sets of rules in P with heads in S, respectively in $\bar{S}$. Moreover, let V be the set of atoms in $\bar{S}$ appearing negatively in P_1^S.*

$[P_1^S]$ is the program obtained from P_1^S by adding, for each $b \in V_S$, the following two rules:

$b \leftarrow not\ ndr(b)$
$ndr(b) \leftarrow not\ b$

E is called conditional answer set of P_1^S iff E is an extension of $[P_1^S]$.

Intuitively, $ndr(b)$ represents the assumption that b is not derivable from P_2^S (since $b \in V_S$ it cannot be derivable from P_1^S anyway). The additional rules allow us to assume b - a condition which we later need to verify. The construction is similar to the one we used for AFs where it was possible to assume that an argument is attacked.

Now, given an answer set E of $[P_1^S]$, we use E to modify P_2^S in the following way. We first use E to simplify P_2^S in exactly the same way this was done by Lifschitz and Turner: we replace atoms in S appearing positively (negatively) in rule bodies of P_2^S with $true$ whenever they are (are not) contained in E. Moreover, we delete each rule with a positive (negative) occurrence of an S-atom in the body which is not (which is) in E. We call the resulting program E-evaluation of P_2^S. Next we add adequate rules (constraints) which guarantee that answer sets generated by the modification of P_2^S match the conditions expressed in the meta-atoms of E. This is captured in the following definition:

Definition 9. *Let P, S, and P_2^S be as in Def. 8, and let E be a conditional answer set of P_1^S. Let $[P_2^S]_E$, the E-modification of P_2^S, be obtained from the E-evaluation of P_2^S by adding the following k rules*

$$\{\leftarrow \mathit{not}\ b \mid b \in E \cap V_S\} \cup \{\leftarrow b \mid ndr(b) \in E\}.$$

E' is called (E, S)-match iff E' is an answer set of $[P_2^S]_E$.

Now we can verify that answer sets of P can be obtained by computing an answer set E_1 of $[P_1^S]$ and an answer set E_2 of the E_1-modification of P_2^S (we just have to eliminate the meta-atoms in E_1).

Theorem 2. *Let P be a normal logic program and let S be a quasi-splitting of P.*

1. *If E is a conditional answer set of P_1^S and F an (E, S)-match, then $(E \cap S) \cup F$ is an answer set of P.*
2. *If H is an answer set of P, then there is a set $X \subseteq \{ndr(a) \mid a \in V_S\}$ such that $E = (H \cap S) \cup X$ is a conditional answer set of P_1^S and $H \cap \bar{S}$ is an (E, S)-match of P.*

Proof. Thanks to the richer syntax of logic programs compared to AFs, the proof of this result is conceptually simpler than the one for Theorem 1. Due to space restrictions, we give here only a sketch. The proof is done in two main steps.

First, given a normal program P and S a quasi-splitting of P, define the program $P_S = [P_1^S] \cup \overline{P}_2^S \cup \{\leftarrow \text{not}\, b', b; \leftarrow b', ndr(b) \mid b \in V_S\}$ where $\overline{P}_2^S$ results from P_2^S by replacing each atom $s \in \bar{S}$ with a fresh atom s'. One can show that P and P_S are equivalent in the following sense: (1) if E is an answer set of P then $X = (E \cap S) \cup \{s' \mid s \in E \cap \bar{S}\} \cup \{ndr(s) \mid s \in V_S \setminus E\}$ is an answer set of P_S; in particular, by the definition of X and $V_S \subseteq \bar{S}$, we have, for each $s \in V_S$, $s' \in X$ iff $s \in X$ iff $ndr(s) \notin X$; (2) if H is an answer set of P_S, then $(H \cap S) \cup \{s \mid s' \in H\}$ is an answer set of P.

Next, we observe that P_S has a proper split T with $T = S \cup \{ndr(s) \mid s \in V_S\}$. With this result at hand, it can be shown that after evaluating the bottom part of this split, i.e. $(P_S)_1^T = [P_1^S]$, the rules $\{\leftarrow \text{not}\, b', b; \leftarrow b', ndr(b) \mid b \in V_S\}$ in P_S play exactly the role of the replacements defined in $[P_2^S]_E$. In other words, we have for each $E \in AS((P_S)_1^T) = AS([P_1^S])$, the E-evaluation of $(P_S)_2^T$ is equal to $([P_2^S]_E)'$, where $([P_2^S]_E)'$ denotes $[P_2^S]_E$ replacing all atoms s by s'. Together with the above relation between answer sets of P and P_S the assertion is now shown in a quite straightforward way. □

Example 5. We follow up on Example 4. To determine the conditional answer sets of P_1^S we use the program

$$a \leftarrow \text{not}\ b$$
$$c \leftarrow a$$
$$b \leftarrow \text{not}\ ndr(b)$$
$$ndr(b) \leftarrow \text{not}\ b$$

This program has two answer sets, namely $E_1 = \{a, c, ndr(b)\}$ and $E_2 = \{b\}$.

The E_1-modification of P_2^S consists of the single rule $\leftarrow b$ and its single answer set $\emptyset$ is an (S, E_1)-match. We thus obtain the first answer set of P, namely $(E_1 \cap S) \cup \emptyset = \{a, c\}$.

The E_2-modification of P_2^S is the program:

$$b$$
$$\leftarrow not\ b$$

Its single answer set $\{b\}$ is an (S, E_2)-match. We thus obtain the second answer set of P, namely $(E_2 \cap S) \cup \{b\} = \{b\}$.

Of course, the example is meant to illustrate the basic ideas, not to show the potential computational benefits of our approach. However, if we find a k-splitting with small k for large programs with hundreds of rules such benefits may be tremendous.

As the thoughtful reader may have recognized our results are stated for normal logic programs while Lifschitz and Turner define splittings for the more general class of disjunctive programs. However, our results can be extended to disjunctive programs in a straightforward way.

5 Algorithms for Quasi-splittings

For the computation of quasi-splittings it is most beneficial to apply some of the existing highly efficient graph algorithms. Since AFs actually are graphs, such algorithms can be directly applied here. For logic programs we have to make a slight detour via their dependency graphs. Intuitively, a dependency graph is a directed graph with two types of links, E_n and E_p, the negative respectively positive links. Recall that the dependency graph of a logic program P is given by

$$(At(P), \{(a, head(r)) \mid a \in neg(r), r \in P\}, \{(a, head(r)) \mid a \in pos(r), r \in P\}).$$

The concepts of quasi-splittings, k-splittings and proper splittings can be defined for dependency graphs in a straightforward way:

Definition 10. *Let $D = (V, E_n, E_p)$ be a dependency graph and $S \subseteq V$. Let $\bar{S} = V \setminus S$, $E = E_n \cup E_p$, $R^S_{\rightarrow} = E \cap (S \times \bar{S})$ and $R^S_{\leftarrow} = E \cap (\bar{S} \times S)$. S is called*

- quasi-splitting *of D, if $R^S_{\leftarrow} \cap E_p = \emptyset$*
- k-splitting *of D, if $|R^S_{\leftarrow}| = k$ and $R^S_{\leftarrow} \cap E_p = \emptyset$.*
- *(proper)* splitting *of D, if $|R^S_{\leftarrow}| = 0$.*

Now it is not difficult to see that each quasi-splitting S of the dependency graph of a program P corresponds to a quasi-splitting of P and vice versa.[4] Since all dependencies

[4] Note, however, that the program quasi-splitting corresponding to a k-splitting of the dependency graph may actually be a k'-splitting for some $k' \neq k$. This is due the different ways to count the size of a splitting. For splittings on the dependency graph we use the number of (negative) edges going form $\bar{S}$ to S while in the definition of program quasi-splittings we used the number of atoms in $\bar{S}$ such that there is an edge to S.

in AFs are negative, we can also identify an AF (A, R) with the dependency graph $(A, R, \emptyset)$.

We now address the problem of finding splittings of a given dependency graph. For proper splittings the distinction between negative and positive dependencies is irrelevant. Proper splittings are given by the strongly connected components (SCCs) of the graph $(V, E_n \cup E_p)$ (see [3,4] for more details). It is well known that the SCCs of a graph can efficiently be computed using, for instance, the Tarjan-algorithm [14].

While proper splittings do not allow splitting within an SCC S, with a k-splitting we can split S as long as the edge-connectivity of S is $\leq k$. However we additionally have to respect the condition $R^S_{\leftarrow} \cap E_p = \emptyset$, i.e. that there are no positive dependencies from $\bar{S}$ to S.

For computing a k-splitting of a dependency graph with minimal k, we can apply existing polynomial-time algorithms for computing minimum cuts in directed graphs (see e.g. [10]). Let $G = (V, E)$ be a directed graph where each arc (i, j) has an associated weight u_{ij}, which is a nonnegative real number. A cut is a partition of the node set into two nonempty parts S and $V \setminus S$. The capacity of the cut $(S, V \setminus S)$ is $\sum_{i \in S, j \in V \setminus S} u_{ij}$, and we denote the capacity of the cut as $u(S, V \setminus S)$. The *minimum unrestricted cut problem* is to find a partition of V into two nonempty parts, S^* and $V \setminus S^*$, so as to minimize $u(S^*, V \setminus S^*)$.

To ensure that minimal cuts do not contain forbidden edges we use the weight function $w : E \mapsto \{1, \infty\}$ such that $w(e) = \infty$ for $e \in E_p$ and $w(e) = 1$ for $e \in E_n \setminus E_p$. Now, if $(S^*, V \setminus S^*)$ is a solution to the problem, then $V \setminus S^*$ is a quasi-splitting of the graph with smallest possible k. More generally, each cut with finite capacity corresponds to a quasi-splitting, and if the minimal cut has weight ∞, then no quasi-splitting exists.

Recursive Splitting. We observe that quasi-splittings allow for a recursive procedure to compute the stable extensions of AFs, resp. the answer-sets of logic programs. This is in contrast to proper splittings, where a decomposition into SCCs is the "best" we can do. To exemplify this observation consider an AF with an even cycle

$$F = (\{a, b, c, d\}, \{(a, b), (b, c), (c, d), (d, a)\}).$$

Then we first can find a quasi split, e.g. $S = \{a, b\}$. If we now consider $[F^S_1]$, we observe that we now find even a proper splitting of this AF, namely $S' = \{a, att(a)\}$. The value of such a recursive approach is even more drastic if we consider a, b, c, d being huge DAGs which are only linked via single edges which however yield a cycle going through all arguments. This suggests the following simple recursive procedure to compute stable extensions of an AF.

Function RS; input is an AF $F = (A, R)$; output is a set of extensions:

1. find non-trivial quasi-splitting S of F (s.t. $|R^S_{\leftarrow}|$ is minimal);
2. if $size([F^S_1]) \geq size(F)$ return[5] $stb(F)$ via some standard method;
3. otherwise, let $\mathcal{E} = \emptyset$ and do for each $E \in RS([F^S_1])$:
   $\mathcal{E} = \mathcal{E} \cup \{(E \cup E') \cap A \mid E' \in RS([F^S_2]_E)\}$.
4. return $\mathcal{E}$.

[5] $size(F)$ denotes the number of arguments in F.

Note that the function terminates since the size of the involved AFs decreases in each recursion. The procedure is directly applicable to splitting of programs, by just replacing F by a program P and $stb(F)$ by $AS(P)$.

6 Discussion

In this paper, we proposed a generalization of the splitting concept introduced by Lifschitz and Turner which we showed to be applicable to two prominent nonmonotonic reasoning formalisms. Compared to other work in the area, the novel contributions of our work are twofold:

1. with the concept of quasi-splitting, we significantly extended the range of applicability of splitting without increasing the computational cost of finding a split;
2. the concept of a modification-based approach allows to evaluate the components of a split within the formalism under consideration.

We believe that the approach we have introduced here is applicable to further formalisms and semantics. In Section 5 we have already discussed some computation methods which might pave the way towards a uniform and general theory of splitting. Future work includes the refinement of our methods in the sense that splitting should, whenever possible, be performed in such a way that one of the resulting components is an easy-to-compute fragment.

Finally, we also want to provide empirical support for our claim that quasi-splittings have computational benefits. Note that quasi-splittings as well as proper splittings, on the one hand, divide the search space into smaller fractions in many cases, but on the other hand this might result in the computation of more models (i.e., stable extensions or answer sets) which turn out to be "useless" when propagated from the first to the second part of the split (i.e. they do not contribute to the models of the entire framework (or program). So from the theoretical side it is not clear how splitting effects the computation times. However for classical splitting we have empirical evidence [4] that splitting improves the average computation time. We thus plan to perform an empirical analysis of the effects of quasi-splitting on computation times in the spirit of [4].

Acknowledgments. We want to thank the reviewer of this paper for various useful remarks which helped to improve the presentation.

References

1. Baroni, P., Caminada, M., Giacomin, M.: An introduction to argumentation semantics. Knowledge Eng. Review 26(4), 365–410 (2011)
2. Baroni, P., Giacomin, M.: Semantics of abstract argument systems. In: Rahwan, I., Simari, G.R. (eds.) Argumentation in Artificial Intelligence, pp. 25–44. Springer (2009)
3. Baumann, R.: Splitting an Argumentation Framework. In: Delgrande, J.P., Faber, W. (eds.) LPNMR 2011. LNCS, vol. 6645, pp. 40–53. Springer, Heidelberg (2011)

4. Baumann, R., Brewka, G., Wong, R.: Splitting Argumentation Frameworks: An Empirical Evaluation. In: Modgil, S., Oren, N., Toni, F. (eds.) TAFA 2011. LNCS, vol. 7132, pp. 17–31. Springer, Heidelberg (2012)
5. Brewka, G., Eiter, T., Truszczynski, M.: Answer set programming at a glance. Commun. ACM 54(12), 92–103 (2011)
6. Dung, P.M.: On the acceptability of arguments and its fundamental role in nonmonotonic reasoning, logic programming and n-person games. Artif. Intell. 77(2), 321–358 (1995)
7. Eiter, T., Gottlob, G., Mannila, H.: Disjunctive Datalog. ACM Transactions on Database Systems 22(3), 364–418 (1997)
8. Gelfond, M., Lifschitz, V.: The stable model semantics for logic programming. In: Logic Programming: Proceedings of the Fifth International Conference and Symposium, pp. 1070–1080. MIT Press, Cambridge (1988)
9. Gelfond, M., Lifschitz, V.: Classical negation in logic programs and disjunctive databases. New Generation Comput. 9(3/4), 365–386 (1991)
10. Hao, J., Orlin, J.B.: A faster algorithm for finding the minimum cut in a directed graph. J. Algorithms 17(3), 424–446 (1994)
11. Janhunen, T., Oikarinen, E., Tompits, H., Woltran, S.: Modularity aspects of disjunctive stable models. J. Artif. Intell. Res. 35, 813–857 (2009)
12. Liao, B.S., Jin, L., Koons, R.C.: Dynamics of argumentation systems: A division-based method. Artif. Intell. 175(11), 1790–1814 (2011)
13. Lifschitz, V., Turner, H.: Splitting a logic program. In: Van Hentenryck, P. (ed.) Proceedings of the Eleventh International Conference on Logic Programming (ICLP 1994), pp. 23–27. MIT Press (1994)
14. Tarjan, R.: Depth-first search and linear graph algorithms. SIAM Journal on Computing 1(2), 146–160 (1972)
15. Turner, H.: Splitting a default theory. In: Clancey, W.J., Weld, D.S. (eds.) Proceedings of the Thirteenth National Conference on Artificial Intelligence and Eighth Innovative Applications of Artificial Intelligence Conference (AAAI/IAAI), vol. 1, pp. 645–651. AAAI Press / The MIT Press (1996)

From Primal Infon Logic with Individual Variables to Datalog

Nikolaj Bjørner[1], Guido de Caso[2], and Yuri Gurevich[1]

[1] Microsoft Research, Redmond, WA, United States
{nbjorner,gurevich}@microsoft.com
[2] DC, FCEyN, Universidad de Buenos Aires, Buenos Aires, Argentina
gdecaso@dc.uba.ar

Abstract. The logic core of Distributed Knowledge Authorization Logic, DKAL, is constructive logic with a quotation construct `said`. This logic is known as the logic of *infons*. The *primal* fragment of infon logic is amenable to linear time decision algorithms when policies and queries are ground. In the presence of policies with variables and implicit universal quantification, but no functions of positive arity, primal infon logic can be reduced to Datalog. We here present a practical reduction of the entailment problem for primal infon logic with individual variables to the entailment problem of Datalog.

Keywords: infon logic, Datalog, PIV, translation.

1 Introduction

The entailment problem for a logic L is a decision problem: Given a finite set H of L formulas (the hypotheses) and one additional L formula q (the query), decide whether H entails q. A *reduction* of logic L_1 to logic L_2 is a reduction of the entailment problem for L_1 to that of L_2.

In [1], the entailment problem for the primal infon logic was reduced to the entailment problem for Datalog. Primal infon logic is called there primal infon logic with variables, in short PIV, to distinguish it from propositional primal infon logic introduced earlier in [5]. We will use the abbreviation "PIV" as well.

Here we develop a more practical PIV-to-Datalog reduction. The reduction itself is more efficient, and the resulting Datalog program runs faster; see § 4.5 in this connection. An implementation of the reduction is found at [3].

The definition of infon logic has been refined over time. Propositional primal infon logic was introduced in [4] and investigated in [5]. Its extension with individual variables and the substitution rule, called PIV, was introduced in [1]. These logics employed two quotation constructs, namely `said` and `implied`. In the meantime, `implied` was retired. The reasons for the original introduction of two quotation constructs and subsequent retirement of one of them are related to the use of infon logic in Distributed Knowledge Authorization Language (DKAL) [2] and will be addressed elsewhere. More precisely we retired `said` and then renamed `implied` to `said`. This detail is irrelevant in the context of the

E. Erdem et al. (Eds.): Correct Reasoning, LNCS 7265, pp. 72–86, 2012.

present paper, but it is relevant in the context of DKAL. In the rest of the present paper, by default, PIV means the simplified version of the original PIV of [1], without the `implied` construct.

In our main construction we take advantage of the retirement of `implied`. But the work reported here started prior to the retirement of `implied`, and we implemented two PIV-to-Datalog reductions; both of them are found at [3]. One of them reduces PIV with `implied` to Datalog, and the other reduces PIV without `implied` to Datalog.

This paper is self-contained, but familiarity with [5], [1] and Datalog may be useful. In §2, we recall the basic definitions of PIV. We also recall Datalog. In §3, we develop a succinct and economical representation of PIV formulas. Finally, in §4 we reduce PIV to Datalog.

2 PIV, Axiomless PIV, and Datalog

We recall PIV and narrow the entailment problem for PIV to that of the axiomless PIV, the fragment of PIV without the axioms. We also recall Datalog.

2.1 PIV

PIV is a logic calculus defined in [1]. In this subsection, we recall the definitions of PIV while making the obvious simplifications to reflect the retirement of `implied`. Also, in contrast to [1], this version of PIV is typed.

Terms and Formulas. Terms are constants or variables. Each term has a type. One required type is "principal". Atomic formulas are formed as usual from relational symbols and terms. Each argument place of a relational symbol has a type and is supposed to be filled in with a term of that type. Compound formulas are built from atomic formulas and $\top$ by the binary connectives of conjunction ($\wedge$) and implication ($\to$) and unary connectives "p `said`" where p is a term of type "principal". Formulas of the form "p `said` α" are *quotation formulas.*

Example 1. Alice `said` friends(Alice, Bob) is a quotation formula. In this case a principal named Alice is saying that Bob (another principal) is a friend of hers. Quotations can be nested, as in Alice `said` Bob `said` friends(Bob, Chuck).

Quotation Prefixes. A *quotation prefix* is a string of the form

$$p_1 \texttt{ said } p_2 \texttt{ said } \ldots p_d \texttt{ said} \qquad (1)$$

where every p_i is a term of type principal. The *depth* d of quotation prefix (1) may be zero in which case the quotation prefix is empty. We use `pref` and π, sometimes with subscripts, to denote quotation prefixes.

Every formula β has a unique presentation of the form $\pi\alpha$ where π is the maximal quotation prefix of β and the quotation prefix of α is empty (though quotations may appear in α, for example α may be a conjunction of quotations). The prefix π is denoted $\Pi(\beta)$ and α is called the *body* of β.

Example 2. Following with our example with principals Alice, Bob and Chuck, $\Pi(\text{Alice } \texttt{said} \text{ Bob } \texttt{said} \text{ friends(Bob, Chuck)}) = \text{Alice } \texttt{said} \text{ Bob } \texttt{said}$.

Now we are ready to define the axioms and rules of inference of PIV. Let α and β range over the formulas, `pref` range over the quotation prefixes, and ξ range over the substitutions of terms for variables.

Axioms.

$$\texttt{pref}\ \top$$

Rules of inference.

$$(\wedge \text{ elimination}) \quad \frac{\texttt{pref}\,(\alpha \wedge \beta)}{\texttt{pref}\,\alpha} \qquad \frac{\texttt{pref}\,(\alpha \wedge \beta)}{\texttt{pref}\,\beta}$$

$$(\wedge \text{ introduction}) \quad \frac{\texttt{pref}\,\alpha \qquad \texttt{pref}\,\beta}{\texttt{pref}\,(\alpha \wedge \beta)}$$

$$(\to \text{ elimination}) \quad \frac{\texttt{pref}\,\alpha \qquad \texttt{pref}\,(\alpha \to \beta)}{\texttt{pref}\,\beta}$$

$$(\to \text{ introduction}) \quad \frac{\texttt{pref}\,\beta}{\texttt{pref}\,(\alpha \to \beta)}$$

$$(\text{substitution}) \quad \frac{\alpha}{\xi\,\alpha}$$

A *derivation* D of a formula q from hypotheses H is a sequence $\alpha_1, \alpha_2, \ldots, \alpha_n$ of formulas such that $\alpha_n = q$ and every α_i is an axiom, a hypothesis or the result of applying a derivation rule to one or two preceding formulas. The formulas α_i are the *members* of D. The number n is the length of D. We write $H \vdash q$ and say that H *entails* q if there is a derivation of q from H.

So the entailment problem for PIV is to decide whether a given finite set H of hypotheses entails a formula q. The pair (H, q) forms an instance of the entailment problem. A substitution ξ for variables is *native* to (H, q) if every constant in the range of ξ occurs in (H, q).

Proposition 3 (Theorem 18 in [1]). *A set H of formulas entails a formula q if and only if there is a set H' of native-substitution instances of formulas in H such that q is deducible from H' without using the substitution rule.*

For a proof, see [1, Theorem 18]. Note that the variables of the query q are treated as constants. Without loss of generality we may assume that q is ground.

2.2 Local Derivations

We adopt the definition of formula components from [5] (though there it was restricted to propositional formulas).

Definition 4 (Components). The *components* of a formula γ are defined by induction:

- γ itself is a component of γ.
- If $\pi(\alpha * \beta)$ is a component of γ, where $*$ is conjunction or implication, then $\pi\alpha$ and $\pi\beta$ are components of γ.

The components of a set of formulas are the components of its members.

Check that a component of a component of γ is a component of γ.

Example 5. The components of

$$\text{Alice } \texttt{said} \text{ (friends(Alice, Bob)} \wedge \text{friends(Bob, Chuck))}$$

are the formula itself as well as formulas Alice `said` friends(Alice, Bob) and Alice `said` friends(Bob, Chuck).

Proposition 6 (Theorem 5.11 in [5]). *If there is a substitution-free derivation of q from H then there is a derivation of q from H where all members are components of $H \cup \{q\}$.*

In [5], the term "local formula" was used in the connection to the `said`/`implied` interplay. In the absence of `implied`, we are free to use the term for a different purpose.

Definition 7 (Local formulas). A formula α is *local* to a formula γ *via a substitution* ξ if $\alpha = \xi\beta$ for some component β of γ. And α is *local* to a set Γ of formulas *via* ξ if it is local to some member of Γ via ξ.

Example 8. If γ = Alice `said` (friends(Alice, Bob) $\wedge$ friends(Bob, y)), then formula Alice `said` friends(Bob, Alice) is local to γ.

Lemma 9. *A component φ of a formula $\xi\gamma'$ local to a formula γ via a substitution ξ is local to γ via ξ.*

Proof. Since γ' is a component of γ, its components are also components of γ. It suffices to show that $\varphi = \xi\beta$ for a component β of γ'. We do that by induction on φ..

The basic case $\varphi = \gamma'$ is obvious. In the induction step, we have a formula $\pi(\alpha_1 * \alpha_2)$, where the operation $*$ is either conjunction or implication, and $\varphi = \pi\,\alpha_i$ for some i, and (by the induction hypothesis) $\pi(\alpha_1 * \alpha_2) = \xi\delta$ for some component δ of γ'. Then δ has the form $\pi'(\delta_1 * \delta_2)$, so that $\pi = \xi\pi'$, $\alpha_i = \xi\delta_i$, and $\varphi = \pi\,\alpha_i = (\xi\pi')(\xi\delta_i) = \xi(\pi'\delta_i)$. So the desired $\beta = \pi'\delta_i$. □

Definition 10 (Local Derivations). A derivation D of q from H is *local* if every member of D is local to (H, q) via a substitution native to (H, q).

Theorem 11. *If $H \vdash q$ then there is a local derivation of q from H.*

Proof. By Proposition 3, there is a set H' of native-substitution instances of the hypotheses such that q is derivable from H' in a substitution-free way. By Proposition 6, there is a derivation D' of q from H' such that all members of D' are components of $H' \cup \{q\}$. By virtue of Lemma 9, every member of D' is local to (H, q) via a substitution native to (H, q). The desired local derivation of q from H is obtained by listing H and then D'. □

2.3 Parse Trees and Parse Forests

For future references, we give a few definitions and introduce some notation. In particular, we will define parse trees of formulas in a way that is convenient for our purposes in this paper. A *labeled tree* is a tree where nodes and edges may have labels. Our trees grow downward, so that the root is the top node. A *forest* is a sequence of disjoint labeled trees. (Making labeled trees disjoint will be no problem as we will be interested in labeled trees only up to isomorphisms.)

The *parse tree* $\mathrm{PT}(\gamma)$ of a formula γ is a labeled tree. We define $\mathrm{PT}(\gamma)$ by induction on γ. If γ is atomic then $\mathrm{PT}(\gamma)$ is a single node labeled with γ. If γ is a quotation formula then $\mathrm{PT}(\gamma)$ is obtained from $\mathrm{PT}(\mathrm{Body}(\gamma))$ by creating an unlabeled parent node u of the root and labeling the new edge with $\Pi(\gamma)$.

Suppose that $\gamma = \alpha * \beta$ where $*$ is conjunction or implication, and let $u = \mathrm{Root}(\mathrm{PT}(\alpha))$, $v = \mathrm{Root}(\mathrm{PT}(\beta))$. The parse tree of γ is obtained by turning the forest

$$(\mathrm{PT}(\alpha),\ \mathrm{PT}(\beta))$$

into a tree by creating a new node w labeled with $*$ (that is with conjunction or with implication) and attaching to it the parse trees for α and β as the left and the right subtrees respectively. The attaching process is as follows.

If α is a quotation formula $\pi\,\alpha'$, then the root u of $\mathrm{PT}(\alpha)$ has a unique child u', and the edge (u, u') is labeled with π. In this case, merge u with w retaining the label $*$ on w and retaining the label π on the edge (w, u'); the node u' becomes the left child of w. Otherwise make u a left child of w and leave the new edge (w, u) unlabeled. The parse tree of β is attached similarly.

That completes the inductive definition of $\mathrm{PT}(\gamma)$. The parse tree of a formula can be constructed in linear time. Note that a node of $\mathrm{PT}(\gamma)$ is unlabeled if only if it is the root and γ is a quotation formula.

Example 12. Figures 1, 2 and 3 contain example parse trees for different PIV formulas.

For every labeled node u on a parse tree $\mathrm{PT}(\gamma)$, we define a quotation prefix $\Pi(u)$ and a formula $\mathbf{F}(u)$. Recall that some edges of $\mathrm{PT}(\gamma)$ are labeled with quotation prefixes and the others are unlabeled. Think of the unlabeled edges as labeled with the empty quotation prefix. To obtain $\Pi(u)$, walk from $\mathrm{Root}(\mathrm{PT}(\gamma))$ down to u and concatenate the labels on your way. To obtain $\mathbf{F}(u)$, let T be the subtree of $\mathrm{PT}(\gamma)$ rooted at u. It is easy to see that T is the parse tree of some formula α; set $\mathbf{F}(u) = \alpha$.

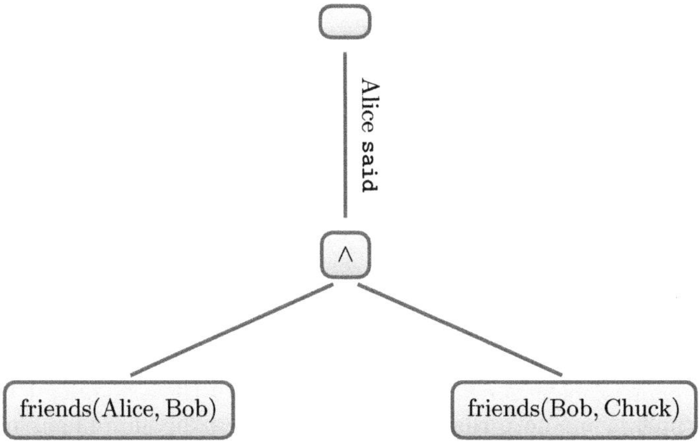

Fig. 1. Parse tree for "Alice said (friends(Alice, Bob) ∧ friends(Bob, Chuck))"

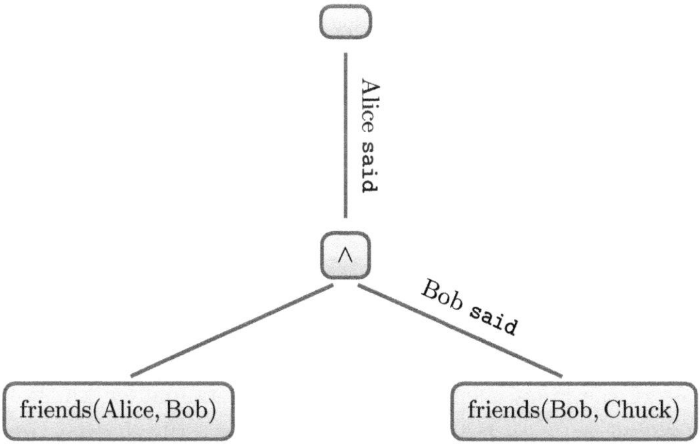

Fig. 2. Parse tree for "Alice said (friends(Alice, Bob) ∧ Bob said friends(Bob, Chuck))"

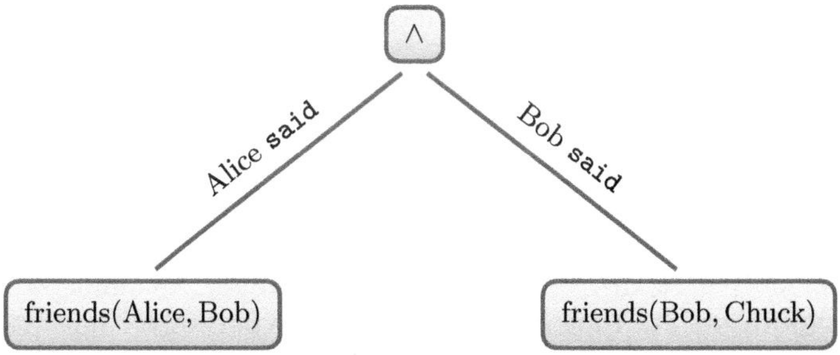

Fig. 3. Parse tree for "(Alice said friends(Alice, Bob)) ∧ (Bob said friends(Bob, Chuck))"

The *parse forest* of a sequence $\gamma_1, \ldots, \gamma_n$ of formulas is the labeled forest $(\mathrm{PT}(\gamma_1), \ldots, \mathrm{PT}(\gamma_n))$.

2.4 From PIV to Axiomless PIV

Datalog, viewed as a calculus (see the next subsection), has no axioms. In that connection, it is convenient (at least for expository purposes) to dispense with the axioms of PIV first and then reduce the axiomless PIV to Datalog.

Definition 13. *Axiomless* PIV is a fragment of PIV obtained by dropping the axioms.

The entailment problem for PIV reduces to that of the axiomless PIV in linear time. But first let us note that instances (H, q) of the entailment problem for PIV that arise in applications are almost invariably "topless" in the sense that they do not contain $\top$.

Proposition 14. *If H entails q in PIV and if $\top$ does not occur in (H, q) then H entails q already in the axiomless PIV.*

Proof. This follows easily from Theorem 11, but here is a direct proof that gives some additional information. By default we work in the original PIV. Formulas, sets of formulas and derivations are *topless* if they have no occurrences of $\top$; otherwise they are *fancy*.

Lemma 15. *A shortest substitution-free derivation of a topless formula from topless hypotheses is topless.*

Proof (of Lemma 15). Proof by contradiction. Let D be a shortest derivation of a topless formula q from topless hypotheses H. Assume that D is fancy and let M be the set of the fancy members of D of the maximal length. We will prove that any member γ of M is redundant which gives the desired contradiction. More exactly, we will prove this: if a derivation rule R uses γ as a premise to produce a formula δ then δ occurs in D before γ.

So suppose that a member γ of M is used as a premise for a derivation rule R. By the length maximality of γ, we have that

(i) either R is conjunction elimination, in which case γ has the form $\texttt{pref}(\alpha \wedge \beta)$ and the conclusion is either $\texttt{pref}\,\alpha$ or $\texttt{pref}\,\beta$,
(ii) or else R is implication elimination, in which case γ is the major premise of the form $\texttt{pref}\,(\alpha \to \beta)$ and the conclusion is $\texttt{pref}\,\beta$.

We consider only case (ii). Since γ is an implication, it cannot be an axiom. Since all hypotheses are topless, γ cannot be a hypothesis. Thus γ is obtained by an application of a derivation rule Q. By the length maximality, Q is an introduction rule. Given the form of γ, Q is implication introduction obtaining γ from $\texttt{pref}\,\beta$, so that $\texttt{pref}\,\beta$ is an earlier member of D. □

To complete the proof of the proposition, suppose that a topless set H of hypotheses entails a topless formula q. By Proposition 3, there exist a set H' of native-substitution instances of formulas in H and a substitution-free derivation of q from H'. Clearly H' is topless. By Lemma 15, any shortest substitution-free derivation of q from H' is topless, and thus H entails q in Axiomless PIV. □

Theorem 16. *There is a linear-time reduction of the entailment problem for PIV to that of Axiomless PIV.*

Proof. The idea is to view $\top$ as just another nullary relation symbol and treat axioms as additional hypotheses. The obvious problem is that there are infinitely many axioms. Fortunately only few of them are relevant to a given instance (H, q) of the PIV entailment problem. Let A be the set of axioms that are components of $H \cup \{q\}$. Since the total number of the components of (H, q) is $O(n)$, the cardinality $|A| = O(n)$. We show that H entails q in PIV if and only $A \cup H$ entails q in Axiomless PIV. The "if" direction is obvious. We prove the "only if" direction.

Suppose that H entails q. It suffices to show that there is a derivation D of q from H such that A entails every axiom in D. By Proposition 3, there is a set H' of native-substitution instances of formulas in H such that q is deducible from H' without using the substitution rule. By Theorem 11, there is a local derivation D of q from H. Every member α' of D is a substitution instance $\xi\alpha$ of a component α of (H, q). If α' is an axiom, then α is an axiom, and thus A entails α'. □

2.5 Datalog

A Datalog program is a finite set of rules. A Datalog rule has the form

$$\delta_0 \quad :- \quad \delta_1, \delta_2, \ldots, \delta_n \tag{2}$$

where each δ_i is an atomic formula in which every term is a constant or variable. δ_0 is the head of the rule, and the sequence $\delta_1, \delta_2, \ldots, \delta_n$ is the body. The length n of the body can be zero. The vocabulary of a Datalog program P consists of the relation symbols and constants that occur in P.

Entailment. Let P be a Datalog program and let r be an atomic formula (a *query*) in the vocabulary of P possibly extended with additional constants. The vocabulary of (P, r) consists of the relation symbols and constants in (P, r). Call a substitution ξ *native* to (P, r) if every constant in the range of ξ occurs in (P, r). Let ξ range over native substitutions. Construct a sequence

$$\Phi_0 \subseteq \Phi_1 \subseteq \Phi_2 \subseteq \ldots$$

of sets of atomic formulas as follows. $\Phi_0 = \emptyset$. If Φ_i is already constructed then, for every rule (2) of P and every substitution ξ, do this: if atomic formulas $\xi\delta_1, \ldots, \xi\delta_n$ belong to Φ_i then put $\xi\delta_0$ into Φ_{i+1}. The program P *entails* the query r if and only if r belongs to $\bigcup_i \Phi_i$.

Lemma 17. *Every Φ_i is closed under native substitutions. In other words, if $\delta \in \Phi_i$ then $\eta\delta \in \Phi_i$ for every native substitution η.*

Proof. The case of $i = 0$ is trivial. We suppose that the claim has been proven for i, and we prove it for $i+1$. Let $\delta \in \Phi_{i+1}$ and η be a native substitution. Then there is a rule (2) and there is a native substitution ξ such that $\xi\delta_1, \dots, \xi\delta_n$ belong to Φ_i and $\delta = \xi\delta_0$. By the induction hypothesis, $\eta\xi\delta_1, \dots, \eta\xi\delta_n$ belong to Φ_i. By the definition of Φ_{i+1}, we have $\eta\delta = \eta\xi\delta_0 \in \Phi_{i+1}$.

3 Succinct Representations of PIV Formulas

In the rest of this paper, by default, PIV is Axiomless PIV. In this section, we fix an instance (H, q) of the PIV entailment problem and develop a succinct representation of PIV formulas local to (H, q) via substitutions native to (H, q). We presume that H is ordered in some way so that the parse forest for the sequence (H, q) of formulas is well defined. In this section, by default, components are components of (H, q), local formulas are local to (H, q), substitutions are native to (H, q), and nodes are nodes of the parse forest for (H, q).

If σ is a formula or quotation prefix then $\mathrm{Var}(\sigma)$ is the list $x_1, \dots, x_k$ of different variables of σ in the order they occur in σ, so that if $i < j$ then the first occurrence of x_i precedes the first occurrence of x_j.

Recall that, according to §2.3, for every labeled node u, we have a quotation prefix $\Pi(u)$ and a formula $\mathbf{F}(u)$.

Lemma 18. *For any labeled node u, $\Pi(u)\mathbf{F}(u)$ is a component with $\mathbf{F}(u)$ being the body.*

Proof. Any such node u belongs to the parse tree of some formula γ in $H \cup \{q\}$. Let u_0 be the root of $\mathrm{PT}(\gamma)$. We prove the lemma by induction on the distance d from u_0 to u.

If $d = 0$, then $u = u_0$. In this case, γ is not a quotation formula, $\Pi(u)$ is empty, and $\mathbf{F}(u) = \Pi(u)\mathbf{F}(u) = \gamma$.

Suppose that $d > 0$ and let v be the parent of u. If v is unlabeled then $v = u_0$, $d = 1$, and γ is a quotation formula. In this case, $\Pi(u) = \Pi(\gamma)$ and $\mathbf{F}(u) = \mathrm{Body}(\gamma)$, so that $\Pi(u)\mathbf{F}(u)$ is again γ.

Suppose that the parent node v is labeled. Then $\mathbf{F}(v)$ has the form $\alpha * \beta$ where $*$ is either conjunction or implication. By the induction hypothesis, $\Pi(v)(\alpha * \beta)$ is a component. We consider the case where u is the left child of v. Then $\Pi(u) = \Pi(v)\Pi(\alpha)$, $\mathbf{F}(u) = \mathrm{Body}(\alpha)$, so that $\Pi(u)\mathbf{F}(u) = \Pi(v)\alpha$ which is a component. □

The formula $\Pi(u)\mathbf{F}(u)$ will be called the *component* of u and denoted $\mathrm{Component}(u)$.

Lemma 19. *For every component φ, there is a labeled node u with*
$\Pi(u) = \Pi(\varphi)$ and $\mathbf{F}(u) = \mathrm{Body}(\varphi)$.

Proof. It suffices to fix a formula γ in $H \cup \{q\}$ and restrict attention to the components φ of γ. Recall Definition 4 of the components of γ.

First suppose that $\varphi = \gamma$. If γ is a quotation formula then the desired u is the unique child of the root of PT(γ); otherwise u is the root itself. Second suppose that ψ has the form $\pi(\alpha * \beta)$ where $*$ is conjunction of implication and φ is either $\pi\alpha$ or else $\pi\beta$. We consider the case when $\varphi = \pi\alpha$. By the induction hypothesis, there is a labeled node v on PT(γ) with $\Pi(v) = \pi$ and $\mathbf{F}(v) = \alpha * \beta$. The desired u is a child of v. We have $\Pi(u) = \pi\Pi(\alpha)$ and $\mathbf{F}(u) = \text{Body}(\alpha)$. □

The depth-first traversal of trees naturally extends to the depth first traversal of forests: traverse the first tree, then jump to the root of the second tree, and so on. As a result we have a linear order on our nodes, namely the depth-first order.

Definition 20 (Lead nodes and components)

- A formula α *dominates* a formula β if β is a substitution instance of α.
- The *lead node of a local formula* α is the labeled node u satisfying the following conditions where φ is the component of u.
  - φ dominates α.
  - If ψ is another component that dominates α then the number of the occurrences of variables in φ is greater than or equal to that of ψ.
  - In the depth-first order of nodes, u is the first labeled node whose component dominates α and has the maximal number of the occurrences of variables.
- A *lead node* is the lead node of some local formula (e.g. its own component).
- The *lead component* Lead(α) of a local formula α is the component of the lead node of α.

Example 21. Figure 4 gives the parse tree for a formula

$$(\text{Alice } \texttt{said} \text{ friends}(\text{Alice}, x) \;\rightarrow\; (\text{Alice } \texttt{said} \text{ friends}(\text{Alice}, \text{Bob})) \wedge$$
$$(\text{Alice } \texttt{said} \text{ friends}(\text{Alice}, y) \;\rightarrow\; (\text{Alice } \texttt{said} \text{ friends}(\text{Alice}, \text{Chuck})).$$

Nodes u, v_1, v_2, w_1 are all lead nodes, and w_1 is the lead nodes of all the leaves.

For every local formula α, the lead node of α and the lead formula are well defined. Indeed α is a substitution instance of and thus dominated by a component. So the set S of nodes whose components dominating α is not empty. A nonempty subset S' of these nodes have components with the maximal possible number of the occurrences of variables. The first node u in S' is the lead node of α, and the component of u is the lead component of α.

Unification. As usual, formulas φ_1, φ_2 without common variables are *unifiable* if there is a substitution ξ such that $\xi\varphi_1 = \xi\varphi_2$. Such a substitution ξ is a *unifier* of φ_1, φ_2. It is a *most general unifier* if it is a substitution instance of any other unifier of φ_1, φ_2.

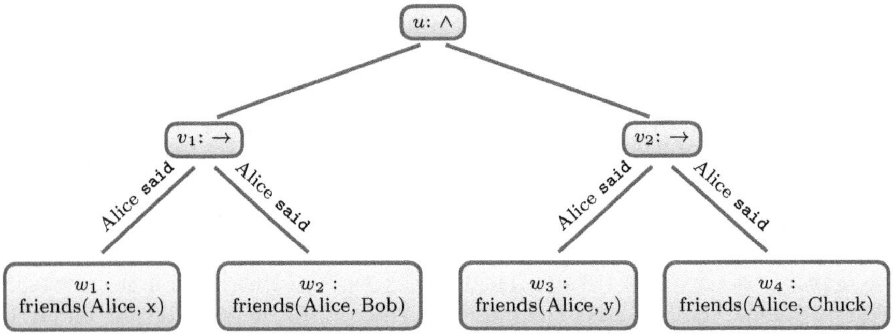

Fig. 4. Domination example

Example 22. Formulas $P(a, y, z_1), P(x, b, z_2)$, where a, b are constants and x, y, z_1, z_2 are variables, are unifiable by means of a substitution ξ such that

$$\xi(x) = a,\ \xi(y) = b,\ \xi(z_1) = z_1,\ \xi(z_2) = z_2.$$

The following proposition is well known.

Proposition 23. *Formulas φ_1, φ_2 are unifiable if they have a common instantiation instance. If they are unifiable, they have a most general unifier.*

Here is a simple construction of a most general unifier for unifiable formulas φ_1, φ_2 with no common variables. Note that φ_1, φ_2 have the same form obtained by replacing all terms with some symbol, e.g. @. Define a graph on the terms (constants and variables) in the two formulas. Two distinct terms form an edge if they occur, in different formulas, at the same position (corresponding to the same occurrence of @ in the form). In Example 22, there are three edges: $(a, x), (b, y), (z_1, z_2)$. Since φ_1, φ_2 are unifiable, every connected component C of the graph contains at most one constant. If C contains a constant c, let $t_C = c$; otherwise let t_C be the lexicographically first variable in C. For every variable z in our formulas, set $\xi(z) = t_C$ where C is the component of z. It is easy to see that $\xi(\varphi_1) = \xi(\varphi_2)$.

4 Reduction to Datalog

Again PIV is by default Axiomless PIV. Given an instance (H, q) of the PIV entailment problem, we construct an instance (P, r) of Datalog such that

- The constants in (P, r) are exactly those in (H, q), so that a substitution is native to (P, r) if and only if it is native to (H, q).
- The set H of hypotheses entails the query q in PIV if and only if the program P entails query r in Datalog using only native substitutions.

Below, by default, components are components of (H, q), local formulas are local to (H, q), substitutions are native to (H, q), and nodes are labeled nodes of the parse forest for (H, q).

4.1 The Vocabulary of (P, r)

We describe the vocabulary of (P, r).

- One relation symbol $\mathcal{D}_u$ for every lead node u. The arity of $\mathcal{D}_u$ is the number of different variables in the component $\Pi(u)\mathbf{F}(u)$ of u.
- The constants that occur in (H, q).

4.2 Rendition of Local Formulas

We translate every PIV formula α local to (H, q) into atomic formula $\mathcal{R}\alpha$, the *rendition* of α, in the vocabulary of (P, r).

Definition 24.

- If α is the component of a lead node u and if $X = \text{Var}(\alpha) = (x_1, \ldots, x_k)$ then $\mathcal{R}\alpha = \mathcal{D}_u(X) = \mathcal{D}_u(x_1, \ldots, x_k)$.
- Let φ be the lead component of α. It follows that $\alpha = \xi\varphi$ for some substitution xi. In this case, $\mathcal{R}\xi\varphi = \xi\mathcal{R}\varphi$.

Lemma 25. *For any local formula α and any native substitution η, if* $\text{Lead}(\alpha) = \text{Lead}(\eta\alpha)$ *then* $\mathcal{R}(\eta\alpha) = \eta\mathcal{R}\alpha$.

Proof. Let φ be the lead component of α. Then $\alpha = \xi\varphi$ for some ξ. We have $\mathcal{R}(\eta\alpha) = \mathcal{R}(\eta\xi\varphi) = \eta\xi\mathcal{R}(\varphi) = \eta\mathcal{R}\alpha$. □

4.3 Program P and Query r

Bodyless Rules. Every hypothesis φ in H is rendered as a bodyless Datalog rule with head $\mathcal{R}\varphi$.

Rules Related to Conjunction. Each lead component γ of the form $\pi(\alpha' \wedge \beta')$ gives rise to three Datalog rules

$$\begin{aligned} \mathcal{R}\gamma &:- \ \mathcal{R}\alpha \ \mathcal{R}\beta, \\ \mathcal{R}\alpha &:- \ \mathcal{R}\gamma \\ \mathcal{R}\beta &:- \ \mathcal{R}\gamma \end{aligned} \tag{3}$$

where $\alpha = \text{Lead}(\pi\alpha')$ and $\beta = \text{Lead}(\pi\beta')$.

Rules Related to Implication. Each lead component γ of the form $\pi(\alpha' \to \beta')$ gives rise to two Datalog rules

$$\begin{aligned} \mathcal{R}\beta &:- \ \mathcal{R}\alpha, \ \mathcal{R}\gamma \\ \mathcal{R}\gamma &:- \ \mathcal{R}\beta \end{aligned} \tag{4}$$

where $\alpha = \text{Lead}(\pi\alpha')$ and $\beta = \text{Lead}(\pi\beta')$.

Unification Rules. In addition to derivation rules related to conjunction and implication, PIV has the substitution rule. Of course Datalog has its own built-in substitution rule. But it does not suffice to establish that $\mathcal{R}(\alpha)$ entails any $\mathcal{R}(\eta\alpha)$ in Datalog. The problem is that α and $\eta\alpha$ may have different lead nodes and so be expressed via different relations. For example, we may have that $\alpha = P(a, y, z_1)$, α is its own lead component with a lead node u, $\eta\alpha = P(a, b, z_1)$, and the lead component of $\eta\alpha$ is $P(x, b, z_2)$ with a lead node v, so that $\mathcal{R}\alpha = \mathcal{D}_u(y, z_1)$ while $\mathcal{R}\eta\alpha = \eta\mathcal{D}_v(x, z_2)$. To this end, we provide program P with additional rules, the unification rules. This would allow us to derive $\mathcal{R}\eta\alpha$ from $\mathcal{R}\alpha$; see Lemma 27.

Every pair of unifiable lead components φ, ψ gives rise to two Datalog rules. We assume without loss of generality that φ and ψ have no common variables. The two rules are

$$\begin{aligned} \xi\mathcal{R}\varphi \ &:- \ \xi\mathcal{R}\psi \\ \xi\mathcal{R}\psi \ &:- \ \xi\mathcal{R}\varphi \end{aligned} \tag{5}$$

where ξ is a most general unifier for φ, ψ.

That completes the construction of P.

Datalog Query. The desired Datalog query $r = \mathcal{R}(q)$.

Remark 26 (On a single Datalog program). It may seem that by converting $\mathcal{D}_u(X)$ into $D(u, X)$ we get a single Datalog program independent from the given instance of the PIV entailment problem. But note that different relation symbols $\mathcal{D}_u$ may have different types and widths (a.k.a. arities). The trick would allows us, however, to use one relation symbol for all relations $\mathcal{D}_u$ of the same type. Besides, there is a prospect of enabling Datalog to deal with sequences of elements.

4.4 Soundness and Completeness

Lemma 27. *By virtue of the unification rules, $\mathcal{R}\alpha$ yields any $\mathcal{R}(\eta\alpha)$ for any local formula α and any native substitution η.*

Proof. If the lead component of $\eta\alpha$ is that of α then, by Lemma 25, $\mathcal{R}\eta\alpha = \eta\mathcal{R}\alpha$, and so $\mathcal{R}\alpha$ yields $\mathcal{R}\eta\alpha$. So suppose that the lead components φ and ψ of α and $\eta\alpha$ respectively are distinct. Without loss of generality, ψ has no variables in common with φ or α.

By the definition of lead components, $\alpha = \eta_0\varphi$ and $\eta\alpha = \eta'\psi$ for some η_0, η'. By the definition of renditions, $\mathcal{R}\alpha = \eta_0\mathcal{R}\varphi$ and $\mathcal{R}(\eta\alpha) = \eta'\mathcal{R}\psi$. Substitutions η and η' have disjoint domains and can be fused into one substitution that we call η. So $\eta\alpha = \eta\psi$. Then $\mathcal{R}(\eta\alpha) = \eta\mathcal{R}\psi$.

Let ξ be a most general unifier for α and ψ, so that $\xi\alpha = \xi\psi$ and $\eta = \chi\xi$ for some χ. We have $\xi\eta_0\varphi = \xi\alpha = \xi\psi$. Clearly $\xi\eta_0$ is a most general unifier for φ and ψ. By the unification rules, $\xi\eta_0\mathcal{R}\varphi$ yields $\xi\eta_0\mathcal{R}\varphi$ which is equal to $\xi\mathcal{R}\psi$. Hence $\xi\mathcal{R}\alpha$ yields $\xi\mathcal{R}\psi$.

We have $\mathcal{R}\alpha \vdash \xi\mathcal{R}\alpha \vdash \xi\mathcal{R}\psi \vdash \chi\xi\mathcal{R}\psi = \eta\mathcal{R}\psi = \mathcal{R}(\eta\alpha)$. □

Theorem 28 (Soundness). *For any local formula* ψ*, if* $H \vdash \psi$ *in PIV then* $P \vdash \mathcal{R}(\psi)$ *in Datalog.*

The proof the soundness theorem proceeds by induction on the given derivation in PIV. The induction step splits into a number of cases depending on the rule used to derive ψ. The proof is rather tedious but routine, and we skip it. Lemma 27 covers the case of substitution rule in the induction step.

Theorem 29 (Completeness). *For every local formula* ψ*, if* $P \vdash \mathcal{R}(\psi)$ *in Datalog then* $H \vdash \psi$ *in PIV.*

Again, the proof is rather tedious but routine, and we skip it.

4.5 Complexity Considerations

Our purpose in this paper was to reduce primal logic with individual variables (PIV) to the standard Datalog so that any any off-the-shell Datalog tool could be applied to the output. Alternatively one may want to design a specialized Datalog-like tool to work directly on PIV but that is a different direction that we may want to take in future.

The reduction time of our algorithm, that is the time it takes to construct an instance of the Datalog entailment problem from a given instance of the PIV entailment problem, is linear in the output size. The size of the output is $O(N \cdot W)$ where N is the number of rules and W is the maximal width W of the Datalog relations $\mathcal{D}_u$. The number $N = O(n^2)$. There are only linear number of rules related to conjunction and implication but the number of unification rules may be quadratic. (We made an attempt to decrease the number of unification rules; that explains "the maximal number of the occurrences of variables" attribute in Definition 20.) W may be linear, so the output size is $O(n^3)$ in the worst case.

At the end we want to solve a given instance of the PIV entailment problem. So we are really interested in the reduction time plus the time to solve the output instance of the Datalog entailment problem. The latter much depends, in general, on the width of the Datalog relations. In our admittedly limited experience, the width of Datalog relations $\mathcal{D}_u$ has been ≤ 6, and there were few unification rules.

Following [1], we could eliminate unification rules altogether, with a side effect of increasing W. To explain the elimination idea, recall the preamble to the introduction of unification rules in §4.3. There we mentioned an example where PIV formulas $P(a, y, z_1)$, $P(x, b, z_2)$ gave rise to binary Datalog relations $\mathcal{D}_u(y, z_1)$ and $\mathcal{D}_v(x, z_2)$. Instead, we could view formulas $P(a, y, z_1)$, $P(x, b, z_2)$ as substitution instances of one formula $P(x, y, z)$ which would lead us to one ternary Datalog relation. Is the elimination idea good? That depends on your applications. If you are interested in scenarios where the input instances of the PIV entailment problem have few occurrences of constants, the price for the elimination of unification rules may be worth paying. In our applications, typically there are many occurrences of constants and few variables, so that unification rules are beneficial.

Finally let us notice that the second of rules (4) is not safe. Recall, however, that we restrict attention to native substitutions. Only the constants in the original instance of the PIV entailment problem can appear in the head $\mathcal{R}\gamma$ of the rule.

Acknowledgment. We are grateful to Andreas Blass and Thomas Eiter for useful comments.

References

1. Blass, A., Gurevich, Y.: Hilbertian deductive systems, infon logic, and Datalog. Bull. of Euro. Assoc. for Theor. Computer Sci. 102, 122–150 (2010), `http://research.microsoft.com/en-us/um/people/gurevich/Opera/204.pdf`
2. Blass, A., Gurevich, Y., Moskal, M., Neeman, I.: Evidential authorization. In: Nanz, S. (ed.) The Future of Software Engineering, pp. 73–99. Springer (2011)
3. DKAL at CodePlex, `http://dkal.codeplex.com/`
4. Gurevich, Y., Neeman, I.: DKAL 2: A simplified and improved authorization language. Tech. rep., MSR-TR-2009-11, Microsoft Research (2009)
5. Gurevich, Y., Neeman, I.: The infon logic. ACM Trans. on Computational Logic 12(2), article 9 (2009), `http://research.microsoft.com/en-us/um/people/gurevich/Opera/198.pdf`

Here and There among Logics for Logic Programming

Alexander Bochman

Computer Science Department,
Holon Institute of Technology, Israel

Abstract. We explore the range of propositional logics suitable for logic programs under the stable semantics, starting with the logic of here-and-there as a primary representative. It will be shown, however, that there are other potential logics in the range. Still, all such logics are based on essentially the same semantics, so their differences are largely due to choice of the underlying language. Our representation suggests a more tolerant answer to the question 'What is the Logic of Logic Programming?', as well as some further expressive opportunities in using logic programs as a general knowledge representation formalism.

1 Introduction

Logic programming has been born with an idea that the language of classical logic can be used directly as a programming language preserving at the same time the declarative meaning of the ubiquitous logical connectives. Thus, the rules of positive (Horn) programs can also be seen as ordinary logical formulas with the usual interpretation of conjunction and implication. Moreover, this classical declarative meaning can be safely extended to positive disjunctive programs, with an additional and quite desirable effect that any classical formula becomes reducible to a logic program.

It is well known, however, that the correspondence between program rules and classical logic breaks down in the presence of negation as failure. The latter cannot be interpreted as a classical negation, and hence relevant program rules cannot be viewed as classical logical formulas. Moreover, the resulting formalism acquires some novel, *nonmonotonic* features which make it distinct from any traditional logical formalism. As a matter of fact, it is these nonmonotonic features that make logic programming a successful competitor of classical logic for problems of artificial intelligence requiring knowledge representation and reasoning.

Facing the discrepancy between logic programming and classical logic, one possible approach that has been pursued amounted to viewing the formalism of logic programs as an independent and self-subsistent knowledge representation formalism that is completely determined by the (restricted) syntax of logic programs, coupled with their (nonmonotonic) semantics. Actually, we will see later that such a view can be given a firm logical justification. However, as we have argued in more details elsewhere (see, e.g., [8, 9]), a more fruitful approach to a

E. Erdem et al. (Eds.): Correct Reasoning, LNCS 7265, pp. 87–101, 2012.

nonmonotonic formalism emerges from representing it as a two-layered system composed of some underlying (monotonic) logic coupled with a nonmonotonic mechanism of choosing intended models. This idea is applicable to logic programming as well. In fact, a first successful realization of this view has been developed by David Pearce (see [17, 18]) who has represented logic programming rules as plain logical formulas in a certain extension of intuitionistic logic called the logic of here-and-there. The logic of here-and-there (HT) is a full-fledged propositional logic with counterparts of all the usual classical connectives, and it can be used for representing and analyzing logic programs of a most general kind (see [15, 11]). Moreover, it has been shown in [14] that two logic programs are strongly equivalent (that is, interchangeable in any larger program without changing the stable semantics) if and only if they are equivalent as formulas in HT. This result has shown, in effect, that HT is a fully adequate logic for reasoning with logic programs under the stable semantics.

Granted the above results, the main question we are going to deal with in this paper is whether HT is the only logic adequate for logic programs under the stable semantics, or there are other possibilities? Our answer to this question will be two-fold. On the one hand, it will be shown that there are other logics that are equally suitable for this task. On the other hand, however, we will see that all these logics are based on the same sematic framework as the models of HT, so the differences between them amount to the choice of logical connectives allowed for representing available information. In particular, it will be shown that there exists a unique maximal logic that subsumes both HT and its possible alternatives, a logic that is expressively complete for the underlying semantic models.

2 The Structural Logic of Logic Programs

Though the logic of here-and-there is a certain extension of intuitionistic logic, it is also, and most importantly, a particular three-valued logic (also called Gödel's three-valued logic). In fact, its three-valued character is determined already by the very choice of the models of HT as pairs (H, T) of interpretations (= sets of atoms) such that $H \subseteq T$ (see [18] for details). In order to see this, we can invoke a general interpretation of four-valued reasoning suggested long ago by Nuel Belnap in [3]. According to the latter, any four-valued interpretation can be represented as a pair of *independent* ordinary interpretations assigning, respectively, truth and falsity to propositions, allowing thereby propositions to be not only true or false, but also neither true nor false or both true and false. Then the four truth-values $\top, \mathbf{t}, \mathbf{f}, \bot$ can be identified with the four *subsets* of the set of classical truth-values $\{t, f\}$, namely with $\{t, f\}$, $\{t\}$, $\{f\}$ and $\emptyset$, respectively. Thus, $\top$ means that a proposition is both true and false (i.e., contradictory), $\mathbf{t}$ means that it is 'classically' true (that is, true without being false), $\mathbf{f}$ means that it is classically false, while $\bot$ means that it is neither true nor false (undetermined). Accordingly, any four-valued interpretation ν is uniquely determined by a pair of ordinary classical assignments, corresponding, respectively, to assignments of truth and falsity to propositions:

$$\nu \vDash A \quad \text{iff} \quad t \in \nu(A) \qquad\qquad \nu \dashv A \quad \text{iff} \quad f \in \nu(A) \tag{1}$$

By the above representation, a four-valued reasoning in general can be seen as reasoning about truth and falsity of propositions, the only distinction from classical reasoning being that the assignments of truth and falsity are independent of each other. Moreover, a three-valued setting appropriate for our subject of stable logic programming can be obtained just by restricting the set of four-valued interpretations to *consistent* interpretations that do not assign the value $\top$ to propositions. In this setting, propositions cannot be both true and false, though they still can be undetermined. From the point of view of the truth and falsity assignments, the restriction amounts to the requirement that truth ($\nu \vDash A$) implies non-falsity ($\nu \not\dashv A$), and it can be easily seen that the pairs of assignments $(\vDash, \not\dashv)$ under this restriction correspond precisely to HT-models (H, T).

A general syntactic counterpart of the above binary representation of four-valued reasoning can be given in terms of biconsequence relations suggested in [4]. Biconsequence relations are sets of *bisequents* - rules of the form $a : b \Vdash c : d$, where a, b, c, d are finite sets of propositions. The intended interpretation of such rules is

> "If all propositions from a are true and all propositions from b are false, then one of the propositions from c is true, or one of the propositions from d is false".

Bisequents are required to satisfy the following *structural rules*:

$$\frac{a : b \Vdash c : d}{a' : b' \Vdash c' : d'}, \quad \text{if } a \subseteq a', b \subseteq b', c \subseteq c', d \subseteq d'. \qquad \text{(Monotonicity)}$$

$$A : \Vdash A : \qquad \text{(Positive Reflexivity)}$$

$$: A \Vdash : A \qquad \text{(Negative Reflexivity)}$$

$$\frac{a : b \Vdash A, c : d \quad A, a : b \Vdash c : d}{a : b \Vdash c : d} \qquad \text{(Positive Cut)}$$

$$\frac{a : b \Vdash c : A, d \quad a : A, b \Vdash c : d}{a : b \Vdash c : d} \qquad \text{(Negative Cut)}$$

A biconsequence relation can be seen as a 'doubled' version of an ordinary sequent calculus reflecting the independence of the truth and falsity assignments. As in the latter, we can extend the notion of a bisequent to arbitrary sets of propositions by accepting the following *compactness condition*:

$$u : v \Vdash w : z \quad \text{iff} \quad a : b \Vdash c : d, \qquad \text{(Compactness)}$$

for some finite sets a, b, c, d such that $a \subseteq u$, $b \subseteq v$, $c \subseteq w$ and $d \subseteq z$.

In what follows, $\overline{u}$ will denote the complement of the set u of propositions. Then the following definition describes 'canonical models' of biconsequence relations.

Definition 1. *A pair of sets of propositions (u, v) is a* bimodel *of a biconsequence relation $\Vdash$ if*

$$u : \overline{v} \nVdash \overline{u} : v.$$

The above condition is equivalent to the following requirement stating that bimodels are closed with respect to the rules of a biconsequence relation.

If $a : b \Vdash c : d$ and $a \subseteq u, b \subseteq \overline{v}$, then either $c \cap u \neq \emptyset$ or $d \cap \overline{v} \neq \emptyset$.

Notice that any bimodel (u, v) can be identified with a four-valued interpretation by taking u to be the set of true propositions and v the set of propositions that are not false. Then the following Representation Theorem can be used to show that biconsequence relations are adequate for their intended four-valued interpretation.

Theorem 1 ((Representation Theorem)). *$a : b \Vdash c : d$ iff, for any bimodel (u, v), if $a \subseteq u$ and $b \subseteq \overline{v}$, then either $c \cap u \neq \emptyset$ or $d \cap \overline{v} \neq \emptyset$.*

Now, a crucial point for our subsequent discussion amounts to the fact that logic programming rules of a general form

$$\mathbf{not}\, D_1 \vee \ldots \vee \mathbf{not}\, D_k \vee C_1 \vee \ldots \vee C_l \leftarrow A_1 \wedge \ldots A_m \wedge \mathbf{not}\, B_1 \wedge \cdots \wedge \mathbf{not}\, B_n$$

can be directly represented as bisequents

$$A_1, \ldots, A_m : B_1, \ldots, B_n \Vdash C_1, \ldots, C_l : D_1, \ldots, D_k.$$

and vice versa, any bisequent in a language without connectives can be viewed as a logic programming rule. In fact, practically all known semantics for logic programs can be described directly in the framework of biconsequence relations. Moreover, it has been shown in [5, 6] that biconsequence relations in their full (four-valued) generality provide an adequate logical framework for a very broad range of semantics suggested for logic programs, including well-founded and partial stable semantics.

For the particular case of logic programs under the stable semantics, however, the formalism of biconsequence relations should be strengthened by adding further structural rules.

A biconsequence relation will be called *consistent* if it satisfies the following structural rule:

Consistency $A : A \Vdash$

Consistency corresponds to the semantic requirement that $u \subseteq v$, for any bimodel (u, v). This constraint reduces, in effect, the formalism of biconsequence relations to a three-valued setting. It provides also a precise syntactic counterpart of the constraint $H \subseteq T$ for HT-models.

A biconsequence relation will be called *regular* if it satisfies the structural rule:

Regularity If $b : a \Vdash a : b$, then $: a \Vdash : b$.

Regularity restricts the binary semantics to a *quasi-reflexive* semantics in which, for every bimodel (u, v), (v, v) is also a bimodel. Note that this constraint is also implicit in the semantics of the logic of here-and-there that identifies, in effect, bimodels of the form (T, T) with ordinary 'classical' models.

It has been shown in [8] that for consistent biconsequence relations, Regularity can be replaced with the following structural rule

(C-Regularity) $$\frac{A, a : b \Vdash : d}{a : b \Vdash : A, d}$$

It turns out that biconsequence relations that are both consistent and regular constitute a maximal structural logic adequate for logic programs under the stable semantics. This fact can be demonstrated by showing that logical equivalence with respect to such biconsequence relations coincides with strong equivalence for logic programs. Thus, the following result has been proved in [8] (see also [10] for a more direct description):

Theorem 2. *Two logic programs are strongly equivalent with respect to the stable semantics if and only if they determine the same consistent and regular biconsequence relation.*

In other words, logic programs Π_1 and Π_2 are strongly equivalent if and only if each program rule of Π_2 is derivable from Π_1 using the structural rules of consistent regular biconsequence relations, and vice versa. The above representation results unanimously suggest that consistent regular biconsequence relations constitute the ultimate structural logic of logic programs under the stable semantics.

A most important consequence of the above representation for our present study is that reasoning about program rules

$$\mathbf{not}\, D_1 \vee \ldots \vee \mathbf{not}\, D_k \vee C_1 \vee \ldots \vee C_l \leftarrow A_1 \wedge \ldots A_m \wedge \mathbf{not}\, B_1 \wedge \cdots \wedge \mathbf{not}\, B_n$$

does *not* depend on the interpretation of the connectives occurring in them (namely conjunction $\wedge$, disjunction $\vee$, negation **not** and implication $\leftarrow$) as *logical* connectives of some logic. Instead, such connectives can be safely viewed simply as suggestive punctuation marks (like commas or parentheses) that determine the structure of the program rule, a structure that is more concisely represented by the corresponding bisequent

$$A_1, \ldots, A_m : B_1, \ldots, B_n \Vdash C_1, \ldots, C_l : D_1, \ldots, D_k.$$

This representation provides, in effect, a solid formal basis for the possibility of viewing logic programming as a 'logically independent' knowledge representation formalism. One of the positive effects of this independence is that the formalism of logic programming acquires freedom of developing its own representation language and constructs that might be more suitable for the problems and tasks it deals with.

Despite all said above, the above structural representation of logic programs leaves some questions unanswered. To begin with, the use of the logical connectives in program rules bears significant heuristic value in the process of transforming 'raw' information about a problem at hand into program rules. In fact, the language of classical logic is pervasive today in informal descriptions of many domains of interest. Moreover, the original logic programming language, Prolog, freely admits compositions of the logical operators, so it treats them essentially as logical connectives. All this obviously creates an incentive for a sound and reasonable extension of the language for logic programs to compound logical formulae. Of course, the fact remains that the paradise of full classical logic is irrevocably lost for representation and reasoning with logic programs. Still, it is worth to inquire how much of it could be preserved in the logic programming reality.

3 The Logic of Here-and-There

To begin with, note that the formalism of biconsequence relations, unlike the majority of other formalisms for many-valued reasoning, does not depend on a particular choice of four-valued or three-valued connectives. In fact, any such connective is expressible in it via introduction and elimination rules as in ordinary sequent calculi, the only distinction being that we have to write a pair of introduction rules and a pair of elimination rules corresponding to two premise sets and two conclusion sets, respectively. Moreover, just as in the classical sequent calculus, these introduction and elimination rules can be used for reducing any bisequent in the extended language to a set of basic bisequents, that is bisequents that involve propositional atoms only. In what follows, we will illustrate this formalization on the logic of here-and-there.

The language of the logic of here-and-there is based on four propositional connectives $\{\wedge, \vee, \rightarrow, \neg\}$[1]. These connectives are definable in the framework of truth and falsity assignments as follows:

$$\nu \vDash A \wedge B \quad \text{iff} \quad \nu \vDash A \text{ and } \nu \vDash B \qquad \nu \dashv A \wedge B \quad \text{iff} \quad \nu \dashv A \text{ or } \nu \dashv B$$

$$\nu \vDash A \vee B \quad \text{iff} \quad \nu \vDash A \text{ or } \nu \vDash B \qquad \nu \dashv A \vee B \quad \text{iff} \quad \nu \dashv A \text{ and } \nu \dashv B$$

$$\nu \vDash \neg A \quad \text{iff} \quad \nu \dashv A \qquad \nu \dashv \neg A \quad \text{iff} \quad \nu \not\dashv A$$

$$\nu \vDash A \rightarrow B \quad \text{iff} \quad \text{if } \nu \vDash A, \text{ then } \nu \vDash B, \text{ and if } \nu \dashv B, \text{ then } \nu \dashv A$$

$$\nu \dashv A \rightarrow B \quad \text{iff} \quad \nu \not\dashv A \text{ and } \nu \dashv B$$

Now, there is a systematic procedure that allows us to transform the above semantic definitions into introduction and elimination rules for the corresponding connectives in the framework of biconsequence relations (see [8] for details). Just as in the classical case, these rules are easily discernible from the above definitions given the intended interpretation of the premises and conclusions of a bisequent.

For our case of HT, these rules are as follows:

Rules for conjunction

$$\frac{a : b \Vdash c, A : d \quad a : b \Vdash c, B : d}{a : b \Vdash c, A \wedge B : d} \qquad \frac{a, A, B : b \Vdash c : d}{a, A \wedge B : b \Vdash c : d}$$

$$\frac{a : b, A \Vdash c : d \quad a : b, B \Vdash c : d}{a : b, A \wedge B \Vdash c : d} \qquad \frac{a : b \Vdash c : d, A, B}{a : b \Vdash c : d, A \wedge B}$$

Rules for disjunction

$$\frac{a, A : b \Vdash c : d \quad a, B : b \Vdash c : d}{a, A \vee B : b \Vdash c : d} \qquad \frac{a : b \Vdash c, A, B : d}{a : b \Vdash c, A \vee B : d}$$

$$\frac{a : b \Vdash c : d, A \quad a : b \Vdash c : d, B}{a : b \Vdash c : d, A \vee B} \qquad \frac{a : b, A, B \Vdash c : d}{a : b, A \vee B \Vdash c : d}$$

[1] It is known, however, that disjunction $A \vee B$ is definable using the rest of the connectives, namely as $((A \rightarrow B) \rightarrow B) \wedge ((B \rightarrow A) \rightarrow A)$.

Rules for negation $\neg$

$$\frac{a : b \Vdash c : d, A}{a : b \Vdash \neg A, c : d} \qquad \frac{a : A, b \Vdash c : d}{a : b \Vdash c : \neg A, d}$$

$$\frac{a : b, A \Vdash c : d}{a, \neg A : b \Vdash c : d} \qquad \frac{a : b \Vdash c : A, d}{a : b, \neg A \Vdash c : d}$$

Rules for implication

$$\frac{a : b, A \Vdash c : d \quad a, B : b \Vdash c : d \quad a : b \Vdash c, A : d, B}{a, A \to B : b \Vdash c : d}$$

$$\frac{a, A : b \Vdash c, B : d \quad a : b, B \Vdash c : d, A}{a : b \Vdash c, A \to B : d}$$

$$\frac{a : b, B \Vdash c : A, d}{a : b, A \to B \Vdash c : d} \qquad \frac{a : b, A \Vdash c : d \quad a : b \Vdash c : d, B}{a : b \Vdash c : d, A \to B}$$

As in the classical sequent calculus, the above rules (applied bottom-up) allow us to reduce any bisequent in the language of HT to a set of bisequents containing atomic propositions only.

Moreover, the language of HT has an important additional property, namely, it allows us to transform any bisequent into a propositional formula. More precisely, the above rules can be used for verifying that any bisequent $a : b \Vdash c : d$ in the language of HT is equivalent to the following bisequent containing a single formula in the conclusions:

$$\Vdash \bigwedge(a \cup \neg b) \to \bigvee(c \cup \neg d) :,$$

where $\neg b$ denotes the set $\{\neg A \mid A \in b\}$. Due to this possibility, any set of bisequents can be represented as a *propositional theory* in HT. Actually, it can be easily verified that, under this correspondence, the above introduction and elimination rules for the connectives of HT correspond precisely to the reduction rules for HT-formulas described in [12].

Summing up the above descriptions and results, the logic of here-and-there fulfils the main desiderata for a sound extension of logic programs to a full-fledged logic. More precisely, it determines a logic which defines the key connectives occurring in logic programming rules as logical connectives, while securing at the same time mutual reducibility of program rules and propositional formulas.

4 Desiderata for a Logic of Logic Programming

The logic of here-and-there has established a certain standard about what could be expected from a potential logic that fulfil the role of logic for logic programming. In this section we will investigate the essential ingredients of this role and requirements imposed by it. On the way we will also single out the range of alternatives that are open for complying with these requirements.

An initial and most basic requirement for such a logic stems from the fact that reasoning about logic programming rules is determined by the three-valued semantics of HT-models. This naturally suggests that any potential logic of this kind should also have a semantic interpretation in terms of such models, which implies, in turn, that it should be some three-valued logic. Accordingly, the choice of a logic reduces, in effect, to the choice of the language, namely to the choice of logical connectives allowable in the three-valued setting. Recall also that any choice of this kind will already secure that any formula or rule of such a logic will be reducible to a logic program.

Remark. It should be noted that the above requirement excludes, in effect, some weaker logics that may still be adequate for logic programs on other counts. Thus, it has been shown in [13] that a weakest intermediate logic that characterizes strong equivalence for logic programs is the logic of weak excluded middle WEM (known also as KC), which is obtained by augmenting intuitionistic logic with the axiom $\neg A \vee \neg\neg A$. As has been noted in [10], this means, in particular, that WEM does not differ from HT on the level of flat (non-nested) logic programs. Still, the semantics of WEM is more general than that of HT, with a side effect that complex logical formulas in WEM are not reducible, in general, to logic programs. This latter fact can be viewed, however, as a sign that the logic WEM goes beyond the logical paradigm behind logic programs.

The stable semantics of logic programs implicitly imposes a further plausible constraint on the set of admissible three-valued connectives. Recall that stable models (equilibrium models in the terminology of HT) are defined as models of the form (H, H) that satisfy some further conditions. In such models, truth coincides with non-falsity, so they determine a purely classical, two-valued logical setting. Accordingly, it is natural to require that admissible connectives of a relevant three-valued logic should behave as ordinary classical connectives in this setting. This requirement amounts to a restriction of three-valued connectives to connectives that give classical truth-values when their arguments receive classical values **t** or **f**. We will call such connectives *conservative* three-valued connectives in what follows.

A final constraint on a potential logic can be formulated as a requirement that the language of such a logic should contain logical counterparts of the connectives that occur in program rules, namely conjunction, disjunction, negation and implication.

In fact, it can be safely claimed that both the conjunction and disjunction of HT constitute natural three-valued counterparts of logical conjunction and disjunction that satisfy practically all the properties of the corresponding classical connectives (such as commutativity, associativity, idempotence and distributivity). Granted this, we can restrict our search of connectives to negation and implication.

4.1 Negations: Gödel versus Lukasiewicz

The negation connective should serve as a logical counterpart of the negation-as-failure operator **not** in logic programs. Consequently, it cannot satisfy all the properties of classical negation. In particular, it should not satisfy the principle of excluded middle $A \vee \mathbf{not}\, A$, since in the logic programming setting a propositional atom may be neither proved, nor rejected (witness the program $p \leftarrow \mathbf{not}\, p$). Nevertheless, the crucial question is what are the properties of classical negation that could be preserved in this setting?

As a matter of fact, the requirements stated earlier do not leave us with too many options. First, a three-valued negation connective $\mathbf{N}$ should behave as the classical negation on the classical truth-values $\mathbf{t}$ and $\mathbf{f}$, that is, it should satisfy

$$\mathbf{N}(\mathbf{t}) = \mathbf{f} \quad \text{and} \quad \mathbf{N}(\mathbf{f}) = \mathbf{t}.$$

Second, in order to be a logical counterpart of **not**, it should satisfy the condition that a bisequent $a : A, b \Vdash c : d$ must be equivalent to $a, \mathbf{N}A : b \Vdash c : d$, while $a : b \Vdash c : A, d$ should be equivalent to $a : b \Vdash c, \mathbf{N}A : d$. This latter constraint completely determines the corresponding truth assignment for $\mathbf{N}$ as the following semantic requirement:

$$\nu \models \mathbf{N}A \quad \text{iff} \quad \nu \dashv A.$$

It turns out that there are precisely *two* three-valued connectives that satisfy the above requirements. The first one is the negation $\neg$ of HT. The second one is the well-known *Lukasiewicz's negation* that we will denote here by $\sim$. It has the following natural semantic definition:

$$\nu \models {\sim}A \quad \text{iff} \quad \nu \dashv A \qquad\qquad \nu \dashv {\sim}A \quad \text{iff} \quad \nu \models A.$$

This fully symmetric description says that ${\sim}A$ is true whenever A is false, while ${\sim}A$ is false if and only if A is true.

A syntactic characterization of this negation is provided by the following introduction and elimination rules:

Rules for $\sim$

$$\frac{a, A : b \Vdash c : d}{a : {\sim}A, b \Vdash c : d} \qquad \frac{a : A, b \Vdash c : d}{a, {\sim}A : b \Vdash c : d}$$

$$\frac{a : b \Vdash c, A : d}{a : b \Vdash c : {\sim}A, d} \qquad \frac{a : b \Vdash c : A, d}{a : b \Vdash c, {\sim}A : d}$$

Both negations of Gödel and Lukasiewicz satisfy the two de Morgan laws with respect to disjunction and conjunction. Still, the main difference between them is that Lukasiewicz's negation satisfies the Double Negation Law:

$${\sim}{\sim}A \equiv A,$$

while $\neg$ satisfies only the Triple Negation Law $\neg\neg\neg A \equiv \neg A$. As a consequence, conjunction and disjunction become inter-definable in the presence of $\sim$:

$$A \wedge B \equiv {\sim}({\sim}A \vee {\sim}B)$$
$$A \vee B \equiv {\sim}({\sim}A \wedge {\sim}B).$$

As a final attractive feature of Lukasiewicz's negation we should mention that it sanctions the reduction rules of the well-known Lloyd-Topor transformation of logic programs with respect to conjunction and disjunction (see [16]).

The differences between these two kinds of negation can be attributed, ultimately, to their different historical origins and associated objectives. Thus, Lukasiewicz's negation has emerged as a most natural generalization of the classical negation for a three-valued setting in which the third truth-value was interpreted as 'undetermined' (neither true, nor false). This kind of negation (and its four-valued extension) is widely used in other parts of logic, for example in relevance logic (see, e.g., [1]).

On the other hand, the HT-negation can be viewed as an offspring of an intuitionistic negation in a three-valued setting. As is well-known, intuitionistic negation does not satisfy the Double Negation Law, for philosophical reasons based on constructivist considerations. Note in this respect that, though natural from the point of view of truth and falsity assignments, the definition of $\sim$ looks very strange in the framework of intuitionistic semantics based on states ordered by a relation of information inclusion. To be more precise, definitions of all the connectives in intuitionistic semantics involve only a current state and its extensions. This implies, in particular, that in an HT-model (H, T), the value of any formula at the 'there' state T depends only on the values of its components in T. In the framework of truth and falsity assignments, however, this amounts to a restriction of three-valued connectives to *negatively local* ones, namely to connectives for which their falsity is defined only in terms of falsity of their arguments. One of the immediate consequences of this fact is that Lukasiewicz's negation is not definable in the language of HT.

Despite the above 'ideological' differences, we will argue below that both kinds of negation can be seen as equally valuable knowledge representation tools. In both cases, given also conjunction and disjunction, logic programming rules are reducible to plain inference rules between logical formulas:

$$a : b \Vdash c : d \;\equiv \bigwedge(a \cup \sim b) : \Vdash \bigvee(c \cup \sim d) : \equiv \bigwedge(a \cup \neg b) : \Vdash \bigvee(c \cup \neg d) : .$$

If we want to transform such inference rules into logical formulas, however, we need a logical implication connective.

4.2 Rules and Implications

Both logic programming rules and their associated bisequents should be primarily viewed as *inference rules* rather than logical formulas. However, in expressive logical formalisms such as classical or intuitionistic logic, inference rules are reducible to logical formulas due to availability of the corresponding implication connective that satisfies the Deduction Theorem: $a, A \vdash B$ iff $a \vdash A \supset B$. In our case, the HT-implication $\to$ satisfies this property, so, as we already mentioned, it allows us to transform any bisequent into a logical formula of HT.

As has been established in the preceding section, the connectives of conjunction, disjunction and negation allows us to transform any bisequent into a rule of the form $A{:}\ \Vdash B{:}$, where A and B are logical formulas. Now, an implication connective $\Rightarrow$ will sanction a reduction of such inference rules to formulas if it will satisfy a condition that $A{:}\ \Vdash B{:}$ is equivalent to $\Vdash A \Rightarrow B{:}$. A semantic counterpart of this condition is the following requirement:

> (R) $\nu \models A \Rightarrow B$ holds for all admissible valuations ν if and only if $\nu \models A$ implies $\nu \models B$ for all such valuations.

Now, the following definition of truth for implication provides the simplest way of complying with the above requirement:

$$\nu \models A \Rightarrow B \quad \text{iff} \quad \nu \not\models A \text{ or } \nu \models B. \tag{R'}$$

It turns out that there are precisely two conservative three-valued connectives that satisfy the above constraint and coincide with classical implication when restricted to the classical truth-values **t** and **f**. Given (R') as a common condition for the truth assignment, these implications are determined, respectively, by adding one of the following falsity assignments:

$$\nu \dashv A \supset B \quad \text{iff} \quad \nu \models A \text{ and } \nu \dashv B$$
$$\nu \dashv A \supset_0 B \quad \text{iff} \quad \nu \models A \text{ and } \nu \not\models B.$$

The first of these implications $\supset$ has been used in [2]. Its corresponding syntactic characterization is provided by the following introduction and elimination rules:

Rules for $\supset$

$$\frac{a : b \Vdash c, A : d \quad a, B : b \Vdash c : d}{a, A \supset B : b \Vdash c : d} \qquad \frac{a, A : b \Vdash c, B : d}{a : b \Vdash c, A \supset B : d}$$

$$\frac{a, A : b, B \Vdash c : d}{a : b, A \supset B \Vdash c : d} \qquad \frac{a : b \Vdash c, A : d \quad a : b \Vdash c : d, B}{a : b \Vdash c : d, A \supset B}$$

In contrast to the above two implications, however, the implication of HT does not satisfy the condition (R'); its corresponding condition of truth is more complex (see above). Still, the adequacy of $\to$ follows from the fact that it satisfies (R), namely $\nu \models A \to B$ holds for all admissible valuations ν if and only if $\nu \models A$ implies $\nu \models B$ for all such valuations[2]. Nevertheless, a stronger condition for truth shows itself in more complex reduction rules for HT implication, as compared, for example, with the above rules for $\supset$.

In fact, in order to evaluate potential alternative candidates on the role of implication in logic programming, it should be taken into account that implication serves not only for reification of program rules, but also, and most importantly, for encoding conditional assertions and if-then-else constructs. What complicates the analysis in this situation is a real possibility that these two roles may conflict with each other. Namely, some implication connectives may be adequate

[2] The semantic property of regularity is essential for this equivalence.

for encoding program rules as formulas, but are less appropriate for representing conditional claims, and vice versa, there are implication connectives that provide a reasonable formalization for conditional assertions, but cannot transform rules into formulas.

As an example of the latter situation, we can consider yet another implication $A \supset_{LT} B$ defined as $\sim A \vee B$. A most attractive feature of this implication is that it is determined by introduction and elimination rules that correspond precisely to *Lloyd-Topor reduction rules* for implication:

Rules for $\supset_{LT}$

$$\frac{a : b, A \Vdash c : d \quad a, B : b \Vdash c : d}{a, A \supset_{LT} B : b \Vdash c : d} \qquad \frac{a : b \Vdash c, B : d, A}{a : b \Vdash c, A \supset_{LT} B : d}$$

$$\frac{a, A : b, B \Vdash c : d}{a : b, A \supset_{LT} B \Vdash c : d} \qquad \frac{a : b \Vdash c, A : d \quad a : b \Vdash c : d, B}{a : b \Vdash c : d, A \supset_{LT} B}$$

Combined with our preceding results for disjunction, conjunction and negation, we even can state the following

Theorem 3. *The language $\{\wedge, \vee, \sim, \supset_{LT}\}$ provides a sound logical representation of logic programs that satisfies the Lloyd-Topor transformation rules with respect to the stable semantics of logic programs.*

Unfortunately, the implication $\supset_{LT}$ is not adequate for transforming program rules into formulas. This follows already from the fact that it does not satisfy reflexivity $A \Rightarrow A$, whereas logic programs under the stable semantics freely admit program rules $p \leftarrow p$.

4.3 A Reconciliation

Facing the above proliferation of potential logics for logic programming, we will suggest in this section a more general approach to the question 'What is a logic of logic programming?'.

Our starting point is based on an observation that all the above alternative logics are based on the same basic three-valued semantics of HT-models. As a result, they are completely determined, in effect, by different choices of conservative three-valued connectives. In fact, all such logics can be viewed simply as alternative *ways of encoding three-valued information.* And just as in the case of classical logic, we can ask whether we can achieve *functional completeness* in our choice of connectives, namely find a set of connectives such that any other connective can be expressed using this set.

As we already mentioned, Lukasiewicz's negation $\sim$ is not expressible in the language of the logic of here-and-there. Accordingly, the language of HT is functionally incomplete in the class of all conservative three-valued functions. However, it turns out that adding $\sim$ to the language of HT will already suffice for achieving functional completeness. In fact, the implication $\rightarrow$ of HT will already be definable in this extended language, so we will obtain the following:

Theorem 4. *The language* $\{\wedge, \neg, \sim\}$ *is functionally complete for the class of all conservative three-valued functions.*

Proof. Using the HT-negation $\neg$, we can define a unary connective $\mathbf{A}A$ as $\neg\neg A$, and then the result follows from a functional completeness of the set $\{\wedge, \sim, \mathbf{A}\}$, proved in [8].

Let us denote by LP3 the logic determined by the language $\{\wedge, \neg, \sim\}$. An axiomatic description of this logic is provided by the introduction and elimination rules for conjunction and the two negations, given earlier. Moreover, the above result shows, in effect, that LP3 is a maximal logic for reasoning about logic programs. In this logic we have full freedom in defining any of the connectives that have been mentioned in this study, and even for defining any other three-valued conservative connective that we could find useful in applications. Consequently, program rules can be encoded as propositional formulas in this logic (in a number of ways), though we still have that any formula of LP3 is reducible, in turn, to a logic program. In this sense, the logic LP3 can be viewed as an ultimate logic for logic programs under the stable semantics.

As a final observation, instead of a formulation of LP3 in the language with two 'competitive' negations, we can use a more 'cooperative' description that employs the implication connective $\supset$, described earlier. Note first that an HT-implication $A \to B$ is definable as $(A \supset B) \wedge (\neg B \supset \neg A)$. Moreover, in the presence of $\sim$, we can define also an HT-negation:

$$\neg A \;\equiv\; \sim(A \supset \sim(A \supset A)).$$

As a result, we immediately obtain the following

Corollary 1. *The language* $\{\wedge, \supset, \sim\}$ *is functionally complete for the class of all conservative three-valued functions.*

Thus, the logic LP3 can also be formulated in the language $\{\wedge, \supset, \sim\}$. As has been established earlier, this language also directly provides all the necessary connectives for a logical representation of logic programs.

5 Conclusions

It has been shown in this study that the range of logics suitable for reasoning with logic programs under the stable model semantics is determined, in effect, by possible choices of propositional connectives definable in the framework of the HT-semantics. As a matter of fact, the idea that a logical variation in reasoning about logic programs is largely confined to the choice of the underlying logical language can actually be extended far beyond the stable semantics. Thus, it has been shown in [5, 6] that practically all semantics suggested for general logic programs can be viewed as instantiations of the same nonmonotonic construction in different logical languages. Even a causal representation of logic programs, described in [7], can be seen as a particular language choice for basically the same semantic interpretation (see also [8] for a more detailed picture).

The approach sketched in the last section above might be considered as a particular elaboration of the claim that logic programming is a logically independent knowledge representation formalism that is permitted to have its own objectives and expressive means. Basically, we suggest to replace the question "What is a logic of logic programs?" (which does not have a unique answer) with a more appropriate question "What are the logical means that are available in representing information and reasoning about logic programs?". According to this view, the choice of a logic amounts, in effect, to a choice of a language used for encoding information in logic programs. In fact, we even do not have to strive for a maximal choice in this respect (provided by the logic LP3), especially if a restricted language turns out to be more efficient from a computational point of view. In any case, we are dealing just with different ways of representing knowledge and information in the formalism of logic programs.

Acknowledgement. Thanks to the reviewer for instructive suggestions and corrections.

References

[1] Anderson, A.R., Belnap Jr., N.D.: Entailment: The Logic of Relevance and Necessity. Princeton University Press, Princeton (1975)
[2] Arieli, O., Avron, A.: Reasoning with logical bilattices. Journal of Logic, Language, and Information 5, 25–63 (1996)
[3] Belnap Jr., N.D.: A useful four-valued logic. In: Dunn, M., Epstein, G. (eds.) Modern Uses of Multiple-Valued Logic, pp. 8–41. D. Reidel (1977)
[4] Bochman, A.: Biconsequence relations: A four-valued formalism of reasoning with inconsistency and incompleteness. Notre Dame Journal of Formal Logic 39(1), 47–73 (1998)
[5] Bochman, A.: A logical foundation for logic programming I: Biconsequence relations and nonmonotonic completion. Journal of Logic Programming 35, 151–170 (1998)
[6] Bochman, A.: A logical foundation for logic programming II: Semantics of general logic programs. Journal of Logic Programming 35, 171–194 (1998)
[7] Bochman, A.: A causal logic of logic programming. In: Dubois, D., Welty, C., Williams, M.-A. (eds.) Proc. Ninth Conference on Principles of Knowledge Representation and Reasoning, KR 2004, pp. 427–437. Whistler (2004)
[8] Bochman, A.: Explanatory Nonmonotonic Reasoning. World Scientific (2005)
[9] Bochman, A.: Logic in nonmonotonic reasoning. In: Brewka, G., Marek, V.W., Truszczynski, M. (eds.) Nonmonotonic Reasoning. Essays Celebrating its 30th Anniversary, pp. 25–61. College Publ. (2011)
[10] Bochman, A., Lifschitz, V.: Yet another characterization of strong equivalence. In: Hermenegildo, M., Schaub, T. (eds.) Technical Communications of the 26th Int'l. Conference on Logic Programming (ICLP 2010). Leibniz International Proceedings in Informatics (LIPIcs), vol. 7, pp. 281–290. Schloss Dagstuhl–Leibniz-Zentrum fuer Informatik, Dagstuhl (2011)
[11] Cabalar, P., Ferraris, P.: Propositional theories are strongly equivalent to logic programs. TPLP 7(6), 745–759 (2007)

[12] Cabalar, P., Pearce, D., Valverde, A.: Reducing Propositional Theories in Equilibrium Logic to Logic Programs. In: Bento, C., Cardoso, A., Dias, G. (eds.) EPIA 2005. LNCS (LNAI), vol. 3808, pp. 4–17. Springer, Heidelberg (2005)
[13] de Jongh, D.H.J., Hendriks, L.: Characterization of strongly equivalent logic programs in intermediate logics. Theory Pract. Log. Program. 3, 259–270 (2003)
[14] Lifschitz, V., Pearce, D., Valverde, A.: Strongly equivalent logic programs. ACM Transactions on Computational Logic 2, 526–541 (2001)
[15] Lifschitz, V., Tang, L.R., Turner, H.: Nested expressions in logic programs. Annals of Mathematics and Artificial Intelligence 25, 369–389 (1999)
[16] Lloyd, J., Topor, R.: Making Prolog more expressive. Journal of Logic Programming 3, 225–240 (1984)
[17] Pearce, D.: A new logical characterization of stable models and answer sets. In: Dix, J., Przymusinski, T.C., Moniz Pereira, L. (eds.) NMELP 1996. LNCS (LNAI), vol. 1216, pp. 57–70. Springer, Heidelberg (1997)
[18] Pearce, D.: Equilibrium logic. Ann. Math. Artif. Intell. 47(1-2), 3–41 (2006)

Causal Logic Programming*

Pedro Cabalar

Department of Computer Science,
University of Corunna, Spain
cabalar@udc.es

Abstract. In this work, we present a causal extension of logic programming under the stable models semantics where, for a given stable model, we capture the alternative causes of each true atom. The syntax is extended by the simple addition of an optional reference label per each rule in the program. Then, the obtained causes rely on the concept of a *causal proof*: an inverted tree of labels that keeps track of the ordered application of rules that has allowed deriving a given true atom.

1 Introduction

Causality is a concept firmly settled in commonsense reasoning. It is present in all kind of human daily scenarios, and has appeared in quite different cultures, both geographically and temporally distant. Paradoxically, although people reveal an innate ability for causal reasoning, the study of causality, or even its very definition, has become a difficult and controversial topic, being tackled under many different perspectives. Philosophers, for instance, have been concerned with the final nature of causal processes and even discussed if there exists so. Logicians have tried to formalise the concept of causal conditionals, trying to overcome counterintuitive effects of material implication. Scientists have informally applied causal reasoning for designing their experiments, but usually disregarded causal information once their formal theories were postulated.

In Artificial Intelligence (AI), we can find two different and almost opposed focusings or currents: (1) *using causal inference*; and (2) *extracting causal knowledge*. Current (1) has been adopted in the area of Reasoning about Actions and Change where most causal approaches have tried to implement some kind of causal derivation in order to solve other reasoning or representational problems. We can cite, for instance, the so-called *causal minimizations* proposed by Lifschitz [1] or by Haugh [2] that were among the first solutions to the well-known Yale Shooting Problem [3], or other later approaches like [4,5,6] applying causal mechanisms to simultaneously solve the frame and ramification problems. All these formalisms are thought to reason *using* causality but not *about* causality. To put an example, we may use a causal rule like "*A causes B*" to deduce that effect B follows from a fact A, but we cannot obtain the information "*A has caused B*." The only concern is that the rule behaves in a directional way: for instance, we do not want to derive $\neg A$ as an effect of fact $\neg B$. A well-studied formalism based on McCain and Turner's work [5] is the approach of *Non-monotonic Causal Theories* [7] developed by V. Lifschitz and his former doctorate students.

* This research was partially supported by Spanish MEC project TIN2009-14562-C05-04.

E. Erdem et al. (Eds.): Correct Reasoning, LNCS 7265, pp. 102–116, 2012.

Current (2), on the contrary, consists in recognising cause-effect relations like "*A has caused B*" from a more elementary, non-causal formalisation[1]. For instance, [10] propose a definition for "*event A is an actual cause of event B in some context C*" in terms of counterfactuals dealing with possible worlds. These possible worlds correspond to configurations of a set of random variables related by so-called *structural equations*. Under this approach, we observe the behaviour of the system variables in different possible situations and try to conclude when "*A has caused B*" using the counterfactual interpretation from [11]: had A not happened, B would not have happened. Recently, [12] refined this definition by considering a ranking function to establish the more "normal" possible worlds as default situations. Under this focusing we cannot, however, describe the system behaviour in terms of assertions like "*A causes B*" as primitive rules or axioms: this must be concluded from the structural equations.

A third and less explored possibility would consist in treating causality in an *epistemological* way, embodied in the semantics as primitive information, so that we can derive causal facts from it. In this case, the goal is both to describe the scenario in terms of rules like "*A causes B*" and derive from them facts like "*A has caused B*". This may look trivial for a single and direct cause-effect relation, but may easily become a difficult problem if we take into account indirect effects and joint interaction of different causes. An approach that followed this focusing was [13] that allowed to derive, from a set of causal rules, which sets of action occurrences were responsible for each effect in a given transition system. This approach was limited in many senses. For instance, only actions could form possible causes, but not intermediate events. The causal semantics was exclusively thought for a single transition. Besides, the implementation of causal rules and the inertia default relied on an additional (and independent) use of the nonmonotonic reasoning paradigm of *answer set programming* (ASP) [14,15], that is, logic programs under the stable model semantics [16].

In this paper we go further and propose to embed causal information *inside* the lower level of ASP. In particular, we are *interested in a formal semantics to capture the causes for each true atom in a given stable model*. To this aim, we extend the syntax by including a label for each rule. Inspired by the *Logic of Proofs* [17], the causes of a given true atom p are then expressed in terms of inverted trees of labels, called *causal proofs*, that reflect the sequence and joint interaction of rule applications that have allowed deriving p as a conclusion. As a result, we obtain a general purpose nonmonotonic formalism that allows both a natural encoding of defaults and, at the same time, the possibility of reasoning about causal proofs, something we may use later to encode high level action languages and extract cause-effect relations among actions and fluents in a more uniform and flexible way.

The rest of the paper is organised as follows. In the next section we explain our motivations and provide a pair of examples. After that, we introduce our semantics for causal proofs, explaining their structure and defining interpretations and valuation of formulas. The next section proceeds to consider positive logic programs explaining how,

[1] Some approaches relying on inductive learning [8,9] also extract causal information from sets of non-causal observations. However, we do not consider them inside current (2) because the learned theory is of type (1), that is, it allows capturing the domain behaviour but not concluding cause-effect relations like "*A has caused B*."

for that case, a concept of model minimality is required. Then, we move to programs with default negation, defining stable models in terms of a straightforward adaptation of the well-known idea of program reduct [16]. Finally, we discuss some related work and conclude the paper.

2 Motivation and Examples

Let us see several examples to describe our understanding of a causal explanation for a given conclusion. Causal explanations (or causal proofs) will be provided in terms of rule labels used to keep track of the possible different ways to obtain a derived fact. For readability, we will use different names for labels (usually a single letter) and propositions, but this restriction is not really required. Sometimes, we will also handle unlabelled rules, meaning that we are not really interested in tracing their application for explaining causal effects.

We begin observing that, in order to explain a given derived atom, we will need to handle causes that are due to the *joint interaction* of multiple events. For instance, suppose we have a row boat with two rowers, one at each side of the boat. The boat will only move forward fwd if both rowers strike at a time. We can encode the program as:

$$p : port \quad s : starb \quad port \wedge starb \rightarrow fwd$$

where we labelled the facts $port$ (port rower made a stroke) and $starb$ (starboard rower made a stroke) respectively using p and s. Suppose that, in this first example, we are only interested in keeping track of actions (in this case, the labelled facts) and that we leave the rule for fwd unlabelled. From this program we expect concluding not only that fwd (the boat moves forward) is true, but also that its cause is $\{p, s\}$, that is, the *simultaneous* interaction of both strokes.

On the other hand, we will also need considering alternative (though equally effective) causes for the same conclusion. For instance, if we additionally have a following wind, the boat moves forward too:

$$w : fwind \qquad fwind \rightarrow fwd$$

so that we have now two alternative and independent ways of explaining fwd: $\{w\}$ and $\{p, s\}$.

From these examples, we conclude that in order to explain a conclusion, we will handle a set of alternative sets of individual events, so that the full explanation for fwd above would be the set $\{\{w\}, \{p, s\}\}$ of its two alternative causes.

Apart from recording labels for facts, we may be interested in a more detailed description that also keeps track of the applied rules. To illustrate the idea, take the following example. Some country has a law l that asserts that driving drunk is punishable with imprisonment. On the other hand, a second law m specifies that resisting arrest has the same effect. The execution e of a sentence establishes that any punishment to imprisonment is made effective unless the accused is exceptionally pardoned. Suppose that some person drove drunk and resisted to be arrested. We can capture this scenario with the next program:

$$\begin{array}{ll} l : drive \wedge drunk \rightarrow punish & d : drive \\ m : resist \rightarrow punish & k : drunk \\ e : punish \wedge \neg pardon \rightarrow prison & r : resist \end{array}$$

We want to conclude that $punish$ holds because of two alternative causes. The first one is the application of law l on the basis of the joint cause $\{d, k\}$. We will denote this as $l \cdot \{d, k\}$. Similarly, the second one would be due to resistance to arrest $m \cdot \{r\}$. These two causes are independent, so the explanation for $punish$ would contain two alternative causes: $\{l \cdot \{d, k\}\}$ and $\{m \cdot \{r\}\}$. Finally, as there is no evidence of $pardon$ we would conclude that the two independent causes for $prison$ are inherited from $punish$ plus the sentence execution e, that is: $\{e \cdot \{l \cdot \{d, k\}\}\}$ and $\{e \cdot \{m \cdot \{r\}\}\}$. We proceed next to formalise these ideas.

3 A Semantics for Causal Proofs

A *signature* is a pair $\langle At, Lb \rangle$ of finite sets that respectively represent the set of *atoms* (or *propositions*) and the set of *labels* (or *causal events*). A formula F is defined by the grammar:

$$F ::= p \mid \bot \mid F_1 \wedge F_2 \mid F_1 \vee F_2 \mid l : F_1 \rightarrow F_2$$

where $p \in At$ is an atom and l can be a label $l \in Lb$ or the *null* symbol $\epsilon \notin Lb$. Symbol ϵ is used when we do not want to label an implication, so that we allow an unlabelled formula $\varphi \rightarrow \psi$ as an abbreviation of $\epsilon : \varphi \rightarrow \psi$. We write $\neg\varphi$ to stand for the implication $\varphi \rightarrow \bot$, and write $\top$ to stand for $\neg\bot$. We also allow labelling non-implicational formulas $l : \varphi$ with some non-null label $l \in Lb$, so that it stands for an abbreviation of $l : \top \rightarrow \varphi$. A *theory* is a finite set of formulas that contains no repeated labels (remember $\epsilon \notin Lb$).

The semantics will rely on the following concept.

Definition 1 (Causal tree). *A* causal tree *for a set of labels Lb is a structure $l \cdot C$ where $l \in Lb$ is a label (the* root*) and C is, in its turn, a (possibly empty) set of causal trees.* □

The informal reading of $l \cdot C$ is that "the set of causal trees in C are used to apply l." We can graphically represent causal trees as regular trees of labels, l being the root and C the child trees, which cannot contain duplications (remember C is a set). We depict trees upside down (the root in the bottom) and with arrows reversed, as in Figure 1, since this better reflects the actual causal direction, as explained before. In the figure, t_1 and t_2 are causal trees but t_3 is not, since there exists a node (the root a) with two identical child trees (the leftmost and rightmost branches). We can deal with usual graph-theoretical terminology for trees so that, for instance, a causal tree with no children $l \cdot \emptyset$ is called a *leaf* (we will just write it l for short). Similarly, the *height* of a causal tree is the length of the longest path to any of its leaves.

Note that, for any non-empty Lb, we will have an infinite set of causal trees. To see why, it suffices to observe that just taking $Lb = \{l\}$ we can build, among others, the infinite sequence of causal trees $l, l \cdot \{l\}, l \cdot \{l \cdot \{l\}\}$, etc. However, as we can see, most

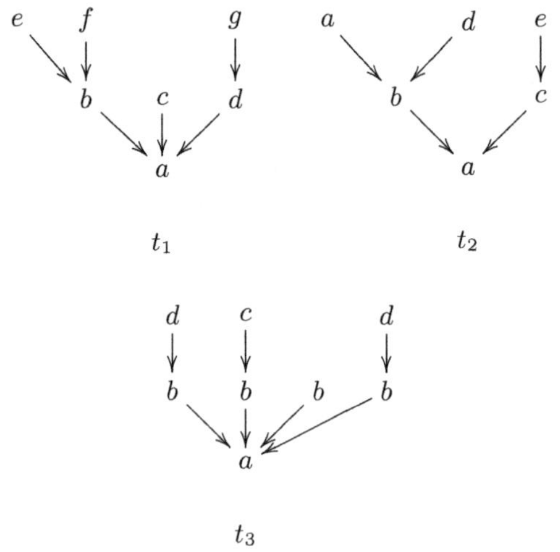

Fig. 1. Three examples of (reversed) trees of labels. t_1 and t_2 are causal trees

trees in $\mathcal{T}$ are not very interesting. Many of them contain some subtree $l \cdot C$ where l occurs in C – this means that we are using l to conclude l. When this happens, we say that $l \cdot C$ is a *self-supported* causal tree. For instance, t_2 in Figure 1 is self-supported. Anything we could explain using t_2 can be also explained using leaf a alone. Any causal tree containing a self-supported subtree is said to be *redundant*.

Definition 2 (Causal proof). *A* causal proof $l \cdot C$ *is a non-redundant causal tree.* □

We write $\mathcal{P}_{Lb}$ to stand for the set of all possible causal proofs for a set of labels Lb. If Lb is finite, $\mathcal{P}_{Lb}$ is also finite and its cardinality is given below.

Proposition 1. *The number of causal proofs $|\mathcal{P}_{Lb}|$ that can be formed with a set Lb of n different labels is given by the recursive function:*

$$f(n) = \begin{cases} 1 & \text{if } n = 1 \\ n\, 2^{f(n-1)} & \text{if } n > 1 \end{cases}$$

□

For instance, with the pair of labels $Lb = \{a, b\}$ we get 4 possible causal proofs $\mathcal{P}_{Lb} = \{a, b, a \cdot \{b\}, b \cdot \{a\}\}$.

We define a *cause* C as any (finite) set of causal proofs, that is, $C \in \mathbf{2}^{\mathcal{P}_{Lb}}$. We write $\mathcal{C}_{Lb} = \mathbf{2}^{\mathcal{P}_{Lb}}$ to refer to the set of all possible causes for a set of labels Lb. An interesting observation is that given any causal proof $l \cdot C$, the set C forms a cause.

As we explained before, the intuitive meaning of a cause is that it collects a set of causal proofs whose joint interaction suffices to explain a given fact or formula. On the other hand, we may have a set of causes that are independent alternative explanations. Our semantics will consist, therefore, in assigning a set of causes (that is, a set of sets of causal proofs) to each formula. However, as happened with redundant trees, a set of causes may easily introduce irrelevant information. Consider the following example.

$$\begin{array}{lll} a : p & p \rightarrow r & r \rightarrow s \\ & b : p \rightarrow q & q \rightarrow s \end{array}$$

Fact s can be obtained following two different paths: one following the implications in the first row, leading to cause $\{a\}$; and the other one following the second row of implications and leading to cause $\{b \cdot \{a\}\}$. The causal proof in the first case, a, actually forms a subtree of $b \cdot \{a\}$. So, from a causal point of view, the latter is not a fully independent alternative, since with the simple application of a it will always *suffice* to get s. Of course, it may be objected that the number of implications for $\{a\}$ is not smaller (it could even be larger). However, all of them are unlabelled, and so, irrelevant for causality steps – we can think of them as "instantaneous." Therefore, we will be interested in dealing with alternative causes that are in some sense minimal (this will be formalised next). Note, however, that inside a cause, we would not want to force minimal causal proofs. For instance, if we modify the previous example as follows:

$$\begin{array}{lll} a : p & p \rightarrow r & q \wedge r \rightarrow s \\ & b : p \rightarrow q & \end{array}$$

now s requires *both* q and r. It seems obvious that b necessarily participates in proving s, so we would get the joint cause $\{a, b \cdot \{a\}\}$ for explaining s, although one of its proofs is a subproof of the other.

Let us capture now these ideas in a formal way. We mutually define relations of *subproof* and *subcause* denoting them, by abuse of notation, with the same symbol $\preceq$.

Definition 3 (subproof/subcause). *Let C, C' denote causes, l, l' labels and t, t' causal proofs. Then:*

- *$l \cdot C$ is a* subproof *of $l' \cdot C'$, written $l \cdot C \preceq l' \cdot C'$, when:*
  - *Either $l = l'$ and $C \preceq C'$;*
  - *or $\{l \cdot C\} \preceq C'$.*
- *C is a* subcause *of C', written $C \preceq C'$, when:*
  for all $t \in C$ there is some $t' \in C'$ such that $t \preceq t'$.

□

From a graphical point of view, t is a subproof of t' if it constitutes a subtree, i.e., any tree formed with a subset of nodes and a subset of edges from t'. We can also see the subcause relation $C \preceq C'$ by understanding that any proof like $l \cdot C$ will be a subtree of $l \cdot C'$ for any l. From this observation, it is quite easy to see that both $\preceq$ are partial order relations. Obviously, $\emptyset \preceq C$ for any cause C, so $\emptyset$ is the smallest subcause. Figure 2 shows three subproofs of t_1 in Figure 1.

Sets of causes $\mathbf{S} \in \mathbf{2}^{\mathcal{C}_{Lb}}$ will be represented with capital boldface letters. By $\min(\mathbf{S})$ we denote the set of $\preceq$-minimal causes from $\mathbf{S}$, formally:

$$\min(\mathbf{S}) \stackrel{\text{def}}{=} \{A \in \mathbf{S} \mid \text{there is no } B \in \mathbf{S} \text{ s.t. } B \preceq A\}$$

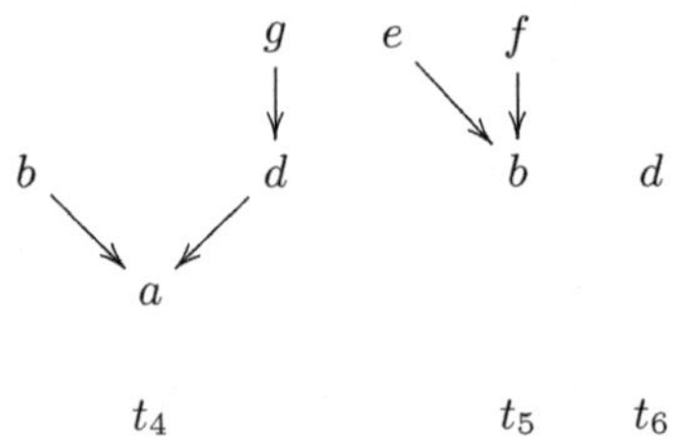

Fig. 2. Three examples of subproofs of t_1

We define the application of $l \in (Lb \cup \epsilon)$ to a set of causes $\mathbf{S}$, written $l \odot \mathbf{S}$, as the set of singleton causes $l \odot \mathbf{S} \stackrel{\text{def}}{=} \{ \{l \cdot C\} \mid C \in \mathbf{S}\}$. For convenience, the expression $\{\epsilon \cdot C\}$ will be understood as an alternative notation for cause C. Using this definition, it is easy to see that $\epsilon \odot \mathbf{S} = \mathbf{S}$.

A *causal value* is a set of causes that are minimal. Formally, the set of causal values $\mathcal{V}_{Lb}$ is defined as:

$$\mathcal{V}_{Lb} \stackrel{\text{def}}{=} \{\mathbf{V} \in \mathbf{2}^{\mathcal{C}_{Lb}} \mid \mathbf{V} = \min(\mathbf{V})\}$$

A *causal interpretation* is a function $I : At \longrightarrow \mathcal{V}_{Lb}$. As $I(p)$ represents the set of alternative causes for p to be *true*, this means that when $I(p) = \emptyset$ (there is no cause for p) we understand that p is *false*[2]. It is easy to see that the minimality condition implies, for instance, that if $\emptyset \in \mathbf{V}$ then $\mathbf{V} = \{\emptyset\}$, for any causal value $\mathbf{V}$. When $I(p) = \{\emptyset\}$ we understand that p is true due to the empty cause $\emptyset$. The empty cause will allow deriving conclusions without tracing their proofs with causal labels and, as we see next, it will represent the concept of "maximal truth." Note the difference between $I(p) = \emptyset$ (p false) and $I(p) = \{\emptyset\}$ (p maximally true).

We define a partial ordering relation '$\sqsubseteq$' on causal values so that for any $\mathbf{V}, \mathbf{V}' \in \mathcal{V}_{Lb}$:

$$\mathbf{V} \sqsubseteq \mathbf{V}' \stackrel{\text{def}}{=} \text{for all } C \in \mathbf{V} \text{ there is some } C' \preceq C \text{ in } \mathbf{V}'$$

The intuitive meaning of $\mathbf{V} \sqsubseteq \mathbf{V}'$ is that $\mathbf{V}'$ makes an atom (or formula) to be *more justified* than with $\mathbf{V}$. For instance, take the particular case $\mathbf{V} \subseteq \mathbf{V}'$ which obviously implies $\mathbf{V} \sqsubseteq \mathbf{V}'$. This means that $\mathbf{V}'$ is offering additional alternative causes to explain a given fact that were not present in $\mathbf{V}$. In the particular case where $\mathbf{V} = \emptyset$, this would mean that $\mathbf{V}'$ makes the fact true (possibly by several causes) whereas $\mathbf{V}$ makes it false. Now, rather than just using a simple inclusion relation, we further specialize it so that each cause in $C \in \mathbf{V}$ is not necessarily present in $\mathbf{V}'$, but there must be some "more justifying cause" $C' \in \mathbf{V}'$ that subsumes C, that is $C' \preceq C$. For instance, take $\mathbf{V} = \{\{a \cdot \{b\}\}, \{c, d\}\}$ and $\mathbf{V}' = \{\{b\}, \{d\}, \{e\}\}$. We have $\mathbf{V} \sqsubseteq \mathbf{V}'$ because in $\mathbf{V}'$, we can find subcauses for all elements of $\mathbf{V}$: $\{b\} \preceq \{a \cdot \{b\}\}$ and $\{d\} \preceq \{c, d\}$.

[2] This is because we will later associate $\neg p$ to *default* negation: there is no cause for p. If we were interested in representing causes for p being false, this would mean introducing a second kind of negation, usually called *explicit* or *strong* negation.

Proposition 2. *$\langle \mathcal{V}_{Lb}, \sqsubseteq \rangle$ constitutes a complete lattice with the following least upper bound (lub) '$\sqcup$' and greatest lower bound (glb) '$\sqcap$':*

$$\mathbf{V} \sqcup \mathbf{V}' \stackrel{\text{def}}{=} \min(\mathbf{V} \cup \mathbf{V}')$$
$$\mathbf{V} \sqcap \mathbf{V}' \stackrel{\text{def}}{=} \min\big(\{ (C \cup C') \mid C \in \mathbf{V}, C' \in \mathbf{V}' \}\big)$$

being the top element $lub(\mathcal{V}_{Lb}) = \{\emptyset\}$ and the bottom element $glb(\mathcal{V}_{Lb}) = \emptyset$. □

Proposition 3. *If $\mathbf{V}$ is a causal value then $l \odot \mathbf{V}$ with $l \in (Lb \cup \epsilon)$ is also a causal value.*

Definition 4 (Valuation of formulas). *Given a causal interpretation I for a signature $\langle At, Lb \rangle$, we define the valuation of a formula φ, by abuse of notation also written $I(\varphi)$, following the recursive rules:*

$$I(\bot) \stackrel{\text{def}}{=} \emptyset$$
$$I(\varphi \wedge \psi) \stackrel{\text{def}}{=} I(\varphi) \sqcap I(\psi)$$
$$I(\varphi \vee \psi) \stackrel{\text{def}}{=} I(\varphi) \sqcup I(\psi)$$
$$I(l : \varphi \to \psi) \stackrel{\text{def}}{=} \begin{cases} \{\emptyset\} & \text{if } l \odot I(\varphi) \sqsubseteq I(\psi) \\ I(\psi) & \text{otherwise} \end{cases}$$

□

As explained before, falsity $\bot$ is understood as absence of cause, and thus, $I(\bot) = \emptyset$. The causes of a conjunction are formed with the joint interaction of pairs of possible causes of each conjunct. That is, if C is a cause for φ and D a cause for ψ then $C \cup D$ together will form a cause for $\varphi \wedge \psi$, provided that $C \cup D$ results minimal among all unions $C' \cup D'$ of that kind. The causes for a disjunction collects (the minimal elements of) the union of causes of both disjuncts. Finally, the most important part is the treatment of implication, as it must act as a *proof constructor*. As we can see, we have two cases. In the first case, the implication is assigned $\{\emptyset\}$ (simply true) when any cause for the antecedent $C \in I(\varphi)$ forms a cause for the consequent, in principle, $\{l \cdot C\} \in I(\psi)$ where, as we can see, we "stamp" the application of l as a prefix. We say "in principle" because $I(\psi)$ can also be $\sqsubseteq$-greater (more true) just because $I(\psi) = \{\emptyset\}$ for instance. If the condition of the first case fails, then the implication inherits the causal value of the consequent $I(\psi)$.

We say that a causal interpretation I is a *causal model* of some theory Γ if for all $\varphi \in \Gamma$, $I(\varphi) = \{\emptyset\}$.

Observation 1. *If $Lb = \emptyset$ then valuation of formulas collapses to classical propositional logic with truth values $\emptyset$ (false) and $\{\emptyset\}$ (true).*

Let us see some particular cases of implications. For instance, when $l = \epsilon$, we get:

$$I(\varphi \to \psi) \stackrel{\text{def}}{=} \begin{cases} \{\emptyset\} & \text{if } I(\varphi) \sqsubseteq I(\psi) \\ I(\psi) & \text{otherwise} \end{cases}$$

When $\psi = \bot$ the implication becomes $l : \neg\varphi$ and the condition $l \odot I(\varphi) \sqsubseteq I(\bot) = \emptyset$ amounts to $I(\varphi) = \emptyset$ obtaining the valuation:

$$I(l : \neg\varphi) \stackrel{\text{def}}{=} \begin{cases} \{\emptyset\} & \text{if } I(\varphi) = \emptyset \\ \emptyset & \text{otherwise} \end{cases}$$

In particular, we can use this to conclude $I(l : \top) = I(l : \neg\bot) = \{\emptyset\}$. Another interesting particular case is $\varphi = \top$, that is, $I(l : \top \to \psi)$ or $I(l : \psi)$ for short. In this case, the set $l \odot I(\varphi)$ becomes $l \odot \{\emptyset\}$ that is $\{\{l \cdot \emptyset\}\} = \{\{l\}\}$. As a result, we obtain:

$$I(l : \psi) \stackrel{\text{def}}{=} \begin{cases} \{\emptyset\} & \text{if } \{\{l\}\} \sqsubseteq I(\psi) \\ I(\psi) & \text{otherwise} \end{cases}$$

A final degenerate case would be $I(\epsilon : \top \to \psi)$ for which $\epsilon \odot \{\emptyset\} = \{\emptyset\}$ and we get the condition:

$$I(\epsilon : \top \to \psi) \stackrel{\text{def}}{=} \begin{cases} \{\emptyset\} & \text{if } \{\emptyset\} \sqsubseteq I(\psi) \\ I(\psi) & \text{otherwise} \end{cases}$$

which trivially collapses into $I(\epsilon : \top \to \psi) = I(\psi)$.

We extend the ordering relation $\sqsubseteq$ to causal interpretations so that given two of them I, J, we write $I \sqsubseteq J$ when $I(p) \sqsubseteq J(p)$ for every atom p.

4 Positive Programs and Minimal Models

Although we will begin focusing on programs without negation, let us first introduce the general syntax of a logic program. As usual, a *literal* is an atom p (*positive literal*) or its negation $\neg p$ (*negative literal*). A *(labelled) logic program* P is a finite set of *rules* of the form:

$$l : B \to H$$

where B is a conjunction of literals (the rule *body*) and H is a disjunction of literals (the rule *head*). The empty conjunction (resp. disjunction) is represented as $\top$ (resp. $\bot$). We write B^+ (resp. B^-) to represent the conjunction of all positive (resp. negative) literals that occur as conjuncts in B. Similarly, H^+ (resp. H^-) represents the disjunction of positive (resp. negative) literals that occur as disjuncts in H. A logic program is *positive* if H^- and B^- are empty for all rules, that is, if it contains no negations. A positive program is further called a *Horn* program if, for all rules, H is an atom. We assume that all the abbreviations seen before are still applicable. Thus, for instance, a rule with empty body $l : \top \to H$ is also written as $l : H$. A rule like $l : p$, with p an atom, is called a *fact*.

Let us see several simple examples. Consider first the program P_1 just consisting of fact $a : p$. The expected behaviour is concluding that p holds because of the only cause $\{a\}$. However, as we saw in the previous section, satisfaction of $a : p$ just requires $\{\{a\}\} \sqsubseteq I(p)$. With one label we can only form one causal proof a, and thus, only two causes $\{a\}$ and $\emptyset$. Since causal values must collect minimal causes, we get exactly three possible causal values $\emptyset \sqsubseteq \{\{a\}\} \sqsubseteq \{\emptyset\}$. This means that $I(p) = \{\emptyset\}$ would also satisfy $a : p$. In fact, it is quite easy to see that, for a positive program, there always exists a model assigning $\{\emptyset\}$ to all atoms in At. It seems obvious that, as happens with standard (non-causal) logic programs, we are interested in a Closed World Assumption, whose reading here would be: "if something is not known to cause a conclusion, it does not cause it." In practice, this means taking $\sqsubseteq$-*minimal* models.

On the other hand, we still want to accept stronger causal values $I(p) = \{\emptyset\}$. This is because other rules could offer more justification for the same atom p. Take, for instance, program P_2 consisting of P_1 plus the (unlabelled) fact p. Now, the only model of $a : p$ and p is $I(p) = \{\emptyset\}$. Informally speaking, an unlabelled fact means that p is "trivially true" and this makes any other rule with p in the head to become redundant (it can be just removed).

Consider now the program P_3:

$$a : p \qquad b : p \rightarrow p$$

From $a : p$ once again we know that $\{\{a\}\} \sqsubseteq I(p)$. The second rule imposes the restriction $b \odot I(p) \sqsubseteq I(p)$. For instance, $b \odot \{\{a\}\}$ corresponds to causal value $\{\{b \cdot \{a\}\}$ and this is $\sqsubseteq$-smaller than $\{\{a\}\}$ (a is a subtree of $b \cdot \{a\}$). So, it can be seen that a $\sqsubseteq$-minimal model should just make $I(p) = \{\{a\}\}$.

Take now program P_4:

$$a : p \;\; b : p \rightarrow q$$
$$c : r \;\; d : q \wedge r \rightarrow s$$

One can easily see that a $\sqsubseteq$-minimal model should still make $I(p) = \{\{a\}\}$ as in P_1, and a similar reason applies to $I(r) = \{\{c\}\}$. In a next step, we proceed to atoms depending on p and r, so from $b : p \rightarrow q$ we may conclude $I(q) = \{\{b \cdot \{a\}\}\}$. Finally, in a last step we would get $I(s) = \{\{d \cdot \{b \cdot \{a\}, c\}\}\}$ so that the single causal proof for s can be graphically depicted as:

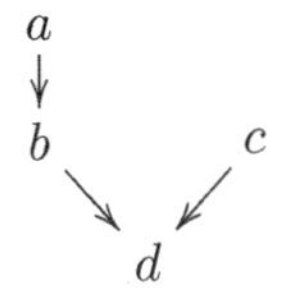

This step by step procedure is well-known in standard logic programming. It is usually obtained from the least fixpoint of a *direct consequences* operator [18] for Horn programs. We define an analogous notion for causal Horn programs as follows:

Definition 5 (Direct consequences). *We define the* direct consequences *operator T_P for a causal Horn logic program P as a mapping from causal interpretations to causal interpretations such that, for any atom p and interpretation I:*

$$T_P(I)(p) \stackrel{\text{def}}{=} \bigsqcup \{\, l \odot I(B) \mid (l : B \rightarrow p) \in P\} \qquad \square$$

That is, we take the least upper bound of all causal values $l \odot I(B)$ obtained from each pair of label l and rule body B for p.

Proposition 4. *Operator T_P is monotonic with respect to ordering $\sqsubseteq$ among interpretations.* □

By Knaster and Tarski's theorem [19], Proposition 4 implies that there exists a greatest and a least fixpoint of T_P, $gfp(T_P)$ and $lfp(T_P)$ respectively. We can thus extrapolate the classical result from [18] to causal programs:

Theorem 1. *A causal Horn program P has a $\sqsubseteq$-least model that coincides with $lfp(T_P)$.* □

We conjecture[3] that T_P is also continuous so it can be computed by iteration on the $\sqsubseteq$-smallest interpretation that makes all atoms false, $I(p) = \emptyset$ for all p.

Finally, to illustrate the effect of disjunction, consider the program P_5 consisting of the single rule $a : p \vee q$. Some models of this rule satisfy $I(p) = \{\emptyset\}$ or $I(q) = \{\emptyset\}$. For the rest of interpretations, we also have models where $\{\{a\}\} \sqsubseteq I(p)$ or $\{\{a\}\} \sqsubseteq I(q)$. The program has two minimal models $I(p) = \{\{a\}\}, I(q) = \emptyset$ and the dual one $I(p) = \emptyset, I(q) = \{\{a\}\}$.

5 Default Negation and Stable Models

Consider now the addition of negation, so that we deal with arbitrary programs. In order to achieve a similar behaviour for default negation to that provided by stable models in the non-causal case, we introduce the following straightforward rephrasing of the traditional program reduct [16].

Definition 6 (Program reduct). *We define the* reduct *of a program P with respect to an interpretation I, written P^I, as the result of the following transformations on P:*

1. *Removing all rules s.t. $I(B^-) = \emptyset$ or $I(H^-) = \{\emptyset\}$;*
2. *Removing all negative literals from the rest of rules.*

Definition 7 (Stable model). *A causal interpretation I is a* stable model *of a causal program P if I is a $\sqsubseteq$-minimal model of P^I.*

As an example, take the program P_6:

$$a : \neg q \rightarrow p \quad b : \neg p \rightarrow q \quad c : p \rightarrow r$$

As we saw in previous sections, negation $\neg\varphi$ is always two-valued: it returns $\emptyset$ if φ has any cause and $\{\emptyset\}$ otherwise. So, when deciding possible reducts, it suffices with considering which atoms, among those negated, will be assigned $\emptyset$. Suppose first we take some I such that $I(p) = \emptyset, I(q) \neq \emptyset$. The reduct P_6^I will correspond to:

$$b : \top \rightarrow q \quad c : p \rightarrow r$$

[3] A formal proof is still under study.

whose least model is $J(p) = \emptyset, J(q) = \{\{b\}\}, J(r) = \emptyset$. In particular, taking $I = J$ is consistent so we obtain a first stable model. Suppose now we take some I' such that $I'(p) \neq \emptyset, I'(q) = \emptyset$. The reduct this time would be:

$$a : \top \rightarrow p \quad c : p \rightarrow r$$

The least model of this program is $J'(p) = \{\{a\}\}, J'(q) = \emptyset, J'(r) = \{c \cdot \{a\}\}$ which is consistent with the assumption $I' = J'$ so that we get a second stable model. Applying a similar reasoning for the remaining cases, we can easily check that P_6 has no more stable models.

6 Related Work

Apart from the different AI approaches and orientations for causality we mentioned in the Introduction, from the technical point of view, the current approach can be classified as a *labelled deductive system* [20]. In particular, the work that has had a clearest and most influential relation to the current proposal has been the *Logic of Proofs* [17] (**LP**). We have borrowed from that formalism (most part of) the notation for our causal proofs and rule labellings and the fundamental idea of keeping track of justifications by considering the rule applications. The syntax of **LP** is that of classical logic extended with the construct $t : F$ where F is any formula and t a *proof polynomial*, a term following the grammar:

$$t ::= a \mid x \mid !t \mid t_1 \cdot t_2 \mid t_1 + t_2$$

where a is a *proof constant* (corresponding to our labels) and x a *proof variable*. The meaning of $t : F$ is that t constitutes a proof for F. **LP** is an axiomatic system containing the axioms:

A0. *Propositional Calculus*
A1. $t : F \rightarrow F$ *"reflection"*
A2. $t : (F \rightarrow G) \rightarrow (s : F \rightarrow (t \cdot s) : G)$ *"application"*
A3. $t : F \rightarrow !t : (t : F)$ *"proof checker"*
A4. $s : F \rightarrow (s + t) : F, \ \ t : F \rightarrow (s + t) : F$ *"sum"*

Without entering into further detail, let us overview the main common points and differences between both formalisms. A first important difference comes from the purpose of each approach. While **LP** is thought for capturing a particular logical system, causal logic programs are thought for dealing with non-logical axioms that allow knowledge representation of specific scenarios. Besides, from a technical point of view, **LP** is an axiomatic system, whereas our formalisation relies on a semantic description.

As we can see, proof polynomials are quite similar to our causal proofs. Axiom **A2** looks like a syntactic counterpart of our semantics for labelled implications. However, there also exist some important differences when comparing proof polynomials and causal proofs. For instance, **LP** is much more expressive in the sense that the $t : F$ construction in our approach is exclusively limited to the case in which t is a label. In other words, we have not specified a syntax for expressing that a given cause is assigned to some formula – this information is only obtained as a semantic by-product. As we explain later, the possibility of adding new operators for inspecting causes is left for future study. Another difference is that, while **LP** represents alternative proofs s and t as the polynomial $s + t$, in our causal proofs the ordering or repetition is irrelevant, and so, we simply handle a set of causes. Note also that axiom **A4** does not make sense under our causal reading: if s is a cause for F, then not any unrelated t will form a cause $s + t$ for F. It is also interesting to observe that the idea of joint causes (that is, the simultaneous interaction of several causal proofs) does not have a syntactic counterpart in **LP**.

Finally, another important difference, especially when thinking about its application to Knowledge Representation, is that **LP** is monotonic whereas our approach allows non-monotonic reasoning and, in fact, is a proper extension of logic programs under the stable model semantics. In this sense, the crucial feature is the introduction of default negation, something that is not present in **LP**.

A preliminary version of the current approach was presented in [21] where most ideas were already present. However, the treatment of causal values and their ordering relation has been considerably improved and generalised now. This has allowed us, for instance, treating disjunction and conjunction respectively as the least-upper and greatest-lower bounds of the causal values lattice. Furthermore, it has also simplified the definition of the direct consequences operator and the proof of its monotonicity.

7 Conclusions

We have introduced an extension of logic programming under the stable model semantics that allows dealing with causal explanations for each derived atom p in a stable model. These explanations are given as sets of alternative, independent causes. In their turn, each cause corresponds to the joint interaction of (one or more) causal proofs, being those used to keep track of the different rule applications that have taken place in the derivation of p.

Many open topics remain for future study. For instance, implementation and a complexity assessment are the next immediate steps. We plan to establish a series of formal results relating regular (non-causal) stable model semantics and the information obtained with causal stable models. These results can be exploited for implementation. Regarding expressivity, an interesting topic is the introduction of new syntactic operators for inspecting causal information. Apart from directly representing whether some cause is an explanation for a given formula, we can imagine many different interesting constructs, like checking the influence of a particular event or label in a conclusion, expressing necessary or sufficient causes, or even dealing with counterfactuals. Another interesting topic is removing the syntactic reduct definition in favour of some full logical treatment of default negation, as happens for (non-causal) stable models and their charaterisation in terms of *Equilibrium Logic* [22]. This may allow extending the definition of causal stable models to an arbitrary syntax and to the first order case, where the use of variables in labels may also introduce new interesting features. Finally, as potential applications, our main concern is designing a high level action language on top of causal logic programs with the purpose of modelling some typical scenarios from the literature on causality in AI. Another possible application domain is trying to establish a relation to relevant approaches [23,24] for debugging in answer set programming.

Acknowledgements. This work is undoubtedly in debt with Vladimir Lifschitz's pioneering research program and his contributions, among others, to two central areas of Knowledge Representation such as Causal Reasoning and Nonmonotonic Reasoning (NMR). Both my PhD advisor, Ramón P. Otero, and I were first introduced to Vladimir as co-speakers in a seminar on Causality organised by Alessandro Provetti in Milano, a pair of days before the 6th International Conference on Principles of Knowledge Representation and Reasoning (KR'98). This conference took place in Trento in June 1998, and during its celebration, Vladimir had the courtesy to help us with our formal work relating Otero's Logic of Pertinence to causal reasoning. With his clean and accurate style, he reformulated our results in one piece of paper which put the basis for what constituted later the central part of my PhD dissertation. Today, KR comes back to Italy (KR'12, Rome) and I am still studying Vladimir's papers on NMR and causality much in the same way as fourteen years ago.

References

1. Lifschitz, V.: Formal theories of action (preliminary report). In: Proc. of the 10th IJCAI, Milan, Italy, pp. 966–972 (1987)
2. Haugh, B.A.: Simple causal minimizations for temporal persistence and projection. In: Proceedings of the 6th National Conference of Artificial Intelligence, pp. 218–223 (1987)
3. Hanks, S., McDermott, D.: Nonmonotonic logic and temporal projection. Artificial Intelligence Journal 33, 379–413 (1987)
4. Lin, F.: Embracing causality in specifying the indirect effects of actions. In: Mellish, C.S. (ed.) Proc. of the Intl. Joint Conf. on Artificial Intelligence (IJCAI), Montreal, Canada. Morgan Kaufmann (1995)
5. McCain, N., Turner, H.: Causal theories of action and change. In: Proc. of the AAAI 1997, pp. 460–465 (1997)
6. Thielscher, M.: Ramification and causality. Artificial Intelligence Journal 1-2(89), 317–364 (1997)
7. Giunchiglia, E., Lee, J., Lifschitz, V., McCain, N., Turner, H.: Nonmonotonic causal theories. Artificial Intelligence 153(1-2), 49–104 (2004)
8. Otero, R.P., Varela, M.: Iaction: a system for learning action descriptions for planning. In: Proc. of the 16th Intl. Conf. on Inductive Logic Programming, ILP 2006 (2006)
9. Balduccini, M.: Learning action descriptions with A-Prolog: Action language $\mathcal{C}$. In: Amir, E., Lifschitz, V., Miller, R. (eds.) Proc. of Logical Formalizations of Commonsense Reasoning (Commonsense 2007) AAAI Spring Symposium (2007)
10. Halpern, J.Y., Pearl, J.: Causes and explana- tions: A structural-model approach. part I: Causes. British Journal for Philosophy of Science 56(4), 843–887 (2005)
11. Hume, D.: An enquiry concerning human understanding (1748); Reprinted by Open Court Press, LaSalle, IL (1958)
12. Halpern, J.Y.: Defaults and normality in causal structures. In: Proc. of the Eleventh International Conference on Principles of Knowledge Representation and Reasoning (KR 2008), pp. 198–208 (2008)
13. Cabalar, P.: A preliminary study on reasoning about causes. In: Proc. of the 6th Intl. Symposium on Logical Formalizations of Commonsense Reasoning (2003)

14. Marek, V., Truszczyński, M.: In: Stable models and an alternative logic programming paradigm, pp. 169–181. Springer (1999)
15. Niemelä, I.: Logic programs with stable model semantics as a constraint programming paradigm. Annals of Mathematics and Artificial Intelligence 25, 241–273 (1999)
16. Gelfond, M., Lifschitz, V.: The stable model semantics for logic programming. In: Kowalski, R.A., Bowen, K.A. (eds.) Logic Programming: Proc. of the Fifth International Conference and Symposium, vol. 2, pp. 1070–1080. MIT Press, Cambridge (1988)
17. Artëmov, S.N.: Explicit provability and constructive semantics. Bulletin of Symbolic Logic 7(1), 1–36 (2001)
18. van Emden, M.H., Kowalski, R.A.: The semantics of predicate logic as a programming language. Journal of the ACM 23, 733–742 (1976)
19. Tarski, A.: A lattice-theoretical fixpoint theorem and its applications. Pacific Journal of Mathematics 5, 285–309 (1955)
20. Broda, K., Gabbay, D., Lamb, L., Russo., A.: Compiled Labelled Deductive Systems: A Uniform Presentation of Non-Classical Logics. Research Studies Press (2004)
21. Cabalar, P.: Logic programs and causal proofs. In: Proc. of the 10th Intl. Symposium on Logical Formalization on Commonsense Reasoning (Commonsense 2011). AAAI Spring Symposium Series (2011)
22. Pearce, D.: Equilibrium logic. Annals of Mathematics and Artificial Intelligence 47(1-2), 3–41 (2006)
23. Gebser, M., Pührer, J., Schaub, T., Tompits, H.: Meta-programming technique for debugging answer-set programs. In: Proc. of the 23rd Conf. on Artificial Inteligence (AAAI 2008), pp. 448–453 (2008)
24. Pontelli, E., Son, T.C., El-Khatib, O.: Justifications for logic programs under answer set semantics. Theory and Practice of Logic Programming 9(1), 1–56 (2009)

On the Interaction of Existential Rules and Equality Constraints in Ontology Querying

Andrea Calì[2,3], Georg Gottlob[1,3,4], Giorgio Orsi[1,4], and Andreas Pieris[1]

[1] Department of Computer Science, University of Oxford, UK
[2] Dept. of Computer Science and Inf. Systems, Birkbeck University of London, UK
[3] Oxford-Man Institute of Quantitative Finance, University of Oxford, UK
[4] Institute for the Future of Computing, Oxford Martin School, UK
andrea@dcs.bbk.ac.uk,
{georg.gottlob,giorgio.orsi,andreas.pieris}@cs.ox.ac.uk

Abstract. Ontological query processing is an exciting research topic in database theory, knowledge representation, and logic programming. In many cases, ontological constraints are expressed over an extensional database by extending traditional Datalog rules to allow existential quantification and equality atoms in the head. The unrestricted use of these features causes undecidability of query answering and, therefore, their interaction must be controlled. This work provides a tutorial-like introduction to the problem of query answering under existential and equality constraints. We survey the most notable (semantic and syntactic) restrictions to such constraints ensuring decidability of query answering, and we discuss their practical application to conceptual modelling.

1 Introduction

During the last decade, the interest of data management researchers and practitioners progressively shifted from tasks such as *storage*, *integration* and *maintenance* to *data analysis* and *automated reasoning*, that are now of paramount importance for modern data-intensive applications. In particular, automated reasoning has proven decisive in areas requiring the analysis of large amounts of semi-structured and incomplete data such as bioinformatics, algorithmic trading, and web search and automation.

The need for scalable reasoning procedures foraged several research activities in database theory [1], knowledge representation [27], and logic programming [24], leading to a progressive convergence of these fields that, for decades, investigated complementary aspects of the same problem. A very challenging reasoning task is certainly *query answering*, to which most of the other reasoning problems can be reduced. Formally, given an extensional database D, a set Σ of ontological constraints, and a *conjunctive query* q of the form $p(\mathbf{X}) \leftarrow \varphi(\mathbf{X}, \mathbf{Y})$, where $\varphi(\mathbf{X}, \mathbf{Y})$ is a conjunction of atoms over a relational schema, the *answer* to q consists of all tuples $\mathbf{t}$ of constants such that, when we replace $\mathbf{X}$ with $\mathbf{t}$, $\exists \mathbf{Y}\, \varphi(\mathbf{X}, \mathbf{Y})$ evaluates to *true* in every model of $D \cup \Sigma$.

E. Erdem et al. (Eds.): Correct Reasoning, LNCS 7265, pp. 117–133, 2012.

Example 1. Consider the following set Σ of constraints, stating that the father of an ancestor of a person P, is also an ancestor of P:

$$\sigma_1 : \forall F \forall P fatherOf(F, P) \rightarrow ancestorOf(F, P)$$
$$\sigma_2 : \forall F \forall A \forall P\ fatherOf(F, A), ancestorOf(A, P) \rightarrow ancestorOf(F, P).$$

Let q be the query asking for all the ancestors of *alice*, that is, $p(X) \leftarrow ancestorOf(X, alice)$, and let $D = \{fatherOf(bob, alice), fatherOf(mark, bob)\}$. Observe that every model of $D \cup \Sigma$ contains the atoms $ancestorOf(bob, alice)$ and $ancestorOf(mark, alice)$. This implies that the answer of q over the logical theory $D \cup \Sigma$ is the set of tuples $\{\langle bob\rangle, \langle mark\rangle\}$. ■

Notice that the set of constraints given above is a plain Datalog program (see, e.g., [1]). Datalog has been used for decades as a counterpart of Prolog for data management; however, its expressive power is often insufficient to model all the necessary constraints one would like to enforce. Therefore, several research activities have been devoted to the problem of extending Datalog with additional features without compromising its good computational properties.

Example 2. Consider the following constraint, asserting that every person necessarily has a father:

$$\sigma : \forall P\ person(P) \rightarrow \exists F\ fatherOf(F, P).$$

Consider also the conjunctive query $q : p(Y) \leftarrow person(Y), fatherOf(X, Y)$, asking for all the persons who have a father. If the extensional database is $D = \{fatherOf(bob, alice), person(alice), person(mark)\}$, then we immediately get that $\langle alice\rangle$ belongs to the answer of q over $D \cup \Sigma$. Furthermore, it is easy to see that $\langle mark\rangle$ is also in the answer of q since σ forces the existence of an atom of the form $fatherOf(z, mark)$ in every model of $D \cup \Sigma$, where z is a variable representing the father of *mark*. ■

Observe that the constraint of Example 2 has an existentially quantified variable in its right-hand side, and thus is not a Datalog rule. Constraints of this form are known as *tuple-generating dependencies (TGDs)* in the database literature. A TGD is an implication of the form $\forall \mathbf{X} \forall \mathbf{Y}\, \varphi(\mathbf{X}, \mathbf{Y}) \rightarrow \exists \mathbf{Z}\, \psi(\mathbf{X}, \mathbf{Z})$, where $\varphi(\mathbf{X}, \mathbf{Y})$ and $\psi(\mathbf{X}, \mathbf{Z})$ are conjunctions of atoms over a relational schema. It is well-known that query answering under TGDs is undecidable [3]. However, by properly restricting the syntactic form of the TGDs, it is possible to regain decidability, while preserving a reasonable expressiveness of the language. Decidable classes of TGDs have been widely adopted for ontological modelling [6,8,22], data integration [23], and data exchange [18], where it is often necessary to state the existence of an (unnamed) object to model incomplete information about a domain of interest.

Another common situation in databases and ontology modelling is the enforcement of functionality constraints over relations, for example, *key dependencies* (see, e.g., [1]) and *identification constraints* [14].

Example 3. Consider the following constraint, stating that each person has at most one father:

$$\sigma : \forall P \forall F_1 \forall F_2 \; \mathit{fatherOf}(F_1, P), \mathit{fatherOf}(F_2, P) \rightarrow F_1 = F_2.$$

Consider also the database $D = \{\mathit{fatherOf}(\mathit{bob}, \mathit{alice}), \mathit{fatherOf}(\mathit{mark}, \mathit{alice})\}$, which states that *bob* and *mark* are fathers of *alice*; obviously D violates σ. ∎

Constraints as the one given above are known as *equality-generating dependencies (EGDs)* in the database literature. An EGD is an expression of the form $\forall \mathbf{X} \, \varphi(\mathbf{X}) \rightarrow X_i = X_j$, where $\varphi(\mathbf{X})$ is a conjunction of atoms over a relational schema, and $\{X_i, X_j\} \subseteq \mathbf{X}$. EGDs are of fundamental importance in database applications such as data integration and data cleaning [19], where it is often necessary to state that two or more objects must necessarily be the same. When it is not possible to satisfy an EGD, like in Example 3, we say that the theory is *inconsistent*, i.e., it has no model, and therefore any tuple is a valid answer to any query. Query answering under TGDs and EGDs is undecidable [16], even in the case of TGDs which guarantee decidability of query answering. In particular, query answering under the simplest type of TGDs, i.e., *inclusion dependencies*, and the simplest type of EGDs, i.e., key dependencies, is undecidable [12]. However, it is possible to identify classes of EGDs for which the interaction with TGDs is "well-behaved", and query answering becomes decidable [12].

Example 4. Consider the following set Σ of constraints; the intuitive meaning of Σ is obvious:

$$\sigma_1 : \forall P \forall F \; \mathit{hasFather}(P, F) \rightarrow \mathit{fatherOf}(F, P)$$
$$\sigma_2 : \forall P \forall F_1 \forall F_2 \; \mathit{hasFather}(P, F_1), \mathit{hasFather}(P, F_2) \rightarrow F_1 = F_2.$$

Consider also the database $D = \{\mathit{hasFather}(\mathit{alice}, \mathit{bob}), \mathit{hasFather}(\mathit{bob}, \mathit{mark})\}$. Observe that σ_1 forces that every model of $D \cup \Sigma$ contains the two atoms $\mathit{fatherOf}(\mathit{bob}, \mathit{alice})$ and $\mathit{fatherOf}(\mathit{mark}, \mathit{bob})$. Moreover, notice that whenever σ_2 is satisfied by D, then it is also satisfied by every model of $D \cup \Sigma$. In other words, the EGD and the TGD do not interact with each other; thus, once the database satisfies the EGD, we can ignore it and consider only the TGD. ∎

The constraints of Example 4 are a case of *separable* TGDs and EGDs, for which query answering is known to be decidable (assuming that the TGDs fall in a decidable class) [6,12] . Moreover, since we are allowed to ignore the EGDs (providing that the extensional database satisfies them), the complexity of query answering under separable TGDs and EGDs is the same as the complexity of query answering under TGDs alone. However, it is easy to construct a non-separable set of dependencies. In this case, the fact that the given database satisfies the set of EGDs, does not guarantee the safe elimination of the EGDs. It is possible that some atoms, which are crucial for query answering purposes, occur in every model of the given logical theory because of the EGDs. This fact is illustrated in the following example.

Example 5. Consider the set Σ of constraints expressing the fact that everyone who works is paid a certain amount per hour, and also has at most one employer. In addition, everyone who is paid by somebody is also employed by her:

$$\sigma_1 : \forall W \forall E\; \mathit{worksFor}(W, E) \rightarrow \exists P \exists A\; \mathit{pays}(P, A, W)$$
$$\sigma_2 : \forall E \forall A \forall W\; \mathit{pays}(E, A, W) \rightarrow \mathit{worksFor}(W, E)$$
$$\sigma_3 : \forall W \forall E_1 \forall E_2\; \mathit{worksFor}(W, E_1), \mathit{worksFor}(W, E_2) \rightarrow E_1 = E_2.$$

Consider the database $D = \{\mathit{worksFor}(\mathit{ann}, \mathit{bill})\}$, and the conjunctive query $q : p(Y) \leftarrow \mathit{pays}(\mathit{bill}, X, Y)$, asking who is paid by *bill*. It is easy to verify that every model of $D \cup \Sigma$ contains an atom of the form $\mathit{pays}(\mathit{bill}, z, \mathit{ann})$, where z represents some unknown value. Therefore, $\langle \mathit{ann} \rangle$ belongs to the answer of q over $D \cup \Sigma$. However, this does not hold if we consider the theory $D \cup \Sigma \setminus \{\sigma_3\}$, i.e, only the TGDs. Notice that the infinite set of atoms

$$\{\mathit{worksFor}(\mathit{ann}, \mathit{bill}), \mathit{pays}(z_0, z_1, \mathit{ann}), \mathit{worksFor}(\mathit{ann}, z_0), \mathit{pays}(z_2, z_3, z_0), \ldots\},$$

where $z_0, z_1, z_2, \ldots$ represent some unknown values, is a model of $D \cup \Sigma \setminus \{\sigma_3\}$, but does not contain an atom with predicate *pays* that has as a first argument the constant *bill*. Hence, the answer to q over $D \cup \Sigma \setminus \{\sigma_3\}$ is the empty set. ■

Unfortunately, deciding whether a set of TGDs and EGDs is separable is undecidable. It is therefore important to study suitable syntactic restrictions which ensure a controlled interaction among dependencies.

Roadmap. This work is a tutorial-like introduction to the problem of query answering under TGDs and EGDs and, in particular, to techniques for controlling their interaction and guarantee decidability. The next section provides the reader with the necessary theoretical background on query answering under TGDs and EGDs. The semantic notion of separability of TGDs and EGDs is formally introduced in Section 3. Section 4 surveys the most notable syntactic conditions that are sufficient for separability, while Section 5 discusses the use of separability in related logic-based formalisms for conceptual modelling.

2 Interaction of TGDs and EGDs in Ontology Querying

In this section, we present the problem of query answering under TGDs and EGDs, and we discuss the difficulties that arise due to the interaction of those constraints. Let us first recall some useful technical notions.

2.1 Technical Definitions

Alphabets. We define the following pairwise disjoint (infinite) sets of symbols: a set Γ of *constants*, that constitute the "normal" domain of a database, a set Γ_N of *labeled nulls*, used as "fresh" skolem terms, which are placeholders for unknown values, and thus can be also seen as (globally) existentially-quantified variables, and a set Γ_V of (regular) *variables*, used in queries and dependencies.

Different constants represent different values (*unique name assumption*), while different nulls may represent the same value. A lexicographic order is defined on $\Gamma \cup \Gamma_N$, such that every value in Γ_N follows all those in Γ. We denote by $\mathbf{X}$ sequences (or sets, with a slight abuse of notation) of variables or constants $X_1, \ldots, X_k$, with $k \geqslant 0$. Throughout, let $[n] = \{1, \ldots, n\}$, for any integer $n \geqslant 1$.

Relational Model. A *relational schema* $\mathcal{R}$ (or simply *schema*) is a set of *relational symbols* (or *predicates*), each with its associated arity. A position $r[i]$, in a schema $\mathcal{R}$, is identified by a predicate $r \in \mathcal{R}$ and its i-th argument. A *term* t is a constant, null, or variable. An *atomic formula* (or simply *atom*) has the form $r(t_1, \ldots, t_n)$, where r is an n-ary relation and $t_1, \ldots, t_n$ are terms. Conjunctions of atoms are often identified with the sets of their atoms. A *relational instance* (or simply *instance*) I for a schema $\mathcal{R}$ is a (possibly infinite) set of atoms of the form $r(\mathbf{t})$, where r is an n-ary predicate of $\mathcal{R}$ and $\mathbf{t} \in (\Gamma \cup \Gamma_N)^n$. We denote by $r(I)$ the set of tuples $\{\mathbf{t} \mid r(\mathbf{t}) \in I\}$. A *database* is a finite relational instance.

Substitutions and Homomorphisms. A *substitution* from one set of symbols S_1 to another set of symbols S_2 is a function $h : S_1 \to S_2$ defined as follows: $\varnothing$ is a substitution (empty substitution), and if h is a substitution, then $h \cup \{X \to Y\}$ is a substitution, where $X \in S_1$ and $Y \in S_2$. If $X \to Y \in h$, then we write $h(X) = Y$. A *homomorphism* that maps a set of atoms A_1 to a set of atoms A_2 is a substitution h from the set of terms of A_1 to the set of terms of A_2 such that: if $t \in \Gamma$, then $h(t) = t$, and if $r(t_1, \ldots, t_n) \in A_1$, then $h(r(t_1, \ldots, t_n)) = r(h(t_1), \ldots, h(t_n)) \in A_2$. The notion of homomorphism naturally extends to sets of atoms.

(Boolean) Conjunctive Queries. A *conjunctive query (CQ)* q of arity n over a schema $\mathcal{R}$, written as q/n, is an assertion the form $p(\mathbf{X}) \leftarrow \varphi(\mathbf{X}, \mathbf{Y})$, where $\varphi(\mathbf{X}, \mathbf{Y})$ is a conjunction of atoms over $\mathcal{R}$, and p is an n-ary predicate that does not occur in $\mathcal{R}$. $\varphi(\mathbf{X}, \mathbf{Y})$ is called the *body* of q, denoted as *body*(q). A *Boolean conjunctive query (BCQ)* is a CQ of arity zero. The *answer* to a CQ q/n over an instance I, denoted as $q(I)$, is the set of all n-tuples $\mathbf{t} \in \Gamma^n$ for which there exists a homomorphism $h : \mathbf{X} \cup \mathbf{Y} \to \Gamma \cup \Gamma_N$ such that $h(\varphi(\mathbf{X}, \mathbf{Y})) \subseteq I$ and $h(\mathbf{X}) = \mathbf{t}$. A BCQ has only the empty tuple $\langle\rangle$ as possible answer, in which case it is said that has positive answer. Formally, a BCQ has *positive* answer over I, denoted as $I \models q$, iff $\langle\rangle \in q(I)$, or, equivalently, $q(I) \neq \varnothing$.

Dependencies. A *tuple-generating dependency (TGD)* σ over a schema $\mathcal{R}$ is a first-order formula $\forall \mathbf{X} \forall \mathbf{Y}\, \varphi(\mathbf{X}, \mathbf{Y}) \to \exists \mathbf{Z}\, \psi(\mathbf{X}, \mathbf{Z})$, where $\varphi(\mathbf{X}, \mathbf{Y})$ and $\psi(\mathbf{X}, \mathbf{Z})$ are conjunctions of atoms over $\mathcal{R}$, called the *body* and the *head* of σ, and denoted as *body*(σ) and *head*(σ), respectively. Henceforth, for brevity, we will omit the universal quantifiers in front of TGDs. Such σ is satisfied by an instance I for $\mathcal{R}$, written as $I \models \sigma$, if whenever there exists a homomorphism h such that $h(\varphi(\mathbf{X}, \mathbf{Y})) \subseteq I$, then there exists an *extension* h' of h (i.e., $h' \supseteq h$) such that $h'(\psi(\mathbf{X}, \mathbf{Z})) \subseteq I$. Notice that *inclusion dependencies (IDs)* are the simplest type of TGDs with just one body-atom and one head-atom, without repetition of variables (neither in the body nor in the head).

An *equality-generating dependency (EGD)* η over $\mathcal{R}$ is a first-order formula of the form $\forall \mathbf{X}\, \varphi(\mathbf{X}) \rightarrow X_i = X_j$, where $\varphi(\mathbf{X})$ is a conjunction of atoms over $\mathcal{R}$, called the *body* and denoted as $body(\eta)$, and $X_i = X_j$ is an equality among variables of $\mathbf{X}$. Henceforth, for brevity, we will omit the universal quantifiers in front of EGDs. Such η is satisfied by an instance I for $\mathcal{R}$ if whenever there exists a homomorphism h such that $h(\varphi(\mathbf{X})) \subseteq I$, then $h(X_i) = h(X_j)$.

A *functional dependency (FD)* over $\mathcal{R}$ is an assertion of the form $r : \mathbf{A} \rightarrow \mathbf{B}$, where $r \in \mathcal{R}$ and $\mathbf{A}, \mathbf{B}$ are sets of attributes of r[1]. Such a FD is satisfied by an instance I if whenever there exist two (distinct) tuples $\mathbf{t_1}, \mathbf{t_2} \in r(I)$ such that $\mathbf{t}_1[\mathbf{A}] = \mathbf{t}_2[\mathbf{A}]$, where $\mathbf{t}[\mathbf{A}]$ is the projection of tuple $\mathbf{t}$ over $\mathbf{A}$, then $\mathbf{t}_1[\mathbf{B}] = \mathbf{t}_2[\mathbf{B}]$. It is not difficult to see that FDs can be identified with sets of EGDs. Formally, a FD ϕ of the from $r : \mathbf{A} \rightarrow \mathbf{B}$ is identified with the set Σ_ϕ of EGDs constructed as follows: for each $i \in \mathbf{B}$, add to Σ_ϕ an EGD η of the form $r(\mathbf{X}, \mathbf{Y}), r(\mathbf{X}, \mathbf{Z}) \rightarrow Y = Z$, where each variable of $\mathbf{X}$ occurs in both atoms of $body(\sigma)$ only once at the same position of $\{r[j] \mid j \in \mathbf{A}\}$, each variable of $\mathbf{Y}$ and $\mathbf{Z}$ occurs in $body(\eta)$ only once, and both $Y \in \mathbf{Y}$ and $Z \in \mathbf{Z}$ occur in $body(\eta)$ at position $r[i]$.

Example 6. The FD $\phi = r : \{1\} \rightarrow \{2, 4\}$, defined on the predicate r of arity four, can be identified with the set of EGDs $\Sigma_\phi = \{r(X, Y_2, Y_3, Y_4), r(X, Z_2, Z_3, Z_4) \rightarrow Y_i = Z_i\}_{i \in \{2,4\}}$. It is easy to see that, $I \models \phi$ iff $I \models \Sigma_\phi$, for every instance I. ■

2.2 Query Answering under TGDs and EGDs

Let us now introduce the crucial problem of evaluating conjunctive queries over databases under TGDs and EGDs. Given a database D, and a set Σ of TGDs and EGDs, the answers we consider are those which are true in *all* models of D w.r.t. Σ, i.e., all instances that contain D and satisfy all the dependencies of Σ. Formally, the *models* of D w.r.t. Σ, denoted as $mods(D, \Sigma)$, is the set of all (finite or infinite) instances I such that $I \supseteq D$ and $I \models \Sigma$. The answer to a CQ q/n w.r.t. D and Σ is the set of n-tuples $ans(q, D, \Sigma) = \{\mathbf{t} \mid \mathbf{t} \in q(I), \text{ for each } I \in mods(D, \Sigma)\}$. The *answer* to a BCQ q w.r.t. D and Σ is *positive*, denoted as $D \cup \Sigma \models Q$, if $\langle\rangle \in ans(Q, D, \Sigma)$, or, equivalently, $ans(q, D, \Sigma) \neq \varnothing$.

An important problem is the decision version of the problem of evaluating queries over databases under TGDs and EGDs. Formally, given a CQ q/n, a database D, a set Σ of TGDs and EGDs, and an n-tuple $\mathbf{t} \in \Gamma^n$, CQAns is defined as the problem of deciding whether $\mathbf{t} \in ans(q, D, \Sigma)$. When the given query is a BCQ, then the above problem is called BCQAns. Notice that CQAns under TGDs and EGDs is undecidable; in fact, this is true even in extremely simple cases such that of inclusion and functional dependencies [16], or inclusion and key dependencies [12]. It is well-known that the above decision problems are LOGSPACE-equivalent; this result is implicit in [15], and stated explicitly in [5]. Henceforth, we thus focus only on BCQAns, and all decidability and complexity results carry over to CQAns.

[1] Such an assertion is called *key dependency (KD)* if the following holds: for each attribute i of r, $i \notin \mathbf{A}$ implies $i \in \mathbf{B}$.

It has been shown that the *chase procedure* (or simply *chase*), introduced for checking implication of dependencies [25], and later for checking query containment [20], is a very useful tool for query answering. Informally, the chase is a process of repairing a database w.r.t. to a set of dependencies so that the resulted instance satisfies the dependencies. By abuse of terminology, we shall use the term "chase" interchangeably for both the procedure and its result. The chase works on an instance through the so called TGD and EGD chase rules.

TGD Chase Rule. Consider an instance I, and a TGD $\sigma = \varphi(\mathbf{X}, \mathbf{Y}) \rightarrow \exists \mathbf{Z}\, \psi(\mathbf{X}, \mathbf{Z})$. If σ is *applicable* to I, i.e., there exists a homomorphism h such that $h(\varphi(\mathbf{X}, \mathbf{Y})) \subseteq I$, but *there is no* $h' \supseteq h$ that maps $\psi(\mathbf{X}, \mathbf{Z})$ to I, then: *(i)* define $h' \supseteq h$ such that $h'(Z_i) = z_i$, for each $Z_i \in \mathbf{Z}$, where $z_i \in \Gamma_N$ is a "fresh" labeled null not occurring in I, and following lexicographically all those occurring in I, and *(ii)* add to I the set of atoms $h'(\psi(\mathbf{X}, \mathbf{Z}))$.

EGD Chase Rule. Consider an instance I, and an EGD $\eta = \varphi(\mathbf{X}) \rightarrow X_i = X_j$. If η is *applicable* to I, i.e., there exists a homomorphism h such that $h(\varphi(\mathbf{X})) \subseteq I$ and $h(X_i) \neq h(X_j)$, then: *(i)* if $h(X_i)$ and $h(X_j)$ are both constants of Γ, then there is a *hard violation* of η, and the chase *fails*, otherwise *(ii)* replace each occurrence of $h(X_j)$ with $h(X_i)$, if $h(X_i)$ precedes $h(X_j)$ in the lexicographic order, or vice-versa otherwise.

Given a database D, and a set Σ of TGDs and EGDs, the (possibly infinite) chase of D w.r.t. Σ, denoted as $chase(D, \Sigma)$, is computed by applying exhaustively (i.e., until a fixpoint is reached): *(i)* the TGD chase rule once, and *(ii)* the EGD chase rule as long as it is applicable. We assume that the chase algorithm is *fair*, i.e., each TGD that must be applied during the construction of the chase is eventually applied. This assumption allows us to show that $chase(D, \Sigma)$ is a *universal model* of D w.r.t. Σ, i.e., for each $I \in mods(D, \Sigma)$, there exists a homomorphism from $chase(D, \Sigma)$ to I (see, e.g., [18]). Using this fact it can be shown that the chase is a fundamental algorithmic tool for query answering under TGDs and EGDs. More precisely, the problem of deciding whether the answer to a BCQ q is positive w.r.t. a database D and a set Σ of TGDs and EGDs, is equivalent to the problem of deciding whether q is entailed by $chase(D, \Sigma)$, providing that the chase does not fail. If the chase fails, then $D \cup \Sigma$ is inconsistent, and thus $mods(D, \Sigma) = \varnothing$ which implies that query answering is trivial since $D \cup \Sigma$ entails every BCQ.

Theorem 1 (implicit in [18]). *Consider a BCQ q, a database D, and a set Σ of TGDs and EGDs. If $chase(D, \Sigma)$ does not fail, then $D \cup \Sigma \models q$ iff $chase(D, \Sigma) \models q$.*

Recall that BCQAns under the simplest type of TGDs, i.e., inclusion dependencies, and the simplest type of EGDs, i.e., key dependencies, is undecidable [12]. In view of the fact that the same problem under inclusion dependencies alone is decidable [20], we conclude that the combination of TGDs (even if they fall in a class which guarantees decidability) with EGDs leads easily to undecidability of query answering. The main reason is the fact that TGDs and EGDs may interact, i.e., the application of the EGD chase rule, during the construction of

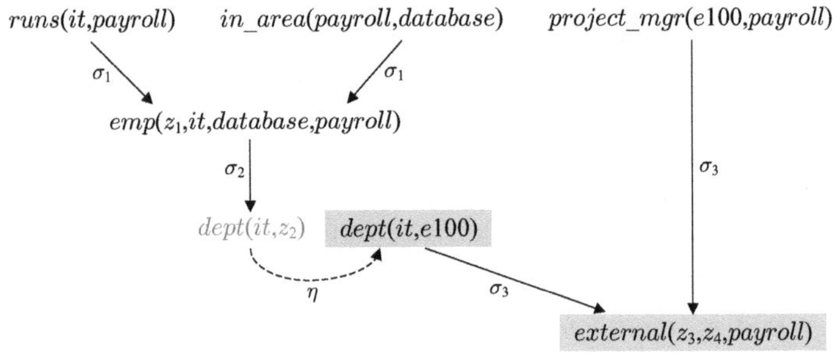

Fig. 1. The chase expansion of Example 7; $z_1, \ldots, z_4$ are nulls of Γ_N

the chase, may cause new applications of the TGD chase rule which were not possible before applying the EGD.

Example 7. Consider the following relational schema:

$$\begin{array}{ll} dept(\mathsf{Dept\_Id}, \mathsf{Mgr\_Id}), & in\_area(\mathsf{Pro\_Id}, \mathsf{Area}), \\ emp(\mathsf{Emp\_Id}, \mathsf{Dept\_Id}, \mathsf{Area}, \mathsf{Pro\_Id}), & project\_mgr(\mathsf{Emp\_Id}, \mathsf{Pro\_Id}), \\ runs(\mathsf{Dept\_Id}, \mathsf{Pro\_Id}), & external(\mathsf{Ext\_Id}, \mathsf{Area}, \mathsf{Pro\_Id}). \end{array}$$

Let Σ be the set of TGDs and EGDs constituted by:

$$\begin{array}{r} \sigma_1 : runs(W, X), in\_area(X, Y) \rightarrow \exists Z\, emp(Z, W, Y, X) \\ \sigma_2 : emp(V, W, X, Y) \rightarrow \exists Z\, dept(W, Z), \\ \sigma_3 : dept(V, W), project\_mgr(W, X) \rightarrow \exists Y \exists Z\, external(Y, Z, X) \\ \eta : dept(W, X), runs(W, Y), project\_mgr(Z, Y) \rightarrow X = Z. \end{array}$$

Consider also the database

$$D = \{runs(it, payroll), in\_area(payroll, database), project\_mgr(e100, payroll)\}.$$

The construction of $chase(D, \Sigma)$ is depicted in Figure 1. The dashed arrow means that the application of the EGD η replaces the atom $dept(it, z_2)$ with the atom $dept(it, e100)$, which in turn triggers σ_3 and the atom $external(z_3, z_4, payroll)$ is obtained. Notice that, if we ignore the EGD η (and consider only the TGDs), there is no way to obtain the shaded atoms during the construction of the chase. Therefore, given the BCQ $q : p \leftarrow external(A, B, payroll)$, it holds that $chase(D, \Sigma) \models q$ but $chase(D, \Sigma \setminus \{\eta\}) \not\models q$. ■

3 Separability of TGDs and EGDs

As already discussed in the previous section, the interaction of TGDs and EGDs is the main reason for which query answering is undecidable. Moreover, while the result of an infinite chase under a set of TGDs is well-defined as the limit of an infinite, monotonically increasing sequence (or, equivalently, as the least fixpoint of a monotonic operator), the sequence of sets obtained in the infinite chase of a database instance under TGDs and EGDs is, in general, neither monotonic nor convergent. Thus, even though the chase procedure under TGDs and EGDs can be formally defined, it is not clear how the result of an infinite chase involving both TGDs and EGDs should be defined.

For the above reasons, the combination of EGDs with existing classes of TGDs (under which query answering is decidable) is a challenging problem. It would be really useful to identify syntactic restrictions which allow us to: *(i)* use the (possibly infinite) chase procedure to obtain a query answering algorithm, and *(ii)* transfer the decidability results and upper complexity bounds, derived for various classes of TGDs, to the extended formalism. A property which guarantees both desiderata is *separability* of TGDs and EGDs. Intuitively, this property implies that there is no interaction between TGDs and EGDs, and query answering is basically insensitive to EGDs. In other words, given a set $\Sigma = \Sigma_T \cup \Sigma_E$, where Σ_T are TGDs and Σ_E are EGDs, if Σ is separable, then we can simply ignore the EGDs (except for some initial computation which is not harder than query answering under TGDs alone), since for every database D that already satisfies Σ_E, $chase(D, \Sigma)$ entails exactly the same set of Boolean conjunctive queries as $chase(D, \Sigma_T)$.

Definition 1 (Separability). *Consider a set $\Sigma = \Sigma_T \cup \Sigma_E$ over a schema $\mathcal{R}$, where Σ_T are TGDs and Σ_E are EGDs. Σ is* separable *if, for every database D for $\mathcal{R}$, the following holds: if $D \models \Sigma_E$, then $chase(D, \Sigma)$ does not fail, and, for every BCQ q over $\mathcal{R}$, $chase(D, \Sigma) \models q$ iff $chase(D, \Sigma_T) \models q$.*

Clearly, the set Σ of TGDs and EGDs given in Example 7 is non-separable. Recall that there exists a database D and a BCQ q such that $chase(D, \Sigma) \models q$ but $chase(D, \Sigma') \not\models q$, where Σ' is obtained from Σ by eliminating the EGDs. Indeed separability of TGDs and EGDs allows us to exploit the (possibly infinite) chase procedure to obtain a query answering algorithm. More precisely, given a BCQ q, a database D, and a separable set $\Sigma = \Sigma_T \cup \Sigma_E$, where Σ_T is a set of TGDs which falls in a class under which query answering is decidable, and Σ_E is a set of EGDs, we can decide whether $D \cup \Sigma \models q$ by applying the following simple algorithm: (1) if $D \not\models \Sigma_E$, then *accept*; (2) if $chase(D, \Sigma_T) \models q$, then *accept*; otherwise *reject*. Interestingly, as shown in [6], the problem of deciding whether the given database satisfies the set of EGDs it is not harder than the problem of query answering in the absence of constraints. In particular, this problem is feasible in AC_0 if the set of EGDs is fixed, and in NP in general. From the above discussion, we conclude that the notion of separability allows us to transfer, not only the decidability results, but also the upper complexity bounds, derived for various classes of TGDs, to the extended formalism.

Theorem 2 ([6]). *Consider a BCQ q, a database D, and a set $\Sigma = \Sigma_T \cup \Sigma_E$, where Σ_T are TGDs and Σ_E are EGDs. If Σ is separable, then deciding whether $D \cup \Sigma \models q$ has the same complexity as deciding whether $D \cup \Sigma_T \models q$.*

Clearly, separability of TGDs and EGDs is a semantic (and not a syntactic) property. In other words, given a set Σ of TGDs and EGDs, it is not possible in general to decide whether Σ is separable just by checking if it satisfies certain syntactic properties. We conclude this section by establishing that this problem is undecidable. We prove this by providing a reduction from query answering under arbitrary TGDs. The idea of the construction is as follows: given a BCQ q, a database D, and a set Σ of TGDs, we combine $D \cup \Sigma$ with a non-separable set Σ' of TGDs and EGDs in such a way that, for every database D', the TGDs of Σ' are triggered during the construction of $chase(D', \Sigma')$ iff $chase(D, \Sigma) \models q$.

Theorem 3. *The problem of deciding whether a set of TGDs and EGDs is separable is undecidable.*

Proof (sketch). The proof is by reduction from BCQAns under arbitrary TGDs. In fact, this problem remains undecidable even if we consider an atomic query $q : p \leftarrow r(c_1, c_2)$, where $\{c_1, c_2\} \subset \Gamma$, and a database D and a set Σ of TGDs such that $r(c_1, c_2) \notin D$ and $r(chase(D, \Sigma)) = \{\langle c_1, c_2 \rangle\}$ (this is implicit in [5]). We construct the set Σ' of TGDs and EGDs from Σ as follows: for each $\underline{a} \in D$, add the TGD $\top \rightarrow \underline{a}$, where $\top$ denotes the constant *true*, add the TGDs σ_1 : $r(c_1, c_2), r^\star(X, Y) \rightarrow \exists Z\, s^\star(X, Z)$ and $\sigma_2 : r(c_1, c_2), s^\star(X, Y) \rightarrow r^\star(X, Y)$, and add the EGD $\eta : r^\star(X, Y), r^\star(X, Z) \rightarrow Y = Z$, where $r^\star$ and $s^\star$ are auxiliary predicates not occurring in Σ. In what follows we show that $chase(D, \Sigma) \models q$ iff Σ' is not separable.

($\Rightarrow$) By hypothesis, $r(c_1, c_2) \in chase(D, \Sigma)$. Now, consider the database $D' = \{r^\star(c, c')\}$, where $\{c, c'\} \subset \Gamma$. Clearly, $D' \models \eta$, and also $chase(D, \Sigma')$ does not fail since at positions $r^\star[2]$ and $s^\star[2]$ only nulls of Γ_N can appear during the construction of the chase. It is easy to see that $s^\star(c, c') \in chase(D, \Sigma')$ but $s^\star(c, c') \notin chase(D, \Sigma' \setminus \{\eta\})$ which implies that Σ' is not separable.

($\Leftarrow$) It is not difficult to verify that if Σ' is not separable, then $r(c_1, c_2) \in chase(D, \Sigma)$; otherwise, σ_1 and σ_2 cannot be triggered, and thus Σ' is separable which contradicts our hypothesis. $\square$

4 Concrete Separable Classes

Theorem 3 implies that it is not possible to define a syntactic class of TGDs and EGDs that captures separability. However, in prior works, efficiently checkable syntactic conditions on a set of TGDs and EGDs have been identified which are sufficient for separability. The aim of this section is to give an overview of the most notable conditions which guarantee separability. For brevity, given a TGD σ, we define the set $\mathbf{U}_\sigma$ of *universal positions* of σ as the set of positions in $head(\sigma)$ at which a $\forall$-variable occurs. Moreover, given an EGD η associated to a FD, we define the set $\mathbf{J}_\eta$ of *joined positions* of η as the set of positions at which a variable that occurs in both atoms of $body(\eta)$ appears.

4.1 Key-Based Inclusion and Key Dependencies

An early separable class of IDs and KDs, called *key-based*, was proposed in the seminal work of Johnson and Klug [20]. In this paper, the problem of conjunctive query containment[2] (which is LOGSPACE-equivalent to conjunctive query answering, see, e.g., [5]) under key-based inclusion and key dependencies has been investigated. The formal definition of the key-based condition follows.

Definition 2 ([20]). *Consider a set $\Sigma = \Sigma_I \cup \Sigma_K$, where Σ_I are IDs and Σ_K are EGDs which identify KDs. Σ is* key-based *if, for each $\langle\sigma,\eta\rangle \in \Sigma_I \times \Sigma_K$, the following conditions hold: (i) $\mathbf{U}_\sigma \subseteq \mathbf{J}_\eta$, and (ii) the set of positions in $body(\sigma)$ at which a variable of $head(\sigma)$ appears is disjoint from $\mathbf{J}_\eta$.*

Example 8. Let Σ be the set (over the schema of Example 7) constituted by σ : $emp(V,W,X,Y) \rightarrow \exists Z\, dept(W,Z)$ and η : $dept(U,V), dept(U,W) \rightarrow V = W$. Clearly, σ is an ID which asserts that each employee works in some department, while η identifies a KD which states that the identifier of each department is unique. Observe that $\mathbf{U}_\sigma = \mathbf{J}_\eta = \{dept[1]\}$, and thus the first condition of Definition 2 is satisfied. Since in Σ there is no EGD expressed on *emp*, the second condition of Definition 2 is satisfied trivially. Hence, Σ is key-based. ∎

The key-based condition guarantees that during the construction of the chase none of the EGDs is triggered. Consider an ID $\sigma = s(\mathbf{X},\mathbf{Y}) \rightarrow \exists \mathbf{Z}\, r(\mathbf{X},\mathbf{Z})$, and an EGD η which belongs to a set which identifies a KD defined on the predicate r. If σ and η satisfy the key-based condition, then:

either $\mathbf{J}_\eta \setminus \mathbf{U}_\sigma$ *is non-empty*, which implies that the application of σ during the chase generates an atom $\underline{a}$ with a "fresh" null at some position of $\mathbf{J}_\eta$, and thus $\underline{a}$ does not violate η,

or $\mathbf{U}_\sigma$ *coincides with* $\mathbf{J}_\eta$, and hence any newly generated atom $\underline{a}$ must have "fresh" distinct nulls at all positions but those of $\mathbf{J}_\eta$. Therefore, if $\underline{a}$ coincides with some existing atom in the chase at the positions of $\mathbf{J}_\eta$, then $\underline{a}$ would not be added since, according to the TGD chase rule, σ is not applicable; hence, again it is not possible to violate η.

From the above informal discussion we conclude that, if the initial database satisfies the given set of EGDs, then the chase does not fail, and we are allowed to proceed with query answering by considering only the IDs. Clearly, the fact that either $\mathbf{J}_\eta \setminus \mathbf{U}_\sigma \neq \varnothing$ or $\mathbf{U}_\sigma = \mathbf{J}_\eta$ holds even if we consider only the first condition of the Definition 2; in fact, the second condition is not really needed to establish that the key-based restriction is sufficient for separability. In [20], the second condition was used to show that the class of key-based IDs and KDs is *finitely controllable*, i.e., that query answering under arbitrary models coincides with query answering under finite models only.

4.2 Non-key-Conflicting Inclusion and Key Dependencies

As discussed in [20], it is reasonable to expect that there will be many cases in practice in which the interaction between the IDs and the KDs is as specified

[2] Given two CQs q_1 and q_2, and a set Σ of TGD and EGDs, the question is whether $q_1(I) \subseteq q_2(I)$, for every instance $I \models \Sigma$.

by the key-based condition. Indeed, the key-based condition allows us to express partially *foreign key dependencies (FKDs)* which are very common in practice. In a nutshell, a FKD is an ID $\sigma : s(\mathbf{X}, \mathbf{Y}) \rightarrow \exists \mathbf{Z}\, r(\mathbf{X}, \mathbf{Z})$ such that $\mathbf{U}_\sigma$ coincides with $\mathbf{J}_\eta$, where η is an EGD which belongs to the set which identifies the KD defined on r. However, as shown in the following example, the key-based condition is not general enough to capture arbitrary FKDs.

Example 9. Consider the set $\Sigma = \{\sigma, \eta\}$ given in Example 8; observe that σ is a FKD. Let $\Sigma' = \Sigma \cup \{\sigma'\}$, where

$$\sigma' : \mathit{dept}(W, X) \rightarrow \exists Y \exists Z\, \mathit{emp}(X, W, Y, Z).$$

Clearly, σ' is an ID which asserts that each department has as manager some employee who works in the same department. It is easy to verify that Σ' is not key-based since the second condition of Definition 2 is violated. In particular, the set of positions of $\mathit{body}(\sigma')$ at which a variable of $\mathit{head}(\sigma')$ appears, that is, $\{\mathit{dept}[1], \mathit{dept}[2]\}$, is a superset (and thus not a disjoint set) of $\mathbf{J}_\eta = \{\mathit{dept}[1]\}$. ■

As illustrated in the above example, the main reason why key-based IDs and KDs are not expressive enough to capture (arbitrary) FKDs, is the restriction on the bodies of the IDs imposed by the second condition of Definition 2. Recall that the main property of key-based IDs and KDs, i.e., the fact that during the construction of the chase the EGD chase rule is not applied, holds even if we drop the (problematic) second condition of Definition 2. Moreover, it is easy to see that the key-based restriction can be slightly extended by allowing the set of universal positions of a TGD to overlap with the set of joined positions of an EGD. The above facts were observed by Calì et al. [12], and the more general class of *non-key-conflicting* IDs and KDs was proposed.

Definition 3 ([12]). *Consider a set $\Sigma = \Sigma_I \cup \Sigma_K$, where Σ_I are IDs and Σ_K are EGDs which identify KDs. Σ is* non-key-conflicting *if, for each $\langle \sigma, \eta \rangle \in \Sigma_I \times \Sigma_K$, it holds that $\mathbf{U}_\sigma \not\supset \mathbf{J}_\eta$.*

It is straightforward to verify that the set Σ' given in Example 9 is non-key-conflicting; in fact, non-key-conflicting IDs and KDs are expressive enough to capture arbitrary FKDs. Interestingly, in [12] was shown that, as soon as we extend slightly the class of IDs and KDs beyond the non-key-conflicting case, query answering becomes undecidable. In particular, the undecidability of query answering under *1-key-conflicting* IDs and KDs was established. This class is obtained by relaxing Definition 3 as follows: for each $\langle \sigma, \eta \rangle \in \Sigma_I \times \Sigma_K$, if $\mathbf{U}_\sigma$ is a strict superset of $\mathbf{J}_\eta$, then $|\mathbf{U}_\sigma \setminus \mathbf{J}_\eta| = 1$, i.e., $\mathbf{U}_\sigma$ is allowed to cover $\mathbf{J}_\eta$ plus at most one attribute of the predicate on which the KD is defined.

4.3 Non-conflicting TGDs and KDs

At the first glance, it may seen that the non-key-conflicting condition, as given in Definition 3, can be employed without further restrictions in order to treat arbitrary TGDs (and not only IDs). As observed in [6], this is not true due to the repeated $\exists$-variables that may appear in the head of a TGD; recall that in IDs it is not possible to have repetition of variables. Let us explain, by means of an example, what is exactly the problem caused by having repeated $\exists$-variables.

Example 10. Consider the set Σ constituted by:

$$\sigma : r(X,Y) \rightarrow \exists Z\, s(X,Z,Z)$$
$$\eta_1 : s(X,Y,Z), s(X,Y',Z') \rightarrow Y = Y'$$
$$\eta_2 : s(X,Y,Z), s(X,Y',Z') \rightarrow Z = Z'.$$

Clearly, since Z appears in $head(\sigma)$ more than once, σ is not an ID. Moreover, the set $\{\eta_1, \eta_2\}$ expresses that the first attribute of s is the key. Observe that the condition given in the Definition 3 is satisfied since $\mathbf{U}_\sigma = \mathbf{J}_{\eta_1} = \mathbf{J}_{\eta_2} = \{s[1]\}$. Consider now the database $D = \{r(a,b), s(a,b,c)\}$. The crucial point is that the TGD σ is applicable, since there exists a homomorphism h that maps $body(\sigma)$ to D, but there is no $h' \supseteq h$ that maps $head(\sigma)$ to D. Thus, the atom $s(a, z_1, z_1)$, where $z_1 \in \Gamma_N$, is generated, and the EGDs are triggered. Moreover, by applying the EGD chase rule, eventually we need to unify the constants b and c, and the chase fails. This implies that Σ is non-separable. It is important to realize that $\sigma' : r(X,Y) \rightarrow \exists Z \exists W\, s(X,Z,W)$ is not applicable since the homomorphism $h' = \{X \rightarrow a, Z \rightarrow b, W \rightarrow c\}$ maps $head(\sigma')$ to D; thus, if we consider σ' there is no way to violate the EGDs, and $\{\sigma', \eta_1, \eta_2\}$ is separable. ∎

In [6], the class of *non-conflicting* TGDs and KDs has been proposed. Notice that in the following definition we assume w.l.o.g. TGDs to have only one head-atom; for more details see [5].

Definition 4 ([6]). *Consider a set $\Sigma = \Sigma_T \cup \Sigma_K$, where Σ_T are TGDs and Σ_K are EGDs which identify KDs. Σ is* non-conflicting *if, for each $\langle \sigma, \eta \rangle \in \Sigma_T \times \Sigma_K$: (i) $\mathbf{U}_\sigma \not\supset \mathbf{J}_\eta$, and (ii) each $\exists$-variable in $head(\sigma)$ occurs just once.*

A slightly more general class which treats arbitrary FDs (and not just KDs), and also forbids the repetition of $\exists$-variables only if the universal positions of a TGD coincide with the joined positions of an EGD, is proposed in [8].

4.4 Non-conflicting TGDs and EGDs

The above condition can be easily extended in order to treat general EGDs (and not just KDs). An EGD η is called *FD-like* if there exists a FD ϕ, an EGD $\eta' \in \Sigma_\phi$, and two atoms $\underline{a}$ and $\underline{b}$ in $body(\eta)$, such that $\{\underline{a}, \underline{b}\}$ is the same (up to bijective variable renaming) with $body(\eta')$; we denote by $\mathsf{f}(\eta)$ the EGD η'.

Example 11. Consider the EGD $\eta : runs(X,Y), runs(X,Z), in\_area(Y, security) \rightarrow Y = Z$ (over the schema of Example 7), which asserts that each department that runs a project which falls in the area of security, runs at most one project. Clearly, η is FD-like due to the atoms $runs(X,Y)$ and $runs(X,Z)$. ∎

An FD-like EGD behaves like an EGD which belongs to a set which identifies a FD. The class of non-conflicting TGDs and FD-like EGDs can be easily defined.

Definition 5. *Consider a set $\Sigma = \Sigma_T \cup \Sigma_E$, where Σ_T are TGDs and Σ_E are FD-like EGDs. Σ is* non-conflicting *if, for each $\langle \sigma, \eta \rangle \in \Sigma_T \times \Sigma_E$, the following hold: (i) $\mathbf{U}_\sigma \not\supset \mathbf{J}_{\mathsf{f}(\eta)}$, and (ii) each $\exists$-variable in $head(\sigma)$ occurs just once.*

During the construction of the chase under non-conflicting TGDs and FD-like EGDs, it is not possible to violate an EGD η since (as for the classes above) there exists a subset of $body(\eta)$ which cannot be mapped to the chase. A more general class which treats arbitrary EGDs is presented in [9].

5 Separability in Conceptual Modelling

In this final section, we present known formalisms for conceptual modelling, which can be translated into separable sets of TGDs and EGDs.

5.1 DL-Lite Family of Description Logics

As shown in [6], every DL-Lite$_X$ TBox, where $X \in \{\mathcal{F}, \mathcal{R}, \mathcal{A}\}$ [13,26], can be translated in LOGSPACE into a set $\Sigma \cup \Sigma_\perp$, where Σ is a non-key-conflicting set of IDs and KDs, and $\Sigma_\perp$ is a set of *negative constraints* of the form $\forall \mathbf{X}\, \varphi(\mathbf{X}) \rightarrow \perp$, where $\perp$ denotes the truth constant *false*. The problem of deciding whether a set of TGDs and EGDs satisfies a set of negative constraints is tantamount to query answering under TGDs and EGDs; for more details see [6].

Example 12. Consider the DL-Lite$_\mathcal{A}$ TBox constituted by

$$\begin{array}{ll} \mathit{Professor} \sqsubseteq \mathit{Member}, & \exists \mathit{leaderOf} \sqsubseteq \mathit{Professor}, \\ \mathit{Member} \sqsubseteq \exists \mathit{worksIn}, & \exists \mathit{leaderOf}^- \sqsubseteq \mathit{Group}, \\ \exists \mathit{worksIn} \sqsubseteq \mathit{Member}, & \mathit{leaderOf} \sqsubseteq \mathit{worksIn}, \\ \exists \mathit{worksIn}^- \sqsubseteq \mathit{Group}, & (\mathsf{funct}\ \mathit{leaderOf}^-), \end{array}$$

which describes a university department. Professors are departmental members who work in at least one (mandatory participation) research group. Also, each research group has at most one leader (functional participation), who is a professor. Finally, each professor works in the same group that (s)he leads (is-a among relationships). The above TBox can be translated into the set of IDs and KDs:

$$\begin{array}{ll} \mathit{Professor}(X) \rightarrow \mathit{Member}(X), & \mathit{leaderOf}(X,Y) \rightarrow \mathit{Professor}(X), \\ \mathit{Member}(X) \rightarrow \exists Y\, \mathit{worksIn}(X,Y), & \mathit{leaderOf}(X,Y) \rightarrow \mathit{Group}(Y), \\ \mathit{worksIn}(X,Y) \rightarrow \mathit{Member}(X), & \mathit{leaderOf}(X,Y) \rightarrow \mathit{workIn}(X,Y), \\ \mathit{worksIn}(X,Y) \rightarrow \mathit{Group}(Y), & \mathit{leaderOf}(Y,X), \mathit{leaderOf}(Z,X) \rightarrow Y = Z. \end{array}$$

Since the predicate *leaderOf* does not occur in the head of any of the IDs, the above set is trivially non-key-conflicting. ■

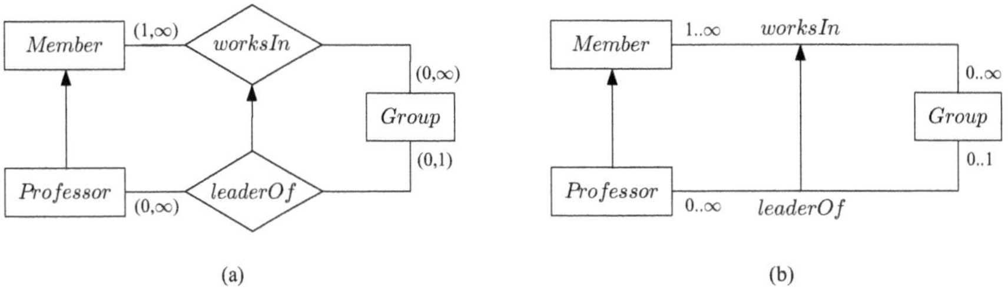

Fig. 2. The ER schema and the UML class diagram for the university scenario

5.2 Entity-Relationship Model

We consider an extended version of the well-known Entity-Relationship (ER) model [17], which comprises is-a constraints among entities and relationships, plus functional and mandatory participation constraints of entities to relationships; for more details on this extended ER model, we refer the reader, e.g., to [10]. It is easy to verify that the following holds: whenever we have an is-a among two relationships, if no functional participation is expressed on the superclass, then the ER schema can be translated into a non-key-conflicting set of IDs and KDs [2]. Such an ER schema is the one depicted in Figure 2(a), which represents the university scenario described in Example 12.

5.3 UML Class Diagrams

Let us now consider UML class diagrams (see, e.g., [4]). By restricting the multiplicity of attributes and associations, and by omitting completeness constraints, it can be shown that a UML class diagram can be translated into a non-conflicting set of *guarded* TGDs and FD-like EGDs [7]; a TGD is guarded if it contains a body-atom that covers all the ∀-variables [5]. In fact, this holds for UML class diagrams which satisfy the following conditions: *(i)* only mandatory and functional participation are expressed (and not arbitrary multiplicity constraints), *(ii)* whenever an association A generalizes some other association, then no functional participation is expressed on A, and *(iii)* there are no completeness constraints. Such a UML class diagram is the one depicted in Figure 2(b).

5.4 F-Logic Lite

F-Logic Lite, introduced in [11], is a small but expressive subset of F-Logic [21], a popular formalism for object oriented deductive databases. Roughly, F-Logic Lite omits negation and default inheritance, and allows only a limited form of cardinality constraints. F-Logic Lite is constituted by twelve deductive rules over a fixed schema. Interestingly, these rules form a non-conflicting set of *weakly-guarded* TGDs, that is, an extension of guarded TGDs introduced in [5], and a single FD-like EGD.

Acknowledgements. This research has received funding from the European Research Council under the European Community's Seventh Framework Programme (FP7/2007-2013) / ERC grant agreement DIADEM no. 246858, and from the Oxford Martin School's grant no. LC0910-019.

References

1. Abiteboul, S., Hull, R., Vianu, V.: Foundations of Databases. Addison-Wesley (1995)
2. Artale, A., Calvanese, D., Kontchakov, R., Ryzhikov, V., Zakharyaschev, M.: Reasoning over Extended ER Models. In: Parent, C., Schewe, K.-D., Storey, V.C., Thalheim, B. (eds.) ER 2007. LNCS, vol. 4801, pp. 277–292. Springer, Heidelberg (2007)
3. Beeri, C., Vardi, M.Y.: The Implication Problem for Data Dependencies. In: Even, S., Kariv, O. (eds.) ICALP 1981. LNCS, vol. 115, pp. 73–85. Springer, Heidelberg (1981)
4. Berardi, D., Calvanese, D., De Giacomo, G.: Reasoning on UML class diagrams. Artif. Intell. 168(1-2), 70–118 (2005)
5. Calì, A., Gottlob, G., Kifer, M.: Taming the infinite chase: Query answering under expressive relational constraints. In: Proc. of KR, pp. 70–80 (2008)
6. Calì, A., Gottlob, G., Lukasiewicz, T.: A general Datalog-based framework for tractable query answering over ontologies. In: Proc. of PODS, pp. 77–86 (2009); To appear in the J. of Web Semantics
7. Calì, A., Gottlob, G., Orsi, G., Pieris, A.: Querying UML Class Diagrams. In: Birkedal, L. (ed.) FOSSACS 2012. LNCS, vol. 7213, pp. 1–25. Springer, Heidelberg (2012)
8. Calì, A., Gottlob, G., Pieris, A.: Advanced processing for ontological queries. PVLDB 3(1), 554–565 (2010)
9. Calì, A., Gottlob, G., Pieris, A.: Querying Conceptual Schemata with Expressive Equality Constraints. In: Jeusfeld, M., Delcambre, L., Ling, T.-W. (eds.) ER 2011. LNCS, vol. 6998, pp. 161–174. Springer, Heidelberg (2011)
10. Calì, A., Gottlob, G., Pieris, A.: Ontological query answering under expressive Entity-Relationship schemata. Inf. Syst. 37(4), 320–335 (2012)
11. Calì, A., Kifer, M.: Containment of conjunctive object meta-queries. In: Proc. of VLDB, pp. 942–952 (2006)
12. Calì, A., Lembo, D., Rosati, R.: On the decidability and complexity of query answering over inconsistent and incomplete databases. In: Proc. of PODS, pp. 260–271 (2003)
13. Calvanese, D., De Giacomo, G., Lembo, D., Lenzerini, M., Rosati, R.: Tractable reasoning and efficient query answering in description logics: The DL-Lite family. J. Autom. Reasoning 39(3), 385–429 (2007)
14. Calvanese, D., De Giacomo, G., Lenzerini, M.: Identification constraints and functional dependencies in description logics. In: Proc. of IJCAI, pp. 155–160 (2001)
15. Chandra, A.K., Merlin, P.M.: Optimal implementation of conjunctive queries in relational data bases. In: Proc. of STOCS, pp. 77–90 (1977)
16. Chandra, A.K., Vardi, M.Y.: The implication problem for functional and inclusion dependencies. SIAM J. of Comput. 14, 671–677 (1985)
17. Chen, P.P.: The Entity-Relationship model: Towards a unified view of data. ACM Trans. Database Syst. 1(1), 124–131 (1976)

18. Fagin, R., Kolaitis, P.G., Miller, R.J., Popa, L.: Data exchange: Semantics and query answering. Theor. Comput. Sci. 336(1), 89–124 (2005)
19. Fan, W., Geerts, F., Jia, X.: A revival of integrity constraints for data cleaning. PVLDB 1(2), 1522–1523 (2008)
20. Johnson, D.S., Klug, A.C.: Testing containment of conjunctive queries under functional and inclusion dependencies. J. Comput. Syst. Sci. 28(1), 167–189 (1984)
21. Kifer, M., Lausen, G., Wu, J.: Logical foundations of object-oriented and frame-based languages. J. ACM 42(4), 741–843 (1995)
22. Krötzsch, M., Rudolph, S.: Extending decidable existential rules by joining acyclicity and guardedness. In: Proc. of IJCAI, pp. 963–968 (2011)
23. Lenzerini, M.: Data integration: A theoretical perspective. In: Proc. of PODS, pp. 233–246 (2002)
24. Lloyd, J.W.: Foundations of logic programming. Springer (1987)
25. Maier, D., Mendelzon, A.O., Sagiv, Y.: Testing implications of data dependencies. ACM Trans. Database Syst. 4(4), 455–469 (1979)
26. Poggi, A., Lembo, D., Calvanese, D., De Giacomo, G., Lenzerini, M., Rosati, R.: Linking data to ontologies. J. Data Semantics 10, 133–173 (2008)
27. Sowa, J.F.: Knowledge representation: Logical, philosophical and computational foundations. Brooks/Cole Publishing Co. (2000)

Extending Action Language $\mathcal{C}+$ by Formalizing Composite Actions*

Xiaoping Chen[1], Guoqiang Jin[1], and Fangkai Yang[2]

[1] Department of Computer Science, University of Science and Technology of China
xpchen@ustc.edu.cn abxeeled@mail.ustc.edu.cn
[2] Department of Computer Science, The University of Texas at Austin
fkyang@cs.utexas.edu

Abstract. This paper extends action language $\mathcal{C}+$ by introducing *composite actions* as sequential execution of primitive actions. Such extension leads to a more intuitive and flexible way to represent action domains, better exploit a general-purpose formalization, and improve the reasoning efficiency for large domains. The semantics of composite actions is defined by a translation to nonmonotonic causal theories. We implement the language by extending CPLUS2ASP, which translates causal theories into answer set programming (ASP) and calls ASP solver.

1 Introduction

The problem of describing changes caused by the execution of actions plays an important role in knowledge representation. Actions may be described

1. by specifying its preconditions and effects, as in STRIPS[1], PDDL-like languages, action languages such as $\mathcal{B}$ and $\mathcal{C}$[2], $\mathcal{C}+$[3], situation calculus[4];
2. in terms of execution of primitive actions, such as programs in GoLog[5], ASP[6], extended event calculus[7], ABStrips[8] and HTN[9]; or
3. as a special case of actions of more general kind, as in MAD[10] and $\mathcal{ALM}$[11].

Actions formalized in the first and third approach are used to automate planning, and more generally, to automate commonsense reasoning tasks such as temporal projection and postdiction, with an emphasis on addressing the problem of generality in AI[12]. However, actions formalized in the second approach are usually used for complementary purposes: they are abstraction or aggregates to characterize the hierarchical structure of the domain and improve search efficiency. This paper extends action language $\mathcal{C}+$ with *composite actions* defined as sequential execution of primary actions, and shows that these composite actions can be used for the purposes of the first and third approaches as well.

The extended $\mathcal{C}+$ has three advantages. First, it has stronger expressivity than $\mathcal{C}+$, by providing one more way of formalizing actions in $\mathcal{C}+$. Second,

* Xiaoping Chen and Guoqiang Jin are supported by the National Hi-Tech Project of China under grant 2008AA01Z150 and the Natural Science Foundations of China under grant 60745002 and 61175057.

E. Erdem et al. (Eds.): Correct Reasoning, LNCS 7265, pp. 134–148, 2012.

composite actions can be defined by exploiting the general purpose formalization of actions and the new language can be seen as a step of addressing the problem of generality in AI. Consider a monkey that can transport a folding ladder of two stairs, climb up one or two stairs of the ladder to pick up bananas hung at different heights. To exploit a general-purpose formalization of *Mount*, such as the one in [13], *ClimbOnLadder* can be defined as executing action *Mount* once or twice. Third, composite actions can be used to characterize the hierarchical structure of problem domain and improve planning efficiency.

To achieve this goal, we introduce a new construct to $\mathcal{C}+$ that defines *composite actions* as sequential executions of primitive actions $a_0, \ldots a_k$ under conditions (written as formulas) $E_0, \ldots E_k$. For instance,

$$\begin{aligned} \mathit{ClimbOnLadder}\ \textbf{is}\ & \mathit{Mount}(\mathit{Monkey}, S_1)\ \textbf{if}\ \mathit{Base}(\mathit{Monkey}) = \mathit{Floor};\\ & \mathit{Mount}(\mathit{Monkey}, S_2)\ \textbf{if}\ \mathit{Base}(\mathit{Monkey}) = S_1. \end{aligned}$$

However, to define the semantics of the construct is not a trivial task. In $\mathcal{C}+$, all actions are assumed to be executed over 1 time interval. This assumption affects the design of both description language and query language: when formalizing action domains, the users don't need to care about the passage of time, leading to a concise representation; when querying the action domain, following the syntax of CCALC[1] query the user can give a temporal projection task such as "*at time 0 the monkey is on the floor; he climbs onto the box at 0 and grasp the banana at 1, does the monkey has banana at time 2?*" — this query also assumes that all actions are executed over one time interval. However, can we define the length of a composite action in terms of the number of primary actions involved? We can, but this will lead to a cumbersome query language. For instance, a similar query may be "*at time 0 the monkey is on the floor; he climbs onto the folding ladder at 0 and grasp the banana at 2, does the monkey has banana at time 3?*" — the user must keep in mind that climbing the folding ladder from the ground needs two time intervals. Even worse, the user must notice that climbing onto the ladder from S_1 costs 1 time interval and formulate the third query accordingly: "*at time 0 the monkey is at S_1; he climbs onto the folding ladder at 0 and grasp the banana at 1, does the monkey has banana at time 2?*" We foresee that specifying queries like these are too complicated.

As a result, we maintain this assumption for composite actions in the new language, in the sense that composite actions b are executed over 1 time instance, such as $(0, 1)$, the same with primary actions, so that the users don't need to care about lengths of composite actions when formalizing action domains, and don't need to distinguish between composite actions and primary actions when giving queries. Alternatively, we describe an execution trajectory of a composite action by a sequence of *primary actions executed at subintervals*, such as $(0, 0.1), (0.1, 0.2), \ldots, (0.k, 1)$ which divide an interval $(0, 1)$. Based on subintervals, we define a precise semantics of an extended action description by rewriting it to nonmonotonic causal theories [3], and show that the resulting causal theories inherit the semantic property of action descriptions: the models

[1] `http://www.cs.utexas.edu/users/tag/cc/`

can be characterized by transition diagrams, which are conservative extensions of the models of the action description without composite actions.

The new language is implemented by extending the software CPLUS2ASP [14] which translates the input into an answer set program (ASP) and computes its models by calling ASP solver ICLINGO[2]. We formalizes a version of monkeys and bananas domain with composite actions, and our experiment shows that composite actions can significantly improve the efficiency.

The work presented in this paper is somewhat similar to [15] but composite actions defined there have fixed and explicitly specified length. Therefore, conditional execution of primitive actions inside a composite action is not allowed.

We dedicate this paper to Professor Vladimir Lifschitz for his 65th birthday.

2 Preliminaries

The review of action language $\mathcal{C}+$ follows from [3]. A (multi-valued) signature is a set σ of symbols, called (multi-valued) constants, along with a non-emtpy finite set $Dom(c)$ of symbols, disjoint from σ, assigned to each constant c. The set $Dom(c)$ is the *domain* of c. Each constant belongs to one of the three groups: *action* constants, *simple fluent* constants and *statically determined fluent* constants.

Consider a fixed multi-valued signature σ. An *atom* is an expression of the form $c = v$ ("the value of c is v") where $c \in \sigma$ and $v \in Dom(c)$. A *formula* is a propositional combination of atoms. An interpretation maps every constant in σ to an element of its domain. A formula is called *fluent formula* if it does not contain action constants, and *action formula* if it contains at least one action constant and no fluent constants.

An *action description* consists of a set of *causal laws* of the form

$$\textbf{caused } F \textbf{ if } G \tag{1}$$

where F and G are formulas. The rule is called *static law* if F and G are fluent formulas, or *action dynamic law* if F is an action formula; and rules of the form

$$\textbf{caused } F \textbf{ if } G \textbf{ after } H \tag{2}$$

where F and G are fluent formulas, and H is a formula, called *fluent dynamic law*.

Many useful constructs are defined as abbreviations for the basic forms (1) and (2) shown above. For instance, the law

$$a \textbf{ causes } F \textbf{ if } G \tag{3}$$

for an action constant a stands for

$$\textbf{caused } F \textbf{ if } \top \textbf{ after } a \wedge G.$$

[2] `http://potassco.sourceforge.net/`

Other useful constructs include

$$\textbf{inertial } c, \qquad \text{for fluent constant } c, \tag{4}$$

which stands for **caused** c **if** c **after** c,

$$\textbf{exogenous } a, \qquad \text{for action constant } a, \tag{5}$$

which stands for **caused** a **if** a, **caused** $\neg a$ **if** $\neg a$,

$$\textbf{default } a, \qquad \text{for an action constant } a, \tag{6}$$

which stands for **caused** a **if** a, and

$$\textbf{nonexecutable } H \textbf{ if } F, \qquad \text{for an action formula } H, \tag{7}$$

which stands for **caused** $\bot$ **after** $H \wedge F$.

A *causal theory* contains a finite set of *causal rules* of the form $F \Leftarrow G$ where F and G are formulas. The semantics of a causal theory is defined in [3]. The semantics of an action description D is defined by a translation to the union of an infinite sequence of causal theories D_m ($m \geq 0$). The signature of D_m consists of pairs of form $i : c$ such that $i \in \{0, \ldots, m\}$ and c is a fluent constant of D, or $i \in \{0, \ldots, m-1\}$ and c is an action constant of D. The rules of D_m are

- $i : F \Leftarrow i : G$, for static law (1) in D and $i \in \{0, \ldots, m\}$, and action dynamic law (1) in D and $i \in \{0, \ldots, m-1\}$;
- $i+1 : F \Leftarrow (i+1 : G) \wedge (i : H)$, for every fluent dynamic law of the form (2) and $i \in \{0, \ldots, m-1\}$;
- $0 : c = v \Leftarrow 0 : c = v$, for simple fluent constant c and $v \in Dom(c)$.

A model of causal theory D_m can be seen as a path of length m in the transition diagram [3, Proposition 8].

Example 1. Suitcase problem in the sense of [16] can be formalized by defining boolean-valued exogenous actions $Toggle_t(l)$ and inertial fluents $Up_t(l)$, $Open_t$, with meta-variable l ranging over $\{L_1, L_2\}$, and action description D^0 consisting of rules

$$\begin{array}{rl} \mathit{Toggle}(l) \textbf{ causes } \mathit{Up}(l) \textbf{ if } \neg \mathit{Up}(l) & \mathit{Toggle}(l) \textbf{ causes } \neg \mathit{Up}(l) \textbf{ if } \mathit{Up}(l) \\ \textbf{caused } \mathit{Open} \textbf{ if } \mathit{Up}(L_1) \wedge \mathit{Up}(L_2) & \textbf{exogenous } \mathit{Toggle}(l) \\ \textbf{nonexecutable } \mathit{Toggle}(L_1) \wedge \mathit{Toggle}(L_2) & \textbf{inertial } \mathit{Up}(l) \quad \textbf{inertial } \mathit{Open} \end{array}$$

A model of D^0_2 can be represented as a path of length 2 in the transition diagram of D^0, which is shown in Figure 1.

3 Defining Composite Actions

3.1 Syntax

In the following, we consider action descriptions containing static laws of the form (1) where F and G are both fluent formulas, action dynamic laws of the form (5) and (6), and fluent dynamic laws of the form (3), (4) and (7).

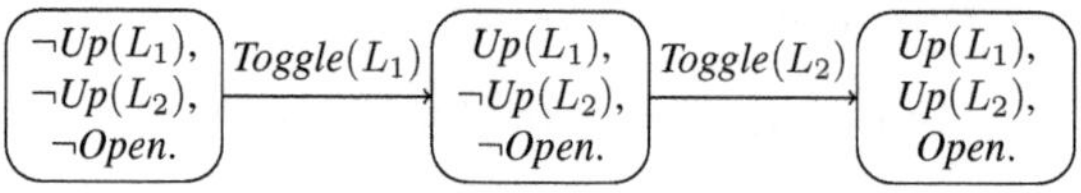

Fig. 1. The path in the transition diagram D

Given an action description D with a set of fluent constants σ^{fl} and a set of action constants σ^{act}, an *extended action description* D^+ is an extension of D by introducing a set of *composite action constants* σ^{comp} and *composite action definition law* of the form

$$b \textbf{ is } (a_0 \textbf{ if } E_0); (a_1 \textbf{ if } E_1); \ldots; (a_k \textbf{ if } E_k) \tag{8}$$

where b is a member of σ^{comp}, known as a *composite action constant*, and $a_0, \ldots, a_k$ are members of σ^{act}, and $E_0, \ldots, E_k$ are fluent formulas. Intuitively, this law means executing composite actions b is defined as executing a_0 if E_0 holds, then executing a_1 if E_1 holds, ..., then executing a_k if E_k holds. If E_i does not hold, action a_i will be skipped.

Example 1, continued. We extend D^0 by introducing an action *Opencase* which makes the suitcase open, as follows

$$\mathit{Opencase} \textbf{ is } \mathit{Toggle}(L_1) \textbf{ if } \neg \mathit{Up}(L_1); \mathit{Toggle}(L_2) \textbf{ if } \neg \mathit{Up}(L_2). \tag{9}$$

Intuitively, action *Opencase* may be executed in four different ways, depending on the initial state where the action is executed: if initially $\neg \mathit{Up}(L_1)$ and $\neg \mathit{Up}(L_2)$, then $\mathit{Toggle}(L_1)$ and $\mathit{Toggle}(L_2)$; if initially if $\neg \mathit{Up}(L_1)$ and $\mathit{Up}(L_2)$, then $\mathit{Toggle}(L_1)$; if initially $\mathit{Up}(L_1)$ and $\neg \mathit{Up}(L_2)$, then $\mathit{Toggle}(L_2)$; doing nothing if initially $\mathit{Up}(L_1)$ and $\mathit{Up}(L_2)$.

3.2 Semantics

For every action a_i occurring in the composite action definition law (8), introduce a new action constant a'_i. Denote the set of newly introduced constant symbols as σ^{aux}.

Given an action description D^+, let k^* denote the maximal value of k's occurring in all laws of form (8). An extended action description D^+ can be translated into an infinite sequence of causal theories D^+_m $(m \geq 0)$.

Since we specify that a composite action is executed in 1 time interval as well as a primitive action, we can only talk about its executing trajectory in a different dimension. As a result, a time interval $(i, i+1)$ is divided by subtime points $i.1, \ldots, i.k^*$ and into k^*+1 subintervals $(i, i.1), (i.1, i.2) \ldots, (i.k^*, i+1)$, and fluents have values in all k^*+1 subintervals. Therefore, the signature of D^+_m contains

- the symbols occurring in the signature of D_m
- for each composite action definition law (8),

- pairs of the form $i : a'_t$ for $i \in \{0, \ldots, m-1\}, a'_t \in \sigma^{aux}$,
- triples of the form $i.j : a'_t$ for $i \in \{0, \ldots, m-1\}, j \in \{1, \ldots, k^*\}, a'_t \in \sigma^{aux}$, and
- triples of the form $i.j : C$ for $i \in \{0, \ldots, m\}, j \in \{1, \ldots, k^*\}$, and C is fluent constants of D^+.

D^+_m is a causal theory containing rules of the following parts.

1. all rules in D_m except rules obtained from (4). That means the primitive actions are executed in 1 time interval.
2. for $i \in \{0, \ldots, m-1\}, j \in \{1, \ldots, k^*\}$ and for each static law (1), rules

$$i.j : F \Leftarrow i.j : G \tag{10}$$

It means that in every sub-interval, the static laws defining the relationship between fluents at time points are also used for subtime points.
3. for $i \in \{0, \ldots m-1\}$, $j \in \{1, \ldots, k^*-1\}$, $c \in Dom(c)$, and for each fluent dynamic law (4), rules

$$\begin{aligned} i.1 : c = v &\Leftarrow (i.1 : c = v) \wedge (i : c = v) \\ i.j{+}1 : c = v &\Leftarrow (i.j{+}1 : c = v) \wedge (i.j : c = v) \\ i{+}1 : c = v &\Leftarrow (i{+}1 : c = v) \wedge (i.k^* : c = v) \end{aligned} \tag{11}$$

The rules state that the original intertial laws form (4) are replaced by a group of inertial laws specifying the values of fluents at subtime points.
4. for each law (8), we introduce a list of auxiliary actions a'_j to simulate the primitive action a_j which is executed in the subinterval,
   4a. for $i \in \{0, \ldots, m-1\}$, rules

$$i.1 : F \Leftarrow (i.1 : G) \wedge (i : H^{a'_0}_{a_0}) \quad i.j{+}1 : F \Leftarrow (i.j{+}1 : G) \wedge (i.j : H^{a'_j}_{a_j}) \tag{12}$$

$$i{+}1 : F \Leftarrow (i{+}1 : G) \wedge (i.k^* : H^{a'_{k^*}}_{a_{k^*}}), \qquad \text{(if } k = k^*) \tag{13}$$

   where a_0, a_j $(1 \leq j \leq k-1)$ and a_k occur in laws (3) or each of them is the only action constant occurring in H of (7). These rules say that the auxiliary action a'_j leads to the same effect in the subinterval as the action a_j when executed as primitive actions. Especially, for a composite action that involves less than $k^*{+}1$ primitive actions, primitive actions will not be executed after $k{+}1$ subintervals.
   4b. for each fluent dynamic rule (7) such that there is at least one action symbol other than a_0 occurs in H, for $i \in \{0, \ldots, m-1\}$, rules

$$\bot \Leftarrow (i : H^b_{a_0}) \wedge (i : F) \tag{14}$$

   It specifies that any action that can not be concurrently executed with the first primitive action of the composite action can also not be executed concurrently with the composite action itself.

4c. for every $i \in \{0, \ldots, m-1\}, j \in \{1, \ldots, k\}, t \in \{0, \ldots, k\}$, rules

$$i : b \Leftarrow i : b \qquad i : \neg b \Leftarrow i : \neg b \tag{15}$$

$$i : a'_0 \Leftarrow (i : b) \wedge (i : E_0) \qquad i.j : a'_j \Leftarrow (i : b) \wedge (i.j : E_j) \tag{16}$$

$$\bot \Leftarrow i : a_t \wedge i : b \tag{17}$$

These rules say that any composite action is exogenous, and its primitive actions can only be "triggered" when the condition E_j is true at subtime point $i.j$. Also, we state that the composite action can not be executed concurrently with its primitive actions.

5. for $i \in \{1, \ldots, m-1\}, j \in \{1, \ldots, k^*\}$, and $a'_t \in \sigma^{aux}$, rules

$$i : \neg a'_t \Leftarrow i : \neg a'_t \qquad i.j : \neg a'_t \Leftarrow i.j : \neg a'_t \tag{18}$$

The rules state that every auxiliary action are by default not executed, so that they can only be "triggered" by b and the condition E_j.

6. for $i \in \{0, \ldots, m\}$, $b_m, b_n \in \sigma^{comp}$, rules

$$\bot \Leftarrow i : b_m \wedge i : b_n \tag{19}$$

It means that composite actions cannot be concurrently executed.

Example 1, continued. $(D^0)^+$ can be rewritten into the causal theories $(D^0)^+_m$:

- all rules except the rules obtained from inertial laws in D^0_m.
- static law **caused** *Open* **if** $Up(L_1)$ is translated into rule

$$i.1 : Open \Leftarrow i.1 : Up(L_1) \wedge i.1 : Up(L_2) \quad (i \in \{1, \ldots, m\})$$

- inertial laws are translated into (11). For instance, **inertial** $Up(l)$ is translated into rules ($i \in \{1, \ldots, m-1\}$)

$$\begin{aligned} i.1 : Up(l) &\Leftarrow i : Up(l) \wedge i.1 : Up(l) \\ i{+}1 : Up(l) &\Leftarrow i.1 : Up(l) \wedge i{+}1 : Up(l) \\ i.1 : \neg Up(l) &\Leftarrow i : \neg Up(l) \wedge i.1 : \neg Up(l) \\ i{+}1 : \neg Up(l) &\Leftarrow i.1 : \neg Up(l) \wedge i{+}1 : \neg Up(l) \end{aligned}$$

- $Toggle(l)$ **causes** $Up(l)$ **if** $\neg Up(l)$ is translated into rules ($i \in \{1, \ldots, m-1\}$)

$$\begin{aligned} i.1 : Up(l) &\Leftarrow i : \neg Up(l) \wedge i : Toggle'(l) \\ i{+}1 : Up(l) &\Leftarrow i.1 : \neg Up(l) \wedge i.1 : Toggle'(l) \end{aligned}$$

- **nonexecutable** $Toggle(L_1) \wedge Toggle(L_2)$ is translated into rule

$$\bot \Leftarrow i : Opencase \wedge i : Toggle(L_2) \quad (i \in \{1, \ldots, m-1\})$$

- from (9) we obtain rules ($i \in \{0, \ldots, m-1\}$)

$$\begin{aligned} i : Opencase \Leftarrow i : Opencase \qquad & i : \neg Opencase \Leftarrow i : \neg Opencase \\ i : \neg Toggle'(l) \Leftarrow i : \neg Toggle'(l) \qquad & i.1 : \neg Toggle'(l) \Leftarrow i.1 : \neg Toggle'(l) \\ \bot \Leftarrow i : Toggle(L_1) \wedge i : Opencase \qquad & \bot \Leftarrow i : Toggle(L_2) \wedge i : Opencase \\ i : Toggle'(L_1) \Leftarrow i &: Opencase \wedge i : \neg Up(L_1) \\ i.1 : Toggle'(L_2) \Leftarrow i &: Opencase \wedge i : \neg Up(L_2) \end{aligned}$$

4 Properties of Extended Action Descriptions

In this section we investigate the properties of the semantics of extended action descriptions by generalizing the notion of using a transition diagram to characterize the model of an action description proposed in [3]. We will identify an interpretation I of a causal theory with the set of atoms that are satisfied by this interpretation, that is to say, with the set of atoms of the form $c = I(c)$. Such a convention allows us to represent a model of an extended action description D_m^+ as

$$\begin{aligned} &(0 : s_0) \cup (0 : e_0) \cup (1 : s_1) \cup \ldots \cup (m : s_m) \\ \cup &\bigcup_{0 \le i \le m-1} ((i : \widehat{e}_i) \cup (i.1 : s_{i.1}) \cup \ldots \cup (i.k^* : s_{i.k^*}) \cup (i.k^* : \widehat{e}_{i.k^*})) \end{aligned} \tag{20}$$

where $e_0, \ldots, e_{m-1}$ are interpretations of $\sigma^{act} \cup \sigma^{comp}$, $s_0, \ldots s_m, s_{i.1}, \ldots, s_{i.k}$ are interpretations of σ^{fl}, and $\widehat{e}_i, \ldots, \widehat{e}_{i.k^*}$ are interpretations of σ^{aux}.

For instance, a model of $(D^0)_1^+$ is

$$\left\{\begin{array}{l} 0{:}\neg\, Up(L_1), 0{:}\neg\, Up(L_2), 0{:}\neg\, Open, 0{:}\neg\, Toggle(L_1), 0{:}\neg\, Toggle(L_2), \\ 0{:}\, Opencase, 0{:}\, Toggle'(L_1), 0{:}\neg\, Toggle'(L_2), \\ 0.1{:}\, Up(L_1), 0.1{:}\neg\, Up(L_2), 0.1{:}\neg\, Open, \\ 0.1{:}\neg\, Toggle'(L_1), 0.1{:}\neg\, Toggle'(L_2), 1{:}\, Up(L_1), 1{:}\, Up(L_2), 1{:}\, Open. \end{array}\right\} \tag{21}$$

which can be represented as

$$\begin{aligned} &(0 : \neg\, Up(L_1), \neg\, Up(L_2), \neg\, Open) \cup (0 : \neg\, Toggle(L_1), \neg\, Toggle(L_2), Opencase) \\ &\cup (1 : Up(L_1), Up(L_2), Open) \cup (0 : Toggle'(L_1), \neg\, Toggle'(L_2)) \\ &\cup (0.1 : Up(L_1), \neg\, Up(L_2), \neg\, Open) \cup (0.1 : \neg\, Toggle'(L_1), Toggle'(L_2)) \end{aligned}$$

A *state* is an interpretation s of σ^{fl} such that $0 : s$ is a model of D_0^+. States are vertexes of the transition diagram represented by D^+.

The transitions are defined by referring to models of D_1^+. For a model of D_1^+, they can be represented as

$$(0 : s) \cup (0 : e) \cup (1 : s') \cup (0 : \widehat{e}_0) \cup (0.1 : s_1) \cup \ldots \cup (0.k^* : s_{k^*}) \cup (0.k^* : \widehat{e}_{k^*}). \tag{22}$$

An *explicit transition* is a triple $\langle s, e, s' \rangle$ where s and s' are interpretations of σ^{fl} and e is an interpretation of $\sigma^{act} \cup \sigma^{comp}$ such that $(0 : s) \cup (0 : e) \cup (1 : s')$ belong to a model of D_1^+. If for some $b \in \sigma^{comp}$, $e(b) = \mathbf{t}$, then $\langle s, e, s' \rangle$ is called a *composite transition*, otherwise it is called a *simple transition*.

An *elaboration* is a tuple of the form

$$\langle s, \widehat{e}_0, s_1, \ldots, s_{k^*}, \widehat{e}_{k^*}, s' \rangle$$

where $\widehat{e}_i$ is an interpretation of σ^{aux} and s_i is an interpretation of σ^{fl}, such that

$$(0 : s) \cup (0 : \widehat{e}_0) \cup (0.1 : s_1) \cup \ldots \cup (0.k^* : s_{k^*}) \cup (0.k^* : \widehat{e}_{k^*}) \cup (1 : s')$$

belongs to a model of D_1^+. An elaboration can be seen as a list of k^*+1 triples

$$\langle s, \widehat{e}_0, s_1 \rangle, \ldots, \langle s_{k^*}, \widehat{e}_{k^*}, s' \rangle.$$

Each of the triples is called an *implicit transition*. If $\widehat{e}_j(a'_j) = \mathbf{f}$ for any a'_j which is the corresponding action symbol of $a_j \in \sigma^{act}$ in σ^{aux} and a_j occurs in (8) for $j \in \{0, \ldots, k\}$, the elaboration is called a *trivial elaboration for* b. The edge of the transition diagram represented by D^+ are the explicit transitions and implicit transitions in the models of D_1^+.

The above definition implicitly relies on the following properties of transitions.

Proposition 1. *For any explicit transition* $\langle s, e, s' \rangle$ *or implicit transition* $\langle s, \widehat{e}_i, s' \rangle$, s *and* s' *are states.*

This proposition is a generalization of Proposition 7 in [3]. Again, the validity of this proposition depends on the fact that statically determined fluents are not allowed to occur in the head of a fluent dynamic law (2).

To relate the model of the causal theory obtained from an extended action description, Proposition 8 of [3] is generalized to include composite transitions and elaborations.

Proposition 2. *For any* $m > 0$*, an interpretation (20) on the signature of* D_m^+ *is a model of* D_m^+ *iff for* $0 \leq i \leq m-1$ *each triple* $\langle s_i, e, s_{i+1} \rangle$ *is an explicit transition, and each tuple* $\langle s_i, \widehat{e}_i, s_{i.1}, \ldots, s_{i.k^*}, \widehat{e}_{i.k^*}, s_{i+1} \rangle$ *is an elaboration.*

Proposition 1 and Proposition 2 allow us to represent an extended action description as a transition graph.

Now we investigate the soundness of introducing composite actions. Following [17], for action description D and action description D' such that the signature of D is a part of the signature of D', D is a *residue* of D' if restricting the states and events of the transition system for D' to the signature of D establishes an isomorphism between the transition system for D' and the transition system for D.

Proposition 3. *Let* D *be an action description of a signature* σ *and* b *be a constant that does not belong to* σ*. If* D' *is an action description of the signature* $\sigma \cup \{c\}$ *obtained from* D *by adding a composite action definition law of* b *in terms of* σ*, then* D *is a residue of* D'*.*

For instance, in the suitcase domain, the transition system represented by $(D_1)^+$ is isomorphic to the transition system represented by D_1, by restricting the events of the transition system for $(D_1)^+$ to the action constants other than *Toggle*$'(L_1)$, *Toggle*$'(L_2)$, *Opencase*.

In addition to showing that an extended action description inherits all "good" things from the original action description, we also show that it doesn't introduce anything "bad": an auxiliary action a'_j, if executed, is the exact simulation of its corresponding primitive action a_j, in the sense that their transitions are in 1-1 correspondence.

Proposition 4. *Each implicit transition* $\langle s, \widehat{e}, s' \rangle$ *of* D^+ *corresponds to a transition* $\langle s, e, s' \rangle$ *of* D*.*

Based on this proposition, it is easy to see that an elaboration in D^+ corresponds to a path of length k^* in the transition diagram of D. Figure 2 shows the transitions of the model (21) of D_1^+, where the implicit transitions are represented as dashed arrows. It can be seen that every implicit transition corresponds to a transition in Figure 1.

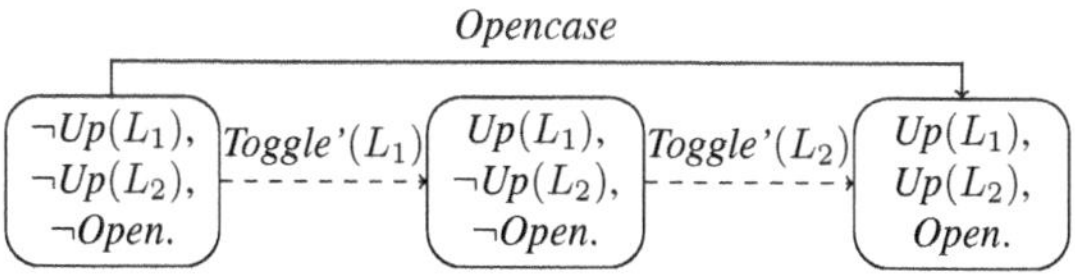

Fig. 2. (21) represented as transitions

An primitive action a occurring in (8) is called *the j-th primitive action of b* if $a_j = a$. The following proposition shows the difference between an auxiliary action a'_j and its corresponding primitive action a_j: instead of being exogenous, a'_j can only be triggered if the composite action of which a_j is the j-th primitive action, is executed.

Proposition 5. *Given an elaboration* $\langle s, \widehat{e}_0, \ldots, \widehat{e}_{k^*}, s' \rangle$, *for* $a' \in \sigma^{aux}$ *and its corresonding primitive action* $a \in \sigma^{act}$ *with some* $j \in \{0, \ldots, k^*\}$ *such that* $\widehat{e}_j(a') = \mathbf{t}$, *there exists a composite transition* $\langle s, e, s' \rangle$ *such that* $e(b) = \mathbf{t}$ *for some composite action b with a is its j-th primitive action.*

In Figure 2, the proposition explains that *Toggle*(L) and *Toggle*(R) are executed only if triggered by *Opencase*.

5 Generalized Monkey and Bananas Domain

5.1 Formalization

In this section, we use composite actions to formalize the generalized monkey and bananas domain (GMB). In the GMB domain, a monkey has to use a folding ladder to grasp bananas hung at different heights. To transport a ladder standing unfolded on the floor, he needs to fold the ladder first, move it to the destination and unfold it. The ladder has two stairs. The monkey can climb onto the first stair of the ladder to grasp a lower banana, or to the second stair of the ladder to grasp a higher banana. He can put a grasped banana in the bag to make him hands free and grasp more bananas. The goal is to collect all bananas.

In the action descriptions below, a fluent constant, if not given its domain, is boolean. All action constants are boolean. To address the problem of generality of AI, we begin with the general-purpose formalization of the primitive actions that depends on their parameters. For any nonempty sets M, O, L, T, A, S of symbols, the action description *LIB*(M, O, L, T, A, S) represents that the mover m (elements of M) moves physical object (elements of O) to location l (elements of L), and the physical object a (elements of A) is mounted to base s

(elements of S) by the tool t (elements of T). The signature and causal laws of $LIB(M, O, L, T, A, S)$ are as follows (where m range over M, o range over O, l range over L, t range over T, a range over A and s range over S):

- inertial fluent constants: $Loc(o)$, $Loc(m)$, $Loc(t)$, $Loc(a)$, with domain L, $Base(t), Base(a)$ with domain S;
- Primitive action constants: $Move(m, o, l)$, $Mount(t, a, s)$
- Causal laws:

$$\begin{array}{l} Move(m,o,l)\ \textbf{causes}\ Loc(m) = l \qquad Move(m,o,l)\ \textbf{causes}\ Loc(o) = l \\ \textbf{nonexecutable}\ Move(m,o,l)\ \textbf{if}\ Loc(o) = l \\ \textbf{nonexecutable}\ Move(m,o,l)\ \textbf{if}\ Loc(m) \neq Loc(o) \\ Mount(t,a,s)\ \textbf{causes}\ Base(a) = s \\ \textbf{nonexecutable}\ Mount(t,a,s)\ \textbf{if}\ Base(a) = s \\ \textbf{nonexecutable}\ Mount(t,a,s)\ \textbf{if}\ Loc(t) \neq Loc(a) \\ \textbf{default}\ \neg Mount(t,a,s) \qquad \textbf{default}\ \neg Move(m,o,l) \end{array}$$

The general-purpose formalization of *Move* and *Mount* are used to define composite actions in the GMB domain. These actions don't have the right to be executed outside composite actions and therefore are not exogenous but by default false.

To describe the GMB domain, we need to conjoin constants and causal laws of action description $Lib(M, O, L, T, A, S)$ such that $M = A = \{Monkey\}$, $O = T = \{Ladder\}$, $L = \{L_1, \ldots, L_n\}$, $S = \{Floor, S_1, S_2\}$ with the description *GMB* defined as follows ($b \in \{B_1, \ldots, B_k\}$, $l \in L$, $s \in S$, $m \in M$, $t \in T$, $o \in O$ and $a \in A$, $c \in \{B_1, \ldots, B_k, Nothing\}$)[3]:

- Simple fluent constants: $Height(b)$ with domain $\{Floor, S_1, S_2\}$, $Hold(c)$, $InBag(b)$, $Folded$.
- Primitive action constants: $Walk(l)$, $Grasp(b)$, $Fold$, $Unfold$, $PutToBag(b)$. Primitive actions are represented in traditional way.
- Three composite action constants $TransportLadder(l)$, $ClimbOnLadder$, $ClimbOffLadder$,
- Constraints that prohibit concurrent execution of actions,
- Composite action definition laws:

$$\begin{array}{l} TransportLadder(l)\ \textbf{is}\ Fold; Move(Monkey, Ladder, l); Unfold \\ ClimbOnLadder\ \textbf{is} \\ \quad Mount(Ladder, Monkey, S_1)\ \textbf{if}\ Base(Monkey) = Floor; \\ \quad Mount(Ladder, Monkey, S_2)\ \textbf{if}\ Base(Monkey) = S_1 \\ \qquad \wedge Loc(b) = Loc(Monkey) \wedge Height(b) = S_2 \\ ClimbOffLadder\ \textbf{is} \\ \quad Mount(Ladder, Monkey, S_1)\ \textbf{if}\ Base(Monkey) = S_2; \\ \quad Mount(Ladder, Monkey, Floor)\ \textbf{if}\ Base(Monkey) = S_1 \end{array}$$

[3] The full action description (including the lib and the domain) can be found at the following url: `http://wrighteagle.org/actiontheory/`.

5.2 Reasoning with Extended Action Descriptions

We implement the language by extending the software CPLUS2ASP to automate answering queries to the GMB domain formalized above. The software parses the input and translates the extended action description into a logic program, which can be further processed by F2LP[4] and ICLINGO to generate answer sets. In the following, assume that there are two bananas (b_1, b_2) and four locations (l_1, l_2, l_3, l_4).

Prediction. *Initially, the monkey is at* l_1*, the banana* b_1 *is at* l_2*, the height of* b_1 *is* s_2*, the banana* b_2 *is at* l_3*, the height of* b_2 *is* s_1*, and the ladder is at* l_4 *staying not folded. The monkey is on the floor. The monkey walks to* l_4 *and then transport the ladder to* l_3*. Does it follow that in the resulting state, the monkey, the banana* b_2 *and the ladder are at the same location?*
We add the following rules into the input of CPLUS2ASP

```
:- query
maxstep :: 2;
0:loc(monkey)=l1, loc(b1)=l2, loc(b2)=l3, loc(ladder)=l4, -folded,
  base(b1)=s2, base(b2)=s1, base(monkey)=floor, base(ladder)=floor,
  -hold(b1), -hold(b2), -inbag(b1), -inbag(b2), hold(nothing),
  walk(l4);
1:transportladder(l3).
2:loc(monkey) \= loc(b2) ++ loc(b2) \= loc(ladder).
```

CPLUSASP return "UNSATISFIABLE", indicating that at time 2, the monkey is at the same location with the banana and the ladder.

Planning. *Given the same initial state as above, find a plan within 10 steps so that the monkey has both bananas in his bag.*

We specify the following query:

```
:- query
maxstep :: 0..10;
0:loc(monkey)=l1, loc(b1)=l2, loc(b2)=l3, loc(ladder)=l4, -folded,
  base(b1)=s2, base(b2)=s1, base(monkey)=floor, base(ladder)=floor,
  -hold(b1), -hold(b2), -inbag(b1), -inbag(b2), hold(nothing);
maxstep:inbag(B).
```

The answer set returned by ICLINGO contains atoms:

```
0:walk(l4) 1:transportladder(l3) 1:fold1 1.1:move1(ladder,l3),
1.2:unfold1 2:climbonladder 2:mount1(monkey,ladder,s1) 3:grasp(b2)
4:puttobag(b2) 5:climboffladder 5:mount1(ladder,monkey,floor)
6:transportladder(l2) 6:fold1 6.1:move1(monkey,ladder,l3)
6.2:unfold1 7:climbonladder 7:mount1(ladder,monkey,s1)
7.1:mount1(ladder,monkey,s2) 8:grasp(b1) 9:puttobag(b1)
```

We have three observations. First, composite actions occur as building blocks of the plan, for example, we see `1:transportladder(l3)`, `2:climbonladder`,

[4] `http://reasoning.eas.asu.edu/f2lp/`

etc in the result. Second, when a composite action is executed, all the details about the executions of the primitive actions are also included, for instance, when `1:transportladder(l2)` is executed, we also have the details `1:fold1`, `1.1:move1(monkey,ladder,l2)` and `1.2:unfold1`. Third, composite actions can have different kinds of execution trajectory, for instance, executing composite action `7:climbonladder` is accompanied with `7:mount1(ladder,monkey,s1)` and `7.1:mount1(ladder,monkey,s2)`, indicating the monkey climbs up the two stairs of the ladder to grasp a high banana `b1`, while `2:climbonladder` is only accompanied with `2:mount1(ladder,monkey,s1)`, because the monkey needs to climb one stair to pick up a lower banana `b2`.

5.3 Performance

We test planning performance by two representations of the domain: a traditional representation GMB_1 without any composite actions, and an extended representation GMB_2 by adding the three composite actions into GMB_1. We consider 206 different domain instances divided into two groups of equal size: for all instances, the numbers of locations and bananas are randomly generated; for Group 1, bananas are hung at either S_1 or S_2, and for Group 2, bananas are all hung at S_2. Setting the goal of collecting all bananas, plans are computed for all instances and for both encodings. We set the longest acceptable length of a plan for an instance using GMB_1 to 50 and time limit for computing to be 30min[5].

The result is shown in Table 1(a) and 1(b). We classify all instances into 6 categories by the length of the plans generated using GMB_1. For each category, the third columns show the number of instances that cannot be computed within time limits using GMB_1. The last columns shows the average ratio of times on computing an instance using GMB_1 and GMB_2. And time-out instances are excluded from computing average ratio. There are no time-outs using GMB_2. In both tables, the ratio is always > 1, showing that adding composite actions leads to improvements on efficiency for instances of different sizes. The improvement is better for Group 2. In Group 2, all bananas are hung at S_2, so plans using GMB_1 contain a lot of consecutive executions of *ClimbTo*, which are composed to *ClimbOnLadder* or *ClimbOffLadder* in the plans generated from GMB_2. Making use of composite actions allows ICLINGO to find the "cumulative effects" at earlier stages of grounding. This improvement is not so apparent in Group 1 because when bananas are hung at S_1, *ClimbOnLadder* and *ClimbOffLadder* only contains one execution of *ClimbTo*, which is equivalent to executing *ClimbTo* without composite actions. Composite actions introduce more rules which may also become overhead of computation. Therefore, when the task domain has a "hierarchical structure" such that its plan consists of many consecutive executions of primitive actions which can compose to an action in a different abstraction space, composite actions may be worthwhile and can improve the efficiency.

Furthermore, we notice that when the plan length increases from ≤ 20 to 31–35, the ratio increases simultaneously, indicating that the composite actions

[5] The detailed representation, instances and logs, as well as the extended CPLUS2ASP system can be found at `http://wrighteagle.org/actiontheory/`

Table 1. The results of two groups

(a) The results of Group 1

Steps	#Nums	#Time-outs	time ratio
≤20	12	0	1.341
21–25	14	0	1.010
26–30	18	0	1.994
31–35	32	4	2.341
36–40	22	3	1.596
41–45	5	1	1.085

(b) The results of Group 2

Steps	#Nums	#Time-outs	time ratio
≤20	9	0	0.721
21–25	9	0	1.733
26–30	9	0	2.928
31–35	17	0	4.853
36–40	39	6	2.417
41–45	20	10	2.214

help improve the efficiency as the complexity of domain tasks increases. However, when the length continues to increase from 31–35 to 41–45, the ratio decreases gradually. This indicates that the one-level composite actions defined in this paper can not withstand the further growth of the complexity and multiple-level composite actions are needed. Allowing composite actions defined in this way is one of our future work.

6 Conclusion

In this paper we introduce composite actions into a fragment of $\mathcal{C}+$, which leads to a more intuitive and flexible way to formalize action domain, and improve efficiency of reasoning and planning by characterizing the hierarchical structure of the problem domain. Extended action descriptions can be processed by the extended CPLUS2ASP.

A direct next step is to apply CPLUS2ASP to real-life large application domain such as the cognitive service robot KEJIA [18] and investigate its representational and computational advantages. In the future, we would like to introduce composite action definitions to MAD, where modular actions can be defined as special cases or sequential executions of actions, by referring to a general-purpose library. Composite actions should also be defined by referring to other composite actions, with richer constructs, and on $\mathcal{C}+$ in its full generality.

Acknowledgement. The authors are grateful for constructive comments from Alfredo Gabaldon, Michael Gelfond, Daniela Inclezan and Vladimir Lifschitz.

References

1. Fikes, R., Nilsson, N.: STRIPS: A new approach to the application of theorem proving to problem solving. Artificial Intelligence 2(3-4), 189–208 (1971)
2. Gelfond, M., Lifschitz, V.: Action languages. Electronic Transactions on Artificial Intelligence 3, 195–210 (1998)
3. Giunchiglia, E., Lee, J., Lifschitz, V., McCain, N., Turner, H.: Nonmonotonic causal theories. Artificial Intelligence 153(1-2), 49–104 (2004)

4. McCarthy, J., Hayes, P.: Some philosophical problems from the standpoint of artificial intelligence. In: Meltzer, B., Michie, D. (eds.) Machine Intelligence, vol. 4, pp. 463–502. Edinburgh University Press, Edinburgh (1969)
5. Levesque, H.J., Reiter, R., Lespérance, Y., Lin, F., Scherl, R.B.: Golog: A logic programming language for dynamic domains. J. Log. Program. 31(1-3), 59–83 (1997)
6. Son, T.C., Baral, C., McIlraith, S.A.: Planning with Different Forms of Domain-Dependent Control Knowledge - An Answer Set Programming Approach. In: Eiter, T., Faber, W., Truszczyński, M. (eds.) LPNMR 2001. LNCS (LNAI), vol. 2173, p. 226. Springer, Heidelberg (2001)
7. Shanahan, M.: Event Calculus Planning Revisited. In: Steel, S. (ed.) ECP 1997. LNCS (LNAI), vol. 1348, pp. 390–402. Springer, Heidelberg (1997)
8. Sacerdott, E.D.: Planning in a hierarchy of abstraction spaces. In: Proceedings of the 3rd International Joint Conference on Artificial Intelligence, IJCAI 1973 (1973)
9. Erol, K., Hendler, J.A., Nau, D.S.: Htn planning: Complexity and expressivity. In: AAAI, pp. 1123–1128 (1994)
10. Lifschitz, V., Ren, W.: A modular action description language. In: Proceedings of National Conference on Artificial Intelligence (AAAI), pp. 853–859 (2006)
11. Gelfond, M., Inclezan, D.: Yet another modular action language. In: Proceedings of the Second International Workshop on Software Engineering for Answer Set Programming, pp. 64–78 (2009)
12. McCarthy, J.: Generality in Artificial Intelligence. Communications of the ACM 30(12), 1030–1035 (1987)
13. Erdoğan, S.T.: A Library of General-Purpose Action Descriptions. PhD thesis, University of Texas at Austin (2008)
14. Casolary, M., Lee, J.: Representing the language of the causal calculator in answer set programming. In: Technical Communications of the 27th International Conference on Logic Programming (ICLP 2011), pp. 51–61 (2011)
15. Inclezan, D., Gelfond, M.: Representing Biological Processes in Modular Action Language ALM. In: Proceedings of the 2011 AAAI Spring Symposium on Formalizing Commonsense, pp. 49–55. AAAI Press (2011)
16. Lin, F.: Embracing causality in specifying the indirect effects of actions. In: Proceedings of International Joint Conference on Artificial Intelligence (IJCAI), pp. 1985–1991 (1995)
17. Erdoğan, S.T., Lifschitz, V.: Actions as special cases. In: Proceedings of International Conference on Principles of Knowledge Representation and Reasoning (KR), pp. 377–387 (2006)
18. Chen, X., Ji, J., Jiang, J., Jin, G., Wang, F., Xie, J.: Developing high-level cognitive functions for service robots. In: Proc. of 9th Int. Conf. on Autonomous Agents and Multi-agent Systems, AAMAS 2010 (2010)

Strong Equivalence of RASP Programs

Stefania Costantini[1], Andrea Formisano[2], and David Pearce[3]

[1] Università di L'Aquila, Italy
stefania.costantini@univaq.it
[2] Università di Perugia, Italy
formis@dmi.unipg.it
[3] Universidad Politècnica de Madrid, Spain
david.pearce@upm.es

Abstract. RASP is a recent extension of Answer Set Programming (ASP) that permits declarative specification and reasoning on consumption and production of resources. In this paper, we extend the concept of strong equivalence (which, as widely recognized, provides an important conceptual and practical tool for program simplification, transformation and optimization) from ASP to RASP programs and discuss its applicability, usefulness and implications in this wider context.

Introduction

Issues related to production, consumption and exchange of resources are at the basis of all human activities, and in particular of economy. "Intelligent" resource management becomes increasingly important in view of sustainability problems that mankind has to face.

In knowledge representation and reasoning, forms of *quantitative* reasoning are possible in Linear Logics [10] and Description Logics [1]. In logic programming, a number of Prolog-like logic programming languages based on linear logic have been proposed (cf. references and discussion in [4]). In Answer Set Programming (ASP for short), a form of resource treatment is described in [17, 16] to model product configuration problems. This framework is based on Weight Constraint Rules, which is a well-known construct encompassing default negation and disjunctive choices [12]. Weight Constraint Rules have a wide applicability in many applications and are able to express costs and limits on costs, where however they do not express directly resource consumption/production. Resources are rendered, in the action description language $\mathcal{CARD}$ [2], through multi-valued fluents and the use of resources is implicitly modeled by the changes in fluents' values caused by actions' executions. The approach emphasizes the use of resources in planning problems and the semantics is given in terms of transition systems (in the spirit of [9]).

RASP (standing for ASP with Resources) [4, 3, 5] is an extension of ASP supporting declarative reasoning on consumption and production of resources. Theoretical and practical results developed for ASP can be extended to RASP: in this paper in fact, we extend the concept of strong equivalence to RASP programs and discuss its usefulness.

E. Erdem et al. (Eds.): Correct Reasoning, LNCS 7265, pp. 149–163, 2012.

Strong equivalence [13, 11], as widely recognized, provides an important conceptual and practical tool for program simplification, transformation and optimization. Even in the case where two theories are formulated in the same vocabulary, they may have the same answer sets yet behave very differently once they are embedded in some larger context. For a robust or modular notion of equivalence one should require that programs behave similarly when extended by any further program. This leads to the concept of strong equivalence, where programs P_1 and P_2 are strongly equivalent if and only if for any S, $P_1 \cup S$ is equivalent to (has the same answer sets as) $P_2 \cup S$. It is easy to see that, whenever P_1 and P_2 are different formulations of a RASP program involving consumption and production of resources, their behaving equivalently in different contexts is of particular importance related to reliability in resource usage. For instance, a designer might be able to evaluate, in terms of strong equivalence, different though analogous processes for producing certain resources, so as to choose one rather than the other in terms of suitable criteria.

In order to extend the notion of strong equivalence to RASP, we need to reformulate the semantics of RASP programs as introduced in [4] (based on a notion of resource "allocation") in a form less elegant but similar to that of plain ASP programs. This is done in Section 2 after an introduction to RASP provided in Section 1. After that, the definition of strong equivalence developed in [11] can be fairly easily extended to RASP (Section 3). However, it turns out that RASP programs behave quite differently from ASP programs as far as strong equivalence is concerned, as interferences in resource usage among rules of P_1, P_2 and S can easily arise. Then, we will argue (Section 4) that a significant notion of strong equivalence for RASP programs requires to state some constraints on S. So done, strong equivalence becomes a more effective notion in the RASP context. Finally, in Section 5 we conclude and outline some possible future directions. We assume a reader to be familiar with both ASP and strong equivalence. The reader may refer for the former to [7] and to the references therein, and for the latter to [15]. An extended version of this papers including proofs (that are omitted here for lack of space) can be found in [6].

1 Background on RASP

RASP [4, 3, 5] is an extension of the ASP framework obtained by explicitly introducing the notion of *resource*. It supports both formalization and quantitative reasoning on consumption and production of amounts of resources. These are modeled by *amount-atoms* of the form $q\!:\!a$, where q represents a specific type of resource and a denotes the corresponding amount. Resources can be produced or consumed (or declared available from the beginning).

The processes that transform some amounts of resources into other resources are specified by *r-rules*, for instance, as in this simple example:

$$computer\!:\!1 \leftarrow cpu\!:\!1, hd\!:\!2, motherboard\!:\!1, ram\_module\!:\!2.$$

where we model the fact that an instance of the resource *computer* can be obtained by "consuming" some other resources, in the indicated amounts.

In their most general form, r-rules may involve plain ASP literals together with amount-atoms. Semantics for RASP programs is given by combining answer set semantics with a notion of *allocation*. While answer sets are used to deal with usual ASP literals, allocations are exploited to take care of amounts and resources. Intuitively, an allocation assigns to each amount-atom a (possibly null) quantity. Quantities are interpreted in an auxiliary algebraic structure that supports comparisons and operations on amounts. Thus, one has to choose a collection Q of *quantities*, the operations to combine and compare quantities, and a mapping that associates quantities to amount-symbols. Admissible allocations are those satisfying, for all resources, the requirement that one can consume only what has been produced. Alternative allocations might be possible. They correspond to different ways of using the same resources. A simple natural choice for Q is the set of integer numbers. In all the examples proposed in the rest of the paper, we implicitly make this choice.

Syntax and semantics of RASP were introduced in [4]. Various extensions, presented in [4] and in [3, 5] (which discuss preferences and complex preferences in RASP) are not considered here. An implementation of RASP is discussed in [5] and is available at `http://www.dmi.unipg.it/formis/raspberry/`.

RASP syntax is based upon partitioning the symbols of the underlying language into program symbols and resource symbols. Precisely, let $\langle \Pi, \mathcal{C}, \mathcal{V} \rangle$ be a structure where $\Pi = \Pi_{\mathcal{P}} \cup \Pi_{\mathcal{R}}$ is a set of predicate symbols such that $\Pi_{\mathcal{P}} \cap \Pi_{\mathcal{R}} = \emptyset$, $\mathcal{C} = \mathcal{C}_{\mathcal{P}} \cup \mathcal{C}_{\mathcal{R}}$ is a set of constant symbols such that $\mathcal{C}_{\mathcal{P}} \cap \mathcal{C}_{\mathcal{R}} = \emptyset$, and $\mathcal{V}$ is a set of variable symbols. The elements of $\mathcal{C}_{\mathcal{R}}$ are said *amount-symbols*, while the elements of $\Pi_{\mathcal{R}}$ are said *resource-predicates*. The elements of $\mathcal{C}_{\mathcal{P}}$ and $\Pi_{\mathcal{P}}$ are constant and predicate symbols like in plain ASP. A *program-term* is either a variable or a constant symbol. An *amount-term* is either a variable or an amount-symbol. The second step is that of introducing amount-atoms in addition to plain ASP atoms, called program-atoms. Let $\mathcal{A}(X, Y)$ denote the collection of all atoms of the form $p(t_1, \ldots, t_n)$, with $p \in X$ and $\{t_1, \ldots, t_n\} \subseteq Y$. Then, a *program-atom* is an element of $\mathcal{A}(\Pi_{\mathcal{P}}, \mathcal{C} \cup \mathcal{V})$. Differently from program-atoms, each *amount-atom* explicitly denotes a resource and an amount. More precisely, an *amount-atom* is an expression of the form $q{:}a$ where $q \in \Pi_{\mathcal{R}} \cup \mathcal{A}(\Pi_{\mathcal{R}}, \mathcal{C} \cup \mathcal{V})$ and a is an amount-term. Let $\tau_{\mathcal{R}} = \Pi_{\mathcal{R}} \cup \mathcal{A}(\Pi_{\mathcal{R}}, \mathcal{C})$. We call elements of τ_R *resource-symbols*.

Expressions such as $p(X){:}V$ where V, X are variable symbols are allowed, as resources amounts can be either directly specified as constants or obtained via some kind of computation. Notice that the set of variables is not partitioned, as the same variable may occur both as a program term and as an amount-term. *Ground* amount- or program-atoms contain no variables. As usual, a *program-literal* L is a program-atom A or the negation $not\, A$ of a program-atom (intended as negation-as-failure).[1] A *resource-literal* is either a program-literal or an amount-atom. Notice that, for reasons discussed in [4], we do not admit negation of amount-atoms.

[1] In this paper we only deal with negation-as-failure. Nevertheless, classical negation of program literals could be used in RASP and treated as usually done in ASP.

Finally, we distinguish between plain rules and rules that involve amount-atoms. In particular, a *program-rule* is defined as a plain ASP rule. Besides program-rules we introduce resource-rules which differ from program rules (which are usual ASP rules) in that they may contain amount-atoms. A *resource-proper-rule* has the form $H \leftarrow B_1, \ldots, B_k$. where $B_1, \ldots, B_k$, are resource-literals and H is either a program-atom or a (non-empty) list of amount-atoms. If H is an amount-atom of the form $q{:}a$ where a is a constant and the body is empty then the rule is called a *resource-fact*. According to the definition then, the amount of an initially available resource has to be explicitly stated. As usual, we often denote the resource-fact $H \leftarrow$ simply by writing H.

In general, we admit several amount-atoms in the head of a rule where the case in which a rule γ has an empty head is admitted only if γ is a program-rule (i.e., γ is an ASP *constraint*). The list of amount-atoms composing the head of an resource-rule has to be understood conjunctively, i.e., as a collection of those resources that are all produced at the same time by *firing*, i.e. applying, the rule.

A *resource-rule* (*r-rule*, for short) can be either a resource-proper-rule or a resource-fact. A RASP program may involve both program rules and resource-rules, i.e., a *RASP-rule* (*rule*, for short) γ is either a program-rule or a resource-rule and a RASP program (*r-program*) is a finite multiset of RASP-rules (because in principle an r-rule may occur more than once in a program: in this case, each "copy" of the rule can be separately applied).

The ground version (or "grounding") of an r-program P is the set of all ground instances of rules of P, obtained through ground substitutions over the constants occurring in P. As customary, in what follows we will implicitly refer to the ground version of P. Intuitively, an interpretation of P is an answer set whenever it satisfies all the program rules in P and all the *fired* r-rules (in the usual way) as concerns their program-literals, and all consumed amounts either were available from resource-facts or have been produced by rule firings.

Example 1. Below is an example of a RASP program.

$g{:}2 \leftarrow q{:}4.$ $\qquad$ $h{:}1 \leftarrow q{:}1.$ $\qquad$ $f{:}3 \leftarrow q{:}2.$ $\qquad$ $q{:}4.$

This program has the following answer sets. The answer set $\{q{:}4, g{:}2, -q{:}4\}$, where we employ (consume) resource $q{:}4$ (as indicated by the notation $-q{:}4$) to *fire* (i.e., apply) the first rule and produce $g{:}2$, with no remainder (the full available amount of q is consumed). The answer set $\{q{:}4, f{:}3, h{:}1, -q{:}3\}$, where we employ (consume) part of resource $q{:}4$ (as indicated by the notation $-q{:}3$) to fire the second and third rule and produce $f{:}3$ and $h{:}1$. In this case, as we do not have consumed the full amount of q, there is a remainder $q{:}1$ that might have been potentially used elsewhere. We cannot produce $g{:}2$ together with $f{:}3$ and/or $h{:}1$ because the available quantity of q is not sufficient. But, we also have the answer sets $\{q{:}4\}$, $\{q{:}4, f{:}3, -q{:}2\}$ and $\{q{:}4, h{:}1, -q{:}1\}$ where all or part of resource $q{:}4$, though available, is left unconsumed.

Notice that the given program does not involve negation. In plain ASP we may have several answer sets only if the program involves negation, and, in particular, cycles on negation. In RASP, we may have several answer sets also in positive (i.e., definite) programs because of different possible allocations of available resources. Notice also that in the present setting each rule can be applied only once, i.e, we cannot for instance use the third rule several times to produce several items of h:1 according to the available qs. Actually, multiple "firings" of rules can be allowed by a suitable specification but we do not consider this extension here.

In [4] we introduce *politics* for resource usage, by extending the semantics so as to allow a programmer to state, for each rule, if the firing is either optional or mandatory. In the rest of this paper, to simplify the discussion, we make the assumption that the firing of rules is mandatory. In the above example, this politics excludes the answer sets $\{q{:}4\}$, $\{q{:}4, f{:}3, -q{:}2\}$ and $\{q{:}4, h{:}1, -q{:}1\}$. In the next section, we introduce a version of the semantics of RASP close to the one originally defined for plain ASP, i.e., in terms of a reduct (for ASP, the so-called Gelfond-Lifschitz reduct, or GL-reduct, introduced in [8]).

2 Reduct-Based RASP Semantics

In order to extend the notion of strong equivalence to RASP, it is useful to devise a semantic definition for RASP as close as possible to the standard answer set semantics as defined in [8]. This will make it easier to extend to RASP the definitions and proofs provided in [11].

In fact, in [4], the formulation of RASP semantics is based on set theory and on a concept of "resource allocation". In this section, we propose a more "practical" version, close to standard ASP. This because, for the sake of conceptual clarity, we intend to define strong equivalence of RASP programs by extending step-by-step the original formalization of [11], which is heavily based upon the notion of reduct as introduced in [8]. We thus introduce for RASP an extended notion of reduct and propose an alternative RASP semantics accordingly, that we prove to be equivalent to the original one.

We base this new semantics on standardized-apart RASP programs, whose definition was originally introduced in [4] in order to evaluate RASP complexity (which turned out to be the same as plain ASP). This involves generating, from a ground r-program, a version where resource-predicates occurring in bodies of rules are associated to the rule where they occur. For the sake of simplicity and without loss of generality, we assume that a resource predicate, say q, may occur more than once in the body of the same rule only if the amounts are different. It may occur instead with either the same or different amounts in the head and body of several rules. Below, let a "program" be a RASP program. The answer sets for a program obtained with the formulation proposed in this section are called *reduct-answer sets* (for short, *r-answer sets*). Specifically, in order to cope with different instances of the same amount-atom, say $q{:}a$, occurring in the body of different rules, we "standardize apart" these occurrences, according to the following definition (reported from [4]).

Definition 1. *Let P be a ground r-program, and let $\gamma_1, ..., \gamma_k$ be the rules in P containing amount-atoms in their body. The standardized-apart version P_s of P*

is obtained from P by renaming each amount-atom q:a in the body of γ_j, $j \leqslant k$ as q^j:a. The q^j's are called the standardized-apart versions of q, or in general standardized-apart resource-predicates.

Example 2. Let P be the following program.

$$
\begin{array}{ll}
g{:}2 \leftarrow q{:}4. & a \leftarrow not\ b. \\
p{:}3 \leftarrow q{:}3, a. & b \leftarrow not\ a. \\
d{:}1 \leftarrow q{:}3, b. & c. \\
q{:}6 \leftarrow c. &
\end{array}
$$

The standardized-apart version P_s of P is as follows.

$$
\begin{array}{ll}
g{:}2 \leftarrow q^1{:}4. & a \leftarrow not\ b. \\
p{:}3 \leftarrow q^2{:}3, a. & b \leftarrow not\ a. \\
d{:}1 \leftarrow q^3{:}3, b. & c. \\
q{:}6 \leftarrow c. &
\end{array}
$$

We let $\mathcal{A}_{P_s}$ be the set of all atoms (both program-atoms and amount-atoms) that can be built from predicate and constant symbols occurring in P_s. Notice that not only the same r-rule might occur more than once in the same program, but also the same resource-predicate might occur more than once in the body of an r-rule.

Definition 2. *A candidate reduct-interpretation $\mathcal{I}_{P_s}$ for P_s is any multiset obtained from a subset of $\mathcal{A}_{P_s}$.*

Referring to Example 2, among the possible candidate interpretations are, e.g., $I_1 = \{p{:}3, q{:}6, q^2{:}3, a, c\}$ and $I_2 = \{p{:}3, q{:}6, q^1{:}4, q^3{:}3, a, c\}$. Standardized-apart amount-atoms occurring in a candidate r-interpretation represent resources that are *consumed.* Plain amount-atoms represent resources that have been produced, or were available from the beginning. For a candidate r-interpretation to be an admissible r-interpretation (or, simply, r-interpretation), consumption has not to exceed production.

Definition 3. *Given multi-set of atoms S and resource-predicate q (possibly standardized-apart) occurring in S, let $f(S)(q)$ be an amount-symbol obtained by summing the quantities related to the occurrences of q. If S contains $q{:}a_1$, $\ldots$, $q{:}a_k$ (or, respectively, $q^j{:}a_1$, $\ldots$, $q^j{:}a_k$) and $a = a_1 + \ldots + a_k$ we will have $f(S)(q) = a$ (or, respectively, $f(S)(q^j) = a$).*

Definition 4. *A candidate reduct-interpretation $\mathcal{I}_{P_s}$ is a reduct-interpretation (for short r-interpretation) if for every resource-predicate q occurring in $\mathcal{I}_{P_s}$, taken all its standardized-apart versions $q^{j_1}, \ldots, q^{j_h}$, $h \geq 0$, also occurring in $\mathcal{I}_{P_s}$, we have $f(\mathcal{I}_{P_s})(q) \geq \sum_{i=1}^{h} f(\mathcal{I}_{P_s})(q^{j_i})$.*

Referring again to Example 2, it is easy to see that I_1 is an r-interpretation, as 6 items of q are produced and just 3 are consumed, while I_2 is not, as 6 items of q are produced but 7 are supposed to be consumed.

We now establish whether an r-interpretation $\mathcal{I}_{P_s}$ is an r-answer set for P_s, and we will then reconstruct from it an r-answer set for P. To this aim, we introduce the following extension to the Gelfond-Lifschitz reduct.

Definition 5 (RASP-reduct). *Given a reduct-interpretation $\mathcal{I}_{P_s}$ for the standardized-apart version P_s of RASP program P, the RASP-reduct $cfp(P_s, \mathcal{I}_{P_s})$ is a RASP program obtained as follows.*

1. *For every standardized-apart amount-atom $A \in \mathcal{I}_{P_s}$, add A to P_s as a fact, obtaining $P_s^+(\mathcal{I}_{P_s})$;*
2. *Compute the GL-reduct of $P_s^+(\mathcal{I}_{P_s})$.*

Let $LM(T)$ be the Least Herbrand Model of theory T. In case T is a RASP program, in computing $LM(T)$ amount-atoms are treated as plain atoms. We may state the main definition:

Definition 6. *Given reduct-interpretation $\mathcal{I}_{P_s}$ for the standardized-apart version P_s of RASP program P, $\mathcal{I}_{P_s}$ is a reduct-answer set (r-answer set) of P_s if $\mathcal{I}_{P_s} = LM(cfp(P_s, \mathcal{I}_{P_s}))$*

Referring again to Example 2, the r-answer sets of P_s are:
$M_1 = \{q{:}6, g{:}2, q^1{:}4, a, c\}$, $M_2 = \{q{:}6, g{:}2, q^1{:}4, b, c\}$,
$M_3 = \{q{:}6, p{:}3, q^2{:}3, a, c\}$, $M_4 = \{q{:}6, d{:}1, q^3{:}3, b, c\}$.

Notice that M_1 and M_2 have the same resource consumption and production but from the even cycle on negation they choose a different alternative (a w.r.t. b). Producing $g{:}2$ excludes being able to produce $p{:}3$ or $d{:}1$ respectively, because the remaining quantity of q is not sufficient. In the terminology of previous section, $g{:}2$ is produced by *firing* the first r-rule, while the second and third ones remain *unfired.* Instead of producing $g{:}2$, one can produce either $p{:}3$ by firing the second r-rule (answer set M_3) if choosing the alternative a or $d{:}1$ by firing the third r-rule (answer set M_4) if choosing the alternative b.

It will be useful in the next sections to define the *set of unfired rules* of a RASP program P w.r.t. any of its answer sets (say M) as the subprogram of P consisting of all r-rules whose head is not in M. We define two RASP programs P_1 and P_2 to be *equivalent* if they have the same r-answer sets and to be *tightly equivalent* if they are equivalent and, for each of their answer sets (say M) they have the same set of unfired rules w.r.t. M.

We now have to prove the equivalence of the above-proposed semantic formulation with the one of [4]. We will prove in particular that there is a bijection between the set of the r-answer sets of the standardized-apart version P_s of RASP program P and the set of RASP answer sets as defined in [4]. To do that, we exploit the part of [4] where, for determining the complexity of RASP, a bijection is introduced between RASP answer sets and *admissible* answer sets (in the usual answer set semantics) of an ASP version of the given RASP program P, called *adapted program* (where admissible answer sets are those satisfying the constraint that resource production must exceed consumption). The adapted program augments a standardized-apart program so as to simulate the allocation of a resource to a rule. Below is the definition, reported from [4].

Definition 7. *The* adapted program *P' for P (corresponding to P_s) is obtained by adding to P_s for each $q^j{:}a$ occurring in the body of some r-rule of P_s and such that $q{:}b$ (for some b) occurs in the head of some r-rule of P_s the following pair of rules (where $no\_q^j{:}a$ is a fresh atom): $q^j{:}a \leftarrow not\ no\_q^j{:}a$. $no\_q^j{:}a \leftarrow not\ q^j{:}a$.*

So, to our aim it suffices to prove that a bijection exists between the answer sets of P_s and the admissible answer sets of P'. This in fact implies that there exists a bijection between the set of RASP answer sets of ground RASP program P and the set of r-answer sets of the standardized-apart version P_s of P.

In order to compare r-answer sets with admissible answer sets we have to make their form compatible. In particular, interpretations of an adapted program will thus contain, for resource q, either $q^j{:}a$ or $no\_q^j{:}a$ to signify availability or, respectively, unavailability of amount a of this resource for consumption by the j-th rule. Below we transform an r-interpretation into this form.

Definition 8. *Given an r-interpretation $\mathcal{I}_{P_s}$ for the standardized-apart version P_s of RASP program P, $ad(\mathcal{I}_{P_s})$ is obtained from $\mathcal{I}_{P_s}$ by adding $no\_q^j{:}a$ for every amount symbol $q^j{:}a$ which occurs in P_s but not in $\mathcal{I}_{P_s}$.*

We can now state the result we where looking for, i.e.,

Theorem 1. *Given an r-interpretation $\mathcal{I}_{P_s}$ for the standardized-apart version P_s of RASP program P, $\mathcal{I}_{P_s}$ is an r-answer set of P_s if and only if $ad(\mathcal{I}_{P_s})$ is an admissible answer set of the adapted program P' corresponding to P_s.*

and, consequently:

Corollary 1. *There exists a bijection between the set of RASP answer sets of ground RASP program P and the set of r-answer sets of the standardized-apart version P_s of P.*

At this stage, as we wish to obtain r-answer sets of P, we can get a more compact form by getting the global consumed/produced quantity of each resource q.

Definition 9. *Given an r-answer set $\mathcal{I}_{P_s}$ of P_s, an r-answer set $\mathcal{M}_P^R$ of P is obtained as follows. For each resource-predicate q occurring in $\mathcal{I}_{P_s}$:*
(i) replace its occurrences $q{:}b_1, \ldots, q{:}b_s$, $s > 0$, with $q{:}b$, for $b = b_1 + \ldots + b_s$;
(ii) replace its standardized-apart occurrences $q^{j_1}{:}a_1, \ldots, q^{j_k}{:}a_k$, $k \geq 0$, with $-q{:}a$, for $a = a_1 + \ldots + a_k$.

By some abuse of notation, we will often interchangeably mention r-answer sets or simply "answer sets" of P or of P_s. For Example 2, the r-answer sets of P are:
$M_1 = \{q{:}6, g{:}2, -q{:}4, a, c\}$, $M_2 = \{q{:}6, g{:}2, -q{:}4, b, c\}$,
$M_3 = \{q{:}6, p{:}3, -q{:}3, c\}$, $M_4 = \{q{:}6, d{:}1, -q{:}3, b, c\}$.

Notice that the above notation does not explicitly report about what is left. Actually, given each r-answer set we can establish which resources are still available after the production/consumption process by computing the difference, for each resource, between what has been produced and what has been consumed. For instance, in M_1 and M_2 we are left with $q{:}2$ and $g{:}2$, in M_3 with $q{:}3$ and $p{:}3$, and in M_4 with $q{:}3$ and $d{:}1$.

3 Strong Equivalence of RASP Programs

In this section, we extend the standard notion of strong equivalence to RASP programs, taking as a basis the definitions that can be found in [11], which provides a characterization of strong equivalence of ground programs in terms of the propositional logic of here-and-there (HT-logic). We remind the reader that the logic of here-and-there is an intermediate logic between intuitionistic logic and classical logic. Like intuitionistic logic it can be semantically characterized by Kripke models, in particular using just two worlds, namely *here* and *there*, assuming that the *here* world is ordered before the *there* world. Accordingly, interpretations (HT-interpretations) are pairs (X, Y) of sets of atoms from given language L, such that $X \subseteq Y$. An HT-interpretation is total if $X = Y$. The intuition is that atoms in X (the *here* part) are considered to be true, atoms not in Y (the *there* part) are considered to be false, while the remaining atoms (from $Y \setminus X$) are undefined. A total HT-interpretation (Y, Y) is called an equilibrium model of a theory T, iff $(Y, Y) \models T$ and for all HT-interpretations (X, Y), such that $X \subset Y$, it holds that $(X, Y) \not\models T$. For an answer set program P, it turns out that an interpretation Y is an answer set of P iff (Y, Y) is an equilibrium model of P reinterpreted as an HT-theory.

We take as a basis the standardized-apart version P_s of RASP program P. Notice that we assume two RASP programs to have the same alphabet (an so to be potentially equivalent and strongly equivalent) if they are defined on the same set Π of predicate symbols. That is, for amount-atoms we allow in the two programs different amounts for the same resource-predicate. This makes the problem of strong equivalence of RASP programs different from the same problem for plain ASP programs.

To account for resource production and consumption, HT-logic must be extended as follows. The set of atoms must be augmented to admit amount-atoms, involving both plain and standardized-apart resource predicates. Like in the RASP semantics, we take for given the choice of an algebraic structure to represent amounts and support operations on them.

The satisfaction relation of HT-logic between an interpretation $I = \langle I^H, I^T \rangle$ and a formula F must be augmented to express that each resource can be produced and consumed in several fragments, but what counts is on the one hand that consumption does not exceed production, and on the other hand which is the total produced quantity. We thus add the following two new axioms (where w is the world, that can be either *here* or *there*).

The first new axiom "distributes" the available quantity of a resource q (obtained by summing the produced quantities) to the formulas that use it.

AR-1
$\langle I^H, I^T, w \rangle \models q^{j_1}{:}a_1 \wedge \ldots \wedge q^{j_k}{:}a_k$ where $k > 0$ and each $j_i > 0$ if
$\langle I^H, I^T, w \rangle \models q{:}b_1 \wedge \ldots \wedge q{:}b_s$, $s > 0$, and $b_1 + \ldots + b_s \geq a_1 + \ldots + a_k$

Notice that, for every HT-interpretation $\langle I_s^H, I_s^T \rangle$ of P_s, AR-1 ensures that the sets I_s^H and I_s^T are, in the terminology of previous section (Definition 4), r-interpretations of P_s.

The second new axiom "computes" the total produced quantity b of each resource q. To this aim, for each resource-predicate q we provisionally introduce a fresh corresponding resource-predicate q^T.

AR-2
$\langle I^H, I^T, w \rangle \models q^T{:}b$ if $\langle I^H, I^T, w \rangle \models q{:}a_1 \wedge \ldots \wedge q{:}a_k$ and
$\langle I^H, I^T, w \rangle \not\models q{:}a,\ a \neq a_1 \wedge \ldots \wedge a \neq a_k$, where $k > 0$ and $b = a_1 + \ldots + a_k$

In order to deal with different though equivalent production patterns that may occur in different RASP programs, we keep in HT-interpretations only the total quantities of produced resources.

Definition 10. *Given an HT-interpretation $\langle I_s^H, I_s^T \rangle$ of P_s, its* normalized version *is obtained by replacing in both I_s^H and I_s^T for each resource-predicate q the set of atoms $q^T{:}b, q{:}a_1, \ldots, q{:}a_k$ with $q : b$.*

In what follows, by some abuse of notation, by "HT-interpretation" we mean its normalized version (the same for HT-models). This stated, it is not difficult to suitably extend to RASP the results introduced in [11]. We introduce the following lemma, so that we can state the main theorem:

Lemma 1. *For any RASP program P and any set I of atoms, the HT-interpretation $\langle I, I \rangle$ is an equilibrium model of P iff I is an r-answer set of P_s.*

Theorem 2. *For any RASP programs P_1 and P_2, and for every RASP program S, $P_1 \cup S$ has the same answer sets of $P_2 \cup S$, i.e., P_1 is strongly equivalent to P_2, if and only if their standardized-apart versions ${P_1}_s$ and ${P_2}_s$ are equivalent in the extended logic of Here-and-There, i.e., have the same HT-models.*

Clearly, two RASP programs are candidates to be equivalent whenever the same total quantity of each resource q is produced. To ensure equivalence consumption must be performed in exactly the same way, which, as we will see, is a heavy limitation. In the rest of this section in fact, we discuss a number of examples to illustrate the subtleties of equivalence and strong equivalence of RASP programs, and emphasize the problems which arise. We will then address these problems in the subsequent section.

Example 3. The following two RASP programs are strongly equivalent.

P_1 :
$q{:}6 \leftarrow not\ c.$

P_2 :
$q{:}3 \leftarrow not\ c.$
$q{:}3 \leftarrow not\ c.$

Their unique equilibrium model is $\langle I, I \rangle$ with $I = \{q : 6\}$ which is the unique r-answer set of both programs. The only difference between the two programs is that the same amount of resource q is produced in P_1 all in once, and in P_2 in two parts. This difference is taken into account by axiom AR-2.

Example 4. The following two RASP programs are, similarly to what would happen in plain RASP, not strongly equivalent.

P_1 :
$q{:}6.$

P_2 :
$q{:}6 \leftarrow not\ c.$

Their unique equilibrium model is $\langle I, I \rangle$ with $I = \{q : 6\}$ which is the unique r-answer set of both programs, but they are not strongly equivalent as can be seen by adding for instance fact c.

In the terms illustrated up to now, it is very difficult for RASP programs to be not only strongly equivalent, but even simply equivalent, as demonstrated by the following examples.

Example 5. The following two standardized-apart RASP programs are, differently from what would happen in plain ASP, not even equivalent. In fact, in the former program there is a number of plainly available resources, while in the latter producing $q{:}4$ requires consuming $p{:}2$.

P_1 : $q{:}4.$ $p{:}2.$ $r{:}4.$ $c.$
Unique answer set: $\{c, q{:}4, p{:}2, r{:}4\}$

P_2 : $q{:}4 \leftarrow p^1{:}2.$ $p{:}2.$ $r{:}4.$ $c.$
Unique answer set: $\{c, q{:}4, p{:}2, r{:}4, p^1{:}2\}$

Example 6. The following two standardized-apart RASP programs are not equivalent, despite that they produce and consume the same resources, though in a different way.

P_1 : $q{:}1 \leftarrow p^1{:}2.$ $p{:}6.$ $r{:}1 \leftarrow p^2{:}3.$ $g{:}1.$
Unique answer set: $\{g{:}1, p{:}6, q{:}1, r{:}1, p^1{:}2, p^2{:}3\}$.

P_2 : $q{:}1 \leftarrow p^1{:}3.$ $p{:}6.$ $r{:}1 \leftarrow p^2{:}2.$ $g{:}1.$
Unique answer set: $\{g{:}1, p{:}6, q{:}1, r{:}1, p^1{:}3, p^2{:}2\}$.

The two programs are however equivalent in terms of compact form of r-answer sets: according to Definition 9, one obtains for both programs the r-answer sets $\{g{:}1, p{:}6, q{:}1, r{:}1, -p{:}5\}$. Yet, even w.r.t. compact r-answer sets the two programs are not strongly equivalent: assume, e.g., to add rule $g{:}2 \leftarrow p{:}4$ (that, standardized-apart, becomes $g{:}2 \leftarrow p^3{:}4$). The additional rule "competes" with the original ones for the use of amounts of resource $p{:}6$. Thus, different choices for employing resource $p{:}6$ become possible. In fact, for the augmented former program the answer sets are:
$M_1 = \{g{:}1, p{:}6, q{:}1, r{:}1, p^1{:}2, p^2{:}3\}$ $M_2 = \{g{:}3, p{:}6, q{:}1, p^1{:}2, p^3{:}4\}$ i.e.,
in compact form, $Mr_1 = \{g{:}1, p{:}6, q{:}1, r{:}1, -p{:}5\}$ $Mr_2 = \{g{:}3, p{:}6, q{:}1, , -p{:}6\}$.
For the latter program they are instead:
$N_1 = \{g{:}1, p{:}6, q{:}1, r{:}1, p^1{:}3, p^2{:}2\}$ $N_2 = \{g{:}3, p{:}6, r{:}1, p^2{:}2, p^3{:}4\}$ i.e.,
in compact form, $Nr_1 = \{g{:}1, p{:}6, q{:}1, r{:}1, -p{:}5\}$ $Nr_2 = \{g{:}3, p{:}6, r{:}1, -p{:}6\}$.

In the two previous examples one may notice that given programs are equivalent w.r.t. what is produced, and differ w.r.t. resources that are consumed. A conceptual tool to recognize some kind of equivalence of the above programs is in order, as a designer would be enabled to assess their similarity and choose the pattern of production/consumption deemed more appropriate in the application at hand. In the next section we will propose a weaker notion of equivalence and strong equivalence than those introduced so far.

4 Strong Equivalence of RASP Programs Revisited

Below we introduce a compact form of HT-models where produced and consumed resources occur in their total quantities, similarly to r-answer sets introduced in Definition 9.

Definition 11. *Given an HT-model* $\langle I_s^H, I_s^T \rangle$ *of* P_s*, a* compact *HT-model (c-HT-model)* $\langle I^H, I^T \rangle$ *of* P *is obtained by replacing, for each resource-predicate* q *occurring in* $\langle I_s^H, I_s^T \rangle$*, its standardized-apart occurrences* $q^{j_1}{:}a_1, \ldots, q^{j_k}{:}a_k$*,* $k \geq 0$*, with* $-q{:}a$*, where* $a = a_1 + \ldots + a_k$*.*

The following definition makes a further simplification by eliminating consumed quantities from r-answers sets and c-HT-models.

Definition 12. *Given an r-answer set* A *of* P *or given a c-HT-model* $\langle I_c^H, I_c^T \rangle$ *of* P_s*, a* production *answer set (p-answer set)* A' *of* P *(resp., a* production *HT-model, or p-HT-model)* $\langle I^H, I^T \rangle$ *of* P_s*) is obtained by removing from* A *(resp., from* I_c^H *and* I_c^T*) all atoms of the form* $-q{:}a$ *for any* q *and* a*.*

In Example 6, the unique equilibrium c-HT-model of both programs is $\langle I, I \rangle$ with $I = \{g{:}1, p{:}6, q{:}1, r{:}1, -p{:}5\}$ where I is the unique r-answer set. The corresponding p-answer set is $I' = \{g{:}1, p{:}6, q{:}1, r{:}1\}$, and the unique equilibrium p-HT-model is $\langle I', I' \rangle$.

In Example 5, the unique r-answer set of P_1 is $M = \{c, q{:}4, p{:}2, r{:}4\}$, which coincides with the p-answer set. The unique equilibrium c- and p-HT-model is $\langle M, M \rangle$. For P_2, the unique r-answer set is $N = \{c, q{:}4, p{:}2, r{:}4, -p{:}2\}$, and the unique equilibrium c-HT-model is $\langle N, N \rangle$. The corresponding p-answer set is $N' = \{c, q{:}4, p{:}2, r{:}4\}$, and the unique equilibrium p-HT-model is $\langle N', N' \rangle$. Thus, in both Example 6 and Example 5 the two given programs are "equivalent" w.r.t. equilibrium p-HT-models (or, equivalently, p-answer sets). We formalize this notion of equivalence below.

Definition 13. *Two RASP theories (standardized-apart programs) are* equivalent on production *(p-equivalent) if their p-HT-models (and, consequently, their p-answer sets) coincide. They are* tightly equivalent on production *if they have the same set of unfired rules w.r.t. any of their p-answer sets. Two RASP theories are* strongly equivalent on production *(p-strongly equivalent) if, after adding whatever RASP theory* S *to both, they are still equivalent on production.*

This definition enlarges the set of RASP programs that can be considered to be equivalent. However, strong equivalence remains problematic.

Example 7. Consider the two programs of Example 5, that are equivalent on production. Assume to add rule: $r{:}1 \leftarrow p^4{:}3$. The c-HT-models and the p-HT-models remain unchanged, and thus the two programs are still p-equivalent. In fact the added rule cannot fire, not being available the needed quantity of p. Assume instead to add rule $r{:}1 \leftarrow p^4{:}2$, which is able to exploit the available resource amount $p{:}2$. In this case, for the augmented P_1 we get the unique r-answer set $\{c, q{:}4, p{:}2, r{:}1, -p{:}2\}$, but for the augmented P_2 the new rule "competes" with pre-existing ones on the use of $p{:}2$: thus, we get the two r-answer sets $\{c, p{:}2, r{:}4, r{:}1, -p{:}2\}$ and $\{c, q{:}4, p{:}2, r{:}4, -p{:}2\}$. Consequently, the updated programs are not p-equivalent.

We may notice that the problems that we have discussed arise when S is a *proper RASP program*, i.e., a RASP program containing amount-atoms. However, Example 4 points out that problems related to the addition of a plain ASP part must also be taken into account. Let a *plain ASP addition* be a RASP program fragment not containing amount-atoms. It is easy to see that:

Proposition 1. *A necessary condition for two RASP programs to be p-strongly equivalent is to be strongly equivalent w.r.t. any plain ASP addition (ASP-strongly-equivalent RASP programs, or ase-RASP programs).*

In order to make p-strong equivalence more widely possible, we may introduce the constraint that whenever the addition S is a proper RASP program, it does not compete on resources with the original program. This appears quite reasonable: in fact, if one intends to enlarge a production/consumption process, preservation of existing processes should be guaranteed. If not, it should be clear that one obtains a different process, with hardly predictable properties.

Definition 14. *A* rational addition *S to a RASP program P is RASP program such that in program $P \cup S$ rules of S do not consume resources produced by rules of P.*

It is easy to get convinced that:

Proposition 2. *A Proper RASP program S is a rational addition if and only if one of the following conditions holds.*

1. *Resources consumed in S are not available in P.*
2. *Resources consumed in S are produced in S.*
3. *Resources consumed in S are produced in $P \cup S$.*
4. *S does not consume resources.*

Referring to Example 5: rule $r{:}1 \leftarrow p^4{:}3$ is a rational addition of kind (1); proper RASP program $r{:}1 \leftarrow p^4{:}3.\ p{:}5.$ is a rational addition of kind (2); proper RASP program $r{:}1 \leftarrow p^4{:}3.\ p{:}5 \leftarrow c.$ is a rational addition of kind (3); rule $r{:}1 \leftarrow c$ is a rational addition of kind (4).

If we restrict p-strong equivalence to p-strong equivalence w.r.t. rational addition, then the notion becomes much more usable in practical cases. In particular for instance, programs P_1 and P_2 of Examples 6 and 5 are p-strongly equivalent w.r.t. rational addition. Notice however that p-strong equivalence between two programs does not guarantee that we are left with the same resources in the two cases. A subject of future work will be that of studying other forms of strong equivalence, e.g. w.r.t. what is left or more particularly what is left for a certain set of resources.

In tightly equivalent ase-RASP programs, resources possibly produced in $P \cup S$ would necessarily be employed in the same way, as the r-rules that might potentially fire are the same. In this case, we consider program atoms (plain

ASP atoms) that may be derived in $P \cup S$ as resources that are available in unlimited quantity. If restricting ourselves to this class of programs, we obtain an interesting sufficient condition.

Proposition 3. *Any two tightly equivalent ase-RASP programs are p-strongly equivalent w.r.t. rational additions.*

5 Conclusions and Future Directions

In this paper, we have extended the notion of strong equivalence from answer set programs to RASP programs. We have seen that this notion takes a quite peculiar flavor in RASP, where strong equivalence (apart from trivial cases) can be ensured at the condition of imposing some requirements on the theory which is added to given one. In fact, interactions in resource usages between two components may be quite involved. Nonetheless, strong equivalence may help a designer to reason about different processes that are strongly equivalent in terms of resources that are produced: a process might be preferred for instance because it consumes less, or consumes smaller quantities of crucial resources. A relevant future direction of this work can be in fact that of introducing a notion strong equivalence of RASP programs taking into account preferences in resource usage, like e.g. those that can be expressed in [3]. Also, in the RASP context an extension of strong equivalence, i.e., synonymy [14], can find interesting applications. Synonymy extends strong equivalence in the sense that two theories may be equivalent even if they are expressed in different languages, if each is bijectively interpretable in the other. In RASP, this might allow one to compare processes formulated in seemingly different ways.

References

[1] Baader, F., Calvanese, D., McGuinness, D., Nardi, D., Patel-Schneider, P.: The Description Logic Handbook. Cambridge University Press (2003)
[2] Chintabathina, S., Gelfond, M., Watson, R.: Defeasible laws, parallel actions, and reasoning about resources. In: Amir, E., Lifschitz, V., Miller, R. (eds.) Logical Formalizations of Commonsense Reasoning: Proceedings of CommonSense 2007. AAAI Press, Menlo Park (2007); Technical report SS-07-05
[3] Costantini, S., Formisano, A.: Modeling preferences and conditional preferences on resource consumption and production in ASP. Journal of Algorithms in Cognition, Informatics and Logic 64(1), 3–15 (2009)
[4] Costantini, S., Formisano, A.: Answer set programming with resources. Journal of Logic and Computation 20(2), 533–571 (2010)
[5] Costantini, S., Formisano, A., Petturiti, D.: Extending and implementing RASP. Fundamenta Informaticae 105(1-2), 1–33 (2010)
[6] Costantini, S., Formisano, A., Petturiti, D.: Strong Equivalence for RASP Programs: Long Version. Tech. Rep. 02-2012 Dip. di Matematica e Informatica, Univ. di Perugia, `http://www.dmi.unipg.it/formis/papers/report2012_02.ps.gz`
[7] Gelfond, M.: Answer sets. In: Handbook of Knowledge Representation, ch.7. Elsevier (2007)

[8] Gelfond, M., Lifschitz, V.: The stable model semantics for logic programming. In: Kowalski, R., Bowen, K. (eds.) Proc. of the 5th Intl. Conference and Symposium on Logic Programming, pp. 1070–1080. The MIT Press (1988)
[9] Gelfond, M., Lifschitz, V.: Action languages. Electronic Transactions on AI 3(16), 193–210 (1998)
[10] Girard, J.-Y.: Linear logic. Theoretical Computer Science 50, 1–102 (1987)
[11] Lifschitz, V., Pearce, D., Valverde, A.: Strongly equivalent logic programs. ACM Transactions on Computational Logic 2, 526–541 (2001)
[12] Niemelä, I., Simons, P., Soininen, T.: Stable Model Semantics of Weight Constraint Rules. In: Gelfond, M., Leone, N., Pfeifer, G. (eds.) LPNMR 1999. LNCS (LNAI), vol. 1730, pp. 317–331. Springer, Heidelberg (1999)
[13] Pearce, D.: A New Logical Characterization of Stable Models and Answer Sets. In: Dix, J., Przymusinski, T.C., Moniz Pereira, L. (eds.) NMELP 1996. LNCS (LNAI), vol. 1216, pp. 55–70. Springer, Heidelberg (1997)
[14] Pearce, D., Valverde, A.: Synonymous theories in answer set programming and equilibrium logic. In: Proc. of 16th Europ. Conf. on Art. Intell., ECAI 2004, pp. 388–390 (2004)
[15] Pearce, D., Valverde, A.: Quantified equilibrium logic and the first order logic of here-and-there. Technical report, Univ. Rey Juan Carlos (2006), `http://www.satd.uma.es/matap/investig/tr/ma06_02.pdf`
[16] Soininen, T., Niemelä, I.: Developing a Declarative Rule Language for Applications in Product Configuration. In: Gupta, G. (ed.) PADL 1999. LNCS, vol. 1551, pp. 305–319. Springer, Heidelberg (1999)
[17] Soininen, T., Niemelä, I., Tiihonen, J., Sulonen, R.: Representing configuration knowledge with weight constraint rules. In: Proceedings of the AAAI Spring 2001 Symposium on Answer Set Programming (ASP 2001): Towards Efficient and Scalable Knowledge. AAAI Press, Menlo Park (2001); Technical report SS-01-01

Considerations on Belief Revision in an Action Theory

James Delgrande

School of Computing Science,
Simon Fraser University,
Burnaby BC, V5A 1S6, Canada
jim@cs.sfu.ca

Among the many and varied areas that Vladimir Lifschitz has worked on is reasoning about action and change, in particular with respect to action languages, where an action language in turn is based on the underlying semantic notion of a transition system. Transition systems have been shown to be an elegant, deceptively simple, yet rich framework from which to address problems of action consequence, causality, planning and the like. In this paper I consider a problem in the interaction between reasoning about action, observations, and the agent's knowledge, specifically when an observation conflicts with the agent's knowledge; and so the agent must revise its knowledge. In particular, it is shown how an agent's initial belief set may be propagated through an action sequence so that, in contrast to previous work, for a revision one does not need to refer back to the initial state of the agent.

1 Introduction

An agent acting in some domain will generally have incomplete and possibly incorrect knowledge regarding that domain. Semantically, an agent's knowledge K may be characterised by a set of interpretations, or possible worlds, consisting of those worlds that, insofar as the agent is concerned, could be the actual world. Assuming that there are no other agents (including a "nature" that might provide stochastic events), there are two ways in which the agent's knowledge may evolve. First, it may execute actions. In this case, the agent's new beliefs can be semantically characterised by the image of each world in K under the executed action. Hence the agent will believe that, if the action preconditions hold, then after execution of the action, the action's effects will hold. One means of specifying the effects of actions is a *transition system*, where a transition system is a directed graph in which vertices are labelled by possible states of the world, and directed edges are labelled by the actions that take one state of the world to another. So after executing action a, the agent's beliefs will be characterized by the a-accessible worlds from worlds in K.

Second, the agent may *sense* or *observe* the environment. Such knowledge-producing actions don't alter the (external) domain, but they do give the agent information concerning the domain. Assuming that the agent's beliefs are in fact *knowledge* (and so the real world is among those in K), the sensing action

E. Erdem et al. (Eds.): Correct Reasoning, LNCS 7265, pp. 164–177, 2012.

that reports that ϕ is true can be characterised semantically by intersecting the K worlds with the ϕ-worlds. This works well enough if the agent's beliefs are correct, but in the case where the agent believes that ϕ is false yet senses that ϕ is true, it will fall into inconsistency.

The obvious solution is to *revise* the agent's beliefs by the result of sensing, rather than simply *expanding* the agent's beliefs by the new information. Such a solution of course presupposes the existence of a revision function whereby, from any knowledge base and formula for revision, a new knowledge base can be determined. However, this still does not resolve all difficulties.

In particular, it seems that if an agent executes an interleaved series of actions and observations, then its beliefs should be determined by iteratively executing the resulting series of actions and belief revisions. That is, one would expect that a *Markovian* process, in which the agent's next belief state depends solely on its previous state together with the relevant action, would be sufficient. However, as we describe in the next section, this naïve approach may lead to incorrect results. These problems have been resolved in an approach called *belief evolution* but, in doing so, the desirable Markovian aspect is lost, in that one must refer back to the agent's initial state of beliefs in order to accommodate the result of an observation.

The goal of this paper is to address this issue. That is, naïvely executing a sequence of actions and revisions leads to problems; and the solution, belief evolution, gives the correct result, but necessitates that each observation must be projected back to the initial state. Here we give a procedure that is equivalent to belief evolution but in which one doesn't have to project each observation back to the initial state. The solution is quite intuitive: in addition to keeping track of the effects of actions via a transition system, one also keeps track of (i.e. *progresses*) information obtained from observations.

In the next section we present the formal framework and discuss related work. Following this we informally but more concretely sketch the problem and solution. The next section gives the formal details. We conclude with a discussion of related work and suggestions for future work.

2 Background

2.1 Transition Systems

The basic definitions of a transition system are taken from [10]. An *action signature* is a pair $\langle \mathbf{F}, \mathbf{A} \rangle$ where $\mathbf{F}, \mathbf{A}$ are disjoint non-empty sets of symbols. $\mathbf{F}$ is the set of *fluent symbols* and $\mathbf{A}$ is the set of *action symbols*. For simplicity we assume that $\mathbf{F}$ and $\mathbf{A}$ are finite.

The fluent symbols in $\mathbf{F}$ are propositional variables. The action symbols in $\mathbf{A}$ denote the actions that an agent may perform. The effects of actions are specified by a transition system.

Definition 1. *A transition system T for an action signature $\sigma = \langle \mathbf{F}, \mathbf{A} \rangle$ is a pair $\langle S, R \rangle$ where*

1. *S is a set of propositional interpretations of* $\mathbf{F}$,
2. $R \subseteq S \times \mathbf{A} \times S$.

S is called the set of *states* and can be regarded as specifying the set of *possible worlds*. R is the *transition relation.* If $(s, a, s') \in R$, then s' is a possible state that could occur as a result of the action a being executed in state s. For formula ϕ, $\|\phi\|$ is the set of states at which ϕ is true, that is $\|\phi\| = \{s \in S \mid s \models \phi\}$.

Transition systems can be represented as directed graphs, where each node is labeled with a state and each edge is labeled with an element of $\mathbf{A}$. We also define for $X \subseteq S$

$$a(X) = \{s' \in S \mid \exists s \in X \text{ and } (s, a, s') \in R\}$$
$$a^{-1}(X) = \{s \in S \mid \exists s' \in X \text{ and } (s, a, s') \in R\}.$$

For $s \in S$, $a(s)$ is used to abbreviate $a(\{s\})$ and similarly for $a^{-1}(s)$. This extends in the obvious way to formulas; that is, we use $a(\phi)$ to mean $a(\|\phi\|)$. Finally, for a sequence of actions $\vec{a} = \langle a_1, \ldots, a_n \rangle$ we extend the above so that we have

$$\vec{a}(S) = a_n(\ldots a_1(S) \ldots)$$
$$\vec{a}^{-1}(S) = a_1^{-1}(\ldots a_n^{-1}(S) \ldots)$$

If there is exactly one possible resulting state s' when a is executed in s for every $s \in S$ and $a \in \mathbf{A}$, then T is *deterministic.* A minor but key point concerning deterministic transition systems is that, while $a(s)$ is a singleton, $a^{-1}(s)$ may not be. We assume throughout this paper that a transition system is deterministic, and that every action is executable in every state. If the transition system does not specify the results of a particular action in a given state, we assume that the state does not change when that action is executed. This is equivalent to adding self loops for every action at every state where no transition is given.

2.2 Belief Revision

The central and best-known approach to belief change is the AGM approach [1,9,19], named after the developers of the approach. In the AGM approach, beliefs of an agent are modelled by a deductively closed set of formulas, or *belief set.* Thus a belief set is a set of formulas K such that $K = Cn(K)$ where $Cn(K)$ is the closure of K under classical logical consequence. It is assumed that the underlying logic subsumes classical propositional logic. Formally, a revision operator $*$ maps a belief set K and formula ϕ to a revised belief set $K * \phi$. The AGM postulates for revision are as follows; the operator $+$ stands for *expansion*, where $K + \phi$ is defined to be $Cn(K \cup \{\phi\})$.

(K*1) $K * \phi = Cn(K * \phi)$
(K*2) $\phi \in K * \phi$
(K*3) $K * \phi \subseteq K + \phi$

(K*4) If $\neg\phi \notin K$ then $K + \phi \subseteq K * \phi$
(K*5) $K * \phi$ is inconsistent only if ϕ is inconsistent
(K*6) If $\phi \equiv \psi$ then $K * \phi = K * \psi$
(K*7) $K * (\phi \wedge \psi) \subseteq K * \phi + \psi$
(K*8) If $\neg\psi \notin K * \phi$ then $K * \phi + \psi \subseteq K * (\phi \wedge \psi)$

See [9,19] for a discussion and motivation of these postulates.

Katsuno and Mendelzon [14] have shown that a necessary and sufficient condition for constructing an AGM revision operator is that there is a function that associates a total preorder on the set of possible worlds with any belief set K, as follows:[1]

Definition 2. *A* faithful assignment *is a function that maps each belief set K to a total preorder $\preceq_K$ on possible worlds such that for any possible worlds w_1, w_2:*

1. *If $w_1, w_2 \in Mod(K)$ then $w_1 \approx_K w_2$*
2. *If $w_1 \in Mod(K)$ and $w_2 \notin Mod(K)$, then $w_1 \prec_K w_2$.*

The resulting preorder is called the *faithful ranking* associated with K. Intuitively, $w_1 \preceq_K w_2$ if w_1 is at least as plausible as w_2 according to the agent. Katsuno and Mendelzon then provide the following representation result, where $t(W)$ is the set of formulas of classical logic true in W:

Theorem 1. *A revision operator $*$ satisfies postulates (K*1)–(K*8) iff there is a faithful assignment that maps each belief set K to a total preorder $\preceq_K$ such that*

$$K * \phi \;=\; t(\min(Mod(\phi), \preceq_K)).$$

Thus the revision of K by ϕ is characterised by those models of ϕ that are most plausible according to the agent.

Various researchers have argued that, in order to address iterated belief revision, it is more appropriate to consider *belief states* (also called *epistemic states*) as objects of revision. A general framework was proposed in [25], while the first systematic exploration of this notion in Artificial Intelligence is reported in [6]. A belief state $\mathcal{K}$ effectively encodes information regarding how the revision function itself changes under a revision. The belief set corresponding to belief state $\mathcal{K}$ is denoted $Bel(\mathcal{K})$. A revision operator $*$ now maps a belief state $\mathcal{K}$ and formula ϕ to a revised belief state $\mathcal{K} * \phi$. The AGM revision postulates can be reformulated by replacing instances of a revision, say $K * \phi$, by the belief set $Bel(\mathcal{K} * \phi)$, and replacing (K*6) by:

(K*6) If $\mathcal{K}_1 = \mathcal{K}_2$ and $\phi \equiv \psi$ then $Bel(\mathcal{K} * \phi) = Bel(\mathcal{K} * \psi)$.

Darwiche and Pearl [6] extend the Katsuno and Mendelzon results as follows:

[1] In [14] (and [6], below), an agent's beliefs are represented by a formula rather than a belief set; hence they adopt a different, but equivalent, set of postulates. Since we deal with finite languages, the difference is immaterial.

Definition 3. *A* faithful assignment *is a function that maps each belief state $\mathcal{K}$ to a total preorder $\preceq_{\mathcal{K}}$ on possible worlds such that for any possible worlds w_1, w_2:*

1. *If $w_1, w_2 \models Bel(\mathcal{K})$ then $w_1 =_{\mathcal{K}} w_2$*
2. *If $w_1 \models Bel(\mathcal{K})$ and $w_2 \not\models Bel(\mathcal{K})$, then $w_1 \prec_{\mathcal{K}} w_2$*

Theorem 2. *A revision operator $*$ satisfies postulates (K*1)–(K*8) iff there exists a faithful assignment that maps each belief state $\mathcal{K}$ to a total preorder $\preceq_{\mathcal{K}}$ such that*

$$Mod(\mathcal{K} * \phi) \;=\; \min(Mod(\phi), \preceq_{\mathcal{K}}).$$

In the above theorem, $Mod(\mathcal{K})$ is understood as $Mod(Bel(\mathcal{K}))$.

2.3 Reasoning about Action and Knowledge

Gelfond and Lifschitz [10] provide an overview of action languages and transition systems. Detailed, specific approaches can be found in, for example, [12,11]. The frameworks developed in these (and other related) papers specify syntactic constructs comprising an *action language*, where the semantics of these constructs can be given in terms of a transition system. In such languages one can then specify the preconditions and effects of actions, along with other related notions, such as persistence of fluent values.

In [2] the base action language $\mathcal{A}$ is extended to allow observations of the truth values of fluents and the actual occurrence of actions, while the entailment relation allows for querying regarding types of hypothetical reasoning. This approach is extended in turn in [3], where it is employed in diagnostic reasoning in an action framework. In [17,24], the action language $\mathcal{A}$ is extended to handle an agent's knowledge and sensing actions. The representation of this in terms of a transition system is clear and intuitive: The agent's beliefs are modelled by a set of states, or possible worlds, K; and in sensing that a formula ϕ is true, all $\neg\phi$ worlds are removed from this set. Since it is assumed that an agent's beliefs are accurate, in that the real world is among those in K, sensing leads to a monotonic refinement of the agent's knowledge. (If nondeterministic actions are allowed, as in [17], the agent's ignorance may increase but it will never be incorrect.)

There has been similar research in other formalisms for reasoning about action, most notably in the *situation calculus* [16]. In brief, the situation calculus is a first-order[2] theory in which fluents take a situation argument, and a function $do(a, s)$ yields the situation resulting from executing action a in situation s. Hence $Red(A, s)$ indicates that object A is *Red* in situation s, while $\neg Red(A, do(paintBlue, A, s))$ indicates that A is not *Red* in the situation resulting from s in which the *paintBlue* action is executed.

Scherl and Levesque [21] extend the basic theory to account for an agent's knowledge, basically by axiomatising the modal logic S5 within the situation

[2] Well, not quite, since there is an induction axiom on situations.

calculus, as well as sensing. [23] extends this approach to allow for a restricted version of belief revision, in that a formula for revision must be true in the domain. Thus, in [23] if one revises by ϕ and then $\neg\phi$, inconsistency results.

3 Revision in Transition Systems

3.1 The Problem

It would seem to be a straightforward matter to address belief revision in a transition system framework, by simply combining an account of reasoning about knowledge with an account of belief revision. This in turn could be accomplished by simply specifying a faithful assignment, as in Definition 2, for every set of states. And indeed it is straightforward to incorporate belief revision in such a manner. However, as [13] points out, iteratively determining the results of actions and observations may yield incorrect results.

Example 1. Assume that there is a beaker containing either an acid (A) or a base ($\neg A$).[3] As well, there is a piece of paper that the agent believes is litmus paper (L). If litmus paper is dipped in acid it turns red (R), and if it is dipped in a base it turns blue (B). The paper is initially white ($\neg R \wedge \neg B$). The only action is to dip the litmus paper into the liquid. The agent initially believes that it is holding litmus paper and that the paper is white.

Consider where the agent dips the paper into the beaker, after which it observes that the paper is white. There are AGM revision operators where in the resulting belief state the agent believes that it is holding a piece of white litmus paper. For example consider the Dalal [5] revision operator: The agent's beliefs are characterized by the possible worlds $A\overline{RB}L, \overline{ARB}L$; the image of these worlds following a *dip* action is $AR\overline{B}L, \overline{AR}BL$. The agent observes that $\neg R \wedge \neg B$ is true. The Dalal operator selects the closest worlds of the formula for revision to the worlds characterising the agent's beliefs, where "closeness" is defined by the Hamming distance. In this case the closest worlds are $A\overline{RB}L, \overline{ARB}L$, so the agent believes that it is holding white litmus paper. The same result obtains with the Satoh [20] operator.[4] Clearly this is an undesirable state, and instead the agent should believe that the paper is not litmus paper.

To deal with such problems, [13] proposes a new operation, *belief evolution*, defined in terms of existing action-update and revision operators. Example 1 illustrates that, if an agent has belief set K, then characterising the result of an action a followed by a revision by ϕ as $K * a(\phi)$ may lead to problems. In belief evolution, the action a followed by a revision by ϕ is expressed as $a(K * a^{-1}(\phi))$. That is, one doesn't revise by ϕ following the action a; rather, given the pair (a, ϕ), one considers those (initial) worlds which, after a is executed, yield ϕ worlds. This set of worlds (that is, $a^{-1}(\phi)$) is used for revising the initial belief

[3] To simplify matters, we disallow the possibility of a neutral pH. We obtain the same results if the example is extended to allow that the liquid may be neutral.

[4] This isn't quite an AGM operator as the last postulate may not hold.

set K, and the result is progressed via a. It is shown that this formulation gives the appropriate results. So in the preceding example, the agent will indeed believe that the paper is not litmus paper. This operator naturally extends to a sequence of actions $\vec{a} = \langle a_1, \ldots, a_n \rangle$, so that a revision by ϕ following this sequence of actions would be computed via the extension $\vec{a}(K * \vec{a}^{-1}(\phi))$.

This is fine, but it implies that the *Markovian* aspect of the naïve procedure (viz. $\vec{a}(K) * \phi$) is lost. Rather, a formula for revision ϕ is projected back through the n actions, a revision is carried out, and the result progressed through the n actions. Informally, it seems at best inconvenient to have to refer to the initial belief state in order to carry out a revision at the end of a sequence of actions; as well, it seems to be unnecessarily inefficient. (It can also be noted that switching to a situation calculus setting, for example, doesn't help, in that *basic action theories* of the situation calculus are set up so that truth of fluents at a situation can be determined by the initial state along with the actions executed.)

3.2 Revision in the Context of Sensing

However, let's (re)examine what's going on in Example 1. The definition of a faithful ranking, Definition 2, stipulates that a total preorder is associated with every set of possible worlds. Arguably, Example 1 illustrates that this is inappropriate in an action context, in that the result of an action will give information that will affect the results of revision. Thus, in Example 1 the agent should not believe that the paper is litmus paper after the dipping action, because the result of the dipping rules this out: litmus paper cannot be white when dipped into a solution known to be non-neutral. Consequently revision, in one form or another, needs to take this into account.

From the consideration that Definition 2 is inappropriate in an action setting, it becomes clear why belief evolution works: one refers to only a single revision operator, that defined by $\preceq_K$. For an observation that follows a sequence of actions, one maps everything back to the original belief set, carries out revision with respect to the initial belief set (and so with respect to the ranking $\preceq_K$), and then progresses the results through the given action sequence.

The question arises as to whether one might be able to do better than with the approach to belief evolution and fortunately, the answer is "yes". The obvious way to proceed is adopt the more general notion of belief state. Then, given an action a in the initial state, one progresses not just the agent's contingent knowledge K, but also the belief state $\mathcal{K}$. It turns out that things are a bit more complicated than what this "obvious" solution suggests. Nonetheless, in the next section we show how one can carry out actions and revisions in a Markovian manner by keeping track of information gained from sensing.

4 The Approach

In what follows, we assume that we are given a deterministic transition system $T = \langle S, R \rangle$ over a finite action signature $\sigma = \langle \mathbf{F}, \mathbf{A} \rangle$. As well, we assume that we are given a belief state $\mathcal{K}$ where $Bel(\mathcal{K}) = K \subseteq S$ is a fixed set of states representing the agent's initial set of beliefs and $\preceq_{\mathcal{K}}$ is a faithful ranking associated with $\mathcal{K}$ giving the agent's initial revision function. We will henceforth understand an agent's (contingent) beliefs to be characterised by a set of worlds; thus the agent's beliefs following a revision will similarly be a set of worlds.

An agent's beliefs may change in one of two ways. It may execute an action, in which case each state in K is mapped to another state. Given the fact that we have a deterministic transition system, there is no uncertainty as to the outcome of an action execution (although, of course, in some states an action may be nonexecutable). Second, the agent may sense that a formula ϕ is true. We assume that the agent believes that sensing is correct, and so the agent will consequently accept that ϕ is true. In this case, the agent would revise its beliefs according to an appropriate faithful ranking and, given this faithful ranking, there is no uncertainty as to the outcome. The key point then is that following any action sequence, we wish to be able to revise the agent's beliefs; and to do this we require, directly or implicitly, a ranking function over possible worlds. We obtain such a ranking function by suitably progressing not just the agent's contingent beliefs, but also the agent's ranking function $\preceq_{\mathcal{K}}$.

The following definition specifies how a plausibility ranking will change following the execution of an action. A complication is that a possible world $w \in a(S)$ may be the image of more than one world in S, in that $a^{-1}(w)$ may not be unique. Consequently, the rank of $w \in a(S)$ is taken as the rank of the minimally-ranked world in $a^{-1}(w)$.

Definition 4. *Let $T = \langle S, R\rangle$ be a transition system over $\sigma = \langle \mathbf{F}, \mathbf{A}\rangle$, and let $\preceq_{\mathcal{K}}$ be a total preorder over S. For $a \in \mathbf{A}$, define $w_1 \preceq_{a(\mathcal{K})} w_2$ iff*
$\exists w_1', w_2' \in S$ where $w_1' \preceq_{\mathcal{K}} w_2'$ and
$w_1' \in \min(a^{-1}(w_1), \preceq_{\mathcal{K}})$, $w_2' \in \min(a^{-1}(w_2), \preceq_{\mathcal{K}})$
Then we can define $Mod(a(\mathcal{K}) * \phi)$ as $\min(Mod(\phi), \preceq_{a(\mathcal{K})})$.

It follows straightforwardly that $\preceq_{a(\mathcal{K})}$ is a total preorder over S with minimum worlds given by $Mod(a(\mathcal{K}))$;[5] we omit the proof.

What would be ideal is if Definition 4 preserved $\preceq$-relations under actions, and so one obtained that

$$Mod(a(\mathcal{K} * \phi)) = Mod(a(\mathcal{K}) * a(\phi)). \qquad (1)$$

However, it is easily shown that this is not the case, as illustrated by Figure 1. On the left hand side we have the total preorder induced by $\mathcal{K}$, and on the right hand side we have the image of this preorder following action a. In both cases the lower a world in a ranking, the more plausible that world is; hence the agent's (contingent) beliefs before and after execution of action a are given by the consequences of $p \wedge q$.

[5] Recall that for belief state $\mathcal{K}$ we define the set of models of the agent's beliefs as $Mod(\mathcal{K}) = Mod(Bel(\mathcal{K}))$.

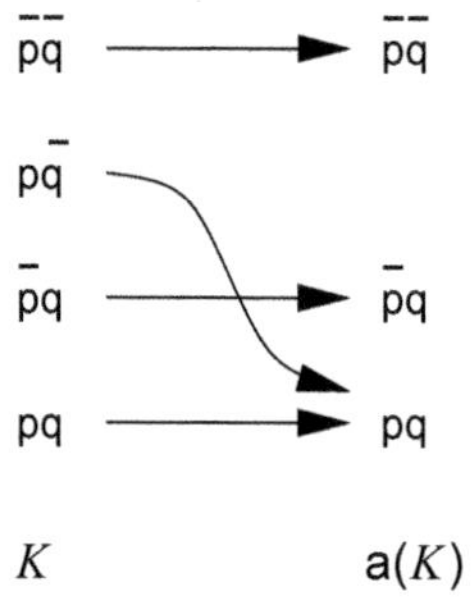

Fig. 1.

Let $\phi = (p \equiv \neg q)$. Then we have that

$$\begin{aligned} Mod(a(\mathcal{K} * \phi)) &= a(\{\neg pq\}) &&= \{\neg pq\} \\ Mod(a(\mathcal{K}) * a(\phi)) &= a(\mathcal{K}) * \{pq, \neg pq\} &&= \{\ \ pq\} \end{aligned}$$

This example shows that neither containment in (1) holds.

However, consider again Example 1, but in the context of Definition 4. Since the liquid is either an acid or a base, then *if* the paper is litmus paper, then it is *impossible* for it to be white after the dipping action. Hence, white-litmus-paper worlds should not take part in any subsequent revision, since they have been ruled out by the action. This helps explain why belief evolution provides the correct results: for an observation (here *white*, expressed as $\neg R \wedge \neg B$) that is inconsistent with the agent's beliefs following an action, it must be the case that the agent's original beliefs are inconsistent with the inverse image of the observation under the action. That is, we have the elementary result:

Proposition 1. *Let* $T = \langle S, R \rangle$ *be a transition system over* $\sigma = \langle \mathbf{F}, \mathbf{A} \rangle$, $a \in \mathbf{A}$, *and let* $\mathcal{K}$ *be a belief state.*
If $Mod(a(\mathcal{K})) \cap \|\phi\| = \emptyset$ *then* $Mod(\mathcal{K}) \cap a^{-1}(\|\phi\|) = \emptyset$.

With belief evolution, an observation ϕ is projected back (via a^{-1}) to the original (pre-action) state of affairs, where revision takes place, thereby adjusting the agent's original, erroneous, set of beliefs. The result is then progressed under the action a, (trivially) yielding a result compatible with a. As described, implementing a reasonable notion of revision then involves regressing an action sequence to the initial state, carrying out revision, and then progressing the same sequence of actions. The fact that one can avoid this effort hinges on the following result.[6]

Proposition 2. $\|\phi\| \cap a(S) \;=\; a(a^{-1}(\phi))$

On the left hand side we have those ϕ-worlds that are compatible with the execution of action a. The right hand side says that this is just the a-regression of

[6] The following results (clearly) assume the same antecedent conditions as Propositoin 1. We omit their statement, for reasons of perspicuity.

ϕ-worlds followed by their a-progression. The next result says that the regression/progression process in belief evolution can be restricted to the formula for revision:

Proposition 3. $Mod(a(\mathcal{K} * a^{-1}(\phi))) \;=\; Mod(a(\mathcal{K}) * a(a^{-1}(\phi)))$

Corollary 1. $Mod(\vec{a}(\mathcal{K} * \vec{a}^{-1}(\phi))) \;=\; Mod(\vec{a}(\mathcal{K}) * \vec{a}(\vec{a}^{-1}(\phi)))$

Proposition 3 is just a weaker version of (1). On the left hand side we have the expression for belief evolution. On the right hand side we have the progression of the belief state, $a(\mathcal{K})$, revised by the regression/progression of the formula for revision. The corollary notes that this, unsurprisingly, extends to a sequence of actions.

Combining the previous two propositions yields the following:

Proposition 4. $Mod(a(\mathcal{K} * a^{-1}(\phi))) \;=\; Mod(a(\mathcal{K}) * (\|\phi\| \cap a(S)))$

Corollary 2. $Mod(\vec{a}(\mathcal{K} * \vec{a}^{-1}(\phi))) \;=\; Mod(\vec{a}(\mathcal{K}) * (\|\phi\| \cap \vec{a}(S)))$

This shows that belief evolution (on the left hand side of the equality) can be expressed as a simple revision (tracked via Definition 4) following a sequence of actions. The (modest) complication is that one needs to also keep track of the context implicit in the sensing action ($a(S)$), and limit the ϕ worlds involved in the revision to these worlds. That is, the proposition shows belief evolution can be computed by progressing the initial revision function, along with the set of possible states (i.e. $a(S)$).

This then restores the Markovian aspect of iterated actions and revisions, in that the right hand side of Proposition 4 makes reference to only the state of affairs following execution of the action a. Conceptually this seems to be more compelling than the original statement of belief evolution (given on the left hand side of Proposition 4). As well, it may offer pragmatic advantages. Consider the following informal argument: Assume that computing action effects, including inverse actions, and revisions have equal, unit cost, and other operations (such as intersection) have negligible cost. Given an initial belief state $\mathcal{K}$, the cost of computing the action/observation sequence $\langle a_1, \phi_1, \ldots, a_n, \phi_n \rangle$ will have cost $n(n+2)$ via belief evolution, but $3n$ via the right hand side of Proposition 4. Hence we go from a quadratic to a linear number of operations. (This argument is admittedly a bit misleading, since belief revision is generally of greater complexity than propositional reasoning [8]; and both approaches to computing the agent's beliefs following an action/observation sequence require n revisions. However, it indicates that in an implementation there may nonetheless be advantages to the latter approach, particularly in an approach to revision with good expected computational properties, such as in Horn formula belief sets [7].)

The above results apply to an agent's belief set. The question arises as to whether one may be able to say something about the agent's belief state. The next result extends Proposition 4 from belief sets to belief states, with respect to the specific approach to revision of [18].

Proposition 5. *Let $T = \langle S, R\rangle$ be a transition system over $\sigma = \langle \mathbf{F}, \mathbf{A}\rangle$. Assume that faithful rankings satisfy the additional conditions:*

(CR1) *If $w_1, w_2 \models \phi$, then $w_1 \preceq_{\mathcal{K}} w_2$ iff $w_1 \preceq_{\mathcal{K}*\phi} w_2$*
(CR2) *If $w_1, w_2 \not\models \phi$, then $w_1 \preceq_{\mathcal{K}} w_2$ iff $w_1 \preceq_{\mathcal{K}*\phi} w_2$*
(Lex) *If $w_1 \models \phi$ and $w_2 \not\models \phi$ then $w_1 \prec_{\mathcal{K}} w_2$*

Then $a(\mathcal{K} * a^{-1}(\phi)) \;=\; a(\mathcal{K}) * (\|\phi\| \cap a(S))$.

The semantic conditions (CR1), (CR2), and (Lex) characterise the specific approach discussed in [18]. (CR1), (CR2) are the first two (of four) conditions for iterated revision from [6], although they were originally employed in the quantitative setting for *ordinal conditional functions*, in [25]. (Lex) in turn implies the conditions (CR3), (CR4) in [6].

This approach [18] gives very high priority to the formula for revision, in that in revising by ϕ, all ϕ worlds are ranked as being more plausible than any $\neg\phi$ world. In return, one obtains an operator that is conceptually simple and, for the present case, compatible with an action framework.

5 Discussion

In this paper we have reformulated an approach to belief revision in an action formalism, *belief evolution*, so that one doesn't need to refer to the initial state of the agent and the domain. To this end, a number of limiting assumptions were made: it was assumed that action preconditions and effects are known, and that actions are deterministic. As well, observations are correct. A fully general account of belief change will need to relax these assumptions of course; however the idea in this paper is to attempt to gain insight into the interaction of actions and observations by considering a more manageable scenario.

5.1 Related Work

The assumptions made here are the same as those made in the account of belief change in the situation calculus in [23]. Interestingly, the problem observed in Example 1 doesn't arise in [23], and we obtain that after observing that the paper is white, the agent believes that the paper is not litmus paper. In the situation calculus, situations are indexed by actions; and in those situations where the agent is holding litmus paper, the paper will turn either red of blue, and those situations where it is not litmus paper, the colour will remain unchanged. That is, since situations record the actions taken, actions are implicitly part of the subject of the revision process. As a result, in observing that $\neg R \wedge \neg B$ is true, it must be that the paper is not litmus paper.

In contrast, in the transition system approach, the link between an action and the resulting state is not retained, in that for a world $w \in a(\mathcal{K})$, $a^{-1}(w)$ is not guaranteed to be a singleton, as it is in the situation calculus. The result is that in the naïve approach, the agent may end up believing that it is holding white litmus paper, since the link between litmus paper and colour after dipping is lost. In essence, the situation calculus approach is finer grained and more nuanced than extant approaches involving transition systems.[7] So this raises the question of whether one should opt for a theory such as the situation calculus, over a simpler approach such as with a transition system.

While there are advantages to the situation calculus, particularly in terms of expressibility, there are also advantages to the simpler approach, namely one might expect it to be easier to implement and to be more computationally efficient, simply because less information is kept track of. Moreover, with the situation calculus, at least with basic action theories, one essentially still needs to regress to the initial state. While there will be cases where one may need to reason among earlier circumstances (e.g.[4]), if one need not, then there will presumably be advantages computationally to adopting a simpler, Markovian, approach.

Regarding other work, the setting described in [3] is broadly similar to that here. In [3], given an action language framework, diagnostic problem solving, based on a set of observations, is developed. That is, given a definition of a *system*, and a set of observations inconsistent with this system, the notion of a *diagnosis* is defined to account for the abnormal behaviour. The setting of [3] is much more specific than that of the present paper, but the overall direction and goals are similar. Consequently, it would be an interesting question to see how one approach may benefit the other. Thus the present approach may help explicate the notion of observation in [3]; as well, by incorporating belief states, one might obtain a more fine-grained diagnostic approach that could accommodate observations and beliefs of varying reliability. On the other hand, by bringing in specific notions (such as that of components, or distinguished sets of literals, or specific action types) from a diagnostic setting, one might be able to provide an account for revision in a specific, practical setting.

5.2 Extending the Approach

There are several ways in which the approach may be generalised. To begin, we've essentially been working with a single observation following an action sequence. The natural extension to a set of observations interleaved with actions implicitly assumes that the observations are, if not correct, at least consistent, taken as a group. Thus, still assuming deterministic actions, the most straightforward means of dealing with a set of observations is to first project all observations to the final state. Under the assumption that this set is consistent, the intersection of the resulting sets of worlds corresponds to the conjunction of these (projected) observations, which can then be used for a revision.

Clearly however, observations may not be correct or compatible, and in belief revision in general for example, the agent may be informed of something that is

[7] Which is to say, there is no obstacle to formulating a situation-calculus like approach involving transition systems, where one keeps track of trajectories of actions and states of the world.

later contradicted. Hence in general one would need to be able to deal with an alternating sequence of actions and observations, where observations may not be correct. Given such a set of (possible incorrect or incompatible) observations, one can still project (or progress) each observation individually through the full sequence of actions, yielding a set of possibly incompatible observations, together with the result of progressing the agent's beliefs. One can then in some fashion *merge* the resulting observations, to give an overall summation of the observations that can then be used to revise the agent's beliefs. This leaves open the question of how to best merge the agent's observations, but in this case there is an extensive literature (for representative work, see for example [15]) and one can treat the problem independently from reasoning about action.[8]

A second extension is to allow more general types of actions. It may be that nondeterminism can be directly incorporated into the approach, provided that a (nondeterministic) action results in equally-probable outcomes. Thus, in the case where the agent tosses a fair coin for example, there are two possible outcomes; while the final outcome is unknown, both outcomes will have the same plausibility. Hence for revision, it may be that in this situation there is no real complication beyond keeping track of the multiple outcomes. If a nondeterministic action allows outcomes of differing likelihood, for example in allowing some actions to occasionally fail or to yield unexpected outcomes, then it is not clear how such outcomes should be reconciled with the agent's plausibility ordering. A second way in which actions can be generalised is in allowing *exogenous actions*. In this case, an approach such as [22] may work here.

References

1. Alchourrón, C., Gärdenfors, P., Makinson, D.: On the logic of theory change: Partial meet functions for contraction and revision. Journal of Symbolic Logic 50(2), 510–530 (1985)
2. Baral, C., Gelfond, M., Provetti, A.: Representing actions: Laws, observations and hypotheses. Journal of Logic Programming 31(1-3), 201–243 (1997)
3. Baral, C., McIlraith, S.A., Son, T.C.: Formulating diagnostic problem solving using an action language with narratives and sensing. In: Proceedings of the International Conference on the Principles of Knowledge Representation and Reasoning, pp. 311–322 (2000)
4. Boutilier, C.: Generalized update: Belief change in dynamic settings. In: Proceedings of the International Joint Conference on Artificial Intelligence, pp. 1550–1556 (1995)
5. Dalal, M.: Investigations into theory of knowledge base revision. In: Proceedings of the AAAI National Conference on Artificial Intelligence, St. Paul, Minnesota, pp. 449–479 (1988)
6. Darwiche, A., Pearl, J.: On the logic of iterated belief revision. Artificial Intelligence 89, 1–29 (1997)

[8] In belief revision, a common assumption, even in static domains, is that the most recent observation should take precedence. The suggetion here is that, unless there are specific reliabilities attached to observations, there is no good reason to prefer one observation over another.

7. Delgrande, J., Peppas, P.: Revising Horn theories. In: Proceedings of the International Joint Conference on Artificial Intelligence, Barcelona, Spain, pp. 839–844 (2011)
8. Eiter, T., Gottlob, G.: On the complexity of propositional knowledge base revision, updates, and counterfactuals. Artificial Intelligence 57(2-3), 227–270 (1992)
9. Gärdenfors, P.: Knowledge in Flux: Modelling the Dynamics of Epistemic States. The MIT Press, Cambridge (1988)
10. Gelfond, M., Lifschitz, V.: Action languages. Electronic Transactions on AI 3 (1998)
11. Giunchiglia, E., Lee, J., Lifschitz, V., McCain, N., Turner, H.: Nonmonotonic causal theories. Artificial Intelligence 153(1-2), 49–104 (2004)
12. Giunchiglia, E., Lifschitz, V.: An action language based on causal explanation: Preliminary report. In: Proceedings of the AAAI National Conference on Artificial Intelligence, pp. 623–630 (1998)
13. Hunter, A., Delgrande, J.P.: Iterated belief change due to actions and observations. Journal of Artificial Intelligence Research 40, 269–304 (2011)
14. Katsuno, H., Mendelzon, A.: Propositional knowledge base revision and minimal change. Artificial Intelligence 52(3), 263–294 (1991)
15. Konieczny, S., Pino Pérez, R.: Merging information under constraints: A logical framework. Journal of Logic and Computation 12(5), 773–808 (2002)
16. Levesque, H.J., Pirri, F., Reiter, R.: Foundations for the situation calculus. Linköping Electronic Articles in Computer and Information Science 3(18) (1998)
17. Lobo, J., Mendez, G., Taylor, S.: Knowledge and the action description language $\mathcal{A}_{\mathcal{K}}$. Theory and Practice of Logic Programming 1(2), 129–184 (2001)
18. Nayak, A.C., Pagnucco, M., Peppas, P.: Dynamic belief revision operators. Artificial Intelligence 146(2), 193–228 (2003)
19. Peppas, P.: Belief revision. In: van Harmelen, F., Lifschitz, V., Porter, B. (eds.) Handbook of Knowledge Representation, pp. 317–359. Elsevier Science, San Diego (2008)
20. Satoh, K.: Nonmonotonic reasoning by minimal belief revision. In: Proceedings of the International Conference on Fifth Generation Computer Systems, Tokyo, pp. 455–462 (1988)
21. Scherl, R., Levesque, H.: Knowledge, action, and the frame problem. Artificial Intelligence 144(1-2), 1–39 (2003)
22. Shapiro, S., Pagnucco, M.: Iterated belief change and exogeneous actions in the situation calculus. In: Proc. ECAI 2004 (2004)
23. Shapiro, S., Pagnucco, M., Lespérance, Y., Levesque, H.J.: Iterated belief change in the situation calculus. Artificial Intelligence 175(1), 165–192 (2011)
24. Son, T., Baral, C.: Formalizing sensing actions: A transition function based approach. Artificial Intelligence 125(1-2), 19–91 (2001)
25. Spohn, W.: Ordinal conditional functions: A dynamic theory of epistemic states. In: Harper, W.L., Skyrms, B. (eds.) Causation in Decision, Belief Change, and Statistics, vol. II, pp. 105–134. Kluwer Academic Publishers (1988)

Approximation Fixpoint Theory and the Semantics of Logic and Answers Set Programs

Marc Denecker, Maurice Bruynooghe, and Joost Vennekens

Department of Computer Science, KULeuven

Abstract. Approximation Fixpoint Theory was developed as a fixpoint theory of lattice operators that provides a uniform formalization of four main semantics of three major nonmonotonic reasoning formalisms. This paper clarifies how this fixpoint theory can define the stable and well-founded semantics of logic programs. It investigates the notion of strong equivalence underlying this semantics. It also shows the remarkable power of this theory for defining natural and elegant versions of these semantics for extensions of logic and answer set programs. In particular, we here consider extensions with general rule bodies, general interpretations (also non-Herbrand interpretations) and aggregates. We also investigate the relationship with the equilibrium semantics of nested answer set programs, on the formal and the informal level.

1 Introduction

In the nineties, Przymusinksi [19], Van Gelder [20] and Fitting [8] applied algebraic techniques to the semantics of Logic Programming. This culminated in a framework proposed by Fitting who demonstrated that the main four semantics of logic programs can be described in abstract algebraic terms of fixpoints of two operators [8]. Motivated by certain analogies between this work and techniques used elsewhere in nonmonotonic reasoning, Denecker, Marek and Truszczyński further generalized this work into an algebraic fixpoint theory defining four types of fixpoints for a bilattice operator [3]. They found that with this theory, the family of four semantics of logic programming can be generated from one operator, namely Fittings (three- or four-valued) immediate consequence operator. They also showed that the fixpoint theory induces isomorphic families including all main and some new semantics for default and autoepistemic logic [4], thus effectively unifying both logics. Thus, this work demonstrated common algebraic foundations in three major nonmonotonic logics.

This paper surveys and explains the application of this approximation fixpoint theory to the semantics of logic programming and answer set programming and generalizations of these. It is fitting to write such a paper for several reasons.

First, while [3] presented the fixpoint theory, it did not detail how to apply it to logic programming. Here we fill this gap and provide theorems and proofs to substantiate the claims of [3] for the first time. The proofs are straightforward. In fact, this is probably one of the main strenghts of the fixpoint theory.

E. Erdem et al. (Eds.): Correct Reasoning, LNCS 7265, pp. 178–194, 2012.

Second, we recall and analyse the stable semantics defined in [22]. There a version of stable semantics was defined through approximation fixpoint theory, for programs with arbitrary first order (FO) rule bodies and arbitrary structures (including non-Herbrand ones). It introduced these generalized versions of stable (and also well-founded) semantics in the context of a technical enquiry of *predicate introduction* but missed any motivation and analysis of the resulting logic from a semantic point of view.

Here, we first recall this formalization, which is very close to the standard way of defining stable semantics, and then show how it can be derived using the four-valued immediate consequence operator. We compare this version of the stable semantics with equilibrium semantics of nested answer set programs [16,17]. We prove a correspondence for a subclass of programs without nested negation. For programs outside this class, the semantics are quite different. We study the underlying notion of equivalence in our semantics (the equivalent of *strong equivalence* of equilibrium semantics) and show that it is much more "classic" than strong equivalence.

We end this paper with an illustration of the flexibility of approximation fixpoint theory to support language extension. Based on the work of [18], we show how to extend the formalism with recursion over aggegrate expressions. Our aim here is to show the remarkable ability of approximation fixpoint theory to define, in a mathematically elegant way, how to build principled and natural semantics for extensions of logic programming and answer set semantics. Moreover, the work recalls how closely related stable and well-founded semantics are.

We dedicate this paper to Vladimir for his 65th anniversary. This paper, as so many other that we wrote has been inspired by his work.

2 Approximation Fixpoint Theory of Lattice Operators

This algebraic fixpoint theory for arbitrary lattice operators was defined in [3]. This theory can be summarized as follows.

A complete lattice $\langle L, \leq \rangle$ is a partial order such that each subset has a least upperbound and greatest lowerbound. It induces a complete bilattice $\langle L^2, \leq_p \rangle$, where $\leq_p$ is the precision order on L^2 defined as follows: $(x, y) \leq_p (u, v)$ if $x \leq u$ and $v \leq y$. Tuples (x, y) such that $x \leq y$ are called *consistent*. Such a tuple can be understood as an approximation of lattice elements u between x and y, i.e., for which $x \leq u \leq y$. Tuples (x, x) approximate only x; they are called *exact*. Exact tuples are the maximally precise consistent pairs. Abusing notation, we will write $(x, y) \leq_p u$ to denote $(x, y) \leq_p (u, u)$ and say "(x, y) approximates u".

Applications of approximation fixpoint theory are initiated by defining one of two sorts of operators. An *approximator* $A : L^2 \to L^2$ is a $\leq_p$-monotone operator that is *symmetric*, i.e., $A(x, y) = (u, v)$ if and only if $A(y, x) = (v, u)$. Let us denote by $A_1, A_2 : L^2 \to L$ the projections of A on the first, respectively second argument; i.e., $A(x, y) = (A_1(x, y), A_2(x, y))$. By symmetry of A, we have that $A_2(x, y) = A_1(y, x)$. Thus, $A(x, y) = (A_1(x, y), A_1(y, x))$.

Table 1. Operators and their fixpoints

Operator	Definition of the operator	(Least) Fixpoint
$A : L^2 \to L^2$	$A(x, y) = (A_1(x, y), A_1(y, x))$	Kripke-Kleene least fixpoint
$O_A : L \to L$	$O_A(x) = A_1(x, x)$	Supported fixpoints
$S_A : L \to L$	$S_A(x) = lfp(A_1(\cdot, x))$	Stable fixpoints
$\Phi_A : L^2 \to L^2$	$\Phi_A(x, y) = (S_A(y), S_A(x))$	Well-founded fixpoint

The second sort of operator is a *monotone-antimonotone* operator $Ap : L^2 \to L$ which is monotone in its first and anti-monotone in its second argument: when $x \leq u$ and $y \geq v$, it holds that $Ap(x, y) \leq Ap(u, v)$.

Approximators and monotone-antimonotone operators are two sides of the same coin. Indeed, for an arbirary operator $Ap : L^2 \to L$, define the operator $A : L^2 \to L^2 : (x, y) \to A(x, y) = (Ap(x, y), Ap(y, x))$. Consequently, A_1 is identical to Ap. The following now holds:

Proposition 1. *Ap is monotone-antimonotone iff A is an approximator.*

As we will see, sometimes it is easier to define Ap, sometimes it is more natural to define A.

Given an approximator A (or equivalently, a monotone-antimonotone Ap), we can define three derived operators $O_A : L \to L$, $S_A : L \to L$ and $\Phi_A : L^2 \to L^2$. The operators, their definition and the names of their (least) fixpoints are shown in Table 1. A and Φ_A are $\leq_p$-monotone and have $\leq_p$-least fixpoints in L^2; S_A is $\leq$-anti-monotone and O_A is arbitrary; both may have 0 or more fixpoints in L.

The operator O_A is the lattice operator approximated by A. Indeed, when $(x, y) \leq_p u$ then $A(x, y) \leq_p O_A(u)$ and $A(x, x) = (O_A(x), O_A(x))$. Fixpoints of O_A are called *supported* and they correspond to exact fixpoints of A.

A crucial operator is the *stable operator* S_A, where $S_A(x)$ is defined as $lfp(A_1(\cdot, x)$ (or $lfp(Ap(\cdot, x))$[1]. This operator is antimonotone. It inherits this property from the anti-monotonicity of A_1 in the second argument. Indeed, consider $u = S_A(x)$ and $v = S_A(y)$ for $x \leq y$. We have that $u = lfp(A_1(\cdot, x))$, hence $u = A_1(u, x)$. By anti-monotonicity of A_1 in its second argument, $u = A_1(u, x) \geq A_1(u, y)$. It follows that u is a *pre-fixpoint* of the monotone operator $A_1(\cdot, y)$. Since the least fixpoint of a monotone operator is also its least pre-fixpoint, it follows that $v = lfp(A_1(\cdot, y)) \leq u$.

An anti-monotone operator has interesting properties. In particular, each fixpoint is $\leq$-minimal. Also, they have a *maximal oscillation pair* (u, v): (u, v) is an oscillation pair (i.e., $S_A(u) = v$, $S_A(v) = u$) and for each oscillation pair (x, y) of S_A, we have that $u \leq x$ and $v \geq y$; hence, $(u, v) \leq_p (x, y)$. Since stable fixpoints w correspond to exact oscillation pairs (w, w), (u, v) is less precise than any stable fixpoint.

The operator Φ_A is called the well-founded operator. It is defined by $\Phi_A(x, y) = (S_A(y), S_A(x))$. It follows from the anti-monotonicity of S_A that Φ_A is

[1] Here, we use $A_1(\cdot, x)$ as a shorthand for $\lambda y A_1(y, x)$.

$\leq_p$-monotone in L^2. Its fixpoints correspond exactly to the oscillation pairs of S_A; its least fixpoint is (u, v), the maximal oscillation pair of S_A; this is called the well-founded fixpoint of A. Fixpoints of Φ_A are also fixpoints of A; indeed, if $x = lfp(A_1(\cdot, y)), y = lfp(A_1(\cdot, x))$ it holds that $x = A_1(x, y)$ and $y = A_1(y, x) = A_2(x, y)$, hence $A(x, y) = (x, y)$.

The names of these fixpoints reflect the well-known semantics of logic programming. Indeed, if we take the four-valued versions of Fitting's three immediate consequence operator for A [7], [3] claimed that the four different types of fixpoints of this operator correspond to four well-known semantics of logic programming: Kripke-Kleene semantics [7], supported model semantics which is the restriction of the completion semantics [2] to Herbrand models, stable semantics [10] and well-founded semantics [21]. However, formal proofs of these results so far did not appear in print. Proofs will be included here for the first time.

3 Relationship to the Stable Model Semantics of Logic Programs

The first step of our enquiry of the applications of approximation fixpoint theory in LP and ASP is its relationship with the stable model semantics [10]. We show it here for the propositional case; in later sections we consider predicate logic programs.

A (propositional) vocabulary Σ is a set of propositional symbols. A Σ-interpretation is a subset of Σ; i.e., it is an element of 2^Σ. A normal rule (over Σ) is of the form:

$$p \leftarrow p_1, \ldots, p_n, \text{not } q_1, \ldots, \text{not } q_m$$

with $p, p_1, .., p_n, q_1, .., q_m \in \Sigma$. A normal logic program Π over Σ is a collection of normal rules over Σ. With a normal logic program Π we associate its immediate consequence operator $\Gamma^\Pi : 2^\Sigma \to 2^\Sigma$ which maps interpretations M to interpretations I consisting of all p such that for some rule

$$p \leftarrow p_1, \ldots, p_n, \text{not } q_1, \ldots, \text{not } q_m \in \Pi,$$

it holds that $p_1, \ldots, p_n \in M$ and $q_1, \ldots, q_m \notin M$.

The Gelfond-Lifschitz reduct Π_M of Π under Σ-interpretation M uses the interpretation M to reduce the normal program Π to a definite program (without negation in bodies). Formally, it is defined as the program consisting of rules:

$$p \leftarrow p_1, \ldots, p_n$$

for which there exists a rule $p \leftarrow p_1, \ldots, p_n, \text{not } q_1, \ldots, \text{not } q_m \in \Pi$ such that $q_1, \ldots, q_n \notin M$.

Π_M is a definite logic program. As a consequence, Γ^{Π_M} is monotone and has a least fixpoint $lfp(\Gamma^{\Pi_M})$. The operator that maps M to $lfp(\Gamma^{\Pi_M})$ is called the Gelfond-Lifschitz operator GL_Π of Π. M is called a stable model of Π if $M = GL_\Pi(M)$, i.e., if $M = lfp(\Gamma^{\Pi_M})$.

The link with the Approximation fixpoint theory is direct.

Definition 1. *Define* $T_1^\Pi : 2^\Sigma \times 2^\Sigma \to 2^\Sigma$ *as the operator that maps* (I, M) *to* $\Gamma^{\Pi_M}(I)$.

We observe that this operator evaluates positive body literals in its first argument, and, due to the construction of the reduct, its negative body literals in its second argument. $T_1^\Pi(I, M)$ is the set K of atoms p such that for some rule $p \leftarrow p_1, \ldots, p_n, \text{not } q_1, \ldots, \text{not } q_m \in \Pi$, $p_1, \ldots, p_n \in I$ and $q_1, \ldots, q_m \notin M$.

An obvious but crucial property is the following.

Proposition 2. T_1^Π *is a monotone-antimonotone operator; i.e., it is monotone in its first and antimonotone in its second argument.*

Definition 2. *Define* $T^\Pi : 2^\Sigma \times 2^\Sigma \to 2^\Sigma \times 2^\Sigma : (I, J) \to (T_1^\Pi(I, J), T_1^\Pi(J, I))$.

Proposition 3. T^Π *is an approximator in the bilattice of* $2^\Sigma, \subseteq$. *Its first component is* T_1^Π. *The stable operator* S_{T^Π} *of* T^Π *is the Gelfond-Lifschitz operator of* Π. *Stable fixpoints of* T^Π *are exactly the stable models of* Π.

Proof. By Proposition 1, T^Π is an approximator with T_1^Π as first component. We have that $GL_\Pi(M) = lfp(\Gamma^{\Pi^M}) = lfp(T_1^\Pi(\cdot, M)) = S_{T^\Pi}(M)$. Hence, stable models of Π are exactly the stable fixpoints of T^Π.

This proposition was informally mentioned in [3], but was never explicitly stated or proven.

Relationship with Well-Founded Semantics. As T^Π is an approximator, the well-founded least fixpoint of T^Π is the maximal oscillating pair of S_{T^Π}. In [20], this maximal oscillating pair was used to characterize the well-founded model of Π. In particular, this pair was proven to be structurally isomorphic with the three-valued well-founded model of Π as defined in [21].

In Section 5, we explain this isomorphism. There we will also show a property that was obvious to the authors of [3] but was never proven and never appeared in print: that T^Π is isomorphic with the three and four-valued immediate consequence operator of Π as defined by Fitting [7,8]. This latter result shows that the four types of semantics of LP (Kripke-Kleene, supported, stable , well-founded) are indeed generated from the four-valued immediate consequence operator through approximation fixpoint theory.

But first, we extend the stable semantics to arbitrary FO rule bodies and arbitrary non-Herbrand structures.

4 Extending the Stable Semantics to Predicate Rule Sets and Non-Herbrand Structures

In this section, we present a version of the stable semantics for rule sets with arbitrary first order logic (FO) formulas in the body. Moreover, this version of the semantics allows stable models to be arbitrary structures, including non-Herbrand ones. The semantic theory defined below was presented for the first time in [22] in the context of an enquiry of *predicate introduction*. However, the resulting semantics was also defined through another semantic theory in [18] as will be shown in the next section.

To define our semantics, we need some standard machinery from first order (FO) logic syntax and semantics.

4.1 Preliminaries: FO Syntax and Semantics

A predicate *vocabulary* Σ is now a finite set of predicate symbols Σ^P and function symbols Σ^F, each such predicate or function symbol with an associated arity. Constants are function symbols with arity 0. We often denote a symbol S with arity n by S/n. Terms and first order FO formulas over a vocabulary Σ are defined in the standard way.

We say that (an occurrence of) a subformula ψ of ϕ is *positive* in ϕ if it occurs in the scope of an even number of negations; it is *negative* otherwise. An occurrence of x in ψ is *bound* if it occurs in the scope of a quantifier, otherwise the occurrence is *free*. A *free variable* of ψ is one with a free occurrence. As usual, we denote a formula φ by $\varphi[\boldsymbol{x}]$ to indicate that the set of free variables of φ is a subset of $\boldsymbol{x}$. A FO formula without free variables is called a *(FO) sentence*.

A Σ*−interpretation* or *structure* I consists of a domain D and an assignment of a relation $P^I \subseteq D^n$ to each predicate symbol $P/n \in \Sigma$ and an assignment of a function $F^I : D^n \to D$ to each function symbol $F/n \in \Sigma$. A *pre-interpretation* of Σ consists of a domain and an interpretation of the function symbols. A (variable) *assignment* θ in D is a mapping from variables to domain elements of D. If I is a Σ-interpretation and $\Sigma' \subseteq \Sigma$, we denote by $I|_{\Sigma'}$ the restriction of I to the symbols of Σ'. If Σ_1 and Σ_2 are two disjoint vocabularies, I a Σ_1-interpretation with domain D and J a Σ_2-interpretation with the same domain, then $I+J$ denotes the unique $(\Sigma_1 \cup \Sigma_2)$-interpretation with domain D such that $(I+J)|_{\Sigma_1} = I$ and $(I+J)|_{\Sigma_2} = J$.

We define the FO satisfaction relation $I, \theta \models \psi$ between structures I, variable assignments θ and FO formulas ψ by the standard recursion. By slight abuse of notation, we often will write $I \models \psi[\bar{d}]$ as a shorthand for $I, \theta \models \psi[\bar{x}]$, where $\theta[x] = \bar{d}$.

Finally, we introduce the two truth values $\mathbf{t}$ and $\mathbf{f}$, and define the strict truth order $\mathbf{f} <_t \mathbf{t}$ and the inverses $(\mathbf{f})^{-1} = \mathbf{t}$ and $(\mathbf{t})^{-1} = \mathbf{f}$. The truth evaluation function $\psi^{I,\theta}$ is defined as follows: $\varphi^{I,\theta} = \mathbf{t}$ if $I, \theta \models \varphi$ and $\varphi^{I,\theta} = \mathbf{f}$ otherwise. For a formula $\psi[\bar{x}]$ and assignment θ such that $\theta(\bar{x}) = \bar{d}$, we often write $\psi[\bar{d}]^I$ instead of $\psi[\bar{x}]^{I,\theta}$. The truth order point-wise extends to interpretations. If I and J are two Σ-interpretations with the same pre-interpretation, then we say that $I \leq_t J$ if for every predicate symbol P and tuple of domain elements $\boldsymbol{d}$ it holds that $P^I(\boldsymbol{d}) \leq_t P^J(\boldsymbol{d})$.

4.2 Generalized Programs and Stable and Well-Founded Semantics

Definition 3. *A* rule *is a formula of the form* $\forall \bar{x}(P(\bar{t}) \leftarrow \varphi[\bar{x}])$ *with* $P/n \in \Sigma^P$, $\bar{t} = (t_1, \ldots, t_n)$ *n terms,* $\bar{x}$ *the set of all free variables in* $P(\bar{t})$ *and* φ, *and* φ *a FO formula. A* program Π *is a set of rules.*

We will often omit the outer universal quantifiers.

We now extend the stable semantics to predicate programs Π and, moreover, also define non-Herbrand stable models. The idea in [22] is to extend the operator $T_1^\Pi(I, M)$ to this general case. The crucial property that needs to be preserved, if we want to maintain the relationship with approximation fixpoint theory, is that the extended operator should be monotone-antimonotone.

In the case for normal programs, these properties were a result of the fact that I was only used to evaluate positive rule literals, and M only negative rule literals. It is fairly straightforward to extend this to arbitrary FO bodies, namely if we use I to interpret atoms that occur positively in rule bodies and M to interpret atoms that occur negatively.

To this aim, we define a satisfaction function that performs such a dual evaluation of atoms in positive and negative contexts.

Definition 4 (Pos-neg evaluation relation φ^{+I-J}). *Let* I_p *be a pre-interpretation of* Σ. *Let* φ *be a* Σ*-formula,* I *and* J *be* Σ*-interpretations extending* I_p *and* θ *an assignment. We define the* pos-neg evaluation *of* φ *in* I *and* J *and* θ, *denoted by* $\varphi^{+I-J,\theta}$, *by induction over the size of* φ:

- *for an atom* $\varphi = P(\mathbf{t})$, $\varphi^{+I-J,\theta} = \varphi^{I,\theta}$;
- *for* $\varphi = \neg\psi$, $\varphi^{+I-J,\theta} = (\psi^{+J-I,\theta})^{-1}$;
- *the normal recursive rules for* $\wedge, \vee, \exists, \forall$.
  E.g., $(\psi \wedge \phi)^{+I-J,\theta} = Min(\psi^{+I-J,\theta}, \phi^{+I-J,\theta})$.

Note that this definition evaluates atoms in I but switches the role of I and J when entering negation. Thus, indeed, positively occurring atoms are evaluated in I, negatively occurring atoms in J. A routine inductive argument shows that the operator is monotone.

Proposition 4. *The pos-neg evaluation* $\psi^{+I-J,\theta}$ *is monotone in* I *and anti-monotone in* J.

Definition 5. *Define the operator* T_1^Π *on all pairs of interpretations* (I, J) *sharing the same pre-interpretation* I_p *as* $T_1^\Pi(I, J) = K$ *if* K *has pre-interpretation* I_p *(the same as* I *and* J*), and moreover, for each* $P/n \in \Sigma^P$ *and tuple of domain elements* $\bar{d}$, $P^K(\bar{d}) = \mathbf{t}$ *iff for some rule* $\forall \bar{x}(P(\bar{t}) \leftarrow \varphi[\bar{x}])$ *and variable assignment* θ, $\bar{t}^{K,\theta} = \bar{d}$ *and* $\varphi[\bar{x}]^{+I-J,\theta} = \mathbf{t}$.

Proposition 5. T_1^Π *is monotone-antimonotone.*

This immediately follows from the monotonicity properties of pos-neg truth evaluation.

Thus, we can again define the operator $T^\Pi(I, J) = (T_1^\Pi(I, J), T_1^\Pi(J, I))$. For each pre-interpretation I_p, the set of Σ-interpretations extending I_p under the truth order $\leq_t$ is a complete lattice.

Definition 6. *A Σ-interpretation M is a stable model of Π if $M = lfp(T^{\Pi}(.,M))$.*

Or equivalently, M is a stable model if it is a fixpoint of the stable operator $S_{T^{\Pi}}$ which is defined as always, $S_{T^{\Pi}}(M) = lfp(T_1^{\Pi}(\cdot, M))$.

The above definition evidently generalizes the standard definition.

Well-Founded Semantics. For each pre-interpretation I_p, the operator $S_{T^{\Pi}}$ is an anti-monotone operator that defines a maximal oscillation pair (I, J). This pair approximates all stable models (since these correspond to exact oscillating pairs). As we shall see in the next section, this pair is structurally isomorphic to a generalized notion of three-valued well-founded model.

Parametrized Stable Semantics. It has become quite common to consider programs with input and output predicates. Initially in answer set programming, one particular form of this idea was found in idea of LP-functions [9]. A different form was introduced in LP modules [11].

Our semantics can be extended to cover parametrized stable semantics by generalizing the notion of a pre-interpretation. Assume that a pre-interpretation now not only provides the domain and interpretation of function symbols but also of certain input or parameter predicate symbols that occur only in rule bodies, not in heads. All above definitions generalize.

Relationship to Equilibrium Semantics. In [16,17], a semantics called *equilibrium semantics* was defined for logic programs and nested answer set programs, based on the notion of the logic of Here and There (HT). We present this semantics and study its relationship to ours.

A formula of HT is defined as in FO. For simplicity, this discussion is limited to the propositional case. The structures of HT are pairs (I, J) such that $I \subseteq J$. The truth function $v_{(I,J)}(\varphi)$ is defined by induction:

- $v_{(I,J)}(p) = p^I$, for $p \in \Sigma$
- the standard rules for $\wedge, \vee$
- $v_{(I,J)}(\neg\psi) = \mathbf{t}$ if $v_{(I,J)}(\psi) = \mathbf{f}$ and $v_{(J,J)}(\psi) = \mathbf{f}$
- $v_{(I,J)}(\psi \rightarrow \phi) = \mathbf{t}$ if $v_{(I,J)}(\psi) = \mathbf{t}$ implies $v_{(I,J)}(\phi) = \mathbf{t}$ and $v_{(J,J)}(\psi) = \mathbf{t}$ implies $v_{(J,J)}(\phi) = \mathbf{t}$.

An interpretation M is an *equilibrium model* of a HT theory T if (i) $v_{(M,M)}(T) = \mathbf{t}$ and (ii) if, for $I \leq M$, it holds that $v_{(I,M)}(T) = \mathbf{t}$ then $I = M$.

For program Π, define $HT(\Pi)$ as the set of formulas $\{\varphi \rightarrow A | A \leftarrow \varphi \in \Pi\}$. It was shown in [16] that for normal programs Π, the standard stable models correspond to the equilibrium models of $HT(\Pi)$. This correspondence extends to the case of nested programs [13].

Let us investigate the relationship to our semantics. First, they disagree for simple programs.

Example 1. Let $\Pi = \{p \leftarrow \neg\neg p\}$. The corresponding HT theory has two equilibrium models {} and {p} but has only one stable model, namely {}. This follows from the fact that $(\neg\neg p)^{+I-J} = p^{+I-J} = p^I$. As a consequence, this program induces the same stable operator as $\{p \leftarrow p\}$ whose only fixpoint is {}.

A striking similary of the two semantics is the use of truth functions based on pairs of interpretations. In some cases these truth functions coincide. That will allows us to prove that under certain circumstances both semantics coincide.

Proposition 6. *Let φ be a formula without nested negations (and no $\rightarrow, \leftrightarrow$). For each $I \subseteq J$, it holds that $v_{I,J}(\varphi) = \varphi^{+I-J}$.*

Proof. The proof is by induction on the structure of φ. In both definitions, the rules for the truth value of atoms, $\wedge$ and $\vee$ are identical. So, we are left with negation. As φ contains no nested negation, it is a positive formula.

We have $v_{(I,J)}(\neg\psi) = \mathbf{t}$ if $v_{(I,J)}(\psi) = \mathbf{f}$ and $v_{(J,J)}(\psi) = \mathbf{f}$ iff (by the induction hypothesis) $\psi^{+I-J} = \mathbf{f}$ and $\psi^J = \mathbf{f}$.

Let us consider this last condition a bit closer. The formula ψ is a positive formula, therefore $\psi^{+J-I} = \psi^J$. Moreover, it always holds that $\psi^{+I-J} \leq \psi^J$. Hence, the condition $\psi^{+I-J} = \mathbf{f}$ and $\psi^J = \mathbf{f}$ is equivalent to $\psi^{+J-I} = \mathbf{f}$ which in turn is equivalent to $\neg\psi^{+I-J} = \mathbf{t}$.

Theorem 1. *If no rule body of a logic program Π contains nested negation, then M is a stable model of Π (as defined in this paper) iff M is an equilibrium model of $HT(\Pi)$.*

Proof. M is an equilibrium model of $HT(\Pi)$ iff (i) $v_{(M,M)}(HT(\Pi)) = \mathbf{t}$ and (ii) $v_{(I,M)}(HT(\Pi)) = \mathbf{t}$ for $I \leq M$ implies $I = M$.

Look at the first condition. With φ a rule body, the truth function $v_{M,M}(\varphi)$ coincides with the standard truth function. By (i), M is a model of $PC(\Pi)$, the set of propositional material implications syntactically identical to $HT(\Pi)$. In turn, this condition is equivalent to M being a pre-fixpoint of the immediate consequence operator of Π. And this is equivalent to $T_1^{\Pi}(M,M) \leq M$.

Now we consider the second condition. When $v_{(I,M)}(HT(\Pi)) = \mathbf{t}$, this means that for each $A \leftarrow \varphi \in \Pi$, $v_{(I,M)}(\varphi) = \varphi^{+I-M} = \mathbf{t}$ implies $v_{(I,M)}(A) = A^I = \mathbf{t}$ and $v_{(M,M)}(\varphi) = \varphi^M = \mathbf{t}$ implies $v_{(M,M)}(A) = A^M = \mathbf{t}$. It follows that $v_{(I,M)}(HT(\Pi)) = \mathbf{t}$ holds iff $T_1^{\Pi}(I,M) \leq I$ and $T_1^{\Pi}(M,M) \leq M$. Thus, the second condition is that if $T_1^{\Pi}(I,M) \leq I$ and $T_1^{\Pi}(M,M) \leq M$ then $I = M$.

Given that $T_1^{\Pi}(M,M) \leq M$ because of (i), we obtain that M is an equilibrium model iff M is a fixpoint of $T_1^{\Pi}(\cdot, M)$ and this operator has no smaller pre-fixpoints. This is equivalent to saying that $M = lfp(T_1^{\Pi}(\cdot, M))$.

Discussion. Equilibrium semantics is defined for a larger class of programs than stable semantics defined here, namely for all of HT, i.e., for all sentences in FO syntax. Whether this is an advantage or not depends on whether it formalizes a natural generalization of the concept of a rule to the full FO formalism. So far no natural applications exist of nested answer set programs beyond the standard rules that we have considered here. To a great extent, the question of whether the above two semantics makes sense depends on the *informal semantics* formalized by each. This issue, the intuitive meaning of language constructs such as negation and the rule operator, and of rules induced by the semantics has not been addressed for either of the semantics. In the next section, we will briefly comment on this issue for the stable semantics defined here.

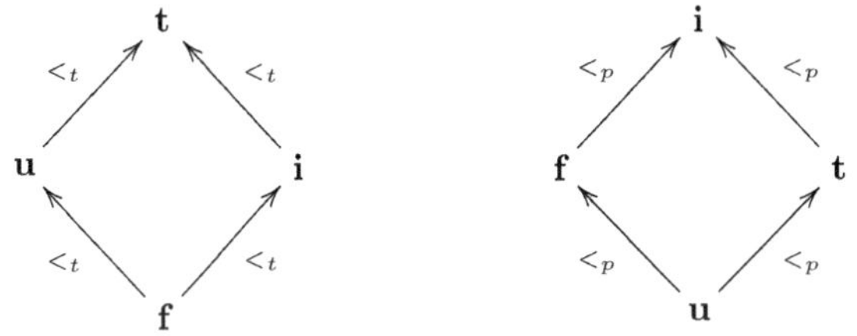

Fig. 1. The truth and precision order

Part of the problem of making intuitive sense of both logics is due to the used truth evaluation function. The evaluation of rules in equilibrium semantics is based on the logic of Here and There. While this logic has a long history, it is nevertheless the case that little or nothing is known about its informal semantics[2]. Questions such as: what is the intuitive interpretation of negation and implication operator in HT, remain unclear to this day. But also the definition of the pos-neg evaluation may seem awkward and its motivation unclear. In the following section, we provide some explanation by laying a simple and tight link between this truth function and the standard Kleene three-valued truth function and Belnap's four-valued extension. This will also clarify the link between T^{Π} and the three- and four-valued immediate consequence operator of Π.

5 Generating Stable and Well-Founded Semantics from Three- and four-Valued Semantics

5.1 The Bilattice View on Three- and Four-Valued Logic

We now present an intimate connection between the approximation of an interpretation by a pair of interpretations and Belnap's four-valued logic [1].

We denote the truth values *true, false, unknown* and *inconsistent* of four-valued logic by respectively $\mathbf{t}, \mathbf{f}, \mathbf{u}$ and $\mathbf{i}$. Define $\mathbf{i}^{-1} = \mathbf{i}, \mathbf{u}^{-1} = \mathbf{u}$. The *truth order* $\leq_t$ and *precision order* $\leq_p$ are defined on these truth values (see Figure 1).

A four-valued relation of arity n on some domain D is a function from D^n to $\{\mathbf{t}, \mathbf{f}, \mathbf{u}, \mathbf{i}\}$. It is three-valued if $\mathbf{i}$ is not in the image. A four-valued (three-valued) interpretation $\mathcal{I}$ of vocabulary Σ consists of a pre-interpretation and, for each predicate symbol $P/n \in \Sigma$ a four-valued (three-valued) relation $P^{\mathcal{I}}$ of arity n in domain $D(\mathcal{I})$.

The truth and precision orders pointwise extend to interpretations. E.g., if $\mathcal{I}$ and $\mathcal{J}$ are two Σ-interpretations sharing the pre-interpretation, then $\mathcal{I} \leq_p \mathcal{J}$ if for every predicate symbol P and tuple of domain elements $\bar{d}$ it holds that $P^{\mathcal{I}}(\bar{d}) \leq_p P^{\mathcal{J}}(\bar{d})$. Similarly, also the truth order is extended to interpretations.

[2] David Pearce, private communication, ASP'03 Workshop, Messina.

Definition 7. *Let $\mathcal{I}$ be a four-valued Σ-structure, θ a variable assignment. For each formula φ over Σ, we define its truth value $\varphi^{\mathcal{I},\theta}$ by essentially the same induction as for 2-valued logic:*

- $P(\bar{t})^{\mathcal{I},\theta} = P^{\mathcal{I}}(\bar{t}^{\mathcal{I}})$;
- *Standard rules for* $\neg, \wedge, \neg\forall, \exists$. *E.g.,* $(\exists x \psi)^{\mathcal{I},\theta} = Max_{\leq_t}\{\psi^{\mathcal{I},\theta[x:d]} | d \in D_{\mathcal{I}}\}$.

This truth evaluation was originally proposed by Belnap as an extension of the standard Kleene evaluation [12] for three-valued structures.

A key property of this truth evaluation is that when $\mathcal{I}$ approximates I, that is, $\mathcal{I} \leq_p I$, then $\varphi^{\mathcal{I},\theta} \leq_p \varphi^{I,\theta}$. This shows that three-valued interpretations can be used as approximations of two-valued ones. Thus, we see that three-valued interpretations could play the same role as consistent pairs in the bilattice, as approximations of exact lattice elements. In fact, both are isomorphic views.

There is a natural isomorphism between Belnap's four truth values and pairs of the two standard truth values: $\tau(\mathbf{t},\mathbf{t}) = \mathbf{t}$; $\tau(\mathbf{f},\mathbf{t}) = \mathbf{u}$; $\tau(\mathbf{t},\mathbf{f}) = \mathbf{i}$; $\tau(\mathbf{f},\mathbf{f}) = \mathbf{f}$. Intuitively, this mapping τ interprets its first argument as an underestimate to the "real" truth value, and its second argument as an overestimate: if the underestimate is **f** and the overestimate is **t**, then the real truth value is indeed unknown; whereas, if the underestimate is **t** and the overestimate if **f**, then there cannot exist a real truth value, since $\mathbf{t} \not\leq \mathbf{f}$, so we end up with inconsistency. This isomorphism τ extends in an obvious way to an isomorphism between pairs (I, J) of two-valued interpretations and four-valued interpretations $\mathcal{I} = \tau(I, J)$ which all share the same pre-interpretations. I.e., for each predicate P/n and tuple $\bar{d} \in D^n$, $P^{\mathcal{I}}(\bar{d}) = \tau(P^I(\bar{d}), P^J(\bar{d}))$.

The tight link between our pos-neg evaluation function ϕ^{+I-J} and Belnap evaluation $\phi^{\mathcal{I}}$ is now as follows.

Proposition 7. *For each four-valued Σ-interpretation $\mathcal{I}$, assignment θ and formula φ over Σ:* $\phi^{\mathcal{I},\theta} = \tau(\phi^{+I-J,\theta}, \phi^{+J-I,\theta})$, *where* $\tau(I, J) = \mathcal{I}$.

This proposition seems to be folk theorem in the area of three- and four-valued logic. The proof is by a routine induction. We did not find a proof but a related result is found in [6]. In the rest of this paper, we will often omit the isomorphism τ, and simply denote the four-valued truth value of a formule ϕ in a pair of interpretations (I, J) as $\phi^{(I,J)}$. An important property, that we already stated above in different notation, is that $\varphi^{(I,J)} \leq_p \varphi^K$ for all $K \in [I, J]$.

What this says about the intuition underlying the pos-neg evaluation, is that this function serves to compute *approximate* truth values for formulas, *both from below and from above.* Indeed, when (I, J) approximates K, then compared to φ^K, φ^{+I-J} underestimates φ^K and φ^{+J-I} overestimates φ^K. To see this, observe that φ^{+I-J} underestimates positive occurring atoms and overestimates negatively occurring atoms. The inverse is true for φ^{+J-I}, leading to an overestimation of φ^K. The link with the four-valued truth evaluation is that the latter performs the same computations (under- and overestimation) simultaneously.

5.2 Semantics of Programs through the Four-Valued Consequence Operator

The (two-valued) immediate consequence operator Γ^{Π} of a program Π extends to three- and four-valued interpretations in an obvious way. The three-valued version was defined first in [7], the four-valued one in [8].

Let Π be a program over Σ. The operator Ψ^{Π} is a mapping of four-valued Σ-interpretations, that maps $\mathcal{I}$ to $\mathcal{J}$ if the following condition holds:

- the pre-interpretation of $\mathcal{I}$ and $\mathcal{J}$ are the same;
- for each predicate P and tuple $\bar{d} \in D^n$, it holds that

$$P^{\mathcal{J}}(\bar{d}) = Max_{\leq_t}\{\varphi^{\mathcal{I},\theta} \mid \text{ there exists a rule } p(\bar{t}) \leftarrow \varphi \in \Pi \text{ and assignment } \theta \text{ such that } \bar{t}^{\mathcal{I},\theta} = \bar{d}\}.$$

We can simplify its definition if we first normalize the program using a well-known procedure akin to predicate completion. In particular, we replace the set of rules $\forall \bar{x}_i(P(\bar{t}_i) \leftarrow \varphi_i)$ with the same predicate P in the head by one rule:

$$\forall \bar{y}(P(\bar{y}) \leftarrow \cdots \vee \exists \bar{x}_i(\bar{t}_i = \bar{y} \wedge \varphi_i) \vee \dots)$$

We obtain a program in which each predicate is defined by one rule $\forall \bar{y}(P(\bar{y}) \leftarrow \varphi_P[\bar{y}])$. For such programs, the definition of the immediate consequence operator simplifies. For $\mathcal{J} = \Psi^{\Pi}(\mathcal{I})$, $P^{\mathcal{J}}$ is defined for all tuples $\bar{d} \in D^n$ as:

$$P^{\mathcal{J}}(\bar{d}) = \varphi[\bar{d}]^{\mathcal{I}}$$

Proposition 8. *For each program Π and four-valued interpretation $\mathcal{I}$, we have that $\Psi^{\Pi}(\mathcal{I})) = \tau(T^{\Pi}(\tau(\mathcal{I})))$.*

Proof. Follows from the isomorphism between between pairs of interpretations four-valued interpretations and the correspondence between pos-neg and Belnaps truth evaluation. In particular, if $\tau(I, J) = \mathcal{I}$, $T^{\Pi}(I, J) = (K, L)$, $\Psi^{\Pi}(\mathcal{I}) = \mathcal{K}$ then $\tau(K, L) = \mathcal{K}$.

Historical Remark. In the late nineties, through the work of Van Gelder, Fitting and Przymusinski, it had become clear that considerable sections of Logic Programming semantics could be "algebraized". For example, Fitting had defined his three- and four-valued immediate consequence operator Ψ^{Π} to characterize Kripke-Kleene fixpoints. He had also introduced the operator T_1^{Π} which had been extended to an operator mapping pairs of 4-valued interpretations to four-valued interpretations to define four-valued stable models. However, the missing link was the relationship between Ψ^{Π} and T_1^{Π} as expressed by Proposition 8. This result is the cornerstone that allows to push all semantic constructions completely to the algebraic setting with the four-valued immediate consequence operator in the centre. This is the theory that was elaborated in [3].

To the authors of [3], the existence of this algebraic relationship between Ψ^{Π} and T_1^{Π} came as a big surprise as it seemed impossible given that the definitions of T_1^{Π} and the stable operator explicitly depend on syntactic details such as the distinction between positive and negative literals; moreover the stable operator treats both in a completely asymmetrical way. On the other hand, the immediate consequence operator seems to treat positive and negative literals in a symmetrical way. It therefore seemed impossible that there could be an algebraic relationship between both operators. That it was possible after all, is due to the fact that the four-valued truth function can be decomposed in two two-valued ones using pos-neg evaluation. Pos-neg evaluation incorporates the asymmetric treatment of positive and negative literals w.r.t. different structures.

5.3 Some Pragmatic Consequences Regarding the Semantics

Equivalence. From a pragmatical viewpoint, equivalence is an important aspect in a logic. When human experts express properties of a domain in a theory, there are typically several ways to express them. Different experts, or the same expert at different times, may express the same properties in different ways. This should lead to equivalent theories. For this to work well, it is necessary that the logic comes with a set of natural well-understood equivalence preserving laws. To illustrate the issue, assume that a condition in a program rule is that symbols P and Q are equivalent. There are two ways to represent this:

$$(P \rightarrow Q) \wedge (Q \rightarrow P) \quad \text{or} \quad (P \wedge Q) \vee (\neg P \wedge \neg Q)$$

In FO, these formulas are equivalent, so it does not matter which one is used. But in other logics, they are not equivalent and the human expert should select the right one to insert in his formula. Knowledge representation without a good understanding of the meaning of both would be seriously hampered.

In the context of the equilibrium semantics, equivalence of programs is based on equivalence in the logic of HT and is called *strong equivalence* [13]: substituting a formula in a body with one that is equivalent (i.e., has the same HT truth value in each pair (I, J)) is equivalence preserving. Most of the standard equivalence preserving transformations in FO do not hold in HT. E.g., the above two formulas for expressing $P \leftrightarrow Q$ are not strongly equivalent. Strong equivalence preserving transformations were investigated in [5,14].

In the context of the semantics presented here, the issue of equivalence has not yet so thoroughly been investigated. Yet, several things are obvious. The underlying equivalence in each of the family of semantics considered here is four-valued equivalence: substituting a formula in a rule body by one that has the same truth value in all four-valued structures preserves the four-valued immediate consequence operator and hence, the four types of semantics. The good news is that almost all standard basic equivalence preserving transformations in FO also hold in four-valued logic: e.g., removing double negation, commutativity of $\wedge, \vee, \leftrightarrow$, distribution laws of $\wedge, \vee, \exists, \forall$ over other connectives, laws of De Morgan. Indeed, left and righthandside of such formulas have the same truth value in all four-valued interpretations. This is important because these laws capture some of the most fundamental "laws of thought" of human thinking.

In contrast, few of these preserve strong equivalence in HT. Standard transformations towards negation normal form or prenex normal form are all equivalence preserving in four-valued logic and hence, can be applied to rule bodies.

Transformations that are not equivalence preserving in four-valued logic are those that introduce reasoning by cases. Examples are FO tautologies such as $\varphi \leftrightarrow \varphi \wedge (\psi \vee \neg\psi)$, $\varphi \leftrightarrow \varphi \vee (\psi \wedge \neg\psi)$ or $\varphi \leftrightarrow (\psi \rightarrow \varphi) \wedge (\neg\psi \rightarrow \varphi)$. This explains why the following programs are not equivalent:

$$\Pi_1 = \{p \leftarrow \mathbf{t}\} \text{ and } \Pi_2 = \{p \leftarrow p \vee \neg p\}$$

Proposition 9. *If Π is a program containing rule $\forall \bar{x}(P(\bar{t}) \leftarrow \varphi)$ and φ' is a formula that has the same truth value in each four-valued interpretation as φ, then $\Pi \setminus \{\forall \bar{x}(P(\bar{t}) \leftarrow \varphi)\} \cup \{\forall \bar{x}(P(\bar{t}) \leftarrow \varphi')\}$ is equivalent in the four semantics.*

The form of equivalence underlying the stable semantics defined here, which also holds for the three other semantics, is much more "standard" than in HT. We believe that this is a considerably advantage from a pragmatic point of view.

Language Extensions and Abstract Semantics. A challenge for a semantics is the ease with which it can be extended to handle new language constructs. A good example where such an extension proved to be quite difficult is the case of logic programming extended with recursion over aggregate expressions.

To accomodate for language extension, one solution is the use of an abstract, syntax independent semantics. This strategy was followed, e.g., in the context of answer set programming with abstract constraint atoms [15]. In this semantics, any new language construct can be added to rule bodies provided that its semantics can be expressed abstractly as "abstract constraint atoms".

The semantics presented here in this paper goes even further in this abstract direction. All that is needed is an approximator on the bilattice, or equivalently, a monotone-antimonotone lattice operator. This is why the Approximation Fixpoint Theory is not only useful to describe LP semantics but also the semantics of Default logic and Autoepistemic reasoning [4].

What needs to be done to add a new language expression in rule bodies of programs (e.g., an aggregate expression)? To extend the family of semantics defined here, it suffices to define a four-valued immediate consequence operator Ψ^{Π} for the extended formalism. The extended operator should satisfy two conditions: it should be $\leq_p$-monotone and it should be symmetric. This will be the case if we can extend the four-valued truth function $\varphi^{\mathcal{I},\theta}$ for the extended formalism of rule bodies such that the following conditions are satisfied:

- $\leq_p$-monotonicity: if $\mathcal{I} \leq_p J$, then $\varphi^{\mathcal{I},\theta} \leq_p \varphi^{\mathcal{J},\theta}$.
- symmetry: if $\mathcal{J}$ can be obtained from $\mathcal{I}$ by switching $\mathbf{i}$ and $\mathbf{u}$, then $\varphi^{\mathcal{J},\theta}$ can be obtained from $\varphi^{\mathcal{I},\theta}$ by switching $\mathbf{i}$ and $\mathbf{u}$. I.e., both are true, or both are false, or one is $\mathbf{u}$ and the other $\mathbf{i}$.

Proposition 10. *If the four-valued truth function is $\leq_p$-monotone and symmetric, so will be Ψ^{Π}.*

It is sometimes even simpler to explain the extension of the semantics in terms of the pos-neg truth evaluation. For the extended formalism of rule bodies, we define $\varphi^{\tau(I,J),\theta} = \tau(\varphi^{+I-J}, \varphi^{+J-I})$ as before and extend the pos-neg evaluation so that the following condition is satisfied:

- monotone-antimonotone: if $I \leq_t K$ and $J \geq_t L$, then $\varphi^{+I-J,\theta} \leq \varphi^{+K-L,\theta}$.

It follows from monotone-antimonotonicity that if $I \leq_t J$ then for every $I \leq_t K \leq_t J$, it holds that $\varphi^{+I-J,\theta} \leq \varphi^{K,\theta} \leq \varphi^{+J-I,\theta}$. As a special case, the truth value $\varphi^{+I-I,\theta}$ denotes the truth value of φ under I, θ and will be denoted $\varphi^{I,\theta}$.

Proposition 11. *A monotone and symmetric four-valued truth function induces a monotone-antimonotone pos-neg truth valuation and vice versa.*

In practice, the pos-neg evaluation is defined by induction on the structure of the formula φ. What needs to be done is to insert a new case in this inductive definition, defining the truth value for the new language construct. Below we illustrate this for the cardinality aggregate. The definitions below stem from [18] where approximation fixpoint theory was used to define the stable and well-founded semantics for logic programs with arbitrary aggregates.

The new language constructs considered here are of the form $\#\{\bar{x} : \varphi\}\ o\ t$ where $o \in \{=, <, >, \leq, \geq\}$, t a numerical term and $\{\bar{x} : \varphi\}$ a set expression.

We need to define $(\#\{\bar{x} : \varphi\}\ o\ t)^{+I-J,\theta}$. This is done in two steps.

- With the set expression $\{\bar{x} : \varphi\}$, we can associate two sets of tuples of domain elements of D:

  $$\{\bar{d} | \varphi^{+I-J,\theta[\bar{x}:\bar{d}]} = \mathbf{t}\} \quad \text{and} \quad \{\bar{d} | \varphi^{+J-I,\theta[\bar{x}:\bar{d}]} = \mathbf{t}\}$$

  In case $I \leq J$, the first will be a subset of the second, due to monotone-antimonotonicity. The first one is an underestimation of the approximated set, the second an overestimation.

- Depending on the operator o, we use one of these sets to compute the truth value of the expression. We illustrate this here for the operator $<$ and $>$. The truth function for the other operators can be defined in terms of these.
  - Define $(\#\{\bar{x} : \varphi\} < t)^{+I-J,\theta} = \mathbf{t}$ iff the number of elements in the set

    $$\{\bar{d} | \varphi^{+J-I,\theta[\bar{x}:\bar{d}]} = \mathbf{t}\}$$

    is strictly smaller than t^I. Thus, for $I \leq_t J$, this value is true if the cardinality of the overestimated set is less than $t^{\mathcal{I}}$.
  - Define $(\#\{\bar{x} : \varphi\} > t)^{+I-J,\theta} = \mathbf{t}$ iff the number of elements in the set

    $$\{\bar{d} | \varphi^{+I-J,\theta[\bar{x}:\bar{d}]} = \mathbf{t}\}$$

    is strictly larger than t^I. Now for $I \leq_t J$, this value is true if the cardinality of the underestimated set is already larger than $t^{\mathcal{I}}$.

Proposition 12 ([18]). $\varphi^{+I-J,\theta}$ *is monotone-antimonotone.*

Thus, this pos-neg truth function induces a monotone-antimonotone operator T_1^{Π}, a symmetric, $\leq_p$-monotone four-valued truth function, an approximator and four types of semantics.

References

1. Belnap, N.D.: A useful four-valued logic. In: Dunn, J.M., Epstein, G. (eds.) Modern Uses of Multiple-Valued Logic, pp. 8–37. Reidel, Dordrecht (1977); Invited papers from the Fifth International Symposium on Multiple-Valued Logic, held at Indiana University, Bloomington, Indiana, May 13-16 (1975)
2. Clark, K.L.: Negation as failure. In: Logic and Data Bases, pp. 293–322. Plenum Press (1978)
3. Denecker, M., Marek, V.W., Truszczyński, M.: Approximating operators, stable operators, well-founded fixpoints and applications in non-monotonic reasoning. In: Logic-based Artificial Intelligence. The Kluwer International Series in Engineering and Computer Science, pp. 127–144. Kluwer Academic Publishers, Boston (2000)
4. Denecker, M., Marek, V.W., Truszczynski, M.: Uniform semantic treatment of default and autoepistemic logics. Artif. Intell. 143(1), 79–122 (2003)
5. Eiter, T., Fink, M., Tompits, H., Traxler, P., Woltran, S.: Replacements in non-ground answer-set programming. In: Doherty, P., Mylopoulos, J., Welty, C.A. (eds.) KR, pp. 340–351. AAAI Press (2006)
6. Feferman, S.: Toward useful type-free theories. Journal of Symbolic Logic 49(1), 75–111 (1984)
7. Fitting, M.: A Kripke-Kleene semantics for logic programs. Journal of Logic Programming 2(4), 295–312 (1985)
8. Fitting, M.: Fixpoint semantics for logic programming a survey. Theoretical Computer Science 278(1-2), 25–51 (2002)
9. Gelfond, M.: Representing Knowledge in A-Prolog. In: Kakas, A.C., Sadri, F. (eds.) Computational Logic: Logic Programming and Beyond. LNCS (LNAI), vol. 2408, pp. 413–451. Springer, Heidelberg (2002)
10. Gelfond, M., Lifschitz, V.: The stable model semantics for logic programming. In: Kowalski, R.A., Bowen, K.A. (eds.) ICLP/SLP, pp. 1070–1080. MIT Press (1988)
11. Janhunen, T., Oikarinen, E., Tompits, H., Woltran, S.: Modularity aspects of disjunctive stable models. J. Artif. Intell. Res (JAIR) 35, 813–857 (2009)
12. Kleene, S.C.: Introduction to Metamathematics. Van Nostrand (1952)
13. Lifschitz, V., Pearce, D., Valverde, A.: Strongly equivalent logic programs. ACM Trans. Comput. Log. 2(4), 526–541 (2001)
14. Lin, F., Chen, Y.: Discovering classes of strongly equivalent logic programs. J. Artif. Intell. Res (JAIR) 28, 431–451 (2007)
15. Marek, V.W., Truszczyński, M.: Logic programs with abstract constraint atoms. In: Proceedings of the 19th National Conference on Artificial Intelligence (AAAI 2004), pp. 86–91. AAAI Press (2004)
16. Pearce, D.: A New Logical Characterisation of Stable Models and Answer Sets. In: Dix, J., Przymusinski, T.C., Moniz Pereira, L. (eds.) NMELP 1996. LNCS, vol. 1216, pp. 57–70. Springer, Heidelberg (1997)
17. Pearce, D.: Equilibrium logic. Ann. Math. Artif. Intell. 47(1-2), 3–41 (2006)
18. Pelov, N., Denecker, M., Bruynooghe, M.: Well-founded and stable semantics of logic programs with aggregates. Theory and Practice of Logic Programming (TPLP) 7(3), 301–353 (2007)
19. Przymusinski, T.C.: The well-founded semantics coincides with the three-valued stable semantics. Fundamenta Informaticae 13(4), 445–463 (1990)

20. Van Gelder, A.: The alternating fixpoint of logic programs with negation. Journal of Computer and System Sciences 47(1), 185–221 (1993)
21. Van Gelder, A., Ross, K.A., Schlipf, J.S.: The well-founded semantics for general logic programs. Journal of the ACM 38(3), 620–650 (1991)
22. Vennekens, J., Mariën, M., Wittocx, J., Denecker, M.: Predicate introduction for logics with a fixpoint semantics. Part I: Logic programming. Fundamenta Informaticae 79(1-2), 187–208 (2007)

Privacy Preservation Using Multi-context Systems and Default Logic

Jürgen Dix[1,⋆], Wolfgang Faber[2,⋆⋆], and V.S. Subrahmanian[3]

[1] Department of Informatics
Clausthal University of Technology
38678 Clausthal, Germany
dix@tu-clausthal.de

[2] Department of Mathematics
University of Calabria
87030 Rende (CS), Italy
wf@wfaber.com

[3] Department of Computer Science
University of Maryland
College Park, MD 20742
vs@cs.umd.edu

Abstract. Preserving the privacy of sensitive data is one of the major challenges the information society has to face. Traditional approaches focused on infrastructures for identifying data which is to be kept private and for managing access rights to these data. However, although these efforts are useful, they do not address an important aspect: While the sensitive data itself can be protected nicely using these mechanisms, related data, which is deemed insensitive per se, may be used to *infer* sensitive data. This inference can be achieved by combining insensitive data or by exploiting specific background knowledge of the domain of discourse. In this paper, we present a general formalization of this problem and two particular instantiations of it. The first supports query answering by means of multi-context systems and hybrid knowledge bases, while the second allows for query answering by using default logic.

1 Introduction

With the advent of the Internet and easy access to huge amounts of data, keeping sensitive data private has become a priority for distributed information systems. An example area in which privacy is at stake are medical information systems.

Most databases have privacy mechanisms which are comparatively simple. Often, this boils down to keeping certain columns of the database hidden from certain types

⋆ The first author acknowledges that this work was partly funded by the NTH School for IT Ecosystems (NTH (Niedersächsische Technische Hochschule) is a joint university consisting of Technische Universität Braunschweig, Technische Universität Clausthal, and Leibniz Universität Hannover).

⋆⋆ Supported by M.I.U.R. within the PRIN project LoDeN. Some of the authors of this paper were funded in part by ARO grants W911NF0910206 and W911NF0910525 and W911NF1110344.

E. Erdem et al. (Eds.): Correct Reasoning, LNCS 7265, pp. 195–210, 2012.

of users. There are many approaches dealing with formalisms for this kind of authorization problem, and we refer to [24] and references in that work, in which aspects of the authorization problem in non-monotonic knowledge bases are discussed. What we are interested in, however, is a somewhat different issue: *Can users infer private information by only asking queries that do not involve such information and then making "common sense" inferences from the answers?*

In this paper, we generalize an earlier definition of the *Privacy Preservation Problem* [10]. This definition imposed several restrictions on the underlying knowledge bases. Most importantly, they had to be first-order theories, because in this way it is easily possible to build a default theory around them. In our new definition, we aim at making as few assumptions about the involved knowledge bases as possible. Essentially we will use the terminology that has been introduced for multi-context systems by Brewka and Eiter in [7]: It only assumes the knowledge bases to have an underlying logic of some sort.

We will show that multi-context systems can be used for implementing a system that computes privacy preserving answers. Essentially, we use contexts and bridge rules that link contexts in order to determine whether an answer violates the privacy requirements of some user. An appealing aspect of this instantiation of the general privacy preservation framework is that efficient systems for reasoning with multi-context systems are beginning to emerge [1], making privacy preserving query answering systems feasible in practice. We will then consider a restriction of the framework, which essentially matches the definitions of [10], and review how default logic can be used in order to obtain a privacy preserving query answering system.

In the following, we first provide a general definition of the privacy preservation problem in Section 2, which allows for heterogeneous knowledge bases. In Section 3 we show how to construct a multi-context system for computing answers for the general privacy preservation problem. In Section 4 we show that the setting of [10] is a special case of the general framework and review how to solve these problems by means of default logic. We conclude with Section 5 and outline future work. This work elaborates on earlier results presented in [10] and [12].

2 Privacy Preservation Problem

In this section, we provide a general formalization of the privacy preservation problem, P3 for short. This development is similar to the one in [5] and some earlier work in [23], with slightly modified terminology. We start with basic concepts for describing knowledge bases, using terminology of [7].

We consider a *logic* L as in [7] to be a triple $(\mathbf{KB}_L, \mathbf{BS}_L, \mathbf{ACC}_L)$ where $\mathbf{KB}_L$ is the set of well-formed knowledge bases of L (each of which is a set as well), $\mathbf{BS}_L$ is the set of possible belief sets, and $\mathbf{ACC}_L$ is a function $\mathbf{KB}_L \rightarrow \mathbf{2}^{\mathbf{BS}_L}$ describing the semantics of each knowledge base. In the following, when mentioning knowledge bases, we do not specify the underlying logic (and drop the subscripts from $\mathbf{KB}$, $\mathbf{BS}$, and $\mathbf{ACC}$): It can just be any logic in the sense just described. Moreover, let the finite set $\mathbf{U}$ contain one user ID for each user in the system under consideration. By abuse of language we use the notation $\mathbf{U} = \{u_1, \ldots, u_{|\mathbf{U}|}\}$.

Definition 1 (main knowledge base $\mathbf{MKB}$). *The* main knowledge base $\mathbf{MKB}$ *is a knowledge base of some logic L.*

The main knowledge base is the one that the users will be querying, and around which the privacy preservation mechanism must be implemented. So the users will query the main knowledge base, and the privacy preservation mechanism might prevent certain answers to be disclosed. This mechanism foresees the availability of a model of each user's knowledge. Thus, at any given instance t in time, each user u has some set of *background knowledge*. This background knowledge may be elicited in many ways: One such source is the set of all information disclosed to the user by the system. For example, a hospital accountant may not be allowed to see patient diagnoses, though she may see billing information about them.

Definition 2 (user model). *The function* $\mathbf{BK}$ *assigns to each user* $u \in \mathbf{U}$ *a* background knowledge base $\mathbf{BK}^t(u)$ *for each timepoint t. The function* $\mathbf{Priv}$ *assigns to each user* $u \in \mathbf{U}$ *a belief set* $\mathbf{Priv}(u)$ *that should be kept private.*

Note that the various knowledge bases need not be of the same logic, but for practical reasons one would assume the belief sets to be homogeneous. It should be pointed out that $\mathbf{BK}^t(u)$ will usually not be the user's own knowledge base, but rather a model of the user's knowledge, maintained by the information system. Note that $\mathbf{BK}^t(u)$ varies as t varies. For example, as the database discloses answers to the user u, the background knowledge associated to u may increase. *Throughout most of this paper, we assume that t is fixed and we address the problem of preserving privacy at a given timepoint.* As a consequence, we usually write $\mathbf{BK}(u)$ and drop the superscript t.

Example 1. Consider a small medical knowledge base MedKB containing information about the symptoms and diseases of some patients. Let this knowledge base describe two predicates $\mathsf{symptom}$ and $\mathsf{disease}$ and let the following be its only belief set S_{MedKB}:

$\mathsf{symptom}(john, s_1)$	$\mathsf{symptom}(jane, s_1)$	$\mathsf{disease}(jane, aids)$
$\mathsf{symptom}(john, s_2)$	$\mathsf{symptom}(jane, s_4)$	$\mathsf{disease}(john, cancer)$
$\mathsf{symptom}(john, s_3)$		$\mathsf{disease}(ed, polio)$

Note that MedKB could very well be just a database. Assume that $john$ and $jane$ are also users of the system and want to keep their diseases private, so $\mathbf{Priv}(john) = \{\mathsf{disease}(john, cancer)\}$, while $\mathbf{Priv}(jane) = \{\mathsf{disease}(jane, aids)\}$. Consider another user *acct* (an accountant). This person may have the following background knowledge base $\mathbf{BK}(acct)$ in the form of rules (so the underlying logic might be answer set programming).

$$\mathsf{disease}(X, aids) \leftarrow \mathsf{symptom}(X, s_1), \mathsf{symptom}(X, s_4)$$
$$\mathsf{disease}(X, cancer) \leftarrow \mathsf{symptom}(X, s_2), \mathsf{symptom}(X, s_3)$$

We now define the concepts of query and answer to a knowledge base. The precise notation of a query is not so important, only the definition of its answer is. So given a *main knowledge base* $\mathbf{MKB}$ wrt. a *logic L*, we assume there is a set $\mathbf{Q}$ consisting of all queries over $\mathbf{MKB}$.

Definition 3 (query and answer). *We assume that there is a mapping which associates to each* query $Q \in \mathbf{Q}$*, each knowledge base and each semantics in* logic L, *a* belief set *of* L. *This belief set is referred to as the* answer *to* Q *and is denoted by* $\mathbf{Ans}(Q)$.

Users pose a query to the main knowledge base, but the privacy preservation mechanism should allow only answers which do not violate the privacy specifications of users after taking into account, the (presumed) knowledge of the user asking the query.

Definition 4 ((maximal) privacy preserving answer). *A* privacy preserving answer *to a query* Q *over* $\mathbf{MKB}$ *posed by* $u_o \in \mathbf{U}$ *with respect to* $\mathbf{BK}$ *and* $\mathbf{Priv}$ *is* $X \subseteq \mathbf{Ans}(Q)$ *such that for all* $u \in \mathbf{U} \setminus \{u_0\}$ *and for all* $p \in \mathbf{Priv}(u)$, *if* $p \notin \mathbf{ACC}(\mathbf{BK}(u_0))$ *then* $p \notin \mathbf{ACC}(X \cup \mathbf{BK}(u_0))$. *A* maximal privacy preserving answer *is a subset maximal privacy preserving answer.*

Note that here we assume that elements of belief sets can be added to knowledge bases, yielding again a knowledge base of the respective logic. We are now ready to formally define the central problem studied in this paper.

Definition 5 (privacy preservation problem). *A privacy preservation problem* P3 *is a tuple* $(\mathbf{MKB}, \mathbf{U}, \mathbf{BK}, \mathbf{Priv}, Q, u_0)$. *Solutions of this problem are all the (maximal) privacy preserving answers to* Q *posed by* u_0 *over* $\mathbf{MKB}$ *with respect to* $\mathbf{BK}$ *and* $\mathbf{Priv}$.

Example 2. Returning to our MedKB example, posing the query $\mathsf{disease}(john, X)$, we would get as an answer the set $\{\mathsf{disease}(john, cancer)\}$. Likewise, the answer to the query $\mathsf{symptom}(john, X)$ is the set $\{\mathsf{symptom}(john, s_1), \mathsf{symptom}(john, s_2), \mathsf{symptom}(john, s_3)\}$.

We assumed that John and Jane want their diseases kept privately. However, the accountant can violate John's privacy by asking the query $\mathsf{symptom}(john, X)$. The answer that *acct* would get from the system is $\{\mathsf{symptom}(john, s_1), \mathsf{symptom}(john, s_2), \mathsf{symptom}(john, s_3)\}$. However, recall that the accountant has some background knowledge including the rule

$$\mathsf{disease}(X, cancer) \leftarrow \mathsf{symptom}(X, s_2), \mathsf{symptom}(X, s_3)$$

which, with the answer of the query, would allow *acct* to infer $\mathsf{disease}(john, cancer)$. Thus the privacy preserving answers to $\mathsf{symptom}(john, X)$ are

$$\begin{aligned}
Ans_1 &= \{\mathsf{symptom}(john, s_1), \mathsf{symptom}(john, s_2)\}\\
Ans_2 &= \{\mathsf{symptom}(john, s_1), \mathsf{symptom}(john, s_3)\}\\
Ans_3 &= \{\mathsf{symptom}(john, s_1)\}\\
Ans_4 &= \{\mathsf{symptom}(john, s_2)\}\\
Ans_5 &= \{\mathsf{symptom}(john, s_3)\}\\
Ans_6 &= \emptyset
\end{aligned}$$

None of these answers allows *acct* to infer the private knowledge $\mathsf{disease}(john, cancer)$. However, except for the answers Ans_1 and Ans_2, which are maximal, all answers yield less information than could be disclosed without infringing privacy requirements. Any system should also provide only one of these answers to the user, because getting for instance both Ans_1 and Ans_2 would again violate John's privacy requirements.

In a practical system, upon disclosing an answer the system should update the respective user's knowledge model in order to avoid privacy infringements by repeated querying. For example, when the system returns Ans_1 to user $acct$, it should modify $\mathbf{BK}(acct)$ in order to reflect the fact that $acct$ now knows $\mathsf{symptom}(john, s_1)$ and $\mathsf{symptom}(john, s_2)$, such that asking the same query again it is made sure that $\mathsf{symptom}(john, s_3)$ will not be disclosed to $acct$.

A related aspect is how the background knowledge base is determined precisely. We do not want to restrict the formalism by making any assumption on this issue, but in practice this will be a system that is maintained dynamically and will derive from both exogenous knowledge (for instance, information provided by an administrator, which may also be information on what knowledge bases a user is actively using) and endogenous knowledge (as in the example above, answers disclosed by the system to a user in the past).

3 Solving Privacy Preservation Problems Using Multi-context Systems and Hybrid Knowledge Bases

The definitions in Section 2 were already slightly geared towards multi-context systems. We recall that a multi-context system in the sense of [7] is a tuple $(C_1, \ldots, C_n)$ where for each i ($1 \leq i \leq n$), $C_i = (L_i, kb_i, br_i)$ where L_i is a logic, kb_i is a knowledge base of L_i and br_i is a set of L_i bridge rules over $\{L_1, \ldots, L_n\}$, where an L_i bridge rule over $\{L_1, \ldots, L_n\}$ is a construct

$$s \leftarrow (r_1 : p_1), \ldots, (r_j : p_j), \text{not } (r_{j+1} : p_{j+1}), \ldots, \text{not } (r_m : p_m)$$

where $1 \leq r_k \leq n$, p_k is an element of a belief set for L_{r_k} and, for each $kb \in \mathbf{KB}_i$, $kb \cup \{s\} \in \mathbf{KB}_i$. Such rules (without negation) were first introduced in [22] and later generalized to include negation (and much more) in [17] and are called "hybrid knowledge bases" based on annotated logic.[1] In the rest of this section, we use multi-construct systems in our syntax simply because a choice has to be made for syntax.

The semantics of a multi-context system is defined by means of *equilibria*. A *belief state* for a multi-context system $(C_1, \ldots, C_n)$ is $S = (S_1, \ldots, S_n)$, where $S_i \in \mathbf{BS}_i$ for $1 \leq i \leq n$. An L_i bridge rule of the form above is applicable in S iff, for $1 \leq k \leq j$, $p_k \in S_{r_k}$ holds and, for $j < k \leq m$, $p_k \notin S_{r_k}$ holds. Let $app(br, S)$ denote the set of all bridge rules in br which are applicable in a belief state S. A belief state $S = (S_1, \ldots, S_n)$ is an equilibrium of a multi-context system $(C_1, \ldots, C_n)$ iff for all $1 \leq i \leq n$, $S_i \in \mathbf{ACC}_i(kb_i \cup \{hd(r) \mid r \in app(br_i, S)\})$, where $hd(r)$ is the head of a bridge rule r, viz. s in the bridge rule schema given above.

---

[1] In [22], the main difference in this syntax was that the $r_i : p_i$'s were instead written $p_i : r_i$. [17] extended this to include not just "annotated" rules in the body, but also many other constructs including references to non-logical data structures and software instead of just logics L_i. However, [7] allows non-atomic constructs in rule bodies. Thus, [7] may be viewed as a generalization of [22] but not of [17].

Given a P3 $(\mathbf{MKB}, \mathbf{U}, \mathbf{BK}, \mathbf{Priv}, Q, u)$, with $\mathbf{U} = \{u_1, \ldots, u_{|\mathbf{U}|}\}$, in order to identify privacy preserving answers, we build a multi-context system $M_{\mathrm{P3}} = (C_1, C_2, C_3, C_4, \ldots, C_{|\mathbf{U}|+3})$, where $C_1 = (L_{\mathbf{MKB}}, \mathbf{MKB}, \emptyset)$, $C_2 = (L_{\mathbf{MKB}}, \emptyset, br_2)$, $C_3 = (L_{\mathbf{MKB}}, \emptyset, br_3)$, $C_4 = (L_{\mathbf{BK}(u_1)}, \mathbf{BK}(u_1), br_4) \ldots, C_{|\mathbf{U}|+3} = (L_{\mathbf{BK}(u_{|\mathbf{U}|})}, \mathbf{BK}(u_{|\mathbf{U}|}), br_{|\mathbf{U}|+3})$. Here L_{kb} is the logic of the knowledge base kb. The meaning is that C_1 provides just the belief sets for $\mathbf{MKB}$ (no bridge rules), C_2 and C_3 are used to identify those belief sets which constitute privacy preserving answers, while $C_4, \ldots, C_{|\mathbf{U}|+3}$ represent the user information, that is, the background knowledge base of the querying user and the privacy requirements of the other users. The important part are the bridge rules, which we will describe next. In many cases, we will create one rule for each symbol that can occur in some belief set of $\mathbf{Ans}(Q)$, so for convenience let $\mathcal{D} = \{p \mid p \in B, B \in \mathbf{Ans}(Q)\}$.

The set br_2 contains one bridge rule $p \leftarrow (1 : p), \mathrm{not}\ (3 : p)$ for each $p \in \mathcal{D}$. Symmetrically, br_3 contains one bridge rule $p \leftarrow (1 : p), \mathrm{not}\ (2 : p)$ for each $p \in \mathcal{D}$. The intuition is that the belief sets of C_2 will be subsets of the belief set of C_1 in any equilibrium, and hence potential privacy preserving answers. C_3 exists only for technical reasons.

For i such that $u_{i-2} = u$, thus for the context C_i of the querying user, we add one bridge rule $p \leftarrow (2 : p)$ for each $p \in \mathcal{D}$. This means that in any equilibrium, the belief set for i will contain all consequences of the privacy preserving answer with respect to u's knowledge base.

For each i where $3 < i \leq |\mathbf{U}| + 3$ such that $u_{i-2} \neq u$, thus for contexts representing non-querying users, br_i contains one bridge rule $p_1 \leftarrow (j : p_1), \ldots, (j : p_l), \mathrm{not}\ (i : p_1)$ for $u_j = u$ and $\{p_1, \ldots, p_l\} \in \mathbf{Priv}(u_{i-2})$. The idea is that no belief state can be an equilibrium, in which the querying user derives information which u_{i-2} wants to keep private.

Note that the tuple $(S_1, S_2, S_3, S_4, \ldots, S_{|\mathbf{U}|+3})$ was constructed in such a way, that S_2 represents the potential privacy preserving answers. The following proposition shows that our construction does indeed reflect this.

Proposition 1. *Given a* P3 $(\mathbf{MKB}, \mathbf{U}, \mathbf{BK}, \mathbf{Priv}, Q, u)$*, each equilibrium belief state* $(S_1, S_2, S_3, S_4, \ldots, S_{|\mathbf{U}|+3})$ *for* M_{P3} *is such that* S_2 *is a privacy preserving answer to* P3*. Also, each privacy preserving answer* S *to* P3 *is the second component of an equilibrium for* M_{P3}.

Example 3. In the example examined above, consider the P3 $(\mathsf{MedKB}, \{john, jane, acct\}, \mathbf{BK}, \mathbf{Priv}, \mathsf{symptom}(john, X), acct)$. Note that we did not define background knowledge bases for users $john$ and $jane$, but their nature is not important for the example, just assume that they exist. We also have not defined any privacy statement for $acct$, but also this is not important for our example and we will assume that it is empty, that is, $acct$ does not require anything to be kept private. We construct a multi-context system $(C_1, C_2, C_3, C_4, C_5, C_6)$ where $C_1 = (L_{\mathsf{MedKB}}, \mathsf{MedKB}, \emptyset)$, $C_2 = (L_{\mathsf{MedKB}}, \emptyset, br_2)$ with bridge rules br_2 being

$$\mathsf{symptom}(john, s_1) \leftarrow (1 : \mathsf{symptom}(john, s_1)), \mathrm{not}\ (3 : \mathsf{symptom}(john, s_1))$$
$$\mathsf{symptom}(john, s_2) \leftarrow (1 : \mathsf{symptom}(john, s_2)), \mathrm{not}\ (3 : \mathsf{symptom}(john, s_2))$$
$$\mathsf{symptom}(john, s_3) \leftarrow (1 : \mathsf{symptom}(john, s_3)), \mathrm{not}\ (3 : \mathsf{symptom}(john, s_3))$$

then $C_3 = (L_{\mathsf{MedKB}}, \emptyset, br_3)$ with bridge rules br_3 being

$$\begin{aligned}
&\mathsf{symptom}(john, s_1) \leftarrow (1 : \mathsf{symptom}(john, s_1)), \mathrm{not}\ (2 : \mathsf{symptom}(john, s_1))\\
&\mathsf{symptom}(john, s_2) \leftarrow (1 : \mathsf{symptom}(john, s_2)), \mathrm{not}\ (2 : \mathsf{symptom}(john, s_2))\\
&\mathsf{symptom}(john, s_3) \leftarrow (1 : \mathsf{symptom}(john, s_3)), \mathrm{not}\ (2 : \mathsf{symptom}(john, s_3))
\end{aligned}$$

then $C_4 = (L_{\mathbf{BK}(john)}, \mathbf{BK}(john), br_4)$ with bridge rules br_4 being

$$\mathsf{disease}(john, cancer) \leftarrow (6 : \mathsf{disease}(john, cancer)), \mathrm{not}\ (4 : \mathsf{disease}(john, cancer))$$

then $C_5 = (L_{\mathbf{BK}(jane)}, \mathbf{BK}(jane), br_5)$ with bridge rules br_5 being

$$\mathsf{disease}(jane, aids) \leftarrow (6 : \mathsf{disease}(jane, aids)), \mathrm{not}\ (5 : \mathsf{disease}(jane, aids)$$

and finally $C_6 = (L_{\mathbf{BK}(acct)}, \mathbf{BK}(acct), br_6)$ with bridge rules br_6 being

$$\begin{aligned}
&\mathsf{symptom}(john, s_1) \leftarrow (2 : \mathsf{symptom}(john, s_1))\\
&\mathsf{symptom}(john, s_2) \leftarrow (2 : \mathsf{symptom}(john, s_2))\\
&\mathsf{symptom}(john, s_3) \leftarrow (2 : \mathsf{symptom}(john, s_3))
\end{aligned}$$

M_{P3} has six equilibria

$$\begin{aligned}
E_1 &= (S_{\mathsf{MedKB}}, Ans_1, \mathbf{Ans}(\mathsf{symptom}(john, X)) \setminus Ans_1, Ans_1, \emptyset, \emptyset)\\
E_2 &= (S_{\mathsf{MedKB}}, Ans_2, \mathbf{Ans}(\mathsf{symptom}(john, X)) \setminus Ans_2, Ans_2, \emptyset, \emptyset)\\
E_3 &= (S_{\mathsf{MedKB}}, Ans_3, \mathbf{Ans}(\mathsf{symptom}(john, X)) \setminus Ans_3, Ans_3, \emptyset, \emptyset)\\
E_4 &= (S_{\mathsf{MedKB}}, Ans_4, \mathbf{Ans}(\mathsf{symptom}(john, X)) \setminus Ans_4, Ans_4, \emptyset, \emptyset)\\
E_5 &= (S_{\mathsf{MedKB}}, Ans_5, \mathbf{Ans}(\mathsf{symptom}(john, X)) \setminus Ans_5, Ans_5, \emptyset, \emptyset)\\
E_6 &= (S_{\mathsf{MedKB}}, Ans_6, \mathbf{Ans}(\mathsf{symptom}(john, X)) \setminus Ans_6, Ans_6, \emptyset, \emptyset)
\end{aligned}$$

where S_{MedKB} is as in Example 1 and the second belief set of each E_i is exactly the respective Ans_i of Example 2 and the third belief set is the complement of Ans_i with respect to $\mathbf{Ans}(\mathsf{symptom}(john, X)) = \{\mathsf{symptom}(john, s_1), \mathsf{symptom}(john, s_2), \mathsf{symptom}(john, s_3)\}$.

We would like to point out that in this construction the original knowledge bases are not changed, we only create contexts and bridge rules. All of the background knowledge bases could be multi-context systems themselves; for instance, if the user model for *acct* foresees that *acct* is aware of SNOMED and PEPID, then *acct*'s background knowledge base could be a multi-context system comprising these two medical knowledge bases.

In order to obtain maximal privacy preserving answers using the described construction, the simplest way is to postprocess all privacy preserving answers. More involved solutions would have to interfere with the underlying multi-context system reasoner, for instance by dynamically changing the multi-context system. It is not clear to us at the moment whether it is possible to modify the construction such that the equilibria of the obtained multi-context system correspond directly to the maximal privacy preserving answers.

We note that the "equilibria" in multi-context systems are similar to the non-monotonic constructs in the prior "hybrid knowledge bases" work of [17] based on annotated logic and so the results of this section also show that hybrid knowledge bases can be used to encode privacy constructs. Hybrid knowledge bases were extensively implemented and used to build a very large number of applications on top of real databases [3].

4 Solving First-Order Privacy Preservation Problems Using Default Logic

In this section, we show that the formalism in [10], called *first-order privacy preservation problem*, is an instance of the formalism defined in Section 2.

4.1 First-Order Privacy Preservation Problems

For defining a first-order language (without equality), we assume the existence of some finite set of constant symbols, function symbols and predicate symbols. As usual, a term is inductively defined as follows: (i) Each constant is a term, (ii) Each variable is a term, and (iii) if f is an n-ary predicate symbol and $t_1, \dots, t_n$ are terms, then $f(t_1, \dots, t_n)$ is a term. A *ground term* is any term that contains no variable symbols. Similarly, if p is an n-ary predicate symbol and $t_1, \dots, t_n$ are terms, then $p(t_1, \dots, t_n)$ is an atom. A *ground atom* is any atom that contains no variable symbols. A well formed formula (wff) is inductively defined as follows. (i) Every atom is a wff, (ii) If F, G are wffs then so are $(F \wedge G), (F \vee G)$ and $\neg F$. The semantics is given as usual (all formulae are considered to be universally quantified, so we do not need to introduce quantifiers).

Definition 6 (first-order privacy preservation problem). *A first-order privacy preservation problem* $(\mathbf{MKB}, \mathbf{U}, \mathbf{BK}, \mathbf{Priv}, Q, u_0)$ *is a* P3 *in which* $\mathbf{MKB}$ *is a set of ground atoms (also called logic database), each* $\mathbf{BK}^t(u)$ *is a set of wffs, and* $\mathbf{Priv}(u)$ *is also a set of wffs, represented by its set of models.*

Now, given a first-order privacy preservation problem $(\mathbf{MKB}, \mathbf{U}, \mathbf{BK}, \mathbf{Priv}, Q, u_0)$, we define a translation trans, which produces a default logic theory $\Delta = (D, W)$ such that there is a bijective correspondence between the solutions to the privacy preservation problem and the extensions of the default theory (restricted to the query) returned by the translation [8]. The consequence of this translation is that standard (and well studied) methods to evaluate default logic theories may be used to preserve privacy effectively, efficiently, and elegantly.

We refer to standard textbooks (e.g. [18,6]) for an introduction to default theories. We denote defaults as usual by $\frac{a\,:\,b}{c}$ *if a holds and it is consistent to assume b then conclude c*. Most of our defaults are supernormal, i.e. of the form $\frac{:\,f}{f}$. A default theory is a pair $\Delta = (D, W)$ where the first component consists of the whole set of defaults and the second is a set of formulae (the classical theory).

Definition 7 (trans). *Let* $(\mathbf{MKB}, \mathbf{U}, \mathbf{BK}, \mathbf{Priv}, Q, u_0)$ *be a first-order privacy preservation problem. The* translation, $\mathsf{trans}(\mathbf{MKB}, \mathbf{U}, \mathbf{BK}, \mathbf{Priv}, Q, u_0)$ *of a privacy preservation problem into default logic is the default logic theory* $\Delta = (D, W)$ *where:*

$$W = \mathbf{BK}(u_0).$$

$$D = \{\frac{: f}{f} \mid f \in \mathbf{MKB}\} \bigcup$$

$$\{\frac{p\ :}{\neg p} \mid (\exists u \in \mathbf{U} - \{u_0\})\, p \in \mathbf{Priv}(u)\ \mathit{and}\ \mathbf{BK}(u_0) \not\models p\}.$$

We now present an example to show how the result of transforming the privacy preservation problem into default logic looks like.

Example 4. Let us return to the case of the accountant. Assume that MedKB of Example 1 is a logic database, that the "rules" of **BK** and **Priv** in Example 1 are wffs, making the problem in the example a first-order privacy preservation problem. In this case, W consists of the following two rules (which need to be written slightly differently so as to comply with the wff's as defined in the beginning of this section):

$$\mathsf{symptom}(X, s_1)\ \&\ \mathsf{symptom}(X, s_4) \rightarrow \mathsf{disease}(X, aids)$$
$$\mathsf{symptom}(X, s_2)\ \&\ \mathsf{symptom}(X, s_3) \rightarrow \mathsf{disease}(X, cancer).$$

In addition, D consists of the following defaults:

$$\frac{: \mathsf{symptom}(john,s_1)}{\mathsf{symptom}(john,s_1)} \quad \frac{: \mathsf{symptom}(john,s_2)}{\mathsf{symptom}(john,s_2)} \quad \frac{: \mathsf{symptom}(john,s_3)}{\mathsf{symptom}(john,s_3)}$$

$$\frac{: \mathsf{symptom}(jane,s_1)}{\mathsf{symptom}(jane,s_1)} \quad \frac{: \mathsf{symptom}(jane,s_4)}{\mathsf{symptom}(jane,s_4)}$$

$$\frac{: \mathsf{disease}(ed,polio)}{\mathsf{disease}(ed,polio)} \quad \frac{: \mathsf{disease}(jane,aids)}{\mathsf{disease}(jane,aids)} \quad \frac{: \mathsf{disease}(john,cancer)}{\mathsf{disease}(john,cancer)}$$

$$\frac{\mathsf{disease}(jane,aids)\ :}{\neg\mathsf{disease}(jane,aids)} \quad \frac{\mathsf{disease}(john,cancer)\ :}{\neg\mathsf{disease}(john,cancer)}$$

Note that we are assuming here that Ed has not marked his disease as being a private fact.

Our translation uses linear space. The time complexity of the translation depends on the complexity of checking entailment. For example, assuming a finite number of constants in our language (reasonable) and assuming that all rules in **BK** are definite clauses (i.e. clauses with exactly one atom), then the translation is implementable in polynomial time. But if **BK** consists of arbitrary first order formulas, then the translation can take exponential time.

We remind the reader of some basic terminology associated with default theories. Given a default $d = \frac{\alpha:\beta}{\gamma}$, we use the notation $pre(d)$ to denote α, $j(d)$ to denote β and $c(d)$ to denote γ. In addition, given any default theory $\Delta = (D, W)$, we may associate with Δ, a mapping Γ_Δ which maps sets of wffs to sets of wffs. $\Gamma_\Delta(Y) = \mathsf{CN}(W \cup \{pre(d) \rightarrow c(d) \mid j(d) \text{ is consistent with } Y\})$. As usual, the function $\mathsf{CN}(X)$

denotes the set of all first order logical consequences of X. A set Y of wffs is an *extension* of Δ iff $Y = \Gamma_\Delta(Y)$.

We are now ready to present a key result linking the privacy preservation problem to default logic extensions. Suppose we consider any privacy preservation problem. The privacy preserving answers to that privacy preservation problem are in a one-one correspondence with the consistent extensions of the translation (restricted to the query) of the privacy preservation problem into default logic (using the translation trans shown in Definition 7).

Theorem 1. *Suppose that Q is an atom and that $(\mathbf{MKB}, \mathbf{U}, \mathbf{BK}, \mathbf{Priv}, Q, u_0)$ is a first-order privacy preservation problem and* $\mathsf{trans}(\mathbf{MKB}, \mathbf{U}, \mathbf{BK}, \mathbf{Priv}, Q, u_0) = \Delta = (D, W)$. *Then: X is a solution to the above privacy preservation problem iff there is a consistent extension E of $\Delta = (D, W)$ such that $X = \{A\theta \mid A\theta \in E \cap \mathbf{MKB}\}$.*

In order to prove Theorem 1, we first formulate a useful abstract lemma.

Lemma 1. *Let W, MKB and P be consistent sets of formulae s.t. $W \cup MKB$ is consistent as well. Let $D_P = \{\frac{p\,:}{\neg p} : p \in P\}$ and $D_{MKB} = \{\frac{:\,f}{f} : f \in MKB\}$.*

Then the consistent extensions of the theory $(D_P \cup D_{MKB}, W)$ are the sets $Cn(W \cup \{f : f \in F\})$ where F is a subset of MKB that is maximal wrt. set inclusion (i.e. there is no larger set F' such that $W \cup \{f : f \in F'\} \not\models p$ for all $p \in P$).

Proof. Clearly the sets $Cn(W \cup \{f : f \in F\})$ where F is a maximal subset of MKB are extensions of the default theory: The defaults in D_P do not apply and we are left with a supernormal default theory (the result follows from well-known characterizations in default logic, see eg. [9,18]).

Conversely, let E be a consistent extension. Then no default in D_P applies. Because extensions are grounded and we are dealing with a supernormal theory, E must have the form $Cn(W \cup \{f : f \in F\})$ for a subset F of MKB. Because E is maximal (no other extension can contain E), the set $Cn(W \cup \{f : f \in F\})$ is maximal in the sense defined in the lemma. □

Now we are able to prove Theorem 1:

Proof. The proof of Theorem 1 is an application of Lemma 1. Suppose X is a solution to $(\mathbf{MKB}, \mathbf{U}, \mathbf{BK}, \mathbf{Priv}, Q, u_0)$ and let $\mathsf{trans}(\mathbf{MKB}, \mathbf{U}, \mathbf{BK}, \mathbf{Priv}, Q, u_0) = \Delta = (D, W)$. Then we let $F := X$, $W := \mathbf{BK}(u_0)$ and $P := \{p : (\exists u \in \mathbf{U} - \{u_0\})\ p \in \mathbf{Priv}(u) \text{ and } \mathbf{BK}(u_0) \not\models p\}$ and apply our lemma. The set $Cn(W \cup \{f : f \in F\})$ is an extension (it is maximal because of (3) and (2) in the definition of a privacy preserving answer).

Conversely let a consistent extension E of $\mathsf{trans}(\mathbf{MKB}, \mathbf{U}, \mathbf{BK}, \mathbf{Priv}, Q, u_0)$ be given and consider $X := \{Q\theta \mid Q\theta \in E \cap \mathbf{MKB}\}$. Our lemma implies that X is a subset of MKB that is maximal. Therefore X is also a privacy preserving answer (if there were a larger X' satisfying (2) in the definition of pp answer, then E would not be maximal and thus not be an extension). □

The preceding theorem applies to *atomic* queries. A straightforward extension of the above proof gives us the following corollary, which applies to arbitrary queries.

Corollary 1. *Suppose that* $(\mathbf{MKB}, \mathbf{U}, \mathbf{BK}, \mathbf{Priv}, Q, u_0)$ *is a privacy preservation problem and that* $\mathsf{trans}(\mathbf{MKB}, \mathbf{U}, \mathbf{BK}, \mathbf{Priv}, Q, u_0) = (D, W)$*. Then:* X *is a solution to the above privacy preservation problem iff there is a consistent extension* E *of* (D, W) *such that* $X = \{Q\theta \mid Q\theta \in E \cap \mathbf{MKB}\}$.

In order to illustrate this theorem, we revisit the example privacy preservation problem and its default logic translation that we presented earlier.

Example 5. Let us return to the MedKB example. Consider the privacy preservation problem of Example 1 and the default logic translation shown in Example 4. As seen in Example 1, there are two privacy preserving answers to this problem. They are:

$$Ans1 = \{\mathsf{symptom}(john, s_1), \mathsf{symptom}(john, s_2)\}$$
$$Ans2 = \{\mathsf{symptom}(john, s_1), \mathsf{symptom}(john, s_3)\}$$

The default logic translation of this privacy preservation problem shown in Example 4 has exactly four consistent extensions $E_1, \ldots, E_4$.

$$\begin{aligned}
E_1 &= \mathsf{CN}(W \cup \{\mathsf{symptom}(john, s_1), \mathsf{symptom}(john, s_2), \\
&\qquad \mathsf{symptom}(jane, s_1), \mathsf{disease}(ed, polio)\}) \\
E_2 &= \mathsf{CN}(W \cup \{\mathsf{symptom}(john, s_1), \mathsf{symptom}(john, s_3), \\
&\qquad \mathsf{symptom}(jane, s_1), \mathsf{disease}(ed, polio)\}) \\
E_3 &= \mathsf{CN}(W \cup \{\mathsf{symptom}(john, s_1), \mathsf{symptom}(john, s_2), \\
&\qquad \mathsf{symptom}(jane, s_4), \mathsf{disease}(ed, polio)\}) \\
E_4 &= \mathsf{CN}(W \cup \{\mathsf{symptom}(john, s_1), \mathsf{symptom}(john, s_3), \\
&\qquad \mathsf{symptom}(jane, s_4), \mathsf{disease}(ed, polio)\})
\end{aligned}$$

However, if we are only interested in answers to the query $\mathsf{symptom}(john, X)$ in the above extensions, then the extensions E_1, E_4 only contain $\{\mathsf{symptom}(john, s_1), \mathsf{symptom}(john, s_2)\}$ while E_2, E_3 only contain $\{\mathsf{symptom}(john, s_1), \mathsf{symptom}(john, s_3)\}$. These restrictions of the extensions are in a one-one correspondence with the privacy preserving answers to the query posed by the accountant.

4.2 Complexity of First-Order Privacy Preservation Problems

Computing a privacy-preserving answer typically involves *guessing* a subset of answers, and subsequently checking it with respect to privacy preservation and maximality. Intuitively, this computational task has a correspondence to common non-monotonic reasoning tasks, because the maximality condition for privacy-preserving answers has its counterpart the minimality conditions in non-monotonic semantics, while guessing a model candidate and checking it on a set of formulae is even more closely related.

It therefore does not come as a surprise that a non-monotonic logic neatly represents the privacy preservation problem. Concerning the complexity analysis, we can indeed leverage the translation trans to use well-known results concerning the complexity of default logic in order to prove membership of various subclasses of first-order privacy preservation problems.

As already shown in [19], default reasoning involving function symbols is undecidable. Note that computing maximal privacy preserving answers involves checking $\mathbf{BK}(u_0) \not\models p$, which is clearly undecidable for arbitrary first-order formulae. We will therefore focus on decidable fragments. In particular, we will assume in our analysis below that problems are restricted to those for which deciding $\mathbf{BK} \not\models p$, $p \in \mathbf{Priv}$ is feasible in polynomial time. We will focus on theories in a Datalog setting, the data complexity (we consider only $\mathbf{MKB}$, i.e. the knowledge base, as input, $\mathbf{BK}$ and $\mathbf{Priv}$ are fixed) of which corresponds to propositional default theories.

Then, membership can be seen by virtue of trans and the form of formulae in $\mathbf{BK}$ and $\mathbf{Priv}$. In particular, brave reasoning for non-disjunctive default theories is NP-complete (see e.g. [16,20] for such classes), while brave reasoning for arbitrary default theories is Σ_2^P-complete, see [14] and [21].
We thus consider first-order privacy preservation problems with the following restrictions:

1. We vary $\mathbf{BK}(u)$ to be an arbitrary theory (without syntactic retrictions), a non-disjunctive theory (as in [16,20]), and a set of facts (a theory containing only ground atoms).
2. We vary $\mathbf{Priv}(u)$ to be a set of arbitrary formulas, a non-disjunctive theory, and a set of facts.

Table 1 summarizes our results on the complexity of privacy preservation in the Datalog case.

Table 1. Data Complexity of First-Order Privacy Preservation Problems

Priv/BK	Facts	Non-disjunctive	Arbitrary
Facts	P	P	Σ_2^P
Non-disjunctive	NP	NP	Σ_2^P
Arbitrary	Σ_2^P	Σ_2^P	Σ_2^P

Theorem 2. *The data complexity for first-order privacy preservation problems without function symbols under various syntactic restrictions are as reported in Table 1. Completeness holds for* NP *and* Σ_2^P *results.*

Next, we will prove some of the hardness results.

Corollary 2. *First-order privacy preservation problems with* $\mathbf{BK}$ *containing non-disjunctive rules and* $\mathbf{Priv}$ *made of facts is hard for* NP.

Proof. We show NP-hardness by a reduction from 3SAT to a first-order privacy preservation problem in which $\mathbf{BK}()$ contains only rules with negation on $\mathbf{MKB}$ predicates and in which $\mathbf{Priv}$ contains only one fact: Given a CNF $\phi = \bigwedge_{i=1}^{n} L_{i,1} \vee L_{i,2} \vee L_{i,3}$, we create a P3 with $\mathbf{MKB} = \{c_i \mid c_i \text{ is an atom in } \phi\} \cup \{q\}$, two users u_0, u_1, $\mathbf{BK}(u_0) = \{L'_{i,1} \wedge L'_{i,2} \wedge L'_{i,3} \rightarrow unsat\}$, where $(\neg x)' = x$ and $x' = \neg x$. Finally, $\mathbf{Priv}(u_1) = \{unsat\}$, and $Q = q$. It is not hard to see that q is an answer iff ϕ is satisfiable: If q is an answer, then a truth assignment can be obtained from the subset $X \subseteq \mathbf{MKB}$ in which exactly the c_i in X are interpreted as true.

As $X \cup \mathbf{BK}(()u_0) \not\models unsat$, no conjunct in ϕ evaluates to false under this assignment, which therefore satisfies ϕ. Conversely, if ϕ is satisfiable, each cardinality maximal satisfying truth assignment induces an $X \subseteq \mathbf{MKB}$, such that $X \cup \mathbf{BK}(()u_0) \not\models unsat$. □

Corollary 3. *First-order privacy preservation problems with empty* $\mathbf{BK}$ *and arbitrary* $\mathbf{Priv}$ *are hard for* Σ_2^P.

Proof. We show Σ_2^P-hardness by a reduction from a $QBF_{2,\exists}$ to a P3 in which $\mathbf{BK}$ is empty and $\mathbf{Priv}$ contains arbitrary formulae. Consider $\psi = \exists x_1 \cdots \exists x_n \forall y_1 \cdots \forall y_m \phi$, where ϕ is a propositional formula. We create a P3 with $\mathbf{MKB} = \{x_1, \ldots, x_n\} \cup \{q\}$, two users u_0, u_1, $\mathbf{Priv}(u_1) = \{\neg\phi\}$, and $Q = q$. An answer X induces a valuation ν of the existentially quantified variables. Then, no extension ν' of ν to the universally quantified variables can exist such that ϕ is false, hence ψ is valid. Conversely, if ψ is valid, each cardinality maximal satisfying truth assignment for $x_1, \ldots, x_n$ induces an answer. □

This proof can easily be adapted so that $\mathbf{BK}(u_0)$ contains the arbitrary formula $(\neg\phi) \rightarrow unsat$ and $\mathbf{Priv}(u_1)$ contains only $unsat$.

All complexity results above refer to propositional theories or data complexity. In our setting this means that only $\mathbf{MKB}$ is considered as input, while especially $\mathbf{BK}$ and $\mathbf{Priv}$ are considered to be fixed. For considering program complexity, i.e. the knowledge base $\mathbf{MKB}$ is fixed but $\mathbf{BK}$ and $\mathbf{Priv}$ are considered as inputs, we can adapt the data complexity results by using techniques from [15]. Due to space constraints, we do not present proofs. It is obvious that allowing programs (not just facts) as input increases the complexity problem. This is shown in Table 2. Allowing function symbols would make all problems undecidable.

Theorem 3. *The program complexity for problems without function symbols under various syntactic restrictions are as reported in the Table 2.*

Table 2. Program Complexity of Privacy Preservation Problems

Priv/BK	Facts	Non-disj.	Arbitrary
Facts	EXPTIME	EXPTIME	$\text{NEXPTIME}^{\text{NP}}$
Non-disj.	NEXPTIME	NEXPTIME	$\text{NEXPTIME}^{\text{NP}}$
Arbitrary	$\text{NEXPTIME}^{\text{NP}}$	$\text{NEXPTIME}^{\text{NP}}$	$\text{NEXPTIME}^{\text{NP}}$

4.3 Algorithm for First-Order Privacy Preservation Problems

We now describe an algorithm that leverages our translation to default logic. First and foremost, we recall the important observation of [2] that Reiter's Γ_Δ operator is anti-monotonic - hence, the operator Γ_Δ^2 that applies Γ_Δ is monotonic. As a consequence, Γ_Δ^2 has both a least fixpoint and a greatest fixpoint, denoted $\mathsf{lfp}(\Gamma_\Delta^2)$ and $\mathsf{gfp}(\Gamma_\Delta^2)$ respectively.

Theorem 4 ([2]). *Recall the following properties:*

1. *If* $Y_1 \subseteq Y_2$ *then* $\Gamma_\Delta(Y_2) \subseteq \Gamma_\Delta(Y_1)$.
2. Γ^2_Δ *has a least and a greatest fixpoint, denoted respectively as* $\mathsf{lfp}(\Gamma^2_\Delta)$ *and* $\mathsf{gfp}(\Gamma^2_\Delta)$.
3. $\Gamma_\Delta(\mathsf{lfp}(\Gamma^2_\Delta)) = \mathsf{gfp}(\Gamma^2_\Delta)$.

An immediate consequence of the above theorem is that one can compute extensions of default theories by first computing $\mathsf{lfp}(\Gamma^2_\Delta)$ and $\mathsf{gfp}(\Gamma^2_\Delta)$. Anything in $\mathsf{lfp}(\Gamma^2_\Delta)$ is true in all extensions, while anything not in $\mathsf{gfp}(\Gamma^2_\Delta)$ is false in all extensions. We can therefore start by computing both $\mathsf{lfp}(\Gamma^2_\Delta)$ and $\mathsf{gfp}(\Gamma^2_\Delta)$. If $\mathsf{lfp}(\Gamma^2_\Delta)$ is not an extension, we nondeterministically add things in $\mathsf{gfp}(\Gamma^2_\Delta)$ to the default theory and iteratively compute the least fixpoint of Γ^2_Δ w.r.t. the modified theory. This algorithm for arbitrary default theories gives rise to the specialization for computing answers depicted in Figure 1.

P3Alg$(\mathbf{MKB}, \mathbf{U}, \mathbf{BK}, \mathbf{Priv}, Q, u_0)$

$\Delta = \mathsf{trans}(\mathbf{MKB}, \mathbf{U}, \mathbf{BK}, \mathbf{Priv}, Q, u_0) = (D, W)$;

$Todo = \mathbf{MKB} \cap (\mathsf{gfp}(\Gamma^2_\Delta) \setminus \mathsf{lfp}(\Gamma^2_\Delta))$;

if $\mathsf{lfp}(\Gamma^2_\Delta) = \Gamma_\Delta(\mathsf{lfp}(\Gamma^2_\Delta))$ **then**

  $done = true$;

while $Todo \neq \emptyset \wedge \neg done$ **do**

  Nondeterministically select an $a \in Todo$;

  Let $\Delta = (D, W \cup \{a\})$;

  if $\mathsf{lfp}(\Gamma^2_\Delta) = \Gamma_\Delta(\mathsf{lfp}(\Gamma^2_\Delta))$ **then**

    $done = true$;

  else

    $Todo = Todo \setminus \{a\}$;

% **end-while**

return $\mathbf{MKB} \cap \mathsf{lfp}(\Gamma^2_\Delta)$;

Fig. 1. Algorithm computing privacy preserving answers

The algorithm proceeds as follows: First the problem is translated to a default theory using trans. Subsequently, the least and greatest fixpoint of Γ^2_Δ are computed. Anything which is in the greatest, but not in the least fixpoint can or cannot be true in some extension, so we store it in $Todo$ to nondeterministically assume its truth.

The crucial point here is that we restrict these nondeterministic choices to $\mathbf{MKB}$, which can dramatically decrease the search space. Then we enter the nondeterministic phase of the algorithm, in which a truth assignment for $Todo$ is generated until a fixpoint (i.e., an extension) is reached, if at all. As a final step, a projection of the extension onto $\mathbf{MKB}$ is generated. The following proposition states that the above algorithm is always guaranteed to return the correct answer.

Proposition 2. *Let* $(\mathbf{MKB}, \mathbf{U}, \mathbf{BK}, \mathbf{Priv}, Q, u_0)$ *be a first-order privacy preservation problem. Then the algorithm* **P3Alg**$(\mathbf{MKB}, \mathbf{U}, \mathbf{BK}, \mathbf{Priv}, Q, u_0)$ *returns* X *iff* X *is a privacy preserving answer to* $(\mathbf{MKB}, \mathbf{U}, \mathbf{BK}, \mathbf{Priv}, Q, u_0)$.

5 Conclusion and Future Work

We have presented a general definition of the privacy preservation problem, which allows for using knowledge bases of different kinds. Finding privacy preserving answers can then be accomplished by building an appropriate multi-context system and computing one of its belief states. Since systems for solving multi-context systems begin to emerge, for example DMCS [1], this also implies that these privacy preserving answers can be effectively computed.

However, usually one is interested in maximal privacy preserving answers. It is unclear to us whether a similar construction to the one presented in this paper can be used for finding privacy preserving answers which are maximal, by just creating appropriate contexts and bridge rules and without modifying the involved knowledge bases or adding new knowledge bases of particular logics. One possible line of investigation is to examine work on diagnosing inconsistent multi-context systems [11,4], since in diagnosis tasks there is an implicit minimization criterion, which could be exploited for encoding maximality.

Furthermore, we showed that the formalism subsumes an earlier definition of the privacy preservation problem, for which it is possible to determine maximal privacy preserving answers by a translation into default logic. For this formalism, we conjecture that a similar transformation to first-order theories interpreted using the stable model semantics [13] exists. In future work, we intend to investigate such a transformation in detail.

References

1. Bairakdar, S.E., Dao-Tran, M., Eiter, T., Fink, M., Krennwallner, T.: The DMCS Solver for Distributed Nonmonotonic Multi-Context Systems. In: Janhunen, T., Niemelä, I. (eds.) JELIA 2010. LNCS, vol. 6341, pp. 352–355. Springer, Heidelberg (2010)
2. Baral, C., Subrahmanian, V.: Dualities Between Alternative Semantics for Logic Programming and Non-Monotonic Reasoning. Journal of Automated Reasoning 10(3), 399–420 (1993)
3. Benton, J., Subrahmanian, V.: Hybrid Knowledge Bases for Missile Siting Applications. In: IEEE Conference on AI Applications, pp. 141–148 (1993)
4. Bögl, M., Eiter, T., Fink, M., Schüller, P.: The MCS-IE System for Explaining Inconsistency in Multi-Context Systems. In: Janhunen, T., Niemelä, I. (eds.) JELIA 2010. LNCS, vol. 6341, pp. 356–359. Springer, Heidelberg (2010)
5. Bonatti, P.A., Kraus, S., Subrahmanian, V.: Foundations of secure deductive databases. IEEE Transactions on Knowledge and Data Engineering 7(3), 406–422 (1995)
6. Brewka, G., Dix, J., Konolige, K.: Nonmonotonic Reasoning: An Overview. CSLI Lecture Notes, vol. 73. CSLI Publications, Stanford (1997)
7. Brewka, G., Eiter, T.: Equilibria in Heterogeneous Nonmonotonic Multi-Context Systems. In: Proceedings of the Twenty-Second National Conference on Artificial Intelligence (AAAI 2007), pp. 385–390. AAAI Press (2007)
8. Cadoli, M., Eiter, T., Gottlob, G.: Default Logic as a Query Language. IEEE Transactions on Knowledge and Data Engineering 9(3), 448–463 (1997)
9. Dix, J.: Default Theories of Poole-Type and a Method for Constructing Cumulative Versions of Default Logic. In: Neumann, B. (ed.) Proc. of 10th European Conf. on Artificial Intelligence ECAI 1992, pp. 289–293. John Wiley & Sons (1992)

10. Dix, J., Faber, W., Subrahmanian, V.: The Relationship between Reasoning about Privacy and Default Logics. In: Sutcliffe, G., Voronkov, A. (eds.) LPAR 2005. LNCS (LNAI), vol. 3835, pp. 637–650. Springer, Heidelberg (2005)
11. Eiter, T., Fink, M., Schüller, P., Weinzierl, A.: Finding Explanations of Inconsistency in Multi-Context Systems. In: Lin, F., Sattler, U., Truszczyński, M. (eds.) Proceedings of the Twelfth International Conference on Knowledge Representation and Reasoning (KR 2010), AAAI Press (2010)
12. Faber, W.: Privacy Preservation Using Multi-Context Systems. In: Mileo, A., Fink, M. (eds.) Proceedings of the 2nd International Workshop on Logic-based Interpretation of Context: Modeling and Applications, May 2011, pp. 45–51 (2011)
13. Ferraris, P., Lee, J., Lifschitz, V.: A New Perspective on Stable Models. In: Twentieth International Joint Conference on Artificial Intelligence (IJCAI 2007), pp. 372–379 (January 2007)
14. Gottlob, G.: Complexity Results for Nonmonotonic Logics. Journal of Logic and Computation 2(3), 397–425 (1992)
15. Gottlob, G., Leone, N., Veith, H.: Succinctness as a Source of Expression Complexity. Annals of Pure and Applied Logic 97(1-3), 231–260 (1999)
16. Kautz, H., Selman, B.: Hard Problems for Simple Default Logics. Artificial Intelligence 49, 243–279 (1991)
17. Lu, J., Nerode, A., Subrahmanian, V.: Hybrid Knowedge Bases. IEEE Transactions on Knowledge and Data Engineering 8(3), 773–785 (1996)
18. Marek, W., Truszczyński, M.: Nonmonotonic Logics; Context-Dependent Reasoning, 1st edn. Springer, Berlin (1993)
19. Reiter, R.: A Logic for Default Reasoning. Artificial Intelligence 13(1-2), 81–132 (1980)
20. Stillman, J.: It's Not My Default: The Complexity of Membership Problems in Restricted Propositional Default Logic. In: Proceedings AAAI 1990, pp. 571–579 (1990)
21. Stillman, J.: The Complexity of Propositional Default Logic. In: Proceedings AAAI 1992, pp. 794–799 (1992)
22. Subrahmanian, V.: Amalgamating Knowedge Bases. ACM Transactions on Database Systems 19(2), 291–331 (1994)
23. Winslett, M., Smith, K., Qian, X.: Formal query languages for secure relational databases. ACM Transactions on Database Systems 19(4), 626–662 (1994)
24. Zhao, L., Qian, J., Chang, L., Cai, G.: Using ASP for knowledge management with user authorization. Data & Knowledge Engineering 69(8), 737–762 (2010)

Simulating Production Rules Using ACTHEX*

Thomas Eiter, Cristina Feier, and Michael Fink

Institute of Information Systems, Vienna University of Technology,
Favoritenstraße 9-11, A-1040 Vienna, Austria
lastname@kr.tuwien.ac.at

Abstract. Production rules are a premier formalism to describe actions which, given that certain conditions are met, change the state of a factual knowledge base and/or effect a change of the external environment in which they are situated, based on an operational semantics. ACTHEX is a recent formalism extending HEX programs, such that the specification of declarative knowledge in the form of logic programming rules can be interleaved with a type of condition-action rules which prescribe the execution of (sequences of) actions that can change the external environment. Under the provision of a specific semantics of conditions, the operational semantics of production rules can be simulated using the model-based semantics of ACTHEX. Given that the latter features abstract access to external sources of computation, it can capture a range of concrete execution semantics and, moreover, facilitate access to heterogeneous information sources.

Keywords: ACTHEX, production rules.

1 Introduction

Production rules are one of the most successful rule paradigms with regard to practical applications. Since more than three decades, they have been deployed to various domains (see e.g. [28] for an overview of early production systems); tools and platforms like JRules, Clips, Jess, or Drools have become popular. They are largely based on theoretical foundations and key technology that has been developed in the rise of the paradigm. In the recent years, there has been a reviving interest in foundational research on production rules, triggered by extensions like the combination of a production rule system (PRS) with ontologies or linked data, which surfaces in the context of the Semantic Web. Formalisms of W3C's Rule Interchange Format (RIF) working group address this, aiming to provide a minimalistic standard for combining rules and ontologies in the web ontology language (OWL) resp. RDF data.

Achieving such combinations is somewhat more difficult than similar combinations of logic-based rules and ontologies (see e.g. [21,9] for surveys). The reason is that production rules have an operational semantics, in which a working memory (roughly, a factual knowledge base) is changed by the firing of rules which are matched against the current state of the working memory; out of the set of fireable rules, one is selected for execution according to some *conflict resolution strategy*. The "result" of the evaluation

* This work is partially supported by the Austrian Science Fund (FWF) under the project P20840, and by the European Commission under the project OntoRule (IST2009231875).

E. Erdem et al. (Eds.): Correct Reasoning, LNCS 7265, pp. 211–228, 2012.

of a PRS is the final state achieved after repeating matching and execution, known as *recognize-act cycle*, as long as possible, provided that it terminates.

Elements of this procedure like a concrete conflict resolution strategy (possibly based on the execution history), and a change mechanism for removing information from the working memory, are challenging for a declarative formalization in standard logic-based formalisms, which lack procedural elements and are subject to logical ramifications: if a fact A is to be removed, presence of a fact B and a clause $B \rightarrow A$ in the background still allows to derive A, so mere physical removal of A is insufficient. Another issue is negation in rule conditions, which refers to the current state.

Several works have considered simulation of PRS in logic-based formalisms, facing these difficulties. E.g., Baral and Lobo [2] used logic programming under stable semantics and situation calculus notation; Kowalski and Sadri [19] resorted in an agent-flavored approach to abductive logic programming combined with reactive rules, on a database with destructive assignments. de Bruijn and Rezk [5] instead employed the mu-calculus and fixpoint logic. Damasio et al. [8] used incremental Answer Set Programming to realize the default semantics of the RIF-PRD dialect. Most recently, aiming at a combination of production rules and ontologies, Rezk and Kifer [24] use transaction logic, while Rosati and Franconi [27] describe a general framework for combining production rules and ontologies, with the purpose of studying termination and complexity for different classes of rules and ontologies.

These proposals often commit to particular settings and ramifying assumptions (e.g., a particular conflict resolution strategy and/or removal strategy), and actual execution of a simulated PRS run to obtain full emulation requires an extra effort. The support of access to other, heterogeneous information sources, or interaction with an environment in which the knowledge base is situated, usually requires an extension.

In this paper, we consider simulation of PRS in the ACTHEX formalism, in which actual execution and the above extensions are readily achieved. ACTHEX [3] is a logic-programming based framework for declarative specification of action execution, using a rule-based language that builds on special action atoms. It is a relative of Gelfond and Lifschitz's action languages [17], in which actions and their effects are typically described in rule-based languages; however, in ACTHEX the effect of actions, especially on the environment, might be implicit via the plugins used. Briefly, ACTHEX allows a) to express and infer a predictable execution order for action atoms; b) to express soft (and hard) preferences among a set of possible action atoms; and c) to actually execute a set of action atoms according to a predictable schedule. ACTHEX extends HEX-programs [11], which in turn extend non-monotonic logic programs under answer set semantics with external atoms. The latter model access to external computation via an abstract interface and a plug-in architecture; more details are provided in Section 2.

Thanks to external and action atoms, ACTHEX is a versatile formalism to simulate PRS. By modeling conflict resolution and fact removal strategies via external atoms, also involved realizations thereof can be elegantly captured. Furthermore, via external atoms access to heterogenous information sources in virtually any format is supported; in particular, to description logic ontologies in OWL, such that an instantiation of the OWL-PR formalism can be accommodated. Since an ACTHEX prototype implementation is available, the PRS simulation can also be effectively realized on top of it.

This work would not exist without the pioneering work of Vladimir Lifschitz on answer-set semantics. In a seminal paper together with Michael Gelfond [16], he coined what has become a predominant formalism for applied nonmonotonic reasoning.

The outline of the rest of this paper is as follows. In the next section, we briefly recall HEX and ACTHEX. We then describe how a generic PRS can be simulated in ACTHEX (Section 3), and consider possible instantiations and properties (Section 4). Related formalisms are discussed in Section 5, while Section 6 concludes the paper.

2 HEX and ACTHEX Programs

2.1 HEX Programs

HEX programs [11] are built over mutually disjoint sets $\mathcal{C}$, $\mathcal{X}$, and $\mathcal{G}$ of *constant*, *variable*, and *external predicate names*, respectively. We follow the convention that elements of $\mathcal{X}$ (resp., $\mathcal{C}$) start with an upper-case (resp., lower-case) letter; elements of $\mathcal{G}$ are prefixed with "&". Constant names serve both as individual and predicate names. Notice, that $\mathcal{C}$ may be infinite. *Terms* are elements of $\mathcal{C} \cup \mathcal{X}$. A (*higher-order*) *atom* is of form $Y_0(Y_1, \ldots, Y_n)$, where Y_i are terms for $1 \leqslant i \leqslant n$, and $n \geqslant 0$ is the *arity* of the atom. The atom is called *ordinary*, if $Y_0 \in \mathcal{C}$. For example, $(x, type, c)$, $node(X)$, and $D(a, b)$, are atoms; the first two are ordinary atoms. Subsequently, we assume that all atoms are ordinary, i.e., of the form $p(Y_1, \ldots, Y_n)$. By $arg(a)$, $var(a)$, $pred(a)$, $arty(a)$, we understand the arguments, the variables, the predicate name, and the arity of an ordinary atom a. An *external atom* is of the form $\&g[\boldsymbol{X}](\boldsymbol{Y})$, where $\boldsymbol{X} = X_1, \ldots, X_n$ and $\boldsymbol{Y} = Y_1, \ldots, Y_m$ are lists of terms (called *input* and *output list*, resp.), and $\&g$ is an *external predicate name*. Such an atom is used to determine the truth value of an atom through an external source of computation. For example, an external atom $\&reach[arc, a](\boldsymbol{Y})$ may capture the nodes of a directed graph arc reachable from node a by querying an external computational source.

HEX-programs (or simply *programs*) are finite sets of *rules* r of the form

$$\alpha_1 \vee \cdots \vee \alpha_k \leftarrow \beta_1, \ldots, \beta_n, not\, \beta_{n+1}, \ldots, not\, \beta_m, \tag{1}$$

where $m, k \geqslant 0$, α_i are atoms, β_j are atoms or external atoms, and "*not*" is *negation as failure* (or *default negation*). If $k = 0$, then r is a *constraint*; if r is variable-free, $k = 1$, and $m = 0$, then r is called a *fact*.

Furthermore, we denote by $H(r) = \{\alpha_1, \ldots, \alpha_k\}$ the *head* of a rule r, and by $B(r) = B^+(r) \cup B^-(r)$ its *body*, where $B^+(r) = \{\beta_1, \ldots, \beta_n\}$ and $B^-(r) = \{\beta_{n+1}, \ldots, \beta_m\}$ are the (sets of) *positive* and *negative body atoms*, respectively. By $cts(P)$ we understand the set of constants which appear in P.

Semantics. Answer sets of ordinary programs [16] are extended to HEX-programs P, using the FLP reduct [13]. The *Herbrand base* $\mathcal{H}_P$ of P is the set of all ground instances of atoms and external atoms occurring in P, obtained by variable substitution over $\mathcal{C}$. The grounding of a rule r, $grnd(r)$, and of P, $grnd(P) = \bigcup_{r \in P} grnd(r)$, is analogous.

An *interpretation of* P is any subset $I \subseteq \mathcal{H}_P$ containing atoms only. A satisfaction relation is defined as follows: I is a *model* of (i) an atom $a \in \mathcal{H}_P$ resp. (ii) a ground external atom $a = \&g[\boldsymbol{x}](\boldsymbol{y})$, denoted $I \models a$, iff (i) $a \in I$ resp. (ii) $f_{\&g}(I, \boldsymbol{x}, \boldsymbol{y}) = 1$, where $f_{\&g}\colon 2^{\mathcal{H}_P} \times \mathcal{C}^{n+m} \to \{0,1\}$ is a (fixed) *oracle function* associated with $\&g$; Intuitively, $f_{\&g}$ tells if $\boldsymbol{y}$ is in the output of the external source $\&g$ provided input $\boldsymbol{x}$. For instance, $f_{\&reach}(I, G, X, Y) = 1$ iff Y is reachable from X in the directed graph encoded by the extension of binary predicate G in I.

For a ground rule r, satisfaction is given by $I \models r$ iff $I \models H(r)$ or $I \not\models B(r)$, where (i) $I \models H(r)$ iff $I \models a$ for some $a \in H(r)$, and (ii) $I \models B(r)$ iff $I \models a$ for every $a \in B^+(r)$ and $I \not\models a$ for all $a \in B^-(r)$. As usual, I is a *model* of P, denoted $I \models P$, iff $I \models r$ for all $r \in grnd(P)$.

The *FLP-reduct* [13] of P w.r.t. an interpretation I, denoted fP^I, is the set of all $r \in grnd(P)$ such that $I \models B(r)$. Eventually, we say that $I \subseteq \mathcal{H}_P$ is an *answer set of* P, iff I is a $\subseteq$-minimal model of fP^I. The set of all answer sets of P is denoted by $\mathcal{AS}(P)$. E.g., let $P_{reach} = \{arc(1,2); arc(2,3); node(X) \leftarrow arc(X,Y); node(Y) \leftarrow arc(X,Y); path(X,Y) \leftarrow \&reach[arc, X](Y), node(X), X \neq Y\}$, then $\mathcal{AS}(P_{reach}) = \{A\}$, such that $\{path(1,2), path(2,3), path(1,3)\} \subseteq A$.

For practical reasons, we assume that each input argument X_i of an external atom $\&g[\boldsymbol{X}](\boldsymbol{Y})$ has a type label *predicate* or *constant*, which is unique for $\&g$. Moreover, we consider external functions to be uniform in the following sense: If I and I' coincide on all the extensions of predicates x_i such that X_i is of type *predicate*, then $f_{\&g}(I, \boldsymbol{x}, \boldsymbol{y}) = f_{\&g}(I', \boldsymbol{x}, \boldsymbol{y})$. Consequently, $f_{\&g}$ depends only on the input of a given by predicate extensions and individuals.

2.2 ACTHEX Programs

ACTHEX [3] is an extension of HEX programs [11] with *action atoms* built using action predicate names $\mathcal{A}$. Unlike dl-atoms in dl-programs [10], which only send and receive inputs to/from ontologies, action atoms are associated to functions capable of actually changing the state of external environments. Such atoms can appear (only) in heads of rules and as such they can be part of answer sets. An *action atom* is of the form

$$\#g\,[Y_1, \ldots Y_n]\,\{o, r\}\,[w : l]$$

where

(i) $\#g$ is an action predicate name and $Y_1, \ldots, Y_n$ is a list of terms (called *input list*), where $n = in(\#g)$ is fixed;
(ii) $o \in \{b, c, c_p\}$ is the *action option*; the action atom is called *brave* (resp., *cautious, preferred cautious*), if $o = b$ (resp., $o = c$, $o = c_p$);
(iii) r and w, the *action precedence* resp. *weight*, range over positive integers, and
(iv) l, the *action level*, ranges over variables.

For instance, an action atom $\#insert[X,Y]\{b, Pr\}$ may be defined to insert paths (pairs of nodes X, Y) into a list of paths. It is a brave atom, whose precedence is given for a respective ground instance by the instantiation of variable Pr.

An ACTHEX rule r is of the form (1) where each α_i can also be an action atom. The notion of constraint, fact etc. and the notation $H(r)$, $B(r)$ etc. naturally extends from HEX to ACTHEX rules. An ACTHEX *program* is a finite set P of ACTHEX rules, and is *ordinary*, if all its rules are ordinary, i.e. contain no external and no action atoms.

As an example consider the ACTHEX program P_{insert} consisting of the ordinary rules of P_{reach} and the rule: $\#insert[X,Y]\{b,Pr\} \leftarrow path(X,Y), Z = X*10, Pr = Z+Y$.

Semantics. Action atoms affect an *external environment* and are executed according to *execution schedules*. Every answer set is associated with one or more *execution schedules*, which are ordered lists containing all action atoms in that particular answer set. The order of execution within a schedule depends on the actions *precedence* attribute. Action atoms allow to specify whether they have to be executed *bravely*, *cautiously* or *preferred cautiously*, respectively, meaning that the atom can get executed if it appears in at least one, all, or all *best cost* answer sets.

More formally, the Herbrand base $\mathcal{H}_P$ of an ACTHEX program P also contains action atoms (in addition to ordinary and external atoms). The grounding of a program is defined as before, and an interpretation I of P is any subset $I \subseteq \mathcal{H}_P$ containing ordinary atoms and action atoms. The satisfaction relation, and eventually the notion of answer sets, both extend straightforwardly by applying to interpretations as above, with a single slight extension:[1] for convenience, we also allow external atoms (computations) to access and take the external environment into account. In particular, we assume the external environment is represented as a finite set E of facts over a suitable language $\mathcal{L}_{env}$. We thus consider an extended oracle function $f_{\&g}: 2^{\mathcal{L}_{env}} \times 2^{\mathcal{H}_P} \times \mathcal{C}^{n+m} \rightarrow \{0,1\}$ associated with any ground external atom $a = \&g[\boldsymbol{x}](\boldsymbol{y})$, and define $I \models a$ iff $f_{\&g}(E, I, \boldsymbol{x}, \boldsymbol{y}) = 1$, for a given external environment $E \subseteq \mathcal{L}_{env}$. For action atoms (and ordinary atoms) a, we say that I is a *model* of a, denoted $I \models a$, iff $a \in I$.

We define the set of *best models* of P, denoted $\mathcal{BM}(P)$, as those answer sets $I \in \mathcal{AS}(P)$, where the objective function $H_P(I) = \Sigma_{i=1}^{l_{max}} (f_P(i) \times \Sigma_{a \in I \wedge l(a)=i} w(a))$ over weights and levels of action atoms in I is minimal. Here, w_{max} and l_{max} are the maximum weight and level of $ground(P)$, and f_P is defined by $f_P(1) = 1$ and $f_P(n) = f_P(n-1) \times |\{a \in ground(P) \mid w(a) \neq 0\}| \times w_{max} + 1$. Intuitively, an answer set I will be a best model if no other answer set yields a strictly lower weight on some level i, while yielding lower or equal weights than I on levels up to i. Here the weight per level is the sum of the weights of all executable actions in I with respective level.

Towards action execution we say, for a given answer set I, that a ground action $a = \#g[y_1, \ldots, y_n]\{o, r\}[w : l]$ is *executable in I* iff (i) a is brave and $a \in I$, or (ii) a is cautious and $a \in B$ for every $B \in \mathcal{AS}(P)$, or (iii) a is preferred cautious and $a \in B$ for every $B \in \mathcal{BM}(P)$. With every answer set of P we associate *execution schedules*: an execution schedule $S_P(I)$ for I is a sequence $[a_1, \ldots, a_n]$ of all actions executable in I, such that a appears before b in in the sequence if $prec(a) < prec(b)$ holds for all action atoms a and b in I. The set of all execution schedules of an answer set I of P is denoted by $\mathcal{ES}_P(I)$. Moreover, if $\mathcal{S}$ is a set of answer sets of P, then $\mathcal{ES}_P(\mathcal{S}) = \bigcup_{I \in \mathcal{S}} \mathcal{ES}_P(I)$.

For an example, observe that the only answer set A of P_{insert} contains the action atoms $\#insert[1,2]\{b,12\}$, $\#insert[2,3]\{b,23\}$, and $\#insert[1,3]\{b,13\}$, giving rise to a single execution schedule $S_{P_{insert}}(A) = [\#insert[1,2]\{b,12\}, \#insert[1,3]\{b,13\}, \#insert[2,3]\{b,23\}]$.

The *execution of an action* on an external environment E is modeled by an action function. We associate with every action predicate name $\#g$ an $(m+2)$-ary

[1] Such an extension has been suggested by Peter Schüller in a different context.

function $f_{\#g}$ with input $(E, I, y_1, \ldots, y_m)$ that returns a new external environment $E' = f_{\#g}(E, I, y_1, \ldots, y_m)$, where $I \subseteq \mathcal{H}_P$. Based on this, given an execution schedule $S_P(I) = [a_1, \ldots, a_n]$ for I, the *execution outcome* of executing $S_P(I)$ on E, is defined as $EX(S_P(I), E) = E_n$, where $E_0 = E$, $E_{i+1} = f_{\#g}(E_i, I, y_1, \ldots, y_m)$, and a_i is of the form $\#g[y_1, \ldots, y_m]\{o, p\}[w : l]$. Intuitively the initial environment $E_0 = E$ is modified by executing every action of $S_P(I)$ in the given order, and the effect of these actions is iteratively taken into account according to the corresponding action function. Given a set $\mathcal{S}$ of answer sets of P, we use $\mathcal{EX}_P(\mathcal{S}, E)$ to denote the set of all possible execution outcomes of P on the (initial) external environment E.

For our example program P_{insert}, executing $S_{P_{insert}}(A)$ from above on an initial environment consisting of an empty list, i.e., $E_0 = []$, results in the execution outcome of an ordered list $E = [(1,2), (1,3), (2,3)]$, as intended. Note that such ordered insertion can not be obtained from a HEX program without post-processing its output.

In practice, one may want only one of the possible execution outcomes of an ACTHEX program P on environment E. Either this can be achieved implicitly by appropriate modeling, such that a single (best) answer set exists, which only allows for a single execution schedule, or one has to provide corresponding selection functions explicitly.

An implementation of ACTHEX programs has been realized and is available[2] as an extension to the dlvhex system[3]. It provides simple (nondeterministic) selection functions for selecting a single answer set (the first computed among the best models) and a single execution schedule (the first computed) for it.

3 Simulating Production Rule Systems Using ACTHEX

3.1 Production Rule Systems

A Production Rule System (PRS) is in the most general case an unordered collection of conditional statements called production rules [15]. They all operate on a global database called *working memory* (WM). The left hand side of a rule (LHS) is a condition in the form of a set of positive and negative patterns, while the right hand side (RHS) contains a set of actions, typically the addition or removal of a set of facts to resp. from the WM. Sometimes, rules have priorities.

The production rule system is 'executed' in cycles, where each cycle contains the following steps:

1. *Match*: The LHS of each production rule is evaluated w.r.t. the current WM. A rule[4] for which the LHS is satisfied is called *fireable*.
2. *Conflict resolution*: From the set of fireable production rules, one is chosen according to a *conflict resolution* strategy. Such a strategy considers the priority of the rules or even the history of the execution of the system to pick a rule for execution.
3. *Act*: The actions in the RHS of the selected production rule are performed.

Such a specification of execution of a PRS is also called operational semantics.

[2] `http://www.kr.tuwien.ac.at/research/systems/dlvhex/actionplugin.html`

[3] `http://www.kr.tuwien.ac.at/research/systems/dlvhex/`

[4] Instance of a rule, in case the rule has variables

Example 1. As an example, we describe some rules which can be used to assess a patient with chronic cough symptoms. The scenario is inspired from the step-by-step procedure described at `http://bestpractice.bmj.com/best-practice/monograph/69/diagnosis/step-by-step.html`.

As chronic cough can be caused by ACE inhibitors, in a first step the patient is asked to stop taking these medicines (in case he takes them) to check whether that is the cause. Alternatively, a set of therapeutic trials can be launched to detect whether the cough is caused by one of the common conditions: asthma, non-asthmatic eosinophilic bronchitis (NAEB), or gastro-oesophogeal reflux disease (GORD).

The scenario can be encoded by means of 4 production rules.

(1) [2]: `if` $has(P, cough)$ `and` $takes(P, acei)$ `then add` $rec(P, stop\_acei)$
(2) [2]: `if` $has(P, cough)$ `and` $has(P, wheezing)$ `then add` $treat(P, asthma)$
(3) [2]: `if` $has(P, cough)$ `then add` $treat(P, naeb)$
(4) [2]: `if` $has(P, cough)$ `and` $has(P, heartburn)$ `then add` $treat(P, gord)$

In order to monitor the state of the patient we introduce two more rules. The patient is asked how he feels: if he feels ok all symptoms are removed from the WM; otherwise, the symptom of the patient is added as a fact to the KB.

(5) [1]: `if` $ask(P, ok)$ `then remove` $has(P, X)$
(6) [1]: `if` $ask(P, X)$ `and` X $\neq$ ok `then add` $has(P, X)$

All rules have attached priorities: rules (1)-(4) have priority 2, while rules (5)-(6) have priority 1. If the conflict resolution strategy decides which rule should be executed solely by considering the priority of fireable rules, rules (1)-(4) will never be executed as always either the condition of (5) or the condition of (6) is fulfilled. As such, conflict resolution strategies are usually more complex: for example, a rule which has already been executed, will not be executed again until its condition is falsified and then becomes true again (i.e., only once for a particular set of bindings, where a binding is maintained until the respective condition is not fulfilled anymore). Thus, if the patient reports the same symptom, e.g. cough, several times, rule (5) will not be reexecuted: instead one of the lower priority rules (1)-(4) will be executed instead. As the lower priority rules have all the same priority, which one is actually chosen depends on satisfaction of their conditions: if more then one condition is satisfied, the rule is chosen nondeterministically (according to the intention of this example; note, however, that some systems use specificity of the condition as a further selection criterion, which would select rule (3) only if the other ones are not in the conflict set).

3.2 Production Rule Systems over HEX Programs

Recently there has been an interest in augmenting Production Rules Systems with more expressive background knowledge, in the form of FOL theories, or DL KBs. The assumption is that patterns are FOL formulas which are evaluated against a KB consisting in the union of the current WM and the underlying FOL theory/DL KB [1].

In this section we introduce PRS over HEX programs. A PRS is augmented with a HEX program which together with the WM offers background knowledge. In an ASP setting, checking brave entailment of atoms, i.e. whether an atom belongs to *some* answer set, is a common reasoning task. Actually, the possibility to express information about alternate states of the world is one of the main features of ASP. As such, the condition part of such production rules is evaluated bravely w.r.t. ASP semantics. The assumption is that for every execution cycle, some answer set A of the corresponding HEX program and current WM is randomly chosen and then all conditions are evaluated w.r.t. A.

In this setting, a *pattern* is a HEX body literal ℓ; it is *positive*, if ℓ is an atom, and *negative* otherwise. In the following, let $\mathbf{L}$ be a set atoms (called labels) such that for every $l_1, l_2 \in \mathbf{L}$: $pred(l_1) \neq pred(l_2)$ and the set $\{pred(l) \mid l \in \mathbf{L}\}$ is disjoint with $\mathcal{C}$.

Definition 1. *Let* $\mathbf{p}$ *be a finite set of patterns, let* $\mathbf{r}$, $\mathbf{a}$, *and* $\mathbf{e}$ *be three finite sets of atoms, and let* $l \in \mathbf{L}$ *such that* $var(l) = var(\mathbf{p}) \cup var(\mathbf{a}) \cup var(\mathbf{r}) \cup var(\mathbf{e})$. *A* HEX*-production rule (PR) is an expression of the form:*

$$[l, pr] \text{ if } \mathbf{p} \text{ then remove } \mathbf{r} \text{ add } \mathbf{a} \text{ execute } \mathbf{e} \tag{2}$$

where pr *is the priority of the rule, a natural number.*

Example 2. The encoding of rules (1)-(6) from example 1 as HEX-production rules is straightforward. For example, rule (1) can be encoded as follows:

$$[r_1(P),2] \text{ if } has(P, cough), takes(P, acei) \text{ then add } rec(P, stop\_acei).$$

We note that the presence of external atoms allows us to express more complex rules whose conditions can be external atoms with bidirectional access to external knowledge sources. For example, an external atom $\&high\_risk$ may have as inputs the extension of the predicate has and a patient, and empty output; it evaluates to `true`, iff the patient has a high risk of complications. High risk patients are referred to the emergency room:

$$[r_7(P),2] \text{ if } \&high\_risk[P, has] \text{ then add } send(P, emergency).$$

Ground instances of production rules are obtained by substitution as usual: for a term t the result of applying a substitution $\sigma : var(t) \to D$ (where D is an arbitrary set of constants) to t is denoted by $t\sigma$, and is obtained by replacing every variable in the term with its image under the substitution. This application naturally extends to sets of terms and rules. An instance of a HEX-production rule (2) is any rule

$$[l\sigma, pr] \text{ if } \mathbf{p}\sigma \text{ then remove } \mathbf{r}\sigma \text{ add } \mathbf{a}\sigma \text{ execute } \mathbf{e}\sigma \tag{3}$$

Next we define the notion of a HEX-based PRS state. The notion is intended to capture the parts of a PRS which change during a run of the system: the working memory and the history of the run itself.

Definition 2. *A* HEX*-based PRS state is a triple* $\langle WM, P, H\rangle$, *where* P *is a finite set of rules, i.e., a* HEX*-program, while* WM *and* H *are finite sets of ground facts: the working memory, and the history, respectively.*

To any set RS of production rules and a HEX-based PRS state $s = \langle WM, P, H\rangle$, we associate a *relevant domain* by $Dom(RS, s) = cts(P \cup WM \cup RS)$. We also say that a ground instance of RS is relevant w.r.t. s iff it is obtained from RS by a substitution to $Dom(RS, s)$. In other words, the set of relevant ground instances of RS w.r.t. s, denoted by $rel(RS, s)$, is obtained by grounding RS over $Dom(RS, s)$.

We now turn to the firing of production rules and first define what it means for a production rule instance to be fireable in a HEX-based PRS state.

Definition 3. *Consider a set* RS *of* HEX*-production rules and a* HEX*-based PRS state* $s = \langle P, WM, H\rangle$ *such that* $P \cup WM$ *is consistent, i.e., it has an answer set, and let* $A \in \mathcal{AS}(P \cup WM)$. *A* HEX*-production rule instance of the form (3) is fireable in* s *w.r.t.* A *if and only if* 1.) $A \models p'\sigma$ *for all* $p' \in \mathbf{p}^+$, *and* 2.) $A \not\models p'\sigma$ *for all* $p' \in \mathbf{p}^-$.

Note that if $l\sigma$ is fireable in s, then it is also relevant w.r.t. s. As for additional notation we use $\mathit{fireable}(RS, s, A)$ to denote the set of all (relevant) instances of production rules from RS that are fireable in s w.r.t. A identified by their labels, i.e., $\mathit{fireable}(RS, s, A) = \{l\sigma \mid l\sigma \in \mathit{rel}(RS, s)$ and $l\sigma$ is fireable in s w.r.t. $A\}$.

Slightly abusing notation, we define $\mathit{fireable}(RS, s) = \mathit{fireable}(RS, s, A)$, for some $A \in \mathcal{AS}(P \cup WM)$ if $P \cup WM$ is consistent (where A is chosen nondeterministically), while $\mathit{fireable}(RS, s) = \emptyset$ otherwise.

A HEX-based PRS comprises besides a set of production rules and an initial HEX-based PRS state, also a conflict resolution function, which selects for every state of the system which PR instance should be executed next (if fireable instances exist); a change function which specifies how the working memory is affected by PR actions; and a bookkeeping function which describes how the history of a run is updated upon transition from one state to another. More specifically,

- $cr(RS_i, H)$ is the conflict resolution function, (a partial function) that given a set of PR instances RS_i and the history H, returns a single PR instance $l\sigma \in RS_i$;
- $ch(WM, P, \mathbf{a}, \mathbf{r}, \mathbf{e})$ is a function which given a set of ground facts representing the WM, a HEX-program P, and three sets of ground atoms, corresponding to assertion, removal, and execute actions, respectively, returns a pair (WM', P') of a set of ground facts and a HEX-program representing the changed working memory WM' and program P' as a result of applying the actions;
- $bk(RS_i, l\sigma, H)$ is a bookkeeping function which given as input a set of PR instances RS_i, a PR instance $l\sigma$, and the history H, returns an updated history H'.

Definition 4. *A* HEX*-based PRS is a quintuple* $\langle RS, s_0, cr, ch, bk\rangle$, *where* RS *is a finite set of* HEX*-production rules of the form (2),* $s_0 = \langle WM_0, P_0, \emptyset\rangle$ *is the initial state of the system, and* cr, ch, *and* bk *are a conflict resolution, a change, and a bookkeeping function, respectively.*

We note that in this definition, a PRS may be non-Markovian w.r.t. to the working memory, i.e., conflict resolution may select from the same conflict set RS_i produced from the same WM different rules for execution, depending on the history. This respects that standard conflict resolution functions, like forward chaining in RIF (see Section 4), take the history into account; in principle, the relevant history information may be stored in WM, and designated rules of the PRS may maintain it, such that the function $cr(RS_i, H)$ can be replaced by some function $cr'(RS_i')$ that is independent of history information H; however, bounds on the size of WM would limit the expressiveness of conflict resolution. For generality and a clean separation between data processing and rule execution management, we use the above definition.

Towards defining runs of a HEX-based PRS in terms of transition functions, let us first consider single transitions. A triple $(s, l\sigma, s')$, where $s = \langle WM, P, H\rangle$ and $s' = \langle WM', P', H'\rangle$ are HEX-based PRS states and $l\sigma$ is the label of a PR instance of the form 3, is a *valid transition* of a PRS $PS = \langle RS, s_0, cr, ch, bk \rangle$ iff (i) $l\sigma = cr(\mathit{fireable}(RS, s), H)$, (ii) $(WM', P') = ch(WM, P, \mathbf{a}, \mathbf{r}, \mathbf{e})$, and (iii) $H' = bk(\mathit{fireable}(RS, s), l\sigma, H)$.

We call a state s *reachable* in (a run of) a PRS PS iff either $s = s_0$ is the initial state of PS, or there exists a valid transition $(s', l\sigma, s)$ such that s' is reachable. Furthermore, we denote by S the set of all states and by $L\Sigma$ the set of all labels of PR instances.

Definition 5. *Let $PS = \langle RS, s_0, cr, ch, bk \rangle$ be a* HEX*-based PRS. A relation $\rightarrow_{PS} \subseteq S \times L\Sigma \times S$ is called a* run *of PS iff $(s, l\sigma, s') \in \rightarrow_{PS}$ implies that $(s, l\sigma, s')$ is a valid transition such that s is reachable.*

Moreover, if there exists $(s, l\sigma, s_f) \in \rightarrow_{PS}$ such that $(s_f, l'\sigma', s') \notin \rightarrow_{PS}$ for all $l'\sigma' \in L\Sigma$ and $s' \in S$, then the run is *finite* (in other words, the run *terminates*), otherwise the run is *infinite*.

3.3 Simulating HEX-Based PRSs in ACTHEX

In this section we show how runs of HEX-based PRSs can be simulated via a translation of such systems to ACTHEX programs. The translation reenacts the operational semantics of HEX-based PRSs in terms of execution schedules of the corresponding ACTHEX programs. While ACTHEX programs do not have an explicit notion of state, they allow for stateful computation via the external environment: a stateful program thus has all state dependent information as a part of the external environment, which is subject to be updated and accessed via action atoms and external atoms.

In our particular case, simulating the behavior of a HEX-based PRS, the state dependent information consists of the WM, the HEX program, and the history of the current run. The facts of the WM and the HEX program rules are part of the actual ACTHEX program which is to be executed for simulation of the PRS behavior. As such, the ACTHEX program is dynamic, i.e., subject to change—the PRS execution cycle is simulated by repeated executions of suitable modifications of the original program (which address just the facts representing the working memory and the HEX program rules). Technically, this is achieved via an action atom $\#execute$ which appears as the last action in every non-empty execution schedule of the ACTHEX program. Its execution results in a recursive call for evaluating the modified program (with updated WM facts and HEX rules).

For a more formal account, consider a HEX-based PRS $PS = \langle RS, s_0, cr, ch, bk \rangle$. Below, we will first give the encoding of the static part of the ACTHEX program which represents (and eventually simulates) the production rules RS. This fixed part of the ACTHEX program will be denoted by Π_{RS}. Furthermore, we will use indices $i \geqslant 0$ to denote the (initial) external environment E_i of iterative evaluations of the ACTHEX program. More specifically, we will use E_i^{WM}, E_i^{HEX}, and E_i^{H} to refer to the different parts of E_i, representing corresponding state information. In slight abuse of notation, we will also use E_i^{WM} and E_i^{HEX} to denote the set of facts and the set of rules that together with Π_{RS} constitute the ACTHEX program to be evaluated (executed) at step i.

There are several issues of concern. To simulate an execution cycle, one has to (i) capture rule fireability conditions, (ii) select a rule for execution (conflict resolution),

(iii) execute the selected rule, and (iv) update the history. After that, one has to (v) move on to the next execution cycle.

(i) The simulation of pattern matching in ACTHEX is straightforward: production rule conditions are captured by bodies of ACTHEX rules: let m be the maximum arity of labels of rules in RS, let *fires* be an ACTHEX predicate of arity $m + 4$. For every production rule of the form (2), we add the following rule to Π_{RS}:

$$\mathit{fires}(\mathit{pred}(l), \mathit{arity}(l), \mathit{arg}(l), pr, 0, \ldots 0) \leftarrow p,$$

where the argument part of *fires* is padded with zeroes up to $m + 4$ arguments.[5] Intuitively, $\mathit{fires}(\mathit{pred}(l), \mathit{arity}(l), \mathit{arg}(l), pr, 0, \ldots 0)$ is satisfied in an answer set of $\Pi_{RS} \cup E_i^{WM} \cup E_i^{\mathrm{HEX}}$ iff there exists a fireable instance $l\sigma$ of the production rule with label l w.r.t. an answer set of $E_i^{WM} \cup E_i^{\mathrm{HEX}}$.

(ii) The conflict resolution strategy is outsourced to an external atom $\&cres[\mathit{fires}](X_1, \ldots, X_{m+2})$. Its external function $f_{\&cres}$ takes the extension of *fires* in the given interpretation I into account as well as the history of the run E_i^H in the environment to select a production rule instance for output. As for *fires*, we use reification to describe a rule instance; hence the output of $\&cres$ has arity $m+2$, where m is again the maximum arity of a label. It represents $cr(\mathit{fireable}(RS, \langle E_i^{WM}, E_i^{\mathrm{HEX}}, E_i^H \rangle, E_i^H)$.

(iii) Once a rule instance is selected, its action part should be executed. For every production rule of form (2) where $\mathbf{a} = \cup_{1 \leqslant i \leqslant n} a_i$, $\mathbf{r} = \cup_{1 \leqslant i \leqslant p} r_i$, and $\mathbf{e} = \cup_{1 \leqslant i \leqslant q} e_i$, let

$$\#action[a_1, arity(a_1), arg(a_1), \ldots, \\ r_1, arity(r_1), arg(r_1), \ldots, e_1, arity(e_1), arg(e_1), \ldots, 0, \ldots, 0]\{b, 1\}$$

be an action atom whose execution is intended to simulate the effect of the execution of the production rule instance: it changes the working memory, and the HEX program, such that their new contents are exactly those given by $ch(E_i^{WM}, E_i^{\mathrm{HEX}}, \mathbf{a}, \mathbf{r}, \mathbf{e})$. Note that the mode of execution for such an action is *brave* and its priority is 1. For simplicity, we will refer in the following to such an atom as act_l. The arity of $\#action$ is $max_{l \in RS}(\sum_{a_i \in \mathbf{a}}(|arg(a_i)| + 2) + \sum_{r_i \in \mathbf{r}}(|arg(r_i)| + 2) + \sum_{e_i \in \mathbf{e}}(|arg(e_i)| + 2))$.

For every production rule with label l, we also add the following rule to Π_{RS}:

$$act_l \leftarrow \&cres[\mathit{fires}](\mathit{pred}(l), \mathit{arity}(l), \mathit{arg}(l), 0, \ldots, 0).$$

(iv) After updating the WM and the HEX program, the history of the run is updated by means of an action atom $\#update$ whose effect is to change the history to the one returned by $bk(\mathit{fireable}(RS, \langle E_i^{WM}, E_i^{\mathrm{HEX}}, E_i^H \rangle), l\sigma, E_i^H)$. It takes the extension of *fires* in I and the input rule instance $l\sigma$ (in reified form; from $\&cres$) into account.

$$\#update[\mathit{fires}, X_1, \ldots, X_{m+2}]\{b, 2\} \leftarrow \&cres[\mathit{fires}](X_1, \ldots, X_{m+2}).$$

(v) Finally, the next execution cycle is triggered by means of an action atom $\#execute$: its effect is to build and execute the ACTHEX program $\Pi_{RS} \cup E_{i+1}^{WM} \cup E_{i+1}^{\mathrm{HEX}}$. Again, this happens only if a production rule action has actually been executed (which means that the external environment has already been changed to contain E_{i+1}^{WM} and E_{i+1}^{HEX} and can thus be used to build the ACTHEX program for the next step).

$$\#execute\{b, 3\} \leftarrow \&cres[\mathit{fires}](X_1, X_2, \ldots, X_{m+2}).$$

[5] Here, for ease of exposition, we use reification to encode a production rule instance as an argument of an action atom. Regarding efficiency, this is suboptimal: rather than padding, one could use different predicates $\#fires_k$ with fixed arity k, for $1 \leqslant k \leqslant m + 4$.

Note that whenever an execution schedule $S_P(I)$ of an ACTHEX program P contains an action atom $\#execute$, whose effect is the execution of another ACTHEX program P', then $S_P(I)$ can be regarded as being interleaved with an execution schedule $S_{P'}(I')$ of P'. Intuitively, $\#execute$ in $S_P(I)$ is replaced with $S_{P'}(I')$. If $S_{P'}(I')$ in turn contains an $\#execute$ atom, and so forth, then $S_P(I)$ is essentially infinite.

In the following let $act_{l\sigma}$ denote $\#action[a_1, arity(a_1), arg(a_1)\sigma, \ldots, r_1, arity(r_1), arg(r_1)\sigma, \ldots, e_1, arity(e_1), arg(e_1)\sigma, \ldots, 0, \ldots, 0]$, and let $\#update_{l\sigma}$ denote $\#update[fires, pred(l), arity(l), arg(l)\sigma, 0, \ldots, 0]$.

Lemma 1. *Given a* HEX*-based PRS* $PS = \langle RS, s_0, cr, ch, bk\rangle$ *such that* $s_0 = \langle WM_0, P_0, \emptyset\rangle$, *let* $E_0^{WM} = WM_0$, $E_0^{\text{HEX}} = P_0$, $E_0^H = \emptyset$, *and let* $\Pi = \Pi_{RS} \cup E_0^{WM} \cup E_0^{\text{HEX}}$ *be an* ACTHEX *program. Then, an execution schedule* S_Π *of* Π *is either empty or has the form:* $[\#act_{l_1\sigma_1}, \#update_{l_1\sigma_1}, \#act_{l_2\sigma_2}, \#update_{l_2\sigma_2}, \ldots,]$. *Moreover, the range of* σ_i *is given by* $cts(E_{i-1}^{WM} \cup E_{i-1}^{\text{HEX}})$, *for* $i > 1$.

The following proposition shows the soundness of the translation: every execution schedule of an ACTHEX program $\Pi_{RS} \cup E_0^{WM} \cup E_0^{\text{HEX}}$ corresponds to a run of PS.

Proposition 1. *Let* $PS = \langle RS, s_0, cr, ch, bk\rangle$ *be a* HEX*-based PRS such that* $s_0 = \langle WM_0, P_0, \emptyset\rangle$. *For every execution schedule* S_Π *of* $\Pi = \Pi_{RS} \cup E_0^{WM} \cup E_0^{\text{HEX}}$ *and corresponding external environments sequence* $(E_i)_{i\geqslant 0}$, *where* $E_i = \langle E_i^{WM}, E_i^{\text{HEX}}, E_i^H\rangle$, *there exists a run* $\rightarrow_{\text{HEX}-PRS}$ *of PS such that the following holds for every* $k \geqslant 1$*:*

- *if* $\#act_{l_k\sigma_k}$ *is in* S_Π, *then there exists* $(s, l\sigma, s') \in \rightarrow_{\text{HEX}-PRS}$ *such that* $E_{k-1} = s$, $E_k = s'$, $l_k = l$, *and* $\sigma_k = \sigma$.

Moreover, the simulation is also complete: for every run of a PRS PS, there exists a counterpart execution schedule of the ACTHEX program $\Pi = \Pi_{RS} \cup E_0^{WM} \cup E_0^{\text{HEX}}$.

Proposition 2. *Let* $PS = \langle RS, s_0, cr, ch, bk\rangle$ *be a* HEX*-based PRS such that* $s_0 = \langle WM_0, P_0, \emptyset\rangle$. *For every run* $\rightarrow_{\text{HEX}-PRS}$ *of PS there exists an execution schedule* S_Π *of* $\Pi = \Pi_{RS} \cup E_0^{WM} \cup E_0^{\text{HEX}}$ *and a corresponding external environments sequence* $(E_i)_{i\geqslant 0}$, *where* $E_i = \langle E_i^{WM}, E_i^{\text{HEX}}, E_i^H\rangle$, *such that the following holds:*

- *for every* $(s, l\sigma, s') \in\rightarrow_{\text{HEX}-PRS}$ *there exists an integer* $k \geqslant 1$ *such that* $s = E_{k-1}$, $s' = E_k$, $l = l_k$, *and* $\sigma = \sigma_k$.

From Propositions 1 and 2, we easily obtain the following:

Corollary 1. *There exists a terminating run of a PRS PS iff there exists a finite execution schedule for* $\Pi_{RS} \cup E_0^{WM} \cup E_0^{\text{HEX}}$.

4 Instantiations and Properties

In Section 3, we provided a general framework for PRSs over HEX programs, in which the conflict resolution strategy, the effects of actions executions, and the history update were generic parameters of a PRS. We now discuss possible ways to instantiate these parameters. As the notions of history and conflict resolution strategy are tightly related, (the strategy uses the history to select a rule for execution), we will treat them together.

Conflict Resolution Strategy/History. In general, a CRS chooses one of the fireable rules for execution. The complexity of a strategy can vary from a simple non-deterministic selection to a multi-tier selection mechanism, as the one given by the `rif:forwardChaining` strategy in RIF-PRD [25]. It uses history related information like the first time a rule instance was in the set of fireable rules, and the last time it did not fire. More specifically, the following rules are applied to select one fireable rule in decreasing order of priority:

- *refraction*: a rule instance which has been previously selected must not be selected again if the reasons that made it eligible for firing in the first place still hold;
- *priority*: only rule instances with the highest priority are maintained;
- *recency*: rule instances are ordered by the number of consecutive system states in which they are fireable, only the most recently fireable ones are eligible for firing;
- for the remaining rules, break the tie somehow.

We discuss how to encode parts of this strategy in ACTHEX. First the $\&update$ action can be detailed such that it stores in `hist` precisely the information needed by the strategy. We assume that `hist` contains for every rule instance $l\sigma$ two counters similar to the $recency$ and $lastPicked$ counters described in the RIF-PRD specification, which indicate the number of consecutive times $l\sigma$ was in the set of fireable rules, and the last time $l\sigma$ fired, respectively.

Next we show how to encode a refraction and priority-based selection in ACTHEX. Let $\&refr$ be an external atom which uses the counters stored in `hist` to indicate refracted rules: the atom $\&refr(pred(l), arity(l), arg(l), pr, 0, \ldots, 0)$ evaluates to true iff a production rule instance $l\sigma$ is refracted[6]. To capture the sets of refracted and non-refracted rule instances, we use for every production rule with label l and priority pr two ACTHEX rules as follows:

$$refr(pred(l), arity(l), arg(l), pr, 0, \ldots 0) \leftarrow fires(pred(l), arity(l), arg(l), pr, 0, \ldots 0),\\ \&refr[pred(l), arity(l), arg(l), pr, 0, \ldots 0)]().$$

$$ref(pred(l), arity(l), arg(l), pr, 0, \ldots 0) \leftarrow fires(pred(l), arity(l), arg(l), pr, 0, \ldots 0),\\ not\ \&refr[pred(l), arity(l), arg(l), pr, 0, \ldots 0)]().$$

The selection among the nonrefracted rules of only those highest priority can be done without accessing the history. For every pair (l, l') of production rules, where l has priority pr and l' has priority pr', we introduce the following ACTHEX rule:

$$spr(pred(l), arity(l), arg(l), pr, 0, \ldots 0) \leftarrow ref(pred(l), arity(l), arg(l), pr, 0, \ldots 0),\\ \&fires(pred(l'), arity(l'), arg(l'), pr', 0, \ldots 0), pr > pr'.$$

Finally, top priority rules (i.e., those kept in) are those not having small priorities:

$$tpr(pred(l), arity(l), arg(l), pr, 0, \ldots 0) \leftarrow ref(pred(l), arity(l), arg(l), pr, 0, \ldots 0),\\ not\ spr(pred(l), arity(l), arg(l), pr, 0, \ldots 0).$$

We note that the last two steps of `rif:forwardChaining`, *recency* and non-deterministic choice, can be encoded similarly: for the former we must access `hist` using an external atom, while the latter can be encoded by non-deterministic selection.

[6] For more information how the counters determine whether a rule is refracted or not please consult the RIF-PRD specification.

Change. Another benefit in terms of versatility of HEX-based PRS and our realization using ACTHEX, is enhanced flexibility of modeling and representing change. A plain PR style instantiation of the function $change(WM, P, \mathbf{a}\sigma, \mathbf{r}\sigma, \mathbf{e}\sigma)$ would execute all of $\mathbf{e}\sigma$ on WM without changing the working memory and return $WM' = (WM \setminus \mathbf{r}\sigma) \cup \mathbf{a}\sigma$.

HEX-based PRS enable richer changes to be realized in a straightforward and often declarative way. By simple encoding techniques, atoms in PR rule heads can represent more sophisticated changes to the working memory. E.g., an atom $remove\_ext(X)$ whose ground instances (where a constant c replaces X), represent the removal of the entire extension of a predicate named c from WM; such predicate retraction has been proposed as an advanced feature in RIF-PRD (see also next section).

By augmenting a PRS with a declarative component such as HEX-rules, more subtle interactions such as logical ramification may have to be respected when updating the working memory. Recalling the simple example from the introduction, if a fact A is to be removed, the presence of another fact B and a rule $B \to A$ in the background still allows to derive A. Problems of this nature have been studied extensively in AI as belief revision and contraction problems (cf. [22] for an overview). Respective solutions and techniques (such as WIDTIO used e.g. in [24]) can be applied and realized via instantiations of *change*, which also has access to the HEX-program P.

Eventually, the augmentation with HEX-programs offers a simple means to create new objects using external atoms. While desirable in modifying the working memory for state of the art PRS, this feature must be used carefully to ensure termination.

Termination. One aspect of encoding PRS in ACTHEX is that in general, there is no guarantee that ACTHEX programs which have recursive evaluation calls using $execute$ terminate. In fact, properties of a PRS like termination, or whether a certain fact holds in some execution/all runs, etc. are not decidable in general, and thus analog properties of the ACTHEX encoding are necessarily undecidable in general. However, under suitable restrictions they are decidable, and consequently the respective properties of PRS; studying such restrictions, guided by [27], remains for future work.

Interfacing with External Sources. Obviously, augmenting PRS with HEX benefits from the fundamental aim of HEX-programs: providing a declarative interface to external information sources and software. To date, ontologies are a common means of representing terminological (background) knowledge that systems can process autonomously and utilize to provide domain specific solutions for various application scenarios. Interfacing an ontology via an external atom is a premier use case of HEX-programs (especially DL-programs [10]). In our example, rather than hard-coding recommendations associated with symptoms in rules, an external medical ontology might be accessed for classifying symptoms and relating them to suitable recommendations, which the PRS then execute.

Clearly, ontologies are only one type of external information that might be relevant for building applications. Through external atoms, HEX-based PRS can incorporate various heterogeneous external sources such as calendars, various databases etc.

5 Discussion

We now briefly address the potential of the ACTHEX simulation w.r.t. RIF, and consider some alternative formalisms using answer set semantics for PRS simulation.

5.1 RIF Potential

The Rule Interchange Format (RIF) working group developed a suite of W3C recommended rule formalisms, including combinations with RDF and OWL.

RIF's production rule dialect, RIF-PRD, is a standard XML serialization format for production rule languages serving as a lingua franca for rule exchange. Roughly, it hosts rules with atomic actions, like *assert fact*, *retract fact*, *retract all slot values*, *retract object*, *execute*, and compound actions, like *modify fact*. The action (then) part of a rule is a sequence of actions preceded by action variable declaration patterns; by the *frame object declaration* pattern, new individuals can be introduced as a side effect of executing an assert action. The condition (if) part is a condition formula, built from atomic formulas using Boolean connectives and existential quantification. In normalized rules, conditions are disjunction-free and compound actions replaced by sequences of atomic actions. Rules can be put in groups, for which priorities and CRS can be defined.

The semantics of atomic actions is specified by the RIF-PRD transition relation: $\rightarrow_{RIF-PRD} \subseteq W \times L \times W$, where W consists of all states of the fact base and L of all ground atomic actions; notably, retraction must respect subclass and class instance relationships in the facts (which are easy to express in HEX background).

RIF-PRD defines PRS semantics in terms of a labeled transition relation $\rightarrow_{PRS} \subseteq S \times L \times S$ on system states S, where the labels L are sequences of ground action atoms and $(s, a, s') \in \rightarrow_{PRS}$ means that $(facts(s), a, facts(s'))$ is in the transitive closure of $\rightarrow_{RIF-PRD}$ and $a = actions(picked(s))$ is from the firing rules selected by the CRS. As default CRS, RIF-PRD defines `RIF:forwardChaining`, but others can be used.

The PRS simulation in ACTHEX outlined above provides a basis for realizing instances of RIF-PRD, where in particular external atoms and actions atoms are helpful to instantiate generic elements of the description, such as $picked(\cdot)$, $actions(\cdot)$ and realization of the transition relation (i.e., realizing $assert(\phi)$, $retract(\phi)$ etc). However, a detailed discussion of how to realize the complex standard is beyond this paper; we just note that answer set semantics has been used to simulate RIF-PRD before (see below).

An important aspect of using ACTHEX programs is that external atoms enable combinations with other formats. Marano et al. [20] showed how to simulate RIF-Core rules combined with OWL2RL ontologies using HEX programs, by casting the ontologies to RIF-Core; in the same vein, RIF-PRD plus OWL2RL may be realized using ACTHEX. Due to the expressiveness of answer set semantics, combinations with other OWL profiles and RDF may be done under suitable assumptions (cf. [4,26]). Finally, a loose-coupling semantics of RIF-OWL à la [10] can easily be forged from the ACTHEX simulation.

5.2 Alternative Approaches Based on Answer Sets

$\mathbb{FDNC}$. Natural candidates are answer set based formalisms which can express a forward notion of time and have well-studied decidable reasoning tasks. Such a formalism are $\mathbb{FDNC}$ programs [12], which are a fragment of ASP with function symbols that achieves decidability via the forest model property, but allows only for unary and binary predicates and restricts the rule syntax. Arbitrary predicate arity is supported in *higher-arity* $\mathbb{FDNC}$, which imposes syntactical restrictions on variables usage to maintain decidability. Algorithms for standard reasoning tasks like deciding program consistency, cautious/brave entailment of atoms, etc. are available. In [12], a translation of the action language $\mathcal{K}$ (which was inspired by the action language $\mathcal{C}$ [18]) to $\mathbb{FDNC}$ is provided. Using a similar translation, potentially infinite PRS runs could be simulated; the reasoning support for $\mathbb{FDNC}$ allows then to check static properties of an encoded PRS. However, due to lacking actions in $\mathbb{FDNC}$, the results of execution runs cannot be materialized. Moreover, the lack of external atoms prevents loosely-coupled interaction with external sources. It remains to explore how $\mathbb{FDNC}$ can be extended with external atoms that allow sending inputs, querying, and modifying external sources.

STLP. Another answer-set based formalism that can simulate a forward time line are Splittable Temporal Logic Programs (STLP) [6]. They are a fragment of Temporal Equilibrium Logic, an extension of ASP with modal temporal operators. An algorithm for reasoning with such programs is provided in [6]; temporal equilibrium models are captured by an LTL formula using two well-known techniques in ASP: program splitting and loop formulas. The algorithm has been implemented using the LTL model checker SPOT [7]. Similar considerations as for $\mathbb{FDNC}$ apply for PRS encodings using STLP.

Incremental ASP. Damasio et al. [8] used ASP to realize a simulation of the default semantics of RIF-PRD. To this end, they described an encoding of RIF-PRD into the incremental ASP solver iClingo,[7] in which roughly a program can be incrementally evaluated, in a stateful manner, where the current program slice is instantiated w.r.t. the current increment value, that takes the already evaluated program slices into account. This mechanism is particularly attractive to generate a (finite) trajectory for the execution of a sequence of (possibly nondeterministic) actions. In particular, [8] presents a nice encoding of the `RIF:forwardChaining` CSR in iClingo. The encoding produces as a result an answer set of the program, which describes an execution run; the real execution, however, must be accomplished separately. In our ACTHEX encoding, action execution is an integral part. In addition, iClingo does not provide access to external sources, nor to an external environment; thus, coupling RIF-PRD with ontologies and linked data, and access to other data sources is unsupported and requires further work.

6 Conclusion

We have discussed how production rule systems (PRS) can be encoded in answer set programs with external source access, and in particular how they can be simulated using ACTHEX programs, which extend HEX programs with actions. Thanks to its generic

[7] `http://potassco.sourceforge.net/#iclingo`

interfacing and plugin architecture, ACTHEX allows to realize a range of conflict resolution and change strategies, and in addition to access and combine PRS with heterogeneous data sources, like ontologies, RDF stores, thesauri etc.; e.g., external atoms make loose coupling with description logic ontologies easy, but also tight coupling as envisaged by RIF may be hosted, extending work of [8,20]. In fact, the formalism offers a smooth integration of three worlds: production rules, logical rules, and ontologies.

Several issues remain for future work. While we have described simulation of PRS, we did not discuss issues like termination and reasoning over ACTHEX programs encoding PRS, nor computational complexity. A detailed study of termination and complexity, guided by [27], is necessary. The general setting of our simulation, in which generic components must be instantiated and also the environment can be changed, covers a large space of concrete settings, and identifying the most relevant ones will be important. With regard to reasoning, it would be interesting to consider properties expressed in temporal logic similar as in STLP [6] and to extend the algorithm and techniques there to suitable settings for ACTHEX programs. Finally, an implementation of the generic PRS simulation as a front end to the ACTHEX prototype remains to be done. In the course of this, also libraries for conflict resolution and change strategies should be built.

Acknowledgement. We are grateful to Jim Delgrande for useful comments and suggestions which helped to improve this work.

References

1. Rezk, M., Nutt, W.: Combining Production Systems and Ontologies. In: Rudolph, S., Gutierrez, C. (eds.) RR 2011. LNCS, vol. 6902, pp. 287–293. Springer, Heidelberg (2011)
2. Baral, C., Lobo, J.: Characterizing production systems using logic programming and situation calculus, `http://www.cs.utep.edu/baral/papers/char-prod-systems.ps`
3. Basol, S., Erdem, O., Fink, M., Ianni, G.: HEX programs with action atoms. In: Tech. Comm. of ICLP 2010. Leibniz International Proc. in Informatics. LIPIcs, vol. 7, pp. 24–33 (2010)
4. de Bruijn, J., Pearce, D., Polleres, A., Valverde, A.: Quantified Equilibrium Logic and Hybrid Rules. In: Marchiori, M., Pan, J.Z., Marie, C.d.S. (eds.) RR 2007. LNCS, vol. 4524, pp. 58–72. Springer, Heidelberg (2007)
5. de Bruijn, J., Rezk, M.: A logic based approach to the static analysis of production systems. In: Polleres and Swift [23], pp. 254–268
6. Aguado, F., Cabalar, P., Pérez, G., Vidal, C.: Loop Formulas for Splitable Temporal Logic Programs. In: Delgrande, J.P., Faber, W. (eds.) LPNMR 2011. LNCS, vol. 6645, pp. 80–92. Springer, Heidelberg (2011)
7. Cabalar, P., Diéguez, M.: STeLP – A Tool for Temporal Answer Set Programming. In: Delgrande, J.P., Faber, W. (eds.) LPNMR 2011. LNCS, vol. 6645, pp. 370–375. Springer, Heidelberg (2011)
8. Damásio, C.V., Alferes, J.J., Leite, J.: Declarative Semantics for the Rule Interchange Format Production Rule Dialect. In: Patel-Schneider, P.F., Pan, Y., Hitzler, P., Mika, P., Zhang, L., Pan, J.Z., Horrocks, I., Glimm, B., et al. (eds.) ISWC 2010, Part I. LNCS, vol. 6496, pp. 798–813. Springer, Heidelberg (2010)

9. de Bruijn, J., Bonnard, P., Citeau, H., Dehors, S., Heymans, S., Pührer, J., Eiter, T.: Combinations of rules and ontologies: State-of-the-art survey of issues. Tech. Rep. Ontorule D3.1, Ontorule Project Consortium (2009), `http://ontorule-project.eu/`
10. Eiter, T., Ianni, G., Lukasiewicz, T., Schindlauer, R., Tompits, H.: Combining answer set programming with description logics for the Semantic Web. Artif. Intell. 172(12/13), 1495–1539 (2008)
11. Eiter, T., Ianni, G., Schindlauer, R., Tompits, H.: A uniform integration of higher-order reasoning and external evaluations in answer-set programming. In: Proc. IJCAI 2005, pp. 90–96. Professional Book Center (2005)
12. Eiter, T., Šimkus, M.: $\mathbb{FDNC}$: Decidable non-monotonic disjunctive logic programs with function symbols. ACM Trans. Computational Logic (TOCL) 11(2), article 14
13. Faber, W., Pfeifer, G., Leone, N.: Semantics and complexity of recursive aggregates in answer set programming. Artif. Intell. 175(1), 278–298 (2011)
14. Feier, C., Aït-Kaci, H., Angele, J., de Bruijn, J., Citeau, H., Eiter, T., Ghali, A.E., Kerhet, V., Kiss, E., Korf, R., Krekeler, T., Krennwallner, T., Heymans, S., (FUB), A.M., Rezk, M., Xiao, G.: Complexity and optimization of combinations of rules and ontologies. Tech. Rep. Ontorule D3.3, Ontorule Project Consortium (2010), `http://ontorule-project.eu/`
15. Forgy, C.: Rete: A fast algorithm for the many patterns/many objects match problem. Artif. Intell. 19(1), 17–37 (1982)
16. Gelfond, M., Lifschitz, V.: Classical Negation in Logic Programs and Disjunctive Databases. New Generation Computing 9, 365–385 (1991)
17. Gelfond, M., Lifschitz, V.: Action languages. Electron. Trans. AI 2(3-4), 193–210 (1998)
18. Giunchiglia, E., Lee, J., Lifschitz, V., McCain, N., Turner, H.: Nonmonotonic Causal Theories. Artif. Intell. 153(1-2), 49–104 (2004)
19. Kowalski, R.A., Sadri, F.: Integrating logic programming and production systems in abductive logic programming agents. In: Polleres and Swift [23], pp. 1–23
20. Marano, M., Obermeier, P., Polleres, A.: Processing RIF and OWL2RL within DLVHEX. In: Hitzler, P., Lukasiewicz, T. (eds.) RR 2010. LNCS, vol. 6333, pp. 244–250. Springer, Heidelberg (2010)
21. Motik, B., Rosati, R.: Reconciling Description Logics and Rules. JACM 57(5), 1–62 (2010)
22. Peppas, P.: Belief revision. In: van Harmelen, F., Lifschitz, V., Porter, B., et al. (eds.) Handbook of Logic in AI and Logic Programming, ch.8, pp. 317–360. Elsevier (2008)
23. Polleres, A., Swift, T. (eds.): RR 2009. LNCS, vol. 5837. Springer, Heidelberg (2009)
24. Rezk, M., Kifer, M.: Formalizing Production Systems with Rule-Based Ontologies. In: Lukasiewicz, T., Sali, A. (eds.) FoIKS 2012. LNCS, vol. 7153, pp. 332–351. Springer, Heidelberg (2012)
25. de Sainte Marie, C., Hallmark, G., Paschke, A. (eds): RIF Production Rule Dialect. Recommendation, W3C, June 22 (2010), `http://www.w3.org/TR/rif-prd/`
26. Rosati, R.: $\mathcal{DL}$+LOG: Tight integration of description logics and disjunctive Datalog. In: Doherty, P., Mylopoulos, J., Welty, C.A. (eds.) Proc. KR 2006, pp. 68–78. AAAI Press (2006)
27. Rosati, R., Franconi, E.: Generalized ontology-based production systems. In: Proc. KR 2012. AAAI Press (to appear, 2012)
28. Waterman, D., Hayes-Roth, F.: Pattern-directed inference systems. Academic Press (1978)

Applications of Action Languages in Cognitive Robotics

Esra Erdem and Volkan Patoglu

Faculty of Engineering and Natural Sciences, Sabancı University
Orhanlı, Tuzla, İstanbul 34956, Turkey
{esraerdem,vpatoglu}@sabanciuniv.edu

Abstract. We summarize some applications of action languages in robotics, focusing on the following three challenges: 1) bridging the gap between low-level continuous geometric reasoning and high-level discrete causal reasoning; 2) embedding background/commonsense knowledge in high-level reasoning; 3) planning/prediction with complex (temporal) goals/constraints. We discuss how these challenges can be handled using computational methods of action languages, and elaborate on the usefulness of action languages to extend the classical 3-layer robot control architecture.

1 Introduction

Action languages are formal models of parts of natural language that are used for describing actions and change, and reasoning about them [34]. The first action language, $\mathcal{A}$ [32,33], was introduced by Michael Gelfond and Vladimir Lifschitz. According to Vladimir Lifschitz [50]:

> Originally, action languages were meant to play an auxiliary role. The primary goal was to represent properties of actions in the less specialized formalisms mentioned above [classical logic, logic programming, nonmonotonic formalisms], and the idea was to present methods for doing that as translations from action languages. Later on, it became clear that such languages, with their limited but concise syntax, can be of interest in their own right. Defining action languages, comparing them and studying their properties help us improve our understanding of the aspects of commonsense knowledge and reasoning related to action.

Indeed, since the first action language $\mathcal{A}$, a series of action languages, such as, $\mathcal{A}_C$ [5], $\mathcal{A}_C^+$ [10,11], $\mathcal{AR}_0$, $\mathcal{AR}$ [45,35], $\mathcal{ARD}$ [37], $\mathcal{AC}$, $\mathcal{B}$ [72], $\mathcal{L}_0$, $\mathcal{L}_1$ [8], $\mathcal{A}_K$ [66], $\mathcal{AL}$ [6], $\mathcal{ALI}$ [7], $\mathcal{ALM}$ [31], $\mathcal{PAL}$ [13], $\mathcal{K}$ [23], causal theories [58,59], $\mathcal{C}$ [38], $\mathcal{C}+$ [36], MAD [53], and query languages, such as $\mathcal{P}$, $\mathcal{Q}$, $\mathcal{R}$ [34] and their generalizations [22,43,16], have been introduced. Each one of them has been studied in detail, relating one to another, as well as the "less specialized formalisms" Vladimir Lifschitz mentioned above.

Due to the close relationships between action languages and the "less specialized formalisms" classical logic and answer set programming (ASP) [56,62,51,52,12], various reasoning systems have been developed to answer queries over action domain descriptions represented in action languages. For instance, the Causal Calculator (CCALC)

E. Erdem et al. (Eds.): Correct Reasoning, LNCS 7265, pp. 229–246, 2012.

Version 1 [57] (resp. Version 2 [36]) allows reasoning over domain descriptions in the definite fragment of the action description language $\mathcal{C}$ (resp. $\mathcal{C}+$); its underlying computational mechanism relies on a SAT solver (e.g., MINISAT [21]), thanks to the transformation from $\mathcal{C}$ (resp. $\mathcal{C}+$) to propositional logic [57,59,38] (resp. [36]). The system DLV$^{\mathcal{K}}$ [23] allows reasoning over domain descriptions in the action description language $\mathcal{K}$; its underlying computational mechanism relies on the ASP solver DLV [24] due to the close relationship between $\mathcal{K}$ and answer set programming [54,23]. The system COALA [28] supports reasoning over a fragment of $\mathcal{C}+$; its underlying computational mechanism relies on the ASP solver ICLINGO [29]. The system CPLUS2ASP [15] on the other hand transforms the input of CCALC into the input language of the ASP solver CLINGO [30]. With the implementation of such reasoning systems, and the advancements of SAT solvers and ASP solvers, action languages have been used to solve reasoning problems over medium-sized action domains [3,22], and applied in various areas, such as wire routing [26], systems biology [4,71,70,68,69,19,20], and robotics [14,25,2,1].

In this chapter, we summarize some applications of action languages in robotics (in the spirit of cognitive robotics [48]), based on our studies. We consider three robotics applications: robotic manipulation for assembly planning, multiple robots cleaning a house, and cognitive factories. While describing these applications, we focus on the following three challenges we have faced: 1) bridging the gap between low-level continuous geometric reasoning with high-level discrete causal reasoning; 2) embedding background/commonsense knowledge in high-level reasoning; and 3) planning/prediction with complex (temporal) goals/constraints. We discuss how these challenges are handled effectively using CCALC. We conclude with an elaboration of how action languages can be used to enhance the classical 3-layer robot control architecture.

Note that there are other logic-based formalisms for reasoning about actions and change, that have applications in cognitive robotics, such as, the situation calculus [60,49], temporal action logic [17], features and fluents [64], and cognitive robotics logic [65], event calculus [46,61], fluent calculus [67]. In this chapter, we do not focus on robotic applications of these formalisms.

2 Robotic Manipulation for Assembly Planning

Manipulation planning aims automatic generation of robot motion sequences for manipulation of movable objects among obstacles to achieve a desired goal configuration. These problems involve objects that can only move when picked up by robots and the order of pick-and-place operations for manipulation may matter to obtain a feasible kinematic solution [47]. Therefore, geometric reasoning and motion planning alone are not sufficient to solve them; and planning of actions such as the pick-and-place operations need to be integrated with the motion planning problem.

Recently, some approaches have been proposed to integrate task and motion planning *at the search level* [39,41,44,63,74]. They take advantage of a forward-search task planner to incrementally build a task plan, while checking its kinematic/geometric feasibility at each step by a motion planner; all these approaches use different methods to utilize the information from the task-level to guide and narrow the search in the configuration space. By this way, the task planner helps focus the search process during motion

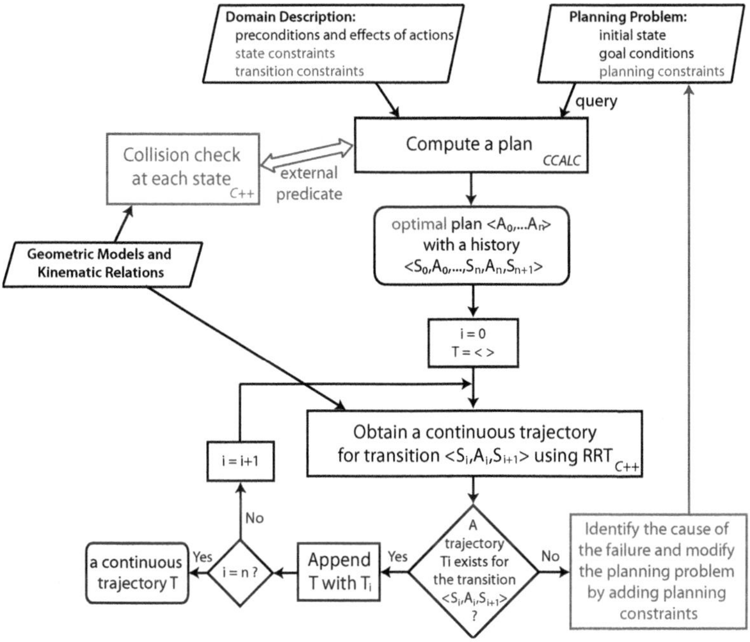

Fig. 1. The overall system architecture for integrating high-level representation and causality-based reasoning with low-level geometric reasoning and motion planning. The components depicted in red signify the important aspects of our approach.

planning. However, each one of these approaches presents a specialized combination of task and motion planning at the search level, and does not consider a general interface between task and motion planning.

We have introduced a method for integrating task and motion planning [25], using CCALC. According to our approach, geometric reasoning is "embedded" in the high-level representation of the action domain so that, while computing a task-plan, CCALC takes into account geometric models and kinematic relations that are defined "externally" (e.g., as a C++ program). In that sense, the geometric reasoner guides the causal reasoner to find feasible kinematic solutions. Also, when a motion planning failure occurs due to some infeasibility not captured by geometric reasoning embedded in the action domain description, the description of the planning problem is modified taking into account some domain-specific information from motion-level (e.g., the causes of infeasibilities), and the causal reasoner is asked to solve a more "relevant" planning problem. Therefore, instead of guiding the task planner at the *search level* by manipulating its search algorithm directly, the motion planner guides the task planner at the *representation level* by presenting to it the "right" planning problem.

The overall architecture of our formal framework for "hybrid planning", that combines high-level representation and causality-based reasoning with low-level geometric reasoning and motion planning is illustrated in Figure 1.

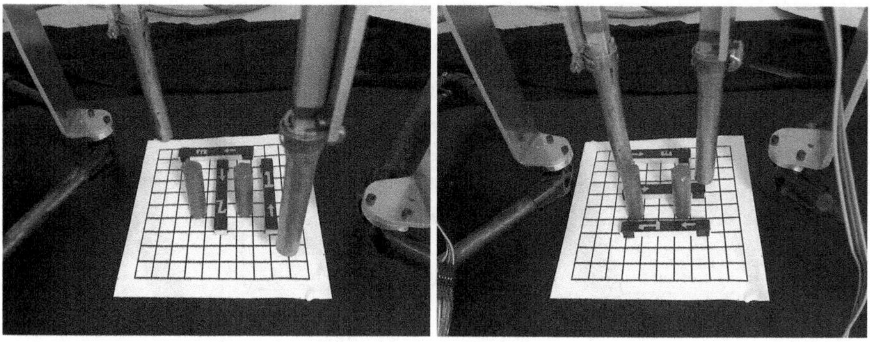

(a) (b)

Fig. 2. A manipulation problem, with an initial state (a) and a goal state (b)

2.1 Example: Two Robots and Multiple Payloads

Consider two robots and multiple payloads on a platform. The payloads can be manipulated by the end effectors of the robots. In particular, the end-effector of each robot can pick (hold and elevate) or drop (release) the payload at one of its end points. None of the robots can carry the payload alone; they have to pick the payload at both ends. Since the payload is elevated from the platform when the robots are holding it, the payload can not collide with the other payloads. However, collisions between payloads may occur if a payload is dropped on top of another one and such collisions are not permitted. Similarly, other types of collisions (robot-robot, payload-obstacle and robot-obstacle) are not permitted either.

Initially, a configuration of the payloads on the platform is given (e.g., as in Figure 2). The goal is to reconfigure the payloads in an optimal manner (by a minimum number of steps). This problem requires payloads to be picked and placed a number of times before they can be positioned into their final configuration. Due to the constraint that a payload can be carried by two robots only and due to the optimality of the plan, this problem requires concurrency. Fortunately, $\mathcal{C}+$ allows representations of such actions and CCALC can compute plans/histories with concurrent actions. Another challenge, meanwhile, is to avoid collisions of the payloads with each other. To handle this challenge, high-level reasoning requires some guidance from the low-level geometric reasoning.

2.2 Embedding Geometric Reasoning in Action Domain Descriptions

In the example above, we view the platform as a grid. We describe the action domain in the input language of CCALC, as in [25].

We embed geometric reasoning in an action domain description in two ways: using state constraints and using external predicates. Let us first consider collisions of payloads with each other. We can identify the conditions under which payloads collide with each other, provided that the orientations and the lengths of the payloads, as well as the positions of their leftmost bottom endpoints are given. For instance, consider two payloads `K1` and `K2` of length `lengthP` on the board, whose orientations are vertical. Suppose that the left bottom endpoints of these payloads are `(minXP(K1),minYP(K1))` and `(minXP(K2),minYP(K2))`. Then these payloads collide with each other if the following holds: `abs(minYP(K1)-minYP(K2))=<lengthP`. Once such collision conditions are identified, we can prevent them:

```
caused false
  if onBoard(K1) & onBoard(K2) & K1@<K2 &
     orientationP(K1)=v & orientationP(K2)=v &
     minXP(K1)=minXP(K2) & abs(minYP(K1)-minYP(K2))<lengthP.
```

Similarly, we can identify conditions for collisions between payloads with different orientations, and add causal laws to prevent such cases.

Next let us consider collisions between the robots, or between a robot and obstacles. To detect this sort of collisions, we need to know the geometric models and kinematic relations; however, such detailed information is not represented at the high-level (otherwise, if we could represent it, the domain description and thus the planning problem would be too large for the causal reasoner). Fortunately, CCALC supports "external predicates", which are functions implemented in some programming language (e.g., C++).

An external predicate takes as input not only some parameters from the action domain description (e.g., the locations of robots) but also detailed information that is not a part of not the action domain description (e.g., geometric models); it returns a truth value. For instance, we check whether a robot located at `(X1,Y1)` collides with another robot at `(X2,Y2)`, by an external predicate `collision(X1,Y1,X2,Y2)` implemented as a C++ program. Then we can add causal laws to ensure that the robots do not collide with each other:

```
caused false
  if xpos(r1)=X1 & ypos(r1)=Y1 & xpos(r2)=X2 & ypos(r2)=Y2
  where collision(X1,Y1,X2,Y2).
```

In addition, an external predicate can accomplish some other tasks as "side-effects". For instance, while checking whether a robot located at `(X1,Y1)` collides with another robot at `(X2,Y2)`, the external predicate `collision(X1,Y1,X2,Y2)` can form a database keeping which locations lead to a collision and which locations do not. Then this database can be reused in the future.

External predicates have been recently introduced into the planning domain description language PDDL [27] and implemented in the planner FF [42], under the name "semantic attachments" [18], also for the purpose of integrating motion planning and task planning.

2.3 Bilateral Interaction between Causal Reasoning and Motion Planning

With the action domain description and the external predicate above, CCALC combines causal reasoning with geometric reasoning to compute task plans without robot-robot or robot-obstacle collisions. Our aim eventually is to compute a complete continuous trajectory for each robot to reach a common goal in an optimal way, considering the possibility of concurrent executions of actions by multiple robots. Such a problem cannot be solved, in general, directly by motion planning because the order of actions matter, in particular with picks/drops. It can be solved, on the other hand, with the help of the causal reasoner: first a task plan and its history is computed, and the motion planner is called to find a continuous collision-free trajectory for each transition.

If the motion planner fails to find (within a given time and number of samples) a continuous collision-free trajectory for a transition $\langle S_i, A_i, S_{i+1}\rangle$, we first try to identify the cause of that failure. In our example, such a failure occurs in three cases: 1) the given time/sample threshold for the task/motion planner is too low, 2) the payload collides with an obstacle during the transition from S_i to S_{i+1} (exclusive) while being carried, or 3) the payload collides with an obstacle at state S_{i+1}. In the first case, motion planning can be modified by increasing the threshold. In the first two cases, task planning can be modified as follows. The cause of the failure can be characterized by the state S_i and the action A_i; and such a failure can be avoided by modifying the planning problem by adding a temporal constraint that expresses "A_i should not be executed at S_i". In the last case, the cause of the failure can be characterized by the state S_{i+1}. Such a failure can be avoided by modifying the planning problem by adding a constraint that expresses "S_{i+1} should not be possible", like in the following query:

```
:- query
% Planning problem
maxstep :: 0..infinity;
0: ...; % Initial state
maxstep: ...; % Goal conditions
% Constraints
T<maxstep ->>
  -((T: xpay(3)=8) && (T: xpay(4)=4) &&
    (T: ypay(3)=5) && (T: ypay(4)=2) && ...).
```

After that, the modified planning problem is solved by CCALC, generating a different optimal task plan that does not cause such failures.

The hybrid planning algorithm that integrates task planning and motion planning is described in [25].

3 Housekeeping with Multiple Robots

Consider a house consisting of three rooms: a bedroom, a living room and a kitchen as shown in Figure 5. There are three cleaning robots in the house. The furniture is stationary and their locations are known to the robots a priori. Other objects are movable. There are three types of movable objects: books (green pentagon shaped objects), pillows (red triangular objects) and dishes (blue circular objects). Some objects are heavy and cannot be moved by one robot only; but the robots do not know which movable objects are heavy. The goal is for the cleaning robots to tidy the house collaboratively in a given number of steps.

This domain is challenging from various aspects. Some challenges are due to robotic manipulation required to clean the house; so all sorts of collisions (e.g., robot-robot,

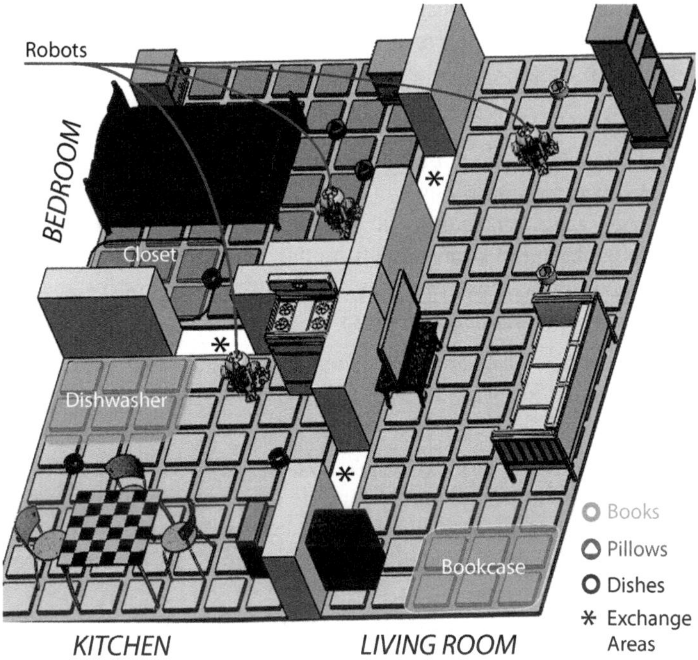

Fig. 3. A simulation of housekeeping robots

robot-stationary object and robot-moveable object collisions) should be avoided. Some challenges are due to background/commonsense knowledge required for robots to behave intelligently; and representing such commonsense knowledge and integrating it with the action domain description (and the reasoner) are challenging. Some challenges are due to execution failure of some tasks (e.g., moving an object may not be possible by one robot, but two robots) that requires collaboration of robots; so robots should be coordinated in such a way to complete all the tasks in a given number of steps.

We handle the challenges due to robotic manipulation, as described in the previous section. Let us describe how we handle the second and the third challenges.

3.1 Embedding Commonsense Knowledge in Action Domain Descriptions

To clean a house, the robots should have an understanding of the following: tidying a house means that the objects are at their desired locations. For that, first we declare a "statically determined fluent" describing that the endpoint of an object is at its expected position in the house, namely `at_desired_location(EP)`, and define it as follows:

```
caused at_desired_location(EP) if at(EP,X,Y)
   where in_place(EP,X,Y).
default -at_desired_location(EP).
```

The second causal law above expresses that normally the movable objects in an untidy house are not at their desired locations. The first causal law formalizes that the endpoint

EP of an object is at its desired location if it is at some "appropriate" position (X,Y) in the right room. Here in_place/3 is defined externally.

After defining at_desired_location/1, we can define tidy by a "macro":

```
:- macros tidy -> [/\EP | at_desired_location(EP)].
```

Finally, the robots need to know that books are expected to be in the bookcase, dirty dishes in the dishwasher, and pillows in the closet. Moreover, a bookcase is expected to be in the living-room, dishwasher in the kitchen, and the closet in the bedroom. We extract such background knowledge from the commonsense knowledge base ConceptNet [55], and describe it externally as a Prolog program. For instance, the external predicate in_place/3 is defined as follows:

```
in_place(EP,X,Y) :- belongs(EP,Obj), type_of(Obj,Type),
   el(Type,Room), area(Room,Xmin,Xmax,Ymin,Ymax),
   X>=Xmin, X=<Xmax, Y>=Ymin, Y=<Ymax.
```

Here belongs(EP,OBJ), type_of(OBJ,Type) describes the type Type of an object Obj that the endpoint EP belongs to, and el(Type,Room) describes the expected room of an object of type Type. The rest of the body of the rule above checks that the endpoint's location (X,Y) is a desired part of the room Room.

3.2 Recovering from Execution Failures via Queries with Complex Goals

To handle the sort of challenges due to execution failures, we introduce a planning and monitoring algorithm shown in Figure 4. The heart of the algorithm relies on replanning with complex temporal goals.

For instance, when the plan fails because the robot attempts to manipulate a heavy object, the robot needs to ask for assistance from other robots so that the heavy object can be carried to its destination. However, in order not to disturb the other robots while they are occupied with their own responsibilities, the call for help is delayed as much as possible.

Such a delay can be achieved by adding a temporal constraint to the goal, as shown in the following query:

```
:- query
maxstep :: 0..k;
% Initial state
0: at(r1,2,3), at(r2,4,5),
   at(book1,3,4), at(book2,5,5);
% Goal
maxstep: tidy, free,
   % Constraints
   [/\T | (T < (maxstep - 4)) ->> T:at(r2,4,5)].
```

Here the last line of the query expresses that the call for help from the robot r2 is delayed until the very last 4 steps of the plan (i.e., the robot r2 remains in his room until then).

Once such a plan is computed, one of the robots who are willing to help gets prepared (e.g., detaches from the object it is carrying, if there is any) and goes to the room of the robot who requests help.

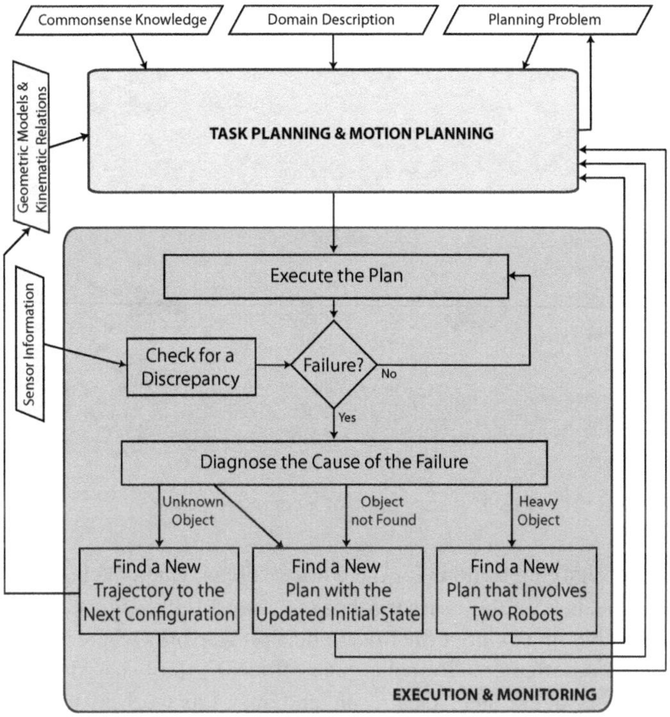

Fig. 4. An execution and monitoring algorithm for housekeeping domain

4 Cognitive Factories

Cognitive factories [75,9] aim to endow manufacturing systems with high-level reasoning capabilities in the style of cognitive robotics, such that these systems become capable of planning their own actions, reconfiguring themselves to allow fabrication of a wide range of parts and to react to change in demands, detecting failures during execution, diagnosing the cause of these failures and recovering from such failures. Since cognitive factories can plan their own actions and self-reconfigure, they can rapidly respond to changing customer needs and customization requests, demonstrating the necessary flexibility while maintaining cost-effectiveness compared to human workshops. Moreover, thanks to fault-awareness, diagnostic reasoning and failure recovery features of cognitive factories, these systems enable a high-degree of reliability comparable to those of mass production systems.

Consider a painting factory (Figure 5) with multiple teams of robots, where each team is located in a separate workspace collectively working toward completion of an assigned task: painting, waxing and stamping a given number of boxes. Each team is composed of two types of robots with different capabilities: worker robots and a single charger robot. Worker robots are self-reconfigurable and can perform different actions (i.e., painting, waxing or stamping) by reconfiguring their end-effectors. Charger robots

Fig. 5. A simulation of a cognitive factory

are designated as charging stations for the worker robots: when the battery of a worker robot drains, it meets with the charger robot and docks for charging. Each workspace contains an assembly line to move the boxes and a pit stop area where the worker robots can change their end-effectors. To make more efficient use of shared resources, teams can exchange robots: at any step, a team can lend one of its worker robots through their pit stop such that after a transportation delay the worker robot shows up next to the pit stop of a borrowing team. Initially, the state of each workspace and the number of boxes to be painted are given; the goal is for all teams to process the specified number of boxes in a minimum number of steps.

The domain of each workspace involves concurrent actions (e.g., worker robots work on different boxes concurrently) and ramifications of actions (e.g., painted boxes dry over several steps). Fortunately, $\mathcal{C}+$ allows representations of such actions and CCALC can compute plans/histories with concurrent actions for each team. In addition to the collision detection problem, discussed in the previous sections as well, there are two other important challenges related to high-level representation and reasoning: finding an optimal decoupled plan for all teams, and diagnosis/repair of execution failures. To handle these challenges we have introduced some algorithms that make use of high-level reasoning; let us focus on these aspects of the algorithms next.

4.1 Communication with Multiple Teams of Robot via Queries with Complex Constraints

The teams act as autonomous cognitive agents; therefore, each team makes its own plan to complete its own designated task. On the other hand, to make more efficient use of shared resources (e.g., robots), teams can exchange robots: at any step, a team can lend one of its worker robots through their pit stop such that after a transportation delay the worker robot shows up in the pit stop of a borrowing team. Therefore, given the initial state of each workspace and the designated tasks for each team (e.g., how many boxes of which colors to paint), the goal is for all the teams to complete these tasks in a minimum number of steps. To handle this challenge, we have developed a semi-centralized algorithm to compute an optimal decoupled plan [73]. According to this algorithm, a centralized agent decides which team lends a robot to which team, based on the teams' responses that she gets to her queries, like "Can your team complete its task in k steps, while also lending a worker robot before step k'?". This query can be represented in the language of CCALC as follows:

```
:- query
maxstep :: k;
0: ...; % Initial state
% Some robot W is available at Step k' for lending
k': [\/W | availableForLending(W)];
maxstep: ... . % Goal
```

According to our approach, teams have different workspaces, and a team does not need to know about other workspaces. Likewise, the central agent does not know about the teams' workspaces. Therefore, the heart of the algorithm lies on communications via queries like the above.

4.2 Diagnostic Reasoning in a Cognitive Factory

Once an optimal decoupled plan is computed, the teams start executing it. However, during a plan execution, it is possible that a robot gets broken so that it can not charge or work on the boxes. In such cases, the goal is to diagnose the cause of the failure or discrepancy, and find an optimal (decoupled) plan for recovery. To handle this challenge, we have developed an execution monitoring algorithm that applies diagnostic reasoning to find which robots may be broken [40].

For diagnostic reasoning, we have modified the domain description as follows. We have introduced a new fluent `broken(R)` to describe that a robot `R` may get broken at any step:

```
caused broken(R) if broken(R) after -broken(R).
```

and then modified the causal laws describing the effects of relevant actions. For instance, we have modified the effects of the action of a robot `C` charging a robot `W`) as follows:

```
charge(C,W) causes charge(C,W) if -broken(C) & -broken(W).
```

Suppose that after a sequence $\langle A_0, ..., A_n\rangle$ of (concurrent) actions is executed at a state S, a discrepancy is observed between the expected state (with respect to the domain description) and the observed state S' (obtained by sensors). In the painting domain, the causes of such discrepancies are due to broken robots; therefore, we can identify possible diagnoses by sets of possibly broken robots. We can find the set C of all minimal sets of at most k broken robots by means of a sequence of CCALC queries.

These queries check, for every subset r of at most $i = 1, 2, ..., k$ robots, whether the execution of $A_0, ..., A_m$ (for $m = n, n-1, ..., 1$) of actions at S leads to S' where the robots in r are broken. If CCALC returns a positive answer to the query, then two important information becomes available: 1) an explanation as to when the robots in r may have got broken during the execution of these actions, 2) which actions in $A_{m+1}, ..., A_n$ are executed.

For instance, consider the execution of a single concurrent action `charge(c1,w3)`, `workOn(w3,1)` ("Robot `c1` charges Robot `w3` while Robot `w3` works on Box 1 on the assembly line") at a state where `w3` is not yet charged and Box 1 is waxed (`workDone(1)=2`) and ready to be stamped. After this action is executed, we observe an unexpected state where Robot `w3`'s battery is empty and Box 2 is stamped. To find a minimal diagnosis, our algorithm first checks whether a single robot might be broken ($n = 1$, $k = 1$) by a CCALC query. For the carrier robot `c1`, the query looks like:

```
% Previous state
0: docked(c1,w3), emptyBattery(w3), workDone(1)=2,...;
% Executed actions
0: charge(c1,w3), workOn(w3,1),
   -[\/ V_A | V_A\=charge(c1,w3) & V_A\=workOn(w3,1)];
% Observed state
1: broken(c1), docked(c1,w3), emptyBattery(w3), workDone(1)=3,... .
```

Here the formula in the line before the observed state description expresses that no other action `V_A` is executed in addition to `charge(c1,w3)` and `workOn(w3,1)`. CCALC returns a positive answer with an explanation that the robot `c1` might be broken initially. Note that, to a similar query for the worker robot `w3`, CCALC returns a negative answer (otherwise work stage would not have progressed); therefore, `w3` is not broken.

It is important to note here that, since broken robots are viewed and formulated in the domain description as "exceptions", specifying these exceptions in queries does not lead to inconsistencies, due to the nonmonotonic semantics of $\mathcal{C}+$.

5 Discussion

We have presented three applications of action languages in robotics, assembly planning, housekeeping, and cognitive factories, focusing on the challenges we have faced. As emphasized in earlier studies on action languages, and as illustrated with many examples, some challenges, like concurrency of actions, ramifications of actions, the frame problem, and the qualification problem can be addressed easily while describing the action domains. So we have focused on some other challenges inherent in robotics applications:

- **Embedding background/commonsense knowledge in high-level reasoning:** In a housekeeping domain, to clean a house, the robots should have an understanding of a "tidy" house according to which objects are at their desired/expected locations. To carry an object, the robots should know that if the object is a glass full of water then the object cannot be carried upside down. In assembly planning, the robots

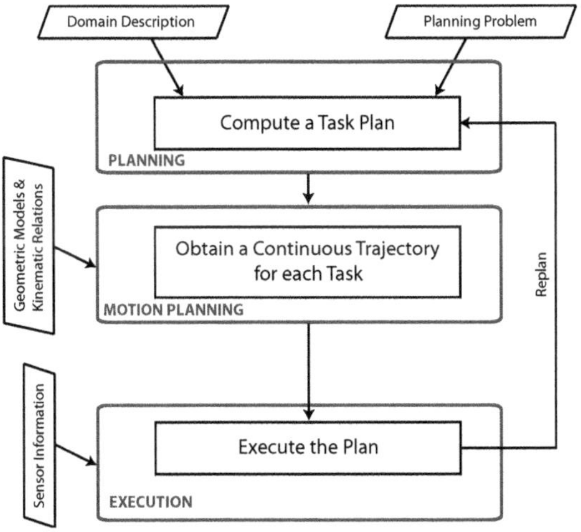

Fig. 6. Classic 3-layer robot control architecture for planning, execution and monitoring

should have an understanding that normally an object cannot be simply put onto a sphere-shaped object, since such a tower of objects may not be stable. Representing such commonsense knowledge and integrating it with the action domain description (and the reasoner) is challenging.

- **Integrating low-level continuous geometric reasoning with high-level discrete causal reasoning:** In all three robotic domains, a robot is allowed to be at the same location with a movable object only if the object is being manipulated; otherwise, collisions between robots, a robot and a stationary object, and a robot and a moveable object are not permitted. Due to these constraints, representing preconditions of (discrete) actions that require (continuous) geometric reasoning for a collision-free execution is challenging.
- **Planning/prediction with complex temporal goals/constraints:** When a plan execution fails, the robots may need to find another plan by taking into account some temporal constraints. For instance, in the housekeeping domain, when a robot cannot move an object because it is heavy, then the robots may want to compute another plan that postpones moving the heavy object to its goal position in the last four steps by the help of another robot. In assembly planning, if a continuous trajectory cannot be computed for a discrete action by a motion planner, then the goals of the planning problem is modified accordingly to find a different discrete plan that avoids the problematic states/actions. Also, planning with complex temporal goals may be useful for robots that collaborate with each other. In cognitive factories, for teams of robots in different workspaces to collaborate with each other, a team needs to know whether another team can lend a robot to complete some specified task, provided that both teams complete their tasks within a given time. Representing and solving such planning problems with temporal constraints and solving them are challenging.

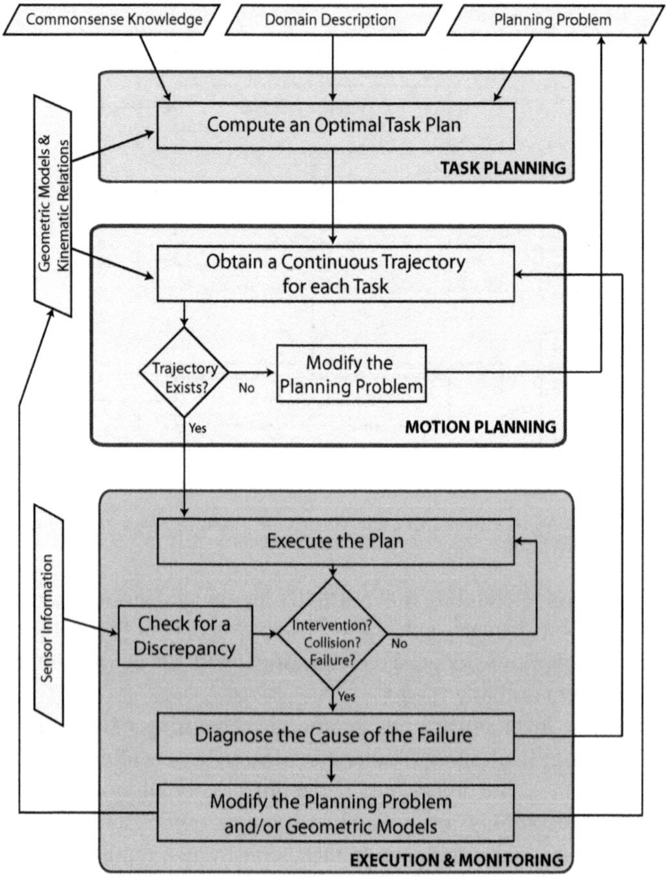

Fig. 7. Proposed framework for planning, execution and monitoring

We have discussed how these challenges can be handled using action languages. The underlying idea of our approach is to embed knowledge representation and automated reasoning in each level of the classical 3-layer robot control architecture (Figure 6), in such a way as to tightly integrate these layers as illustrated in Figure 7. We have utilized the expressive language of $\mathcal{C}+$ and the features of CCALC for this purpose as follows.

- **Embedding External Knowledge/Computation via External Predicates** External predicates are not part of the signature of the domain description (i.e., they are not fluent or action constants); they are defined and evaluated externally, for instance, by a C++ program. We have made use of external predicates for the first two challenges above. We have represented commonsense knowledge (possibly extracted from available commonsense knowledge bases, such as ConceptNet) as a logic program in Prolog and used the predicates defined in the logic program as external predicates in causal laws. Similarly, we have implemented collision/stability checks as a function in the programming language C++, and used these functions as external functions in causal laws. In this way, we have closely coupled commonsense knowledge and geometric reasoning into the discrete reasoner (first layer).

- **Reasoning via Logical Queries with Complex Goals/Constraints** For the third challenge, we have made use of queries that allow us to represent planning/prediction problems with complex temporal goals/constraints. These queries can be used for collaboration/coordination of multiple teams of robots (first layer). They can be used for finding discrete plans with feasible continuous trajectories; hence, high-level reasoning is involved in the motion planning (second layer). Also, for safe execution of plans (third layer), such queries can be used for recovery from plan failures (e.g., by replanning or by predictions for diagnostic reasoning).

Cognitive robotics presents further challenges to action languages, such as embedding sensor information into high-level representation and reasoning. Investigation of such challenges will not only enhance action languages and reasoners but also lead to various robotics applications.

Acknowledgments. Thanks to Gerhard Lakemeyer for his useful comments on an earlier draft of this paper. This work has been partially supported by Sabancı University IRP Grant and TUBITAK Grant 111E116.

References

1. Aker, E., Erdogan, A., Erdem, E., Patoglu, V.: Causal Reasoning for Planning and Coordination of Multiple Housekeeping Robots. In: Delgrande, J.P., Faber, W. (eds.) LPNMR 2011. LNCS, vol. 6645, pp. 311–316. Springer, Heidelberg (2011)
2. Aker, E., Erdogan, A., Erdem, E., Patoglu, V.: Housekeeping with multiple autonomous robots: Representation, reasoning and execution. In: Proc. of Commonsense (2011)
3. Akman, V., Erdogan, S.T., Lee, J., Lifschitz, V., Turner, H.: Representing the zoo world and the traffic world in the language of the causal calculator. Artificial Intelligence 153(1-2), 105–140 (2004)
4. Baral, C., Chancellor, K., Tran, N., Tran, N.: Representing and reasoning about signal networks: an illustration using nfkappab dependent signaling pathways. In: Proc. of CSB, pp. 623–628 (2003)
5. Baral, C., Gelfond, M.: Representing concurrent actions in extended logic programming. In: Proc. of IJCAI, pp. 866–873 (1993)
6. Baral, C., Gelfond, M.: Reasoning agents in dynamic domains, pp. 257–279. Kluwer Academic Publishers (2000)
7. Baral, C., Gelfond, M.: Reasoning about intended actions. In: Proc. of AAAI, pp. 689–694 (2005)
8. Baral, C., Gelfond, M., Provetti, A.: Representing actions: Laws, observations and hypotheses. Journal of Logic Programming 31(1-3), 201–243 (1997)
9. Beetz, M., Buss, M., Wollherr, D.: Cognitive Technical Systems — What Is the Role of Artificial Intelligence? In: Hertzberg, J., Beetz, M., Englert, R. (eds.) KI 2007. LNCS (LNAI), vol. 4667, pp. 19–42. Springer, Heidelberg (2007)
10. Bornscheuer, S.E., Thielscher, M.: Representing Concurrent Actions and Solving Conflicts. In: Dreschler-Fischer, L., Nebel, B. (eds.) KI 1994. LNCS, vol. 861, pp. 16–27. Springer, Heidelberg (1994)

11. Bornscheuer, S.E., Thielscher, M.: Representing concurrent actions and solving conflicts. Logic Journal of the IGPL 4(3), 355–368 (1996)
12. Brewka, G., Eiter, T., Truszczynski, M.: Answer set programming at a glance. Communications of ACM 54(12), 92–103 (2011)
13. Cabalar, P.: Pertinence for Causal Representation of Action Domains. Ph.D. thesis, University of Corunna (2001)
14. Caldiran, O., Haspalamutgil, K., Ok, A., Palaz, C., Erdem, E., Patoglu, V.: Bridging the Gap between High-Level Reasoning and Low-Level Control. In: Erdem, E., Lin, F., Schaub, T. (eds.) LPNMR 2009. LNCS, vol. 5753, pp. 342–354. Springer, Heidelberg (2009)
15. Casolary, M., Lee, J.: Representing the language of the causal calculator in answer set programming. In: Proc. of ICLP (Technical Communications), pp. 51–61 (2011)
16. Delgrande, J.P., Schaub, T., Tompits, H.: An extended query language for action languages and its application to aggregates and preferences. In: Proc. of NMR, pp. 362–370 (2006)
17. Doherty, P., Gustafsson, J., Karlsson, L., Kvarnström, J.: Tal: Temporal action logics language specification and tutorial. ETAI 2, 273–306 (1998)
18. Dornhege, C., Eyerich, P., Keller, T., Trüg, S., Brenner, M., Nebel, B.: Semantic attachments for domain-independent planning systems. In: Proc. of ICAPS (2009)
19. Dworschak, S., Grell, S., Nikiforova, V.J., Schaub, T., Selbig, J.: Modeling biological networks by action languages via answer set programming. Constraints 13(1-2), 21–65 (2008)
20. Dworschak, S., Grote, T., König, A., Schaub, T., Veber, P.: The system bioc for reasoning about biological models in action language c. In: Proc. of ICTAI (1), pp. 11–18 (2008)
21. Eén, N., Sörensson, N.: An Extensible SAT-solver. In: Giunchiglia, E., Tacchella, A. (eds.) SAT 2003. LNCS, vol. 2919, pp. 502–518. Springer, Heidelberg (2004)
22. Eiter, T., Erdem, E., Fink, M., Senko, J.: Updating action domain descriptions. Artificial Intelligence 174(15), 1172–1221 (2010)
23. Eiter, T., Faber, W., Leone, N., Pfeifer, G., Polleres, A.: A logic programming approach to knowledge-state planning, II: The DLV^{k} system. Artificial Intelligence 144(1–2), 157–211 (2003)
24. Eiter, T., Leone, N., Mateis, C., Pfeifer, G., Scarcello, F.: A Deductive System for Nonmonotonic Reasoning. In: Fuhrbach, U., Dix, J., Nerode, A. (eds.) LPNMR 1997. LNCS, vol. 1265, pp. 363–374. Springer, Heidelberg (1997)
25. Erdem, E., Haspalamutgil, K., Palaz, C., Patoglu, V., Uras, T.: Combining high-level causal reasoning with low-level geometric reasoning and motion planning for robotic manipulation. In: Proc. of ICRA, pp. 4575–4581 (2011)
26. Erdem, E., Lifschitz, V., Wong, M.D.F.: Wire Routing and Satisfiability Planning. In: Palamidessi, C., Moniz Pereira, L., Lloyd, J.W., Dahl, V., Furbach, U., Kerber, M., Lau, K.-K., Sagiv, Y., Stuckey, P.J. (eds.) CL 2000. LNCS (LNAI), vol. 1861, pp. 822–836. Springer, Heidelberg (2000)
27. Fox, M., Long, D.: Pddl2.1: An extension to pddl for expressing temporal planning domains. J. Artif. Intell. Res (JAIR) 20, 61–124 (2003)
28. Gebser, M., Grote, T., Schaub, T.: Coala: A Compiler from Action Languages to ASP. In: Janhunen, T., Niemelä, I. (eds.) JELIA 2010. LNCS, vol. 6341, pp. 360–364. Springer, Heidelberg (2010)
29. Gebser, M., Kaminski, R., Kaufmann, B., Ostrowski, M., Schaub, T., Thiele, S.: Engineering an Incremental ASP Solver. In: Garcia de la Banda, M., Pontelli, E. (eds.) ICLP 2008. LNCS, vol. 5366, pp. 190–205. Springer, Heidelberg (2008)
30. Gebser, M., Kaufmann, B., Kaminski, R., Ostrowski, M., Schaub, T., Schneider, M.T.: Potassco: The potsdam answer set solving collection. AI Communications 24(2), 107–124 (2011)

31. Gelfond, M., Inclezan, D.: Yet another modular action language. In: Proc. of SEA, pp. 64–78 (2009)
32. Gelfond, M., Lifschitz, V.: Representing actions in extended logic programming. In: Proc. of the Joint International Conference and Symposium on Logic Programming, pp. 559–573 (1992)
33. Gelfond, M., Lifschitz, V.: Representing action and change by logic programs. Journal of Logic Programming 17(2/3&4), 301–321 (1993)
34. Gelfond, M., Lifschitz, V.: Action languages. Electron. Trans. Artif. Intell. 2, 193–210 (1998)
35. Giunchiglia, E., Kartha, G.N., Lifschitz, V.: Representing action: Indeterminacy and ramifications. Artificial Intelligence 95(2), 409–438 (1997)
36. Giunchiglia, E., Lee, J., Lifschitz, V., McCain, N., Turner, H.: Nonmonotonic causal theories. Artificial Intelligence 153(1–2), 49–104 (2004)
37. Giunchiglia, E., Lifschitz, V.: Dependent fluents. In: Proc. of IJCAI, pp. 1964–1969 (1995)
38. Giunchiglia, E., Lifschitz, V.: An action language based on causal explanation: Preliminary report. In: Proc. of AAAI/IAAI, pp. 623–630 (1998)
39. Gravot, F., Cambon, S., Alami, R.: aSyMov:A Planner That Deals with Intricate Symbolic and Geometric Problems. In: Robotics Research the Eleventh International Symposium. Springer Tracts in Advanced Robotics, vol. 15, pp. 100–110. Springer (2005)
40. Haspalamutgil, K.: Multi-Robot Systems in Cognitive Factories: Representation, Reasoning, Execution and Monitoring. Master's thesis, Sabanci University, Istanbul, Turkey (2011)
41. Hauser, K., Latombe, J.C.: Integrating task and PRM motion planning: Dealing with many infeasible motion planning queries. In: Workshop on Bridging the Gap between Task and Motion Planning at ICAPS (2009)
42. Hoffmann, J., Nebel, B.: The ff planning system: Fast plan generation through heuristic search. J. Artif. Intell. Res (JAIR) 14, 253–302 (2001)
43. Hopton, L., Cliffe, O., De Vos, M., Padget, J.: A*QL*: A Query Language for Action Domains Modelled Using Answer Set Programming. In: Erdem, E., Lin, F., Schaub, T. (eds.) LPNMR 2009. LNCS, vol. 5753, pp. 437–443. Springer, Heidelberg (2009)
44. Kaelbling, L.P., Lozano-Perez, T.: Hierarchical planning in the now. In: Proc. of ICRA Workshop on Mobile Manipulation (2010)
45. Kartha, G.N., Lifschitz, V.: Actions with indirect effects (preliminary report). In: Proc. of KR, pp. 341–350 (1994)
46. Kowalski, R., Sergot, M.: A logic-based calculus of events. New Gen. Comput. 4(1), 67–95 (1986)
47. Latombe, J.C.: Robot Motion Planning. Kluwer Academic, Dordrecht (1991)
48. Levesque, H., Lakemeyer, G.: Cognitive robotics. In: Handbook of Knowledge Representation. Elsevier (2007)
49. Levesque, H.J., Pirri, F., Reiter, R.: Foundations for the situation calculus. ETAI 2, 159–178 (1998)
50. Lifschitz, V.: Two components of an action language. Annals of Mathematics in Artificial Intelligence 21(2–4), 305–320 (1997)
51. Lifschitz, V.: Action languages, answer sets and planning. In: The Logic Programming Paradigm: a 25-Year Perspective, pp. 357–373. Springer (1999)
52. Lifschitz, V.: What is answer set programming? In: Proc. of. AAAI, pp. 1594–1597 (2008)
53. Lifschitz, V., Ren, W.: A modular action description language. In: Proc. of AAAI (2006)
54. Lifschitz, V., Turner, H.: Representing Transition Systems by Logic Programs. In: Gelfond, M., Leone, N., Pfeifer, G. (eds.) LPNMR 1999. LNCS (LNAI), vol. 1730, pp. 92–106. Springer, Heidelberg (1999)
55. Liu, H., Singh, P.: ConceptNet: A practical commonsense reasoning toolkit. BT Technology Journal 22 (2004)

56. Marek, V., Truszczyński, M.: Stable models and an alternative logic programming paradigm. In: The Logic Programming Paradigm: a 25-Year Perspective, pp. 375–398. Springer (1999)
57. McCain, N.: Causality in Commonsense Reasoning about Actions. Ph.D. thesis, University of Texas at Austin (1997)
58. McCain, N., Turner, H.: A causal theory of ramifications and qualifications. In: Proc. of IJCAI, pp. 1978–1984 (1995)
59. McCain, N., Turner, H.: Causal theories of action and change. In: Proc. of AAAI/IAAI, pp. 460–465 (1997)
60. McCarthy, J.: Situations, actions, and causal laws. Tech. rep., Stanford University (1963)
61. Miller, R., Shanahan, M.: The event calculus in classical logic - alternative axiomatisations. ETAI 3(A), 77–105 (1999)
62. Niemelä, I.: Logic programs with stable model semantics as a constraint programming paradigm. Annals of Mathematics and Artificial Intelligence 25, 241–273 (1999)
63. Plaku, E., Hager, G.D.: Sampling-based motion and symbolic action planning with geometric and differential constraints. In: Proc. of ICRA, pp. 5002–5008 (2010)
64. Sandewall, E.: Features and Fluents: A Systematic Approach to the Representation of Knowledge about Dynamical Systems. Oxford University Press (1994)
65. Sandewall, E.: Cognitive robotics logic and its metatheory: Features and fluents revisited. ETAI 2, 307–329 (1998)
66. Son, T.C., Baral, C.: Formalizing sensing actions a transition function based approach. Artificial Intelligence 125(1–2), 19–91 (2001)
67. Thielscher, M.: Introduction to the fluent calculus. ETAI 2, 179–192 (1998)
68. Tran, N., Baral, C.: Reasoning about non-immediate triggers in biological networks. Ann. Math. Artif. Intell. 51(2–4), 267–293 (2007)
69. Tran, N., Baral, C.: Hypothesizing about signaling networks. J. Applied Logic 7(3), 253–274 (2009)
70. Tran, N., Baral, C., Nagaraj, V.J., Joshi, L.: Knowledge-Based Integrative Framework for Hypothesis Formation in Biochemical Networks. In: Ludäscher, B., Raschid, L. (eds.) DILS 2005. LNCS (LNBI), vol. 3615, pp. 121–136. Springer, Heidelberg (2005)
71. Tran, N., Baral, C., Shankland, C.: Issues in reasoning about interaction networks in cells: Necessity of event ordering knowledge. In: Proc. of AAAI, pp. 676–681 (2005)
72. Turner, H.: Representing actions in logic programs and default theories: A situation calculus approach. Journal of Logic Programming 31(1–3), 245–298 (1997)
73. Uras, T.: Applications of AI Planning in Genome Rearrangement and in Multi-Robot Systems. Master's thesis, Sabanci University, Istanbul, Turkey (2011)
74. Wolfe, J., Marthi, B., Russell, S.: Combined task and motion planning for mobile manipulation. In: International Conference on Automated Planning and Scheduling (2010)
75. Zaeh, M., Beetz, M., Shea, K., Reinhart, G., Bender, K., Lau, C., Ostgathe, M., Vogl, W., Wiesbeck, M., Engelhard, M., Ertelt, C., Rühr, T., Friedrich, M., Herle, S.: The cognitive factory. In: Changeable and Reconf. Manufacturing Systems, pp. 355–371 (2009)

The Intelligent Grounder of DLV*

Wolfgang Faber, Nicola Leone, and Simona Perri

Department of Mathematics, University of Calabria,
P.te P. Bucci, Cubo 30B, I-87036 Rende, Italy
{faber,leone,perri}@mat.unical.it

Abstract. In this work, we give an overview of the DLV *Intelligent Grounder*, one of the most popular Answer Set Programming instantiators, and a very strong point of the DLV system. Based on a variant of semi-naive evaluation, it also includes several advanced optimization techniques and supports a number of application-oriented features which allow for the successful exploitation of DLV in real-world contexts, also at an industrial level.

1 Introduction

Answer Set Programming (ASP) [18,19,11,32] is a powerful logic-based programming language which is enjoying increasing interest within the scientific community also thanks to the availability of a number of efficient implementations [27,15,23,29,30,2]. DLV [27] is one of the most successful and widely used ASP systems, which has stimulated some interest also in industry. DLV's implementation is based on solid theoretical foundations. It relies on advanced optimization techniques and sophisticated data structures.

The computation of answer sets in DLV is characterized by two phases, namely *program instantiation (grounding)* and *answer set search*. The former transforms the input program into a semantically equivalent one with no variables (ground) and the latter applies propositional algorithms on the instantiated program to generate answer sets.

Grounding in DLV is much more than a simple replacement of variables by all possible ground terms: It partially evaluates relevant program fragments, and efficiently produces a ground program which has precisely the same answer sets as the full one, but is much smaller in general. In order to highlight these features, we qualify it as Intelligent Grounder. Notably, it has the power of a full-fledged deductive database system, able to completely solve deterministic programs, most notably normal stratified programs. Moreover, it allows for dealing with recursive function symbols, and thus for expressing every computable function. More in detail, the Intelligent Grounder is able to finitely evaluate every program belonging to the powerful class of *finitely-ground ($\mathcal{FG}$)* programs with recursive functions defined in [5].

* Partially supported by the Regione Calabria and the EU under POR Calabria FESR 2007-2013 within the PIA project of DLVSYSTEM s.r.l.

E. Erdem et al. (Eds.): Correct Reasoning, LNCS 7265, pp. 247–264, 2012.

The DLV grounder plays a key role for the successful deployment of DLV in real-world contexts. Indeed, it incorporates many algorithms for improving the performance (see Section 5), including database optimization strategies and parallel evaluation techniques allowing for dealing with data-intensive applications. Moreover, it is endowed with a number of mechanisms that meet the requirement of real-world applications and make its usage feasible in practice: *database interoperability* is possible by means of an ODBC interface [25,38] which allows for both importing input data from and exporting answer set data to an external database; *plugin functions* [4] provide a framework for integrating application specific functions in logic rules and dealing with external sources of computation; *non-ground queries* allow for advanced reasoning.

In this paper we overview the DLV Intelligent Grounder, focusing on its input language, the main evaluation strategy, and recalling the most relevant optimization techniques. While the software has been available for quite some time, this work provides its first comprehensive description, including all features up to the recent release of 2011-12-21.

2 The DLV System and Its Applications

In this section we provide an overview of the DLV system, in which the Intelligent Grounder is embedded, focussing on its use within projects and applications. The DLV project has been active for more than fifteen years, encompassing first the development and later on the continuous enhancement of the DLV system.

The DLV system offers a range of advanced knowledge modeling features, providing support for declarative problem solving. Its language extends basic Answer Set Programming (ASP) with a number of constructs, including aggregates [14], weak constraints [27], functional terms [5]. The latter considerably increase the expressiveness of the language, which is important in several real-world contexts. In addition, the system incorporates several front-ends for dealing with specific applications. Concerning efficiency, DLV is competitive with the most advanced systems in the area of ASP, as confirmed also by the results of the First and Second ASP System Competitions [16,10], in which DLV won the MGS (Modeling, Grounding, Solving) category and the class of decision problems in P, respectively. DLV did not participate in the most recent competition [6], as the project team was organizing the event.

DLV is widely used by researchers all over the world: it is used for educational purposes in courses on Databases and Artificial Intelligence, both in European and American universities; it has been employed at CERN, the European Laboratory for Particle Physics, for a deductive database application; the Polish company Rodan Systems S.A. has exploited DLV in a tool for the detection of price manipulations and unauthorized use of confidential information, used by the Polish Securities and Exchange Commission. The European Commission funded a project on Information Integration, which produced a sophisticated and efficient data integration system based on DLV, called INFOMIX[24].

Notably, DLV has stimulated quite some interest also in industry. Most industrial applications of DLV are currently supervised by two spin-off companies of the University of Calabria, EXEURA and DLVSYSTEM. EXEURA uses DLV in its line of knowledge management products intended for resale, which includes OntoDLV [35], a system for ontology specification and reasoning, OLEX [37], a corporate classification system supporting the entire content classification life-cycle, and HıLεX [36], a system for ontology-based information extraction from unstructured documents. DLVSYSTEM, on the other hand, maintains the DLV system itself and supervises direct deployment of DLV in industrial applications by means of consulting. The main industrial applications that directly employ DLV currently are IDUM [22], an intelligent e-tourism system, and a system for *Team Building at the seaport of Gioia Tauro* [20], used by the transshipment company ICO BLG. For more details on applications of DLV, see [21].

3 The Input Language

In this section we first provide syntax and semantics of the core language of DLV (disjunctive logic programs with functional terms) and then overview some linguistic extensions. A number of examples illustrate the knowledge modeling features of the language.

Core Language
A *term* is either a *simple term* or a *functional term*. A *simple term* is either a constant or a variable. If $t_1 \dots t_n$ are terms and f is a function symbol of arity n, then $f(t_1, \dots, t_n)$ is a *functional term*. If $t_1, \dots, t_k$ are terms and p is a *predicate symbol* of arity k, then $p(t_1, \dots, t_k)$ is an *atom*. A *literal* l is of the form a or not a, where a is an atom; in the former case l is *positive*, otherwise *negative*[1]. A *rule* r is of the form $\alpha_1 \,\mathrm{v} \cdots \mathrm{v}\, \alpha_k \texttt{:-}\ \beta_1, \dots, \beta_n, \mathrm{not}\, \beta_{n+1}, \dots, \mathrm{not}\, \beta_m.$ where $m \geq 0$, $k \geq 0$; $\alpha_1, \dots, \alpha_k$ and $\beta_1, \dots, \beta_m$ are atoms. We define $H(r) = \{\alpha_1, \dots, \alpha_k\}$ (the *head* of r) and $B(r) = B^+(r) \cup B^-(r)$ (the *body* of r), where $B^+(r) = \{\beta_1, \dots, \beta_n\}$ (the *positive body* of r) and $B^-(r) = \{\mathrm{not}\ \beta_{n+1}, \dots, \mathrm{not}\ \beta_m\}$ (the *negative body* of r). If $H(r) = \emptyset$ then r is a *(strong) constraint*; if $B(r) = \emptyset$ and $|H(r)| = 1$ then r is a *fact*.

A rule r is safe if each variable of r has an occurrence in $B^+(r)$. A DLV program is a finite set P of safe rules. A program (a rule, a literal) is said to be *ground* if it contains no variables. A predicate is defined by a rule if the predicate occurs in the head of the rule. A predicate defined only by facts is an *EDB* predicate, the remaining predicates are *IDB* predicates. The set of all facts in P is denoted by $Facts(P)$; the set of instances of all EDB predicates in P is denoted by $EDB(P)$.

Given a program P, the *Herbrand universe* of P, denoted by $U_{\mathcal{P}}$, consists of all (ground) terms that can be built combining constants and function symbols appearing in P. The *Herbrand base* of P, denoted by $B_{\mathcal{P}}$, is the set of all ground atoms obtainable from the atoms of P by replacing variables with elements from $U_{\mathcal{P}}$. A *substitution* for a rule $r \in P$ is a mapping from the set of variables of r to

[1] Note that the DLV language also supports strong negation; however, for simplicity, in this paper we do not consider it, since it is irrelevant for the instantiation process.

the set $U_{\mathcal{P}}$ of ground terms. A *ground instance* of a rule r is obtained applying a substitution to r. The *instantiation (grounding)* $Ground(\mathcal{P})$ of P is defined as the set of all ground instances of its rules over $U_{\mathcal{P}}$. An *interpretation* I for P is a subset of $B_{\mathcal{P}}$. A positive literal a (resp., a negative literal not a) is true w.r.t. I if $a \in I$ (resp., $a \notin I$); it is false otherwise. Given a ground rule r, we say that r is satisfied w.r.t. I if some atom appearing in $H(r)$ is true w.r.t. I or some literal appearing in $B(r)$ is false w.r.t. I. Given a ground program P, we say that I is a *model* of P, iff all rules in $Ground(\mathcal{P})$ are satisfied w.r.t. I. A model M is *minimal* if there is no model N for P such that $N \subset M$. The *Gelfond-Lifschitz reduct* [19] of P, w.r.t. an interpretation I, is the positive ground program P^I obtained from $Ground(\mathcal{P})$ by: (i) deleting all rules having a negative literal false w.r.t. I; (ii) deleting all negative literals from the remaining rules. $I \subseteq B_{\mathcal{P}}$ is an *answer set* for a program P iff I is a minimal model for P^I. The set of all answer sets for P is denoted by $AS(P)$.

It is worthwile noting that, even disregarding the extensions that will be presented in the next subsection, the DLV core language is quite expressive. Indeed, its function-free fragment allows us to express, in a precise mathematical sense, every property of finite structures over a function-free first-order structure that is decidable in nondeterministic polynomial time with an oracle in NP [11] (i.e., it captures the complexity class Σ_2^P). Thus, even this fragment allows for encoding problems that cannot be translated to SAT in polynomial time. Importantly, the encoding of a large variety of problems is very concise, simple, and elegant.

Example 1. Consider the following problem, called EXAM-SCHEDULING, which consists of scheduling examinations for courses. In particular, we want to assign exams to time slots such that no two exams are assigned for the same time slot if the respective courses have a student in common (we call such courses "incompatible"). Supposing that there are three time slots available, namely, ts_1, ts_2 and ts_3, we express the problem by the following program P_{sch}:

$$r_1: \ assign(X, ts_1) \vee assign(X, ts_2) \vee assign(X, ts_3) :\!-\ course(X).$$
$$s_1: \ :\!-\ assign(X, S), assign(Y, S), incompatible(X, Y).$$

Here we assume that the courses and the pair of incompatible courses are specified by a set F of input facts with predicate *course* and *incompatible*, respectively. Rule r_1 says that every course is assigned to one of the three time slots; strong constraint s_1 (a rule with empty head) expresses that no two incompatible courses can be overlapped, that is, they cannot be assigned to the same time slot. There is a one-to-one correspondence between the solutions of the EXAM-SCHEDULING problem and the answer sets of $P_{sch} \cup F$.

Linguistic Extensions

An important feature of the DLV language are *weak constraints* [27], which allow for expressing optimization problems. A weak constraint is denoted like a strong constraint, but using the symbol :~ instead of :- . Intuitively, weak constraints allow for expressing conditions that *should* be satisfied, but not necessarily have to be. The informal meaning of a weak constraint :~ B. is "B should preferably be false". Additionally, a weight and a priority level for the weak constraint may be specified enclosed in square brackets (by means of positive integers or variables). When not specified, these values default to 1. Optimal answer sets are those minimizing the sum of weights of the violated weak constraints in the highest priority level and, among them, those which minimize the sum of weights of the violated weak constraints in the next lower level, and so on. Weak constraints allow us to express "desiderata" and are very useful in practice, since they allow for obtaining a solution (answer set) also when the usage of strong constraints would imply that there is no answer set.

Example 2. In specific instances of EXAM-SCHEDULING, there could be no way to assign courses to time slots without having some overlapping between incompatible courses. However, in real life, one is often satisfied with an approximate solution, that is, one in which constraints are satisfied as much as possible. In this light, the problem at hand can be restated as follows (APPROX-SCHEDULING): "assign exams to time slots trying to not overlap incompatible courses". This can be expressed by the program P_{asch} using weak constraints:

$$r_1: \ assign(X, ts_1) \, \text{v} \, assign(X, ts_2) \, \text{v} \, assign(X, ts_3) :\!-\, course(X).$$
$$w_1: \ :\sim assign(X, S), assign(Y, S), incompatible(X, Y).$$

An informal reading of the above weak constraint w_1 is: "preferably, do not assign the exams X and Y to the same time slot if they are incompatible". Note that the above two programs P_{sch} and P_{asch} have exactly the same answer sets if all incompatible courses can be assigned to different time slots. However, when P_{sch} has no answer set, P_{asch} provides answer sets corresponding to ways to satisfy the problem constraints "as much as possible".

The DLV language also supports *aggregate atoms* [14], allowing for representing in a simple and natural manner also properties that require the use of arithmetic operators on (multi-)sets, often arising in real-world applications. Aggregate atoms consist of an aggregation function (currently one of cardinality, sum, product, maximum, minimum), evaluated over a multiset of terms, the content of which depend on the truth of non-aggregate atoms. The syntax is $L \prec_1 \mathbf{F}\{Vars : Conj\} \prec_2 U$ where $\mathbf{F}$ is a function among `#count`, `#min`, `#max`, `#sum`, and `#times`, $\prec_1, \prec_2 \in \{=, <, \leq, >, \geq\}$, L and U are integers or variables, called guards, and $\{Vars : Conj\}$ is a symbolic set, which intuitively represents the set of values for $Vars$ for which the conjunction $Conj$ is true. For instance, the symbolic set $\{X, Y{:}a(X, Y, Z), \text{not } p(Y)\}$ stands for the set of pairs (X, Y) satisfying the conjunction $a(X, Y, Z), \text{not } p(Y)$, i.e., $S = \{(X, Y) \mid \exists Z : a(X, Y) \wedge \text{not } p(Y) \textit{ is true}\}$. When evaluating an aggregate function over it, the projection on the first elements of the pairs is considered, which yields a multiset in general. The value yielded by the function evaluation is compared against the guards, determining the truth value of the aggregate.

Example 3. Consider, for instance, a TEAM-BUILDING problem, where a project team has to be built according to the following specifications:

(p_1) The team consists of a certain number of employees.
(p_2) At least a given number of different skills must be present in the team.
(p_3) The sum of the salaries of the employees working in the team must not exceed the given budget.
(p_4) The salary of each individual employee is within a specified limit.
(p_5) The team must include at least a given number of female employees.

Information on the employees is provided by a number of facts of the form $emp(EmpId, Sex, Skill, Salary)$. The size of the team, the minimum number of different skills in the team, the budget, the maximum salary, and the minimum number of female employees are given by facts $nEmp(N)$, $nSkill(N)$, $budget(B)$, $maxSal(M)$, and $women(W)$. We then encode each property p_i above by an aggregate atom A_i, and enforce it by an integrity constraint containing not A_i.

$$
\begin{array}{ll}
r_1: & in(I) \lor out(I) :\!- \; emp(I, Sx, Sk, Sa). \\
s_1: & :\!- \; nEmp(N), \text{not } \#\texttt{count}\{I : in(I)\} = N. \\
s_2: & :\!- \; nSkill(M), \text{not } \#\texttt{count}\{Sk : emp(I, Sx, Sk, Sa), in(I)\} \geq M. \\
s_3: & :\!- \; budget(B), \text{not } \#\texttt{sum}\{Sa, I : emp(I, Sx, Sk, Sa), in(I)\} \leq B. \\
s_4: & :\!- \; maxSal(M), \text{not } \#\texttt{max}\{Sa : emp(I, Sx, Sk, Sa), in(I)\} \leq M. \\
s_5: & :\!- \; women(W), \text{not } \#\texttt{count}\{I : emp(I, f, Sk, Sa), in(I)\} \geq W.
\end{array}
$$

Intuitively, r_1 "guesses" whether an employee is included in the team or not, while each constraint s_1-s_5 corresponds one-to-one to a requirement p_1-p_5.

4 Basic Grounding Methods

All currently competitive ASP systems mimic the definition of the semantics as given in Section 3 by first creating a ground program without variables. This phase is usually referred to as *grounding* or *instantiation*. The program created is usually a subset of the ground program as defined in Section 3. Still, this task is computationally expensive (see [11,9]), and its efficiency is important for the performance of the entire system. Indeed, the grounding frequently forms a bottleneck and is crucial in real-world applications involving large input data.

In this Section we give a general description of the DLV grounder. We first describe the algorithm for instantiating programs of the DLV core language and then briefly discuss the linguistic extensions. Note that the DLV core language also permits function symbols, which can imply non-termination of the instantiation. We hence examine *finitely-ground* programs [5] for which the DLV grounder is guaranteed to terminate and explain how to identify programs of this class.

4.1 Dependency and Component Graphs

Given an input program $\mathcal{P}$, the DLV grounder creates a subset of $Ground(\mathcal{P})$, whose ground rules only contain literals that can potentially become true. To this end, structural information of the input program is analyzed. The *Dependency Graph* of a program $\mathcal{P}$ is a directed graph $G_{\mathcal{P}} = \langle N, E \rangle$, where N is the set of

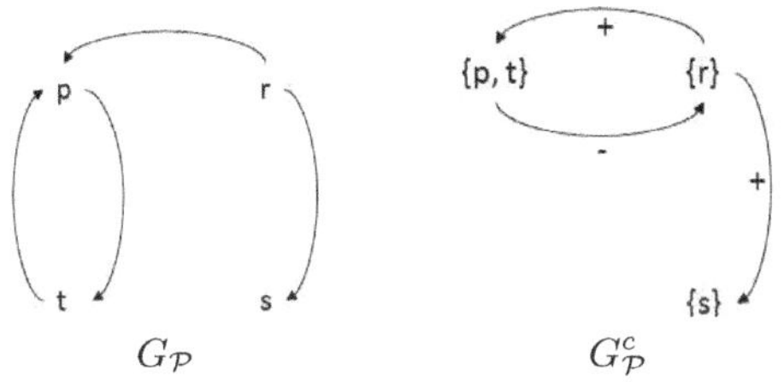

Fig. 1. Dependency and Component Graphs

IDB predicates of $\mathcal{P}$, and E contains an arc (p, q) if there is a rule r in $\mathcal{P}$ such that q occurs in the head of r and p occurs in a positive literal of the body of r. The graph $G_{\mathcal{P}}$ induces a partition of $\mathcal{P}$ into subprograms (also called *modules*) allowing for a modular evaluation: For each strongly connected component (SCC) C of $G_{\mathcal{P}}$ (a set of predicates), the set of rules defining the predicates in C is called *module* of C and is denoted by $\mathcal{P}_C$. A rule r occurring in a module $\mathcal{P}_C$ (i.e., defining some predicate $q \in C$) is said to be *recursive* if there is a predicate $p \in C$ in the positive body of r; otherwise, r is said to be an *exit rule*.

Example 4. Consider the following program $\mathcal{P}$, where a is an EDB predicate:

$$a(g(1)). \quad t(X, f(Y)) \,\text{:-}\, p(X, Y), a(Y). \quad p(g(X), Y) \vee s(Y) \,\text{:-}\, r(X), r(Y).$$
$$p(X, Y) \,\text{:-}\, r(X), t(X, Y). \qquad r(X) \,\text{:-}\, a(g(X)), not\ t(X, f(X)).$$

Graph $G_{\mathcal{P}}$ is illustrated in Figure 1; the strongly connected components of $G_{\mathcal{P}}$ are $\{s\}$, $\{r\}$ and $\{p, t\}$. They correspond to the three following modules:

$$\mathcal{P}_{\{s\}} = \{p(g(X), Y) \vee s(Y) \,\text{:-}\, r(X), r(Y).\ \}$$
$$\mathcal{P}_{\{r\}} = \{r(X) \,\text{:-}\, a(g(X)), not\ t(X, f(X)).\ \}$$
$$\mathcal{P}_{\{p,t\}} = \{p(g(X), Y) \vee s(Y) \,\text{:-}\, r(X), r(Y). \quad p(X, Y) \,\text{:-}\, r(X), t(X, Y).$$
$$t(X, f(Y)) \,\text{:-}\, p(X, Y), a(Y).\ \}$$

Moreover, $\mathcal{P}_{\{s\}}$ and $\mathcal{P}_{\{r\}}$ do not contain recursive rules, while $\mathcal{P}_{\{p,t\}}$ contains one exit rule ($p(g(X), Y) \vee s(Y) \,\text{:-}\, r(X), r(Y).$) and two recursive rules.

The *Component Graph* of a program $\mathcal{P}$ is a directed labeled graph $G^c_{\mathcal{P}} = \langle N, E, lab \rangle$, where N is the set of strongly connected components of $G_{\mathcal{P}}$, and E contains an arc (B, A) with $lab((B, A)) =$"+", if there is a rule r in $\mathcal{P}$ such that $q \in A$ occurs in the head of r and $p \in B$ occurs in a positive literal of the body of r, and E contains an arc (B, A), with $lab((B, A)) =$"-", if there is a rule r in $\mathcal{P}$ such that $q \in A$ occurs in the head of r and $p \in B$ occurs in a negative literal of the body of r, and there is no arc e' in E, with $lab(e') =$"+".

The Component Graph induces a partial ordering among the SCCs of the Dependency Graph as follows. For any pair of nodes A, B of $G^c_{\mathcal{P}}$, A *positively precedes* B in $G^c_{\mathcal{P}}$ (denoted $A \prec_+ B$) if there is a *path* in $G^c_{\mathcal{P}}$ from A to B in which all arcs are labeled with "+"; A *negatively precedes* B (denoted $A \prec_- B$), if there is a path in $G^c_{\mathcal{P}}$ from A to B in which at least one arc is labeled with "-". This ordering induces *admissible component sequences* $C_1, \dots, C_n$ of SCCs of $G_{\mathcal{P}}$ such that for each $i < j$, i) $C_j \not\prec_+ C_i$; ii) if $C_j \prec_- C_i$ then there is a cycle in $G^c_{\mathcal{P}}$ from C_i to C_j(i.e. either $C_i \prec_+ C_j$ or $C_i \prec_- C_j$). Several such sequences exist in general.

Example 5. Given the program $\mathcal{P}$ of Example 4 its Component Graph is illustrated in Figure 1. It easy to see that $\{r\} \prec_+ \{p,t\}$, $\{r\} \prec_+ \{s\}$, while $\{p,t\} \prec_- \{r\}$ and $\{p,t\} \prec_- \{s\}$. An admissible component sequence would be $\{r\}$, $\{p,t\}$, $\{s\}$.

Intuitively, this ordering allows incremental grounding, one module at a time. If a module A positively precedes a module B then A must be evaluated before B. If A negatively precedes B then A should be possibly evaluated before B. Negative precedences are only overridden for unstratified components.

4.2 Instantiation Procedure

The procedure *Instantiate* shown in Figure 2 takes as input both a program $\mathcal{P}$ to be instantiated and the Component Graph $G^c_{\mathcal{P}}$, and outputs a set Π of ground rules containing only atoms which can possibly be derived from $\mathcal{P}$, such that $ANS(\mathcal{P}) = ANS(\Pi \cup EDB(\mathcal{P}))$. As already pointed out, the input program $\mathcal{P}$ is divided into modules corresponding to the nodes of $G^c_{\mathcal{P}}$(i.e. the SCCs of the Dependency Graph $G_{\mathcal{P}}$), and these modules are evaluated one at a time following an admissible component sequence.

The algorithm keeps a set of significant atoms S, a subset of the Herbrand Base, such that instantiated rules contain only atoms from S. Initially, $S = EDB(\mathcal{P})$, and $\Pi = \emptyset$. Then, an admissible component sequence $(C_1, \ldots, C_n)$ is created, and each module corresponding to C_i is grounded by invoking *InstantiateModule. Instantiate* runs until all components have been considered.

Procedure *InstantiateModule* handles the grounding of one module. Its inputs are the component C to be grounded and S, and it computes those ground instances for each r in the module for C that contain only atoms from S. It also updates the set S with the atoms occurring in the heads of rules in Π. The grounding of single rules is handled by the procedure *InstantiateRule*: Given the set of atoms that are known to be significant up to now, it builds all the significant ground instances of r, adds them to Π, and adds the head atoms of the newly generated ground rules to the significant ones. The evaluation of r is essentially performed by evaluating the relational join of the positive body literals. Since the rule is safe, each variable occurring either in a negative literal or in the head of the rule appears also in some positive body literal, thus the instantiation of positive literals implies that all rule variables have been instantiated (details about this procedure can be found in [34]). Moreover, before being added to Π, each ground rule is simplified by removing from the body those (positive and negative) literals which are already known to be true. Those rules whose head is already true, or where a negative body literal is already known to be false are not added to Π. This mechanism will be described in detail in Section 4.3.

Note that a disjunctive rule r may appear in the program modules of two different components. Thus, before processing r, *InstantiateRule* checks whether

Procedure *Instantiate*($\mathcal{P}$: Program; $G^c_{\mathcal{P}}$: ComponentGraph; **var** Π: GroundProgram)
  var S: SetOfAtoms, $(C_1, \ldots, C_n)$: List of nodes of $G^c_{\mathcal{P}}$;
  $S = EDB(\mathcal{P})$; $\Pi := \emptyset$;
  $(C_1, \ldots, C_n) := OrderedNodes(G^c_{\mathcal{P}})$; /* *admissible component sequence* */
  for i = 1 ... n **do** *InstantiateModule*$(\mathcal{P}, C_i, S, \Pi)$;

Procedure *InstantiateModule* ($\mathcal{P}$: Program; C: SetOfPredicates;
  var S: SetOfAtoms; **var** Π: GroundProgram)
  var $\mathcal{NS}$: SetOfAtoms, ΔS: SetOfAtoms;
  $\mathcal{NS} := \emptyset$; $\Delta S := \emptyset$;
  for each $r \in Exit(C, \mathcal{P})$ **do** *InstantiateRule*$(r, S, \Delta S, \mathcal{NS}, \Pi)$;
  do
    $\Delta S := \mathcal{NS}$; $\mathcal{NS} = \emptyset$;
    for each $r \in Recursive(C, \mathcal{P})$ **do** *InstantiateRule*$(r, S, \Delta S, \mathcal{NS}, \Pi)$;
    $S := S \cup \Delta S$;
  while $\mathcal{NS} \neq \emptyset$

Procedure *InstantiateRule*(r: rule; S: SetOfAtoms; ΔS: SetOfAtoms;
  var $\mathcal{NS}$: SetOfAtoms; **var** Π: GroundProgram)
/* *Given S and ΔS builds the ground instances of r, simplifies them (see Sec. 4.3), adds them to Π, and add to $\mathcal{NS}$ the head atoms of the generated ground rules.* */

Fig. 2. The DLV Instantiation Procedure

it has been already grounded during the instantiation of another component. This ensures that a rule is actually processed only within one program module.

Recursive rules are processed several times using a variant of the semi-naïve evaluation technique [39], in which at each iteration n only the significant information derived during iteration $n-1$ is used. This is implemented by partitioning the significant atoms into three sets: ΔS, S, and $\mathcal{NS}$. $\mathcal{NS}$ is filled with atoms computed during the current iteration (say n); ΔS contains atoms computed during the previous iteration (say $n-1$); and S contains those computed earlier (up to iteration $n-2$). Initially, ΔS and $\mathcal{NS}$ are empty, and the exit rules contained in the program module of C are evaluated by a single call to procedure *InstantiateRule*; then, the recursive rules are evaluated (do-while loop). At the beginning of each iteration, $\mathcal{NS}$ is assigned to ΔS, i.e. the new information derived during iteration n is considered as the significant information for iteration $n+1$. Then, *InstantiateRule* is invoked for each recursive rule r, and, at the end of each iteration, ΔS is added to S (since it has already been dealt with). The procedure stops whenever no new information has been derived (i.e. $\mathcal{NS} = \emptyset$). Intuitively, the instantiation procedure of DLV allows for dynamically computing extensions of predicates; head atoms resulting from a rule instantiation immediately become members of the domains for the next iteration, even during the instantiation of the same recursive component.

Note that the algorithm described here does not take into account strong constraints, since they do not belong to any module of the input. Since their evaluation does not produce new significant atoms to be added to S, they are processed when the instantiation of all program modules has terminated, by means of a simplified version of procedure *InstantiateRule* for which sets ΔS and $\mathcal{NS}$ are useless. We remark that, as ground rules, also ground constraints are simplified, possibly resulting in constraints with empty body, and thus violated. In this case the computation is aborted since the input program is inconsistent.

It can be proved that the ground program generated by the DLV instantiation algorithm has the same answer sets as the non ground input program.

Proposition 1. *Let $\mathcal{P}$ be an ASP program, and Π be the ground program generated by the algorithm* Instantiate. *Then $ANS(\mathcal{P}) = ANS(\Pi \cup EDB(\mathcal{P}))$ (i.e. $\mathcal{P}$ and $\Pi \cup EDB(\mathcal{P})$ have the same answer sets).* □

The proof is a generalization of the one provided in [13] for function-free programs and is omitted for space reasons.

4.3 Instance Simplifications

Each ground rule generated by procedure *InstantiateRule* is examined and possibly simplified or even eliminated. In particular, body literals (positive and negative ones) which are already known to be true can be dropped. Moreover, since *InstantiateRule* computes variable substitutions by considering only positive body variables (sufficient because of safety), it may occur that some negative literal in the created rule instance is already known to be false. In this case the rule instance is already satisfied and need not be considered further.

For formalising these ideas, we partition the set S of significant ground atoms into two subsets: S^T, containing those significant ground atoms that are already known to be true, and S^{PT}, containing those significant ground atoms that can become true ("potentially true"). S^T is initialized with the input facts and then extended by those heads of instantiated rules which have been transformed into facts once the simplification below has been applied (essentially when all positive atoms are in S^T and all negative literals are known to be true as well). The heads of all other instantiated rules belong to S^{PT} (essentially all atoms from disjunctive heads and rules in which the body is not known to be true yet).

Once a rule instance R is generated, the following actions are carried out for simplifying the program: i) if a positive literal $Q \in B^+(R)$ and $Q \in S^T$, then delete Q from $B(R)$; ii) if a negative body literal not Q over predicate q is in $B(R)$, $Q \notin S$, and all the rules defining q have been already instantiated, then delete not Q from $B(R)$; iii) if a negative body literal not Q is in $B(R)$ and $Q \in S^T$, then remove the ground instance R.

Note that, while for positive literals it suffices to check whether it is in S^T for deciding its truth, for negative literals it is not sufficient to check whether its atom is not in S, but it should also not be added later. In case the input program is non-disjunctive and stratified,the modular evaluation (which respects the ordering previously described) together with the simplification above, allows the DLV grounder for completely evaluating the program.

To formalize this, we say that a literal with predicate q is *solved* if (i) q is defined solely by non-disjunctive rules (i.e., all rules with q in the head are non-disjunctive), and (ii) q does not depend (even transitively) on any unstratified predicate [3] or disjunctive predicate (i.e., a predicate defined by a disjunctive rule). The component ordering obtained by the Component Graph ensures that when a rule with a solved body predicate q is instantiated, the rules defining q have been instantiated previously; thus the extension of q has already been determined and, moreover, it completely belongs to the S^T component of S. That is, the truth values of all ground literals that are instances of solved predicates are fully determined by the instantiator.

It follows that, after the simplification, none of the solved predicates occur in the rules of the ground instantiation Π produced by the instantiator; rather, all the predicates occurring in the rules of Π will be not solved and will be evaluated during the answer set search phase. In case the input program is non-disjunctive and stratified, all predicates are solved; thus all generated rule instances are either simplified to facts and added to S^T or deleted. The program has a single answer set, coinciding with the set S^T.

4.4 Dealing with Weak Constraints and Aggregates

We now provide an overview of how the instantiation process handles the two major linguistic extensions, aggregates and weak constraints.

Concerning aggregates, in the following we suppose that programs respect aggregate stratification as defined in [14], which intuitively forbids recursion through aggregates. As previously described, the instantiation proceeds bottom-up following the dependencies among predicates. In the presence of aggregates, admissible component sequences must also conform with the aggregate stratification. Then, the instantiation of a rule with aggregates is performed by first evaluating non-aggregate body literals, and then applying variable substitutions to aggregates.

In more detail, let r be the rule $H \,\texttt{:-}\, B, aggr.$, where H is the head of the rule, B is the conjunction of the non-aggregate body literals, and $aggr$ is an aggregate literal over a symbolic set $\{Vars{:}Conj\}$. A variable appearing in r is said to be *local* if it appears solely in $aggr$, otherwise it is said to be *global*. The instantiation of r proceeds by first evaluating the instantiation of the literals in B, thus computing a substitution θ for the global variables of $Conj$. Then, the (partially bound) conjunction $\theta(Conj)$ is instantiated by using the extensions of predicates appearing in $Conj$ (since the instantiation process respects also aggregate stratification, all extensions are already available). Thus, a set of pairs $\{\langle\theta_1(Vars) : \theta_1(\theta(Conj))\rangle, \ldots, \langle\theta_n(Vars) : \theta_n(\theta(Conj))\rangle\}$is generated, where each θ_i is a possible substitution for the local variables in $\theta(Conj)$.

Note that, similar to rule simplification, we materialize only those pairs whose truth value cannot be determined yet (that is, instances of unsolved literals) and process the others dynamically, (partially) evaluating the aggregate already during instantiation. The same process is repeated for all further substitutions of the literals in B.

Instantiation of weak constraints, similar to that of strong contraints, is performed after the evaluation of all rules, basically computing the relational join of literals and simplifying the produced ground weak constraints as described in Section 4.3. Note that for a weak constraint also a weight and a level could be specified, each of them can either be an integer or a variable. In case of variables, the instantiation of the body literals also provides a substitution for them. Note also that the body of a weak constraint could become empty after the simplification step, just like for strong constraints. This means that the weak constraint is unconditionally violated, but differently from strong constraints this does not cause the program to be inconsistent, but only causes the penalty of this weak constraint to be present for each answer set. Therefore the violated weak constraint is stored in a dedicated structure in order to be treated later on when computing the costs of each answer set.

4.5 Finitely Ground Programs

The presence of recursive function symbols within DLV programs has a strong impact on the grounding process, which might even not terminate. All common reasoning tasks on such programs are indeed undecidable, in the general case. Despite this, the DLV instantiation procedure does allow for dealing with recursive function symbols, and it is guaranteed to terminate on the class of *finitely-ground* ($\mathcal{FG}$) programs defined in [5]. Intuitively, for each program $\mathcal{P}$ in this class, there exists a finite ground program $\mathcal{P}'$ having exactly the same answer sets as $\mathcal{P}$. $\mathcal{P}'$ is computable for $\mathcal{FG}$ programs, thus answer sets of $\mathcal{P}$ are computable as well. Moreover, each computable function can be expressed by a $\mathcal{FG}$ program. Since $\mathcal{FG}$ programs express any computable function, membership in this class is obviously not decidable, but it has been proved to be semi-decidable [5].

$\mathcal{FG}$ programs are defined by exploiting the fix-point Φ^{∞} of an operator Φ [2] that acts on a module of a program $\mathcal{P}$ in order to: (i) select only those ground rules whose positive body is contained in a set of ground atoms consisting of the heads of a given set of rules; (ii) perform further simplifications by deleting all those rules whose body is certainly false or whose head is certainly already true w.r.t. a given set of ground atoms A, and simplifies the remaining rules by removing from the bodies all literals that are true w.r.t. A. The proper composition of consecutive applications of Φ^{∞} to all program modules according to one admissible component sequence γ (that is, an ordering which respects dependencies induced by the Component Graph) produces an instantiation $I_{\gamma}(\mathcal{P})$ of $\mathcal{P}$ which drops many useless rules w.r.t. answer sets computation. The program $\mathcal{P}$ is finitely-ground if $I_{\gamma}(\mathcal{P})$ is finite for every admissible component ordering γ.

The way in which the instantiation $I_{\gamma}(\mathcal{P})$ is computed has a number of relevant similarities with the DLV instantiation approach. First of all, the application of the operator Φ is performed by considering the components of the Dependency Graph one at a time and following one of the orderings induced by the Component Graph, exactly as in the case of the bottom-up evaluation performed by the DLV instantiator. Moreover, for every component C, the ground rules

[2] For details we refer the reader to [5].

produced by the application of Φ only contain ground atoms appearing in the heads of ground rules produced by the evaluation of the previous modules. In the DLV approach this corresponds to the use of the set S of ground atoms significant for the instantiation (see the algorithm in Figure 2). The operator Φ also performs a simplification on the produced ground rules (which possibly become new facts) by taking into account facts and ground rules previously determined, similarly to the simplification performed by DLV described in Section 4.3. This gives the intuition that the ground program produced by DLV coincides with the instantiation $I_\gamma(\mathcal{P})$ if γ is the ordering exploited by DLV. However, in some cases, the DLV instantiation can be actually smaller than $I_\gamma(\mathcal{P})$. Indeed, in case of components with recursive rules, the computation of Φ^∞ simulates the semi-naive approach of DLV, in which head atoms resulting from a rule instantiation immediately become members of the domains for the next iteration; but the simplification step applied by Φ only considers information coming from previous components, while the DLV simplification also considers information derived during the evaluation of the current component, in previous iterations. Summarizing, the ground program Π generated by the algorithm *Instantiate*, according to a component ordering γ, is not bigger than $I_\gamma(P)$. Hence, if $I_\gamma(P)$ is finite, Π is finite as well, thus proving the following result.

Proposition 2. *Let $\mathcal{P}$ be a* DLV *program, and Π be the ground program generated by the algorithm* Instantiate. *Then, if $\mathcal{P}$ is a $\mathcal{FG}$ program, Π is finite.* □

Note that for applications in which termination needs to be guaranteed a priori, the DLV grounder has been endowed with a checker which allows the user to statically recognize if the input program belongs to a class for which the grounding process terminates, the class of argument-restricted programs [28]. However, if the user is confident that the program can be grounded in finite time, even if it does not belong to the class of argument-restricted programs, then she can disable the checker by specifying a command-line option. Moreover, the DLV grounder provides another way for guaranteeing termination: the possibility to specify, by means of another command-line option, the maximum allowed nesting level for functional terms.

5 Optimization Techniques

Much effort has been spent on sophisticated algorithms and optimization techniques aimed at improving the performance of the DLV instantiator. In the following we briefly recall the most relevant ones, providing references to detailed descriptions of the respective techniques.

Some of the techniques exploited for optimizing the instantiation procedure descend from the database field. For instance, the DLV instantiator implements a **program rewriting** [12] strategy descending from query optimization techniques in relational algebra. According to this technique, program rules are automatically rewritten by pushing projections and selections down the execution tree as much as possible; this allows for reducing in many cases the size of the program instantiation. Another rewriting-based optimization technique used in DLV are **dynamic magic sets** [1], an extension of the Magic Sets technique originally defined for standard Datalog for optimizing query answering over logic programs. The Magic Sets technique rewrites the input program for identifying a subset of the program instantiation which is sufficient for answering the query. The restriction of the instantiation is obtained by means of additional "magic" predicates, whose extensions represent relevant atoms w.r.t. the query. Dynamic Magic Sets, specifically conceived for disjunctive programs, inherit the benefits provided by standard magic sets and additionally allow for exploiting the information provided by the magic predicates also during the nondeterministic answer set search.

Another group of techniques descending from databases concerns the instantiation process of each rule of the program. In particular, since rule instantiation is essentially performed by evaluating the relational join of the positive body literals, an optimal ordering of literals in the body is a key issue for the efficiency of the instantiation procedure, just like for join computation. Indeed, a good ordering may dramatically affect the overall instantiation time. The DLV instantiator exploits a well-motivated **body reordering** criterion [26], which determines the position in the body of each literal by taking into account two factors: one is a measure of how much the choice of a literal L reduces the search space for possible substitutions and the other takes into account the binding of the variables of L (since preferring literals with already bound variables, possible inconsistencies may be detected quickly).

Moreover, to guarantee good performance also in case of problems with huge amount of input data, the DLV instantiator exploits an efficient main-memory indexing technique [8]. In particular, it implements a kind of **on demand indexing**, where a generic argument can be indexed (not necessarily the first one), and indices are computed during the evaluation and only if they can really be exploited. Moreover, the argument to be indexed is not predetermined, but is established during the computation according to a heuristic. For optimizing the rule instantiation task, a **backjumping algorithm** [34] is employed. In particular, given a rule r to be grounded, this algorithm exploits both the semantical and the structural information about r for computing efficiently the ground instances of r, avoiding the generation of "useless" rules. That is, from each rule only a relevant subset of its ground instances are computed, avoiding the generation of "useless" instances, but fully preserving the semantic of the program.

In the last few years,in order to make use of modern multi-core/multi-processor computers, a parallel version of the DLV instantiator has been realized, based on a number of strategies [7,33] specifically conceived for the instantiation task. More in detail, the **parallel instantiator** is based on three levels of parallelism: *components*, *rules* and *single rule* level. The first level allows for instantiating in parallel subprograms of the program in input: it is especially useful when handling programs containing parts that are, somehow, independent. The second one allows for the parallel evaluation of rules within a given subprogram: it is useful when the number of rules in the subprograms is large. The third one allows for the parallel evaluation of a single rule: it is crucial for the parallelization of programs with few rules, where the first two levels are almost not applicable. Moreover, the parallel instantiator is endowed with mechanisms for dealing with two important issues that may strongly affect the performance of a real implementation: *load balancing* and *granularity control.* Indeed, if the workload is not uniformly distributed to the available processors then the benefits of parallelization are not fully obtained; moreover, if the amount of work assigned to each parallel processing unit is too small then the (unavoidable) overheads due to creation and scheduling of parallel tasks might overcome the advantages of parallel evaluation.

6 Related Work

In this section we briefly discuss some of the main differences and similarities of the DLV Intelligent Grounder with respect to the other two most popular ASP instantiators, namely, lparse [31], and gringo [17].

Concerning lparse, it accepts a different class of input programs, and follows different strategies for the computation. Indeed, lparse accepts logic programs respecting *domain restrictions.* This condition enforces each variable in a rule to occur in a positive body literal, called domain literal, which (i) is not mutually recursive with the head, and (ii) is neither unstratified nor dependent (also transitively) on an unstratified literal. For instance, the program consisting of rules $\mathcal{P} = \{a(X) :\!-\, b(X), c(X).\quad b(X) :\!-\, a(X).\}$ is not accepted by lparse. To instantiate a rule r, lparse employs a nested loop that scans the extensions of the domain predicates occurring in the body of r, and generates ground instances accordingly. It is therefore a comparatively simple and fast instantiation method, at least for applications with few domains or for domains with small extensions. However, lparse may generate useless rules as they may contain non-domain body literals that are not derivable by the program. The DLV instantiator incorporates several database optimization techniques and builds the domains dynamically, hence the instantiation generated by DLV is generally a subset of that generated by lparse. Thus, in case of applications where the size of domain extensions are very large (as in many industrial applications), lparse may take significantly more time and produce a larger instantiation than DLV.

Concerning gringo, versions up to 3.0 also accepted only domain restricted programs; however, the notion of domain literal was an extension of that of lparse, so gringo could handle all the programs accepted by lparse but not vice versa. For example, program $\mathcal{P}$ above was accepted by gringo, while the following one, encoding reachability, could not be handled prior to version 3.0: $\{r(X,Y) :\!-\, arc(X,Y).\quad r(X,Y) :\!-\, arc(X,U), r(U,Y).\}$. The current gringo releases (since version 3.0) removed domain restrictions and instead requires programs to be safe as in DLV, and evaluate them according to a grounding algorithm based on the semi-naive schema, very similar to the one in the DLV instantiator. It is worth noting that, passing from domain restrictedness to the more general notion of safety, also the gringo grounding process may not terminate, just like for DLV. However, while gringo leaves the responsibility to check whether the input program has a finite grounding to the user, DLV implements some checks for guaranteeing termination (see Section 4.5), and the user can choose to disable them.

References

1. Alviano, M., Faber, W.: Dynamic Magic Sets and super-coherent answer set programs. AI Communications 24(2), 125–145 (2011)
2. Anger, C., Konczak, K., Linke, T.: *NoMoRe*: A System for Non-Monotonic Reasoning under Answer Set Semantics. In: Eiter, T., Faber, W., Truszczyński, M. (eds.) LPNMR 2001. LNCS (LNAI), vol. 2173, pp. 406–410. Springer, Heidelberg (2001)
3. Apt, K.R., Blair, H.A., Walker, A.: Towards a Theory of Declarative Knowledge. In: Minker, J. (ed.) Foundations of Deductive Databases and Logic Programming, Washington DC, pp. 89–148 (1988)
4. Calimeri, F., Cozza, S., Ianni, G.: External sources of knowledge and value invention in logic programming. AMAI 50(3-4), 333–361 (2007)
5. Calimeri, F., Cozza, S., Ianni, G., Leone, N.: Computable Functions in ASP: Theory and Implementation. In: Garcia de la Banda, M., Pontelli, E. (eds.) ICLP 2008. LNCS, vol. 5366, pp. 407–424. Springer, Heidelberg (2008)
6. Calimeri, F., Ianni, G., Ricca, F., Alviano, M., Bria, A., Catalano, G., Cozza, S., Faber, W., Febbraro, O., Leone, N., Manna, M., Martello, A., Panetta, C., Perri, S., Reale, K., Santoro, M., Sirianni, M., Terracina, G., Veltri, P.: The Third Answer Set Programming Competition: Preliminary Report of the System Competition Track. In: Delgrande, J.P., Faber, W. (eds.) LPNMR 2011. LNCS, vol. 6645, pp. 388–403. Springer, Heidelberg (2011)
7. Calimeri, F., Perri, S., Ricca, F.: Experimenting with Parallelism for the Instantiation of ASP Programs. J. of Algorithms 63(1-3), 34–54 (2008)
8. Catalano, G., Leone, N., Perri, S.: On demand indexing techniques for the dlv instantiator. In: Proceedings of the Workshop on Answer Set Programming and Other Computing Paradigms (ASPOCP 2008), Udine, Italy (2008)
9. Dantsin, E., Eiter, T., Gottlob, G., Voronkov, A.: Complexity and Expressive Power of Logic Programming. ACM Computing Surveys 33(3), 374–425 (2001)
10. Denecker, M., Vennekens, J., Bond, S., Gebser, M., Truszczyński, M.: The Second Answer Set Programming Competition. In: Erdem, E., Lin, F., Schaub, T. (eds.) LPNMR 2009. LNCS, vol. 5753, pp. 637–654. Springer, Heidelberg (2009)
11. Eiter, T., Gottlob, G., Mannila, H.: Disjunctive Datalog. ACM TODS 22(3), 364–418 (1997)
12. Faber, W., Leone, N., Mateis, C., Pfeifer, G.: Using Database Optimization Techniques for Nonmonotonic Reasoning. In: INAP Organizing Committee (ed.) DDLP 1999, pp. 135–139. Prolog Association of Japan (September 1999)
13. Faber, W., Leone, N., Perri, S., Pfeifer, G.: Efficient Instantiation of Disjunctive Databases. Tech. Rep. DBAI-TR-2001-44, TU Wien, Austria (November 2001), `http://www.dbai.tuwien.ac.at/local/reports/dbai-tr-2001-44.pdf`
14. Faber, W., Pfeifer, G., Leone, N., Dell'Armi, T., Ielpa, G.: Design and implementation of aggregate functions in the dlv system. TPLP 8(5-6), 545–580 (2008)
15. Gebser, M., Kaufmann, B., Neumann, A., Schaub, T.: Conflict-driven answer set solving. In: IJCAI 2007, pp. 386–392 (January 2007)

16. Gebser, M., Liu, L., Namasivayam, G., Neumann, A., Schaub, T., Truszczyński, M.: The First Answer Set Programming System Competition. In: Baral, C., Brewka, G., Schlipf, J. (eds.) LPNMR 2007. LNCS (LNAI), vol. 4483, pp. 3–17. Springer, Heidelberg (2007)
17. Gebser, M., Schaub, T., Thiele, S.: GrinGo: A New Grounder for Answer Set Programming. In: Baral, C., Brewka, G., Schlipf, J. (eds.) LPNMR 2007. LNCS (LNAI), vol. 4483, pp. 266–271. Springer, Heidelberg (2007)
18. Gelfond, M., Lifschitz, V.: The Stable Model Semantics for Logic Programming. In: ICLP/SLP 1988, pp. 1070–1080. MIT Press, Cambridge (1988)
19. Gelfond, M., Lifschitz, V.: Classical Negation in Logic Programs and Disjunctive Databases. NGC 9, 365–385 (1991)
20. Grasso, G., Iiritano, S., Leone, N., Lio, V., Ricca, F., Scalise, F.: An ASP-Based System for Team-Building in the Gioia-Tauro Seaport. In: Carro, M., Peña, R. (eds.) PADL 2010. LNCS, vol. 5937, pp. 40–42. Springer, Heidelberg (2010)
21. Grasso, G., Iiritano, S., Leone, N., Ricca, F.: Some DLV Applications for Knowledge Management. In: Erdem, E., Lin, F., Schaub, T. (eds.) LPNMR 2009. LNCS, vol. 5753, pp. 591–597. Springer, Heidelberg (2009)
22. Ielpa, S.M., Iiritano, S., Leone, N., Ricca, F.: An ASP-Based System for e-Tourism. In: Erdem, E., Lin, F., Schaub, T. (eds.) LPNMR 2009. LNCS, vol. 5753, pp. 368–381. Springer, Heidelberg (2009)
23. Janhunen, T., Niemelä, I., Seipel, D., Simons, P., You, J.H.: Unfolding Partiality and Disjunctions in Stable Model Semantics. ACM TOCL 7(1), 1–37 (2006)
24. Leone, N., Gottlob, G., Rosati, R., Eiter, T., Faber, W., Fink, M., Greco, G., Ianni, G., Kałka, E., Lembo, D., Lenzerini, M., Lio, V., Nowicki, B., Ruzzi, M., Staniszkis, W., Terracina, G.: The INFOMIX System for Advanced Integration of Incomplete and Inconsistent Data. In: SIGMOD 2005, pp. 915–917. ACM Press (June 2005)
25. Leone, N., Lio, V., Terracina, G.: DLV^{DB}: Adding Efficient Data Management Features to ASP. In: Lifschitz, V., Niemelä, I. (eds.) LPNMR 2004. LNCS (LNAI), vol. 2923, pp. 341–345. Springer, Heidelberg (2004)
26. Leone, N., Perri, S., Scarcello, F.: Improving ASP Instantiators by Join-Ordering Methods. In: Eiter, T., Faber, W., Truszczyński, M. (eds.) LPNMR 2001. LNCS (LNAI), vol. 2173, pp. 280–294. Springer, Heidelberg (2001)
27. Leone, N., Pfeifer, G., Faber, W., Eiter, T., Gottlob, G., Perri, S., Scarcello, F.: The DLV System for Knowledge Representation and Reasoning. ACM TOCL 7(3), 499–562 (2006)
28. Lierler, Y., Lifschitz, V.: One More Decidable Class of Finitely Ground Programs. In: Hill, P.M., Warren, D.S. (eds.) ICLP 2009. LNCS, vol. 5649, pp. 489–493. Springer, Heidelberg (2009)
29. Lierler, Y., Maratea, M.: Cmodels-2: SAT-based Answer Set Solver Enhanced to Non-tight Programs. In: Lifschitz, V., Niemelä, I. (eds.) LPNMR 2004. LNCS (LNAI), vol. 2923, pp. 346–350. Springer, Heidelberg (2004)
30. Lin, F., Zhao, Y.: ASSAT: computing answer sets of a logic program by SAT solvers. AI 157(1-2), 115–137 (2004)
31. Syrjänen, T.: Lparse 1.0 User's Manual (2002), `http://www.tcs.hut.fi/Software/smodels/lparse.ps.gz`
32. Marek, V.W., Truszczyński, M.: Stable Models and an Alternative Logic Programming Paradigm. In: Apt, K.R., Marek, V.W., Truszczyński, M., Warren, D.S. (eds.) The Logic Programming Paradigm – A 25-Year Perspective, pp. 375–398 (1999)
33. Perri, S., Ricca, F., Sirianni, M.: Parallel instantiation of ASP programs: techniques and experiments. In: TPLP (2012)

34. Perri, S., Scarcello, F., Catalano, G., Leone, N.: Enhancing DLV instantiator by backjumping techniques. AMAI 51(2-4), 195–228 (2007)
35. Ricca, F., Gallucci, L., Schindlauer, R., Dell'Armi, T., Grasso, G., Leone, N.: OntoDLV: an ASP-based system for enterprise ontologies. Journal of Logic and Computation (2009)
36. Ruffolo, M., Manna, M.: HiLeX: A System for Semantic Information Extraction from Web Documents. ICEIS (Selected Papers). LNBIP, vol. 3, pp. 194–209 (2008)
37. Rullo, P., Cumbo, C., Policicchio, V.L.: Learning rules with negation for text categorization. In: ACM Symposium on Applied Computing, pp. 409–416. ACM (2007)
38. Terracina, G., Leone, N., Lio, V., Panetta, C.: Experimenting with recursive queries in database and logic programming systems. TPLP 8, 129–165 (2008)
39. Ullman, J.D.: Principles of Database and Knowledge Base Systems. Computer Science Press (1989)

Bi-state Logic

Luis Fariñas del Cerro[1,*], David Pearce[2,*], and Agustín Valverde[3]

[1] Université Paul Sabatier, Toulouse, France
farinas@irit.fr
[2] Universidad Politécnica de Madrid, Spain
david.pearce@upm.es
[3] Universidad de Málaga, Málaga, Spain
a_valverde@ctima.uma.es

Abstract. This paper proposes an answer to a question recently posed by Vladimir Lifschitz about which logical system would be appropriate for reasoning about logic programs with intensional functions (IF-programs for short), a type of causal logic program introduced by him in [2]. As an appropriate system we propose *bi-state* logic, a four-valued logic that has apparently not been previously studied. We characterize bi-state models and their logic and show how a concept of *superstable* (bi-state) model corresponds in the propositional case to the semantics of IF-programs. We also relate bi-state logic to classical logic and suggest its possible application in the area of program updates.

1 Introduction

It is a pleasure to dedicate this paper to our friend and colleague, Vladimir Lifschitz, on the occasion of his 65th birthday. The paper is also devoted thematically to his work on answer set programming, in fact to a very recent development in the theory of stable models.[1] In [2] Lifschitz has introduced the idea of logic programs with *intensional functions*, or IF-programs for short. These are closely related to causal logic programs. The semantics of IF-programs is defined in [2] via a form of second-order stable model and gives rise to a non-monotonic form of inference. The question arises whether this semantics can be understood in terms of preferred models of an underlying monotonic logic, in the same way that ordinary stable models can be understood as preferred or minimal models in the logic **HT** of here-and-there [4].

In this paper we introduce *bi-state logic*, another useful four-valued logic for applications in artificial intelligence, especially in knowledge representation and reasoning. In fact, we suggest that bi-state logic is an adequate logic for dealing with the foundations of Lifschitz's IF-programs. However, at present we shall deal only with the propositional version of bi-state logic and therefore we shall

---

* Corresponding authors.

[1] This goes to show, if any proof were needed, that VL continues to be source of inspiration in this as in many other areas of computation and logic.

E. Erdem et al. (Eds.): Correct Reasoning, LNCS 7265, pp. 265–278, 2012.

not consider IF-programs in their full generality.[2] We can nevertheless show how the semantics of propositional versions of IF-programs can be understood in terms of bi-state logic.

Bi-state logic, denoted by **BiS**, is a system in which there is a separation between the interpretation of negation and that of other connectives. It can be presented as a four-valued logic or, equivalently, as a logic based on two independent worlds or states of interpretation, hence the name bi-state logic. Although four-valued, **BiS** has interesting relations to classical logic as well as to the logic of here-and-there that provides a foundation for ordinary logic programs under stable model semantics. We study these relations later in the paper.

In the next section we introduce bi-state logic by giving equivalent formulations in terms of semantics, an axiomatic system and a Gentzen style sequent calculus. In Section 3 we study a form of preferred models for bi-state logic that we call *superstable* models and relate this to the semantics of Lifschtiz's IF-programs. We also provide a strong equivalence theorem for superstable models. In Section 4 we compare bi-state logic to the usual logics studied in the foundations of answer set programming: the logic of here-and-there and its non-monotonic extension, equilibrium logic. Section 5 relates bi-state models to a notion of RE-model that has recently been proposed by Slota and Leite [5] as a suitable basis for defining logic program updates in a semantical framework. We conclude by stating a simple relationship that holds between bi-state and classical logic, and by summarizing the main properties established for bi-state models.

2 Bi-state Logic

We consider a propositional language $\mathcal{L}$, over a set P, of propositional variables, with connectives '$\vee$', '$\wedge$', '$\rightarrow$', '$\neg$', and auxiliary parentheses '(','$)$'.

A **BiS**-*interpretation* is a pair $\langle I_0, I_1\rangle$, of sets of atoms. The subscripts 0, 1, refer to the *states* s_0 and s_1; the *satisfaction* relation between a **BiS**-interpretation $\mathcal{I} = \langle I_0, I_1\rangle$, a state s_i and a formula φ, is defined recursively: for every $i = 0, 1$,

- $\mathcal{I}, s_i \models p$ if $p \in I_i$,
- $\mathcal{I}, s_i \models \varphi \wedge \psi$ if $\mathcal{I}, s_i \models \varphi$ and $\mathcal{I}, s_i \models \psi$,
- $\mathcal{I}, s_i \models \varphi \vee \psi$ if $\mathcal{I}, s_i \models \varphi$ or $\mathcal{I}, s_i \models \psi$,
- $\mathcal{I}, s_i \models \varphi \rightarrow \psi$ if, either $\mathcal{I}, s_i \not\models \varphi$ or $\mathcal{I}, s_i \models \psi$,
- $\mathcal{I}, s_i \models \neg\varphi$ if $I, s_1 \not\models \varphi$.

We write $\mathcal{I} \models \varphi$ if $I, s_0 \models \varphi$ and $I, s_1 \models \varphi$; in such a case, we say that I *satisfies* φ or I is a model of φ. A formula φ is *valid*, in symbols $\models \varphi$, if every interpretation is a model of φ; this defines the *bi-state logic*, denoted by **BiS**. Two formulas φ and ψ are said equivalent if $\varphi \leftrightarrow \psi$ is valid; equivalently, two formulas φ and ψ are equivalent if and only if they have the same **BiS**-models. For any set Γ of formulas and any formula φ, we write $\Gamma \models \varphi$ if for every **BiS**-interpretation $\mathcal{I}$ and every state s: $\mathcal{I}, s \models \Gamma$ implies $\mathcal{I}, s \models \varphi$. For later use, let us

[2] First-order bi-state logic and its relation to IF-programs in the full sense will be the subject of future work.

say that a **BiS**-interpretation $\langle I_0, I_1\rangle$ is *consistent* if $I_0 \subseteq I_1$. This terminology is justified by the fact that in a consistent interpretation the case that both p and $\neg p$ are true is excluded.

2.1 Axiomatization

A sound and complete axiomatization can be constructed as follows:

Axioms: The usual axioms for positive logic:
P1 $\varphi \to (\psi \to \varphi)$
P2 $(\varphi \to (\psi \to \phi)) \to ((\varphi \to \psi) \to (\varphi \to \phi))$
P3 $(\varphi \wedge \psi) \to \varphi$
P4 $(\varphi \wedge \psi) \to \psi$
P5 $\varphi \to (\psi \to (\varphi \wedge \psi))$
P6 $(\varphi \to \phi) \to ((\psi \to \phi) \to ((\varphi \vee \psi) \to \phi))$
P7 $\varphi \to (\varphi \vee \psi)$
P8 $\psi \to (\varphi \vee \psi)$
And the following axioms:
B1 $\varphi \vee (\varphi \to \psi)$
B2 $\neg(\varphi \vee \psi) \leftrightarrow (\neg\varphi \wedge \neg\psi)$
B3 $\neg(\varphi \wedge \psi) \leftrightarrow (\neg\varphi \vee \neg\psi)$
B4 $\neg(\varphi \to \psi) \leftrightarrow (\neg\neg\varphi \wedge \neg\psi)$
B5 $\neg\varphi \vee \neg\neg\varphi$
B6 $\neg\neg\varphi \to (\neg\varphi \to \psi)$
Inference rule: *Modus Ponens*, from φ and $\varphi \to \psi$, conclude ψ.

Theorem 1 (Soundness and completeness). *If $\vdash$ is the inference relation defined by the axiomatic system, then $\Gamma \models \varphi$ if and only if $\Gamma \vdash \varphi$ for every set of formulas Γ and every formula φ.*

Proof: Soundness is straightforward and to prove completeness we use the standard Henkin method. Let us assume that $\Gamma \nvdash \varphi$. Let Δ_0 be the theory such that

1. $\Gamma \subseteq \Delta_0$, Δ_0 is closed for $\vdash$, and $\Delta_0 \nvdash \varphi$.
2. If $\alpha \vee \beta \in \Delta_0$, then either $\alpha \in \Delta_0$ or $\beta \in \Delta_0$. The axiom P6 guarantees that, for every formula $\alpha \vee \beta$, either α or β does not allow to deduce φ if it is added to Γ.

Let Δ_1 be another theory such that:

1. $\Gamma \cup \{\neg\varphi\} \subseteq \Delta_1$ and Δ_1 is closed for $\vdash$.
2. Δ_1 is maximal consistent, that is, there is no ψ such that $\Delta_1 \vdash \psi$ and $\Delta_1 \vdash \neg\psi$, and there is no a greater theory with the same property.

We consider the BiS-interpretation $\mathcal{I} = \langle I_0, I_1\rangle$ where I_0 is the set of atoms in Δ_0 and I_1 is the set of atoms in Δ_1. We will show the following properties, which allow us to complete the proof:

$$\mathcal{I}, s_1 \models \psi \quad \text{iff} \quad \Delta_1 \vdash \psi \tag{1}$$

$$\mathcal{I}, s_1 \models \neg\psi \quad \text{iff} \quad \Delta_0 \vdash \neg\psi \tag{2}$$

$$\mathcal{I}, s_0 \models \psi \quad \text{iff} \quad \Delta_0 \vdash \psi \tag{3}$$

For (1), we can conclude that $\mathcal{I}, s_1 \models \Gamma$ and for (3), we can conclude that $\mathcal{I}, s_0 \models \Gamma$ and $\mathcal{I}, s_0 \not\models \varphi$. That is, $\mathcal{I}$ is a model of Δ but it is not a model of φ, what establishes completeness.
Proof of (1), by induction:

- $\mathcal{I}, s_1 \models \psi_1 \wedge \psi_2 \iff \mathcal{I}, s_1 \models \psi_1$ and $\mathcal{I}, s_1 \models \psi_2$, $\overset{\text{IH}}{\iff}$ $\iff \Delta_1 \vdash \psi_1$ and $\Delta_1 \vdash \psi_2$, $\iff \Delta_1 \vdash \psi_1 \wedge \psi_2$.
  The last equivalence makes use of the axioms P3, P4, and P5.
- $\mathcal{I}, s_1 \models \psi_1 \vee \psi_2 \iff \mathcal{I}, s_1 \models \psi_1$ or $\mathcal{I}, s_1 \models \psi_2$, $\overset{\text{IH}}{\iff}$ $\iff \Delta_1 \vdash \psi_1$ or $\Delta_1 \vdash \psi_2$, $\overset{(*)}{\iff} \Delta_1 \vdash \psi_1 \vee \psi_2$.
  The left-to-right direction in (*) is a consequence of P7 and P8 and the right-to-left direction is a consequence of the maximal consistency property.
- $\mathcal{I}, s_1 \models \psi_1 \to \psi_2 \iff \mathcal{I}, s_1 \not\models \psi_1$ or $\mathcal{I}, s_1 \models \psi_2$, $\overset{\text{IH}}{\iff}$ $\iff \Delta_1 \nvdash \psi_1$ or $\Delta_1 \vdash \psi_2$, $\overset{(*)}{\iff} \Delta_1 \vdash \psi_1 \to \psi_2$.
  The right-to-left direction in (*) is a consequence of Modus Ponens and the left-to-right direction is a consequence of the maximal condition.
- $\mathcal{I}, s_1 \models \neg\psi, \iff \mathcal{I}, s_1 \not\models \psi, \iff \Delta_1 \nvdash \psi_1 \iff \Delta_1 \vdash \neg\psi_1$.
  The last equivalence is a consequence of the consistency of Δ_1.

Proof of (2), by induction:

- $\mathcal{I}, s_1 \models \neg(\psi_1 \vee \psi_2) \iff \mathcal{I}, s_1 \models \neg\psi_1$ and $\mathcal{I}, s_1 \models \neg\psi_2$, $\overset{\text{IH}}{\iff}$ $\iff \Delta_0 \vdash \neg\psi_1$ and $\Delta_0 \vdash \neg\psi_2$, $\iff \Delta_0 \vdash \neg(\psi_1 \vee \psi_2)$.
  The last equivalence is a consequence of the axioms B2, P3, P4 y P5.
- $\mathcal{I}, s_1 \models \neg(\psi_1 \wedge \psi_2) \iff \mathcal{I}, s_1 \models \neg\psi_1$ or $\mathcal{I}, s_1 \models \neg\psi_2$, $\overset{\text{IH}}{\iff}$ $\iff \Delta_0 \vdash \neg\psi_1$ or $\Delta_0 \vdash \neg\psi_2$, $\overset{(*)}{\iff} \Delta_0 \vdash \neg(\psi_1 \wedge \psi_2)$.
  The left-to-right direction in (*) is a consequence of axioms B3, P7 y P8, and the right-to-left direction is a consequence of axiom B3 and condition 2 in the definition of Δ_0.
- $\mathcal{I}, s_1 \models \neg\neg\psi \iff \mathcal{I}, s_1 \not\models \neg\psi$, $\overset{\text{IH}}{\iff} \Delta_0 \nvdash \neg\psi$, $\overset{(*)}{\iff} \Delta_0 \vdash \neg\neg\psi$.
  (*) is a consequence of axiom B5 and condition 2 in the definition of Δ_0.
- $\mathcal{I}, s_1 \models \neg(\psi_1 \to \psi_2) \iff \mathcal{I}, s_1 \models \neg\neg\psi_1$ and $\mathcal{I}, s_1 \models \neg\psi_2$, $\overset{\text{IH}}{\iff}$ $\iff \Delta_0 \vdash \neg\neg\psi_1$ and $\Delta_0 \vdash \neg\psi_2$, $\iff \Delta_0 \vdash \neg(\psi_1 \to \psi_2)$.
  The last equivalence is a consequence of axioms B4, P3, P4 and P5.

Proof of (3), by induction:

- $\mathcal{I}, s_0 \models \psi_1 \wedge \psi_2 \iff \mathcal{I}, s_0 \models \psi_1$ and $\mathcal{I}, s_0 \models \psi_2$, $\overset{\text{IH}}{\iff}$ $\iff \Delta_0 \vdash \psi_1$ and $\Delta_0 \vdash \psi_2$, $\iff \Delta_0 \vdash \psi_1 \wedge \psi_2$.
  The last equivalence is a consequence of axioms P3, P4, and P5.

- $\mathcal{I}, s_0 \models \psi_1 \vee \psi_2 \iff \mathcal{I}, s_0 \models \psi_1$ or $\mathcal{I}, s_0 \models \psi_2, \overset{\text{IH}}{\iff}$

$\iff \Delta_0 \vdash \psi_1$ or $\Delta_0 \vdash \psi_2, \overset{(*)}{\iff} \Delta_0 \vdash \psi_1 \vee \psi_2$.

The left-to-right direction in (*) is a consequence of axioms P7 and P8 and the right-to-left direction is a consequence of condition 3 in the definition of Δ_0.

- $\mathcal{I}, s_0 \models \psi_1 \to \psi_2 \iff \mathcal{I}, s_0 \not\models \psi_1$ or $\mathcal{I}, s_0 \models \psi_2, \overset{\text{IH}}{\iff}$

$\iff \Delta_0 \nvdash \psi_1$ or $\Delta_0 \vdash \psi_2, \overset{(*)}{\iff} \Delta_0 \vdash \psi_1 \to \psi_2$.

The right-to-left direction in (*) is a consequence of Modus Ponens; the left-to-right direction is proved as follows: if $\psi_2 \in \Delta_0$, then $\psi_1 \to \psi_2 \in \Delta_0$ by axiom P1, $\psi_2 \to (\psi_1 \to \psi_2)$; on the other hand, if $\psi_2 \notin \Delta_0$, then $\psi_1 \to \psi_2 \in \Delta_0$ by axiom B1 and property 2 in the definition of Δ_0.

- $\mathcal{I}, s_0 \models \neg\psi \iff \mathcal{I}, s_1 \models \neg\psi, \iff \Delta_0 \vdash \neg\psi_1$.

The last equivalence is the property (2). ⊣

2.2 Gentzen System

We can also provide a Gentzen system, more suitable to check validity in **BiS**. The system is cut-free and therefore it can be described as a tableau system which may be used, for example, to check the *strong* equivalence of formulas, defined in Section 3.

The axioms of the system are sequents $\Gamma \vdash \Delta$ such that $\Gamma \cap \Delta \neq \varnothing$ and the rules of the system are:

$$\frac{\Gamma \vdash \Delta, \alpha \qquad \Gamma \vdash \Delta, \beta}{\Gamma \vdash \Delta, \alpha \wedge \beta} \qquad \frac{\Gamma, \alpha, \beta \vdash \Delta}{\Gamma, \alpha \wedge \beta \vdash \Delta}$$

$$\frac{\Gamma \vdash \Delta, \alpha, \beta}{\Gamma \vdash \Delta, \alpha \vee \beta} \qquad \frac{\Gamma, \alpha \vdash \Delta \qquad \Gamma, \beta \vdash \Delta}{\Gamma, \alpha \vee \beta \vdash \Delta}$$

$$\frac{\Gamma, \alpha \vdash \Delta, \beta}{\Gamma \vdash \Delta, \alpha \to \beta} \qquad \frac{\Gamma \vdash \alpha, \Delta \qquad \Gamma, \beta \vdash \Delta}{\Gamma, \alpha \to \beta \vdash \Delta}$$

$$\frac{\Gamma \vdash \Delta, \neg\alpha \qquad \Gamma \vdash \Delta, \neg\beta}{\Gamma \vdash \Delta, \neg(\alpha \vee \beta)} \qquad \frac{\Gamma, \neg\alpha, \neg\beta \vdash \Delta}{\Gamma, \neg(\alpha \vee \beta) \vdash \Delta}$$

$$\frac{\Gamma \vdash \Delta, \neg\alpha, \neg\beta}{\Gamma \vdash \Delta, \neg(\alpha \wedge \beta)} \qquad \frac{\Gamma, \neg\alpha \vdash \Delta \qquad \Gamma, \neg\beta \vdash \Delta}{\Gamma, \neg(\alpha \wedge \beta) \vdash \Delta}$$

$$\frac{\Gamma, \neg\alpha \vdash \Delta \qquad \Gamma \vdash \Delta, \neg\beta}{\Gamma \vdash \Delta, \neg(\alpha \to \beta)} \qquad \frac{\Gamma, \neg\beta \vdash \Delta, \neg\alpha}{\Gamma, \neg(\alpha \to \beta) \vdash \Delta}$$

$$\frac{\Gamma, \neg\alpha \vdash \Delta}{\Gamma \vdash \Delta, \neg\neg\alpha} \qquad \frac{\Gamma \vdash \Delta, \neg\alpha}{\Gamma, \neg\neg\alpha \vdash \Delta}$$

Theorem 2 (Soundness and completeness). *$\Gamma \models \varphi$ if and only if $\Gamma \vdash \varphi$.*

3 Superstable Models and IF-Programs

If I is a classical model of a formula φ, then, trivially, $\langle I, I\rangle$ is a **BiS**-model of φ; and vice versa, if $\langle I, I\rangle$ is a **BiS**-model of φ, then I is a classical model of φ. We will call these kinds of models *total models.* We can now introduce a kind of preferred model that allows us to define a non-monotonic logic based on **BiS** and obtain a characterization of the semantics of IF-programs.

Definition 1. *A total* **BiS**-*model of Π, $\langle I, I\rangle$, is said to be* superstable *if there does not exist another model $\langle I_0, I\rangle$ of Π such that $I_0 \neq I$ and I_0 only contains atoms occurring in Π.*

For example, $\langle\{p, q\}, \{p, q\}\rangle$ is a superstable model of $p \wedge q$. However, $\langle\varnothing, \varnothing\rangle$ is the unique total model of $\neg p \wedge \neg q$, and it is not superstable.

The logic induced by superstable models is non-monotonic.[3] For example, $\varphi = \neg p \wedge q$ does not have superstable models. $\langle\{q\}, \{q\}\rangle$ and $\langle\{p, q\}, \{q\}\rangle$ are **BiS**-models of φ; however, $\{\neg p \wedge q, p \to \neg q\}$ has a superstable model: $\langle\{q\}, \{q\}\rangle$.

Notice that we add the condition that the model $\langle I_0, I\rangle$ must contain atoms from Π, because otherwise the definition of superstable would make no sense: if q is a variable not in φ and $\langle I, I\rangle$ is a total model of φ, then $\langle I \cup \{q\}, I\rangle$ is also a model of φ and thus, $\langle I, I\rangle$ would never be superstable.

Lifschitz introduces in [2] a new semantics for a logic programming, called IF-programs, which can be considered as causal theories. We can show how the logic **BiS** can characterize Lifschitz's semantics for the propositional case. Moreover, **BiS** also yields a characterization of the strong equivalence relation for superstable models.

If $\boldsymbol{p} = p_1 \dots p_n$ is the list of propositional variables in φ, and $\boldsymbol{q} = q_1 \dots q_n$ is a list of variables not occurring in φ, then $\boldsymbol{q} \doteq \boldsymbol{p}$ stands for

$$\bigwedge_{i=1\dots n} q_i \leftrightarrow p_i$$

Lifschitz defines a second order formula which he uses to provide a new concept of stable model. Although his definition applies to first order formulas with function symbols, the corresponding propositional version would be

$$SM[\varphi] = \forall \boldsymbol{q}(\varphi^{\diamond}[\boldsymbol{p}/\boldsymbol{q}] \leftrightarrow \boldsymbol{q} \doteq \boldsymbol{p})$$

where $\varphi^{\diamond}[\boldsymbol{p}/\boldsymbol{q}]$ is the formula obtained by replacing each nonnegated occurrence of each member p_i with the variable q_i. A stable model of a program Π is a model of the quantified boolean formula $SM[\Pi]$.

Theorem 3. *I is a model of $SM[\varphi]$ iff $\langle I, I\rangle$ is a superstable model of φ.*

[3] Non-monotonic inference is not our main topic here, however we might define a non-monotonic entailment relation in the usual way by saying that a theory entails a formula φ if that formula is true in all its superstable models.

Proof:

($\Rightarrow$) Let us assume that I is a model of $SM[\varphi]$. Trivially, I is a model φ, because I is a model of $\varphi^\diamond[\boldsymbol{p}/\boldsymbol{p}] \leftrightarrow \boldsymbol{p} \doteq \boldsymbol{p}$ and thus it is a model of $\varphi^\diamond[\boldsymbol{p}/\boldsymbol{p}] = \varphi$. Therefore, $\langle I, I\rangle$ is a **BiS**-model of φ.

Let us suppose that $\langle I, I\rangle$ is not superstable; then there exists another model $\langle J, I\rangle$ of φ such that $J \neq I$. Let p_{i_0} be such that $I(p_{i_0}) \neq J(p_{i_0})$, and let $\overline{J}$ be the interpretation defined as follows:

$$\overline{J}(p_i) = I(p_i), \qquad \overline{J}(q_i) = J(p_i)$$

It is easy to prove by induction that $\overline{J}(\varphi^\diamond[\boldsymbol{p}/\boldsymbol{q}]) = 1$ iff $\langle J, I\rangle, s_0 \models \varphi$. Therefore, $\overline{J}(\varphi^\diamond[\boldsymbol{p}/\boldsymbol{q}]) = 1$ and $\overline{J}(\varphi^\diamond[\boldsymbol{p}/\boldsymbol{q}] \leftrightarrow \boldsymbol{q} \doteq \boldsymbol{p}) = 0$, which contradicts the assumption that I is a model of $SM[\varphi]$.

($\Leftarrow$) The other direction is analogous. ⊣

BiS logic also allows us to characterize the strong equivalence concept associated with superstable models.

Definition 2. *Two sets of formulas, Π_1 and Π_2 are said to be strongly equivalent if, for every set of formulas Δ, the sets $\Pi_1 \cup \Delta$ and $\Pi_2 \cup \Delta$ have the same superstable models.*

Theorem 4 (Strong equivalence). *Π_1 and Π_2 are strongly equivalent if and only if Π_1 and Π_2 are equivalent in* **BiS**.

Lemma 1. *If $\langle I_0, I_1\rangle \models \varphi$, then $\langle I_1, I_1\rangle \models \varphi$.*

Proof: The statement is a consequence of the following properties:

$$\begin{array}{ccc} \langle I_0, I_1\rangle, s_1 \models \varphi & \Leftrightarrow & \langle I_1, I_1\rangle, s_1 \models \varphi \\ \langle I_1, I_1\rangle, s_0 \models \varphi & \Leftrightarrow & \langle I_1, I_1\rangle, s_1 \models \varphi \end{array}$$

The proof is easy and left to the reader. ⊣

Proof of theorem 4:

- Let us assume that Π_1 and Π_2 are equivalent in **BiS**; in particular, they have the same total models. Let Δ be another set of formulas and $\langle I, I\rangle$ a superstable model of $\Pi_1 \cup \Delta$; then it is also a model of $\Pi_2 \cup \Delta$. Moreover, it is superstable, because if $\langle I_0, I\rangle$ was a model of Π_2 and Δ, then it would be a model of Π_1, and thus of $\Pi_1 \cup \Delta$, what is not possible, because $\langle I, I\rangle$ be a superstable model of $\Pi_1 \cup \Delta$.
- Let us assume that Π_1 and Π_2 are strongly equivalent. Let Q be the set of atoms occurring in Π_1 or Π_2 and let $\langle I_0, I_1\rangle$ be a model of Π_1 such that $I_0 \subseteq Q$, $I_1 \subseteq Q$.

1. If $I_0 = I_1$, we consider the formulas

$$\Delta_0 = \{p \vee \neg p \mid p \in I_0\}, \qquad \Delta_1 = \{q \rightarrow \neg\neg q \mid q \in Q \setminus I_0\},$$

   It is easy to check that $\langle I_0, I_0\rangle$ is a model of $\Pi_1 \cup \Delta_0 \cup \Delta_1$ and there is no model $\langle I_0', I_0\rangle$ such that $I_0' \neq I_0$.

   Therefore, $\langle I_0, I_0\rangle$ is a superstable model of $\Pi_1 \cup \Delta_0 \cup \Delta_1$ and of $\Pi_2 \cup \Delta_0 \cup \Delta_1$, and in particular, it is a model of Π_2.
2. If $I_0 \subset I_1$, then by lemma 1 $\langle I_1, I_1\rangle$ is also a model of Π_1, and by the previous item, $\langle I_1, I_1\rangle$ is also a model of Π_2. Then, let us consider the set

$$\Delta = I_0 \cup \{p \rightarrow q \mid p, q \in I_1 \setminus I_0\}$$

   It is easy to check that $\langle I_0, I_1\rangle$ and $\langle I_1, I_1\rangle$ are the unique models of Δ with I_1 as s_1 part. Therefore, $\langle I_1, I_1\rangle$ is not a superstable model neither of $\Pi_1 \cup \Delta$ nor $\Pi_2 \cup \Delta$. For $\langle I_0, I_1\rangle$ is the unique model of Δ with $I_0 \neq I_1$, necessarily $\langle I_0, I_1\rangle$ must be a model of Π_2.
3. If $I_0 \supset I_1$, then by lemma 1 $\langle I_1, I_1\rangle$ is also a model of Π_1, and by previous item, $\langle I_1, I_1\rangle$ is also a model of Π_2. Then, let us consider the set

$$\Delta = I_1 \cup \{p \rightarrow q \mid p, q \in I_0 \setminus I_1\}$$

   It is easy to check that $\langle I_0, I_1\rangle$ and $\langle I_1, I_1\rangle$ are the unique models of Δ with I_1 as s_1 part. Therefore, $\langle I_1, I_1\rangle$ is not a superstable model neither of $\Pi_1 \cup \Delta$ nor $\Pi_2 \cup \Delta$. For $\langle I_0, I_1\rangle$ is the unique model of Δ with $I_0 \neq I_1$, necessarily $\langle I_0, I_1\rangle$ must be a model of Π_2.

Analogously, we can prove that every model of Π_2 is a model of Π_1. ⊣

This therefore answers at least at the propositional level a question left open in [2], namely: Which transformations of IF-programs preserve stability in this new, stronger sense? As Lifschitz suggests, the "logic of IF-programs" should be intermediate between positive logic and classical logic. As Theorems 3 and 4 show, transformations that preserve the (strong) equivalence of IF-programs are precisely those that preserve ordinary logical equivalence in **BiS**.

4 Relation with Equilibrium Logic

4.1 Relation with the Logic of Here-and-There

The basic framework of answer set programming, without intensional functions, can be understood in terms of *equilibrium logic*, a non-monotonic extension of the non-classical logic of *here-and-there* [4,3], denoted by **HT**. Let us briefly recall the main ideas of these logics.

An *HT-interpretation* is a pair $\langle I_h, I_t\rangle$, of sets of atoms. The subscripts h, t, refer to *states* or 'worlds' h and t; interpretations are just Kripke models for intuitionistic logic with a simple, two-world structure. The *satisfaction* relation between an HT-interpretation $\mathcal{I} = \langle I_h, I_t\rangle$, a state x (where x is h or t) and a formula φ, is defined recursively: for $x = h, t$,

- $\mathcal{I}, x \models p$ if $p \in I_x$,
- $\mathcal{I}, x \models \varphi \wedge \psi$ if $\mathcal{I}, x \models \varphi$ and $\mathcal{I}, x \models \psi$,
- $\mathcal{I}, x \models \varphi \vee \psi$ if $\mathcal{I}, x \models \varphi$ or $\mathcal{I}, x \models \psi$,
- $\mathcal{I}, t \models \varphi \rightarrow \psi$ if, either $\mathcal{I}, t \not\models \varphi$ or $\mathcal{I}, t \models \psi$,
- $\mathcal{I}, h \models \varphi \rightarrow \psi$ if $\mathcal{I}, t \models \varphi \rightarrow \psi$, and either $\mathcal{I}, h \not\models \varphi$ or $\mathcal{I}, h \models \psi$,
- $\mathcal{I}, x \models \neg\varphi$ if $\mathcal{I}, t \not\models \varphi$.

Notation and terminology are similar to those for bistate logic.

However when we need to distinguish the two logics, we use the subscript HT for satisfaction and entailment in **HT**. Thus we define truth in an interpretation by setting $\mathcal{I} \models_{HT} \varphi$ if $\mathcal{I}, h \models_{HT} \varphi$ (this implies that also $\mathcal{I}, t \models_{HT} \varphi$). For any set Γ of formulas and any formula φ, we write $\Gamma \models_{HT} \varphi$ if every HT-interpretation satisfying all formulas in Γ satisfies φ also. A formula φ is *valid*, in symbols $\models_{HT} \varphi$, if every interpretation is a model of φ; this defines *here-and-there logic*, denoted by **HT**. Two formulas φ and ψ are said to be equivalent if $\varphi \leftrightarrow \psi$ is valid in **HT**; equivalently, two formulas φ and ψ are equivalent if and only if they have the same HT-models.

At first sight, bi-state logic, in symbols **BiS**, looks to be a much weaker logic than here-and-there, **HT**. In fact, in terms of theorems or tautologies, the two systems are not comparable. Each has theorems that are not valid in the other system.

On the other hand between **HT** and **BiS** models we do have a simple inclusion relation. For notation, we write **HT** and **BiS** models in the same way, as pairs of sets of atoms. The only difference is that for **BiS** we do not require that the first element of the pair is a subset of the second; ie. not all interpretations need be consistent.

In either case, we use lower-case h and t to denote the two worlds of evaluation corresponding to $\models_{HT}$ or $\models_{BiS}$, and we write $\mathcal{M}, h \models \varphi$ and $\mathcal{M}, t \models \varphi$ to indicate that a formula φ is true in $\mathcal{M}$ at the corresponding world.

Proposition 1. *Let φ be a formula and let $\mathcal{I}$ be an* **HT**-*model of φ. Then $\mathcal{I}$ is a* **BiS**-*model of φ.*

The proof is by induction and uses two lemmas. The first is straightforward and stated without proof.

Lemma 2. *Let $\mathcal{I}$ be a consistent interpretation. Then for any φ, $\mathcal{I}, t \models_{HT} \varphi$ if and only if $\mathcal{I}, t \models_{BiS} \varphi$.*

Lemma 3. *Let $\mathcal{I}$ be a consistent interpretation. Then for any φ, $\mathcal{I}, h \models_{HT} \varphi$ implies $\mathcal{I}, h \models_{BiS} \varphi$.*

Proof. By induction on φ. For an atom p the claim is immediate. Conjunction and disjunction are obvious. Let φ have the form $\neg\psi$. Then $\mathcal{I}, h \models_{HT} \varphi$ iff $\mathcal{I}, t \not\models_{HT} \psi$ iff $\mathcal{I}, t \not\models_{BiS} \psi$ (Lemma 2) iff $\mathcal{I}, h \models_{BiS} \neg\psi$ (**BiS**-semantics).

Let φ have the form $\alpha \rightarrow \beta$. Then $\mathcal{I}, h \models_{HT} \varphi$ iff (i) $\mathcal{I}, h \models_{HT} \alpha \Rightarrow \mathcal{I}, h \models_{HT} \beta$ and (ii) $\mathcal{I}, t \models_{HT} \alpha \Rightarrow \mathcal{I}, t \models_{HT} \beta$. (i) implies (i)' $\mathcal{I}, h \models_{BiS} \alpha \Rightarrow \mathcal{I}, h \models_{BiS} \beta$

(ind. hyp.) and (ii) is equivalent to $\mathcal{I}, t \models_{BiS} \alpha \Rightarrow \mathcal{I}, t \models_{BiS} \beta$ by Lemma 2. The last two conditions imply $\mathcal{I}, h \models_{BiS} \varphi$, which we wanted to prove. ⊣

Proposition 1 follows from Lemmas 2 and 3.

Notice that even if $\mathcal{I}$ is a consistent interpretation, the converse of Proposition 1 does not hold.

Example 1. Let p, q be atoms. Consider the formula $\varphi := p \vee p \to q$ and let $\mathcal{I}$ be the **HT**-interpretation $\langle \varnothing, \{p\} \rangle$. Then $\mathcal{I}, h \not\models_{HT} \varphi$ while $\mathcal{I}, h \models_{BiS} \varphi$. Consequently, the interpretation $\mathcal{I}$ is a **BiS**-model of φ but does not satisfy φ in **HT**. Notice that by axiom B1 φ is actually a tautology in **BiS** while it is not a valid formula in **HT**.

4.2 Equilibrium Models

We recall the definition of equilibrium model of a formula φ.

Definition 3. *A total HT-model of φ, $\langle I, I \rangle$, is said to be an* equilibrium *model of φ if there is no other HT-model $\langle I', I \rangle$ with $I' \subset I$.*[4]

It is well-known that for logic programs (see below) equilibrium models coincide with answer sets or stable models. We can mimic the equilibrium model construction in **BiS** by saying that a total **BiS**-model $\langle I, I \rangle$ of φ is an *optimal* model of φ if there is no **BiS**-model $\langle I', I \rangle$ of φ such that $I' \subset I$. Evidently a superstable model is also optimal, but the converse is not guaranteed. Example 1 shows that some equilibrium models are not optimal and hence not superstable. Let $\mathcal{J}$ be the structure $\langle \{p\}, \{p\} \rangle$. Then $\mathcal{J}$ is an equilibrium model of $p \vee (p \to q)$ because the structure $\mathcal{I}$ in Example 1 is not an **HT** model of $p \vee (p \to q)$. However, since $\mathcal{I} \models_{BiS} p \vee (p \to q)$, $\mathcal{J}$ is not optimal.

Proposition 2. *Let $\mathcal{I}$ be an optimal model of φ. Then $\mathcal{I}$ is an equilibrium model of φ.*

Proof. Suppose that $\mathcal{I} = \langle T, T \rangle$ is an optimal but not an equilibrium model of φ. Then there is an **HT**-model $\langle H, T \rangle$ of φ with $H \subset T$. This is contradicted by Proposition 1. ⊣

It follows that superstable models are also equilibrium models.

The formulas of a (generalized) logic program have the shape

$$b_1 \wedge \ldots \wedge b_m \wedge \neg b_{m+1} \wedge \ldots \wedge \neg b_n \to a_1 \vee \ldots \vee a_k \vee \neg a_{k+1} \vee \ldots \vee \neg a_l \qquad (4)$$

where the a_i, b_j are atoms.

Lemma 4. *Let $\mathcal{I} = \langle I_0, I_1 \rangle$ be a consistent interpretation and φ a formula of form (4). Then if $\mathcal{I} \models_{BiS} \varphi$ also $\mathcal{I} \models_{HT} \varphi$.*

[4] We use '$\subset$' to denote strict subset.

Proof. Assume the hypothesis. Then since $\mathcal{I}, s_1 \models_{BiS} \varphi$ also $\mathcal{I}, t \models_{HT} \varphi$ by Lemma 1. Now $\mathcal{I}, s_0 \models_{BiS} \varphi$ iff at least one of the following holds: (i) $a_i \in I_0$ for some $i \leq k$; (ii) $a_j \notin I_1$ for some j, $k+1 \leq j \leq l$; (iii) $b_i \notin I_0$ for some $i \leq m$; (iv) $b_j \in I_1$ for some j, $m+1 \leq j \leq n$. But both (i) and (ii) imply that $\mathcal{I}, h \models_{HT} a_1 \vee \ldots \vee a_k \vee \neg a_{k+1} \vee \ldots \vee \neg a_l$ and both (iii) and (iv) imply that $\mathcal{I}, h \not\models_{HT} b_1 \wedge \ldots \wedge b_m \wedge \neg b_{m+1} \wedge \ldots \wedge \neg b_n$. Given that $\mathcal{I}, t \models_{HT} \varphi$, either of these conditions implies that $\mathcal{I}, h \models_{HT} \varphi$, and therefore $\mathcal{I} \models_{HT} \varphi$. ⊣

Proposition 3. *Let Π be a (generalized) logic program and $\mathcal{I} = \langle T, T \rangle$ a total interpretation. Then $\mathcal{I}$ is an equilibrium model of Π iff it is an optimal model of Π.*

Proof. One direction is Proposition 2. For the other direction, suppose that $\mathcal{I} = \langle T, T \rangle$ is an equilibrium model of Π and that it is not an optimal model of Π. Clearly, $\mathcal{I} \models_{BiS} \Pi$ and there is a model $\mathcal{I}' = \langle H, T \rangle$ with H a proper subset of T such that $\mathcal{I}' \models_{BiS} \varphi$ for each formula $\varphi \in \Pi$, while by the equilibrium property there must be a formula $\psi \in \Pi$ such that $\mathcal{I}' \not\models_{HT} \psi$. But the latter is impossible by Lemma 4, contradicting the assumption that $\mathcal{I}$ is not optimal. ⊣

One consequence of this is a partial strong equivalence theorem for logic programs. For ordinary logic programs strong equivalence is defined as in Definition 1 where superstable model is replaced by stable or equilibrium model [3]. From Proposition 3 we obtain the corollary that two programs are strongly equivalent if they are equivalent (have the same models) in bi-state logic.

Notice that the converse does not hold. If two programs are strongly equivalent then they have the same **HT**-models, but their **BiS**-models may differ since some of them may not be consistent interpretations.

In particular, it allows one to distinguish some formulas that seem to be update sensitive but are equivalent in **HT**, while it still enables one to capture equilibrium models and hence the answers sets of logic programs.

5 Bi-state Logic and Updates

After completing most of our work on bi-state logic and its non-monotonic extensions we learnt of a very recent paper by Slota and Leite [5]. This work aims to provide a suitable semantic treatment of updates for logic programs under stable model semantics. Slota and Leite propose to use as an underlying semantical basis for updates, not **HT**-models, but rather a variation of these which they call RE-models. These models are defined for generalized logic programs and they fulfil several properties that are arguably desirable for a semantic treatment of updates.

One of the desiderata suggested in [5] is that in a dynamic context of updates it may be important to distinguish between formulas that seem to carry the same meaning in a static context. For instance in logic programming the constraint

$$\leftarrow p, q \tag{5}$$

(in logical notation we might write it as $p \wedge q \rightarrow \bot$) has the meaning that p and q cannot both be true. In the logic **HT** we could re-write (5) by either of

$$p \rightarrow \neg q, \quad q \rightarrow \neg p \tag{6}$$

since in **HT** the three formulas are all equivalent. However Slota and Leite suggest that in a dynamic setting the rules $\neg q \leftarrow p$ and $\neg p \leftarrow q$ should be treated differently since the truth of one atom "gives a *reason* for the other atom to *become false*" ([5] section 3). In other words, in an update context the idea seems to be to treat these expressions not simply as logical statements as in (6) but rather as rules having a *justificational* or perhaps even a *causal* force. One of the properties of RE-models is that they distinguish between the three formulas mentioned. This means that by regarding an update as an operation on a program viewed as a set of RE-models, these expressions will in general behave differently.

Slota and Leite do not define RE-models for arbitrary formulas nor do they study the 'logic' of RE-models. However, we can easily compare them to bi-state models. In [5] RE-models are consistent interpretations defined in terms of program reducts. It is easy to reformulate the definition in terms of our semantics for bi-state models and verify the following.

Proposition 4. *Let φ be a formula of form (4). An RE-model of φ is a consistent interpretation $\mathcal{I} = \langle I_0, I_1 \rangle$ such that $\mathcal{I}, s_0 \models_{BiS} \varphi$.*

It follows that every consistent interpretation that is a **BiS** model of a formula φ is also an RE-model of φ and by Lemma 3 every **HT** model of φ is an RE-model.

Suppose we extend the optimal model construction to cover RE-models by saying that a total RE-model $\langle J, J \rangle$ of φ is RE-optimal if there is no RE-model of φ of the form $\langle I, J \rangle$ with $I \subset J$. Then it is easy to check that for any logic program Π, a total interpretation is RE-optimal if and only if it is optimal. It follows from Proposition 3 that RE-optimal models coincide with equilibrium models and hence stable models. This is the content of [5], Proposition 9.

This suggests that bi-state logic may also be of interest in the context of the semantics of updates. For instance, the formulas in (6) are also distinguishable in bi-state logic: the interpretation $\langle \{p, q\}, \{p\} \rangle$ is a **BiS**-model of $p \rightarrow \neg q$ but is not a **BiS**-model of $q \rightarrow \neg p$. Hence **BiS** fulfils at least some of the desiderata proposed by [5] for the semantic treatment of updates. We hope to pursue this line of thought in future work.

6 Relation to Classical Logic

There is a simple relation between bi-state logic and classical logic. We mention it here as it may help to shed light on the nature of negation in **BiS**.

Let $p_1, \ldots, p_n$ be the propositional variables in $\varphi \in \mathcal{L}$ and let $p_1^*, \ldots, p_n^*$ distinct variables not occurring in φ. Then we denote by φ^* the formula obtained from φ by replacing any variable p_i not in the scope of a negation, by p_i^*. Let $\models_{Cl}$ denote validity in classical logic.

Theorem 5. $\models_{BiS} \varphi$ *iff* $\models_{Cl} \varphi^*$.

Proof:

($\Leftarrow$) Suppose that φ^* is a classical tautology. Let $\mathcal{I} = \langle I_0, I_1 \rangle$ be a bi-state model and let us consider the interpretation I such that: $I(p) = I_1(p)$ and $I(p^*) = I_0(p)$ for every p. Then, it is easy to prove by induction that $\mathcal{I}, s_0 \models \varphi$ iff $I(\varphi^*) = 1$ and $\mathcal{I}, s_1 \models \varphi$ iff $I(\varphi) = 1$, which are the case because both φ and φ^* are tautologies; therefore φ is valid in **BiS**.

($\Rightarrow$) Suppose that φ is valid in **BiS**. Let I be a classical interpretation and let us consider the bi-state model $\langle I_0, I_1 \rangle$ defined as: $I_1(p) = I(p)$ and $I_0(p) = I(p^*)$ for every p. Then, it is easy to prove by induction that $I(\varphi^*) = 1$ iff $\langle I_0, I_1 \rangle, s_0 \models \varphi$, which is the case because φ is valid in **BiS**; therefore φ^* is a classical tautology. $\dashv$

7 Summary and Conclusions

Let us briefly summarize the main properties and relations established so far. We have presented bi-state logic and shown how to describe its proof theory in axiomatic and in Gentzen style. We have seen how to define a non-monotonic extension of bi-state logic using the idea of superstable model. In the propositional case, superstable models coincide with the stable model semantics for IF-programs recently studied in [2]. Moreover we have a strong equivalence theorem for this non-monotonic extension, since formulas are strongly equivalent under the superstable semantics if and only if they are equivalent in **BiS**. This therefore answers a question raised by Lifschitz in [2] about the appropriate logic for IF-programs.

A weaker kind of preferred model is given by the concept of optimal model. Superstable models are optimal but it is easy to see that the converse does not hold. Although **BiS** is quite different from the logic **HT** of here-and-there, **HT**-models are also **BiS**-models and on generalized logic programs optimal models and equilibrium models actually coincide. Comparing **BiS**-models to the RE-models introduced in [5], we have seen that if a consistent interpretation is a **BiS**-model of a formula of a logic program then it is also an RE-model of that formula. Moreover, optimal and RE-optimal models coincide. This suggests that the logic **BiS** may also be of interest in the setting studied in [5], namely that of logic programming updates.

In [2] Lifschitz shows how programs with intensional functions whose rules are quantifier-free can be transformed into equivalent causal theories, understood according to the causal logic of [1]. He also shows how IF-programs can provide a concise means to describe the effects of actions on fluents. This suggests that bi-state logic may also play an interesting role in the study of causal theories and reasoning about actions. We hope to explore these directions in the future and consider a full first-order version of bi-state logic and its relation to IF-programs.

References

1. Lifschitz, V.: On the logic of causal explanation (research note). Artif. Intell. 96(2), 451–465 (1997)
2. Lifschitz, V.: Logic programs with intensional functions (preliminary report). In: Workshop on Answer Set Programming and Other Computing Paradigms (2011)
3. Lifschitz, V., Pearce, D., Valverde, A.: Strongly equivalent logic programs. ACM Tr. on Computational Logic 2(4), 526–541 (2001)
4. Pearce, D.: A New Logical Characterization of Stable Models and Answer Sets. In: Dix, J., Przymusinski, T.C., Moniz Pereira, L. (eds.) NMELP 1996. LNCS, vol. 1216, pp. 57–70. Springer, Heidelberg (1997)
5. Slota, M., Leite, J.: Robust equivalence models for semantic updates of answer-set programs. In: KR 2012 (to appear, 2012)

An Equational Approach to Logic Programming

Dov M. Gabbay

[1] Bar Ilan University, Israel
[2] King's College London, UK
[3] University of Luxembourg, Luxembourg

Abstract. In this paper we follow ideas from our Equational approach to argumentation, [3,4], and develop the Equational approach to Logic programs. We regard a logic program P as a template for generating a system of equations $Eq(P)$, where the literals are considered variables ranging over the unit interval $[0, 1]$, and where the solutions to the equations give us the logical meaning of the logic program. We show soundness of the equational approach with respect to traditional Prolog computation and with respect to answer set programming. We prove completeness of answer sets for P with respect to $\{0, 1\}$ solutions of $Eq(P)$ for programs with only negated atoms in the body of clauses. We offer equational semantics for logic programs with negation as failure in the spirit of Clark's completion.

1 Equational Approach to Logic Programs

This section will present the equational approach to logic programs. We begin with purely formal definitions. The examples will come afterwards.

Consider a propositional language with propositional atoms $\{q_1, q_2, q_3, \ldots\}$ and the connectives $\wedge, \vee, \to$ and $\neg$. $\neg$ is supposed to be negation as failure and $\to$ causal implication.

We may later use other connectives like $\equiv$ (if and only if) or $\leftrightarrow$ (which also stands for if and only if).

Definition 1 (Prolog goals, clauses and computation)

1. *Any atomic q is both a goal and a clause.*
2. *If A and B are goals so are $A \wedge B$ and $\neg A$.*
3. *If A is a goal q atomic then $A \to q$ is a clause. q is said to be the* head *of the clause and A is the* body *of the clause.*
4. *Given a program P and a goal G, we define the notion of success (failure) of G from P, notation $P?G = 0$ or 1.*
   (a) *If $G = q$, q atomic, then q succeeds if q is in P or if for some clause $A \to q$ in P, A succeeds. q fails if it is not the head of any clause in P, or if for each clause $A \to q$ in P, A fails.*
   (b) *If $G = A \wedge B$ then it succeeds if both conjuncts succeed and fails if at least one conjunct fails.*
   (c) *$\neg G$ succeeds (fails) iff G fails (succeeds).*

E. Erdem et al. (Eds.): Correct Reasoning, LNCS 7265, pp. 279–295, 2012.

Definition 2

Let P be a set of clauses as defined in Definition 1. We write P in the following form

$$P = \bigcup_c P(c)$$

where c ranges over all atomic literals appearing in P, and $P(c)$ is the set of all clauses in P with head c.

Note that for the sake of uniformity of mathematical notation, we write

- $P(c) = \varnothing$, *if there are no clauses with head c*
- $\top \wedge \neg\bot \to c$ *if the clause is just c*
- $\top \wedge \bigwedge_k \neg b_k \to c$ *if the clause if $\bigwedge_k \neg b_k \to c$, and*
- $\bigwedge_i a_i \wedge \neg\bot \to c$, *if the clause is $\bigwedge_i a_i \to c$.*

Thus if c is the head of some clauses in P then $P(c)$ is the set of clauses of the form

$$\begin{array}{l} \bigwedge_j a_{i,j} \wedge \bigwedge_k \neg b_{i,k} \to c \\ i = 1, \ldots, r(c) \\ j = 1, \ldots, J(i,c) \\ k = 1, \ldots, K(i,c). \end{array}$$

1. *We consider P as a syntactic object generating equations in the compact unit real interval $[0,1]$. The type of equations that P generates can be $Eq_{\text{inverse}}(P)$ or $Eq_{\max}$ or other types. The equations themselves, for any proram P, are denoted by $Eq_{\text{inverse}}(P)$ or $Eq_{\max}(P)$. The literals of P are considered the variables of the equations.*
   We define

$$Eq(P) = \bigcup_c Eq(P(c))$$

   and we define the following equations for the variables/literals in P:
   - $\top = 1$
   - $\bot = 0$
   - $c = 0$ *if* $P(c) = \varnothing$
   - *If $P(c) \neq \varnothing$ then the equation for $P(c)$ is the following for the case of $Eq_{\text{inverse}}(P(c))$:*

$$c = \mathbf{h}_{\text{inverse}}(c) = 1 - \prod_{i=1}^{r(c)} (1 - \prod_{j=1}^{J(i,c)} a_{i,j} \cdot \prod_{k=1}^{K(i,c)} (1 - b_{i,k}))$$

   where, as we said, $c, a_{i,j}, b_{i,k}$ are considered variables ranging over $[0,1]$, and $\top$ is 1 and $\bot$ is 0.
2. *We define $Eq_{\max}(P)$ as follows. $Eq_{\max}(P(c))$ is*
   - $c = 0$ *if* $P(c) = \varnothing$
     $c = \mathbf{h}_{\max}(c) = \min(1 - \max_{j,k}(1 - a_{i,j}, b_{i,k}))$, *otherwise*

We use the following abbreviations when we talk about $Eq(P(c))$.

$$\prod_k \textit{ refers to } \prod_{k=1}^{K(i,c)}(1-b_{i,k})$$
$$\prod_j \textit{ refers to } \prod_{j=1}^{J(i,c)} a_{i,j}$$
$$\prod_i \textit{ refers to} \prod_{i=1}^{r(c)}(1-\prod_j \prod_k).$$

Example 1 1. Consider the program $P_1 = \{a \to b, \neg a \to b, \neg b \to c, a \to a\}$.
The Eq_{inverse} and $Eq_{\max}$ equations are (both types are) the same for this program. They are as follows:
(a) $b = 1 - (1-a)a$
(b) $c = 1 - b$
(c) $a = a$
From (a) and (b) we get
(d) $c = (1-a)a$
The solutions are $c = (1-a)a, b = 1-(1-a)a$ and $a \in [0,1]$ is arbitrary.

2. Consider the program $P_2 = \{\neg c \to c\}$.
The equation is

$$c = 1 - (1 - (1-c)) = 1 - c$$

The solution is $c = \frac{1}{2}$.

3. Consider the program $P_3 = \{a \to c, \neg c \to a\}$.
The equations are
(a) $c = 1 - (1-a) = a$
(b) $a = 1 - (1-(1-c)) = 1 - c$
The solution is $c = a = \frac{1}{2}$.

4. Consider the program $P_4 = \{d \wedge \neg p \to p, \neg d \to r, \neg r \to d\}$.
The equations are (using Eq_{inverse}):
(a) $p = 1 - (1 - d(1-p))$
(b) $r = 1 - (1 - (1-d)) = 1 - d$
(c) $d = 1 - (1-(1-r)) = 1 - r$
The solution is $p = \frac{d}{1+d}, r = 1-d, d$ arbitrary in $[0,1]$.
If we use $Eq_{\max}$ the first equation becomes
(m1) $p = (1 - \max(p, 1-d)) = \min(d, 1-p)$

To solve the equations, we distinguish two cases.

Case 1. $1 - p \leq d$.
Then $p = d$ and $r = 1-d$ and d is arbitrary.

Case 2. $d \leq 1-p$.
then $p = \frac{1}{2}$ and $r = 1 - d$ and d equals any value $\leq \frac{1}{2}$.

Theorem 1 (Existence). *Let P be a program and let $Eq_{\text{inverse}}(P)$ or $Eq_{\max}(P)$ be the associated system of equations. then there exists at least one function* $\mathbf{f}$: *Literals of $P \mapsto [0,1]$ which solves the equations.*

Proof. Consider the vector $(c_1, \dots, c_n)$ listing all the literals in P. Consider the vector function $\mathbf{F}$ from $[0,1]^n \mapsto [0,1]^n$ defined as follows:

$$\mathbf{F}(c_1, \dots, c_n) = (F_1(c_1, \dots, c_n), \dots, F_n(c_1, \dots, c_n))$$

where

$$F_i = \begin{cases} 0, \text{ if } P(c_i) = 0 \\ \mathbf{h}_{\text{inverse}}(c_i) \\ (\text{or resp. } \mathbf{h}_{\max}(c_i)), \text{ if } P(c_i) \neq \varnothing \end{cases}$$

$i = 1, \dots, n$.

This function is continuous on $[0,1]^n$ and therefore by Brouwer fixed point theorem [8], has at least one fixed point solution $\mathbf{f}$.

$$(\mathbf{f}(c_1), \dots, \mathbf{f}(c_n)) = F_1(\mathbf{f}(c_1), \dots, \mathbf{f}(c_n)), \dots, F_n(\mathbf{f}(c_1), \dots, \mathbf{f}(c_n)).$$

Theorem 2 (Soundness). *Let P be a program and let $Eq_{\text{inverse}}(P)$ be its equational system. Let $\mathbf{f}$ be a solution to the equations. Then following the Prolog computation of Definition 1 we have for any literal c*

1. *If $P?c = 1$ then $\mathbf{f}(c) = 1$.*
2. *If $P?c = 0$ (i.e. $P?\neg c = 1$) then $\mathbf{f}(c) = 0$.*

Proof. By induction on the depth of the computation of Definition 1 (i.e. the depth of the Prolog computation). We write c for $\mathbf{f}(c)$, to simplify our notation.

Case 1
If $P?c = 1$ in one step then the clause c is in P. The equation for Eq_{inverse} for c is

$$Eq(c) = c = 1 - \prod_i (1 - \prod_j a_{i,j} \cdot \prod_k (1 - b_{i,k})).$$

Since $c \in P$, we have the clause $\top \wedge \neg\bot \to c$ being used in constructing $\prod_i$. Say it contributes the ith clause. The factor for it in $\prod_i$ is

$$1 - 1 \cdot (1 - 1) = 0.$$

Therefore $\prod_i = 0$ and so $c = 1$.

If $P?c = 0$ in one stage, then c is not a head of any clause and the equation for c is $c = 0$

Case $m + 1$
Assume $P?c = 1$ in $m + 1$ steps. Then for some clause (c, i):

$$\bigwedge_j a_{i,j} \wedge \bigwedge_k \neg b_{i,k} \to c$$

we have that

$$P?a_{i,j} = 1 \text{ for all } j$$

and

$$P?b_{i,k} = 0 \text{ for all } k$$

By the induction hypothesis, we have $\mathbf{f}(a_{i,j}) = 1$ for all j and $\mathbf{f}(b_{i,k}) = 0$ for all k.

Substituting these values in the equation $Eq(c)$ for the factor in $\prod_i$ corresponding to clause (c, i) we get

$$1 - \prod_j 1 \cdot \prod_k (1 - 0) = 0$$

Thus $c = 1 - 0 = 1$.

Assume now that $P?c = 0$. This means, according to the Prolog computation, that for each clause (c, i) for c, for $i = 1, \ldots, r(c)$, there exists either a $j(i)$ or a $k(i)$ such that either $P?a_{i,j(i)} = 0$ or $P?b_{i,k(i)} = 1$.

This means that by the induction hypothesis, for each factor of $\prod_i$ we have that it is equal to one of the two forms

$$1 - 0 \cdot \prod_k = 1$$

or

$$1 - \prod_j \cdot 0 = 1$$

thus $\prod_i = 1$ and so $c = 1 - \prod_i = 0$.

Example 2. The converse of Theorem 2 does not hold. If we look at program P_1 of Example 1, it has a solution $b = 1, c = 0, a = 0$ but $P?a$ is not 0.

The reader may ask what if $\mathbf{f}(c) = 1$ (resp. $\mathbf{f}(c) = 0$) in *every* solution $\mathbf{f}$ of the equations $Eq(P)$, does this imply that $P?c = 1$ (resp. $P?c = 0$)? The answer is negative as P_6 of Example 3 shows.

Example 3 (Comparing Eq_{inverse} and Eq_{max}). Consider the program $P_6 = \{\neg a \wedge \neg b \to b, \neg b \to a\}$.

The Eq_{inverse} equations are

1. $b = 1 - (1 - (1 - a)(1 - b)) = (1 - a)(1 - b)$
2. $a = 1 - b$

From (1) and (2) we get

3. $b = (1 - b)b$

The only solution is $a = 1, b = 0$.

The Eq_{max} equations are

1. $b = 1 - \max(a, b)$
2. $b = 1 - a$.

From (1) and (2) we get

3. $b = 1 - \max(1 - b, b)$

Hence $a = b = \frac{1}{2}$.

Remark 1. Let P be a program with negation as failure in the body of clauses. Then we consider $Eq(P)$ as the Equational semantics/completion for P. We consider any solution $\mathbf{f}$ as a model for P.

2 Comparison with Answer Set Semantics

We begin by introducing answer set programming, see [5,9].

Definition 3. *Let P be a program as in Definition 1. Let X be a set of positive literals. Let P^X be the following program obtained from P using X.*

1. *Delete from P any rule of the form*
   (*) $\bigwedge_j a_{i,j} \wedge \bigwedge_k \neg b_{i,k} \to c$
   for which some $b_{i,k} \in X$.
2. *Replace any remaining rule (after the deletions in (1)) by its positive part, i.e. if (*) is such that $b_{i,k} \in X$ for all k then we replace (*) by the rule $(*X)$*
   $(*X)$ $\bigwedge_j a_{i,j} \to c$
3. *P^X is obtained from P and X by executing (1) and (2) above.*

Definition 4

1. *Let P be a program, and let X be a set of positive atoms appearing in P. Consider P^X as defined in Definition 3. P^X is a positive program. Define a set $Y(P^X)$ of atoms out of X and P^X as follows:*
   (a) *Let $Y_0 = \{a | a \in P^X\}$*
   (b) *Assume Y_n has been defined. Let $Y_{n+1} = Y_n \cup \{c | \bigwedge_j a_{i,j} \to c$ is in P^X and $a_{i,j} \in Y_n$ for all $j\}$.*
   (c) *Let $Y(P^X) = \bigcup_n Y_n$.*
2. *We say that X is an answer set for the program P if $X = Y(P^X)$*
   In words: $Y(P^X)$ is the minimal model of P^X and so for X being an answer set means that X is being the minimal model of P^X.
3. *Note that if X is an answer set for P, then since X equals Y then the elements of x of X are ranked by the minimal n such that x is in Y_n. This comes in useful in proofs by induction involving X.*

Example 4. 1. Let $P_5 = \{\neg b \to a, \neg a \to b\}$.
   Then $P_5^{\{a\}} = a$ and $P_5^{\{b\}} = b$.
   The $\{a\}$ and $\{b\}$ are two answer sets. $\{a, b\}$ is not an answer set because $P_5^{\{a,b\}} = \varnothing$ and its minimal model is $\varnothing$.
2. Let $P_6 = \{\neg a \wedge \neg b \to b, \neg b \to a\}$.
   Then $P_6^{\{a\}} = \{a\}$ and $P_6^{\{b\}} = P_6^{\{a,b\}} = \varnothing$.
   Thus only $X = \{a\}$ is an answer set.
   Compare with Example 3. The only Eq_{inverse} solution there is $a = 1, b = 0$ agreeing with $\{a\}$ being the only answer set. The only $Eq_{\max}$ solution does not agree with $\{a\}$ being an answer set.

Theorem 3 (Soundness w.r.t. answer sets). *Let P be a program and let X be an answer set for P. Define a function $\mathbf{f}_X$ by $\mathbf{f}_X(c) = 1$ iff $c \in X$.*
Then $\mathbf{f}_X$ is a solution to $Eq_{\text{inverse}}(P)$.

Proof. 1. If c is not a head of any clause in P then both $\mathbf{f}_X(c) = 0$ and the equation for c is $c = 0$.

2. If $c \in P$, then the equation for c is $c = 1$, but also since X is a minimal model for P^X and $c \in P^X$, then $\mathbf{f}_X(c) = 1$.
3. Consider the equation for c, using

$$c = 1 - \prod_i (1 - \prod_j a_{i,j} \cdot \prod_k (1 - b_{i,k}))$$

the clauses in $P(c)$ are

$$\text{clause } (c, i) = \bigwedge_j a_{i,j} \wedge \bigwedge_k \neg b_{i,k} \to c.$$

Case 1
In clause (c, i) some $b_{i,k} \in X$. Then $\mathbf{f}_X(b_{i,k}) = 0$ and so under $\mathbf{f}_X$, the ith conjunct in $\prod_i$ is 1.
Let I_0 be the set of all such indices i.

Case 2
In clause (c, i) all the $b_{i,k}$ are not in X. Thus under $\mathbf{f}_X$ the ith conjunct in $\prod_i$ is $1 - \prod_j a_{i,j}$.
Let I_1 be the set of all such indices i. Thus under $\mathbf{f}_X$ we have

$$\mathbf{f}_X(c) = 1 - \prod_{i \in I_1} (1 - \prod_j \mathbf{f}_X(a_{i,j})).$$

4. Assume $c \in X$. We now prove by induction on the rank of c (since we assumed $c \in X$, it has a rank as explained in item 3 of Definition 4), that $\mathbf{f}_X(c) = 1$. For rank 1, i.e. $c \in P^X$ we have $\mathbf{f}_X(c) = 1$ from item (1) above. For rank $m + 1$, we have that for some i_0

$$\prod_j a_{i_0,j} \to c$$

is in P^X and we have that $a_{i_0,j} \in X$ and $a_{i_0,j}$ are of lower rank. Thus by the induction hypothesis $\mathbf{f}_X(a_{i_0,j}) = 1$.
From item (3) above we have that

$$\mathbf{f}_X(c) = 1 - \prod_{i \in I_1} (1 - \prod_j \mathbf{f}_X(a_{i,j})).$$

If $i_0 \in I_1$ then we are finished, because then we would have $\prod_{i \in I_1} = 0$.
Let us show that indeed $i_o \in I_1$. We ask: How did $\bigwedge_j a_{i,j} \to c$ get into P^X? This was because all $b_{i,k}$ were not in X. But this is the same condition for i_o to get into I_1. Thus we get $\mathbf{f}_X(c) = 1$.
5. Assume $c \notin X$. then $\mathbf{f}_X(c) = 0$. We also have that c has no rank. This means that we never have that for some i

$$\bigwedge_j a_{i,j} \to c \in P^X$$

and for all $j, a_{i,j} \in X$.
Thus for each i, there is a $j(i)$ such that $a_{i,j(i)} \notin X$, i.e. $\mathbf{f}_X(a_{i,j(i)}) = 0$.

We now check whether the equation associated with $P(c)$ is satisfied by $\mathbf{f}_X$. We need to check whether

$$\mathbf{f}_X(c) =?1 - \prod_i (1 - \prod_j \mathbf{f}_X(a_{i,j}) \cdot \prod_k (1 - \mathbf{f}_X(b_{i,k})))$$

Let us concentrate on the right hand side of the equation. Since for each i there is a $j(i)$ such that $\mathbf{f}_X(a_{i,j(i)}) = 0$, we get that $\prod_j = 0$ for each i. Hence $\prod_i = 1$ and so the right hand side equals 0. So $\mathbf{f}_X(c)$ should be 0, which is indeed the case. We indeed get $0 = 0$.

So $\mathbf{f}_X$ solves this equation also for the case $c \notin X$.

From (4) and (5) we get the theorem.

Example 5. The converse of Theorem 3 is not true. Consider the program $P = \{\neg c \wedge a \to b, a \to x, x \to a\}$. The equations for P are

$$\begin{aligned} c &= 0 \\ b &= 1 - (1 - a(1 - c)) \\ a &= x \end{aligned}$$

Consider the function $\mathbf{f}$ such that

$$\begin{aligned} &\mathbf{f}(c) = 0 \\ &\mathbf{f}(a) = \mathbf{f}(x) = \mathbf{f}(b) = 1 \end{aligned}$$

We get for b

$$\begin{aligned} 1 &= 1 - (1 - (1 - 0) \cdot 1 \\ &= 1 - (1 - 1) \\ &= 1 \end{aligned}$$

Let $X_{\mathbf{f}} = \{x | \mathbf{f}(x) = 1\} = \{x, a, b\}$. Hence $P^{\{a,b,x\}} = \{a \to b, b \to x, x \to a\}$. The answer set for P is therefore $\varnothing$.

It is not $\{a, b, x\}$.

Thus, although every answer set X for P yields a solution function $\mathbf{f}_X$ with values $\{0, 1\}$, not every such solution function yields an answer set.

Example 6.

1. Consider the program P_4 of Example 1. The only answer set for P_4 is $X = \{r\}$.
   Indeed for the solution choice of $d = 0$ we get $r = 1$ and $p = 1$. This corresponds to the $\{r\}$ answer set.
2. The program $\neg c \to c$ has no answer sets, but its equation

$$\begin{aligned} c &= 1 - (1 - (1 - c)) \\ &= 1 - c \end{aligned}$$

   does have solutions, e.g. the unique solution $c = \frac{1}{2}$.
3. The program $\{\neg p \to q, p \to p\}$ has $\{q\}$ as the only answer set. $\{p\}$ is not an answer set, even though the function $p = 1, q = 0$ is a minimal $[0, 1]$ function.

Theorem 4 (Completeness for programs containing only negated atoms in the bodies of its clauses). *Let P be a program containing only negated atoms in the bodies of its clauses and let $\mathbf{f}$ be a solution to the system $Eq_{\text{inverse}})(P)$, such that $\mathbf{f}(c) \in \{0,1\}$ for each atom c appearing in P.*

Let $X_\mathbf{f}$ be $\{c | \mathbf{f}(c) = 1\}$. Then $X_\mathbf{f}$ is an answer set for the program P.

Proof. Let c be any atom appearing in P.

1. If c is not the head of any clause in P then certainly $\mathbf{f}(c) = 0$ and certainly c is not the head of any clause in P^X for any X and so c is not an element of any answer set of P.
2. Let us focus on c which is a head of some clauses in P. If $c \in P$ then $c \in P^X$ for any X and $\mathbf{f}(c) = 1$ always for any solution $\mathbf{f}$. So there is also agreement for this case.
3. Assume c is the head of some clauses and list them as all clauses of the form
$$\text{clause}(c, i) : \bigwedge_k \neg b_{i,k} \to c, \text{ for } i = 1, 2, \ldots$$
The equation for c is as follows, where we regard the atoms of P as variables in the equation
$$c = 1 - \prod_i (1 - \prod_k (1 - b_{i,k})) \qquad (*)$$
Let us analyse what can happen with this equation:
(a) If $\mathbf{f}(c) = 1$ then $\prod_i$ must be 0. To be 0, we must have for some i_0 that
$$\prod_k (1 - \mathbf{f}(b_{i_0,k})) = 1.$$
So $\mathbf{f}(b_{i_0,k}) = 0$ for all k.
Thus $b_{i_0,k} \notin X_\mathbf{f}$ for all k.
This means that c is in $P^{X_\mathbf{f}}$.
(b) If $\mathbf{f}(c) = 0$, then $\prod_i$ must be 1 and so for each i in equation (*) we must have that
$$\prod_k (1 - b_{i,k}) = 0.$$
So for each i, we must have a $k(i)$ such that
$$\mathbf{f}(b_{i,k(i)}) = 1$$
Hence c is not in $P_\mathbf{f}^X$, because all the clauses with head c are ignored.
4. We now summarise our situation from the points of view of atoms and clauses in $P^{X_\mathbf{f}}$
(a) If c is not a head of any clause in P, then c is not a head of any clause in $P^{X_\mathbf{f}}$.
(b) If $c \in P$, then $c \in P^{X_\mathbf{f}}$
(c) If c has some clauses in P for which it is head, then
i. If $\mathbf{f}(c) = 1$, i.e. $c \in X_\mathbf{f}$ then because of some i_o, we have that c is in $P^{X_\mathbf{f}}$.
ii. If $\mathbf{f}(c) = 0$ then c is not in $P^{X_\mathbf{f}}$.

5. It is now clear that $X_{\mathbf{f}}$ is an answer set for P, because we got that $P^{X_{\mathbf{f}}} = \{c | \mathbf{f}(c) = 1\}$.

Theorem 5. *Let P be a program containing only negated atoms in the bodies of its clauses. Then the answer sets X for P are exactly the characteristic sets $X_{\mathbf{f}}$ of functions $\mathbf{f}$ such that $\mathbf{f}$ is a $\{0,1\}$ solution for $Eq_{\text{inverse}}(P)$.*

Proof. Follows from Theorems 4 and 3.

Remark 2. Theorem 5 cannot be stronger in view of item 3 of Example 6.

Theorem 6. *Let P be a program with clauses of the form*

$$\textit{clause } (c, i) : \bigwedge_j a_{i,j} \wedge \bigwedge_k \neg b_{i,k} \to c.$$

Let the Clark completion of P be the set of all clauses

$$[\bigvee_i (\bigwedge_j a_{i,j} \wedge \bigwedge_k \neg b_{i,k})] \leftrightarrow c \qquad (*c)$$

if c is a head of some clauses in P and

$$\neg c \qquad (*\neg c)$$

if c appears in P, but is not the head of any clause in P.

Then the $\{0,1\}$ solutions to $Eq_{\text{inverse}}(P)$ are exactly the $\{0,1\}$ models of $Comp(P)$.

Proof. Let $\mathbf{f}$ be a solution to the equations. Then we have

$$\mathbf{f}(c) = 1 - \prod_i (1 - \prod_j \mathbf{f}(a_{i,j}) \cdot \prod_k (1 - \mathbf{f}(b_{i,k}))) \qquad (\sharp c)$$

when c is the head of some clauses in P and

$$\mathbf{f}(c) = 0 \qquad (\sharp\neg c)$$

when c appears in P but is not the head of any clause in QP.

We write $\mathbf{f}(c) = 0$ or $\mathbf{f}(c) = 1$, when we regard $\mathbf{f}$ as a $\{0,1\}$ solution to the equations $Eq_{\text{inverse}}(P)$ and we write $\mathbf{f} \vDash c$ or $\mathbf{f} \vDash \neg c$ when we regard $\mathbf{f}$ as a $\{0,1\}$ model to Comp(P).

We now prove the equivalence.

We have

$$\mathbf{f} \vDash c$$

iff, by definition

$$\mathbf{f}(c) = 1,$$

iff for some i

$$1 = \prod_j \mathbf{f}(a_{i,j}) \prod_k (1 - \mathbf{f}(b_{i,k}))$$

iff for some i and all j and all k

$$\mathbf{f}(a_{i,j}) = 1 \text{ and } \mathbf{f}(b_{i,k}) = 0$$

iff for some i and for all j and all k

$$\mathbf{f} \vDash a_{i,j} \text{ and } \mathbf{f} \vDash \neg b_{i,k}$$

iff for some i

$$\mathbf{f} \vDash \bigwedge_j a_{i,j} \wedge \bigwedge_k \neg b_{i,k}$$

iff

$$\mathbf{f} \vDash \bigvee_i (\bigwedge_j a_{i,j} \wedge \bigwedge_k \neg b_{i,k}).$$

So we have that $\mathbf{f}$ solves the equations iff for all c, $(\sharp c)$ and $(\sharp\neg c)$ holds for $\mathbf{f}$. If $(\sharp c)$ holds for $\mathbf{f}$, i.e. c is the head of some clauses in P, then the above proof shows that

$$\mathbf{f} \vDash c \text{ iff } \mathbf{f}(c) = 1.$$

If c is not the head of any clause in P, then clearly by definition of $Eq_{\text{inverse}}(P)$ and of Comp(P) we have $\mathbf{f}(c) = 0$ (i.e. $(\sharp\neg c)$) and $(*\neg c)$ is in Comp(P). So we do get for this case that

$$\mathbf{f} \vDash \neg c \text{ iff } \mathbf{f}(c) = 0.$$

We thus get

$$\mathbf{f} \text{ solves the equations iff } \mathbf{f} \vDash \text{Comp}(P)$$

3 Comparison with Argumentation Networks

An argumentation network has the form $\mathcal{A} = (S, R)$, where S is a non-empty set of points called arguments, and $R \subseteq S \times S$, called the attack relation. If $(x, y) \in R$, we say x attacks y.

The argumentation community is interested in subsets E of S called admissible extensions, satisfying the following:

1. If x is not attacked then $x \in E$
2. E is conflict free, i.e. if $x, y \in E$ then (x, y) is not in R, i.e. x does not attack y.
3. E protects itself, namely if z attacks x and $x \in E$ then for some $y \in E$, y attacks z.

The research in this area looks at different extensions for various networks and investigates their properties. See [6] and [7] for more infomation. For example, a stable extension E is an admissible set such that for all $x \notin E$ there is a $y \in E$ s.t. y attacks x.

The object level connection with logic programming we are interested in, first introduced in [11], see also [10], is as follows: Given $\mathcal{A} = (S, R)$ regard any $x \in S$ as an atom in a logic program $P = P(\mathcal{A})$. For each $x \in S$, let the following clause C_x be in P.

$$C_x : \bigwedge_{k=1}^{m(x)} \neg y_k \to x$$

in case x does have attackers and where $y_1, \dots, y_{m(x)}$ are all the attackers of x in (S, R).

If x has no attackers then the clause is $\neg\bot \to x$.

A logic program P can be identified as (arising from) argumentation network based on the atoms of P if the following holds

1. $\bot$ is also considered an atom.
2. All the clauses in P have the form $\bigwedge \neg y_k \to x$.
3. Each atom x has exactly one clause C_x in P for which it is head.

We can define (S, R) from P as follows:

4. S is the set of atoms of P excluding $\bot$.
5. yRx iff $y \neq \bot$ and $\neg y$ appears in the body of the unique clause of C_x of x.

In our papers [3,4] we introduced the equational approach to argumentation and used, among others, Eq_{inverse} and Eq_{max}.

For $x \in S$ we write the equations for Eq_{inverse}:

- $x = \prod_{k=1}^{m(x)} (1 - y_k)$ where $y_1, \dots, y_{m(x)}$ are the attackers of x
- $x = 1$, if x is not attacked.

If we compare the above equations with the equations we offered for a logic program, we see they are the same. The equation for the unique C_x in P, namely for

$$\bigwedge_k \neg y_k \to x$$

is

$$\begin{aligned} x &= 1 - (1 - \textstyle\prod_k (1 - y_k)) \\ &= \textstyle\prod_k (1 - y_k) \end{aligned}$$

For unattacked x the clause is $\neg\bot \to x$ and we get $x = 1 - (1 - (1 - 0)) = 1$.

For Eq_{max} we write

- $x = 1 - \max(y_1, \dots, y_k)$
- $x = 1$ if it has no attackers.

In [3] we prove the following:

Theorem 7. *1. If we use $Eq_{\text{max}}(\mathcal{A})$ then the solutions $\mathbf{f}$ correspond exactly to the Dung extensions of A. Namely*
- *$\mathbf{f}(x) = 1$ corresponds to $x = in$*
- *$\mathbf{f}(x) = 0$ corresponds to $x = out$*
- *$0 < \mathbf{f}(x) < 1$ corresponds to $x = undecided$.*

The actual value in $[0, 1]$ reflects the degree of odd looping involving x.

2. If we use Eq_{inverse}, we give more sensitivity to loops. For example the more undecided elements y attack x, the closer to 0 (out) its value gets.

Remark 3. Note for example that an answer set for this program $P(\mathcal{A})$ yields a stable extension for the original argumentation system $\mathcal{A}$. In fact the stable extensions of $\mathcal{A}$ are the same as the answer sets of $P(\mathcal{A})$. Further note the interesting Corollary 1 below.

Corollary 1. *Let $\mathcal{A}$ be any argumentation system. The following holds: A function* $\mathbf{f}$ *is a* $\{0,1\}$ *solution of* $Eq_{\max}(\mathcal{A})$ *iff it is a* $\{0,1\}$ *solution of* $Eq_{\text{inverse}}(\mathcal{A})$.

Proof. Follows from Theorem 5 used in conjunction with Theorem 7.

A general program P can be translated into an argumentation network using auxiliary additional variables. We need to overcome two obstacles:

1. Deal with clauses of the form $\bigwedge_j a_j \wedge \bigwedge_k \neg b_k \rightarrow x$, i.e. where un-negated atoms apear in the body.
2. Deal with the case where a head x have more than one clause for which it is head.

This is dealt with in [3]. Let us give a quick explanation.

For clauses like

$$a \wedge \neg b \rightarrow c$$

we add an auxiliary atom a' and write

$$\neg a \rightarrow a'$$
$$\neg a' \wedge \neg b \rightarrow c.$$

If c is the head of two clauses such as

$$A \rightarrow c$$
$$B \rightarrow c$$

we add the new auxiliary atoms c_A and c_B and c' and write

$$A \rightarrow c_A$$
$$B \rightarrow c_B$$
$$\neg c_A \rightarrow c'$$
$$\neg c_B \rightarrow c'$$
$$\neg c' \rightarrow c$$

For details of the actual translation, see [3].

Remark 4. 1. It is instructive to see what happens with the program of item 3 of Example 6.

The program is P

$$\neg p \rightarrow q$$
$$p \rightarrow p$$

The answer set for this program is $\{q\}$.

The equations are

$$q = 1 - p$$
$$p = p$$

The Clark completion is

$$p \leftrightarrow \neg q$$
$$p \leftrightarrow p$$

The equations have the two solutions $\{p = 1, q = 0\}$ and $\{p = 0, q = 1\}$ in agreement with the two models of the completion, as predicted in Theorem 6. Let us now eliminate the clause $p \to p$, as indicated in this section. We add a new auxiliary atom p' and write a new program P'.

$$\neg p \to q$$
$$\neg p' \to p$$
$$\neg p \to p'$$

The equations are now

$$q = 1 - p$$
$$p = 1 - p'$$
$$p' = 1 - p$$

The solutions remain the same on $\{p, q\}$. The solutions are

$$\{q = 0, p = 1, p' = 0\} \text{ and } \{q = 1, p = 0, p' = 1\}.$$

The answer sets for P' must correspond now to the $\{0, 1\}$ solutions to the equations of $Eq_{\text{inverse}}(P')$, by Theorem 5.
They are

$$\{q, p'\} \text{ and } \{p\}$$

Indeed they correspond to the P solutions (if we ignore p'). Thus the additional non-answer set $\{0, 1\}$ solutions for P became answer set retracts in P'.

2. It is worthwhile to have a general formulation of this phenomenon.
Let P be a logic program. Then there exists a logic program $P' \supseteq P$ such that the following holds:
(a) X is an answer set for P' iff X is a model of Comp(P').
(b) Comp(P) is logically equivalent to Comp(P') $\upharpoonright P$
(c) If X is an answer set for P then X is a retract of a unique answer set X' of P'.
(d) The move from P to P' is functorial, it translates the language of P into the language of P', and does not make use of the logical content of P. So we have

$$(P + P_1)' = P' + P_1'$$

(e) In fact let Q be the atoms to be used in P or any of its possible extensions. Let us add the atom $\top$, and for any program P and any atom c in the language of P, let us add the clause

$$\neg\top \to c.$$

Let us have the commitment that $\top$ always succeeds and it numerical value is always 1.

This gives us a new program P^*, in the augmented language with $\top$. The program P^* has the same logical contents as P, but it does have the additional property that any literal in P^* is the head of a clause. This property will facilitate the translation from P^* into P'^*. Under the above notation and assumptions on P and P^*, we can translate the clauses of P^* as follows:
Let $\mathcal{Q}'$ be the set of the new atoms $\{x'|x \in \mathcal{Q}\}$, not that $\top' = \bot$. Let

$$C = \bigwedge x_i \wedge \bigwedge \neg y_j \to z$$

be a clause in the language of $\mathcal{Q}$.
Then the following set of clauses is the translation C' of C

$$\begin{array}{l} \bigwedge \neg x_i' \wedge \bigwedge \neg y_j \to z \\ \neg x_i \to x_i' \end{array}$$

Any program P^* of the language of $\mathcal{Q}$ is translated into a program P'^* of the language $\mathcal{Q} + \mathcal{Q}'$ by translating its clauses as above. Note that in the translation no new clauses are added which have heads in $\mathcal{Q}$, the language of P^*.

Theorem 8. *Let P^*, P'^* be two programs related as in item (2e) of Remark 4. then the following holds:*

1. *$Eq_{\text{inverse}}(P'^*)$ reduced to the language of P^* are the same as $Eq_{\text{inverse}}(P^*)$.*
2. *Let $\mathbf{f}$ be any solution of $Eq_{\text{inverse}}(P^*)$. Then $\mathbf{f}$ can be extended uniquely to a solution $\mathbf{f}'$ of $Eq_{\text{inverse}}(P'^*)$.*
3. *Let $\mathbf{f}$ be any $\{0,1\}$ solution to $Eq_{\text{inverse}}(P^*)$. Let $\mathbf{f}'$ be its unique extension as in (2) above. Then $\mathbf{f}'$ is a $\{0,1\}$ function and $X_{\mathbf{f}'} = \{y \text{ in } P'^* | \mathbf{f}(y) = 1\}$ is an answer set for P'^*.*

Proof. 1. Let c be a literal in P^* and assume it is the head of the clauses

$$\text{clause } (c, i) : \bigwedge_j a_{i,j} \wedge \bigwedge_k \neg b_{i,k} \to c.$$

The equations for c are in $Eq_{\text{inverse}}(P^*)$ are

$$c = 1 - \prod_i (1 - \prod_j a_{i,j} \cdot \prod_k (1 - b_{i,k} \to c))$$

Clause (c, i) is traslated in P'^* into clauses$'(c, i)$:
- $\bigwedge_j \neg a'_{i,j} \wedge \bigwedge_k \neg b_{i,k} \to c$
- $\neg a_{i,j} \to a'i, j$

The equations for clauses$'(c, i)$ are in $Eq_{\text{inverse}}(P'^*)$ are:
- $c = 1 - \prod_i (1 - \prod_j (1 - a'_{i,j}) \cdot \prod_k (1 - b_{i,k}))$
- $a'_{i,j} = 1 - a_{i,j}$
- $c' = 1 - c$

It is clear that since $a'_{i,j} = 1 - a_{i,j}$ that we get the same equations.

2. Follows from the proof of (1)
3. Let $\mathbf{f}$ be a $\{0,1\}$ solution of $Eq_{\text{inverse}}(P^*)$. Clearly its extension $\mathbf{f}'$ is a $\{0,1\}$ solution of the equations of $Eq_{\text{inverse}}(P'^*)$.
   We now show that

$$X_{\mathbf{f}'} = \{y \text{ im } \mathcal{Q} \cup \mathcal{Q}' | \mathbf{f}'(y) = 1\}$$

   is an answer set for P'^*.
   We show that

$$P'^{*X_{\mathbf{f}'}} = X_{\mathbf{f}'} \qquad (*)$$

   (a) Let $c \in X_{\mathbf{f}'}$ and assume c is in the language of P^*. The only way that c is kept out of $P'^{*X_{\mathbf{f}'}}$ is that all clauses with head c are deleted from being candidates for inclusion in $P'^{*X_{\mathbf{f}'}}$. This means that for every i, there is a $j(i)$ or a $k(i)$ such that either $a'_{i,j(i)} \in X_{\mathbf{f}'}$ or $b_{i,k(i)} \in X_{\mathbf{f}'}$.
   This implies that for each i, either $\mathbf{f}(a_{i,j(i)}) = 0$ or $\mathbf{f}(b_{i,k(i)}) = 1$.
   From the equation for c we get that this implies $\mathbf{f}(c) = 0$. But since we are given that $\mathbf{f}'(c) = 1$, we must have that for some i_0, all $a'_{i_0,j}$ for all j and all $b_{i_0,k}$ for all k are not in $X_{\mathbf{f}'}$. In this case we have $c \in P'^{*X_{\mathbf{f}'}}$.
   (b) Assume $c' \in X_{\mathbf{f}'}$ and c' is in the language of P'^*. This means that $c \notin X_{\mathbf{f}'}$, therefore $c' \in P'^{*X_{\mathbf{f}'}}$, because the only clause with head c' is the clause $\neg c \to c'$ and this clause is not deleted if $c \notin X_{\mathbf{f}'}$, and its head c' is put in $P'^{*X_{\mathbf{f}'}}$.
   (c) Assume, for the other direction of the equality (*), that $c \in P'^{*X_{\mathbf{f}'}}$. If c is in the language of P^* then the only way c can get into $P'^{*X_{\mathbf{f}'}}$ is that for some clause (c, i)

$$\bigwedge_j \neg a'_{i,j} \wedge \bigwedge_k \neg b_{ik} \to c$$

   we have that $a'_{i,j} \notin X_{\mathbf{f}'}$, for all j and $b_{i,k} \notin X_{\mathbf{f}'}$ for all k. This means that $\mathbf{f}(a_{i,j}) = 1$ for all j an $\mathbf{f}(b_{i,k}) = 0$ for all k.
   But in this case we get from the equations that $\mathbf{f}$ satisfies that $\mathbf{f}(c) = 1$, i.e. $c \in X_{\mathbf{f}'}$.
   (d) Assume $c' \in P'^{*X_{\mathbf{f}}}$ and that c' is in the language of P'^*. The only clause which can let c' into $P'^{*X_{\mathbf{f}}}$ is $\neg c \to c'$. This means that $c \notin X_{\mathbf{f}'}$, i.e. $\mathbf{f}(c) = 0$, so $\mathbf{f}'(c') = 1$ ad $c \in X_{\mathbf{f}'}$.
   From (*) it is clear that $X_{\mathbf{f}'}$ is an answer set for P'^*.

4 Conclusion

We introduced the equational approach to logic programs and showed its soundness. This is part of a general methodological drive of applying the equational approach to argumentation, modal logic, default logic, logic programming, liar paradoxes and more. In the case of logic programming, we can regard the equational approach as offering new semantics, each solution to the equation to be considered a model. Note that the problem of the inconsistency of Clark completion for programs with negation as failure in the body of clauses does not arise in the equational semantics! We also mention that there is need to research the correspondence between properties of the solutions of the equations $Eq(P)$ and properties/answer sets/models of the program P.

Acknowledgement. I am grateful to Alexander Bochman for valuable comments and criticism. Research done under ISF project Integrating Logic and Network Reasoning.

References

1. Lloyd, J.W.: Foundations of Logic Programming, 2nd edn. Springer (1987)
2. Clark, K.: Negation as failure. Originally published in 1978, and reproduced in Readings in nonmonotonic reasoning. Morgan Kaufmann Publishers, pp. 311–325 (1987)
3. Gabbay, D.: An Equational Approach to Argumentation Networks, p. 107 (February 2011). To Appear in Argumentation and Computation (2012); Special double issue on numerical and equational argumentation networks
4. Gabbay, D.M.: Introducing Equational Semantics for Argumentation Networks. In: Liu, W. (ed.) ECSQARU 2011. LNCS (LNAI), vol. 6717, pp. 19–35. Springer, Heidelberg (2011)
5. Lifschitz, V.: What is answer set programming? (2008), `http://www.cs.utexas.edu/~vl/papers/wiasp.pdf`
6. Caminada, M., Gabbay, D.: A logical account of formal argumentation. Studia Logica 93(2-3), 109–145 (2009)
7. Rahwan, I., Simari, G.R.: Argumentation in Artificial Intelligence. Springer (2009)
8. Sobolev, V.I.: Brouwer theorem. In: Hazewinkel, M. (ed.) Encyclopaedia of Mathematics. Springer (2001), For Brouwer Fixed Point Theorem, `http://en.wikipedia.org/wiki/Brouwer_fixed_point_theorem`
9. Son, T.C.: Answer Set Programming Tutorial (October 2005), `http://www.cs.nmsu.edu/~tson/tutorials/asp-tutorial.pdf`
10. Gabbay, D.: Fibring argumentation frames. Studia Logica 93(2-3), 231–295 (2009)
11. Gabbay, D., d'Avila Garcez, A.: Logical modes of attack in argumentation networks. Studia Logica 93(2-3), 199–230 (2009)

Gearing Up for Effective ASP Planning

Martin Gebser, Roland Kaufmann, and Torsten Schaub*

Universität Potsdam

Abstract. We elaborate upon incremental modeling techniques for ASP Planning, a term coined by Vladimir Lifschitz at the end of the nineties. Taking up this line of research, we argue that ASP needs both a dedicated modeling methodology and sophisticated solving technology in view of the high practical relevance of dynamic systems in real-world applications.

1 Introduction

The stable models semantics was born more than two decades ago, fathered by Michael Gelfond and Vladimir Lifschitz in [1]. Since then, it has seen a pretty rough childhood. Initially facing the greatly dominating elder brother Prolog, it made its way despite many fights with first and second grade cousins in the area of Logic Programming and Nonmonotonic Reasoning. Being now in its early adulthood, under the pseudonym of Answer Set Programming (ASP; [2]), it entertains a competitive yet extremely fruitful relationship with Satisfiability Testing (SAT; [3]), an offspring of a house with a certain veil of antique nobility, viz. classical logic.

However, the rivalry between ASP and SAT has turned out to be extremely productive for ASP. And in fact ASP often followed in the footsteps of SAT. This is particularly true as regards computational issues, where the Davis-Putman-Logemann-Loveland procedure [4,5] led the way for the first effective implementation of ASP, namely the *smodels* system [6]. Similarly, current ASP solvers like *clasp* [7] largely benefit from the technology of advanced Boolean constraint solving boosted to great success in the area of SAT (cf. [3]).

Looking at the success stories of SAT, among which the most shiny ones are arguably Automated Planning [8] and Model Checking [9], we notice that both deal with dynamic applications, whose complexity seems to be a priori out of reach of SAT. In both cases the key idea was to reduce the complexity from PSPACE to NP by treating these problems in a bounded way and to consider in turn one problem instance after another by gradually increasing the bound on the solution size. This idea can be seen as the major driving force behind the extension of SAT solvers with incremental interfaces (cf. [10,11]) which constitute nowadays a key technology in many SAT-based real-world applications.

Similarly, there were early attempts to apply ASP to Automated Planning in [12,13] based upon which Vladimir Lifschitz put forward ASP Planning in [14,2] as a knowledge-intense alternative to SAT Planning. In fact, ASP's rich modeling language

* Affiliated with the School of Computing Science at Simon Fraser University, Canada, and the Institute for Integrated and Intelligent Systems at Griffith University, Australia.

E. Erdem et al. (Eds.): Correct Reasoning, LNCS 7265, pp. 296–310, 2012.

offers an attractive alternative to the encoding of planning problems via imperative programming languages, which is common and actually unavoidable in SAT. So far, however, ASP Planning is no real match for SAT Planning. For one thing, ASP modeling techniques for dynamic domains focus on knowledge representation issues but neglect the development of design patterns aiming at search space reductions, as found in the SAT Planning literature [15] (eg. forward expansion, mutex analysis, or operator splitting). A first yet incomplete attempt to address this problem was done in [16], where a selection of such SAT Planning techniques was modeled and studied in the context of ASP. This approach is summarized in Section 6.

Another and more general reason why ASP is lagging behind SAT in terms of dynamic applications is that incremental grounding and solving techniques have not yet found the same proliferation as in SAT. On the one hand, SAT has its focus on solving, while ASP is additionally concerned with grounding in view of its modeling language. Hence, it is a more complex endeavor to come up with an ASP system addressing both incremental grounding and solving. On the other hand, now that a first incremental ASP system, viz. *iclingo* [17], is available since a couple of years, we find it important to elaborate upon the differences in modeling and employment with respect to a static setting in order to foster its usage and thus to open up dynamic applications to ASP.

This is also our essay's topic. After laying some formal foundations in Section 2, we start from a blocks world planning example stemming from Vladimir Lifschitz' work on ASP Planning and transfer it into an incremental setting in Section 3 and 4. For a complement, we address in Section 5 the "Towers of Hanoi" problem in order to deepen the introduction to modeling in incremental ASP. Finally, we return to the initial motivation of Vladimir Lifschitz' work and sketch a first prototype for PDDL-based ASP Planning.

In what follows, we presuppose some familiarity with the syntax and semantics of logic programs in the framework of ASP. A general introduction to ASP can be found in [18]; one focusing on the theme of this essay is given in [17].

2 Incremental Logic Programs

For capturing dynamic systems, we take advantage of *incremental logic programs* [17], consisting of triples (B, P, Q) of logic programs, among which P and Q contain a (single) parameter t ranging over the natural numbers. In view of this, we sometimes denote P and Q by $P[t]$ and $Q[t]$. The base program B is meant to describe static knowledge, independent of parameter t. The role of P is to capture knowledge accumulating with increasing t, whereas Q is specific for each value of t. Provided all programs are "modularly composable" (cf. [17]), we are interested in finding an answer set of the program

$$B \cup \left(\bigcup_{1 \leq j \leq i} P[k/j]\right) \cup Q[k/i] \tag{1}$$

for some (minimum) natural number $i \geq 1$.

Such an answer is traditionally found by appeal to iterative deepening search. That is, one first checks whether $B \cup P[1] \cup Q[1]$ has an answer set, if not, the same is done for $B \cup P[1] \cup P[2] \cup Q[2]$ and so on. For a given i, this approach re-processes B

for i times and $(i{-}j{+}1)$ times each $P[j]$, where $1 \leq j \leq i$, while each $Q[j]$ is dealt with only once. Unlike this, incremental ASP solving computes these answers sets in an incremental fashion, starting from B but then gradually dealing only with the program slices $P[i]$ and $Q[i]$ rather than the entire program in (1). However, B and the previously processed slices $P[j]$ and $Q[j]$, $1 \leq j < i$, must be taken into account when dealing with $P[i]$ and $Q[i]$: while the rules in $P[j]$ are accumulated, the ones in $Q[j]$ must be discarded. For accomplishing this, an ASP system has to operate in a "stateful way." That is, it has to maintain its previous state for processing the current program slices. In this way, all components, B, $P[j]$, and $Q[i]$, of (1) are dealt with only once, and duplicated work is avoided when increasing i.

However, it is important to note that an incremental proceeding leads to a slightly different semantics than obtained in a static setting. Foremost, we must realize that we deal with an infinite set of terms containing all natural numbers. Unlike this, an incremental proceeding aims at providing a finite grounding at each step. On the one hand, we may thus never obtain a complete finite representation of the overall program. And on the other hand, each incremental step can only produce a grounding relative to the (finite) set of terms that were up to that point encountered by the grounder. The stable models semantics must thus falsify all atoms that have so far not been derived, although they might become true at future steps. We refer the interested reader to [17] for a formal elaboration of this phenomenon along with its formal semantics.

However, given that an ASP system is composed of a grounder and a solver, an incremental ASP solver gains on both ends. As regards grounding, it reduces efforts by avoiding reproducing previous ground rules. Regarding solving, it reduces redundancy, in particular, if a learning ASP solver is used, given that previously gathered information on heuristics, conflicts, or loops (cf. [7]), respectively, remains available and can thus be continuously exploited.

For illustration, consider the following example enumerating even and odd natural numbers.

$$
\begin{aligned}
B &= \{\ \mathit{even}(0)\ \} \\
P[k] &= \left\{\begin{array}{l}
\mathit{odd}(k) \leftarrow \mathit{even}(k-1) \\
\mathit{even}(k) \leftarrow \mathit{odd}(k-1) \\
\mathit{opooo}(k) \leftarrow \mathit{odd}(k), k = M * N * O, \mathit{odd}(M), \mathit{odd}(N), \mathit{odd}(O)
\end{array}\right\} \\
Q[k] &= \{\ \leftarrow \{\ \mathit{opooo}(K) \mid K = 1..k\ \} \leq 2\ \}
\end{aligned}
$$

The goal of this program is to find the first triple *opooo* number, that is, the smallest number k such that there are 3 odd numbers $k' \leq k$ that equal the product of 3 odd numbers.

This program is represented in the language of the incremental ASP system *iclingo* in Listing 1.

The partition of rules into B, $P[k]$, and $Q[k]$ is done by appeal to the directives `#base`, `#cumulative`, and `#volatile` (all of which may appear multiple times in a program), respectively.

Passing the program in Listing 1 to *iclingo* yields an answer set at Step 27:

Listing 1. An incremental program computing the triple *opooo* number (`opooo.lp`)

```
1  #base.

3  even(0).

5  #cumulative k.

7   odd(k) :- even(k-1).
8  even(k) :-  odd(k-1).

10 opooo(k) :- odd(k), k==M*N*O, odd(M), odd(N), odd(O), M<N, N<O.

12 #volatile k.

14 :- { opooo(K) : K=1..k } 2.
```

```
nix> iclingo opooo.lp
Answer: 1
even(0) odd(1) even(2) odd(3) even(4) odd(5) even(6) odd(7) even(8)    \
odd(9) even(10) odd(11) even(12) odd(13) even(14) odd(15) opooo(15)    \
even(16) odd(17) even(18) odd(19) even(20) odd(21) opooo(21) even(22) \
odd(23) even(24) odd(25) even(26) odd(27) opooo(27)
SATISFIABLE

Models       : 1
Total Steps  : 27
Time         : 0.000
  Prepare    : 0.000
  Prepro.    : 0.000
  Solving    : 0.000
```

Observe that *iclingo* launched 26 solving processes before the above answer set was found in the 27th step. We get three opooo numbers, viz. 15, 21, and 27. Rather than re-grounding and re-solving each time from scratch, *iclingo* only grounded each time the necessary program slice. For instance, at Step 25 only 2 rules are sent to the solver:

```
odd(25).
:-.
```

The first rule is the instantiation of Line 7 in Listing 1 in view of the fact that `even(24)` was obtained at Step 24. And the second rule is the instantiation of the volatile integrity constraint in Line 14 in Listing 1. This is because the cardinality constraint is instantiated as '`{opooo(15),opooo(21)} 2`' and then evaluated to true and thus removed from the body of the integrity constraint.

3 Blocks World Planning

Let us begin with addressing the problem of blocks world planning following the approach taken by Vladimir Lifschitz in [14,2].

A planning problem consists of three parts. An initial situation, a set of actions, and a goal situation (or formula characterizing goal situations). Given such a problem description, a solution is given by a sequence of actions leading from the initial situation to a goal situation.

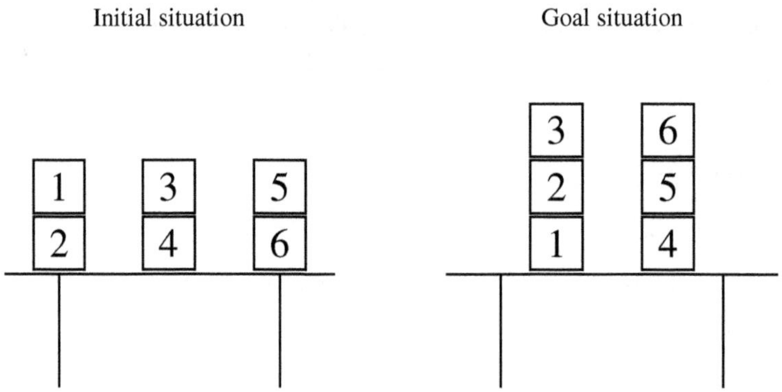

Fig. 1. The initial and goal situation for blocks world planning

Listing 2. Initial and goal situation (`blocks.lp`)

```
on(1,2,0).
on(2,table,0).
on(3,4,0).
on(4,table,0).
on(5,6,0).
on(6,table,0).

:- not on(3,2,lasttime).
:- not on(2,1,lasttime).
:- not on(1,table,lasttime).
:- not on(6,5,lasttime).
:- not on(5,4,lasttime).
:- not on(4,table,lasttime).
```

The initial and desired final situation of a simple blocks world problem is given in Figure 1. In each situation, we consider six blocks on a table, yet in different arrangements. Listing 2 gives the representation provided in [14,2]. An atom like `on(2,table,0)` expresses that Block 2 is on the table at timepoint `0`. Note that the initial and goal situation are represented differently. While the initial situation is given and thus represented as facts, the goal situation is represented as conditions on the final state (at `lasttime`) that must be generated by a successful plan. In this simple example, we consider a single action, `move`, that allows us to move a block on a location at a certain timepoint. A location can be a block or the table.

Listing 3 gives the encoding of blocks world planning given by Vladimir Lifschitz in [14,2], yet adapted to the current language of the ASP grounder *gringo*. For this purpose, we eliminated (nowadays) obsolete domain predicates, added the symbol # in front of directives, and finally provide a simpler display expression in terms of `#hide` and `#show` directives. (The formatting of Listing 2 and 3 is done in accord with the incremental ones in Listing 4 and 5, respectively.)

Listing 3. Blocks world planning: Vladimir Lifschitz' encoding (`planning.lp`)

```
1  #const lasttime=3.
2  #const grippers=2.

5  time(0..lasttime).
6  block(1..6).

8  location(B) :- block(B).
9  location(table).

13 { move(B,L,T) : block(B) : location(L) } grippers :- time(T), T<lasttime.

15 on(B,L,T+1) :- move(B,L,T), T<lasttime.
16 on(B,L,T+1) :- on(B,L,T), not onp(B,L,T+1), T<lasttime.

18 onp(B,L1,T) :- on(B,L,T), L!=L1, location(L1).

20 :- on(B,L,T), onp(B,L,T).
21 :- 2 { on(B1,B,T) : block(B1) }, block(B), time(T).
22 :- move(B,L ,T), on(B1,B,T),   T<lasttime.
23 :- move(B,B1,T), move(B1,L,T), T<lasttime.

25 #hide.
26 #show move/3.
```

Vladimir Lifschitz' encoding consists of five parts. Line 1 and 2 are directives fixing default values for the last time step as well as the number of grippers. The very first part of the actual program begins in Line 5 and ends in Line 9 and provides the basic *data*. The second part is concentrated in Line 13 and deals with the *generation* of all possible sequences of move actions. The third part furnishes the *definition* of the successor states in terms of the fluents *on* and its negation *onp*.[1] Line 15 specifies the effect of moving a block. Line 16 is a frame axiom for fluent *on*. And Line 18 addresses the uniqueness of locations, stating that once a block is on a location it cannot be on any other location. The following integrity constraints provide a *test* series, eliminating invalid solution candidates. Line 20 makes sure that fluent *onp* is the negation of *on*. Line 21 ensures that two blocks cannot be on top of the same block. Line 22 makes sure that a block cannot be moved unless it is clear. And finally Line 23 forbids that a block is moved onto a block that is also being moved. Line 25 and 26 can be regarded as the *display* part, directing the solver to project answer sets onto the instances of *move*/3.

Although there are no answer sets for `lasttime=1,2`, that is, no plans of length one or two, we get a plan of length three as shown next.

```
nix>  clingo -c lasttime=3 planning.lp blocks.lp
Answer: 1
move(6,5,2) move(3,2,2)       move(5,4,1)       \
move(2,1,1) move(3,table,0) move(1,table,0)
SATISFIABLE

Models       : 1
Time         : 0.000
  Prepare    : 0.000
  Prepro.    : 0.000
  Solving    : 0.000
```

[1] *onp* stands for *on*′.

Listing 4. Initial and goal situation: Incremental encoding (`blocksInc.lp`)

```
1  #base.

3  on(1,2,0).
4  on(2,table,0).
5  on(3,4,0).
6  on(4,table,0).
7  on(5,6,0).
8  on(6,table,0).

10 #volatile lasttime.

12 :- not on(3,2,lasttime).
13 :- not on(2,1,lasttime).
14 :- not on(1,table,lasttime).
15 :- not on(6,5,lasttime).
16 :- not on(5,4,lasttime).
17 :- not on(4,table,lasttime).
```

Looking at the statistics we note that 2492 rules were grounded for `lasttime=3`. Adding the 687 and 1577 ground rules obtained for the two unsatisfiable programs obtained for `lasttime=1,2`, respectively, we needed to ground in total 4731 rules in order to find the above plan. In addition, we had to re-launch *clingo* three times and no (learned) information could be passed from one attempt to the next.

4 Incremental Blocks World Planning

Let us now turn to an incremental setting. To begin with, let us adapt the logic program giving the initial and goal situation in Listing 2. The result is shown in Listing 4.

We note that the actual program is unaffected. The only change concerns the addition of two directives. The first one, `#base`, declares the initial situation (in Line 3-8) as static information that is grounded only once and stays within the solver. In contrast to this, the statement `#volatile` directs the grounder to reground the integrity constraints (in Line 12-17) expressing the goal situation at each step, while withdrawing the previous instantiation of the constraints from the solver.

Listing 5 provides an incremental version of the encoding in Listing 3. The `#base` part is almost identical to the one in Listing 3. In fact, Line 6, 8, and 9 are identical in both listings. However, the unary `time/1` predicate (along with the declaration of the default value of the constant `lasttime`) in Line 5 (and 1) have vanished in Listing 3. This actually applies to all occurrences of the predicate `time/1` in Listing 3 because the instantiation of time steps is now handled via the incremental parameters and the corresponding directives.

The adaption of the remaining non-incremental encoding in Listing 3 is less straightforward. In fact, looking at the idealized program in (1), we observe that the unfolding of the cumulative program part starts with 1. The idea is that static knowledge, often attached with time step 0, belongs to the static case (that is, the `#base` part). This semantics is also accounted for in the incremental solver *iclingo*, where the parameters like `t` declared by '`#cumulative t.`' or '`#volatile t.`' are instantiated beginning with 1. Unlike this, the time steps in the original encoding — bound by `time(T)`

Listing 5. Blocks world planning: Incremental encoding (`planningInc.lp`)

```
2  #const grippers=2.

4  #base.

6  block(1..6).

8  location(B) :- block(B).
9  location(table).

11 #cumulative t.

13 { move(B,L,t-1) : block(B) : location(L) } grippers.

15 on(B,L,t) :- move(B,L,t-1).
16 on(B,L,t) :- on(B,L,t-1), not onp(B,L,t).

18 onp(B,L1,t) :- on(B,L,t), L!=L1, location(L1).

20 :- on(B,L,t), onp(B,L,t).
21 :- 2 { on(B1,B,t) : block(B1) }, block(B).
22 :- move(B,L ,t-1), on(B1,B,t-1).
23 :- move(B,B1,t-1), move(B1,L,t-1).

25 #hide.
26 #show move/3.
```

— range from `0` to `lasttime` (yet often limited to `T<lasttime`) in Listing 3. This difference has major consequences. First of all, the facts of the initial situation are implicitly verified by the constraints in Listing 3, while this is not the case in Listing 5. To do so, the corresponding constraints had to be replicated with time stamp `0`. Moreover, the respective time stamps have to be adapted to the shift by one. This can be accomplished as follows. For each rule in Listing 3 having body literal '`T<lasttime`', decrement the terms including `T` by one and substitute `T` by `t`. Otherwise, simply replace `T` by `t`. As a consequence, the application of move/3 actions is aligned in both encodings, although the generation in Line 13 refers to different relative time steps, viz `T` and `t-1`.

As a side-effect, our proceeding has also resolved a major problem that had been obtained by a straightforward replacement of `T` by `t` in Listing 3. Recall that an incremental solver unfolds the cumulative part stepwisely. Now inspecting Rule 16 in Listing 3, we observe that the literal `onp(B,L,T+1)` refers to time stamp `T+1`. The only rule deriving instances of onp/3 is given in Line 18 of Listing 3. However, this rule's head atom `onp(B,L1,T)` refers to time stamp `T`. Hence, when the nth program slice is grounded, the overall program may only contain instances of `onp(B,L1,T)` for `T` $= 1..n$ and none for `T` $= n+1$. As a consequence, all instances of the body literal `onp(B,L,T+1)` would be false when producing the nth program slice, simply because they refer to the yet unavailable future. Such phenomena cannot arise in a non-incremental setting given that all program slices are grounded at once. See [17] for a formal elaboration of this and a module based account of incremental grounding and solving.

Finally, launching *iclingo* on the incremental programs in Listing 4 and 5, yields the following result. Note that we take advantage of *iclingo*'s option *--istats* in order to get some insight into the intermediate steps as well.

```
nix> iclingo planningInc.lp blocksInc.lp --istats
=============== step 1 ===============

Models   : 0
Time     : 0.000 (g: 0.000, p: 0.000, s: 0.000)
Rules    : 656
Choices  : 0
Conflicts: 0
=============== step 2 ===============

Models   : 0
Time     : 0.000 (g: 0.000, p: 0.000, s: 0.000)
Rules    : 904
Choices  : 0
Conflicts: 0
=============== step 3 ===============
Answer: 1
move(3,table,0) move(1,table,0) move(5,4,1) \
move(2,1,1)     move(6,5,2)     move(3,2,2)

Models   : 1
Time     : 0.000 (g: 0.000, p: 0.000, s: 0.000)
Rules    : 904
Choices  : 7
Conflicts: 5
=============== Summary ===============
SATISFIABLE

Models      : 1+
Total Steps : 3
Time        : 0.000
  Prepare   : 0.000
  Prepro.   : 0.000
  Solving   : 0.000
```

In total, *iclingo* grounds 2464 rules, 656 in the first step and 904 in the second and third step. Also, the solver is initiated only once and updated twice with new information. Whenever a solving process is engaged it thus benefits from the information gathered during the previous solving attempt.

5 Towers of Hanoi

For further illustration, we now discuss a rather compact encoding of a related planning problem that was trimmed to produce a linear number of ground rules (during the 2011 ASP competition).

The towers of Hanoi problem is a simple puzzle game very similar to the blocks world planning problem presented above. The differences are that instead of a table there are pegs on which discs are put rather than blocks. In addition, discs are of different sizes and can only be put on either a peg or a disk of larger size. Given an initial placement of discs on pegs, the goal is to find a plan that establishes another such placement.

A towers of Hanoi instance consists of a set of pegs given by predicate `peg/1`, a set of discs given by predicate `disk/1`, the initial situation specifying which disk is on which peg at time step zero via predicate `on/3`, and finally the predicate `goal/2` specifying which disk has to be on which peg in the goal situation. Note that in contrast to the description of blocks world instances, we are just specifying on which peg a

Listing 6. Towers of Hanoi instance

```
peg(a;b;c).

disk(1..6).

on(1,a,0).
on(2,b,0).
on(3..6,c,0).

goal_on(3;4,a).
goal_on(6,b).
goal_on(1;2;5,c).
```

disk is because the ordering of discs on a peg is implicitly given by the discs' sizes. Given that there are typically only three pegs and a much larger number of discs, this allows for representing a state with a linear number of fluents instead of the quadratic representation chosen in the blocks world setting. Listing 6 gives an instance with six discs and three pegs, which is depicted in Figure 2.

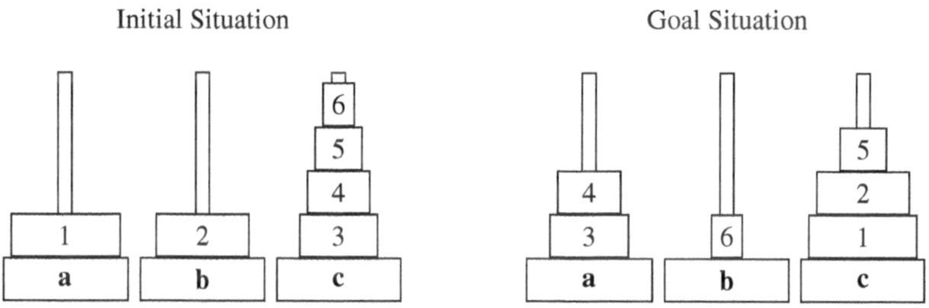

Fig. 2. The initial and goal situation for the towers of Hanoi problem

Listing 7 shows the towers of Hanoi encoding. It incorporates the same ideas as the encoding used in the last ASP competition. Hence, it is optimized for use with ASP solvers. The rule in Line 3 of the cumulative part of the encoding guesses a move. As in the instance, we just select the target peg. This way we reduce the number of atoms used to represent moves and keep the branching factor low. Note that we do not allow for parallel moves here. In principal this would easily be possible but we just have instances with three pegs. Hence, parallel moves are impossible anyway. In the consecutive line, the target is projected out to just capture which disc has been moved. The idea here is to avoid a general frame axiom as in the blocks world encoding and rather to use the moves directly to specify the state transition in lines 6 and 7. This way the grounding is kept more compact because we do not write rules involving the cross-product of all discs. The number of ground rules per step here are directly proportional to number of discs (assuming a constant number of pegs). The rules in lines 9 and 10 specify which positions on a peg are blocked. Again the number of ground rules is directly proportional to the number of discs. The last block of rules in the cumulative part eliminates incorrect moves and adds some domain knowledge in Line 14 to speed up solving. The number of resulting ground rules is again proportional to the number of discs. Finally, the goal situation is checked in the volatile block in Line 17 and the answer set is projected onto the moves in lines 19 and 20.

Listing 7. Towers of Hanoi encoding

```
#cumulative t.

1 { move(D,P,t) : disk(D) : peg(P) } 1.
move(D,t) :- move(D,_,t).

on(D,P,t) :- on(D,P,t-1), not move(D,t).
on(D,P,t) :- move(D,P,t).

blocked(D-1,P,t) :- on(D,P,t-1), D > 0.
blocked(D-1,P,t) :- blocked(D,P,t), D > 0.

:- move(D,t), on(D,P,t-1), blocked(D,P,t).
:- move(D,P,t), blocked(D-1,P,t).
:- not 1 { on(D,P,t) : peg(P) } 1, disk(D).

#volatile t.
:- goal_on(D,P), not on(D,P,t).

#hide.
#show move/3.
```

All in all, the number of rules per time step is directly proportional to the number of discs. Thus we get a very compact encoding that can be used to solve instances requiring large plan lengths. For example a plan for the instance given in Figure 2, which requires 34 moves, can be found in less than a second with *iclingo*.

6 Towards PDDL-Based ASP Planning

Finally, let us sketch how incremental solving can be used for PDDL-based ASP planning. The prototypical system, *plasp*, follows the approach of *SATPlan* [8,19] in translating a planning problem from the Planning Domain Definition Language (PDDL; [20]) into Boolean constraints. Unlike *SATPlan*, however, *plasp* aims at keeping the actual compilation simple in favor of modeling planning techniques by meta-programming in ASP. Although the compilations and meta-programs made available by *plasp* do not (yet) match the sophisticated approaches of dedicated planning systems, they allow for applying ASP systems to available planning problems. In analogy to the previous sections, *plasp* also makes use of the incremental ASP system *iclingo* [17], supporting the step-wise unrolling of problem horizons.

As illustrated in Figure 3, *plasp* translates a PDDL problem instance to ASP and runs it through a solver producing answer sets. The latter represent solutions to the initial

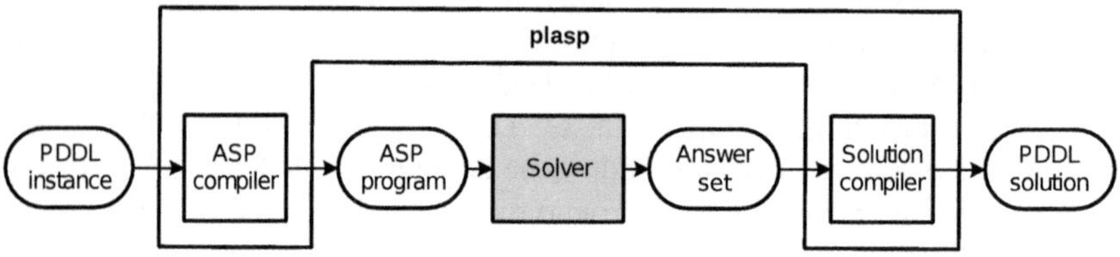

Fig. 3. Architecture of the *plasp* system

planning problem. To this end, a plan is extracted from an answer set and output in PDDL syntax. *plasp* thus consists of two modules, viz., the ASP and Solution compilers. The *ASP compiler* is illustrated in Figure 4.

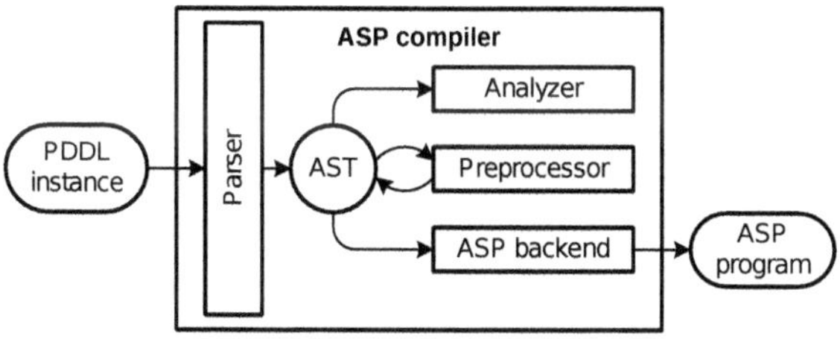

Fig. 4. Architecture of the *ASP compiler*

First, a parser reads the PDDL description as input and builds an internal representation, also known as Abstract Syntax Tree (AST). Then, the *Analyzer* gathers information on the particular problem instance. For example, it determines predicates representing fluents. Afterwards, the *Preprocessor* modifies the instance and enhances it for the translation process. Finally, the *ASP backend* produces an ASP program using the data gathered before. The *Solution compiler* constructs a plan from an answer set output by the solver. This is usually just a syntactic matter, but it becomes more involved in the case of parallel planning where an order among the actions must be re-established. Afterwards, the plan is verified and output in PDDL syntax.

In order to give an idea of the resulting ASP programs, let us sketch the most basic planning encoding relying on meta-programming. To this end, a PDDL domain description is mapped onto a set of facts built from predicates $init$, $goal$, $action$, $demands$, $adds$, and $deletes$ along with their obvious meanings. Such facts are then combined with the meta-program in Figure 5. Note that this meta-program is treated incrementally by the ASP system *iclingo*, as indicated in lines (1), (3), and (10). While the facts resulting from the initial PDDL description along with the ground rules of (2) in Figure 5 are processed just once (and passed to the ASP solver), the rules in (4)–(9) are successively grounded for increasing values of t and accumulated in *iclingo*'s solving component. Finally, goal conditions are expressed by volatile rules, contributing ground rules of (11) and (12) only for the current step t. From a representational perspective, it is interesting to observe that ASP allows for omitting a frame axiom (like the one in line (9)) for negative information, making use of the fact that instances of *holds* are false by default, that is, unless they are explicitly derived to be true. Otherwise, the specification follows closely the semantics of STRIPS [21].

Beyond the meta-program in Figure 5, *plasp* offers planning with concurrent actions. The corresponding modification of the rule in (4) is shown in Figure 6. While (4′) drops the uniqueness condition on applied actions, the additional integrity constraints stipulate that concurrent actions must not undo their preconditions, nor have conflicting effects. The resulting meta-program complies with the ∀-step semantics in [22]. Furthermore, *plasp* offers operator splitting as well as forward expansion. The goal of operator splitting [23] is to reduce the number of propositions in the representation of a planning problem by decomposing action predicates. For instance, an action $a(X, Y, Z)$

(1) **#base.**
(2) $holds(F,0) \leftarrow init(F).$
(3) **#cumulative t.**
(4) $1\,\{apply(A,t) : action(A)\}\,1.$
(5) $\leftarrow apply(A,t), demands(A,F,true), not\ holds(F,t{-}1).$
(6) $\leftarrow apply(A,t), demands(A,F,false), holds(F,t{-}1).$
(7) $holds(F,t) \leftarrow apply(A,t), adds(A,F).$
(8) $del(F,t) \leftarrow apply(A,t), deletes(A,F).$
(9) $holds(F,t) \leftarrow holds(F,t{-}1), not\ del(F,t).$
(10) **#volatile t.**
(11) $\leftarrow goal(F,true), not\ holds(F,t).$
(12) $\leftarrow goal(F,false), holds(F,t).$

Fig. 5. Basic ASP encoding of STRIPS planning

(4′) $1\,\{apply(A,t) : action(A)\}.$
(4′a) $\leftarrow apply(A_1,t), apply(A_2,t), A_1 \neq A_2, demands(A_1,F,true), deletes(A_2,F).$
(4′b) $\leftarrow apply(A_1,t), apply(A_2,t), A_1 \neq A_2, demands(A_1,F,false), adds(A_2,F).$
(4′c) $\leftarrow apply(A_1,t), apply(A_2,t), A_1 \neq A_2, adds(A_1,F), deletes(A_2,F).$

Fig. 6. Adaptation of the basic ASP encoding to parallel STRIPS planning

can be represented in terms of $a_1(X), a_2(Y), a_3(Z)$. Forward expansion (without mutex analysis [24]) instantiates schematic actions by need, viz., if their preconditions have been determined as feasible at a time step, instead of referring to statically given instances of the *action* predicate. This can be useful if initially many instances of a schematic action are inapplicable, yet it requires a domain-specific compilation; meta-programming is difficult to apply because *action* instances are not represented as facts. For further details on the compilation techniques supported by *plasp*, we refer the interested reader to [21,25]. Finally, *plasp* supports combinations of forward expansion with either concurrent actions or operator splitting. Regardless of whether forward expansion is used, concurrent actions and operator splitting can currently not be combined; generally, both techniques are in opposition, although possible solutions have recently been proposed [26].

7 Discussion

ASP Planning was put forward by Vladimir Lifschitz in [14,2] as a knowledge-intense alternative to SAT Planning. Although ASP's modeling language offers an attractive alternative to the encoding of planning problems via imperative programming languages in SAT, so far, ASP Planning is no real match for SAT Planning in terms of performance. On the one hand, ASP lacks modeling techniques aiming at search space reductions in dynamic domains. First attempts to take advantage of incremental grounding and solving ASP techniques were conducted in the areas of Automated Planning [16], Action Languages [27], Finite Model Generation [28], and Stream Reasoning [29,30]. And on the other hand, we take too little advantage of incremental ASP solving when addressing dynamic domains. We discussed these issues and sketched first attempts to rectify this situation. However, dynamic systems are omnipresent in real-world applications. Hence, it is important to equip ASP with an adequate methodology and technology for addressing such highly demanding applications. This is not only important in offline settings, like ASP Planning, but moreover in online settings in view of the emergence of pervasive and ubiquitous computing. A first step in this direction is done in [29,30].

Acknowledgments. This work was partially funded by the German Science Foundation (DFG) under grant SCHA 550/8-1/2. We are grateful to Son Cao Tran and Oliver Ray for comments on an earlier draft of this paper.

References

1. Gelfond, M., Lifschitz, V.: The stable model semantics for logic programming. In: Kowalski, R., Bowen, K. (eds.) Proceedings of the Fifth International Conference and Symposium of Logic Programming (ICLP 1988), pp. 1070–1080. MIT Press (1988)
2. Lifschitz, V.: Answer set programming and plan generation. Artificial Intelligence 138(1-2), 39–54 (2002)
3. Biere, A., Heule, M., van Maaren, H., Walsh, T. (eds.): Handbook of Satisfiability. Frontiers in Artificial Intelligence and Applications, vol. 185. IOS Press (2009)
4. Davis, M., Putnam, H.: A computing procedure for quantification theory. Journal of the ACM 7, 201–215 (1960)
5. Davis, M., Logemann, G., Loveland, D.: A machine program for theorem-proving. Communications of the ACM 5, 394–397 (1962)
6. Simons, P., Niemelä, I., Soininen, T.: Extending and implementing the stable model semantics. Artificial Intelligence 138(1-2), 181–234 (2002)
7. Gebser, M., Kaufmann, B., Neumann, A., Schaub, T.: Conflict-driven answer set solving. In: Veloso, M. (ed.) Proceedings of the Twentieth International Joint Conference on Artificial Intelligence (IJCAI 2007), pp. 386–392. AAAI Press/The MIT Press (2007)
8. Kautz, H., Selman, B.: Planning as satisfiability. In: Neumann, B. (ed.) Proceedings of the Tenth European Conference on Artificial Intelligence (ECAI 1992), pp. 359–363. John Wiley & Sons (1992)
9. Clarke, E., Biere, A., Raimi, R., Zhu, Y.: Bounded model checking using satisfiability solving. Formal Methods in System Design 19(1), 7–34 (2001)
10. Whittemore, J., Kim, J., Sakallah, K.: SATIRE: a new incremental satisfiability engine. In: Proceedings of the Thirty-eighth Conference on Design Automation (DAC 2001), pp. 542–545. ACM Press (2001)
11. Eén, N., Sörensson, N.: Temporal induction by incremental SAT solving. Electronic Notes in Theoretical Computer Science 89(4) (2003)
12. Subrahmanian, V., Zaniolo, C.: Relating stable models and AI planning domains. In: Proceedings of the Twelfth International Conference on Logic Programming, pp. 233–247. MIT Press (1995)
13. Dimopoulos, Y., Nebel, B., Köhler, J.: Encoding Planning Problems in Nonmonotonic Logic Programs. In: Steel, S., Alami, R. (eds.) ECP 1997. LNCS (LNAI), vol. 1348, pp. 169–181. Springer, Heidelberg (1997)
14. Lifschitz, V.: Answer set planning. In: de Schreye, D. (ed.) Proceedings of the International Conference on Logic Programming (ICLP 1999), pp. 23–37. MIT Press (1999)
15. Rintanen, J.: Planning and SAT. In: [3], ch.15, pp. 483–504

16. Gebser, M., Kaminski, R., Knecht, M., Schaub, T.: plasp: A prototype for PDDL-based planning in ASP. In: [31], pp. 358–363
17. Gebser, M., Kaminski, R., Kaufmann, B., Ostrowski, M., Schaub, T., Thiele, S.: Engineering an Incremental ASP Solver. In: Garcia de la Banda, M., Pontelli, E. (eds.) ICLP 2008. LNCS, vol. 5366, pp. 190–205. Springer, Heidelberg (2008)
18. Baral, C.: Knowledge Representation, Reasoning and Declarative Problem Solving. Cambridge University Press (2003)
19. Kautz, H., Selman, B.: Pushing the envelope: Planning, propositional logic, and stochastic search. In: Shrobe, H., Senator, T. (eds.) Proceedings of the National Conference on Artificial Intelligence (AAAI), pp. 1194–1201. AAAI Press (1996)
20. McDermott, D.: PDDL — the planning domain definition language. Technical Report CVC TR-98-003/DCS TR-1165, Yale Center for Computational Vision and Control (1998)
21. Nau, D., Ghallab, M., Traverso, P.: Automated Planning: Theory and Practice. Morgan Kaufmann Publishers (2004)
22. Rintanen, J., Heljanko, K., Niemelä, I.: Parallel Encodings of Classical Planning as Satisfiability. In: Alferes, J.J., Leite, J. (eds.) JELIA 2004. LNCS (LNAI), vol. 3229, pp. 307–319. Springer, Heidelberg (2004)
23. Kautz, H., McAllester, D., Selman, B.: Encoding plans in propositional logic. In: Aiello, L., Doyle, J., Shapiro, S. (eds.) Proceedings of the Fifth International Conference on Principles of Knowledge Representation and Reasoning (KR 1996), pp. 374–384. Morgan Kaufmann Publishers (1996)
24. Blum, A., Furst, M.: Fast planning through planning graph analysis. Artificial Intelligence 90(1-2), 279–298 (1997)
25. Knecht, M.: Efficient domain-independent planning using declarative programming. M.Sc. thesis, Institute for Informatics, University of Potsdam (2009)
26. Robinson, N., Gretton, C., Pham, D., Sattar, A.: SAT-based parallel planning using a split representation of actions. In: Gerevini, A., Howe, A., Cesta, A., Refanidis, I. (eds.) Proceedings of the Nineteenth International Conference on Automated Planning and Scheduling (ICAPS 2009), pp. 281–288. AAAI Press (2009)
27. Gebser, M., Grote, T., Schaub, T.: Coala: A Compiler from Action Languages to ASP. In: Janhunen, T., Niemelä, I. (eds.) JELIA 2010. LNCS, vol. 6341, pp. 360–364. Springer, Heidelberg (2010)
28. Gebser, M., Sabuncu, O., Schaub, T.: An incremental answer set programming based system for finite model computation. AI Communications 24(2), 195–212 (2011)
29. Gebser, M., Grote, T., Kaminski, R., Schaub, T.: Reactive answer set programming. In: [31], pp. 54–66
30. Gebser, M., Grote, T., Kaminski, R., Obermeier, P., Sabuncu, O., Schaub, T.: Stream reasoning with answer set programming: Preliminary report. In: Eiter, T., McIlraith, S. (eds.) Proceedings of the Thirteenth International Conference on Principles of Knowledge Representation and Reasoning (KR 2012). AAAI Press (to appear, 2012)
31. Delgrande, J.P., Faber, W. (eds.): LPNMR 2011. LNCS (LNAI), vol. 6645. Springer, Heidelberg (2011)
32. oclingo, `http://www.cs.uni-potsdam.de/oclingo`

Toward Question Answering in Travel Domains

Yana Todorova and Michael Gelfond

Computer Science Department,
Texas Tech University,
Lubbock TX USA
{yana.todorova,michael.gelfond}@ttu.edu

Abstract. The paper gives Answer Set Prolog axiomatizations of knowledge needed to answer questions about the content of simple travel stories. We assume that the background knowledge needed to understand these stories contains a hierarchy of classes relevant to them and concentrate on answering questions about locations of movers and cardinalities of different groups of movers. The axiomatizations allow to properly answer such questions for stories with various forms of incompleteness.

1 Introduction

This paper belongs to the line of work, which investigates the applicability of Answer Set Programming (ASP) [10,15,16] to question answering from natural language ([2]). We are interested in reasoning about simple travel stories, with the emphasis on the locations of participants and the cardinality of groups. The previous work [3,4] on answering questions about travel in ASP was able to answer rather sophisticated questions about locations of participants, given complete information about the travel domain. No attempt, however, was made to deal with cardinality and with stories containing only partial information. In this work, we remove these restrictions. In addition, we assume that the background knowledge, needed to understand travel stories, contains a hierarchy of classes[1] of movable objects described by the stories. Movement of such an object into an area[2] changes not only its position, but also the cardinality of the sets of objects from different classes located in this (and other) areas. This adds an extra level of complexity not present in the previous work. The following examples will be used throughout the paper for illustrative purposes.

[1] By *hierarchy* we mean a collection of classes connected by arrows, which indicate the subclass relation between the classes; Children of a class are disjoint; *instance of a hierarchy* is a set of objects called the *universe* of objects of the hierarchy, and a mapping of class names into subsets of the universe, which respects the hierarchy's subclass relation.

[2] We assume that areas in the stories are disjoint. Removing this restriction will require defining some areas as points and adding several axioms including rules summing up numbers of elements of a given class located in all the points belonging to a larger area. This is not feasible due to the space restrictions.

E. Erdem et al. (Eds.): Correct Reasoning, LNCS 7265, pp. 311–326, 2012.

Example 1. [Basic Travel Story]
Professor D and two of his students, A and B, entered an empty room. They were immediately followed by professor C. Is A in the room? How many people are in the room? How many students? How many professors?

The hierarchy needed to understand this story and the relevant questions consists of the classes *person*, *professor*, and *student* with natural subclass relations between them. The story describes a trajectory of a discrete dynamic system[3]. Initially, the system is in the state in which the room is empty. After the first action, the state changes. Now the room contains A, B, and D. After the second action, they are joined by C. The questions, which refer to the last state of the trajectory, are answered by *yes*, 4, 2 and 2, respectively. Since the story gives complete information about locations of people and their positions in the inheritance hierarchy, the cardinality questions are answered by a single number each. A small modification of existing axioms was sufficient to find the desired trajectory and to answer the corresponding questions. The next example shows that the situation changes when we do not have a complete knowledge about our domain.

Example 2. [Uncertain group affiliation]
Professor D and two of his students, A and B, entered the empty room. They were immediately followed by professor C. How many freshmen are in the room?

The hierarchy of classes, pertinent to the story from Example 2, includes *freshman*, *sophomore*, *junior*, and *senior* which are subclasses of the class *student*. In contrast to the previous example, we do not have complete knowledge about classes to which the entities discussed in the text belong to. This implies that there is a number of trajectories compatible with the story. An analysis of these trajectories allows us to produce an expected answer: *at most two*. The next example illustrates another type of incompleteness. This time, we do not even know the exact number and names of people, initially located in the room.

Example 3. [Uncertainty in the initial sizes of groups]
There were less than two people in the room. How many people are in the room, after it has been entered by a student named John?

Again the story is compatible with multiple trajectories. Their analysis allows us to produce the correct answer: *between* 1 *and* 3. Finally, the following example:

Example 4. [Uncertainty in the number of movers]
There were two professors and four students in the room. They were joined by at least two more students. How many professors, students, freshmen, and people are in the room?

The story only specifies the lower bound of people of a given class involved in the movement. There are multiple models of this story, containing multiple moving

[3] We assume that such system is described by a transition diagram, whose nodes represent possible states of the system, and whose arcs are labeled by actions.

objects and multiple trajectories, but the questions can be uniquely answered by 2, *between* 6 *and* max_size, *between* 0 *and* max_size, and *between* 8 *and* max_size.

The above stories have several characteristic features. They describe trajectories of some dynamic system and are concerned with questions about positions of objects and about cardinality (number of objects from a class of some inheritance hierarchy located in a given area). The last three stories also deal with various types of incompleteness of knowledge. These features cause difficulties for the reasoning parts of existing question answering systems. The method discussed in this paper is able to overcome these difficulties in the context of simple travel stories. Hopefully it will also be applicable to more general domains.

2 Travel Logic Form

We follow a logic based approach to question answering, in which a text-question pair $\langle T, Q\rangle$ is translated into a logical representation, called *logic form* of $\langle T, Q\rangle$. This form (sometimes together with the background knowledge) is then used to find answer to the question. A specific feature of our approach is the use of a particular logic form, suitable for reasoning about travel stories. We refer to it as *travel logic form* (TLF).

Definition 1. *[TLF]*
A TLF consists of:

1. Description of the relevant hierarchy:

   (a) A tree of classes:

$$root(C) \qquad class(C) \qquad c\_link(C_1, C_2)$$

   The last statement says that in the class hierarchy of the story, class C_1 is a child of class C_2;

   (b) An instance of the hierarchy:

$$object(O) \qquad m\_link(O, C)$$

   The last statement places an object O into a class C of the hierarchy;

   (c) Cardinality of the universe:

$$card = k$$

2. Collection of areas:

$$area(A)$$

   We refer to this part of logic form as *static.*

3. History of the travelers' domain described by the story, which is represented by collection of statements of the form:

$$hpd(a, i) \qquad obs(f, v, i)$$

   where v is a boolean value; the first statement means that action a happened at step i of the system's trajectory; the second one states that at step i fluent[4] f was observed to have truth value v. (For simplicity we restrict ourselves to histories, which only contain observations of fluents made at time 0). The actions of a simple travel domain are of the form

$$enter(O, A) \qquad enter(X, N, C, A)$$

   where X is min, max, or ex – *minimum, maximum, or exactly N members of class C entered area A.* Similarly for actions *leave*. The fluent

$$in(O, A)$$

   read as *object O is located in area A* describes a property of an individual object. Other fluents describe properties of *populations* — groups of object of class C located in area A. We will need:

$$lb(P, N) \qquad ub(P, N)$$

   read as *N is the lower (upper) bound of the size of population P.* Action $enter(O, A)$ and fluent $in(O, A)$ will be called *basic*. Other actions and fluents will be called *extended.*
4. Collection of queries of the form:

$$query(in(O, A)) \quad -- \quad \textit{Is object } O \textit{ in the area } A?$$

$$query(where(O)) \quad -- \quad \textit{Where is } O?$$

$$query(who(A)) \quad -- \quad \textit{Who is located in area } A?$$

$$query(how\_many(C, A)) \quad -- \quad \textit{How many members of class } C \textit{ are in } A?$$

   The questions are referring to the values of the fluents at the end of the trajectory.

A TLF can be viewed as a theory defining a collection of *models.* To define this notion, let us consider a TLF, LF. By $\mathcal{H}(LF)$ we denote the hierarchy described by statements (1a) of LF. An instance, $\mathcal{I}(LF)$, of $\mathcal{H}(LF)$ consists of the universe U of cardinality k containing all the objects defined in LF, and a mapping from classes of $\mathcal{H}(LF)$ to subsets of U such that for every statement $c\_link(c_1, c_2)$ of LF, class c_1 is mapped into a subset of c_2 and the root is mapped into U. By *encoding* of $\mathcal{I}$ with the universe U, we mean the set

$$e(\mathcal{I}) = \{object(o) : o \in U\}.$$

[4] A fluent is a property of the domain, whose truth value can be changed by actions. Other properties are called *statics.*

A model of LF consists of an instance $\mathcal{I}$ of the LF's hierarchy, a *transition diagram* T (describing effects of actions $enter(O, A)$ and $leave(O, A)$ on locations of movers from $\mathcal{I}$), and a collection P of paths of T, compatible with the TLF's history. T and P will be defined by an instance $\mathcal{I}$ and an ASP program, $\mathcal{M}^n$, where n is the maximum number of steps in the story's history. The program contains general knowledge about travel and about inheritance hierarchies.

Definition of $\mathcal{M}^n$: The program consists of the following rules. (Possibly indexed variables O, A, F and I range over objects, areas, fluents, and steps of the system's trajectory, respectively; n is the length of the story's history);
Dynamic causal law:

$$holds(in(O, A), I + 1) \leftarrow occurs(enter(O, A), I). \tag{1}$$

which says that $in(O, A)$ is a direct effect of action $enter(O, A)$;
State constraint:

$$\neg holds(in(O, A_2), I) \leftarrow holds(in(O, A_1), I), A_1 \neq A_2. \tag{2}$$

which says that an object can not be located in two disjoint areas;
Executability condition:

$$\leftarrow occurs(enter(O, A), I), holds(in(O, A), I). \tag{3}$$

which says that it is impossible for O to enter area A, if it is already there;
Inertia axioms:

$$\begin{array}{rl} holds(F, I+1) \leftarrow & fluent(inertial, F), \\ & holds(F, I), \\ & \text{not } \neg holds(F, I+1) \\ \neg holds(F, I+1) \leftarrow & fluent(inertial, F), \\ & \neg holds(F, I), \\ & \text{not } holds(F, I+1) \end{array} \tag{4}$$

which say that inertial fluents tend to stay unchanged;
Membership of the class hierarchy:

$$\begin{array}{l} member(O, C) \ \ \leftarrow m\_link(O, C). \\ member(O, C2) \leftarrow c\_link(C1, C2), member(O, C1). \end{array} \tag{5}$$

which defines *member* as the *transitive closure of relation m_link*;
Disjointness axiom:

$$\begin{array}{rl} \neg member(O, C2) \leftarrow & member(O, C1), C1 \neq C2, \\ & c\_link(C1, C), c\_link(C2, C). \end{array} \tag{6}$$

stating that the children of a class are disjoint;
Completeness of the hierarchy axioms:

$$\begin{array}{ll} \neg leaf(C2) & \leftarrow c\_link(C1, C2). \\ leaf(C) & \leftarrow \text{ not } \neg leaf(C). \\ is\_defined(O) & \leftarrow leaf(C), member(O, C). \\ & \leftarrow \text{ not } is\_defined(O). \end{array} \tag{7}$$

stating that every object of the domain belongs to a leaf of the hierarchy; and *Axioms for observations in the initial situation*:

$$\begin{array}{ll} holds(F,0) & \leftarrow obs(F,true,0). \\ \neg holds(F,0) & \leftarrow obs(F,false,0). \end{array} \tag{8}$$

This completes the definition of $\mathcal{M}^n$.

Now we define the transition diagram T, given by an instance $\mathcal{I}$ of a travel logic form LF. The signature of T consists of the objects of the universe of U, inertial fluent $in(O,A)$, statics $object(O)$, $area(A)$, $root(C)$, $class(C)$, $m\_link(O,C)$, $c\_link(C_1,C_2)$, and $member(O,C)$, as well as actions $enter(O,A)$ and $leave(O,A)$.

A *state* of T consists of the encoding $e(\mathcal{I})$, the collection, *stat*, of static statements of LF, and a complete and consistent collection of literals formed by relation $in(O,A)$, which satisfies rule 2 of $\mathcal{M}^1$. A triple $\langle \sigma_0, a, \sigma_1 \rangle$ is a *transition* of T iff there exists an answer set S of the program:

$$\mathcal{M}^1 \cup e(\mathcal{I}) \cup \{holds(f,0) : f \in \sigma_0\} \cup \{\neg holds(f,0) : \neg f \in \sigma_0\} \cup \{occurs(e,0) : e \in a\},$$

such that

$$\sigma_1 = stat \cup \{f : holds(f,1) \in S\} \cup \{\neg f : holds(f,1) \in S\}.$$

Finally, we define the set P of all possible trajectories of T, which are compatible with the recorded history H_n of LF (we refer to them as models of H_n). A trajectory $M = \langle \sigma_0, a_0, \sigma_1, \ldots, a_{n-1}, \sigma_n \rangle$ of T is a *model* of H_n if:

- if $obs(f,true,i) \in H_n$ then $f \in \sigma_i$.
- if $obs(f,false,i) \in H_n$ then $\neg f \in \sigma_i$.
- $hpd(e,i) \in H_n$ iff $e \in a_i$.

A history is *consistent*, if it has a model. This completes our definition of a model $\langle \mathcal{I}, T, P \rangle$ of a travel logic form LF. A travel story is *consistent*, if its logic form is consistent, i.e., has a model. A statement Q is *entailed* by a travel story with travel logic form LF, if Q is true in all models of LF.

3 Complete Travel Stories

In this section we assume that the logic form, constructed from a text-question pair of a travel story is *complete*. This will be defined as follows:

Definition 2. *[Complete TLF]* A travel logic form LF is called *complete*, if it has the following properties:

1. $card = k \in LF$ iff $k = |\{o : object(o) \in LF\}|$.
2. Every movable object O of LF is linked by m_link relation with the leaf of the story's class hierarchy.
3. For every movable object O and area A, such that O is initially located in A, the logic form contains $obs(in(O,A), true, 0)$.
4. The only fluents and actions mentioned in the logic form are basic.

A travel story is called *complete*, if it has a complete TLF.

Proposition 1. *[Uniqueness of model for complete TLF]*
A complete and consistent TLF has a unique model.

As usual in ASP, computing this model and answering our queries will be reduced to finding answer set of a logic program. To describe this process, we need the following definitions:
A relation p is *defined by* a set of ground literals S, if: $\bar{a} \in p$ iff $p(\bar{a}) \in S$ and $\bar{a} \notin p$ iff $\neg p(\bar{a}) \in S$. A trajectory $\langle \sigma_0, a_0, \sigma_1, \ldots, a_{n-1}, \sigma_n \rangle$ is *defined by* S, if:

- $\sigma_i = \{f \mid holds(f,i) \in S\} \cup \{\neg f \mid \neg holds(f,i) \in S\}$, for any $1 \le i \le n$; and
- $a_i = \{a \mid occurs(a,i) \in S\}$, for any $1 \le i < n$.

Now let us expand our program $\mathcal{M}^n$ (where n is the length of story's history), by the rules defining answers to our queries. Here are some examples:

$$answer(O, is\_in, A) \leftarrow query(where(O), n), holds(in(O,A), n).$$
$$answer(O, is\_not\_in, A) \leftarrow query(where(O), n), \neg holds(in(O,A), n).$$

$$answer(N, members\_of, C, in, A) \leftarrow query(how\_many(C,A), n),$$
$$N = \#count\{holds(in(X,A), n) : member(X,C)\}.$$

(Here we use an extension of the original ASP by aggregates [18].) Other queries are added in a similar way. We denote the resulting program by $\mathcal{P}_1^n$; $\mathcal{P}_1^n(LF)$ is the union of $\mathcal{P}_1^n$ and LF.

Proposition 2. *[Correctness of reasoning with complete stories]* The model of a complete and consistent travel story LF is defined by the unique answer set of program $\mathcal{P}_1^n(LF)$. Moreover, the *answer* literal, contained in this answer set, gives the correct answer to the story's query.

This proposition can be used to answer queries from the first example of the introduction.

Example 5. [Example 1, revisited]
The logic form of the example story will contain description of movable objects a, b, c, and d, area *room*, together with statements:
$card = 4$
$root(person).$
$c\_link(prof, person).$ $c\_link(student, person).$
$m\_link(a, student).$ $m\_link(b, student).$ $m\_link(c, prof).$ $m\_link(d, prof).$
describing the instance of the hierarchy; the initial situation:
$obs(in(O, room), false, 0).$
and actions:
$hpd(enter(d, room), 0).$ $hpd(enter(a, room), 0).$
$hpd(enter(b, room), 0).$ $hpd(enter(c, room), 1).$
Consider a text-question pair with the question: *How many students are in the room?* The corresponding logic form will contain:
$query(how\_many(student, room), 2).$

Combination of this logic form and $\mathcal{M}^2$ constitutes program $\mathcal{P}_1^2(LF)$. As expected, the answer set of this program contains:

$answer(there\_are, 2, members\_of\_class, student, in, room)$.
An answer set solver (in our case *clingo* [7]), returns the answers instantaneously. The other questions from Example 1 can be answered in a similar way.

4 Uncertain Group Affiliation

Now we discuss answering questions about travel stories, similar to that from Example 2. They contain complete knowledge of the class hierarchy, the locations of objects in the initial state, and the actions up to step n. However, they only have *partial knowledge about the class membership of objects.* More precisely,

Definition 3. *[TLF with incomplete class membership]*
A logic form is *incomplete with respect to class membership of the hierarchy* if:

1. $card = k \in LF$ iff $k = |\{o : object(o) \in LF\}|$.
2. For every object O from the logic form, there is a unique class C of the hierarchy, such that $m\_link(O, C)$ belongs to the logic form.
3. For every movable object O and area A, such that O is initially located in A, the logic form contains $obs(in(O, A), true, 0)$.
4. The only fluents and actions mentioned in the logic form are basic.

This only differs from Definition 2 by clause (2) – objects of the domain do not have to be linked to the leaves of the hierarchy. To illustrate the definition, consider the logic form for Example 2. It includes statements from the logic form for Example 1, together with the new classes $freshman$, $sophomore$, $junior$, and $senior$, included in the hierarchy by the statements:

$c\_link(freshman, student)$. $c\_link(sophomore, student)$.
$c\_link(junior, student)$. $c\_link(senior, student)$.

The corresponding question has the form:
$query(how\_many(freshman, room), 2)$.

Since m_link does not connect students a and b with leaves of the hierarchy, the previous question answering algorithm, justified by Proposition 4, is not applicable. Indeed, the attempt to run the corresponding program, will return the answer set with 0 freshmen located in the room. The problem is that even though the history of Example 2 is the same as that of Example 1 (and hence is represented by the encoding described in Example 5), it does not have a unique model. Instead, it has 16 models, corresponding to 16 possible instances of the hierarchy compatible with our knowledge. All models have the same universe $\{a, b, c, d\}$, but the objects can be placed into different classes. For instance, in the first instance, both a and b can be juniors, in the second, a can be a freshman and b a sophomore, etc.

Let us notice that models of travel logic form LF, incomplete with respect to class membership of the hierarchy, coincide on atoms of the form $holds(in(O, A), n)$, but differ on atoms of the form $member(O, C)$. So the definition of answers to queries containing "where" and "who" are not going to change. *But the answer to a query containing "how_many" should be redefined. This time the answer should be given by an interval, defining lower and upper bound for the cardinality of the corresponding set.* More precisely,

Definition 4. *[Answer to a query how_many for stories with multiple models]* Let LF be a travel logic form with multiple models. We say that an interval $[l, u]$ is the LF's *answer* to a query of the type $how\_many(C, A)$ for a class C and area A if:

1. For every model of LF the number K of elements of the class C located in area A at step n in this model belongs to the interval $[l, u]$.
2. There is a model of LF, such that the number of elements of the class C, located in area A at step n in this model is l.
3. There is a model of LF, such that the number of elements of the class C, located in area A at step n in this model is u.

Our next step is to present a logic program $\mathcal{P}_2^n$, which would be able to properly answer our questions.

Definition of $\mathcal{P}_2^n$: The program will consists of:
Rules of $\mathcal{M}^n$.
Definition of the notion of *population* (The population of members of C located in A will be denoted by $r(C, A)$).

$$\begin{array}{l} population(r(C,A)). \\ population\_class(r(C,A),C). \\ population\_area(r(C,A),A). \end{array} \tag{9}$$

The *uniqueness of value* rule

$$\begin{array}{rl} \neg holds(lb(P,N2),I) \leftarrow & holds(lb(P,N1),I), \\ & N1 \mathrel{!=} N2. \\ \neg holds(ub(P,N2),I) \leftarrow & holds(ub(P,N1),I), \\ & N1 \mathrel{!=} N2. \end{array} \tag{10}$$

which states that the lower bound is a function, i.e., it has a unique value N. Similarly for the upper bound.
Another collection of rules deals with the incompleteness of our stories.

Class membership uncertainty is captured by relation $maybe(O, C)$, which holds if there is an instance of the hierarchy, compatible with the membership relation, defined by the logic form of our story,

$$\begin{array}{l} maybe(O,C) \leftarrow member(O,C). \\ maybe(O,C_1) \leftarrow subclass(C_1,C_2), m\_link(O,C_2). \end{array} \tag{11}$$

and relation $maybe\_member(O, r(C, A), I)$, which holds if at step I, object O might be a member of class C and is located in area A:

$$\begin{array}{rl} maybe\_member(O,r(C,A),0) \leftarrow & maybe(O,C), \\ & holds(in(O,A),0). \end{array} \tag{12}$$

Relation *subclass*:

$$\begin{array}{l} subclass(C1, C2) \leftarrow c\_link(C1, C2). \\ subclass(C1, C2) \leftarrow c\_link(C1, C3), subclass(C3, C2). \\ subclass(C, C). \end{array} \tag{13}$$

The next collection of rules defines the upper bound of the set of members of C, initially located in A.

$$holds(ub(P, N), T) \leftarrow N = \#count\{maybe\_member(Y, P, T) : object(Y)\}. \tag{14}$$

The lower bound is given by the rule:

$$\begin{array}{rl} holds(lb(P, N), T) \leftarrow & population\_class(P, U), population\_area(P, V), \\ & N = \#count\{holds(in(Y, V), T) : member(Y, U)\}. \end{array} \tag{15}$$

Finally, we need an auxiliary rule:

$$occurs(X, T) \leftarrow hpd(X, T). \tag{16}$$

and *the definition of answer* for our new domain. This consists of the old definitions for queries not containing "how many" and the rule:

$$\begin{array}{rl} answer(between, N1, and, N2, C, in, A) \leftarrow & query(how\_many(C, A), n), \\ & holds(lb(r(C, A), N1), n), \\ & holds(ub(r(C, A), N2), n). \end{array} \tag{17}$$

This completes the construction of program $\mathcal{P}_2^n$. As before, by $\mathcal{P}_2^n(LF)$ we denote the union of $\mathcal{P}_2^n$ and the logic form LF.

Proposition 3. *[Correctness of reasoning with incomplete information about class membership]*
If a consistent travel story with the logic form LF is incomplete with respect to class membership of the story's hierarchy, then program $\mathcal{P}_2^n(LF)$ has exactly one answer set, S, and:

1. For every class c and area a, interval $[l, u]$ is the answer to a question $how\_many(c, a)$ iff $answer(between, l, and, u, c, in, a) \in S$ iff $holds(lb(r(c, a), l), n), holds(ub(r(c, a), u), n) \in S$;
2. For every object o, area a is the answer to a query $where(o, a)$ iff $answer(o, is\_in, a) \in S$. Similarly for the other queries.

Example 6. [Example 2, revisited]
It is not difficult to check that the answers to queries:
$query(how\_many(person, room), 2).$
$query(how\_many(professor, room), 2).$
$query(how\_many(freshman, room), 2).$
$query(how\_many(student, room), 2).$

are
$answer(there\_are\_between, 4, and, 4, person, in\_the, room).$
$answer(there\_are\_between, 2, and, 2, professor, in\_the, room).$
$answer(there\_are\_between, 0, and, 2, freshman, in\_the, room).$
$answer(there\_are\_between, 2, and, 2, student, in\_the, room).$

5 Uncertain Identity of Objects in the Initial Situation

Now consider stories similar to that of Example 3. In addition to uncertainty about the class membership of John this story does not have *information about identity of other movers and the initial size of the domain's populations.* This means that the closed domain assumption is no longer applicable, the corresponding hierarchy will have instances with multiple universes, and hence, multiple, universe dependent models. The TFL for such stories will be defined as follows:

Definition 5. *[TLF with incomplete identity of object in initial situation]*
A travel logic form is *incomplete with respect to identity of movers* if:

1. If $card = k \in LF$, then k is sufficiently big to be compatible with the story (i.e., it is bigger than the number of objects explicitly or implicitly mentioned in the story).
2. For every object O from the logic form, there is a unique class C of the hierarchy, such that $m\_link(O, C)$ belongs to the logic form.
3. The initial situation is given by observations of fluents $in(O, A)$, $lb(P, N)$, and $ub(P, N)$.
4. The only actions mentioned in the logic form are basic.
5. There are no concurrent actions. (The condition was added to simplify the presentation.)

Example 7. [Example 3, revisited]
The logic form for this example consists of statements:

$card = 2.$
$object(john).$
$m\_link(john, student).$
$obs(lb(r(person, room), 0), true, 0).$
$obs(ub(r(person, room), 1), true, 0).$
$hpd(enter(john, room), 0).$

together with representation of the area and the hierarchy (as in Example 2). (Note that the cardinality can be any number larger than 2. This will not change answers to our queries in which this number will be replaced by symbolic constant max_size.)

The answers to queries for travel stories incomplete with respect to identity of movers will be computed using a logic program $\mathcal{P}_3^n(LF)$ defined as follows:

Definition of $\mathcal{P}_3^n$: The program consists of rules of $\mathcal{P}_3^n$ together with

$$occurs(leave(O, A_2), I) \leftarrow occurs(enter(O, A_1), I), \quad holds(in(O, A_2), I). \tag{18}$$

$$holds(ub(r(C, A), N1 + 1), I + 1) \leftarrow occurs(enter(O, A), I), \quad maybe(O, C), \quad holds(ub(r(C, A), N1), I). \tag{19}$$

$$holds(lb(r(C,A),N1+1),I+1) \leftarrow occurs(enter(O,A),I),\; member(O,C),\; holds(lb(r(C,A),N1),I). \tag{20}$$

$$holds(ub(r(C,A),N1-1),I+1) \leftarrow occurs(leave(O,A),I),\; member(O,C),\; holds(ub(r(C,A),N1),I),\; N1>0. \tag{21}$$

$$holds(lb(r(C,A),N1-1),I+1) \leftarrow occurs(leave(O,A),I),\; maybe(O,C),\; holds(lb(r(C,A),N1),I),\; N1>0. \tag{22}$$

In addition, the definition 17 of answer will be replaced by a new definition which accommodates the unknown cardinality of the domain.

$$\begin{aligned} answer(between, N1, and, N2, C, in, A) \leftarrow\ & query(how\_many(C,A),n), \\ & holds(lb(r(C,A),N1),n), \\ & holds(ub(r(C,A),N2),n), \\ & N2 \neq k \\ answer(between, N1, and, max\_size, C, in, A) \leftarrow\ & query(how\_many(C,A),n), \\ & holds(lb(r(C,A),N1),n), \\ & holds(ub(r(C,A),N2),n), \\ & N2 = k \end{aligned} \tag{23}$$

where k is the cardinality of the domain. This completes the definition of $\mathcal{P}_3^n$.

Proposition 4. *[Correctness of reasoning with incomplete identity of movers]* If a consistent travel story with the logic form LF is incomplete with respect to class membership of the story's hierarchy, then program $\mathcal{P}_3^n(LF)$ has exactly one answer set, S, and:

1. For every class c and area a, interval $[l,u]$ is the answer to a question $how\_many(c,a)$ iff $answer(between, l, and, u, c, in, a) \in S$ iff $holds(lb(r(c,a),l),n), holds(ub(r(c,a),u),n) \in S$;
2. For every object o, area a is the answer to a query $where(o,a)$ iff $answer(o, is\_in, a) \in S$. Similarly for the other queries.

It is not difficult to verify that the answers to queries:
$query(how\_many(person, room), 1).$ $query(how\_many(professor, room), 1).$
$query(how\_many(freshman, room), 1).$ $query(how\_many(student, room), 1).$
are
$answer(there\_are\_between, 1, and, max\_size, person, in\_the, room).$
$answer(there\_are\_between, 0, and, 1, professor, in\_the, room).$
$answer(there\_are\_between, 0, and, max\_size, freshman, in\_the, room).$
$answer(there\_are\_between, 1, and, max\_size, student, in\_the, room).$

6 Uncertainty in the Number of Movers

Finally, we consider stories similar to those given in Example 4. Such stories have neither information about identities of movers in the domain nor their precise number. All we know is the limits for the sizes of the corresponding populations in the initial situation and the number of people from such populations involved in the moves. In other words we are interested in stories with the following logic form:

Definition 6. *[TLF with uncertainty in the number of movers.]*
A travel logic form is *incomplete with respect to number of movers* if:

1. If $card = k \in LF$ then k is sufficiently big to be compatible with the story.
2. The logic form contains no basic actions and fluents.
3. There are no concurrent actions.

We illustrate this by example Example 4.

Example 8. [Example 4 revisited]
The logic form will have representation of the areas and the hierarchy (as in Example 2) together with statements:
$card = 10$ $\quad$ $hpd(enter(min, 2, student, room), 0)$
$obs(lb(r(student, room), 4), true, 0)$ $\quad$ $obs(ub(r(student, room), 4), true, 0)$
$obs(lb(r(professor, room), 2), true, 0)$ $\quad$ $obs(ub(r(professor, room), 2), true, 0)$

As in the previous example the value of *card* can be any number greater than or equal to 8.

This is the first time when we consider a logic form of travel story containing extended actions. This seems like a substantial change which may require us to change our previous framework. We do not even have a notion of model defined for such logic forms — so far we only considered transition diagrams describing effects of actions $enter(O, A)$ and $leave(O, A)$. To deal with the problem we translate a logic form LF with uncertainty in the number of movers into a collection of complete logic forms, called *instances* of LF whose models will be viewed as models of LF. First we need the following definition.

Definition 7. *[Instance of a logic form with extended history]*
Let LF be logic form with extended history. Let $inst(LF)$ be a logic form obtained from LF by

1. Expending the signature of LF by new constant symbols $x_1, x_2, \ldots, x_m$ where m is the cardinality of the domain.
2. Adding statements $object(x_1), \ldots, object(x_m)$ and a collection of statements of the form $m\_link(x_i, c)$ such that for every $0 \leq i \leq m$ object x_i is allocated into some leaf c of the domain hierarchy,
3. Adding a collection of statements of the form $obs(in(x_i, area), true, 0)$ placing each x_i into some area in the initial situation.

4. Replacing every occurrence of a statement $hpd(a, i)$ where a is an extended action $enter(rel, k, c, area)$ by a collection of basic actions $\{occurs(enter(x_1, area), i), \dots occurs(enter(x_n, area), i)\}$ where $x_1, \dots, x_n$ are elements of class c and n and k satisfy the relation rel. Similarly for *leave*.
5. Removing all statements containing occurrences of lb and ub.

It is easy to see that $inst(LF)$ is a complete logic form. We say that $inst(LF)$ is an *instance* of LF if it is consistent and satisfies all the observations of LF made in the initial situation.
By *models* of LF we mean models of its instances.

Now Definition 4 becomes applicable. The answers will be computed with the help of logic program $\mathcal{P}_4^n(LF)$ defined as follows:

Definition of $\mathcal{P}_4^n$: The program consists of rules of $\mathcal{P}_3^n$ together with the following rules. Direct effect of $enter(min, N1, C1, A)$:

$$\begin{aligned} holds(lb(r(C2, A), N1 + N2), I + 1) \leftarrow\ & occurs(enter(min, N1, C1, A), I), \\ & subclass(C1, C2), \\ & holds(lb(r(C2, A), N2), I). \end{aligned} \tag{24}$$

$$\begin{aligned} holds(ub(r(C2, A), k), I + 1) \leftarrow\ & occurs(enter(min, N1, C1, A), I), \\ & subclass(C1, C2). \end{aligned} \tag{25}$$

where k is the cardinality of the domain.
Direct effect of $enter(ex, N1, C1, A)$:

$$\begin{aligned} holds(lb(r(C2, A), N1 + N2), I + 1) \leftarrow\ & occurs(enter(ex, N1, C1, A), I), \\ & holds(lb(r(C2, A), N2), I), \\ & subclass(C1, C2). \end{aligned} \tag{26}$$

$$\begin{aligned} holds(ub(r(C2, A), N1 + N2), I + 1) \leftarrow\ & occurs(enter(ex, N1, C1, A), I), \\ & holds(ub(r(C2, A), N2), I), \\ & subclass(C1, C2). \end{aligned} \tag{27}$$

Similarly for other actions. This completes the definition of $\mathcal{P}_4^n$.

Proposition 5. *[Correctness of reasoning with unknown number of movers]*
If a consistent travel story with the logic form LF is incomplete with respect to number of movers then program $\mathcal{P}_4^n(LF)$ has exactly one answer set, S, and for every class c and area a, interval $[l, u]$ is the answer to a question $how\_many(c, a)$ iff $answer(between, l, and, u, c, in, a) \in S$ iff $holds(lb(r(c, a), l), n) \in S$ and $holds(ub(r(c, a), u), n) \in S$;

Example 9. [Example 4 revisited]
It is not difficult to verify that the answers to queries:
$query(how\_many(person, room), 1)$. $query(how\_many(professor, room), 1)$.
$query(how\_many(freshman, room), 1)$. $query(how\_many(student, room), 1)$.

are
$answer(there\_are\_between, 8, and, max\_size, person, in\_the, room).$
$answer(there\_are\_between, 2, and, 2, professor, in\_the, room).$
$answer(there\_are\_between, 0, and, max\_size, freshman, in\_the, room).$
$answer(there\_are\_between, 6, and, max\_size, student, in\_the, room).$

7 Discussion

The axiomatization of travel domains presented in this paper is based on extensive research on the relationship between reasoning about actions and Answer Set Prolog. This work, which started in [11,20], led to the development of rich theory and multiple applications [6]. Reasoning about various types of motion, including travel, was often used to test this theory. In the state of the art approach the background knowledge about actions is normally represented in action languages [12]. In fact, there is a small collection of modules containing axioms for various actions built in modular action languages (see, for instance, [13,14,1]). These theories are automatically translated into ASP which allows solutions of various problems using efficient answer set solvers like *smodels* [17], *dlv* [5], *clingo* [8] and others. In our extended work we also use a modular action language $\mathcal{ALM}$ [9] but this was omitted to save space. We believe that results presented in this paper will, eventually, be useful for the design of real question-answering systems. Of course to make this happen we need to develop translations from natural language which will be able to classify a text into a travel story and translate it into the ASP based logic form. First steps towards this were made in [19] in which this was done for a simple controlled language. However, much more research is needed to properly combine natural language processing and reasoning parts of such future systems. Still we believe that our work helps to better understand different types of incompleteness and their impact on question answering which contributes to this effort.

Acknowledgements. We would like to thank M. Balduccini, C. Baral and V. Lifschitz for early discussions on the subject of this paper, and D. Inclezan for useful comments on the current version. We also would like to acknowledge NSF grant IIS-1018031.

References

1. Akman, V., Erdogan, S.T., Lee, J., Lifschitz, V., Turner, H.: Representing the zoo world and the traffic world in the language of the causal calculator. Artif. Intell. 153(1-2), 105–140 (2004)
2. Balduccini, M., Baral, C., Lierler, Y.: Handbook of Knowledge Representation. In: Knowledge Representation and Question Answering, ch.1. Elsevier (2007)
3. Baral, C., Gelfond, M., Gelfond, G., Scherl, R.: Textual Inference by Combining Multiple Logic Programming Paradigms. In: AAAI 2005 Workshop on Inference for Textual Question Answering (2005)

4. Baral, C., Gelfond, M., Scherl, R.: Using answer set programming to answer complex queries. In: Workshop on Pragmatics of Question Answering at HLT-NAAC 2004 (2004)
5. Leone, N., Pfeifer, G., Faber, W., Calimeri, F., Dell'Armi, T., Eiter, T., Gottlob, G., Ianni, G., Ielpa, G., Koch, C., Perri, S., Polleres, A.: The DLV System. In: Flesca, S., Greco, S., Leone, N., Ianni, G. (eds.) JELIA 2002. LNCS (LNAI), vol. 2424, pp. 537–540. Springer, Heidelberg (2002)
6. Baral, C.: Knowledge Representation, Reasoning and Declarative Problem Solving, ch.5. Cambridge University Press (2003)
7. Gebser, M., Kaminski, R., Kaufmann, B., Ostrowski, M., Schaub, T., Thiele, S.: A User's Guide to gringo, clasp, clingo, and iclingo. Unpublished draft (2008), `http://downloads.sourceforge.net/potassco/guide.pdf`
8. Gebser, M., Kaufmann, B., Neumann, A., Schaub, T.: Conflict-Driven Answer Set Enumeration. In: Baral, C., Brewka, G., Schlipf, J. (eds.) LPNMR 2007. LNCS (LNAI), vol. 4483, pp. 136–148. Springer, Heidelberg (2007)
9. Gelfond, M., Inclezan, D.: Yet another modular action language. In: Proceedings of the Second International Workshop on Software Engineering for Answer Set Programming, pp. 64–78 (2009)
10. Gelfond, M., Lifschitz, V.: Classical Negation in Logic Programs and Disjunctive Databases. New Generation Computing 9, 365–385 (1991)
11. Gelfond, M., Lifschitz, V.: Representing Actions in Extended Logic Programs. In: Joint International Conference and Symposium on Logic Programming, pp. 559–573. MIT Press (1992)
12. Gelfond, M., Lifschitz, V.: Action Languages. Electronic Transactions on AI 3 (1998)
13. Lifschitz, V., McCain, N., Remolina, E., Tacchella, A.: Getting to the airport: the oldest planning problem in ai. In: Minker, J. (ed.) Logic-Based Artificial Intelligence, pp. 147–165. Kluwer (2000)
14. Lifschitz, V., Ren, W.: A modular action description language. In: AAAI (2006)
15. Marek, V.W., Truszczynski, M.: Stable models and an alternative logic programming paradigm. In: The Logic Programming Paradigm: a 25-Year Perspective, pp. 375–398. Springer, Berlin (1999)
16. Niemela, I.: Logic Programs with Stable Model Semantics as a Constraint Programming Paradigm. In: Proceedings of the Workshop on Computational Aspects of Nonmonotonic Reasoning, pp. 72–79 (June 1998)
17. Niemela, I., Simons, P.: Smodels - An Implementation of the Stable Model and Well-founded Semantics for Normal logic Programs. In: Fuhrbach, U., Dix, J., Nerode, A. (eds.) LPNMR 1997. LNCS, vol. 1265, pp. 420–429. Springer, Heidelberg (1997)
18. Niemela, I., Simons, P.: Extending the Smodels System with Cardinality and Weight Constraints. In: Logics in Artificial Intelligence. Kluwer Academic Publishers (2000)
19. Todorova, Y.: Answering questions about dynamic domains from natural language using ASP. PhD Dissertation (2011)
20. Turner, H.: Representing Actions In Logic Programs And Default Theories. Journal of Logic Programming, 245–298 (1997)

Algorithms for Solving Satisfiability Problems with Qualitative Preferences

Enrico Giunchiglia and Marco Maratea

DIST, Università di Genova, Viale Causa, 13 – 16145 Genova, Italy
{enrico,marco}@dist.unige.it

Abstract. In this work we present a complete picture of our work on computing optimal solutions in satisfiability problems with qualitative preferences. With this task in mind, we first review our work on computing optimal solutions by imposing an ordering on the way the search space is explored, e.g., on the splitting heuristic in case the DPLL algorithm is used. The main feature of this approach is that it guarantees to compute all and only the optimal solutions, i.e., models which are not optimal are not even computed: For this result, it is essential that the splitting heuristic of the solver follows the partial order on the expressed preferences. However, for each optimal solution, a formula that prunes non-optimal solutions needs to be retained, thus this procedure does not work in polynomial space when computing all optimal solutions.

We then extend our previous work and show how it is possible to compute optimal solutions using a generate-and-test approach: Such a procedure is based on the idea to first compute a model and then check for its optimality. As a consequence, no ordering on the splitting heuristic is needed, but it may compute also non-optimal models. This approach does not need to retain formulas indefinitely, thus it does work in polynomial space.

We start from a simple setting in which a preference is a partial order on a set of literals. We then show how other forms of preferences, i.e., quantitative, qualitative on formulas and mixed qualitative/quantitative can be captured by our framework, and present alternatives for computing "complete" sets of optimal solutions. We finally comment on the implementation of the two procedures on top of state-of-the-art satisfiability solvers, and discuss related work.

1 Introduction

The problem of finding an optimal solution in a satisfiability (SAT) problem with qualitative preferences has attracted a lot of researchers in Artificial Intelligence in general, and in the constraint and logic programming community in particular. As a consequence, several approaches for expressing and reasoning with SAT problems with preferences have been proposed, and viable solutions exist, especially for finding one optimal solution. However, in some cases, it is not desirable to find just one solution. Indeed, it might be desirable to be able to compute more, and possibly all, solutions, e.g., for comparatively evaluate them on the basis of other criteria not captured by the preferences. See, e.g., [4, 34, 8, 6, 25, 10, 18, 49, 3] for approaches for finding one and all optimal solutions.

E. Erdem et al. (Eds.): Correct Reasoning, LNCS 7265, pp. 327–344, 2012.

A simple approach for finding optimal solutions consists in first enumerating all (non necessarily optimal) solutions, and then eliminating a solution μ if there exists another solution μ' which is "preferred" to μ. The first obvious drawback of this approach is that it requires the computation of all solutions, even the non optimal ones. The second drawback is that each solution has to be stored and compared with the others. In [5], in the context of CP-nets [4], the authors noticed, that by imposing an ordering on the splitting heuristic used for searching solutions, it is possible to mitigate the second drawback by comparing a solution only with the previously generated ones, which are already guaranteed to be optimal: In this way, only the so far generated optimal solutions need to be stored. Still, the number of optimal solutions can be exponential and all the solutions (even the non-optimal ones) are computed. Further, it is well known that imposing an ordering on the splitting heuristic may lead to a significant degradation in the performances of the solver used for finding solutions [38, 39].

In this work we present two procedures, based on the Davis-Putnam-Logemann-Loveland (DPLL) algorithm [16, 15], for computing optimal solutions of a SAT problem with qualitative preferences. In our setting, a qualitative preference is a partially ordered set of literals $\langle S, \prec\rangle$: S is the set of literals that we would like to have satisfied, and $\prec$ is a (strict) partial order on S expressing the relative importance of fulfilling each literal in S. The first procedure is guaranteed to compute all and only the optimal solutions, i.e., models which are not optimal are not even computed. For this result, it is essential that the splitting heuristic of the solver follows the partial order on the expressed preferences [34]: As we already said, imposing such ordering can lead to significant degradation in the performances of the solver, though this is not the case for many applications, see, e.g., [35, 45] in the context of satisfiability planning [42] and Answer Set Programming [30, 31]. However, for each optimal solution this approach needs to retain a formula that prunes non-optimal solutions: Thus, such a procedure works in polynomial space when searching for a bounded number of optimal solutions, but not in the general case [20]. The second procedure is based on the idea to first compute a model and then check for its optimality: The check consists in determining whether a better model exists and this task is reduced again to a SAT problem. As a consequence, no ordering on the splitting heuristic is needed. Of course, this second procedure may compute models which are not optimal, but is guaranteed to work in polynomial space given there is no need to retain formulas indefinitely. The solving procedure for finding one optimal solution has been presented in [19].

We then show how qualitative preferences on formulas and quantitative preferences on literals or formulas can be reduced to the basic framework of qualitative preferences on literals: This allows us to use our procedures also in these extended settings and, further, for solving problems with mixed qualitative and quantitative preferences. Our procedures compute "complete" set of optimal solutions, and different complete sets of optimal solutions may exist: We also present alternatives for computing such sets. We finally comment on the implementation of the two procedures on top of state-of-the-art satisfiability solvers, like MINISAT [24], and discuss related work.

The paper is structured as follows. In Section 2 we review the basic definitions and terminology about qualitative preferences on literals. In Section 3 we present the two procedures for computing optimal models, while how to deal with other forms of preferences and with other concepts of complete sets of optimal models is showed in Section 4. Section 5 discusses implementation and related work, and we conclude the paper in Section 6.

2 Satisfiability and Qualitative Preferences

Consider a finite set P of *variables*. A *literal* is a variable x or its negation $\neg x$. A *formula* is either a variable or a finite combination of formulas using the n-ary connectives $\wedge$, $\vee$ for conjunction and disjunction ($n \geq 0$), and the unary connective $\neg$ for negation. We use the symbols $\bot$ and $\top$ to denote the empty disjunction and conjunction, respectively. If l is a literal, we write $\overline{l}$ for $\neg l$ and we assume $\overline{\overline{x}} = x$. This notation is extended to sets S of literals, i.e., $\overline{S} = \{\overline{l} : l \in S\}$.

Formulas are used to express hard constraints that have to be satisfied. For example, given the 4 variables *Fish*, *Meat*, *RedWine*, *WhiteWine*, the formula

$$(\overline{\mathit{Fish}} \vee \overline{\mathit{Meat}}) \wedge (\overline{\mathit{RedWine}} \vee \overline{\mathit{WhiteWine}}) \qquad (1)$$

models the fact that we cannot have both fish (*Fish*) and meat (*Meat*), both red (*RedWine*) and white (*WhiteWine*) wine.

An *assignment* μ is a consistent set of literals. If $l \in \mu$, we say that both l and $\overline{l}$ are *assigned* by μ. An assignment μ is *total* if each literal l is assigned by μ. A total assignment μ *satisfies*

- a literal l if $l \in \mu$,
- a disjunction $(\varphi_1 \vee \ldots \vee \varphi_n)$ $(n \geq 0)$ if and only if μ satisfies at least one disjunct φ_i with $1 \leq i \leq n$,
- a conjunction $(\varphi_1 \wedge \ldots \wedge \varphi_n)$ $(n \geq 0)$ if and only if μ satisfies all the φ_i with $1 \leq i \leq n$,
- the negation of a formula $\neg\psi$ if and only if μ does not satisfy ψ.

A *model* of a formula φ is an assignment satisfying φ. A formula φ *entails* a formula ψ ($\varphi \models \psi$) if the models of φ are a subset of the models of ψ. For instance, (1) has 9 models. In the following, we represent a total assignment with the set of variables assigned to true in it. For instance, $\{$*Fish*, *WhiteWine*$\}$ represents the total assignment in which the only variables assigned to true are *Fish* and *WhiteWine*, i.e., the situation in which we have fish and white wine.

A *(qualitative) preference (on literals)* is a partially ordered set of literals, i.e., a pair $\langle S, \prec \rangle$ where

- S is a set of literals, called the *set of preferences*: Intuitively, S represents the set of literals that we would like to have satisfied; and
- $\prec$ is a (strict) partial order on S: Intuitively, $l \prec l'$ models the fact that we prefer l to l'.

For example,

$$\{\mathit{Fish}, \mathit{Meat}, \overline{\mathit{RedWine}}\}, \{\mathit{Fish} \prec \mathit{Meat}\} \qquad (2)$$

models the case in which we prefer to have both fish and meat, and avoid red wine; in the case in which it is not possible to have both fish and meat, we prefer to have fish over having meat.

A qualitative preference $\langle S, \prec \rangle$ on literals can be extended to the set of total assignments as follows [49]: Given two total assignments μ and μ', we say that μ *is preferred to* μ' ($\mu \prec \mu'$) if and only if[1]

1. there exists a literal $l \in S$ with $l \in \mu$ and $\bar{l} \in \mu'$; and
2. for each literal $l' \in S \cap (\mu' \setminus \mu)$, there exists a literal $l \in S \cap (\mu \setminus \mu')$ such that $l \prec l'$.

From the definition, it is clear that for any two total assignments μ and μ':

1. If $S \cap \mu = S \cap \mu'$ then $\mu \not\prec \mu'$: In particular, if the set S of preferences is empty, every model is optimal.
2. If $S \cap \mu' \subset S \cap \mu$ then $\mu \prec \mu'$: Every optimal model has a maximal intersection with S. In the case $\prec$ is empty, every model with a maximal intersection with S is optimal.

$\langle S, \prec \rangle$ induces a partial order on the set of total assignments, as stated by the following theorem.

Theorem 1. *Let $\langle S, \prec \rangle$ be a qualitative preference on literals. The relation $\prec$ extended to the set of total assignments is a partial order.*

This theorem has been presented and proved as Theorem 7 in [49] and Theorem 1 in [20].

A model μ of a formula φ is *optimal* if it is a minimal element of the partially ordered set of models of φ. A model μ *dominates* a model μ' if $\mu \prec \mu'$. For instance, considering the qualitative preference (2), the formula (1) has only two optimal models, i.e., $\{Fish\}$ and $\{Fish, WhiteWine\}$. We call $\{\{Fish\}, \{Fish, WhiteWine\}\}$ a complete, or "P-complete", set of optimal models.

3 Computing All Optimal Solutions in a SAT Problem with Preferences

Given a formula φ and a preference, we now show how it is possible to compute all optimal models of φ by extending the famous DPLL procedure [16, 15]. In principle, we could use any complete backtrack-search algorithm that can find all satisfying assignment of φ. For presenting our algorithms, we have chosen DPLL for clarity. However, DPLL does not directly handle arbitrary formulas, but finite sets of clauses, where a *clause* is a finite set of literals to be interpreted disjunctively. This is not a limitation because of well known clause form transformation procedures (see, e.g., [59, 51, 37]). In the following, we will continuously switch between formulas and sets of clauses, intuitively meaning the same thing. We remind that deciding whether a formula belongs to an optimal solution is in Σ_p^2 (see, e.g., Theorem 14 in [49]).

[1] It is easy to see that in the case in which the partial order is empty, our definition corresponds to the standard Pareto's optimality, while, in the case in which the partial order is not empty, it corresponds to the "Inter criterial Pareto Optimality" as defined in [22].

3.1 Computing All Optimal Solutions by Pruning Non-optimal Models

Consider a formula φ and a preference $\langle S, \prec \rangle$. The problem of computing all optimal models of φ wrt $\langle S, \prec \rangle$ can be solved by

1. determining and printing an optimal model μ of φ by imposing an ordering on the splitting heuristic, as in, e.g., [34];
2. adding to the input formula a new formula which prunes the models which are dominated by μ; and
3. returning FALSE in order to continue the search for other optimal models.

Crucial for the above procedure is a condition which enables us to say which are the total assignments that are dominated by μ (wrt $\langle S, \prec \rangle$). We therefore define a formula whose models are dominated by μ: From our definition such formula is

$$(\vee_{l \in S \cap \mu} \overline{l}) \wedge (\wedge_{l \in S \cap \overline{\mu}} (\overline{l} \vee \vee_{l' \in S \cap \mu, l' \prec l} \overline{l'})). \quad (3)$$

The total assignment μ dominates a total assignment μ' wrt $\langle S, \prec \rangle$ iff μ' satisfies Eq. (3), as stated by the following theorem.

Theorem 2. *Let $\langle S, \prec \rangle$ be a qualitative preference on literals. A total assignment μ dominates a total assignment μ' wrt $\langle S, \prec \rangle$ if and only if μ' satisfies the formula in Eq. (3) wrt $\langle S, \prec \rangle$.*

This theorem has been presented and proved as Theorem 3 in [20].
For example,

1. if $\mu_1 = \{Fish\}$ and $\langle S, \prec \rangle$ is as in (2), then (3) is

$$(\overline{Fish} \vee RedWine) \wedge (\overline{Meat} \vee \overline{Fish})$$

which is equivalent to

$$\overline{Fish} \vee (RedWine \wedge \overline{Meat})$$

Any total assignment which satisfies $\overline{Fish}$ or $(RedWine \wedge \overline{Meat})$ is dominated by $\{Fish\}$.
2. if $\mu_2 = \{Meat\}$ and $\langle S, \prec \rangle$ is as in (2), then (3) is

$$(\overline{Meat} \vee RedWine) \wedge \overline{Fish}$$

Any total assignment which satisfies $\overline{Fish}$ and at least one between *RedWine* and $\overline{Meat}$) is dominated by $\{Meat\}$.

Notice that if μ_1 dominates μ_2 and ψ_1 (resp. ψ_2) is the formula (3) computed for μ_1 (resp. μ_2), then $\psi_2 \models \psi_1$, i.e., the models of ψ_2 are a subset of the models ψ_1: This is a simple consequence of the fact that if $\mu_1 \prec \mu_2$ then μ_1 dominates a superset of the total assignments dominated by μ_2.

As general examples consider the following particular cases:

1. If $S \cap \mu = \emptyset$, then formula (3) is equivalent to the empty disjunction, i.e., FALSE: Indeed, if μ does not satisfy any preference, no assignment is dominated by μ;

$\langle S, \prec \rangle$:= a qualitative preference on literals;
$\psi := \emptyset$;

function nOPT-DLL$_1(\varphi \cup \psi, \mu)$

1 **if** $(\bot \in (\varphi \cup \psi)_\mu)$ **return** FALSE;

2 **if** (μ is total)

3   *Print*$(\mu \cap (P \cup \overline{P}))$;

4    $\psi := \psi \cup$ *Reason*(μ);

5   **return** FALSE;

6 **if** $(\{l\} \in (\varphi \cup \psi)_\mu)$ **return** nOPT-DLL$_1(\varphi \cup \psi, \mu \cup \{l\})$;

7 $l :=$ *ChooseLiteral*$_1(\varphi \cup \psi, \mu)$;

8 **return** nOPT-DLL$_1(\varphi \cup \psi, \mu \cup \{l\})$ **or**
nOPT-DLL$_1(\varphi \cup \psi, \mu \cup \{\bar{l}\})$.

Fig. 1. The algorithm of nOPT-DLL$_1$

2. If $S \subseteq \mu$, then formula (3) is equivalent to
$$\vee_{l \in S} \bar{l}.$$
Each assignment which does not satisfy all the preferences is dominated by μ;
3. If $\prec = \emptyset$, then formula (3) is equivalent to
$$\vee_{l \in S \cap \mu} \bar{l} \wedge \wedge_{l \in S \cap \overline{\mu}} \bar{l}.$$
Each assignment satisfying a strict subset of the set of preferences satisfied by μ, is dominated by μ.

Given a system *SYS* for computing an optimal model of a formula φ wrt a preference $\langle S, \prec \rangle$, Theorem 2 allows us to compute a complete set of optimal models using *SYS* as a black box, according to the following procedure:

1. *SYS* is invoked with input φ and the preference $\langle S, \prec \rangle$;
2. If *SYS* returns that φ is unsatisfiable then all optimal models have been already computed and the procedure stops;
3. If *SYS* returns an optimal model μ, the negation of the formula (3) is computed and added to φ;
4. Go to Step 1.

The resulting procedure, which generalizes the DPLL-based procedure presented in [34] for computing one optimal model, is represented in Figure 1 and returns a complete set of optimal models.

In the figure,[2]

- it is assumed that the input formula φ is a set of clauses; μ is an assignment; ψ is an initially empty set of clauses;
- $(\varphi \cup \psi)_\mu$ is the set of clauses obtained from $\varphi \cup \psi$ by (i) deleting the clauses $C \in \varphi \cup \psi$ with $\mu \cap C \neq \emptyset$, and (ii) substituting the other clauses $C \in \varphi \cup \psi$ with $C \setminus \{\bar{l} : l \in \mu\}$;

[2] We assume left-associativity for the **or** at line 8 of the procedure.

- *Reason*(μ) returns a set of clauses equivalent to the negation of (3): Let P be the signature of φ, *Reason*(μ) is a finite set of clauses —possibly in a signature P' extending P— such that
  1. for each total assignment μ satisfying the negation of (3), there exists one assignment μ' in P' extending μ and satisfying *Reason*(μ);
  2. for each total assignment μ' in P' satisfying *Reason*(μ), the restriction of μ' to P satisfies the negation of (3).

  Such a set of clauses can be computed starting from the negation of (3) using the already mentioned clause form transformations [59, 51, 37].
- *ChooseLiteral*$_1(\varphi \cup \psi, \mu)$ returns an unassigned literal l such that
  - if there exists a literal in S which is not assigned by μ, then each literal l' with $l' \prec l$ has to be assigned by μ, and
  - is an arbitrary literal occurring in $\varphi \cup \psi$, otherwise.

nOPT-DLL$_1$ has to be invoked with φ and μ set to the input formula and the empty set, respectively. It is easy to see that if there are no preferences, the computation performed by nOPT-DLL$_1$ for computing the first (optimal) model is the same as the one performed by DPLL. nOPT-DLL$_1$ prints all and only the optimal models of φ wrt $\langle S, \prec\rangle$, as stated by the following theorem.

Theorem 3. *Let $\langle S, \prec\rangle$ be a qualitative preference on literals. Let φ be a set of clauses. nOPT-DLL$_1(\varphi, \emptyset)$ returns all and only the optimal models for φ wrt $\langle S, \prec\rangle$.*

This theorem has been presented and proved as Theorem 4 in [20]. Notice that if the number of optimal models is polynomial, so is the space requirement of nOPT-DLL$_1$, and it is easy to modify nOPT-DLL$_1$ by introducing a bound on the number of optimal models to be generated. However, even in practice we did not experience many problems due to excessive space requirements on most of the benchmarks and applications we considered, in general there can be exponentially many optimal models and thus nOPT-DLL$_1$ is not ensured to run in polynomial space.

3.2 Computing All Optimal Solutions via Generate-and-Test

As we have already anticipated, nOPT-DLL$_1$ has two drawbacks: In principle, it may have exponential space requirements and it imposes an ordering on the splitting heuristic. In order to be sure to run in polynomial space, a procedure for computing all optimal models of a formula φ has to give up the idea of storing information about the previously computed optimal models. However, this has the consequence that we are no longer ensured that a generated model is also optimal, even by designing the splitting heuristic as in nOPT-DLL$_1$. Thus, it is necessary to test for optimality of a generated model μ, and this test has to be performed by taking into account only the model μ, the formula φ and the preference $\langle S, \prec\rangle$. In other words, we need a condition enabling us to determine if a model μ of a formula φ is optimal wrt $\langle S, \prec\rangle$, i.e., if there exists another model μ' of φ with $\mu' \prec \mu$. The *preference formula for μ (wrt $\langle S, \prec\rangle$)* is

$$(\vee_{l \in S \cap \overline{\mu}}\, l) \wedge (\wedge_{l' \in S \cap \mu}(\vee_{l \in S \cap \overline{\mu}, l \prec l'}\, l \vee l')). \tag{4}$$

A total assignment μ' is preferred to μ wrt $\langle S, \prec\rangle$ iff μ' satisfies (4), as stated by the following theorem.

Theorem 4. *Let $\langle S, \prec\rangle$ be a qualitative preference on literals. A total assignment μ' is preferred to a total assignment μ wrt $\langle S, \prec\rangle$ if and only if μ' satisfies the preference formula for μ wrt $\langle S, \prec\rangle$.*

The theorem can be proved from the definition of dominance between total assignments, as for Theorem 2.

For example,

1. if $\mu_1 = \{Fish\}$ and $\langle S, \prec\rangle$ is as in (2), then the preference formula for μ_1 is

$$(Meat \wedge Fish \wedge \overline{RedWine}).$$

   The two total assignments satisfying $(Meat \wedge Fish \wedge \overline{RedWine})$ are preferred to μ_1.
2. if $\mu_2 = \{Meat\}$ and $\langle S, \prec\rangle$ is as in (2), then the preference formula for μ_2 is

$$Fish \wedge ((Meat \vee Fish) \wedge \overline{RedWine})$$

   equivalent to $Fish \wedge \overline{RedWine}$: The four total assignments satisfying $Fish \wedge \overline{RedWine}$ are preferred to μ_2.

Notice that since $\mu_1 \prec \mu_2$, the preference formula (4) for μ_1 entails the preference formula for μ_2: The set of total assignments which are preferred to μ_1 is a subset of the set of total assignments which are preferred to μ_2. As general examples consider the following particular cases:

1. If $S \subseteq \mu$ (e.g., because $S = \emptyset$), then (4) is equivalent to $\bot$ meaning that there is no assignment which is preferred to μ, i.e., that μ is optimal.
2. If $\prec = \emptyset$, then (4) becomes

$$(\vee_{l \in S \cap \overline{\mu}}\, l) \wedge \wedge_{l' \in S \cap \mu}\, l',$$

   meaning that a total assignment μ' is preferred to μ if and only if $\mu \cap S \subset \mu' \cap S$.

Thanks to Theorem 4 we can check if a model μ of a formula φ is optimal by checking the satisfiability of φ and the preference formula ψ for μ. We can thus easily generate a complete set of optimal solutions by modifying DPLL in order to

1. compute a (not necessarily optimal) model μ of φ;
2. test if μ is optimal, in which case μ is printed; and
3. return FALSE in order to continue the search for other (possibly optimal) models.

In Figure 2 we maintain the same assumptions and notations used in Figure 1, extended with:

- *NewReason*(μ, ψ) returns a subset of the clauses in *Reason*$(\mu) \cup \psi$;
- *Prefwff*(μ) returns the set of clauses equivalent to the preference formula for μ;
- $UNSAT(\varphi \cup$ *Prefwff*$(\mu))$ is an invocation to a SAT solver returning TRUE if the input set of clauses is unsatisfiable, and FALSE otherwise;
- *ChooseLiteral*$_2(\varphi \cup \psi, \mu)$ returns an arbitrary unassigned literal l.

$\langle S, \prec \rangle$:= a qualitative preference on literals;
$\psi := \emptyset$;

function nOPT-DLL$_2$($\varphi \cup \psi, \mu$)
1 **if** ($\bot \in (\varphi \cup \psi)_\mu$) **return** FALSE;
2 **if** (μ is total)
3   ψ := *NewReason*(μ, ψ);
4   **if** ($UNSAT$($\varphi \cup$ *Prefwff*(μ))) *Print*(μ);
5   **return** FALSE;
6 **if** ($\{l\} \in (\varphi \cup \psi)_\mu$) **return** nOPT-DLL$_2$($\varphi \cup \psi, \mu \cup \{l\}$);
7 l := *ChooseLiteral*$_2$($\varphi \cup \psi, \mu$);
8 **return** nOPT-DLL$_2$($\varphi \cup \psi, \mu \cup \{l\}$) **or**
            nOPT-DLL$_2$($\varphi \cup \psi, \mu \cup \{\bar{l}\}$).

Fig. 2. The algorithm of nOPT-DLL$_2$

The nOPT-DLL$_2$ algorithm in Figure 2 has to be invoked with φ and μ set to the input formula and the empty set, respectively. It is easy to see that if there are no preferences, the computation performed by nOPT-DLL$_2$ for computing the first (optimal) model is the same as the one performed by DPLL. nOPT-DLL$_2$ prints all optimal models, as stated by the following theorem.

Theorem 5. *Let $\langle S, \prec \rangle$ be a qualitative preference on literals. Let φ be a set of clauses. nOPT-DLL$_2$($\varphi, \emptyset$) prints all optimal models for φ.*

Proof. The theorem follows from:

1. The correctness and completeness of DPLL as models enumerator, and
2. the correctness of the $UNSAT$($\varphi \cup$ *Prefwff*(μ)) function.

The first point is proved in, e.g., [33], while the second point holds by definition of *Prefwff*(μ).

As an optimization of the above procedure, when a model μ is computed, we can add to the input formula a subset of the clauses in *Reason*(μ) $\cup\ \psi$ at line 3 of nOPT-DLL$_2$, e.g., the ones corresponding to the negation of (3). The goal of these clauses is to prune the models of μ which are guaranteed not to be optimal because dominated by μ: They are not needed for the correctness of the procedure and can be removed at any time.

No formula is needed to be retained indefinitely in this algorithm, thus if *NewReason* computes a polynomial number of clauses, then nOPT-DLL$_2$ is guaranteed to work in polynomial space.

4 Extensions

In this section we describe two extensions of our initial setting of (i) computing P-complete sets of optimal solutions (ii) of SAT problems with qualitative preferences on literals. Subsection 4.1 shows how to deal with an alternative concept of "complete" set of optimal models, while Subsection 4.2 shows how problems with quantitative preferences, or with qualitative preferences defined on formulas, or with mixed qualitative/quantitative preferences, can be captured by our basic setting (ii). This last part has been already presented in [20].

4.1 Alternative Complete Sets of Optimal Models

The two procedures we have presented compute what we have called a P-complete set of optimal models: Considering the formula (1) and the preference (2), a P-complete set of optimal models for this problem is $\{\{Fish\}, \{Fish, WhiteWine\}\}$. Given the task to compute all optimal models, it can be the case that it is not interesting to distinguish between the two optimal models $\{Fish\}$ and $\{Fish, WhiteWine\}$ given that they differ only for the truth value assigned to *WhiteWine*, and the set of preferences says nothing about the desired truth value assigned to *WhiteWine*.

More formally, consider a formula φ, a qualitative preference $\langle S, \prec\rangle$ and a set Γ of optimal models of φ, Γ is *P-complete* if it contains all the optimal models of φ: Indeed, there can be only one P-complete set of optimal models. An alternative form, we call *S-complete*, considers that for each optimal model μ of φ there exists exactly one model μ' in Γ with $\mu \cap S = \mu' \cap S$. Intuitively, any two models in Γ have to differently evaluate some of the literals in S. There can be more than one S-complete sets of optimal models, for example, the sets of models $\{\{Fish\}\}$ and $\{\{Fish, WhiteWine\}\}$ are both S-complete for (1), assuming $\langle S, \prec\rangle$ is (2).

Some updates are needed in order to find an S-complete set of optimal models. First, the definition of dominance: A model μ dominates a model μ' if either $\mu \prec \mu'$ or $\mu \cap S = \mu' \cap S$.

Then, the formula (3) that defines which are the total assignments dominated by a given total assignment μ becomes

$$\wedge_{l \in S \cap \overline{\mu}} \ (\ \overline{l} \vee \vee_{l' \in S \cap \mu, l' \prec l} \overline{l'}\ ). \tag{5}$$

As general examples consider the following particular cases:

1. If $S \subseteq \mu$ (e.g., because $S = \emptyset$), then (5) is equivalent to $\top$ meaning that all assignments are dominated by μ, i.e. $\{\mu\}$ is S-complete.
2. If $\prec = \emptyset$, then (5) becomes
$$(\wedge_{l \in S \cap \overline{\mu}} \overline{l})$$
meaning that a total assignment μ is preferred to μ' if and only if $\mu' \cap S \subseteq \mu \cap S$.

In our example,

1. if $\mu_1 = \{Fish\}$ and $\langle S, \prec\rangle$ is as in (2), then (5) is
$$(\overline{Meat} \vee \overline{Fish}).$$
Any total assignment which satisfies $\overline{Fish}$ or $\overline{Meat}$ is dominated by $\{Fish\}$.
2. if $\mu_2 = \{Meat\}$ and $\langle S, \prec\rangle$ is as in (2), then (5) is
$$\overline{Fish}.$$
Any total assignment which satisfies $\overline{Fish}$ is dominated by $\{Meat\}$.

Similar changes hold for the preference formula (4). Moreover, in the second algorithm the generation of an S-complete set of models is more difficult than computing a P-complete set. Indeed, we cannot have two optimal models which satisfy the same set of preferences. If μ is an already determined optimal model, in order to avoid the generation of models satisfying the preferences of μ (i.e., the literals in $S \cap \mu$) we could add a clause containing the negation of the literals in $S \cap \mu$, as soon as μ is determined to be optimal. However, the resulting procedure is no longer guaranteed to run in polynomial space. A simple solution that guarantees the polynomial space requirement is to force DPLL in order to first split on the literals l such that either $l \in S$ or $\bar{l} \in S$: When a model μ is found, regardless of whether it is optimal or not, a set of clauses corresponding to the negation of (5) is added to the input formula. The goal of these clauses is to force the procedure to backtrack up to one of the literals in S, in this way avoiding the generation of models which satisfy the same preferences as μ. Once the procedure backtracks to one such literal, these clauses can be removed, thus guaranteeing the polynomial space property of the procedure. Thus, the definition of *ChooseLiteral*$_2$ needs to be updated in this case: *ChooseLiteral*$_2$ returns (i) a literal l with $l \in S$ or $\bar{l} \in S$ if not all the literals in S are assigned by μ, and (ii) an arbitrary unassigned literal otherwise.

All theorems and results can be restated in terms of S-complete set of models.

4.2 Quantitative and Qualitative Preferences on Formulas and Their Mixing

Quantitative Preferences on Literals. Given a set of preferences S and a formula ψ, if it is not possible to satisfy both S and ψ, an alternative approach to model the relative importance of the preferences in S is to define a function $c : S \mapsto \mathbb{N}^+$: Intuitively, $c(l)$ is the reward for satisfying $l \in S$. A pair $\langle S, c\rangle$ is a *quantitative preference* and a model μ of ψ is *optimal* if it maximizes the *objective function* defined as[3]

$$\sum_{l \in S \cap \mu} c(l). \tag{6}$$

Consider a quantitative preference $\langle S', c\rangle$ and a satisfiable set of clauses φ'.

The problem of finding a complete set of optimal models of φ' wrt $\langle S', c\rangle$ can be solved again using nOPT-DLL$_1$ or nOPT-DLL$_2$ as core engine. The basic idea is to encode the value of the objective function (6) as a sequence of bits $b_{n-1}, \ldots, b_0$ and then consider the qualitative preference $\langle\{b_{n-1}, \ldots, b_0\}, \{b_i \prec b_j : 0 \leq j < i < n\}\rangle$. In more details, let *adder*(S', c) be a set of clauses such that:

1. If $n = \lceil log_2(\sum_{l \in S'} c(l)+1)\rceil$, *adder*$(S', c)$ contains n new variables $b_{n-1}, \ldots, b_0$; and
2. A total assignment μ satisfies φ' iff there exists a unique total assignment μ' to the variables in φ' and in *adder*(S', c) such that
   (a) μ' extends μ and satisfies both φ' and *adder*(S', c), and

[3] Assuming we want $c(l) < 0$ for some $l \in S$, we can replace l with $\bar{l}$ in S and define $c(\bar{l}) = -c(l)$: The set of optimal models does not change. Given $\langle S, c\rangle$ and assuming we are interested in minimizing the objective function (6), we can consider the quantitative preference $\langle \overline{S}, c'\rangle$ with $c'(l) = c(\bar{l})$, and then look for a model maximizing $\sum_{l \in \overline{S} \cap \mu} c'(l)$.

(b) $\sum_{l \in S' \cap \mu} c(l) = \sum_{i=0}^{n-1} \mu'(b_i) \times 2^i$, where $\mu'(b_i)$ is 1 if $b_i \in \mu'$, and is 0 otherwise.

If the above conditions are satisfied, we say that *adder*(S', c) is a *Boolean encoding of* $\langle S', c \rangle$ *with output* $b_{n-1}, \ldots, b_0$. *adder*(S', c) can be realized in polynomial time in many ways, see, e.g., [61]. In the above hypotheses, if

1. φ is the set of clauses in φ' or in *adder*(S', c), and
2. $\langle S, \prec \rangle$ is the qualitative preference $\langle \{b_{n-1}, \ldots, b_0\}, \{b_i \prec b_j : 0 \leq j < i < n\} \rangle$

then nOPT-DLL$_1$ and nOPT-DLL$_2$ return a complete set of optimal solutions of φ' wrt $\langle S', c \rangle$. The following theorem formally states this result.

Theorem 6. *Let φ' be a set of clauses and let $\langle S', c \rangle$ be a quantitative preference on literals. Let adder(S', c) be a Boolean encoding of $\langle S', c \rangle$ with output $b_{n-1}, \ldots, b_0$. If*

1. *φ is the set of clauses in φ' or in adder(S', c),*
2. *$\langle S, \prec \rangle$ is the qualitative preference $\langle \{b_{n-1}, \ldots, b_0\}, \{b_i \prec b_j : 0 \leq j < i < n\} \rangle$, and*
3. *M is the set of models of φ printed by nOPT-DLL$_1$ in Figure 1, or by nOPT-DLL$_2$ in Figure 2,*

then the models in M, restricted to the signature of φ', are all the optimal models of φ' wrt $\langle S', c \rangle$.

This theorem has been presented and proved as Theorem 5 in [20].

Qualitative and Quantitative Preferences on Formulas. So far, a preference is a literal, and we have seen how it is possible to use DPLL to find optimal models wrt both qualitative and quantitative preferences on literals. We now show that the hypothesis that preferences are literals can be waved, i.e., that it is possible to generalize the previous concepts and results from literals to arbitrary formulas. The basic idea is to introduce definitions [59] or "names" [51] for the formulas at hand.

First, we define a *qualitative preference on formulas* to be a pair $\langle S, \prec \rangle$ where S is a finite set of formulas and $\prec$ is a (strict) partial order on S. The set S of preferences does not need to be consistent. Then, as in Section 2, the partial order on S induces a partial order on the sets of total assignments according to which, if μ and μ' are two total assignments, $\mu \prec \mu'$ if and only if

1. there exists a formula $\psi \in S$ satisfied by μ and not by μ'; and
2. for each formula $\psi' \in S$ satisfied by μ' and not by μ, there exists a formula $\psi \in S$ satisfied by μ and not by μ' such that $\psi \prec \psi'$.

It is easy to see that if the formulas in S are literals, then the above definition coincides with the one given in Section 2. It is also straightforward to generalize the result of Theorem 1 saying that the if $\langle S, \prec \rangle$ is a qualitative preference on formulas, the relation $\prec$ extended to the set of total assignments is a partial order.

A model μ of a formula ψ is *optimal wrt a qualitative preference on formulas* $\langle S, \prec \rangle$ if μ is a minimal element of the partial order on the models of ψ.

Consider a formula ψ and a qualitative preference on formulas $\langle S, \prec \rangle$. Instead of ψ and $\langle S, \prec \rangle$ we can consider

1. the qualitative preference on literals $\langle L_s, \prec_S \rangle$, where
   - L_S has a newly introduced variable x_α for each formula $\alpha \in S$, and
   - $x_\alpha \prec_S x_\beta$ if and only if $\alpha \prec \beta$; and
2. the formula

$$\psi \wedge \bigwedge_{\alpha \in S}(x_\alpha \equiv \alpha). \tag{7}$$

Then, if

$$\mu_S = \mu \cup \{x_\alpha : \alpha \in S, \mu \models \alpha\} \cup \{\neg x_\alpha : \alpha \in S, \mu \not\models \alpha\}$$

it is straightforward to see that a model μ of ψ is optimal wrt the qualitative preference on formulas $\langle S, \prec \rangle$ iff μ_S is an optimal model of (7) wrt the qualitative preference on literals $\langle L_S, \prec_S \rangle$. It is also easy to see that (7) can be simplified to

$$\psi \wedge \bigwedge_{\alpha \in S}(\neg x_\alpha \vee \alpha) \tag{8}$$

and we obtain again the desired correspondence between the models of ψ and (8).

Introducing definitions [59] or "names" [51] for the formulas in the preferences allows us also to reduce quantitative preferences on formulas (defined in the obvious way) to qualitative preferences on literals. Further, it allows us to use nOPT-DLL$_1$ and nOPT-DLL$_2$ as core engines for computing optimal models of ψ given a qualitative/quantitative preference on formulas.

An advantage of reducing quantitative preferences to qualitative ones is that it makes also possible to mix the two, e.g., we can ask (we assume $b_{n-1}, \ldots, b_0$ to be the output bits of *adder*(S', c)):

1. Which among the optimal models according to a qualitative preference $\langle S, \prec \rangle$ are optimal according to a quantitative preference $\langle S', c \rangle$: Such assignments correspond to the optimal models of $\psi \wedge$ *adder*(S', c) wrt the qualitative preference

   $$\langle S \cup \{b_{n-1}, \ldots, b_0\}, \prec \cup \{b_i \prec b_j : 0 \leq j < i < n\} \cup \{\alpha \prec b_i : \alpha \in S, 0 \leq i < n\} \rangle.$$

   This preference, e.g., forces nOPT-DLL$_1$ to consider first $\langle S, \prec \rangle$ and then $\langle S', c \rangle$,
2. or which among the optimal models according to a quantitative preference $\langle S', c \rangle$, are optimal according to a qualitative preference $\langle S, \prec \rangle$: Such assignments correspond to the optimal models of $\psi \wedge$ *adder*(S', c) wrt the qualitative preference

   $$\langle S \cup \{b_{n-1}, \ldots, b_0\}, \prec \cup \{b_i \prec b_j : 0 \leq j < i < n\} \cup \{b_i \prec \alpha : \alpha \in S, 0 \leq i < n\} \rangle.$$

5 Discussion and Related Work

Our procedures have been implemented on top of MINISAT [24], the 2005 version, winner of the SAT 2005 competition on the industrial benchmarks category (together with the SAT/CNF minimizer SATELITE [23]). We have used MINISAT as models generator in both algorithms, given it is a CDCL [48, 57, 29] solver and thus satisfies the terms of Section 3. We also rely on MINISAT for the SAT test at line 4 of nOPT-DLL$_2$. Experimental analysis of our procedures for finding both one optimal solution and a complete set of optimal solutions, on both randomly generated and real-world SAT problems, with both qualitative and quantitative preferences, can be found in [19–21].

In the context of SAT and Constraint Satisfaction (CSP) problems with qualitative preferences, the idea of computing "optimal" (according to some given definition) models by modifying the heuristic in order to follow the expressed preferences on literals has been already proposed in [13] for SAT and in [5] for acyclic CP-nets [4]. [13] introduced the idea to compute all optimal models by adding constraints pruning the models dominated by the already computed optimal models: Other works which exploit further techniques to eliminate previously computed solutions in SAT include [46, 54, 41, 40] in the context of symbolic model checking [47]. CP-nets [4] (where CP stands for *Conditional Preference*) are a well-known and powerful method for expressing and graphically representing qualitative preferences. In [5] the authors have presented an algorithm, SEARCHCP, for finding more than one optimal solution. The algorithm, similarly to nOPT-DLL$_1$, follows the given partial order on qualitative preferences, but it is backtracking-free. From the computation point of view, if compared with nOPT-DLL$_1$, SEARCHCP computes also non-optimal models that has to be tested with all previously computed optimal solutions and, if compared with nOPT-DLL$_2$, it does not run in polynomial space when looking for all solutions. Moreover, as far as we know, no related implementation is available. Other differences wrt out work and the underlying formalisms used in [13, 5] for expressing preferences are (i) in the language: Both [13] and [5] allow for expressing preferences on literals, but in these approaches it is not possible to rank the preferences according to a partial order; and (ii) in the semantics: Even considering the case in which preferences are expressed as a consistent set S of literals, the order on models induced by S in [13, 5] is different from our (see [20] for details). On the other hand, [5] can deal with non-Boolean domains. As far as the generate-and-test approach is concerned, the idea of adding a constraint that forces a new solution to be better than the current one has been previously employed in, e.g., [26, 52] in the context of constraint optimization problem and constraint logic programming, respectively.

In the context of ASP, several works have dealt with qualitative preferences: In [49], a similar way, in comparison with our approach, of extending preferences on literals to total assignments is used. In [18], several preference handling approaches, not restricted to ASP, are reviewed and compared. Logic Programs with Ordered Disjunction [6] is an extension of normal logic programs with a connective which allows representing alternative, ranked options for problem solutions in the heads of ASP rules: An implementation based on the SMODELS ASP system [58] is presented in [6, 9]. Answer Set Optimization (ASO) programs [10] are another extension of normal logic program for representing qualitative preferences on rule heads, also allowing for formulas in the heads. Extensions of ASO are presented in, e.g., [7, 55], allowing for "complex preferences" and aggregates in ASO programs. Another approach for computing preferred answer sets has been followed in [25], where meta-interpreters are used to implement different combinations of ASP and preferential information, i.e., the approaches in [8, 17, 60] on top of the DLV ASP system [43]. Recently, in [28], another framework based on meta-interpreters to various forms of qualitative preferences among answer sets, e.g., inclusion-based minimization or Pareto efficiency, is presented.

In the literature of quantitative SAT and CSP, the kind of problem solved in (6) is also known as Binate Covering Problem [14], recently generalized in [44] to Weighted

Boolean Optimization problems. In the context of ASP, quantitative preferences are taken into account in, e.g., [12], for computing weighted solutions, [50] for solving Max-ASP problems, [11] with weak constraints, solving pseudo-Boolean problems with CLASP [29] and ASP under multi-criteria optimization [27].

Similar modeling approaches for reducing preferences on formulas to preferences on literals, by introducing definitions [59] or "names" [51], have been presented in, e.g., [36, 53, 2, 1].

6 Conclusions

In this paper we have presented a complete picture of our work on computing optimal solutions in satisfiability problems with preferences, by reviewing some results and presenting new ones. In particular, we have presented two solving procedures, different forms of preferences, ranging from qualitative on literals to mixed qualitative/quantitative on formulas, for finding two types of complete sets of optimal models.

The system implementing the presented procedures is available at `http://www.star.dist.unige.it/~emanuele/sat&pref/`.

Acknowledgement. The authors would like to thank Emanuele Di Rosa for the implementation of the system, and Torsten Schaub for useful comments on the topic of the paper.

References

1. Aloul, F.A., Ramani, A., Markov, I.L., Sakallah, K.A.: Generic ILP versus specialized 0-1 ILP: an update. In: Pileggi, L.T., Kuehlmann, A. (eds.) Proc. of the 2002 IEEE/ACM International Conference on Computer-aided Design (ICCAD 2002), pp. 450–457. ACM (2002)
2. Amgoud, L., Cayrol, C., LeBerre, D.: Comparing arguments using preference ordering for argument-based reasoning. In: Proc. of the 8th International Conference on Tools with Artificial Intelligence (ICTAI 1996), pp. 400–403. IEEE Computer Society (1996)
3. Bienvenu, M., Lang, J., Wilson, N.: From preference logics to preference languages, and back. In: Lin, F., Sattler, U., Truszczynski, M. (eds.) Proc. of the 12th International Conference on Principles of Knowledge Representation and Reasoning (KR 2010). AAAI Press (2010)
4. Boutilier, C., Brafman, R.I., Domshlak, C., Hoos, H.H., Poole, D.: CP-nets: A tool for representing and reasoning with conditional ceteris paribus preference statements. Journal of Artificial Intelligence Research 21, 135–191 (2004)
5. Boutilier, C., Brafman, R.I., Domshlak, C., Hoos, H.H., Poole, D.: Preference-based constrained optimization with CP-nets. Computational Intelligence 20(2), 137–157 (2004)
6. Brewka, G.: Logic programming with ordered disjunction. In: Dechter, R., Sutton, R.S. (eds.) Proc. of the 18th National Conference on Artificial Intelligence (AAAI 2002), pp. 100–105. AAAI Press / The MIT Press (2002)
7. Brewka, G.: Complex preferences for answer set optimization. In: Dubois, D., Welty, C.A., Williams, M.-A. (eds.) Proc. of the 9th International Conference on Principles of Knowledge Representation and Reasoning (KR 2004), pp. 213–223. AAAI Press (2004)
8. Brewka, G., Eiter, T.: Preferred answer sets for extended logic programs. Artificial Intelligence 109(1-2), 297–356 (1999)

9. Brewka, G., Niemelä, I., Syrjänen, T.: Logic programs with ordered disjunction. Computational Intelligence 20(2), 335–357 (2004)
10. Brewka, G., Niemelä, I., Truszczynski, M.: Answer set optimization. In: Gottlob, G., Walsh, T. (eds.) Proc. of the 18th International Joint Conference on Artificial Intelligence (IJCAI 2003), pp. 867–872. Morgan Kaufmann (2003)
11. Buccafurri, F., Leone, N., Rullo, P.: Strong and Weak Constraints in Disjunctive Datalog. In: Fuhrbach, U., Dix, J., Nerode, A. (eds.) LPNMR 1997. LNCS, vol. 1265, pp. 2–17. Springer, Heidelberg (1997)
12. Çakmak, D., Erdem, E., Erdoğan, H.: Computing Weighted Solutions in Answer Set Programming. In: Erdem, E., Lin, F., Schaub, T. (eds.) LPNMR 2009. LNCS, vol. 5753, pp. 416–422. Springer, Heidelberg (2009)
13. Castell, T., Cayrol, C., Cayrol, M., Le Berre, D.: Using the Davis and Putnam procedure for an efficient computation of preferred models. In: Wahlster, W. (ed.) Proc. of the 12th European Conference on Artificial Intelligence (ECAI 1996), pp. 350–354. John Wiley and Sons, Chichester (1996)
14. Coudert, O.: On solving covering problems. In: Pennino, T., Yoffa, E.J. (eds.) Proc. of the 33rd Conference on Design Automation (DAC 1996), pp. 197–202. ACM Press (1996)
15. Davis, M., Logemann, G., Loveland, D.W.: A machine program for theorem proving. Communication of ACM 5(7), 394–397 (1962)
16. Davis, M., Putnam, H.: A computing procedure for quantification theory. Journal of the ACM 7, 201–215 (1960)
17. Delgrande, J.P., Schaub, T.: Expressing preferences in default logic. Artificial Intelligence 123(1-2), 41–87 (2000)
18. Delgrande, J.P., Schaub, T., Tompits, H., Wang, K.: A classification and survey of preference handling approaches in nonmonotonic reasoning. Computational Intelligence 20(2), 308–334 (2004)
19. DiRosa, E., Giunchiglia, E., Maratea, M.: A new approach for solving satisfiability problems with qualitative preferences. In: Ghallab, M., Spyropoulos, C.D., Fakotakis, N., Avouris, N.M. (eds.) Proc. of the 18th European Conference on Artificial Intelligence (ECAI 2008). Frontiers in AI and Applications, vol. 178, pp. 510–514. IOS Press (2008)
20. DiRosa, E., Giunchiglia, E., Maratea, M.: Solving satisfiability problems with preferences. Constraints 15(4), 485–515 (2010)
21. DiRosa, E., Giunchiglia, E., O'Sullivan, B.: Optimal stopping methods for finding high quality solutions to satisfiability problems with preferences. In: Chu, W.C., Eric Wong, W., Palakal, M.J., Hung, C.-C. (eds.) Proc. of the 2011 ACM Symposium on Applied Computing (SAC 2011), pp. 901–906. ACM (2011)
22. Doyle, J., Junker, U.: Preferences. In: Tutotial at the 19th National Conference on Artificial Intelligence, AAAI 2004 (2004)
23. Eén, N., Biere, A.: Effective Preprocessing in SAT Through Variable and Clause Elimination. In: Bacchus, F., Walsh, T. (eds.) SAT 2005. LNCS, vol. 3569, pp. 61–75. Springer, Heidelberg (2005)
24. Eén, N., Sörensson, N.: An Extensible SAT-solver. In: Giunchiglia, E., Tacchella, A. (eds.) SAT 2003. LNCS, vol. 2919, pp. 502–518. Springer, Heidelberg (2004)
25. Eiter, T., Faber, W., Leone, N., Pfeifer, G.: Computing preferred answer sets by meta-interpretation in answer set programming. Theory and Practice of Logic Programming 3(4-5), 463–498 (2003)
26. Gavanelli, M.: Partially Ordered Constraint Optimization Problems. In: Walsh, T. (ed.) CP 2001. LNCS, vol. 2239, p. 763. Springer, Heidelberg (2001)
27. Gebser, M., Kaminski, R., Kaufmann, B., Schaub, T.: Multi-criteria optimization in answer set programming. In: Gallagherand, J.P., Gelfond, M. (eds.) Technical Communications of

the 27th International Conference on Logic Programming (ICLP 2011). LIPIcs, vol. 11, pp. 1–10. Schloss Dagstuhl - Leibniz-Zentrum fuer Informatik (2011)
28. Gebser, M., Kaminski, R., Schaub, T.: Complex optimization in answer set programming. Theory and Practice of Logic Programming 11(4-5), 821–839 (2011)
29. Gebser, M., Kaufmann, B., Neumann, A., Schaub, T.: Conflict-driven answer set solving. In: Veloso, M.M. (ed.) Proc. of the 20th International Joint Conference on Artificial Intelligence (IJCAI 2007), pp. 386–391 (2007)
30. Gelfond, M., Lifschitz, V.: The stable model semantics for logic programming. In: Kowalski, R., Bowen, K. (eds.) Proc. of the 5th International Conference and Symposium on Logic Programming (ICLP/SLP 1988), pp. 1070–1080 (1988)
31. Gelfond, M., Lifschitz, V.: Classical negation in logic programs and disjunctive databases. New Generation Computing 9, 365–385 (1991)
32. Gent, I., Van Maaren, H., Walsh, T. (eds.): SAT 2000. Satisfiability Research in the Year 2000. IOS Press (2000)
33. Giunchiglia, E., Giunchiglia, F., Tacchella, A.: SAT-based decision procedures for classical modal logics. Journal of Automated Reasoning 28, 143–171 (2002), Reprinted in [32]
34. Giunchiglia, E., Maratea, M.: Solving optimization problems with DLL. In: Brewka, G., Coradeschi, S., Perini, A., Traverso, P. (eds.) Proc. of the 17th European Conference on Artificial Intelligence (ECAI 2006). Frontiers in Artificial Intelligence and Applications, vol. 141, pp. 377–381. IOS Press (2006)
35. Giunchiglia, E., Massarotto, A., Sebastiani, R.: Act, and the rest will follow: Exploiting determinism in planning as satisfiability. In: Mostow, J., Rich, C. (eds.) Proc. of the 15th National Conference on Artificial Intelligence (AAAI 1998), pp. 948–953. AAAI Press / The MIT Press (1998)
36. de Givry, S., Larrosa, J., Meseguer, P., Schiex, T.: Solving Max-SAT as Weighted CSP. In: Rossi, F. (ed.) CP 2003. LNCS, vol. 2833, pp. 363–376. Springer, Heidelberg (2003)
37. Jackson, P., Sheridan, D.: Clause Form Conversions for Boolean Circuits. In: Hoos, H.H., Mitchell, D.G. (eds.) SAT 2004. LNCS, vol. 3542, pp. 183–198. Springer, Heidelberg (2005)
38. Järvisalo, M., Junttila, T., Niemelä, I.: Unrestricted vs restricted cut in a tableau method for Boolean circuits. Annals of Mathematics and Artificial Intelligence 44(4), 373–399 (2005)
39. Järvisalo, M., Junttila, T.A.: Limitations of restricted branching in clause learning. Constraints 14(3), 325–356 (2009)
40. Jin, H., Han, H., Somenzi, F.: Efficient Conflict Analysis for Finding All Satisfying Assignments of a Boolean Circuit. In: Halbwachs, N., Zuck, L.D. (eds.) TACAS 2005. LNCS, vol. 3440, pp. 287–300. Springer, Heidelberg (2005)
41. Jin, H., Somenzi, F.: Prime clauses for fast enumeration of satisfying assignments to Boolean circuits. In: Joyner Jr., W.H., Martin, G., Kahng, A.B. (eds.) Proc. of the 42nd Design Automation Conference (DAC 2005), pp. 750–753. ACM (2005)
42. Kautz, H., Selman, B.: Planning as satisfiability. In: Neumann, B. (ed.) Proc. of the 10th European Conference on Artificial Intelligence (ECAI 1992), pp. 359–363. John Wiley and Sons (1992)
43. Leone, N., Pfeifer, G., Faber, W., Eiter, T., Gottlob, G., Perri, S., Scarcello, F.: The DLV system for knowledge representation and reasoning. ACM Transactions on Computational Logic 7(3), 499–562 (2006)
44. Manquinho, V., Marques-Silva, J., Planes, J.: Algorithms for Weighted Boolean Optimization. In: Kullmann, O. (ed.) SAT 2009. LNCS, vol. 5584, pp. 495–508. Springer, Heidelberg (2009)
45. Maratea, M., Ricca, F., Veltri, P.: DLV^{MC} Enhanced Model Checking in DLV. In: Janhunen, T., Niemelä, I. (eds.) JELIA 2010. LNCS, vol. 6341, pp. 365–368. Springer, Heidelberg (2010)

46. McMillan, K.L.: Applying SAT Methods in Unbounded Symbolic Model Checking. In: Brinksma, E., Larsen, K.G. (eds.) CAV 2002. LNCS, vol. 2404, pp. 250–264. Springer, Heidelberg (2002)
47. McMillan, K.L.: Symbolic Model Checking: an Approach to the State Explosion Problem. Kluwer Academic Publishers (1993)
48. Mitchell, D.G.: A SAT solver Primer. Bulletin of the EATCS 85, 112–132 (2005)
49. Van Nieuwenborgh, D., Vermeir, D.: Preferred answer sets for ordered logic programs. Theory and Practice of Logic Programming 6(1-2), 107–167 (2006)
50. Oikarinen, E., Järvisalo, M.: Max-ASP: Maximum Satisfiability of Answer Set Programs. In: Erdem, E., Lin, F., Schaub, T. (eds.) LPNMR 2009. LNCS, vol. 5753, pp. 236–249. Springer, Heidelberg (2009)
51. Plaisted, D.A., Greenbaum, S.: A structure-preserving clause form translation. Journal of Symbolic Computation 2, 293–304 (1986)
52. Prestwich, S.: Three implementation of branch-and-cut in CLP. In: Proc. of the 4th Compulog-Net Workshop on Parallelism and Implementation Technologies (1996)
53. Ramírez, M., Geffner, H.: Structural Relaxations by Variable Renaming and Their Compilation for Solving MinCostSAT. In: Bessiere, C. (ed.) CP 2007. LNCS, vol. 4741, pp. 605–619. Springer, Heidelberg (2007)
54. Ravi, K., Somenzi, F.: Minimal Assignments for Bounded Model Checking. In: Jensen, K., Podelski, A. (eds.) TACAS 2004. LNCS, vol. 2988, pp. 31–45. Springer, Heidelberg (2004)
55. Saad, E., Brewka, G.: Aggregates in Answer Set Optimization. In: Delgrande, J.P., Faber, W. (eds.) LPNMR 2011. LNCS, vol. 6645, pp. 211–216. Springer, Heidelberg (2011)
56. Siekmann, J., Wrightson, G. (eds.): Automation of Reasoning: Classical Papers in Computational Logic 1967–1970, vol. 1-2. Springer (1983)
57. Marques Silva, J.P., Lynce, I., Malik, S.: Conflict-driven clause learning SAT solvers. In: Biere, A., Heule, M., van Maaren, H., Walsh, T. (eds.) Handbook of Satisfiability. Frontiers in Artificial Intelligence and Applications, vol. 185, pp. 131–153. IOS Press (2009)
58. Simons, P., Niemelä, I., Timo, S.: Extending and implementing the stable model semantics. Artificial Intelligence 138(1–2), 181–234 (2002)
59. Tseitin, G.: On the complexity of proofs in propositional logics. Seminars in Mathematics 8 (1970) Reprinted in [56]
60. Wang, K., Zhou, L., Lin, F.: Alternating Fixpoint Theory for Logic Programs with Priority. In: Lloyd, J., Dahl, V., Furbach, U., Kerber, M., Lau, K.-K., Palamidessi, C., Moniz Pereira, L., Sagiv, Y., Stuckey, P.J. (eds.) CL 2000. LNCS (LNAI), vol. 1861, pp. 164–178. Springer, Heidelberg (2000)
61. Warners, J.P.: A linear-time transformation of linear inequalities into conjunctive normal form. Information Processing Letters 68(2), 63–69 (1998)

Oscillating Behavior of Logic Programs

Katsumi Inoue[1] and Chiaki Sakama[2]

[1] National Institute of Informatics,
2-1-2 Hitotsubashi, Chiyoda-ku, Tokyo 101-8430, Japan
[2] Department of Computer and Communication Sciences, Wakayama University,
Sakaedani, Wakayama 640-8510, Japan

Abstract. We examine oscillation behavior of normal logic programs. Both the Gelfond-Lifschitz operator and the T_P operator are used to update Herbrand interpretations, and any interpretation finally reaches in an oscillator. It has been shown that the supported model semantics of normal logic programs can characterize point attractors of Boolean networks. We here newly define supported classes of normal logic programs to investigate periodic oscillation induced by the T_P operator, and apply them to characterize cycle attractors of Boolean networks. We also relate stable classes and supported classes of normal logic programs.

1 Introduction

A logic program can be viewed as a state transition system, in which each rule in the program represents how an entity (atom) is affected by other entities. Given an Herbrand interpretation as an initial state of the entities, a logic program defines the next state as an Herbrand interpretation through an operator associated with the program. It has been observed in [5,14] that both the T_P operator [26,3] and the Gelfond-Lifschitz operator [12,6] exhibit oscillating behavior for normal logic programs. This paper investigates such behavior in detail.

For a definite program P, van Emden and Kowalski [26] considered the T_P *operator* for P. This T_P operator is monotone, so that any interpretation finally reaches a fixpoint. In particular, the empty set $\emptyset$ reaches the least fixpoint, $T_P \uparrow \omega$, which is the *least model* of P. For a normal logic program P, however, T_P is not monotone. Apt, Blair and Walker [3] showed that a fixpoint of T_P for a normal logic program P is a *supported model* of P, and vice versa.

Given an Herbrand interpretation I, Baral and Subrahmanian [5,6] defined an operator for a normal logic program P called the F_P *operator* such that $F_P(I) = T_{P^I} \uparrow \omega$, where P^I is the *Gelfond-Lifschitz reduct* of P with respect to I [12]. By definition, a fixpoint of F_P is a *stable model* of P. This F_P is anti-monotone, so ${F_P}^2$ is monotone. Then, [5] defined a *stable class* of P, which is a set $\mathcal{S}$ of Herbrand interpretations such that $\mathcal{S} = \{F_P(I) \mid I \in \mathcal{S}\}$. A stable model corresponds to a singleton stable class, i.e., $|\mathcal{S}| = 1$. It has been proved that every normal logic program has at least one stable class [5] and that the *well-founded semantics* [27] corresponds to a stable class that is minimal with respect to the Hoare ordering [6].

E. Erdem et al. (Eds.): Correct Reasoning, LNCS 7265, pp. 345–362, 2012.

Recently, Inoue [14] revealed that the T_P operator for a normal logic program P precisely captures the synchronous update of *Boolean networks*, which have been used as a mathematical model of genetic networks and complex adaptive systems [18,19]. The stable states and dynamics of Boolean networks are characterized by their *attractors*. Then, the supported model semantics of normal logic programs captures the *point attractors* of Boolean networks. On the other hand, *cycle attractors* of Boolean networks represent periodic oscillation of the T_P operator. By this way, [14] observes the similarity between normal logic programs and Boolean networks. Actually, any normal logic program P can be converted to a Boolean network whose point attractors correspond to the supported models of P. Yet, [14] has not presented to what classes of interpretations cycle attractors precisely correspond in the semantics of logic programs.

In this paper, we first revisit the stable class semantics of normal logic programs, and analyze the oscillation behavior of them. Next, the *supported classes* of normal logic programs are newly defined to extend the supported models so that the supported models correspond to the singleton supported classes. This extension is made in a similar way that the stable classes are defined by extending the stable models in [5,6]. Then, we characterize both point attractors and cycle attractors of Boolean networks by supported classes of corresponding logic programs. This result also extends the previous result in [14], which characterizes point attractors by supported models. We also investigate the relationships between stable classes and supported classes of normal logic programs, thereby illustrating different oscillating behaviors of programs. Moreover, stable classes of a program can be shown to be translated into supported classes of a prerequisite-free program, which enables us to compute stable classes via computation of attractors of the corresponding Boolean network.

In the rest of this paper, Section 2 revisits the stable class semantics of normal logic programs and characterizes it in a different way. Section 3 defines the supported class semantics of normal logic programs and shows its relation to supported models. Section 4 considers attractors of Boolean networks and their relations to supported classes of logic programs. Section 5 presents more relationships between stable classes and supported classes of normal logic programs, and discusses their computational issues.

2 Stable Classes

We consider a first-order language and denote the Herbrand base (the set of all ground atoms) as $\mathcal{B}$. A *normal logic program* (NLP) is a set of rules of the form

$$A \leftarrow A_1 \wedge \cdots \wedge A_m \wedge \neg A_{m+1} \wedge \cdots \wedge \neg A_n \tag{1}$$

where A and A_i's are atoms ($n \geq m \geq 0$). For any rule R of the form (1), the atom A is called the *head* of R and is denoted as $h(R)$, and the conjunction to the right of $\leftarrow$ is called the *body* of R and we represent the positive and negative literals in the body as $b^+(R) = \{A_1, \ldots, A_m\}$ and $b^-(R) = \{A_{m+1}, \ldots, A_n\}$, respectively. An NLP is also called a *logic program* or a *program* in this paper. An NLP P is a *definite program* if $b^-(R) = \emptyset$ for every rule R in P.

Let $ground(P)$ be the set of ground instances of all rules in a logic program P. An (*Herbrand*) *interpretation* I is a subset of $\mathcal{B}$, and is called an (*Herbrand*) *model* of P if I *satisfies* all ground rules from P, that is, for any rule $R \in ground(P)$, $b^+(R) \subseteq I$ and $b^-(R) \cap I = \emptyset$ imply $h(R) \in I$.

For a definite program P, there exists a unique minimal model [26], i.e., the *least model* of P. It is characterized by the *immediate consequence operator* (or T_P *operator*), which is defined as a mapping $T_P : 2^{\mathcal{B}} \rightarrow 2^{\mathcal{B}}$:

$$T_P(I) = \{\, h(R) \mid R \in ground(P), \text{ the body of } R \text{ is true in } I \,\}. \tag{2}$$

If P is a definite program, then $T_P(I)$ for an Herbrand interpretation I becomes

$$T_P(I) = \{\, h(R) \mid R \in ground(P),\, b^+(R) \subseteq I \,\}. \tag{3}$$

The ordinal powers of T_P are defined as:

$$\begin{aligned} T_P \uparrow 0 &= \emptyset, \\ T_P \uparrow n+1 &= T_P(T_P \uparrow n), \\ T_P \uparrow \omega &= \textstyle\bigcup_{n \in \omega} T_P \uparrow n, \end{aligned}$$

where n is a successor ordinal and ω is a limit ordinal. Note that the mapping T_P is monotone for any definite program P. Then $T_P \uparrow \omega$ is the least fixpoint of T_P, which is exactly the least model of P [26].

The stable model semantics was defined by Gelfond and Lifschitz [12] through the reduct of a program. Given a logic program P and an Herbrand interpretation I, the *reduct* of P relative to I is defined as the definite program:

$$P^I = \left\{ \left(h(R) \leftarrow \bigwedge_{B \in b^+(R)} B \right) \,\middle|\, R \in ground(P),\, b^-(R) \cap I = \emptyset \right\}.$$

An Herbrand model I is a *stable model* [12] of P if I is the least model of P^I, i.e., $T_{P^I} \uparrow \omega = I$. Since $P^I = P$ holds for any definite program P and any Herbrand interpretation I, the unique stable model of a definite program is its least model.

Definition 2.1 (Baral and Subrahmanian [5,6]). Given a logic program P and an Herbrand interpretation I, the *Gelfond-Lifschitz operator* (or the F_P *operator*) is defined as:

$$F_P(I) = T_{P^I} \uparrow \omega. \tag{4}$$

A non-empty set $\mathcal{S}$ of Herbrand interpretations[1] is a *stable class* of P iff it holds that

$$\mathcal{S} = \{F_P(I) \mid I \in \mathcal{S}\}. \tag{5}$$

A stable class $\mathcal{S}$ of P is *strict* iff no proper subset of $\mathcal{S}$ is a stable class of P.

[1] The non-emptiness condition on $\mathcal{S}$ is necessary, since $\mathcal{S} = \emptyset$ satisfies (5). This condition is stated in [30]. On the other hand, the definition in [6] imposes the condition that $\mathcal{S}$ is finite to avoid an infinite transition. We can allow an infinite $\mathcal{S}$ in this section, but later the finiteness is required in Section 4.

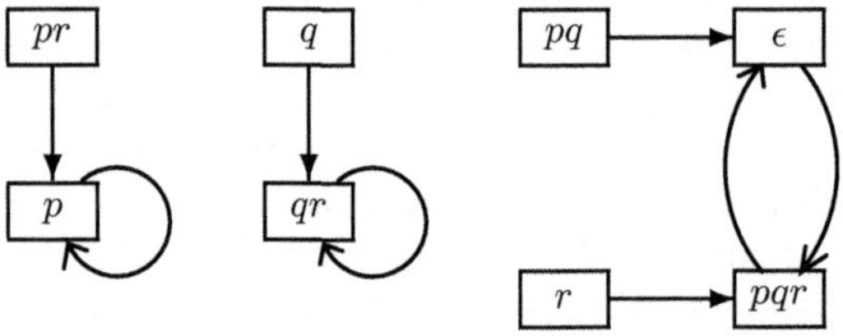

Fig. 1. State transition graph induced by F_{P_1}

A stable model corresponds to a singleton stable class $\mathcal{S}$, i.e., $|\mathcal{S}| = 1$. According to [5], every NLP has at least one stable class. It is easy to see that the union of two stable classes of P is also a stable class of P. Hence, strict stable classes are meaningful to represent such minimal cores.

Example 2.1. Consider the logic program P_1:

$$p \leftarrow \neg q,$$
$$q \leftarrow \neg p,$$
$$r \leftarrow q.$$

There are three strict stable classes of P_1:

$$S_1 = \{\{p\}\}, \quad S_2 = \{\{q, r\}\}, \quad S_3 = \{\emptyset, \{p, q, r\}\}.$$

S_1 and S_2 correspond to the stable models of P. These stable classes can be graphically represented [6] as cycles in a *state transition graph* in which nodes are Herbrand interpretations[2] and there is a directed arc from interpretation I to interpretation J iff $J = F_P(I)$. The state transition graph induced by F_{P_1} is depicted in Figure 1. The stable classes S_1 and S_2 respectively correspond to the self-loops connecting to p and qr, and S_3 is represented by the non-singleton cycle $\epsilon \to pqr \to \epsilon$.

We now give an alternative characterization for the strict stable classes. A sequence of applications of an operator on the Herbrand interpretations is called an *orbit* [7]. Given a logic program P and an interpretation I, the *orbit* of I with respect to the T_P operator is the sequence $\langle {T_P}^k(I) \rangle_{k \in \omega}$, where ${T_P}^0(I) = I$ and ${T_P}^{k+1}(I) = T_P({T_P}^k(I))$ for $k = 0, 1, \ldots$. Similarly, we can now define the *orbit* of I with respect to the F_P operator as the sequence $\langle {F_P}^k(I) \rangle_{k \in \omega}$. Put

$$\mathcal{F}_P(I) = \{{F_P}^k(I) \mid k \in \omega\}. \tag{6}$$

Theorem 2.1. *A non-empty set $\mathcal{S}$ of Herbrand interpretations is a strict stable class of a logic program P iff $\mathcal{F}_P(I) = \mathcal{S}$ for every $I \in \mathcal{S}$.*

Proof. For any $I \in \mathcal{S}$, $F_P(I) = {F_P}^1(I) \in \mathcal{F}_P(I)$ holds. Then, $\{F_P(I) \mid I \in \mathcal{S}\} \subseteq \bigcup_{I \in \mathcal{S}} \mathcal{F}_P(I)$. Suppose that $\mathcal{F}_P(I) = \mathcal{S}$ for every $I \in \mathcal{S}$. Then, $\bigcup_{I \in \mathcal{S}} \mathcal{F}_P(I) =$

[2] Each interpretation is represented as a sequence of atoms instead of a set of atoms in the graph, e.g., pq means $\{p, q\}$ and the empty string ϵ means $\emptyset$.

$\bigcup_{I\in\mathcal{S}} \mathcal{S} = \mathcal{S}$. Hence, $\{F_P(I) \mid I \in \mathcal{S}\} \subseteq \mathcal{S}$. Assume that $\mathcal{S} \setminus \{F_P(I) \mid I \in \mathcal{S}\} \neq \emptyset$. Then, there exists $I \in \mathcal{S}$ such that $I \neq F_P(J)$ for every $J \in \mathcal{S}$. Since $J \in \mathcal{S}$, $I \in \mathcal{F}_P(J) = \mathcal{S}$, then $I = {F_P}^k(J)$ for some $k > 1$. But $I = F_P({F_P}^{k-1}(J))$ and ${F_P}^{k-1}(J) \in \mathcal{S}$, a contradiction. Hence, $\{F_P(I) \mid I \in \mathcal{S}\} = \mathcal{S}$. Therefore, $\mathcal{S}$ is a stable class of P. Now assume that there exists a subset $\mathcal{S}' \subset \mathcal{S}$ such that $\mathcal{S}'$ is a stable class of P, i.e., $\mathcal{S}' = \{F_P(I) \mid I \in \mathcal{S}'\}$. Take any $I \in \mathcal{S}'$. By $I \in \mathcal{S}$, $\mathcal{F}_P(I) = \mathcal{S}$ holds. There must be $J \in \mathcal{S} \setminus \mathcal{S}'$, but $J = {F_P}^k(I)$ holds for some $k > 1$. Then, ${F_P}^{k-1}(I) \notin \mathcal{S}'$, since otherwise J belongs to $\mathcal{S}$. Similarly, ${F_P}^{k-2}(I) \notin \mathcal{S}'$ must hold. Repeating this inference we reach to the conclusion that ${F_P}^1(I) \notin \mathcal{S}'$, a contradiction. Hence, $\mathcal{S}$ is a strict stable class of P.

Conversely, suppose that $\mathcal{S}$ is a strict stable class of P. Since $\mathcal{S}$ is a stable class of P, $\mathcal{S} = \{F_P(I) \mid I \in \mathcal{S}\}$ holds. By ${F_P}^0(I) = I \in \mathcal{F}_P(I)$, $\mathcal{S} \subseteq \bigcup_{I\in\mathcal{S}} \mathcal{F}_P(I)$ holds. Assume that there exists $J \in \bigcup_{I\in\mathcal{S}} \mathcal{F}_P(I) \setminus \mathcal{S}$. Then, $J = {F_P}^k(I)$ for some $I \in \mathcal{S}$ and $k > 1$. Then, ${F_P}^{k-1}(I) \notin \mathcal{S}$, since otherwise J belongs to $\mathcal{S}$. Similarly, ${F_P}^{k-2}(I) \notin \mathcal{S}$ must hold. Repeating this inference we reach to the conclusion that ${F_P}^1(I) \notin \mathcal{S}$, a contradiction. Hence, $\mathcal{S} = \bigcup_{I\in\mathcal{S}} \mathcal{F}_P(I)$.

Now assume that $\mathcal{F}_P(I) \neq \mathcal{S}$ for some $I \in \mathcal{S}$. By $\mathcal{S} = \bigcup_{J\in\mathcal{S}} \mathcal{F}_P(J)$, ${F_P}^k(I)$ must belong to $\mathcal{S}$ for every $k \geq 0$. Hence, $\mathcal{F}_P(I) \subset \mathcal{S}$ holds. Let $\mathcal{S}' = \mathcal{S} \setminus \mathcal{F}_P(I)$. Take any $J \in \mathcal{S}'$. Since $J \notin \mathcal{F}_P(I)$, $F_P(J) \notin \mathcal{F}_P(I)$ holds too. Then, $F_P(J) \in \mathcal{S}'$. Hence, $\mathcal{S}' = \{F_P(J) \mid J \in \mathcal{S}'\}$ holds. This means that $\mathcal{S}'$ is a stable class of P. However this is impossible, since $\mathcal{S}$ is a strict stable class of P. Therefore, $\mathcal{F}_P(I) = \mathcal{S}$ for every $I \in \mathcal{S}$. □

Theorem 2.1 gives us a new insight into strict stable classes. The original definition of strict stable classes [5] is based on the minimality of stable classes with respect to set inclusion of interpretations. Such minimality is guaranteed if no redundant interpretation is contained in a stable set. The irredundancy of a strict stable class $\mathcal{S}$ is explained in Theorem 2.1 by the property that those interpretations appearing in the orbit of any interpretation in $\mathcal{S}$ exactly coincide with $\mathcal{S}$. Hence, a strict stable class $\mathcal{S}$ composes a *connected component* in the state transition graph.[3] On the other hand, a non-strict stable class must consist of multiple connected components. Hence, a strict stable class represents a minimal oscillation between interpretations.

Since the mapping F_P is deterministic for any NLP P, we can further guarantee that the orbit of any interpretation belonging to a *finite* strict stable class $\mathcal{S}$ repeats a sequence of the interpretations appearing in $\mathcal{S}$ always in the same order. In other words, the state transition graph for $\mathcal{S}$ becomes a *directed cycle*, which is shown in the following strengthened result.[4]

Theorem 2.2. *Let P be a logic program, and $\mathcal{S}$ a finite set of Herbrand interpretations of P. Then, $\mathcal{S}$ is a strict stable class of P iff there is a directed cycle*

[3] In other words, $\mathcal{S}$ is the set of interpretations that are *reachable* from every interpretation in $\mathcal{S}$ in the state transition graph. This property is inspired by the definition of *attractors* in Boolean networks [11,14], and we adapt the notion into stable classes.

[4] Theorem 2.2 is essentially equivalent to [5, Theorem 3]. We here give a proof which can be applied to a similar result for supported classes in Section 3.

$I_1 \to I_2 \to \cdots \to I_k \to I_1$ $(k \geq 1)$ in the state transition graph induced by F_P such that $\{I_1, I_2, \ldots, I_k\} = \mathcal{S}$.

Proof. If there is a directed cycle satisfying the condition of the proposition, then $\mathcal{F}_P(I_i) = \mathcal{S}$ holds for every $I_i \in \mathcal{S}$ $(i = 1, \ldots, k)$. Then, $\mathcal{S}$ is a strict stable class of P by Theorem 2.1.

Conversely, let $\mathcal{S}$ be a strict stable class of P such that $\mathcal{S} = \{I_1, I_2, \ldots, I_k\}$ $(k > 0)$. Then, $\mathcal{F}_P(I_i) = \mathcal{S}$ for every $i = 1, \ldots, k$ by Theorem 2.1. Suppose further that, for each $i = 1, \ldots, k$, $F_P(I_i) = I_{s(i)} \in \mathcal{S}$ for some $1 \leq s(i) \leq k$. Since $\mathcal{S}$ is strict, $\{I_{s(i)} \mid 1 \leq i \leq k\} = \mathcal{S}$ and all $I_{s(i)}$'s are different from each other. Then, there is a 1-1 correspondence between $\{I_{s(i)} \mid 1 \leq i \leq k\}$ and $\mathcal{S}$, that is, $\mathcal{S}$ is a cyclic group, which constitutes a directed cycle $I_1 \to I_{s(1)} \to I_{s(s(1))} \to \cdots \to I_{s^k(1)} \to I_1$ in the state transition graph induced by F_P. □

Note that the condition being a strict stable class in Theorem 2.1 is weaker than that in Theorem 2.2, since the former is stated in terms of an unordered set. Then, equivalence of strict stable classes in two programs does not imply equivalence of their state transition graphs.[5]

Example 2.2. Consider the logic program P_2 containing a cycle with three negations:

$$p \leftarrow \neg q,$$
$$q \leftarrow \neg r,$$
$$r \leftarrow \neg p.$$

P_2 has no stable model but has two strict stable classes:

$$S_3 = \{\emptyset, \{p, q, r\}\}, \quad S_4 = \{\{p\}, \{p, q\}, \{q\}, \{q, r\}, \{r\}, \{p, r\}\}.$$

Let us consider the logic program P_3 obtained by taking the contrapositive of each rule in P_2:

$$q \leftarrow \neg p,$$
$$r \leftarrow \neg q,$$
$$p \leftarrow \neg r.$$

P_3 has exactly the same stable classes as P_2. However, the directed cycle for S_2 in P_2 is $p \to pq \to q \to qr \to r \to pr \to p$, while that in P_3 is in the reverse order, i.e., $p \to pr \to r \to qr \to q \to pq \to p$.

Since all meaningful stable classes are strict, from now on we simply call each strict stable class as a *stable class* as long as there is no confusion. Each (strict) stable class is minimal in the sense of set inclusion over the sets of stable classes. Over the sets of strict stable classes of a logic program, however, we can further define preference relations. For example, we can prefer those minimal interpretations containing as few atoms as possible. Based on this intuition, stable classes have been used to represent several semantics for NLPs as follows.

[5] To remedy this problem, we could define a stable class as a directed cycle satisfying the condition in Theorem 2.2, while we follow the original definition of [5] here.

- Baral and Subrahmanian [5] prefer the stable classes that are minimal with respect to the *Smyth ordering* $\preceq_s$.[6] For Example 2.1, S_1 and S_2 are the $\preceq_s$-minimal (strict) stable classes, which correspond to the stable model semantics in this case.
- Baral and Subrahmanian [6] show that the *well-founded semantics* [27] corresponds to a stable class that is minimal with respect to the *Hoare ordering* $\preceq_h$. For Example 2.1, S_3 is the $\preceq_h$-minimal (strict) stable classes, in which the truth values of p, q, r are undefined, that is, they are true in $\{p, q, r\} \in S_3$ and are false in $\emptyset \in S_3$.
- You and Yuan [30] use results from [16] and show that a $\preceq_s$-minimal stable class $\mathcal{S}$ such that (i) $\mathcal{S}$ is a maximal fixpoint of the ${F_P}^2$ operator, and that (ii) $\mathcal{S} = \{I, F_P(I)\}$ for some $I \in 2^{\mathcal{B}}$ satisfying $I \subseteq F_P(I)$ corresponds to a *partial stable model* [23], a *preferred extension* [9], and a *regular model* [29].

These correspondences with various semantics of logic programming are an important aspect of the stable class semantics. In this paper, we further focus on another feature that has never been explored in detail. That is, we regard that the oscillating behavior is very useful in representing dynamic systems. This aspect will be highlighted in the following sections where supported classes are defined and are applied to represent dynamic systems.

3 Supported Classes

An Herbrand interpretation $I \in 2^{\mathcal{B}}$ is *supported* in an NLP P if for any ground atom $A \in I$, there exists a rule $R \in ground(P)$ such that $h(R) = A$, $b^+(R) \subseteq I$, and $b^-(R) \cap I = \emptyset$. I is a *supported model* of P if I is a model of P and is supported in P [3]. It is known that every stable model is a supported model [21], but not vice versa. For example, the logic program $\{\, p \leftarrow p,\ q \leftarrow \neg p \,\}$, has the supported models $\{p\}$ and $\{q\}$, but only the latter is its stable model.

For a logic program P and an Herbrand interpretation I, Apt *et al.* [3] have defined the T_P operator $T_P : 2^{\mathcal{B}} \rightarrow 2^{\mathcal{B}}$ as

$$T_P(I) = \{\, h(R) \mid R \in ground(P),\ b^+(R) \subseteq I,\ b^-(R) \cap I = \emptyset \}. \tag{7}$$

Actually, equation (7) is equivalent to equation (2), and is a generalization of (3). Then, I is a model of P iff I is a pre-fixed point of T_P, i.e., $T_P(I) \subseteq I$. By definition, I is supported iff $I \subseteq T_P(I)$. Hence, I is a supported model of P iff I is a fixpoint of T_P, i.e., $T_P(I) = I$. Moreover, I is a model of $Comp(P)$, which is the Clark's *completion* of P, iff $T_P(I) = I$. This means that the supported models of P are precisely the models of $Comp(P)$.

Now we give the definition of the supported class semantics. Remember that I is a stable model of P iff $F_P(I) = I$ and that a stable class is defined as a fixpoint over sets of interpretations. The supported classes are then defined

[6] Given a pre-ordered set $(D, \preccurlyeq)$ and $X, Y \subseteq D$, the *Smyth order* is defined as $X \preceq_s Y$ iff $(\forall x \in X)(\exists y \in Y)\, x \preccurlyeq y$, and the *Hoare order* is defined as $X \preceq_h Y$ iff $(\forall y \in Y)(\exists x \in X)\, x \preccurlyeq y$ [6]. Note that these orders are defined reversely in [13].

in the same way as the stable classes using the T_P operator instead of the F_P operator in (5).

Definition 3.1. A *supported class* of a logic program P is defined as a non-empty set $\mathcal{S}$ of Herbrand interpretations satisfying the fixpoint equation:

$$\mathcal{S} = \{T_P(I) \mid I \in \mathcal{S}\}. \tag{8}$$

A supported class $\mathcal{S}$ of P is *strict* if no proper subset of $\mathcal{S}$ is a supported class of P.[7]

Alternatively, we can define the strict supported classes in the same way as Theorem 2.1. Given a logic program P and an Herbrand interpretation I, let $\mathcal{T}_P(I)$ be the set of Herbrand interpretations appearing in the orbit $\langle {T_P}^k(I)\rangle_{k\in\omega}$ of I with respect to T_P:

$$\mathcal{T}_P(I) = \{{T_P}^k(I) \mid k \in \omega\}. \tag{9}$$

Theorem 3.1. *A non-empty set $\mathcal{S}$ of Herbrand interpretations is a strict supported class of a logic program P iff $\mathcal{T}_P(I) = \mathcal{S}$ for every $I \in \mathcal{S}$.*

Proof. The proof of Theorem 2.1 can be applied here by substituting $F_P(I)$ and $\mathcal{F}_P(I)$ in Theorem 2.1 with $T_P(I)$ and $\mathcal{T}_P(I)$, respectively. □

As in the case of strict stable classes, Theorem 3.1 can be further strengthened by taking the cyclic group into account.

Theorem 3.2. *Let P be a logic program, $\mathcal{S}$ a finite set of Herbrand interpretations of P. Then, $\mathcal{S}$ is a strict supported class of P iff there is a directed cycle $I_1 \to I_2, \to \cdots \to I_k \to I_1$ $(k \geq 1)$ in the state transition graph induced by T_P such that $\{I_1, I_2, \ldots, I_k\} = \mathcal{S}$.*

Proof. The proof of Theorem 2.2 can be applied here by respectively substituting $F_P(I)$ and $\mathcal{F}_P(I)$ in Theorem 3.1 with $T_P(I)$ and $\mathcal{T}_P(I)$. □

Example 3.1. Consider the program P_1 in Example 2.1. There are three strict supported classes of P_1:

$$S_1 = \{\{p\}\}, \quad S_2 = \{\{q, r\}\}, \quad S_5 = \{\{p, q\}, \{r\}\}.$$

S_1 and S_2 are also stable classes of P, but the stable class $S_3 = \{\emptyset, \{p, q, r\}\}$ is now replaced by S_5. The state transition graph induced by T_{P_1} is depicted in Figure 2.

The next proposition states that two strict supported classes are orthogonal.

Proposition 3.3. *Suppose $\mathcal{S}$ and $\mathcal{S}'$ are strict supported classes of a logic program P that has a finite Herbrand base. Then, $\mathcal{S} \neq \mathcal{S}'$ iff $\mathcal{S} \cap \mathcal{S}' = \emptyset$.*

---

[7] Again, the union of any two sets of interpretations satisfying (8) satisfies (8).

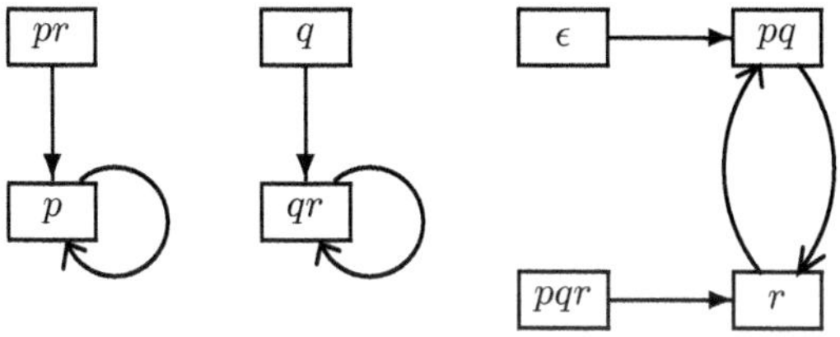

Fig. 2. State transition graph induced by T_{P_1}

Proof. The if direction is obvious. To prove the only-if direction, assume that $\mathcal{S} \cap \mathcal{S}' \neq \emptyset$ and there exists an Herbrand interpretation $I \in \mathcal{S} \cap \mathcal{S}'$. Applying Theorem 3.1 twice, we have $\mathcal{T}_P(I) = \mathcal{S}$ and $\mathcal{T}_P(I) = \mathcal{S}'$, and thus $\mathcal{S} = \mathcal{S}'$. □

As in the case of stable classes, all meaningful supported classes are strict. Hence, we will simply call each strict supported class as a *supported class* as long as there is no confusion.

Proposition 3.4. *I is a supported model of a logic program P iff* $\{I\}$ *is a supported class of P.*

Proof. $\{I\}$ is a supported class of P iff $\mathcal{T}_P(I) = \{I\}$ iff $T_P(I) = I$ iff I is a supported model of P. □

Since the T_P operator is the immediate consequence operator, the utility of the supported class semantics can be seen in representing state transition systems, in which inference of stepwise changes is simulated by the T_P operator.

Example 3.2. Consider the logic program P_4:

$$\begin{aligned} &produce \leftarrow \neg stock, \\ &stock \leftarrow produce, \end{aligned}$$

which represents that a shortage of stock triggers an additional production and that a production causes a stock. Neither stable model nor supported model exists for P_4. Both the stable class $S_4 = \{\emptyset, \{produce, stock\}\}$ and the supported class $S_5 = \{\emptyset, \{produce\}, \{produce, stock\}, \{stock\}\}$ of P_4 can represent continuous changes of stocks. While S_4 represents the cycle $\epsilon \rightarrow produce{\cdot}stock \rightarrow \epsilon$, S_5 is a more refined cycle $\epsilon \rightarrow produce \rightarrow produce{\cdot}stock \rightarrow stock \rightarrow \epsilon$. Hence, supported classes can be used to represent time delay occurring in positive inference, while stable classes infer all consequences of the reduct at once.

4 Boolean Networks

In this section, we will see that the supported class semantics can be well applied to *Boolean networks*, which was proposed as a mathematical model of genetic networks and complex adaptive systems [18,19], and has been used as a discrete model of gene regulatory, signal transduction and protein interaction networks. *Cellular automata* [28] are regarded as special cases of Boolean networks. Inoue [14] has shown that the T_P operator is useful to characterize the dynamics of synchronous Boolean networks. Here, we extend the result of [14] and show that the attractors of Boolean networks can be completely characterized by supported classes of associated logic programs.

A *Boolean network* (BN) is a pair $N = (V, F)$, where $V = \{v_1, \ldots, v_n\}$ is a finite set of nodes and $F = \{f_1, \ldots, f_n\}$ is a corresponding set of Boolean functions.[8] Let $v_i(t)$ denote the value of v_i at time t, which takes either 1 or 0. The overall expression level of all nodes in N at time step t is called a *state* of N at t, and is expressed as a vector $\mathbf{v}(t) = (v_1(t), \ldots, v_n(t))$. The value of node v_i at the next time step $t+1$ is determined by $v_i(t+1) = f_i(v_{i_1}(t), \ldots, v_{i_k}(t))$, where $v_{i_1}, \ldots, v_{i_k}$ are the set of *input nodes* of v_i, and the number k is called the *indegree* of v_i. In this paper, we consider Boolean networks in which the value of each node is updated *synchronously*.[9]

A consecutive sequence of states obtained by state transitions is called a *trajectory* of N. Since any state transition at any time step is *deterministic*, the trajectory starting from any state is uniquely determined. Let $w \in \{0,1\}^n$ be a state, and $R_N(w)$ be the states reachable in the trajectory of N starting from w. Then, a set S of states is an *attractor* of N if $R_N(w) = S$ holds for every $w \in S$ [11]. Any trajectory from a node in an attractor S composes a single loop, $w_0, \ldots, w_{p-1}, w_p (= w_0)$, where $p = |S|$ $(1 \leq p \leq 2^n)$. The length p is also called the *period* of the attractor S, and S is called a *point attractor* (or *singleton attractor*) if $p = 1$; Otherwise $(p > 1)$, it is called a *cycle attractor*. The set of states that reach the same attractor is called its *basin of attraction* [19].

A Boolean network is often represented graphically with two types of edges, which are positive and negative, in which $u \longrightarrow v$ means that $u(t)$ positively takes part in the regulation function for $v(t+1)$ and $u \dashv v$ means that $u(t)$ negatively takes part in the regulation function for $v(t+1)$.[10]

Example 4.1. Consider the Boolean network $N_1 = (V_1, F_1)$, where $V_1 = \{p, q, r\}$ and F_1 is as follows.

$$p(t+1) = q(t),$$
$$q(t+1) = p(t) \wedge r(t),$$
$$r(t+1) = \neg p(t).$$

---

[8] In a gene regulation network, each node $v_i \in V$ represents a *gene* and each $f_i \in F$ is called the *regulation function* of v_i. A node $v_i \in V$ takes the value 1 if the gene is *expressed*, and takes the value 0 if it is not expressed.

[9] There are also *asynchronous Boolean networks* [11], in which not all nodes are necessarily updated at a time. Some asynchronous BNs can be encoded in ASP [14].

[10] A positive edge of the form $u \longrightarrow v$ is often called a *trigger* or an *activator* of v, and a negative edge of the form $u \dashv v$ is called an *inhibitor* or a *repressor* of v. Note that the exact Boolean function $f_i \in F$ for a node $v_i \in V$ is not captured with this graphical representation. Hence the set F must be always shown with such a graph.

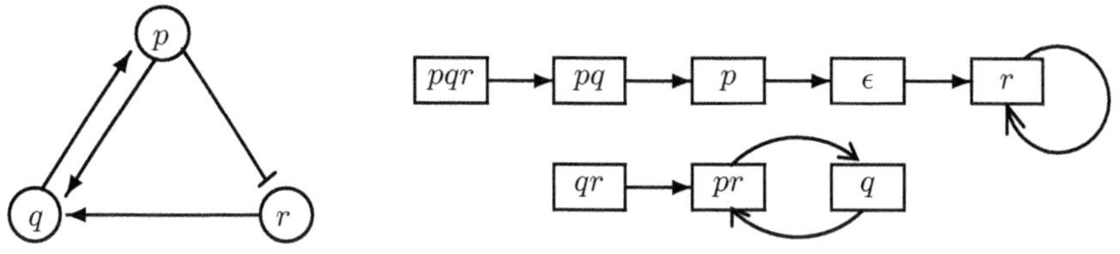

Fig. 3. Boolean network N_1 and its state transition diagram

The Boolean network N_1 is represented in Figure 3 (left). Starting from the initial state $\mathbf{v}(0) = (0,1,1)$, the trajectory becomes $(0,1,1)$, $(1,0,1)$, $(0,1,0)$, $(1,0,1)$, ..., and $pr \to q \to pr$ is a cycle attractor (Figure 3, right below).[11] N_1 has another, point attractor $r \to r$ (Figure 3, right above) whose basin of attraction is $\{pqr, pq, p, \epsilon, r\}$.

Note that any state in a Boolean network deterministically belongs to the basin of attraction of only one attractor. In applications to biological networks [19,24], each attractor represents a cell type, a type of memory, or a cellular state such as proliferation, apoptosis and differentiation.

4.1 From Boolean Networks to Logic Programs

We here show a translation of Boolean networks into normal logic programs. Given a Boolean network $N = (V, F)$, each Boolean function $f_i \in F$ for a node $v_i \in V$ is to be embedded into rules in a logic program. Then, f_i should be transformed in disjunctive normal form (DNF). Since this is always possible, we assume that each $f_i \in F$ for a node $v_i \in V$ is already written as a DNF formula:

$$v_i(t+1) = \bigvee_{j=1}^{l_i} B_{i,j}(t), \quad B_{i,j}(t) = \bigwedge_{k=1}^{m_j} v_{i,j,k}(t) \;\wedge \bigwedge_{k=m_j+1}^{n_j} \neg v_{i,j,k}(t), \tag{10}$$

where $v_{i,j,k} \in V$ and $n_j \geq m_j \geq 0$ for $j = 1, \ldots, l_i$. Note that l_i (and j) can be 0 for a node v_i, so that the indegree of v_i is 0. In this case, v_i is called a *constant node*, and cannot change its value. Let $V_C \subseteq V$ be the constant nodes of N.

According to [14], we can associate the *propositional* logic program $\pi(N)$ for a Boolean network N as:

$$\pi(N) = \{\, (v_i \leftarrow B_{i,j}) \mid v_i \in (V \setminus V_C),\ 1 \leq j \leq l_i \,\} \cup \{\, (v_i \leftarrow v_i) \mid v_i \in V_C \,\}, \tag{11}$$

where $B_{i,j}$ is the conjunction of literals obtained from $B_{i,j}(t)$ in (10) by deleting the time argument (t) appearing in every $v_{i,j,k}(t)$ $(k = 1, \ldots, n_j)$ in it. For any state $\mathbf{v}(t) = (v_1(t), \ldots, v_n(t))$ at time step t, the interpretation $I^t \subseteq V$ is defined as $I^t = \{v_i \in V \mid v_i(t) = 1\}$. Then, it holds that $I^{t+1} = T_{\pi(N)}(I^t)$.

[11] As in the case of state transition for logic programs, each state is represented as a sequence of nodes whose values are 1, e.g., pq means $(p, q, r) = (1, 1, 0)$ and the empty string ϵ means $(0, 0, 0)$ in the state transition diagram for a Boolean network.

Proposition 4.1. [14] *Let N be a Boolean network, and $\mathbf{v}(t)$ a state at some time step t. Then, the orbit of I^t with respect to $T_{\pi(N)}$ is precisely the trajectory of N starting from $\mathbf{v}(t)$. That is, $\mathcal{T}_{\pi(N)}(I^t) = R_N(\mathbf{v}(t))$ holds.*

Proposition 4.1 implies that every attractor can be obtained as an attracting cycle appearing in an orbit of I^0 that corresponds to some initial state $\mathbf{v}(0)$, and in particular that a point attractor corresponds to a fixed point in such an orbit.

Example 4.2. For the Boolean network N_1 in Example 4.1, the logic program $\pi(N_1)$ is given as:

$$\begin{aligned} &p \leftarrow q, \\ &q \leftarrow p \wedge r, \\ &r \leftarrow \neg p. \end{aligned} \tag{12}$$

Then, starting from the state $\mathbf{v}(0) = (0, 1, 1)$, the orbit $\langle I^k \rangle_{k\in\omega}$ of I^0 with respect to $T_{\pi(N_1)}$ is $\{q, r\}$, $\{p, r\}$, $\{q\}$, $\{p, r\}$, ..., which is exactly the trajectory of N_1 from $\mathbf{v}(0)$. Among them, the repeat $pr \rightarrow q \rightarrow pr$ represents the cycle attractor of N_1. On the other hand, starting from $(1, 1, 1)$, the orbit of $\{p, q, r\}$ reaches the fixed point $\{r\}$, which corresponds to the point attractor $r \rightarrow r$ of N_1.

We often identify a state $\mathbf{v}(t)$ with an interpretation I^t, and will denote it as I whenever the time step t is not important.

Proposition 4.2. [14] *Let $N = (V, F)$ be a Boolean network. Then, $\{I\}$ is a point attractor of N iff I is a supported model of $\pi(N)$.*

Proposition 4.2 characterizes the set of all point attractors of a Boolean networks in terms of a single logic program. All supported models of $\pi(N)$ can be enumerated as the models of its completion:

$$Comp(\pi(N)) \equiv \bigwedge_{v_i \in (V \setminus V_C)} \left(v_i \leftrightarrow \bigvee_{j=1}^{l_i} B_{i,j} \right). \tag{13}$$

Using a SAT solver, computation of point attractors can be automated by computing the models of the formula (13).

We now generalize Proposition 4.2 to characterize the set of all attractors of a Boolean network.

Theorem 4.3. *Let $N = (V, F)$ be a Boolean network. Then, S is an attractor of N iff S is a supported class of $\pi(N)$.*

Proof. S is an attractor of N iff $R_N(I) = S$ for every $I \in S$ (by definition) iff $\mathcal{T}_{\pi(N)}(I) = S$ for every $I \in S$ (by Proposition 4.1) iff S is a supported class of $\pi(N)$ (by Theorem 3.1). □

Theorem 4.3 now characterizes both cycle and point attractors of Boolean networks. In fact, Proposition 4.2 is derived as a corollary of Theorem 4.3 using Theorem 3.4. For Example 4.2, we see that there are two supported classes of $\pi(N_1)$, $\{\{r\}\}$ and $\{\{p, r\}, \{q\}\}$, which respectively correspond to the point attractor and the cycle attractor of N_1. Remember that $\{r\}$ is the unique supported model of $\pi(N_1)$, which represents the point attractor by Proposition 4.2.

4.2 From Logic Programs to Boolean Networks

Here we show a converse translation from logic programs to Boolean networks. We here assume that the Herbrand base $\mathcal{B}$ is finite. By setting $\mathcal{B}$ as the nodes of a Boolean network, any interpretation $I \in 2^{\mathcal{B}}$ can be identified with a state at some time step t, that is, $A_i(t) = 1$ iff $A_i \in I$ and $A_i(t) = 0$ iff $A_i \notin I$ for any $A_i \in \mathcal{B}$. According to [14], given a propositional logic program P, we can construct the Boolean network $\nu(P) = (\mathcal{B}, F(P))$, where $F(P)$ is defined as follows. For each $A_i \in \mathcal{B}$, suppose the set of rules in P whose heads are A_i is precisely given by $\{(A_i \leftarrow \Gamma_{i,1}), \ldots, (A_i \leftarrow \Gamma_{i,i_k})\}$, where each $\Gamma_{i,j}$ $(1 \leq j \leq i_k)$ is a conjunction of literals. The Boolean function for A_i is then defined as $A_i(t+1) = (\Gamma_{i,1}(t) \vee \cdots \vee \Gamma_{i,i_k}(t))$ if $i_k \geq 1$, and is assigned 0 if $i_k = 0$ (A_i is a 0-*node*[12]).

Proposition 4.4. [14] *Let P be a propositional logic program. Then, I is a supported model of P iff $\{I\}$ is a point attractor of $\nu(P)$.*

Here, we can generalize Proposition 4.4 as follows.

Theorem 4.5. *Let P be a propositional logic program. Then, S is a supported class of P iff S is an attractor of $\nu(P)$.*

Proof. Each Boolean function $f_i \in F(P)$ for a node $A_i \in \mathcal{B}$ in $\nu(P) = (\mathcal{B}, F(P))$ can be written as $f_i = (\Gamma_{i,1} \vee \cdots \vee \Gamma_{i,i_k})$. Then, for a time step t, $A_i(t+1) = 1$ iff $f_i(t) = 1$ iff $(\exists j)\Gamma_{i,j}(t) = 1$. Suppose an interpretation $I \in 2^{\mathcal{B}}$ such that $(A_i(t) = 1$ iff $A_i \in I)$ and $(A_i(t) = 0$ iff $A_i \notin I)$ hold for any $A_i \in \mathcal{B}$. Then, $J = T_P(I)$ iff I for each $A_i \in J$ there exists a rule $(A_i \leftarrow \Gamma_{i,j})$ in P such that $\Gamma_{i,j}$ is true in I iff I satisfies f_i for every $A_i \in J$ iff J is the next state of I for the Boolean network $\nu(P)$. Then, S is a supported class of P iff $\mathcal{T}_P(I) = S$ for any $I \in S$ (by Theorem 3.1) iff $R_{\nu(P)}(I) = S$ for any $I \in S$ (by Proposition 4.1) iff S is an attractor of $\nu(P)$. □

Note that, given a Boolean network N, it may hold that $\nu(\pi(N)) \neq N$. This is because for any constant node v_i in N, no Boolean function is defined for v_i in N. However, the rule $(v_i \leftarrow v_i)$ is included in $\pi(N)$, which is then kept in $\nu(\pi(N))$ as the Boolean function $f_i{}' = v_i$. Nevertheless, we can identify a Boolean network N and its corresponding logic program $\pi(N)$ and identify a logic program P and its corresponding Boolean network $\nu(P)$ under the supported class semantics.

5 Between Stable and Supported Classes

We have seen in Section 2 that the stable class semantics can represent several important semantics of logic programs including the stable model semantics [12] and the well-founded semantics [27].

[12] In a Boolean network, a 0-node can be graphically illustrated as a node that has a single incoming edge from $\perp$ representing the value 0.

On the other hand, the supported class semantics defined in Section 3 is suitable to represent dynamics of state transition systems including Boolean networks [19] as shown in Section 4. Then, another merit of the supported class semantics is that computation of supported classes is possible via algorithms to compute attractors of Boolean networks. For example, attractors are searched on state transition diagrams for Boolean networks with bounded model checking [8], in which the length of trajectories is incrementally varied. Particular focuses are put on point attractors [25,2] based on elaborate translations of Boolean networks into SAT through completion (13). There are also some efficient algorithms to compute cycle attractors with period 2 when Boolean networks are unate [1]. These procedures to compute attractors of Boolean networks can thus be applied to compute supported classes of logic programs. On the other hand, there has been no procedure to compute stable classes except that singleton stable classes, i.e., stable models, can be computed in ASP.

Given those merits of each semantics, we now investigate relationships between stable and supported classes. At first, recall that any stable model of a logic program P is a supported model of P [21]. Any stable model also comprises a singleton stable class [5], and any supported model forms a singleton supported class (Proposition 3.4). Hence, we have the following immediate property.

Proposition 5.1. *Let P be a logic program, I a stable model of P. Then, $\{I\}$ is both a stable class and a supported class of P.*

Next we would expect that this result could be generalized so that any stable class of P is a supported class of P. However, as shown in Examples 2.1 and 3.1, this property does not hold. Then, it appears that a supported class might have some delay compared with a corresponding stable class, due to the difference between the T_P and F_P operators applied to reducts, as explained in Example 3.2. Unfortunately, this does not hold either.

Example 5.1. Consider the program P_2 in Example 2.2, which has two stable classes S_3 and S_4. The supported classes of P_2 are exactly the same as these, corresponding to cycle attractors with period 2 and period 6, respectively.[13] Now, consider the next program P_5 obtained from P_2 by adding one rule $(p \leftarrow p)$:

$$\begin{aligned} p &\leftarrow p, \\ p &\leftarrow \neg q, \\ q &\leftarrow \neg r, \\ r &\leftarrow \neg p. \end{aligned}$$

P_5 has the same stable classes as P_2, i.e., S_3 and S_4, but there is the unique supported class of P_5: $S_6 = \{\{p, q\}\}$. In fact, P_5 has the unique supported model $\{p, q\}$, and has no cycle attractor in the corresponding Boolean network.

[13] The Boolean network corresponding to P_2 is made of three repressors hooked up in a cycle to form a negative feedback loop, and is called a *repressilator* [10]. Such circuits often exhibit very complex oscillations.

The next proposition shows that stable classes and supported classes coincide for logic programs without "prerequisites". A rule is called *prerequisite-free* if $b^+(R) = \emptyset$, and a logic program P is *prerequisite-free* if every rule in P is prerequisite-free.

Proposition 5.2. *Let P be a prerequisite-free logic program, and $\mathcal{S}$ a set of interpretations. Then, $\mathcal{S}$ is a stable class of P iff $\mathcal{S}$ is a supported class of P.*

Proof. Let I be any interpretation. When P is prerequisite-free, it holds that $P^I = \{h(R) \mid R \in ground(P),\ b^-(R) \cap I = \emptyset\}$. Hence, $F_P(I) = T_{P^I} \uparrow \omega = T_{P^I}(I)$. By [21, Theorem 2], $T_{P^I}(I) = T_P(I)$. Therefore, $F_P(I) = T_P(I)$. Hence, for any $I \in \mathcal{S}$, $\mathcal{F}_P(I) = \mathcal{T}_P(I)$ holds. By Theorems 2.1 and 3.1, $\mathcal{S}$ is a stable class of P iff $\mathcal{S}$ is a supported class of P. □

Proposition 5.2 gives a bridge between stable classes and supported classes. If we find a translation of a program P into a prerequisite-free program Q without changing the stable classes of P, then we can compute supported classes of Q that are equivalent to stable classes of Q (and P) by Proposition 5.2. Fortunately, we can use *unfolding* for this purpose.

Let R be a ground rule of the form (1):

$$A \leftarrow A_1 \wedge \cdots \wedge A_m \wedge \neg A_{m+1} \wedge \cdots \wedge \neg A_n.$$

Suppose that R_i is a ground rule of the form $A_i \leftarrow \Gamma_i$ for $i = 1, \ldots, m$, where Γ_i is a conjunction of literals. Then, $U_R(R_1, \ldots, R_m)$ is a ground rule:

$$A \leftarrow \Gamma_1 \wedge \cdots \wedge \Gamma_m \wedge \neg A_{m+1} \wedge \cdots \wedge \neg A_n.$$

Given an NLP P and a prerequisite-free program Q, Aravindan and Dung [4] have defined unfolding of the rules in $ground(P)$ with prerequisite-free rules in Q via the following operator S_P:

$$S_P(Q) = \{U_R(R_1, \ldots, R_m) \mid R \in ground(P),\ R_i \in Q,\ 1 \leq i \leq m\}.$$

Note that any $U_R(R_1, \ldots, R_m) \in S_P(Q)$ is a prerequisite-free rule, and that $S_P(\emptyset) = \{R \in ground(P) \mid b^+(R) = \emptyset\}$ is the set of prerequisite-free rules in $ground(P)$. Then the *semantic kernel* of P, denoted as $SK(P)$, is defined as the prerequisite-free program $S_P \uparrow \omega$, where

$$\begin{aligned} S_P \uparrow 0 &= \emptyset, \\ S_P \uparrow n+1 &= S_P(S_P \uparrow n), \\ S_P \uparrow \omega &= \textstyle\bigcup_{n \in \omega} S_P \uparrow n. \end{aligned}$$

Proposition 5.3. [4, Theorem 3.1] *Let P be an NLP, and $SK(P)$ its semantic kernel. Then, P and $SK(P)$ have the same stable models.*

Proposition 5.3 can be generalized as follows. In [4], it has been shown that P and $SK(P)$ have the same preferred extensions, the same regular models, and the same partial stable models. Hence, we add one more property here.

Lemma 5.4. *Let P be an NLP, and $SK(P)$ its semantic kernel. For any atom $A \in \mathcal{B}$, $A \in T_P \uparrow n$ for some $n \in \omega$ iff there is a prerequisite-free rule $Q \in S_P \uparrow n$ such that $h(Q) = A$ and $I \cap b^-(Q) = \emptyset$.*

Proof. We prove the lemma by induction on n. When $n = 0$, it is obvious. Assume that the lemma holds for $n \leq k$, and consider the case of $n = k + 1$. Suppose that A is derived at the ordinal $k+1$, i.e., $A \in T_{P^I} \uparrow k+1$. Then, there is a rule $R \in ground(P)$ such that $h(R) = A$ and $b^-(R) \cap I = \emptyset$. For this R, the reduct R' exists in P^I such that $h(R') = h(R) = A$, $b^+(R') = b^+(R)$ and $b^-(R') = \emptyset$. Moreover, $A_i \in T_P \uparrow k$ holds for every $A_i \in b^+(R')$. By the induction hypothesis, there is a rule $Q_i \in S_P \uparrow k$ such that $h(Q_i) = A_i$, $b^+(Q_i) = \emptyset$ and $I \cap b^-(Q_i) = \emptyset$. Then, by unfolding, the rule $Q = U_R(Q_1, \ldots, Q_m) \in S_P \uparrow k+1$ such that $h(Q) = A$, $b^+(Q) = \emptyset$ and $I \cap b^-(Q) = I \cap (b^-(Q_1) \cup \cdots \cup b^-(Q_m) \cup b^-(R)) = (I \cap b^-(Q_1)) \cup \cdots \cup (I \cap b^-(Q_m)) \cup (I \cap b^-(R)) = \emptyset$. □

Theorem 5.5. *Let P be an NLP, and $SK(P)$ its semantic kernel. Then, P and $SK(P)$ have the same stable classes.*

Proof. We prove that $F_P(I) = F_{SK(P)}(I)$ holds for any interpretation I. Since $SK(P)$ is prerequisite-free, $SK(P)^I = \{h(R) \mid R \in SK(P), b^-(R) \cap I = \emptyset\}$. Then, $F_{SK(P)}(I) = T_{SK(P)^I} \uparrow \omega = SK(P)^I$.

Now, let A be any ground atom. Then, $A \in F_P(I)$
iff $A \in T_{P^I} \uparrow \omega$ iff $A \in T_{P^I} \uparrow n$ for some $n \geq 1$
iff there is a prerequisite-free rule $Q \in S_P \uparrow n$ such that $h(Q) = A$ and $I \cap b^-(Q) = \emptyset$ (by Lemma 5.4)
iff there is $Q \in SK(P)$ such that $h(Q) = A$ and $I \cap b^-(Q) = \emptyset$
iff $A \in SK(P)^I$ iff $A \in F_{SK(P)}(I)$. □

Hence, computing stable classes is now possible through translation of a logic program P into $SK(P)$ (Theorem 5.5) and computing supported classes of $SK(P)$ (Proposition 5.2) through attractor computation (Theorem 4.5). On the other hand, $SK(P)$ does not preserve the supported models as well as the supported classes of P, e.g., $P = \{p \leftarrow p\}$ and $SK(P) = \emptyset$.

As for computational complexity, however, we see below that stable classes and supported classes have the same complexity on their existence. As explained in previous sections, existence of stable/supported classes is always guaranteed.

Proposition 5.6. *Any logic program has at least one stable class as well as one supported class.*

The next property is easily obtained by complexity results for existence of stable/supported models of logic programs.

Proposition 5.7. (1) *Deciding if there is a singleton stable class is NP-complete.* (2) *Deciding if there is a singleton supported class is NP-complete.*

Proof. (1) is obtained by [22, Theorem 6.7]. (2) is equivalent to the problem that $Comp(P)$ is consistent for an NLP P, which is NP-complete. □

Our interest here is a program that has no stable/supported model. Such a program is regarded as inconsistent in general, but has a meaning under the stable/supported class semantics. A program P is called *F_P-periodic* (resp. *T_P-periodic*) if the size of minimum stable (resp. supported) classes of P is more than 1. Then, the next property holds by Propositions 5.6 and 5.7.

Theorem 5.8. *Deciding if a logic program P is F_P-periodic (or T_P-periodic) is coNP-complete.*

As the final remark, notice that the difference between the definition of stable classes and that of supported classes only lies in the deterministic operators, F_P and T_P, on $2^{\mathcal{B}}$. Hence, the essence in the proofs of Theorems 2.1 and 2.2 can be directly applied to the proofs of Theorems 3.1 and 3.2, respectively. Both the F_P operator and T_P operator are reasonable as deterministic operators that map over Herbrand interpretations, and are useful to characterize semantic and dynamic aspects of logic programs. It is open whether any other interesting deterministic operator exists for normal logic programs.

For the class of *disjunctive logic programs*, we might need a *nondeterministic* operator like [15,20], which is a mapping $2^{\mathcal{B}} \rightarrow 2^{2^{\mathcal{B}}}$, yet Kalinski [17] has defined stable classes for disjunctive programs by extending the definition (6) with the notion of *model filters*. Moreover, to characterize *asynchronous Boolean networks*, the use of nondeterministic operators has also been suggested in [14]. These generalizations are future works.

References

1. Akutsu, T., Melkman, A.A., Tamura, T.: Singleton and 2-periodic attractors of sign-definite Boolean networks. Information Processing Letters 112, 35–38 (2012)
2. Akutsu, T., Melkman, A.A., Tamura, T., Yamamoto, M.: Determining a singleton attractor of a Boolean network with nested canalyzing functions. Journal of Computational Biology 18, 1275–1290 (2011)
3. Apt, K.R., Blair, H.A., Walker, A.: Towards a theory of declarative knowledge. In: Minker, J. (ed.) Foundations of Deductive Databases and Logic Programming, pp. 89–148. Morgan Kaufmann (1988)
4. Aravindan, C., Dung, P.M.: On the correctness of unfold/fold transformation of normal and extended logic programs. Journal of Logic Programming 24, 201–217 (1995)
5. Baral, C., Subrahmanian, V.S.: Stable and extension class theory for logic programs and default logics. Journal of Automated Reasoning 8, 345–366 (1992)
6. Baral, C., Subrahmanian, V.S.: Dualities between alternative semantics for logic programming and nonmonotonic reasoning. Journal of Automated Reasoning 10, 399–420 (1993)
7. Blair, H.A., Dushin, F., Humenn, P.R.: Simulations between Programs as Cellular Automata. In: Fuhrbach, U., Dix, J., Nerode, A. (eds.) LPNMR 1997. LNCS (LNAI), vol. 1265, pp. 115–131. Springer, Heidelberg (1997)
8. Dubrova, E., Teslenko, M.: A SAT-based algorithm for finding attractors in synchronous Boolean networks. IEEE/ACM Transactions on Computational Biology and Bioinformatics 8(5), 1393–1399 (2011)

9. Dung, P.M.: Negations as hypotheses: An abductive foundation for logic programming. In: Proceedings of ICLP 1991, pp. 3–17. MIT Press (1991)
10. Elowitz, M.B., Leibler, S.: A synthetic oscillatory network of transcriptional regulators. Nature 403(6767), 335–338 (2000)
11. Garg, A., Di Cara, A., Xenarios, I., Mendoza, L., De Micheli, G.: Synchronous versus asynchronous modeling of gene regulatory networks. Bioinformatics 24(17), 1917–1925 (2008)
12. Gelfond, M., Lifschitz, V.: The stable model semantics for logic programming. In: Proceedings of ICLP 1988, pp. 1070–1080. MIT Press (1988)
13. Gunter, C.A., Scott, D.S.: Semantic domains. In: van Leeuwen, J. (ed.) Handbook of Theoretical Computer Science, vol. B, pp. 633–674. North-Holland (1990)
14. Inoue, K.: Logic programming for Boolean networks. In: Proceedings of IJCAI 2011, pp. 924–930 (2011)
15. Inoue, K., Sakama, C.: A fixpoint characterization of abductive logic programs. Journal of Logic Programming 27(2), 107–136 (1996)
16. Kakas, A.C., Mancarella, P.: Preferred extensions are partial stable models. Journal of Logic Programming 14, 341–348 (1992)
17. Kalinski, J.: Stable Classes and Operator Pairs for Disjunctive Programs. In: Marek, V.W., Truszczyński, M., Nerode, A. (eds.) LPNMR 1995. LNCS (LNAI), vol. 928, pp. 358–371. Springer, Heidelberg (1995)
18. Kauffman, S.A.: Metabolic stability and epigenesis in randomly constructed genetic nets. Journal of Theoretical Biology 22(3), 437–467 (1969)
19. Kauffman, S.A.: The Origins of Order: Self-Organization and Selection in Evolution. Oxford University Press (1993)
20. Marek, V.W., Niemelä, I., Truszczyński, M.: Logic programs with monotone abstract constraint atoms. Theory and Practice of Logic Programming 8(2), 167–199 (2007)
21. Marek, W., Subrahmanian, V.S.: The relationship between stable, supported, default and autoepistemic semantics for general logic programs. Theoretical Computer Science 103(2), 365–386 (1992)
22. Marek, W., Truszczyński, M.: Autoepistemic logic. Journal of the ACM 38(3), 588–619 (1991)
23. Saccà, D., Zaniolo, C.: Stable models and non-determinism in logic programs with negation. In: Proceedings of the 9th ACM SIGMOD-SIGACT Symposium on Principles of Database Systems, pp. 205–217 (1990)
24. Shmulevich, I., Dougherty, E.R., Zhang, W.: From Boolean to probabilistic Boolean networks as models of genetic regulatory networks. Proceedings of the IEEE 90(11), 1778–1792 (2002)
25. Tamura, T., Akutsu, T.: Detecting a singleton attractor in a Boolean network utilizing SAT algorithms. IEICE Trans. 92-A(s), 493–501 (2009)
26. van Emden, M.H., Kowalski, R.A.: The semantics of predicate logic as a programming language. Journal of the ACM 23(4), 733–742 (1976)
27. Van Gelder, A., Ross, K., Schlipf, J.S.: The well-founded semantics for general logic programs. Journal of the ACM 38(3), 620–650 (1991)
28. Wolfman, S.: Cellular Automata And Complexity: Collected Papers. Westview Press (1994)
29. You, J.H., Yuan, L.: A three-valued semantics for deductive database and logic programs. Journal of Computer and System Sciences 49, 334–361 (1994)
30. You, J.H., Yuan, L.: On the equivalence of semantics for normal logic programs. Journal of Logic Programming 22(3), 212–222 (1995)

Applying Visible Strong Equivalence in Answer-Set Program Transformations*

Tomi Janhunen and Ilkka Niemelä

Aalto University
Department of Information and Computer Science
P.O. Box 15400, FI-00076 Aalto, Finland
{Tomi.Janhunen,Ilkka.Niemela}@aalto.fi

Abstract. Strong equivalence is one of the basic notions of equivalence that have been proposed for logic programs subject to the answer-set semantics. In this paper, we propose a new generalization of strong equivalence which takes the visibility of atoms into account and we characterize it in terms of revised SE-models. Our design resembles (relativized) strong equivalence but is essentially different due to the strict correspondence of models adopted from the notion of visible equivalence. We illustrate the use of visible strong equivalence when showing correct program transformations introducing lots of auxiliary atoms. Moreover, we present a translation which enables us to automate the task of verifying the visible strong equivalence of SMODELS programs having enough visible atoms.

1 Introduction

Answer-set programming (ASP) [1] is a declarative problem solving paradigm where the solutions of a problem are determined by computing *answer sets* [10,11,17], originally coined as *stable models* [9], for a logic program representing the problem. The rapid improvement of answer-set *solvers* has made ASP a viable way to solve search problems arising in a variety of applications. The development and implementation of answer-set programs involves different kinds of rule-level transformations such as normalization and optimization of rules. The soundness of such transformations is highly important but nontrivial to establish due to the global nature of answer-set semantics.

The notion of *strong equivalence* introduced by Lifschitz et al. [18] provides a solid foundation for such considerations (see, e.g., [4]) as it insists on the same meaning of programs in all possible contexts and it can be characterized in terms of superintuitionistic logic [7,18,23] and strong equivalence models [26,27]. The global nature of answer sets has also been addressed by compositionality results [15,19,22] which relate the answer sets of an entire program with the answer sets of its parts meeting certain criteria. A respective notion of *modular equivalence* is well-suited for inter-module comparisons but not really applicable to intra-module transformations, e.g., when a rule is substituted by others in a definition. In contrast, strong equivalence covers rule-level substitutions as it is a congruence relation for program union.

* The support from the Finnish Centre of Excellence in Computational Inference Research (COIN) funded by the Academy of Finland (under grant #251170) is gratefully acknowledged.

E. Erdem et al. (Eds.): Correct Reasoning, LNCS 7265, pp. 363–379, 2012.

Most programming languages provide mechanisms for hiding unnecessary details when constructing complex pieces of software. The input language of the SMODELS system [25] with its `hide` and `show` statements is not an exception in this respect. In fact, the use of auxiliary predicates typically favors the compactness of encodings but the interpretations of auxiliary predicates are not that interesting when answer sets are inspected. Then the question is how hiding auxiliary atoms should affect the notions of program equivalence. In this respect, there are a few existing approaches. The notion of *visible equivalence* [12] takes the user's perspective, i.e., the answer sets printed out by the solver, as the starting point. Due to high worst-case computational complexity[1], this notion has only been implemented in a limited setting [14] where hidden non-determinism is ruled out. There are also derivatives of strong equivalence [6,24,29,28] to support auxiliary predicates. The *relativized* variants of strong equivalence constrain context programs in terms of subsidiary signatures. However, this does not exactly amount to hiding auxiliary atoms in programs subject to comparison (see Examples 2 and 3 in Section 2). A potential solution to this aspect can be found in [6,24] where the projections of answer sets are introduced, but multiple copies of answer sets having identical projections are neglected in contrast to visible equivalence [12].

In this paper, we explore the middle ground between visible equivalence and the previous generalizations of strong equivalence. The goal is to pinpoint a notion which can be viewed as a relaxation of both visible and strong equivalence and which is applicable to a wider variety of program transformations. In particular, we aim to support transformations introducing auxiliary atoms and to establish their correctness in arbitrary contexts not referring to the auxiliary atoms in question. In the long run, we plan to partly automate verification steps required to check output produced by different translators. The rest of this paper is organized as follows. Some basic concepts of logic programs and definitions of equivalence relations are first recalled in Section 2. A new variant of strong equivalence is then worked out in Section 3 in close connection with relativized strong equivalence. To further motivate the reconstruction, we illustrate its potential for showing answer-set program transformations correct in Section 4. In Section 5, we concentrate on the problem of verifying whether two answer-set programs are visibly strongly equivalent in analogy to [14]. We present a translation which enables the use of answer-set solvers for the verification task. The contrast with other notions of equivalence is then briefly discussed in Section 6. The paper is concluded in Section 7.

2 Background

This section has a number of objectives. First, in Section 2.1, we recall several kinds of rules used to form logic programs in ASP. The resulting standard classes of programs are also defined. The semantics based on stable models is then defined in Section 2.2, giving rise to the basic notions of equivalence, viz. weak and strong equivalence, which are then reviewed in Section 2.3. Finally, we pave the way for a new *visibility-based* generalization of strong equivalence by reviewing previous approaches in Section 2.4.

[1] If all atoms are hidden, visible equivalence reduces to model counting—a #P-hard problem.

2.1 Frequently Used Classes of Logic Programs

In the sequel, we will address *propositional logic programs*, i.e., finite sets rules of the forms (1)–(5) where a, a_i's, b_j's, and c_k's are *propositional atoms* (or *atoms* for short) and $\sim$ denotes *default negation*. The intuition behind a *normal* rule of the form (1) is that the *head* atom a can be derived whenever the *body conditions* of the rule are satisfied, i.e., when the *positive* body atoms $b_1, \ldots, b_n$ are derivable by the other rules in the program but none of the *negative* body atoms $c_1, \ldots, c_m$ are. An abbreviation $a \leftarrow B, \sim C$ of (1) where $B = \{b_1, \ldots, b_n\}$ and $C = \{c_1, \ldots, c_m\}$ will also be used.

$$a \leftarrow b_1, \ldots, b_n, \sim c_1, \ldots, \sim c_m. \tag{1}$$

$$\{a_1, \ldots, a_h\} \leftarrow b_1, \ldots, b_n, \sim c_1, \ldots, \sim c_m. \tag{2}$$

$$a \leftarrow l \leq \{b_1, \ldots, b_n, \sim c_1, \ldots, \sim c_m\}. \tag{3}$$

$$a \leftarrow w \leq \{b_1 = w_{b_1}, \ldots, b_n = w_{b_n}, \sim c_1 = w_{c_1}, \ldots, \sim c_m = w_{c_m}\}. \tag{4}$$

$$a_1 \mid \ldots \mid a_h \leftarrow b_1, \ldots, b_n, \sim c_1, \ldots, \sim c_m. \tag{5}$$

The other rule types (2)–(5) extend the idea of a normal rule as follows. The head $\{a_1, \ldots, a_h\}$ of a *choice rule* (2) denotes a choice to be made when the body of the rule is satisfied: any of a_i's can be derived. A *cardinality rule* (3) is similar to a normal rule but its body becomes already satisfied whenever the number of satisfied body conditions is at least l. More generally, the body of a *weight rule* (4) is satisfied if the sum of weights (denoted by w_{b_j}'s and w_{c_k}'s above) of satisfied body conditions is at least w. Finally, the head $a_1 \mid \ldots \mid a_h$ of a *disjunctive rule* (5) must be satisfied, i.e., at least one of the head atoms is (minimally) derived, if the body is satisfied. We use analogous set-based shorthands for the extended rule types like $a \leftarrow w \leq \{B = W_B, \sim C = W_C\}$ for a weight rule (4) and $A \leftarrow B, \sim C$ for a disjunctive rule (5).

Typical (syntactic) classes of logic programs are as follows. *Normal logic programs* (NLPs) solely consist of normal rules (1). The fragment internally supported by the SMODELS system, also known as SMODELS programs, is based on the forms (1)–(4). The class of *weight constraint programs* (WCPs) allows more liberal use of cardinality and weight constraints but WCPs are easy to translate into SMODELS programs using auxiliary atoms. Last, the class of *disjunctive logic programs* (DLPs) have disjunctive rules (5) as their building blocks; or normal rules (1) as their special case ($h = 1$). In the sequel, is not that crucial which class of logic programs is considered and thus we use the term *logic program* (or *program* for short) to refer to any finite set of rules—even allowing for hybrid programs that mix the rule types above. A rule is *positive* if $m = 0$ and it is of the forms (1), or (3)–(5). A program P is positive if its rules are all positive.

2.2 Stable Model Semantics

To define the formal semantics of programs, we write $\mathrm{At}(P)$ for the *signature*[2] of a program P, i.e., a set of atoms to which all atoms occurring in P belong to. An *interpretation* $I \subseteq \mathrm{At}(P)$ of P determines which atoms $a \in \mathrm{At}(P)$ are *true* ($a \in I$) and which atoms are *false* ($a \in \mathrm{At}(P) \setminus I$). Atoms are also called *positive literals*. Any

[2] Some references assume a global universe $\mathcal{U}$ of atoms that serves as $\mathrm{At}(P)$ if necessary.

negative literal $\sim c$ where c is an atom is treated classically, i.e., $\sim c$ is satisfied in I, denoted $I \models \sim c$, iff $I \not\models c$. The satisfaction relation $\models$ extends for other syntax as follows. For a body $B \cup \sim C$ of a normal/choice/disjunctive rule, let $I \models B \cup \sim C$ iff $I \models b$ for each $b \in B$ and $I \models \sim c$ for each $c \in C$. Quite similarly, the body $l \leq \{B, \sim C\}$ of a cardinality rule is satisfied in I iff $l \leq |B \cap I| + |C \setminus I|$. This can be generalized for the body $w \leq \{B = W_B, \sim C = W_C\}$ of a weight rule—satisfied in I iff the *weight sum* $\mathrm{WS}_I(B = W_B, \sim C = W_C) = \sum_{b \in B \cap I} w_b + \sum_{c \in C \setminus I} w_c$ is at least w. A rule r is satisfied in I, denoted $I \models r$, iff the satisfaction of its body implies the satisfaction of its head. As special cases, the head $\{A\}$ of a choice rule is always satisfied in I, and the head A of a disjunctive rule is satisfied in I iff $A \cap I \neq \emptyset$. An interpretation $I \subseteq \mathrm{At}(P)$ is a (*classical*) *model* of a program P, denoted $I \models P$, iff $I \models r$ for each rule $r \in P$. A model $M \models P$ is a $\subseteq$-*minimal model* of a program P iff there is no $M' \models P$ such that $M' \subset M$. The set of minimal models of P is denoted by $\mathrm{MM}(P)$. If P is positive and it has no disjunctive rules (5), then $|\mathrm{MM}(P)| = 1$.

Definition 1 (Reduct). *Given a program P and an interpretation $I \subseteq \mathrm{At}(P)$, the* reduct *of P with respect to I, denoted by P^M, contains*

1. *a rule $a \leftarrow B$ for each normal rule $a \leftarrow B, \sim C$ in P such that $I \models \sim C$, and for each choice rule $\{A\} \leftarrow B, \sim C$ in P such that $a \in A \cap I$ and $I \models \sim C$;*
2. *a rule $a \leftarrow l' \leq \{B\}$ for each cardinality rule $a \leftarrow l \leq \{B, \sim C\}$ in P where $l' = \max(0, l - |C \setminus I|)$;*
3. *a rule $a \leftarrow w' \leq \{B = W_B\}$ for each weight rule*
$$a \leftarrow w \leq \{B = W_B, \sim C = W_C\}$$
in P where $w' = \max(0, w - \mathrm{WS}_I(\sim C = W_C))$; and
4. *a rule $A \leftarrow B$ for each disjunctive rule $A \leftarrow B, \sim C$ in P such that $I \models \sim C$.*

It is worth noting that P^M is always a positive program so that $\mathrm{MM}(P^M) \neq \emptyset$. The following generalizes the respective definitions of stable models from [9,11,25].

Definition 2 (Stable Model). *An interpretation $M \subseteq \mathrm{At}(P)$ of a* logic program *P is a* stable model *of P if and only if $M \in \mathrm{MM}(P^M)$.*

The number of stable models of P, also known as the *answer sets* of P, can vary in general and we let $\mathrm{SM}(P)$ stand for the set of stable models associated with P.

2.3 Basic Notions of Equivalence

The formal semantics provided by stable models gives rise to a straightforward notion of equivalence. Given two logic programs P and Q, they are defined to be *weakly equivalent*, denoted $P \equiv Q$, if and only if $\mathrm{SM}(P) = \mathrm{SM}(Q)$, i.e., the answer sets of P and Q are exactly the same subsets of $\mathrm{At}(P)$ and $\mathrm{At}(Q)$, respectively. The syntactic class of programs is not crucial for the definition so that even inter-class comparisons using $\equiv$ make sense. The definition of strong equivalence [18], however, assumes a context program R which makes its definition specific to a particular class of programs. So, given logic programs P and Q from the class of interest, they are *strongly equivalent*, denoted

$P \equiv_s Q$, if and only if $P \cup R \equiv Q \cup R$ for any logic program R from the same class. By setting $R = \emptyset$, it is easy to see that $P \equiv_s Q$ implies $P \equiv Q$. The converse does not hold in general, e.g., $P \equiv Q$ and $P \not\equiv_s Q$ hold for $P = \{a.\}$ and $Q = \{a \leftarrow {\sim}b.\}$ as witnessed by the context $R = \{b.\}$. In contrast to weak equivalence, strong equivalence allows for substitutions of mutually equivalent programs in arbitrary contexts. Hence $\equiv_s$ is a *congruence relation* for $\cup$, i.e., $P \equiv_s Q$ implies $P \cup R \equiv_s Q \cup R$ for any context program R from the class under consideration.

It is possible to characterize strong equivalence without explicitly referring to context programs [26,27]. A *strong equivalence model* (SE-model for short) of a program P is a pair $\langle X, Y \rangle$ of interpretations where $X \subseteq Y \subseteq \mathrm{At}(P)$ such that $Y \models P$ and $X \models P^Y$. The set of SE-models of P is denoted by $\mathrm{SE}(P)$. It follows for any programs P and Q that $P \equiv_s Q$ if and only if $\mathrm{SE}(P) = \mathrm{SE}(Q)$. This characterization makes the notion of strong equivalence independent of the class of programs under consideration—enabling the substitution of P by Q, or vice versa, as long as the respective unions of programs are well-defined in the context. Moreover, if $P \not\equiv_s Q$ holds, the space of witnessing contexts R, for which $\mathrm{SM}(P \cup R) \neq \mathrm{SM}(Q \cup R)$ holds, appears to be much larger than that of counter-models certifying $\mathrm{SE}(P) \neq \mathrm{SE}(Q)$. However, there are results [18,29] indicating that only contexts consisting of *unary* rules are sufficient. In our case, such rules are obtained as special cases of (1)–(5) when $n = 1$ and $m = 0$.

2.4 Visibility-Based Variants

A typical answer-set program involves auxiliary atoms that formalize some secondary concepts for the problem being solved. They are not directly needed in order to inspect the solution(s) of the problem and hence it is customary to hide them from the user whereas the rest of atoms remain visible. To formalize this idea, we follow the approach of [12] and write $\mathrm{At_v}(P)$ and $\mathrm{At_h}(P)$ for the *visible* and *hidden* signatures of P, respectively, so that $\mathrm{At}(P) = \mathrm{At_v}(P) \cup \mathrm{At_h}(P)$. The point is that given $M \in \mathrm{SM}(P)$ only $M \cap \mathrm{At_v}(P)$ is visible to the user and relevant when comparing P with other programs. Given a program P, an interpretation $I \subseteq \mathrm{At}(P)$ and a set of atoms $A \subseteq \mathrm{At}(P)$, we write $I|_A$ for the *projection* $I \cap A$ of the interpretation I over A and, in particular, I_v and I_h for the respective projections $I|_{\mathrm{At_v}(P)}$ and $I|_{\mathrm{At_h}(P)}$. We extend these notations for sets of interpretations $S \subseteq \mathbf{2}^{\mathrm{At}(P)}$ by $S|_A = \{I|_A \mid I \in S\}$, $S_\mathrm{v} = \{I_\mathrm{v} \mid I \in S\}$, and analogously for S_h. Thus, e.g., $\mathrm{SM}(P)_\mathrm{v}$ consists of M_v for each $M \in \mathrm{SM}(P)$.

The basic relations $\equiv$ and $\equiv_s$ introduced in Section 2.3 count on all atoms being visible, i.e., $\mathrm{At_v}(P) = \mathrm{At}(P)$ and $\mathrm{At_h}(P) = \emptyset$ hold for programs subject to comparison. The notion of *visible equivalence* [12], denoted by $\equiv_\mathrm{v}$, generalizes $\equiv$ for comparisons where the visibility of atoms really matters. Projections are compared as follows.

Definition 3. *Given logic programs P and Q such that $\mathrm{At_v}(P) = \mathrm{At_v}(Q)$ and sets of interpretations $S_1 \subseteq \mathbf{2}^{\mathrm{At}(P)}$ and $S_2 \subseteq \mathbf{2}^{\mathrm{At}(Q)}$, the sets S_1 and S_2 are* visibly equal, *denoted by $S_1 =_\mathrm{v} S_2$, if and only if there is a bijection $f : S_1 \to S_2$ such that (i) for every $I \in S_1$, $I_\mathrm{v} = f(I)_\mathrm{v}$ and (ii) for every $I, J \in S_1$, $I_\mathrm{h} = J_\mathrm{h}$ implies $f(I)_\mathrm{h} = f(J)_\mathrm{h}$.*

Definition 4 (Visible Equivalence [12]). *Logic programs P and Q are* visibly equivalent, *denoted by $P \equiv_\mathrm{v} Q$, if and only if $\mathrm{At_v}(P) = \mathrm{At_v}(Q)$ and $\mathrm{SM}(P) =_\mathrm{v} \mathrm{SM}(Q)$.*

It is straightforward to show that both $=_{\mathrm{v}}$ and $\equiv_{\mathrm{v}}$ are equivalence relations in their respective domains. The strict (bijective) correspondence of stable models underlying $\equiv_{\mathrm{v}}$ goes back to formalizing the user's view in the presence of hidden atoms: it is possible that a particular projection of stable models is printed out by the solver multiple times because the mutual differences concern only hidden atoms. From a more theoretical perspective, such a tight relationship preserves the different reasoning modes of ASP such as *brave* and *cautions* reasoning up to counting answer sets.

Example 1. If $\mathrm{SM}(P) = \{\{a\}, \{b\}\}$ and $\mathrm{SM}(Q) = \{\emptyset, \{b\}\}$, then $P \equiv_{\mathrm{v}} Q$ holds if $\mathrm{At}_{\mathrm{v}}(P) = \{b\} = \mathrm{At}_{\mathrm{v}}(Q)$, i.e., a is hidden. It is easy to see that b is only a brave but not a cautious consequence with respect to both P and Q. However, if a is made visible a bijective mapping between stable models in the sense of $=_{\mathrm{v}}$ becomes impossible. ■

Definition 4 treats the visible projections of $\mathrm{SM}(P)$ and $\mathrm{SM}(Q)$ as multisets, i.e., the number of copies of each projection with respect to $\mathrm{At}_{\mathrm{v}}(P)$ and $\mathrm{At}_{\mathrm{v}}(Q)$ matter. Indeed, the condition $\mathrm{SM}(P) =_{\mathrm{v}} \mathrm{SM}(Q)$ differs from $\mathrm{SM}(P)_{\mathrm{v}} = \mathrm{SM}(Q)_{\mathrm{v}}$ which would lead us to the *projective notions* of equivalence addressed in [6]. The condition (ii) in Definition 3 strengthens the notion from [12] and it ensures that the mapping f is *coherent*, i.e., interpretations having the same hidden part over $\mathrm{At}_{\mathrm{h}}(P)$ are mapped by f as a group: their images must accordingly have equal hidden parts over $\mathrm{At}_{\mathrm{h}}(Q)$. It is also worth pointing out that the definition of $\equiv_{\mathrm{v}}$ is independent of the syntax of programs which enables natural comparison of programs belonging to different syntactic classes.

There are also existing generalizations of strong equivalence [18] which take the visibility of atoms into account. For instance, the idea behind a *relativized* version of strong equivalence [28] is to constrain potential contexts R using a fixed set of atoms A such that $\mathrm{At}(R) \subseteq A$. The concept can be further refined [29] by introducing distinct sets of atoms H and B to constrain head and body atoms appearing in the rules of context programs, respectively. But, when H and B coincide, the more general notion is thus reduced to relativized strong equivalence whose definition recalled next.

Definition 5 (Relativized Strong Equivalence [28]). *Logic programs P and Q are strongly equivalent relative to A, denoted by $P \equiv_{\mathrm{s}}^{A} Q$, if and only if* $\mathrm{SM}(P \cup R) = \mathrm{SM}(Q \cup R)$ *for all context programs R such that* $\mathrm{At}(R) \subseteq A$.

At first glance Definitions 4 and 5 look incompatible. However, we obtain an interesting special case by assuming $\mathrm{At}_{\mathrm{v}}(P) = A = \mathrm{At}_{\mathrm{v}}(Q)$. In this setting, the context program R may interact with P and Q through visible atoms only.

Example 2. Consider a logic program P consisting of a single choice rule $\{a\} \leftarrow {\sim}b$ and let Q be its tentative translation into *normal* rules $a \leftarrow {\sim}\overline{a}, {\sim}b$ and $\overline{a} \leftarrow {\sim}a$ where $\overline{a}$ is an auxiliary atom to be hidden. So, let $\mathrm{At}_{\mathrm{v}}(P) = \{a, b\} = \mathrm{At}_{\mathrm{v}}(Q)$ and $\overline{a} \in \mathrm{At}_{\mathrm{h}}(Q)$. For the context $R = \emptyset$, we obtain $\mathrm{SM}(P \cup R) = \{\emptyset, \{a\}\}$ and $\mathrm{SM}(Q \cup R) = \{\{\overline{a}\}, \{a\}\}$ so that $P \not\equiv_{\mathrm{s}}^{\{a,b\}} Q$. Thus $\equiv_{\mathrm{s}}^{\{a,b\}}$ does not capture our intuition about the translation Q, i.e., it should be equivalent with P in any context respecting the definition of $\overline{a}$. ■

This example suggests potential relaxations of Definition 5, allowing stable models to differ over atoms in $\mathrm{At}_{\mathrm{h}}(P)$ and $\mathrm{At}_{\mathrm{h}}(Q)$. Designing such a variant shall be the topic of Section 3. Before that we recall the characterization of $\equiv_{\mathrm{s}}^{A}$ in terms of A-SE-models defined below, i.e., $P \equiv_{\mathrm{s}}^{A} Q$ holds iff $A\text{-SE}(P) = A\text{-SE}(Q)$.

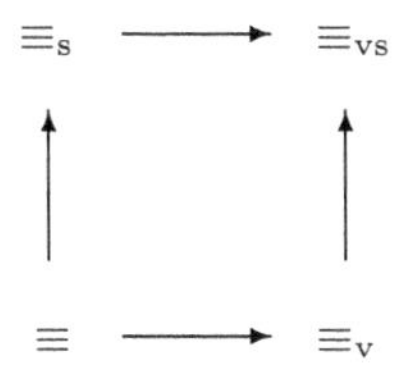

Fig. 1. Orthogonal Generalizations of Weak Equivalence (≡)

Definition 6 (Relativized SE-Models [28]). *A pair $\langle X, Y\rangle$ of interpretations is an A-SE-interpretation of P if and only if $Y \subseteq \mathrm{At}(P)$ and either $X = Y$ or $X \subseteq Y|_A$.*

Moreover, an A-SE-interpretation $\langle X, Y\rangle$ of P is an A-SE-model of P if and only if (i) $Y \models P$, (ii) there is no $Y' \subset Y$ such that $Y'|_A = Y|_A$ and $Y' \models P^Y$, and (iii) if $X \subset Y$, then there is $X' \subseteq Y$ such that $X'|_A = X$ and $X' \models P^Y$.

The idea is that Y is a $\subseteq$-minimal model of P^Y when the interpretation of the atoms in A, i.e., $Y|_A$, is kept *fixed* in the sense of *parallel circumscription* [16,21]. The third condition ensures that a *non-total* $X \subset Y$ can be extended to a model X' of P^Y such that $X'|_A = X$. Note that $Y \models P$ implies $Y \models P^Y$ by the fact that taking the reduct P^Y partially evaluates the negative body literals of P with respect to Y. Thus, given an A-SE-model $\langle X, Y\rangle$, being a model of P^Y is an essential property since Y has it and X can be extended to have it by assigning values to atoms residing outside A.

Example 3. Recall the program $P = \{\{a\} \leftarrow {\sim}b.\ \}$ of Example 2 and its potential normalization $Q = \{a \leftarrow {\sim}\overline{a}, {\sim}b.\ \ \overline{a} \leftarrow {\sim}a.\ \}$ subject to $A = \{a, b\}$. Due to the choice rule of P any subset Y of $\mathrm{At}(P) = \{a, b\}$ is a model of P. The reduct $P^Y = \emptyset$ except when $Y = \{a\}$ which implies $P^Y = \{a.\ \}$. Thus the A-SE-models of P are essentially $\langle\{a\}, \{a\}\rangle$ and for $Y \neq \{a\}$, $\langle X, Y\rangle$ where $X \subseteq Y$.

The classical models $Y \subseteq \mathrm{At}(Q) = \{a, \overline{a}, b\}$ of Q that satisfy the first two conditions of Definition 6 are $Y_1 = \{\overline{a}\}$, $Y_2 = \{a\}$, $Y_3 = \{\overline{a}, b\}$, and $Y_4 = \{a, b\}$. Note that $\{a, \overline{a}\}$ and $\{a, \overline{a}, b\}$ are not minimal due to presence of both a and $\overline{a}$. For Y_1, we obtain $Q^{Y_1} = \{\overline{a}.\ \}$ and an $\{a, b\}$-SE-model $\langle\emptyset, \{\overline{a}\}\rangle$. Similarly, $Q^{Y_2} = \{a.\ \}$ giving rise to $\langle\{a\}, \{a\}\rangle$. The reduct $Q^{Y_3} = \{\overline{a}.\ \}$ results in $\langle X_3, Y_3\rangle$ with $X_3 \subseteq \{b\}$ and, finally, Q^{Y_4} in $\langle X_4, Y_4\rangle$ where $X_4 \subseteq \{a, b\}$. The $\{a, b\}$-SE-models $\langle\emptyset, \{\overline{a}\}\rangle$, $\langle\emptyset, \{\overline{a}, b\}\rangle$, and $\langle\{b\}, \{\overline{a}, b\}\rangle$ of Q make the difference with respect to $\{a, b\}$-SE(P). Again, the difference is due to the hidden atom $\overline{a}$ involved in Q and its interpretations. ■

3 Visible Strong Equivalence

In this section, we restrict ourselves to a special case of the framework [28,29] and refine the corresponding notion of strong equivalence. The general objective is to relax some limitations of $\equiv_{\mathrm{s}}^A$ and to prove a stronger characterization theorem in order to establish wider applicability for the resulting variant of strong equivalence.

Our strategy is illustrated in Figure 1 where weak equivalence $\equiv$ is orthogonally being generalized as $\equiv_{\mathrm{s}}$ and $\equiv_{\mathrm{v}}$. The question is whether these ways to generalize

$\equiv$ can actually meet—hence arriving at a new relation $\equiv_{\mathrm{vs}}$ in the upper right corner. We use relativized strong equivalence $\equiv_{\mathrm{s}}^{A}$ as a starting point for the reconstruction. As hinted in Section 2.4, the mutual compatibility of $\equiv_{\mathrm{v}}$ and $\equiv_{\mathrm{s}}^{A}$ leads us to assume $\mathrm{At_v}(P) = A = \mathrm{At_v}(Q)$ for any programs P and Q subject to comparison. Given this assumption, it is possible to directly specialize Definitions 5 and 6 for a pair of programs P and Q, but as illustrated by Examples 2 and 3 there are programs which would not be strongly equivalent although one could intuitively argue the contrary.

In what follows, we propose a reconstruction of relativized strong equivalence to make it more generally applicable. A part of our solution is to restrict context programs on the basis of hidden atoms. We say that logic programs P and Q *mutually respect* their hidden atoms iff $\mathrm{At}(P) \cap \mathrm{At_h}(Q) = \emptyset$ and $\mathrm{At_h}(P) \cap \mathrm{At}(Q) = \emptyset$.

Definition 7 (Visible Strong Equivalence). *Programs P and Q are* visibly strongly equivalent, *denoted by $P \equiv_{\mathrm{vs}} Q$, if and only if $\mathrm{SM}(P \cup R) =_{\mathrm{v}} \mathrm{SM}(Q \cup R)$ for any context R that mutually respects the hidden atoms of P and Q.*

It should be emphasized that Definition 7 does not require that P and Q mutually respect their hidden atoms. Thus $\mathrm{At_h}(P)$ and $\mathrm{At_h}(Q)$ may overlap and the respective definitions of (shared) hidden atoms in P and Q need not coincide. For instance, Q could be a rewrite of P permuting the names of hidden atoms. Moreover, the context R may utilize hidden atoms if appropriate. Given $M \models P$, we say that M is $\mathrm{At_h}(P)$-minimal if and only if there is no $N \models P$ such that $N_{\mathrm{v}} = M_{\mathrm{v}}$ but $N_{\mathrm{h}} \subset M_{\mathrm{h}}$.

Definition 8. *A VSE-model of a logic program P is a pair $\langle X, Y\rangle$ of interpretations where $X \subseteq Y \subseteq \mathrm{At}(P)$ and both X and Y are $\mathrm{At_h}(P)$-minimal models of P^{Y}.*

The set of VSE-models of P is denoted by $\mathrm{VSE}(P)$. The intuition of a VSE-model $\langle X, Y\rangle$ is that the second component Y represents a context for P against which the rules of P are reduced (to form P^{Y}). Any visible atoms are interpreted classically whereas hidden ones are false by default. The first component X is a model capturing a potential closure of P^{Y} also defined to be minimal with respect to $\mathrm{At_h}(P)$.

It is worth pointing out the two extreme cases of Definitions 7 and 8. If $\mathrm{At_h}(P) = \emptyset$, then $\mathrm{VSE}(P) = \mathrm{SE}(P)$ and $\equiv_{\mathrm{vs}}$ coincides with $\equiv_{\mathrm{s}}$. If $\mathrm{At_v}(P) = \emptyset$, then $\mathrm{VSE}(P) = \{\langle M, M\rangle \mid M \in \mathrm{SM}(P)\}$ and $\equiv_{\mathrm{vs}}$ coincides with $\equiv_{\mathrm{v}}$ subject to $\mathrm{At_v}(P) = \emptyset$, i.e., comparing the numbers of stable models is then of interest.

Lemma 1. *For a program P and $I \subseteq \mathrm{At}(P)$, $I \models P$ if and only if $I \models P^{I}$.*

Proposition 1. *If $\langle X, Y\rangle \in \mathrm{VSE}(P)$, then $Y \models P$ and $X_{\mathrm{v}} = Y_{\mathrm{v}}$ implies $X = Y$.*

Our next objective is to define when two sets of VSE-models can be considered to be the same. In contrast to [28,29], we partly disregard hidden information from VSE-interpretations at this point. Given a set S of SE-interpretations, we define the projections $[S]_1 = \{X \mid \langle X, Y\rangle \in S\}$ and $[S]_2 = \{Y \mid \langle X, Y\rangle \in S\}$.

Definition 9. *Given programs P and Q such that $\mathrm{At_v}(P) = \mathrm{At_v}(Q)$, the respective sets $\mathrm{VSE}(P)$ and $\mathrm{VSE}(Q)$* visibly match, *denoted $\mathrm{VSE}(P) \stackrel{\mathrm{v}}{=} \mathrm{VSE}(Q)$, if and only if $[\mathrm{VSE}(P)]_2 =_{\mathrm{v}} [\mathrm{VSE}(Q)]_2$ via a bijection f and for each $Y \in [\mathrm{VSE}(P)]_2$,*

$$\{X_{\mathrm{v}} \mid \langle X, Y\rangle \in \mathrm{VSE}(P)\} = \{X_{\mathrm{v}} \mid \langle X, f(Y)\rangle \in \mathrm{VSE}(Q)\}. \tag{6}$$

Lemma 2. *If* $\mathrm{VSE}(P) \stackrel{\mathrm{v}}{=} \mathrm{VSE}(Q)$ *for programs* P *and* Q*, then* $P \equiv_{\mathrm{v}} Q$*.*

Lemma 3. *If programs* P_1 *and* P_2 *mutually respect their hidden atoms, then* $\mathrm{VSE}(P_1 \cup P_2) = \mathrm{VSE}(P_1) \bowtie \mathrm{VSE}(P_2)$ *where the* join $\mathrm{VSE}(P_1) \bowtie \mathrm{VSE}(P_2)$ *is the set of pairs* $\langle X_1 \cup X_2, Y_1 \cup Y_2 \rangle$ *for each* $\langle X_1, Y_1 \rangle \in \mathrm{VSE}(P_1)$ *and each* $\langle X_2, Y_2 \rangle \in \mathrm{VSE}(P_2)$ *such that (i)* $X_1 \cap \mathrm{At_v}(P_2) = X_2 \cap \mathrm{At_v}(P_1)$ *and (ii)* $Y_1 \cap \mathrm{At_v}(P_2) = Y_2 \cap \mathrm{At_v}(P_1)$*.*

The conditions (i) and (ii) of Lemma 3 essentially require $\langle X_1, Y_1 \rangle$ and $\langle X_2, Y_2 \rangle$ to be *compatible* [22], i.e., they assign the same truth values to their shared visible atoms. Hidden atoms do not affect compatibility since they are distinct by assumption.

Proof. Let $\langle X_1, Y_1 \rangle$ such that $X_1 \subseteq Y_1 \subseteq \mathrm{At}(P_1)$ and $\langle X_2, Y_2 \rangle$ such that $X_2 \subseteq Y_2 \subseteq \mathrm{At}(P_2)$ be compatible—making $X_1 \cup X_2$ and $Y_1 \cup Y_2$ disjoint so that X_1, X_2, Y_1, and Y_2 can be extracted as simple projections over $\mathrm{At}(P_1)$ and $\mathrm{At}(P_2)$. Then $Y_1 \cup Y_2 \models (P_1 \cup P_2)^{Y_1 \cup Y_2}$ iff $Y_1 \cup Y_2 \models P_1 \cup P_2$ (Lemma 1) iff $Y_1 \models P_1$ and $Y_2 \models P_2$ iff $Y_1 \models P_1^{Y_1}$ and $Y_2 \models P_2^{Y_2}$ (Lemma 1). Slightly more directly, we have $X_1 \cup X_2 \models (P_1 \cup P_2)^{Y_1 \cup Y_2}$ iff $X_1 \cup X_2 \models P_1^{Y_1} \cup P_2^{Y_2}$ iff $X_1 \models P_1^{Y_1}$ and $X_2 \models P_2^{Y_2}$. Moreover, as P_1 and P_2 mutually respect each other's hidden atoms, $\mathrm{At_h}(P_1 \cup P_2)$ is the disjoint union of $\mathrm{At_h}(P_1)$ and $\mathrm{At_h}(P_2)$. It follows that $Y_1 \cup Y_2$ is a $\mathrm{At_h}(P_1 \cup P_2)$-minimal model of $(P_1 \cup P_2)^{Y_1 \cup Y_2} = P_1^{Y_1} \cup P_2^{Y_2}$ iff Y_1 is a $\mathrm{At_h}(P_1)$-minimal model of $P_1^{Y_1}$ and Y_2 is a $\mathrm{At_h}(P_2)$-minimal model of $P_2^{Y_2}$. In summary, we have shown that $\langle X_1 \cup X_2, Y_1 \cup Y_2 \rangle \in \mathrm{VSE}(P_1 \cup P_2)$ if and only if $\langle X_1, Y_1 \rangle \in \mathrm{VSE}(P_1)$ and $\langle X_2, Y_2 \rangle \in \mathrm{VSE}(P_2)$. □

Our next goal is to characterize $\equiv_{\mathrm{vs}}$ in terms of VSE-models and in analogy to a number of results [27, Theorem 1], [20, Theorem 1], and [5, Theorem 4.5]. In our case, the bijective relationship of models plays its particular role in the result.

Theorem 1. *For programs* P *and* Q *with* $\mathrm{At_v}(P) = \mathrm{At_v}(Q)$*,* $\mathrm{VSE}(P) \stackrel{\mathrm{v}}{=} \mathrm{VSE}(Q)$ *implies* $P \equiv_{\mathrm{vs}} Q$*.*

Proof. Recall that by Definition 8, the sets $[\mathrm{VSE}(P)]_2$ and $[\mathrm{VSE}(Q)]_2$ are the $\mathrm{At_h}(P)$-minimal models Y of P^Y and the $\mathrm{At_h}(Q)$-minimal models Y' of $Q^{Y'}$, respectively.

Let $\mathrm{VSE}(P) \stackrel{\mathrm{v}}{=} \mathrm{VSE}(Q)$ via a bijection f from $[\mathrm{VSE}(P)]_2$ to $[\mathrm{VSE}(Q)]_2$. Then consider any context program R which mutually respects the hidden atoms of P and Q and the set $\mathrm{VSE}(R)$ associated with the context. It follows by Lemma 3 that $\mathrm{VSE}(P \cup R) = \mathrm{VSE}(P) \bowtie \mathrm{VSE}(R)$ and $\mathrm{VSE}(Q \cup R) = \mathrm{VSE}(Q) \bowtie \mathrm{VSE}(R)$. Then consider any $Y \in [\mathrm{VSE}(P \cup R)]_2$ for which there is $\langle X, Y \rangle \in \mathrm{VSE}(P \cup R)$. It follows that $\langle X_1, Y_1 \rangle \in \mathrm{VSE}(P)$ and $\langle X_2, Y_2 \rangle \in \mathrm{VSE}(R)$ where $X_1 = X \cap \mathrm{At}(P)$, $Y_1 = Y \cap \mathrm{At}(P)$, $X_2 = X \cap \mathrm{At}(R)$, and $Y_2 = Y \cap \mathrm{At}(R)$. Since $Y_1 \in [\mathrm{VSE}(P)]_2$, we can map it to $Y_1' = f(Y_1) \in [\mathrm{VSE}(Q)]_2$ such that $(Y_1')_{\mathrm{v}} = (Y_1)_{\mathrm{v}}$. Thus Y_1' is compatible with Y_2 as Y_1 is. By (6), there is $X_1' \subseteq Y_1'$ such that $\langle X_1', Y_1' \rangle \in \mathrm{VSE}(Q)$ and $(X_1')_{\mathrm{v}} = (X_1)_{\mathrm{v}}$. This makes X_1' compatible with X_2 as X_1 is. It follows that $\langle X', Y' \rangle \in \mathrm{VSE}(Q \cup R)$ for $X' = X_1' \cup X_2$ and $Y' = Y_1' \cup Y_2$. Thus $Y' \in [\mathrm{VSE}(Q \cup R)]_2$ and we have obtained a function $f'(Y) = Y' = Y_1' \cup Y_2 = f(Y \cap \mathrm{At}(P)) \cup (Y \cap \mathrm{At}(R))$ which is bijective and coherent as f is. To establish (6) in the presence of R, we have to analyze $X_{\mathrm{v}} \subseteq Y_{\mathrm{v}}$ such that $\langle X, Y \rangle \in \mathrm{VSE}(P \cup R)$. Using the same line of reasoning as above, we obtain $\langle X', Y' \rangle \in \text{VSE}(Q \cup R)$. A simple calculation yields $X'_\text{v} = (X'_1)_\text{v} \cup (X_2)_\text{v} = (X_1)_\text{v} \cup (X_2)_\text{v} = X_\text{v}$. This shows one half of (6) and the other follows by symmetry using the inverse of f. Thus $\text{VSE}(P \cup R) \stackrel{\text{v}}{=} \text{VSE}(Q \cup R)$ via f'. It follows by Lemma 2 that $\text{SM}(P \cup R) =_\text{v} \text{SM}(Q \cup R)$. Since R was an arbitrary context program mutually respecting the hidden atoms of both P and Q, we obtain $P \equiv_\text{vs} Q$ as desired. □

To establish the converse of Theorem 1, we need a sophisticated context program which is specific to a given $\text{At}_\text{h}(P)$-minimal model Y of P^Y. The goal is to capture (6) by detecting (i) each $X^i_\text{v} \subset Y_\text{v}$ for which there is $\langle X, Y \rangle \in \text{VSE}(P)$ such that $X_\text{v} = X^i_\text{v}$ and (ii) each $Z^j_\text{v} \subset Y_\text{v}$ for which there is no $\langle Z, Y \rangle \in \text{VSE}(P)$ such that $Z_\text{v} = Z^j_\text{v}$. Assuming that $X^1_\text{v}, \ldots, X^n_\text{v}$ and $Z^1_\text{v}, \ldots, Z^m_\text{v}$ are all such sets, i.e., $n + m = 2^{|Y_\text{v}|} - 1$, we write $\text{ctx}(Y_\text{v}; X^1_\text{v}, \ldots, X^n_\text{v}; Z^1_\text{v}, \ldots, Z^m_\text{v})$ for the context program specified below. New atoms $t_1, \ldots, t_n$ are used to activate tests associated with $X^1_\text{v}, \ldots, X^n_\text{v}$ individually whereas t activates analogous tests for $Z^1_\text{v}, \ldots, Z^m_\text{v}$ simultaneously. The atom u denotes inconsistency—the derivation of which implies the derivation of Y_v to stabilize Y.

$$
\begin{array}{rl}
t_1 \mid \ldots \mid t_n \mid t. & \\
x \mid u \leftarrow t_i. & (1 \leq i \leq n \text{ and } x \in X^i_\text{v}) \\
y_1 \mid u \leftarrow y_2, t_i. & (1 \leq i \leq n,\ y_1 \in Y_\text{v} \setminus X^i_\text{v}, \text{ and } y_2 \in Y_\text{v} \setminus X^i_\text{v}) \\
z \mid u_j \leftarrow t. & (1 \leq j \leq m \text{ and } z \in Z^j_\text{v}) \\
z_1 \mid u_j \leftarrow z_2, t. & (1 \leq j \leq m,\ z_1 \in Y_\text{v} \setminus Z^j_\text{v}, \text{ and } z_2 \in Y_\text{v} \setminus Z^j_\text{v}) \\
u \leftarrow u_1, \ldots, u_m, t. & \\
u_j \leftarrow u, t. & (1 \leq j \leq m) \\
u \leftarrow Y_\text{v}. & \\
y \leftarrow u. & (y \in Y_\text{v})
\end{array}
$$

Lemma 4. *Let P be a program, $Y \subseteq \text{At}(P)$ an interpretation, $X^1_\text{v}, \ldots, X^n_\text{v}$ and $Z^1_\text{v}, \ldots, Z^m_\text{v}$ all proper subsets of Y_v, and R the respective disjunctive context program $\text{ctx}(Y_\text{v}; X^1_\text{v}, \ldots, X^n_\text{v}; Z^1_\text{v}, \ldots, Z^m_\text{v})$ with $\text{At}_\text{v}(R) = Y_\text{v} \cup \{t, t_1, \ldots, t_n, u, u_1, \ldots, u_m\}$, $\text{At}_\text{h}(R) = \emptyset$, and R respecting the hidden atoms of P. Then*

1. *$Y \cup \{t, u, u_1, \ldots, u_m\} \in \text{SM}(P \cup R)$ iff Y is a $\text{At}_\text{h}(P)$-minimal model of P^Y and no Z^j_v is extendible to a model $Z \models P^Y$ such that $Z \subset Y$ and $Z_\text{v} = Z^j_\text{v}$, and*
2. *for any $1 \leq i \leq n$, $Y \cup \{t_i, u\} \in \text{SM}(P \cup R)$ iff Y is a $\text{At}_\text{h}(P)$-minimal model of P^Y and X^i_v is not extendible to a model $X \models P^Y$ such that $X \subset Y$ and $X_\text{v} = X^i_\text{v}$.*

Theorem 2. *For programs P and Q with $\text{At}_\text{v}(P) = \text{At}_\text{v}(Q)$, $P \equiv_\text{vs} Q$ implies $\text{VSE}(P) \stackrel{\text{v}}{=} \text{VSE}(Q)$.*

Proof. Let $P \equiv_\text{vs} Q$ hold, i.e., for any context R that is mutually compatible with P and Q, we have $\text{SM}(P \cup R) =_\text{v} \text{SM}(Q \cup R)$ which is induced by a context-specific bijection, say f_R. To show $\text{VSE}(P) \stackrel{\text{v}}{=} \text{VSE}(Q)$ let us consider any $Y \in [\text{VSE}(P)]_2$, i.e., Y is a $\text{At}_\text{h}(P)$-minimal model of P^Y. Let $X^1_\text{v}, \ldots, X^n_\text{v}$ be the proper subsets of Y_v which are extendible to $\text{At}_\text{h}(P)$-minimal models $X^1 \subset Y, \ldots, X^n \subset Y$ of P^Y and for which $\langle X^1, Y \rangle \in \text{VSE}(P), \ldots, \langle X^n, Y \rangle \in \text{VSE}(P)$. Define $Z^1_\text{v}, \ldots, Z^m_\text{v}$ as the proper subsets of Y_v none of which is extendible to a model $Z \subset Y$ of P^Y such that $Z_\text{v} = Z^j_\text{v}$. Then let R be the respective context program $\text{ctx}(Y_\text{v}; X^1_\text{v}, \ldots, X^n_\text{v}; Z^1_\text{v}, \ldots, Z^m_\text{v})$ with $\text{At}_\text{v}(R) = Y_\text{v} \cup T \cup U$, $T = \{t, t_1, \ldots, t_n\}$, $U = \{u, u_1, \ldots, u_m\}$, and $\text{At}_\text{h}(R) = \emptyset$. It follows by the first item of Lemma 4 that $V = Y \cup \{t\} \cup U \in \text{SM}(P \cup R)$. Then there is

$V' = f_R(V) \in \mathrm{SM}(Q \cup R)$ such that $V'_{\mathrm{v}} = V_{\mathrm{v}}$ over $\mathrm{At}_{\mathrm{v}}(P \cup R) = \mathrm{At}_{\mathrm{v}}(P) \cup T \cup U = \mathrm{At}_{\mathrm{v}}(Q) \cup T \cup U = \mathrm{At}_{\mathrm{v}}(Q \cup R)$, i.e., $V' \cap (T \cup U) = \{t\} \cup U$ and $Y'_{\mathrm{v}} = Y_{\mathrm{v}}$ for $Y' = V' \cap \mathrm{At}(Q)$. It follows that $R = \mathrm{ctx}(Y'_{\mathrm{v}}; X^1_{\mathrm{v}}, \ldots, X^n_{\mathrm{v}}; Z^1_{\mathrm{v}}, \ldots, Z^m_{\mathrm{v}})$. The first part of Lemma 4 implies the $\mathrm{At}_{\mathrm{h}}(Q)$-minimality of Y' so that $Y' \in [\mathrm{VSE}(Q)]_2$.

Additionally, no Z^j_{v} with $1 \leq j \leq m$ is extendible to $Z' \models Q^{Y'}$ such that $Z' \subset Y'$ and $Z'_{\mathrm{v}} = Z^j_{\mathrm{v}} \subset Y'_{\mathrm{v}}$, i.e., $\mathrm{VSE}(Q)$ does not contain a respective pair $\langle Z', Y' \rangle$. This implies the $\supseteq$-part of the equality (6). To show the $\subseteq$-part, let us consider any $\langle X, Y \rangle \in \mathrm{VSE}(P)$ such that $X_{\mathrm{v}} \subset Y_{\mathrm{v}}$. Thus $X_{\mathrm{v}} = X^i_{\mathrm{v}}$ for some $1 \leq i \leq n$ and X^i_{v} is clearly extendible a model $X \subset Y$ of P^Y such that $X_{\mathrm{v}} = X^i_{\mathrm{v}}$. It follows by the second item of Lemma 4 that $Y \cup \{t_i, u\} \notin \mathrm{SM}(P \cup R)$. Assuming that $Y' \cup \{t_i, u\} \in \mathrm{SM}(P \cup R)$ leads to a contradiction by the coherence of f_R^{-1} implied by the coherence of f_R. Thus $Y' \cup \{t_i, u\} \notin \mathrm{SM}(P \cup R)$ and the second part of Lemma 4 implies that X^i_{v} is extendible to a model $X' \models Q^{Y'}$ such that $X' \subset Y'$ and $X'_{\mathrm{v}} = X^i_{\mathrm{v}}$. Without loss of generality, we may assume that X' is also $\mathrm{At}_{\mathrm{h}}(Q)$-minimal so that $\langle X', Y' \rangle \in \mathrm{VSE}(Q)$ and $X'_{\mathrm{v}} = X^i_{\mathrm{v}}$ is contained in the right hand side of (6). The overall mapping $f : Y \mapsto Y'$ can be defined by $Y' = f(Y) = f_R(Y \cup \{t\} \cup U) \cap \mathrm{At}(Q)$ where the bijection $f_R : \mathrm{SM}(P \cup R) \to \mathrm{SM}(Q \cup R)$ is selected for each Y in turn. This ensures that f is both bijective and coherent as each individual mapping f_R is. □

4 Application in Program Transformations

In this section, we illustrate the use of visible strong equivalence in a practical setting. For instance, when translating answer-set programs into classical logic [13] the *normalization* of extended rule types (2)–(4) becomes an issue. In what follows, we will address the cases of choice and cardinality rules as illustrative examples. It should be emphasized that standard strong equivalence [18] and relativized strong equivalence [28,29] are not directly applicable due to hidden atoms and restricted unions of context programs (recall Example 2). In contrast, we use VSE-models and the correspondence established in Theorem 1 to argue for the correctness of normalization.

As presented in [13], a choice rule of the form (2) can be turned into a normal rule $d \leftarrow b_1, \ldots, b_n, \sim c_1, \ldots, \sim c_m$ where the head has been replaced by a new atom d denoting that the body of the rule is satisfied. Moreover, we need $2h$ normal rules

$$a_1 \leftarrow d, \sim\overline{a_1}. \qquad \overline{a_1} \leftarrow \sim a_1. \qquad \ldots \qquad a_h \leftarrow d, \sim\overline{a_h}. \qquad \overline{a_h} \leftarrow \sim a_h.$$

with new atoms $\overline{a_1}, \ldots, \overline{a_h}$ that denote the complements of $a_1, \ldots, a_h$, respectively.

Example 4. Consider a program P consisting of a single choice rule $\{a\} \leftarrow b, \sim c$ such that $\mathrm{At}_{\mathrm{v}}(P) = \{a, b, c\}$ and $\mathrm{At}_{\mathrm{h}}(P) = \emptyset$. The translation $Q = \{a \leftarrow d, \sim\overline{a}.\ d \leftarrow b, \sim c.\ \overline{a} \leftarrow \sim a.\ \}$ such that $\mathrm{At}_{\mathrm{v}}(Q) = \mathrm{At}_{\mathrm{v}}(P)$ and $\mathrm{At}_{\mathrm{h}}(Q) = \{\overline{a}, d\}$. Any subset $Y \subseteq \mathrm{At}(P)$ satisfies P. The reduct P^Y contains $a \leftarrow b$ iff $a \in Y$ and $c \notin Y$. Thus only $Y = \{a, b\}$ gives rise to exceptional VSE-models $\langle \emptyset, \{a, b\} \rangle$, $\langle \{a\}, \{a, b\} \rangle$, $\langle \{a, b\}, \{a, b\} \rangle$ whereas all other VSE-models based on $Y \neq \{a, b\}$ take the form $\langle X, Y \rangle$ with any $X \subseteq Y$. A summary of the VSE-models is given in the table below. Any model $Y \subseteq \mathrm{At}(P)$ of P (and P^Y) can be turned into a $\mathrm{At}_{\mathrm{h}}(Q)$-minimal model Y' of Q (resp. Q^Y) by adding $d \in Y'$ iff $b \in Y$ and $c \notin Y$, and by adding $\overline{a} \in Y'$ iff $a \notin Y$. The respective $\mathrm{At}_{\mathrm{h}}(Q)$-minimal models X' of $Q^{Y'}$ are listed in the final column of the table.

Y	P^Y	X	Y'	$Q^{Y'}$	X'
$\emptyset$		$\emptyset$	$\{\overline{a}\}$	$d \leftarrow b.\ \overline{a}.$	$\{\overline{a}\}$
$\{a\}$	$a \leftarrow b.$	$\emptyset \ldots \{a\}$	$\{a\}$	$a \leftarrow d.\ d \leftarrow b.$	$\emptyset \ldots \{a\}$
$\{b\}$		$\emptyset \ldots \{b\}$	$\{\overline{a}, b, d\}$	$d \leftarrow b.\ \overline{a}.$	$\{\overline{a}\}, \{\overline{a}, b, d\}$
$\{c\}$		$\emptyset \ldots \{c\}$	$\{\overline{a}, c\}$	$\overline{a}.$	$\{\overline{a}\}, \{\overline{a}, c\}$
$\{a, b\}$	$a \leftarrow b.$	$\emptyset, \{a\}, \{a, b\}$	$\{a, b, d\}$	$a \leftarrow d.\ d \leftarrow b.$	$\emptyset, \{a\}\ \{a, b, d\}$
$\{a, c\}$		$\emptyset \ldots \{a, c\}$	$\{a, c\}$	$a \leftarrow d.$	$\emptyset \ldots \{a, c\}$
$\{b, c\}$		$\emptyset \ldots \{b, c\}$	$\{\overline{a}, b, c\}$	$\overline{a}.$	$\{\overline{a}\} \ldots \{\overline{a}, b, c\}$
$\{a, b, c\}$		$\emptyset \ldots \{a, b, c\}$	$\{a, b, c\}$	$a \leftarrow d.$	$\emptyset \ldots \{a, b, c\}$

The sets $[\mathrm{VSE}(P)]_2$ and $[\mathrm{VSE}(Q)]_2$ are in one-to-one correspondence and coincide up to $\mathrm{At_v}(P) = \mathrm{At_v}(Q) = \{a, b, c\}$. It is also easy to check (6) for each pair Y and Y'. Thus $\mathrm{VSE}(P) \stackrel{\mathrm{v}}{=} \mathrm{VSE}(Q)$ and $P \equiv_{\mathrm{vs}} Q$ by Theorem 1. In other words, the choice rule and its translation behave identically in any context not referring to d and $\overline{a}$.

Finally, let us note that SE-models of P coincide with VSE-models. The relativized $\{a, b, c\}$-SE-models of Q can be obtained using the respective projections of X'. ■

Proposition 2. *Let P be a program consisting of a choice rule $\{A\} \leftarrow B, {\sim}C$ and Q its normalization in the way described above. Then* $\mathrm{VSE}(P) \stackrel{\mathrm{v}}{=} \mathrm{VSE}(Q)$.

Cardinality rules are much harder to normalize succinctly. In [13], we present a transformation following an approach introduced in the context of satisfiability checking [2]. To represent (3) in general, a total of $l \times (n + m - l + 1)$ new atoms $d_{i,j}$ are required. Here $1 \leq i \leq l$ is the count of satisfied literals and $l - i + 1 \leq j \leq n + m - i + 1$ points to the jth literal (either b_j or ${\sim}c_{j-n}$) in the body of (3). The reading of $d_{i,j}$ is that the number of satisfied literals, from the jth up to the $(n + m)^{\text{th}}$ literal, is at least i. Then $d_{l,1}$ captures the intended condition for the head a of (3). The rules are as follows:

$$
\begin{array}{ll}
a \leftarrow d_{l,1}. & \\
d_{i,j} \leftarrow d_{i,j+1}. & (1 \leq i \leq l \text{ and } l - i + 1 \leq j < n + m - i + 1) \\
d_{i,j} \leftarrow d_{i-1,j+1}, b_j. & (1 < i \leq l \text{ and } l - i + 1 \leq j \leq n) \\
d_{i,j} \leftarrow d_{i-1,j+1}, {\sim}c_{j-n}. & (1 < i \leq l \text{ and } \max(l, n+1) \leq j \leq n + m - i + 1) \\
d_{1,j} \leftarrow b_j. & (l \leq j \leq n) \\
d_{1,j} \leftarrow {\sim}c_{j-n}. & (\max(l, n+1) \leq j \leq n + m)
\end{array}
$$

The rules formalize a kind of a *counting grid* where vertical moves (up) increase i upon a satisfaction of a literal. Horizontal moves (left) are possible by default when a literal is not satisfied—decreasing j. The case $l = n = m = 1$ is further analyzed below.

Example 5. Consider a program P consisting of $a \leftarrow 1 \leq \{b, {\sim}c\}$ and its translation $Q = \{\ a \leftarrow d_{1,1}.\ d_{1,1} \leftarrow d_{1,2}.\ d_{1,1} \leftarrow b.\ d_{1,2} \leftarrow {\sim}c.\ \}$. Let $\mathrm{At_v}(P) = \mathrm{At_v}(Q) = \{a, b, c\}$, $\mathrm{At_h}(P) = \emptyset$, and $\mathrm{At_h}(Q) = \{d_{1,1}, d_{1,2}\}$. There are five classical models $Y \subseteq \mathrm{At}(P)$ of P and the reduct P^Y contains $a \leftarrow 1 \leq \{b\}$ if $c \in Y$, and $a \leftarrow 0 \leq \{b\}$ if $c \notin Y$. Each $Y \models P$ can be turned into a $\mathrm{At_h}(Q)$-minimal model Y' of Q by adding $d_{1,2} \in Y'$ iff $c \notin Y$, and by adding $d_{1,1} \in Y'$ iff $b \in Y$ or $c \notin Y$. The reduct $Q^{Y'}$ contains the first three rules of Q and $d_{1,2}$ as a fact iff $c \notin Y'$. The respective $\mathrm{At_h}(Q)$-minimal models X' are reported below:

Y	P^Y	X	Y'	X'
$\{a\}$	$a \leftarrow 0 \leq \{b\}$	$\{a\}$	$\{a, d_{1,1}, d_{1,2}\}$	$\{a, d_{1,1}, d_{1,2}\}$
$\{c\}$	$a \leftarrow 1 \leq \{b\}$	$\emptyset \ldots \{c\}$	$\{c\}$	$\emptyset \ldots \{c\}$
$\{a, b\}$	$a \leftarrow 0 \leq \{b\}$	$\{a\}, \{a, b\}$	$\{a, b, d_{1,1}, d_{1,2}\}$	$\{a, d_{1,1}, d_{1,2}\}$, $\{a, b, d_{1,1}, d_{1,2}\}$
$\{a, c\}$	$a \leftarrow 1 \leq \{b\}$	$\emptyset \ldots \{a, c\}$	$\{a, c\}$	$\emptyset \ldots \{a, c\}$
$\{a, b, c\}$	$a \leftarrow 1 \leq \{b\}$	$\emptyset \ldots \{a, c\}$, $\{a, b\}, \{a, b, c\}$	$\{a, b, c, d_{1,1}\}$	$\emptyset \ldots \{a, c\}$, $\{a, b, d_{1,1}\}, \{a, b, c, d_{1,1}\}$

Again, the bijective relationship of $Y \in [\text{VSE}(P)]_2$ with $Y' \in [\text{VSE}(Q)]_2$ is easy to inspect and, furthermore, (6) holds for each such pair of Y and $Y' = f(Y)$. Thus $\text{VSE}(P) \stackrel{\text{v}}{=} \text{VSE}(Q)$ and $P \equiv_{\text{vs}} Q$ follows by Theorem 1. ■

Proposition 3. *Let P be a program consisting of a cardinality rule $a \leftarrow l \leq \{B, {\sim}C\}$ and Q its normalization in the way described above. Then* $\text{VSE}(P) \stackrel{\text{v}}{=} \text{VSE}(Q)$.

5 Translation-Based Verification

The goal of this section is to develop a translation-based method to check whether $P \equiv_{\text{vs}} Q$ holds for two programs P and Q. We will restrict ourselves to the case of SMODELS programs and use SMODELS-compatible solvers (or solving mechanisms) for actual computations. To realize this, we have to further constrain the class of programs under consideration, i.e., we assume that each program has *enough visible atoms* (so called EVA property [14]). This means that given $I \subseteq \text{At}(P)$, the hidden part of P relative to I, denoted by P_{h}/I, has a unique stable model. Thus each $\text{At}_{\text{h}}(P)$-minimal model Y of P^Y becomes unique up to $\text{At}_{\text{v}}(P)$. This reduces the complexity of verifying $\equiv_{\text{vs}}$ to a level where actual SMODELS-compatible solvers can be used.

The overall translation for the verification task is devised in two steps. First we translate an SMODELS program P into another program $\text{Tr}_{\text{vs}}(P)$ which has the VSE-models of P as its stable models. The VSE-models of Q are analogously captured by $\text{Tr}_{\text{vs}}(Q)$. After this we can apply the existing translation $\text{Tr}_{\text{eq}}(\cdot, \cdot)$ for the verification of weak equivalence [14] to finalize our approach: $P \equiv_{\text{vs}} Q$ iff $\text{Tr}_{\text{vs}}(P) \equiv \text{Tr}_{\text{vs}}(Q)$ iff the symmetric translations $\text{Tr}_{\text{eq}}(\text{Tr}_{\text{vs}}(P), \text{Tr}_{\text{vs}}(Q))$ and $\text{Tr}_{\text{eq}}(\text{Tr}_{\text{vs}}(Q), \text{Tr}_{\text{vs}}(P))$ have no stable models. The translation $\text{Tr}_{\text{vs}}(P)$ (see below) introduces a new atom $a^\bullet$ for each atom $a \in \text{At}(P)$. These atoms are required to represent the unique *least model* $X = \text{LM}(P^Y)$ given a $\text{At}_{\text{h}}(P)$-minimal model Y of P^Y. For an arbitrary set $S \subseteq \text{At}(P)$, define the renamed version of S by setting $S^\bullet = \{a^\bullet \mid a \in S\}$.

Definition 10. *The translation* $\text{Tr}_{\text{vs}}(P)$ *extends an* SMODELS *program P with*

1. *choice rules $\{a\}$ and $\{a^\bullet\} \leftarrow a$ for each visible atom $a \in \text{At}_{\text{v}}(P)$;*
2. *a constraint $\leftarrow a^\bullet, {\sim}a$ for each visible atom $a \in \text{At}_{\text{v}}(P)$;*
3. *a rule $a^\bullet \leftarrow B^\bullet, {\sim}C$ for each normal rule $a \leftarrow B, {\sim}C$ in P;*
4. *a rule $a^\bullet \leftarrow B^\bullet \cup \{a\}, {\sim}C$ for each choice rule $\{A\} \leftarrow B, {\sim}C$ in P and each head atom $a \in A$; and*

5. *a rule* $a^\bullet \leftarrow l \leq \{B^\bullet, {\sim}C\}$ *for each cardinality rule* $a \leftarrow l \leq \{B, {\sim}C\}$ *in* P*;*
6. *a rule* $a^\bullet \leftarrow w \leq \{B^\bullet = W_{B^\bullet}, {\sim}C = W_C\}$ *for each weight rule* $a \leftarrow w \leq \{B = W_B, {\sim}C = W_C\}$ *in* P*.*

Let $\mathrm{At_v}(\mathrm{Tr_{vs}}(P)) = \mathrm{At_v}(P) \cup \mathrm{At_v}(P)^\bullet$ *and* $\mathrm{At_h}(\mathrm{Tr_{vs}}(P)) = \mathrm{At_h}(P) \cup \mathrm{At_h}(P)^\bullet$.

Theorem 3. *Let* P *be an* SMODELS *program with the EVA property and* $\mathrm{Tr_{vs}}(P)$ *its translation to capture the VSE-models of* P*. Then for any* $X \subseteq Y \subseteq \mathrm{At}(P)$, $\langle X, Y\rangle \in \mathrm{VSE}(P)$ *if and only if* $M = Y \cup X^\bullet \in \mathrm{SM}(\mathrm{Tr_{vs}}(P))$.

Proof. Consider any $\langle X, Y\rangle$ with $X \subseteq Y \subseteq \mathrm{At}(P)$ and the respective interpretation $Y \cup X^\bullet \subseteq \mathrm{At}(\mathrm{Tr_{vs}}(P))$. The reduct $\mathrm{Tr_{vs}}(P)^{Y \cup X^\bullet}$ consists of P^Y, the fact a for each $a \in Y_\mathrm{v}$, the rule $a^\bullet \leftarrow a$ for each $a \in X_\mathrm{v}$, the constraint $\leftarrow a^\bullet$ for each $a \in \mathrm{At_v}(P) \backslash Y_\mathrm{v}$, and $(P^Y)^\bullet$. It follows that $Y \cup X^\bullet = \mathrm{LM}(\mathrm{Tr_{vs}}(P)^{Y \cup X^\bullet})$ iff Y is a $\mathrm{At_h}(P)$-minimal model of P^Y, $X \subseteq Y$, and X is a $\mathrm{At_h}(P)$-minimal model of P^Y. Hence the result. □

Due to EVA property, the verification of the key condition (6) gets simpler. Given $Y \in [\mathrm{VSE}(P)]_2$ and $Y' \in [\mathrm{VSE}(P)]_2$, $Y'_\mathrm{v} = Y_\mathrm{v}$ implies $Y' = Y$. By this observation, the translation-based method for weak/visible equivalence [14] implies the following.

Corollary 1. *Let* P *and* Q *be* SMODELS *programs with the EVA property. Then* $P \equiv_\mathrm{vs} Q$ *iff* $\mathrm{Tr_{eq}}(\mathrm{Tr_{vs}}(P), \mathrm{Tr_{vs}}(Q))$ *and* $\mathrm{Tr_{eq}}(\mathrm{Tr_{vs}}(Q), \mathrm{Tr_{vs}}(P))$ *have no stable models.*

We have implemented the translation $\mathrm{Tr_{vs}}(\cdot)$ as additional functionality to a tool called CLASSIC[3] for computing classical models of SMODELS programs. We did some preliminary experiments using LP2NORMAL [13], LPEQ [14], and CLASP [8]. A random choice rule of 1000 literals can be proved to be visibly strongly equivalent with its normalization in 3.52 seconds. This is quite amazing, since a 12-literal choice rule has already 531 376 VSE-models. Similarly, a random cardinality rule of 30 literals can be proved visibly strongly equivalent with its translation in 12.33 seconds. For the sake of comparison, a random 12-literal cardinality rule has 13 745 VSE-models. In the future, we aim to automatically check that the output of LP2NORMAL is correct (for debugging purposes) by considering each rule of the input program and its translation in turn.

6 Related Work

The approach taken in this paper is closely related to [28]. The definitions of A-SE-models and VSE-models are very close to each other: the main difference is in the X-part. The original definition (given as Definition 6) records only the (visible) projection with respect to A and hence distinguishes the *total* case $X = Y$ from *non-total* ones $X \subset Y$. In contrast, Definition 8 makes the roles of X and Y analogous. This reflects the idea that $\mathrm{At_h}(P)$-minimal models act as natural representatives of classical models in the presence of hidden atoms. The hidden parts are concealed when comparing sets of VSE-models using the correspondence (6). The correspondences of answer sets are also different, i.e., $\mathrm{SM}(P \cup R) = \mathrm{SM}(Q \cup R)$ versus $\mathrm{SM}(P \cup R) \overset{\mathrm{v}}{=} \mathrm{SM}(Q \cup R)$.

[3] Published under `http://research.ics.aalto.fi/software/asp/`

The signatures of programs are made explicit in our approach—favoring the counting of models if appropriate. Numbers of models can become very large or even infinite if some background signature (such as $\mathcal{U}$ in [28,29,6]) is fixed for programs of interest.

The general framework based on *equivalence frames* [6] generalizes relativized strong equivalence, parameterized by the set A, by incorporating a further parameter set B for answer-set projection (as further analyzed in [24]). However, projections are treated differently from $=_{\mathrm{v}}$. It is required for programs P and Q in a context R with $\mathrm{At}(R) \subseteq A$ that $\mathrm{SM}(P \cup R)\,|_B = \mathrm{SM}(Q \cup R)\,|_B$. For instance, the copies of answer sets which are created when a disjunctive rule $a \mid b$ (or the respective normal rules $a \leftarrow {\sim}b$ and $a \leftarrow {\sim}b$ obtained via shifting) with $a, b \in A \setminus B$ is added, cannot necessarily be distinguished. There are also differences in corner cases: $\mathrm{At}_{\mathrm{v}}(P) = \emptyset$ implies model counting for $\equiv_{\mathrm{vs}}$ but $B = \emptyset$ means checking whether answer sets exist on an equal basis. It is also worth pointing out that the two approaches coincide in the case of SMODELS programs having the EVA property as used in Section 5. However, knowing that $P \equiv_{\mathrm{vs}} Q$ brings us more information about P and Q than just knowing that P and Q are strongly equivalent relative to A and B (subject to $\mathrm{At}_{\mathrm{v}}(P) = A = B = \mathrm{At}_{\mathrm{v}}(Q)$).

The preservation of strong and *uniform equivalence* [3] under program transformations is addressed in [4]. A number of rule-level transformations from the literature, such as TAUT, RED^{-}, NONMIN, WGPPE, and CONTRA, are considered. These transformations do not involve auxiliary atoms and hence the original versions of strong and uniform equivalence are sufficient for the analysis.

7 Conclusions

In this paper, we explore the interconnection of strong equivalence [18] and visible equivalence [12] and propose *visible strong equivalence* as a reconstruction of relativized strong equivalence [28]. The characterization based on VSE-models suggests that the reconstruction is successful. In view of previous generalizations of strong equivalence, we have restricted ourselves to an interesting special case by fixing the relevant *parameter sets* (such as $\mathcal{U}$, $A \subseteq \mathcal{U}$, and $B \subseteq \mathcal{U}$ in [6]) with respect to the program's interface. The motivation of this goes back to practical tool development and the needs arising in that respect. We believe that strong visible equivalence will have both theoretical and practical value. As illustrated in Section 4, the notion can be used to prove translations introducing new auxiliary atoms generally correct in a very strict sense (formalized by $\equiv_{\mathrm{v}}$ and $\overset{\mathrm{v}}{=}$ in the paper). Moreover, the implementation described in Section 5 provides a basis for the systematic verification and debugging of rule-level translators. The EVA property is necessary to trade off computational complexity so that a polynomial translation is achievable and answer-set solvers themselves can be used for computations. The ground programs produced by front-ends, such as LPARSE and GRINGO, have this property by default unless too many atoms are intentionally hidden.

As regards future work, there is call for a rigorous complexity analysis of $\equiv_{\mathrm{vs}}$ in terms of $\#P$-oracles. Moreover, the close interconnection of *uniform equivalence* [3] and strong equivalence, as studied in [5], suggests an analogous extension for our approach using sets of facts rather than arbitrary programs as contexts.

References

1. Brewka, G., Eiter, T., Truszczynski, M.: Answer set programming at a glance. Communications of the ACM 54(12), 92–103 (2011)
2. Eén, N., Sörensson, N.: Translating pseudo-Boolean constraints into SAT. Journal on Satisfiability, Boolean Modeling and Computation 2(1–4), 1–26 (2006)
3. Eiter, T., Fink, M.: Uniform Equivalence of Logic Programs under the Stable Model Semantics. In: Palamidessi, C. (ed.) ICLP 2003. LNCS, vol. 2916, pp. 224–238. Springer, Heidelberg (2003)
4. Eiter, T., Fink, M., Tompits, H., Woltran, S.: Simplifying Logic Programs Under Uniform and Strong Equivalence. In: Lifschitz, V., Niemelä, I. (eds.) LPNMR 2004. LNCS (LNAI), vol. 2923, pp. 87–99. Springer, Heidelberg (2003)
5. Eiter, T., Fink, M., Woltran, S.: Semantical characterizations and complexity of equivalences in answer set programming. ACM Transactions on Computational Logic 8(3) (2007)
6. Eiter, T., Tompits, H., Woltran, S.: On solution correspondences in answer-set programming. In: Proceedings of the Nineteenth International Joint Conference on Artificial Intelligence, IJCAI 2005, pp. 97–102. Professional Book Center (2005)
7. Fink, M.: A general framework for equivalences in answer-set programming by countermodels in the logic of here-and-there. Theory and Practice of Logic Programming 11(2-3), 171–202 (2011)
8. Gebser, M., Kaufmann, B., Schaub, T.: The Conflict-Driven Answer Set Solver *clasp*: Progress Report. In: Erdem, E., Lin, F., Schaub, T. (eds.) LPNMR 2009. LNCS, vol. 5753, pp. 509–514. Springer, Heidelberg (2009)
9. Gelfond, M., Lifschitz, V.: The stable model semantics for logic programming. In: Proceedings of the 6th International Conference on Logic Programming, ICLP 1988, pp. 1070–1080 (1988)
10. Gelfond, M., Lifschitz, V.: Logic programs with classical negation. In: Proceedings of the 7th International Conference on Logic Programming, ICLP 1990, pp. 579–597 (1990)
11. Gelfond, M., Lifschitz, V.: Classical negation in logic programs and disjunctive databases. New Generation Computing 9, 365–385 (1991)
12. Janhunen, T.: Some (in)translatability results for normal logic programs and propositional theories. Journal of Applied Non-Classical Logics 16(1–2), 35–86 (2006)
13. Janhunen, T., Niemelä, I.: Compact Translations of Non-disjunctive Answer Set Programs to Propositional Clauses. In: Balduccini, M., Son, T.C. (eds.) Logic Programming, Knowledge Representation, and Nonmonotonic Reasoning. LNCS, vol. 6565, pp. 111–130. Springer, Heidelberg (2011)
14. Janhunen, T., Oikarinen, E.: Automated verification of weak equivalence within the Smodels system. Theory and Practice of Logic Programming 7(6), 697–744 (2007)
15. Janhunen, T., Oikarinen, E., Tompits, H., Woltran, S.: Modularity aspects of disjunctive stable models. Journal of Artificial Intelligence Research 35, 813–857 (2009)
16. Lifschitz, V.: Computing circumscription. In: Proceedings of the 9th International Joint Conference on Artificial Intelligence, Los Angeles, California, USA, pp. 121–127. Morgan Kaufmann (August 1985)
17. Lifschitz, V.: Answer set planning. In: Proceedings of the 16th International Conference on Logic Programming, ICLP 1999, pp. 23–37 (1999)
18. Lifschitz, V., Pearce, D., Valverde, A.: Strongly equivalent logic programs. ACM Transactions on Computational Logic 2(4), 526–541 (2001)
19. Lifschitz, V., Turner, H.: Splitting a logic program. In: Proceedings of the 11th International Conference on Logic Programming, ICLP 1994, Santa Margherita Ligure, Italy, pp. 23–37. MIT Press (1994)

20. Liu, L., Truszczynski, M.: Properties and applications of programs with monotone and convex constraints. Journal of Artificial Intelligence Research 27, 299–334 (2006)
21. McCarthy, J.: Applications of circumscription to formalizing commonsense knowledge. Artificial Intelligence 28, 89–116 (1986)
22. Oikarinen, E., Janhunen, T.: Achieving compositionality of the stable model semantics for smodels programs. Theory and Practice of Logic Programming 8(5-6), 717–761 (2008)
23. Pearce, D.: Equilibrium logic. Annals of Mathematics and Artificial Intelligence 47(1-2), 3–41 (2006)
24. Pührer, J., Tompits, H.: Casting Away Disjunction and Negation under a Generalisation of Strong Equivalence with Projection. In: Erdem, E., Lin, F., Schaub, T. (eds.) LPNMR 2009. LNCS, vol. 5753, pp. 264–276. Springer, Heidelberg (2009)
25. Simons, P., Niemelä, I., Soininen, T.: Extending and implementing the stable model semantics. Artificial Intelligence 138(1–2), 181–234 (2002)
26. Turner, H.: Strong Equivalence for Logic Programs and Default Theories (Made Easy). In: Eiter, T., Faber, W., Truszczyński, M. (eds.) LPNMR 2001. LNCS (LNAI), vol. 2173, pp. 81–92. Springer, Heidelberg (2001)
27. Turner, H.: Strong equivalence made easy: nested expressions and weight constraints. Theory and Practice of Logic Programming 3(4-5), 609–622 (2003)
28. Woltran, S.: Characterizations for Relativized Notions of Equivalence in Answer Set Programming. In: Alferes, J.J., Leite, J. (eds.) JELIA 2004. LNCS (LNAI), vol. 3229, pp. 161–173. Springer, Heidelberg (2004)
29. Woltran, S.: A common view on strong, uniform, and other notions of equivalence in answer-set programming. Theory and Practice of Logic Programming 8(2), 217–234 (2008)

From Turner's Logic of Universal Causation to the Logic of GK

Jianmin Ji and Fangzhen Lin

Department of Computer Science and Engineering
The Hong Kong University of Science and Technology
Clear Water Bay, Kowloon, Hong Kong
jijianmin@cse.ust.hk, flin@cs.ust.hk

Abstract. Logic of knowledge and justified assumptions, also known as logic of grounded knowledge (GK), was proposed by Lin and Shoham as a general logic for nonmonotonic reasoning. To date, it has been used to embed in it default logic, autoepistemic logic, and general logic programming under stable model semantics. Besides showing the generality of GK as a logic for nonmonotonic reasoning, these embeddings shed light on the relationships among these other logics. Along this line, we show that Turner's logic of universal causation can be naturally embedded into logic of GK as well.

1 Introduction

Lin and Shoham [1] proposed a logic with two modal operators **K** and **A**, standing for knowledge and assumption, respectively. The idea is that one starts with a set of assumptions (those true under the modal operator **A**), computes the minimal knowledge under this set of assumptions, and then checks to see if the assumptions were justified in that they agree with the resulting minimal knowledge. For instance, consider $\mathbf{A}p \supset \mathbf{K}p$. If one assumes p, then one can conclude $\mathbf{K}p$, thus the assumption that p holds is justified, and one gets a GK model where both $\mathbf{A}p$ and $\mathbf{K}p$ are true. However, there is no GK model of $\neg\mathbf{A}p \equiv \mathbf{K}p$ as one cannot deduce $\mathbf{K}p$ when assuming p but gets $\mathbf{K}p$ when not assuming p.

To date, there have been embeddings from default logic [2] and autoepistemic logic [3] to the logic of GK [1], as well as from general logic programs [4,5] to logic of GK [6]. Among others, these embeddings shed new lights on nonmonotonic reasoning, and have led to an interesting characterization of strong equivalence in logic programming [7,6], and helped relate logic programming to circumscription [1] as the semantics of GK is just a minimization together with an identity checking after the minimization. Here we add to this repertoire by providing an embedding from Turner's logic of universal causation [8] to logic of GK.

This paper is organized as follows. Section 2 reviews logic of GK and Turner's logic. Section 3 shows how Turner's logic can be embedded in GK. Finally, Section 4 concludes this paper.

E. Erdem et al. (Eds.): Correct Reasoning, LNCS 7265, pp. 380–385, 2012.

2 Preliminaries

2.1 Propositional Languages

We assume a propositional language with two zero-place logical connectives $\top$ for tautology and $\bot$ for contradiction. We denote by *Atoms* the set of atoms, the signature of our language, and *Lit* the set of literals: $Lit = Atoms \cup \{\neg a \mid a \in Atoms\}$. A set I of literals is called *complete* if for each atom a, exactly one of $\{a, \neg a\}$ is in I.

In this paper we identify an interpretation with a complete set of literals. Thus if I is a complete set of literals, we use it as an interpretation when we say that it is a model of a formula, and we use it as a set of literals when we say that it entails a formula. In particular, we denote by $Th(I)$ the logical closure of I (considered to be a set of literals).

2.2 The Logic of GK

The language of GK proposed by Lin and Shoham [1] is a modal propositional language with two modal operators, **K**, for knowledge, and **A**, for assumption. GK *formulas* are propositional formulas with **K** and **A**. A GK *theory* is a set of GK formulas.

GK is a nonmonotonic logic, and its semantics is defined using the standard Kripke possible world interpretations. Informally speaking, a GK model is a Kripke interpretation where what is true under **K** is minimal and exactly the same as what is true under **A**. The intuition here is that given a GK formula, one first makes some assumptions (those true under **A**), then one minimizes the knowledge thus entailed, and finally checks to make sure that the initial assumption is justified in the sense that the minimal knowledge is the same as the initial assumption.

Formally, a *Kripke interpretation* M is a tuple $\langle W, \pi, R_K, R_A, s\rangle$, where W is a nonempty set of *possible worlds*, π a function that maps a possible world to an interpretation, R_K and R_A binary relations over W representing the accessibility relations for **K** and **A**, respectively, and $s \in W$, called the *actual world* of M. The *satisfaction relation* $\models$ between a Kripke interpretation $M = \langle W, \pi, R_K, R_A, s\rangle$ and a GK formula F is defined in a standard way as follows:

- $M \not\models \bot$,
- $M \models a$ if $a \in \pi(s)$, where a is an atom,
- $M \models \neg F$ iff $M \not\models F$,
- $M \models F \wedge G$ iff $M \models F$ and $M \models G$,
- $M \models F \vee G$ iff $M \models F$ or $M \models G$,
- $M \models F \supset G$ iff $M \not\models F$ or $M \models G$,
- $M \models \mathbf{K}F$ iff $\langle W, \pi, R_K, R_A, \omega\rangle \models F$ for any $\omega \in W$, such that $(s, \omega) \in R_K$,
- $M \models \mathbf{A}F$ iff $\langle W, \pi, R_K, R_A, \omega\rangle \models F$ for any $\omega \in W$, such that $(s, \omega) \in R_A$.

Note that, for any $\omega \in W$, $\pi(\omega)$ is an interpretation. We say that a Kripke interpretation M is a *model* of a GK formula F if M satisfies F, M is a *model* of a GK theory T if M satisfies every GK formula in T.

The modal logic that we have just defined corresponds to $\mathcal{K}$ [9], with two independent modal operators $\mathbf{K}$ and $\mathbf{A}$. In the following, we write $T \models \varphi$ if the modal formula φ is entailed by T in $\mathcal{K}$.

In the following, given a Kripke interpretation M, we let

$$\mathbf{K}(M) = \{\, \phi \mid \phi \text{ is a propositional formula and } M \models \mathbf{K}\phi \,\},$$
$$\mathbf{A}(M) = \{\, \phi \mid \phi \text{ is a propositional formula and } M \models \mathbf{A}\phi \,\}.$$

Notice that $\mathbf{K}(M)$ and $\mathbf{A}(M)$ are always closed under classical logical entailment.

Given a GK formula T, a Kripke interpretation M is a minimal model of T if M is a model of T and there does not exist another model M_1 of T such that $\mathbf{A}(M_1) = \mathbf{A}(M)$ and $\mathbf{K}(M_1) \subset \mathbf{K}(M)$. We say that M is a GK *model* of T if M is a minimal model of T and $\mathbf{K}(M) = \mathbf{A}(M)$.

We consider only a special kind of GK formulas. An $\mathbf{A}$-*atom* is a formula of the form $\mathbf{A}\phi$ and a $\mathbf{K}$-*atom* is a formula of the form $\mathbf{K}\phi$, where ϕ is a propositional formula. An $\mathbf{A}$-*literal* ($\mathbf{K}$-*literal*) is an $\mathbf{A}$-atom ($\mathbf{K}$-atom) or the negation of it. Both $\mathbf{A}$-atoms and $\mathbf{K}$-atoms are called GK-*atoms*. A GK-*literal* is a GK-atom or the negation of a GK-atom. A GK formula is called a *pure* GK *formula* if it is formed from GK-atoms and propositional connectives. A *pure* GK *theory* is a set of pure GK formulas. Similarly, a $\mathbf{K}$-*formula* is a GK formula formed from $\mathbf{K}$-atoms and propositional connectives and a $\mathbf{K}$-*theory* is a set of $\mathbf{K}$-formulas. Note that there is no nested occurrences of modal operators in pure GK theories or $\mathbf{K}$-theories.

So far in the applications of GK, only pure GK formulas are used. For instance, a (propositional) default theory $\Delta = (W, D)$ is translated into pure GK formulas in the following way:

1. Translate each $\phi \in W$ to $\mathbf{K}\phi$.
2. Translate each default $(\phi : \psi_1, \ldots, \psi_n / \varphi) \in D$ to

$$\mathbf{K}\phi \wedge \neg\mathbf{A}\neg\psi_1 \wedge \cdots \wedge \neg\mathbf{A}\neg\psi_n \supset \mathbf{K}\varphi \in \Delta_{GK}.$$

Similarly, a disjunctive logic program rule

$$p_1 \vee \cdots \vee p_k \leftarrow p_{k+1}, \ldots, p_t, \mathit{not}\, p_{t+1}, \ldots, \mathit{not}\, p_m,$$

where p's are atoms, corresponds to the following pure GK formula:

$$\mathbf{K}p_{k+1} \wedge \cdots \wedge \mathbf{K}p_t \wedge \neg\mathbf{A}p_{t+1} \wedge \cdots \wedge \neg\mathbf{A}p_m \supset \mathbf{K}p_1 \vee \cdots \vee \mathbf{K}p_k.$$

In this paper, we show how Turner's logic of universal causation can be embedded in GK.

2.3 Turner's Logic of Universal Causation

Turner's logic of universal causation [8], called UCL, is a nonmonotonic modal logic that generalizes McCain and Turner's causal action theories [10]. We first briefly review it here and then show how it can be embedded in GK.

The language of UCL is a modal propositional language with one modal operator **C**. Semantically, a UCL *structure* is a pair $(I, \mathcal{S})$, where $\mathcal{S}$ is a set of interpretations, and $I \in \mathcal{S}$. The satisfaction relation between UCL sentences and UCL structures is defined as follows:

$$(I, \mathcal{S}) \models a \text{ iff } I \models a \quad \text{(for any atom } a)$$
$$(I, \mathcal{S}) \models \mathbf{C}\phi \text{ iff for all } I' \in \mathcal{S},\ (I', \mathcal{S}) \models \phi$$

and the usual definition of propositional connectives.

Given a UCL theory T, we write $(I, \mathcal{S}) \models T$ to mean that $(I, \mathcal{S}) \models \phi$, for every $\phi \in T$. In this case, $(I, \mathcal{S})$ is said to be a *model* of T. We also say that $(I, \mathcal{S})$ is an *I-model* of T, emphasizing the distinguished interpretation I.

The semantics of UCL is defined by so-called causally explained interpretations: an interpretation I is *causally explained* by a theory T if $(I, \{I\})$ is the unique I-model of T.

Notice that this semantics is language-sensitive. For example, assuming that p is the only atom in the language, $\mathbf{C}p$ has a unique causally explained model $\{p\}$. However, if there is another atom, say q, then $\mathbf{C}p$ has no causally explained models.

It is easy to see that under this definition, for any theory T, I is causally explained by T iff it is causally explained by the theory obtained from T by removing all occurrences of **C** that are under the scope of another **C**. Thus, in the rest of the paper, we consider only UCL formulas that do not have a nested occurrence of **C**.

3 Embedding Turner's Logic of Universal Causation to GK

Now we show that Turner's logic can be embedded into GK by providing a translation from UCL theories to pure GK theories.

Given a UCL formula F without nested occurrences of **C**, let $tr_{GK}(F)$ be the pure GK formula obtained from F by replacing every occurrence of **C** by **K** and adding **A** before each atom which is not in the range of **C** in F. Given a UCL theory T, let $tr_{GK}(T) = \{tr_{GK}(F) \mid F \in T\}$. For example, if F is $(a \wedge \neg b) \supset \mathbf{C}(a \wedge \neg b)$, then $tr_{GK}(F)$ is $(\mathbf{A}a \wedge \neg \mathbf{A}b) \supset \mathbf{K}(a \wedge \neg b)$.

Given that causally explained interpretations depend on the underlying language used but GK models do not, it is clear that our translation from UCL to GK needs to have a language dependent component as well. In the following, if *Atoms* is the set of atoms in the language, we let

$$tr_{GK}(Atoms) = \{\mathbf{A}a \vee \mathbf{A}\neg a \mid a \in Atoms\}.$$

Our following result shows that in GK, $tr_{GK}(T) \cup tr_{GK}(Atoms)$ captures causally explained interpretations of T.

Theorem 1. *Let T be a UCL theory. If I is a causally explained interpretation of T, then there exists a GK model M of $tr_{GK}(T) \cup tr_{GK}(Atoms)$ such that $\mathbf{A}(M) = Th(I)$. Conversely, if M is a GK model of $tr_{GK}(T) \cup tr_{GK}(Atoms)$, then some interpretation I, $\mathbf{A}(M) = \mathbf{K}(M) = Th(I)$, and I is a causally explained interpretation of T.*

Proof. Given a pure GK theory T', if M is a model of $T' \cup tr_{GK}(Atoms)$, then $\mathbf{A}(M) = Th(I)$ for some interpretation I.

Given a UCL structure $(I, \mathcal{S})$, we can always create a Kripke interpretation M such that $\mathbf{A}(M) = Th(I)$ and $\mathbf{K}(M) = \bigcap_{I' \in \mathcal{S}} Th(I')$. Note that $I \in \mathcal{S}$, thus $\mathbf{K}(M) \subseteq \mathbf{A}(M)$, if $\{I\} \subset \mathcal{S}$, then $\mathbf{K}(M) \subset \mathbf{A}(M)$. From the definition of $tr_{GK}(T)$, if $(I, \mathcal{S})$ is a model of T, then M is a model of $tr_{GK}(T)$.

Given a Kripke interpretation M such that $\mathbf{A}(M) = Th(I)$ for some interpretation I and $\mathbf{K}(M) \subseteq \mathbf{A}(M)$, we can always create a UCL structure $(I, \mathcal{S})$ such that

$$\mathcal{S} = \{\, I' \mid \text{interpretation } I' \text{ satisfies every propositional formula in } \mathbf{K}(M) \,\}.$$

Note that $\mathbf{K}(M) \subseteq \mathbf{A}(M)$, thus $I \in \mathcal{S}$, if $\mathbf{K}(M) \subset \mathbf{A}(M)$, then $\{I\} \subset \mathcal{S}$. From the definition of $tr_{GK}(T)$, if M is a model of $tr_{GK}(T) \cup tr_{GK}(Atoms)$ such that $\mathbf{K}(M) \subseteq \mathbf{A}(M)$, then $\mathbf{A}(M) = Th(I)$ for some interpretation I and $(I, \mathcal{S})$ is a model of T.

From the above results, if I is a causally explained interpretation of T, then $(I, \{I\})$ is a model of T and there does not exist another model $(I, \mathcal{S})$ such that $\{I\} \subset \mathcal{S}$. We can create a Kripke interpretation M such that $\mathbf{A}(M) = \mathbf{K}(M) = Th(I)$. As $(I, \{I\})$ is a model of T, then M is a model of $tr_{GK}(T)$. There does not exist another model $(I, \mathcal{S})$ such that $\{I\} \subset \mathcal{S}$, then there does not exists another model M' of $tr_{GK}(T)$ such that $\mathbf{A}(M') = Th(I)$ and $\mathbf{K}(M') \subset \mathbf{A}(M')$, thus M is a GK model of $tr_{GK}(T)$, M is a GK model of $tr_{GK}(T) \cup tr_{GK}(Atoms)$.

If M is a GK model of $tr_{GK}(T) \cup tr_{GK}(Atoms)$, then $\mathbf{A}(M) = \mathbf{K}(M) = Th(I)$, where $I = (\mathbf{A}(M) \cap Atoms) \cup (\mathbf{A}(M) \cap \neg Atoms)$. Clearly, $(I, \{I\})$ is a model of T and there does not exist another model $(I, \mathcal{S})$ such that $\{I\} \subset \mathcal{S}$, thus I is a causally explained interpretation of T.

Let us call a GK model M *unary* if for some interpretation I we have that $\mathbf{A}(M) = Th(I)$. Thus by the above theorem, GK theories translated from UCL theories have only unary GK models.

Consider again the simple UCL theory $\{\mathbf{C}p\}$. If $Atoms = \{p\}$, then its GK translation is $\{\mathbf{K}p, \mathbf{A}p \vee \mathbf{A}\neg p\}$. This GK theory has a GK model and if M is such a GK model, then $\mathbf{A}(M) = \mathbf{K}(M) = Th(\{p\})$. However, if $Atoms = \{p, q\}$, then the GK translation is $\{\mathbf{K}p, \mathbf{A}p \vee \mathbf{A}\neg p, \mathbf{A}q \vee \mathbf{A}\neg q\}$, and there is no GK model for this theory as one could not deduce $\mathbf{K}q$ if $\mathbf{A}q$ is assumed, neither could one deduce $\mathbf{K}\neg q$ when $\mathbf{A}\neg q$ is assumed.

4 Conclusion

Logic of GK was proposed as a general framework for nonmonotonic reasoning. Like circumscription [11,12], it is based on minimization. To date, it has been shown to be able to embed fixed-point nonmonotonic logics such as default logic. In this paper, we show that it can embed Turner's logic of universal causation as well. One potential use of this result is to work as a bridge to connect fixed-point based causal action theories such as McCain and Turner's with minimization-based ones such as that in [13,14]. However, this remains future work.

Acknowledgements. We want to thank Vladimir Lifschitz for his pioneering work in nonmonotonic logic and reasoning about action that makes this work possible. In particular logic of GK was part of the second author's PhD thesis and Vladimir was on the thesis committee, and logic of universal causation was part of Hudson Turner's PhD thesis supervised by Vladimir. It should surprise no one that the two logics should be connected.

References

1. Lin, F., Shoham, Y.: A logic of knowledge and justified assumptions. Artificial Intelligence 57(2-3), 271–289 (1992)
2. Reiter, R.: A logic for default reasoning. Artificial Intelligence 13, 81–132 (1980)
3. Moore, R.: Semantical considerations on nonmonotonic logic. Artificial Intelligence 25(1), 75–94 (1985)
4. Ferraris, P.: Answer Sets for Propositional Theories. In: Baral, C., Greco, G., Leone, N., Terracina, G. (eds.) LPNMR 2005. LNCS (LNAI), vol. 3662, pp. 119–131. Springer, Heidelberg (2005)
5. Ferraris, P., Lee, J., Lifschitz, V.: A new perspective on stable models. In: Proceedings of International Joint Conference on Artificial Intelligence (IJCAI 2007), pp. 372–379 (2007)
6. Lin, F., Zhou, Y.: From answer set logic programming to circumscription via logic of gk. Artificial Intelligence 175(1), 264–277 (2011)
7. Lin, F.: Reducing strong equivalence of logic programs to entailment in classical propositional logic. In: Proceedings of the 8th International Conference on Principles and Knowledge Representation and Reasoning (KR 2002), pp. 170–176 (2002)
8. Turner, H.: Logic of universal causation. Artificial Intelligence 113(1), 87–123 (1999)
9. Chellas, B.: Modal logic. Cambridge University Press (1980)
10. McCain, N., Turner, H.: Causal theories of action and change. In: Proceedings of the 14th National Conference on Artificial Intelligence (AAAI 1997), pp. 460–465 (1997)
11. McCarthy, J.: Circumscription – a form of non-monotonic reasoning. Artificial Intelligence 13, 295–323 (1980)
12. McCarthy, J.: Applications of circumscription to formalizing commonsense knowledge. Artificial Intelligence 28, 89–118 (1986)
13. Lin, F.: Embracing causality in specifying the indirect effects of actions. In: Proceedings of International Joint Confernence on Artificial Intelligence (IJCAI 1995), pp. 1985–1993 (1995)
14. Lin, F., Soutchanski, M.: Causal theories of actions revisited. In: Proceedings of the 2011 AAAI Spring Symposium on Logical Formalization of Commonsense Reasoning (2011), `http://commonsensereasoning.org/2011/proceedings.html`

Lifschitz and Circumscription

Neelakantan Kartha

25750 SE 41st Street
Issaquah, WA 98029
gnkartha@yahoo.com

Abstract. This note provides a brief overview of Lifschitz's contributions to the definition of circumscription and to its application in commonsense reasoning.

1 Introduction

Circumscription, introduced by John McCarthy, is a technique for applying non-monotonic reasoning in first order logic. It has found application in a number of areas such as knowledge representation and the semantics of logic programs. Apart from McCarthy, the name most associated with circumscription is that of Vladimir Lifschitz.

2 McCarthy's Definition of Circumscription

The earliest reference to circumscription is from McCarthy's paper titled "Epistemological Problems of Artificial Intelligence" [McCarthy1977] . There, he wanted to formalize the intuition that sometimes we want to conclude that the known objects in a certain class are *all* the objects in that class. For example, assume that the object a satisfies the predicate P, and the function f maps objects satisfying P to other objects satisfying P. This can be formalized as

$$P(a) \wedge \forall x(P(x) \supset P(f(x))). \tag{1}$$

To formalize the intuition that these are *all* the objects satisfying P, McCarthy introduced the following sentence schema:

$$\Phi(a) \wedge \forall x(\Phi(x) \supset \Phi(f(x))) \supset \forall x(P(x) \supset \Phi(x)). \tag{2}$$

In this schema, Φ is a predicate variable for which any predicate may be substituted. Intuitively, schema (2) states that if there is an predicate Φ such that the object a satisfies the predicate Φ, and the function f maps objects satisfying Φ to other objects satisfying Φ, then the extent of P is a subset of the extent of Φ. In other words, the extent of P consists of just those objects satisfying (1). This version of circumscription came to be called domain circumscription.

The paper [McCarthy1980] defines a new version of circumscription called predicate circumscription. It is defined as follows. Let us denote by $A(P)$ a

E. Erdem et al. (Eds.): Correct Reasoning, LNCS 7265, pp. 386–389, 2012.

sentence in first order logic containing a predicate symbol[1] P and let $A(\Phi)$ denote the result of replacing all occurrences of P in $A(P)$ with Φ. Then the following schema is defined to be the circumscription of P in $A(P)$:

$$A(\Phi) \wedge \forall x(\Phi(x) \supset P(x)) \supset \forall x(P(x) \supset \Phi(x)) \tag{3}$$

Informally, (3) states that if Φ satisfies the conditions satisfied by P and its extent is a subset of the extent of P, then the extents of P and Φ coincide. Put another way, (3) states the the extent of P is minimal. The paper [McCarthy1980] also relates domain circumscription and predicate circumscription and gives several examples of how to apply predicate circumscription for knowledge represenation.

In [McCarthy1986], McCarthy proposes a generalization called formula circumscription that allows minimizing a formula, in contrast to predicate circumscription, which minimizes a predicate. Since formula circumscription has not found wide use in knowledge representation, we will not discuss it further.

3 Lifschitz's Definition of Circumscription

Lifschitz substantially refined and extended the formal treatment of circumscription in his 1985 paper titled "Computing Circumscription" [Lifschitz1985]. The definition given there is as follows. Let $A(P, Z)$ denote a sentence, where P is a tuple of predicate constants and Z a tuple of function and/or predicate constants disjoint with P. The circumscription of P in $A(P, Z)$ with variable Z is defined as the second order sentence

$$A(P, Z) \wedge \neg\exists p, z(A(p, z) \wedge p < P). \tag{4}$$

The $<$ symbol in the above expression is defined as follows: If U and V are n-ary predicates, $U \leq V$ stands for $\forall x_1 \ldots x_n(U(x_1, \ldots, x_n) \supset V(x_1, \ldots, x_n))$. $U = V$ stands for $U \leq V$ and $V \leq U$ and finally, $U < V$ stands for $U \leq V \wedge \neg(V \leq U)$. These definitions are extended to tuples of predicates in the obvious fashion.

The above definition is noteworthy for several reasons.

1. It uses a second order formula to define circumscription, instead of using a first order schema[2].
2. It minimizes several predicates, while at the same time allowing other predicates and functions to vary. This flexibility is crucial in applying circumscription to commonsense reasoning (see, for instance, [Baker1991],[Kartha1993]).
3. It makes it easy to see the relationship between circumscription and minimal models.

[1] For simplicity, we assume that the predicate symbol P has arity one. The generalization to predicates of higher arity is straightforward.

[2] Using a second order formula to define circumscription is also suggested in [McCarthy1977]

In the same paper, Lifschitz also defines a class of formulas called separable formulas, and shows that the circumscription of a separable first order sentence is first order sentence. This theorem allows one to easily compute circumscriptions of large classes of formulas that arise in practise. This was quite important, because prior to this development, obtaining the circumscription of a sentence was a non-trivial mathematical exercise.

Subsequently, Lifschitz defined several interesting variations of circumscription. For example, in "pointwise circumscription" [Lifschitz1987b], instead of a single minimality condition, the circumscription expresses the minimality of a predicate "at every point". It is interesting that this variation has proven quite useful in studying the properties of the standard definition of circumscription. As another example, [Lifschitz1989] introduces a version of circumscription that is similar to autoepistemic logic [Moore1985].

4 Lifschitz's Contributions to Applications of Circumscription

In addition to his work on defining circumscription and studying its properties, Lifschitz's work on applying circumscription has been quite influential. He brings his characteristic clarity and rigor to this important task, giving careful definitions and complete proofs. An early example is his paper on formal theories of action [Lifschitz1987a], where circumscription is applied to the task of formalizing reasoning about the effects of action. The formalization is novel in that it uses an axiomatization based on the causal connection between actions and effects. In contrast to many of the papers from that era, [Lifschitz1987a] carefully states the underlying assumptions and gives complete proofs.

Over the last two decades, Lifschitz has played leading role in applying nonmonotonic formalisms (including circumscription) to the task of knowledge representation. For instance, [Lifschitz1991] formulates theories of action in a general circumscriptive framework and proves theorems applicable not just to one theory, but a class of theories. [Kartha and Lifschitz1995] propose new formalization of action that is more amenable to automated techniques of computing circumscription. [Lifschitz1997] provides a circumscriptive framework for causal reasoning. More recently, he and colleagues have applied the notions of circumscription to give an alternate definition for the stable model semantics of logic programs [Ferraris *et al.*2011]. These examples show that in Lifschitz's hands, circumscription continues to be a versatile tool that provides valuable theoretical and practical insights into complex problems in commonsense reasoning.

References

[Baker1991] Baker, A.: Nonmonotonic reasoning in the framework of situation calculus. Artificial Intelligence 49, 5–23 (1991)

[Ferraris *et al.*2011] Ferraris, P., Lee, J., Lifschitz, V.: Stable models and circumscription. Artificial Intelligence 175, 236–263 (2011)

[Kartha and Lifschitz1995] Neelakantan Kartha, G., Lifschitz, V.: A simple formalization of actions using circumscription. In: Proc. of IJCAI 1995, pp. 1970–1975 (1995)

[Kartha1993] Neelakantan Kartha, G.: Soundness and completeness theorems for three formalizations of action. In: Proc. of IJCAI 1993, pp. 724–729 (1993)

[Lifschitz1985] Lifschitz, V.: Computing circumscription. In: Proc. of IJCAI 1985, pp. 121–127 (1985)

[Lifschitz1987a] Lifschitz, V.: Formal theories of action. In: Brown, F.M. (ed.) Proc. of the 1987 Workshop on The Frame Problem in Artificial Intelligence, pp. 35–58 (1987)

[Lifschitz1987b] Lifschitz, V.: Pointwise circumscription. In: Ginsberg, M. (ed.) Readings in Nonmonotonic Reasoning, pp. 179–193. Morgan Kaufmann, San Mateo (1987)

[Lifschitz1989] Lifschitz, V.: Between circumscription and autoepistemic logic. In: Brachman, R., Levesque, H., Reiter, R. (eds.) Proc. of the First Int'l Conf. on Principles of Knowledge Representation and Reasoning, pp. 235–244 (1989)

[Lifschitz1991] Lifschitz, V.: Towards a metatheory of action. In: Allen, J., Fikes, R., Sandewall, E. (eds.) Proc. of the Second Int'l Conf. on Principles of Knowledge Representation and Reasoning, pp. 376–386 (1991)

[Lifschitz1997] Lifschitz, V.: On the logic of causal explanations. Artificial Intelligence 96, 451–465 (1997)

[McCarthy1977] McCarthy, J.: Epistemological problems of artificial intelligence. In: Proc. of IJCAI 1977, pp. 1038–1044 (1977)

[McCarthy1980] McCarthy, J.: Circumscription—a form of non-monotonic reasoning. Artificial Intelligence 13(1–2), 27–39 (1980)

[McCarthy1986] McCarthy, J.: Applications of circumscription to formalizing common sense knowledge. Artificial Intelligence 28(1), 89–116 (1986)

[Moore1985] Moore, R.: Semantical considerations on nonmonotonic logic. Artificial Intelligence 25(1), 75–94 (1985)

Towards Formalizing Non-monotonic Reasoning in Physics: Logical Approach Based on Physical Induction and Its Relation to Kolmogorov Complexity

Vladik Kreinovich

University of Texas at El Paso, El Paso, TX 79968, USA
vladik@utep.edu
http://www.cs.utep.edu/vladik

Abstract. To formalize some types of non-monotonic reasoning in physics, researchers have proposed an approach based on Kolmogorov complexity. Inspired by Vladimir Lifschitz's belief that many features of reasoning can be described on a purely logical level, we show that an equivalent formalization can be described in purely logical terms: namely, in terms of physical induction.

One of the consequences of this formalization is that the set of not-abnormal states is (pre-)compact. We can therefore use Lifschitz's result that when there is only one state that satisfies a given equation (or system of equations), then we can algorithmically find this state. In this paper, we show that this result can be extended to the case of approximate uniqueness.

Keywords: non-monotonic reasoning, physical induction, uniqueness implies computability, approximate uniqueness

1 Non-monotonic Features of Physics Reasoning and Their Formalization Based on Kolmogorov Complexity

Non-monotonic Features of Physics Reasoning. Many areas of physics – ranging from quantum physics (the physics of microscopic objects) to cosmology (the physics of very large-scale objects) – have well-defined well-studied mathematical equations and models. At first glance, one may get an impression that these equations are all we need to make conclusions about the physical world. In practice, however, in addition to equations and precise logical conclusions, physicists also use intuitive informal reasoning – some of which is non-monotonic. Specifically, they believe that not all solutions to the corresponding equations are physically meaningful – only those solutions which are, in some reasonable sense, "typical" ("not abnormal"). Let us give a few examples of such reasoning; for details, see, e.g., [2].

First Example: Statistical Physics. The first example comes from the study of micro-objects, namely, from statistical physics. According to modern physics,

E. Erdem et al. (Eds.): Correct Reasoning, LNCS 7265, pp. 390–404, 2012.

all the molecules that form a gas are constantly in random motion. It is, in principle, possible that due to this motion, all the molecules of a gas will concentrate in one half of a vessel. The probability of this event is very low, but still positive; so, from the purely mathematical viewpoint, this event may occur – we just have to wait a very long time. Physicists, however, believe that such an event is simply not possible at all (see, e.g., [2], Vol. 1, Ch. 44). Their argument is that while mathematically, such an event is possible, this event is abnormal (atypical), and we should only consider not-abnormal (typical) situations.

This physicists' belief may sound unusual, but actually it is in good accordance with common sense. Indeed, if we toss a fair coin many times, then from the purely mathematical viewpoint, it is possible to have heads a hundred or even a million times in a row: the probability of this event is small, but if we wait long enough, it will happen. Similarly, in a state lottery, it is mathematically possible that the same person wins several times in a row. However, in practice, if the same individual wins a state lottery several times in a row, then every person using common sense will conclude that the lottery is rigged.

Second Example: Cosmology. Our second example comes from cosmology, the study of very large objects. According to modern physics, the large-scale state of the Universe is described by the equations of General Relativity. In principle, these equations allow many different types of solutions. Some of these solutions correspond to "generic" initial conditions, some to specific "degenerate" situations. It turns out that all solutions corresponding to the generic initial conditions have the same asymptotic. Because of this, physicists conclude that the actual space-time has this same asymptotic – this is the usual picture of the expansion following the Big Bang. The physicists' argument is that degenerate solutions are abnormal, and the actual solution should be not-abnormal; see, e.g., [10].

Third Example: General Physical Reasoning. One of the most productive way of making conclusions in physics is to use linearized versions of different equations. In general, the dependence $y = f(x_1, \ldots, x_n)$ of different physical quantities on each other is non-linear, but when the values x_i are close to some values $x_i^{(0)}$, we can expand the dependence $f(x_1, \ldots, x_n) = f(x_1^{(0)} + \Delta x_1, \ldots, x_n^{(0)} + \Delta x_n)$ into Taylor series in terms of the differences $\Delta x_i = x_i - x_i^{(0)}$ and retain only linear terms in this expansion. The physicists' usual argument (see, e.g., [2], Vol. 1, Section 9.6; Vol. 2, Chapters 6 an 19) is that quadratic terms are proportional to $\Delta x_i \cdot \Delta x_j$ and, since the differences Δx_i are small, these quadratic terms can be safely ignored.

For example, the non-linear differential equation describing a pendulum are usually approximated by a linear equation (that allows the known sinusoidal solutions). This approximation does not work when a pendulum is swinging with a large enough arc; in this case, we need to take quadratic and higher order terms into account. However, as long as the arc is small (e.g., smaller than 0.1 radian $\approx 6°$), we expect the predictions of the linear theory to be accurate proportional to the ignored quadratic terms $0.1^2 \approx 0.01$.

Of course, the Taylor series contain each quadratic term with a numerical factor. From the purely mathematical viewpoint, this factor can be huge, in which case we can no longer ignore the corresponding quadratic term. The physicists' argument is that such situations are abnormal, and in not-abnormal situations, each factor is reasonably small.

How to Formalize Such Reasoning: Let us Start with the Simplified Version of the Statistical Case. Let us start our description with the simplified version of the above statistical case. Crudely speaking, the above case means that if an event has a very small probability, then it cannot happen. Of course, we cannot take this statement literally: for example, we believe that it is not possible to have 1000 heads in a row when tossing a coin, but every other sequence of 1000 heads and tails has the same probability 2^{-1000}, and surely one of these sequences will appear if we toss a coin 1000 times.

The simplified statement is that if an event has probability 0, then it cannot happen. This statement may also sound unusual, but it is an implicit basis of all real-life conclusions about random events. For example, we usually believe that for a fair coin, in the limit, the frequency of heads tends to $1/2$. How do we justify this belief? From the purely mathematical viewpoint, the only conclusion that we can make is that the frequency of heads converges to $1/2$ with probability 1, i.e., that the probability that the frequency *does not* converge to $1/2$ is 0. So, when we transition from this mathematically justified conclusion to a belief that for the fair coin, the frequency tends to $1/2$, we implicitly use the statement that events with probability 0 cannot happen.

Similarly, we believe that deviations of the frequency from $1/2$ are (asymptotically) normally distributed – based on the mathematical result that this asymptotical behavior occurs with probability 1.

The above implicit statement – that events with probability 0 cannot occur – is the basis of Kolmogorov-Martin-Löf formalization of the notion of a random sequence (and, more generally, a random object); see, e.g., [7]. The need for such a definition comes from the fact that in traditional statistics, there is no definition of a random sequence, while from the physics viewpoint, some sequences are random and some are not. What we want from this definition is the ability to conclude that the random sequence satisfies all the laws of probability: that the frequency tends to $1/2$, that deviations from the frequency are asymptotically normally distributed, etc. It is therefore reasonable to define a random sequence as a sequence that satisfies all the corresponding probability laws.

A probability law can be defined as a statement which is true with probability 1 – and whose negation is true with probability 0. Thus, crudely speaking, a sequence is random if it belongs to every set of probability measure 1 – or, equivalently, does not belong to every set of probability measure 0. Of course, this cannot be literally true since for every infinite sequence x, the set $\{x\}$ consisting of this very sequence has probability measure 0. To make the above definition consistent, we must therefore restrict ourselves to sets which are *definable* in some reasonable language. So, we arrive at the first definition of randomness: *an element x of a probability space (X, p) is random$_{\rm A}$ if x is not an element of any* *definable set $Y \subseteq X$ of p-measure 0.* Every language has only countably many words, so if we require that an element does not belong to any definable set of measure 0, then we dismiss countably many set of measure 0 – i.e., a set of total measure 0. As a result, almost all sequences are random in this sense.

There are different versions of Kolmogorov-Martin-Löf (KM) complexity, depending on how we define definable sets. For example, if we consider sets which are computable (in some reasonable sense), then we get an equivalent definition in terms of Kolmogorov complexity $K(s)$ – the shortest length of a program that generates a string s. Intuitively, a sequence which is not random – such as 0101...01 – can be generated by a simple for-loop, while to generate a truly random sequence, we have to print the corresponding sequence of symbols one by one – and no shorter program can produce the given random sequence. Thus, for random strings, the Kolmogorov complexity is close to their length, while for non-random strings s, the Kolmogorov complexity is much smaller than the length $\text{len}(s)$: $K(s) \ll \text{len}(s)$. It turns out that an infinite sequence $x = x_1 x_2 \ldots$ is random if and only if, in some reasonable sense, $K(x_1 \ldots x_n) \approx \text{len}(x_1 \ldots x_n) = n$ for all n; see [7] for details.

From Simplified Version to a Full Statistical Case. The above notion of randomness formalizes the idea that events with probability 0 do not occur, but it still allows events with very small probability. For example, if we place million zeros in front of a KM-random sequence, the result is still KM-random. However, from the physicists' viewpoint, a sequence of coin toss results that starts with million heads cannot be truly random.

How can we formalize this? How can we formalize the physicists' idea that an event with a very small probability cannot occur? We have already mentioned that we cannot describe this idea by simply fixing some threshold p_0 and requiring that all events with probability $< p_0$ cannot occur. Instead, it is natural to use the following idea: for every definable decreasing sequence of events $A_1 \supseteq A_2 \supseteq A_3 \supseteq \ldots$, if the probability $P(A_n)$ tends to 0, then there exists an index N for which the probability is so small that this event cannot occur.

For example, for coin tosses, A_n is the set of all of the sequences for which the first n tosses resulted in all heads. Here, clearly, $A_n \supseteq A_{n+1}$ and $P(A_n) = 2^{-n} \to 0$, so there exists an N for which having N heads in a row is not possible.

In general, if we have a set X with a probability measure P, then a set $\mathcal{R} \subseteq X$ is called a *set-of-random-elements* if for every definable sequence of sets $A_n \subseteq X$ for which $A_n \supseteq A_{n+1}$ and $P(A_n) \to 0$, there exists an integer N for which $A_N \cap \mathcal{R} = \emptyset$ – i.e., for which no element from the atypical set A_N can be viewed as truly random. There are many sets that satisfy this condition, it is up to the physicists to find out which is the correct one – e.g., which which sequences of coin toss results are physically possible. Once such a set-of-random-elements $\mathcal{R}$ has been selected for a given probability space (X, p), we can then say that *an element $x \in X$ is random$_B$ if it belongs to the set $\mathcal{R}$.*

It is easy to prove that this new definition of randomness is indeed a refinement of the previous one, in the sense that every random$_B$ element is random$_A$. To prove this, for every definable set A of measure 0, we take $A_n = A$ for all n; then we can conclude that a random$_B$-element x does not belong to A – and is thus, random$_A$.

We can prove that this definition is not trivial, that there are infinite sets-of-random-elements. Specifically, for every $\varepsilon > 0$, there exists a set-of-random-elements of measure $\geq 1 - \varepsilon$. Indeed, there are countably many definable sequences of sets A_n with $p(A_n) \to 0$. Let us denote k-th such sequence by $A^k = \{A^k_n\}_n$. For each k, let n_k be the first index for which $p(A^k_{n_k}) \leq 2^{-k} \cdot \varepsilon$. Then, as the desired set $\mathcal{R}$, we can take the complement to the union $\bigcup\limits_k A^k_{n_k}$.

From Statistical Case to the General Description. In our other two examples, we do not have probabilities. However, we can raise a similar argument. For example, in our third example, we do not know beforehand how large the factors need to be for the situation to become abnormal, but we are confident that some values are too large to be typical. Similarly, we may not know which human heights are abnormal, but we know that some heights are too large to be normal.

In all these cases, we can consider the set A_n of all situations in which (the absolute values of) some factors exceed n. Here, $A_n \supseteq A_{n+1}$ and $\cap A_n = \emptyset$, and we conclude that there exists an integer N for which none of the elements of the set A_N are typical. Thus, we arrive at the following definition; see, e.g., [3,4,5]. For this definition, we need to select a theory $\mathcal{L}$ which is rich enough to contain all physicists' arguments and at the same time weak enough so that we will be able to formally talk about definability in $\mathcal{L}$; for a detailed discussion, see Appendix.

Definition 1. *Let $\mathcal{L}$ be a theory, and let $P(x)$ be a formula from the language of the theory $\mathcal{L}$, with one free variable x for which, in the theory $\mathcal{L}$, there exists a set $\{x \mid P(x)\}$. We will then call the set $\{x \mid P(x)\}$* $\mathcal{L}$-definable.

Comment. In the following text, we will assume that the language $\mathcal{L}$ is fixed, so we will simply talk about definability.

Definition 2. *Let X be a set. We say that a subset $\mathcal{T}$ is a* set-of-typical(not-abnormal)-elements *if for every definable sequence A_n for which $A_n \supseteq A_{n+1}$ and $\cap A_n = \emptyset$, there exists an integer N for which $A_N \cap \mathcal{T} = \emptyset$.*

Similarly to the random$_B$-case, there are many sets $\mathcal{T}$ that satisfy this condition; it is up to the physicists to find out which is the correct one. Once such a set-of-typical-elements $\mathcal{R}$ has been selected for a given probability space (X, p), we can then say that *an element $x \in X$ is typical (or random$_C$) if it belongs to the set $\mathcal{T}$.*

One can easily see that every set-of-random-elements is also a set-of-typical elements. So, each result about sets-of-typical-elements is applicable to sets-of-random-elements as well. The inverse is not always true: e.g., on the interval $[0, 1]$ with the usual probability measure, the set $\{0, 1\}$ is a set-of-typical-elements, but it is *not* a set-of-random-elements, since its elements 0 and 1 are not random$_A$.

Physical Induction: An Important Consequence of the above Definition. As a consequence of the above definition, we get an explanation of *physical induction:* the principle that when we have observed some property A sufficiently many times, then this property must be always true. This is how physical laws are confirmed: we perform a large number of experiments and/or observations, and if the hypothetic law is confirmed in all these experiments and observations, we consider it valid.

The principle of physical induction becomes a theorem if we assume that the state of the world s is not abnormal. Let $A(s,k)$ mean that the property A was confirmed during the k-th measurement. Then, physical induction means that there exists a natural number N_A (depending on A) such that if we have $A(s,1)$, $A(s,2)$, ..., $A(s,N_A)$, then $A(s,n)$ holds for every natural number n.

Proposition 1. *Let S be a set; its elements are called states of the world. Let $\mathcal{T} \subseteq S$ be a set of not-abnormal elements. Then, for every definable property A, there exists an integer N_A such that, if the state s is not abnormal (i.e., $s \in \mathcal{T}$) and the property $A(s,n)$ holds for all $n \le N_A$, then the property $A(s,n)$ holds for all natural numbers n.*

Comment. Physical induction can be described in purely logical terms, as the following deduction rule: $\dfrac{A(s,1), A(s,2), \ldots, A(s,N_A), \neg ab(s)}{A(s,n)}$, where $ab(s)$ means that $s \notin \mathcal{T}$.

Proof of Proposition 1. To prove this proposition, let us consider the the following sequence of sets $A_n \stackrel{\text{def}}{=} \{s : A(s,1) \,\&\, \ldots \,\&\, A(s,n) \,\&\, \neg\forall m\, A(s,m)\}$. One can easily see that this sequence is definable, that $A_n \supseteq A_{n+1}$, and that $\cap A_n = \emptyset$. Thus, by definition of a set of not-abnormal elements, there exists an integer N for which $A_N \cap \mathcal{T} = \emptyset$. This means that if $s \in \mathcal{T}$, then $s \notin A_N$. So, if $s \in \mathcal{T}$ and we have $A(s,1)$, ..., $A(s,N)$, then we cannot have $\neg\forall m\, A(s,m)$. Therefore, when $s \in \mathcal{T}$, we have the desired property $\forall m\, A(s,m)$.

Another Important Property: Every Set-of-Typical-Elements Is Pre-Compact and so, Inverse Problems become Well-Defined. Another important consequence of the above definition is related to the fact that usually, we do not directly observe the state of the world $s \in S$, we observe the result $r = f(s)$ of applying some transformation to this state. We would like to reconstruct the state s from this observation, as the state s for which $f(s) = r$, i.e., as the value $f^{-1}(r)$, where f^{-1} denotes an inverse function. This reconstruction problem is known in physics as an *inverse problem*.

One of the main challenges related to the inverse problem is that measurements are never absolutely accurate. As a result, instead of observing the exact combination of values $r = f(s)$, we observe a combination of values $\widetilde{r}$ which is *close* to r. It would be nice to be able to conclude that the corresponding reconstructed state $f^{-1}(\widetilde{r})$ is close to the actual state s – but for that, we need the inverse function f^{-1} to be continuous.

Most physical functions are continuous, so it is reasonable to assume that the function f is continuous. However, the inverse to a continuous function is, in general, not continuous. As a result, small changes in the measurement results can, in principle, lead to drastic changes in the reconstructed state. This discontinuity is described by saying that the inverse problem is *ill-defined*; see, e.g., [13].

To make a definite state reconstruction, physicists often make additional assumptions about the state: e.g., if we are reconstructing a signal $x(t)$, we assume certain bounds on the value of the signal and bounds on its derivative. The set of all the functions that satisfy these bounds form a compact set, and it is known that for a continuous function f from a compact set, its inverse f^{-1} is also continuous. Thus, once we impose such a restriction, the inverse problem becomes well-defined.

We will show that, in principle, there is no need to come up with artificial compactness restrictions: the mere suggestion that the state s is not abnormal (in the above precise sense) is sufficient to conclude that the corresponding set is compact. Let us describe this in precise terms.

Definition 3. *By a definable separable metric space, we mean a set X with a definable metric $d(x, y)$ and a definable sequence $\{x_n\}$ which is everywhere dense in the set X.*

Proposition 2. *Let X be a definable separable metric space, and let $\mathcal{T} \subseteq X$ be a set-of-typical-elements. Then, the closure $\overline{\mathcal{T}}$ of this set is a compact set.*

Proof of Proposition 2. In a separable metric space, a set C is compact if and only if it is closed and for each $\varepsilon > 0$, it has a finite ε-net, i.e., a finite set $c_1, \ldots, c_N$ for which every point $c \in C$ is $\leq \varepsilon$-close to one of these points c_i: $\forall c_{\in C}\, \exists i\, (d(c, c_i) \leq \varepsilon)$. The property that the points c_i form an ε-net is equivalent to the condition that the set C is covered by the union of the corresponding balls: $C \subseteq \cap B_\varepsilon(c_i)$, where $B_\varepsilon(c) \stackrel{\text{def}}{=} \{x : d(x, c) \leq \varepsilon\}$.

It is sufficient to prove the existence of an ε-net for rational values $\varepsilon > 0$ (actually, it is sufficient to prove it, e.g., for $\varepsilon = 2^{-k}$).

So, to prove that the closure $\overline{\mathcal{T}}$ is a compact set, it is sufficient to prove that for every rational number $\varepsilon > 0$, the set $\mathcal{T}$ has a finite ε-net. To prove this, let us consider the following sequence of sets: $A_n = X - \bigcup\limits_{i=1}^{n} B_\varepsilon(x_i)$. This sequence is definable – we have just given a definition, and it is easy to prove that $A_n \supseteq A_{n+1}$ and that $\cap A_n = \emptyset$. Thus, there exists an integer N for which $A_N \cap \mathcal{T} = \emptyset$, i.e., for which $\mathcal{T} \subseteq \bigcup\limits_{i=1}^{N} B_\varepsilon(x_i)$. Therefore, the elements $x_1, \ldots, x_N$ form a finite ε-net for the set $\mathcal{T}$. The proposition is proven.

Comment. One can show that a similar result does not hold if we use random$_A$ instead of random$_B$: e.g., on the real line with a normal distribution, the closure of the set of all random$_A$ elements is the whole real line – and is, thus, not compact. Thus, we cannot use a simpler definition random$_A$, we do need a more complex definition random$_B$.

2 First Result: Reformulating the above Definition of Typical Elements in Purely Logical Terms

Need for a Logical Formalization. Our objective is to formalize an important feature of the physicists' *reasoning*. Since logic is what describes reasoning, it is therefore natural to expect a formalization in terms of *logic*. Instead, we have a formalization in terms of sets. It is thus desirable to provide an equivalent formulation of the above definition in terms of logic.

Possibility of a Logical Formalization? In searching for such a logical reformulation, I was inspired by the experience of Vladimir Lifschitz who, via his numerous papers, showed that many important things related to human reasoning can be reformulated in logical terms. First, he worked in constructive mathematics, the analysis of algorithmic computability of different mathematical objects; in his research, among other things, he analyzed what can be expressed in the corresponding (intuitionistic) logic. Then, he started working in logic programming and in the formalization of commonsense reasoning; here, he also showed that many complex formalisms can be equivalently reformulated in terms of the corresponding logics.

Towards Our Result. In our case, there is already a logical consequence: physical induction. What we will prove here is that physical induction is not just a *consequence* of the above non-logical definition, it is actually *equivalent* to this definition.

Definition 4. *Let X be a set. We say that a property $ab(x)$* describes abnormality *if and only if for every definable property A, the following rule is valid for an some integer N_A (depending on A):* $\dfrac{A(x,1), A(x,2), \ldots, A(x,N_A), \neg ab(x)}{A(x,n)}$.

Theorem 1. *For every set X and for every property $ab(x)$, the following two conditions are equivalent to each other:*

- *the property $ab(x)$ describes abnormality (in the sense of Definition 4), and*
- *the set $\{x : \neg ab(x)\}$ is a set-of-typical-elements (in the sense of Definition 2).*

Proof of Theorem 1. We have already proven that if the set $\mathcal{T}$ is a set-of-typical-elements in the sense of Definition 2, then the corresponding property $ab(x) \Leftrightarrow x \notin \mathcal{T}$ describes abnormality in the sense of Definition 4. So, to complete our proof, we need to show that vice versa, if the property $ab(x)$ describes abnormality, then the set $\mathcal{T} \stackrel{\text{def}}{=} \{x : \neg ab(x)\}$ is a set-of-typical-elements.

Indeed, let A_n be a definable sequence of sets for which $A_n \supseteq A_{n+1}$ and $\cap A_n = \emptyset$. Let us take $A(x,k) \stackrel{\text{def}}{=} x \in A_k$. The general physical induction rules means that if we have $A(x,1), \ldots, A(x,N_A)$, and $\neg ab(x)$, then we have $\forall n\, A(x,n)$. In our case, this means that if $x \in A_1, \ldots, x \in A_{N_A}$, and $x \in \mathcal{T}$, then for every n, we have $x \in A_n$, i.e., we have $x \in \cap A_n$. Since $\cap A_n = \emptyset$, this means that it is not possible to have $x \in A_1, \ldots, x \in A_{N_A}$, and $x \in \mathcal{T}$. Thus, if we already know that $x \in \mathcal{T}$, then we cannot have $x \in A_1, \ldots$, and $x \in A_{N_A}$, i.e., we must have $x \notin A_k$ for some $k \le N_A$. For all such k, we have $A_k \supseteq A_{N_A}$, so $x \notin A_k$ implies $x \notin A_{N_A}$. Thus, $x \in \mathcal{T}$ implies that $x \notin A_{N_A}$, i.e., $\mathcal{T} \cap A_{N_A} = \emptyset$. The theorem is proven.

Comment. It is important to emphasize that physical induction is a *meta-rule*, a sequence of rules corresponding to different *definable* properties A. In general, it cannot be equivalently reformulated as a rule of second-order logic – which would mean that this implication holds for *all* properties A. Indeed, as we will show, the corresponding second-order logical statement

$$\forall A\, \exists N\, \forall x\, ((A(x,1)\,\&\, \ldots\, \&\, A(x,N)\,\&\, \neg ab(x)) \Rightarrow \forall n\, A(x,n))$$

implies that only finitely many elements are not-abnormal.

Indeed, let us assume that there are infinitely many not-abnormal elements. Then, we can find countably many among them. Let us denote these not-abnormal elements by $x_1, \ldots, x_n, \ldots$ Let us select the following property $A(x,k)$: $A(x,k)$ holds if and only if $x = x_i$ and $k \le i$. According to the above second-order formula, for this property A, there exists an integer N for which, for every not-abnormal element x, the condition $A(x,1)\,\&\, \ldots\, \&\, A(x,N)$ implies that $A(x,n)$ holds for every integer n. In particular, this implication is true for a not-abnormal element x_N. For this element, by definition of the property A, we have $A(x_N,1), \ldots, A(x_N,N)$, and $\neg ab(x_N)$. Thus, we should be able to conclude that $A(x_N,n)$ holds for every integer n, but by definition of the property A, the property $A(X_N,n)$ does not hold already for $n = N+1$.

This contradiction proves that under the second-order reformulation of physical induction, there are indeed only finitely many not-abnormal elements – and thus, that this reformulation is not adequate for describing physicists' intuition.

Comment. Our idea is similar to J. Pearl's ε-semantics for non-monotonic logic (see, e.g., [11]); once we require that the actual values are typical, the prerequisites for Pearl-type arguments automatically appear.

3 Second Result: Computability from Uniqueness to Approximate Uniqueness

Uniqueness Implies Computability: Reminder. In Section 2, we have shown that the closure of every set-of-typical-elements is compact. One computational advantage of compactness, as we have mentioned, is that inverse problems become well-defined.

Compactness also has another computational advantage: in a compact set, if we know that there is only one element with a certain property – e.g., the property that $F(x) = 0$ for some computable function f – then we can algorithmically find this element x. For example, if we are reconstructing the state s from measurement results $f(s) = (f_1(s), \ldots, f_m(s)) = (r_1, \ldots, r_m) = r$, then as the desired function $F(x)$ we can take the sum of the squares $F(x) = \sum\limits_{i=1}^{m} (f_i(x) - r_i)^2$.

To describe this result – originally proven by V. Lifschitz [8] – in precise terms, let us recall the definitions of computable numbers, computable functions, and computable compact sets; see, e.g., [12,14] (see also [1,6,9]).

Definition 5. *A real number x is called* computable *if there exists an algorithm (program) that transforms an arbitrary natural number k into a rational number r_k which is 2^{-k}-close to x. It is said that this algorithm* computes *the real number x.*

When we say that a computable real number is given, we mean that we are given an algorithm that computes this real number.

Definition 6. *A sequence of real numbers* $x_1, x_2, \ldots, x_n, \ldots$ *is called* computable *if there exists an algorithm (program) that transforms arbitrary natural numbers* n *and* k *into a rational number* r_{nk} *which is* 2^{-k}*-close to* x_n. *It is said that this algorithm* computes *the sequence* x_n.

When we say that a computable sequence of real numbers is given, we mean that we are given an algorithm that computes this sequence.

Definition 7. *By a* a computable metric space, *we mean a triple* $(X, d, \{x_n\})$, *where* (X, d) *is a metric space,* $\{x_1, x_2, \ldots, x_n, \ldots\}$ *is a dense subset of* X, *and there exists an algorithm that, given two natural numbers* i *and* j, *computes the distance* $d(x_i, x_j)$.

In other words, we have an algorithm that, given i, j, and an accuracy k, computes the 2^{-k}-rational approximation to $d(x_i, x_j)$.

Definition 8. *A point* $x \in X$ *of a computable metric space* $(X, d, \{x_n\})$ *is called* computable *if there exists an algorithm that transforms an arbitrary natural number* k *into a natural number* i *for which* $d(x, x_i) \leq 2^{-k}$. *It is said that this algorithm* computes *the point* x.

A space is a compact set if there is an algorithm that, given $\varepsilon = 2^{-k}$, computes the ε-net:

Definition 9. *A computable metric space* $(X, d, \{x_n\})$ *is called* a computable compact space *if there exists an algorithm that, given an arbitrary natural number* k, *returns a finite set of indices* $F_k \subset \{1, 2, \ldots, n, \ldots\}$ *such that for every* i *there is a* $f \in F_k$ *for which* $d(x_i, x_f) \leq 2^{-k}$.

Many real-life quantities x, y are related by an (efficiently computable) functional relation $y = F(x)$. For example, the volume V of a cube is equal to the cube of its linear size s: $V = F(s) = s^3$. This means that, once we know the linear size, we can compute the volume.

At every moment of time, we can only know an approximate value of the actual quality $x \in X$. Thus, to be able to compute $F(x)$ with a given accuracy 2^{-k}, we must:

- be able to tell with what accuracy we need to know x, and then
- be able to use the corresponding approximation to compute $F(x)$.

We thus arrive at the following definition.

Definition 10. *A function* $F : X \to X'$ *from a computable metric space* $(X, d, \{x_n\})$ *to a computable metric space* $(X', d', \{x'_n\})$ *is called* computable *if there exist two algorithms* U_F *and* φ *with the following properties:*

- *the algorithm* φ *takes a natural number* k *and produces a natural number* $\ell = \varphi(k)$ *such that* $d(x, y) \leq 2^{-\ell}$ *implies that* $d'(F(x), F(y)) \leq 2^{-k}$;
- U_F *takes two natural numbers* n *and* k *and produces a* 2^{-k}*-approximation to* $F(x_n)$, *i.e., a point* x'_ℓ *for which* $d'(x'_\ell, F(x_n)) \leq 2^{-k}$.

Several computability results are known for computable functions on computable compact spaces.

Proposition 3. *There exists an algorithm that, given a computable compact spaces X and a computable function $F : X \to R$ from X to real numbers, compute its maximum and its minimum on X.*

Proof. Indeed, to compute $M \stackrel{\text{def}}{=} \max F(x)$ with the accuracy 2^{-k}, we must first use the fact that F is computable and find with what accuracy $2^{-\ell}$ we must compute x to be able to estimate $F(x)$ with the accuracy $2^{-(k+1)}$. Then, we use the fact that X is a computable compact space to find a finite $2^{-\ell}$-net. For each point x_i from this $2^{-\ell}$-net, we compute the $2^{-(k+1)}$-approximation $\widetilde{F}(x_i)$ to the value $F(x_i)$. Then, $\widetilde{M} \stackrel{\text{def}}{=} \max \widetilde{f}(x_i)$ is the desired 2^{-k}-approximation to $M = \max f(x)$. Indeed, since $f(x_i) \geq \widetilde{F}(x_i) - 2^{-(k+1)}$, we have

$$M = \max F(x) \geq \max F(x_i) \geq \max \widetilde{F}(x_i) - 2^{-(k+1)} = \widetilde{M} - 2^{-(k+1)}.$$

On the other hand, since the values x_i form a $2^{-\ell}$-net, for every value x, there is an x_i for which $d(x, x_i) \leq 2^{-\ell}$ and hence $|F(x) - F(x_i)| \leq 2^{-(k+1)}$; therefore, $F(x) \leq \max F(x_i) + 2^{-(k+1)}$ for all x and $M = \max F(x) \leq \max F(x_i) + 2^{-(k+1)}$. Here, $F(x_i) \leq \widetilde{F}(x_i) + 2^{-(k+1)}$ so $M \leq \max \widetilde{F}(x_i) + 2^{-(k+1)} + 2^{-(k+1)} \leq \widetilde{M} + 2^{-k}$. The proposition is proven.

Proposition 4. [1] *If $G : X \to R$ is a computable mapping from a computable compact space X into real numbers, then, for every two rational numbers r and r' for which $r < r' \leq \max G(x)$, we can algorithmically produce a computable number $\alpha \in [r, r']$ for which the pre-image $\{x : G(x) \geq \alpha\}$ is also constructively compact (and the corresponding 2^{-k}-nets are also algorithmically produced).*

Now, we are ready to reproduce (and prove) Lifschitz's result that uniqueness implies algorithmic computability:

Proposition 5. [8] *There exists an algorithm that, given a computable function $F : X \to \mathbb{R}$ that has exactly one root x_0 (for which $F(x_0) = 0$) on a computable compact space X, computes this root x_0.*

Comment. While the result was first proven in [8], we will provide a different proof of this result, a proof that will be easy to modify to cover our new result as well.

Proof of Proposition 5. Let us show how to compute the root x_0 with a given accuracy $\delta > 0$. Let us take $\eta = \dfrac{\delta}{8}$, and build an η-net $\{p_1, \ldots, p_k\}$ for the computable compact space X. Let us compute the distances $d(p_i, p_j)$ between the points p_i with accuracy η. As a result, we get the values $\widetilde{d}(p_i, p_j)$ for which $\left|\widetilde{d}(p_i, p_j) - d(p_i, p_j)\right| \leq \eta$.

According to Proposition 4, for each $i = 1, \ldots, k$, there exists a value $\eta_i \in [\eta, 2\eta]$ for which the ball $B_i \stackrel{\text{def}}{=} B_{\eta_i}(p_i) = \{x : d(x, p_i) \leq \eta_i\}$ is a computable compact. Due to Proposition 3, we can compute each minimum $m_i = \min\limits_{x \in B_i} |F(x)|$

with an arbitrary accuracy 2^{-k}. In other words, given an integer k, we can compute a rational value $\widetilde{m}_{ik}$ for which $|\widetilde{m}_{ik} - m_i| \le 2^{-k}$.

For each $k = 0, 1, 2, \ldots$ we compute these values $\widetilde{m}_{ik}$ until for all points p_i and p_j for which $\widetilde{m}_{ik} \le 2^{-k}$ and $\widetilde{m}_{jk} \le 2^{-k}$, we get $\widetilde{d}(p_i, p_j) \le 5\eta$. Once such a k is reached, we return one of the points p_i for which $\widetilde{m}_{ik} \le 2^{-k}$ as the desired δ-approximation to the desired root x_0.

Let us prove that this algorithm always converges, and that once it converges, the produced point p_i is indeed a δ-approximation to x_0. Let us start with the second statement. Let us assume that the process converged. Since the points p_i form an η-net, there exists an index j for which $d(x_0, p_j) \le \eta$. Since $\eta \le \eta_j$, the root x_0 is within the ball $B_j = B_{\eta_j}(p_j)$ and thus, due to $|F(x_0)| = 0$ and $|F(x)| \ge 0$ for all x, we have $m_j = \min\limits_{x \in B_j} |F(x)| = 0$. Hence, for the 2^{-k}-approximation $\widetilde{m}_{jk}$ to the actual minimum $m_j = 0$, we get $\widetilde{m}_{jk} \le 2^{-k}$. So, according to our algorithm, we then have $\widetilde{d}(p_i, p_j) \le 5\eta$. Since $\widetilde{d}(p_i, p_j)$ is an η-approximation to the distance $d(p_i, p_j)$, we conclude that $d(p_i, p_j) \le \widetilde{d}(p_i, p_j) \le 5\eta + \eta = 6\eta$. From $d(x_0, p_j) \le \eta$, we can now get $d(x_0, p_i) \le d(x_0, p_j) + d(p_j, p_i) \le \eta + 6\eta \le 7\eta$. Since $\eta = \frac{\delta}{8}$, this implies that $d(x, p_i) < \delta$, i.e., that p_i is indeed the desired δ-approximation to the root x_0.

To complete the proof, let us show that the algorithm converges. Indeed, since x_0 is the only root, for every ball B_i that does not contain x_0, the actual minimum m_i is positive. Let m be the smallest of these positive values, and let k be such that $3 \cdot 2^{-k} \le m$. We will show that for this k, the above algorithm will converge. Indeed, for balls that do not contain x_0, we have $m_i \ge m \ge 3 \cdot 2^{-k}$. Since the estimate $\widetilde{m}_{ik}$ of the actual minimum m_i is 2^{-k}-close to m_i, we get $\widetilde{m}_{ik} \ge m_i - 2^{-k} \ge 3 \cdot 2^{-k} - 2^{-k} = 2 \cdot 2^{-k} > 2^{-k}$. Thus, the only points p_i which will be selected by our algorithm as having $\widetilde{m}_{ik} \le 2^{-k}$ are the points for which the corresponding ball $B_i = B_{\eta_i}(p_i)$ contains x_0. Thus, for every selected point p_i, we have $d(x_0, p_i) \le \eta_i$. Since $\eta_i \le 2\eta$, we get $d(x_0, p_i) \le 2\eta$.

Let p_i and p_j be two such points. Then, we have $d(x_0, p_i) \le 2\eta$ and $d(x_0, p_j) \le 2\eta$ and thus, $d(p_i, p_j) \le d(p_i, x_0) + d(x_0, p_j) \le 2\eta + 2\eta = 4\eta$. Hence, the value $\widetilde{d}(p_i, p_j)$, which is an η-approximation to the actual distance $d(p_i, p_j)$, satisfies the inequality $\widetilde{d}(p_i, p_j) \le d(p_i, p_j) + \eta \le 4\eta + \eta = 5\eta$. Thus, the algorithm indeed stops for this value k (if it has not stopped earlier). The proposition is proven.

From Uniqueness to Approximate Uniqueness. In practice, we may not be sure that the desired value is unique, we may only be sure that it is *approximately* unique – in the sense that for some $\varepsilon > 0$, all the roots are ε-close. Our second result extends the above computability from the uniqueness case to this approximate uniqueness case.

Theorem 2. *There exists an algorithm that, given a computable function $F : X \to \mathbb{R}$, a rational number $\varepsilon > 0$ for which all roots of F are ε-close, and the desired accuracy $\delta > 0$, returns a finite list of points $\ell_1, \ldots, \ell_m$ for which $d(\ell_i, \ell_j) \le \varepsilon + \delta$ and for which every root of F is δ-close to one of these points ℓ_i.*

Proof of Theorem 2. Similarly to the proof of Proposition 5, let us take $\eta = \frac{\delta}{8}$, and build an η-net $\{p_1, \ldots, p_k\}$ for the computable compact space X. Let us compute the distances $d(p_i, p_j)$ between the points p_i with accuracy η. As a result, we get the values $\widetilde{d}(p_i, p_j)$ for which $\left|\widetilde{d}(p_i, p_j) - d(p_i, p_j)\right| \le \eta$.

Similarly for the previous proof, for each $i = 1, \ldots, k$, there exists a value $\eta_i \in [\eta, 2\eta]$ for which the ball $B_i \stackrel{\text{def}}{=} B_{\eta_i}(p_i) = \{x : d(x, p_i) \le \eta_i\}$ is a computable compact. We can therefore compute each minimum $m_i = \min\limits_{x \in B_i} |F(x)|$ with an arbitrary accuracy 2^{-k}. In other words, given an integer k, we can compute a rational value $\widetilde{m}_{ik}$ for which $|\widetilde{m}_{ik} - m_i| \le 2^{-k}$.

For each $k = 0, 1, 2, \ldots$ we compute these values $\widetilde{m}_{ik}$ until for all points p_i and p_j for which $\widetilde{m}_{ik} \le 2^{-k}$ and $\widetilde{m}_{jk} \le 2^{-k}$, we get $\widetilde{d}(p_i, p_j) \le \varepsilon + 5\eta$. Once such a k is reached, we return all the points p_i for which $\widetilde{m}_{ik} \le 2^{-k}$ as the desired list of points $\ell_1, \ldots, \ell_m$.

Let us prove that this algorithm always converges, and that once it converges, the produced list has the desired properties. Let us start with the second statement. Let us assume that the process converged. Since for selected points, we have $\widetilde{d}(p_i, p_j) \le \varepsilon + 5\eta$, and the estimate $\widetilde{d}(p_i, p_j)$ is an η-approximation to the actual distance $d(p_i, p_j)$, we conclude that

$$d(p_i, p_j) \le \widetilde{d}(p_i, p_j) + \eta \le (\varepsilon + 5\eta) + \eta = \varepsilon + 6\eta.$$

Since $\eta = \frac{\delta}{8}$, this inequality implies that $d(p_i, p_j) < \varepsilon + \delta$.

Let us now show that each root x_0 is δ-close to one of the selected points p_j. Indeed, since the points p_i form an η-net, for each root x_0 there exists an index j for which $d(x_0, p_j) \le \eta$. Since $\eta \le \eta_j$, the root x_0 is within the ball $B_j = B_{\eta_j}(p_j)$ and thus, due to $|F(x_0)| = 0$ and $|F(x)| \ge 0$ for all x, we have $m_j = \min\limits_{x \in B_j} |F(x)| = 0$. Hence, for the 2^{-k}-approximation $\widetilde{m}_{jk}$ to the actual minimum $m_j = 0$, we get $\widetilde{m}_{jk} \le 2^{-k}$. So, the point p_j will indeed be selected. For this point, the inequality $d(x_0, p_j) \le \eta$ implies that $d(x_0, p_j) \le 8\eta = \delta$.

To complete the proof, let us show that the algorithm converges. Indeed, for every ball B_i that does not contain any root, the actual minimum m_i is positive. Let m be the smallest of these positive values, and let k be such that $3 \cdot 2^{-k} \le m$. We will show that for this k, the above algorithm will converge. Indeed, for balls that do not contain any root, we have $m_i \ge m \ge 3 \cdot 2^{-k}$. Since the estimate $\widetilde{m}_{ik}$ is 2^{-k}-close to the actual minimum m_i, we get

$$\widetilde{m}_{ik} \ge m_i - 2^{-k} \ge 3 \cdot 2^{-k} - 2^{-k} = 2 \cdot 2^{-k} > 2^{-k}.$$

Thus, the only points p_i which will be selected by our algorithm as having $\widetilde{m}_{ik} \le 2^{-k}$ are the points for which the corresponding ball $B_i = B_{\eta_i}(p_i)$ contains a root x_0. For this root, $d(x_0, p_i) \le \eta_i$. Since $\eta_i \le 2\eta$, we get $d(x_0, p_i) \le 2\eta$.

Let p_i and p_j be two selected points. Then, we have two roots x_0 and x_0' for which $d(x_0, p_i) \le 2\eta$ and $d(x_0', p_j) \le 2\eta$. Since every two roots are ε-close to each other, we get $d(x_0, x_0') \le \varepsilon$ and thus,

$$d(p_i, p_j) \le d(p_i, x_0) + d(x_0, x_0') + d(x_0', p_j) \le 2\eta + \varepsilon + 2\eta = \varepsilon + 4\eta.$$

Hence, the value $\widetilde{d}(p_i, p_j)$, which is an η-approximation to the actual distance $d(p_i, p_j)$, satisfies the inequality $\widetilde{d}(p_i, p_j) \le d(p_i, p_j) + \eta \le (\varepsilon + 4\eta) + \eta = \varepsilon + 5\eta$. Since $5\eta < 8\eta = \delta$, for every two selected points p_i, we indeed have $\widetilde{d}(p_i, p_j) \le \varepsilon + \delta$. Thus, the algorithm indeed stops for this value k (if it has not stopped earlier). The theorem is proven.

Acknowledgments. This work was supported in part by the National Science Foundation grants HRD-0734825 and DUE-0926721, by Grant 1 T36 GM078000-01 from the National Institutes of Health. The author is thankful to the anonymous referee for valuable suggestions.

References

1. Bishop, E., Bridges, D.S.: Constructive Analysis. Springer, New York (1985)
2. Feynman, R.P., Leighton, R.B., Sands, M.: Feynman Lectures on Physics. Addison-Wesley, Boston (1963)
3. Finkelstein, A.M., Kreinovich, V.: Impossibility of hardly possible events: physical consequences. Abstracts of the 8th International Congress on Logic, Methodology and Philosophy of Science, Moscow 5(2), 25–27 (1987)
4. Kreinovich, V.: Toward formalizing non-monotonic reasoning in physics: the use of Kolmogorov complexity. Revista Iberoamericana de Inteligencia Artificial 41, 4–20 (2009)
5. Kreinovich, V., Finkelstein, A.M.: Towards applying computational complexity to foundations of physics. Notes of Mathematical Seminars of St. Petersburg Department of Steklov Institute of Mathematics 316, 63–110 (2004); reprinted in Journal of Mathematical Sciences 134(5), 2358–2382 (2006)
6. Kushner, B.A.: Lectures on Constructive Mathematical Analysis. Amer. Math. Soc., Providence (1984)
7. Li, M., Vitányi, P.: An Introduction to Kolmogorov Complexity and Its Applications. Springer, New York (2008)
8. Lifschitz, V.A.: Investigation of constructive functions by the method of filling. J. Soviet Math. 1, 41–47 (1973)
9. Lifschitz, V.: Constructive assertions in an extension of classical mathematics. J. Symb. Log. 47(2), 359–387 (1982)
10. Misner, C.W., Thorne, K.S., Wheeler, J.A.: Gravitation. Freeman, San Francisco (1973)
11. Pearl, J.: Probabilistic Reasoning in Intelligence Systems: Networks of Plausible Inference. Morgan Kaufmann, San Francisco (1988)
12. Pour-El, M.B., Richards, J.I.: Computability in Analysis and Physics. Springer, Berlin (1989)
13. Tikhonov, A.N., Arsenin, V.Y.: Solutions of Ill-Posed Problems. V. H. Winston & Sons, Washington, DC (1977)
14. Weihrauch, K.: Computable Analysis. Springer, Berlin (2000)

A Definability: A Detailed Discussion

To make formal definitions, we must fix a formal theory $\mathcal{L}$ that has sufficient expressive power and deductive strength to conduct all the arguments and calculations necessary for working physics. For simplicity, in the arguments presented in this paper, we consider ZF, one of the most widely used formalizations of set theory.

A formal definition of definability is given by Definition 1. The set of all real numbers, the set of all solutions of a well-defined equation, every set that we can describe in mathematical terms is $\mathcal{L}$-definable. This does not mean, however, that *every* set is $\mathcal{L}$-definable: indeed, every $\mathcal{L}$-definable set is uniquely determined by formula $P(x)$, i.e., by a text in the language of set theory. There are only denumerably many words and therefore, there are only denumerably many $\mathcal{L}$-definable sets. Since, e.g., in a standard model of set theory ZF, there are more than denumerably many sets of integers, some of them are thus not $\mathcal{L}$-definable.

Our objective is to be able to make mathematical statements about $\mathcal{L}$-definable sets. Therefore, in addition to the theory $\mathcal{L}$, we must have a stronger theory $\mathcal{M}$ in which the class of all $\mathcal{L}$-definable sets is a set – and it is a countable set.

For every formula F from the theory $\mathcal{L}$, we denote its Gödel number by $\lfloor F \rfloor$. A Gödel number of a formula is an integer that uniquely determines this formula. For example, we can define a Gödel number by describing what this formula will look like in a computer. Specifically, we write this formula in LaTeX, interpret every LaTeX symbol as its ASCII code (as computers do), add 1 at the beginning of the resulting sequence of 0s and 1s, and interpret the resulting binary sequence as an integer in binary code.

Definition A1. *We say that a theory* $\mathcal{M}$ *is* stronger *than* $\mathcal{L}$ *if it contains all formulas, all axioms, and all deduction rules from* $\mathcal{L}$*, and also contains a special predicate* $\mathrm{def}(n, x)$ *such that for every formula* $P(x)$ *from* $\mathcal{L}$ *with one free variable, the formula* $\forall y\,(\mathrm{def}(\lfloor P(x) \rfloor, y) \leftrightarrow P(y))$ *is provable in* $\mathcal{M}$*.*

The existence of a stronger theory can be easily proven:

Proposition A1. [5] *For* $\mathcal{L}$=*ZF, there exists a stronger theory* $\mathcal{M}$*.*

Comments. In this paper, we assume that a theory $\mathcal{M}$ that is stronger than $\mathcal{L}$ has been fixed; proofs will mean proofs in this selected theory $\mathcal{M}$.

An important feature of a stronger theory $\mathcal{M}$ is that the notion of an $\mathcal{L}$-definable set can be expressed within the theory $\mathcal{M}$: a set S is $\mathcal{L}$-definable if and only if $\exists n \in \mathbb{N}\,\forall y(\mathrm{def}(n, y) \leftrightarrow y \in S)$.

In the paper, when we talk about definability, we mean this property expressed in the theory $\mathcal{M}$. So, all the statements involving definability (e.g., the Definition 2) become statements from the theory $\mathcal{M}$ itself, *not* statements from metalanguage.

Reformulating Action Language $\mathcal{C}$+ in Answer Set Programming

Joohyung Lee

School of Computing, Informatics and Decision Systems Engineering
Arizona State University
Tempe, AZ, 85287, USA
joolee@asu.edu

Abstract. Action language $\mathcal{C}$+ is a high level notation of nonmonotonic causal logic for describing properties of actions. The definite fragment of $\mathcal{C}$+ is implemented in Version 2 of the Causal Calculator (CCALC) based on the reduction of nonmonotonic causal logic to propositional logic. On the other hand, here we present two reformulations of the definite fragment of $\mathcal{C}$+ in terms of different versions of the stable model semantics. The first reformulation is in terms of the recently proposed stable model semantics of formulas with intensional functions, and can be encoded in the input language of CSP solvers. The second reformulation is in terms of the stable model semantics of propositional logic programs, which can be encoded in the input language of ASP systems. The second one is obtained from the first one by eliminating intensional functions in favor of intensional predicates.

1 Introduction

Action languages are formal models of parts of natural language that are used for describing properties of actions. Among them, language $\mathcal{C}$+ [1] and its predecessor $\mathcal{C}$ [2] are based on nonmonotonic causal logic. The definite fragment of nonmonotonic causal logic can be turned into propositional logic by the literal completion method, which resulted in an efficient way to compute $\mathcal{C}$+ using propositional satisfiability (SAT) solvers. The Causal Calculator (CCALC) is an implementation of this idea. Version 1 of CCALC, which accepts $\mathcal{C}$ as input, was created by McCain as part of his Ph.D. thesis under Vladimir Lifschitz's supervision [3]. Version 2 is an enhancement that accepts $\mathcal{C}$+ as input, as described in Lee's Ph.D. thesis also under Lifschitz's supervision [4]. Language $\mathcal{C}$+ has many features that are not available in $\mathcal{C}$, such as being able to represent multi-valued formulas, defined fluents, additive fluents, rigid constants and defeasible causal laws.

Nonmonotonic causal logic is closely related to logic programs under the stable model semantics [5,6]. Proposition 6.7 from [3] states how a fragment of Boolean-valued causal logic can be turned into logic programs under the stable model semantics [6]. This result was extended to non-definite theories and to first-order causal theories in [7]. Based on these embeddings, Casolary and Lee [8] show how to represent the language of CCALC in the input language of ASP systems following these steps: (i)

E. Erdem et al. (Eds.): Correct Reasoning, LNCS 7265, pp. 405–421, 2012.

turn the given $\mathcal{C}$+ action description D into the corresponding multi-valued causal theory D_m; (ii) turn D_m into a Boolean-valued causal theory D'_m; (iii) turn D'_m into formulas with intensional predicates under the stable model semantics; (iv) turn the result further into an answer set program. The prototype implementation CPLUS2ASP reported there takes the advantage of answer set solvers to yield efficient computation that is orders of magnitude faster than CCALC on several benchmark examples.

In this note, we provide an alternative reformulation of $\mathcal{C}$+ in answer set programming. Instead of step (ii) above, we turn D_m into multi-valued propositional formulas under the stable model semantics, which is a special case of first-order formulas with intensional functions [9]. The resulting theory can be encoded in the input language of CSP solvers, or it can be further turned into the input language of ASP systems by eliminating intensional functions in favor of intensional predicates.

2 Preliminaries

2.1 Multi-valued Propositional Formulas

We first review the definition of a multi-valued propositional formula from [1], where atomic parts of a formula can be equalities of the kind found in constraint satisfaction problems.

A *(multi-valued propositional) signature* is a set σ of symbols called *constants*, along with a nonempty finite set *Dom*(c) of symbols, disjoint from σ, assigned to each constant c. We call *Dom*(c) the *domain* of c. A *Boolean* constant is one whose domain is the set $\{\text{TRUE}, \text{FALSE}\}$. An *atom* of a signature σ is an expression of the form $c\!=\!v$ ("the value of c is v") where $c \in \sigma$ and $v \in$ *Dom*(c). A *(multi-valued propositional) formula* of σ is a propositional combination of atoms.

A *(multi-valued propositional) interpretation* of σ is a function that maps every element of σ to an element in its domain. An interpretation I *satisfies* an atom $c\!=\!v$ (symbolically, $I \models c\!=\!v$) if $I(c) = v$. The satisfaction relation is extended from atoms to arbitrary formulas according to the usual truth tables for the propositional connectives.

2.2 Nonmonotonic Causal Theories and $\mathcal{C}$+

Let σ be a multi-valued propositional signature. A *(multi-valued propositional) causal rule* is an expression of the form

$$F \Leftarrow G\,, \tag{1}$$

where F and G are multi-valued propositional formulas. A *(multi-valued propositional) causal theory* is a finite set of causal rules.

Let T be a causal theory, and let I be a multi-valued propositional interpretation of its signature. The *reduct* of T relative to I, denoted by T^I, is the set of the heads of all rules in T whose bodies are satisfied by I. We say that I is a *(causal) model* of T if I is the unique model of T^I.

A causal theory is called *definite* if the heads of the rules are either an atom or $\bot$.

Language $\mathcal{C}$+ is a high level notation for causal theories that was designed for describing transition systems—directed graphs whose vertices represent states and edges are labeled by actions that affect the states. In C+, constants in σ are partitioned into the set σ^{fl} of *fluent* constants and the set σ^{act} of *action* constants. Fluent constants are further partitioned into *simple* and *statically determined* fluents. A *fluent formula* is a formula where all constants occurring in it are fluent constants. An *action formula* is a formula that contains at least one action constant and no fluent constants. A *static law* is an expression of the form

$$\textbf{caused } F \textbf{ if } G \tag{2}$$

where F and G are fluent formulas. An *action dynamic law* is an expression of the form (2) in which F is an action formula and G is a formula. A *fluent dynamic law* is an expression of the form

$$\textbf{caused } F \textbf{ if } G \textbf{ after } H \tag{3}$$

where F and G are fluent formulas and H is a formula, provided that F does not contain statically determined fluent constants. A *causal law* is a static law, or an action dynamic law, or a fluent dynamic law. An *action description* is a set of causal laws.

The semantics of C+ in [1] is described via a translation into causal logic. For any action description D and any nonnegative integer m, the causal theory D_m is defined as follows. The signature of D_m consists of the pairs $i\!:\!c$ such that

- $i \in \{0, \dots, m\}$ and c is a fluent constant of D, or
- $i \in \{0, \dots, m-1\}$ and c is an action constant of D.

The domain of $i : c$ is the same as the domain of c. By $i : F$ we denote the result of inserting $i\!:$ in front of every occurrence of every constant in a formula F, and similarly for a set of formulas. The rules of D_m are

$$i\!:\!F \Leftarrow i\!:\!G \tag{4}$$

for every static law (2) in D and every $i \in \{0, \dots, m\}$, and for every action dynamic law (2) in D and every $i \in \{0, \dots, m-1\}$;

$$i{+}1\!:\!F \Leftarrow (i{+}1\!:\!G) \wedge (i\!:\!H) \tag{5}$$

for every fluent dynamic law (3) in D and every $i \in \{0, \dots, m-1\}$;

$$0\!:\!c{=}v \Leftarrow 0\!:\!c{=}v \tag{6}$$

for every simple fluent constant c and every $v \in \mathit{Dom}(c)$.

The causal models of D_m correspond to the paths of length m in a transition system — a directed graph whose vertices represent the states and edges are labeled by actions that affect the states. A *state* is an interpretation s of σ^{fl} such that $0\!:\!s$ is a model of D_0. States are the vertices of the transition system represented by D. A *transition* is a triple $\langle s, e, s' \rangle$, where s and s' are interpretations of σ^{fl} and e is an interpretation of σ^{act}, such that $0\!:\!s \cup 0\!:\!e \cup 1\!:\!s'$ is a model of D_1. Transitions correspond to the edges of the transition system: for every transition $\langle s, e, s' \rangle$, it contains an edge from s to s' labeled e. These labels e are called *events*.

Notation: b, b_1, b_2 range over the blocks in the domain
l ranges over the locations (the blocks and the table)

Simple fluent constant:	Domain:
$\mathit{Loc}(b)$	the set of locations
Action constant:	Domain:
$\mathit{Move}(b,l)$	Boolean

Causal laws:

constraint $\neg(\mathit{Loc}(b_1)=b \wedge \mathit{Loc}(b_2)=b)$ for $b_1 \neq b_2$

$\mathit{Move}(b,l)$ **causes** $\mathit{Loc}(b)=l$
nonexecutable $\mathit{Move}(b,l)$ **if** $\mathit{Loc}(b_1)=b$
nonexecutable $\mathit{Move}(b,b_1) \wedge \mathit{Move}(b_1,l)$

exogenous $\mathit{Move}(b,l)$

inertial $\mathit{Loc}(b)$

Fig. 1. Blocks World in $\mathcal{C}$+

Example 1. Figure 1 shows a description of the Blocks World in $\mathcal{C}$+. The semantics of $\mathcal{C}$+ turns the causal laws in Figure 1 into a causal theory D_m:

$$\begin{array}{rcl}
\bot & \Leftarrow & j:(\mathit{Loc}(b_1)=b \wedge \mathit{Loc}(b_2)=b) \qquad (b_1 \neq b_2)\\
i+1:\mathit{Loc}(b)=l & \Leftarrow & i:\mathit{Move}(b,l)=\mathrm{TRUE}\\
\bot & \Leftarrow & i:(\mathit{Move}(b,l)=\mathrm{TRUE} \wedge \mathit{Loc}(b_1)=b)\\
\bot & \Leftarrow & i:(\mathit{Move}(b,b_1)=\mathrm{TRUE} \wedge \mathit{Move}(b_1,l)=\mathrm{TRUE})\\
i:\mathit{Move}(b,l)=\mathrm{TRUE} & \Leftarrow & i:\mathit{Move}(b,l)=\mathrm{TRUE}\\
i:\mathit{Move}(b,l)=\mathrm{FALSE} & \Leftarrow & i:\mathit{Move}(b,l)=\mathrm{FALSE}\\
i+1:\mathit{Loc}(b)=l & \Leftarrow & i+1:\mathit{Loc}(b)=l \wedge i:\mathit{Loc}(b)=l\\
0:\mathit{Loc}(b)=l & \Leftarrow & 0:\mathit{Loc}(b)=l
\end{array} \tag{7}$$

$(0 \leq j \leq m,\ 0 \leq i \leq m-1)$.

3 Stable Model Semantics

We review two versions of the stable model semantics. One is the stable model semantics for propositional formulas defined by Ferraris [10]. The other is the stable model semantics for multi-valued propositional formulas defined by Bartholomew and Lee [9]. We understand propositional logic programs (multi-valued logic programs, respectively) as an alternative notation of some special syntactic class of propositional formulas (multi-valued propositional formulas, respectively).

3.1 Stable Models of a Propositional Formulas

The following definition is from [10]. For any propositional formula F, the *reduct* F^X of F relative to a set X of atoms is the formula obtained from F by replacing each maximal subformula that is not satisfied by X with $\bot$. We say that X is a *(propositional) stable model* of F if X is a minimal set of atoms satisfying F^X.

By a *propositional* logic program, we denote a set of rules that have the form

$$F \leftarrow G \tag{8}$$

where F and G are propositional formulas that do not contain implications. We identify a logic program with the conjunction of propositional formulas $G \rightarrow F$ for each rule (8) in it.

3.2 Stable Models of a Multi-valued Propositional Logic Programs

Bartholomew and Lee [9] define stable models of first-order formulas containing intensional functions. There, stable models of a multi-valued propositional formula are understood as a special case of stable models of a first-order formula with intensional functions. We review the stable model semantics of multi-valued propositional formulas by using the notion of a reduct that is similar to the reduct in the previous section.

Let F be a multi-valued propositional formula of signature σ, and let I be a multi-valued propositional interpretation of σ. The reduct F^I of a multi-valued propositional formula F relative to a multi-valued propositional interpretation I is the formula obtained from F by replacing each maximal subformula that is not satisfied by I with $\bot$. I is a *(multi-valued) stable model* of F if I is the unique multi-valued interpretation of σ that satisfies F^I.

By a *multi-valued logic program*, we denote the set of rules that have the form

$$F \leftarrow G \tag{9}$$

where F and G are multi-valued propositional formulas as defined in Section 2.1. We identify a multi-valued logic program with the conjunction of multi-valued propositional formulas $G \rightarrow F$ for each rule (9) in it.

3.3 Turning Multi-valued Propositional Formulas into Propositional Formulas under the Stable Model Semantics

Note that even when we restrict attention to Boolean constants only, the stable model semantics for multi-valued propositional formulas does not coincide with the stable model semantics for propositional formulas. Syntactically, they are different (one uses an expression of the form $c = \text{TRUE}$, $c = \text{FALSE}$ and the other uses the usual notion of an atom). Semantically, the former relies on the uniqueness of (Boolean)-functions, while the latter relies on the minimization on sets of atoms. Nonetheless there is a simple reduction from the former to the latter.

Begin with a multi-valued propositional signature σ. By σ^p we denote the signature consisting of Boolean constants $c(v)$ for all constants c in $\mathbf{c}$ and all $v \in \mathit{Dom}(c)$.

For any multi-valued propositional formula F of σ, by F_σ we denote the propositional formula that is obtained from F by replacing each occurrence of a multi-valued atom $c\!=\!v$ with $c(v)$, and adding the formulas

$$\neg(c(v) \wedge c(v')) \tag{10}$$

for all $v, v' \in \mathit{Dom}(c)$ such that $v \neq v'$, and also adding

$$\neg\neg \bigvee_{v \in \mathit{Dom}(c)} c(v). \tag{11}$$

For any interpretation I of σ, by I_σ we denote the interpretation of σ^P that is obtained from I by defining $c(I(c))^I = \text{TRUE}$ iff $c^I = I(c)$.

The following proposition is a special case of Corollary 2 of [9].

Theorem 1. *Let F be a multi-valued propositional formula of a signature σ such that, for every constant c in σ, $Dom(c)$ has at least two elements. (i) An interpretation I of σ is a multi-valued stable model of F iff I_σ is a propositional stable model of F_σ. (ii) An interpretation J of σ^P is a propositional stable model of F_σ iff $J = I_\sigma$ for some multi-valued stable model I of F.*

4 Representing Definite $\mathcal{C}$+ in Multi-valued Propositional Formulas under SM

4.1 Turning Definite Causal Theories into Multi-valued Logic Programs

For any definite causal theory T, by *cl2mvlp*(T) we denote the multi-valued logic program consisting of rules

$$F \leftarrow \neg\neg G$$

for each rule (1) in T. The causal models of such T coincide with the multi-valued stable models of *cl2mvlp*(T).

The following theorem is a special case of Theorem 13 from [9].

Theorem 2. *For any definite causal theory T of a signature σ, a multi-valued interpretation I of σ is a causal model of T iff it is a multi-valued stable model of cl2mvlp(T).*

4.2 Reformulating Definite $\mathcal{C}$+ in Multi-valued Logic Programs

We consider a finite definite $\mathcal{C}$+ description D of signature σ, where the heads of the rules are either an atom or $\bot$. Without loss of generality, we assume that, for any constant c in σ, *Dom*(c) has at least two elements. Description D can be turned into a logic program following these steps: (i) turn D into the corresponding multi-valued causal theory D_m (as explained in Section 2.2); (ii) turn D_m into a logic program with multi-valued constants *cl2mvlp*(D_m); (iii) Eliminate multi-valued atoms in favor of propositional atoms. The resulting program can be executed by ASP solvers.

For any definite action description D and any nonnegative integer m, the logic program Π_m is defined as follows. The signature of Π_m consists of the pairs $i : c$ such that

- $i \in \{0, \ldots, m\}$ and c is a fluent constant of D, or
- $i \in \{0, \ldots, m-1\}$ and c is an action constant of D.

The domain of $i : c$ is the same as the domain of c. By $i : F$ we denote the result of inserting i: in front of every occurrence of every constant in a formula F, and similarly for a set of formulas. The rules of Π_m are:

$$i:F \leftarrow \neg\neg\,(i:G) \tag{12}$$

for every static law (2) in D and every $i \in \{0, \ldots, m\}$, and for every action dynamic law (2) in D and every $i \in \{0, \ldots, m-1\}$;

$$i+1:F \leftarrow \neg\neg(i+1:G) \wedge (i:H) \tag{13}$$

for every fluent dynamic law (3) in D and every $i \in \{0, \ldots, m-1\}$;

$$0:c=v \leftarrow \neg\neg\,(0:c=v) \tag{14}$$

for every simple fluent constant c and every $v \in \mathit{Dom}(c)$.

Example 2. In view of Theorem 2, the causal theory D_m in Example 1 can be represented in multi-valued logic programs as follows.

$$\begin{array}{rcll}
\bot & \leftarrow & \neg\neg(j:(\mathit{Loc}(b_1)=b \wedge \mathit{Loc}(b_2)=b)) & (b_1 \neq b_2)\\
i+1:\mathit{Loc}(b)=l & \leftarrow & i:\mathit{Move}(b,l)=\mathrm{TRUE} & \\
\bot & \leftarrow & \neg\neg(i:(\mathit{Move}(b,l)=\mathrm{TRUE} \wedge \mathit{Loc}(b_1)=b)) & \\
\bot & \leftarrow & \neg\neg(i:(\mathit{Move}(b,b_1)=\mathrm{TRUE} \wedge \mathit{Move}(b_1,l)=\mathrm{TRUE}) & \\
i:\mathit{Move}(b,l)=\mathrm{TRUE} & \leftarrow & \neg\neg(i:\mathit{Move}(b,l)=\mathrm{TRUE}) & \\
i:\mathit{Move}(b,l)=\mathrm{FALSE} & \leftarrow & \neg\neg(i:\mathit{Move}(b,l)=\mathrm{FALSE}) & \\
i+1:\mathit{Loc}(b)=l & \leftarrow & \neg\neg(i+1:\mathit{Loc}(b)=l) \wedge i:\mathit{Loc}(b)=l & \\
0:\mathit{Loc}(b)=l & \leftarrow & \neg\neg(0:\mathit{Loc}(b)=l) &
\end{array} \tag{15}$$

$(0 \leq j \leq m; 0 \leq i \leq m-1)$.

According to the theorem on strong equivalence in [9], replacing a rule $\bot \leftarrow \neg\neg F$ with $\bot \leftarrow F$ does not affect the stable models.

Let Π be a multi-valued logic program of signature σ such that the heads of the rules are either an atom or $\bot$. The *dependency graph* of Π, denoted by $\mathrm{DG}[\Pi]$, is the directed graph that

- has all multi-valued constants of σ as its vertices, and
- has an edge from c to d if, for some rule $F \leftarrow G$ of Π, c occurs in F and d has a positive occurrence in G that is not in the scope of any negation.

We say that Π is *tight* if the graph $\mathrm{DG}[\Pi]$ is acyclic. For example, program (15) is tight. Indeed, it is not difficult to check that $\mathit{cl2mvlp}(T)$ for any definite causal theory T is tight.

Any tight multi-valued logic programs can be turned into "completion," which is similar to Clark's completion [11]. We say that a multi-valued logic program Π is in *Clark normal form* if it is a conjunction of sentences of the form

$$c=v \leftarrow F \tag{16}$$

one for each pair of c and v, and sentences of the form

$$\bot \leftarrow F. \tag{17}$$

The *(functional) completion* of a multi-valued logic program Π is obtained from Π by replacing each conjunctive term (16) in Π with $c{=}v \leftrightarrow F$ and (17) with $\neg F$.

Theorem 3. *Let Π be a multi-valued logic program such that for each multi-valued constant c, Dom(c) has at least two elements. For any multi-valued interpretation I, I is a multi-valued stable model of Π iff I is a model of the completion of Π.*

Example 3. The following theory is the completion of this program. Its stable models are the same as the models of the completion according to Theorem 3.

$$\begin{array}{ll}
i{+}1: Loc(b){=}l \leftrightarrow i{:}Move(b,l){=}\text{TRUE} \vee\ (i{+}1: Loc(b){=}l \wedge i{:}Loc(b){=}l) & \\
j{:}(Loc(b_1){=}b \wedge Loc(b_2){=}b) & (b_1 \neq b_2)\\
i{:}(Move(b,l){=}\text{TRUE} \wedge Loc(b_1){=}b) & \\
i{:}(Move(b,b_1){=}\text{TRUE} \wedge Move(b_1,l){=}\text{TRUE}) &
\end{array}$$

$(0 \le j \le m;\ 0 \le i \le m{-}1)$.

The completion can be computed by CSP solvers, as shown in [9].

4.3 Reformulating Definite $\mathcal{C}$+ in Propositional Logic Programs

Multi-valued logic program Π_m in the previous section can be further turned into propositional logic program $(\Pi_m)_\sigma$, as described in Section 3.3. We abbreviate a rule $F \leftarrow \neg\neg F \wedge G$ as $\{F\} \leftarrow G$.

The rules of $(\Pi_m)_\sigma$ are:

$$i{:}F_\sigma \leftarrow \neg\neg\,(i{:}G_\sigma) \tag{18}$$

for every static law (2) in D and every $i \in \{0,\ldots,m\}$, and for every action dynamic law (2) in D and every $i \in \{0,\ldots,m-1\}$;

$$i{+}1{:}F_\sigma \leftarrow \neg\neg(i{+}1{:}G_\sigma) \wedge (i{:}H_\sigma) \tag{19}$$

for every fluent dynamic law (3) in D and every $i \in \{0,\ldots,m-1\}$;

$$\{0{:}c(v)\} \tag{20}$$

for every simple fluent constant c and every $v \in Dom(c)$. Also, we add rules

$$\bot \leftarrow i{:}(c(v) \wedge c(v')) \tag{21}$$

$$\bot \leftarrow i:\Big(\bigwedge_{v \in Dom(c)} \neg c(v)\Big). \tag{22}$$

for all $c \in \mathbf{c}$ and all $v, v' \in Dom(c)$ such that $v \neq v'$.

Example 4. Action description D in Figure 1 is represented by the following propositional logic program:

$$
\begin{array}{rll}
\bot \leftarrow & j\!:\!(Loc(b_1,b) \wedge Loc(b_2,b)) & (b_1 \neq b_2)\\
i{+}1\!:\!Loc(b,l) \leftarrow & i\!:\!Move(b,l,\textsc{true}) & \\
\bot \leftarrow & i\!:\!(Move(b,l,\textsc{true}) \wedge Loc(b_1,b)) & \\
\bot \leftarrow & i\!:\!(Move(b,b_1,\textsc{true}) \wedge Move(b_1,l,\textsc{true})) & \\
\{i\!:\!Move(b,l,\textsc{true})\} & & \\
\{i\!:\!Move(b,l,\textsc{false})\} & & \\
\{i{+}1\!:\!Loc(b,l)\} \leftarrow & i\!:\!Loc(b,l) & \\
\{0\!:\!Loc(b,l)\} & & \\
\\
\bot \leftarrow & i : (Loc(b,l) \wedge Loc(b,l')) & (l \neq l')\\
\bot \leftarrow & i : (Move(b,l,\textsc{true}) \wedge Move(b,l,\textsc{false})) & \\
\\
\bot \leftarrow & i : (\bigwedge_{l \in Locations} \neg Loc(b,l)) & \\
\bot \leftarrow & i : (\neg Move(b,l,\textsc{true}) \wedge \neg Move(b,l,\textsc{false})) &
\end{array}
\quad (23)
$$

We can simplify some rules containing Boolean constants. Replace $Move(b,l,\textsc{true})$ with $Move(b,l)$ and $Move(b,l,\textsc{false})$ with $\neg Move(b,l)$. We also drop rules that contain $Move(b,l,\textsc{false})$ from program (23).

$$
\begin{array}{rll}
\bot \leftarrow & j\!:\!(Loc(b_1,b) \wedge Loc(b_2,b)) & (b_1 \neq b_2)\\
i{+}1\!:\!Loc(b,l) \leftarrow & i\!:\!Move(b,l) & \\
\bot \leftarrow & i\!:\!(Move(b,l) \wedge Loc(b_1,b)) & \\
\bot \leftarrow & i\!:\!(Move(b,b_1) \wedge Move(b_1,l)) & \\
\{i\!:\!Move(b,l)\} & & \\
\{i{+}1\!:\!Loc(b,l)\} \leftarrow & i\!:\!Loc(b,l) & \\
\{0\!:\!Loc(b,l)\} & & \\
\\
\bot \leftarrow & i : (Loc(b,l) \wedge Loc(b,l')) & (l \neq l')\\
\bot \leftarrow & i : (\bigwedge_{l \in Locations} \neg Loc(b,l)) &
\end{array}
\quad (24)
$$

4.4 Representing Definite C+ in the Language of ASP

The logic program representation of C+ introduced in the previous section can be encoded in the input language of ASP grounders.

We rewrite $i : G$ as $h(G,i)$, where $h(G,i)$ is obtained from $i : G$ by replacing every atomic formula $i : c(v)$ in it by

- $h(c(v),i)$ if c is non-Boolean,
- $h(c,i)$ if c is Boolean and v is TRUE, and
- $\sim h(c,i)$ if c is Boolean and v is FALSE. (' $\sim$' is the symbol for strong negation.)

Each rule (4) is represented by

$$h(F_\sigma,i) \leftarrow \neg\neg h(G_\sigma,i)\ ;$$

Each rule (5) is represented by

$$h(F_\sigma,i{+}1) \leftarrow \neg\neg h(G_\sigma,i) \wedge h(H_\sigma,i)\ ;$$

Each rule (6) is represented by

$$\{h(c(v), 0)\}.$$

Rules (21) and (22) can be succinctly represented by cardinality constraints [12]. If c is nonBoolean, rule (21) can be encoded as

$$\leftarrow 2\{h(c(v), i) : \mathit{Domain}(v)\}$$

(*Domain* is a domain predicate that defines the range of variable v) and rule (22) can be encoded as

$$\bot \leftarrow \{c(v) : \mathit{Domain}(v)\}0.$$

If c is Boolean, rule (22) can be encoded as

$$\bot \leftarrow \{h(c, i), \sim h(c, i)\}0.$$

and we do not need to represent rule (10).

Example 5. Program (24) can be encoded in the input language of GRINGO as follows:

```
step(0..maxstep).                   astep(0..maxstep-1) :- maxstep > 0.

#domain step(ST).                   #domain astep(T).
#domain block(B).                   #domain block(B1).
#domain location(L).

% every block is a location
location(B) :- block(B).

% the table is a location
location(table).

% two blocks can't be on the same block at the same time
:- 2{h(loc(BB,B),ST): block(BB)}.

% direct effect
h(loc(B,L),T+1) :- h(move(B,L),T).

% preconditions
:- h(move(B,L),T) , h(loc(B1,B),T).
:- h(move(B,B1),T) , h(move(B1,L),T).

{h(loc(B,L),0)}.
{h(move(B,L),T)}.
{h(loc(B,L),T+1)} :- h(loc(B,L),T).

% existence constraint
:- {h(loc(B,LL),ST): location(LL)}0.

% uniqueness constraint
:- 2{h(loc(B,LL),ST): location(LL)}.
```

5 Monkey and Bananas in the Language of F2LP

The Monkey and Bananas domain is the main example used in [1] to illustrate the expressivity of definite C+. The C+ action description *MB* from that paper is reproduced in Figure 2. The propositional logic program representation of *MB* may not be directly accepted by an ASP solver as it may contain syntactically complex formulas. For example, the causal rule

$$\textbf{nonexecutable}\ \mathit{PushBox}(l)\ \textbf{if}\ \neg\Big(\bigvee_{l'\in\{L_1,L_2,L_3\}}\big(\mathit{Loc}(\mathit{Monkey})=l'\wedge \mathit{Loc}(\mathit{Box})=l'\big)\Big)$$

is turned into [1]

$$\bot\leftarrow i:\Big(\mathit{PushBox}(l)\wedge\neg\Big(\bigwedge_{l'\in\{L_1,L_2,L_3\}}\mathit{Loc}(\mathit{Monkey})=l'\wedge \mathit{Loc}(\mathit{Box})=l'\Big)\Big).$$

In order to handle this, we use system F2LP [13] ("*f*ormulas *to l*ogic *p*rograms")[2], a front-end that allows ASP solvers to compute stable models of the general programs defined in [14,15]. Figure 3 is the propositional logic program representation of *MB* in the input language of F2LP. We show how planning, prediction, and postdiction problems can be answered by using the combination of F2LP and CLINGO[3].

Planning

Find the shortest sequence of actions that would allow the monkey to have the bananas.

The problem can be formalized as follows: Find an answer set of the propositional logic program $(MB_m)_\sigma$, where σ is the underlying signature, that satisfies the initial conditions

$$0{:}\mathit{Loc}(\mathit{Monkey})=L_1,\ 0{:}\mathit{Loc}(\mathit{Bananas})=L_2,\ 0{:}\mathit{Loc}(\mathit{Box})=L_3 \qquad (25)$$

and the goal

$$m{:}\mathit{HasBananas} \qquad (26)$$

where m is the smallest number for which such a model exists. To solve this problem, we take consecutively $m = 0, 1, \ldots$ and look for an answer set of $(MB_m)^{\mathrm{c}}$ that satisfies the constraint in File `planning`. Such an interpretation will be first found for $m = 4$.

[1] In multi-valued propositional logic, $\mathit{Loc}(\mathit{Monkey}) = \mathit{Loc}(\mathit{Box})$ is shorthand for $\bigvee_{l'\in\{L_1,L_2,L_3\}}(\mathit{Loc}(\mathit{Monkey})=l'\wedge \mathit{Loc}(\mathit{Box})=l')$.

[2] `http://reasoning.eas.asu.edu/f2lp`

[3] `http://potassco.sourceforge.net`

Notation: x ranges over $\{Monkey, Bananas, Box\}$; l ranges over $\{L_1, L_2, L_3\}$.

Simple fluent constants:	Domains:
$Loc(x)$	$\{L_1, L_2, L_3\}$
HasBananas, *OnBox*	Boolean

Action constants:	Domains:
$Walk(l)$, $PushBox(l)$, *ClimbOn*, *ClimbOff*, *GraspBananas*	Boolean

Causal laws:

caused $Loc(Bananas) = l$ **if** $HasBananas \wedge Loc(Monkey) = l$
caused $Loc(Monkey) = l$ **if** $OnBox \wedge Loc(Box) = l$

$Walk(l)$ **causes** $Loc(Monkey) = l$
nonexecutable $Walk(l)$ **if** $Loc(Monkey) = l$
nonexecutable $Walk(l)$ **if** *OnBox*

$PushBox(l)$ **causes** $Loc(Box) = l$
$PushBox(l)$ **causes** $Loc(Monkey) = l$
nonexecutable $PushBox(l)$ **if** $Loc(Monkey) = l$
nonexecutable $PushBox(l)$ **if** *OnBox*
nonexecutable $PushBox(l)$ **if** $Loc(Monkey) \neq Loc(Box)$

ClimbOn **causes** *OnBox*
nonexecutable *ClimbOn* **if** *OnBox*
nonexecutable *ClimbOn* **if** $Loc(Monkey) \neq Loc(Box)$

ClimbOff **causes** $\neg OnBox$
nonexecutable *ClimbOff* **if** $\neg OnBox$

GraspBananas **causes** *HasBananas*
nonexecutable *GraspBananas* **if** *HasBananas*
nonexecutable *GraspBananas* **if** $\neg OnBox$
nonexecutable *GraspBananas* **if** $Loc(Monkey) \neq Loc(Bananas)$

nonexecutable $Walk(l) \wedge PushBox(l)$
nonexecutable $Walk(l) \wedge ClimbOn$
nonexecutable $PushBox(l) \wedge ClimbOn$
nonexecutable $ClimbOff \wedge GraspBananas$

exogenous c for every action constant c

inertial c for every simple fluent constant c

Fig. 2. Action description *MB*

```
% File: mb

step(0..maxstep).
astep(0..maxstep-1) :- maxstep > 0.

#domain step(ST).                          #domain astep(T).
#domain thing(TH).

thing(monkey;bananas;box).

#domain location(L).

location(l1;l2;l3).

% state description
h(loc(bananas,L),ST) <- h(hasBananas,ST) & h(loc(monkey,L),ST).
h(loc(monkey,L),ST) <- h(onBox,ST) & h(loc(box,L),ST).


%% effect and preconditions of actions
h(loc(monkey,L),T+1) <- h(walk(L),T).
<- h(walk(L),T) & h(loc(monkey,L),T).
<- h(walk(L),T) & h(onBox,T).

h(loc(box,L),T+1) <- h(pushBox(L),T).
h(loc(monkey,L),T+1) <- h(pushBox(L),T).
<- h(pushBox(L),T) & h(loc(monkey,L),T).
<- h(pushBox(L),T) & h(onBox,T).
<- h(pushBox(L),T) & - (?[L]: (h(loc(monkey,L),T) & h(loc(box,L),T))).

h(onBox,T+1) <- h(climbOn,T).
<- h(climbOn,T) & h(onBox,T).
<- h(climbOn,T) & - (?[L]: (h(loc(monkey,L),T) & h(loc(box,L),T))).

-h(onBox,T+1) <- h(climbOff,T).
<- h(climbOff,T) & -h(onBox,T).

h(hasBananas,T+1) <- h(graspBananas,T).
<- h(graspBananas,T) & h(hasBananas,T).
<- h(graspBananas,T) & -h(onBox,T).
<- h(graspBananas,T) & - (?[L]: (h(loc(monkey,L),T) & h(loc(bananas,L),T))).

% no concurrency
<- h(walk(L),T) & h(pushBox(L),T).
<- h(walk(L),T) & h(climbOn,T).
<- h(pushBox(L),T) & h(climbOn,T).
<- h(climbOff,T) & h(graspBananas,T).


% fluents are initially exogenous
{h(hasBananas,0), -h(hasBananas,0)}.       {h(onBox,0), -h(onBox,0)}.
{h(loc(TH,L),0)}.

% actions are exogenous
{h(walk(LL),T): location(LL)}.             {h(pushBox(LL),T): location(LL)}.
{h(climbOn,T)}.       {h(climbOff,T)}.     {h(graspBananas,T)}.

% commonsense law of inertia
{h(hasBananas,T+1)} <- h(hasBananas,T).    {-h(hasBananas,T+1)} <- -h(hasBananas,T).
{h(onBox,T+1)} <- h(onBox,T).              {-h(onBox,T+1)} <- -h(onBox,T).
{h(loc(TH,L),T+1)} <- h(loc(TH,L),T).

% Eliminating multi-valued constants
<- {h(onBox,ST), -h(onBox,ST)}0.           <- {h(hasBananas,ST), -h(hasBananas,ST)}0.
<- {h(loc(TH,LL),ST): location(LL)}0.

<- 2{h(loc(TH,LL),ST): location(LL)}.
```

Fig. 3. Action description *MB* in ASP

```
% File: planning

% initial condition
<- not (-h(hasBananas,0) & -h(onBox,0) & h(loc(monkey,l1),0) &
        h(loc(box,l3),0) & h(loc(bananas,l2),0)).

% goal
<- not h(hasBananas,maxstep).
```

The following is the trace of the program. AS2TRANSITION [4] is a utility program that displays answer sets in the format of a transition system.

```
$ f2lp mb planning | clingo -c maxstep=4 | as2transition
Solution 1:

0:  h(loc(bananas,l2),0)  h(loc(box,l3),0)  h(loc(monkey,l1),0)

  ACTIONS:  h(walk(l3),0)

1:  h(loc(bananas,l2),1)  h(loc(box,l3),1)  h(loc(monkey,l3),1)

  ACTIONS:  h(pushBox(l2),1)

2:  h(loc(bananas,l2),2)  h(loc(box,l2),2)  h(loc(monkey,l2),2)

  ACTIONS:  h(climbOn,2)

3:  h(loc(bananas,l2),3)  h(loc(box,l2),3)  h(loc(monkey,l2),3)
h(onBox,3)

  ACTIONS:  h(graspBananas,3)

4:  h(hasBananas,4)  h(loc(bananas,l2),4)  h(loc(box,l2),4)
h(loc(monkey,l2),4)  h(onBox,4)


Models      : 1
Time        : 0.000  (Parsing: 0.000)
```

Prediction

Initially, the monkey is at L_1, the bananas are at L_2, and the box is at L_3. The monkey walks to L_3 and then pushes the box to L_2. Does it follow that in the resulting state the monkey, the bananas and the box are at the same location?

[4] http://reasoning.eas.asu.edu/cplus2asp/downloads.html

This question can be formalized as follows: Determine whether every answer set of $(MB_2)_\sigma$ satisfies the following formula:

$$\begin{array}{l}[(0{:}Loc(Monkey)=L_1) \wedge (0{:}Loc(Bananas)=L_2) \wedge (0{:}Loc(Box)=L_3) \\ \quad \wedge (0{:}Walk(L_3)) \wedge (1{:}PushBox(L_2))] \\ \qquad \rightarrow 2{:}(Loc(Monkey)=Loc(Bananas) \wedge Loc(Bananas)=Loc(Box)).\end{array} \tag{27}$$

This is equivalent to checking if MB_2 conjoined with the negation of the formula above has no answer sets. The negation of the formula above can be represented in the input language of F2LP as follows: [5]

```
% File: prediction

not
(h(loc(monkey,l1),0) & h(loc(bananas,l2),0) & h(loc(box,l3),0) &
 h(walk(l3),0) &  h(pushBox(l2),1)
 -> ?[L]:(h(loc(monkey,L),2) & h(loc(bananas,L),2) & h(loc(box,L),2))).
```

The following command is used to answer the prediction query.

```
$ f2lp mb prediction | clingo -c maxstep=2 | as2transition
```

CLINGO returns no answer set as expected.

Postdiction

The monkey walked to location L_3 and then pushed the box. Does it follow that the box was initially at L_3?

This question can be formalized as follows: Determine whether $(MB_2)_\sigma$ entails the formula

$$\left[(0{:}Walk(L_3)) \wedge \left(1{:}\bigvee_l PushBox(l)\right)\right] \rightarrow 0{:}Loc(Box)=L_3. \tag{28}$$

It can be reduced to the satisfiability problem in the same way as the prediction problem above. The answer to this question is yes. Similarly, the negation of the query can be represented as follows.

```
% File: postdiction

not (h(walk(l3),0) & ?[L]: h(pushBox(L),1) -> h(loc(box,l3),0)).
```

[5] F2LP allows us to represent a formula of the form $\neg F$ where F is an arbitrary formula, including implication (`->`), and quantifiers (`?` for $\exists$, `!` for $\forall$).

6 Discussion

Based on the theoretical result that turns nonmonotonic causal logic into the stable model semantics, we presented a method that represents the definite fragment of $\mathcal{C}$+ in the language of answer set programming.

Our reformulation always yields a tight logic program due to the use of double negations, and in this sense the use of SAT solvers and ASP solvers are not distinguishable. However, it is worthwhile to note that the reformulation in terms of the stable model semantics may provide a way to extend language $\mathcal{C}$+ by allowing recursive definitions. For instance, one may consider extending static causal laws to

$$\textbf{caused } F \textbf{ if } G \textbf{ assuming } H \ ,$$

which can be translated into propositional logic program rules

$$i\!:\!F_\sigma \leftarrow i\!:\!(G_\sigma \wedge \neg\neg H_\sigma) \ .$$

In the absence of **if** G, this is essentially the translation (18). In the absence of **assuming** H, this is close to the treatment in language $\mathcal{B}$ [16].

Acknowledgements. The work presented here would not have been possible without having the chances to work with Vladimir Lifschitz. The extension of $\mathcal{C}$ to $\mathcal{C}$+, and the implementation of Version 2 of CCALC was my thesis work under his supervision. His recent proposal of logic programs with intensional functions inspired a new perspective on the relationship between causal logic and logic programs, which benefited this work.

The work here also benefited from collaborations with Michael Bartholomew, Michael Casolary and Ravi Palla. Martin Gebser gave numerous useful comments on the draft of this paper. This work was partially supported by the National Science Foundation under Grant IIS-0916116.

References

1. Giunchiglia, E., Lee, J., Lifschitz, V., McCain, N., Turner, H.: Nonmonotonic causal theories. Artificial Intelligence 153(1–2), 49–104 (2004)
2. Giunchiglia, E., Lifschitz, V.: An action language based on causal explanation: Preliminary report. In: Proceedings of National Conference on Artificial Intelligence (AAAI), pp. 623–630. AAAI Press (1998)
3. McCain, N.: Causality in Commonsense Reasoning about Actions. PhD thesis, University of Texas at Austin (1997), `ftp://ftp.cs.utexas.edu/pub/techreports/tr97-25.ps.gz`
4. Lee, J.: Automated Reasoning about Actions. PhD thesis, University of Texas at Austin (2005), `http://peace.eas.asu.edu/joolee/papers/dissertation.pdf`
5. Gelfond, M., Lifschitz, V.: The stable model semantics for logic programming. In: Kowalski, R., Bowen, K. (eds.) Proceedings of International Logic Programming Conference and Symposium, pp. 1070–1080. MIT Press (1988)
6. Gelfond, M., Lifschitz, V.: Classical negation in logic programs and disjunctive databases. New Generation Computing 9, 365–385 (1991)

7. Ferraris, P., Lee, J., Lierler, Y., Lifschitz, V., Yang, F.: Representing first-order causal theories by logic programs. Theory and Practice of Logic Programming (2011), Available on CJO 2011, doi:10.1017/S1471068411000081
8. Casolary, M., Lee, J.: Representing the language of the Causal Calculator in answer set programming. In: ICLP (Technical Communications), pp. 51–61 (2011)
9. Bartholomew, M., Lee, J.: Stable models of formulas with intensional functions. In: Proceedings of International Conference on Principles of Knowledge Representation and Reasoning, KR (to appear, 2012)
10. Ferraris, P.: Answer Sets for Propositional Theories. In: Baral, C., Greco, G., Leone, N., Terracina, G. (eds.) LPNMR 2005. LNCS (LNAI), vol. 3662, pp. 119–131. Springer, Heidelberg (2005)
11. Clark, K.: Negation as failure. In: Gallaire, H., Minker, J. (eds.) Logic and Data Bases, pp. 293–322. Plenum Press, New York (1978)
12. Simons, P., Niemelä, I., Soininen, T.: Extending and implementing the stable model semantics. Artificial Intelligence 138, 181–234 (2002)
13. Lee, J., Palla, R.: System F2LP – Computing Answer Sets of First-Order Formulas. In: Erdem, E., Lin, F., Schaub, T. (eds.) LPNMR 2009. LNCS, vol. 5753, pp. 515–521. Springer, Heidelberg (2009)
14. Ferraris, P., Lee, J., Lifschitz, V.: A new perspective on stable models. In: Proceedings of International Joint Conference on Artificial Intelligence (IJCAI), pp. 372–379 (2007)
15. Ferraris, P., Lee, J., Lifschitz, V.: Stable models and circumscription. Artificial Intelligence 175, 236–263 (2011)
16. Gelfond, M., Lifschitz, V.: Action languages. Electronic Transactions on Artificial Intelligence 3, 195–210 (1998), http://www.ep.liu.se/ea/cis/1998/016/

The Truth about Defaults

Hector J. Levesque[1] and Gerhard Lakemeyer[2]

[1] Dept. of Computer Science, University of Toronto
Toronto, Canada, M5S 3A6
[2] Dept. of Computer Science, RWTH Aachen University
52056 Aachen, Germany

It is a great honour and a pleasure to be able to offer this paper in celebration of Vladimir Lifschitz's sixty-fifth birthday. His work has been an inspiration to both of us since we first started reading his papers in the 1980s. At a time when many papers and presentations in AI were either very abstract on the one hand, or tied to specific systems on the other, Vladimir has consistently found a sweet spot that emphasized clarity and rigour, while maintaining a strong connection to AI practice. His work, in a nutshell, has been a model of how to do AI research, of great value to new students and to older researchers like us. So this is our chance to say thank you, Vladimir, and happy birthday!

1 Introduction

It is somewhat surprising that much of logic-based AI does not deal explicitly with a notion of *truth*. The idea of a sentence being true or false in a model has been at the root of how we understand logic and entailment since the pioneering work of Tarski [21]. Yet Tarski structures (and their many variants) are almost never seen in AI papers involving quantified logic. In some cases, this may be explained by the fact that the objects of study lie below the level of sentences, such as the descriptions found in description logic [1], which are more like noun phrases. In other cases, this may be explained by the fact that the required notion of truth is already obvious and does not require further elaboration, as in the work on satisfiability [6]. But what remains surprising is that *new formalisms* involving new forms of inference over sentences are proposed that completely bypass the notion of truth and jump directly to logical consequence (or entailment).

Consider for example, the sort of default rules first defined by Reiter [20]. Formally, a default theory T is a pair $\langle F, D\rangle$ where F is a set of ordinary sentences and D is a set of (closed) default rules of the form

$$\frac{\alpha : \beta_1, \ldots, \beta_n}{\gamma}.$$

where α, the β_i and γ are all ordinary sentences. Informally, this default rule is read as follows: If α is believed, and each β_i can be consistently believed, then infer that γ is true. Reiter specifies how to reason with a default theory by specifying the *extensions* of T, that is, the sets of sentences considered to be reasonable sets of beliefs, given T. There are actually two modes of reasoning:

E. Erdem et al. (Eds.): Correct Reasoning, LNCS 7265, pp. 422–435, 2012.

in *credulous reasoning*, we are to be content with any extension of a theory; in *skeptical reasoning* we are to find what is common to all extensions of a theory.

So the notion of logical inference is tied to the notion of extension. In fact, two very different forms of extension have been considered in the literature, one due to Reiter and another due to Moore [19].[1] The exact technical details of these definitions are unimportant here. Suffice it to say that Reiter extensions are minimal sets of sentences that contain the given facts F, are closed under logical entailment, and have applied the defaults in D as much as possible. Moore extensions (which he calls "stable expansions") are sets of sentences that start with the facts F and the defaults in D (represented as modal sentences), and are closed under logical entailment, as well as positive and negative introspection.

What is missing in both these accounts is any appeal to the *truth* of the sentences. Although both definitions make reference to logical entailment, this is only one part of a complex minimization. As a result, the analysis of default reasoning is done using extra-logical notions like fixpoints, partial orders, closure operations, stable sets, and so on. What is missing, in other words, is a *semantic model* of a default theory where one can ask: what is true? what is believed? what is all that is believed?

This paper proposes to remedy this situation. In section 2, we consider the notion of truth and argue for a very simple semantic basis. In section 3, we extend the logical language to deal with beliefs and defaults. In section 4, the concept of only knowing is introduced and then generalized in section 5. In section 6, an axiomatic account of the language is considered. Finally, conclusions and future work are presented in section 7. Almost all the technical material presented here derives from earlier work of ours, especially [16,12,13].

2 Truth and Semantics

Perhaps one of the reasons Tarski structures do not show up in AI papers, and that Kripke structures for belief [8,5] typically appear only in the propositional case is that they both end up being too cumbersome to work with in practice.[2] To be workable, semantic models and the associated definition of truth need to take the following two observations into account:

1. Many semantic arguments require mathematical induction over sentences. It should be possible to do induction over sentences that include quantifiers, without having to deal with open formulas and elements of the domain.
2. Many semantic arguments about belief require assembling a new model from a combination of other ones. It should be possible to do so easily without having to deal with different domains of quantification.

Both of these suggest that we should put aside the idea of a domain of quantification in our semantic models and use a different generalization of the truth assignments and truth tables from propositional logic.

[1] We will also see a third one due to Konolige [10].

[2] See [11] for some of the difficulties with using standard Tarski semantics for work in the situation calculus.

Perhaps the simplest way to do this is to assume that beyond any function and predicate symbols, a first-order language contains a countably infinite set of special terms called *standard names*. The idea is that the models of the language can then be *truth assignments*, functions from primitive atoms to $\{0, 1\}$, where a primitive atom is of the form $P(n_1, \ldots, n_k)$, where P is a predicate symbol and each n_i is a standard name. Informally, a quantified formula $\forall x \alpha$ is then considered true iff each of its instances α^x_n is considered true. More formally, we have a first-order language called $\mathcal{L}$ with the following semantics:[3]

> Let W be the set of all truth assignments and let $w \in W$. We define what it means for a sentence α of $\mathcal{L}$ to be true wrt w, which we write as $w \models \alpha$, as follows:
> 1. $w \models P(n_1, \ldots, n_k)$ iff $w[P(n_1, \ldots, n_k)] = 1$;
> 2. $w \models (n_1 = n_2)$ iff n_1 and n_2 are the same standard name;
> 3. $w \models \neg\alpha$ iff $w \not\models \alpha$;
> 4. $w \models (\alpha \wedge \beta)$ iff $w \models \alpha$ and $w \models \beta$;
> 5. $w \models \forall x.\alpha$ iff $w \models \alpha^x_n$ for every standard name n;
>
> We say that α is *valid*, written $\models \alpha$, when $w \models \alpha$ for every $w \in W$.

Is this version of truth for a quantified logic equivalent to the classical one? Almost. In the Tarski definition, the $=$ symbol is just another predicate, the domain of quantification is any non-empty set, and there may be elements of the domain that are unnamed by any term of the language. The main difference is the second one. For example in $\mathcal{L}$, we have the following: $\models \exists x \exists y\, (x \neq y)$. This sentence is not valid in Tarski logic (even if $=$ is interpreted as identity), since there can be models with just one element. The simplification of having what amounts to a single countably infinite domain of discourse makes the logic much easier to work with. Moreover, the restriction is not a serious one. First, it is well known that any satisfiable set of sentences is satisfiable in a countable domain, so the restriction to countability is without loss of generality. Furthermore, it is possible in $\mathcal{L}$ to deal with finite sets of objects in the domain by using a predicate. For example, to say that there are at most two objects in the world, we could use the following sentence: $\exists x \exists y \forall z. (Obj(z) \supset z = x \vee z = y)$, where *Obj* is the predicate for objects.

3 Belief and Defaults

The notion of a default from Reiter [20] appeals to the concept of *belief*. The thinking might go along the following lines:

> Suppose all we are told about Tweety is that she is a bird. Then we believe *Bird*(*tweety*), but we do not believe ¬*Fly*(*tweety*) (nor do we believe its negation). It will thus be consistent to believe *Fly*(*tweety*). Therefore, ...

[3] For simplicity, we omit constants and function symbols from the language $\mathcal{L}$. The only terms will be variables and standard names. We also assume that the connectives $\vee$, $\supset$, $\equiv$ and the quantifier $\exists$ are introduced as abbreviations in the usual way.

This suggests two additions to the language: $\mathbf{K}\alpha$, read as, "α is believed," and $\mathbf{M}\alpha$, read as "it is consistent to believe α." We can identify a state of belief e with a set of truth assignments, $e \subseteq W$, with the understanding that $\mathbf{K}\, Bird(tweety)$ will be true in state e iff $Bird(tweety)$ is true for every $w \in e$, and $\mathbf{M}\, Bird(tweety)$ will be true in state e iff $Bird(tweety)$ is true for some $w \in e$. Overall, we have a new logic $\mathcal{KL}$ with the following truth conditions:

> Let $w \in W$ and $e \subseteq W$. We define what it means for a sentence α to be true wrt e and w, which we write as $e, w \models \alpha$, as follows:
> 1. $e, w \models P(n_1, \ldots, n_k)$ iff $w[P(n_1, \ldots, n_k)] = 1$;
> 2. $e, w \models (n_1 = n_2)$ iff n_1 and n_2 are the same standard name;
> 3. $e, w \models \neg\alpha$ iff $e, w \not\models \alpha$;
> 4. $e, w \models (\alpha \wedge \beta)$ iff $e, w \models \alpha$ and $e, w \models \beta$;
> 5. $e, w \models \forall x.\alpha$ iff $e, w \models \alpha^x_n$ for every standard name n;
> 6. $e, w \models \mathbf{K}\alpha$ iff $e, w' \models \alpha$ for every $w' \in e$;
> $e, w \models \mathbf{M}\alpha$ iff $e, w' \models \alpha$ for some $w' \in e$.
>
> We say that α is *valid*, written $\models \alpha$, when $e, w \models \alpha$ for every e and w.

Note that this is the same semantics as for $\mathcal{L}$, but carrying around the additional e argument, used for the rules for $\mathbf{K}$ and $\mathbf{M}$.[4] Is this account of truth equivalent to the one in classical modal logic [9,2]? Almost. In the classical possible-world definition of modal truth (going back to Kripke), each world gets to have its own set of accessible worlds and its own domain of quantification. In our case, e behaves like a fixed, universally accessible set of worlds and the set of standard names again behaves like a fixed domain of quantification. This implies that our logic has the following introspection properties:

$$\models \mathbf{K}\alpha \supset \mathbf{KK}\alpha$$
$$\models \neg\mathbf{K}\alpha \supset \mathbf{K}\neg\mathbf{K}\alpha$$

We also have the property of belief generalization:

$$\models \mathbf{K}\forall x\alpha \equiv \forall x\mathbf{K}\alpha.$$

Once again, these simplifications make the logic much easier to work with. However, because of the fixed domain of quantification, if we want to model worlds where there are additional or fewer objects than in the real world, we would again use a predicate *Obj* whose extension would vary from world to world.

Once we have a notion of belief, we can follow Konolige [10] and interpret a default as a sentence: the (possibly open) default rule

$$\frac{\alpha\ :\ \beta_1, \ldots, \beta_n}{\gamma}.$$

can be written in $\mathcal{KL}$ as the sentence

$$\forall \boldsymbol{x}.\ \mathbf{K}\,\alpha \wedge \mathbf{M}\,\beta_1 \wedge \cdots \wedge \mathbf{M}\,\beta_n \supset \gamma.$$

[4] We could have defined $\mathbf{M}\alpha$ as an abbreviation for $\neg\mathbf{K}\neg\alpha$. However in the treatment of Reiter defaults later, it will be convenient to have two separate modalities.

From now on we will use this encoding for defaults, and treat a default theory as a set of $\mathcal{KL}$ sentences. For example, let T_0 be the following sentences (with *tweety* and *chilly* assumed to be standard names):

$$\begin{array}{l} \mathit{Bird}(\mathit{tweety}) \\ \mathit{Bird}(\mathit{chilly}) \\ \neg \mathit{Fly}(\mathit{chilly}) \\ \forall x.\, \mathbf{K}\mathit{Bird}(x) \wedge \mathbf{M}\mathit{Fly}(x) \supset \mathit{Fly}(x). \end{array}$$

The question then is how to reason with such a theory and obtain by default the conclusion $\mathit{Fly}(\mathit{tweety})$, as desired.

First, observe that we do not want to simply calculate the logical entailments of this modal theory. In fact, we can see that T_0 can be true without $\mathit{Fly}(\mathit{tweety})$ being true. (Let $e = W$ and let w be such that no bird flies: $w[\mathit{Bird}(n)] = 1$ and $w[\mathit{Fly}(n)] = 0$, for every n.)

Next, observe that T_0 can be believed without $\mathit{Fly}(\mathit{tweety})$ being believed. (Let $e = \{w : w[\mathit{Bird}(n)] = 1$ and $w[\mathit{Fly}(n)] = 0$, for all $n\}$. Then we have that $e \models \mathbf{K}\forall x \mathit{Bird}(x)$ and $e \models \mathbf{K}\forall x \neg \mathit{Fly}(x)$.) But note that for T_0 to be believed without $\mathit{Fly}(\mathit{tweety})$ being believed, we need to have other independent beliefs beyond T_0, like the fact that no bird flies.

But finally, suppose that T_0 is *all* that is believed, that is, that there is no additional information beyond what is stated in T_0. In this case, it can be seen that $\mathit{Fly}(\mathit{tweety})$ will be believed. The reason, informally, is this: Suppose e is a state where only T_0 is believed. Then $e \not\models \mathbf{K}\neg \mathit{Fly}(\mathit{tweety})$, since there is nothing in T_0 that would lead to a non-flying belief. It follows that $e \models \mathbf{M}\mathit{Fly}(\mathit{tweety})$ and so $e \models \mathbf{KM}\mathit{Fly}(\mathit{tweety})$. We also have that $e \models \mathbf{K}\mathit{Bird}(\mathit{tweety})$ and so $e \models \mathbf{KK}\mathit{Bird}(\mathit{tweety})$. Finally, $e \models \mathbf{K}\forall x.\, \mathbf{K}\mathit{Bird}(x) \wedge \mathbf{M}\mathit{Fly}(x) \supset \mathit{Fly}(x)$, and so we have that $e \models \forall x.\, \mathbf{KK}\mathit{Bird}(x) \wedge \mathbf{KM}\mathit{Fly}(x) \supset \mathbf{K}\mathit{Fly}(x)$. The conclusion: $e \models \mathbf{K}\mathit{Fly}(\mathit{tweety})$.

So to draw the appropriate conclusions from a default theory, we need to know what is believed and we also need to know that this is *all* that is believed.

4 Only Knowing: The Simple Case

This suggest another addition to the language, $\mathbf{O}\alpha$, read as, "α is all that is believed." Depending on how we characterize the truth of these sentences, we will obtain different treatments of defaults.

Here is the simplest case. Suppose ϕ is an objective sentence.[5] Then $e \models \mathbf{K}\phi$ holds iff $e \subseteq \{w : w \models \phi\}$. Acquiring additional information means moving from e to a subset e'. For example, if we find out in e' that ψ is also true, we have

$$e' \models (\mathbf{K}\phi \wedge \mathbf{K}\psi) \text{ iff } e' \subseteq \{w : w \models \phi\} \cap \{w : w \models \psi\}.$$

So we can say that ϕ is all that is believed when there is no additional information and so e is as large as it can be: $e = \{w : w \models \phi\}$. More generally, we can say

[5] A sentence is *objective* when it contains no modal operators and *subjective* if all the predicate symbols are within the scope of a modal operator.

that $e \models \mathbf{O}\alpha$ iff for every w', if $w' \in e$, then $e, w' \models \alpha$ (that is, α is believed) and for every w', if $e, w' \models \alpha$, then $w' \in e$ (that is, nothing else is).

Overall, this leads to a new logic $\mathcal{OL}$ with the following truth conditions:

Let $w \in W$ and $e \subseteq W$. We define what it means for a sentence α to be true wrt e and w, which we write as $e, w \models \alpha$, as follows:
1. $e, w \models P(n_1, \ldots, n_k)$ iff $w[P(n_1, \ldots, n_k)] = 1$;
2. $e, w \models (n_1 = n_2)$ iff n_1 and n_2 are the same standard name;
3. $e, w \models \neg\alpha$ iff $e, w \not\models \alpha$;
4. $e, w \models (\alpha \wedge \beta)$ iff $e, w \models \alpha$ and $e, w \models \beta$;
5. $e, w \models \forall x.\alpha$ iff $e, w \models \alpha^x_n$ for every standard name n;
6. $e, w \models \mathbf{K}\alpha$ iff $e, w' \models \alpha$ for every $w' \in e$;
   $e, w \models \mathbf{M}\alpha$ iff $e, w' \models \alpha$ for some $w' \in e$.
7. $e, w \models \mathbf{O}\alpha$ iff for every $w' \in W$, $e, w' \models \alpha$ iff $w' \in e$.

We say that α is *valid*, written $\models \alpha$, when $e, w \models \alpha$ for every e and w.

This is the same semantics as for the previous logic $\mathcal{KL}$ with the addition of the new rule for the $\mathbf{O}$ operator.

We already observed the following:

$\not\models T_0 \supset \mathit{Fly}(\mathit{tweety})$,
$\not\models \mathbf{K}T_0 \supset \mathbf{K}\mathit{Fly}(\mathit{tweety})$.

Now we can prove that only knowing T_0 gets Tweety off the ground:

$\models \mathbf{O}T_0 \supset \mathbf{K}\mathit{Fly}(\mathit{tweety})$.

Proof: Suppose $e \models \mathbf{O}T_0$. We will prove that $e \models \mathbf{M}\mathit{Fly}(\mathit{tweety})$, from which the argument that $e \models \mathbf{K}\mathit{Fly}(\mathit{tweety})$ was presented above. First, let w^* be such that $w^*[\rho] = 1$ for all atoms ρ except $\mathit{Fly}(\mathit{chilly})$. Since $e \models \neg\mathbf{M}\mathit{Fly}(\mathit{chilly})$, $e, w^* \models \forall x.\mathbf{K}\mathit{Bird}(x) \wedge \mathbf{M}\mathit{Fly}(x) \supset \mathit{Fly}(x)$. Hence, $e, w^* \models T_0$. Since $e \models \mathbf{O}T_0$, we have that $w^* \in e$. Then, since $w^* \in e$ and $w^*[\mathit{Fly}(\mathit{tweety})] = 1$, we have that $e \models \mathbf{M}\mathit{Fly}(\mathit{tweety})$.

So in the context of the logic $\mathcal{OL}$, the pattern for skeptical reasoning is this: given (the modal encoding of) a default theory T, we believe any α such that $(\mathbf{O}T \supset \mathbf{K}\alpha)$ is valid. The pattern for credulous reasoning is this: given (the modal encoding of) a default theory T, select an e such that $e \models \mathbf{O}T$, and we believe every α such that $e \models \mathbf{K}\alpha$.

Levesque [15] showed that this characterization aligned precisely with Moore's autoepistemic logic (see Theorem 3.9, p. 281):

Theorem 1. *E is a Moore extension of T iff for some e such that $e \models \mathbf{O}T$, $E = \{basic\ \alpha : e \models \mathbf{K}\alpha\}$.*[6]

But what about other forms of default reasoning? In the next section, we replace the $\mathbf{O}$ operator by three others: $\mathbf{O}_M, \mathbf{O}_K, \mathbf{O}_R$, for Moore, Konolige and Reiter respectively, and we show in each case that the only-knowing captures the idea of the extension for the logic. (In fact, we will only deal with two new versions of only-knowing since $\mathbf{O}_M$ is precisely the $\mathbf{O}$ operator defined above.)

[6] A sentence is *basic* if it does not contain $\mathbf{O}$ operators.

5 Only Knowing: Three Variants

One question to ask is this: does $\mathbf{O}_M\alpha$ really capture the fact that α is all that is believed? Is it possible that $\mathbf{O}_M\alpha$ is true, but that even less can be known? Consider the case where α is $(\neg\mathbf{K}p \vee p)$ for some atomic sentence p. This has two Moore extensions, and therefore two epistemic states only know it:

1. Let $e_t = W$. Then $e_t \models \mathbf{O}_M(\neg\mathbf{K}p \vee p)$.
2. Let $e_p = \{w : w \models p\}$. Then $e_p \models \mathbf{O}_M(\neg\mathbf{K}p \vee p)$.

Yet, $e_p \subsetneq e_t$, and so e_p is a belief state that knows more than it needs to.

Following Konolige [10], we therefore define E to be a Konolige extension of a default theory T iff E is a Moore extension with a minimal set of objective beliefs. Informally then, we will say that $\mathbf{O}_K\alpha$ is true when $\mathbf{O}_M\alpha$ is true but $\mathbf{O}_M\alpha$ is false for all less informed epistemic states. We will see below that

$$e_t \models \mathbf{O}_K(\neg\mathbf{K}p \vee p), \text{ but } e_p \not\models \mathbf{O}_K(\neg\mathbf{K}p \vee p).$$

This takes care of Konolige extensions. But what about Reiter extensions? Consider δ which is the conjunction of the following two defaults:

$$\begin{array}{l} \mathbf{K}p \wedge \mathbf{M}\text{TRUE} \supset p \\ \mathbf{K}\text{TRUE} \wedge \mathbf{M}\neg p \supset p. \end{array}$$

Because $\mathbf{K}$ is equivalent to $\neg\mathbf{M}\neg$, we have that $\models \delta \equiv p$ and so $\models \mathbf{O}_M\delta \equiv \mathbf{O}_M p$. So this default theory has exactly one Moore extension (and so one Konolige one too) corresponding to e_p.

But in Reiter's default logic, there is an argument that δ should have *no* extensions: the first default cannot be used to provide support for p since it requires belief in p as a prerequisite (it is ungrounded); the second default is nonsensical, since it says that we can conclude p when $\neg p$ is consistent with what is believed.

The difference between Reiter and the autoepistemic logics is that for Reiter, $\mathbf{K}$ and $\mathbf{M}$ are not considered to be duals [18]. So the $\mathbf{K}p$ in the first default is not considered to be the negation of the $\mathbf{M}\neg p$ in the second. There is, consequently, no way in default logic to combine the two defaults to obtain p, as there is in autoepistemic logic.[7]

Looking at the technical details of Reiter extensions, it can be seen that the definition looks to minimize beliefs from a set of sentences S, while always checking consistency wrt S itself. So the consistency testing is done with respect to a *fixed* set of sentences even as the beliefs grow. Informally then, we will say that $\mathbf{O}_R\alpha$ is true when $\mathbf{O}_K\alpha'$ is true, where α' is α with subformulas $\mathbf{M}\beta$ replaced by their truth values (and thus held fixed). We will see below that $\models \neg\mathbf{O}_R\delta$, that is, the δ above has no Reiter extensions.

Putting all the pieces into place, we have a new logic $\mathcal{O}_3\mathcal{L}$ with the following truth conditions:

[7] Denecker *et al* [4] tell an alternate story about default logic where the duality of $\mathbf{K}$ and $\mathbf{M}$ are preserved, but the conclusion about p is avoided by giving up some other properties of classical logic.

Let $w \in W$ and $e \subseteq W$. We define what it means for a sentence α to be true wrt e and w, which we write as $e, w \models \alpha$, as follows:

1. $e, w \models P(n_1, \ldots, n_k)$ iff $w[P(n_1, \ldots, n_k)] = 1$;
2. $e, w \models (n_1 = n_2)$ iff n_1 and n_2 are the same standard name;
3. $e, w \models \neg\alpha$ iff $e, w \not\models \alpha$;
4. $e, w \models (\alpha \wedge \beta)$ iff $e, w \models \alpha$ and $e, w \models \beta$;
5. $e, w \models \forall x.\alpha$ iff $e, w \models \alpha^x_n$ for every standard name n;
6. $e, w \models \mathbf{K}\alpha$ iff $e, w' \models \alpha$ for every $w' \in e$;
   $e, w \models \mathbf{M}\alpha$ iff $e, w' \models \alpha$ for some $w' \in e$.
7. $e, w \models \mathbf{O}_M\alpha$ iff for every $w' \in W$, $e, w' \models \alpha$ iff $w' \in e$.
8. $e, w \models \mathbf{O}_K\alpha$ iff for every e' such that $e \subseteq e'$, $e', w \models \mathbf{O}_M\alpha$ iff $e' = e$.
9. $e, w \models \mathbf{O}_R\alpha$ iff $e, w \models \mathbf{O}_K\alpha'$, where α' is like α except that any $\mathbf{M}\beta$ in it is replaced by TRUE if $e \models \mathbf{M}\beta$ and by FALSE otherwise.[8]

We say that α is *valid*, written $\models \alpha$, when $e, w \models \alpha$ for every e and w.

This logic is the same as $\mathcal{OL}$ with two new rules for $\mathbf{O}_K$ and $\mathbf{O}_R$.

The following is shown in [12] (see Theorem 10, p. 636):

Theorem 2. *Let T be (the modal encoding of) a closed default theory. Then*

1. *E is a Moore extension of T iff there is an e such that $e \models \mathbf{O}_M T$ and $E = \{\,$basic $\alpha : e \models \mathbf{K}\alpha\,\}$;*
2. *E is a Konolige extension of T iff there is an e such that $e \models \mathbf{O}_K T$ and $E = \{\,$basic $\alpha : e \models \mathbf{K}\alpha\,\}$;*
3. *E is a Reiter extension of T iff there is an e such that $e \models \mathbf{O}_R T$ and $E = \{\,$objective $\alpha : e \models \mathbf{K}\alpha\,\}$.*

Corollary 1. *Let T be (the modal encoding of) a closed default theory and ψ be an objective sentence. Then ψ is an element of every Moore / Konolige / Reiter extension of T iff $\mathbf{K}\psi$ is logically entailed by $\mathbf{O}_M T$ / $\mathbf{O}_K T$ / $\mathbf{O}_R T$.*

What we have, in other words, is a single monotonic logic with a well-defined notion of truth where it is possible to compare what is believed in the presence of defaults according to Moore, Konolige, and Reiter.

Unfortunately, this does not tell us which treatment of defaults is the best one, or indeed if any of them are any good. Rather, it appears that each of the three proposals has faults and limitations.

Consider, for example, the treatment of *open defaults* by Reiter. Reiter suggests that these should be treated as abbreviations for its set of ground instances. So for example, from $Bird(favouritePet(oldestFriend(george)))$, one concludes by default $Fly(favouritePet(oldestFriend(george)))$. This suggests that one need not know the *identity* of a bird to be able to use the default. However, this is not applied consistently. If we had started with $\exists x.\, OnBranch(x) \wedge Bird(x)$, we would not be able to apply the default to the unknown bird on the branch.[9]

[8] This version of the semantics does not allow "quantifying in," that is, formulas of the form $\mathbf{O}_R(\ldots\forall x(\ldots\mathbf{M}(\ldots x\ldots)))$. See section 6.4 for discussion.

[9] To do so, it would be necessary to first *Skolemize* the existential, which itself raises further concerns.

Similarly, from $Bird(c) \wedge (c = tweety \vee c = spike)$, one can conclude by default that $(Fly(tweety) \vee Fly(spike))$, but this same conclusion is not sanctioned in default logic from $(Bird(tweety) \vee Bird(spike))$.

6 An Axiomatic Account

Let us put aside the advantages and disadvantages of the three proposals for now, and turn instead to default reasoning from a more proof-theoretic perspective. Given that $\mathcal{O}_3\mathcal{L}$ is a classical truth-theoretic logic, we can consider looking for a set of axioms and rules of inference that generate all and only the valid sentences of the logic. These proof-theoretic characterizations may provide additional insight into the behaviour of the logic and therefore of defaults.

In the case of $\mathcal{O}_3\mathcal{L}$, moreover, an axiom system will allow us to consider step-by-step monotonic *derivations* for skeptical reasoning. In a nutshell, instead of starting with a default theory like T_0 and looking for some nonmonotonic steps that will lead us to $Fly(tweety)$, we start with $\mathbf{O}T_0$ and look for classical monotonic steps that will take us to $\mathbf{K}Fly(tweety)$.

In what follows, we will develop an axiomatic proof theory for $\mathcal{O}_3\mathcal{L}$ under the following three restrictions:

1. we consider the propositional subset of the language only;
2. we exclude **O** operators within the scope of a **K**, **M**, or **O** operator;
3. we exclude **K** and **M** operators within the scope of a **K** or **M** operator.

We will comment on the restriction to the propositional subset in section 6.4. (The other limitations should be thought of as simply needing more work.)

6.1 Moore

A proof theory for the $\mathbf{O}_M$ operator already appeared in [15]. It was based on using another modal operator **N** whose truth condition was as follows:

$$e, w \models \mathbf{N}\alpha \text{ iff for every } w' \notin e,\ e, w' \models \alpha.$$

Just as $\mathbf{K}\alpha$ can be read as "I know at least that α is true," $\mathbf{N}\alpha$ can be read as "I know at most that α is false." It turns out that **N** behaves like a classical **K45** modal operator and that $\mathbf{O}_M$ can be defined in terms of it and **K**. This then leads to a proof theory that starts with a variant of the modal system **K45**:

Rule of Inference:
From α and $(\alpha \supset \beta)$, derive β.

Axioms: (Duplicate the axioms below for $\mathbf{L} = \mathbf{K}$ and $\mathbf{L} = \mathbf{N}$)
1. The axioms of propositional logic
2. $\mathbf{L}\alpha$, where α is an axiom of propositional logic
3. $\mathbf{L}(\alpha \supset \beta) \supset (\mathbf{L}\alpha \supset \mathbf{L}\beta)$
4. $\sigma \supset \mathbf{L}\sigma$, where σ is any subjective sentence
5. $\mathbf{M}\alpha \equiv \neg\mathbf{K}\neg\alpha$

We then add two new axioms:

Axioms:

6. $\mathbf{O}_M\alpha \equiv \mathbf{K}\alpha \wedge \mathbf{N}\neg\alpha$
7. $\mathbf{N}\neg\phi \supset \mathbf{M}\phi$, where ϕ is any satisfiable objective sentence of propositional logic

There is a proof in [15] that this system is sound and complete for the non-quantified part of $\mathcal{OL}$. (However, it is worth noting that contrary to a conjecture by Levesque, the quantified version of these axioms was proven to be incomplete by Halpern and Lakemeyer [7].)

The heart of default reasoning in a modal setting is arriving at the conclusion $\mathbf{M}\phi$ for some objective ϕ, and then using classical modal logic from there.

For example, consider a propositional version of T_0, $(F \wedge D)$, where F is the objective facts $Bird(tweety)$, $Bird(chilly)$, $\neg Fly(chilly)$, and where D is the ground instances of the default:

$$\mathbf{K}Bird(tweety) \wedge \mathbf{M}Fly(tweety) \supset Fly(tweety) \quad \wedge$$
$$\mathbf{K}Bird(chilly) \wedge \mathbf{M}Fly(chilly) \supset Fly(chilly).$$

Here then is a formal derivation that if $(F \wedge D)$ is all that is believed, then Tweety is believed to fly:[10]

1. $\mathbf{O}_M(F \wedge D)$	Assumption.
2. $\mathbf{K}(F \wedge D)$	1; defn. of $\mathbf{O}_M$ (Axiom 6).
3. $\mathbf{K}\neg Fly(tweety) \vee \mathbf{K}Fly(tweety)$	2; K45.
4. $\mathbf{N}\neg\mathbf{M}\,Fly(chilly)$	2; K45.
5. $\mathbf{N}\neg(F \wedge D)$	1; defn. of $\mathbf{O}_M$ (Axiom 6).
6. $\mathbf{N}\neg(F \wedge Fly(tweety))$	4, 5; K45.
7. $\mathbf{M}(F \wedge Fly(tweety))$	6; **N** vs. **M** (Axiom 7).
8. $\mathbf{M}\,Fly(tweety)$	7; K45.
9. $\mathbf{K}\,Fly(tweety)$	3, 8; K45.

This is non-trivial modal reasoning, and there are many large steps indicated by the K45 annotation. But in terms of default reasoning, the key move here is in line (7) where the Axiom 7 is used to conclude $\mathbf{M}(F \wedge Fly(tweety))$. To take this step, it was necessary for the objective sentence $(F \wedge Fly(tweety))$ to be satisfiable, that is, for $Fly(tweety)$ to be consistent with the given objective facts F. Modal reasoning does all the rest.

6.2 Konolige

We now augment the axiom system for $\mathbf{O}_M$ to obtain one for the $\mathbf{O}_K$ operator as well. To do so, we use the following result of [16] (see Corollary 9.5.6, p. 154):

[10] A justification of K45 in the derivation indicates that the conclusion follows in the classical modal logic **K45**.

Theorem 3. *Let α be a basic sentence without quantifiers. Then there is a finite set of objective sentences, $\{\phi_1, \ldots, \phi_n\}$ such that* $\models \mathbf{O}_M\alpha \equiv (\mathbf{O}_M\phi_1 \vee \cdots \vee \mathbf{O}_M\phi_n)$

It then turns out that $\mathbf{O}_K\alpha$ is equivalent to the disjunction of the "minimal" of these $\mathbf{O}_M\phi_i$. This can then be captured proof-theoretically (although somewhat awkwardly) as follows:

Axiom:
$(\mathbf{O}_K\alpha \supset \mathbf{O}_M\alpha)$

Rules of Inference:
1. From $(\mathbf{O}_M\psi \supset \mathbf{O}_M\alpha)$, $(\mathbf{O}_M\phi \supset \mathbf{O}_M\alpha)$, $(\mathbf{O}_M\psi \supset \mathbf{K}\phi)$, $(\mathbf{O}_M\phi \supset \neg\mathbf{K}\psi)$, derive $(\mathbf{K}\psi \supset \neg\mathbf{O}_K\alpha)$.
2. From $(\mathbf{O}_M\alpha \supset \mathbf{O}_M\psi \vee \bigvee \mathbf{O}_M\phi_i)$, $(\mathbf{O}_M\psi \supset \mathbf{O}_M\alpha)$, $(\mathbf{O}_M\psi \supset \bigwedge \neg\mathbf{K}\phi_i)$, derive $(\mathbf{O}_M\psi \supset \mathbf{O}_K\alpha)$.

The first rule of inference deals with the case where the ψ is not minimal, and so knowing it precludes $\mathbf{O}_K\alpha$; the second rule deals with the case where the ψ is one of the minimal disjuncts, where the conclusion is the opposite.

6.3 Reiter

Finally we turn to the $\mathbf{O}_R$ operator corresponding to Reiter's default logic. The starting point is the work by Lin and Shoham [18] showing that in default logic, the **K** and **M** operators are not duals. Then we get to use a fundamental result of Vladimir Lifschitz dating back to 1994. This result, which appeared in [17] and was taken up again by Denecker *et al* in [3], established that Reiter's default logic was similar to autoepistemic logic except that it held the **M** fixed. We exploited this fact already in the semantic characterization of $\mathbf{O}_R$, and a similar move can be done axiomatically:

Axioms:
1. $(\mathbf{O}_R\alpha \equiv \mathbf{O}_K\alpha)$, when α has no **M** operators.
2. $\mathbf{M}\phi \supset (\mathbf{O}_R\alpha \equiv \mathbf{O}_R\alpha')$, where α' is α with $\mathbf{M}\phi$ replaced by TRUE.
3. $\neg\mathbf{M}\phi \supset (\mathbf{O}_R\alpha \equiv \mathbf{O}_R\alpha')$, where α' is α with $\mathbf{M}\phi$ replaced by FALSE.

What these axioms say is that for Reiter's default logic, we can systematically replace every $\mathbf{M}\phi$ in α by either TRUE or FALSE and then use the Konolige version of only-knowing.

The main result, then, is shown in [13] (see Theorems 2 and 3, p. 266):

Theorem 4. *Let α be any sentence of $\mathcal{O}_3\mathcal{L}$ subject to the restrictions noted. Then α is valid iff it is derivable according to the given axioms and rules of inference.*

6.4 The First-Order Case

The proof theory above only works for the propositional subset of the language, and therefore, only for closed defaults. The semantic theory for defaults presented above allows quantified defaults in the case of $\mathbf{O}_M$ and $\mathbf{O}_K$. For example, we have that $\models (\mathbf{O}_K T_0 \supset \mathbf{K}\mathit{Fly}(\mathit{tweety}))$. In the case of $\mathbf{O}_R$, however, only closed defaults are allowed: in replacing the subformulas $\mathbf{M}\beta$ by their truth values, the β must not contain free variables.

It is possible to extend the definition $\mathbf{O}_R$ to handle quantifying-in. Instead of replacing subformulas $\mathbf{M}\beta$ by their truth values (to keep the $\mathbf{M}$ fixed), a second epistemic state can be used for this purpose. (The details appear in [12].) However, while this would allow quantified defaults within the scope of $\mathbf{O}_R$, these defaults would not be handled the same way Reiter handles open defaults. Moreover, it is unlikely that there are axioms and rules of inference that would work for these quantified defaults.

Consider the following example. Let D consist of a single quantified default of the simplest sort, normal and prerequisite-free: $\forall x.\, \mathbf{M}\neg Ab(x) \supset \neg Ab(x)$. Let F consist of the following objective facts:

$$\forall x.\, \neg R(x,x)$$
$$\forall x,y,z.\, R(x,y) \wedge R(y,z) \supset R(x,z)$$
$$\exists x.\, Ab(x)$$
$$\forall x.\, Ab(x) \supset \exists y.\, R(x,y) \wedge Ab(y)$$

This default theory has no Moore extensions: $\models \neg\mathbf{O}_M(F \wedge D)$. Consequently, it has no Konolige or Reiter extensions either. Intuitively, what is happening here is that D is insisting that the extension of Ab be minimal, whereas F is insisting that it be infinite (using an irreflexive, transitive relation R). No belief state e can satisfy both. It is unlikely that there are axioms and rules of inference that would lead to this conclusion, however, as they would need to confirm the impossibility of a minimal infinite set. It is interesting to note that in Reiter's default logic, this theory (now using an open default) would have a single extension: a theory that insists that there are infinitely many Ab individuals, but that contains $\neg Ab(t)$ for every possible term t.

7 Conclusion

What we have attempted to show in this paper is that it is possible to consider default reasoning from the standpoint of truth. We can look at a model of a default theory (a belief state e and a world state w) and ask what is true, what is believed, what is all that is believed. Default reasoning, in other words, does not need to be limited to a proof-theoretic analysis.

The exercise also reveals interesting connections among the versions of default reasoning proposed by Moore, Konolige, and Reiter. By formulating these three accounts within a monotonic logic of belief, we also get sentence-by-sentence derivations that correspond precisely to each form of default reasoning. The whole machinery of fixpoints, stable sets, and so on is still there in the background, of course, but we are no longer forced to use it.

In terms of future work, many questions remain. The axioms for the Konolige extensions are quite clumsy and should be reformulated. The use of quantified defaults and its connection to open defaults needs to be further investigated. Other forms of default reasoning, based on circumscription and nonmonotonic modal systems, for instance, should be incorporated into some sort of grand unified theory. One step in this direction was recently made in [14]. Finally, other forms of logic-based AI may stand to benefit from the truth-oriented perspective advocated here.

References

1. Baader, F., Calvanese, D., McGuinness, D.L., Nardi, D., Patel-Schneider, P.F. (eds.): The Description Logic Handbook: Theory, Implementation, and Applications. Cambridge University Press (2003)
2. Chellas, B.: Modal logic. Cambridge University Press (1980)
3. Denecker, M., Marek, V.W., Truszczynski, M.: Uniform semantic treatment of default and autoepistemic logics. Artif. Intell. 143(1), 79–122 (2003)
4. Denecker, M., Marek, V., Truszczynski, M.: Reiter's default logic is a logic of autoepistemic reasoning and a good one, too. In: Brewka, G., Marek, V., Truszczynski, M. (eds.) Nonmonotonic Reasoning – Essays Celebrating Its 30th Anniversary, pp. 111–144. College Publications (2011)
5. Fagin, R., Halpern, J.Y., Moses, Y., Vardi, M.Y.: Reasoning About Knowledge. The MIT Press (1995)
6. Gomes, C.P., Kautz, H., Sabharwal, A., Selman, B.: Satisfiability Solvers. In: Frank van Harmelen, V.L., Porter, B. (eds.) Handbook of Knowledge Representation. Foundations of Artificial Intelligence, vol. 3, ch.2, pp. 89–134. Elsevier (2008)
7. Halpern, J., Lakemeyer, G.: Multi-agent only knowing. Journal of Logic and Computation 11(1), 41 (2001)
8. Hintikka, J.: Knowledge and belief: an introduction to the logic of the two notions. Cornell University Press (1962)
9. Hughes, G.E., Cresswell, M.J.: An introduction to modal logic. Methuen London (1972)
10. Konolige, K.: On the relation between default and autoepistemic logic. Artif. Intell. 35(3), 343–382 (1988)
11. Lakemeyer, G., Levesque, H.J.: Situations, si! situation terms, no? In: Dubois, D., Welty, C.A., Williams, M.A. (eds.) KR, pp. 516–526. AAAI Press (2004)
12. Lakemeyer, G., Levesque, H.J.: Only-knowing: Taking it beyond autoepistemic reasoning. In: Veloso, M.M., Kambhampati, S. (eds.) AAAI, pp. 633–638. AAAI Press / The MIT Press (2005)
13. Lakemeyer, G., Levesque, H.J.: Towards an axiom system for default logic. In: AAAI. AAAI Press (2006)
14. Lakemeyer, G., Levesque, H.J.: Only-knowing meets nonmonotonic modal logic. In: Brewka, G., Eiter, T., McIlraith, S. (eds.) KR. AAAI Press (2012)
15. Levesque, H.J.: All i know: A study in autoepistemic logic. Artif. Intell. 42(2-3), 263–309 (1990)
16. Levesque, H.J., Lakemeyer, G.: The logic of knowledge bases. MIT Press (2000)
17. Lifschitz, V.: Minimal belief and negation as failure. Artif. Intell. 70(1-2), 53–72 (1994)

18. Lin, F., Shoham, Y.: Epistemic semantics for fixed-points non-monotonic logics. In: Parikh, R. (ed.) TARK, pp. 111–120. Morgan Kaufmann (1990)
19. Moore, R.C.: Semantical considerations on nonmonotonic logic. Artif. Intell. 25(1), 75–94 (1985)
20. Reiter, R.: A logic for default reasoning. Artificial Intelligence 13(1-2), 81–132 (1980)
21. Tarski, A.: Logic, Semantics, Metamathematics: Papers from 1923 to 1938. Hacket (1956)

Parsing Combinatory Categorial Grammar via Planning in Answer Set Programming

Yuliya Lierler[1] and Peter Schüller[2]

[1] Department of Computer Science, University of Kentucky
yulia@cs.uky.edu
[2] Institut für Informationssysteme, Technische Universität Wien
ps@kr.tuwien.ac.at

Abstract. Combinatory categorial grammar (CCG) is a grammar formalism used for natural language parsing. CCG assigns structured lexical categories to words and uses combinatory rules to combine these categories to parse a sentence. In this work we propose and implement a new approach to CCG parsing that relies on a prominent knowledge representation formalism, answer set programming (ASP) — a declarative programming paradigm. We formulate the task of CCG parsing as a planning problem and use an ASP computational tool to compute solutions that correspond to valid parses. Compared to other approaches, there is no need to implement a specific parsing algorithm using such a declarative method. Our approach aims at producing all semantically distinct parse trees for a given sentence. From this goal, normalization and efficiency issues arise, and we deal with them by combining and extending existing strategies. We have implemented a CCG parsing tool kit — ASPCCGTK— that uses ASP as its main computational means. The C&C supertagger can be used as a preprocessor within ASPCCGTK, which allows us to achieve wide-coverage natural language parsing.

1 Introduction

The task of parsing, i.e., recovering the internal structure of sentences, is an important task in natural language processing. Combinatory categorial grammar (CCG) is a popular grammar formalism used for this task. It assigns basic and complex lexical categories to words in a sentence and uses a set of combinatory rules to combine these categories to parse the sentence. In this work we propose and implement a new approach to CCG parsing that relies on a prominent knowledge representation formalism, answer set programming (ASP) — a declarative programming paradigm. Our aim is to create a wide-coverage[1] parser which returns all semantically distinct parse trees for a given sentence.

One major challenge of natural language processing is ambiguity of natural language. For instance, many sentences have more than one plausible internal structure, which often provide different semantics to the same sentence. Consider a sentence

John saw the astronomer with the telescope.

[1] The goal of wide-coverage parsing is to parse sentences that are not within a controlled fragment of natural language, e.g., sentences from newspaper articles.

E. Erdem et al. (Eds.): Correct Reasoning, LNCS 7265, pp. 436–453, 2012.

It can denote that John used a telescope to see the astronomer, or that John saw an astronomer who had a telescope. It is not obvious which meaning is the correct one without additional context. Natural language ambiguity inspires our goal to return *all semantically distinct* parse trees for a given sentence.

CCG-based systems OPENCCG [31] and TCCG [1, 3] (implemented in the LKB toolkit) can provide multiple parse trees for a given sentence. Both use chart parsing algorithms with CCG extensions such as modalities or hierarchies of categories. While OPENCCG is primarily geared towards generating sentences from logical forms, TCCG targets parsing. However, both implementations require lexicons[2] with specialized categories. Generally, crafting a CCG lexicon is a time–consuming task. An alternative method to using a hand-crafted lexicon has been implemented in a wide-coverage CCG parser — C&C [6, 7]. C&C relies on machine learning techniques for tagging an input sentence with CCG categories as well as for creating parse trees with a chart algorithm. As training data, C&C uses CCGbank— a corpus of CCG derivations and dependency structures [20] based on the translation of the Penn Treebank[3] using CCG. It pairs syntactic derivations with sets of word-word dependencies which approximate the underlying predicate-argument structure. The parsing algorithm of C&C returns a *single* most probable parse tree for a given sentence[4].

In the approach that we describe in this paper we formulate the task of CCG parsing as a planning problem. Then we solve it using answer set programming [24, 26]. ASP is a declarative programming formalism based on the answer set semantics of logic programs [18]. The idea of ASP is to represent a given computational problem by a program whose answer sets correspond to solutions, and then use an answer set solver to generate answer sets for this program. Utilizing ASP for CCG parsing allows us to control the parsing process with declarative descriptions of constraints on combinatory rule applications and parse trees. Moreover, there is no need to implement a specific parsing algorithm, as an answer set solver is used as a computational vehicle of the method. In our ASP approach to CCG parsing we formulate a problem in such a way that multiple parse trees are computed.

An important issue inherent to CCG parsing are spurious parse trees: a given sentence may have many distinct parse trees which yield the same semantics. Various methods for eliminating such spurious parse trees have been proposed [6, 12, 32]. We adopt some of these syntactic methods in this work.

We implemented our approach in an ASPCCGTK toolkit. The toolkit equips a user with two possibilities for assigning plausible categories to words in a sentence: it can either use a given (hand-crafted) CCG lexicon or it can take advantage of the C&C supertagger [7] for this task. The second possibility provides us with wide-coverage CCG parsing capabilities. The ASPCCGTK toolkit computes best-effort parses in cases where no full parse can be achieved with CCG, resulting in parse trees for as many phrases of a sentence as possible. This behavior is more robust than completely failing in producing

---

[2] A CCG lexicon is a mapping from each word that can occur in the input to one or more CCG categories.

[3] `http://www.cis.upenn.edu/~treebank/`

[4] Parser C&C defines "most probable" based on categories co-occurrence statistics derived from CCGbank corpus.

a parse tree. It is also useful for development, debugging, and experimenting with rule sets and normalizations. In addition to producing parse trees, ASPCCGTK contains a module for visualizing CCG derivations. The following table compares ASPCCGTK to CCG parsers discussed earlier.

Properties	OPENCCG	TCCG	C&C	ASPCCGTK
multiple parses	✓	✓		✓
wide-coverage			✓	✓

A number of theoretical characterizations of CCG parsing exists. They differ in their use of specialized categories, their sets of combinatory rules, or specific conditions on applicability of rules. We see an ASP approach to CCG parsing implemented in ASPCCGTK as a basis of a generic tool for encoding different CCG category and rule sets in a declarative and straightforward manner. Such a tool provides a test-bed for experimenting with different theoretical CCG frameworks without the need to craft specific parsing algorithms.

The structure of this paper is as follows: we start by reviewing planning, ASP, and CCG. We describe our new approach to CCG parsing by formulating this task as a planning problem in Section 3. The implementation and framework for realizing this approach using ASP technology is the topic of Section 4. We conclude with a discussion of future work directions and challenges.

2 Preliminaries

2.1 Planning

Automated planning [5] is a widely studied area in Artificial Intelligence. In *planning*, given knowledge about

(a) available actions, their executability, and effects,
(b) an initial state, and
(c) a goal state,

the task is to find a sequence of actions that leads from the initial state to the goal state. A number of special purpose planners have been developed in this sub-area of Artificial Intelligence. Answer set programming provides a viable alternative to special-purpose planning tools [13, 23, 26].

2.2 Answer Set Programming (for Planning)

Answer set programming (ASP) [24, 26] is a declarative programming formalism based on the answer set semantics of logic programs [18, 19]. The idea of ASP is to represent a given computational problem by a program whose answer sets correspond to solutions, and then use an answer set solver to generate answer sets for this program. In this work we use the CLASP[5] system with its front-end (grounder) GRINGO [16], which is currently one of the most widely used answer set solvers.

[5] `http://potassco.sourceforge.net/`

A common methodology to solve a problem in ASP is to design GENERATE, DEFINE, and TEST [23] parts of a program. The GENERATE part defines a large collection of answer sets that could be seen as potential solutions. The TEST part consists of rules that eliminate the answer sets of the GENERATE part that do not correspond to solutions. The DEFINE section expresses additional concepts and connects the GENERATE and TEST parts.

A typical logic programming rule has the form of a Prolog rule. For instance, program

$$p.$$
$$q \leftarrow p,\ not\ r.$$

is composed of such rules. This program has one answer set $\{p, q\}$. In addition to Prolog rules, GRINGO also accepts rules of other kinds — "choice rules" and "constraints". For example, rule

$$\{p, q, r\}.$$

is a choice rule. Answer sets of this one-rule program are arbitrary subsets of the atoms $p,\ q,\ r$. Choice rules are typically the main members of the GENERATE part of the program. Constraints often form the TEST section of a program. Syntactically, a constraint is the rule with an empty head. It encodes the conditions on the answer sets that have to be met. For instance, the constraint

$$\leftarrow p,\ not\ q.$$

eliminates the answer sets of a program that include p and do not include q.

System GRINGO allows the user to specify large programs in a compact way, using rules with schematic variables and other abbreviations. A detailed description of its input language can be found in the online manual [16]. Grounder GRINGO takes a program "with abbreviations" as an input and produces its propositional counterpart that is then processed by CLASP. Unlike Prolog systems, the inference mechanism of CLASP is related to that of Propositional Satisfiability (SAT) solvers [17].

The GENERATE-DEFINE-TEST methodology is suitable for modeling planning problems. To illustrate how ASP programs can be used to solve such problems, we present a simplified part of the encoding of a classic toy planning domain *blocks world* given in [23]. In this domain, blocks are moved by a robot. There are a number of restrictions including the fact that a block cannot be moved unless it is clear.

Lifschitz [23] models the blocks world domain by means of five predicates: *time/1*, *block/1*, *location/1*, *move/3*, *on/3*; a location is a *block* or the *table*. The constant *maxsteps* is an upper bound on the length of a plan. States of the domain are modeled by the ground atoms of the form *on(b,l,t)* stating that block b is at location l at time t. Actions are modeled by ground atoms *move(b,l,t)* stating that block b is moved to location l at time t.

The GENERATE section of a program consists of a single rule

$$\{move(B, L, T)\} \leftarrow block(B),\ location(L),\ time(T),\ T < maxsteps.$$

that defines a potential solution to be an arbitrary set of *move* actions executed before *maxsteps*.

The fact that moving a block to a position at time T forces a block to be at this position at time $T{+}1$ is encoded in DEFINE part of the program by the rule

$$on(B, L, T{+}1) \leftarrow move(B, L, T),\ block(B),\ location(L),\ time(T),\ T{<}maxsteps.$$

The rule below specifies the commonsense law of inertia for a predicate *on* stating that unless we know that the block is no longer at the same position it remains where it was:

$$\begin{aligned} on(B, L, T{+}1) \leftarrow\ & on(B, L, T),\ not\ \neg on(B, L, T{+}1),\ block(B),\ location(L),\\ & time(T),\ T < maxsteps. \end{aligned}$$

The following constraint in TEST encodes the restriction that a block cannot be moved unless it is clear

$$\begin{aligned} \leftarrow\ & move(B, L, T),\ on(B1, B, T),\ block(B),\ block(B1),\\ & location(L),\ time(T),\ T < maxsteps. \end{aligned}$$

Given the rest of the encoding and the description of an initial state and of the goal state, answer sets of the resulting program represent plans. The ground atoms of the form *move(b,l,t)* present in an answer set form the list of actions of a corresponding plan.

2.3 Combinatory Categorial Grammar

Combinatory Categorial Grammar (CCG) [29] is a linguistic grammar formalism. CCG uses a small set of combinatory rules – combinators – to combine rich lexical categories of words.

Categories in CCG are either atomic or complex. For instance, noun N, noun phrase NP, and sentence S are atomic categories. Complex categories are functors that specify the type and direction of the arguments and the type of the result. A complex category

$$S\backslash NP$$

is a category for English intransitive verbs (such as *walk, hug*), which states that a noun phrase is required to the left, resulting in a sentence. A category

$$(S\backslash NP)/NP$$

for English transitive verbs (such as *like* and *bite*) specifies that a noun phrase is required to the right and yields the category of an English intransitive verb, which (as before) requires a noun phrase to the left to form a sentence.

Given a sentence and a lexicon containing a set of word-category pairs, we can replace words in the sentence by appropriate categories. For example, for a sentence

$$\textit{The dog bit John} \qquad (1)$$

and a lexicon containing pairs

$$\textit{The} \text{ - } NP/N;\ \textit{dog} \text{ - } N;\ \textit{bit} \text{ - } (S\backslash NP)/NP;\ \textit{John} \text{ - } NP \qquad (2)$$

we obtain

$$\frac{\mathit{The}}{NP/N} \qquad \frac{\mathit{dog}}{N} \qquad \frac{\mathit{bit}}{(S\backslash NP)/NP} \qquad \frac{\mathit{John}}{NP}\,.$$

Words may have multiple categories, e.g., "bit" is also an intransitive verb and a noun. To simplify the presentation of parsing in this paper we limit out attention to the case when there is a unique category corresponding to each word. Nevertheless, our framework is able to handle multiple categories by considering all combinations of word categories.

To parse English sentences a number of combinators are required [29]: forward and backward application (> and <, respectively), forward and backward *composition* (>**B** and <**B**), forward and backward *type raising* (>**T** and <**T**), backward *cross composition*, backward *cross substitution*, and *coordination*. Specifications of some of these combinators follow:

$$\frac{A/B \quad B}{A}> \qquad \frac{A/B \quad B/C}{A/C}>\mathbf{B} \qquad \frac{A}{B/(B\backslash A)}>\mathbf{T}$$

$$\frac{B \quad A\backslash B}{A}< \qquad \frac{B\backslash C \quad A\backslash B}{A\backslash C}<\mathbf{B} \qquad \frac{A}{B\backslash(B/A)}<\mathbf{T}$$

where A, B, C are variables that can be substituted by CCG categories such as N or $S\backslash NP$. An *instance* of a CCG combinator is obtained by substituting CCG categories for variables. For example,

$$\frac{NP/N \quad N}{NP}> \tag{3}$$

is an instance of the forward application combinator (>). A CCG combinatory rule combines one or more adjacent categories and yields exactly one output category. To parse a sentence is to apply instances of CCG combinators so that the final category S is derived at the end. A sample CCG derivation for sentence (1) follows

$$\begin{array}{lcccccl}
 & \mathit{The} & \mathit{dog} & \mathit{bit} & \mathit{John} & & \\
\text{initial state (time 0)} & NP/N & N & (S\backslash NP)/NP & NP & & \\
 & \multicolumn{2}{c}{\rule{2cm}{0.4pt}>} & \multicolumn{2}{c}{\rule{3cm}{0.4pt}>} & & \text{two > actions at time 0} \\
\text{state (time 1)} & \multicolumn{2}{c}{NP} & \multicolumn{2}{c}{S\backslash NP} & & \\
 & \multicolumn{4}{c}{\rule{5cm}{0.4pt}<} & & \text{one < action at time 1} \\
\text{goal state (time 2)} & \multicolumn{4}{c}{S} & &
\end{array} \tag{4}$$

On the left and right side of the derivation we give an intuition about how we translate the CCG parsing task into action planning. Section 3.1 gives a formal definition of this translation.

Type Raising and Spurious Parses: CCG restricted to application combinators generates the same language as CCG restricted to application, composition, and type raising rules [10, 27]. One of the motivations for type raising are non-constituent coordination constructions[6] that can only be parsed with the use of raising [2, Example (2)] and the additional coordination rule shown below (coordinating words such as "and" receive category *CONJ*).

$$\frac{A \; CONJ \; A}{A} \; \mathbf{\Phi}$$

Unrestricted applications of composition and type raising combinators often create spurious parse trees which are semantically equivalent to parse trees derived using application rules only. Eisner [12, Example (3)] presents a sample sentence with 12 words and 252 parses but only 2 distinct meanings. An example of a spurious parse for sentence (1) is the following derivation

$$\cfrac{\cfrac{\cfrac{\cfrac{\cfrac{The}{NP/N} \quad \cfrac{dog}{N}}{NP}\,>}{S/(S\backslash NP)}\,>\mathbf{T} \quad \cfrac{bit}{(S\backslash NP)/NP}}{S/NP}\,>\mathbf{B} \quad \cfrac{John}{NP}}{S}\,> \qquad (5)$$

which utilizes application, type raising, and composition combinators. Both derivations (4) and (5) have the same semantic value (in a sense, the difference between (4) and (5) is not essential for subsequent semantic analysis).

In this work we aim at the generation of parse trees that have different semantic values so that they reflect a real ambiguity of natural language, and not a spurious ambiguity that arises from the underlying CCG formalism. Various methods for dealing with spurious parses have been proposed such as limiting type raising only to certain categories [6], normalizing branching direction of consecutive composition rules by means of predictive combinators [32] or restrictions on parse tree shape [12]. We combine and extend these ideas to pose restrictions on generated parse trees within our framework. Details about normalizations and type raising limits that we implement are discussed in Section 3.3.

3 CCG Parsing via Planning

3.1 Problem Statement

We start by defining precisely the task of *CCG parsing*. We then state how this task can be seen as a planning problem.

A *sentence* is a sequence of words. An *abstract sentence representation* (ASR) is a sequence of categories annotated by a unique id. Recall that given a lexicon, we can replace words in the sentence by appropriate categories. As a result we can turn any sentence into ASR using a lexicon. For instance, for sentence (1) and lexicon (2) a sequence

$$[NP/N^1,\ N^2,\ (S\backslash NP)/NP^3,\ NP^4]. \qquad (6)$$

[6] E.g, in the sentence "We gave Jan a record and Jo a book", neither "Jan a record" nor "Jo a book" is a linguistic constituent of the sentence. With raising we can produce meaningful categories for these non-constituents and subsequently coordinate them using "and".

is an ASR of (1). We refer to categories annotated by id's as *annotated categories*. Members of (6) are annotated categories.

Recall that an instance of a CCG combinator C has a general form

$$\frac{X_1, \ldots, X_n}{Y}\, C.$$

We say that the sequence $[X_1, \ldots, X_n]$ is a *precondition* sequence of C, whereas Y is an *effect* of applying C. The precondition sequence and the effect of instance (3) of the combinator $>$ are $[NP/N, N]$ and NP, respectively.

Given an instance C of a CCG combinator we may annotate it by

- assigning a distinct id to each member of its precondition sequence, and
- assigning the id of the left most annotated category in the precondition sequence to its effect.

We call such an instance an *annotated (combinator) instance*. For example,

$$\frac{NP/N^1 \quad N^2}{NP^1} > \tag{7}$$

is an annotated instance w.r.t. (3).

An annotated instance C is applied to an ASR sequence A by replacing the substring of A corresponding to the precondition sequence of C by its effect. For example, applying (7) to (6) yields ASR $[NP^1, (S\backslash NP)/NP^3, NP^4]$. In the following we will often say annotated combinator in place of annotated instance.

To view CCG parsing as a planning problem we need to specify states and actions of this domain. In CCG planning, states are ASRs and actions are annotated combinators. So the task is given the initial ASR, e.g., $[X_1^1, \ldots, X_n^n]$, to find a sequence of annotated combinators that leads to the goal ASR — $[S^1]$.

Let $\mathcal{C}_1$ denote annotated combinator (7), $\mathcal{C}_2$ denote

$$\frac{(S\backslash NP)/NP^3 \quad NP^4}{S\backslash NP^3} >,$$

and $\mathcal{C}_3$ denote

$$\frac{NP^1 \quad S\backslash NP^3}{S^1} >.$$

Given ASR (6) a sequence of actions $\mathcal{C}_1$, $\mathcal{C}_2$, and $\mathcal{C}_3$ forms a plan:

$$\begin{array}{ll} \text{Time 0:} & [NP/N^1,\ N^2,\ (S\backslash NP)/NP^3,\ NP^4] \\ \quad \text{action: } \mathcal{C}_1 & \\ \text{Time 1:} & [NP^1,\ (S\backslash NP)/NP^3,\ NP^4], \\ \quad \text{action: } \mathcal{C}_2 & \\ \text{Time 2:} & [NP^1,\ S\backslash NP^3], \\ \quad \text{action: } \mathcal{C}_3 & \\ \text{Time 3:} & [S^1]. \end{array} \tag{8}$$

This plan corresponds to parse tree (4) for sentence (1). On the other hand, a plan formed by a sequence of actions $\mathcal{C}_2$, $\mathcal{C}_1$, and $\mathcal{C}_3$ also corresponds to (4).

In planning the notion of *serializability* is important. Often given a plan, applying several consecutive actions in the plan in any order or in parallel does not change the effect of their application. Such plans are called *serializable*. Consequently, by allowing parallel execution of actions one may represent a class of plans by a single one. This is a well-known optimization in planning. For example, plan

Time 0: $[NP/N^1,\ N^2,\ (S\backslash NP)/NP^3,\ NP^4]$
  actions: $\mathcal{C}_1, \mathcal{C}_2$
Time 1: $[NP^1,\ S\backslash NP^3]$,
  action: $\mathcal{C}_3$
Time 2: $[S^1]$

may be seen as an abbreviation for a group of plans, i.e., itself, plan (8), and a plan formed by a sequence $\mathcal{C}_2$, $\mathcal{C}_1$, and $\mathcal{C}_3$. In CCG parsing as a planning problem, we are interested in finding plans of this kind, i.e., plans with concurrent actions.

Next we present the ASP encoding of the planning problem. In order to enforce normalizations that limit spurious parses, in the encoding the planning problem presented so far is extended further to eliminate some redundant plans.

3.2 ASP Encoding

In an ASP approach to CCG parsing, the goal is to encode the planning problem as a logic program so that its answer sets correspond to plans. As a result answer sets of this program will contain the sequence of annotated combinators (actions, possibly concurrent) such that the application of this sequence leads from a given ASR to the ASR composed of a single category S. We present a part of the encoding `ccg.asp`[7] in the GRINGO language that solves a CCG parsing problem by means of ideas presented in Section 2.2.

First, we need to decide how we represent states — ASRs — by sets of ground atoms. To this end, we introduce symbols called "positions" that encode annotations of ASR members. In `ccg.asp`, relation $posCat(p, c, t)$ states that a category c is annotated with (position) p at time t. Relation

$$posAdjacent(p_L, p_R, t)$$

states that a position p_L is adjacent to a position p_R at time t. In other words, a category annotated by p_L immediately precedes a category annotated by p_R in an ASR that corresponds to a state at time t (intuitively, L and R denote left and right, respectively.) These relations allow us to encode states of a CCG planning domain. For example, given an ASR (6) as the initial state, we can encode this state by the following set of facts

$$\begin{array}{l} posCat(1, \mathit{rfunc}(\text{"}NP\text{"}, \text{"}N\text{"}), 0).\ \ posCat(2, \text{"}N\text{"}, 0). \\ posCat(3, \mathit{rfunc}(\mathit{lfunc}(\text{"}S\text{"}, \text{"}NP\text{"}), \text{"}NP\text{"}), 0).\ \ posCat(4, \text{"}NP\text{"}, 0). \\ posAdjacent(1, 2, 0).\ \ posAdjacent(2, 3, 0).\ \ posAdjacent(3, 4, 0). \end{array} \tag{9}$$

[7] The complete listing of `ccg.asp` is available at
`http://www.kr.tuwien.ac.at/staff/ps/aspccgtk/ccg.asp`

Next we need to choose how we encode actions. The combinators mentioned in Section 2.3 are of two kinds: the ones whose precondition sequence consists of a single element (i.e., $>\mathbf{T}$ and $<\mathbf{T}$) and of two elements (e.g., $>$ and $<$). Coordination combinator is of a third type, i.e., its precondition sequence contains three elements. We simplify the presentation of the encoding by omitting the details of this case. We call the combinators from Section 2.3 *unary* and *binary* respectively. Reification of actions is a technique used in planning that allows us to talk about common properties of actions in a compact way. To utilize this idea, we first introduce relations $unary(a)$ and $binary(a)$ for every unary and binary combinator a respectively. For a unary combinator a, a relation $occurs(a, p, c, t)$ states that a type raising action a occurring at time t raises a category identified with position p (at time t) to category c. For a binary combinator a a relation $occurs(a, p, t)$ states that an action a applied to positions p (and the position adjacent to p to the right) occurs at time t. For instance, given the initial state (9)

- $occurs(ruleFwdTypeR, 4, (S\backslash NP)/NP, 0)$ represents an application of the annotated combinator
$$\frac{NP^4}{(S\backslash NP)/NP^4} >\mathbf{T}$$
to (9) at time 0,
- $occurs(ruleFwdAppl, 1, 0)$ represents an application of (7) to (9) at time 0.

Given an atom $occurs(a, p, c, t)$ or $occurs(a, p, t)$ we often say that action a *modifies* position p at time t.

Recall that solutions of this formalization correspond to parse trees so that each application of a combinator forms an edge (or a set of edges) in a tree. We introduce an auxiliary action named
$$placeEdgeTag(p, t, tag),$$
which states that there is an edge placed at position p at time t tagged by a tag $unary$ or $binary$. Intuitively occurrence of an atom $placeEdgeTag(p, t, unary)$ (or $placeEdgeTag(p, t, binary)$) in a solution guarantees that an atom of the form $occurs(a, p, c, t)$ (or $occurs(a, p, t)$) is also present in the solution. In other words, some unary (or binary) action *modifies* a position p at time t. Introducing this auxiliary relation allows us to state some constraints on solutions by referring only to the type of combinators (i.e., $unary$ or $binary$) rather than their kind (i.e., $ruleFwdTypeR$ or $ruleFwdAppl$).

The GENERATE section of `ccg.asp` contains a choice rule

$$0\{placeEdgeTag(P, T, TAG) : type(TAG)\}1 \leftarrow posASR(P, T), time(T),\ T < maxsteps.$$

where $posASR$ is an auxiliary relation specifying that a position p is part of an ASR encoded by a state at time t. This rule states that for "ASR" positions it is possible to place a single edge either of type unary or binary. Another sample GENERATE rule

$$1\{occurs(A, P, T) : binary(A)\}1 \leftarrow placeEdgeTag(P, T, binary).$$

specifies that if a binary edge is placed at position P then one of the binary actions must occur at this time modifying P. Such choice rules describe a potential solution to the planning problem as an arbitrary set of actions executed before *maxsteps*.

In order to state effects of actions and executability conditions the DEFINE part of a program introduces an auxiliary relation *precCat* for each action corresponding to a CCG combinator. For example,

$$\begin{aligned} \mathit{precCat}(\mathit{ruleFwdAppl}, L, T, A) \leftarrow\ & \mathit{posAdjacent}(L, R, T),\ \mathit{time}(T), \\ & \mathit{posCat}(L, \mathit{rfunc}(A, B), T),\ \mathit{posCat}(R, B, T). \end{aligned}$$

states that if there are two adjacent positions such that the category of the left and right positions are A/B and B respectively then preconditions of binary action *ruleFwdAppl* are satisfied and the resulting category of applying *ruleFwdAppl* to this position is A.

A rule that models effects of actions in the CCG parsing domain using the *precCat* relation follows

$$\mathit{posCat}(P, C, T{+}1) \leftarrow \mathit{precCat}(A, P, T, C),\ \mathit{occurs}(A, P, T),\ \mathit{time}(T).$$

It states that an application of a combinator A at time T causes a category annotated by P to be C at the next time point. Note that this rule takes advantage of reification and provides means for compact encoding of common effects of all binary actions. On the other hand, following rules

$$\begin{aligned} &\mathit{prec}(A, L, T) \leftarrow \mathit{precCat}(A, L, T, C). \\ &\leftarrow \mathit{occurs}(A, P, T),\ \mathit{not}\ \mathit{prec}(A, P, T). \end{aligned}$$

formulate executability conditions by forbidding a combinator A to occur modifying position P at time T unless its preconditions are satisfied.

The following rule characterizes another effect of combinators and defines the *posAffected* concept which is useful in stating several normalization conditions described in Section 3.3:

$$\mathit{posAffected}(P, T{+}1) \leftarrow 1\{\mathit{placeEdgeTag}(P, T, TAG) : \mathit{type}(TAG)\}\ \mathit{time}(T),\ T < \mathit{maxsteps}.$$

Relation $\mathit{posAffected}(P, T{+}1)$ holds if the element annotated by P in the ASR was modified by a combinator at time T. Note that this rule takes advantage of auxiliary relation *placeEdgeTag* that provides means for compact encoding of common effects of all unary, binary (and ternary) actions. Furthermore, *posAffected* is used to state the law of inertia for the predicate *posCat*

$$\begin{aligned} \mathit{posCat}(P, C, T{+}1) \leftarrow\ & \mathit{posCat}(P, C, T),\ \mathit{not}\ \mathit{posAffected}(P, T{+}1), \\ & \mathit{time}(T),\ T < \mathit{maxsteps}. \end{aligned}$$

stating that a category of a position stays the same unless it is affected.

In the TEST section of the program we encode such restrictions as no two combinators may modify the same position simultaneously and the fact that the goal has to be reached. We allow two possibilities for specifying a goal. In one case, the goal is to reach an ASR composed of a single category S by $maxsteps$. In another case, the goal is to reach the shortest possible ASR sequence by $maxsteps$.

The TEST section also includes a set of constraints modeling conditions when it is impossible for an action a to modify position p at time t. These rules form the main mechanism by which normalization techniques are encoded in `ccg.asp`. For instance, a rule

$$\leftarrow occurs(ruleFwdAppl, P, T),\ occurs(ruleFwdRaise, P, X, TLast-1),\\ posLastAffected(P, TLast, T),\ time(TLast), time(T),\ T < maxsteps.$$

states that a forward application modifying position P may not *occur* at time T if the last action modifying P was forward type raising (*posLastAffected* is an auxiliary predicate that helps to identify the last action modifying an element of the ASR). This corresponds to one of the normalization rules discussed in [12] and reviewed in the following subsection.

We pose additional restrictions, which ensure that only a single plan is produced when multiple serializable plans correspond to the same parse tree.

Finally, we devised punctuation specific combinators which have been described in [8, Appendix A] and are based on Sections 02-21 of CCGbank.

Given `ccg.asp` and the set of facts describing the initial state (ASR representation of a sentence) and the goal state (ASR containing a single category S), answer sets of the resulting program encode plans corresponding to parse trees. The ground atoms of the form $occurs(a, p, t)$ and $occurs(a, p, c, t)$ present in an answer set form the list of actions of a matching plan.

3.3 Normalizations

Currently, `ccg.asp` implements a number of normalization techniques and strategies for improving efficiency and eliminating spurious parses:

- One of the techniques used in C&C to improve its efficiency is to limit type raising to certain categories *based on the most commonly used type raising rule instantiations in Sections 2-21 of CCGbank* [6]. We adopt this idea by limiting type raising to be applicable only to noun phrases, NP, so that NP can be raised using categories S, $S\backslash NP$, or $(S\backslash NP)/NP$. This technique reduces the size of the ground program for `ccg.asp` and subsequently the performance of `ccg.asp` considerably. We plan to extend limiting type raising to the full set of categories used in C&C that proved to be suitable for wide-coverage parsing.
- We normalize branching direction of subsequent functional composition operations [12]. This is realized by disallowing functional forward composition to apply to a category on the left side that has been created by functional forward composition. (And similar for backward composition.)
- We disallow some combinations of rule applications if the same result can be achieved by other rule applications as shown in the following

$$\dfrac{\dfrac{X/Y \quad Y/Z}{X/Z}{\scriptstyle >\mathsf{B}} \quad Z}{X}{\scriptstyle >} \;\overset{\text{normalize}}{\Rightarrow}\; \dfrac{X/Y \quad \dfrac{Y/Z \quad Z}{Y}{\scriptstyle >}}{X}{\scriptstyle >} \qquad\qquad \dfrac{\dfrac{X}{Y/(Y\backslash X)}{\scriptstyle >\mathsf{T}} \quad Y\backslash X}{Y}{\scriptstyle >} \;\overset{\text{normalize}}{\Rightarrow}\; \dfrac{X \quad Y\backslash X}{Y}{\scriptstyle <}$$

where the left-hand side is the spurious parse and the right-hand side the normalized parse. These two normalizations (plus analogous normalizations for backward composition and backward type raising) eliminate spurious parses like (5) and have been discussed in [3, 12].

4 ASPCCG Toolkit

We have implemented ASPCCGTK— a python[8] framework for using `ccg.asp`. The framework is available online[9], including documentation and examples.

Figure 1 shows a block diagram of ASPCCGTK. We use GRINGO and CLASP for ASP solving and control these solvers from python using a modified version of the BioASP library [14]. BioASP is used for calling ASP solvers as subtasks, parsing answer sets, and writing these answer sets to temporary files as facts.

Input for parsing can be

- a natural language sentence given as a string, or
- a sequence of words and a dictionary providing possible categories for each word, both given as ASP facts.

In the first case, the framework uses C&C supertagger[10] [7] to tokenize and tag this sentence. The result of supertagging is a sequence of words of the sentence, where each word is assigned a set of likely CCG categories. From the C&C supertagger output, ASPCCGTK creates a set of ASP facts representing the sequence of words and a corresponding set of likely CCG categories. This set of facts is passed to `ccg.asp` as the initial state. In the second case the input can be processed directly by `ccg.asp`. The maximum parse tree depth (i.e., the maximum plan length – *maxsteps*) currently has to be specified by the user. Auto detection of useful depth values is subject of future work.

ASPCCGTK first attempts to find a "strict" parse which requires that the resulting parse tree yields a category S (by $maxsteps$). If this is impossible, we do "best-effort" parsing using CLASP optimization features to minimize the number of categories left by the time $maxsteps$. For instance, consider a lexicon that provides a single category for "bit", namely $(S\backslash NP)/NP$, then the following derivation

$$\dfrac{\dfrac{\dfrac{\dfrac{\mathit{The}}{NP/N} \quad \dfrac{\mathit{dog}}{N}}{NP}{\scriptstyle >}}{S/(S\backslash NP)}{\scriptstyle >\mathsf{T}} \quad \dfrac{\mathit{bit}}{(S\backslash NP)/NP}}{S/NP}{\scriptstyle >\mathsf{B}} \tag{10}$$

corresponds to a best-effort parse.

[8] http://www.python.org/

[9] http://www.kr.tuwien.ac.at/staff/ps/aspccgtk/

[10] http://svn.ask.it.usyd.edu.au/trac/candc

Answer sets resulting from `ccg.asp` represent parse trees. ASPCCGTK passes them to a visualization component, which invokes GRINGO+CLASP on another ASP encoding `ccg2idpdraw.asp`.[11] The resulting answer sets of `ccg2idpdraw.asp` contain drawing instructions for the IDPDraw tool [33], which is used to produce a two-dimensional image for each parse tree. Figure 2 demonstrates an image generated by IDPDraw for parse tree (4) of sentence (1). If multiple parse trees exist, IDPDraw allows to switch between them.

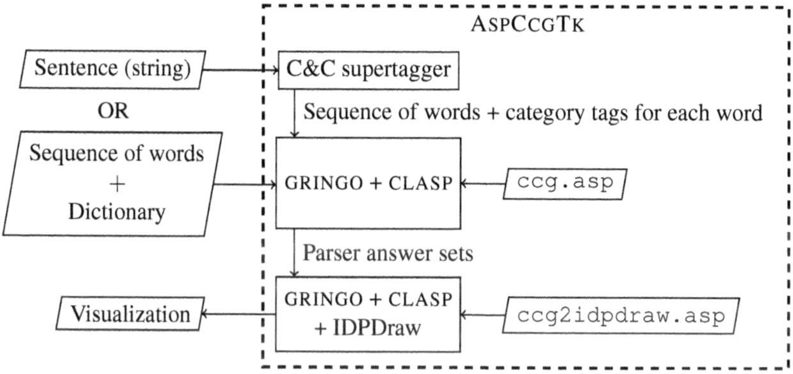

Fig. 1. Block diagram of the ASPCCG framework. (Arrows indicate data flow.)

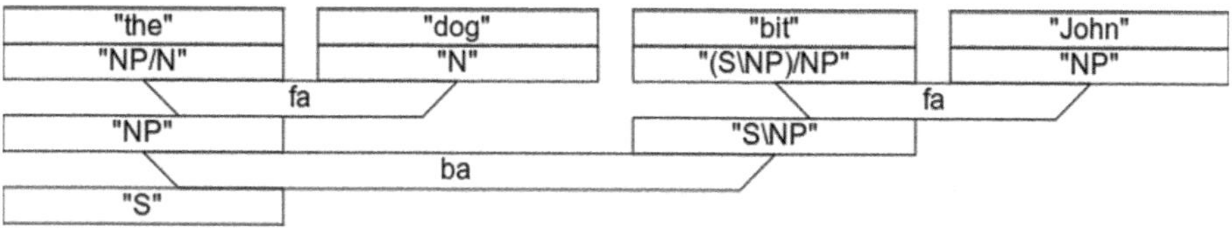

Fig. 2. Visualization of parse tree (4) for sentence (1) using IDPDraw

5 Experimental Evaluation

We evaluated the efficiency of `ccg.asp` on Section 00 of CCGbank [20] (about 2000 sentences). CCGbank contains a gold-standard parse tree for each sentence where words are annotated by unique categories. We extracted these categories and used them as input for `ccg.asp`. This method for evaluating parsing performance is used in [8, 9] as well. Figure 3 presents the experimental results that summarize the efficiency of `ccg.asp`. The experiments were run on Xeon X5355 @ 2.66GHz. The runtimes presented account for solving time of CLASP v 2.0.2 on `ccg.asp`. The timeout was set to 1200 seconds. Furthermore, in the experiments we only considered the task of finding a single parse tree. We present the results by splitting the sentences from Section 00

[11] This visualization component could be put directly into `ccg.asp`. However, for performance reasons it has proved crucial to separate the parsing calculation from the drawing calculations.

of CCGbank into 8 groups depending on the number of words occurring in them (any punctuation symbol is also treated as a word). The second line in Figure 3 specifies how many sentences each of the groups contains. The third line presents average number of words in the sentences of the corresponding group. The fourth line accounts for average *maxsteps* parameter of a plan to be searched for. We used the height of gold-standard parse tree from CCGbank as *maxsteps* for a corresponding instance. The last four lines present average runtime and number of timeouts for two configurations of CLASP that we denote CLASP^d and CLASP^t. The configuration CLASP^d is the default call to the system, whereas CLASP^t stands for a commandline

```
clasp --sat-p=-1,-1,120,-1,0 --backprop=1 --eq=1 --trans-ext=dynamic \
--seed=-1 --save-progress=0 --local-restarts=1 --initial-lookahead=-1 \
--strengthen=yes --del=1.5,1.1,3.0 --loops=no --reduce-on-restart=0 \
--otfs=0 --rand-watches=0 --heuristic=Vsids --contraction=120 \
--restarts=100,1.5,10000 --reverse-arcs=0 --rand-freq=0.02 \
--recursive-str=1
```

The automatic algorithm configuration tool PARAMILS[12] [21] (version 2.3.5) was used to inspect numerous parameter settings of CLASP resulting in configuration CLASP^t attuned to instances in our domain. The portfolio toolkit BORG[13] was used to evaluate the CLASP^t configuration together with 25 configurations of CLASP used in portfolio answer set solver CLASPFOLIO v 1.0.1 [14] in order to select the best performing one. CLASP^t proved to be the best configuration. The details on the described evaluation are presented in [28].

Groups: Number of Words		1-10	11-15	16-20	21-25	26-30	31-35	36-40	41+
Number of Sentences		191	282	342	319	278	217	114	118
Average Number of Words		7.3	13.2	18.1	22.9	27.9	33.0	37.8	47.3
Average Maxsteps		6.6	10.0	11.6	13.7	15.2	16.2	17.8	19.3
CLASP^d	Average Time	0.13	2.78	24.41	134.87	364.74	529.82	609.14	655.86
	Number of Timeouts	0	0	0	4	58	123	99	111
CLASP^t	Average Time	0.09	0.95	5.61	28.36	97.58	228.36	457.78	560.18
	Number of Timeouts	0	0	0	0	1	8	28	73

Fig. 3. Experimental results on CLASP using `ccg.asp` on Section 00 of CCGbank

These experiments demonstrate that for sentences of length 20 and less, the presented approach to CCG parsing is viable.

6 Discussion and Future Work

To increase parsing efficiency of ASPCCGTK we consider to reformulate the CCG parsing problem as a "configuration" problem. This might improve performance. At the

[12] `http://www.cs.ubc.ca/labs/beta/Projects/ParamILS/`

[13] `http://nn.cs.utexas.edu/pages/research/borg/`

[14] `http://potassco.sourceforge.net/`

same time the framework would keep its beneficial declarative nature. Investigating applicability of incremental ASP [15] to enhance system's performance is another direction of future research. Furthermore, deciding whether a sentence is in the language of a given CCG grammar can be done in polynomial time [30] (if there is unique category for each word in the sentence). In [30] the authors described a recognition algorithm for CCG grammar based on the Cocke-Younger-Kasami (CYK) chart parsing algorithm for Context Free grammars. In the future, we would like to mimic the algorithm in [30] by means of ASP so that the task of enumerating CCG parse trees would rely on its result. We expect substantial performance gains by adopting this approach. Both OPENCCG and C&C rely on variants of CYK algorithm. Also Drescher and Walsh [11] described ASP-based formulation of CYK algorithm for Context Free grammar. Extending the recognition algorithm in [30] to multiple categories makes the problem computable in nondeterministic polynomial time.

It might seem tempting to realize the planning task described in this work in a planning language such as PDDL [25] and use specialized planning tools to compute all parse trees. However CCG parsing requires objects with inner structure, i.e., nested forward and backward slashes in fluent constants, that is cumbersome to encode in planning languages. Furthermore, it is unclear how executability conditions on actions enforcing normalizations maybe stated using standard planing languages.

Preliminary experiments on using the C&C supertagger as a front-end of ASPCCGTK yielded promising results for achieving wide-coverage parsing. The supertagger of C&C not only provides a set of likely category assignments for the words in a given sentence but also includes probability values for assigned categories. C&C uses a dynamic tagging strategy for parsing. First only very likely categories from the tagger are used for parsing. If this yields no result then less likely categories are also taken into account. In the future, we will implement a similar approach in ASPCCGTK.

Creating semantic representations for sentences is an important task in natural language processing. Boxer [4] is a tool which accomplishes this task, given a CCG parse tree from C&C. To take advantage of this advanced computational semantics tool, we aim at creating an output format for ASPCCGTK that is compatible with Boxer.

As our framework is a generic parsing framework, we can easily compare different CCG rule sets with respect to their efficiency and normalization behavior. We also suspect that improving scalability of `ccg.asp` is possible using an alternative combinatory rule set in place of the one currently implemented in `ccg.asp`. Type raising is a core source of nondeterminism in CCG parsing and is one of the reasons for spurious parse trees and long parsing times. In the future we would like to evaluate an approach that partially eliminates type raising by pushing it into all non-type-raising combinators. A similar strategy has been proposed for composition combinators by Wittenburg [32].[15] Combining CCG rules this way creates more combinators, however these rules contain fewer nondeterministic guesses about raising categories. The reduced nondeterminism should improve solving efficiency without losing any CCG derivations.

[15] Wittenburg introduced a new set of combinatory rules by combining the functional composition combinators with other combinators. By omitting the original functional composition combinators, certain spurious parse trees can no longer be derived.

Acknowledgments. We would like to thank John Beavers and Vladimir Lifschitz for valuable detailed comments on the workshop paper that presented the preliminary results on this work [22]. We are especially grateful to Bryan Silverthorn for sharing with us the experimental results presented in Figure 3. We are indebted to Jason Baldridge, Marcello Balduccini, Johan Bos, Esra Erdem, Michael Fink, Michael Gelfond, Joohyung Lee, and Miroslaw Truszczynski for useful discussions and comments related to the topic of this work. Yuliya Lierler was supported by a CRA/NSF 2010 Computing Innovation Fellowship. Peter Schüller was supported by the Vienna Science and Technology Fund (WWTF) project ICT08-020.

References

1. Beavers, J.: Documentation: A CCG implementation for the LKB. Tech. rep., Stanford University, Center for the Study of Language and Information (2003)
2. Beavers, J., Sag, I.: Coordinate ellipsis and apparent non-constituent coordination. In: International Conference on Head-Driven Phrase Structure Grammar (HPSG 2004), pp. 48–69 (2004)
3. Beavers, J.: Type-inheritance combinatory categorial grammar. In: International Conference on Computational Linguistics, COLING 2004 (2004)
4. Bos, J.: Wide-coverage semantic analysis with boxer. In: Bos, J., Delmonte, R. (eds.) Semantics in Text Processing. STEP 2008 Conference Proceedings, pp. 277–286. Research in Computational Semantics, College Publications (2008)
5. Cimatti, A., Pistore, M., Traverso, P.: Automated planning. In: van Harmelen, F., Lifschitz, V., Porter, B. (eds.) Handbook of Knowledge Representation. Elsevier (2008)
6. Clark, S., Curran, J.R.: Log-linear models for wide-coverage CCG parsing. In: SIGDAT Conference on Empirical Methods in Natural Language Processing, EMNLP 2003 (2003)
7. Clark, S., Curran, J.R.: Parsing the WSJ using CCG and log-linear models. In: Proceedings of the 42nd Annual Meeting of the Association for Computational Linguistics (ACL 2004), Barcelona, Spain, pp. 104–111 (2004)
8. Clark, S., Curran, J.R.: Wide-coverage efficient statistical parsing with CCG and log-linear models. Computational Linguistics 33(4), 493–552 (2007)
9. Djordjevic, B., Curran, J.R.: Efficient combinatory categorial grammar parsing. In: Proceedings of the 2006 Australasian Language Technology Workshop (ALTW), pp. 3–10 (2006)
10. Dowty, D.: Type raising, functional composition, and non-constituent conjunction. In: Oehrle, R.T., Bach, E., Wheeler, D. (eds.) Categorial Grammars and Natural Language Structures, vol. 32, pp. 153–197. Reidel, Dordrecht (1988)
11. Drescher, C., Walsh, T.: Modelling grammar constraints with answer set programming. In: Gallagher, J.P., Gelfond, M. (eds.) Technical Communications of the 27th International Conference on Logic Programming, ICLP 2011, vol. 11, pp. 28–39 (2011)
12. Eisner, J.: Efficient normal-form parsing for combinatory categorial grammar. In: Proceedings of the 34th Annual Meeting on Association for Computational Linguistics (ACL 1996), pp. 79–86 (1996)
13. Eiter, T., Faber, W., Leone, N., Pfeifer, G., Polleres, A.: A logic programming approach to knowledge-state planning: Semantics and complexity. ACM Trans. Comput. Logic 5, 206–263 (2004)
14. Gebser, M., König, A., Schaub, T., Thiele, S., Veber, P.: The BioASP library: ASP solutions for systems biology. In: 22nd IEEE International Conference on Tools with Artificial Intelligence (ICTAI 2010), vol. 1, pp. 383–389 (2010)

15. Gebser, M., Kaminski, R., Kaufmann, B., Ostrowski, M., Schaub, T., Thiele, S.: Engineering an Incremental ASP Solver. In: Garcia de la Banda, M., Pontelli, E. (eds.) ICLP 2008. LNCS, vol. 5366, pp. 190–205. Springer, Heidelberg (2008)
16. Gebser, M., Kaminski, R., Kaufmann, B., Ostrowski, M., Schaub, T., Thiele, S.: A user's guide to gringo, clasp, clingo, and iclingo (2010), `http://sourceforge.net/projects/potassco/files/potassco_guide/2010-10-04/guide.pdf`
17. Gebser, M., Kaufmann, B., Neumann, A., Schaub, T.: Conflict-driven answer set solving. In: Proceedings of 20th International Joint Conference on Artificial Intelligence (IJCAI 2007), pp. 386–392. MIT Press (2007)
18. Gelfond, M., Lifschitz, V.: The stable model semantics for logic programming. In: Kowalski, R., Bowen, K. (eds.) Proceedings of International Logic Programming Conference and Symposium (ICLP 1988), pp. 1070–1080. MIT Press (1988)
19. Gelfond, M., Lifschitz, V.: Classical negation in logic programs and disjunctive databases. New Generation Computing 9, 365–385 (1991)
20. Hockenmaier, J., Steedman, M.: CCGbank: A corpus of CCG derivations and dependency structures extracted from the Penn Treebank. Comput. Linguist. 33, 355–396 (2007)
21. Hutter, F., Hoos, H., Leyton-Brown, K., Stützle, T.: ParamILS: An automatic algorithm configuration framework. Journal of Artificial Intelligence Research 36, 267–306 (2009)
22. Lierler, Y., Schüller, P.: Parsing combinatory categorial grammar with answer set programming: Preliminary report. In: Workshop on Logic programming, WLP (2011)
23. Lifschitz, V.: Answer set programming and plan generation. Artificial Intelligence 138, 39–54 (2002)
24. Marek, V., Truszczyński, M.: Stable models and an alternative logic programming paradigm. In: The Logic Programming Paradigm: a 25-Year Perspective, pp. 375–398. Springer (1999)
25. McDermott, D., et al.: PDDL — the Planning Domain Definition Language. Tech. rep., Yale Center for Computational Vision and Control (1998), CVC TR-98-003/DCS TR-1165
26. Niemelä, I.: Logic programs with stable model semantics as a constraint programming paradigm. Annals of Mathematics and Artificial Intelligence 25, 241–273 (1999)
27. Partee, B., Rooth, M.: Generalized conjunction and type ambiguity. In: Baeuerle, R., Schwarze, C., von Stechov, A. (eds.) Meaning, Use, and Interpretation, pp. 361–383 (1983)
28. Silverthorn, B., Lierler, Y., Schneider, M.: Surviving solver sensitivity: An asp practitioner's guide (2012) (under review)
29. Steedman, M.: The syntactic process. MIT Press, London (2000)
30. Vijay-Shanker, K., Weir, D.J.: Polynomial time parsing of combinatory categorial grammars. In: Proceedings of the 28th Annual Meeting on Association for Computational Linguistics, ACL 1990, pp. 1–8 (1990)
31. White, M., Baldridge, J.: Adapting chart realization to CCG. In: European Workshop on Natural Language Generation, EWNLG 2003 (2003)
32. Wittenburg, K.: Predictive combinators: a method for efficient processing of combinatory categorial grammars. In: 25th Annual Meeting of the Association for Computational Linguistics (ACL 1987), pp. 73–80 (1987)
33. Wittocx, J.: IDPDraw (2009), Katholieke Universiteit Leuven, `http://dtai.cs.kuleuven.be/krr/software/download`

Declarative Distributed Computing*

Jorge Lobo[1], Jiefei Ma[2], Alessandra Russo[2], and Franck Le[1]

[1] IBM T.J. Watson Research Center
[2] Imperial College London

Abstract. In this paper we present a language to write distributed applications. We provide an operational semantics of a single computational node based on Datalog. We then introduce a framework that can capture the semantics of a network of computational nodes working together. The framework can express several communication models (e.g. synchronous vs. asynchronous) and can be used to check many properties of the distributed computation under the different communication models. The framework is developed using Answer Set Programs.

1 Introduction

With a very simple conceptual extension, enforcing that the first argument of every predicate in a Datalog program must represent a *physical* location (defined as an IP address or a URI or something similar), Loo in [1] introduced a programming model to describe and implement network routing protocols. Intuitively, nodes or routers in a network have a copy of the same set of Datalog rules and given an extensional database of ground atoms, the atoms are distributed around the nodes according to their first argument. Computation starts independently bottom-up in each node, nodes send generated ground predicates to the appropriate nodes again based on the first argument of the predicate and other nodes may request information to other nodes to complete the evaluation of their rules. At the end of the computation each node has locally a routing table. Many routing algorithms are based on shortest path computations or other graph properties that are easily expressible using logic programs. Hence, logic programming makes the specification of complex network protocols and distributed algorithms very concise and intuitive, and the language can be executed using algorithms for distributed query processing. This computational model is known as *Declarative Networking*. There are several implementations of languages based on this concept [2,3], and the implementations of protocols in these languages compare well with implementations of the same protocols in

* Research was sponsored by the U.S. Army Research Laboratory and the U.K. Ministry of Defence under Agreement Number W911NF-06-3-0001. The views and conclusions are those of the authors and do not represent the U.S. Army Research Laboratory, the U.S. Government, the U.K. Ministry of Defence or the U.K. Government. The U.S. and U.K. Governments are authorized to reproduce and distribute reprints for Government purposes notwithstanding copyright notation.

E. Erdem et al. (Eds.): Correct Reasoning, LNCS 7265, pp. 454–470, 2012.

C or C++. These implementations, however, need to accommodate typical network changes (e.g. links coming up or down, communication delays, etc.) into their operational semantics outside logic. The reason behind this limitation is that state changes must be tracked and the Datalog semantics is too poor to express state changes. To address this limitation, Alvaro et al [4] have proposed a new Declarative Networking language, called Dedalus, where all predicates are extended with an extra argument that represents *time*. With the time argument, states can now be captured: changes of state can be reflected in changes of truth values of predicates over *time*. With this extension Declarative Networking becomes a very general distributed computational model. Based on these ideas, we have been working on our own declarative language. Alvaro et al [4] did not think in terms of state machine transitions, and because of the way time was modelled, in order to avoid limiting the expressiveness of the language, their semantics allows predicates, sent from one node to another, to arrive at the receiving node as if the predicate had been sent from the future. Our language does not have these peculiarities, and may also allow different computational nodes to have different rule sets. We will present, in Section 2, the main features of our language and describe its operational semantics in terms of state transition systems similar to the transition systems defined by action description languages [5]. As in action languages, specifications written in our language define a state transition function. It is standard to use logic programs to define the semantics of action domains. We are going to follow the same pattern. However, given that we can define a collection of *distributed state machines* (DSM) that can exchange information, if we want to do analysis of these machines our description must also include axioms that capture the semantics of the communication model. We will show in Section 3 how different communication models can be easily expressed in answer set programs (ASP). We will also show examples of properties of distributed algorithms that can be proved using an ASP solver. We will do an informal presentation but try to provide sufficient detail so that readers with knowledge of logic programming and answer set programming can grasp the formal foundation of the computational model.

2 Declarative Description of Distributed State Machines

2.1 The Language

Our computational model consists of a network of nodes where each node (e.g., host, router) on the network is abstracted as an *input/output automaton*, and the nodes can exchange messages. Thus, the nodes form a collection of *distributed state machines* (DSM). In each node a set of *named tuples* in the form of $\mathtt{p}(\mathtt{a}_1, \ldots, \mathtt{a}_n)$, where $\mathtt{p}$ is the tuple name and $\mathtt{a}_1, \ldots, \mathtt{a}_n$ is a list of constants, is stored. These tuples represent the automaton's current state, and hence are called *state tuples*. A node can input tuples to the state machine it is hosting (e.g. the router informing the machine who are the physical neighbours, or a sensor node sensing temperature and passing the information to the machine). We will call these tuples *input tuples*. Tuples can been sent by other nodes as messages. Tuples in messages will be called *transport tuples*. The different sets of tuple names are assumed to be mutually exclusive.

Each state transition in an automaton is triggered when the automaton receives input or transport tuples. During the state transition, a set ADD of state tuples, a set DEL of state tuples and a set $SEND$ of transport tuples are computed based on the existing state tuples and the tuples received. Let OLD and NEW be the set of state tuples stored by the automaton before and after the state transition, respectively, then

$$NEW = (OLD \setminus DEL) \cup ADD$$

At the end of the state transition, all tuples in $SEND$ will be placed in the outgoing communication channel by the automaton. These tuples will be accompanied by the destination address of the tuple. In practice, it is often useful to allow a set of temporary tuples to be derived to support the computation of ADD, DEL and $SEND$. We call these *transient tuples* as they are not stored by the automaton after the state transition.

The state transition functions are defined using *declarative rules* and *tuple schemas*. In our language, these rules do not need to be the same at each node. In routing protocols, for instance, nodes may have different path selection or filtering policies. A tuple schema looks very much like a tuple $\mathtt{p}(\mathtt{t}_1, \ldots, \mathtt{t}_n)$ with the difference that each $\mathtt{t}_i$ is either a constant, a variable or an expression involving constants and variables. Rules that compute a tuple in ADD are of the form:

$$\mathtt{H}\ \textbf{after}\ \mathtt{L}_1, \ldots, \mathtt{L}_n, \mathtt{c}_1, \ldots, \mathtt{c}_m \tag{1}$$

where $\mathtt{H}$ is a tuple schema for a state tuple, and each $\mathtt{L}_i$ $(0 < i \leq n)$ is either a *positive* tuple schema (i.e., a tuple schema) or a *negative* tuple schema in the form of **not** $\mathtt{p}(\mathtt{t}_1, \ldots, \mathtt{t}_k)$, for an input, state, transient or transport tuple. Each $\mathtt{c}_i$ $(0 \leq i \leq m)$ is an expression of the form $\mathtt{l} \otimes \mathtt{r}$ where $\mathtt{l}$ and $\mathtt{r}$ are either a constant, a variable or an arithmetic or string expression of constants and variables, and $\otimes$ is one of $\{=, !=, <, <=, >, >=\}$. $\mathtt{H}$ is called the *head* and $\mathtt{L}_1, \ldots, \mathtt{L}_n, \mathtt{c}_1, \ldots, \mathtt{c}_m$ is called the *body* of the rule. In fact, a rule with variables is a generalisation of the set of all rules obtained by replacing each variable with all possible constants. This is with the exception of rules where arguments use aggregate operators, as described later in this section. In order to guarantee the states to be finite, it is required that every variable that appears either in the head, a $\mathtt{c}_i$, or a negative tuple schema in the body of a rule, it should also appear in a positive tuple schema in the body of that rule. An informal reading of rule (1) is: if we find all the tuples in the current state (including the received and the transient tuples) that match each tuple in the body of the rule, no tuple that matches the negative tuples, and all $\mathtt{c}_i$ are satisfied, then the body of the rule is *satisfied* and the state tuple that matches the head will be in ADD (and hence will be stored in NEW).

Rules that compute tuples in DEL are of the form:

$$\textbf{forget}\ \mathtt{H}\ \textbf{if}\ \mathtt{L}_1, \ldots, \mathtt{L}_n, \mathtt{c}_1, \ldots, \mathtt{c}_m \tag{2}$$

where H is a tuple schema for a state tuple, and $L_1, \ldots, L_n, c_1, \ldots, c_m$ is defined as in (1). An informal reading of this rule is: if the body of the rule is satisfied with respect to the current state then the state tuple that matches the head will be in *DEL* (and hence will not be "copied" to *NEW*).

Similarly, rules that compute transient tuples are of the form:

$$\texttt{H}\ \textbf{if}\ L_1, \ldots, L_n, c_1, \ldots, c_m \tag{3}$$

where H is a tuple schema for a transient tuple, and $L_1, \ldots, L_n, c_1, \ldots, c_m$ is defined as in (1) except that $n \geq 0$ (i.e., it can have an empty body). An informal reading of this rule is: if the body of the rule is satisfied with respect to the current state, then the transient tuple that matches the head must also be considered part of the current state. Note that if this rule has an *empty* body (i.e., $n = m = 0$), then the tuple that matches the head will temporarily be in every state.

Recall that transport tuples are exchanged between nodes and can be either the input or the output of a state transition. We require that every transport tuple (schema) that appears in a rule must have a suffix of the form @ID, where ID is either a constant representing a node's identifier, or a variable whose possible constant values are node identifiers. When a transport tuple (schema) $p(t_1, \ldots, t_n)$@ID appears in the body of a rule, it represents a transport tuple received (i.e., as the input of the state transition), and ID indicates the sender of the tuple. Transport tuple schemas appear only in the head of rules that compute tuples in *SEND*. These rules are of the form:

$$\textbf{send}\ \texttt{H@N}\ \textbf{after} L_1, \ldots, L_n, c_1, \ldots, c_m \tag{4}$$

where H is a tuple schema for a transport tuple, and $L_1, \ldots, L_n, c_1, \ldots, c_m$ is defined as in (1). In contrast to transport tuple schemas appearing in the body of rules, the ID in the head of a rule indicates the destination of the tuple. An informal reading of this rule is: if the body of the rule is satisfied with respect to the current state, then the transport tuple that matches the head will be in *SEND*.

As an example consider the following Colour Voting algorithm. Given a mesh network, we initially assign one of two colours, red or blue, to each node in the network. The nodes exchange information of their current colours with their neighbors, and decide their new colours based on the majority colour of their neighbors. We will use the following schemas to specify this algorithm in our language:

input	**init_neighbour**(X)	set X to be a neighbour of the node.
	init_colour(C)	set C to be the initial colour of the node.
state	**my_colour**(C)	the node's current colour is C.
	neighbour_colour(X, C)	the currently stored colour of neighbour X is C.
	neighbour(X)	X is a neighbour.
transient	**new_colour**(C)	the node needs to update its colour to C.
	latest_colour(X, C)	the latest colour of neighbour X is C.
	num_reds(N)	the number of red neighbours is N.
	num_blues(N)	the number of blue neighbours is N.
transport	**vote_colour**(C)	the sender's latest colour is C.

We will assume that the network topology does not change during the algorithm execution, i.e., once a neighbour is added it cannot be removed. Thus, there is only one rule defining `neighbour(X)`:

$$\texttt{neighbour(X)}\ \textbf{after}\ \texttt{init\_neighbour(X)}. \tag{5}$$

The `new_colour(C)` schema used next is a schema for transient tuples that it will help us compute changes of colour to the local node. The node then stores this colour in the state using the state tuple (schema) `my_colour(C)` and informs its neighbours of the change using the transport tuple (schema) `vote_colour(C)`. The relevant rules are:

$$\texttt{new\_colour(C)}\ \textbf{if}\ \texttt{init\_colour(C)}, \textbf{not}\ \texttt{my\_colour(red)}, \textbf{not}\ \texttt{my\_colour(blue)}. \tag{6}$$

$$\texttt{new\_colour(red)}\ \textbf{if}\ \texttt{num\_reds(N)}, \texttt{num\_blues(M)}, \texttt{N} >= \texttt{M}, \texttt{my\_colour(blue)}. \tag{7}$$

$$\texttt{new\_colour(blue)}\ \textbf{if}\ \texttt{num\_reds(N)}, \texttt{num\_blues(M)}, \texttt{N} < \texttt{M}, \texttt{my\_colour(red)}. \tag{8}$$

$$\texttt{my\_colour(C)}\ \textbf{after}\ \texttt{new\_colour(C)}. \tag{9}$$

$$\textbf{forget}\ \texttt{my\_colour(OldC)}\ \textbf{if}\ \texttt{my\_colour(OldC)}, \texttt{new\_colour(C)}. \tag{10}$$

$$\textbf{send}\ \texttt{vote\_colour(C)@X}\ \textbf{after}\ \texttt{new\_colour(C)}, \texttt{neighbour(X)}. \tag{11}$$

In addition to storing its own colour, the local node also stores the colour of its neighbours:

$$\texttt{neighbour\_colour(X, C)}\ \textbf{after}$$
$$\quad \texttt{vote\_colour(C)@X}, \textbf{not}\ \texttt{neighbour\_colour(X, C)}. \tag{12}$$

$$\textbf{forget}\ \texttt{neighbour\_colour(X, OldC)}\ \textbf{if}$$
$$\quad \texttt{neighbour\_colour(X, OldC)}, \texttt{vote\_colour(C)@X}, \texttt{OldC} \mathrel{!=} \texttt{C}. \tag{13}$$

Finally, the number of red and blue neighbours are calculated using the transient tuple (schema) `latest_colour(X, C)`. The latest colour of the current node is the colour currently stored at that node[1]. The latest colour of neighbour `X` is either the one received from a transport tuple sent by `X`, or the one stored at the current state if no transport tuple is received from `X`. The relevant rules are:

$$\texttt{latest\_colour(X, C)}\ \textbf{if}\ \texttt{current\_host(X)}, \texttt{my\_colour(C)}. \tag{14}$$

$$\texttt{latest\_colour(X, C)}\ \textbf{if}\ \texttt{vote\_colour(C)@X}. \tag{15}$$

$$\texttt{latest\_colour(X, C)}\ \textbf{if}$$
$$\quad \texttt{neighbour\_colour(X, C)},$$
$$\quad \textbf{not}\ \texttt{vote\_colour(red)@X}, \textbf{not}\ \texttt{vote\_colour(blue)@X}. \tag{16}$$

$$\texttt{num\_reds(\#count(X))}\ \textbf{if}\ \texttt{latest\_colour(X, red)}. \tag{17}$$

$$\texttt{num\_blues(\#count(X))}\ \textbf{if}\ \texttt{latest\_colour(X, blues)}. \tag{18}$$

---

[1] This is expressed by the type predicate `current_host(X)`.

In the above last two rules, the operator $\#\texttt{count}(\texttt{X})$ is used. This is an example of an expression involving a variable in the argument of a tuple schema. $\#\texttt{count}$ is an *aggregation* operation. In the last rule, $\#\texttt{count}(\texttt{X})$ is equal to the total number of constant values for X extracted from the tuples matching latest_colour(X, blue) in the current state. Other aggregation operations supported by our language are $\#\texttt{sum}(\texttt{X})$, $\#\texttt{min}(\texttt{X})$ and $\#\texttt{max}(\texttt{X})$, which return the sum, the smallest value and the biggest value of X, respectively (in these cases the possible values for X must be numerical). The other operators allowed in expressions are arithmetic operations with their standard semantics.

The full specification for the Colour Voting algorithm is therefore the set of rules (5)–(18). Each node that participates in executing the algorithm will be running a copy of these rules.

2.2 Formal Semantics

The semantics of a single node can be described by a (Datalog+time) logic program by mapping each tuple to a *predicate* with new arguments representing location and time. First, we introduce two *sorts*: the *identifier* sort (used to uniquely identify a node in the network) and the *time* sort (which is the set of non-negative integers plus a special constant null), expressed by the predicate time. Secondly, for each tuple type we introduce one or two corresponding predicates. This is illustrated in Table 1, where $\overline{a}$ represents a list of terms.

The predicate receive_p with the extra time argument will be useful for the specification of the *communication model* which will be described in Section 3.1. With these predicates, each declarative rule (i.e., (1)–(4)) can be translated into Datalog+time rules. Let $\texttt{B} = \texttt{l}_1(\overline{\texttt{V}_1}), \ldots, \texttt{l}_n(\overline{\texttt{V}_n}), \texttt{c}_1, \ldots, \texttt{c}_m$ be the body of a declarative rule. The translated body $\texttt{B}(\texttt{ID}, \texttt{T})$ is obtained from B by translating each $\texttt{l}_i(\overline{\texttt{V}_i})$ as follows. If $\texttt{p}(\overline{\texttt{V}})$ is a non-transport tuple schema of $\texttt{l}_i(\overline{\texttt{V}_i})$, then it is replaced with the predicate $\texttt{p}(\texttt{ID}, \overline{\texttt{V}}, \texttt{T})$; otherwise let $\texttt{p}(\overline{\texttt{V}})@\texttt{Src}$ be the transport tuple schema of $\texttt{l}_i(\overline{\texttt{V}_i})$, it is replaced with the predicate $\texttt{receive\_p}(\texttt{ID}, \overline{\texttt{V}}, \texttt{T})$. Note that in $\texttt{B}(\texttt{ID}, \texttt{T})$ all predicates have the same first argument (i.e., the location) and last argument (i.e., the time).

The declarative rule $\texttt{p}(\overline{\texttt{V}})$ **after** B for a state tuple schema $\texttt{p}(\overline{\texttt{V}})$ is translated to a Datalog+time rule:

$$\texttt{p}(\texttt{ID}, \overline{\texttt{V}}, \texttt{T}+1) \leftarrow \texttt{B}(\texttt{ID}, \texttt{T}) \tag{19}$$

and the rule **forget** $\texttt{p}(\overline{\texttt{V}})$ **if** B is translated to a Datalog+time rule:

$$\texttt{forget\_p}(\texttt{ID}, \overline{\texttt{V}}, \texttt{T}) \leftarrow \texttt{B}(\texttt{ID}, \texttt{T}) \tag{20}$$

Similarly, the declarative rule $\texttt{p}(\overline{\texttt{V}})$ **if** B for a transient tuple schema $\texttt{p}(\overline{\texttt{V}})$ is translated to a Datalog+time rule:

$$\texttt{p}(\texttt{ID}, \overline{\texttt{V}}, \texttt{T}) \leftarrow \texttt{B}(\texttt{ID}, \texttt{T}) \tag{21}$$

Table 1. Corresponding Predicates for Tuples

Tuple Type	Tuple	Predicate	Intuitive Meaning
state	$\mathtt{p}(\bar{\mathtt{a}})$	$\mathtt{p}(\mathtt{id}, \bar{\mathtt{a}}, \mathtt{t})$	it holds iff $\mathtt{p}(\bar{\mathtt{a}})$ is stored by node `id` at the state associated with time `t`.
		$\mathtt{forget\_p}(\mathtt{id}, \bar{\mathtt{a}}, \mathtt{t})$	it holds iff $\mathtt{p}(\bar{\mathtt{a}})$ is in the set DEL of node `id` at the state associated with time `t`.
input	$\mathtt{p}(\bar{\mathtt{a}})$	$\mathtt{p}(\mathtt{id}, \bar{\mathtt{a}}, \mathtt{t})$	it holds iff $\mathtt{p}(\bar{\mathtt{a}})$ is manually inserted to node `id` at the state associated with time `t`.
transient	$\mathtt{p}(\bar{\mathtt{a}})$	$\mathtt{p}(\mathtt{id}, \bar{\mathtt{a}}, \mathtt{t})$	it holds iff $\mathtt{p}(\bar{\mathtt{a}})$ is derived by node `id` at the state associated with time `t`.
transport	$\mathtt{p}(\bar{\mathtt{a}})@\mathtt{id1}$	$\mathtt{send\_p}(\mathtt{id}, \bar{\mathtt{a}}, \mathtt{id1}, \mathtt{t})$	it holds iff $\mathtt{p}(\bar{\mathtt{a}})$ (in the head) with destination `id1` is in the set $SEND$ of node `id` at the state associated with time `t`.
		$\mathtt{receive\_p}(\mathtt{id}, \bar{\mathtt{a}}, \mathtt{id1}, \mathtt{t1}, \mathtt{t})$	it holds iff $\mathtt{p}(\bar{\mathtt{a}})$ (in the body) is sent by node `id1` at `id1`'s state associated with (send) time `t1` and received by node `id` at `id`'s state associated with (receive) time `t`.
		$\mathtt{receive\_p}(\mathtt{id}, \bar{\mathtt{a}}, \mathtt{id1}, \mathtt{t})$	it holds iff the predicate $\mathtt{receive\_p}(\mathtt{id}, \bar{\mathtt{a}}, \mathtt{id1}, \mathtt{t1}, \mathtt{t})$ holds (i.e., it simply drops the send time `t1`).

To capture the default persistence nature of state tuples, for each state tuple schema $\mathtt{p}(\overline{\mathtt{V}})$ where $\overline{\mathtt{V}}$ are all variables an *inertia* rule is added:

$$\mathtt{p}(\mathtt{ID}, \overline{\mathtt{V}}, \mathtt{T}+1) \leftarrow \mathtt{p}(\mathtt{ID}, \overline{\mathtt{V}}, \mathtt{T}), \mathbf{not}\ \mathtt{forget\_p}(\mathtt{ID}, \overline{\mathtt{V}}, \mathtt{T}) \tag{22}$$

There is no such *inertia* rule for transient tuples.

Finally, the declarative rule **send** $\mathtt{p}(\overline{\mathtt{V}})@\mathtt{Dest}$ **after** `B` for a transport tuple schema $\mathtt{p}(\overline{\mathtt{V}})$ is translated to a Datalog+time rule:

$$\mathtt{send\_p}(\mathtt{ID}, \overline{\mathtt{V}}, \mathtt{Dest}, \mathtt{T}+1) \leftarrow \mathtt{B}(\mathtt{ID}, \mathtt{T}) \tag{23}$$

Let $\mathcal{M}_{id}$ be the set of Datalog+time rules associated with a node identified by *id*, and $\mathcal{M}$ the union of all the rules $\mathcal{M}_{id}$ for all the *id*. Note that if the set of rules is the same in every node then $\mathcal{M} = \mathcal{M}_{id}$.

Computations in a Single Machine: We are going to assume that the standard definition of stratification over negation and aggregation applies to the collection of logic programming rules defining transient tuples (i.e. tuples defined by (21))[2]. The (local) stratification of the other rules is instead guaranteed because the heads of the rules are always in a different time (+1) than the literals

[2] This is assumed to be guaranteed by the programmer.

in the body. Hence, given an OLD set of state tuples in a node identified by id at time t, and a set of input tuples I and transport tuples M that are received by node id at time t, the set NEW can be calculated as follows:

1. Let $OLD(id,t) = \{p(id,\overline{a},t)|p(\overline{a}) \in OLD\}$.
2. Let $I(id,t) = \{p(id,\overline{a},t)|p(\overline{a}) \in I\}$.
3. Let $M(id,t) = \{p(id,\overline{a},id',t)|p(\overline{a})@id' \in \mathcal{M}\}$.
4. Let A be the unique answer set associated with $\mathcal{M}_{id} \cup OLD(id,t) \cup I(id,t) \cup M(id,t)$.
5. $NEW = \{p(\overline{a})|p(id,\overline{a},t+1) \in A, p$ a state predicate$\}$.
6. $SEND = \{(p(\overline{a})@id,id')|send\_p(id,\overline{a},id',t+1) \in A\}$.

The reader can observe that the evaluation of the transition function can be done using a simple Datalog program with aggregates since there are only two states mentioned in the rules, the current state and the successor state.[3] Hence, instead of having a generic time argument we can use two constants, one for the current state and a second one for the successor state. However, our goal is to provide a semantics for the overall system of distributed state machines so that we can do analysis of distributed programs. For that we need to create a bridge between the rules of nodes with different identifiers. This bridge is done through the `receive_p` predicates and the `send_p` predicates as follows: for each transport tuple schema $\mathtt{p}(\overline{\mathtt{V}})$ where $\overline{\mathtt{V}}$ are all variables the following two rules are added:

$$\begin{aligned}&\mathtt{receive\_p(Dest,\overline{V},Src,SendT,RecvT)} \leftarrow \\ &\quad \mathtt{send\_p(Src,\overline{V},Dest,SendT),choice((Src,\overline{V},Dest,SendT),(RecvT))}. \quad (24)\\ &\mathtt{receive\_p(Dest,\overline{V},Src,RecvT)} \leftarrow \\ &\quad \mathtt{receive\_p(Dest,\overline{V},Src,SendT,RecvT)}. \quad (25)\end{aligned}$$

With these new domain independent axioms we are leaving Datalog+time by introducing non-deterministic computations. The *choice* operator in the first rule is the standard choice operation of Datalog extensions and encoded in answer set programming (ASP) as multiple answer sets [6,7]. Theoretically the choice is made over an infinite domain, the non-negative integers plus `null`. In practice, for analysis as it will be explained later, a finite domain will be used. The rule non-deterministically assigns a value of the time sort to `RecvT` based on the values of $\mathtt{Src},\overline{\mathtt{V}},\mathtt{Dest},\mathtt{SendT}$. Because of the choice operator now we will have multiple (and in some cases an infinite number of) answer sets, each one corresponding to a different communication sequence among the nodes. Note that in the case when `RecvT` is assigned the special value `null`, it is equivalent to saying that the tuple was lost during communication. Note also that `SendT` is a local time to node `Src`, and `RecvT` is a local time to node `Dest`. Thus, depending on the communication model (e.g., synchronous or asynchronous) assumed for the algorithm execution, it does not necessarily hold that `RecvT` > `SendT`. Different

[3] Supported by this observation, we have an implementation of a DSM system in which we have used a relational database as the core of the rule evaluation engine.

communication models will be defined by imposing constraints on the ground instances of receive_p(Dest, $\overline{\text{V}}$, Src, SendT, RecvT) that can be part of an answer set.

3 An Analysis Framework for Distributed Algorithms

The declarative specification of a distributed algorithm using our language can not only be executed directly but also be analysed using off-the-shelf logic programming tools for ASP such as [8,9,10]. However, in order to perform analysis, two extra components are needed: a *communication model* and a *query language*, which allows the initial domain state (of each node) and various system properties to be specified. In this section we will informally describe these two components using the Colour Voting example.

3.1 Communication Models

The main purpose of a communication model is to describe how the send tuples and the receive tuples are related. Various assumptions can be made for the communication channel, such as whether a message can be lost, duplicated or received out of order. There are two basic models for distributed algorithms: *synchronous* and *asynchronous*. In a synchronous communication model, all the nodes' local clocks are synchronised (i.e., each local clock is the same as a global clock), and all the nodes send out tuples, receive tuples and update states at the same time, respectively. In an asynchronous communication model nodes' local clocks are not synchronised.

The communication model assumptions are often specified using *integrity constraints*. Implementations of ASP solvers require finite domains. However, this is not our case since the time sort has an infinite number of possible values. To restrict this for algorithm analysis, we assume that there is a pre-specified special value #maxtime such that the time sort (for analysis) is the set of integers between 0 and #maxtime (i.e., no need for the special constant null). The algorithm execution (during analysis) is affected by #maxtime as follows. Each node can go through at most #maxtime state transitions, which are indexed from 0 to #maxtime − 1. A node may receive tuples at a *terminating state* indexed with #maxtime, but these tuples do not trigger a new state transition (i.e., the tuples are considered to be received too late and ignored, or be lost during communication). A node may also send tuples at #maxtime (i.e., the transport tuples in $SEND$ computed at #maxtime − 1), but these tuples will not be received by the destination node (or received at time #maxtime local to the destination). Note that the terminating state of each node is particularly useful when we perform analysis on algorithm convergence, e.g., the algorithm converges when there are no tuples sent or received at each node's terminating state (i.e., all the communication channels are empty). This will be further discussed in Section 3.2. Next, we will describe how the synchronous and the asynchronous communication models are specified in ASP.

Interfacing Predicates The specification for a distributed algorithm and the specification for the adopted communication model are loosely coupled through a set of *interfacing predicates*, which are summarised as follows:

Predicate	Meaning
communication(Src, Dest, SendT, RecvT)	it holds iff a transport tuple is sent by Src at Src's local time SendT, and is received by Dest at Dest's local time RecvT.
message_sent(X, T)	it holds iff node X sends a transport tuple at its local time T.
message_received(X, T)	it holds iff node X receives a transport tuple at its local time T.

These interfacing predicates are defined using the transport predicates (i.e., the corresponding predicate for transport tuple schema) from the algorithm specification. For example, for each transport predicate $\mathtt{receive\_p}(\mathtt{ID}, \overline{\mathtt{V}}, \mathtt{ID1}, \mathtt{T1}, \mathtt{T})$ there is a rule:

$$\mathtt{communication}(\mathtt{ID}, \mathtt{ID1}, \mathtt{T1}, \mathtt{T}) \leftarrow \mathtt{receive\_p}(\mathtt{ID}, \overline{\mathtt{V}}, \mathtt{ID1}, \mathtt{T1}, \mathtt{T}) \quad (26)$$

and a rule:

$$\mathtt{message\_received}(\mathtt{ID}, \mathtt{T}) \leftarrow \mathtt{receive\_p}(\mathtt{ID}, \overline{\mathtt{V}}, \mathtt{ID1}, \mathtt{T1}, \mathtt{T}) \quad (27)$$

Similarly, for each transport predicate $\mathtt{send\_p}(\mathtt{ID}, \overline{\mathtt{V}}, \mathtt{ID1}, \mathtt{T})$ there is a rule:

$$\mathtt{message\_sent}(\mathtt{ID}, \mathtt{T}) \leftarrow \mathtt{send\_p}(\mathtt{ID}, \overline{\mathtt{V}}, \mathtt{ID1}, \mathtt{T}) \quad (28)$$

A communication model is a set of rules and integrity constraints that are specified based on these predicates plus the transport predicates.

Synchronous Model. The simplest communication model is a synchronous model, in which all the nodes' local clocks are the same and each message sent will be received at the same state. Note that the transport tuples are computed in the state right before that in which they are sent, so we may assume the messages sent are delivered immediately. This model has only one integrity constraint:

$$\leftarrow \mathtt{communication}(\mathtt{Src}, \mathtt{Dest}, \mathtt{SendT}, \mathtt{RecvT}), \mathtt{RecvT} \mathrel{!=} \mathtt{SendT}. \quad (29)$$

This integrity constraint effectively forces the implementation of the *choice* predicate in (24) to assign the value SendT to RecvT.

If we want to allow a message to be lost during transmission, it can be easily done by modifying (29) to be:

$$\begin{aligned} \leftarrow\ & \mathtt{communication}(\mathtt{Src}, \mathtt{Dest}, \mathtt{SendT}, \mathtt{RecvT}), \\ & \mathtt{RecvT} \mathrel{!=} \mathtt{SendT}, \mathtt{RecvT} \mathrel{!=} \#\mathtt{maxtime}. \end{aligned} \quad (30)$$

Thus, an synchronous communication model, $\mathcal{C}$, is defined by the set of rules and integrity constraints {(24), (25), (26), (27), (28), (29)} or the set {(24), (25), (26), (27), (28), (30)}.

Note that in the synchronous model, a node's local clock may advance by 1 even though it does not receive any transport or input tuple.

Asynchronous Model. The main difference between an asynchronous model and a synchronous model is that in the former the nodes' local clocks are not synchronised. Each node's local time is understood by that node only. Therefore, we cannot guarantee at what state a node may receive a tuple that is sent to it. This poses significant challenges in the modelling.

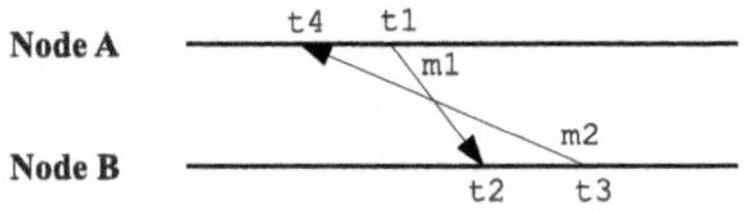

Fig. 1. An Invalid Communication Log: Node A sends a message $m1$ at local time $t1$ to Node B. Node B receives $m1$ at local time $t2$, which triggers a message $m2$ to be sent at a later local time $t3$ to Node A. Node A receives $m2$ at a local time before $t1$.

First of all, if one wants to guarantee that the *choice* predicate assigns the right values for message delivery time so that no node can receive a message that is sent in the future (see Figure 1), we need to implement the Lamport timestamps [11]. This can be easily specified through the following rules:

$$\texttt{local\_state\_ts(ID,T)} \leftarrow \texttt{message\_received(ID,T),T !=}\ \#\texttt{maxtime}. \tag{31}$$

$$\texttt{local\_state\_ts(ID,T)} \leftarrow \texttt{message\_sent(ID,T),T !=}\ \#\texttt{maxtime}. \tag{32}$$

$$\tag{33}$$

$$\texttt{globally\_precedes(ID,LT1,ID,LT2)} \leftarrow$$
$$\texttt{local\_state\_ts(ID,LT1),local\_state\_ts(ID,LT2),LT1} < \texttt{LT2}. \tag{34}$$

$$\texttt{globally\_precedes(ID1,LT1} - \texttt{1,ID2,LT2)} \leftarrow$$
$$\texttt{communication(ID1,ID2,LT1,LT2)}. \tag{35}$$

$$\texttt{globally\_precedes(ID1,LT1,ID2,LT2)} \leftarrow$$
$$\texttt{globally\_precedes(ID1,LT1,ID3,LT3),}$$
$$\texttt{globally\_precedes(ID3,LT3,ID2,LT2)}. \tag{36}$$

The first rules simply collect the local state timestamps as a set of (identifier, time) pairs, based on the interactions between the nodes. The predicate

$$\texttt{globally\_precedes(ID1,LT1,ID2,LT2)}$$

can be interpreted as the event with timestamp (ID1, LT1) is *logically before* the event with timestamp (ID2, LT2). This is defined by three cases: First, (34) says that the a local event globally precedes another local event if the former occurs before the latter at the same node (i.e. having a smaller local time). Second, (35) says that if there is a message passing between two nodes, then the send event globally precedes the receive event. Note that in the head of (35), the use of LT1 − 1 instead of LT1 for the second argument is due to the fact that transport tuples are sent at the next state after they are computed. By using LT1 − 1 we allow a node to receive and process a transport tuple at the same time it sends out transport tuples computed at the previous state. Third, (36) computes the transitive closure of $\texttt{globally\_precedes}$. Finally, the integrity constraint for guaranteeing correct local time assignments by *choice* is:

$$\leftarrow \texttt{globally\_precedes(ID, LT, ID, LT)}. \tag{37}$$

which means no event can globally precede itself.

With the above integrity constraint, several communication invariants can be specified. For example, the assumption that *"a message sent too late by a node (i.e., at local time* #**maxtime***) will not be processed by the destination"* is:

$$\leftarrow \texttt{communication(Src, Dest, maxtime, RecvT), RecvT} \mathrel{!=} \texttt{\#maxtime}. \tag{38}$$

The assumption that *"messages sent by a source node to a destination node must be delivered in order"* is:

$$\begin{aligned}\leftarrow\ & \texttt{communication(Sender, Receiver, SendTime1, RecvTime1)},\\ & \texttt{communication(Sender, Receiver, SendTime2, ReceiveTime2)},\\ & \texttt{SendTime1} < \texttt{SendTime2}, \texttt{RecvTime2} \mathrel{!=} \texttt{\#maxtime},\\ & \texttt{RecvTime1} >= \texttt{RecvTime2}.\end{aligned} \tag{39}$$

The assumption that *"between any two nodes, the ordering of the messages sent must be the same as that of the messages received"* is:

$$\begin{aligned}\leftarrow\ & \texttt{message\_received(Receiver, RecvTime)},\\ & \texttt{time(SomeTime)},\\ & \texttt{SomeTime} < \texttt{RecvTime},\\ & \textbf{not}\ \texttt{message\_received(Receiver, SomeTime)}.\end{aligned} \tag{40}$$

Depending on the desired properties, an asynchronous communication model, $\mathcal{C}$, will add to the set of rules {(24), (25), (26), (27), (28), (37)} any specific set of rules and constraints (e.g., {(38), (39), (40)}) that corresponds to the appropriate model.

3.2 Query Language

The query language for algorithm analysis allows *narratives* and *queries* to be specified. Narratives are observations made from a node state. Queries are either hypothetical assertions about the effects of the distributed algorithm execution based on the observations, or assertions about the past states which the algorithm has executed.

The basic components of narratives and queries are called *axiom schemas*, which are expressions of one of the following four forms:

$$\begin{aligned}&\texttt{P}\ \textbf{holds at}\ \texttt{ID.T}\\ &\texttt{I}\ \textbf{inserted at}\ \texttt{ID.T}\\ &\texttt{M}\ \textbf{from}\ \texttt{ID}'\ \textbf{received at}\ \texttt{ID.T}\\ &\texttt{M}\ \textbf{to}\ \texttt{ID}'\ \textbf{sent at}\ \texttt{ID.T}\end{aligned}$$

where P is a either a state or transient tuple schema, I is an input tuple schema, M is a transport tuple schema, ID and ID′ are constants or variables of the *identifier* sort, and T is a constant or variable of the *time* sort.

A *narrative axiom* is a variable-free axiom schema and a *narrative* is a finite collection of narrative axioms. For a concrete example of a narrative axiom (or axiom to simplify notation), let us consider again the Colour Voting algorithm, which is to be analysed (for convergence) with respect to a network configuration shown in Figure 2.

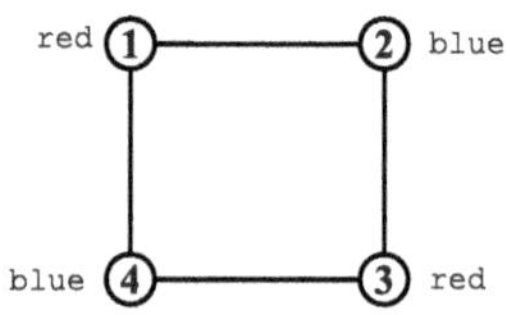

Fig. 2. A network with four nodes: Each line represents a bidirectional communication channel between two nodes. Node 1 and Node 3 are initially assigned to red; Node 2 and Node 4 are initially assigned to blue.

The set of axioms describing such network configuration is given below:

```
neighbour(2) holds at 1.0
neighbour(4) holds at 1.0
my_colour(red) holds at 1.0
vote_colour(red) to 2 sent at 1.0
vote_colour(red) to 4 sent at 1.0
⋮
```

A *query definition rule* is a rule for the form:

$$\mathtt{H}\ \textbf{given}\ \mathtt{L}_1, \ldots, \mathtt{L}_n, \mathtt{c}_1, \ldots, \mathtt{c}_m$$

where H is a *query predicate* different from any predicate introduced by the algorithm specification and the communication model. Query predicates are essentially auxiliary predicates used to easy the computation of analysis queries. In the query definition rule, each $\mathtt{L}_i$ is either a positive or negative literal formed from an axiom schema or a query predicate, and each $\mathtt{c}_j$ is a constraint expression. It is also required that all variables appearing in the head of a query definition rule must also appear in at least one positive $\mathtt{L}_i$.
Finally, a query is an expression of the form:

$$quantifier_{max}\ \mathtt{L}_1, \ldots, \mathtt{L}_n$$

where $quantifier$ is one of {**always**, **never**, **sometimes**}, max is a non-negative integer value for specifying #maxtime, and each $\mathtt{L}_i$ is a positive or negative query predicate or axiom schema, and is variable-free.

Consider again the Colour Voting example. We say that the algorithm *converges* (i.e., is terminating) within `#maxtime` if and only if each node will no longer change its colour in fewer than `#maxtime` steps. To check this property it is sufficient to check whether the communication channels are empty at `#maxtime` for each node, i.e., no node sends or receives a message at its local time `#maxtime`. To specify a query for checking such property, the following query definition rules may be used:

```
has_unprocessed_message given
    vote_colour(C)@Dest sent at ID.#maxtime.
has_unprocessed_message given
    vote_colour(C)@Src received at ID.#maxtime.
converged given not has_unprocessed_message.
```

where `has_unprocessed_message` and `converged` are query predicates. Therefore, three different queries **always**$_{\mathtt{m}}$ `converged`, **sometimes**$_{\mathtt{m}}$ `converged` and **never**$_{\mathtt{m}}$ `converged` can be asked to check whether the algorithm can always converge, sometimes converge or never converge, respectively, within m steps given a particular communication model and network configuration (as a narrative).

3.3 Formal Semantics of Narratives and Queries

Narratives and queries can also be translated into Datalog+time rules to describe their semantics.

First, each axiom schema, `S`, can be translated to a corresponding predicate, `tr(S)`, using the following table:

Schema Axiom	Predicate
$\mathtt{p}(\overline{\mathtt{V}})$ **holds at** ID.T	$\mathtt{p}(\mathtt{ID}, \overline{\mathtt{V}}, \mathtt{T})$
$\mathtt{p}(\overline{\mathtt{V}})$ **inserted at** ID.T	$\mathtt{p}(\mathtt{ID}, \overline{\mathtt{V}}, \mathtt{T})$
$\mathtt{p}(\overline{\mathtt{V}})$ **from** ID$'$ **received at** ID.T	$\mathtt{receive\_p}(\mathtt{ID}, \overline{\mathtt{V}}, \mathtt{ID}', \mathtt{T})$
$\mathtt{p}(\overline{\mathtt{V}})$ **to** ID$'$ **sent at** ID.T	$\mathtt{send\_p}(\mathtt{ID}, \overline{\mathtt{V}}, \mathtt{ID}', \mathtt{T})$

Each narrative axiom, `L`, can then be translated into a *fact,* *tr*(`L`), (i.e., a rule with an empty body) following the table mapping. Similarly, each query definition rule can be translated into a rule by simply replacing **given** with $\leftarrow$ and translating each schema axiom in the body according to the table. Given a narrative N and a set of query definition rules, Q, denote by $tr(N)$ and $tr(Q)$, the set of facts and logic programming rules that result from the translation.

Definition 1. *Let $\mathcal{M}$ be the set of rules associated with a collection of DSM programs, $\mathcal{C}$ a communication model with* `#maxtime` $= \mathtt{m}$*, N a narrative and Q a set of query definition rules. Let $\Pi = \mathcal{M} \cup \mathcal{C} \cup tr(N) \cup tr(Q)$.*

- *A query* **sometimes**$_{\mathtt{m}}$ $\mathtt{L}_1, \ldots, \mathtt{L}_\mathtt{n}$ *is true if and only if there exists an answer set* $\mathbf{M}$ *of* Π *such that* $\mathbf{M} \models tr(L_1), \ldots, tr(L_n)$.
- *A query* **always**$_{\mathtt{m}}$ $\mathtt{L}_1, \ldots, \mathtt{L}_\mathtt{n}$ *is true if and only if for every answer set* $\mathbf{M}$ *of* Π *it holds that* $\mathbf{M} \models tr(L_1), \ldots, tr(L_n)$.
- *A query* **never**$_{\mathtt{m}}$ $\mathtt{L}_1, \ldots, \mathtt{L}_\mathtt{n}$ *is true if and only if the query* **sometimes**$_{\mathtt{m}}$ $\mathtt{L}_1, \ldots, \mathtt{L}_\mathtt{n}$ *is false.*

3.4 Example Analysis

There are many queries that can be asked regarding properties of individual nodes using the language, but the most interesting queries are related to the global behaviour of a collection of DSMs. For example, take the Colour Voting algorithm and the queries **sometimes**$_{\mathtt{m}}$ `converged` and **always**$_{\mathtt{m}}$ `converged`. The query result may vary depending on the communication model, *synchronous* vs. *asynchronous*. As a specific example, take the network in Figure 2. For both communication models, if we assume that the communication is reliable (i.e., no message can be lost or duplicated), both queries are false regardless of the value of `m`, as each node alternates its colour between state transitions.[4] In the asynchronous case, if orderly communication and continuous message processing are further assumed (i.e., using (38), (39) and (40)) within $\mathtt{m} \geq 4$, the query **sometimes**$_{\mathtt{m}}$ `converged` is true and the query **always**$_{\mathtt{m}}$ `converged` is false. For each computed model, an *execution trace* (that contains inter-node messages and node colours) can be extracted. One of the traces in which the algorithm converged with $\mathtt{m} = 4$ is illustrated in Figure 3.

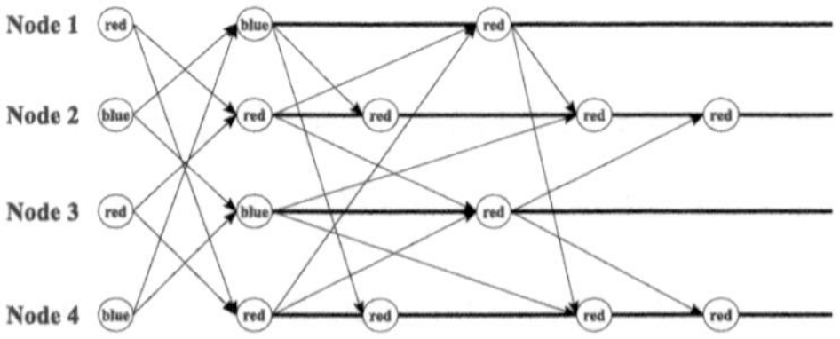

Fig. 3. A converged execution trace within #`maxtime` = 4: all nodes become red

4 Related Work

We have already mentioned in the introduction that our work builds on the programming language Dedalus of Alvaro et al [4]. In [12], Dedalus is used as the basis for a programming language that mixes declarative and imperative specifications and some high level analysis of concurrency and synchronisation is done. Several analysis systems have been developed for declarative networking. They are limited by the restricted semantics of declarative networking languages as in the work described in [13] and in many cases they are specific for the analysis of routing protocols as in [14] and [15]. Datalog has been used to analyze distributed discrete event systems described as Petri nets [16]. This is an interesting area to explore next. The description of transition systems using logic rules is not limited to action languages. Relational transducers [17] have been used to define state transition systems mainly with the goal of describing web-services and service composition and not distributed computing. We are the first ones to use ASP and we believe that our model and ASP are a very good combination for the study of many distributed programs.

[4] In the synchronous case, only (29) is needed in the communication model.

5 Final Remarks

We implemented a parser which translates DSM specifications and queries into their corresponding answer set program and integrity constraints. Clingo [10] was used as the underlying ASP solver for model computation. We have also used this implementation to check properties of two different classes of network routing protocols: path-vector based protocols and link state protocols [18,19]. In path vector protocols we are able to prove protocol convergence under conditions for which no analytical conditions for convergence are known [20], and checking the convergence manually is virtually impossible.

There are many directions of research that can be followed. We will mention a few. Our query language still has several drawbacks. The query definition rules are very general but the model does not provide too much guidance to the programmer about what kind of rules are needed and how to write them. Adding explicitly temporal operators might be useful. We are also investigating queries that incorporate some type of abductive reasoning [21]. For example, an interesting query for the voting algorithm is to find assignments of colours for the nodes of a given network so that the algorithm converges, or even automatically generate the network. Good methods to detect loops (i.e. state repetitions) are also needed. We also need a good library of communication models for programmers to use, and adding probability to describe communication models will be very useful. Visualisation of computation is also needed. Probabilistic queries can also be of interest. For example, finding the likelihood of certain properties to emerge, say, the nodes of a given region in the graph are mostly red, are questions of interest for an analyst.

References

1. Loo, B.T.: The Design and Implementation of Declarative Networks. PhD thesis, EECS Department, University of California, Berkeley (December 2006)
2. Loo, B.T., Condie, T., Garofalakis, M.N., Gay, D.E., Hellerstein, J.M., Maniatis, P., Ramakrishnan, R., Roscoe, T., Stoica, I.: Declarative networking: language, execution and optimization. In: SIGMOD Conference, pp. 97–108 (2006)
3. Li, X., Muthukumar, S.C., Liu, C., Kopena, J.B., Oprea, M., Correa, R., Loo, B.T., Basu, P.: A demonstration of the rapidmesh development toolkit. In: Proceedings of the 4th ACM International Workshop on Experimental Evaluation and Characterization, WINTECH 2009, pp. 89–90. ACM, New York (2009)
4. Alvaro, P., Marczak, W.R., Conway, N., Hellerstein, J.M., Maier, D., Sears, R.: DEDALUS: Datalog in Time and Space. In: de Moor, O., Gottlob, G., Furche, T., Sellers, A. (eds.) Datalog 2010. LNCS, vol. 6702, pp. 262–281. Springer, Heidelberg (2011)
5. Gelfond, M., Lifschitz, V.: Action languages. Electron. Trans. Artif. Intell. 2, 193–210 (1998)
6. Greco, S., Zaniolo, C.: Greedy algorithms in datalog. Theory Pract. Log. Program. 1, 381–407 (2001)
7. Baral, C.: Knowledge Representation, Reasoning, and Declarative Problem Solving. Cambridge University Press, New York (2003)

8. Leone, N., Pfeifer, G., Faber, W., Eiter, T., Gottlob, G., Perri, S., Scarcello, F.: The dlv system for knowledge representation and reasoning. ACM Trans. Comput. Logic 7, 499–562 (2006)
9. Simons, P., Niemelá, I., Soininen, T.: Extending and implementing the stable model semantics. Artif. Intell. 138, 181–234 (2002)
10. Gebser, M., Kaminski, R., Kaufmann, B., Ostrowski, M., Schaub, T., Schneider, M.: Potassco: The Potsdam answer set solving collection 24(2), 105–124 (2011)
11. Lamport, L.: Time clocks, and the ordering of events in a distributed system. Commun. ACM 21, 558–565 (1978)
12. Alvaro, P., Conway, N., Hellerstein, J., Marczak, W.R.: Consistency analysis in bloom: a calm and collected approach. In: CIDR, pp. 249–260 (2011)
13. Deng, Y., Grumbach, S., Monin, J.-F.: A Framework for Verifying Data-Centric Protocols. In: Bruni, R., Dingel, J. (eds.) FMOODS/FORTE 2011. LNCS, vol. 6722, pp. 106–120. Springer, Heidelberg (2011)
14. Ren, Y., Zhou, W., Wang, A., Jia, L., Gurney, A.J.T., Loo, B.T., Rexford, J.: Fsr: formal analysis and implementation toolkit for safe inter-domain routing. In: SIGCOMM, pp. 440–441 (2011)
15. Wang, A., Talcott, C., Jia, L., Loo, B.T., Scedrov, A.: Analyzing BGP Instances in Maude. In: Bruni, R., Dingel, J. (eds.) FMOODS/FORTE 2011. LNCS, vol. 6722, pp. 334–348. Springer, Heidelberg (2011)
16. Abiteboul, S., Abrams, Z., Haar, S., Milo, T.: Diagnosis of asynchronous discrete event systems: datalog to the rescue! In: PODS, pp. 358–367 (2005)
17. Abiteboul, S., Vianu, V., Fordham, B.S., Yesha, Y.: Relational transducers for electronic commerce. J. Comput. Syst. Sci. 61(2), 236–269 (2000)
18. Griffin, T., Wilfong, G.T.: A safe path vector protocol. In: INFOCOM, pp. 490–499 (2000)
19. Clausen, T., Jacquet, P.: Optimized link state routing protocol (OLSR). RFC 3236 (October 2003)
20. Griffin, T.G., Shepherd, F.B., Wilfong, G.: The stable paths problem and interdomain routing. IEEE/ACM Trans. Netw. 10, 232–243 (2002)
21. Kakas, A.C., Kowalski, R.A., Toni, F.: Abductive logic programming. J. Log. Comput. 2(6), 719–770 (1992)

Disjunctive Programs with Set Constraints

Victor W. Marek[1] and Jeffrey B. Remmel[2]

[1] Department of Computer Science, University of Kentucky, Lexington, KY 40506
[2] Departments of Mathematics and Computer Science,
University of California at San Diego, La Jolla, CA 92903
marek@cs.uky.edu, jremmel@ucsd.edu

To Vladimir Lifschitz on the occasion of his 65-th birthday: in recognition of his many contributions to Nonmonotonic Reasoning which have inspired so many researchers in the field.

Abstract. We study an extension of disjunctive logic programs called *set constraint disjunctive (SCD) programs* where the clauses of the program are allowed to have a disjunction of monotone set constraints in their head and arbitrary monotone and antimonotone set constraints in their body. We introduce new class of models called selector stable models which represent all models which can be computed by an analogue the Gelfond-Lifschitz transform. We show that the stable models of disjunctive logic programs can be defined in terms of selector stable models and then extend this result to *SCD* logic programs. Finally we show that there is a natural proof theory associated with selector stable models.

1 Introduction

The answer-set semantics for disjunctive programs both resembles and differs from the answer set semantics for normal logic programs. On the one hand, it is based on the notion of the Gelfond-Lifschitz reduct [6]. On the other hand, it involves an additional element, namely, the minimality of a model. This conjoining of two seemingly different notions results of the increased expressibility. That is, propositional disjunctive programs capture the class of Σ_2^P problems [3]. In this paper, we investigate a class of programs, called *set constraint disjunctive (SCD) logic programs*, which generalize disjunctive logic programs [11] and set constraint logic programs [13]. Clauses in *SCD* logic programs are allowed to have heads which are a disjunction of monotone set constraints and bodies which are conjunctions of monotone and antimonotone set constraints.

We define a natural class of models called *selector stable models* which can be constructed via an analogue of the standard method of constructing stable models for normal logic programs based on the Gelfond-Lifschitz reduct. Selector stable models are based on an underlying *selector function* f which selects for each *SCD* clause C in a *SCD* program D, a specific set of atoms $f(C)$ such that $f(C)$ satisfies at least one monotone constraint that occurs in the head of the C.

E. Erdem et al. (Eds.): Correct Reasoning, LNCS 7265, pp. 471–486, 2012.

When D is an *SCD* program which has no antimonotone set constraints in the body of its clauses, then D behaves like a Horn program in that we can assign an analogue of the one-step provability operator $T_{f,D}$ to D and f. $T_{f,D}$ is always a monotone operator whose least fixpoint is a model of P. Conversely, each model M of such a Horn-like program determines a canonical function f so that the least fixpoint of $T_{f,D}$ is included in M. We can then define the notion of a selector stable model for D and f via the usual Gelfond-Lifschitz transform assuming that the selector function f satisfies a simple coherence condition which assures that $f(C_1) = f(C_2)$ whenever the Horn parts of clauses C_1 and C_2 coincide.

In the special case of disjunctive logic programs, we will show that a stable model is just a minimal selector stable model. A similar result holds for general *SCD* programs. We will also show that selector stable models have a natural proof theory associated with them.

The outline of this paper is as follows. In Section 2, we shall define the basic notions of set constraints and *SCD* programs. In Section 3, we shall show how stable models of disjunctive logic programs can be defined via selector stable models and define a proof theory of selector stable models. In Section 4, we will show how the results of Section 3 naturally extend to *SCD* logic programs. In Section 5, we will state our conclusions and perspectives for further research.

2 Preliminaries

Given any set X, we let 2^X denote the set of all subsets of X. Let At be a set of propositional variables. A *set constraint* over At is a pair $\langle X, F\rangle$ where X is a finite subset of At and $F \subseteq 2^X$. A set constraint $\langle X, F\rangle$ is called *monotone* if whenever $Y \in F$ and $Y \subseteq Z \subseteq X$, $Z \in F$. $\langle X, F\rangle$ is called *antimonotone* if whenever $Y \in F$ and $Z \subseteq Y$, $Z \in F$. Set constraints were introduced by the authors in [13] and were further studied in [9,12]. The semantics for programs with set constraints introduced in [13] was a natural generalization of the proposal of [18]. An alternative semantics for those constraints (with the name *abstract* constraints) was studied in [19]. A more general proposal for the semantics of abstract constraints was introduced in [10] which included a set of postulates that should be satisfied by any reasonable semantics for abstract constraints.

Given a set constraint $S = \langle X, F\rangle$, we define the monotonic closure of S to be the set constraint $\overline{S} = \langle X, \overline{F}\rangle$ where $A \in \overline{F}$ if and only if $A \subseteq X$ and there is a $B \in F$ such that $B \subseteq A$. Similarly, we define the antimonotonic closure of S to be the set constraint $\underline{S} = \langle X, \underline{F}\rangle$ where $A \in \underline{F}$ if and only if there is a $B \in F$ such that $A \subseteq B$. We say a subset M of At is a model of $\langle X, F\rangle$, written $M \models \langle X, F\rangle$, if $M \cap X \in F$. One advantage of monotone constraints $\langle X, F\rangle$ is that if $M \subseteq N \subseteq At$ and $M \models \langle X, F\rangle$, then $N \models \langle X, F\rangle$, Among the monotone constraints, a special role is played by monotone cardinality constraints and by *cones* i.e., constraints of the form $C_Z = \langle X, \{Y : Z \subseteq Y \subseteq X\}\rangle$. In particular, every monotone constraint and every monotone cardinality constraint can be represented as union of cones. An analogous result holds for antimonotone constraints [12].

Set constraints or abstract constraints are a common generalization of constraints pervasive in ASP literature such as cardinality constraints, weight constraints, parity constraints, SQL constraints (i.e., those using constructs such as min,max avg, etc.) One complaint about the practicality of set constraints is that when a set constraint is represented explicitly the size of such representation may be exponential in $|X|$. While this is true in general, there are many set constraints which have exponential size when written out explicitly, but still can be processed efficiently. For example, the monotone cardinality constraint $\{Y : |Y| \geq .5 * |X|\}$ has exponential size when written out explicitly. Nevertheless, cardinality constraints and weight constraints that have been implemented effectively. That is, we write $kX\ell$ for the set constraint such that $M \models kX\ell$ if and only if $k \leq |M \cap X| \leq \ell$. Thus $kX\ell = \langle X, F\rangle$ where F is the family of sets $A \subseteq X$ such that $k \leq |A| \leq \ell$. Even though explicitly representing $kX\ell$ in set form can be exponential in $|X|$, the reason one can build effective systems in ASP which allow for cardinality constraints is that there is is an efficient algorithm to test whether $M \models kX\ell$. That is, given a total order $<$ on At, and $X = \{x_1 < \ldots < x_n\}$, then we can represent $M \cap X$ as a sequence $s_{M\cap X} = s_1 \ldots s_n$ in $\{0,1\}^n$ where $s_i = 1$ if and only if $x_i \in M$. Given $s_{M\cap X}$ and k and ℓ, it is simple to determine if $M \models kX\ell$ by taking one pass through $s_{M\cap X}$. In fact, every set constraint $\langle X, F\rangle$ where $X = \{x_1 < \ldots < x_n\}$ can be thought of a Boolean function over $\{0,1\}^n$ where $f(s_1 \ldots s_n) = 1$ if and only if $\{x_i : s_i = 1\} \in F$. Thought of in this way, set constraints can be given a variety of representations, for instance as CNFs, DNFs, ROBDDs, Boolean polynomials, etc., which allow for efficient processing. The topic of such representations will be studied in [14].

In this paper, we shall define an answer set or stable model semantics for an extension of disjunctive logic programs [11] and set constraint programs [13] which we call set constraint disjunctive (*SCD*) logic programs. An *SCD* clause is a clause of the form

$$C = H_1 \vee \ldots \vee H_k \leftarrow K_1, \ldots, K_n, L_1, \ldots, L_m \tag{1}$$

where $H_1, \ldots, H_k, K_1, \ldots K_n$ are monotone constraints and $L_1, \ldots, L_m$ are antimonotone constraints. We refer to $H_1 \vee \ldots \vee H_k$ as the head of C and $K_1 \wedge \ldots \wedge K_n \wedge L_1 \wedge \ldots \wedge L_m$ as the body of C and write $concl(C) = \{H_1, \ldots, H_k\}$, $prem(C) = \{K_1, \ldots, K_n\}$ and $constr(C) = \{L_1, \ldots, L_m\}$. We say that C is a Horn clause if $constr(C) = \emptyset$. If $M \subseteq At$, then we say that M satisfies the body of C if and only if $M \models K_i$ and $M \models L_j$ for all i and j and M satisfies the head of C if there is at least one i such that $M \models H_i$. We say that M is model of C if and only if either M does not satisfy the body of C or M satisfies the head of C. An *SCD*-program P is a collection of *SCD* clauses. M is model of P if and only if M is model of every clause in P.

3 Selector Stable Models for Disjunctive Logic Programs

A disjunctive logic programming clause is a clause of the form

$$C = a_1 \vee a_2 \vee \ldots \vee a_n \leftarrow b_1, \ldots, b_n, \neg c_1, \ldots, \neg c_m \quad (2)$$

where $a_1, \ldots, a_k, b_1, \ldots, b_n, c_1, \ldots, c_m$ are atomic formulas in a first order language. We call $a_1 \vee a_2 \vee \ldots \vee a_k$ the head of C, $b_1, \ldots, b_n$ the premises of C, $c_1, \ldots, c_m$ the constraints of C, $b_1 \wedge \ldots \wedge b_n \wedge \neg c_1 \wedge \ldots \wedge \neg c_m$ the body of C, and write $concl(C) = \{a_1, \ldots, a_k\}$, $prem(C) = \{b_1, \ldots, b_n\}$, $constr(C) = \{c_1, \ldots, c_m\}$. C is called a (disjunctive) Horn clause if $constr(C) = \emptyset$, i.e., if C has no negated atoms in its body. C is a ground clause if C has no free variables. If C has no disjunctions in the head, i.e., if $k = 1$, the C is a normal logic programming clause.

A disjunctive logic program D is a set of clauses of the form (2). D is said to be a Horn program if all its clauses are Horn clauses. A ground instance of a clause is a clause obtained by substituting ground terms (terms without free variables) for all the free variables of the clause. We let $ground(D)$ denote the disjunctive propositional logic program consisting of all the ground instances of the clauses in D. The Herbrand base of D, $H(D)$, is the set of all ground atoms that are instances of atoms that appear in D. If $M \subseteq H(D)$ and

$$C = a_1 \vee a_2 \vee \cdots \vee a_k \leftarrow b_1, \ldots, b_m, \neg c_1, \ldots, \neg c_n \in ground(D),$$

then we say that M is a model of D if either M does not satisfy the body of C or M satisfies the head of C. M is a model of D if M is a model of all clauses in $ground(D)$. Thus, as usual, one can reduce models and stable models from predicate disjunctive logic programs and to models and stable model of their grounded versions. That is, the semantics of predicate logic programs can be reduce to the semantics of propositional logic programs. Thus for the rest of this section, we shall focus on propositional disjunctive logic programs.

One of the significant differences between disjunctive logic programs and normal logic programs is that disjunctive Horn programs have multiple intended models. In disjunctive logic programming, one takes the point of view of that models which are minimal with respect to inclusion are the preferred models. We let $mm(D)$ denote the set of minimal models of D.

Example 1. Let D be the propositional disjunctive logic program consisting of the following two clauses.
$C_1 = a \vee b \leftarrow .$
$C_2 = c \vee d \leftarrow b.$
Then is is easy to check that the models of D are $M_1 = \{a\}$, $M_2 = \{b, c\}$, $M_3 = \{b, d\}$, $M_4 = \{b, c, d\}$, $M_5 = \{a, b, c\}$, $M_6 = \{a, b, d\}$, and $M_7 = \{a, b, c, d\}$. Thus $mm(D) = \{M_1, M_2, M_3\}$. □

Given a disjunctive propositional logic program D and a set $M \subseteq H(D)$, we define the Gelfond-Lifschitz reduct D^M by first removing all clauses $C \in D$ such that $constr(C) \cap M \neq \emptyset$ and then for each of the remaining clauses C, replacing C by the clause $a_1 \vee a_2 \vee \ldots \vee a_k \leftarrow b_1, \ldots, b_n$ where $a_1 \vee a_2 \vee \ldots \vee a_k$ is the conclusion of C and $prem(C) = \{b_1, \ldots, b_n\}$. Clearly D^M will always be a disjunctive logic Horn program. Then we say that M is a *stable model* (answer set) of D if $M \in mm(D^M)$.

The main goal of this section is define an alternative approach to defining models and stable models of disjunctive logic programs that can be extended to a much larger class of programs. Our approach is to use what we call selector functions.

Let us suppose that D is a disjunctive propositional logic Horn program. We say that $f : D \to 2^{H(D)}$ is a *selector function* for D if for each clause $C \in D$, $f(C)$ is a non-empty subset of $concl(C)$. This given, we can then define an analogue of the one-step provability operator relative to D and f. That is, for $M \subseteq H(D)$, we define

$$T_{f,D}(M) = \bigcup \{A : (\exists C \in D)(prem(C) \subseteq M \ \&\ A = f(C)\}.$$

The idea is that one cannot define a one-step provability operator for propositional disjunctive logic programs because if $M \subseteq H(D)$ and C is a clause of the form

$$C = a_1 \vee a_2 \vee \ldots \vee a_k \leftarrow b_1, \ldots, b_n$$

where $\{b_1, \ldots, b_n\} \subseteq M$ and $k \geq 2$, then we do not know which elements from $a_1, \ldots, a_k$ that we should put into $T_D(M)$ for the clause C. The selector function overcomes this difficulty in that it says that elements from $a_1, \ldots, a_k$ that we should put into $T_{f,D}(M)$ are precisely the elements in $f(C)$. It is easy to see that the usual proof that the one-step provability operator T_P for propositional Horn programs is monotone and continuous [20] also applies to the operators $T_{f,D}$. Thus, $T_{f,D}$ is monotone and continuous and $T_{f,D}$ reaches the fixpoint in at most ω steps. This given, then we define the *selector model $M_{f,D}$ of D relative to f* to be

$$M_{f,D} = T_{f,D} \uparrow_\omega (\emptyset) = \bigcup_{n \geq 0} T^n_{f,D}(\emptyset)$$

where for any $S \subseteq H(D)$, $T^0_{f,D}(S) = S$ and $T^{n+1}_{f,D}(S) = T_{f,D}(T^n_{f,D}(S))$.

For example, consider the program D in Example 1. We have 3 choices for the value of selector function f on C_1, namely, we can have $f(C_1) = \{a\}$, $f(C_1) = \{b\}$, or $f(C_1) = \{a, b\}$. Similarly, we have 3 choices for the value of selector function f on C_2, namely, we can have $f(C_1) = \{c\}$, $f(C_2) = \{d\}$, or $f(C_2) = \{c, d\}$. Now if $f_1(C_1) = \{a\}$, then it is easy to see that $M_{f_1,D} = \{a\} = M_1$ no matter what the value of $f_1(C_2)$ is. If $f_2(C_1) = \{b\}$, then it is easy to see that $M_{f_2,D} = \{b, c\} = M_2$ if $f_2(C_2) = \{c\}$, $M_{f_2,D} = \{b, d\} = M_3$ if $f_2(C_2) = \{d\}$, and $M_{f_2,D} = \{b, c, d\} = M_4$ if $f_2(C_2) = \{c, d\}$. If $f_3(C_1) = \{a, b\}$, then it is easy to see that $M_{f_3,D} = \{a, b, c\} = M_5$ if $f_3(C_2) = \{c\}$, $M_{f_3,D} = \{a, b, d\} = M_6$ if $f_3(C_2) = \{d\}$, and $M_{f_3,D} = \{b, c, d\} = M_7$ if $f_3(C_2) = \{c, d\}$.

Theorem 1. *Suppose that D is a propositional disjunctive logic Horn program. Then*
1. *for all selector functions $f : D \rightarrow 2^{H(D)}$, $M_{f,D}$ is a model of D and*
2. *for every minimal model M of D, $M = M_{g,D}$ where for any clause $C \in D$, $g(C) = M \cap concl(C)$ if $prem(C) \subseteq M$ and $g(C) = concl(C)$ otherwise.*

Proof: For (1), note that we have observed that $T_{f,D}$ is a monotone operator. Thus if $A \subseteq B \subseteq H(D)$, then $T_{f,D}(A) \subseteq T_{f,D}(B)$. It then easily follows that for all n, $T^n_{f,D}(\emptyset) \subseteq T^{n+1}_{f,D}(\emptyset)$. Now suppose that $C = a_1 \vee a_2 \vee \ldots \vee a_k \leftarrow b_1, \ldots, b_m$ is a clause in D. Now if $\{b_1, \ldots, b_m\} \subseteq M_{f,D}$, then for each i, there is stage n_i such that $b_i \in T^{n_i}_{f,D}(\emptyset)$. Thus if $n = max(\{n_1, \ldots, n_k\})$, then $\{b_1, \ldots, b_m\} \subseteq T^n_{f,D}(\emptyset)$. But then $f(C) \subseteq T^{n+1}_{f,D}(\emptyset)$. Since we are assuming that $f(C) \neq \emptyset$, it follows that $f(C) \subseteq M_{f,D} \cap \{a_1, \ldots, a_k\}$ so that $M_{f,D}$ is a model of C. Hence $M_{f,D}$ is a model of D.

For (2), it is easy to prove by induction that $T^n_{g,D}(\emptyset) \subseteq M$ for all n so that $M_{g,D} \subseteq M$. That is, $T^1_{g,D}(\emptyset) = \{g(C) : C \in D \ \& \ prem(C) \subseteq \emptyset\}$. But if $prem(C) = \emptyset$, then C must be of the form $a_1 \vee \ldots \vee a_k \leftarrow$ and since M is a model of C, $g(C) = \{a_1, \ldots, a_k\} \cap M$. Thus $g(C)$ is a nonempty subset of M. Hence $T^1_{g,D}(\emptyset) \subseteq M$. Now by induction, suppose that $T^n_{g,D}(\emptyset) \subseteq M$. Then

$$T^{n+1}_{g,D}(\emptyset) = \{g(C) : C \in D \ \& \ prem(C) \subseteq T^n_{g,D}(\emptyset)\}.$$

Now if $prem(C) \subseteq T^n_{g,D}(\emptyset)$, then $prem(C) \subseteq M$ so that $g(C) = M \cap concl(C)$. It follows that $T^{n+1}_{g,D}(\emptyset) \subseteq M$. Hence $M_{g,D} = T_{g,D} \uparrow_\omega (\emptyset) \subseteq M$. But by (1), $M_{g,D}$ is model of D so that $M_{g,D} = M$ since M is a minimal model of D. □

We note that the hypothesis that M is a minimal model in part 2 of Theorem 1 is necessary. That is, suppose that $\overline{D}$ consists of the clauses C_1 and C_2 from Example 1 plus the clause

$$C_3 = e \vee k \leftarrow g.$$

Then it is to see $M = \{a, b, c, e\}$ is model of $\overline{D}$, but that M cannot be of the form $M_{f,\overline{D}}$ for any selector function. That is, since g is not in the head of any clause of $\overline{D}$, it follows that it is impossible that e could be derived in process of computing $T_{f,\overline{D}} \uparrow_\omega (\emptyset)$ no matter how one defines the selector function f. In fact, in this case, it is easy to see that the selector models of D from Example 1 and $\overline{D}$ are the same.

We can also define selector stable models for disjunctive propositional logic programs admitting negation in the body as follows. Suppose D is such disjunctive propositional logic program. We say that $f : D \rightarrow 2^{H(D)}$ is a *selector function* for D if it satisfies the following two properties.

1. If C is a clause in D, then $f(C)$ is a non-empty subset of $concl(C)$.
2. If C_1 and C_2 are clauses in D such that $concl(C_1) = concl(C_2)$ and $prem(C_1) = prem(C_2)$, then $f(C_1) = f(C_2)$.

Now suppose that we are given a subset M of $H(P)$ and a selector function f. We define the *Gelfond-Lifschitz reduct* of D, D^M, via the following two step process. In Step 1, we eliminate all clauses $C \in D$ such that $constr(C) \cap M \neq \emptyset$. In Step 2, for each remaining clause

$$C = a_1 \vee a_2 \vee \ldots \vee a_k \leftarrow b_1, \ldots, b_n, \neg c_1, \ldots, \neg c_m,$$

we replace C by

$$C_M = a_1 \vee a_2 \vee \ldots \vee a_k \leftarrow b_1, \ldots, b_n.$$

The resulting program D^M is a disjunctive propositional Horn program. We then let f_M be the selector function for D^M defined by letting $f_M(C_M) = f(C)$. Note that condition (2) of our definition of a selector function for D ensures that f_M is a well defined function from D^M into $2^{H(D)}$. Then we say that M is a *selector stable model of D relative to f* if $M = M_{f_M, D^M}$. We say that M is a *selector stable model* if M is a selector stable model relative to f for some selector function for D. We let $SS(D)$ denote the set of selector stable models of D. Then we say that M is a *minimal selector stable model of D* if and only if M is a minimal element of $SS(D)$ relative to inclusion.

We then have the following theorem.

Theorem 2. *Let D be disjunctive logic program. Then M is a stable model of D if and only if M is a minimal selector stable model of D.*

Proof: First assume that M is a stable model of D. Then M is a minimal model of D^M. Since D^M is a disjunctive propositional logic Horn program, it follows from Theorem 1 that there is selector function g_M for M such that $M = M_{g_M, D^M}$ where for any clause $C \in D$, $g_M(C) = M \cap concl(C)$ if $prem(C) \subseteq M$ and $g_M(C) = concl(C)$ otherwise. Then we define $f : D \rightarrow 2^{H(D)}$ by letting $f(C) = g_M(E)$ if there is a clause $E \in D^M$ such that $concl(C) = concl(E)$ and $prem(C) = prem(E)$ and defining $f(C) = concl(C)$, otherwise. It is easy to see that f is a selector function for D and that $f_M = g_M$. It follows that $M_{f_M, D^M} = M$ so that M is a selector stable model.

Now suppose that N is a selector model and $N \subseteq M$. Then we know that $D^M \subseteq D^N$ and N is a model of D^N. But then N is a model of D^M. Since M is a minimal model of D^M, it follows that $N = M$. Hence M is a minimal selector stable model.

Next suppose that N is a minimal selector stable model of D. Then N is a model of D^N by Theorem 1. We claim that N is a minimal model of D^N so that N is stable model of D. That is, suppose that $M \subset N$ and M is a minimal model of D^N. Then by Theorem 1, there is a selector function g for D^N such that $M_{g, D^N} = M$. Then as above, we define $f : D \rightarrow 2^{H(D)}$ by letting $f(C) = g(E)$ if there is a clause $E \in D^N$ such that $concl(C) = concl(E)$ and $prem(C) = prem(E)$ and defining $f(C) = concl(C)$, otherwise. Then f is a selector function for D such that $f_N = g$. It follows that $M_{f_N, D^N} = M$ so that M is a selector stable model which violates the fact that N was a minimal selector stable model. Thus it must be the case that N is a minimal model of D^N so that N is a stable model. □

We view the collection of selector stable models of a disjunctive logic program D as the collection of models that can reasonably be computed from D. Since selector stable models are intrinsic to D, we can use the set of selector stable models to define alternative stable logic semantics for D. For example, one might prefer models that are minimal with respect to cardinality rather than just models that are minimal with respect to inclusion. It is easy to see that our proof of Theorem 1 also shows that M is minimal model of a disjunctive propositional logic Horn program with respect to cardinality, then it will be of the form $M_{f,D}$ for some selector program. This allows to define "cardinality stable models" of a disjunctive logic program by defining it to a selector stable model of minimal cardinality.

One advantage of selector stable models is that there is a natural proof theory associated with them. That is, recall [15] that normal propositional logic programs P have an associated collection of P-proof schemes. That is, given a normal propositional logic program P, the notion of a P-proof scheme is defined by induction on its length n. Specifically, the set of P-proof schemes are defined inductively by declaring that

(I) $\langle\langle C_1, p_1\rangle, U\rangle$ is a P-proof scheme of length 1 if $C_1 \in P$, p_1 is the head of C_1, $prem(C_1) = \emptyset$, and $U = constr(C_1)$ and
(II) for $n > 1$, $\langle\langle C_1, p_1\rangle, \ldots, \langle C_n, p_n\rangle, U\rangle$ is a P-proof scheme of length n if $\langle\langle C_1, p_1\rangle, \ldots, \langle C_{n-1}, p_{n-1}\rangle, \bar{U}\rangle$ is a P-proof scheme of length $n-1$ and C_n is a clause in P such that p_n is the head of C_n, $prem(C_n) \subseteq \{p_1, \ldots, p_{n-1}\}$ and $U = \bar{U} \cup constr(C_n)$.

If $S = \langle\langle C_1, p_1\rangle, \ldots, \langle C_n, p_n\rangle, U\rangle$ is a P-proof scheme of length n, then we let $supp(S) = U$ and $concl(S) = p_n$.

Example 2. Let P be the normal propositional logic program consisting of the following four clauses:

$$C_1 = p \leftarrow,\ C_2 = q \leftarrow p, \neg r,\ C_3 = r \leftarrow \neg q, \text{ and } C_4 = s \leftarrow \neg t.$$

Then we have the following useful examples of P-proof schemes:

(a) $\langle\langle C_1, p\rangle, \emptyset\rangle$ is a P-proof scheme of length 1 with conclusion p and empty support.
(b) $\langle\langle C_1, p\rangle, \langle C_2, q\rangle, \{r\}\rangle$ is a P-proof scheme of length 2 with conclusion q and support $\{r\}$.
(c) $\langle\langle C_1, p\rangle, \langle C_3, r\rangle, \{q\}\rangle$ is a P-proof scheme of length 2 with conclusion r and support $\{q\}$.
(d) $\langle\langle C_1, p\rangle, \langle C_2, q\rangle, \langle C_3, r\rangle, \{q, r\}\rangle$ is a P-proof scheme of length 3 with conclusion r and support $\{q, r\}$.

In this example we see that the proof scheme in (c) had an unnecessary item, the first term, while in (d) the proof scheme was supported by a set containing q, one of atoms that were proved on the way to r. □

A P-proof scheme differs from the usual Hilbert-style proofs in that it carries within itself its own applicability condition. In effect, a P-proof scheme is a *conditional* proof of its conclusion. It becomes applicable when all the constraints collected in the support are satisfied. Formally, for a set M of atoms, we say that a P-proof scheme S is M-*applicable* or that M *admits* S if $M \cap supp(S) = \emptyset$. The fundamental connection proved in between proof schemes and stable models is given by the following proposition which is proved in [15].

Proposition 1. *For every normal propositional logic program P and every set M of atoms, M is a stable model of P if and only if*
(i) for every $p \in M$, there is a P-proof scheme S with conclusion p such that M admits S and
(ii) for every $p \notin M$, there is no P-proof scheme S with conclusion p such that M admits S.

We can define an analogous notion of selector proof schemes for disjunctive logic programs. Suppose that we are given a disjunctive propositional logic program D and a selector function f for D. Then we can define a (D, f)-proof scheme by induction on its length n. Specifically, the set of (D, f)-proof schemes are defined inductively by declaring that

(I) $\langle\langle C_1, f(C_1)\rangle, U\rangle$ is a (D, f)-proof scheme of length 1 if $C_1 \in D$, $prem(C_1) = \emptyset$, and $U = constr(C_1)$ and
(II) for $n > 1$, $\langle\langle C_1, f(C_1)\rangle, \ldots, \langle C_n, f(C_n)\rangle, U\rangle$ is a (D, f)-proof scheme of length n if $\langle\langle C_1, f(C_1)\rangle, \ldots, \langle C_{n-1}, f(C_{n-1})\rangle, \bar{U}\rangle$ is a (D, f)-proof scheme of length $n - 1$ and C_n is a clause in D such that $prem(C_n) \subseteq \bigcup_{i=1}^{n-1} f(C_i)$ and $U = \bar{U} \cup constr(C_n)$

If $S = \langle\langle C_1, f(C_1)\rangle, \ldots, \langle C_n, f(C_n)\rangle, U\rangle$ is a (D, f)-proof scheme of length n, then we let $supp(S) = U$ and $concl(S) = \bigcup_{i=1}^{n} f(C_i)$.

Example 3. Let D be the normal propositional logic program consisting of the following four clauses:

$$C_1 = p \vee q \leftarrow,\ C_2 = a \vee b \leftarrow p, \neg r,\ C_3 = r \leftarrow a, b, \neg q, \text{ and } C_4 = s \vee t \leftarrow \neg t.$$

and $f(C_1) = \{p\}$, $f(C_2) = \{a, b\}$, $f(C_3) = \{r\}$, and $f(C_4) = \{t\}$. Then

(a) $\langle\langle C_1, \{p\}\rangle, \emptyset\rangle$ is a (D, f)-proof scheme of length 1 with conclusion $\{p\}$ and empty support.
(b) $\langle\langle C_1, \{p\}\rangle, \langle C_2, \{a, b\}\rangle, \{r\}\rangle$ is a (D, f)-proof scheme of length 2 with conclusion $\{p, a, b\}$ and support $\{r\}$.
(c) $\langle\langle C_1, \{p\}\rangle, \langle C_2, \{a, b\}\rangle, \langle C_3, \{r\}\rangle, \{q, r\}\rangle$ is a (D, f)-proof scheme of length 3 with conclusion $\{p, a, b, r\}$ and support $\{q, r\}$. □

For a set M of atoms, we say that a (D, f)-proof scheme S is M-*applicable* or that M *admits* S if $M \cap supp(S) = \emptyset$. Then we have the following analogue of Proposition 1.

Proposition 2. *For every disjunctive propositional logic program D, every selector function f for D, and every set M of atoms, $M = M_{f_M, D^M}$ is the selector stable model of D relative to the selector function f if and only if*
(i) for every $p \in M$, there is a (D, f)-proof scheme S with $p \in concl(S)$ such that M admits S and
(ii) for every $p \notin M$, there is no (D, f)-proof scheme S such that $p \in concl(S)$ and M admits S.

Proof: First suppose that $M = M_{f,D}$ is a selector stable model. It is easy to see by induction on the length of (D,f) proof schemes that if S is a (D,f)-proof scheme admitted by M, then $concl(S) \subseteq M$. That is, if $S = \langle\langle C_1, f(C_1)\rangle, U\rangle$ is a (D,f)-proof scheme of length 1 which is admitted by M, then $C_1 \in D$, $prem(C_1) = \emptyset$, and $U = constr(C_1)$ is such that $U \cap M = \emptyset$. It then follows that $(C_1)_M$ is of the form $a_1 \vee \ldots \vee a_k \leftarrow$ and $f_M((C_1)_M) = f(C_1)$. Thus $concl(S) = f(C_1) \subseteq T^1_{f_M,D^M}(\emptyset) \subseteq M$.

Next suppose that $n > 1$ and $S = \langle\langle C_1, f(C_1)\rangle, \ldots, \langle C_n, f(C_n)\rangle, U\rangle$ is a (D,f)-proof scheme of length n admitted by M. Then

$$\overline{S} = \langle\langle C_1, f(C_1)\rangle, \ldots, \langle C_{n-1}, f(C_{n-1})\rangle, \bar{U}\rangle$$

is a (D,f)-proof scheme of length $n-1$ admitted by M and C_n is a clause in D such that $prem(C_n) \subseteq \bigcup_{i=1}^{n-1} f(C_i)$ and $U = \bar{U} \cup constr(C_n)$. By induction, $\bigcup_{i=1}^{n-1} f(C_i) \subseteq M$. Hence there is a q such that $\bigcup_{i=1}^{n-1} f(C_i) \subseteq T^q_{f_M,D^M}(\emptyset)$. Then it is easy to see that C_n will witness that $f(C_n) \subseteq T^{q+1}_{f_M,D^M}(\emptyset)$.

Vice versa, it is also easy to prove by induction that for all $n \geq 1$, if $p \in T^n_{f_M,D^M}(\emptyset)$, then there is a (D,f)-proof scheme S such that $p \in concl(S)$ and M admits S. That is, if $p \in T^1_{f_M,D^M}(\emptyset)$, there there must be a clause B of the form $a_1 \vee \ldots \vee a_k \leftarrow$ and belonging to D^M such that $p \in f_M(B)$. But then there is a clause $C \in D$ such that $C_M = B$ which means that C is of the form

$$a_1 \vee \ldots \vee a_k \leftarrow \neg c_1, \ldots, \neg c_m$$

where $M \cap \{c_1, \ldots, c_m\} = \emptyset$. Since in the case $f(C) = f_M(B)$, it follows that $S = \langle\langle C, f(C)\rangle, \{c_1, \ldots, c_m\}\rangle$ is (D,f) proof scheme of length 1 with $p \in concl(S)$.

Next assume that $p \in T^{n+1}_{f_M,D^M}(\emptyset) \setminus T^n_{f_M,D^M}(\emptyset)$. Then there must be a clause B of the form

$$a_1 \vee \ldots \vee a_k \leftarrow b_1, \ldots, b_p \in D^M$$

such that $p \in f(B)$ and $b_1, \ldots, b_p \in T^n_{f_M,D^M}(\emptyset)$. But then there are (f,D)-proof schemes $S_1, \ldots, S_p$ admitted by M such that $b_i \in f(S_i)$ and a clause C in D of the form

$$a_1 \vee \ldots \vee a_k \leftarrow b_1, \ldots, b_p, \neg c_1, \ldots, \neg c_m$$

such that $M \cap \{c_1, \ldots, c_m\} = \emptyset$ and $f(C) = f_M(B)$. It follows that we if take the proof scheme S which combines the proof schemes $S_1, \ldots, S_p$ followed by the $\langle C, f(C)\rangle, \{c_1, \ldots, c_m\} \cup \bigcup_{i=1}^{n-1} supp(S_i)\rangle$, then S will be a (D,f) admitted by M such that $p \in concl(S)$. Thus (i) and (ii) hold.

Now if (i) and (ii) hold, our arguments show that $M = T_{f_M,D^M} \uparrow_\omega (\emptyset)$ so that M is a selector stable model. □

4 A Stable Model Semantics for *SCD* Programs

In this section, we shall extend the ideas of Section 2 to define a stable model semantics for *SCD* programs.

We start by defining the notion of a selector functions. Suppose D is an *SCD* Horn program, i.e., D has no antimonotone constraints appearing in the body of any of its clauses, and $C \in D$ is an *SCD* Horn clause with head $H_1 \vee \ldots \vee H_k$ where each H_i is a monotone set constraint of the form $\langle X_i, F_i \rangle$. To avoid trivialities, we shall always assume that there is no i such that $F_i = 2^{X_i}$ since otherwise every M is a model of $H_1 \vee \ldots \vee H_k$. Thus, in particular, we assume that $\emptyset \notin F_i$ for all i. The Herbrand base $H(D)$ of D is the set of all atoms that appear in some set constraint which occurs in a clause in D. A selector function f for D is a map from D into $2^{H(D)}$ where for each such clause C, $f(C)$ is a non-empty subset of $X_1 \cup \ldots \cup X_k$ such that there is at least one i such that $f(C) \cap X_i \in F_i$.

Suppose that D is an *SCD* propositional Horn program and $f : D \to 2^{H(D)}$ is a selector function for D. Then we can define the one-step provability operator $T_{D,f} : 2^{H(D)} \to 2^{H(D)}$ for D relative to f by defining for $S \subseteq H(D)$,

$$T_{f,D}(S) = \bigcup \{f(C) : (\exists C \in D)(S \text{ satisfies the body of } C)\}.$$

Again, it is easy to see that the usual proof that the one-step provability operator T_P for propositional Horn programs is monotone and continuous [20] also applies to the operators $T_{f,D}$. Thus, $T_{f,D}$ is monotone and continuous and $T_{f,D}$ reaches the fixpoint in at most ω steps. We then define the *selector model* $M_{f,D}$ *of* D *relative to* f to be

$$M_{f,D} = T_{f,D} \uparrow_\omega (\emptyset) = \bigcup_{n \geq 0} T^n_{f,D}(\emptyset)$$

where for any $S \subseteq H(D)$, $T^0_{f,D}(S) = S$ and $T^{n+1}_{f,D}(S) = T_{f,D}(T^n_{f,D}(S))$.

Theorem 3. *Suppose that D is an SCD propositional Horn program. Then*
1. *for all selector functions $f : D \to 2^{H(D)}$, $M_{f,D}$ is a model of D and*
2. *for every minimal model M of D, $M = M_{g,D}$ where for any clause $C \in D$ whose head is of the form $\langle X_1, F_1 \rangle \vee \ldots \vee \langle X_k, F_k \rangle$, $g(C) = M \cap (X_1 \cup \ldots \cup X_k)$ if M satisfies the body of C and $g(C) = X_1 \cup \ldots \cup X_k$ otherwise.*

Proof: For (1), observe that since $T_{f,D}$ is a monotone operator, $T^n_{f,D}(\emptyset) \subseteq T^{n+1}_{f,D}(\emptyset)$ for all n. Now suppose that $C = H_1 \vee H_2 \vee \ldots \vee H_k \leftarrow K_1, \ldots, K_m$ is an *SCD* Horn clause in D and that $M_{f,D} \models K_i = \langle Y_i, G_i \rangle$ for each $i \leq m$. Then $M \cap Y_i \in G_i$ for each i. Thus there must be a stage n_i such that $M \cap Y_i \subseteq T^{n_i}_{f,D}(\emptyset)$. Thus if $n = max(\{n_1, \ldots, n_k\})$, then $T^n_{f,D}(\emptyset)$ satisfies the body of C. But then $f(C) \subseteq T^{n+1}_{f,D}(\emptyset)$. Since we are assuming that $f(C) \models H_j$ for at least one j, it follows that $M_{f,D} \models H_j$ since $f(C) \subseteq M_{f,D}$ and H_j is monotone constraint. Thus $M_{f,D}$ is a model of C. It follows that $M_{f,D}$ is a model of D.

For (2), it is easy to prove by induction that $T^n_{g,D}(\emptyset) \subseteq M$ for all n so that $M_{f,D} \subseteq M$. That is, $T^1_{g,D}(\emptyset) = \{g(C) : C \in D \ \& \ prem(C) \subseteq \emptyset\}$. But if $prem(C) = \emptyset$, then C must be of the form: $H_1 \vee \ldots \vee H_k \leftarrow$, where each H_i is a monotone constraint of the form $\langle X_i, F_i \rangle$. Since M is a model of C, $g(C) = M \cap (X_1 \cup \ldots \cup X_k)$. Thus $g(C)$ is a nonempty subset of M. Hence $T^1_{g,D}(\emptyset) \subseteq M$. Now by induction, suppose that $T^n_{g,D}(\emptyset) \subseteq M$. Then

$$T^{n+1}_{g,D}(\emptyset) = \{g(C) : C \in D \ \& \ T^n_{g,D}(\emptyset) \text{ satisfies the body of } C\}.$$

Now if $T^n_{g,D}(\emptyset)$ satisfies the body of C, then M must satisfy the body of C since all the elements in the body of C are monotone constraint. If the head of C is of the form $H_1 \vee \ldots \vee H_k \leftarrow$ where each $H_i = \langle X_i, F_i \rangle$ is a monotone constraint, then $g(C) = M \cap (X_1 \cup \ldots \cup X_k)$. It follows that $T^{n+1}_{g,D}(\emptyset) \subseteq M$. Hence $M_{g,D} = T_{g,D} \uparrow_\omega (\emptyset) \subseteq M$. But by (1), $M_{g,D}$ is model of D so that $M_{g,D} = M$ since M is a minimal model of D. □

We define selector stable models for SCD propositional logic programs as follows. Suppose D is a SCD propositional logic program. We say that $f : D \rightarrow 2^{H(D)}$ is a selector function for D if it satisfies the following two properties.

1. If C is a clause in D whose head is of the form $\langle X_1, F_1 \rangle \vee \ldots \vee \langle X_k F_k \rangle$, then $f(C)$ is a non-empty subset of $X_1 \cup \ldots \cup X_k$ such that there is at least one i such that $f(C) \cap X_i \in F_i$.
2. If C_1 and C_2 are clauses in D such that $concl(C_1) = concl(C_2)$ and $prem(C_1) = prem(C_2)$, then $f(C_1) = f(C_2)$.

Now suppose that we are given a subset M of $H(P)$ and a selector function f. We define the *Gelfond-Lifschitz reduct* of D, D^M, via the following two step process. Suppose that C is a SCD clause in D of the form

$$C = H_1 \vee H_2 \vee \ldots \vee H_k \leftarrow K_1, \ldots, K_n, L_1, \ldots, L_m$$

where $H_1, \ldots, H_k, K_1, \ldots, K_m$ are monotone constraints and $L_1, \ldots, L_n$ are antimonotone constraints. In Step 1, we eliminate all clauses $C \in D$ such that M does not satisfy L_i for some i, $1 \leq i \leq m$. In Step 2, if C was not eliminated in Step I, then we replace C by

$$C_M = H_1 \vee H_2 \vee \ldots \vee H_k \leftarrow K_1, \ldots, K_n.$$

The resulting program D^M is an SCD propositional disjunctive Horn program. We then let f_M be the selector function for D^M defined by letting $f_M(C_M) = f(C)$. Note that condition (2) of our definition of a selector function for D ensures that f_M is a well defined function from D^M into $2^{H(D)}$. Then we say that M is a *selector stable model of D relative to f* if $M = M_{f_M, D^M}$. We say that M is a *selector stable model* if M is a selector stable model relative to f for some selector function for D. We let $SS(D)$ denote the set of selector stable models of D. Then we say that M is a *minimal selector stable model of* D if and only if M is a minimal element of $SS(D)$ relative to inclusion. Finally, we say that M is stable model of D if and only if M is minimal model of D^M.

We then have the following theorem.

Theorem 4. *Let D be SCD propositional logic program. Then M is a stable model of D if and only if M is a minimal selector stable model of D.*

Proof: First assume that M is a stable model of D. Then M is a minimal model of D^M. Since D^M is an SCD propositional Horn program, it follows from Theorem 3 that there is selector function g_M for D^M such that $M = M_{g_M, D^M}$ where for any clause $C \in D^M$ whose head is of the form $\langle X_1, F_1 \rangle \vee \ldots \vee \langle X_k, F_k \rangle$,

$g_M(C) = M \cap (X_1 \cup \ldots \cup X_k)$ if M satisfies the body of C and $g_M(C) = X_1 \cup \ldots \cup X_k$, otherwise. Then we define $f : D \to 2^{H(D)}$ by letting $f(C) = g_M(E)$ if there is a clause $E \in D^M$ such that $concl(C) = concl(E)$ and $prem(C) = prem(E)$ and defining $f(C) = X_1 \cup \ldots \cup X_k$ if M does not satisfy the body of C and the head of C is of the form $\langle X_1, F_1 \rangle \vee \ldots \vee \langle X_k, F_k \rangle$. It is easy to see that f is a selector function for D and that $f_M = g_M$. It follows that $M_{f_M,D^M} = M$ so that M is a selector stable model.

Now suppose that N is a selector model and $N \subseteq M$. Then we know that $D^M \subseteq D^N$ and N is a model of D^N. But then N is a model of D^M. Since M is a minimal model of D^M, it follows that $N = M$. Hence M is a minimal selector stable model.

Next suppose that N is a minimal selector stable model of D. Then N is a model of D^N by Theorem 3. We claim that N is a minimal model of D^N so that N is stable model of D. That is, suppose that $M \subset N$ and M is a minimal model of D^N. Then by Theorem 3, there is a selector function g for D^N such that $M_{g,D^N} = M$. Then as above, we define $f : D \to 2^{H(D)}$ by letting $f(C) = g(E)$ if there is a clause $E \in D^N$ such that $concl(C) = concl(E)$ and $prem(C) = prem(E)$ and defining $f(C) = X_1 \cup \ldots \cup X_k$ if there is no such clause $E \in D^M$ and the head of C is of the form $\langle X_1, F_1 \rangle \vee \ldots \vee \langle X_k, F_k \rangle$, otherwise. Then f is a selector function for D such that $f_N = g$. It follows that $M_{f_N,D^N} = M$ so that M is a selector stable model which violates the fact that N was a minimal selector stable model. Thus it must be the case that N is a minimal model of D^N so that N is a stable model. □

We can also define a notion of selector proof schemes for *SCD* propositional logic programs. Suppose that we are given a disjunctive propositional logic program D and a selector function f for D. Then we can define a (D, f)-proof scheme by induction on its length n. Specifically, the set of (D, f)-proof schemes are defined inductively by declaring that

(I) $\langle \langle C_1, f(C_1) \rangle, U \rangle$ is a (D, f)-proof scheme of length 1 if $C_1 \in D$, $prem(C_1) = \emptyset$, and $U = constr(C_1)$ and

(II) for $n > 1$, $\langle \langle C_1, f(C_1) \rangle, \ldots, \langle C_n, f(C_n) \rangle, U \rangle$ is a (D, f)-proof scheme of length n if $\langle \langle C_1, f(C_1) \rangle, \ldots, \langle C_{n-1}, f(C_{n-1}) \rangle, \bar{U} \rangle$ is a (D, f)-proof scheme of length $n - 1$ and C_n is a clause in D such that $\bigcup_{i=1}^{n-1} f(C_i)$ is a model of all the premises of C_n and $U = \bar{U} \cup constr(C_n)$

If $S = \langle \langle C_1, f(C_1) \rangle, \ldots, \langle C_n, f(C_n) \rangle, U \rangle$ is a (D, f)-proof scheme of length n, then we let $supp(S) = U$ and $concl(S) = \bigcup_{i=1}^{n} f(C_i)$.

For a set M of atoms, we say that a (D, f)-proof scheme S is *M-applicable* or that *M admits S* if M is a model of all antimonotone constraints in $supp(S)$. Then we have the following analogue of Proposition 2.

Proposition 3. *For SCD propositional logic program D, every selector function f for D, and every set M of atoms, $M = M_{f_M,D^M}$ is the selector stable model of D relative to the selector function f if and only if*

(i) for every $p \in M$, there is a (D, f)-proof scheme S with $p \in concl(S)$ such that M admits S and

(ii) for every $p \notin M$, there is no (D, f)-proof scheme S such that $p \in concl(S)$ and M admits S.

Proof: First assume that $M = M_{f,D}$ is selector stable model. It is easy to see by induction on the length of (D, f) proof schemes that if S is a (D, f)-proof scheme admitted by M, then $concl(S) \subseteq M$. That is, if $S = \langle\langle C_1, f(C_1)\rangle, U\rangle$ is a (D, f)-proof scheme of length 1 which is admitted by M, then $C_1 \in D$, $prem(C_1) = \emptyset$, and $U = constr(C_1)$ is such that M satisfies every antimonotone constraint in U. It then follows that $(C_1)_M$ is of the form $H_1 \vee \ldots \vee H_k \leftarrow$ and $f_M((C_1)_M) = f(C_1)$. Thus $concl(S) = f(C_1) \subseteq T^1_{f_M,D^M}(\emptyset) \subseteq M$.

Next suppose that $n > 1$ and $S = \langle\langle C_1, f(C_1)\rangle, \ldots, \langle C_n, f(C_n)\rangle, U\rangle$ is a (D, f)-proof scheme of length n admitted by M. Then

$$\overline{S} = \langle\langle C_1, f(C_1)\rangle, \ldots, \langle C_{n-1}, f(C_{n-1})\rangle, \bar{U}\rangle$$

is a (D, f)-proof scheme of length $n - 1$ admitted by M and C_n is a clause in D such that $prem(C_n) \subseteq \bigcup_{i=1}^{n-1} f(C_i)$ and $U = \bar{U} \cup constr(C_n)$. By induction, $\bigcup_{i=1}^{n-1} f(C_i) \subseteq M$. Hence there is a q such that $\bigcup_{i=1}^{n-1} f(C_i) \subseteq T^q_{f_M,D^M}(\emptyset)$. Then it is easy to see that C_n will witness that $f(C_n) \subseteq T^{q+1}_{f_M,D^M}(\emptyset)$.

Vice versa, it is also easy to prove by induction that for all $n \geq 1$, if $p \in T^n_{f_M,D^M}(\emptyset)$, then there is a (D, f)-proof scheme S such that $p \in concl(S)$ and M admits S. That is, if $p \in T^1_{f_M,D^M}(\emptyset)$, there there must be a clause B of the form $H_1 \vee \ldots \vee H_k \leftarrow$ belonging to D^M such that $p \in f_M(B)$. But then there is a clause $C \in D$ such that $C_M = B$ which means that C is of the form

$$H_1 \vee \ldots \vee H_k \leftarrow L_1, \ldots, L_m$$

where each L_i is an antimonotone constraint such that $M \models L_i$. Since in the case $f(C) = f_M(B)$, it follows that $S = \langle\langle C, f(C)\rangle, \{L_1, \ldots, L_m\}\rangle$ is (D, f) proof scheme of length 1 with $p \in concl(S)$.

Next assume that $p \in T^{n+1}_{f_M,D^M}(\emptyset) - T^n_{f_M,D^M}(\emptyset)$. Then there must be a clause B of the form

$$H_1 \vee \ldots \vee H_k \leftarrow K_1, \ldots, K_p \in D^M$$

such that $p \in f(B)$ and $T^n_{f_M,D^M}(\emptyset)$ is a model of $K_i = \langle Y_i, G_i\rangle$ for $i = 1, \ldots, p$. But then there are (f, D)-proof schemes $S_1, \ldots, S_r$ admitted by M such that for each b such that there exists an i with $b \in M \cap Y_i$, there exists a j with $b \in concl(S_j)$ and a clause C of the form

$$H_1 \vee \ldots \vee H_k \leftarrow K_1, \ldots, K_p, L_1, \ldots, L_m$$

where $L_1, \ldots, L_m$ are antimonotone constraints such that $M \models L_i$ for $i = 1, \ldots, m$ and $f(C) = f_M(B)$. It follows that we if take the proof scheme S which combines the proof schemes $S_1, \ldots, S_p$ followed by the $\langle\langle C, f(C)\rangle, \{L_1, \ldots, L_m\} \cup \bigcup_{i=1}^{n-1} supp(S_i)\rangle$, then S will be a (D, f) admitted by M such that $p \in concl(S)$. Thus (i) and (ii) hold.

If (i) and (ii) hold, then our proofs show that $M = T_{f,D} \uparrow_\omega (\emptyset)$ so that M is a selector stable model. □

5 Conclusions and Further Research

In this paper, we introduced the notion of selector stable models for a class of programs called set constraint logic (*SCD*) programs which are a common generalization of disjunctive logic programs and set constraint logic programs. We defined a collection of selector stable models which we view as the set of models that can reasonably be computed from the program via natural analogues of the Gelfond-Lifschitz transform. Selector stable models have a natural proof theory and can be used to define classical stable models of disjunctive logic programs.

Selector stable models are based on the notion of selector functions which specifies of a way to satisfy the head of any *SCD* clause. A moment reflection shows that such selector functions are present even in the standard normal logic programming. In that case, the selector function just specifies the head of the clause so it is completely trivial. Moreover, it is not difficult to see in hindsight that selector functions are implicit in the paper by Niemelä and his collaborators [18] on weight constraint programs and in our generalization of their construction in [13] on set constraint programs. That is, the selector function was hidden in the translation of the SNS-reduct to the clauses with single-atom heads. But since this translation produced groups of clauses that fire simultaneously, the selector function is just the abstraction from that idea. By that same argument the selector functions generalize the approach of [13].

We believe that selector functions play a crucial role whenever constructions admitting disjunctions of conditions are studied. Moreover, our work opens up several topics for further research. For example, it would be interesting to see how the analysis of Ferraris and Lifschitz [5] of the relationship of weight constraints and nested expressions relates to the present context. Our work also suggests that a natural notion of equivalence of two *SCD* programs is that they have the same set of selector stable models. Thus it should be interesting to study analogues of the notions of equivalence of normal logic programs and its variations such as those in [8] for *SCD* programs.

Our work suggests that one can explore alternative algorithms to the standard "guess-and-check" search method to computing stable models in the context of selector stable models of *SCD* programs. For example, in the case of normal logic programs, there is a forward chaining algorithm of [16] or a Metropolis-type algorithm due to Brik and Remmel [2]. One should also study a number of complexity issues associated with *SCD* programs such as the complexity of finding stable models under limitations of the asymptotic complexity of selector function that are allowed in the process. Finally, it is possible to extend our approach to programs which allow arbitrary set constraints in the bodies and to predicate logic versions of *SCD* programs.

References

1. Baral, C.: Knowledge Representation, Reasoning and Declarative Problem Solving. Cambridge University Press (2003)
2. Brik, A., Remmel, J.B.: Computing Stable Models of Logic Programs Using Metropolis Type Algorithms. In: Proceedings of Workshop on Answer Set Programming and Other Computing Paradigms (ASPOCP) 2011, paper no. 6, 15 pgs (2011)
3. Eiter, T., Gottlob, G.: On the Computational Cost of Disjunctive Logic Programming: Propositional Case. Ann. Math. Artif. Intell. 15, 289–323 (1995)
4. Eiter, T., Faber, W., Leone, N., Pfeifer, G.: Declarative Problem-solving in DLV. In: Minker, J. (ed.) Logic-based Artificial Intelligence, pp. 79–103 (2000)
5. Ferraris, P., Lifschitz, V.: Weight constraints as nested expressions. Theor. Pract. Logic Prog. 5, 45–74 (2005)
6. Gelfond, M., Lifschitz, V.: The stable semantics for logic programs. In: Proceedings 5th Int'l. Symp. Logic Programming, pp. 1070–1080. MIT Press (1988)
7. Gelfond, M., Lifschitz, V.: Classical negation in logic programs and disjunctive databases. New Gen. Comput. 9, 365–385 (1991)
8. Lifschitz, V., Pearce, D., Valverde, A.: Strongly equivalent logic programs. ACM Trans. Comput. Log. 2, 526–541 (2001)
9. Liu, L., Truszczynski, M.: Properties and Applications of Programs with Monotone and Convex Constraints. J. Artif. Intell. Res. 27, 299–334 (2006)
10. Liu, L., Pontelli, E., Son, T.C., Truszczynski, M.: Logic Programs with Abstract Constraint Atoms – the Role of Computations. Artif. Intell. 174, 295–315 (2010)
11. Lobo, J., Minker, J., Rajasekar, A.: Foundations of Disjunctive Logic Programming. MIT Press (1992)
12. Marek, V.W.: Introduction to Mathematics of Satisfiability. CRC Press (2009)
13. Marek, V.W., Remmel, J.B.: Set Constraints in Logic Programming. In: Lifschitz, V., Niemelä, I. (eds.) LPNMR 2004. LNCS (LNAI), vol. 2923, pp. 167–179. Springer, Heidelberg (2003)
14. Marek, V.W., Remmel, J.B.: Effective Set Constraints (in preparation)
15. Marek, W., Nerode, A., Remmel, J.B.: Nonmonotonic rule systems I. Ann. Math. Artif. Intell. 1, 241–273 (1990)
16. Marek, W., Nerode, A., Remmel, J.B.: Logic Programs, Well-orderings, and Forward Chaining. Ann. Pure App. Logic 96, 231–276 (1999)
17. Minker, J.: Overview of Disjunctive Logic Programming. Ann. Math. Artif. Intell. 12, 1–24 (1994)
18. Niemelä, I., Simons, P., Soininen, T.: Stable Model Semantics of Weight Constraint Rules. In: Gelfond, M., Leone, N., Pfeifer, G. (eds.) LPNMR 1999. LNCS (LNAI), vol. 1730, pp. 317–331. Springer, Heidelberg (1999)
19. Son, T.C., Pontelli, E., Tu, P.H.: Answer Sets for Logic Programs with Arbitrary Abstract Constraint Atoms. J. Artif. Intell. Res. 29, 353–389 (2007)
20. van Emden, M.H., Kowalski, R.A.: The semantics of predicate logic as a programming language. J. ACM 23, 733–742 (1976)

The Gödel-Tarski Translations of Intuitionistic Propositional Formulas

Grigori Mints

Stanford University, Stanford CA 94305, USA
gmints@stanford.edu
http://philosophy.stanford.edu/profile/Grigori+Mints/

Abstract. The Gödel-Tarski operation that prefixes the necessity symbol to every subformula is a sound and faithful translation of intuitionistic propositional logic into modal logic S4. We characterize modal formulas equivalent in S4 to Gödel-Tarski translations of intuitionistic propositional formulas. It would be interesting to obtain a similar characterization for intuitionistic predicate formulas.

Keywords: modal logic, intuitionistic logic, Gödel-Tarski translation.

1 Introduction

This paper is dedicated to Vladimir Lifschitz with whom we discussed so many things logical and non-logical.

The Gödel-Tarski operation that prefixes the necessity symbol to every subformula is a sound and faithful translation of intuitionistic propositional logic into modal logic S4. We characterize modal formulas equivalent in S4 to Gödel-Tarski translations of intuitionistic propositional formulas. It would be interesting to obtain a similar characterization for intuitionistic predicate formulas.

Let us fix terminology.

An intuitionistic formula is a formula of intuitionistic propositional logic constructed from propositional variables and the constant $\bot$ by $\&, \vee, \supset$. The negation is defined as $(\alpha \supset \bot)$.

A *modal formula* is a formula of the propositional modal logic in the language $\bot, \wedge, +$(disjunction)$, \rightarrow, \Box$ with other connectives including $\neg$(negation) and $\Diamond$ defined.

INT denotes intuitionistic propositional logic.

Definition 1. *The* Gödel-Tarski translation *of an intuitionistic formula* α *is the result* $\alpha^{\Box}$ *of prefixing* $\Box$ *to all subformulas of* α.

For example

$$(p \vee \neg p)^{\Box} := \Box(\Box p + \Box(\Box p \rightarrow \Box\bot))$$

which is S4-equivalent to $\Box(\Box p + \Box\neg\Box p)$.

Gödel [1] announced and McKinsey and Tarski [2] proved the following result.

E. Erdem et al. (Eds.): Correct Reasoning, LNCS 7265, pp. 487–491, 2012.

Theorem 1. *An intuitionistic formula* α *is derivable in* INT *iff* $\alpha^{\Box}$ *is derivable in S4.*

Equivalent reformulation given in [2] prefixes $\Box$ only to atomic formulas and implications. We prove that it is possible to "box" only propositional variables and the whole formula.

Notation $\alpha(p_1, \ldots, p_n)$ is used when $p_1, \ldots, p_n$ is the list of all propositional variables in α.

Our main result is the following statement.

Theorem 2. *A modal propositional formula* $\alpha(p_1, \ldots, p_n)$ *is equivalent in S4 to a formula of the form* $\phi^{\Box}$ *iff in S4*

$$\alpha(p_1, \ldots, p_n) \equiv \Box\alpha(\Box p_1, \ldots, \Box p_n) \tag{1}$$

Let's give a more local form of the same criterion.

Theorem 3. *A modal propositional formula* $\alpha(p_1, \ldots, p_n)$ *is equivalent in S4 to a formula of the form* $\phi^{\Box}$ *iff* $S4 \vdash \alpha \equiv \Box\alpha$ *and for every* $i \in \{1, \ldots, n\}$

$$\alpha(p_1, \ldots, p_i, \ldots, p_n) \equiv \alpha(p_1, \ldots, \Box p_i, \ldots, p_n)$$

A need for some result of this kind arose in the process of proving that some formulas of predicate modal logic are not equivalent to modal translation of intuitionistic formulas. The idea (used in the proof below) to consider first Boolean combinations of modal translations belongs to A. Urquhart.

Unfortunately Theorem 2 does not extend to predicate logic: modal formula $\Box\exists x(\Box Px \wedge \neg\Box Qx)$ is not equivalent to a modal translation of an intuitionistic predicate formula. This was proved by G. Olkhovikov [6] using his much more sophisticated criterion in terms of some analogue of bisimulation.

In section 2 below we reproduce a proof that the Gödel-Tarski translation is sound and faithful, then prove Theorem 2. Section 3 presents a similar result for a familiar translation of modal propositional formulas into first order logic.

Discussions with Grigory Olkhovikov and Alasdair Urquhart helped in preparation of this work.

2 Gödel-Tarski Translation

Soundness of the Gödel-Tarski translation is easy to prove.

Lemma 1. *If* INT $\vdash \alpha$ *then* $S4 \vdash \alpha^{\Box}$.

Induction on derivations in INT. $\vdash$

Let's recall three proofs of faithfulness of the Gödel-Tarski translation available in the literature. All three generalize to the predicate case and there is a hope that one of them may be of help in finding a simple criterion generalizing Theorem 2.

Lemma 2. *For every intuitionistic formula* α

$$S4 \vdash \alpha^{\Box} \textit{ implies } \mathrm{INT} \vdash \alpha. \tag{2}$$

Proof. 1. A proof via Kripke models. Suppose INT $\not\vdash \alpha$. Then there exists intuitionistic Kripke model M and a world $w \in M$ such that $M, w \not\models \alpha$. Then induction on α shows that $M, w \not\models \alpha^{\Box}$ for M treated as an S4-model, as required.

2. A proof via topological models. Recall that a topological model V for INT in a topological space X assigns open sets of X to propositional variables p_i. Values for composite formulas are open sets of X defined as follows:

$$V(\alpha\&\beta) = V(\alpha) \cap V(\beta);\ \ V(\alpha \vee \beta) = V(\alpha) \cup V(\beta);$$

$$V(\alpha \supset \beta) = Int(CV(\alpha) \cup V(\beta));\ \ V(\bot) = \emptyset,$$

where C denotes complement and Int is topological interior.

An S4-topological model V assigns arbitrary subsets of a space X to propositional variables. Values for composite formulas are defined as follows:

$$V(\alpha \wedge \beta) = V(\alpha) \cap V(\beta);\ \ V(\alpha + \beta) = V(\alpha) \cup V(\beta);$$

$$V(\Box\alpha) = Int(V(\alpha));\ \ V(\bot) = \emptyset$$

After that the proof of faithfulness for the Gödel-Tarski translation is the same as for Kripke models.

3. Deductive (and effective) proof. Suppose $S4 \vdash \alpha^{\Box}$. Consider a cut-free derivation of $\alpha^{\Box}$ in a Gentzen-type cut-free formulation of S4. By a standard inversion argument this derivation can be transformed so that every propositional connective is introduced immediately before the inference introducing corresponding occurrence of a $\Box$. For example $\Box(\alpha \wedge \beta)$ is introduced into the antecedent as follows:

$$\dfrac{\dfrac{\alpha, \beta, \Gamma \Rightarrow \Delta}{(\alpha \wedge \beta), \Gamma \Rightarrow \Delta}}{\Box(\alpha \wedge \beta), \Gamma \Rightarrow \Delta}$$

Moving up the $\Box$-inferences introducing $\Box p$ for atomic p we can eliminate all such inferences. Indeed each $\Box p$-antecedent inference in the resulting derivation is a part of a figure

$$\dfrac{\dfrac{\Box p, \Box\Gamma \Rightarrow p}{\Box p, \Box\Gamma \Rightarrow p}}{\Box p, \Box\Gamma \Rightarrow \Delta, \Box p}$$

This whole figure can be replaced by an axiom so that the resulting derivation can be easily transformed into an intuitionistic derivation of the original formula α. ⊢

To make the induction in the next proof go, we prove that a modal formula is equivalent in S4 to a Boolean combination of a formulas of the form $\phi^{\Box}$ iff every occurrence of an atomic subformula is prefixed with a $\Box$. More precisely,

Lemma 3. *Any modal formula of the form*

$$\alpha(\Box p_1, \ldots, \Box p_n) \tag{3}$$

is S4-equivalent to a Boolean combination of formulas of the form $\phi^{\Box}$. *Moreover, if* $\alpha(\Box p_1, \ldots, \Box p_n)$ *begins with a* $\Box$ *then it is S4-equivalent to a formula of the form* $\phi^{\Box}$.

Proof. We use induction on α. The induction base $\alpha \equiv \Box p$ is obvious. The induction step for Boolean connectives follows from the inductive assumption since α is again a Boolean combination. Assume now

$$\alpha \equiv \Box\gamma \text{ where } \gamma \equiv \wedge_i D_i$$

and each D_i is a disjunction of the formulas $\phi^{\Box}$ or their negations. We have

$$\Box\gamma \iff \Box \wedge_i \ ((\phi_1^{\Box} \wedge \ldots \phi_k^{\Box}) \to (\psi_1^{\Box} + \ldots + \psi_l^{\Box}))$$

and the r.h.s. is S4-equivalent to a formula of the required form

$$((\phi_1 \wedge \ldots \phi_k) \supset (\psi_1 \vee \ldots \vee \psi_l))^{\Box}$$

since $S4 \vdash (\Box\delta + \Box\theta) \iff \Box(\Box\delta + \Box\theta)$. $\vdash$

Proof of Theorem 2. An easy induction on ϕ proves that every formula of the form $\phi^{\Box}$ is of the form $\Box\alpha(\Box p_1, \ldots, \Box p_n)$, therefore condition (3) is satisfied. In the other direction use Lemma 3.

3 Predicate Translations

The *standard translation* of a modal formula α with predicate symbols $p_1, \ldots p_n$ (cf. for example [4]) is a first order formula (α, w) with an additional free individual variable w and predicates $P_1, \ldots, P_n, R$ expressing the statement:

α is true at the world w of an arbitrary Kripke model with the accessibility relation R and predicates p_i evaluated by P_i.

Definition 2. *For any propositional formulas* φ, ψ *and individual variable* w *we define:*

$$\begin{array}{ll} (p, w) & := P(w) \\ (\varphi \wedge \psi, w) & := (\varphi, w) \wedge (\psi, w) \\ (\varphi + \psi, w) & := (\varphi, w) + (\psi, w) \\ (\Box\varphi, w) & := \forall w'(R(w, w') \to (\varphi, w')) \\ (\bot, w) & := \bot \end{array} \tag{4}$$

where w' *is a fresh individual variable.*

Let

$$Ref :\equiv \forall w Rww, \qquad Tr :\equiv \forall u \forall v \forall w (Ruv \& Rvw \to Ruw)$$

It is well-known (cf. [3]) that

$$\models (\phi, w) \iff K \vdash \phi \text{ and}$$

$$Ref \& Tr \models (\phi, w) \iff S4 \vdash \phi.$$

A similar definition for intuitionistic formulas which we do not use here builds in Ref,Tr and the monotonicity condition for atomic formulas and implications. Let P^+ denote the monotonic version of the predicate P:

$$P^+(w) :\equiv \forall w'(Rww' \rightarrow P(w'))$$

Definition 3. *We say that a first order formula Φ with predicates $P_1, \ldots, P_n, R$ and a variable w is Ref, Tr-monotonic if the following statements are valid:*

$$Ref, Tr \models \Phi \iff \forall w'(Rww' \rightarrow \Phi[w/w'])$$

$$Ref, Tr \models \Phi(P_1, \ldots, P_n, R) \iff \Phi(P_1^+, \ldots, P_n^+, R).$$

These relations are first-order counterparts of the conditions from Theorem 2. The next theorem characterizes modal translations of intuitionistic formulas.

Theorem 4. *Under assumptions Ref, Tr a first order formula Φ is equivalent to a standard translation of a modal formula of the form $\alpha^\Box$ iff*
(i) Φ is stable under bisimulation (cf. [7]) and
(ii) Φ is Ref, Tr-monotonic with respect to some variable w.

Proof. Every Φ equivalent under assumptions Ref, Tr to a standard translation of $\alpha^\Box$ is easily seen to be Ref, Tr-monotonic and stable under bisimulation.

Assume now that under the same assumptions Φ is monotonic and stable under bisimulation. Stability under bisimulation implies [7] that ϕ is equivalent to a formula (α, w) where α is a modal formula:

$$Ref, Tr \models \Phi(P_1, \ldots, P_n) \iff (\alpha(p_1, \ldots, p_n), w).$$

By monotonicity the l.h.s. is equivalent to

$$\forall w'(Rww' \rightarrow \Phi(P_1^+, \ldots, P_n^+)[w/w']$$

which is the translation of $\Box\alpha(\Box p_1, \ldots, \Box p_n)$. Now apply Theorem 2. $\dashv$

References

1. Gödel, K.: Eine Interpretation des intuitionischen Aussagenkalküls. Ergebnisse Math. Colloq. 4, 39–40 (1933)
2. McKinsey, J., Tarski, A.: Some theorems about the sentential calculi of Lewis and Heyting. J. Symb. Log. 13, 1–15 (1948)
3. Mints, G.: Embedding operations related to S. Kripke's semantics. Seminars in Mathematics, V.A. Steklov Math. Inst. 4, 60–62 (1969)
4. Mints, G.: A Short Introduction to Intuitionistic Logic. Kluwer Publishers (2000)
5. Mints, G.: A Short Introduction to Modal Logic. CSLI Publications, Stanford (1992)
6. Olkhovikov, G.: Model-theoretic characterization of predicate intuitionistic formulas, arxiv:1202.1195 (2012)
7. van Benthem, J.: Modal Logic for Open Minds. CSLI Publications (2010)

Stepwise Debugging of Description-Logic Programs*

Johannes Oetsch, Jörg Pührer, and Hans Tompits

Technische Universität Wien, Institut für Informationssysteme 184/3,
Favoritenstraße 9-11, A-1040 Vienna, Austria
{oetsch,puehrer,tompits}@kr.tuwien.ac.at

Abstract. *Description-logic programs* (or *DL-programs* for short) combine logic programs under the answer-set semantics with description logics for semantic-web reasoning. In order for a wider acceptance of the formalism among semantic-web engineers, it is vital to have adequate tools supporting the program development process. In particular, methods for debugging DL-programs are needed. In this paper, we introduce a framework for interactive stepping through a DL-program as a means for debugging which builds on recent results on stepping for standard answer-set programs. To this end, we provide a computation model for DL-programs using states based on the rules that a user considers as active in the program and the resulting intermediate interpretation. During the course of stepping, the interpretations of the subsequent states evolve towards an answer set of the overall program. Compared to the case of standard answer-set programs, we need more involved notions of states and computations in the presence of DL-atoms. In particular, if non-convex DL-atoms are involved, we have to allow for non-stable computations. Intuitively speaking, we realise this by allowing the user to assume the truth of propositional atoms which must be justified in subsequent states. To keep track of these additional atoms, we extend the well-known notion of an unfounded set for DL-programs.

1 Introduction

Description-logic programs (or *DL-programs* for short) [1] have been proposed as a powerful formalism to couple answer-set programming (ASP) [2] and description logics (DLs) [3] for semantic-web reasoning. Indeed, DL-programs realise a promising way of integrating the rules with the ontology layer in the semantic-web architecture. However, as the formalism is quite recent, it still lacks methods that support semantic-web engineers in developing DL-programs. In particular, no debugging tools for DL-programs are available.

In this paper, we introduce a stepping approach for DL-programs that allows for interactive rule-based debugging. As it is based on a sound and complete characterisation of the semantics of DL-programs, it is suited to detect all derivations from the expected to the actual semantics of a DL-program. Hence, it is not limited to detecting the source for contradictions in the case of the absence of answer sets, but it also allows for handling cases where literals are missing or are superfluous in an answer set.

* This work was partially supported by the Austrian Science Fund (FWF) under project P21698 and by the European Commission under project IST-2009-231875 (OntoRule).

E. Erdem et al. (Eds.): Correct Reasoning, LNCS 7265, pp. 492–508, 2012.

Step-by-step execution of a program is a standard technique in procedural programming languages, where developers can debug and investigate the behaviour of their programs in an incremental way. As DL-programs have a genuine declarative semantics lacking any control flow, it is not obvious how stepping can be realised. Our approach builds on recent results on stepping of standard logic programs under the answer-set semantics [4]. Similar to that approach, we introduce a computation model for DL-programs that is based on states which represent the ground DL-rules that a user considers as active in the program and the resulting intermediate interpretation. The approach for answer-set programs was based on a simple computation model in which, at each intermediate state, the interpretation that is induced by the considered rules is guaranteed to be an answer set of these rules. As this is in general not possible for DL-programs, we have to extend the previous notions of a state and of the successor relation determining how to step from one state to another to deal with the presence of DL-atoms. For achieving this goal, we define the notions of an unfounded set and of the external support for DL-programs that allow us to keep track of literals that still need to be justified by a defining rule at a later step in a computation.

Our stepping approach is *interactive* and *incremental*, letting the semantic-web engineer choose which rules are added at each step. In our framework, states may serve as *breakpoints* from which stepping can be started. We discuss how the user can generate breakpoints that can be used to jump directly to interesting situations. We also show how ground rules that are subsequently considered active can be quickly obtained from the non-ground source code using filtering techniques. Due to the interactive nature of our proposed approach, the search for bugs can easily be guided by the intuitions of a developer about which part of the DL-program is likely to be the source of an error.

2 Preliminaries

Intuitively, a DL-program is a combination of a standard DL knowledge base and a logic program augmented with dedicated atoms realising the coupling. We first recall syntax and semantics of DLs and then introduce DL-programs based on that.

2.1 Description Logics

As our stepping approach is to a large extent independent of a specific DL, we only provide background for the basic description logic $\mathcal{ALC}$ and refer the interested reader to the literature [3] for more information on language features beyond $\mathcal{ALC}$.

By a *DL-signature* we understand a triple $\Sigma = \langle \mathcal{C}, \mathcal{R}, \mathcal{I} \rangle$, where $\mathcal{C}$, $\mathcal{R}$, and $\mathcal{I}$ are pairwise disjoint (denumerable) sets of *atomic concepts*, *role names*, and *individual names*, respectively. *Concepts* are inductively defined thus: (i) each atomic concept $A \in \mathcal{C}$, $\top$ (the *universal concept*), and $\bot$ (the *empty concept*) are concepts; (ii) if C and D are concepts and $R \in \mathcal{R}$ is a role name, then $C \sqcap D$ (the *intersection of C and D*), $C \sqcup D$ (the *union of C and D*), $\neg C$ (the *negation of C*), $\exists R.C$ (the *existential restriction of C by R*), and $\forall R.C$ (the *universal restriction of C by R*) are also concepts.

A *(DL) knowledge base* $\Phi = \langle \mathcal{T}, \mathcal{A} \rangle$, also referred to as a *(DL) ontology*, consists of a *TBox* $\mathcal{T}$, which constitutes the terminological part of the knowledge base, and its assertional part $\mathcal{A}$, called *ABox*, which consists of assertions about actual individuals. A TBox is a finite set of *concept inclusion axioms* of the form $C \sqsubseteq D$ (expressing that the extension of C is a subset of the extension of D) or $C \equiv D$ (meaning that both $C \sqsubseteq D$ and $D \sqsubseteq C$ holds) with C and D being concepts. An ABox is a finite set of *concept assertions* of the form $C(a)$ and *role assertions* of the form $R(a, b)$, where $a, b \in \mathcal{I}$ are individual names, C is a concept, and $R \in \mathcal{R}$ is a role name.

An *interpretation* $I = \langle \Delta^I, \cdot^I \rangle$ consists of a nonempty *domain* Δ^I and a mapping $\cdot^I$ that assigns to each atomic concept $C \in \mathcal{C}$ a subset of Δ^I, to each individual $o \in \mathcal{I}$ an element of Δ^I, and to each role $R \in \mathcal{R}$ a subset of $\Delta^I \times \Delta^I$. The mapping $\cdot^I$ is inductively defined as follows, where C and D are concepts and $R \in \mathcal{R}$ is a role name:

- $\top^I = \Delta^I$ and $\bot^I = \emptyset$;
- $(C \sqcap D)^I = C^I \cap D^I$;
- $(C \sqcup D)^I = C^I \cup D^I$;
- $(\neg C)^I = \Delta^I \setminus C^I$;
- $(\forall R.C)^I = \{x \in \Delta^I \mid \forall y \colon \langle x, y \rangle \in R^I \rightarrow y \in C^I\}$; and
- $(\exists R.C)^I = \{x \in \Delta^I \mid \exists y \colon \langle x, y \rangle \in R^I \wedge y \in C^I\}$.

The *satisfaction relation* $\models$ between an interpretation I and a concept inclusion axiom $C \sqsubseteq D$, a concept assertion $C(a)$, or a role assertion $R(a, b)$ is defined as follows: (i) $I \models C \sqsubseteq D$ iff $C^I \subseteq D^I$; (ii) $I \models C(a)$ iff $a^I \in C^I$; and (iii) $I \models R(a, b)$ iff $\langle a^I, b^I \rangle \in R^I$. An interpretation I is a *model* of a TBox $\mathcal{T}$, symbolically $I \models \mathcal{T}$, iff $I \models t$ for all $t \in \mathcal{T}$. Moreover, I is a model of an ABox $\mathcal{A}$, symbolically $I \models \mathcal{A}$, iff $I \models a$ for all $a \in \mathcal{A}$. Finally, I is a model of an $\mathcal{ALC}$ knowledge base $\Phi = \langle \mathcal{T}, \mathcal{A} \rangle$ iff $I \models \mathcal{T}$ and $I \models \mathcal{A}$. An axiom or assertion F is a *logical consequence* of Φ, denoted by $\Phi \models F$, iff every model of Φ satisfies F.

2.2 DL-Programs

In the following, we briefly summarise syntax and semantics of DL-programs.

A *signature* $\Sigma = \langle \mathcal{C}, \mathcal{R}, \mathcal{P}, \mathcal{I} \rangle$ for DL-programs consists of pairwise disjoint (denumerable) sets $\mathcal{C}$, $\mathcal{R}$, $\mathcal{P}$, and $\mathcal{I}$, where $\langle \mathcal{C}, \mathcal{R}, \mathcal{I} \rangle$ is a DL-signature and $\mathcal{P}$ is a set of predicate symbols. By a *term* we understand an individual name from $\mathcal{I}$ or a variable. A (*classical*) *literal* is an atom a or its *strong negation* $\sim a$. For a literal l, we define $\mathrm{Lit}_l = \{l\}$. A *query*, $Q(\mathbf{t})$, is either (i) a concept inclusion axiom F or its negation $\neg F$, (ii) an expression of form $C(t)$ or $\neg C(t)$, where C is a concept and t is a *term*, or (iii) an expression of form $R(t_1, t_2)$ or $\neg R(t_1, t_2)$, where R is a role and t_1, t_2 are terms.

Informally, a DL-program over $\Sigma = \langle \mathcal{C}, \mathcal{R}, \mathcal{P}, \mathcal{I} \rangle$ consists of an ontology Φ over $\Sigma_o = \langle \mathcal{C}, \mathcal{R}, \mathcal{I} \rangle$ and a normal logic program Π over Σ possibly containing queries to Φ. In formal terms, a *DL-atom* $a(\mathbf{t})$ *over* Σ is defined as an expression of form

$$\mathrm{DL}[S_1 \; op_1 \; p_1, \ldots, S_m \; op_m \; p_m; \; Q](\mathbf{t}), \qquad m \geq 0, \tag{1}$$

where each S_i is either a concept from $\mathcal{C}$ or a role predicate from $\mathcal{R}$, $op_i \in \{\uplus, \cup\!\!\!-, \cap\!\!\!-\}$, p_i is a unary or binary predicate symbol from $\mathcal{P}$, respectively, and $Q(\mathbf{t})$ is a query. We call $S_1 \; op_1 \; p_1, \ldots, S_m \; op_m \; p_m$ the *input signature* and $p_1, \ldots, p_m$ the *input predicate symbols* of $a(\mathbf{t})$. Moreover, literals over input predicate symbols are *input literals*. We denote the set of input literals of a DL-atom A by Lit_A. Intuitively, $\uplus$ (resp., $\cupdot$) increases S_i (resp., $\neg S_i$) by the extension of p_i, while $\cap\!\!\!-$ constrains S_i to p_i. A *DL-rule* r *over* Σ has the form

$$a \leftarrow b_1, \ldots, b_k, not\ b_{k+1}, \ldots, not\ b_m\,, \qquad m \geq k \geq 0\,, \tag{2}$$

where a is a literal and any $b_1, \ldots, b_m$ is a literal or a DL-atom. We call $B(r) = \{b_1, \ldots, b_k, not\ b_{k+1}, \ldots, not\ b_m\}$ the *body* of r and $H(r) = a$ the *head* of r. Moreover, we distinguish between the *positive body* $B^+(r) = \{b_1, \ldots, b_k\}$ and the *negative body* $B^-(r) = \{b_{k+1}, \ldots, b_m\}$ of r. By Lit_r we denote the set $\{a\} \cup \bigcup_{1 \leq i \leq m} \mathrm{Lit}_{b_i}$. A DL-rule with $B(r) = \emptyset$ is called a *fact*. DL-rules without a head are also allowed and are called *constraints*. These are used to filter out every answer-set candidate that satisfies their bodies. Finally, a *description-logic program*, or a *DL-program, over* $\Sigma = \langle \mathcal{C}, \mathcal{R}, \mathcal{P}, \mathcal{I} \rangle$ is a pair $\mathcal{KB} = \langle \Phi, \Pi \rangle$ consisting of a DL ontology Φ over $\Sigma_o = \langle \mathcal{C}, \mathcal{R}, \mathcal{I} \rangle$ and a finite set of DL-rules Π over Σ.

For defining the semantics of DL-programs, let in what follows $\mathcal{KB} = \langle \Phi, \Pi \rangle$ be a DL-program over $\Sigma = \langle \mathcal{C}, \mathcal{R}, \mathcal{P}, \mathcal{I} \rangle$, where $\Phi = \langle \mathcal{T}, \mathcal{A} \rangle$, and $\Sigma_{ASP} = \langle \mathcal{P}, \mathcal{I} \rangle$. By $gr(\Pi)$ we denote the *grounding* of Π with respect to $\mathcal{I}$, i.e., the set of all ground rules originating from DL-rules in Π by uniformly replacing, per DL-rule, all variables by each possible combination of constants in $\mathcal{I}$.

An *interpretation* I *over* Σ_{ASP} is a consistent subset of literals over Σ_{ASP}. We say that I *satisfies* a literal l under Φ, denoted by $I \models^{\Phi} l$, iff $l \in I$. Furthermore, I satisfies a ground DL-atom $a = DL[S_1\, op_1\, p_1, \ldots, S_m\, op_m p_m; Q](\mathbf{c})$ under Φ, denoted by $I \models^{\Phi} a$, if $\langle \mathcal{T}, \mathcal{A} \cup \tau^I(a) \rangle \models Q(\mathbf{c})$, where $\tau^I(a) = \bigcup_{i=1}^{m} A_i(I)$ is the extension of a under I and

- $A_i(I) = \{S_i(\mathbf{t}) \mid p_i(\mathbf{t}) \in I\}$, for $op_i = \uplus$;
- $A_i(I) = \{\neg S_i(\mathbf{t}) \mid p_i(\mathbf{t}) \in I\}$, for $op_i = \cupdot$; and
- $A_i(I) = \{\neg S_i(\mathbf{t}) \mid p_i(\mathbf{t}) \notin I\}$, for $op_i = \cap\!\!\!-$.

An interpretation I satisfies $not\ b$ under Φ, where b is a literal or a DL-atom, symbolically $I \models^{\Phi} not\ b$, if $I \not\models^{\Phi} b$. Let S be a set of literals and DL-atoms, each of which possibly default negated. Then, I satisfies S under Φ, symbolically $I \models^{\Phi} S$, if $I \models^{\Phi} l$ for each $l \in S$. A DL-rule r is *active under* I *and* Φ iff $I \models^{\Phi} B(r)$. For a ground DL-rule r under Φ not being a constraint, I satisfies r, symbolically $I \models^{\Phi} r$, if $I \models^{\Phi} B(r)$ implies $I \models^{\Phi} H(r)$. Furthermore, I is a model of a DL-program $\mathcal{KB} = \langle \Phi, \Pi \rangle$, denoted by $I \models \mathcal{KB}$, if $I \models^{\Phi} r$ for all $r \in gr(\Pi)$.

We base the semantics of DL-programs on a reduct construction introduced by Faber, Leone, and Pfeifer [5], which we sometimes refer to as the *FLP-semantics*. We consider this semantics rather than the weak or strong semantics of Eiter et al. [1] because it is the one implemented in DLVHEX[1], the state-of-the-art solver for HEX-programs [6] which generalise DL-programs.

Definition 1. *Let* $\Sigma = \langle \mathcal{C}, \mathcal{R}, \mathcal{P}, \mathcal{I} \rangle$ *be a signature for DL-programs,* Φ *a DL ontology over* $\langle \mathcal{C}, \mathcal{R}, \mathcal{I} \rangle$, Π *a set of ground DL-rules over* Σ, *and* I *an interpretation over*

[1] `http://www.kr.tuwien.ac.at/research/systems/dlvhex/`

$\Sigma_{ASP} = \langle \mathcal{P}, \mathcal{I} \rangle$. *Then, the* FLP-reduct of Π under Φ relative to I *is the set*

$$\Pi_{\Phi}^{I} = \{r \in \Pi \mid I \models^{\Phi} B(r)\}.$$

We first define answer sets of sets of DL-rules with respect to a DL knowledge base.

Definition 2. *Let $\Sigma = \langle \mathcal{C}, \mathcal{R}, \mathcal{P}, \mathcal{I} \rangle$ be a signature for DL-programs, Φ a DL ontology over $\langle \mathcal{C}, \mathcal{R}, \mathcal{I} \rangle$, Π a set of DL-rules over Σ, and I an interpretation over $\Sigma_{ASP} = \langle \mathcal{P}, \mathcal{I} \rangle$. Then, I is an* answer set *of Π* with respect to Φ *if it is a minimal model of $gr(\Pi)_{\Phi}^{I}$. The set of all answer sets of Π with respect to Φ is denoted by* $\mathrm{AS}(\Pi)^{\Phi}$.

Based on that, we define answer sets for DL-programs as follows.

Definition 3. *Let $\mathcal{KB} = \langle \Phi, \Pi \rangle$ be a DL-program. An interpretation I is an* answer set *of $\mathcal{KB}$ if it is is an answer set of Π with respect to Φ. The set of all answer sets of $\mathcal{KB}$ is denoted by* $\mathrm{AS}(\mathcal{KB})$.

In the absence of DL-atoms in a DL-program $\mathcal{KB} = \langle \Phi, \Pi \rangle$, Π corresponds to a non-disjunctive extended logic program whose answer sets as defined by Gelfond and Lifschitz [7,8] coincide with the answer sets of $\mathcal{KB}$. If $\mathcal{KB}$ contains neither DL-atoms nor strong negation, Π is a normal logic program and the answer sets of $\mathcal{KB}$ are the stable models of Π as defined earlier by Gelfond and Lifschitz [9]. Also note that the semantics we use coincides with the strong answer-set semantics when all DL-atoms are *monotonic* [6]:

Definition 4. *For a DL-program $\mathcal{KB} = \langle \Phi, \Pi \rangle$, a ground DL-atom a is* monotonic relative to $\mathcal{KB}$ *if for all interpretations I and J with $I \subseteq J$, $I \models^{\Phi} a$ implies $J \models^{\Phi} a$.*

Moreover, we need the related notion of *convex* DL-atoms:

Definition 5. *For a DL-program $\mathcal{KB} = \langle \Phi, \Pi \rangle$, a ground DL-atom a is* convex relative to $\mathcal{KB}$ *if for all interpretations I, J, and K, if $I \subset J \subset K$, then, whenever $I \models^{\Phi} a$ and $K \models^{\Phi} a$ jointly hold, then also $J \models^{\Phi} a$ holds.*

3 A Stepping Framework for DL-Programs

In this section, we introduce our framework for stepping through DL-programs. As noted in the introduction, our approach builds on ideas of previous work on stepping for normal logic programs under the answer-set semantics [4]. To illustrate the basic idea of stepping, we first briefly discuss the intuitions of the previous stepping approach.

The general idea is to first take a part of a program and an answer set of this part. Then, step by step, rules are added by the user such that, at every step, the literal derived by the new rule is added to the interpretation which remains to be an answer set of the evolving program part. Hereby, the user only adds rules he or she thinks are active in the final answer set. The interpretation grows monotonically until it is eventually guaranteed to be an answer set of the overall program, otherwise the programmer is informed why and at which step something went wrong. This way, one can in principle without any backtracking direct the computation towards an expected or an unintended actual answer set. The individual steps of a computation, referred to as *states* of the program, are represented by a set of ground rules which the user considers as active along with an interpretation that constitutes a partial answer set of the program.

Example 1. Let Π be the normal logic program consisting of the rules

$$r_1 : p_1(c) \leftarrow not\ p_2(c), \quad r_2 : p_2(c) \leftarrow not\ p_1(c), \quad \text{and} \quad r_3 : p_3(c) \leftarrow p_1(c).$$

Following the intuitions above, we express states by pairs $\langle \Pi', I' \rangle$, where Π' are the rules considered active and I' is the interpretation derived by those rules. First, we consider no rule to be active, and hence no atom is derived—the corresponding state is $\langle \emptyset, \emptyset \rangle$. Under the current interpretation $\emptyset$, two unconsidered rules are active: r_1 and r_2. We choose to consider r_1 first and arrive at state $\langle \{r_1\}, \{p_1(c)\} \rangle$, as $p_1(c)$ is derived when r_1 is assumed to be active. At this point, only r_3 is active under $\{p_1(c)\}$. Hence, we finally reach state $\langle \{r_1, r_3\}, \{p_1(c), p_3(c)\} \rangle$ whose interpretation $\{p_1(c), p_3(c)\}$ is an answer set of Π. □

Note that in the example, and generally in the case of normal logic programs, stepping can be done in such a way that every intermediate state in a computation is *stable*. This means that the atoms I' derived by the currently considered set Π' of rules form an answer set of Π'. This is in general not possible for DL-programs in the presence of non-convex DL-atoms. Thus, the previous method for standard logic programs cannot be applied straightforwardly when DL-atoms are involved, as illustrated next.

Example 2.
Consider the DL-program $\mathcal{KB} = \langle \Phi, \Pi \rangle$ where $\Phi = \langle \{A \sqcap B \sqsubseteq Q, \neg C \sqcap \neg D \sqsubseteq Q\}, \emptyset \rangle$ and Π consists of the DL-rules

$$\begin{aligned} &r_1 : p_1(c) \leftarrow \mathrm{DL}[A \uplus p_1, B \uplus p_2, C \cap\!\!\!\!- p_3, D \cap\!\!\!\!- p_2;\ Q](c), \\ &r_2 : p_2(c) \leftarrow p_1(c), \quad \text{and} \\ &r_3 : p_1(c) \leftarrow p_2(c), \end{aligned}$$

having unique answer set $\{p_1(c), p_2(c)\}$. The DL-atom involved is non-convex relative to Φ as it is true under $\emptyset$ and $\{p_1(c), p_2(c)\}$ but not under $\{p_1(c)\}$ or $\{p_2(c)\}$. Now, assume we want to start stepping from the empty interpretation. At the beginning, only r_1 is applicable under $\emptyset$, which derives $p_1(c)$. We arrive at a state which is not stable as $\{p_1(c)\}$ is not an answer set of $\langle \Phi, \{r_1\} \rangle$. Next, we can only choose r_2 as next DL-rule to be considered active. The two active DL-rules already derive the answer set $\{p_1(c), p_2(c)\}$ of Π, but $\{p_1(c), p_2(c)\}$ is no answer set of $\langle \Phi, \{r_1, r_2\} \rangle$ because $\{p_2(c)\}$ is a smaller model of $\langle \Phi, \{r_1, r_2\} \rangle$. However, the computation becomes stable again when we add r_3. □

The example shows that a stepping approach for DL-programs under the FLP-semantics must allow for non-stable computations. Intuitively, we realise this by allowing the user to assume the truth of propositional literals which must be justified in subsequent states. Technically, we use the theory of unfounded sets for guaranteeing stability at a later point in the computation. To this end, we next introduce the notions of external support and unfounded sets for DL-programs.

3.1 External Support and Unfounded Sets for DL-Programs

Intuitively, each set of literals in an answer set must be "supported" by an active DL-rule deriving one of the literals in a non-cyclic way, i.e., the reason for the DL-rule to be active does not depend on the literal it derives. We call such DL-rules *external supports*.

Definition 6. *Let r be a ground DL-rule, Φ a DL knowledge base, I an interpretation, and X a set of literals. Then, r is an* external support for X with respect to I and Φ *if (i) $I \models^{\Phi} B(r)$, (ii) $I \setminus X \models^{\Phi} B(r)$, and (iii) $H(r) \in (X \cap I)$.*

Next, we show how answer sets can be characterised in terms of external supports.

Theorem 1. *Let $\mathcal{KB} = \langle \Phi, \Pi \rangle$ be a DL-program and I an interpretation. Then, I is an answer set of $\mathcal{KB}$ iff $I \models^{\Phi} gr(\Pi)$ and every X with $\emptyset \subset X \subseteq I$ has an external support $r \in gr(\Pi)$ with respect to I and Φ.*

We express the absence of an external support in an interpretation by adapting the concept of an *unfounded set* [10,11] to DL-programs.

Definition 7. *Let X be a set of literals, Π a set of DL-rules, Φ a DL knowledge base, and I an interpretation. Then, X is* unfounded in Π with respect to I and Φ *if there is no DL-rule $r \in \Pi$ that is an external support for X with respect to I and Φ.*

Note that $\emptyset$ is an unfounded set independent of which DL-rules, interpretations, or DL knowledge base is chosen. Theorem 1 immediately implies the following result:

Corollary 1. *Let $\mathcal{KB} = \langle \Phi, \Pi \rangle$ be a DL-program and I an interpretation. Then, I is an answer set of $\mathcal{KB}$ iff $I \models^{\Phi} gr(\Pi)$ and there is no X with $\emptyset \subset X \subseteq I$ that is unfounded in Π with respect to I.*

3.2 States and Computations

Our stepping framework is based on sequences of states, reassembling computations, in which an increasing number of ground DL-rules are considered that build up a monotonically growing interpretation. Besides that interpretation, states also capture literals which cannot become true in subsequent steps and sets that currently lack external support in the state's interpretation.

Definition 8. *A* state structure *is a tuple $\langle \Pi, I, I^{-}, \Upsilon \rangle$, where Π is a set of ground DL-rules, I and I^{-} are disjoint interpretations, and Υ is a set of sets of literals.*

Given a DL knowledge base Φ, a state structure $\langle \Pi, I, I^{-}, \Upsilon \rangle$ is a state with respect to Φ *if (i) $I \models^{\Phi} B(r) \cup H(r)$ for every $r \in \Pi$, (ii) $\mathrm{Lit}_r \subseteq I \cup I^{-}$ for every $r \in \Pi$, and (iii) $\Upsilon = \{X \subseteq I \mid X$ is unfounded in Π with respect to I and $\Phi\}$.*

Now we are ready to formally state what we understand by the stability of a state.

Definition 9. *A state $\langle \Pi, I, I^{-}, \Upsilon \rangle$ with respect to an DL knowledge base Φ is* Φ-stable *if $I \in \mathrm{AS}(\Pi)^{\Phi}$.*

Note that a state is Φ-stable exactly when $\Upsilon = \{\emptyset\}$.

In what follows, we show how we can proceed forward in a computation, i.e., which states might follow a given state. This is expressed in the successor relation defined next.

Definition 10. *For a state $S = \langle \Pi, I, I^{-}, \Upsilon \rangle$ with respect to DL knowledge base Φ and a state structure $S' = \langle \Pi', I', I'^{-}, \Upsilon' \rangle$, S' is a* Φ-successor of S *if there is a DL-rule $r \in \Pi' \setminus \Pi$ and sets $\Delta, \Delta^{-} \subseteq \mathrm{Lit}_r$ such that (i) $\Pi' = \Pi \cup \{r\}$, (ii) $I' = I \cup \Delta$, $I'^{-} = I^{-} \cup \Delta^{-}$, and $(I \cup I^{-}) \cap (\Delta \cup \Delta^{-}) = \emptyset$, (iii) $\mathrm{Lit}_r \subseteq (I' \cup I'^{-})$, (iv) $I \models^{\Phi} B(r)$, (v) $I' \models^{\Phi} B(r) \cup H(r)$, and (vi) $X' \in \Upsilon'$ iff $X' = X \cup \Delta'$, where $X \in \Upsilon$, $\Delta' \subseteq \Delta$, and r is not an external support for X' with respect to I' and Φ.*

Condition (i) ensures that a successor state considers exactly one DL-rule more to be active. Conditions (ii) and (iii) express that the interpretations I and I^- are extended by the so far unconsidered literals in Δ and Δ^- appearing in the new DL-rule r. Note that from S' being a state structure we get that Δ and Δ^- are distinct. A requirement for considering r as next DL-rule is that it is active under the current interpretation I, expressed by Condition (iv). Moreover, r must be satisfied and still be active under the succeeding interpretation, as required by Condition (v). The final condition ensures that the unfounded sets of the successor are extensions of the previously unfounded sets that are not externally supported by the new DL-rule.

Here, it is interesting that only extended previous unfounded sets can be unfounded sets in the extended program Π' and that r is the only rule which could provide external support for them in Π' with respect to the new interpretation I' and Φ, as seen next.

Theorem 2. *Let $S = \langle \Pi, I, I^-, \Upsilon \rangle$ be a state with respect to DL knowledge base Φ and $S' = \langle \Pi \cup \{r\}, I', I'^-, \Upsilon' \rangle$ a Φ-successor of S, where $\Delta = I' \setminus I$. Moreover, let X' be a set of literals with $\emptyset \subset X' \subseteq I'$. Then, the following statements are equivalent:*
(i) X' is unfounded in $\Pi \cup \{r\}$ with respect to I' and Φ.
(ii) $X' = \Delta' \cup X$, where $\Delta' \subseteq \Delta$, $X \in \Upsilon$, and r is not an external support for X' with respect to I' and Φ.

The result shows that determining the unfounded sets in a computation after adding a further DL-rule r can be done locally, i.e., only supersets of previously unfounded sets can be unfounded sets, and if such a superset has some external support then it is externally supported by r. The result also implies that the successor relation suffices to "step" from one state to another.

Corollary 2. *Let S be a state with respect to DL knowledge base Φ and S' a Φ-successor of S. Then, S' is a state with respect to Φ.*

Next, we define computations based on the notion of a state.

Definition 11. *Let Φ be a DL ontology. A* Φ-computation *is a sequence $C = S_0, \ldots, S_n$ of states with respect to Φ such that S_{i+1} is a Φ-successor of S_i, for all $0 \leq i < n$.*

The following result guarantees the soundness of our stepping framework.

Theorem 3. *Let $\mathcal{KB} = \langle \Phi, \Pi \rangle$ be a DL-program and $C = S_0, \ldots, S_n$ a Φ-computation such that $S_n = \langle gr(\Pi)^I_\Phi, I, I^-, \{\emptyset\} \rangle$. Then, I is an answer set of $\mathcal{KB}$.*

The computation model is also complete in the following sense:

Theorem 4. *Let $S_0 = \langle \Pi, I, I^-, \Upsilon \rangle$ be a state with respect to Φ, $\mathcal{KB} = \langle \Phi, \Pi' \rangle$ a DL-program with $\Pi \subseteq gr(\Pi')$, and I' an answer set of $\mathcal{KB}$ with $I \subseteq I'$ and $I' \cap I^- = \emptyset$. Then, there is a Φ-computation $S_0, \ldots, S_n$ such that $S_n = \langle gr(\Pi)^{I'}_\Phi, I', I'^-, \{\emptyset\} \rangle$.*

As the empty state, $\langle \emptyset, \emptyset, \emptyset, \{\emptyset\} \rangle$, trivially is a state, we can make the completeness aspect of the previous result more apparent in the following corollary:

Corollary 3. *Let $\mathcal{KB} = \langle \Phi, \Pi \rangle$ be a DL-program and $I \in \mathrm{AS}(\mathcal{KB})$. Then, there is a Φ-computation $S_0, \ldots, S_n$ with $S_0 = \langle \emptyset, \emptyset, \emptyset, \{\emptyset\} \rangle$ and $S_n = \langle gr(\Pi)^{I'}_\Phi, I', I'^-, \{\emptyset\} \rangle$.*

Example 3. Consider $\mathcal{KB} = \langle \Phi, \Pi \rangle$ from Example 2. Then, the sequence

$$\langle \emptyset, \emptyset, \emptyset, \{\emptyset\} \rangle,\ \langle \{r_1\}, \{p_1(c), p_2(c)\}, \emptyset, \{\emptyset, \{p_1(c)\}, \{p_2(c)\}\} \rangle,$$
$$\langle \{r_1, r_2\}, \{p_1(c), p_2(c)\}, \emptyset, \{\emptyset, \{p_1(c)\}\} \rangle,\ \langle \{r_1, r_2, r_3\}, \{p_1(c), p_2(c)\}, \emptyset, \{\emptyset\} \rangle$$

is a Φ-computation, constituting a derivation for the answer set $\{p_1(c), p_2(c)\}$ of $\mathcal{KB}$. The first and the last state in this computation are Φ-stable whereas the other two are not, as indicated by the presence of non-empty unfounded sets. □

Indeed, the DL-program of Example 2 can be seen as an unlikely worst-case scenario in which computations are required to be unstable. In fact, whenever a DL-program does not involve recursion through DL-atoms or contains only convex DL-atoms then computations with stable states only are sufficient to compute all answer sets. That is, in such a setting, it is sufficient to add at most a single classical literal to the emerging interpretation in every subsequent state. Note that DL-atoms that do not involve the rarely used $\cap\!\!\!\!-$-operator are always convex.

4 Applying Stepping

In this section, we outline how the stepping framework can be applied in practice. As it allows for stepwise constructing interpretations following a user's intuition on which DL-rule instances to become active next, one may also reach states where there is no answer set of the overall DL-program extending the state's interpretation under which the DL-rules considered active are indeed active. Then, every continuation would reach a sate where adding a further DL-rule would require to add literals that are inconsistent with previously chosen active rules. The possibility of such dead-ends is intentional, as reaching such a point—which can be automatically detected—indicates that and why the DL-program's semantics differs from the semantics expected by the user.

In our approach, the user always has two options how to proceed: (i) (re-)initialise stepping and start a computation with a new state as breakpoint, or (ii) extend the current computation by adding a further active DL-rule. We first describe the technical aspects of how to obtain a breakpoint and how ground DL-rule instances can be chosen. Then, we discuss how stepping can be applied for debugging.

As an example, we consider a situation where a car model should undergo multiple crash tests under different conditions. We assume that the manufacturer has an ontology Φ_{ex} about possible test conditions regarding the car which also contains information on which conditions cannot hold at the same time. The knowledge base is given as follows:

$$\begin{aligned}\Phi_{ex} = \{\{ & \mathit{TestableCond} \equiv \mathit{Testable} \sqcap \mathit{Cond}\},\\ \{ & \mathit{Cond}(\mathit{engine\_running}),\ \mathit{Cond}(\mathit{engine\_off}),\ \mathit{Cond}(\mathit{battery\_on}),\\ & \mathit{Cond}(\mathit{battery\_off}),\ \mathit{Cond}(\mathit{front\_seat\_adult}),\\ & \mathit{Cond}(\mathit{front\_seat\_child}),\ \mathit{Cond}(\mathit{front\_seat\_empty}),\\ & \mathit{Cond}(\mathit{extreme\_temperature}),\ \mathit{Cond}(\mathit{low\_temperature}),\\ & \mathit{Incompatible}(\mathit{engine\_running}, \mathit{engine\_off}),\\ & \mathit{Incompatible}(\mathit{battery\_on}, \mathit{battery\_off}),\\ & \mathit{Incompatible}(\mathit{engine\_running}, \mathit{battery\_off}),\\ & \mathit{Incompatible}(\mathit{front\_seat\_adult}, \mathit{front\_seat\_child}),\\ & \mathit{Incompatible}(\mathit{front\_seat\_adult}, \mathit{front\_seat\_empty}),\end{aligned}$$

$$\textit{Incompatible}(\textit{front\_seat\_child}, \textit{front\_seat\_empty}),$$
$$\textit{Incompatible}(\textit{extreme\_temperature}, \textit{low\_temperature})\}\}.$$

The axiom states that a testable condition is both in the extension of *Testable* and *Cond*, where *Testable* is a concept for which the ontology does not assert any individuals. The remaining assertions list the conditions that can be set for testing as well as specify which conditions are incompatible in the sense that they cannot hold at the same time.

The task now is to write DL-rules such that the resulting DL-program creates a fixed number n of different test configurations in which every compatible pair of testable conditions is tested at least once in some configuration. Moreover, it should also be expressed by the DL-rules which conditions are considered testable. However, only those conditions which are also known in the ontology should be used for testing. Assume the set Π_{ex}, comprising the following DL-rules, realises this task:

$$\begin{aligned}
r_1 &: \textit{testNo}(1..n) \leftarrow, \\
r_2 &: \textit{testable}(\textit{engine_running}) \leftarrow, \\
r_3 &: \textit{testable}(\textit{engine_off}) \leftarrow, \\
r_4 &: \textit{testable}(\textit{battery_on}) \leftarrow, \\
r_5 &: \textit{testable}(\textit{battery_off}) \leftarrow, \\
r_6 &: \textit{testable}(\textit{front_seat_adult}) \leftarrow, \\
r_7 &: \textit{testable}(\textit{front_seat_child}) \leftarrow, \\
r_8 &: \textit{testable}(\textit{front_seat_empty}) \leftarrow, \\
r_9 &: \textit{testable}(\textit{roof_opened}) \leftarrow, \\
r_{10} &: \textit{testable}(\textit{roof_closed}) \leftarrow, \\
r_{11} &: \textit{testcond}(M) \leftarrow \mathrm{DL}[\textit{Testable} \uplus \textit{testable};\ \textit{TestableCond}](M), \\
r_{12} &: \textit{incompatible}(X,Y) \leftarrow \mathrm{DL}[;\ \textit{Incompatible}](X,Y), \\
r_{13} &: \textit{incompatible}(X,Y) \leftarrow \textit{incompatible}(Y,X), \\
r_{14} &: \textit{test}(T,S) \leftarrow \textit{testcond}(S), \textit{testNo}(T), \textit{not}\ {\sim}\textit{test}(T,S), \\
r_{15} &: {\sim}\textit{test}(T,S) \leftarrow \textit{testcond}(S), \textit{testNo}(T), \textit{not}\ \textit{test}(T,S), \\
r_{16} &: \textit{combination}(S_1,S_2) \leftarrow \textit{testcond}(S_1), \textit{testcond}(S_2), \\
&\qquad\qquad \textit{not}\ \textit{incompatible}(S_1,S_2), S_1 < S_2, \\
r_{17} &: \textit{combinationTested}(S_1,S_2) \leftarrow \textit{combination}(S_1,S_2), \\
&\qquad\qquad \textit{test}(T,S_1), \textit{test}(T,S_2), \\
r_{18} &: \leftarrow \textit{combination}(S_1,S_2), \textit{not}\ \textit{combinationTested}(S_1,S_2), \\
r_{19} &: \leftarrow \textit{test}(T,S_1), \textit{test}(T,S_2), \textit{not}\ \textit{combination}(S_1,S_2), S_1 < S_2.
\end{aligned}$$

Intuitively, r_1 assigns the numbers 1 to n as indices of single tests in any solution while r_2 to r_{10} define testable conditions. Note that not all conditions in Φ_{ex} are testable, and conversely not all testable conditions are conditions in Φ_{ex}. The DL-rule r_{11} states which conditions of the ontology are testable. For that, we send information about which conditions we consider testable to the ontology and query for the extension of the *TestableCond* concept. Due to the axiom in the ontology, we collect the intersection of conditions in Φ_{ex} and testable conditions of Π_{ex} in the *testcond* predicate. The DL-rule r_{12} imports incompatible conditions from Φ_{ex} and r_{13} ensures symmetry of the *incompatible* relation. The DL-rules r_{14} and r_{15} non-deterministically choose whether a given condition holds with respect to a given test case. The *combination* predicate collects pairs of testable conditions that may occur in the same test case, as realised by

r_{16}. The combinations of testable conditions covered by some test case are derived by r_{17}. This information is used in constraint r_{18} which eliminates answer-set candidates with a combination of testable conditions not tested by any test case. Finally, constraint r_{19} filters out candidates in which two incompatible conditions are jointly tested.

Obtaining a Breakpoint. Every state may serve as a potential starting point for a stepping session. Hence, analogous to stepwise debugging in procedural programming languages, we can consider a state as a breakpoint from which stepping is started. Having a suitable breakpoint at hand will often allow for finding a bug in just a few steps. As mentioned earlier, the empty state $\langle \emptyset, \emptyset, \emptyset, \{\emptyset\}\rangle$ is a trivial state. Besides that, $\langle F, F, \emptyset, \{\emptyset\}\rangle$, where F is the set of all facts in a DL-program, is also ensured to be a state (except for the practically irrelevant case when a literal and its strong negation are jointly asserted).

Example 4. Let us consider the case $n = 7$ in our running example, and let F be the set of facts in Π_{ex}, given thus:

$$\begin{aligned}F = \{&\mathit{testNo}(1), \mathit{testNo}(2), \mathit{testNo}(3), \mathit{testNo}(4), \mathit{testNo}(5), \mathit{testNo}(6), \mathit{testNo}(7),\\ &\mathit{testable}(\mathit{engine\_running}), \mathit{testable}(\mathit{engine\_off}), \mathit{testable}(\mathit{battery\_on}),\\ &\mathit{testable}(\mathit{battery\_off}), \mathit{testable}(\mathit{front\_seat\_adult}), \mathit{testable}(\mathit{front\_seat\_child}),\\ &\mathit{testable}(\mathit{front\_seat\_empty}), \mathit{testable}(\mathit{roof\_opened}), \mathit{testable}(\mathit{roof\_closed})\}.\end{aligned}$$

Note that $S_0 = \langle F, F, \emptyset, \{\emptyset\}\rangle$ is a state. From here, we can start stepping by choosing, e.g., the ground DL-rule $r = \mathit{state}(\mathit{engine\_running}) \leftarrow \mathrm{DL}[\mathit{Testable} \uplus \mathit{testable}; \mathit{TestableCond}](\mathit{engine\_running})$, being an instance of r_{11} and active under F and Φ_{ex}, as next rule to be added. We obtain the Φ_{ex}-computation $C = S_0, S_1$ with $S_1 = \langle F \cup \{r\}, F \cup \{\mathit{state}(\mathit{engine\_running})\}, \emptyset, \{\emptyset\}\rangle$. □

Often, it is useful to have states other than the empty or the fact-based state as starting points for stepping, since to reach an answer set I of a DL-program, the minimum length of a computation starting from the empty state is $|I|$. We now discuss how to generate states that may serve as breakpoints using conditions the user finds relevant.

Stable states can be obtained by computing an answer set I of a trusted subset of the DL-rules (or their grounding) and selecting rule instances active under I.

Proposition 1. *Let $\mathcal{KB} = \langle \Phi, \Pi \rangle$ be a DL-program and $\Pi' \subseteq \Pi \cup gr(\Pi)$ such that $I \in \mathrm{AS}(\Pi')^{\Phi}$. Then, $\langle gr(\Pi')^I_{\Phi}, I, \bigcup_{r \in gr(\Pi')} \mathrm{Lit}_r \setminus I, \{\emptyset\}\rangle$ is a state.*

Hence, it suffices to find an appropriate Π' in order to get breakpoints. One option for doing so is to let the user manually specify Π' as a subset of Π (including facts).

Example 5. Assume we want to step through the DL-rules that derive the $\mathit{test}/2$ atoms. The respective definitions rely on the available testable conditions of the car. Hence, we use a breakpoint where all instances of DL-rule r_{11}, deriving $\mathit{testcond}/1$-atoms, were already applied. Following Proposition 1, we calculate an answer set of program $\Pi'_{ex} = F \cup \{r_{11}\}$ with respect to Φ_{ex}. The unique answer set of Π'_{ex} is

$$\begin{aligned}I_3 = F \cup \{&\mathit{testcond}(\mathit{front\_seat\_empty}), \mathit{testcond}(\mathit{front\_seat\_child}),\\ &\mathit{testcond}(\mathit{front\_seat\_adult}), \mathit{testcond}(\mathit{battery\_off}),\\ &\mathit{testcond}(\mathit{battery\_on}), \mathit{testcond}(\mathit{engine\_off}), \mathit{testcond}(\mathit{engine\_running})\}.\end{aligned}$$

The desired breakpoint for subsequent stepping is $S_3 = \langle gr(\Pi'_{ex})^{I_3}_{\Phi_{ex}}, I_3, \emptyset, \{\emptyset\}\rangle$. □

Note that if the subprogram Π' for breakpoint generation has more than one answer set, the selection of the set $I \in \mathrm{AS}(\Pi')^{\Phi}$ is based on the programmer's intuition, similar to selecting the next DL-rule in stepping.

Another use of Proposition 1 is *jumping* from one state to another by considering further non-ground DL-rules. This makes sense, e.g., in a debugging situation where the user initially started with a breakpoint S that is considered as an early state in a computation. After few steps, reaching state $S' = \langle \Pi_{S'}, I_{S'}, I_{S'}^{-}, \Upsilon_{S'} \rangle$, the user realises that the computation from S to S' is as intended and wants to proceed to a point where more literals have already been derived, i.e., after applying a selection Π'' of non-ground DL-rules from Π on top of the interpretation $I_{S'}$. Then, Π' from Proposition 1 is given by $\Pi' = \Pi_{S'} \cup \Pi''$. Note that, for an arbitrary answer set I of $\mathrm{AS}(\Pi')^{\Phi}$, it is not ensured that there is a computation starting from S' that ends with the state $gr(\Pi')^{I}_{\Phi}$ because there might be DL-rules in $\Pi_{S'}$ that are not active under I. For assuring that there is a computation of Π starting from S' and ending with $gr(\Pi')^{I}_{\Phi}$, Π' can be joined with $Con_{S'} = \{\leftarrow not\ l \mid l \in B^{+}(r), r \in \Pi_{S'}\} \cup \{\leftarrow l \mid l \in B^{-}(r), r \in \Pi_{S'}\}$.

Example 6. Starting from state S_3 obtained in Example 5, we start stepping through the DL-rules that derive the $test/2$ atoms, i.e., instances of DL-rule r_{14}. Hence, as next DL-rule to be added, we choose

$$r' : test(1, engine\_running) \leftarrow testcond(engine\_running), testNo(1), \\ not\ {\sim}test(engine\_running, 1)$$

and obtain as succeeding state

$$S_4 = \langle \Pi_4, I_3 \cup \{test(1, engine\_running)\}, \{{\sim}test(1, engine\_running)\}, \{\emptyset\} \rangle,$$

where $\Pi_4 = gr(\Pi'_{ex})^{I_3}_{\Phi_{ex}} \cup \{r'\}$. As the DL-rule instance works as expected, we now want to apply the full non-ground DL-rule r_{14}. We use Proposition 1 by first computing an answer set of $\Pi_5 = \Pi_4 \cup \{r_{14}\}$, e.g.,

$$\begin{aligned} I_5 = I_3 \cup \{&test(1, engine\_off), test(1, engine\_running), test(1, front\_seat\_adult), \\ &test(2, battery\_on), test(2, engine\_running), \\ &test(2, front\_seat\_empty), test(3, battery\_off), \\ &test(4, battery\_on), test(4, engine\_running), test(4, front\_seat\_child), \\ &test(5, battery\_off), test(5, engine\_off), test(5, front\_seat\_child), \\ &test(6, battery\_off), test(6, front\_seat\_adult), \\ &test(7, battery\_off), test(7, engine\_off), test(7, front\_seat\_empty)\}. \end{aligned}$$

The new state is $S_5 = \langle gr(\Pi_5)^{I_5}_{\Phi_{ex}}, I_5, I_5^{-}, \{\emptyset\} \rangle$, where

$$\begin{aligned} I_5^{-} = \{&{\sim}test(1, engine\_off), {\sim}test(1, engine\_running), \\ &{\sim}test(1, front\_seat\_adult), {\sim}test(2, battery\_on), \\ &{\sim}test(2, engine\_running), {\sim}test(2, front\_seat\_empty), \\ &{\sim}test(3, battery\_off), {\sim}test(4, battery\_on), {\sim}test(4, engine\_running), \\ &{\sim}test(4, front\_seat\_child), {\sim}test(5, battery\_off), {\sim}test(5, engine\_off), \\ &{\sim}test(5, front\_seat\_child), {\sim}test(6, battery\_off), \\ &{\sim}test(6, front\_seat\_adult), {\sim}test(7, battery\_off), {\sim}test(7, engine\_off), \\ &{\sim}test(7, front\_seat\_empty)\}. \end{aligned}$$

□

Assisted Stepping. To obtain a Φ-successor of a given state $S = \langle \Pi_S, I, I^-, \Upsilon \rangle$ in the context of a DL-program $\mathcal{KB} = \langle \Phi, \Pi \rangle$, by Definition 10 we need a DL-rule $r \in gr(\Pi) \setminus \Pi_S$ such that $S' = \langle \Pi_S \cup \{r\}, I \cup \Delta, I^- \cup \Delta^-, \Upsilon' \rangle$ is also a state, where $\Delta \cup \Delta^- \subseteq \mathrm{Lit}_r$. One can proceed in the following fashion: First, a non-ground DL-rule $r \in \Pi$ with $H(r) \neq \emptyset$ is selected for instantiation. Then, the user assigns constants to the variables occurring in r. Both steps can be assisted by filtering techniques. Information which non-ground DL-rules in Π have instances that are active under I but not contained in Π_S can be done, e.g., by using the formalism of DL-programs itself, through meta-programming techniques like tagging transformations [12,13].

Example 7. When a computation reached state S_5 of our running example, only ground instances of r_{12}, r_{15}, r_{16}, and r_{19} are active under I_5 but not contained in Π_5. Thus, they can be pre-filtered for the user's disposal. □

Assistence can also be given when the variables in r are assigned one after the other. Then, the domains of the remaining ones can be accordingly restricted such that there is still a compatible ground instance of r that is active under I. Consider a partial substitution ϑ assigning constants in Π to some variables in r. When fixing the assignment of a further variable X occurring in $B(r)$, where $\vartheta(X)$ is yet undefined, we may choose only a constant c such that there is a substitution ϑ' with $\vartheta'(X') = \vartheta(X')$, where $\vartheta(X')$ is defined, $\vartheta'(X) = c$, and $I \models^{\Phi} B(r)\vartheta'$. A simple meta-DL-program can be used to compute potential values of $\vartheta'(X)$, given r, ϑ, and I, checking the above conditions and whether $r\vartheta' \notin \Pi_S$. This is computationally not harder than evaluating the DL-program to debug and in practice often easier, as no guessing is needed in the meta-DL-program.

Once a substitution ϑ for all variables in r is found, Δ and Δ^- must be determined. Again, a system assisting the stepping process can identify respective subsets of $\mathrm{Lit}_r \setminus (I \cup I^-)$ such that the obtained state satisfies the final condition of Definition 10, i.e., that all DL-rules in the potential successor state of S are active.

Example 8. For obtaining a successor of state S_5, we like to apply an instance of

$$r_{12} = \mathit{incompatible}(X, Y) \leftarrow \mathrm{DL}[;\ \mathit{Incompatible}](X, Y).$$

Two variables are contained in r_{12}, X and Y. Assume we already assigned the constant *front_seat_adult* to variable X. Then, a filtering system can help to find a substitution for Y where $I_5 \models^{\Phi} B(r_{12})\vartheta'$. This amounts to querying for *Incompatible*-successors in Φ_{ex}. The resulting choices for Y are *front_seat_child* and *front_seat_empty*. □

Stepping-Based Debugging. Besides getting insights into the interplay of DL-rules of a DL-program, stepping is beneficial when it comes to detecting the reason for an error, i.e., an unexpected outcome, of a DL-program. After a user detected unintended semantics of his or her program, e.g., answer sets that are not expected or missing answer sets, stepping can be started from a state that considers only a trusted subset of the current DL-program. In particular, during development, states obtained in previous stepping sessions can often be reused for extended versions of the evolving DL-program.

Example 9. Let us assume that Π'_{ex} is identical to Π_{ex} except that it does not contain DL-rule r_{13} that ensures the symmetry of the *incompatible* predicate. Forgetting this

DL-rule can be considered a typical programming mistake. It turns out that Π'_{ex} has an answer set $I_{\Pi'_{ex}}$ such that $I_5 \subseteq I_{\Pi'_{ex}}$. This is in contradiction to our expectations as I_5 contains both $test(1, engine\_off)$ and $test(1, engine\_running)$, stating that in test 1 the engine of the car is off and running at the same time. Constraint

$$r_{19} = \leftarrow test(T, S_1), test(T, S_2), not\ \ combination(S_1, S_2), S_1 < S_2$$

is meant to eliminate such answer sets. To find the bug, we start stepping at state S_5 and instantiate r_{19}, replacing T by 1, S_1 by *engine_off*, and S_2 by *engine_running*. Now, the user sees that the grounded DL-rule is active under I_5 and Φ_{ex}. We have an indication that the atom $combination(engine\_off, engine\_running)$ must become true in subsequent steps, as we know that this rule is not active under $I_{\Pi'_{ex}}$ and continue with

$$\begin{aligned} r_{16} = combination(S_1, S_2) \leftarrow\ & testcond(S_1), testcond(S_2), \\ & not\ \ incompatible(S_1, S_2), S_1 < S_2\,, \end{aligned}$$

the only DL-rule in Π'_{ex} that derives atoms of the *combination* predicate, and substitute S_1 and S_2 like before. Indeed, the resulting ground DL-rule is applicable under I_5 and DL_{ex} as $incompatible(engine\_off, engine\_running)$ is not in I_5 which should not be the case in an answer set. Finally, we check the instance

$$\begin{aligned} & incompatible(engine\_off, engine\_running) \leftarrow \\ & \qquad \mathrm{DL}[;\ Incompatible](engine\_off, engine\_running) \end{aligned}$$

of DL-rule r_{12} being the only one in the grounding of Π'_{ex} that might derive the atom $incompatible(engine\_off, engine\_running)$. Here, a query to the ontology reveals that $Incompatible(engine\_off, engine\_running)$ is not a consequence of Φ_{ex}. Instead, only $Incompatible(engine\_running, engine\_off)$ is asserted in Φ_{ex}. Now it is obvious that the encoding does not enforce the expected symmetry of predicate *incompatible*. □

5 Related Work

There has been little work on debugging DL-programs. In fact, we are only aware of one approach that aims for diagnosing minimal sets of ground DL-atoms in an inconsistent DL-program that would restore consistency when the Boolean results of the query of these DL-atoms are inverted [14]. Besides that, a refined semantics for DL-programs to overcome counter-intuitive results that may emerge when input literals of DL-atoms cause inconsistency in the ontology was presented by Pührer et al. [15].

Within the last years, there has been a considerable amount of work on debugging answer-set programs. The idea of stepping, adapted in this paper for DL-programs, was initially introduced for normal logic programs [4]. Other debugging methods related to stepping are, on the one hand, finding reasons why some interpretation is not an answer set of a program by identifying unfounded loops or unsatisfied rules [12] and, on the other hand, explaining why a program yields no answer sets at all by means of pinpointing unintentionally active constraints [16]. Brain and De Vos [17] used a simple algorithm to recursively find active rules that explain why an atom is in some answer set or why no such rules exist. Similar debugging questions have been considered by Brain et al. [13] using a meta-programming approach based on ASP itself. While our approach is independent of a concrete solver implementation, a method to directly trace derivations for atoms was realised for the ASP solver DLV [18].

The notion of computations for stepping is related to work by Pontelli et al. [19] who used justifications for similar purposes. Justifications are labelled directed graphs that explain the truth value of a literal l in some answer set in terms of truth values of literals l depends on. Computations in our sense, however, are more related to progressions of active rules, which can be identified in a program following a programmer's intuition that explain how partial interpretations evolve towards answer sets. Quite in the spirit of our notion of computation is that of Liu et al. [20] introduced for characterising the answer sets of logic programs with arbitrary abstract constraints as a sequence of evolving interpretations. As DL-programs can be seen as abstract constraint programs [21], the framework of Liu et al. [20] is, in turn, relevant for our work. Besides differences in the semantics, our notion of computations explicitly takes the rules that are active in some state into account since our motivation is debugging and program analysis.

There exists work focussing on efficient evaluation of restricted classes of DL-programs by rewriting them to datalog with negation [22]. In principle, for this type of DL-programs, the result of this transformation can be used for stepping also through the DL-part of the DL-program. Clearly, this requires the user's familiarity with the translation. In general, for a debugging approach that covers also the ontology part, our approach for stepping of DL-rules can be combined with work on finding faults in DLs. Such methods include explaining concept subsumption [23,24,25], i.e., giving reasons why for given concepts C and D, $C^I \subseteq D^I$ hold for every model I of a TBox $\mathcal{T}$. Subsumption checking can be used to identify incoherent concepts, i.e., concepts that can be proven to have no satisfying instances. Moreover, it can be used to check whether two concepts C and D are equivalent and thus one of them can be regarded as redundant. Another approach is axiom pinpointing [26], where axioms causing a concept to be unsatisfiable with respect to a TBox are detected.

6 Conclusion

We presented a framework for stepping through DL-programs that can be used for debugging based on the intuitions of the user on which DL-rules to apply next. It rests on a computation model where rules are subsequently added to a state. Moreover, we introduced unfounded sets and the notion of external support for DL-programs. We discussed how to obtain states that may serve as breakpoints from which stepping is started. By keeping these breakpoints during development, stepping sessions can be quickly initiated from situations the semantic-web engineer is already familiar with.

As a debugging methodology, our approach focuses on the rules part of a DL-program as the DL ontology is treated as a black box. For future work, it would be interesting to explore how our method can be combined with existing explanation techniques for DLs. That is, when during stepping a DL-atom is or is not satisfied although the opposite is expected, a hybrid debugging approach could provide reasons in terms of axioms and assertions in the DL knowledge base.

References

1. Eiter, T., Ianni, G., Lukasiewicz, T., Schindlauer, R., Tompits, H.: Combining answer set programming with description logics for the semantic web. Artificial Intelligence 172(12-13), 1495–1539 (2008)
2. Lifschitz, V.: What is answer set programming? In: Proceedings of the 23rd AAAI Conference on Artificial Intelligence (AAAI 2008), pp. 1594–1597. AAAI Press (2008)
3. Baader, F., Calvanese, D., McGuinness, D., Nardi, D., Patel-Schneider, P.: The Description Logic Handbook: Theory, Implementation and Applications. Cambridge University Press (2003)
4. Oetsch, J., Pührer, J., Tompits, H.: Stepping through an Answer-Set Program. In: Delgrande, J.P., Faber, W. (eds.) LPNMR 2011. LNCS, vol. 6645, pp. 134–147. Springer, Heidelberg (2011)
5. Faber, W., Pfeifer, G., Leone, N.: Semantics and complexity of recursive aggregates in answer set programming. Artificial Intelligence 175(1), 278–298 (2011)
6. Eiter, T., Ianni, G., Schindlauer, R., Tompits, H.: A uniform integration of higher-order reasoning and external evaluations in answer-set programming. In: Proceedings of the 19th International Joint Conference on Artificial Intelligence (IJCAI 2005), Professional Book Center, pp. 90–96 (2005)
7. Gelfond, M., Lifschitz, V.: Logic programs with classical negation. In: Proceedings of the 7th International Conference on Logic Programming (ICLP 1990), pp. 579–597 (1990)
8. Gelfond, M., Lifschitz, V.: Classical negation in logic programs and disjunctive databases. New Generation Computing 9(3/4), 365–386 (1991)
9. Gelfond, M., Lifschitz, V.: The stable model semantics for logic programming. In: Kowalski, R.A., Bowen, K. (eds.) Proceedings of the 5th International Conference on Logic Programming (ICLP 1988), Seattle, WA, USA, pp. 1070–1080. MIT Press (1988)
10. Leone, N., Rullo, P., Scarcello, F.: Disjunctive stable models: Unfounded sets, fixpoint semantics, and computation. Information and Computation 135(2), 69–112 (1997)
11. Faber, W.: Unfounded Sets for Disjunctive Logic Programs with Arbitrary Aggregates. In: Baral, C., Greco, G., Leone, N., Terracina, G. (eds.) LPNMR 2005. LNCS (LNAI), vol. 3662, pp. 40–52. Springer, Heidelberg (2005)
12. Oetsch, J., Pührer, J., Tompits, H.: Catching the Ouroboros: On debugging non-ground answer-set programs. Theory and Practice of Logic Programming 10(4-5), 513–529 (2010)
13. Brain, M., Gebser, M., Pührer, J., Schaub, T., Tompits, H., Woltran, S.: Debugging ASP Programs by Means of ASP. In: Baral, C., Brewka, G., Schlipf, J. (eds.) LPNMR 2007. LNCS (LNAI), vol. 4483, pp. 31–43. Springer, Heidelberg (2007)
14. Pührer, J., El Ghali, A., Chniti, A., Korf, R., Schwichtenberg, A., Lévy, F., Heymans, S., Xiao, G., Eiter, T.: D2.3 Consistency maintenance. Intermediate report. Technical report, ONTORULE IST-2009-231875 Project (2010)
15. Pührer, J., Heymans, S., Eiter, T.: Dealing with Inconsistency When Combining Ontologies and Rules Using DL-Programs. In: Aroyo, L., Antoniou, G., Hyvönen, E., ten Teije, A., Stuckenschmidt, H., Cabral, L., Tudorache, T. (eds.) ESWC 2010. LNCS, vol. 6088, pp. 183–197. Springer, Heidelberg (2010)
16. Syrjänen, T.: Debugging inconsistent answer set programs. In: Proceedings of the 11th International Workshop on Non-Monotonic Reasoning (NMR 2006), Clausthal, Germany, Institut für Informatik, Technische Universität Clausthal, Technical Report, pp. 77–83 (2006)
17. Brain, M., De Vos, M.: Debugging logic programs under the answer-set semantics. In: Proceedings of the 3rd Workshop on Answer Set Programming: Advances in Theory and Implementation, ASP 2005. CEUR Workshop Proceedings, CEUR-WS.org, vol. 142, pp. 140–152 (2005)

18. Calimeri, F., Leone, N., Ricca, F., Veltri, P.: A visual tracer for DLV. In: Proceedings of the 2nd Workshop on Software Engineering for Answer Set Programming (SEA 2009), Technical Report 2009-20, University of Bath, pp. 79–93 (2009)
19. Pontelli, E., Son, T.C., El-Khatib, O.: Justifications for logic programs under answer set semantics. Theory and Practice of Logic Programming 9(1), 1–56 (2009)
20. Liu, L., Pontelli, E., Son, T.C., Truszczyski, M.: Logic programs with abstract constraint atoms: The role of computations. Artificial Intelligence 174(3-4), 295–315 (2010)
21. Wang, Y., You, J.H., Yuan, L.Y., Shen, Y.D., Zhang, M.: The loop formula based semantics of description logic programs. Theoretical Computer Science 415, 60–85 (2012)
22. Heymans, S., Eiter, T., Xiao, G.: Tractable reasoning with dl-programs over datalog-rewritable description logics. In: Proceedings of the 19th European Conference on Artificial Intelligence (ECAI 2010). Frontiers in Artificial Intelligence and Applications, vol. 215, pp. 35–40. IOS Press (2010)
23. McGuinness, D.L., Borgida, A.: Explaining subsumption in description logics. In: Proceedings of the 14th International Joint Conference on Artificial Intelligence (IJCAI 1995), pp. 816–821. Morgan Kaufmann (1995)
24. Borgida, A., Franconi, E., Horrocks, I.: Explaining ALC subsumption. In: Proceedings of the 1999 International Workshop on Description Logics (DL 1999). CEUR Workshop Proceedings, CEUR-WS.org, vol. 22, pp. 33–36 (1999)
25. Deng, X., Haarslev, V., Shiri, N.: A resolution based framework to explain reasoning in description logics. In: Proceedings of the 2005 International Workshop on Description Logics (DL 2005). CEUR Workshop Proceedings, CEUR-WS.org, vol. 147 (2005)
26. Schlobach, S., Cornet, R.: Non-standard reasoning services for the debugging of description logic terminologies. In: Gottlob, G., Walsh, T. (eds.) Proceedings of the Eighteenth International Joint Conference on Artificial Intelligence (IJCAI 2003), pp. 355–362. Morgan Kaufmann (2003)

Answer Set Programming and Planning with Knowledge and World-Altering Actions in Multiple Agent Domains

Enrico Pontelli[1], Tran Cao Son[1], Chitta Baral[2], and Gregory Gelfond[2]

[1] Department of Computer Science
New Mexico State University
{epontell,tson}@cs.nmsu.edu
[2] Department of Computer Science & Engineering
Arizona State University
{chitta,ggelfond}@asu.edu

Abstract. This paper discusses the planning problem in multi-agent domains, in which agents may execute not only world-altering actions, but also epistemic actions. The paper reviews the concepts of Kripke structures and update models, as proposed in the literature to model epistemic and ontic actions; it then discusses the use of *Answer Set Programming (ASP)* in representing and reasoning about the effects of actions on the world, the knowledge of agents, and planning. The paper introduces the $m\mathcal{A}_0$ language, an action language for multi-agent domains with epistemic and ontic actions, to demonstrate the proposed ASP model.

1 Introduction

The literature on multi-agent planning has grown at a fast pace in recent years. A large part of the literature deals with coordination between agents [5,11,7,6,8,16] and their actions. While these issues are important, what is challenging, but less frequently addressed, is the issue of agents' knowledge about each other's knowledge and beliefs, and the manipulation of such knowledge/beliefs to achieve goals. Indeed, while logistics and coordination is important in multi-agent scenarios, such as those dealing with warfare, history provides myriad examples of battles where smaller armies have outsmarted better equipped ones, partly through the use of misinformation. Intelligence and counter-intelligence actions play important roles in such operations.

Thus, within a multi-agent setting, an important and difficult aspect is planning that involves the manipulation of the knowledge of agents, and not just about the physical world, but about each other's knowledge. In this paper, we take steps towards addressing these issues. In particular, we are interested in planning scenarios where agents reason about each others knowledge, perform actions to manipulate such knowledge, and develop plans that can guarantee awareness/ignorance of certain properties of the world by different agents to reach their own objectives. Consider the following example.

Example 1 (The Strongbox Domain). Agents A, B, and C are in a room. In the room there is a box containing a coin. It is common knowledge amongst them that:

- No one knows whether the coin is showing heads or tails.
- The box is locked and one needs a key to open it.

E. Erdem et al. (Eds.): Correct Reasoning, LNCS 7265, pp. 509–526, 2012.

- Only agent A has the key of the box.
- To determine the face of the coin one can peek into the box, if the box is open.
- If one is looking at the box and someone peeks into it, he will be able to conclude that the agent who peeked knows which face of the coin is showing—but without knowing the state of the coin himself.
- Distracting an agent causes this agent not to look at the box.
- Signaling an agent to look causes that agent to look at the box.
- Announcing that the status of the coin will cause everyone to know this fact.

Suppose that agent A wishes to know which face of the coin is up, and that he would like agent B to become aware of the fact that he knows, while keeping agent C in the dark. Intuitively, agent A could achieve his goal by: (*i*) distracting C, keeping him from looking at the box; (*ii*) signaling B to look at the box; (*iii*) opening the box; and finally (*iv*) peeking into the box.

This simple scenario poses a number of challenges for research in multi-agent planning. The domain contains several classes of actions: *(1)* Actions that allow the agents to change the state of the world (e.g., open the box, signal/distract the agents); *(2)* Actions that change the knowledge of the agents (e.g., peek into the box, announce head/tail); *(3)* Actions that manipulate the beliefs of other agents (e.g., peek while other agents observe). In order for agent A to realize that steps *(i)*–*(iv)* will achieve his goal, he must be able to reason about the effects of actions:

- ◦ On the state of the world (e.g., opening the box causes the box to be open; distracting causes an agent to not look at the box); and
- ◦ On the knowledge of agents about her own knowledge (e.g., someone following her actions would know what she knows).

In this paper, we address the aforementioned problems by developing a high-level action language for representing and reasoning about actions in multi-agent domains. The semantics of an action theory is defined by the *answer sets* of a corresponding logic program. Our approach shows that *Answer Set Programming (ASP)* approaches which have been investigated for single-agent domains can be naturally generalized to multi-agent ones. The advantage of this approach stems from the fact that ASP can be used both as a specification and implementation language; an ASP encoding of an action theory can be used for various reasoning tasks, e.g., hypothetical reasoning, planning, and diagnosis. As such, it becomes an indispensable tool to explore epistemic action languages for multi-agent systems and validate the design of action theories.

2 Preliminaries

2.1 Answer Set Programming

Let us assume a collection of propositional variables $\mathcal{P}$. An answer set program (ASP) over $\mathcal{P}$ [10,2] is a set of rules of the form: $a_0 \leftarrow a_1, \ldots, a_m, not\ \ a_{m+1}, \ldots, not\ \ a_n$, where $0 \leq m \leq n$, each a_i is an atom of $\mathcal{P}$[1], and not represents *negation-as-failure*. A naf-literal has the form $not\ \ a$, where a is an atom. Given a rule of this form, the

[1] A rule with variables is viewed as a shorthand for the set of its ground instances.

left and right hand sides are called the *head* and *body*, respectively. A rule may have either an empty head or an empty body, but not both. Rules with an empty head are called *constraints*—the empty head is implicitly assumed to represent false—while those with an empty body are known as *facts*.

A set of ground atoms X satisfies the body of a rule if $\{a_{m+1}, \ldots, a_n\} \cap X = \emptyset$ and $\{a_1, \ldots, a_m\} \subseteq X$. A rule with a non-empty head is satisfied if either its body is not satisfied by X, or $a_0 \in X$. A constraint is *satisfied* by X if its body is not satisfied by X. Given a program Π and a set of ground atoms X, the *reduct* of Π w.r.t. X (denoted by Π^X) is the program obtained from the set of all ground instances of Π by:

1. Deleting all the rules that have a naf-literal $not\ \ a$ in the body where $a \in X$, and
2. Removing all naf-literals in the bodies of the remaining rules.

A set of ground atoms X is an *answer set* of a program Π if X is the subset-minimal set of atoms that satisfies all the rules in the program Π^X.

A program Π is said to be *consistent* if it has an answer set, and *inconsistent* otherwise. To make answer set programming easier, Niemelä et al. [13] introduced a new type of rule, called a *cardinality constraint rule*, where each atom in the rule can be a *choice atom*. A choice atom has the form $l\{b_1, \ldots, b_k\}u$, where each b_j is an atom, and l and u are integers such that $l \leq u$. Choice atoms can be also written as $l\{p(\bar{X}) : q(\bar{X})\}u$, where $\bar{X}$ is a set of variables—this is shorthand for the choice atom $l\{p(\bar{s}_1, \ldots, p(\bar{s}_k\}u$, where $\{\bar{s}_1, \ldots, \bar{s}_k\}$ are all the ground instances of $\bar{X}$ such that $q(\bar{X})$ is true. A set of atoms X satisfies a choice atom $l\{b_1, \ldots, b_k\}u$ if $l \leq |X \cap \{b_1, \ldots, b_k\}| \leq u$. The semantics of logic programs which contain such rules is given in [13].

The fact that a program can have multiple (or no) answer sets, encourages an alternative method of solving problems via logic programming [12,13]. In this approach, we develop logic programs whose answer sets have a one-to-one correspondence with the solutions of the particular problem being modeled. Typically an ASP program consists of *(1)* Rules to enumerate the possible solutions of a problem as *candidate* answer sets; and *(2)* Constraints to eliminate answer sets not representing solutions of the problem.

2.2 Belief Formulae and Kripke Structures

Let us consider an environment with n agents $\mathcal{AG} = \{1, \ldots, n\}$. The state of the world may be described by a set $\mathcal{F}$ of propositional variables, called *fluents*. Following [9], we associate with each agent i a modal operator $\mathbf{B}_i$, and represent the beliefs of an agent as belief formulae in a logic extended by these operators:

- *Fluent formulae:* a fluent formula is a propositional formula built using the atomic formulae in $\mathcal{F}$ and the traditional propositional connectives $\vee$, $\rightarrow$, $\neg$, etc. A *fluent literal* is either a fluent atom $f \in \mathcal{F}$ or its negation $\neg f$.
- *Belief formulae:* a belief formula is a formula which has one of the following forms: *(1)* a fluent formula; *(2)* a formula of the form $\mathbf{B}_i\varphi$ where φ is a belief formula; *(3)* A formula of the form $\varphi_1 \wedge \varphi_2$, $\varphi_1 \vee \varphi_2$ or $\neg\varphi_1$ where φ_1 and φ_2 are belief formulae.

In addition, given a belief formula, φ, and a non-empty set $\alpha \subseteq \mathcal{AG}$, we call $\mathbf{E}_\alpha\varphi$ and $\mathbf{C}_\alpha\varphi$ *group formulae.* Furthermore, we use the shorthand form $\mathbf{C}\varphi$ to denote $\mathbf{C}_{\mathcal{AG}}\varphi$. In the following sections, we will simply use the term formula instead of belief formula. We denote with $\mathcal{L}_{\mathcal{AG}}$ the set of all formulae over $\mathcal{F}$ and $\mathcal{AG}$.

Definition 1 (Kripke Structure). A *Kripke structure* with respect to[2] an $\mathcal{F}$ and $\mathcal{AG}$ is a tuple $\langle S, \pi, \mathcal{B}_1, \ldots, \mathcal{B}_n \rangle$, where S is a set of state symbols, π is a function that associates an interpretation of $\mathcal{F}$ to each element of S, and $\mathcal{B}_i \subseteq S \times S$ for $1 \leq i \leq n$. A *pointed Kripke structure* is defined as a pair (M, s) where $M = \langle S, \pi, \mathcal{B}_1, \ldots, \mathcal{B}_n \rangle$ is a Kripke structure and $s \in S$ (referred to as the *real state* of the world).

Given a Kripke structure, $M = \langle S, \pi, \mathcal{B}_1, \ldots, \mathcal{B}_n \rangle$, and a state symbol, $s \in S$, the satisfaction relation between belief formulae and a pointed Kripke structure (M, s) is defined as follows:

- $(M, s) \models \varphi$ if φ is a fluent formula and $\pi(s) \models \varphi$;
- $(M, s) \models \mathbf{B}_i\varphi$ if $\forall t \in S$ s.t. $(s, t) \in \mathcal{B}_i$, $(M, t) \models \varphi$;
- $(M, s) \models \neg\varphi$ if $(M, s) \not\models \varphi$;
- $(M, s) \models \varphi_1 \vee \varphi_2$ if $(M, s) \models \varphi_1$ or $(M, s) \models \varphi_2$;
- $(M, s) \models \mathbf{E}_\alpha\varphi$ if $(M, s) \models \mathbf{B}_i\varphi$ for every $i \in \alpha$.
- $(M, s) \models \mathbf{C}_\alpha\varphi$ if $(M, s) \models E^k_\alpha\varphi$ for every $k \geq 0$ where: $E^1_\alpha\varphi = E_\alpha\varphi$ and $E^{k+1}_\alpha = E_\alpha(E^k_\alpha\varphi)$.

We often view a Kripke structure M as a directed labeled graph, with S as its nodes and with an arc of the form (s, i, t) if and only if $(s, t) \in \mathcal{B}_i$. We use $M[S]$, $M[\pi]$, and $M[i]$, to denote the components S, π, and $\mathcal{B}_i$ of M, respectively.

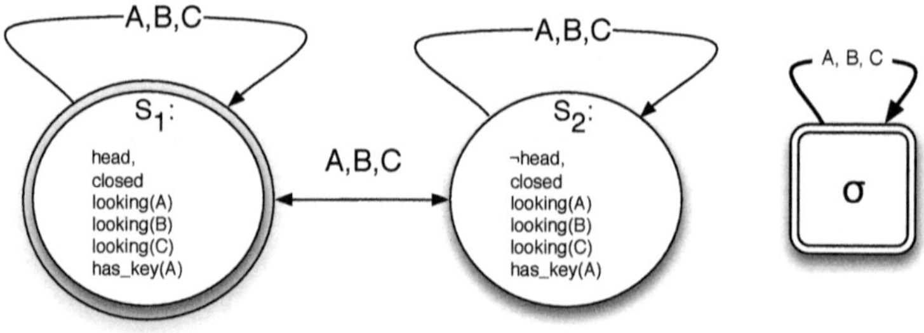

Fig. 1. An Example of a Pointed Kripke Structure and an Update Model

Consider a simplified version of the initial state in Example 1. None of the agents A, B, and C is aware of the state of the coin, and this is common knowledge. The box is closed. All the agents are aware that the box is closed, everyone is looking, and everyone knows that agent A has the key. Assume that the coin is showing heads. The knowledge of the agents together with the real world is captured by the pointed Kripke structure shown in Fig. 1. In the figure, a circle represents a state, and is labeled by its name and interpretation. Arcs denote the belief relations captured by the structure. Lastly, the double circle represents the real physical state of the world.

Intuitively, a Kripke structure denotes the possible worlds envisioned by the agents, with multiple worlds denoting uncertainty and the presence of different beliefs. The relation $(s_1, s_2) \in \mathcal{B}_i$ captures the notion that agent i when at the world s_1 can not distinguish between the state described by the world s_1 and the one described by the

[2] When it is clear from the context we may not explicitly mention the associated $\mathcal{F}$ and $\mathcal{AG}$ of a Kripke structure.

world s_2. Thus, $M[\pi](s_1) \models \varphi$ and $M[\pi](s_2) \models \neg\varphi$, indicates that agent i is uncertain about the truth of φ.

We are often interested in Kripke structures with certain properties; for example, a Kripke structure $\langle S, \pi, \mathcal{B}_1, \ldots, \mathcal{B}_n \rangle$ is **S5** if, for each agent i and formulae φ and ψ the following axioms hold: **(K)** $(\mathbf{B}_i\varphi \wedge \mathbf{B}_i(\varphi \Rightarrow \psi)) \Rightarrow \mathbf{B}_i\psi$; **(T)** $\mathbf{B}_i\psi \Rightarrow \psi$; **(4)** $\mathbf{B}_i\psi \Rightarrow \mathbf{B}_i\mathbf{B}_i\psi$; and **(5)** $\neg\mathbf{B}_i\psi \Rightarrow \mathbf{B}_i\neg\mathbf{B}_i\psi$.

2.3 Update Models

Program models are used to represent action occurrences, using structures similar to pointed Kripke structures; they describe the effects of an action on states using an update operator. The original proposal [1] deals with sensing and announcement actions, later extended to world-altering (a.k.a. ontic) actions [15] (and called update models).

An $\mathcal{L}_{\mathcal{AG}}$-substitution is a set $\{p_1 \rightarrow \varphi_1, \ldots, p_n \rightarrow \varphi_n\}$, where each p_i is a distinct fluent and each φ_i is a formula in $\mathcal{L}_{\mathcal{AG}}$. We will assume that for each $p \in \mathcal{F} \setminus \{p_1, \ldots, p_n\}$, the substitution contains $p \rightarrow p$. The set of all $\mathcal{L}_{\mathcal{AG}}$-substitutions is denoted with $SUB_{\mathcal{L}_{\mathcal{AG}}}$.

Definition 2. *An* update model $\mathbf{\Sigma}$ *is a tuple* $(\Sigma, \{R_i \mid i \in \mathcal{AG}\}, pre, sub)$ *where*

- Σ *is a set, whose elements are called* events*;*
- $R_i \subseteq \Sigma \times \Sigma$ *for each* $i \in \mathcal{AG}$*;*
- $pre : \Sigma \rightarrow \mathcal{L}_{\mathcal{AG}}$ *is a function mapping each event* $a \in \Sigma$ *to a formula in* $\mathcal{L}_{\mathcal{AG}}$*;*
- $sub : \Sigma \rightarrow SUB_{\mathcal{L}_{\mathcal{AG}}}$.

A update instance ω *is a pair* $(\mathbf{\Sigma}, e)$ *where* $\mathbf{\Sigma}$ *is an update model* $(\Sigma, \{R_i \mid i \in \mathcal{AG}\}, pre, sub)$ *and* e*, referred to as a* designated event*, is a member in* Σ*.*

Intuitively, an update model represents different views of an action occurrence which are associated with the observability of agents. Each view is represented by an event in Σ. The designated event is the one that agents who are aware of the action occurrence will observe. The relation R_i describes agent i's uncertainty on action execution—i.e., if $(\sigma, \tau) \in R_i$ and event σ is performed, then agent i may believe that event τ is executed instead. pre defines the action precondition and sub specifies the changes of fluent values after the execution of an action. Update models and instances are graphically represented similarly to (pointed) Kripke structures. The update instance on the right of Fig. 1 is $(\mathbf{\Sigma}_1, \sigma)$ where $\mathbf{\Sigma}_1 = (\{\sigma\}, \{R_A, R_B, R_C\}, pre_1, sub_1)$ and $R_A = R_B = R_C = \{(\sigma, \sigma)\}$, $pre_1(\sigma) = true$, and $sub_1(\sigma) = \{closed \rightarrow false\}$.

Definition 3. *Given a Kripke structure* M *and an update model* $\mathbf{\Sigma} = (\Sigma, \{R_i \mid i \in \mathcal{AG}\}, pre, sub)$*, the* update operator *defines a Kripke structures* $M' = M \otimes \mathbf{\Sigma}$*, where*

- $M'[S] = \{(s, \tau) \mid s \in M[S], \tau \in \Sigma, (M, s) \models pre(\tau)\}$,
- $((s, \tau), (s', \tau')) \in M'[i]$ *iff* $(s, s') \in M[i]$ *and* $(\tau, \tau') \in R_i$*, and*
- *For each* $f \in \mathcal{F}$*,* $M'[\pi]((s, \tau)) \models f$ *iff* $f \rightarrow \varphi \in sub$ *and* $(M, s) \models \varphi$*.*

Intuitively, the Kripke structure M' is obtained from the component-wise cross-product of the old structure M and the update model $\mathbf{\Sigma}$, by keeping only those new states (s, τ) s.t. (M, s) satisfies the action precondition.

Example 2. Continuing with the previous examples, let us compute $M' = M_1 \otimes \mathbf{\Sigma}_1$:

- $M'[S]=\{(s_1,\sigma),(s_2,\sigma)\}$. Let $u=(s_1,\sigma)$ and $v=(s_2,\sigma)$.
- $M'[A] = M'[C] = \{(u,u),(v,v)\}$ and $M'[B] = \{(u,u),(v,v),(u,v),(v,u)\}$.
- $M'[\pi](u) = \{head, \neg closed\}$ and $M'[\pi](v) = \{\neg head, \neg closed\}$. □

An update template is a pair $(\mathbf{\Sigma}, \Gamma)$ where $\mathbf{\Sigma}$ is an update model with the set of events Σ and $\Gamma \subseteq \Sigma$. The update of a state (M,s) given a update template $(\mathbf{\Sigma}, \Gamma)$ is a set of states, denoted by $(M,s) \otimes (\mathbf{\Sigma}, \Gamma)$, where for each $(M', s') \in (M,s) \otimes (\mathbf{\Sigma}, \Gamma)$, it holds that $M' = M \otimes \mathbf{\Sigma}$ and $s' = (s, \tau)$ where $\tau \in \Gamma$ and $s' \in M'[S]$.

Observe that the discussion in this section focuses on the changes caused by an update model $\mathbf{\Sigma}$ (resp. update template $(\mathbf{\Sigma}, \Gamma)$) on a state (M,s). It does not place any requirement (e.g. **S5**) on the Kripke structure M of the state. In a dynamic environment, agents might be unaware of action occurrences and thus could have false beliefs. For instance, the agent C (Example 1) would still believe that agent A does not know the status of the coin after A executes the action sequence (i)-(iv). As such, it will be interesting to investigate the properties of the Kripke structures after an update by an update model. We leave this as an important future research topic as it is outside the scope of this paper.

3 Basic ASP Encodings

In this section, we will present the ASP rules encoding the update operator. The encoding is general and does not assume any properties of the underlying Kripke structures.

Encoding Kripke Structures in ASP: Each fluent and belief formula of interest (i.e., used in the domain specification) φ is represented by a corresponding term $\tau(\varphi)$, defined in the natural recursive manner:

- if φ is true, then $\tau(\varphi) = top$
- if φ is a fluent, then $\tau(f) = f$
- if φ is the literal $\neg f$, then $\tau(\neg f) = neg(f)$
- if φ is the formula $\varphi_1 \vee \varphi_2$, then $\tau(\varphi) = or(\tau(\varphi_1), \tau(\varphi_2))$
- if φ has the form $\mathbf{B}_i\varphi_1$, then $\tau(\varphi) = b(i, \tau(\varphi_1))$

In order to represent a Kripke structure, we need to describe its three components: the state symbols, their associated interpretations, and the accessibility relations. We will assume that each pointed Kripke structure has a name—represented by a term; we will use *pointedKS*(t) to assert that t is the name of a pointed Kripke structure. The components of each pointed Kripke structure (M,s) A pointed Kripke structure (M,s), named $t_{(M,s)}$, is described by atoms of the form:

- *state*$(u, t_{(M,s)})$ denoting the fact that $u \in M[S]$;
- *real*$(s, t_{(M,s)})$ denoting that s is the real state of the world in the Kripke structure;
- $r(i, u, v, t_{(M,s)})$ denoting the fact that $(u,v) \in M[i]$;
- $holds(\tau(\ell), u, t_{(M,s)})$ denoting the fact that $M[\pi](u) \models \ell$ for a fluent literal ℓ.

The following constraints are useful to guarantee core properties of a Kripke structure: for each $f \in \mathcal{F}$, $u \in M[S]$

$$\leftarrow holds(\tau(f), u, t_{(M,s)}), holds(\tau(\neg f), u, t_{(M,s)})$$
$$\leftarrow not\ holds(\tau(f), u, t_{(M,s)}), not\ holds(\tau(\neg f), u, t_{(M,s)})$$

The predicate $holds(\tau(\varphi), s, t_{(M,s)})$ expresses the truth value of a formula φ with respect to a pointed Kripke structure (M, s) (i.e., $(M, s) \models \varphi$), and is defined recursively on the structure of φ. For example:

- if φ is a literal, then its definition comes from the pointed Kripke structure;
- if φ is of the form $\varphi_1 \vee \varphi_2$ then:

$$holds(or(\tau(\varphi_1), \tau(\varphi_2)), S, T) \leftarrow holds(\tau(\varphi_1), S, T)$$
$$holds(or(\tau(\varphi_1), \tau(\varphi_2)), S, T) \leftarrow holds(\tau(\varphi_2), S, T)$$

- if φ is of the form $\mathbf{B}_i\varphi_1$ then:

$$n\_holds(b(i, \tau(\varphi)), S, T) \leftarrow r(i, S, S_1, T), not\ holds(\tau(\varphi_1), S_1, T)$$
$$holds(b(i, \tau(\varphi)), S, T) \leftarrow not\ n\_holds(b(i, \tau(\varphi)), S, T)$$

- if φ is of the form $E_\alpha\varphi_1$ then:

$$n\_holds(\tau(\varphi), S, T) \leftarrow not\ holds(b(i, \tau(\varphi_1)), S, T) \qquad \text{for each } i \in \alpha$$
$$holds(\tau(\varphi), S, T) \leftarrow not\ n\_holds(\tau(\varphi), S, T)$$

- if φ is of the form $C_\alpha\varphi_1$ then:

$$connect(S, S_1, \alpha, T) \leftarrow r(i, S, S_1, T) \qquad \text{for each } i \in \alpha$$
$$connect(S_1, S_2, \alpha, T) \leftarrow connect(S_1, S_3, \alpha, T), connect(S_3, S_2, \alpha, T)$$
$$n\_holds(\tau(\varphi), S, T) \leftarrow connect(S, S_1, \alpha, T), not\ holds(\tau(\varphi_1), S_1, T)$$
$$holds(\tau(\varphi), S, T) \leftarrow not\ n\_holds(\tau(\varphi), S, T)$$

Observe that the above encoding utilizes the following property: $(M, s) \models C_\alpha\varphi$ iff $(M, s') \models \varphi$ for every state $s' \in M[S]$ such that there exist a sequence of agent $i_1, \ldots, i_k \in \alpha$ and a sequence of states $s_1, \ldots, s_k$ such that $s_1 = s$, $s_k = s'$, and $s_{i+1} \in M[i]$ for $1 \leq i < k$.

For a formula φ, let Π^T_φ denote the set of rules defining $holds(\tau(\varphi), S, T)$ (including the rules for the sub-formulae of φ). For a pointed Kripke structure (M, s), let $\kappa\rho^t(M, s)$ be the following set of facts:

- $real(s, t)$;
- $state(u, t)$ for each $u \in M[S]$;
- $r(a, u, v, t)$ if $(u, v) \in M[a]$;
- $holds(\ell, u, t)$ if $(M, u) \models \ell$, for each fluent literal ℓ.

Proposition 1. *$\Pi(M, s, t) = \kappa\rho^t(M, s) \cup \Pi^t_\varphi$ has a unique answer set S and $(M, u) \models \varphi$ iff $holds(\tau(\varphi), u, t) \in S$.*

Encoding Update Models and Update Templates: The encoding of an update model and update template follows an analogous structure as a Kripke structure; given an update template $(\boldsymbol{\Sigma}, \Gamma)$ where $\boldsymbol{\Sigma} = (\Sigma, \{R_i \mid i \in \mathcal{AG}\}, pre, sub)$, we introduce a fact of the form $updateT(t)$ to indicate that t is the term naming the update template. The description of $(\boldsymbol{\Sigma}, \Gamma)$ contains the rules $\upsilon\mu^t(\boldsymbol{\Sigma}, \Gamma)$:

- $actual(e, t)$ for each $e \in \Gamma$;
- $event(e, t)$ for each $e \in \Sigma$;
- $acc(a, e, e', t)$ if $(e, e') \in R_a$;
- $pre(e, \tau(\varphi), t)$ if $pre(e) = \varphi$;
- $sub(e, \tau(f), \tau(\varphi), t)$ and $sub(e, \tau(\neg f), \tau(\neg\varphi), t)$ if $(f \rightarrow \varphi) \in sub(e)$ and $\varphi \not\equiv f$.

In the case of an update instance, $\upsilon\mu^t(\mathbf{\Sigma}, \Gamma)$ will contain a single fact of $actual$.

Encoding Update Operators in ASP: The outcome of the update operation between a pointed Kripke structure and an update instance is a new pointed Kripke structure; the rules encoding the update operation will thus define the relations describing the components of the new pointed Kripke structure.[3] Let us introduce the fact $occ(t_K, t_\Sigma)$ to identify the application of an update instance to a given pointed Kripke structure. The following rules are used to determine the pointed Kripke structure resulting from the application of an update mode.

The identification of the new pointed Kripke structure comes from the rule

$$pointedKS(app(KS, UT)) \leftarrow pointedKS(KS), updateT(UT), occ(KS, UT)$$

The states of the new Kripke structure are defined as follows:

$$\begin{array}{rl} state(st(S, E), app(KS, UT)) \leftarrow & occ(KS, UT), state(S, KS), event(E, UT), \\ & pre(E, F, UT), holds(F, S, KS) \end{array}$$

The accessibility relation of the new pointed Kripke structure is a direct consequence of the accessibility relations of the Kripke structure and the update model:

$$\begin{array}{rl} r(Ag, st(S1, E1), st(S2, E2), app(KS, UT)) \leftarrow & occ(KS, UT), \\ & state(st(S1, E1), app(KS, UT)), \\ & state(st(S2, E2), app(KS, UT)), \\ & r(Ag, S1, S2, KS), acc(Ag, E1, E2, UT) \end{array}$$

The real state of the world is defined by

$$\begin{array}{rl} real(st(S, E), app(KS, UT)) \leftarrow & occ(KS, UT), state(st(S, E), app(KS, UT)), \\ & real(S, KS), actual(E, UT) \end{array}$$

Finally, we need to determine the interpretations associated to the various states:

$$\begin{array}{rl} complement(F, neg(F)) & \leftarrow fluent(F) \\ complement(neg(F), F) & \leftarrow fluent(F) \\ holds(L, st(S, E), app(KS, UT)) & \leftarrow occ(KS, UT), state(st(S, E), app(KS, UT)), literal(L), \\ & \quad sub(E, L, Form, UT), holds(Form, S, KS) \\ holds(L, st(S, E), app(KS, UT)) & \leftarrow occ(KS, UT), state(st(S, E), app(KS, UT)), literal(L), \\ & \quad complement(L, L1), holds(L, S, KS), \\ & \quad not\ holds(L1, st(S, E), app(KS, UT)) \end{array}$$

Let us denote this set of rules with $\alpha\pi$. To prepare for the following proposition, let us introduce some notations. Given an update model $\mathbf{\Sigma} = (\Sigma, \{R_i \mid i \in \mathcal{AG}\}, pre, sub)$, let us define $\Phi(\mathbf{\Sigma}) = \{\varphi \mid \exists e \in \Sigma.\ (f \rightarrow \varphi) \in sub(e)\} \cup \{pre(e) \mid e \in \Sigma\}$.

[3] The code has been simplified for readability—e.g., by removing some domain predicates.

Proposition 2. *Let (M, s) be a pointed Kripke structure and let $(\mathbf{\Sigma}, \Gamma)$ be an update template. Let t_1 be the term denoting the name given to (M, s) and t_2 the term denoting the name given to $(\mathbf{\Sigma}, \Gamma)$. Let*

$$\Pi((M,s),t_1,(\mathbf{\Sigma},\Gamma),t_2) = \alpha\pi \cup \kappa\rho^{t_1}(M,s) \cup \upsilon\mu^{t_2}(\mathbf{\Sigma},\Gamma) \cup \bigcup_{\varphi \in \Phi(\mathbf{\Sigma})} \Pi_{\varphi}^{t_1} \cup \{occ(t_1,t_2)\}.$$

Let S be an answer set of $\Pi((M,s),t_1,(\mathbf{\Sigma},\Gamma),t_2)$. Then
- $(u,e) \in (M \otimes \mathbf{\Sigma})[S]$ *iff* $state(st(u,e), app(t_1,t_2)) \in S$
- $((u,e),(u',e')) \in (M \otimes \mathbf{\Sigma})[i]$ *iff* $r(i, st(u,e), st(u',e'), app(t_1,t_2)) \in S$
- $(M \otimes \mathbf{\Sigma}, (u,e)) \models \psi$ *iff* $holds(\tau(\psi), st(u,e), app(t_1,t_2)) \in S$
- $(M \otimes \mathbf{\Sigma}, (u,e)) \in (M,s) \otimes (\mathbf{\Sigma},\Gamma)$ *iff* $real(st(u,e), app(t_1,t_2)) \in S$

4 An Application in Multi-agent Planning

In this section we instantiate the generic principles illustrated above to the case of a multi-agent action language—the language $m\mathcal{A}_0$ [14]. We review the syntax of $m\mathcal{A}_0$ and illustrate the specific encoding of some of its actions using ASP.

4.1 Syntax

The action language $m\mathcal{A}_0$ is based on the same logic language introduced in Section 2.2. We extend the language signature with a set $\mathcal{A}$ of *actions*.

For the Strongbox domain, the set $\mathcal{AG} = \{A, B, C\}$, the set of fluents contains the fluents $head$ (the coin is head's up), $closed$ (the box is closed), $looking(i)$ (agent i is looking at the box), and $key(i)$ (agent i has a key), and the set of actions include actions like $open(i)$ (agent i opens the box), $peek(i)$ (agent i peeks into the box), and $announce(i, \varphi)$ (agent i announces that the formula φ is true).

Each action is associated to exactly one executability law of the form

$$\textbf{executable } a \textbf{ if } \psi \tag{1}$$

indicating that the action $a \in \mathcal{AG}$ can be executed only if the formula ψ is satisfied. We distinguish three types of actions in $m\mathcal{A}_0$, i.e., $\mathcal{A} = \mathcal{A}_o \uplus \mathcal{A}_s \uplus \mathcal{A}_a$:

- *Ontic* actions are used to modify properties of the world; they are described by statements of the form
$$a \textbf{ causes } \ell \textbf{ if } \psi \tag{2}$$
indicating that the action $a \in \mathcal{A}_o$ will make the literal ℓ true if the action is executed and the formula ψ is satisfied. For example, the action $open(i)$ is described by:
$$open(i) \textbf{ causes } \neg closed \textbf{ if } true$$
- *Sensing* actions enable agents to observe unknown properties of the world, refining their knowledge. Each sensing action $a \in \mathcal{A}_s$ is described by a statement
$$a \textbf{ determines } f \tag{3}$$
where $f \in \mathcal{F}$ is the property being observed. For example, the $peek(i)$ action is described by: $peek(i)$ **determines** $head$.

- *Announcement* actions are used by an agent to share knowledge with other agents; each announcement action $a \in \mathcal{A}_a$ is described by a statement of the form

$$a \textbf{ announces } \varphi \tag{4}$$

where φ is a formula describing the knowledge being shared. For example, the action $announce(i, \neg head)$ is described by:

$$announce(i, \neg head) \textbf{ announces } \neg head$$

Another distinct feature of $m\mathcal{A}_0$ is action observability; the effects of each action on a pointed Kripke structure is dependent on which agents can observe the execution of the action and its effects. This is a dynamic property which is handled explicitly in the domain description through statements of the form:

$$ag \textbf{ observes } a \textbf{ if } \varphi \tag{5}$$

$$ag \textbf{ partially\_observes } a \textbf{ if } \varphi \tag{6}$$

where $a \in \mathcal{A}$ and φ is a formula. For example (for $X, Y \in \mathcal{AG}$):

$$X \textbf{ observes } peek(X) \textbf{ if } true$$
$$X \textbf{ partially\_observes } peek(Y) \textbf{ if } X \neq Y \wedge looking(X)$$

A domain description $\mathcal{D}$ is a collection of statements of the type (1)-(6). For simplicity, we assume that each action has one statement of type (1); we also assume that each sensing and announcement action is described by one statement of type (3) or (4).

The semantics of $m\mathcal{A}_0$ has been introduced in [3,4] and it relies on the definition of a transition function $\Phi_D(a, B)$ which determines the result of executing an action a in a set of pointed Kripke structures B (a.k.a. a *belief state*)—as a new belief state.

4.2 Modeling $m\mathcal{A}_0$ Actions in ASP

Executability. We envision actions being executed in a state of the world/knowledge described by a pointed Kripke structure. Actions can be executed only if their executability condition is met; if a is an action and **executable** a **if** ψ is its executability law, then we add to $\epsilon\varsigma^t$ the constraint

$$\leftarrow occ(t, a), real(s, t), not\ holds(\tau(\psi), s, t)$$

Observability. Let us introduce three ASP predicates that will capture the observability properties of an action: *obs* indicating that an agent is fully knowledgeable of the effects of the action, *pobs* indicating that the agent is only aware of the action execution but not its effects, and *obv* denoting that the agent is oblivious about the action execution. The rules defining these predicates compose the logic program $o\beta^t$. For each action a, if i **observes** a **if** φ is in $\mathcal{D}$, then $o\beta^t$ contains

$$obs(i, a, t) \leftarrow real(s, t), occ(t, a), holds(\tau(\varphi), s, t)$$

If $\mathcal{D}$ contains i **partially_observes** a **if** φ, then $o\beta^t$ contains

$$pobs(i, a, t) \leftarrow real(s, t), occ(t, a), holds(\tau(\varphi), s, t)$$

Finally, we need to add to $o\beta^t$ the rules

$$obv(i, a, t) \leftarrow occ(t, a), not\ obs(i, a, t), not\ pobs(i, a, t)$$

For the sake of the discussion in the following subsections, given an action a and a pointed Kripke structure (M, s), we define

$$\begin{array}{rcl}\alpha(a, M, s) & = & \{i \mid (i \textbf{ observes } a \textbf{ if } \varphi) \in \mathcal{D}, (M, s) \models \varphi\} \\ \beta(a, M, s) & = & \{i \mid (i \textbf{ observes } a \textbf{ if } \varphi) \in \mathcal{D}, (M, s) \models \varphi\} \\ \gamma(a, M, s) & = & \mathcal{AG} \setminus (\alpha(a, M, s) \cup \beta(a, M, s))\end{array}$$

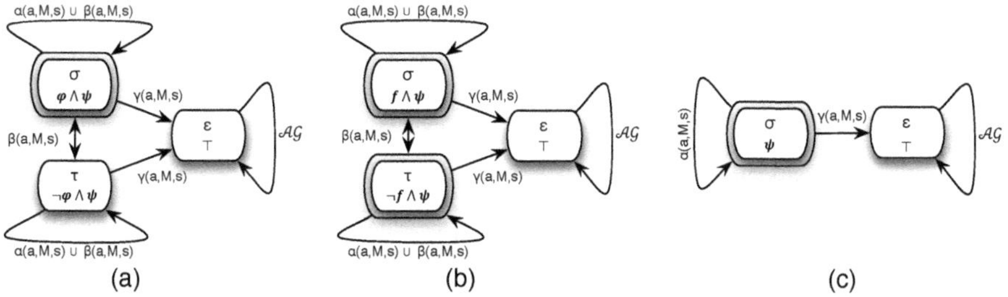

Fig. 2. Graphical Representations of the Update Templates

Announcements Actions. Let us consider an announcement action a described by the law a **announces** φ. This action can be captured by an update template which is schematically summarized in Figure 2(a) (the double circle denotes the real event, the formulae inside the circles represent the precondition pre). For this update model, $sub(e) = \emptyset$ for each $e \in \Sigma$. The intuition behind this update model is as follows: σ represents the actual announcement, which will make all agents in $\alpha(a, M, s)$ aware that φ is true; the agents in $\beta(a, M, s)$ will partially observe the action, thus learning that all agents in $\alpha(a, M, s)$ are aware of the value of φ, but unable to know whether φ or $\neg\varphi$ is true—and thus they cannot distinguish between the even σ and the event τ (that announces $\neg\varphi$. The agents in $\gamma(a, M, s)$ are unaware of the action execution and thus do not see any change of beliefs (this is encoded by the event ϵ).

Let us denote this update model by $a_\varphi(T) = (\Sigma_a(T), \Gamma_a(T))$, where T is the identification of the pointed Kripke structure in which the update model is performed and a is the e action. This behavior is coded in ASP by the following collection of facts:

- The actual event is described by $actual(\sigma, a_\varphi(T))$
- The collection of events is $\{event(\sigma, a_\varphi(T)), event(\tau, a_\varphi(T)), event(\epsilon, a_\varphi(T))\}$.
- The accessibility relations among events are described as follows:

$$\begin{array}{lcl} acc(Agent, S_1, S_1, a_\varphi(T)) & \leftarrow & S_1 \in \{\tau, \sigma, \epsilon\}, obs(Agent, a, T) \\ acc(Agent, S_1, S_1, a_\varphi(T)) & \leftarrow & S_1 \in \{\tau, \sigma, \epsilon\}, pobs(Agent, a, T) \\ acc(Agent, \epsilon, \epsilon, a_\varphi(T)) & \leftarrow & obv(Agent, a, T) \\ acc(Agent, \sigma, \tau, a_\varphi(T)) & \leftarrow & pobs(Agent, a, T) \\ acc(Agent, \tau, \sigma, a_\varphi(T)) & \leftarrow & pobs(Agent, a, T) \\ acc(Agent, S_1, \epsilon, a_\varphi(T)) & \leftarrow & S_1 \in \{\sigma, \tau\}, obv(Agent, a, T) \end{array}$$

Sensing Actions. Let us consider a sensing action s described by the law s **determines** f. This action can be captured by an update template which is schematically summarized in Figure 2(b). For this update model, $sub(e) = \emptyset$ for each $e \in \Sigma$. The intuition is similar to the case of announcement actions; σ represents the the sensing action detecting that the fluent f is true, while τ is the sensing action detecting the fluent f being false; the action ϵ is viewed by the agents that are oblivious of the action execution.

Let us denote this update model by $s_f(T) = (\mathbf{\Sigma}_s(T), \Gamma_s(T))$, where T is the identification of the pointed Kripke structure in which the update model is performed and s is the name of the action. This behavior is coded in ASP by the following facts:

- The actual event is described by $actual(\sigma, s_f(T))$
- The collection of events is $\{event(\sigma, s_f(T)), event(\tau, s_f(T)), event(\epsilon, s_f(T))\}$.
- The accessibility relations among events are described as follows:

$$\begin{array}{ll} acc(Agent, S_1, S_1, s_f(T)) & \leftarrow S_1 \in \{\tau, \sigma, \epsilon\}, obs(Agent, s, T) \\ acc(Agent, S_1, S_1, s_f(T)) & \leftarrow S_1 \in \{\tau, \sigma, \epsilon\}, pobs(Agent, s, T) \\ acc(Agent, \epsilon, \epsilon, s_f(T)) & \leftarrow obv(Agent, s, T) \\ acc(Agent, \sigma, \tau, s_f(T)) & \leftarrow pobs(Agent, s, T) \\ acc(Agent, \tau, \sigma, s_f(T)) & \leftarrow pobs(Agent, s, T) \\ acc(Agent, S_1, \epsilon, s_f(T)) & \leftarrow S_1 \in \{\sigma, \tau\}, obv(Agent, s, T) \end{array}$$

Ontic Actions. Let us consider an ontic action o described by the set of laws o **causes** ℓ_1 **if** $\varphi_1, \ldots, o$ **causes** ℓ_n **if** φ_n. For the sake of simplicity, we assume here that the various ℓ_i are simply literals (i.e., a fluent or its negation). This action can be captured by an update template which is schematically summarized in Figure 2(c). For this update model, $sub(\epsilon) = \emptyset$ while

$$sub(\sigma) = \{f \rightarrow \varphi \vee f \mid (o \textbf{ causes } f \textbf{ if } \varphi) \in D\} \cup \{f \rightarrow \neg\varphi \wedge f \mid (o \textbf{ causes } \neg f \textbf{ if } \varphi) \in D\}$$

Intuitively, the event σ denotes the actual world-changing event, seen by all agents witnessing the action execution, while ϵ is the event witnessed by all other agents.

Let us denote this update model by $o(T) = (\mathbf{\Sigma}_o(T), \Gamma_o(T))$, where T is the identification of the pointed Kripke structure in which the update model is performed and o is the name of the action. This behavior is coded in ASP by the following facts:

- The actual event is described by $actual(\sigma, o(T))$
- The collection of events is $\{event(\sigma, o(T)), event(\epsilon, o(T))\}$.
- The accessibility relations among events are described as follows:

$$\begin{array}{ll} acc(Agent, S_1, S_1, o(T)) & \leftarrow S_1 \in \{\sigma, \epsilon\}, obs(Agent, o, T) \\ acc(Agent, \epsilon, \epsilon, o(T)) & \leftarrow obv(Agent, o, T) \\ acc(Agent, \sigma, \epsilon, o(T)) & \leftarrow obv(Agent, o, T) \end{array}$$

- The substitution is described by all facts of the form $(1 \leq i \leq n)$

$$\begin{array}{ll} sub(\sigma, f_i, \tau(\varphi_i \vee f_i), o(T)) & \ell_i \textit{ is the fluent } f_i \\ sub(\sigma, f_i, \tau(\neg\varphi_i \wedge f_i), o(T)) & \ell_i \textit{ is the literal } \neg f_i \end{array}$$

To conclude this section, it is possible to show that, for each type of action described, the following property holds.

Proposition 3. *Let a be an action described by the update model $\eta(T)$ and let (M, s) be a pointed Kripke structure. Let us consider the program $\Pi((M, s), t_1, \eta(M, s), t_2)$. Then for each formula ψ the following holds: for each pointed Kripke structure $(M', s') \in \Phi_D(a, \{(M, s)\})$, $(M', s') \models \psi$ iff there exists an answer set A of $\Pi((M, s), t_1, \eta(M, s), t_2)$ such that $real(x, v) \in A$ and $holds(\tau(\psi), x, v) \in A$.*

4.3 ASP for Reasoning in $m\mathcal{A}_0$

Various forms of reasoning can be realized using the set of rules described earlier. We illustrate some of these next.

Projection. Given a sequence of actions $a_1, \ldots, a_k$ and a pointed Kripke structure (M, s), let us denote with $\Phi^*_D([a_1, \ldots, a_k], (M, s))$ the set of pointed Kripke structures derived from the execution of the given sequence of actions starting in the pointed Kripke structure (M, s). Let us denote with $ut(a_i)$ the update model of the action a_i. Let us generalize the definition of Π given earlier as

$$\begin{array}{rcl}
\Pi^0((M,s),t_0,ut(a_1),t_1,\ldots,ut(a_k),t_k) & = & \alpha\pi \cup \kappa\rho^{t_0}(M,s) \\
R^0((M,s),t_0,ut(a_1),t_1,\ldots,ut(a_k),t_k) & = & t_0 \\
\Pi^j((M,s),t_0,ut(a_1),t_1,\ldots,ut(a_k),t_k) & = & \Pi^{j-1}((M,s),t_0,ut(a_1),t_1,\ldots,ut(a_k),t_k)\cup \\
 & & \upsilon\mu^{t_j}(ut(a_j)) \cup \bigcup_{\varphi\in\Phi(ut(a_j))} \Pi_\varphi^{t_j-1} \cup \\
 & & \{occ(R^{j-1}((M,s),t_0,ut(a_1),t_1,\ldots,ut(a_k),t_k),t_j)\} \\
R^j((M,s),t_0,ut(a_1),t_1,\ldots,ut(a_k),t_k) & = & app(R^{j-1}((M,s),t_0,ut(a_1),t_1,\ldots,ut(a_k),t_k),t_j) \\
\Pi((M,s),t_0,ut(a_1),t_1,\ldots,ut(a_k),t_k) & = & \Pi^k((M,s),t_0,ut(a_1),t_1,\ldots,ut(a_k),t_k)
\end{array}$$

A *projection query* has the form φ **after** $a_1, \ldots, a_k$; the query is entailed w.r.t. (M, s) if for each $(M', s') \in \Phi^*([a_1, \ldots, a_k], (M, s))$ we have that $(M', s') \models \varphi$.

A program to answer the projection query can be realized by adding to $\Pi((M, s), t_0, ut(a_1), t_1, \ldots, ut(a_k), t_k)$ the rules

$$\begin{array}{l}
\leftarrow real(s, R^k((M,s),t_0,ut(a_1),t_1,\ldots,ut(a_k),t_k)), \\
\quad not\ holds(\tau(\varphi), s, R^k((M,s),t_0,ut(a_1),t_1,\ldots,ut(a_k),t_k))
\end{array}$$

Let us denote with $Prj_\varphi((M, s), t_0, ut(a_1), t_1, \ldots, ut(a_k), t_k)$ this program.

Proposition 4. *The program $Prj_\varphi((M, s), t_0, ut(a_1), t_1, \ldots, ut(a_k), t_k)$ has an answer set A iff the projection query φ* **after** *$a_1, \ldots, a_k$ is entailed w.r.t. (M, s).*

Planning. The generalization of projection queries to planning is simple. Let us consider the case of planning with a finite horizon k and let us consider a formula φ representing the planning goal. The rules to generate occurrences of actions

$$\begin{array}{l}
current(t_0, 0). \\
1\{occ(M, A) : action(A)\}1 \leftarrow current(M, T). \\
current(app(M, A), T+1) \leftarrow occ(M, A), current(M, T)
\end{array}$$

The validation of the goal can be described by the constraint

$$\leftarrow current(M, k), real(S, M), holds(\tau(\varphi), S, M).$$

Let us consider the program $Plan_\varphi((M, s), t_0, k)$ containing the following rules:

- The rules $\alpha\pi$;
- The rules $\kappa\rho^{t_0}(M, s)$;

- The rules $\upsilon\mu^{t_i}(ut(a_i))$ for each action a_i with update model $ut(a_i)$;
- The rules $\bigcup_{\phi \in \Phi(ut(a_i))} \Pi^T_\varphi$ for each action a_i; and
- The described rules for action occurrence generation and for goal validation.

Proposition 5. *Let (M, s) be a pointed Kripke structure, an horizon k, and a formula φ. Then, the program $Plan_\varphi(M, s, t_0, k)$ has an answer set iff there is a sequence of actions $a_1, \ldots, a_k$ such that (M, s) entails φ* **after** $a_1, \ldots, a_k$.

4.4 From Theory to Practice

Towards a More Practical ASP Encoding. In this section, we will discuss practical issues that we have to address in order to derive a workable implementation from the ideas presented in the previous sections. We will assume that the initial pointed Kripke structure is given and is encoded following the description in Section 3. The standard components of an ASP program for plan generation are not changed with respect to the description in the previous section. Since we are working with one pointed Kripke structure at a time and the execution of an action in a pointed Kripke structure results in a pointed Kripke structure, the naming of Kripke structures can be simplified by using the time step of the planning problem (Subsection 4.3).

Because the answer set solver `clingo` accepts λ-restricted programs we can identify formulae by themselves, providing that they are defined by the predicate $formula/1$. The following code defines the types of formulae that we will be considered in the program. To make the program λ-restricted, we consider only formulae that contain at most m operators and connectives.

```
2 {formula(F), length(F, 1)}:- fluent(F).
2 {formula(neg(F)), length(neg(F), 1)}:- fluent(F).
2 {formula(knows(A,F)), length(knows(A,F), L+1)}:-
       formula(F), length(F, L), L < m, agent(A).
2 {formula(and(F1,F2)), length(and(F1,F2), L1+L2)}:-
       formula(F1), formula(F2), length(F1, L1),
       length(F2, L2), L1+L2 < m.
2 {formula(or(F1,F2)), length(or(F1,F2), L1+L2)}:-
       formula(F1), formula(F2), length(F1, L1),
       length(F2, L2), L1+L2 < m.
2 {formula(neg(F)), length(neg(F), L+1)}:-
      formula(F), length(F, L), L < m.
```

The encoding of the updates caused by the update models on pointed Kripke structures can also be simplified by observing that there are at most three events (σ, τ, and ϵ, see Subsection 4.2) in each update model. Since the update models corresponding to the actions are known, it is possible to specialize the code that implements the update operations w.r.t these known update models. For example, let us consider the action $open(X)$ from the Strongbox domain. Since this is an ontic action, we deal with two events σ and ϵ. State symbols $o(S, E)$ for the next pointed Kripke structure are computed as follows:

```
state(o(S, sigma),T+1) :-
    occ(open(X), T),
    ontic(open(X)),time(T), T < n,
    state(S, T), connected(S, T),
    holds(has_key(X), S, T).
```

```
state(o(S, epsilon), T+1) :-
    occ(open(X), T),
    ontic(open(X)), time(T),
    T < n, state(S, T),
    connected(S, T).
```

The first rule states that `o(S,sigma)` is a new state symbol of the pointed Kripke structure at time step $T+1$ if S is a state symbol of the structure at time step T and the action $open(X)$ is performed at time T. Note that n denotes the length of the desired plan.

The accessibility relation is defined as follows:

```
r(X,o(S1,sigma),o(S2,sigma),T+1):- time(T), T < n,
    state(o(S1, sigma), T+1), state(o(S2, sigma), T+1),
    obs(X, T),  r(X, S1, S2, T).
r(X, o(S1, epsilon), o(S2, epsilon), T+1):- time(T), T < n,
    state(o(S1, epsilon), T+1), state(o(S2, epsilon), T+1),
    agent(X), r(X, S1, S2, T).
r(X, o(S1, sigma), o(S2, epsilon), T+1):- time(T), T < n,
    state(o(S1, sigma), T+1), state(o(S2, epsilon), T+1),
    obv(X, T), r(X, S1, S2, T).
```

The encoding of the interpretation can also be simplified as follows:

```
holds(F, o(S, sigma), T+1):- time(T), T < n,
    state(o(S, sigma), T+1),
    ontic(open(X)), occ(open(X), T), holds(F, S, T).
holds(opened, o(S, sigma), T+1):- time(T), T < n,
    state(o(S, sigma), T+1), ontic(open(X)), occ(open(X), T).
holds(F, o(S, epsilon), T+1) :- time(T), T < n,
    state(o(S, epsilon), T+1), holds(F, S, T).
```

The first two rules define the interpretation for the new state `o(S, sigma)`. The first one encodes the inertial axiom and the second encodes a positive effect of $open(a)$. The last rule encodes the interpretation for the state `o(S, epsilon)`, which is the same as that of S.

The encoding can be used for two purposes: projection and planning. To verify the executability of an action sequence, we can add the action occurrences as facts and verify whether an answer set exists. To compute a plan, we need to add the goal as a constraint; e.g., for the goal of having a to know the state of the coin and both b and c be oblivious, we can use the following code:

```
goal :- real(S, n), holds(b(a, head), S, n),
  holds(b(b, neg(or(b(a, head), b(a, neg(head))))),S,n),
  holds(b(c, neg(or(b(a, head), b(a, neg(head))))),S,n),
:- not goal.
```

Some Experimental Results. We have experimented the above mentioned encoding with the Strongbox domain used earlier and a more complicated domain, called the Prison domain. In the latter, we have agents a, b, and c, where agent a, a friend of c

(a double agent in the organization of b), is in the custody of an hostile agent b. a needs c's help to escape. a needs to take the key without b knowing about it, and make c aware that he has the key. He cannot do that while b is watching. c can only be aware of a's action if he is watching a. c can make a aware of his presence by making noise (e.g., shouting). a could also look around for c.

All experiments have been performed a Mac OS machine with an Intel Core i7 2.8 GHz processor and 16 GB memory. The codes used in the experiments are available for download. A detailed discussion on the Prison domain can be found in [4]. The ASP solver used for the experiments is `clingo` version 3.0.3 (based on `clasp` version 1.3.5).

Our initial experiments with the code reveal that, even with $m = 3$ (the maximal length of formula), `clingo` uses most of the time for grounding the formulae and the related rules. For example, `clingo` was not able to return a plan for the Strongbox domain goal described earlier (i.e., a is aware of the state of the coin while b and c are not) within 1 hour. To this end, we simplify the encoding using a preprocessing step, which extracts all the formulae that are used in the goal and in the action descriptions, and specializes the encoding to focus exclusively on this set of formulae. With this optimization, `clingo` was able to generate plans in just a few minutes.

In the Strongbox domain, with the initial pointed Kripke structure of Figure 1, the solver was able to generate a total of 12 plans of length 4 (in 25 seconds) for the goal mentioned earlier. The first group of plans consists of two actions for a—aimed at distracting b and c ($distract(a, b)$ and $distract(a, c)$)—an action to open the box ($open(a)$), and then an action to peek into the box ($peek(a)$). The first three actions can be in any order, leading to 8 plans. A sample plan is:

```
occ(distract(a,c),0); occ(open(a),1); occ(distract(a,b),2);
                                      occ(peek(a),3)
```

The other group of plans represents interesting aspects of multi-agent planning. A plan in this group contains a distract action between b and c ($distract(b, c)$ or $distract(c, b)$), a distract action between a and the executor of the previous action, and the $open(a)$ and $peek(a)$ actions. This group contains four plans, e.g.,

```
occ(distract(b,c),0); occ(open(a),1); occ(distract(a,b),2);
                                      occ(peek(a),3)
```

In the Prison domain, we used an initial pointed Kripke structure where a, b, and c know that a is in the custody of b, b is watching a, both a and b are present, and a does not have a key. a and b do not know whether c is present. In the real state of the world, c is present. We experiment with the goal

```
goal :- real(S, n), holds(b(a, has_key(a)),S,n),
  holds(b(c, has_key(a)),S,n),
  holds(b(b, neg(has_key(a))),S,n).
:- not goal.
```

The goal is related to a: obtaining the key, making c aware of this while keeping b in the dark. This requires that c announces his presence ($shouting(c)$) or a looks around for c, a distracts b ($distract(a, b)$) and signals c ($signal(a, c)$), and a takes the key

$(get\_key(a))$. The solver was able to return the first plan within one minute. It found all possible plans in 76 seconds (the problem admits two possible plans).

To test the scalability of the approach, we introduce a new action called $free(c, a, b)$, whose precondition is a conjunction of $B_a(has\_key(a) \wedge present(c))$, $B_c(has\_key(a))$, and $B_{a,c}(\neg looking(b))$ and whose effect is $\neg custody(a, b)$. The minimal plan that achieves the goal $\neg custody(a, b)$ has length 5. The solver is able to generate the first two plans in 627 seconds:

```
occ(shout(c),0); occ(signal(a,c),1); occ(distract(a,b),2);
                    occ(get_key(a),3); occ(free(c,a,b),4)
occ(lookAround(a,c),0); occ(signal(a,c),1); occ(distract(a,b),2);
                    occ(get_key(a),3); occ(free(c,a,b),4)
```

We aborted the computation of all plans for this goal after 30 minutes without being able to identify any additional solutions.

5 Conclusion and Future Work

In this paper, we demonstrated the use of ASP as a technology to model and encode multi-agent planning domains where agents can perform both ontic as well as epistemic actions. The use of ASP enables us to provide a clear semantics to this type of action languages—providing a very high level and executable encoding of actions and their effects on the pointed Kripke structures used to represent the state of the world. ASP allows us also to validate models—supporting the use of different forms of reasoning, such as projection and planning. We illustrated this possibility in two sample domains, with encouraging results.

The work presented in this paper is aimed at laying the foundations for a large breadth investigation in high level action languages for epistemic and ontic multi-agent domains. In particular, there are several aspects in the design of a suitable action language that need to be considered—such as how to embed in the action languages more refined views of visibility of action execution (e.g., allow agents to view agents viewing actions being executed) and how to handle actions related to dishonesty (e.g., telling lies). Another aspect that needs to be considered is the task of planning and/or projection with respect to some initial specification since the present work assumes that the initial state, in the form of a pointed Kripke structure, is given. The experimental steps presented in this paper have also highlighted strengths and weaknesses of ASP in this type of applications. In particular, it is clear that grounding remains a great concern—indeed, in order to obtain an usable program it became necessary to devise an encoding in ASP that restricts the set of formulae to be analyzed—something that would require a smart translator from action theories to ASP. These aspects will be the focus of our future work.

Acknowledgement. Chitta Baral acknowledges the support by ONR-MURI and IARPA. Enrico Pontelli and Tran Cao Son acknowledge the support by NSF-IIS 0812267 grant.

References

1. Baltag, A., Moss, L.: Logics for Epistemic Programs. Synthese (2004)
2. Baral, C.: Knowledge Representation, reasoning, and declarative problem solving with Answer sets. Cambridge University Press, Cambridge (2003)
3. Baral, C., Gelfond, G.: On Representing Actions in Multi-agent Domains. In: Balduccini, M., Son, T.C. (eds.) Gelfond Festschrift. LNCS (LNAI), vol. 6565, pp. 213–232. Springer, Heidelberg (2011)
4. Baral, C., Gelfond, G., Pontelli, E., Son, T.C.: An Action Language for Multi-agent Domains, Technical Report, New Mexico State University (2011)
5. Cox, J.S., Durfee, E.H.: An Efficient Algorithm for Multi-agent Plan Coordination. In: 4th International Joint Conference on Autonomous Agents and Multi-agent Systems (AAMAS 2005), Utrecht, The Netherlands, July 25-29, pp. 828–835. ACM (2005)
6. de Weerdt, M., ter Mors, A., Witteveen, C.: Multi-agent Planning: An Introduction to Planning and Coordination. In: Handouts of the European Agent Summer School, pp. 1–32 (2005)
7. de Weerdt, M., Witteveen, C.: Multi-agent Planning: Problem Properties that Matter. In: Proceedings of the AAAI Spring Symposium on Distributed Plan and Schedule Management, number SS-06-04, pp. 155–156. AAAI (2006)
8. Durfee, E.H.: Distributed Problem Solving and Planning. In: Multi-agent Systems: A Modern Approach to Distributed Artificial Intelligence, pp. 121–164. MIT Press (1999)
9. Fagin, R., Halpern, J., Moses, Y., Vardi, M.: Reasoning about Knowledge. The MIT press (1995)
10. Gelfond, M., Lifschitz, V.: The Stable Model Semantics for Logic Programming. In: Logic Programming: Proceedings of the Fifth International Conf. and Symp., pp. 1070–1080 (1988)
11. Cox, J.S., Durfee, E.H., Bartold, T.: A Distributed Framework for Solving the Multi-agent Plan Coordination Problem. In: AAMAS, pp. 821–827. ACM Press (2005)
12. Marek, V., Truszczyński, M.: Stable Models as an Alternative Logic Programming Paradigm. In: The Logic Programming Paradigm: a 25-year Perspective, pp. 375–398. Springer (1999)
13. Niemelä, I.: Logic Programming with Stable Model Semantics as a Constraint Programming Paradigm. Annals of Mathematics and Artificial Intelligence 25(3,4), 241–273 (1999)
14. Pontelli, E., Son, T.C., Baral, C., Gelfond, G.: Logic Programming for Finding Models in the Logics of Knowledge and its Applications: A Case Study. Theory and Practice of Logic Programming 10(4-6), 675–690 (2010)
15. van Benthem, J., van Eijck, J., Kooi, B.P.: Logics of communication and change. Inf. Comput. 204(11), 1620–1662 (2006)
16. van der Hoek, W., Wooldridge, M.: Tractable Multi-agent Planning for Epistemic Goals. In: Proceedings of the First International Joint Conference on Autonomous Agents & Multiagent Systems, AAMAS 2002, Bologna, Italy, July 15-19, pp. 1167–1174. ACM (2002)

A Language for Default Reasoning about Actions

Hannes Strass[1] and Michael Thielscher[2]

[1] Computer Science Institute, University of Leipzig
strass@informatik.uni-leipzig.de
[2] School of Computer Science and Engineering, The University of New South Wales
mit@cse.unsw.edu.au

Abstract. Action languages allow for a concise representation of actions and their effects while at the same time being easily readable and writable for humans. In this paper, we introduce $\mathcal{D}$, the first action language that centres around *default* reasoning about actions and change. It allows to specify normal Reiter-style defaults and provides a semantics that has at its core the groundedness of conclusions. This is not only of use for default conclusions, but also for $\mathcal{D}$'s solution to the ramification problem. Additionally, our language does not suffer from Yale Shooting-like counterexamples since it uses different mechanisms for default persistence and default change. The answer set programming paradigm is used as the basis of $\mathcal{D}$'s implementation, which we prove sound and complete with respect to the language's semantics. We finally present a showcase application for the language: its straightforward solution to the qualification problem.

1 Introduction

Action languages are simple declarative languages for describing actions and their effects on the world. The first ever action language, $\mathcal{A}$ [1], was introduced in 1993 by Vladimir Lifschitz, to whom we dedicate this article on the occasion of his 65th birthday, and his colleague Michael Gelfond to enhance the traditionally example-oriented mode of operation of reasoning about actions research.

This original language $\mathcal{A}$ allowed only for very basic action descriptions, and so was soon extended to $\mathcal{B}$ [2], which handles indirect effects through static laws. A further extension came with $\mathcal{C}$ [3], enabling convenient description of concurrency and non-determinism. The language $\mathcal{E}$ [4] then introduced an explicit notion of time into action languages, which had hitherto only possessed an implicit time structure defined through state transition systems.

In this paper, we introduce the action language $\mathcal{D}$ for *default* reasoning about actions. It is a useful addition to the existing $\mathcal{A}$, $\mathcal{B}$, $\mathcal{C}$ and $\mathcal{E}$ – but not just as "yet another action language": it is the first language that centres around default reasoning about actions. We argue that this is of practical relevance for agents with incomplete knowledge about their domain.

Two existing action languages do allow for some forms of default reasoning, $\mathcal{C}+$ [5] and $\mathcal{K}$ [6]. Alas, in both languages defaults can be at odds with the solution of the frame problem, since the same mechanism is used for static defaults

E. Erdem et al. (Eds.): Correct Reasoning, LNCS 7265, pp. 527–542, 2012.

and temporal persistence defaults. We have found that certain intuitive ways of modelling a domain do not yield the intuitively expected answers: As an example, imagine a simple domain where two inertial fluents, Bird and Flies, express whether there is a bird in the domain and whether it flies. We want to state that birds fly by default and look at the interaction of this default with temporal persistence. A seemingly straightforward $\mathcal{C}+$ specification of this domain is

inertial Bird
inertial Flies
default Flies **if** Bird

Now consider an abnormal initial time point 0 where Bird is true and Flies is false, $\{0{:}\mathsf{Bird}, 0{:}\neg\mathsf{Flies}\}$. What holds at the next time point when no action occurs at 0? Intuition suggests that the world does not change when nothing happens, hence ¬Flies should still hold. However, $\mathcal{C}+$ does not conform with this intuition in that it admits – along with the model where Flies still does not hold after waiting (due to persistence) – an additional model where the abnormal bird magically learns to fly (by default).[1] In $\mathcal{D}$, the straightforward specification of this simple domain will yield the intuitively expected inference that abnormality persists when not caused otherwise.

Another observation we made is that some conclusions in $\mathcal{C}+$ circularly justify themselves and are thus not grounded: The statements

default Rain **if** Wet
default Wet **if** Rain

say that rain and wet grass usually go hand in hand. For time point 0, they expand to the formulas $0{:}\mathsf{Rain} \Leftarrow 0{:}\mathsf{Rain} \wedge 0{:}\mathsf{Wet}$ and $0{:}\mathsf{Wet} \Leftarrow 0{:}\mathsf{Wet} \wedge 0{:}\mathsf{Rain}$ of nonmonotonic causal logic [5]. If nothing further is known about the time point, $\{0{:}\mathsf{Rain}, 0{:}\mathsf{Wet}\}$ is a model for the two formulas, where rain and wet grass appear without any evidence for either. In contrast, all conclusions in $\mathcal{D}$ are grounded in the sense that they have a non-cyclic derivation from definite knowledge. For the same reason, $\mathcal{D}$ also offers a solution to the ramification problem that can deal with cyclic effect dependencies.[2]

Together with our new action language $\mathcal{D}$, we introduce a query language for prediction. We present $\mathcal{D}$'s implementation, which uses answer set programming (ASP) as back-end, and is provably sound and complete for the semantics of $\mathcal{D}$. Finally, we demonstrate the capabilities of $\mathcal{D}$ by developing a solution for the qualification problem [7] entirely inside the language itself.

---

[1] Of course, this does not suggest that the domain cannot otherwise be modelled in $\mathcal{C}+$. If the cause of the bird's abnormality is explicitly named in the language (say, by inertial fluent AbBird) and 0:AbBird is added to the domain along with the static law **caused** ¬Flies **if** AbBird, then $\mathcal{C}+$ treats the example right.

[2] It is even possible to use more general ramification rules than the ones considered here. Ramification is however not our main topic here, so we keep that simple.

2 Action Language $\mathcal{D}$

We assume a sorted logical signature that contains the sorts FLUENT (for domain properties that change over time) and ACTION (for actions that affect the state of the world). Like its predecessor $\mathcal{A}$, the language $\mathcal{D}$ assumes inertia for all fluent properties unless there is an explicit cause for change.

2.1 Syntax

A specification of an action domain in $\mathcal{D}$ consists of two parts: the first part contains general knowledge about the domain – action preconditions, action effects, ramifications, state defaults. The second part contains information about the initial time point of a specific domain instance. The vocabulary to describe a domain is given by non-empty sets FLUENT and ACTION of constant symbols.

Definition 1. *Assume a fixed logical signature with sorts* FLUENT *and* ACTION. *For a fluent F, a* fluent literal *is of the form F or $\neg F$. Define $\overline{F} \stackrel{\text{def}}{=} \neg F$ and $\overline{\neg F} \stackrel{\text{def}}{=} F$, and extend this notation to sets of fluent literals.*

Let A be an ACTION, *F be a* FLUENT, *K, L be fluent literals and C be a finite set of fluent literals. A* statement *can be:*

- *a* precondition statement*:* <u>`possible`</u> A <u>`if`</u> C
- *a* direct effect statement*:* <u>`action`</u> A <u>`causes`</u> L <u>`if`</u> C
- *an* indirect effect statement*:* <u>`effect`</u> K <u>`causes`</u> L <u>`if`</u> C
- *a* default statement*:* <u>`normally`</u> L <u>`if`</u> C

An initial state axiom *is of the form* <u>`initially`</u> L. *An* action domain specification, *or* domain *for short, is a finite set $\Sigma = \Upsilon \cup \Omega$ where Υ is a set of statements and Ω is a set of initial state axioms.*

In statements of the above form, we will refer to literal L as the *consequent.* If $C = \emptyset$ for a statement, we omit the <u>`if`</u> part in writing. To illustrate $\mathcal{D}$, we use the following running example throughout the paper.

Example 2 (Swipe Card Domain). Imagine an office building where some parts have restricted access through swipe cards. It is possible for an agent who has a card to swipe it through the reader. Normally, the agent has a card, and swiping the card through the reader unlocks the door. Subsequently pushing an unlocked door opens it, unless it is jammed, which may be caused by pushing a locked door. In $\mathcal{D}$, the domain specification of this environment is as follows:

$$
\begin{aligned}
\Upsilon_{\mathbb{D}} = \{&\underline{\texttt{possible}}\ \mathsf{Swipe}\ \underline{\texttt{if}}\ \{\mathsf{HasCard}\},\\
&\underline{\texttt{normally}}\ \mathsf{HasCard},\\
&\underline{\texttt{action}}\ \mathsf{Swipe}\ \underline{\texttt{causes}}\ \mathsf{Swiped},\\
&\underline{\texttt{normally}}\ \neg\mathsf{Locked}\ \underline{\texttt{if}}\ \mathsf{Swiped},\\
&\underline{\texttt{action}}\ \mathsf{Push}\ \underline{\texttt{causes}}\ \mathsf{Open}\ \underline{\texttt{if}}\ \{\neg\mathsf{Locked}, \neg\mathsf{Jammed}\},\\
&\underline{\texttt{action}}\ \mathsf{Push}\ \underline{\texttt{causes}}\ \mathsf{Jammed}\ \underline{\texttt{if}}\ \{\mathsf{Locked}\}\}
\end{aligned}
$$

There is no precondition statement for Push, we thus take it to be the trivial one – possible Push if $\emptyset$. At an initial time point, the door is locked and not jammed, and the card has not been swiped:

$$\Omega_{\mathbb{D}} = \{\underline{\texttt{initially}}\ \mathsf{Locked}, \underline{\texttt{initially}}\ \neg\mathsf{Jammed}, \underline{\texttt{initially}}\ \neg\mathsf{Swiped}\}$$

This concludes the specification of the swipe card domain $\Sigma_{\mathbb{D}} = \Upsilon_{\mathbb{D}} \cup \Omega_{\mathbb{D}}$.

$\mathcal{D}$ domains state how the world normally behaves. Due to their syntax being close to natural language, we already have an intuitive understanding of their meaning. In the next section, we will develop a mathematical semantics for $\mathcal{D}$.

2.2 Semantics

Traditional action languages use transition systems to interpret action domains and a Tarski-style entailment relation over so-called histories to solve reasoning problems in these domains [2]. In $\mathcal{D}$, we pay special attention to the *groundedness* of conclusions and thus use a fixed-point based semantics much in the spirit of default logic [8]. The time structure of $\mathcal{D}$'s semantics as defined below is branching. However, this is only for the purpose of this paper and all the definitions we give here can be adjusted to the case of more general time structures.

Definition 3. *Assume a fixed logical signature with sorts* FLUENT *and* ACTION. *An* action sequence α *is a word over the alphabet of* ACTIONs*, that is, either* ε *(the empty sequence) or of the form* $\alpha' A$ *for an action sequence* α'.

A scenario S *is a set of pairs* (α, L) *where* α *is an action sequence and* L *is a fluent literal. A scenario* S *is* consistent *iff* $\{(\alpha_1, F), (\alpha_2, \neg F)\} \subseteq S$ *implies* $\alpha_1 \neq \alpha_2$ *for all fluents* F.

Intuitively, a pair (α, L) in a scenario means that L holds after execution of α. For a scenario S and an action sequence α, we use the notation $S(\alpha) \stackrel{\text{def}}{=} \{L \mid (\alpha, L) \in S\}$ to refer to the set of fluent literals to which α is related. Read as a mapping, the alternative notation $S(\alpha)$ assigns to each action sequence a (possibly incomplete) knowledge state [6], where incompleteness of the state only reflects incomplete knowledge about the real world. Consider again the example:

Example 2 (Continued). In the first scenario S_1, everything works as expected: swiping the card unlocks an initially not jammed door which is then opened by pushing it. Had the agent initially pushed the locked door, it would be jammed.

$$\begin{aligned}
S_1(\varepsilon) &= \{\mathsf{HasCard}, \neg\mathsf{Open}, \mathsf{Locked}, \neg\mathsf{Jammed}, \neg\mathsf{Swiped}\} \\
S_1(\mathsf{Swipe}) &= \{\mathsf{HasCard}, \neg\mathsf{Open}, \neg\mathsf{Locked}, \neg\mathsf{Jammed}, \mathsf{Swiped}\} \\
S_1(\mathsf{SwipePush}) &= \{\mathsf{HasCard}, \mathsf{Open}, \neg\mathsf{Locked}, \neg\mathsf{Jammed}, \mathsf{Swiped}\} \\
S_1(\mathsf{Push}) &= \{\mathsf{HasCard}, \neg\mathsf{Open}, \mathsf{Locked}, \mathsf{Jammed}, \neg\mathsf{Swiped}\}
\end{aligned}$$

In scenario S_2, the card reader does not work and the door remains locked:

$$\begin{aligned}
S_2(\varepsilon) &= \{\mathsf{HasCard}, \neg\mathsf{Open}, \mathsf{Locked}, \neg\mathsf{Jammed}, \neg\mathsf{Swiped}\} \\
S_2(\mathsf{Swipe}) &= \{\mathsf{HasCard}, \neg\mathsf{Open}, \mathsf{Locked}, \neg\mathsf{Jammed}, \mathsf{Swiped}\}
\end{aligned}$$

While scenarios talk about states of the world after execution of actions, there is yet no mention of changes due to action effects. In the following, we define how to determine these effects from the statements of a domain specification. This is easy in the case of direct and indirect effects. For the case of default effects, we use an additional scenario T, which represents a particular context against which default conclusions are checked. We first define when statements are considered applicable in a scenario S with respect to context scenario T.

Definition 4. *Let Σ be a domain, S, T be scenarios for Σ's signature, α be an action sequence and A an action with precondition statement* <u>`possible`</u> *A* <u>`if`</u> *P. A statement $\sigma \in \Sigma$ is* applicable in S after αA *iff $P \subseteq S(\alpha)$ and*

- *$\sigma =$ <u>`action`</u> A <u>`causes`</u> L <u>`if`</u> C and $C \subseteq S(\alpha)$; or*
- *$\sigma =$ <u>`effect`</u> K <u>`causes`</u> L <u>`if`</u> C and $\overline{K} \in S(\alpha)$, $K \in S(\alpha A)$, $C \subseteq S(\alpha)$; or*
- *$\sigma =$ <u>`normally`</u> L <u>`if`</u> C and (a) $C \subseteq S(\alpha A)$, (b) $\overline{L} \notin T(\alpha A)$ and (c) one of $\overline{C} \cap S(\alpha) \neq \emptyset$ or $L \in S(\alpha)$.*

The direct effects $\Delta_\Sigma^{Dir}(S, \alpha A)$, indirect effects $\Delta_\Sigma^{Ind}(S, \alpha A)$ *and* default effects $\Delta_{\Sigma,T}^{Def}(S, \alpha A)$ of A after α in S *are the sets of consequent literals L of direct and indirect effect and default statements from Σ that are applicable in S after αA.*

$$\Delta_{\Sigma,T}(S, \alpha A) \stackrel{\text{def}}{=} \Delta_\Sigma^{Dir}(S, \alpha A) \cup \Delta_\Sigma^{Ind}(S, \alpha A) \cup \Delta_{\Sigma,T}^{Def}(S, \alpha A)$$

The set $\Delta_{\Sigma,T}(S, \alpha A)$ contains all the effects of the action A when it is executed in the state $S(\alpha)$ of domain Σ. Direct effects occur whenever their precondition C was satisfied in the starting state. Indirect effects materialise when the precondition C was satisfied and additionally the trigger literal K changed its truth value during action execution. A default effect L appears whenever the precondition C was satisfied after executing A, the effect is consistent with the context scenario T and the starting state was not abnormal with respect to this default. Note that default effects are the only ones that require the context scenario T.

Example 2 (Continued). For scenario S_1, where the world behaves normally, we obtain $\Delta_\Sigma^{Dir}(S_1, \mathsf{Swipe}) = \{\mathsf{Swiped}\}$ and $\Delta_\Sigma^{Ind}(S_1, \mathsf{Swipe}) = \emptyset$ along with $\Delta_{\Sigma,S_1}^{Def}(S_1, \mathsf{Swipe}) = \{\neg\mathsf{Locked}\}$. But note that using S_2 as a context scenario yields $\Delta_{\Sigma,S_2}^{Def}(S_1, \mathsf{Swipe}) = \emptyset$, since $\mathsf{Locked} \in S_2(\mathsf{Swipe})$. For the empty scenario we have $\Delta_\Sigma^{Dir}(\emptyset, \mathsf{Swipe}) = \emptyset$ since the action precondition $\mathsf{HasCard}$ of Swipe is not satisfied.

Next, we define the set of *non-effects* of an action. Intuitively, the set $\Delta_{\Sigma,T}(S, \alpha A)$ just defined contains all the fluent literals that are guaranteed to hold in S after αA. The non-effects of an action, on the other hand, will contain all the fluent literals that are guaranteed to never possibly hold. For example, if for a fluent F there is no indirect effect statement with F as effect, no default statement that concludes F and also no direct effect statement with effect F for an action A, then we can be sure that A will never make F true. The next definition formalises this intuition. Note that "inapplicable" below is not the negation of applicable – it rather means "not applicable now or ever."

In addition, (in)applicability of a statement is only meaningful for time-points that are connected by applicable actions, that is, actions whose preconditions are fulfilled in the starting state.

Definition 5. *Let Σ be a domain, S be a scenario for Σ's signature, α be an action sequence and A be an action. A statement $\sigma \in \Sigma$ is* inapplicable in S after αA *iff one of*

- $\sigma = \underline{\texttt{action}}\ A\ \underline{\texttt{causes}}\ L\ \underline{\texttt{if}}\ C$ *and* $\overline{C} \cap S(\alpha) \neq \emptyset$*; or*
- $\sigma = \underline{\texttt{effect}}\ K\ \underline{\texttt{causes}}\ L\ \underline{\texttt{if}}\ C$ *and one of: (a)* $K \in S(\alpha)$ *or (b)* $\overline{K} \in S(\alpha A)$ *or (c)* $\overline{C} \cap S(\alpha) \neq \emptyset$*; or*
- $\sigma = \underline{\texttt{normally}}\ L\ \underline{\texttt{if}}\ C$ *and one of (a)* $\overline{C} \cap S(\alpha A) \neq \emptyset$ *or (b)* $\overline{L} \in S(\alpha A)$ *or (c)* $C \subseteq S(\alpha)$ *and* $\overline{L} \in S(\alpha)$*.*

The non-effects of A after α in S *are* $\Psi_\Sigma^{Dir}(S, \alpha A)$, $\Psi_\Sigma^{Ind}(S, \alpha A)$ *and* $\Psi_\Sigma^{Def}(S, \alpha A)$, *defined as containing those literals L for which all direct and indirect effect and default statements with consequent L are inapplicable in S after αA. Then*

$$\Psi_\Sigma(S, \alpha A) \stackrel{\text{def}}{=} \Psi_\Sigma^{Dir}(S, \alpha A) \cap \Psi_\Sigma^{Ind}(S, \alpha A) \cap \Psi_\Sigma^{Def}(S, \alpha A)$$

In particular, $\Psi_\Sigma(S, \alpha A)$ will contain a literal L if there is no statement with consequent L. With the presumptions of the previous definition, we finally use the set of non-effects to solve the frame problem: whenever we know F holds before executing A and A cannot make F false, it will still hold afterwards. We thus conclude persistence only in light of evidence that change is impossible.

Definition 6. *Let Σ be a domain, S be a scenario for Σ's signature, α be an action sequence and A an action with precondition statement* $\underline{\texttt{possible}}\ A\ \underline{\texttt{if}}\ P$*. The* persisting fluents of A after α in S *are*

$$\Delta_\Sigma^{Frame}(S, \alpha A) \stackrel{\text{def}}{=} \left\{(\alpha A, L) \;\middle|\; (\alpha, L) \in S, P \subseteq S(\alpha), \overline{L} \in \Psi_\Sigma(S, \alpha A)\right\}$$

This very cautious treatment of persistence is rooted in allowing incomplete knowledge while dealing with defaults. If we allowed to conclude persistence solely on the fact that the contrary effect did not occur in the context scenario, then undesired interaction between persistence and defaults would be supported as described in the introduction. Taken together, the two previous definitions constitute $\mathcal{D}$'s solution to the frame problem in the presence of defaults.

Example 2 (Continued). In S_1, $\underline{\texttt{action}}$ Push $\underline{\texttt{causes}}$ Jammed $\underline{\texttt{if}}$ $\{\mathsf{Locked}\}$ is inapplicable after $\mathsf{SwipePush}$ since $\neg\mathsf{Locked} \in S_1(\mathsf{Swipe})$, which implies that $\mathsf{Jammed} \in \Psi_\Sigma^{Dir}(S_1, \mathsf{SwipePush})$. Since there are no indirect effect or default statements with consequent Jammed, we get $\mathsf{Jammed} \in \Psi_\Sigma(S, \mathsf{SwipePush})$, which means that Jammed is a non-effect of the action Push after Swipe. Now $\neg\mathsf{Jammed}$ holds after Push in S_1 – formally, $\neg\mathsf{Jammed} \in S_1(\mathsf{Push})$ – and therefore $\neg\mathsf{Jammed} \in \Delta_{\Sigma,S_1}^{Frame}(S_1, \mathsf{SwipePush})$.

The next definition provides the main "workhorse" for $\mathcal{D}$'s semantics. It is an operator that takes a scenario as argument and transforms it into another scenario using statements and axioms from an action domain specification. We will see later that this operator corresponds to the one-step consequence operator from logic programming. First, the set Δ_Ω puts together the information about the initial state of the domain. Then, $\Delta^{\alpha}_{\Sigma,T}(S)$ computes the additional domain information about action sequence α that can be derived from S and the statements in the domain. There, $\Delta^{\varepsilon}_{\Sigma,T}(S)$ applies default statements to the initial state of S, while $\Delta^{\alpha A}_{\Sigma,T}(S)$ computes all pairs of action sequences and fluent literals that hold due to application of action A after α in S – be they direct effects, indirect effects, default effects or persisting fluents. Finally, $\Gamma_{\Sigma,T}(S)$ accumulates the world knowledge and puts it into the resulting scenario. The additional scenario T is the context against which default application is checked.

Definition 7. *Let $\Sigma = \Upsilon \cup \Omega$ be a $\mathcal{D}$ action domain specification and S and T be scenarios.*

$$\begin{aligned}
\Delta_\Omega &\stackrel{\text{def}}{=} \{(\varepsilon, L) \mid \underline{\texttt{initially}}\ L \in \Omega\} \\
\Delta^{\varepsilon}_{\Sigma,T}(S) &\stackrel{\text{def}}{=} \left\{(\varepsilon, L) \,\middle|\, \underline{\texttt{normally}}\ L\ \underline{\texttt{if}}\ C \in \Sigma, C \subseteq S(\varepsilon),\ \overline{L} \notin T(\varepsilon)\right\} \\
\Delta^{\alpha A}_{\Sigma,T}(S) &\stackrel{\text{def}}{=} \left\{(\alpha A, L) \mid L \in \Delta_{\Sigma,T}(S, \alpha A)\right\} \cup \Delta^{Frame}_{\Sigma}(S, \alpha A) \\
\Gamma_{\Sigma,T}(S) &\stackrel{\text{def}}{=} \Delta_\Omega \cup \bigcup_{\alpha \in \text{ACTION}^*} \Delta^{\alpha}_{\Sigma,T}(S)
\end{aligned}$$

It is tedious but not hard to show that $\Gamma_{\Sigma,T}$ is a monotone operator for any given Σ, T. We are now ready to define *possible scenarios*, the central notion of $\mathcal{D}$'s semantics. As we will see later on, it corresponds to the notion of an answer set of a logic program. A possible scenario can be reconstructed from the initial state specification using the domain rules at hand.

Definition 8. *Let Σ be a domain. A scenario S is* possible for Σ *iff it is consistent and the least fixed point of $\Gamma_{\Sigma,S}$.*

It is a direct consequence of this definition that possible scenarios of a given domain Σ need not be unique and need not necessarily exist at all.

Example 2 (Continued). Our example scenario S_1 for the swipe card domain can be extended to a scenario S_1^* that is possible for $\Sigma_{▯}$ by repeatedly applying $\Gamma_{\Sigma_{▯},S_1}$ until reaching a fixed point. S_2, on the other hand, cannot be extended to a possible scenario. Roughly, one cannot explain $\mathsf{Locked} \in S_2(\mathsf{Swipe}) \subseteq S_2^*(\mathsf{Swipe})$ for any potential candidate S_2^*: there is no statement with consequent Locked, hence persistence would be the only possibility. However, the default statement $\underline{\texttt{normally}}$ $\neg\mathsf{Locked}$ $\underline{\texttt{if}}$ Swiped is not inapplicable after Swipe in S_2^*, thus $\neg\mathsf{Locked} \notin \Psi_{\Sigma_{▯}}(S_2^*, \mathsf{Swipe})$. The intuition here is that in S_2 the world does not behave normally: the default effect of unlocking the door might materialise, but has not done so in the context. Indeed, S_1^* is the only possible scenario of $\Sigma_{▯}$.

Our action language $\mathcal{D}$ shares with its predecessors $\mathcal{A}$ and $\mathcal{B}$ the principle that the semantics solves the frame problem [2].[3] Domain specifications in $\mathcal{A}$ consist solely in effect statements (written as A **causes** L **if** C), and the semantics is defined by a state transition system that obeys these effect laws and otherwise assumes inertia. Lack of space does not permit to go into details, but it is easy to verify that $\mathcal{D}$ is a proper generalisation of $\mathcal{A}$ in the following sense.

Theorem 9. *Consider a domain in which all statements are of the form* <u>action</u> A <u>causes</u> L <u>if</u> C*, then any possible scenario (in the sense of* $\mathcal{D}$*) corresponds to a sequence of state transitions (in the sense of* $\mathcal{A}$*) and vice versa.*

2.3 Query Answering

In $\mathcal{D}$, we do not ask what definitely holds after a sequence of actions in a domain, but instead what *normally* holds. We next introduce the *normality* version of the query language $\mathcal{P}$ [2].

Definition 10. *Let* Σ *be a* $\mathcal{D}$ *action domain description,* α *be an action sequence and* L *be a fluent literal. A* query *is of the form* <u>normally</u> L <u>after</u> α*. We say that* Σ entails *the query and write* $\Sigma \mathrel{|\!\approx}$ <u>normally</u> L <u>after</u> α *if and only if* $L \in S(\alpha)$ *for all possible scenarios* S *of* Σ*.*

When solving projection problems for a domain Σ, we specify an initial state and then ask what is true after a sequence of actions has been performed.

Example 2 (Continued). Possible queries about the swipe card domain $\Sigma_{\mathbb{D}}$ are "does the agent initially have a swipe card?" – <u>normally</u> HasCard <u>after</u> ε, or "is the door open after swiping the card and pushing the door?" – <u>normally</u> Open <u>after</u> SwipePush. Both queries are entailed by $\Sigma_{\mathbb{D}}$ since they hold in the only possible scenario S_1.

3 Implementation

We now present the implementation of action language $\mathcal{D}$. It is based on logic programming, more specifically the answer set semantics, which has also been conceived by Vladimir Lifschitz together with his colleague Michael Gelfond [9]. The translation we define below transforms $\mathcal{D}$ action domain specifications into extended logic programs. These rules will contain first-order variables, thereby representing the set of the rule's well-sorted ground instances. Before delving into the technical details, we recall the necessary notions.

Definition 11. *Let* $\mathfrak{P}$ *be a propositional signature. An* extended logic program rule *is of the form*

$$L_0 \leftarrow L_1, \ldots, L_m, \mathit{not}\ L_{m+1}, \ldots, \mathit{not}\ L_{m+n} \tag{1}$$

[3] Language $\mathcal{C}$ deviates from this principle in that it assumes explicit inertia statements to be included in a domain specification [3].

where $L_0, L_1, \ldots, L_{m+n}$ *are literals over* $\mathfrak{P}$ *and* $m, n \geq 0$. *A program rule is* definite *iff* $n = 0$. *For a set* P *of definite rules and a set* M *of literals, define*

$$\Gamma_P(M) \stackrel{\text{def}}{=} \{L_0 \mid L_0 \leftarrow L_1, \ldots, L_m \in P, \{L_1, \ldots, L_m\} \subseteq M\}$$

For a set P *of extended logic program rules and a set* M *of literals, define the* Gelfond-Lifschitz reduct P^M *as the logic program obtained from* P *by*

1. *eliminating each rule containing an expression not* L *with* $L \in M$, *and*
2. *deleting all expressions not* L *from the remaining clauses.*

M *is an* answer set for P *iff* M *is consistent and the least fixed point of* Γ_{P^M}.

Note that this definition of answer sets requires consistency, while [9] admitted the set of all literals as an answer set for inconsistent programs. There will be no difference for query entailment, since this depends on containment in *all* answer sets. Additionally, in practice we are naturally only interested in possible *consistent* belief states for an agent.

For specifying the extended logic program P_Σ with variables for a domain Σ, we assume a sorted, first-order logical language Π. To the sorts FLUENT and ACTION used by a $\mathcal{D}$ domain, we add the sort TIME for time-points along with the predicates $Holds(f, t)$ (saying that fluent f is true at time-point t) and $Poss(a, s, t)$ (saying that it is possible to execute an action from time-point s to t). The notation $(\neg)F[\tau]$ for a fluent F and term τ : TIME abbreviates $(\neg)Holds(F, \tau)$. For a set $C = \{L_1, \ldots, L_m\}$ of fluent literals, $C[\tau]$ denotes the rule body $L_1[\tau], \ldots, L_m[\tau]$. We use a term-based encoding of action sequences in the logic program: for an action sequence α, its *ending time-point* τ_α is defined inductively by $\tau_\varepsilon \stackrel{\text{def}}{=} \varepsilon$ and $\tau_{\alpha A} \stackrel{\text{def}}{=} \tau_\alpha \cdot A$.

The answer set program defined below implements the principle of universal causation by reifying possible causes. In accord with $\mathcal{D}$'s semantics (cf. Definition 7), there is a pair of predicates for each type of effect: $DirT(f, a, s, t)$ and $DirF(f, a, s, t)$, e.g., express that f is a positive (negative) direct effect of action a from s to t. $Dir(L, a, s, t)$ for a fluent literal L then abbreviates $DirF(F, a, s, t)$ if $L = \neg F$ for a fluent F and $DirT(L, a, s, t)$ otherwise. Predicates $Frame(L, s, t)$, $Ind(L, s, t)$ and $Def(L, s, t)$ are used for the other causes.

The effect rules below now simply say that a fluent holds (or does not hold) after an action was possible leading to the time-point if there was a cause for the fluent to have its respective truth value. These causes, in turn, are derived from additional rules: for persistence, two special rules expressing what persistence means; the rules for direct effects are created from $\mathcal{D}$ direct effect statements and implement an explanation closure assumption; default effects are derived by rules using negation as failure. Disjunction ";" in rule bodies is syntactic sugar for multiplying out its arguments into multiple rules with the same head.

Definition 12. *Let* Υ *be a set of statements and* f : FLUENT, a : ACTION, s, t : TIME *be fresh variables and assume w.l.o.g.* $C = \{C_1, \ldots, C_n\}$ *for sets of fluent literals. The extended logic program* P_Υ *contains the following.*

For each <u>`possible`</u> A <u>`if`</u> $C \in \Upsilon$, *the rules*

$$Poss(A, s, s \cdot A) \leftarrow C[s] \tag{2}$$
$$\neg Poss(A, s, s \cdot A) \leftarrow \overline{C_1}[s]; \ldots; \overline{C_n}[s] \tag{3}$$

For each <u>`action`</u> A <u>`causes`</u> L <u>`if`</u> $C \in \Upsilon$, *the rules*

$$Dir(L, A, s, t) \leftarrow Poss(A, s, t),\ C[s] \tag{4}$$
$$\neg Dir(L, A, s, t) \leftarrow \overline{C_1}[s]; \ldots; \overline{C_n}[s] \tag{5}$$

For each <u>`effect`</u> K <u>`causes`</u> L <u>`if`</u> $C \in \Upsilon$, *the rules*

$$Ind(L, s, t) \leftarrow Poss(a, s, t),\ \overline{K}[s],\ K[t],\ C[s] \tag{6}$$
$$\neg Ind(L, s, t) \leftarrow K[s]; \overline{K}[t]; \overline{C_1}[s]; \ldots; \overline{C_n}[s] \tag{7}$$

For each <u>`normally`</u> L <u>`if`</u> $C \in \Upsilon$, *the rules*

$$L[\varepsilon] \leftarrow C[\varepsilon],\ not\ \overline{L}[\varepsilon] \tag{8}$$
$$Def(L, s, t) \leftarrow Poss(a, s, t),\ C[t],\ (\overline{C_1}[s]; \ldots; \overline{C_n}[s]; L[s]),\ not\ \overline{L}[t] \tag{9}$$
$$\neg Def(L, s, t) \leftarrow \overline{C_1}[t]; \ldots; \overline{C_n}[t]; \overline{L}[t]; (C[s],\ \overline{L}[s]) \tag{10}$$

Finally, the rules

$$\begin{aligned} FrameT(f, s, t) \leftarrow{} & Poss(a, s, t),\ Holds(f, s), \\ & \neg DirF(f, a, s, t),\ \neg IndF(f, s, t),\ \neg DefF(f, s, t) \end{aligned} \tag{11}$$
$$\begin{aligned} FrameF(f, s, t) \leftarrow{} & Poss(a, s, t),\ \neg Holds(f, s), \\ & \neg DirT(f, a, s, t),\ \neg IndT(f, s, t),\ \neg DefT(f, s, t) \end{aligned} \tag{12}$$
$$\begin{aligned} Holds(f, t) \leftarrow{} & FrameT(f, s, t); DirT(f, a, s, t); \\ & IndT(f, s, t); DefT(f, s, t) \end{aligned} \tag{13}$$
$$\begin{aligned} \neg Holds(f, t) \leftarrow{} & FrameF(f, s, t); DirF(f, a, s, t); \\ & IndF(f, s, t); DefF(f, s, t) \end{aligned} \tag{14}$$

along with facts $\neg Dir(L, A, s, t)$ *for each* A : ACTION *and fluent literal* L *without direct effect statement; and facts* $\neg Ind(L, s, t)$ *and* $\neg Def(L, s, t)$ *for all fluent literals* L *that do not appear as consequent of an indirect effect statement or default statement, respectively.*

As a last but one step, we define how to transform a set Ω of $\mathcal{D}$ axioms into a set P_Ω of ground facts: initial state axioms just become ground *Holds* literals in the initial time-point ε.

Definition 13. *Let* Ω *be a set of* $\mathcal{D}$ *axioms.* $P_\Omega \stackrel{\text{def}}{=} \{L[\varepsilon] \mid$ <u>`initially`</u> $L \in \Omega\}$.

Example 2 (Continued). For the swipe card domain $\Upsilon_{\mathbb{D}}$, the translation yields

$$
\begin{aligned}
Poss(\mathsf{Swipe}, s, s \cdot \mathsf{Swipe}) &\leftarrow Holds(\mathsf{HasCard}, s) \\
\neg Poss(\mathsf{Swipe}, s, s \cdot \mathsf{Swipe}) &\leftarrow \neg Holds(\mathsf{HasCard}, s) \\
Poss(\mathsf{Push}, s, s \cdot \mathsf{Push}) & \\
DirT(\mathsf{Swiped}, \mathsf{Swipe}, s, t) &\leftarrow Poss(\mathsf{Swipe}, s, t) \\
DirT(\mathsf{Open}, \mathsf{Push}, s, t) &\leftarrow Poss(\mathsf{Push}, s, t), \\
&\qquad \neg Holds(\mathsf{Locked}, s),\ \neg Holds(\mathsf{Jammed}, s) \\
DirT(\mathsf{Jammed}, \mathsf{Push}, s, t) &\leftarrow Poss(\mathsf{Push}, s, t),\ Holds(\mathsf{Locked}, s) \\
Holds(\mathsf{HasCard}, \varepsilon) &\leftarrow not\ \neg Holds(\mathsf{HasCard}, \varepsilon) \\
DefT(\mathsf{HasCard}, s, t) &\leftarrow Poss(a, s, t), \\
&\qquad Holds(\mathsf{HasCard}, s),\ not\ \neg Holds(\mathsf{HasCard}, t) \\
\neg Holds(\mathsf{Locked}, \varepsilon) &\leftarrow Holds(\mathsf{Swiped}, \varepsilon),\ not\ Holds(\mathsf{Locked}, \varepsilon) \\
DefF(\mathsf{Locked}, s, t) &\leftarrow Poss(a, s, t), \\
&\qquad \neg Holds(\mathsf{Swiped}, s),\ not\ Holds(\mathsf{Locked}, t) \\
DefF(\mathsf{Locked}, s, t) &\leftarrow Poss(a, s, t), \\
&\qquad \neg Holds(\mathsf{Locked}, s),\ not\ Holds(\mathsf{Locked}, t)
\end{aligned}
$$

along with $\neg Dir(L, A, s, t)$ for all fluent literals L and actions A without direct effect statement, $\neg Ind(L, s, t)$ for all fluent literals L and (11–14). The initial state axioms $\Omega_{\mathbb{D}}$ become $\{Holds(\mathsf{Locked}, \varepsilon), \neg Holds(\mathsf{Jammed}, \varepsilon), \neg Holds(\mathsf{Swiped}, \varepsilon)\}$.

To complete our translation, we have to make sure the resulting program admits only groundings that are well-sorted with respect to the first-order language Π. Consequently, we define a fresh predicate name Q_σ for each sort σ of Π; we add a set of ASP rules that define the domain of each Q_σ; lastly, for all (first-order) variables $x : \sigma$ occurring in rules, we add the atom $Q_\sigma(x)$ to the rule body. So for a $\mathcal{D}$ action domain specification $\Sigma = \Upsilon \cup \Omega$, its ASP translation P_Σ is simply $P_\Upsilon \cup P_\Omega$ along with the rules for the sort domains. Since the signature Π contains function symbols of positive arity (e.g. in terms of the form $\tau_\alpha \cdot A$), the well-sorted grounding of P_Σ is obviously infinite. In the actual implementation, we introduce a finite horizon, that is, a maximal term depth to which the program is grounded.

The most remarkable property of the translation we presented above is that Υ (general workings of the domain) and Ω (a specific starting time-point for an agent in the domain) can be translated completely independently. This has the advantage that for any given domain, we need to compile the general domain knowledge only when it changes, which should arguably happen less often. In particular, the rules in P_Υ make no mention of actual states and can therefore easily be extended by any P_Ω. Information about actual domain instances (which arguably changes more often during online control of an agent) can be translated to ASP in linear time, which is immediate from Definition 13.

When posing a query to a $\mathcal{D}$ action domain, it is straightforward to reduce sceptical query entailment to answer set existence: we add an integrity constraint that forbids L being true at the ending time point τ_α of the action sequence.

Definition 14. *Let* ζ = <u>`normally`</u> L <u>`after`</u> α *be a query. Its corresponding extended logic program is* $P_\zeta \stackrel{\text{def}}{=} \{Q \leftarrow L[\tau_\alpha], \textit{not } Q\}$ *for a fresh predicate* Q.

Now for a query ζ = <u>`normally`</u> L <u>`after`</u> α, the literal $L[\tau_\alpha]$ is contained in every answer set of P iff $P \cup P_\zeta$ admits no answer set.

3.1 Proof of Correctness

In this section, we take the propositional signature $\mathfrak{P}$ to contain all ground instances of predicates from the signature Π of the previous section, hence P_Σ represents its ground instantiation. The proof now establishes a one-to-one correspondence between possible scenarios of Σ and answer sets of P_Σ.

To develop the correspondence, we first define how to obtain a scenario from a given set of literals. For a set M of literals over the domain signature of a domain specification Σ, we define a scenario $S_M \stackrel{\text{def}}{=} \{(\alpha, L) \mid L[\tau_\alpha] \in M, \alpha \in \text{ACTION}^*\}$. The scenario and M now agree on all fluent literals at all time-points (i.e., after all action sequences). Our first formal result states that the one-step consequence operators for domain Σ and program P_Σ agree likewise during their iterations, adjusted for a small difference/lag due to action applicability. For an operator Γ on sets, define $\Gamma^0 \stackrel{\text{def}}{=} \emptyset$, for $i \geq 0$ set $\Gamma^{i+1} \stackrel{\text{def}}{=} \Gamma(\Gamma^i)$ and $\Gamma^\infty \stackrel{\text{def}}{=} \bigcup_{i=0}^{\infty} \Gamma^i$.

Theorem 15. *Let* $\Sigma = \Upsilon \cup \Omega$ *be a domain,* M *be a set of literals,* α *be an action sequence and* L *be a fluent literal. For all* $i \geq 0$,

1. $L[\tau_\alpha] \in \Gamma^i_{P^M_\Sigma}$ *implies* $(\alpha, L) \in \Gamma^i_{\Sigma, S_M}$, *and*
2. $(\alpha, L) \in \Gamma^i_{\Sigma, S_M}$ *implies there is a* $j \geq i$ *with* $L[\tau_\alpha] \in \Gamma^j_{P^M_\Sigma}$.

As an immediate corollary, we obtain that the least fixed points of the two operators coincide with respect to literals after all action sequences.

Corollary 16. *Let* Σ *be a domain,* M *be a set of literals,* α *be an action sequence and* L *be a fluent literal. Then* $(\alpha, L) \in \Gamma^\infty_{\Sigma, S_M}$ *iff* $L[\tau_\alpha] \in \Gamma^\infty_{P^M_\Sigma}$.

Our main result now states that computing the answer sets of the logic program P_Σ as a matter of fact computes the possible scenarios of the action domain specification Σ.

Theorem 17. *Let* Σ *be a* $\mathcal{D}$ *action domain specification.*

1. *For each answer set* M *for* P_Σ, *scenario* S_M *is possible for* Σ.
2. *For each possible scenario* S *for* Σ, *there exists an answer set* M *for* P_Σ *such that* $S_M = S$.

Proof. 1. *Let α be an action sequence and L be a ground literal. We have*

$$\begin{aligned}
&(\alpha, L) \in \Gamma^{\infty}_{\Sigma,S_M} \\
&\textit{iff } L[\tau_\alpha] \in \Gamma^{\infty}_{P_\Sigma^M} && \textit{(Corollary 16)} \\
&\textit{iff } L[\tau_\alpha] \in M && \textit{(M is an answer set for } P_\Sigma\textit{)} \\
&\textit{iff } (\alpha, L) \in S_M && \textit{(Definition of } S_M\textit{)}
\end{aligned}$$

This yields $\Gamma^{\infty}_{\Sigma,S_M} = S_M$ and hence S_M is a possible scenario for Σ.

2. *Define $M^0 \stackrel{\text{def}}{=} \{L[\tau_\alpha] \mid (\alpha, L) \in S\}$ and $M^\infty \stackrel{\text{def}}{=} \Gamma^{\infty}_{P_\Sigma^{M^0}}$. We prove that M^∞ is an answer set for P_Σ, that is, $\Gamma^{\infty}_{P_\Sigma^{M^\infty}} = M^\infty = \Gamma^{\infty}_{P_\Sigma^{M^0}}$ by showing $P_\Sigma^{M^\infty} = P_\Sigma^{M^0}$. Observe that all default-negated literals in P_Σ are of the form "not $L[\tau]$" for some time-point τ, hence it suffices to show that M^0 and M^∞ agree on all literals of the form $L[\tau_\alpha]$ for an action sequence α:*

$$\begin{aligned}
&L[\tau_\alpha] \in M^0 \\
&\textit{iff } (\alpha, L) \in S && (S = S_{M^0}) \\
&\textit{iff } (\alpha, L) \in \Gamma^{\infty}_{\Sigma,S} && \textit{(S is possible)} \\
&\textit{iff } L[\tau_\alpha] \in \Gamma^{\infty}_{P_\Sigma^{M^0}} && \textit{(Corollary 16)} \\
&\textit{iff } L[\tau_\alpha] \in M^\infty && \textit{(Definition of } M^\infty\textit{)}
\end{aligned}$$

Additionally, this shows that $S_{M^\infty} = S$ and concludes the proof. □

The main result implies as an immediate corollary the correctness of our implementation of query answering in $\mathcal{D}$.

Corollary 18. *Let Σ be a $\mathcal{D}$ action domain specification, and consider a query $\zeta =$ <u>`normally`</u> L <u>`after`</u> α, then $\Sigma \approx\!\!\!\!\mid\; \zeta$ if and only if $L[\tau_\alpha]$ is contained in each answer set of P_Σ.*

The one-to-one correspondence of possible scenarios and answer sets gives us important information about the type of nonmonotonic reasoning performed by $\mathcal{D}$: there is a similar one-to-one correspondence between answer sets of extended logic programs and extensions of Reiter's default logic [9]. Combining these two results, we can see that the action language presented here indeed allows for Reiter-style default reasoning.

4 The Qualification Problem

In $\mathcal{D}$ as defined so far, we make the simplifying assumption that necessary preconditions of actions are fully known. This is unrealistic insofar as there are potentially infinitely many circumstances that can prevent the successful execution of an action, which cannot be foreseen let alone specified [7]. For practical reasoning, this constitutes at least two tasks: (1) assume away all of the unlikely circumstances that prevent action execution and (2) correctly predict action disqualification if an exceptional circumstance is known to arise.

Moreover, an action might not always downright fail, but only *fail to produce a certain outcome*, for which Vladimir Lifschitz and his colleagues coined the term *weak* qualification [10] (vs. *strong* qualification, which means that an action fails altogether).

To solve the strong qualification problem in $\mathcal{D}$, we introduce a new function symbol $\mathsf{Disqualified} : \text{ACTION} \rightarrow \text{FLUENT}$ with the obvious intuitive meaning [11]. For each action A, we turn its precondition P_A into $P_A \cup \{\neg\mathsf{Disqualified}(A)\}$ – that is, to the known, definite preconditions we add another one that represents all additional conceivable preconditions. These are then assumed away by default through the statement $\underline{\texttt{normally}}$ $\neg\mathsf{Disqualified}(A)$. An action A is then possible after α iff $\Sigma \approx$ $\underline{\texttt{normally}}$ L $\underline{\texttt{after}}$ α for all $L \in P_A$. Particular causes for disqualification of A can now be expressed modularly by adding ramification rules $\underline{\texttt{effect}}$ K $\underline{\texttt{causes}}$ $\mathsf{Disqualified}(A)$ $\underline{\texttt{if}}$ C.

For weak qualification, we introduce a similar function symbol $\mathsf{Ab} : \text{FLUENT} \rightarrow \text{FLUENT}$. The term $\mathsf{Ab}(F)$ now says that fluent F is abnormally disqualified at a time-point. For each direct effect statement $\underline{\texttt{action}}$ A $\underline{\texttt{causes}}$ $(\neg)F$ $\underline{\texttt{if}}$ C we add $\neg\mathsf{Ab}(F)$ to the effect's precondition C. This expresses that effect $(\neg)F$ only occurs if there was nothing abnormal about F at the starting time point. As before, abnormality is assumed away by default using the statements $\underline{\texttt{normally}}$ $\neg\mathsf{Ab}(F)$ for all fluents F.

Notice that $\mathcal{D}$'s solution to the qualification problem is formulated entirely within the language itself and requires no language extension or external machinery.

5 Discussion

We introduced the action language $\mathcal{D}$ for default reasoning about actions. The language solves the frame problem in the presence of defaults as well as the ramification and qualification problems. $\mathcal{D}$ is efficiently implemented, which makes it immediately applicable for practical problems.

Our work can be seen as a restriction of [12] where the restriction is solely for computational benefits: in a domain with n fluents, there are potentially $O(2^n)$ knowledge states, all of which we would have to inspect for query answering. What we trade off here, however, is expressiveness: the version of $\mathcal{D}$ presented in this paper is essentially "disjunction-free." For example, from the statements $\underline{\texttt{action}}$ A $\underline{\texttt{causes}}$ G $\underline{\texttt{if}}$ $\{F\}$ and $\underline{\texttt{action}}$ A $\underline{\texttt{causes}}$ G $\underline{\texttt{if}}$ $\{\neg F\}$, we cannot conclude $\underline{\texttt{normally}}$ G $\underline{\texttt{after}}$ A.[4] This is however common for the implementation of action languages [1]. In particular, $\mathcal{A}$ and $\mathcal{E}$ only come with translations to logic programming that are sound but incomplete. In our case of a nonmonotonic formalism, this would not work since incompleteness is bound to lead to unsoundness (imagine a default being wrongly applicable because a justification could not be derived due to incompleteness).

[4] In $\mathcal{A}$, such a pair of statements would not even be admissible for translation [1].

Generally speaking, surprisingly few approaches exist that deal with default reasoning about actions. The Discrete Event Calculus [13] offers simple default reasoning about time using circumscription, which however allows for default conclusions with circular justifications. Action language $\mathcal{C}+$ [5] provides the default statements we have seen in the introduction, which however have an underlying intuition that is different from ours. Additionally, $\mathcal{C}+$ also allows the circularly justified conclusions we have seen in the introduction. [14] use a modal variant of the Situation Calculus to define a semantics for reasoning about actions in the presence of defaults. They however "forget" default conclusions and re-apply defaults after each action without keeping track of extensions. Also, there is no mention of an implementation. [15] offer an argumentation-based semantics for what they call "knowledge qualification." There, each piece of knowledge about a domain is encoded as an argument in favor of some conclusion. Preferences between different kinds of arguments determine what is believed about the domain. These preferences are declared by the axiomatiser and are themselves arguments, which makes the formalism quite complex and delegates the specification of the semantics to the user. An implementation is not mentioned in the paper. [16] extend modal logics with preferences in order to incorporate defeasible inferences into modal-based formalisms for reasoning about actions. However, they do not provide a solution to the frame problem in this framework nor an implementation.

There are many implemented systems that employ answer set programming for reasoning about actions – [1,6,17,18,19] to name only a few. However, none of these systems aspire to combine temporal reasoning with default reasoning. They use the nonmonotonicity of ASP to implement the explanation closure assumption, to solve the frame problem or compute circumscription.

Acknowledgements. This paper is based entirely on Vladimir Lifschitz's groundbreaking research in knowledge representation, reasoning about actions and logic programming. None of what we described would have been possible without his seminal work on action languages and the foundations for answer set programming that he laid, for which we thank him profoundly! We also thank our second reader Fangkai Yang for the for helpful comments on an earlier version of this paper.

This research was supported under Australian Research Council's (ARC) *Discovery Projects* funding scheme (project number DP 120102144) The second author is the recipient of an ARC Future Fellowship (project number FT 0991348). He is also affiliated with the University of Western Sydney.

References

1. Gelfond, M., Lifschitz, V.: Representing Action and Change by Logic Programs. Journal of Logic Programming 17(2/3&4), 301–321 (1993)
2. Gelfond, M., Lifschitz, V.: Action Languages. Electronic Transactions on Artificial Intelligence 3 (1998)

3. Giunchiglia, E., Lifschitz, V.: An Action Language Based on Causal Explanation: Preliminary Report. In: Proceedings of the Fifteenth National Conference on Artificial Intelligence (AAAI 1998), pp. 623–630. American Association for Artificial Intelligence, Menlo Park (1998)
4. Kakas, A., Miller, R.: A Simple Declarative Language for Describing Narratives with Actions. Journal of Logic Programming 31(1–3), 157–200 (1997); Reasoning about Actions and Change
5. Giunchiglia, E., Lee, J., Lifschitz, V., McCain, N., Turner, H.: Nonmonotonic Causal Theories. Artificial Intelligence 153(1-2), 49–104 (2004)
6. Eiter, T., Faber, W., Leone, N., Pfeifer, G., Polleres, A.: A Logic Programming Approach to Knowledge-State Planning: Semantics and Complexity. ACM Transactions on Computational Logic 5, 206–263 (2004)
7. McCarthy, J.: Epistemological Problems of Artificial Intelligence. In: Proceedings of the Fifth International Joint Conference on Artificial Intelligence (IJCAI 1977), pp. 1038–1044 (1977)
8. Reiter, R.: A Logic for Default Reasoning. Artificial Intelligence 13, 81–132 (1980)
9. Gelfond, M., Lifschitz, V.: Classical Negation in Logic Programs and Disjunctive Databases. New Generation Computing 9, 365–385 (1991)
10. Gelfond, M., Lifschitz, V., Rabinov, A.: What Are the Limitations of the Situation Calculus? In: Boyer, R.S., Pase, W. (eds.) Automated Reasoning. Automated Reasoning Series, vol. 1, pp. 167–179. Springer, Netherlands (1991)
11. Thielscher, M.: Causality and the Qualification Problem. In: Proceedings of the International Conference on Principles of Knowledge Representation and Reasoning (KR), Cambridge, MA, pp. 51–62 (November 1996)
12. Baumann, R., Brewka, G., Strass, H., Thielscher, M., Zaslawski, V.: State Defaults and Ramifications in the Unifying Action Calculus. In: Proceedings of the Twelfth International Conference on the Principles of Knowledge Representation and Reasoning, Toronto, Canada, pp. 435–444 (May 2010)
13. Mueller, E.: Commonsense Reasoning. Morgan Kaufmann (2006)
14. Lakemeyer, G., Levesque, H.: A Semantical Account of Progression in the Presence of Defaults. In: Proceedings of the Twenty-first International Joint Conference on Artificial Intelligence (IJCAI 2009), pp. 842–847 (2009)
15. Michael, L., Kakas, A.: A Unified Argumentation-Based Framework for Knowledge Qualification. In: Davis, E., Doherty, P., Erdem, E. (eds.) Proceedings Commonsense, Stanford, CA (March 2011)
16. Britz, K., Meyer, T., Varzinczak, I.: Preferential Reasoning for Modal Logics. Electronic Notes in Theoretical Computer Science 278, 55–69 (2011)
17. Kim, T.W., Lee, J., Palla, R.: Circumscriptive Event Calculus as Answer Set Programming. In: IJCAI, pp. 823–829 (July 2009)
18. Lee, J., Palla, R.: Situation Calculus as Answer Set Programming. In: Proceedings of the Twenty-Fourth Conference on Artificial Intelligence (AAAI 2010), pp. 309–314 (July 2010)
19. Casolary, M., Lee, J.: Representing the Language of the Causal Calculator in Answer Set Programming. In: Proceedings of the Twenty-Seventh International Conference on Logic Programming (ICLP 2011) (July 2011)

Connecting First-Order ASP and the Logic FO(ID) through Reducts

Miroslaw Truszczynski

Department of Computer Science, University of Kentucky, Lexington, KY 40506-0633, USA

In honor of Vladimir Lifschitz on his 65th birthday!

Abstract. Recently, an answer-set programming (ASP) formalism of logic programing with the answer-set semantics has been extended to the full first-order setting. Earlier an extension of first-order logic with inductive definitions, the logic FO(ID), was proposed as a knowledge representation formalism and developed as an alternative ASP language. We present characterizations of these formalisms in terms of concepts of infinitary propositional logic. We use them to find a direct connection between the first-order ASP and the logic FO(ID) under some restrictions on the form of theories (programs) considered.

1 Introduction

Answer-set programming (*ASP*, for short) is a paradigm for modeling and solving search problems and their optimization variants. To model a search problem, one constructs a theory in some logic language so that once the theory is appended with an encoding of a problem instance, its models represent in some direct fashion solutions to that instance of the problem. The paradigm was first formulated in these terms by Marek and Truszczyński [14] and Niemelä [16] for the formalism of logic programming with the stable-model semantics by Gelfond and Lifschitz [10,11], a nonmonotonic knowledge representation formalism with informal roots in epistemic interpretations of the negation as failure and closely connected to the default logic by Reiter [20]. Logic programming with the stable-model semantics and its extensions with the semantics of *answer sets* [11] are to this day the most broadly used dialects of ASP.

These formalisms were originally introduced with the syntax limited to *rules* and the semantics restricted to Herbrand interpretations. Recently researchers have sought to address these limitations. In particular, Pearce and Valverde [19] introduced the quantified equilibrium logic. That logic is a first-order extension of the equilibrium logic by Pearce [18], a propositional logic with the semantics of equilibrium models. For a class of theories that correspond to programs, equilibrium models and answer sets coincide and so, the quantified equilibrium logic is indeed a generalization of logic programming with the answer-set semantics to the full first-order setting. Ferraris, Lee and Lifschitz [8], proposed an alternative approach within the language of second-order logic. They introduced an operator SM that assigns a second-order sentence to a first-order one (incidentally, the operator SM closely resembles the one used to define circumscription). For a first-order sentence F, Ferraris et al. [8] proposed models of $SM[F]$ as *answer*

E. Erdem et al. (Eds.): Correct Reasoning, LNCS 7265, pp. 543–559, 2012.

sets of F and showed that the concept generalizes that of an answer set of a propositional formula. They also proved that the semantics of sentences provided by answer sets coincides with that of the quantified equilibrium logic.

While papers on ASP often bring up the default negation operator in logic programming as the key element to its success as a modeling language, the fact is that in most applications the default negation *not* is used as if it were a classical one. Arguably, the main appeal of logic programming with the answer-set semantics as an ASP formalism comes from its capability to capture inductive definitions. The importance of inductive definitions for knowledge representation was argued by Denecker [1,2], who proposed an extension of the first-order logic with inductive definitions, the logic FO(ID), as a knowledge representation formalism. A version of that language can be used according to the ASP paradigm and there are fast tools to support that use of the logic FO(ID).[1] The semantics of definitions in the logic FO(ID) is given by the well-founded semantics extended to the case of arbitrary interpretations. As the well-founded and answer-set semantics are related, the question arises about the relation between the first-order extensions of ASP that we discussed earlier and the logic FO(ID).

In this work we show a class of FO(ID) theories for which the relationship is quite direct. Under a simple translation of FO(ID) theories into programs, models of the FO(ID) theories in that class are precisely answer sets of the program resulting from the translation. In this way, we resolve in positive a conjecture by Vladimir Lifschitz[2]. We point out that a converse embedding is possible as well.

As the main technical device in our arguments we use characterizations of the first-order ASP and FO(ID) in the infinitary propositional logic. They are based on extensions to the infinitary case of the notion of reduct [7] on the one hand, and of the algebraic approach to stable and well-founded semantics [4] of general programs on the other. For the class of theories that we call programs, the concept of the reduct can be extended in two ways. We use one of them as a bridge to the first-order ASP as developed by Pearce and Valverde [19] and Ferraris et al. [8]. We use the other as the connection to the logic FO(ID), and note here in passing that it also provides an alternative characterization of a version of the first-order ASP proposed by Denecker et al. [3].

2 Stable Models in Infinitary Propositional Logic

Let A be a *propositional signature*, that is, a set of 0-ary relation symbols (or propositions). We assume the existence of a 0-ary predicate constant $\bot$, different from all symbols in A, and define sets $\mathcal{F}_0, \mathcal{F}_1, \ldots$ by induction as follows:

1. $\mathcal{F}_0 = A \cup \{\bot\}$
2. $\mathcal{F}_{i+1}$, where $i \geq 0$, consists of expressions $\mathcal{H}^\vee$ and $\mathcal{H}^\wedge$, for all subsets $\mathcal{H}$ of $\mathcal{F}_0 \cup \ldots \cup \mathcal{F}_i$, and of expressions $F \to G$, where $F, G \in \mathcal{F}_0 \cup \ldots \cup \mathcal{F}_i$.

We define $\mathcal{L}_A^{inf} = \bigcup_{i=0}^{\infty} \mathcal{F}_i$. We call elements of $\mathcal{L}_A^{inf}$ *infinitary formulas* (over A). Each formula $F \in \mathcal{L}_A^{inf}$ belongs to at least one set $\mathcal{F}_i$. We call the least index i of a set $\mathcal{F}_i$ containing F the *rank* of F.

[1] The IDP system, `http://dtai.cs.kuleuven.be/krr/software/idp3`

[2] The conjecture was communicated to me by Yulia Lierler.

The primary connectives of the language are $\{\}^\vee$, $\{\}^\wedge$ and $\to$. We define the boolean connectives $\wedge$, $\vee$, $\leftrightarrow$ and $\neg$, as well as another 0-ary predicate constant $\top$, as shorthands: $F \vee G ::= \{F, G\}^\vee$; $F \wedge G ::= \{F, G\}^\wedge$; $F \leftrightarrow G ::= (F \to G) \wedge (G \to F)$; $\neg F ::= F \to \bot$; and $\top ::= \neg\bot$.

The standard semantics of propositional logic extends to the case of infinitary formulas. An *interpretation* of A is a subset of A (atoms in the subset are *true* and all the other ones are *false*). We denote the set of all interpretations of A by Int_A. For an interpretation I of A, and an infinitary formula F, we define the relation $I \models F$ by induction on the rank of a formula as follows:

1. $I \not\models \bot$
2. For every $p \in A$, $I \models p$ if $p \in I$
3. $I \models \mathcal{H}^\vee$ if there is a formula $F \in \mathcal{H}$ such that $I \models F$
4. $I \models \mathcal{H}^\wedge$ if for every formula $F \in \mathcal{H}$, $I \models F$
5. $I \models F \to G$ if $I \not\models F$ or $I \models G$.

The concept of the *reduct* proposed by Ferraris [7] for the standard propositional logic can be extended to sets of infinitary formulas. The inductive definition follows:

1. $\bot^I = \bot$
2. For $p \in A$, $p^I = \bot$ if $I \not\models p$; otherwise $p^I = p$
3. $(\mathcal{H}^\wedge)^I = \bot$ if $I \not\models \mathcal{H}^\wedge$; otherwise, $(\mathcal{H}^\wedge)^I = \{G^I \mid G \in \mathcal{H}\}^\wedge$
4. $(\mathcal{H}^\vee)^I = \bot$ if $I \not\models \mathcal{H}^\vee$; otherwise, $(\mathcal{H}^\vee)^I = \{G^I \mid G \in \mathcal{H}\}^\vee$
5. $(G \to H)^I = \bot$ if $I \not\models G \to H$; otherwise $(G \to H)^I = G^I \to H^I$.

If $\mathcal{F}$ is a set of infinitary formulas, we define the reduct $\mathcal{F}^I$ by $\mathcal{F}^I = \{F^I \mid F \in \mathcal{F}\}$.

Definition 1. *Let $\mathcal{F} \subseteq \mathcal{L}_A^{inf}$ be a set of infinitary formulas. An interpretation $I \in Int_A$ is a* stable model *of $\mathcal{F}$ if I is a minimal model of $\mathcal{F}^I$.*

The use of the term *model* in *stable model* is justified. That is, stable models are models. This is evident from the following more general property.[3]

Proposition 1. *For every set $\mathcal{F} \subseteq \mathcal{L}_A^{inf}$ and every interpretation $I \in Int_A$, $I \models \mathcal{F}$ if and only if $I \models \mathcal{F}^I$.*

If a set $\mathcal{F}$ of finitary formulas has no negative occurrences of variables, it has minimal models and each of these models is a stable model of the formula. This property does not hold in the case of infinitary formulas. Let $F_i = \{p_i, p_{i+1}, \ldots\}^\vee$, $i = 0, 1, \ldots$, and let $\mathcal{F} = \{F_0, F_1, \ldots\}$ (we assume here that $A = \{p_0, p_1, \ldots\}$). It is easy to see that there is no finite set $M \subseteq A$ such that $M \models \mathcal{F}$. On the other hand, every infinite set $M \subseteq A$ is a model of $\mathcal{F}$. It follows that $\mathcal{F}$ has no minimal models. It is also easy to show that $\mathcal{F}$ has no stable models.

Next, we extend the semantics of HT-interpretations to (sets of) infinitary formulas. Our goal is to extend the equilibrium logic [18] to the infinitary case and show that equilibrium models and stable models coincide.

[3] The proofs of this result and the next two closely follow those of the corresponding results in the finitary case [7] and we omit them.

Definition 2. *An* HT-interpretation *is a pair* $\langle X, Y\rangle$*, where* $X, Y \in Int_A$ *and* $X \subseteq Y$*. The satisfiability relation* $\models_{ht}$ *is specified by induction as follows:*

1. $\langle X, Y\rangle \not\models_{ht} \bot$
2. *For* $p \in A$, $\langle X, Y\rangle \models_{ht} p$ *if* $p \in X$
3. $\langle X, Y\rangle \models_{ht} \mathcal{H}^\vee$ *if there is* $G \in \mathcal{H}$ *such that* $\langle X, Y\rangle \models_{ht} G$
4. $\langle X, Y\rangle \models_{ht} \mathcal{H}^\wedge$ *if for every* $G \in \mathcal{H}$, $\langle X, Y\rangle \models_{ht} G$
5. $\langle X, Y\rangle \models_{ht} G \to H$ *if* $Y \models G \to H$*; and* $\langle X, Y\rangle \not\models_{ht} G$ *or* $\langle X, Y\rangle \models_{ht} H$.

If $\langle X, Y\rangle \models_{ht} F$*, then we say that* $\langle X, Y\rangle$ *is an* HT-model *of* F*. The concept of a model and the relation* $\models_{ht}$ *extend in a standard way to* sets *of infinitary formulas.*

The following result gathers important properties of the relation $\models_{ht}$. They extend the corresponding properties of that relation in the standard finitary setting [7,9].

Theorem 1. *For every formula* F *and every interpretations* $X, Y \in Int_A$ *such that* $X \subseteq Y$ *we have:*

1. $\langle X, Y\rangle \models_{ht} F$ *implies* $Y \models F$
2. $\langle X, Y\rangle \models_{ht} \neg F$ *if and only if* $Y \not\models F$
3. $\langle Y, Y\rangle \models_{ht} F$ *if and only if* $Y \models F$.

The next result characterizes the relation $\models_{ht}$ in terms of the standard satisfiability relation and the reduct.

Theorem 2. *For every set* $\mathcal{F} \subseteq \mathcal{L}_A^{inf}$ *of infinitary formulas and for every interpretations* $X, Y \in Int_A$ *such that* $X \subseteq Y$, $\langle X, Y\rangle \models_{ht} \mathcal{F}$ *if and only if* $X \models \mathcal{F}^Y$.

Let $\mathcal{F} \subseteq \mathcal{L}_A^{inf}$ be a set of infinitary formulas. Directly extending the definition from the finitary case, we say that an HT-interpretation $\langle Y, Y\rangle$ is an *equilibrium* model of $\mathcal{F}$ if $\langle Y, Y\rangle \models_{ht} \mathcal{F}$ and there is no proper subset X of Y such that $\langle X, Y\rangle \models_{ht} \mathcal{F}$. The following result connects stable and equilibrium models and follows directly from Theorem 1(3) and Theorem 2.

Theorem 3. *An interpretation* $Y \in Int_A$ *is a stable model of a set* $\mathcal{F}$ *of infinitary formulas from* $\mathcal{L}_A^{inf}$ *if and only if* $\langle Y, Y\rangle$ *is an equilibrium model of* $\mathcal{F}$.

3 Stable Models in First-Order Logic

Let σ be a signature of a language of first-order logic and let U be a set. By σ^U we denote the signature obtained by adding to σ distinct symbols u^* (*names*) for every $u \in U$.

Next, let I be an interpretation of σ, that is, a *structure* comprising a non-empty *domain*, written as $|I|$, and for each relation and function symbol in σ, a relation or function on $|I|$, of the same arity, to interpret it. We denote by $A_{\sigma,I}$ the set of all those atomic formulas of the first order language $\mathcal{L}_{\sigma^{|I|}}$ that are built of relation symbols in σ and the names of elements in $|I|$. We identify an interpretation I of σ with its extension I' to $\sigma^{|I|}$ defined by setting $I'(s) = I(s)$, for every $s \in \sigma$, and $I'(u^*) = u$ for every

$u \in |I|$. From now on, we use the same symbol for an interpretation I of σ and for its (unique) extension to $\sigma^{|I|}$ defined above. We represent an interpretation I of σ (and its extension to $\sigma^{|I|}$) by a pair $\langle I^f, I^r \rangle$, where I^f is an interpretation of the part of σ (or equivalently, of $\sigma^{|I|}$) that consists of constant and function symbols in σ, and I^r is a subset of $A_{\sigma,I}$ that describes in the obvious way the relations in I (the interpretation of new constants is determined and does not need to be explicitly represented). We write Int_σ for the set of all interpretations of σ (extended as described above).

Let F be a sentence in the language $\mathcal{L}_{\sigma^{|I|}}$. We define the relation $I \models F$ following the approach used, for instance, by Doets [6] (the definition of the value t^I of a term t in I is standard, we assume the reader is familiar with it):

1. $I \not\models \bot$
2. $I \models p(t_1, \ldots, t_k)$ if $p((t_1^I)^*, \ldots, (t_k^I)^*) \in I^r$
3. $I \models t_1 = t_2$ if $t_1^I = t_2^I$
4. $I \models F \vee G$ if $I \models F$ or $I \models G$ (the case of $\wedge$ is analogous)
5. $I \models F \rightarrow G$ if $I \not\models F$ or $I \models G$
6. $I \models \exists x F(x)$ if for some $u \in |I|$, $I \models F(u^*)$
7. $I \models \forall x F(x)$ if for every $u \in |I|$, $I \models F(u^*)$.

Let I be an interpretation of σ and F be a sentence in $\mathcal{L}_{\sigma^{|I|}}$. We define the *grounding of F with respect to I*, $gr_I(F)$, as follows:

1. $gr_I(\bot) = \bot$
2. $gr_I(p(t_1, \ldots, t_k)) = p((t_1^I)^*, \ldots, (t_k^I)^*)$
3. $gr_I(t_1 = t_2)) = \top$, if $t_1^I = t_2^I$, and $\bot$, otherwise
4. If $F = G \vee H$, $gr_I(F) = gr_I(G) \vee gr_I(H)$ (the case of $\wedge$ is analogous)
5. If $F = G \rightarrow H$, $gr_I(F) = gr_I(G) \rightarrow gr_I(H)$
6. If $F = \exists x G(x)$, $gr_I(F) = \{gr_I(G(u^*)) \mid u \in |I|\}^\vee$
7. If $F = \forall x G(x)$, $gr_I(F) = \{gr_I(G(u^*)) \mid u \in |I|\}^\wedge$.

In addition, if $\mathcal{F}$ is a set of sentences from the language $\mathcal{L}_{\sigma^{|I|}}$, we define $gr_I(\mathcal{F}) = \{gr_I(F) \mid F \in \mathcal{F}\}$. It is clear that for every sentence F in $\mathcal{L}_{\sigma^{|I|}}$, $gr_I(F)$ is an infinitary propositional formula in the signature $A_{\sigma,I}$. It is important to note that $gr_I(F)$ depends only on I^f and not on I^r.

There is a simple connection between the first-order satisfiability relation and the one we defined earlier for the infinitary propositional logic.

Proposition 2. *Let I be an interpretation of σ and F a sentence from $\mathcal{L}_{\sigma^{|I|}}$. Then $I \models F$ if and only if $I^r \models gr_I(F)$.*

Proof. The basis of the induction is evident. For example, let us assume that F has the form $t_1 = t_2$. By the definition, if $I \models t_1 = t_2$ then $t_1^I = t_2^I$. It follows that $gr_I(F) = \top$ and $I^r \models gr_I(F)$. Conversely, if $I^r \models gr_I(F)$, then $gr_I(F) \neq \bot$. Thus, $t_1^I = t_2^I$ and $I \models t_1 = t_2$.

The inductive step is simple, too. For example, let us assume that $F = \forall x G(x)$. By the definition, $I \models F$ if and only if $I \models G(u^*)$, for every $u \in |I|$. By the induction hypothesis (as F is a sentence, each $G(u^*)$ is a sentence, too), this condition is equivalent to $I^r \models gr_I(G(u^*))$, for all $u \in |I|$ which, in turn, is equivalent to $I^r \models \{gr_I(G(u^*)) \mid u \in |I|\}^\wedge$. Noting that $\{gr_I(G(u^*)) \mid u \in |I|\}^\wedge = gr_I(F)$ completes the argument. The other cases for F can be handled in a similar way. □

With the notion of grounding in hand, we now define stable models of a set of first-order sentences.

Definition 3. *Let σ be a signature. An interpretation $I = \langle I^f, I^r \rangle$ of σ is a* stable model *of a set $\mathcal{F}$ of sentences from $\mathcal{L}_\sigma$ if I^r is a stable model of $gr_I(\mathcal{F})$.*

This concept of stability is well defined as formulas in $gr_I(\mathcal{F})$ are infinitary propositional formulas over the signature $A_{\sigma,I}$ and for every interpretation I of σ, $I^r \subseteq A_{\sigma,I}$.

By the definition of a stable model of a set of infinitary formulas over $A_{\sigma,I}$ we have the following direct characterization of stable models.

Proposition 3. *Let σ be a signature and let $\mathcal{F}$ be a set of sentences from $\mathcal{L}_\sigma$. An interpretation I of σ is a stable model of $\mathcal{F}$ if and only if I^r is a minimal model of the reduct $[gr_I(\mathcal{F})]^{I^r}$.*

Ferraris et al. [8] introduced an operator *SM* that assigns to each first-order sentence F (in signature σ) a second-order formula $SM[F]$. The details of the definition are immaterial to our subsequent discussion and we omit them. Ferraris et al. defined an interpretation $I \in Int_\sigma$ to be a *stable model* of F if I is a model of $SM[F]$. We show that our definition of stable models of a sentence is equivalent to the one based on the operator *SM*. We proceed in a roundabout way through a connection between our concept of stability and that based on the quantified logic *here-and-there* [19].

Following Ferraris et al. [8], we define an *HT-interpretation* of a first-order signature σ as a triple $I = \langle I^f, I^h, I^t \rangle$, where I^f is an interpretation of the part of σ that consists of constant and function symbols, and I^h and I^t are subsets of $A_{\sigma,I}$ such that $I^h \subseteq I^t$. Moreover, we define the relation $I \models_{ht} F$, where F is a sentence from $\mathcal{L}_{\sigma^{|I|}}$, follows:

1. $I \not\models_{ht} \bot$
2. $I \models_{ht} p(t_1, \ldots, t_k)$ if $p((t_1^I)^*, \ldots, p(t_k^I)^*) \in I^h$
3. $I \models_{ht} t_1 = t_2$ if $t_1^I = t_2^I$
4. $I \models_{ht} G \vee H$ if $I \models G$ or $I \models H$ (the case of $\wedge$ is analogous)
5. $I \models_{ht} G \rightarrow H$ if $\langle I^f, I^t \rangle \models G \rightarrow H$; and $I \not\models_{ht} G$ or $I \models_{ht} H$.
6. $I \models_{ht} \forall x G(x)$ if for every $u \in |I|$, $I \models_{ht} G(u^*)$
7. $I \models_{ht} \exists x G(x)$ if for some $u \in |I|$, $I \models_{ht} G(u^*)$.

An HT-interpretation $I = \langle I^f, I^h, I^t \rangle$ is an *equilibrium* model of a sentence F [19] if $I \models_{ht} F$, $I^h = I^t$, and for every *proper* subset X of I^h, $\langle I^f, X, I^t \rangle \not\models_{ht} F$. Ferraris et al. [8] proved the following result.

Theorem 4 (Ferraris et al. [8]). *An HT-interpretation $I = \langle I^f, I^h, I^h \rangle$ is an equilibrium model of F if and only if $\langle I^f, I^h \rangle$ is a stable model of F (a model of $SM[F]$).*

The key step in showing that these two notions of stability coincide with the one we introduced in Definition 3 consists of showing that the first-order relation $\models_{ht}$ can be expressed in terms of the relation $\models_{ht}$ of the infinitary propositional logic.

Proposition 4. *Let I be an HT-interpretation of σ and F a sentence from $\mathcal{L}_{\sigma^{|I|}}$. Then, $I \models_{ht} F$ if and only if $\langle I^h, I^t\rangle \models_{ht} gr_I(F)$.*

Proof. The basis of the induction is evident. For example, let us assume that $F = p(t_1, \ldots, t_k)$. Then $I \models_{ht} F$ if and only if $p((t_1^I)^*, \ldots, (t_k^I)^*) \in I^h$. Since $gr_I(F) = p((t_1^I)^*, \ldots, (t_k^I)^*)$, that condition is equivalent to $\langle I^h, I^t\rangle \models_{ht} gr_I(F)$.

The induction step is also simple. For instance, let $F = G \to H$ and let us assume that $I \models_{ht} G \to H$. It follows that $\langle I^f, I^t\rangle \models G \to H$ and, also, that $I \not\models_{ht} G$ or $I \models_{ht} H$. By Proposition 2 and by the induction hypothesis, we obtain $I^t \models gr_I(G \to H)$, and $\langle I^h, I^t\rangle \not\models_{ht} gr_I(G)$ or $\langle I^h, I^t\rangle \models_{ht} gr_I(H)$. Since $gr_I(G \to H) = gr_I(G) \to gr_I(H)$, it follows that $\langle I^h, I^t\rangle \models_{ht} gr_I(G) \to gr_I(H)$ and, consequently, that $\langle I^h, I^t\rangle \models_{ht} gr_I(G \to H)$. The converse implication and other cases for F can be reasoned in a similar way. □

We now state and prove the result showing the equivalence of the three definitions of stable models of a first-order sentence.

Theorem 5. *The following definitions of a stable model of a sentence F are equivalent:*

1. *the definition in terms of the operator SM*
2. *the definition in terms of equilibrium models*
3. *the definition in terms of ground programs (Definition 3).*

Proof. (1) and (2) are equivalent by Theorem 4. We will prove the equivalence of (2) and (3). Let I be an interpretation of σ such that $\langle I^f, I^r, I^r\rangle$ is an equilibrium model of F. It follows that $\langle I^f, I^r, I^r\rangle \models_{ht} F$ and for every proper subset X of I^r, $\langle I^f, X, I^r\rangle \not\models_{ht} F$. The first property and Proposition 4 imply that $\langle I^r, I^r\rangle \models_{ht} gr_I(F)$. The second property and Proposition 4 imply that for every proper subset X of I^r, $\langle X, I^r\rangle \not\models_{ht} gr_I(F)$. Thus, by Theorem 3, I is a stable model of $gr_I(F)$ and, consequently, a stable model of F according to Definition 3.

Conversely, let us assume that I is a classical interpretation of σ such that I^r is a stable model of $gr_I(F)$. It follows (Theorem 3) that $\langle I^r, I^r\rangle \models_{ht} gr_I(F)$ and there is no proper subset X of I^r such that $\langle X, I^r\rangle \models_{ht} gr_I(F)$. Using Proposition 4, we obtain that I is an equilibrium model of F. □

We note that the definitions of stable models of sentences given here and in terms of equilibrium models extend to infinite collections of sentences. The definition in terms of the operator *SM* does not lend itself in any obvious way to such an extension.

4 Programs

A *program* (in the language of the infinitary propositional logic) is a set of *program clauses*, that is, formulas $F \to p$, where $F \in \mathcal{L}_A^{inf}$ and $p \in A$. For consistency with the standard logic programming notation, we write a clause $F \to p$ as $p \leftarrow F$. We call p the *head* of the clause $p \leftarrow F$.

Let Π be a program in the signature A. We denote by A^{out}_{Π} the set of all atoms that appear in the heads of clauses in Π and define $A^{in}_{\Pi} = A \setminus A^{out}_{\Pi}$. If the program Π is clear from the context, we drop "Π" from the notation. We call atoms in A^{in}_{Π} and A^{out}_{Π} *input* and *output* atoms, respectively.[4]

For programs we can generalize the concept of a stable model by taking into account a given interpretation of its input atoms.

Definition 4. *Let Π be a program in a signature A. An interpretation I of A is an* input stable model *of Π if I is a stable model of $\Pi \cup (I \cap A^{in})$.*

The concept of an input stable model was introduced and studied by Lierler and Truszczynski [13] as the basis for the formalism SM(ASP). It is closely related to models of modular logic programming systems [12,17,3].

Input stable models have an elegant direct characterization in terms of stable models that extends the corresponding characterization for the finitary case given by Lierler and Truszczynski [13]. Let Π be a program. We define $\Pi^{in} = \Pi \cup \{a \leftarrow \neg\neg a \mid a \in A^{in}\}$. The proof of the characterization below is similar to the one for the finitary case and we omit it.

Proposition 5. *Let Π be a program in a signature A. An interpretation I of σ is an input stable model of Π if and only if I is a stable model of Π^{in}.*

For programs one can introduce an alternative notion of a reduct. Let $F \in \mathcal{L}^{inf}_{A}$ and $I \in Int_A$. We define F_I to be the formula obtained by replacing each atom p that occurs negatively in F with $\bot$, if $I \not\models p$, and with $\top$, otherwise.[5] For a program Π, we define $\Pi_I = \{p \leftarrow F_I \mid p \leftarrow F \in \Pi\}$.

We note that formulas F_I have only positive occurrences of atoms. Thus, for any two interpretations $J, J' \in Int_A$ such that $J \subseteq J'$, if $J \models F_I$ then $J' \models F_I$. In particular, it follows that for every program Π and every interpretation I, Π_I has a least model denoted by $LM(\Pi_I)$. This observation gives rise to the notion of an *ID-stable* model of a program. We introduce it below, together with the related notion of an *input* ID-stable model.

Definition 5. *Let Π be a program in a signature A. An interpretation I of A is an* ID-stable model *of a program Π if $I = LM(\Pi_I)$. An interpretation I of A is an* input ID-stable model *of Π if I is an ID-stable model of $\Pi \cup (I \cap A^{in})$.*

It is clear that $I \models \Pi$ if and only if $I \models \Pi_I$. Thus, ID-stable models of Π are models of Π and the use of the term "model" in "ID-stable model" (and so, also in "input ID-stable model") is justified.

[4] One can consider a slightly more general setting in which we define A^{out}_{Π} as a subset of A that contains the heads of all rules in Π (but, possibly, also some other atoms). That setting reduces in a simple way to the one we consider. One just needs to extend Π with rules of the form $a \leftarrow \bot$, for every $a \in A^{out}_{\Pi}$ that is not the head of any rule in Π.

[5] The only connectives in the language are $\{\cdot\}^{\vee}$ (generalized $\vee$), $\{\cdot\}^{\wedge}$ (generalized $\wedge$), and $\rightarrow$. Thus, the notions of a positive and negative occurrence of a propositional atom in a formula are well defined.

In general, stable models and ID-stable models of programs do not coincide. For instance, let $\Pi = \{p \leftarrow \neg\neg p\}$. One can check that $I = \emptyset$ and $J = \{p\}$ are stable models of Π. On the other hand, since p occurs positively in Π, $\Pi_I = \Pi_J = \Pi$. The least model of Π is $\emptyset$. Thus, I is an ID-stable model of Π but J is not!

We will now show a class of programs for which the two concepts coincide. Let $\mathcal{N}$ be the set of all formulas F that satisfy the following property: every occurrence of the implication in F has $\bot$ as the consequent and no occurrence of implication in its antecedent. The first requirement says that all occurrences of the implication operator can be replaced with the negation operator, the second requirement says that the negation operator cannot be nested.

Lemma 1. *Let Π be a program in signature A and I an interpretation of A such that $I \models \Pi$. Then $\Pi^I \equiv \{p \leftarrow F^I \mid p \leftarrow F \in \Pi\}$.*

Proof. Let $p \leftarrow F \in \Pi$. Since $I \models p \leftarrow F$,

$$(p \leftarrow F)^I = \begin{cases} p^I \leftarrow \bot & \text{if } I \not\models F \\ p \leftarrow F^I & \text{if } I \models F \text{ and } I \models p \end{cases}$$

while

$$p \leftarrow F^I = \begin{cases} p \leftarrow \bot & \text{if } I \not\models F \\ p \leftarrow F^I & \text{if } I \models F \text{ and } I \models p. \end{cases}$$

Thus the assertion follows. □

Lemma 2. *For every formula $F \in \mathcal{N}$, and every interpretation I, F^I and F_I have the same models contained in I.*

Proof. The proof is by induction on the rank of a formula. If $F = \bot$, then $F^I = \bot = F_I$ and the claim is evident. If $F = p$, and $I \models p$, then $p^I = p$ and $p_I = p$. If $I \not\models p$, then $p^I = \bot$ and $p_I = p$. In each case, the formulas p^I and p_I have the same models that are subsets of I.

For the inductive step there are several cases to consider. First, let us assume that $F = \mathcal{H}^\vee$. If $I \not\models F$, $F^I = \bot$ and it has no models contained in I. Moreover, for every $G \in \mathcal{H}$, $I \not\models G$. By the induction hypothesis, the formulas G^I and G_I have the same models contained in I. Since $G^I = \bot$, no G_I has models contained in I and, consequently, $F_I = \{G_I \mid G \in \mathcal{H}\}^\vee$ has no models contained in I. Thus, let us assume that $I \models F$. It follows that $(\mathcal{H}^\vee)^I = \{G^I \mid G \in \mathcal{H}\}^\vee$ and $(\mathcal{H}^\vee)_I = \{G_I \mid G \in \mathcal{H}\}^\vee$. By the induction hypothesis, for every $G \in H$, G^I and G_I have the same models contained in I. Thus, $(\mathcal{H}^\vee)^I$ and $(\mathcal{H}^\vee)_I$ have that property, too.

The argument for the case $F = \mathcal{H}^\wedge$ is similar. So, let us assume that $F = G \rightarrow \bot$. Since $F \in \mathcal{N}$, G has no occurrences of implication and, consequently, all occurrences of atoms in G are negative in F. It follows that if $I \not\models G$ then $F_I \equiv \bot \rightarrow \bot \equiv \top$ and, otherwise (if $I \models G$) $F_I \equiv \top \rightarrow \bot \equiv \bot$.

Moreover, if $I \not\models G$, then $I \models F$. Thus, $F^I = G^I \rightarrow \bot = \bot \rightarrow \bot \equiv \top \equiv F_I$. Similarly, if $I \models G$ then $I \not\models F$ and, consequently, $F^I = \bot$. Thus, also in this case $F_I \equiv F^I$ and the assertion follows. □

Theorem 6. *Let Π be a program such that for every clause $p \leftarrow G \in \Pi$, $G \in \mathcal{N}$. Then stable and ID-stable models of Π coincide, and input stable and input ID-stable models coincide.*

Proof. Reasoning in each direction we have that I is a model of Π. By Lemmas 1 and 2, Π^I and Π_I have the same models contained in I. Thus, if I is the least model of Π_I, I is the least model (and, in particular, a minimal model) of Π^I. Conversely, if I is a minimal model of Π^I, then I is a minimal model of Π_I and so, the least model of Π_I. These two observations imply the first part of the assertion. The second part follows from the first part and from the definitions. □

The discussion above extends in a straightforward way to the first-order case. Let us consider a first-order signature σ. A *program clause* is a formula $\forall \boldsymbol{X}\,(G \rightarrow p(\boldsymbol{t}))$, where $\boldsymbol{t}$ is a tuple of terms of the arity equal to the arity of p, and $\boldsymbol{X}$ is a tuple of all free variables in $G \rightarrow p(\boldsymbol{t})$. A *program* is a collection of clauses. As before, we write a clause $\forall \boldsymbol{X}\,(G \rightarrow p(\boldsymbol{t}))$ as $\forall \boldsymbol{X}\,(p(\boldsymbol{t}) \leftarrow G)$ or even as $p(\boldsymbol{t}) \leftarrow G$.

First, we generalize to the first-order setting the results concerning input stable models.

Definition 6. *Let Π be a program in a first-order signature σ. An interpretation $I \in Int_\sigma$ is an input stable model of Π if I^r is an input stable model of $gr_I(\Pi)$.*

For a program Π in a first-order signature σ, we define σ_Π^{out} to be the set of all relation symbols occurring in the heads of clauses in Π and σ_Π^{in} to be the set of all other relation symbols in Π. Whenever there is no ambiguity, we drop Π from the notation. We set $\Pi^{in} = \Pi \cup \{p(\boldsymbol{X}) \leftarrow \neg\neg p(\boldsymbol{X}) \mid p \in \sigma^{in}\}$. We have the following result, which can be obtained by lifting through grounding the corresponding result from the infinitary propositional setting (Proposition 5).

Theorem 7. *Let Π be a program in a first-order signature σ. An interpretation $I \in Int_\sigma$ is an input stable model of Π if and only if I is a stable model of Π^{in}.*

The concepts of ID-stable and input ID-stable models can similarly be lifted to the first-order setting.

Definition 7. *If Π is a program in a first-order signature σ, an interpretation $I \in Int_\sigma$ is an (input)* ID-stable model *of Π if I^r is an (input) ID-stable model of $gr_I(\Pi)$.*

The definition of the class $\mathcal{N}$ extends literally to the first-order language. We define the class $\mathcal{N}^{fo}$ to consist of all first-order formulas F such that every occurrence of $\rightarrow$ in F has $\bot$ in its consequent and no occurrence of $\rightarrow$ in its antecedent (elements of $\mathcal{N}^{fo}$ may contain free variables). Since grounding formulas form $\mathcal{N}^{fo}$ results in infinitary propositional formulas from $\mathcal{N}$, Theorem 6 lifts to the first-order setting.

Theorem 8. *Let Π be a program over a first-order signature σ such that for every clause $p(\boldsymbol{t}) \leftarrow G \in \Pi$, $G \in \mathcal{N}^{fo}$. Then (input) stable and (input) ID-stable models of Π coincide.*

5 Logics PC(ID) and FO(ID)

We now consider the logic FO(ID) introduced by Denecker [2] and investigated in detail by Denecker and Ternovska [5]. Our goal is to relate that logic to the formalism of first-order programs under the stable model semantics. To this end, we first relate the logic FO(ID) with the logic of (first-order) programs under the semantics of ID-stable models. Next, we apply Theorem 8 to obtain the result we are interested in.

We start by extending the logic PC(ID), the propositional version of FO(ID), to the infinitary propositional case. Our approach consists of a straightforward extension to the infinitary setting of the algebraic approach developed by Denecker et al. [4].

Let A be a propositional signature and Π a program in $\mathcal{L}_A^{inf}$. The *Fitting* operator for Π, $\Phi_\Pi\colon Int_A \times Int_A \to Int_A$, is defined by

$$\Phi_\Pi(I,J) = \{p \mid p \leftarrow F \in \Pi \text{ and } I \models F_J\}.$$

The key monotonicity properties of the operator Φ_Π in the finitary setting extend in a direct way to the infinitary one.

Proposition 6. *For every program Π, the operator Φ_Π is monotone in the first argument and antimonotone in the second.*

We recall that for a program Π in the signature A we write A_Π^{out} for the set of all atoms that appear in the heads of clauses in Π and A_Π^{in} for $A \setminus A_\Pi^{out}$. We also omit Π from the notation whenever it is clear from the context.

For every interpretation $K \in Int_{A^{in}}$, we set $Int_{A,K} = \{I \in Int_A \mid I \cap A^{in} = K\}$. Given a program Π and an interpretation $K \in Int_{A^{in}}$, we define the *Fitting operator with input* K, $\Phi_{\Pi,K}\colon Int_{A,K} \times Int_{A,K} \to Int_{A,K}$, by setting

$$\Phi_{\Pi,K}(I,J) = K \cup \Phi_\Pi(I,J),$$

where $I,J \in Int_{A,K}$. The operator $\Phi_{\Pi,K}$ is well defined, that is, to every pair of interpretations from $Int_{A,K}$ it assigns an interpretation from $Int_{A,K}$. It is easy to see that for every $I,J \in Int_A$ $(= Int_{A,\emptyset})$, $\Phi_{\Pi,\emptyset}(I,J) = \Phi_\Pi(I,J)$. Moreover, by the previous result, $\Phi_{\Pi,K}$ is monotone in the first argument and antimonotone in the second.

Definition 8. *Let Π be a program in signature A and $K \in Int_{A^{in}}$ an interpretation. The* stable operator with input K, *$St_{\Pi,K}\colon Int_{A,K} \to Int_{A,K}$, is defined by*

$$St_{\Pi,K}(J) = \mathit{lfp}(\Phi_{\Pi,K}(\cdot,J)) \quad (\textit{where } J \in Int_{A,K}).$$

We note that input ID-stable models that we introduced in the previous section can be characterized in terms of the operator $St_{\Pi,K}$.

Proposition 7. *Let Π be a program in a signature A. An interpretation $I \in Int_A$ is an input ID-stable model of Π if and only if $St_{\Pi,I\cap A^{in}}(I) = I$.*

The operator $St_{\Pi,K}$ is a stepping stone to the fundamental concept of the logic PC(ID): the *well-founded model* based on an interpretation of input atoms. To introduce it, we define an operator $W_{\Pi,K}$ on $Int_{A,K} \times Int_{A,K}$ by setting:

$$W_{\Pi,K}(I,J) = (St_{\Pi,K}(J), St_{\Pi,K}(I)) \quad (\text{where } I,J \in Int_{A,K}).$$

By Proposition 6 and the definitions of the operators $\Phi_{\Pi,K}$ and $St_{\Pi,K}$, for every $K \in Int_{A^{in}}$ the operator $St_{\Pi,K}$ is antimonotone. It follows that the operator $W_{\Pi,K}$ is monotone with respect to the *precision order* $\leq_P$ defined as follows:

$$(I, J) \leq_P (I', J') \quad \text{if and only if} \quad I \subseteq I' \text{ and } J' \subseteq J.$$

The precision order is a partial order that imposes on $Int_{A,K} \times Int_{A,K}$ the structure of a complete lattice, with the pair (K, A) as its least element. By the Tarski-Knaster theorem, $W_{\Pi,K}$ has a least fixpoint, and this fixpoint is the limit of the transfinite sequence $\{W^{\alpha}_{\Pi,K}(K, A)\}_{\alpha}$, where iterations $W^{\alpha}_{\Pi,K}(K, A)$ of the operator $W_{\Pi,K}$ over (K, A) are defined in the standard way. If $I, J \in Int_{A,K}$, $I \subseteq J$, and $W_{\Pi,K}(I, J) = (I', J')$, then $I' \subseteq J'$. Thus, for every element (I, J) in the sequence $\{W^{\alpha}_{\Pi,K}(K, A)\}_{\alpha}$, $I \subseteq J$ and the limit (the least fixpoint of $W_{\Pi,K}$), satisfies the same property.

Let us assume that (I_0, J_0) is that limit. Then, we have $I_0 \subseteq J_0$ and

$$(I_0, J_0) = W_{\Pi,K}(I_0, J_0) = (St_{\Pi,K}(J_0), St_{\Pi,K}(I_0)).$$

It follows that $I_0 = St_{\Pi,K}(J_0)$ and $I_0 \subseteq St_{\Pi,K}(I_0)$. We call the pair $(I_0, St_{\Pi,K}(I_0))$ the *well-founded model of Π based on input K*.[6] Atoms in I_0 are *true* in the model and those not in $St_{\Pi,K}(I_0)$ are *false*. All the other atoms are *unknown*. If $I_0 = St_{\Pi,K}(I_0)$, then we call the well-founded model *total*, as no atoms are *unknown* in it.

Before we proceed, we note two results generalizing well-known properties of stable and well-founded models of standard finitary programs to the present setting. The first one states that the well-founded model of Π based on input K approximates all input ID-stable models of Π such that $I \cap A^{in} = K$. The second one relates total well-founded and stable models.

Proposition 8. *If (I_0, J_0) is the well-founded model of Π based on the input K, and I is an input ID-stable model of Π such that $I \cap A^{in} = K$, then $I_0 \subseteq I \subseteq J_0$.*

Proposition 9. *Let Π be a program and $K \in Int_{A^{in}}$. If the well-founded model of Π based on input K is total, then it is of the form (I, I), where $I \cap A^{in} = K$ and I is an input ID-stable model of Π.*

The well-founded models based on a specified input form the basis of the logic PC(ID). We introduce this logic here in a form adapted to the infinitary setting.

Definition 9. *Let A be a propositional signature. A* PC(ID) theory *is a pair (F, Π), where $F \subseteq \mathcal{L}^{inf}_A$ and Π is a program in A. An interpretation $I \in Int_A$ is an* ID-model *of (F, Π) if I is a model of F and (I, I) is the well-founded model of Π based on input $I \cap A^{in}$.*

One can define a PC(ID) theory as consisting of a propositional theory in $\mathcal{L}^{inf}_A$ and a set of programs. The concept of an ID-model extends directly to that more general setting. However, all salient features of the logic PC(ID) are captured by theories with a single program (cf. Denecker et al. [15]), which is the reason for the restriction we adopted.

[6] The concept of the well-founded model in the finitary propositional setting is due to Van Gelder et al. [21].

A program Π in a signature A is *total* if for every $K \in Int_{A^{in}}$, the well-founded model of Π based on the input K is total. Total programs are also called *definitions*. A PC(ID) theory is *total* if its program is total. PC(ID) theories that arise naturally in knowledge representation applications are total. From now on we focus on total PC(ID) theories and study the connection between the concepts of ID-models and ID-stable models.

To this end, we extend the class of programs we consider. Namely, we allow programs to contain *constraints*, that is, clauses of the form $\bot \leftarrow \varphi$, where $\varphi \in \mathcal{L}_A^{inf}$.

Definition 10. *Let Π be an infinitary program in a signature A and let Π' and Π'' consist of all non-constraint and constraint clauses in Π, respectively. An interpretation I is an* input ID-stable model *of Π if I is an input ID-stable model of Π' and a model of Π''*

Remark. Constraints can also be handled directly in the language of programs as we introduced them earlier. Let Π be a program (without constraints). An atom f such that every clause in Π with f in the head is of the form $f \leftarrow \varphi \wedge \neg f$ is an *effective contradiction* for Π. Clauses in Π with heads that are effective contradictions for Π are called *effective constraints* in Π. Here, as in the finitary case, effective constraints work as constraints. Specifically, let Π be a program without constraints (but, possibly, with effective constraints), and let Π' be a program with constraints obtained from Π by replacing each effective constraint $f \leftarrow \varphi \wedge \neg f$ with the constraint $\bot \leftarrow \varphi$. One can show that an interpretation $I \in Int_A$ is an input ID-stable model of Π if and only if I is an input ID-stable model of Π' according to Definition 10. □

Let $F \subseteq \mathcal{L}_A^{inf}$. Formulas in F can be written as constraints. Namely, we define

$$F^{\leftarrow} = \{\bot \leftarrow \neg\varphi \mid \varphi \in F\}.$$

It is clear that F and $F^{\leftarrow}$ have the same models (are equivalent). We have the following connection between total PC(ID) theories and programs with constraints.

Theorem 9. *Let F be a set of formulas from $\mathcal{L}_A^{inf}$ and Π a definition in A (without constraints). An interpretation $I \in Int_A$ is an ID-model of (F, Π) if and only if I is an input ID-stable model of $\Pi \cup F^{\leftarrow}$.*

Proof. Let I be an ID-model of (F, Π). Then I is a model of F, and (I, I) is the well-founded model of Π based on the input $I \cap A^{in}$. By Proposition 9, I is an input ID-stable model of Π. By Definition 10, I is an input ID-stable model of $\Pi \cup F^{\leftarrow}$.

Conversely, let I be an input ID-stable model of $\Pi \cup F^{\leftarrow}$. By Definition 10, I is a model of F and an input ID-stable model of Π. Let (I_0, J_0) be the well-founded model of Π based on input $I \cap A^{in}$. By Proposition 8, $I_0 \subseteq I \subseteq J_0$. Since Π is total, $I_0 = J_0$ and so, (I, I) is the well-founded model of Π based on input $I \cap A^{in}$. Thus, I is an ID-model of (F, Π). □

Input stable and input ID-stable models coincide for the class of programs whose rules have formulas from $\mathcal{N}$ as their bodies (Theorem 6). Under the restriction to that class of programs, Theorem 9 implies the following connection between ID-models of PC(ID) theories and stable models of infinitary programs.

Theorem 10. *Let $F \subseteq \mathcal{L}_A^{inf}$ and Π be a definition (without constraints) in A such that for every clause $p \leftarrow G \in \Pi$, $G \in \mathcal{N}$. Then an interpretation I is an ID-model for (F, Π) if and only if I is a stable model of $\Pi^{in} \cup F^{\leftarrow}$.*

Proof. Let I be an ID-model for (F, Π). By Theorem 9, I is an input ID-stable model of $\Pi \cup F^{\leftarrow}$. By the definitions and Theorem 6, I is an input stable model of $\Pi \cup F^{\leftarrow}$ and so, by Proposition 5, a stable model of $(\Pi \cup F^{\leftarrow})^{in} = \Pi^{in} \cup F^{\leftarrow}$ (it is straightforward to see that Proposition 5 extends to the case of programs with constraints). All these implications can be reversed and so, the converse implication follows. □

We now move on to the first-order case. An *FO(ID) theory* in a first-order signature σ is a pair (F, Π), where F is a set of sentences in σ and Π is a program in σ. We define the semantics of FO(ID) theories by lifting the semantics of the infinitary PC(ID) theories. One can show that this definition is equivalent to the original one [5].

Definition 11. *Let (F, Π) be an FO(ID) theory in a signature σ. An interpretation $I = \langle I^f, I^r \rangle$ of σ is an* ID-model *of (F, Π) if I^r is an ID-model of the PC(ID) theory $(gr_I(F), gr_I(\Pi))$ (in the propositional signature $A_{\sigma,I}$).*

A definition Π is *total*, if for every interpretation $I = \langle I^f, I^r \rangle$, the well-founded model of $gr_I(\Pi)$ based on the input $I^r \cap A_{\sigma^{in},I}$ is total. In particular, it follows that if Π is total then $gr_I(\Pi)$ is total.

Theorem 11. *Let σ be a first-order signature and let (F, Π) be an FO(ID) theory such that Π is total. An interpretation I is an ID-model of (F, Π) if and only if I is an input ID-stable model of $\Pi \cup F^{\leftarrow}$.*

Proof. The following statements are equivalent:

1. I is an ID-model of (F, Π)
2. I^r is an ID-model of $(gr_I(F), gr_I(\Pi))$
3. I^r is an input ID-model of $gr_I(\Pi) \cup [gr_I(F)]^{\leftarrow}$
4. I^r is an input ID-model of $gr_I(\Pi) \cup gr_I(F^{\leftarrow}) = gr_I(\Pi \cup F^{\leftarrow})$
5. I is an input ID-stable model of $\Pi \cup F^{\leftarrow}$.

The equivalences (1) ≡ (2) and (4) ≡ (5) follow from the corresponding definitions. The equivalence (2) ≡ (3) follows from Theorem 9 and the equivalence (3) ≡ (4) from the identity $[gr_I(\varphi)]^{\leftarrow} = gr_I(\varphi^{\leftarrow})$, which is a direct consequence of the definition of the operators $gr_I(\cdot)$ and $\{\cdot\}^{\leftarrow}$. □

The next result connects ID-models of an FO(ID) theory whose program is a definition consisting of rules with bodies in $\mathcal{N}^{fo}$ and stable models of a certain program.

Theorem 12. *Let σ be a first-order signature and let (F, Π) be an FO(ID) theory such that Π is total and for every $\forall \boldsymbol{X}\ (p(\boldsymbol{X}) \leftarrow G) \in \Pi$, $G \in \mathcal{N}^{fo}$. An interpretation I is an ID-model of (F, Π) if and only if I is a stable model of $\Pi^{in} \cup F^{\leftarrow}$.*

Proof. The following statements are equivalent:

1. I is an ID-model of (F, Π)
2. I is an input ID-stable model of $\Pi \cup F^{\leftarrow}$
3. I is an input stable model of $\Pi \cup F^{\leftarrow}$
4. I is a stable model of $\Pi^{in} \cup F^{\leftarrow}$.

The equivalence (1) $\equiv$ (2) follows by Theorem 11. The equivalence (2) $\equiv$ (3) follows from the fact that Π has the same input stable and input ID-stable models (Theorem 8), and from the definitions of input stable and input ID-stable models of programs with constraints. Finally, the equivalence (3) $\equiv$ (4) follows from Theorem 7. □

If F and Π are finite, Theorem 12 can be restated in terms of the operator SM.

Corollary 1. *Let σ be a first-order signature and let (F, Π) be an FO(ID) theory such that Π is total and for every rule $\forall \boldsymbol{X}\,(p(\boldsymbol{X}) \leftarrow G) \in \Pi$, $G \in \mathcal{N}^{fo}$. An interpretation I is an ID-model of (F, Π) if and only if I is a model of $SM[\Pi^{in} \cup F^{\leftarrow}]$.*

A representation of programs in terms of FO(ID) theories is also possible. We will outline it below. We omit proofs as they are similar to other proofs we constructed in the paper. Let σ be a first-order signature. By σ^* we denote the extension of σ with relation symbol p^* for every relation symbol $p \in \sigma$ (p^* must be of the same arity as p). For a program Π, we define Π^* to be the program obtained by replacing each negative occurrence of an atom $p(\boldsymbol{t})$ in the body of a rule in Π by $p^*(\boldsymbol{t})$. It is easy to see that Π^* is total. Next, we define $F_\sigma = \{\forall \boldsymbol{X}\,(p(\boldsymbol{X}) \leftrightarrow p^*(\boldsymbol{X})) \mid p \text{ is a relational symbol in } \sigma\}$. Finally, for an interpretation $I \in Int_\sigma$, we define I^* to be an interpretation of σ^* that has the same domain as I, coincides with I on all symbols common to the two interpretations, and interprets every relation symbol p^* in the same way as p. One can prove the following results.

Theorem 13. *Let Π be a program in a first-order signature σ. An interpretation $I \in Int_\sigma$ is an ID-stable model of Π if and only if the interpretation I^* is an ID-model of (F_σ, Π^*).*

Corollary 2. *Let Π be a program in a first-order signature σ such that for every rule $\forall \boldsymbol{X}\,(p(\boldsymbol{X}) \leftarrow G) \in \Pi$, $G \in \mathcal{N}^{fo}$. An interpretation I of σ is a stable model of Π if and only if I^* is an ID-model of (F_σ, Π^*).*

6 Conclusions

We introduced characterizations of several first-order ASP logics in terms of reducts of infinitary propositional theories. We used these characterizations to relate these logics. Under some restrictions on program components in total FO(ID) theories, these theories can be encoded as programs so that their ID-models correspond precisely with answer-sets of the programs resulting from the translation. The restricted class of theories contains, in particular, theories that arise naturally in practical applications — their definitions are represented by standard stratified logic programs. A converse encoding (under similar syntactic restrictions) is possible, too. Thus, for theories arising in the ASP practice, there is no formal difference between the logic FO(ID) and the full first-order extension of logic programming with the answer-set semantics proposed in the literature.

Acknowledgments. I am grateful to Yulia Lierler for discussions and comments related to the topic of this work.

References

1. Denecker, M.: The Well-Founded Semantics Is the Principle of Inductive Definition. In: Dix, J., Fariñas del Cerro, L., Furbach, U. (eds.) JELIA 1998. LNCS (LNAI), vol. 1489, pp. 1–16. Springer, Heidelberg (1998)
2. Denecker, M.: Extending Classical Logic with Inductive Definitions. In: Palamidessi, C., Moniz Pereira, L., Lloyd, J.W., Dahl, V., Furbach, U., Kerber, M., Lau, K.-K., Sagiv, Y., Stuckey, P.J. (eds.) CL 2000. LNCS (LNAI), vol. 1861, pp. 703–717. Springer, Heidelberg (2000)
3. Denecker, M., Lierler, Y., Truszczynski, M., Vennekens, J.: A Tarskian semantics for Answer Set Programming (2012) (a manuscript)
4. Denecker, M., Marek, V., Truszczyński, M.: Approximations, stable operators, well-founded fixpoints and applications in nonmonotonic reasoning. In: Minker, J. (ed.) Logic-Based Artificial Intelligence, pp. 127–144. Kluwer Academic Publishers (2000)
5. Denecker, M., Ternovska, E.: A logic for non-monotone inductive definitions. ACM Transactions on Computational Logic 9(2) (2008)
6. Doets, K.: From Logic to Logic Programming. Foundations of Computing Series. MIT Press, Cambridge (1994)
7. Ferraris, P.: Answer Sets for Propositional Theories. In: Baral, C., Greco, G., Leone, N., Terracina, G. (eds.) LPNMR 2005. LNCS (LNAI), vol. 3662, pp. 119–131. Springer, Heidelberg (2005)
8. Ferraris, P., Lee, J., Lifschitz, V.: Stable models and circumscription. Artif. Intell. 175(1), 236–263 (2011)
9. Ferraris, P., Lifschitz, V.: Mathematical foundations of answer set programming. In: Artëmov, S., Barringer, H., d'Avila Garcez, A., Lamb, L.C., Woods, J. (eds.) We Will Show Them! Essays in Honour of Dov Gabbay, pp. 615–664. College Publications (2005)
10. Gelfond, M., Lifschitz, V.: The stable semantics for logic programs. In: Proceedings of the 5th International Conference on Logic Programming (ICLP 1988), pp. 1070–1080. MIT Press (1988)
11. Gelfond, M., Lifschitz, V.: Classical negation in logic programs and disjunctive databases. New Generation Computing 9, 365–385 (1991)
12. Gelfond, M.: Representing Knowledge in A-Prolog. In: Kakas, A.C., Sadri, F. (eds.) Computat. Logic (Kowalski Festschrift) . LNCS (LNAI), vol. 2408, pp. 413–451. Springer, Heidelberg (2002)
13. Lierler, Y., Truszczynski, M.: Transition systems for model generators - a unifying approach. Theory and Practice of Logic Programming 11(4-5), 629–646 (2011)
14. Marek, V., Truszczyński, M.: Stable models and an alternative logic programming paradigm. In: Apt, K., Marek, W., Truszczyński, M., Warren, D. (eds.) The Logic Programming Paradigm: a 25-Year Perspective, pp. 375–398. Springer, Berlin (1999)
15. Mariën, M., Wittocx, J., Denecker, M., Bruynooghe, M.: SAT(ID): Satisfiability of Propositional Logic Extended with Inductive Definitions. In: Kleine Büning, H., Zhao, X. (eds.) SAT 2008. LNCS, vol. 4996, pp. 211–224. Springer, Heidelberg (2008)
16. Niemelä, I.: Logic programming with stable model semantics as a constraint programming paradigm. Annals of Mathematics and Artificial Intelligence 25(3-4), 241–273 (1999)
17. Oikarinen, E., Janhunen, T.: Achieving compositionality of the stable model semantics for Smodels programs. Theory and Practice of Logic Programming 5-6, 717–761 (2008)

18. Pearce, D.: A New Logical Characterisation of Stable Models and Answer Sets. In: Dix, J., Przymusinski, T.C., Moniz Pereira, L. (eds.) NMELP 1996. LNCS, vol. 1216, pp. 57–70. Springer, Heidelberg (1997)
19. Pearce, D., Valverde, A.: Quantified Equilibrium Logic and Foundations for Answer Set Programs. In: Garcia de la Banda, M., Pontelli, E. (eds.) ICLP 2008. LNCS, vol. 5366, pp. 546–560. Springer, Heidelberg (2008)
20. Reiter, R.: A logic for default reasoning. Artificial Intelligence 13(1-2), 81–132 (1980)
21. Van Gelder, A., Ross, K., Schlipf, J.: The well-founded semantics for general logic programs. Journal of the ACM 38(3), 620–650 (1991)

A New Incarnation of Action Language H

Sandeep Chintabathina[1] and Richard Watson[2]

[1] University of Arkansas at Pine Bluff, Pine Bluff AR 71601, USA
chintabathinas@uapb.edu
[2] Texas Tech University, Lubbock TX 79409, USA
richard.watson@ttu.edu

Abstract. In this paper we present a new version of action language H which is more expressive and powerful than its previous version. We enhanced the syntax to include triggers which allows us to reason about natural actions. The new version is capable of modeling a variety of domains, demonstrating that it is a good language for knowledge representation. We present the syntax and semantics of the language and show how it can be used to model the behavior of a bouncing ball.

1 Introduction

An intelligent agent is a software entity capable of reasoning, planning and acting on its own. To act intelligently, the agent must have knowledge about its environment and its own capabilities and goals. There are several approaches to representing and reasoning about such knowledge. In this paper, we use *Action languages* - high-level languages for representing and reasoning about actions and their effects [9]. This approach is applicable if the dynamic system which includes the agent and its environment is viewed as a transition diagram whose states correspond to possible physical states of the system and whose arcs are labeled by actions. A transition, $\langle \sigma, a, \sigma' \rangle$, of a diagram denotes that action a is possible in state σ and that after the execution of a the system may move to state σ'. The diagram consists of all possible trajectories of the system. A theory written in some action language (often called an *action description*) describes a transition diagram that contains all possible trajectories of a given dynamic system.

Currently there are several action languages that are used to study different features of dynamic domains. For instance action language $\mathcal{AL}$ [2,19] is simply an extension of action language $\mathcal{A}$ [8] by state constraints which express causal relations between *fluents*[1]. The semantics of $\mathcal{AL}$ formalize McCarthy's *Principle of inertia* which says that "*Things tend to stay the same unless they are changed by actions*" [11]. $\mathcal{AL}$ was designed to capture fluents such as the position of a switch which changes when the switch is flipped. However, it was not designed to capture properties such as the *height* of a falling brick which changes continuously with time. In this paper, properties of domain that change

[1] Functions whose values depend on a state and may change as a result of actions.

E. Erdem et al. (Eds.): Correct Reasoning, LNCS 7265, pp. 560–575, 2012.

continuously with time will be referred to as *process fluents*. Domains consisting of both process and non-process fluents are called *hybrid domains*.

We have logic-based formalisms such as Situation Calculus and Event Calculus that are capable of reasoning about process fluents. Reiter and fellow researchers extended the language of situation calculus (sitcalc) [16] to incorporate time, concurrency and other features. Shanahan [17] extended event calculus to be able to reason about process fluents. Both approaches demonstrate via examples how their approach can be used for reasoning about process fluents. However, in both approaches, it is difficult to express causal relations between fluents. We will demonstrate this using an example presented later on in this paper. There is an action language called $\mathcal{ADC}$ [3] for reasoning about process fluents. However, this language is based on action language $\mathcal{A}$ and does not support state constraints.

In this paper we are interested in modeling hybrid domains. Language H (*Hybrid*) is an action language based approach for modeling hybrid domains. We presented an earlier version of H in [4]. However, in this paper we redesigned H by extending the signature of $\mathcal{AL}$ with

- a collection of numbers for representing time
- a collection of functions defined over time (*processes*)
- fluents with non-boolean values including fluents defined by functions of time (process fluents).

and adding *triggers* which allows us to specify conditions under which actions are triggered. The semantics of $\mathcal{AL}$ is based on the McCain-Turner equation [10]. We modify this equation slightly to define the semantics of H. In this way both languages are based on the same underlying intuition. However, there is a major difference between the transition diagrams described by action descriptions of $\mathcal{AL}$ and those described by action descriptions of H. A state of a transition diagram described by action description of $\mathcal{AL}$ is a snapshot of the world. Whereas in H, a state represents continuous evolution of fluents over a time interval represented as $[start, end]$. Intuitively, the length of a time interval denotes the time elapsed between two consecutive actions. The lower bound of the interval, *start*, denotes the time at which an action initiates a state and the upper bound, *end*, denotes the time at which an action terminates a state. We assume that actions are instantaneous i.e. the actual duration is negligible with respect to the duration of units of time in our domain.

In the previous version of H [4], every state was assigned an interval of the form $[0, end]$. Thus, every state had its own local (internal) clock which was later mapped to global time for reasoning purposes. The new version of H presented in this paper only uses global time which is convenient for reasoning. In the previous version, properties that changed continuously with time were treated differently from fluents. In the new version, properties that change continuously with time are nothing but fluents defined by functions of time. As a result, the syntax of the new version is much simpler than the syntax of the previous version. Also, the new version allows triggers which was not allowed in the previous version. This allows us to model domains that could not be modeled properly in the past. In [5], we show that the new version is able to reason about a variety of domains involving natural actions, resources, actions with durations or delayed effects and default behavior. We compared action descriptions of H with logical theories of situation calculus and discovered that action descriptions of H are simpler, concise and elaboration tolerant.

In this paper, we discuss the new syntax and semantics of H followed by a brief section on methodology. We present an example of using H for reasoning about natural actions and talk about the solvers used in the implementation of H.

2 Syntax

By *sort* we mean a non-empty countable collection of strings in some fixed alphabet. A *sorted signature* Σ is a collection of sorts and function symbols.

A *process signature* is a sorted signature with special sorts *time*, *action*, and *process*. Sort *time* is normally identified with one of the standard numerical sorts with the exception that it contains an ordinal ω such that for any $x \in time \setminus \{\omega\}$, $\omega > x$. No operations are defined over ω. If time is discrete, elements of $time \setminus \{\omega\}$ may be viewed as non-negative integers, otherwise they can be interpreted as either rational numbers, constructive real numbers, etc.

Sort *process* contains strings of the form $\lambda T.f(T)$ where T is a variable ranging over *time* and $f(T)$ is a mathematical expression (possibly) containing T. A string $\lambda T.f(T)$ represents a function defined over *time*. The λ is said to bind T in $f(T)$. If the expression, $f(T)$, does not contain any variables for time then $\lambda T.f(T)$ is said to denote a constant function. For e.g. $\lambda T.0$ denotes the constant function 0. For simplicity we assume that all functions from *process* have the same range denoted by the sort *range*(*process*). An example of a function from sort *process* is $\lambda T.h - (g/2) * (T - t)^2$ which defines the height in meters, at time T, of a freely falling object dropped from a height h, $T - t$ seconds before. The symbol g denotes the Earth's average gravitational acceleration which is equal to 9.8 $meters/sec^2$. From now onwards we will replace $g/2$ by 4.9.

Sort *action* is divided into subsorts *agent* and *exogenous*. Elements of *agent* are actions performed by an agent and elements of *exogenous* are actions that are not performed by an agent. Both agent and exogenous actions will be referred to as actions.

The collection of function symbols includes names for fluents and standard numerical functions. Each fluent name is associated with an *arity* - a number indicating the number of arguments. Intuitively, *fluents* are properties that may change as a result of actions. For example, the *height* of a brick held at a certain position above the ground could change when it is dropped. Every process signature contains reserved fluents *start* and *end* of sort *time*.

A *term of sort s* is defined as follows:

1. A string $y \in s$ is a term of sort s;
2. If $t_1, \ldots, t_n$ are terms of sorts $s_1, \ldots, s_n$ respectively and $f : s_1 \times \ldots \times s_n \to s$ is a function symbol then $f(t_1, \ldots, t_n)$ is a term of sort s.

Notice that if $f(\bar{x})$ is a term of sort *process* and t is a term of sort *time* then $f(\bar{x})(t)$ is a term of sort *range(process)*. For example, to represent the height of brick b we can introduce a fluent $height(b)$ of sort *process*. Then by $height(b)(10)$ we denote the height of b at time 10. Similarly, $\lambda T.200-4.9*(T-5)^2(10)$ denotes the value of the function at $T = 10$ which is equal to 77.5.

An *atom* of Σ is a statement of the form $t = y$ where t is a term of some sort s and $y \in s$. Examples of atoms are $end = 10$, $2+3 = 5$ etc. If t is a term built from fluent symbols then such an atom is called a *fluent atom*. Examples of fluent atoms are $height(b) = \lambda T.100 - 4.9 * (T-5)^2$, $height(b)(5) = 100$ etc.

A *literal* of Σ is an atom $t = y$ or its negation $\neg(t = y)$. Negation of $=$ will be often written as $\neq$. If t is a term of Boolean sort then $t = true$ ($t \neq false$) is often written as t and $t = false$ ($t \neq true$) is often written as $\neg t$. For example, the atom $4 < 5 = true$ will be written as $4 < 5$.

Language, H, is parameterized by a process signature Σ with standard interpretations of numerical functions and relations (such as $+, <, \leq, \neq$, etc).

Definition 1. An *action description* of $H(\Sigma)$ is a collection of statements of the form:

$$l_0 \text{ if } l_1, \ldots, l_n. \quad (1)$$

$$e \text{ causes } l_0 \text{ if } l_1, \ldots, l_n. \quad (2)$$

$$\text{impossible } e_1, \ldots, e_m \text{ if } l_1, \ldots, l_n. \quad (3)$$

$$l_1, \ldots, l_n \text{ triggers } e. \quad (4)$$

where e's are elements of *action*, l_0's are fluent atoms and $l_1, \ldots, l_n$ are literals of the signature of H. l_0 is referred to as the *head* of a statement and $l_1, \ldots, l_n$ are referred to as the *body* of a statement.

A statement of the form (1) is called a *state constraint*. It guarantees that any state satisfying $l_1, \ldots, l_n$ also satisfies l_0. A statement of the form (2) is called a *dynamic causal law* and it states that if action e were executed in a state satisfying literals $l_1, \ldots, l_n$ then any successor state would satisfy l_0. A statement of the form (3) is called an *executability condition* and it states that actions $e_1, \ldots, e_m$ cannot be executed in a state satisfying $l_1, \ldots, l_n$. If $n = 0$ then *if* is dropped from statements (1), (2) and (3). A statement of the form (4) is called a *trigger* and it states that action e is triggered in any state satisfying $l_1, \ldots, l_n$.

By ground instantiations of a variable of sort s, we mean the elements of s. From the description of the syntax, the only variable that appears in the statements of H is the variable T ranging over time. However, variables ranging over other sorts are allowed in the statements as long as those statements are viewed as a shorthand for the collection of statements obtained by replacing each occurrence of a variables other than T by its corresponding ground instantiations.

As we can see, statements of H are very similar to statements of $\mathcal{AL}$. In fact, all statements except for statements of the form (4) are similar to statements of $\mathcal{AL}$. One more difference is that H allows both boolean and non-boolean fluents whereas $\mathcal{AL}$ allows only boolean fluents. For example, literals such as $f = 5$ and $p = \lambda T.T^2$ where f and p are fluents are allowed to appear in the statements of H. However, this is not allowed in $\mathcal{AL}$. The following proposition specifies conditions under which an action description of H is syntactically equivalent to an action description of $\mathcal{AL}$.

Proposition 1. An action description of H that does not contain triggers and whose statements contain only literals built from boolean fluents is an action description of $\mathcal{AL}$.

3 Semantics

The semantics of language H is based on a slightly modified McCain-Turner equation [10]. An action description, AD, of H(Σ) describes a transition diagram, $TD(AD)$, whose nodes correspond to possible physical states of a system and whose arcs are labeled by actions. A transition $\langle s, a, s' \rangle$ of the diagram denotes that action a is possible in s and as a result of execution of a the system may move to state s'. It is important to note that an action description of H can be either *deterministic* (i.e. for any state-action pair there is at most one successor state [2]) or *non-deterministic* (i.e. there is a state-action pair with more than one successor state). In this section we will give a formal definition for a state and a transition of $TD(AD)$. We begin with interpreting symbols of Σ.

Definition 2. Given an action description AD of $H(\Sigma)$, an *interpretation* I of Σ is a mapping defined as follows.

- for every non-process sort, s, and every string $y \in s$, I maps y into itself i.e. $y^I = y$.
- standard interpretation is used for the sort *process* and other standard numerical functions and relations.
- I maps every fluent into a properly typed function.

Often an interpretation I of Σ is identified with a collection, $s(I)$, of atoms of the form $t = y$ such that $t^I = y$ where t and y are terms of some sort. In other words, $s(I) = \{t = y \mid t^I = y\}$.

Before we give the definition of a state of $TD(AD)$ let us consider the following definitions.

A set, s, of atoms is said to be *consistent* if for every atom $t = y_1 \in s$, $\neg\exists y_2$ such that $t = y_2 \in s$ and $y_1 \neq y_2$.

Let us define what it means for a literal to be true w.r.t a set of atoms of Σ.

Definition 3. Given a consistent set, L, of atoms of Σ

- An atom $t = y$ is *true in* L (symbolically $L \models t = y$) iff $t = y \in L$.
- A literal $t \neq y$ is *true in* L ($L \models t \neq y$) iff $L \models t = y_0$ and $y \neq y_0$.

We will now define what it means for a set of atoms to be closed under state constraints of AD.

Definition 4. A *set L of atoms is closed under the state constraint*

$$l_0 \text{ if } l_1, \ldots, l_n$$

of AD if, whenever $L \models l_i$ for every i, $1 \leq i \leq n$, $L \models l_0$.

A *set L of atoms is closed under state constraints* of AD if L is closed under every state constraint of AD.

Next, we define what it means for a set of atoms to satisfy a trigger of AD.

Definition 5. A *set L of atoms of H satisfies a trigger*

$$l_1, \ldots, l_n \text{ triggers } e$$

of AD iff $L \models l_i$ for every i such that $1 \leq i \leq n$.

Intuitively, if a set of atoms satisfies a trigger it means that the corresponding action will take place at some time point. The next definition characterizes sets of atoms that define the earliest possible occurrence times of triggered actions.

Definition 6. A *set L of atoms of H is closed under triggers* of AD iff $\neg\exists\ L'$ such that L' satisfies at least one trigger of AD and $L \setminus L' = \{end = t_2\}$ and $L' \setminus L = \{end = t_1\}$ and $t_1 < t_2$.

Now we are ready to give the definition of a state of $TD(AD)$.

Definition 7. Given an interpretation I of Σ, $s(I)$ is a *state* of $TD(AD)$ if each of the following holds.

- $s(I)$ is a collection of atoms of the form $t = y$ such that $t^I = y$ where t and y are terms of the same sort.
- $s(I)$ is closed under the state constraints of AD.
- If $s(I) \models start = t_1$ and $s(I) \models end = t_2$ then $t_1 \leq t_2 \wedge t_1 < \omega$.
- $s(I)$ is closed under the triggers of AD.
- If $s(I) \models p = \lambda T.f(T)$ where p is a fluent of sort *process* then $\lambda T.f(T)$ is defined over the domain $\{t \mid start^I \leq t \leq end^I \wedge t < \omega\}$.
- If p is a fluent of sort *process* and t is a term of sort *time* then $s(I) \models p(t) = x$ iff $s(I) \models p = \lambda T.f(T)$ and $\lambda T.f(T)(t^I) = x$.

By definition of interpretation every symbol is mapped uniquely. Therefore, states of $TD(AD)$ are complete and consistent. Whenever convenient the parameter I will be dropped from $s(I)$.

Intuitively, a state can be viewed as a collection of functions of time defined over an interval. The endpoints of the interval are implicitly defined by the reserved fluents *start* and *end*. The domain of each function is the set $\{t \mid start \leq t \leq end \wedge t < \omega\}$. We say that a state is defined over an interval of the form $[start, end]$ iff $end \neq \omega$. There is at least one arc labeled by an action leading out of such a state. We say that a state is defined over an interval of the form $[start, end)$ iff $end = \omega$. There is no arc leading out of such a state. States that begin at time 0 are called *initial states*. They define the initial conditions of a domain.

Now that we have defined what a state is we will define what is means for an action to be possible in a state.

Definition 8. Action a is *possible* in state s if for every non-empty subset a_0 of a, there is no executability condition

$$\text{impossible } a_0 \text{ if } l_1, \dots, l_n.$$

of AD such that $s \models l_i$ for every i, $1 \leq i \leq n$.

Given a state s and action e let us define what are the direct effects of executing e in s.

Definition 9. Let e be an elementary action that is possible in state s. By $E_s(e)$ we denote the set of all *direct effects of* e w.r.t s.

$$E_s(e) = \{l_0 \mid e \text{ causes } l_0 \text{ if } l_1, \dots, l_n \in AD \wedge s \models l_i \text{ for every } i, 1 \leq i \leq n\}$$

If a is a compound action then $E_s(a) = \bigcup_{e \in a} E_s(e)$.

The following definition allows us to identify sets of literals with adjacent intervals.

Definition 10. Let x, y, and z be elements of sort *time* such that $x \leq y \leq z \wedge y < \omega$ and s and s' be sets of literals of H. We say that s' *follows* s iff $s \models \{start = x, end = y\}$ and $s' \models \{start = y, end = z\}$.

Given two sets of literals s and s', the function $T_s(s')$ is defined as follows.

$$T_s(s') = \begin{cases} \{start = t_1, end = t_2\} \text{ if } s' \text{ follows } s \wedge \{start = t_1, end = t_2\} \subseteq s'. \\ \emptyset \text{ otherwise.} \end{cases}$$

In other words, the function returns the interval of s' if s' follows s; otherwise it returns an empty set.

The consequences of a set of atoms w.r.t a set of state constraints is defined as follows.

Definition 11. Given a set S of atoms and a set Z of state constraints of AD the set, $Cn_Z(S)$, of *consequences of S under Z* is the smallest set of atoms (w.r.t set theoretic inclusion) containing S and closed under Z.

Definition 12. *Action a is complete w.r.t a set of literals* s if for every trigger r of the form

$$l_1, \dots, l_n \text{ triggers } e$$

$e \in a$ iff s satisfies r.

We know that a state contains arbitrary atoms of Σ. However, for the next definition we will focus our attention on fluent atoms and atoms formed from *start* and *end*. Other atoms belonging to a state will be ignored because they are either universally true or could be derived from fluent atoms.

Definition 13. A transition diagram $TD(AD)$ is a tuple $\langle \phi, \psi \rangle$ where

- ϕ is the set of states.
- ψ is the set of all transitions $\langle s, a, s' \rangle$ such that each of the following holds.
  - a is complete w.r.t s
  - a is possible in s
  - s' is closed under the triggers of AD
  - $$s' = Cn_Z(E_s(a) \cup (s \cap s') \cup T_s(s')) \tag{1}$$

    where Z is the set of state constraints of AD.

The set, $E_s(a)$, consists of direct effects of a while the set, $s \cap s'$, consists of facts preserved by inertia. $T_s(s')$ projects the *start* and *end* of s'. The application of Cn_Z to the union of these sets adds the indirect effects.

4 Methodology

After working with a number of examples we came up with a methodology for writing action descriptions of H. Here are some guidelines to writing decent action descriptions of H.

- Do not allow reserved fluents such as *start* and *end* to appear in the heads of dynamic causal laws.
- Currently, there are no restrictions on the type of actions allowed in the triggers. However, an action classified as an agent action should not be part of a trigger.
- Avoid writing action descriptions that contain both a trigger as well as an executablity condition involving the same action. This is because if the bodies of both laws are satisfied then it implies that the action is triggered and impossible at the same time. We can avoid such situations by combining the executability condition with the trigger to obtain a collection of triggers. In this way we end up with only one type of statements and avoid conflicts with other statements. For example, if A is an action description of H containing only the statements

  $$l_1, \ldots, l_n \text{ triggers } e$$

  $$\text{impossible } e \text{ if } k_1, \ldots, k_m$$

  then A' is an action description of H similar to A obtained by combining these statements into a collection of triggers

  $$l_1, \ldots, l_n, \neg k_1 \text{ triggers } e$$

  $$\ldots\ldots\ldots$$

  $$l_1, \ldots, l_n, \neg k_m \text{ triggers } e$$

  The resulting action description avoids the possibility of impossible actions being triggered. Action e is never triggered if the preconditions of the original executability condition hold.

5 An Example of Using H to Represent Hybrid Domains

We now illustrate the use of H through an example. Consider an agent acting in a domain consisting of a ball. The ball is held above the ground by the agent. The actions available to the agent are *drop* and *catch*. Dropping the ball causes the *height* of the ball to change continuously with time as defined by Newton's laws of motion. As the ball accelerates towards the ground it gains velocity. If the ball is not caught before it reaches the ground it hits the ground with velocity v and bounces up into the air with velocity $r * v$ where r is the rebound coefficient. The bouncing ball reaches a certain height and falls back towards the ground due to gravity. Therefore, we have two natural actions *bounce* and $fall$. Let us see how we can use language H to determine the height of the ball as various actions take place.

Let $\mathcal{A}_0$ be an action description of H. The corresponding signature $\Sigma(\mathcal{A}_0)$ consists of fluent $status$, process fluents $height$ and $velocity$, agent actions *drop* and *catch* and natural actions *bounce* and $fall$. Fluent $status$ denotes the status of the ball and ranges over $\{descending, ascending, stationary\}$. We assume that all fluents are inertial. Let sort $process$ contain functions of time ranging over $\mathcal{R}$. Therefore, $process = \{\lambda T.max(0, 20 - 4.9 * (T-1)^2), \ldots, \lambda T.max(0, 10 - 4.9 * (T-5)^2), \ldots, \}$. The corresponding causal laws are as follows.

$$
\begin{array}{ll}
drop \text{ causes } status = descending & (1) \\
fall \text{ causes } status = descending & (2) \\
\text{impossible } drop \text{ if } status \neq stationary & (3) \\
drop \text{ causes } velocity = \lambda T.9.8 * (T - T_0) \text{ if } end = T_0 & (4) \\
drop \text{ causes } height = \lambda T.max(0, X - 4.9 * (T - T_0)^2) \text{ if} & (5) \\
\qquad height(end) = X, end = T_0. & \\
fall \text{ causes } velocity = \lambda T.9.8 * (T - T_0) \text{ if } end = T_0 & (6) \\
fall \text{ causes } height = \lambda T.max(0, X - 4.9 * (T - T_0)^2) \text{ if} & (7) \\
\qquad height(end) = X, end = T_0. & \\
catch \text{ causes } status = stationary & (8) \\
\text{impossible } catch \text{ if } status = stationary & (9) \\
\text{impossible } catch \text{ if } height(end) = 0. & (10) \\
\text{impossible } drop \text{ if } height(end) = 0. & (11) \\
catch \text{ causes } velocity = \lambda T.0 & (12) \\
catch \text{ causes } height = \lambda T.X \text{ if } height(end) = X. & (13) \\
bounce \text{ causes } status = ascending & (14) \\
bounce \text{ causes } velocity = \lambda T.max(0, X * 0.8 - 9.8 * (T - T_0)) \text{ if} & (15) \\
\qquad velocity(end) = X, end = T_0. & \\
bounce \text{ causes } height = \lambda T.(X * 0.8) * (T - T_0) - 4.9 * (T - T_0)^2 \text{ if} & (16) \\
\qquad velocity(end) = X, end = T_0. & \\
status = descending,\ height(end) = 0,\ velocity(end) > 0 \text{ triggers } bounce & (17) \\
status = ascending,\ velocity(end) = 0,\ height(end) > 0 \text{ triggers } fall & (18)
\end{array}
$$

In the above causal laws, we use Newton's laws of motion to define $height$ and $velocity$. Dynamic laws (1),(4) and (5) capture the effects of *drop* on fluents *status*, *velocity* and *height* respectively. Similarly, causal laws (2), (6) and (7) capture the direct effects of *fall* on *status*, *velocity* and *height* respectively. As we can see, both *drop* and *fall* have the same direct effects. Executability condition (3) specifies conditions under which *drop* is impossible. Similarly, (9) specifies conditions under which *catch* is impossible. Executability conditions (10) and (11) state that *catch* and *drop* cannot be executed if the height of the ball (at the end of a state) is zero. We talk about the end of a state because it is the only time at which an action can take place. Dynamic laws (8), (12) and (13) capture the direct effects of *catch* on fluents *status*, *velocity*, and *height* respectively. Causal laws (14), (15) and (16) capture the effects of *bounce* on fluents *status*, *velocity* and *height* respectively. We assume the rebound coefficient to be 0.8. So when the ball strikes the ground with velocity v it rebounds with a velocity $v * 0.8$. Causal laws (15) and (16) capture this change in velocity by multiplying the *velocity* at the end of previous state by 0.8. Triggers (17) and (18) state conditions under which actions *bounce* and *fall* are triggered respectively. The transition diagram, $TD(\mathcal{A}_0)$, contains an infinite number of states and transitions. We will look at a particular trajectory of this diagram with initial state s_0 defined as follows.

$$\begin{aligned} s_0 = \{&height = \lambda T.500, status = stationary, velocity = \lambda T.0, \\ &start = 0, end = 5\} \end{aligned}$$

Action *drop* is possible in s_0. There are several successor states of s_0 w.r.t *drop* all of which differ in the value of *end*. Let us consider the following candidate for a successor state.

$$\begin{aligned} s_1 = \{&height = \lambda T.max(0, 500 - 4.9 * (T - 5)^2), status = descending, \\ &velocity = \lambda T.9.8 * (T - 5), start = 5, end = 8\} \end{aligned}$$

Let us check whether s_1 satisfies the modified McCain-Turner equation. The direct effects of *drop* are encoded by the set $E_{s_0}(drop)$.

$$\begin{aligned} E_{s_0}(drop) = \{&height = \lambda T.max(0, 500 - 4.9 * (T - 5)^2), status = descending, \\ &velocity = \lambda T.9.8 * (T - 5)\} \end{aligned}$$

As we can see nothing is carried over by inertia from state s_0 to s_1. We also have

$$T_{s_0}(s_1) = \{start = 5, end = 8\}$$

Since there are no state constraints in $\mathcal{A}_0$, the consequences of $E_{s_0}(drop) \cup T_{s_0}(s_1)$ w.r.t state constraints will be nothing more than the union of these two sets. Therefore, we get

$$\begin{aligned} \{&height = \lambda T.max(0, 500 - 4.9 * (T - 5)^2), status = descending, \\ &velocity = \lambda T.9.8 * (T - 5), start = 5, end = 8\} \end{aligned}$$

which is the same as s_1. So s_1 satisfies the modified McCain-Turner equation. Hence, we conclude that $\langle s_0, drop, s_1 \rangle$ is a transition of $TD(\mathcal{A}_0)$.

Now consider the state s_1. Action *catch* is possible in s_1 and a successor, s_2, of s_1 w.r.t *catch* is determined using the approach described above. The trajectory $\langle s_0, drop, s_1, catch, s_2\rangle$ of $TD(\mathcal{A}_0)$ is depicted in figure 1. For space reasons, we ignore *velocity* and use h and s as abbreviations for *height* and *status* respectively.

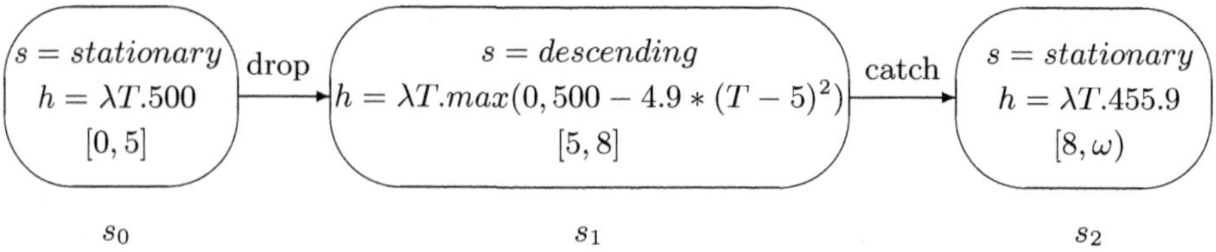

Fig. 1. Transitions caused by *drop* and *catch*

As we can see, each state has an interval associated with it and fluents are mapped into functions defined over this interval. This is a major difference between transition diagrams described by H and $\mathcal{AL}$.

The interval $[8, \omega)$ associated with state s_2 implies that no actions take place in s_2 and the domain remains in s_2 for a very long time. We also see that the end of one state coincides with the start of the next state. For this reason when an action changes the value of a fluent it is possible that the fluent has one value at the end of the current state and another value at the start of the successor state. This implies that the fluent is not uniquely defined at the shared time point. We consider these time points as the transition points for a fluent. In figure 1 it is possible to see that time points 5 and 8 are transition points for *status*.

5.1 Comparison with Sitcalc and Event Calculus

Consider a space shuttle capable of carrying objects including people. The status of a space shuttle can be represented using the fluent *status*(*shuttle*) ranging over the set R=$\{ascending, descending, orbiting\}$. Suppose we are given a list of crew members aboard the space shuttle for e.g. member(mccool,shuttle), member(chawla,shuttle) etc. We can define the status of a crew member using a state constraint of H written as follows.

$$\begin{aligned} status(M) = X \text{ if } & status(P) = X, \\ & member(M, P). \end{aligned}$$

where variable M ranges over names of crew members, P ranges over $\{shuttle\}$ and X ranges over R. Let us see how we can write this definition in Sitcalc and Event Calculus. Both formalisms are usually formulated in first or higher order logic. A direct way of representing this causal relation in either formalism would be

$$status(p, s) = x \wedge member(m, p) \supset status(m, s) = x$$

where letter s denotes situations and p, m, and x are as defined above. The drawback of this representation is that the contrapositive is also true and this can lead to unintuitive conclusions. To address this problem, Reiter and Lin [16] suggested a sitcalc solution in which instead of writing state constraints separately, we write them as part of successor state axioms. However, it is possible to have a collection of state constraints for which there are no corresponding successor state axioms. Hence, the problem persists. In Event Calculus, state constraints must be used with caution; otherwise it leads to contradiction. State constraints are most useful when fluents are divided into *primitive* and *derived*. Effect axioms are used to describe the primitive fluents and state constraints are used to describe the derived fluents in terms of the primitive ones [18]. As we can see, H does not have such limitations.

6 Implementing H

We know that an action description of H describes a transition diagram that contains an infinite number of states and transitions. However, given an initial state and a history of events that took place there are only a finite number of paths that are valid. In order to reason about properties of a domain it is enough to identify these valid paths. In the first subsection, we will see how to specify history in *H* and identify valid paths.

An action description of H can be viewed as a specification of a dynamically changing system. Given such a specification a user can implement it in several ways. One way to implement an action description is to translate it into an equivalent logic program such that there is a one-to-one correspondence between models of the logic program and models of the specification. In this way various tasks of an agent are reduced to computing models of logic programs. In our research we use *Answer Set Prolog* - a class of logic programs under answer set semantics [6,7] to implement action descriptions of H. The reason for choosing answer set prolog is its ability to represent and reason with recursive definitions, defaults and their exceptions, causal relations and incomplete information. Due to lack of space we will not discuss the details of the translation here. We will, however, discuss the solvers used for computing models of the resulting translations in the second subsection.

6.1 Specifying History

In addition to the action description, the agents knowledge base may contain the domain's *recorded history* - observations made by the agent together with a record of its own actions.

The recorded history defines a collection of paths in the diagram which, from the standpoint of the agent, can be interpreted as the system's possible pasts. If the agent's knowledge is complete (e.g., it has complete information about the initial state and the occurrences of actions) and the action description is deterministic then there is only one such path. Here is a formal definition.

Definition 14. Given an action description AD of domain $\mathcal{D}$ and an integer $n > 0$, the *recorded history*, Γ_n, of $\mathcal{D}$ upto moment n is a pair $\langle \mathcal{O}, \mathcal{H} \rangle$ where $\mathcal{O}$ is a collection of statements of the form

$$obs(p, i, t, y)$$

where p is a fluent, $y \in range(p)$, $t \in time$, and integer $i \in [0, n]$ and $\mathcal{H}$ is a collection of statements of the form

$$hpd(a, i, t)$$

where a is an elementary action, $t \in time$ and integer $i \in [0, n)$.

Integer i, often referred to as a *step*, denotes the order in which states and actions appear in a trajectory. Intuitively, the statement $hpd(a, i, t)$ means that action a was observed to have happened at time t in step i. The statement $obs(p, i, t, y)$ means that fluent p was observed to have the value y at time t in step i. Observations of the form $obs(p, 0, 0, y)$ define the initial values of fluents.

Definition 15. Given an action description AD and a recorded history Γ_n of domain $\mathcal{D}$, the pair $\langle AD, \Gamma_n \rangle$ is called a *domain description* of $\mathcal{D}$.

The following definition identifies all those paths that are compatible with agent's observations.

Definition 16. Given a domain description $\langle AD, \Gamma_n \rangle$ and the transition diagram, $TD(AD)$, described by AD, a path

$$\langle s_0, a_0, s_1, \ldots, a_{n-1}, s_n \rangle \in TD(AD)$$

is a *model of* Γ_n if each of the following holds.

1. For every i, $0 \leq i < n$, $a_i = \{a \mid hpd(a, i, t) \in \Gamma_n\}$
2. For every i, $0 \leq i < n$, if $hpd(a, i, t) \in \Gamma_n$ then $s_i \models end = t$
3. For every i, $0 \leq i \leq n$, if $obs(p, i, t, y) \in \Gamma_n$ and
   - p is a process fluent then $\exists \lambda T.f(T) \in process$ such that
   $$s_i \models p = \lambda T.f(T) \wedge \lambda T.f(T)(t) = y$$
   - p is a non-process fluent then
   $$s_i \models p = y$$
4. For every i, $0 \leq i \leq n$, if $obs(p, i, t, y) \in \Gamma_n$ then $\exists t_1, t_2 \in time$ such that $s_i \models start = t_1 \wedge s_i \models end = t_2 \wedge t_1 \leq t \leq t_2 \wedge t < \omega$.

In order to understand the above definition let us look at the example from section 5 about the bouncing ball. Let Γ_1 be a recorded history of this domain consisting of statements

$$\begin{array}{l} obs(status, 0, 0, stationary). \\ obs(height, 0, 0, 500). \\ hpd(drop, 0, 5). \\ obs(height, 1, 10, 377.5). \end{array}$$

According to these statements the agent observes that the ball is stationary at a *height* of 500 units at time 0. At t=5 seconds the agent drops the ball and observes that the height is 377.5 units at t=10 seconds in the resulting state. Now consider the following trajectory $P \in TD(\mathcal{A}_0)$.

$$\langle\{status = stationary, height = \lambda T.500, velocity = \lambda T.0, start = 0, end = 5\},$$
$$drop,$$
$$\{status = descending, height = \lambda T.max(0, 500 - 4.9 * (T - 5)^2),$$
$$velocity = \lambda T.9.8 * (T - 5), start = 5, end = 15\}\rangle$$

Upon careful observation it is possible to see that P is indeed a model of Γ_1.

6.2 Solvers for H

In the past few years researchers [1,13] have focused on integrating answer set programming(ASP) and Constraint logic programming(CLP). They came up with new systems that achieve significant improvement in performance over existing ASP solvers. The following such systems are available: *ACsolver*[12] (and it's successor *L*una[15]); *EZCSP*[2]; and *Clingcon*[3]. Each has its own strengths and weaknesses. *ACsolver* was developed as a prototype solver for the *AC* language. The implementation was more of a proof of concept than a production level effort, hence we focus on it's successor, *L*una. *Clingcon* is arguably the most developed of these solvers, however the underlying constraint solver only deals with finite domains which is a limitation when dealing with continuous functions. This makes it less than ideal for use with H.

Both *L*una and *EZCSP* allow for the infinite domains needed by H. The primary difference in approach between the solvers is how they couple the answer set solver with the constraint solver. In *L*una the constraint solver is tightly coupled with the answer set solver. As a result, solutions from the constraint solver can be used by the answer set solver to make new inferences. *EZCSP*, on the other hand, is loosely coupled. The ASP programs are written in such a way that their answer sets encode a constraint satisfaction problem. The system calls the answer set solver, translates the resulting answer sets into the input language of the constraint solver, calls the constraint solver and combines the solutions returned by both solvers. Therefore, unlike *Luna*, it is not possible to use the solutions from the constraint solver to make new inferences on the ASP side.

The coupling in the solvers also effects the input languages for the solvers and hence the translation of H. We have separate, provenly correct translations from H into the input languages used by both *L*una and *EZCSP*. While the translations for the solvers are very similar, there are cases where the *EZCSP* translation is both more complex and the resulting code is more computationally expensive than it is in the *L*una translation.

[2] `http://marcy.cjb.net/ezcsp/index.html`
[3] `http://www.cs.uni-potsdam.de/clingcon/`

From the above observations it would seem that *L*una would be the obvious choice. In theory this is true, however implementation issues also arise. Due to its loose coupling, the *EZCSP* approach makes it relatively easy to swap the solvers being used. The current version uses gringo+clasp[4] by default as the ASP solver and SICSTUS Prolog as the constraint solver. Both solvers are state-of-the-art and very fast. It also allows the use of ASP solvers such as lparse+smodels[5]. The implementation of *L*una requires modification of the source of both the ASP and the constraint solver. Not only does this limit the choice of solvers, it also makes upgrading more difficult. The current implementation of *L*una uses the constraint solver *clp(r)* and the ASP solver *Surya*[14] (which is similar to, but less efficient than, Smodels).

As a result of these implementation issues, we found that in many cases *EZCSP* performs better than *L*una. It should be noted that, while *L*una improved *ACsolver* using several modifications described in [15], it did not implement all the proposed improvements, nor did it use the proposed, more expressive version of language *AC*. There is reason to believe that a full and more efficient implementation of algorithms from [15] would be far superior to the current options.

Regardless, the use of H for tasks such as projection and planning was successfully tested using these ststems. As expected, projection is much quicker than planning since, with H, the planning task is not just determining which action to perform, but when they should happen. In essence it is both planning and scheduling. Performance for planning was reasonable for domains such as the bouncing ball example in this paper where a plan might consist of dropping the ball and then catching it at a given goal height. Further investigation is needed before we can comment on the use of these solvers for larger planning problems.

7 Conclusions and Future Work

The new version of action language H allows us to elegantly describe hybrid domains. Compared to other approaches we are able to come up with simpler, concise and elaboration tolerant action descriptions. Thanks to our translations and solvers such as EZCSP we are able to solve problems that could not be solved in the past. Our future goals include solving complex planning problems in H. We will continue to test the existing solvers and based on the outcome we will suggest improvements. Another area for future work is to improve the input language of the solvers to make it more suitable for knowledge representation.

Acknowledgements. The authors would like to give a special thanks to Vladimir Lifschitz for being an inspirational leader in this field and for laying a fertile groundwork for us to work in. The work presented here involves both ASP and Action Languages, two areas that, together with Michael Gelfond, Vladimir helped pioneer. He has been, and continues to be, a great scientist and teacher. We have both had the pleasure of attending his talks - they are among the best we have ever experienced.

[4] `http://potassco.sourceforge.net/`

[5] `http://www.tcs.hut.fi/Software/smodels/`

References

1. Balduccini, M.: Representing constraint satisfaction problems in answer set programming. In: ICLP 2009 Workshop on Answer Set Programming and Other Computing Paradigms (ASPOCP 2009) (July 2009)
2. Baral, C., Gelfond, M.: Reasoning agents in dynamic domains. In: Minker, J. (ed.) Logic-Based Artificial Intelligence, pp. 257–279. Kluwer Academic Publishers (2000)
3. Baral, C., Son, T., Tuan, L.: A transition function based characterization of actions with delayed and continuous effects. In: Proc. of KR 2002, pp. 291–302 (2002)
4. Chintabathina, S., Gelfond, M., Watson, R.: Modeling hybrid domains using process description language. In: Proc. of ASP 2005, pp. 303–317 (2005)
5. Chintabathina, S.: Towards Answer Set Progamming Based Architectures for Intelligent Agents. PhD Dissertation. Texas Tech University (December 2010)
6. Gelfond, M., Lifschitz, V.: The stable model semantics for logic programming. In: Kowalski, R., Bowen, K. (eds.) Proc. of ICLP 1988, pp. 1070–1080. The MIT Press, Cambridge (1988)
7. Gelfond, M., Lifschitz, V.: Classical negation in logic programs and disjunctive databases. New Generation Computing 9(3/4), 365–386 (1991)
8. Gelfond, M., Lifschitz, V.: Representing action and change by logic programs. Journal of Logic Programming 17, 301–321 (1993)
9. Gelfond, M., Lifschitz, V.: Action languages. Electronic Transactions on AI 3(16) (1998)
10. McCain, N., Turner, H.: A causal theory of ramifications and qualifications. In: Mellish, C. (ed.) Proc. of IJCAI 1995, pp. 1978–1984. Morgan Kaufmann (1995)
11. McCarthy, J., Hayes, P.: Some philosophical problems from the standpoint of artificial intelligence. Machine Intelligence 4, 463–502 (1969)
12. Mellarkod, V.: Integrating ASP and CLP Systems: Computing Answer Sets from Partially Ground Programs. Texas Tech University (2007)
13. Mellarkod, V., Gelfond, M., Zhang, Y.: Integrating Answer Set Programming and Constraint Logic Programming. In: Proc. of ISAIM 2008 (2008), `http://isaim2008.unl.edu/index.php`
14. Mellarkod, V.: Optimizing The Computation Of Stable Models Using Merged Rules. Masters Thesis. Texas Tech University (May 2002)
15. Ricardo Morales, A.: Improving Efficiency of Solving Computational Problems with ASP. PhD Dissertation. Texas Tech University (December 2010)
16. Reiter, R.: Knowledge in Action: Logical Foundations for Specifying and Implementing Dynamical Systems. MIT Press (2001)
17. Shanahan, M.: Solving the frame problem. MIT Press (1997)
18. Shanahan, M.: The event calculus explained. In: Artificial Intelligence Today, pp. 409–430 (1999)
19. Turner, H.: Representing actions in logic programs and default theories: A situation calculus approach. Journal of Logic Programming 31(1-3), 245–298 (1997)

Well-Supported Semantics for Logic Programs with Generalized Rules

Jia-Huai You[1], Yi-Dong Shen[2], and Kewen Wang[3]

[1] Department of Computing Science, University of Alberta, Canada
[2] State Key Laboratory of Computer Science, Chinese Academy of Sciences, China
[3] School of Computing and Information Technology, Griffith University, Australia

Abstract. Logic programming under the stable model semantics has been extended to arbitrary formulas. A question of interest is how to characterize the property of well-supportedness, in the sense of Fages, which has been considered a cornerstone in answer set programming. In this paper, we address this issue by considering *general logic programs*, which consist of disjunctive rules with arbitrary propositional formulas in rule bodies. We define the justified stable semantics for these programs, propose a general notion of well-supportedness, and show the relationships between the two. We address the issue of computational complexity for various classes of general programs. Finally, we show that previously proposed well-supported semantics for aggregate programs and description logic programs are rooted in the justified stable semantics of general programs.

1 Introduction

Logic programs under the stable model semantics have been extended to general forms of formulas, for which various semantics have been defined, including answer sets for nested expressions [13,18], general stable models [14], and the FLP-semantics for various kinds of logic programs [2,9,11,29]. These extensions are in part motivated by the need to provide a semantic account for logic programs with aggregates, and by supporting external atoms in combination of answer set programming (ASP) with other reasoning formalisms.

For normal programs, the notion of well-supportedness is well understood [12]. It can be informally described as non-circular justification of atoms in answer sets. Intuitively, this means that no atoms in an answer set may solely depend on the truth of themselves in derivations by rules. However, when more general forms of formulas are introduced, question arises as what could be a suitable notion of well-supportedness. This has contributed to the question what exactly a phrase like *self-supporting loop* means. Recall that latter was introduced in [8] to describe a seemingly counterintuitive behavior of weak answer sets for description logic programs (i.e., dl-programs).

The problem is non-trivial when disjunction is involved. One difficulty is, when disjunction appears in the body of a rule, it is not clear how to capture the notion of dependency. Another difficulty is due to the uniform treatment of logic implication in arbitrary formulas: when a formula contains several implications, we may have to view the formula as one with nested rules in it. An interesting alternative is recently proposed [2],

E. Erdem et al. (Eds.): Correct Reasoning, LNCS 7265, pp. 576–591, 2012.

where rules are of the form $H \leftarrow F$, with H and F being arbitrary (first-order) formulas. For the semantics, circumscription is applied in such a way that only the implication between H and F is strengthened to behave like a rule.

In this paper, we consider the class of propositional logic programs, called *general programs*, in which a rule has a disjunction of atoms in the head and an arbitrary formula in the body. We define a semantics for these programs by formulating the notion of *justified stable models*, propose the notion of well-supportedness, and address the issue of computational complexity for various classes of general programs. We show that the justified stable semantics for general programs provides a uniform representation framework for the family of well-supported semantics currently known in the literature. It is capable of representing the well-supported semantics for aggregate programs, known as the the answer set semantics based on *conditional satisfaction* [26,27], or alternatively the equivalent semantics defined under the theory of approximating operators on bilattices [6,21,26].[1] This work was reported earlier in [25]. In this paper, we further show that the justified stable semantics for general programs is capable of representing the well-supported semantics of dl-programs, recently proposed in [24].

The paper is organized as follows. Following the preliminaries, we define the justified stable semantics for general programs and propose a general notion of well-supportedness. Then we present the complexity results, and discuss related work. This is followed by a sketch of how well-supported semantics for dl-programs may be captured by justified stable models of general programs. The paper is concluded by final remarks and questions for further investigation.

2 Preliminaries

We restrict attention to a propositional language, as we consider only Herbrand interpretations so that the first-order case reduces to a propositional one via grounding. We assume a propositional language, $\mathcal{L}_\Sigma$, determined by a fixed countable set Σ of propositional *atoms*.

Formulas are built from atoms using standard (classical) connectives $\neg$, $\wedge$, $\vee$, $\supset$, and $\equiv$. A *literal* is an atom or a negated atom. A *theory* is a set of formulas.

A *rule* r is of the form: $\alpha_1; \ldots; \alpha_k \leftarrow F$, where $k \geq 1$ and each α_i is an atom and F a formula. We use $head(r)$ and $body(r)$ to refer to the head set $\{\alpha_1, \ldots, \alpha_k\}$ and the body formula F of r, respectively.

A *general program* (or *program*) Π is a set of rules. Π is called *non-disjunctive* if the head of every rule in Π consists of a single atom.

A *disjunctive (logic) program* is a program in which each rule body is a conjunction of literals. A *normal program* is a disjunctive program whose rule heads consist of a single atom. Traditionally in normal and disjunctive programs we use default negation not, but in general programs we replace it with $\neg$.

An *interpretation* is a subset of Σ. We say that an interpretation I *satisfies* an atom α if $\alpha \in I$; $\neg\alpha$ if $\alpha \notin I$. The satisfaction of a formula F by an interpretation I is defined

[1] As shown in [26], the answer set semantics for aggregate programs coincides with the two-valued stable model semantics defined by the fixpoint operator Φ_P^{appr}, when the approximating aggregate used in Φ_P^{appr} is the *ultimate approximating aggregate* [21].

as in propositional logic. I satisfies a rule r if it satisfies $head(r)$ or it does not satisfy $body(r)$. I is a *model* of a program Π if it satisfies all rules in Π. A *minimal model* is a model none of whose proper subsets is also a model. For any expression E, we say E is *true* (resp. *false*) in I if and only if I satisfies (resp. does not satisfy) E.

For an interpretation I, let $I^- = \{\neg a \mid a \in \Sigma \setminus I\}$.

For any two theories F and G, F *entails* G, denoted $F \models G$, if G is true in all models of F. Note that an interpretation I satisfying F is different from I entailing F (i.e., $I \models F$ where I is treated as the conjunction of atoms in I). The former amounts to the entailment $I \cup I^- \models F$.

Given a disjunctive program Π and an interpretation I, the standard *Gelfond-Lifschitz reduct* of Π w.r.t. I, written as Π^I, is obtained from Π by performing two operations: (1) remove from Π all rules whose bodies contain a negative literal $\neg a$ with $a \in I$, and (2) remove from the remaining rules all negative literals. The *standard ASP semantics* defines I to be a stable model (also called an answer set) of Π if it is a minimal model of Π^I [15].

3 Logic Programs with Generalized Rules

We define the notion of *deductive closure*.

Definition 1. *Let Π be a program and I an interpretation. A* deductive closure *of Π and I is a minimal set X of atoms satisfying the condition: for any rule $\alpha_1; \ldots; \alpha_k \leftarrow F \in \Pi$, if $X \cup I^- \models F$, then for some α_i $(1 \leq i \leq k)$, $\alpha_i \in X$.*

We denote by $\Omega(\Pi, I)$ the set of all deductive closures of Π and I. Note that this set is non-empty as the set of all atoms satisfies the condition and it contains minimal subsets that satisfy the condition.

Notice also that I^- above is fixed in determining if X is minimal. That is, that X is minimal satisfying the stated condition means there exists no $X' \subset X$ such that for any $r \in \Pi$, if $X' \cup I^- \models body(r)$ then there exists an $\alpha \in head(r)$ such that $\alpha \in X'$.

Definition 2. *Let Π be a program and I an interpretation. I is a* justified stable model *of Π if I is a deductive closure Π and I.*

Intuitively, a justified stable model is a minimal set of atoms satisfying the closure property where the entailed body of a rule derives at least one head atom.

Example 1. Consider the following disjunctive program, Π_1:

$$a; b \leftarrow \qquad a \leftarrow b \qquad d \leftarrow \neg b$$

Under the standard ASP semantics, the only stable model of Π_1 is $I_1 = \{a, d\}$, which is also the unique justified stable model of Π_1. Note that $I_2 = \{a, b\}$ is not a justified stable model of Π_1, since it is not a minimal set satisfying the stated condition in Definition 1, as the proper subset $\{a\}$ satisfies the condition.

Example 2. As an example beyond the class of disjunctive programs, consider Π_2:

$$a \leftarrow b \qquad\qquad b \leftarrow \neg b \vee a$$

The only model of Π_2 is $I = \{a, b\}$, which is a minimal model of Π_2, but not a justified stable model of Π_2. In terms of Definition 1, I is not a minimal set satisfying the stated condition, as the empty set satisfies the condition. This shows that not all minimal models are justified in the sense of Definition 2.

With a clear understanding that I^- is fixed in the minimization of a set, we can combine Definitions 1 and 2 to arrive at an even simpler yet equivalent definition.

Definition 3. *Given a program Π and an interpretation I, I is a justified stable model of Π if I is a minimal set X satisfying the condition, for any $r \in \Pi$, if $X \cup I^- \models body(r)$ then there exists $\alpha \in head(r)$, such that $\alpha \in I$.*

The justified stable semantics extends the stable model semantics for disjunctive logic programs, as it is easy to check that in this case the definition coincides with the standard one.

Theorem 1. *For a disjunctive logic program Π, an interpretation I is a justified stable model of Π iff I is a stable model of Π under the standard ASP semantics.*

It is also easy to show that justified stable models are minimal models.

Proposition 1. *A justified stable model of a program Π is a minimal model of Π.*

The justified stable semantics also extends the *progression semantics*, from disjunctive logic programs [32] to general programs, for the propositional case. That is, there is an iterative definition of justified stable model, which extends the concept of *progression*, based on expansions by *hitting sets*.

Definition 4. *Let S be a set of atoms and $\xi = \{S_1, ..., S_i, ...\}$ a collection of sets of atoms such that $S_i \subseteq S$, for all i. A subset $H \subseteq S$ is said to be a* hitting set *of ξ if for all i, $H \cap S_i \neq \emptyset$. Furthermore, H is said to be a* minimal hitting set *of ξ if H is a hitting set of ξ and there is no $H' \subset H$ such that H' is also a hitting set.*

Definition 5. *Let Π be a program and I a model of Π. An* evolution sequence *of Π* based on *I, is a sequence of sets of atoms $\sigma_I^0(\Pi), \sigma_I^1(\Pi), ..., \sigma_I^k(\Pi), ...,$ denoted as $\sigma_I(\Pi)$ (or simply as σ when the context is clear), such that*

1. *$\sigma_I^0(\Pi) = \emptyset$, and*
2. *For $i \geq 0$, $\sigma_I^{i+1}(\Pi) = \sigma_I^i(\Pi) \cup H_i$, if there exists $H_i \subseteq I$ such that H_i is a minimal hitting set of the sets,*

$$head(r),$$

where $r \in \Pi$, $head(r) \cap \sigma_I^i(\Pi) = \emptyset$, and $\sigma_I^i(\Pi) \cup I^- \models body(r)$; otherwise $\sigma_I^{i+1}(\Pi) = \sigma_I^i(\Pi)$.

As commented in [32], the basic idea in an evolution sequence is that we start with the fixed I^- and progress by nondeterministically selecting a minimal hitting set at each step, from heads of the rules whose bodies are logically entailed by I^- and the set of atoms already derived. The condition $H_i \subseteq I$ ensures that the construction is guarded, and the condition $head(r) \cap \sigma_I^i(\Pi) = \emptyset$ only allows the rule heads that are not already satisfied to be considered.

Lemma 1. *Let Π be a program and I a model of Π. Then, for any evolution sequence ρ, $\rho_I^\infty(\Pi) \subseteq I$.*

If interpretation I above is not a model, then atoms not in I may be derived by a derivation sequence, which could result in a set of atoms that are inconsistent with I - some atoms interpreted to be false in I now must be true. When an evolution sequence ρ of Π based on I satisfies $\rho_I^\infty(\Pi) \subseteq I$, we say ρ is *consistent*. If I is a model of Π, it is guaranteed that any evolution sequence of Π based on I is consistent.

The interest in the following theorem is two-fold. On the one hand, it shows a constructive definition of justified stable models, and on the other hand, along with Theorem 1, it shows that for propositional disjunctive programs, the progression semantics [32] has a much simpler definition (i.e., Definition 2), without resorting to the concept of evolution sequence. In addition, as we will see shortly, an evolution sequence serves a witness for justified stable models to be well-supported, in a native manner.

Theorem 2. *Let Π be a program and I a model of Π. I is a justified stable model of Π iff there exists at least one evolution sequence of Π based on I, and for all evolution sequences $\sigma_I(\Pi)$, $\sigma_I^\infty(\Pi) = I$.*

Proof. (Sketch) ($\Rightarrow$) Let I be a justified stable model of Π. Then I is a deductive closure of Π and I, i.e., $I \in \Omega(\Pi, I)$. It can be shown that I induces an evolution sequence $\sigma_I(\Pi)$ such that $I = \sigma_I^\infty(\Pi)$. We show that this is the case for all evolution sequences of Π based on I. Now suppose there is some evolution sequence δ such that $\delta_I^\infty(\Pi) \neq I$. It follows from Lemma 1 that $\delta_I^\infty(\Pi) \subset I$. By construction, $\delta_I^\infty(\Pi)$ satisfies the condition in Definition 1, i.e., for any rule $r \in \Pi$ such that $\delta_I^\infty(\Pi) \cup I^- \models body(r)$, for some $\alpha \in head(r)$, $\alpha \in \delta_I^\infty(\Pi)$. As $\delta_I^\infty(\Pi) \subset I$, I is not a minimal set satisfying the stated condition, as $\delta_I^\infty(\Pi)$ also satisfies the condition. This is a contradiction. Hence the evolution sequence δ does not exist. Thus, for all evolution sequences σ of Π based on I, we have $\sigma_I^\infty(\Pi) = I$.

($\Leftarrow$) Assume there is some evolution sequence σ such that $\sigma_I^\infty(\Pi) = I$, and this is the case for all evolution sequences of Π based on I. Since σ is consistent, all rules in Π are satisfied by I, hence I is a model of Π, Towards a contradiction, assume I is not a justified stable model of Π. Then, for any deductive closure $X \in \Omega(\Pi, I)$, $X \neq I$. If for every deductive closure $X \in \Omega(\Pi, I)$ there exists an atom $a \notin I$ and $a \in X$, then some rule in Π is not satisfied by I. This is not possible since I is a model of Π. It follows that for some deductive closure $X \in \Omega(\Pi, I)$, we have $X \subset I$, for which there is a corresponding evolution sequence $\rho_I(\Pi)$ such that $\rho_I^\infty(\Pi) = X$. Since $X \neq I$, it follows $\rho_I^\infty(\Pi) \neq I$. Contradiction.

3.1 A Generalized Notion of Well-Supportedness

The notion of well-supportedness is introduced in [12]: For a normal program Π, an interpretation I is *well-supported* if there exists a strict well-founded partial order $\prec$ on I such that for any $a \in I$, there is a rule $a \leftarrow body(r)$ in Π such that I satisfies $body(r)$ and for every positive literal b in $body(r)$, $b \prec a$. A binary relation $\prec$ is *well-founded* if there is no infinite decreasing chain $a_0 \succ a_1 \succ \cdots$. Intuitively, a well-supported interpretation I guarantees that every positive conclusion in I has a non-circular justification, i.e., I is free of self-supporting loops.

There are two problems when attempting to apply this definition to general programs. Firstly, the definition does not handle disjunctive rules. Secondly, when the body of a rule is an arbitrary formula, the condition "I satisfies $body(r)$ and for every positive literal b in $body(r)$, $b \prec a$" is no longer applicable. For example, for the program $\{a \leftarrow a \vee b,\ b \leftarrow\}$, the interpretation $\{a, b\}$ is a justified stable model, but a blind application would require $a \prec a$ to be in a partial order, which cannot be well-founded.

We propose a generalized notion of well-supportedness.

Definition 6. *Let Π be a program and I an interpretation. I is* well-supported *if there exists a strict well-founded partial order $\prec$ on I such that for any atom $a \in I$, there exist a rule $a_1; \ldots; a; \cdots; a_k \leftarrow body(r) \in \Pi$ and a subset $S \subset I$ such that $S \cup I^- \models body(r)$ and for every $b \in S$, $b \prec a$.*

Following the literature, we call such a well-founded partial order a *level mapping*. As for any justified stable model there is at least one corresponding evolution sequence, which serves as a witness of well-supportedness, we have

Proposition 2. *Any justified stable model of a general program is well-supported.*

Recall that according to [12], the stable models of a normal program P are precisely well-supported models of P. This can easily be extended to non-disjunctive general programs under the generalized notion of well-supportedness, by a routine proof.

Proposition 3. *Let Π be a non-disjunctive program and I an interpretation. I is a justified stable model of Π iff I is a model of Π and is well-supported.*

The iff statement in this proposition is important. It answers the question, given a non-disjunctive program, what if a model (which could be a stable model defined in a different way) is not a justified stable model - then we know that it does not possess a level mapping as defined in Definition 6, and therefore necessarily incurs the phenomenon that some atoms in it depend on the truth of themselves.

From now on, we can say that a model M of a non-disjunctive program is *self-supporting*, or M has *self-supporting loops*, if and only if M is not well-supported. Due to Proposition 3, this is a formal statement.

4 Complexity

In this section, we address the computational complexity of the justified stable semantics for general programs. The following three problems will be considered:

- *Consistency*: The problem of deciding whether a justified stable model exists.
- *Credulous reasoning*: The problem of deciding whether an atom is in a justified stable model.
- *Skeptical reasoning*: The problem of deciding whether an atom is in all justified stable models.

Recall that $\Delta_2^p = P^{NP}$ is the class of problems that are *deterministically* decidable in polynomial time with the help of an NP oracle; $\Sigma_2^p = NP^{NP}$ is the class of problems that are *nondeterministically* decidable in polynomial time with the help of an NP oracle; $\Pi_2^p = \text{co-}NP^{NP}$ is the class of problems such that the complementary problem is in Σ_2^p.

Our main complexity results for the justified stable semantics are summarized in Table 1.

We need to define the class of basic programs, which are motivated from representing aggregate programs by non-disjunctive general programs [25]. In this paper, for notational convenience, we assume that an aggregate is a constraint whose semantics can be defined by an *abstract constraint* (or a *c-atom*) of the form (D, S), where D is a set of atoms serving as the *domain* and S is a set of subsets of D representing *admissible solutions* of the aggregate.

Definition 7. *Let $A = (D, S)$ be a c-atom, where $S = \{\phi_1, ..., \phi_m\}$, $\phi_i = \{a_1, ..., a_k\}$, and $D \setminus \phi_i = \{b_1, ..., b_l\}$. Define $\tau(A)$ to be the formula: $\tau(A) = false$ when $m = 0$, otherwise $\tau(A) = C_1 \vee ... \vee C_m$, where each C_i is the conjunction $a_1 \wedge ... \wedge a_k \wedge \neg b_1 \wedge ... \wedge \neg b_l$.*

That is, $\tau(A)$ is a special type of DNF, where all conjunctions are formed from the same set of atoms; in each conjunction, an atom in this set appears either positively or negatively. Let us call this type of DNFs *complete DNFs*.

Definition 8. *A* basic program *is a non-disjunctive general program consisting of rules whose bodies are a conjunction of complete DNFs and their negations.*

In other words, a basic program is a general program that corresponds to an aggregate program under the translation τ, where each admissible solution is listed explicitly as a conjunction.

From Table 1, it is interesting to observe that the complexity for general programs is on the same level of the polynomial hierarchy as the complexity for non-disjunctive programs which is also on the same level as the complexity for disjunctive logic programs.

Table 1. Complexity of justified stable semantics (entries are completeness results)

program Π	basic	disjunctive	non-disjunctive	general
Consistency	NP	Σ_2^p	Σ_2^p	Σ_2^p
Credulous	NP	Σ_2^p	Σ_2^p	Σ_2^p
Skeptical	co-NP	Π_2^p	Π_2^p	Π_2^p

However, for the class of basic programs, which is a subclass of non-disjunctive general programs, the complexity drops to the first level. This requires some explanation.

Given an aggregate program P, we can show that its conditional satisfaction-based semantics coincides with the justified stable semantics of $\tau(P)$. If we write an aggregate program as a logic program with abstract constraint atoms, that is, if we explicitly list the domain and admissible solutions of an aggregate, the complexity under the conditional satisfaction-based semantics is NP-complete, for consistency [31].[2] Thus, the complexity for basic programs under the justified stable semantics is NP-complete for both consistency and credulous reasoning. By a similar proof, it is easy to show that for skeptical reasoning the complexity is co-NP-complete.

For disjunctive programs, the justified stable semantics agrees with the standard ASP semantics (Theorem 1). So the complexity for the justified stable semantics is the same as that for the standard ASP semantics, which is Σ_2^p-complete for consistency and credulous reasoning, and Π_2^p-complete for skeptical reasoning [5,7].

For non-disjunctive and general programs, the complexity for the justified stable semantics is formally stated as follows.

Theorem 3. *(1) The problem* Consistency *is Σ_2^p-complete for general programs. (2) The problem* Credulous reasoning *is Σ_2^p-complete for general programs. (3) The problem* Skeptical reasoning *is Π_2^p-complete for general programs. (4) These problems for non-disjunctive programs are still complete on the second level of the polynomial hierarchy.*

Note that, for the non-disjunctive case, while the complexity for basic programs is on the first level of the polynomial hierarchy, if we allow rule bodies to be arbitrary formulas, the complexity rises to the second level.

The main idea in the proof of this theorem is the following. We can show that general programs can be mapped to default theories by a polynomial translation. We recall that the Σ_2^p-membership of Reiter's default logic for Consistency is shown by guessing a set of generating defaults for a given default theory first and then testing if this set determines an extension of the default theory [16]. However, this algorithm cannot be directly lifted to the justified stable semantics for general programs, because we need also to nondeterministically determine a subset of the head atoms for each rule in the general program. However, by the results in [23,28], the complexity for the nonmonotonic modal logic S4F is on the second level and each general program can be equivalently transformed into a theory in the nonmonotonic modal logic S4F in polynomial time. Thus, the justified stable semantics for general programs is on the second level.

We now give the details.

Proof of Theorem 3: We first prove the statements (1)-(3) and then the statement (4).

Hardness for general programs: By Theorem 1, the justified stable semantics coincides with standard stable model semantics for disjunctive programs. It is shown in [7] that

[2] For logic programs with aggregates where aggregates are written as *aggregate atoms*, constructed from the standard aggregate functions (SUM, MIN, MAX, COUNT, AVG) and relations ($=, \geq, >, \leq, <, \neq$), the complexity of the answer set existence problem is at the second level of the polynomial hierarchy [26].

the complexity for the latter is hard on the second level (i.e. *Consistency* and *Credulous reasoning* are Σ_2^p-hard while *Skeptical reasoning* is Π_2^p-hard). Therefore, the justified stable semantics for general programs is at least as hard as problems on the second level of the polynomial hierarchy.

Membership for general programs: It can be obtained by combining results in [23,28]. The basic idea is to embed general programs into nonmonotonic logic S4F.

Let $\mathcal{L}$ be the classical propositional language. The language of autoepistemic logic $\mathcal{L}_{ae}$ is the propositional language obtained from $\mathcal{L}$ by augmenting a unary modal operator L. For a formula ϕ in $\mathcal{L}_{ae}$, $L\phi$ means that "ϕ is believed". A theory T is a finite subset of $\mathcal{L}_{ae}$. Let $\models_{S4F}$ be the consequence relation in modal logic S4F and $cons_{S4F}(T)$ denotes the set of consequences of T in S4F.

Lemma 2. *The problem of deciding $T \models_{S4F} \phi$ for a theory T and a formula ϕ in S4F is in Δ_2^p.*

A deterministic algorithm can be designed similar to the algorithm in [16] (page 12). The algorithm is polynomial with a polynomial number of queries to NP-oracle.

Let Δ be a theory in S4F. A theory E is an *S4F expansion* of Δ iff $E = cons_{S4F}(\Delta \cup \{\neg L\phi \mid \phi \notin E\})$. Based on the above result, the following lemma can be proven [23].

Lemma 3. *(1) The problem of deciding whether a theory T has an S4F expansion is in Σ_2^p.*
(2) The problem of deciding whether a formula is in an S4F expansion is in Σ_2^p.
(3) The problem of deciding whether a formula is in all S4F expansions is in Π_2^p.

Given a general P, each rule r of the form $a_1|\cdots|a_k \leftarrow body(r)$ can be transformed into a formula $tr(r)$ in S4F:

$$L\,body(r) \rightarrow La_1 \vee \cdots \vee La_k.$$

Denote $T_P = \{tr(r) \mid r \in P\} \cup \{L\neg La \rightarrow L\neg a \mid a \in \Sigma\}$. Then T_P is a theory in $\mathcal{L}_{ae}$.

The following lemma is a special case of the result in [28].

Lemma 4. *Let P be a general program and I be an interpretation. I is a justified answer set of P iff there exists an S4F expansion E of $tr(P)$ such that I coincides with the set of atoms in E.*

By Lemmas 3 and 4, it is easy to see that *Consistency* and *Credulous reasoning* for general programs under the justified stable semantics are in Σ_2^p while *Skeptical reasoning* is in Π_2^p.

We then show that the justified stable semantics for non-disjunctive programs is still complete on the second level.

Membership for non-disjunctive programs: While the membership can be seen from the above argument for general programs, here we present a direct proof by providing a Σ_2^p-algorithm for deciding whether a program has a justified stable set: Let P be a non-disjunctive program. Guess an interpretation I, the literal closure $\Sigma(P, I)$ can be computed in polynomial time using the NP-oracle of verifying the validity of propositional consequences. Then check if $I = \Sigma(P, I)$. If yes, I is a justified stable model of P. Since only a linear number of queries to NP-oracle are used, the problem is in Σ_2^p.

Hardness for non-disjunctive programs: The hardness is not straightforward. We prove it by a polynomial transformation from $QBF_{2,\exists}$. That is, we construct a polynomial time transformation mapping each QBF $Q = \exists p_1 \cdots \exists p_n \forall q_1 \cdots \forall q_m E$ to a program P_Q such that Q is valid for a truth assignment iff P_Q has an answer set. Here E is a propositional formula made of the atoms $p_1, \ldots, p_n, q_1, \ldots, q_m$. We introduce $n+3$ new atoms: $p'_1, \ldots, p'_n, f, f'$ and g. Denote $P_i = \{p'_i \leftarrow \neg p_i.\ p_i \leftarrow \neg p'_i.\ f \leftarrow p \wedge p' \wedge \neg f\}$ for $i = 1, \ldots, n$ and $P' = \{f' \leftarrow \neg q_j \wedge \neg f' \mid 1 \leq j \leq m\}$.

Let $P_Q = \{g \leftarrow \neg F \wedge \neg g\} \cup P' \cup \bigcup_{1 \leq i \leq n} P_i$.

The sub-program P_i is to guess a truth value for each p_i. By the definition of the justified stable semantics, the CWA automatically applies to every negative literals. However, we do not intend to apply the CWA on the set $\{\neg q_1, \ldots, \neg q_m\}$ and thus P' is used here.

The program P_Q can be constructed from Q in polynomial time. Also, each truth assignment to $p_1, \ldots, p_n$, under which Q is true, corresponds to a justified stable model of P. That is, Q is valid iff P_Q has justified stable model. Therefore, *Consistency* for program is Σ_2^p-hard.

In a similar way, it can be shown that *Credulous reasoning* is Σ_2^p-hard. As a result, *Skeptical reasoning* is Π_2^p-hard. □

5 Related Work

5.1 Well-Supportedness

The idea of *unfounded sets* for normal programs [30] has been applied to logic programs with monotone and antimonotone aggregates [3]. But this approach only provides a necessary condition when extended to arbitrary aggregates [19], i.e., an answer set is unfounded-free, but a model being unfounded-free is not guaranteed to be an answer set. In [26], the existence of a level mapping w.r.t. a model is shown to be a necessary condition for the model to be an answer set. The notion of well-supportedness formulated in this paper is a necessary condition in general, and a necessary and sufficient condition for non-disjunctive programs.

5.2 Relation with the FLP-Semantics

The FLP-semantics [10,11] is a simple and elegant semantics for aggregate programs, which has been extended to languages that combine ASP with external atoms [9], to arbitrary propositional formulas [29], and to first-order general programs [2].

The key idea in the original formulation of FLP-semantics is the notion of *reduct* that keeps the rules whose bodies are satisfied by an interpretation I. Then, I is an FLP-stable model if I is a minimal model of the reduct. For aggregate programs, the difference between the FLP-semantics and the conditional satisfaction-based semantics has been studied in [25]. For programs with arbitrary formulas, let us consider propositional general programs defined in this paper, for which the FLP-semantics is also defined. In the sequel, FLP-semantics refers to the one defined in [2].

Let Π be a general program, where a rule is denoted by $H \leftarrow B$. Tailored to the propositional case, let $\mathbf{p}$ be the list of distinct predicate constants $(p_1, \ldots, p_n)$ appearing in Π (i.e., they are 0-ary predicates corresponding to atoms). By $\mathbf{FLP}[\Pi, \mathbf{p}]$, we denote the seconde-order sentence

$$\Pi \wedge \neg\exists\mathbf{u}((\mathbf{u} < \mathbf{p}) \wedge \Pi^\star(\mathbf{u})) \tag{1}$$

where $\mathbf{u} = (u_1, \ldots, u_n)$ is a list of n distinct predicate variables, and $\Pi^\star(\mathbf{u})$ is the conjunction of

$$H(\mathbf{u}) \leftarrow B \wedge B(\mathbf{u}) \tag{2}$$

for all rules in Π, where $G(\mathbf{u})$ denotes the formula obtained from formula G by replacing all occurrences of the atoms from $\mathbf{p}$ with the corresponding atom variables from $\mathbf{u}$. For propositional logic, $\mathbf{u} < \mathbf{p}$ is a shorthand for $(u_1, \ldots, u_n) < (p_1, \ldots, p_n)$, which means $u_i \leq p_i$ for all i and there exists some k $(1 \leq k \leq n)$ such that $u_k < p_k$, where the truth value $true$ is 1 and $false$ is 0.

An *FLP-stable model* of Π is defined as a model of $\mathbf{FLP}[\Pi, \mathbf{p}]$.

We can show the following proposition.

Proposition 4. *Let Π be a general program and I a model of Π. If I is a justified stable model of Π then it is an FLP-stable model of Π, but not vice versa.*

Example 3. Consider again $\Pi_2 = \{a \leftarrow b,\ b \leftarrow \neg b \vee a\}$. It can be verified that the interpretation $I = \{a, b\}$ is an FLP-stable model of Π_2.

$$\begin{aligned}&\mathbf{FLP}[\Pi_2, a, b] = \\ &\Pi_2 \wedge \neg\exists(a^*, b^*)((a^*, b^*) < (a, b)) \wedge \Pi_2^\star(a^*, b^*)\end{aligned}$$

where $\Pi_2^\star(a^*, b^*)$ is

$$(a^* \leftarrow b \wedge b^*) \wedge (b^* \leftarrow (\neg b \vee a) \wedge (\neg b^* \vee a^*))$$

Since I is a model of $\mathbf{FLP}[\Pi_2, a, b]$, it is an FLP-stable model of Π_2. But I is not a justified stable model of Π_2. By Proposition 3, we know that, for any non-disjunctive program, any model that is not justified does not possess a level mapping. We see that this is the case for I, which incurs a self-supporting loop.

5.3 Relation with Aggregate Programs

We note that programs studied in [25] correspond to non-disjunctive programs of this paper. The definition of answer set there is tied to the notion of default extensions, but the semantics coincides with the justified stable semantics of this paper, for non-disjunctive programs. It is shown in [25] that the conditional satisfaction-based semantics for aggregate programs [26] can be captured by non-disjunctive general programs. However, the complexity issue is completely absent, and the notion of well-supportedness is only discussed informally. In this paper, not only this is defined formally for the class of all general programs, but is also shown to be a sufficient and necessary condition for a model to be a justified stable model, for non-disjunctive programs. In doing so, we are able to answer the question, formally, what if a model of an aggregate program is not a justified stable model - then we know that it is necessarily the case that the model does not possess a level mapping, and as a result, some atoms in it depend on the truth of themselves.

To see further that the conditional satisfaction-based semantics [26], or alternatively the equivalent semantics defined under the approximation theory [20], is rooted on the justified stable semantics, we can define a semantics for *general programs with aggregates*, in which the body of a rule is built from atoms and aggregate atoms using standard (classical) connectives. We extend the mapping τ in Definition 7 to arbitrary formulas as follows: Given a general program with aggregates Π, $\tau(\Pi)$ is the general program obtained from Π where each aggregate A in Π is replaced by $\tau(A)$. Then, we define the justified stable semantics of Π via the justified stable semantics of $\tau(\Pi)$. Immediately, we have

Proposition 5. *Let Π be a general program with aggregates.*

- *Justified stable models of Π are well-supported.*
- *If Π is an aggregate program, justified stable models of Π are precisely the answer sets of Π as defined in [26].*

Note that, aggregates in a general program with aggregates can be defined in the form of [26]. We use the form of abstract atoms only for semantic purposes. As such, the complexity results presented in this paper for general programs do not automatically apply to general programs with aggregates.

6 Well-Supported Answer Sets for DL-Programs

We assume that the reader has some familiarity with description logics (DLs) [1], which are decidable fragments of first order logic.

A *dl-program* is a pair $\mathcal{K} = (L, R)$, where L is a DL knowledge base and R is a rule base. In [8] *weak* and *strong* answer sets are defined, and it is commented that the reason to introduce the latter is because there may exist self-supporting loops in weak answer sets. Later, it is also found that even strong answer sets may incur self-supporting loops. To circumvent this problem, the well-supported semantics for dl-programs is proposed [24]. We can show that the well-supported semantics for dl-programs is rooted in the justified stable semantics of general programs. This is sketched below.

A rule in a dl-program $\mathcal{K} = (L, R)$ is of the form

$$H \leftarrow A_1 \wedge \cdots \wedge A_m \wedge not\ B_1 \wedge \cdots \wedge not\ B_n \qquad (3)$$

where H is an atom, and A_i and B_i are atoms or *dl-atoms*,[3] which are of the form

$$DL[S_1 op_1 p_1, \cdots, S_m op_m p_m; Q](\mathbf{t}) \qquad (4)$$

[3] For simplicity, we assume that equality doesn't appear in rules.

in which S_i is a concept or role from the vocabulary of L, $op_i \in \{\uplus, \cup\!\!\!\!-, \cap\!\!\!\!-\}$, p_i is a predicate symbol only appearing in R whose arity matches that of S_i, and $Q(\mathbf{t})$ is a dl-query.[4]

In this paper, we assume that rules in R are ground.

The *Herbrand base* of R, denoted HB_R, is the set of all ground atoms $p(t_1, ..., t_m)$, where p appears in R and t_i is a constant. Any subset of HB_R is an *interpretation* of R.

Definition 9. Let $\mathcal{K} = (L, R)$ be a dl-program and I an interpretation (of R). The *satisfaction relation under* L, denoted $\models_L$, is defined as:

1. $I \models_L \top$ and $I \not\models_L \bot$.[5]
2. For any atom $a \in HB_R$, $I \models_L a$ if $a \in I$.
3. For any dl-atom $A{=}DL[S_1op_1p_1, \cdots, S_mop_mp_m; Q](\mathbf{c})$ occurring in $ground(R)$, $I \models_L A$ if $L \cup \bigcup_{i=1}^{m} A_i \models Q(\mathbf{c})$, where

$$A_i = \begin{cases} \{S_i(\mathbf{e}) \mid p_i(\mathbf{e}) \in I\}, & \text{if } op_i = \uplus; \\ \{\neg S_i(\mathbf{e}) \mid p_i(\mathbf{e}) \in I\}, & \text{if } op_i = \cup\!\!\!\!-; \\ \{\neg S_i(\mathbf{e}) \mid p_i(\mathbf{e}) \notin I\}, & \text{if } op_i = \cap\!\!\!\!-. \end{cases}$$

4. For any ground atom or dl-atom A, $I \models_L not\ A$ if $I \not\models_L A$.

Given a dl-program $\mathcal{K} = (L, R)$, we map a dl-atom to a c-atom, which can then be translated to a propositional formula. The resulting program is a general program.[6]

Let A be a dl-atom in R. We represent A by a c-atom (D, C), produced by a mapping β, i.e., $\beta(A) = (D, C)$, where D is a set of atoms appearing in R, and $C = \{I \subseteq HB_R \mid I \models_L A\}$.

Definition 10. *Let $\mathcal{K} = (L, R)$ be a dl-program and denote by $\xi_L(R)$ the general program obtained from R by (1) replacing any dl-atom A in R by $\tau \circ \beta(A)$, (2) replacing the default negation symbol not by $\neg$, (3) replacing $\bot$ by $false$ and $\top$ by $true$.*

We refer the reader to [24] for the definition of well-supported answer set, which, as stated in the following theorem, is rooted on the justified stable semantics.

Theorem 4. *Let $\mathcal{K} = (L, R)$ be a dl-program and $I \subseteq HB_R$ an interpretation. I is a (strongly) well-supported answer set of $\mathcal{K}$ iff I is a justified stable model of the general program $\xi_L(R)$.*

7 Final Remarks

For normal and disjunctive programs, there exist a number of different ways to define the same semantics (cf. [17]). However, beyond normal and disjunctive logic programming, this agreement begins to depart in two different directions in the literature. One

[4] A *dl-query* is of the form $Q(\mathbf{t})$, where $\mathbf{t}$ is a list of terms, and Q is a concept, a role, or a concept inclusion axiom, built from the vocabulary of L.

[5] In DL, $\top$ is the most general concept and $\bot$ is the empty concept.

[6] The complexity of this translation depends on the underlying DL.

is based on minimal models in terms of a reduct or modified circumscription. This approach is mathematically elegant, and general enough to deal with arbitrary formulas, including first-order formulas. The other is the family of the semantics defined by fixpoints of a monotonic operator. Such a definition typically carries a form of justified reasoning, natively.

Minimization in the forms mentioned above and justified reasoning are two related but separate issues. The former does not guarantee the latter. Unfortunately, this issue has not received sufficient attention in the recent literature.

Under this circumstance, in this paper we define the justified stable semantics for general programs, formulate the notion of well-supportedness for these programs, and present the complexity results for the semantics. Furthermore, perhaps most interestingly, the work is not only about a specific semantics for a specific class of programs. The framework is unifying in that the semantics for various kinds of logic programs, known to be well-supported in the literature, are all rooted in the justified stable semantics of general programs.

The two approaches mentioned above are closely related, in the sense that the well-supported stable models are always FLP-stable models but not vice versa - when they differ, we now have a precise understanding of what exactly the difference is: for an aggregate program/dl-program/general program with aggregates, any FLP-stable model that is not a justified stable model is not well-supported, i.e., it is necessarily the case that some atoms in it depend on the truth of themselves.

There are several interesting questions that require further investigation. In this paper we only showed that a justified stable model is well-supported. A question is how to characterize justified stable models in terms of well-supportedness, for general programs where rules may have a disjunctive head. That is, we would be interested in a sufficient and necessary condition between justified stable models and well-supportedness, for the class of all general programs. Another question is what would be the counterpart of justified stable models for first-order general programs. Finally, although we do not expect a huge impact on implementation techniques, since the justified stable semantics is closely related to default logic [22], it is interesting to observe that recent effort in implementing the latter is by adopting ASP techniques [4].

Acknowledgement. We would like to thank the reader of this paper, Miroslaw Truszczynski, for detailed suggestions on improving the paper. Jia-Huai You is supported by a discovery grant from Natural Sciences and Engineering Research Council of Canada (NSERC), Yi-Dong Shen is supported in part by the National Natural Science Foundation of China (NSFC) grants 60970045 and 60833001, and the work of Kewen Wang was partially supported by the Australia Research Council (ARC) grants DP1093652 and DP110101042.

References

1. Baader, F., Calvanese, D., McGuinness, D., Nardi, D., Patel-Schneider, P.F.: The Description Logic Handbook: Theory, Implementation and Applications. Cambridge University Press (2003)

2. Bartholomew, M., Lee, J., Meng, Y.: First-order extension of the flp stable model semantics via modified circumscription. In: Proc. IJCAI 2011, pp. 724–730 (2011)
3. Calimeri, F., Faber, W., Leone, N., Perri, S.: Declarative and computational properties of logic programs with aggregates. In: Proc. IJCAI 2005, Edinburgh, Scotland, UK, pp. 406–411. Professional Book Center (2005)
4. Chen, Y., Wan, H., Zhang, Y., Zhou, Y.: dl2asp: Implementing default logic via answer set programming. In: Proceedings 12th European Conference on Logics in Artificial Intelligence, pp. 104–116 (2010)
5. Dantsin, E., Eiter, T., Gottlob, G., Voronkov, A.: Complexity and expressive power of logic programming. ACM Computing Survey 33(3), 374–425 (2001)
6. Denecker, M., Marek, V.W., Truszczynski, M.: Ultimate approximation and its application in nonmonotonic knowledge representation systems. Information and Computation 192(1), 84–121 (2004)
7. Eiter, T., Gottlob, G.: On the computational cost of disjunctive logic programming: Propositional case. Annals of Mathematics and Artificial Intelligence 15(3-4), 289–323 (1995)
8. Eiter, T., Ianni, G., Lukasiewicz, T., Schindlauer, R., Tompits, H.: Combining answer set programming with description logics for the semantic web. Artifical Intelligence 172(12-13), 1495–1539 (2008)
9. Eiter, T., Ianni, G., Schindlauer, R., Tompits, H.: A uniform integration of higher-order reasoning and external evaluations in answer-set programming. In: Proc. IJCAI 2005, Edinburgh, Scotland, UK, pp. 90–96. Professional Book Center (2005)
10. Faber, W., Leone, N., Pfeifer, G.: Recursive Aggregates in Disjunctive Logic Programs: Semantics and Complexity. In: Alferes, J.J., Leite, J. (eds.) JELIA 2004. LNCS (LNAI), vol. 3229, pp. 200–212. Springer, Heidelberg (2004)
11. Faber, W., Pfeifer, G., Leone, N.: Semantics and complexity of recursive aggregates in answer set programming. Artificial Intelligence 175(1), 278–298 (2011)
12. Fages, F.: Consistency of clark's completion and existence of stable models. Journal of Methods of Logic in Computer Science 1, 51–60 (1994)
13. Ferraris, P.: Answer Sets for Propositional Theories. In: Baral, C., Greco, G., Leone, N., Terracina, G. (eds.) LPNMR 2005. LNCS (LNAI), vol. 3662, pp. 119–131. Springer, Heidelberg (2005)
14. Ferraris, P., Lee, J., Lifschitz, V.: Stable models and circumscription. Artificial Intelligence 175(1), 236–263 (2011)
15. Gelfond, M., Lifschitz, V.: Classical negation in logic programs and disjunctive databases. New Generation Computing 9, 365–385 (1991)
16. Gottlob, G.: Complexity results for nonmonotonic logics. Journal of Logic and Computation 2(3), 397–425 (1992)
17. Lifschitz, V.: Twelve Definitions of a Stable Model. In: Garcia de la Banda, M., Pontelli, E. (eds.) ICLP 2008. LNCS, vol. 5366, pp. 37–51. Springer, Heidelberg (2008)
18. Lifschitz, V., Tang, L.R., Turner, H.: Nested expressions in logic programs. Annals of Mathematics and Artificial Intelligence 25(3-4), 369–389 (1999)
19. Liu, G., You, J.-H.: Lparse Programs Revisited: Semantics and Representation of Aggregates. In: Garcia de la Banda, M., Pontelli, E. (eds.) ICLP 2008. LNCS, vol. 5366, pp. 347–361. Springer, Heidelberg (2008)
20. Pelov, N., Denecker, M., Bruynooghe, M.: Well-founded and stable semantics of logic programs with aggregates. Theory and Practice of Logic Programming 7, 301–353 (2007)
21. Pelov, N., Denecker, M., Bruynooghe, M.: Partial Stable Models for Logic Programs with Aggregates. In: Lifschitz, V., Niemelä, I. (eds.) LPNMR 2004. LNCS (LNAI), vol. 2923, pp. 207–219. Springer, Heidelberg (2003)
22. Reiter, R.: A logic for default reasoning. Artificial Intelligence 13(1-2), 81–132 (1980)

23. Schwarz, G., Truszczynski, M.: Nonmonotonic reasoning is sometimes simpler! Journal of Logic and Computation 6(2), 295–308 (1996)
24. Shen, Y.-D.: Well-supported semantics for description logic programs. In: Proc. IJCAI 2011, IJCAI/AAAI, pp. 1081–1086, Barcelona, Spain (2011)
25. Shen, Y.-D., You, J.-H.: A Default Approach to Semantics of Logic Programs with Constraint Atoms. In: Erdem, E., Lin, F., Schaub, T. (eds.) LPNMR 2009. LNCS, vol. 5753, pp. 277–289. Springer, Heidelberg (2009)
26. Son, T.C., Pontelli, E.: A constructive semantic characterization of aggregates in answer set programming. Theory and Practice of Logic Programming 7, 355–375 (2007)
27. Son, T.C., Pontelli, E., Tu, P.H.: Answer sets for logic programs with arbitrary abstract constraint atoms. Journal of Artificial Intelligence Research 29, 353–389 (2007)
28. Truszczynski, M.: Modal interpretations of default logic. In: Proc. IJCAI 1991, pp. 393–398 (1991)
29. Truszczynski, M.: Reducts of propositional theories, satisfiability relations, and generalizations of semantics of logic programs. Artificial Intelligence 174(16-17), 1285–1306 (2010)
30. Van Gelder, A., Ross, K.A., Schlipf, J.S.: The well-founded semantics for general logic programs. J. ACM 38(3), 620–650 (1991)
31. You, J.-H., Yuan, L.-Y., Liu, G., Shen, Y.-D.: Logic Programs with Abstract Constraints: Representaton, Disjunction and Complexities. In: Baral, C., Brewka, G., Schlipf, J. (eds.) LPNMR 2007. LNCS (LNAI), vol. 4483, pp. 228–240. Springer, Heidelberg (2007)
32. Zhou, Y., Zhang, Y.: Progression semantics for disjunctive logic programs. In: Proc. AAAI 2011, pp. 286–291 (2011)

Author Index

GPSR Compliance

The European Union's (EU) General Product Safety Regulation (GPSR) is a set of rules that requires consumer products to be safe and our obligations to ensure this.

If you have any concerns about our products, you can contact us on ProductSafety@springernature.com

In case Publisher is established outside the EU, the EU authorized representative is:

Springer Nature Customer Service Center GmbH
Europaplatz 3
69115 Heidelberg, Germany

Batch number: 09473985

Printed by Printforce, the Netherlands